Understanding Human Behavior

3rd edition

UNDERSTANDING HUMAN BEHAVIOR

An Introduction to Psychology

James V. McConnell
The University of Michigan

3rd edition

Holt, Rinehart, and Winston

New York Chicago San Francisco Dallas
Montreal Toronto London Sydney

Associate Publisher   Richard C. Owen
Development Editors   Johnna Barto
    Charlyce Jones
Managing Editor   Jeanette Ninas Johnson
Senior Project Editor   Françoise D. Bartlett
Production Manager   Victor Calderon
Art Director   Robert Kopelman
Text Designer   A Good Thing, Inc.
Cover   Infield, D'astolfo Associates
Photo Research   Susan Yount
Cartoons   Steve Fritsch

Dedication

For Johnna and Louise,
For Tim and Al,
For Brian and Chris and Lauren,
And most of all, with great thanks to all the students . . .

Library of Congress Cataloging in Publication Data

McConnell, James V
    Understanding human behavior.

    Bibliography
    Includes indexes.
    1. Psychology.   I. Title.
BF121.M18   1980   150   79-24039
ISBN 0-03-044411-X

For permission to use copyrighted materials the authors are indebted to the following:

Chapter 1:   p. 6, photo courtesy of Michael Weisbrot / p. 15, photo courtesy of J. Brian King / p. 21, photo courtesy of Kenneth Karp.

Part 1,   left photo courtesy of Kenneth Karp/right photo courtesy of Arthur Sirdofsky.

(continued on p. 786)

Preface

Early in 1979, when I was spending about 60 hours a week preparing this edition of *Understanding Human Behavior*, a colleague asked me why I was working so hard. "After all," she said, "you just published the second edition in 1977. How can you have so much new to say?"

A good question, but one that's fairly easy to answer. First, psychology is a rapidly-changing discipline, and introductory textbooks must be constantly updated if they are to remain abreast of current developments. Second, the success of *Understanding Human Behavior* is built on feedback from instructors and students, and since the publication of the second edition, we've received comments and suggestions for improvement from hundreds of people who have used the book in the classroom. We simply couldn't wait any longer to put these suggestions into practice. Last but not least, there have been many recent advances in the technology of *producing* textbooks that we could no longer ignore.

Thus *UHB-3* is significantly better than *UHB-1* and *-2* in at least two important ways. First, there is a great deal of information in the third edition that didn't appear in the first two editions, mostly because the data simply weren't available by 1977. Second, thanks to suggestions from readers, we have found better and more effective ways to present much of the old material. In fact, for reasons I will shortly make clear, I rewrote every page of the book this time around. At the strong urging of most of the "users" of *UHB-2*, however, we have deliberately kept intact those elements of the first two editions that students and teachers found particularly valuable.

In discussing *UHB-3*, then, I would like to describe three things: (1) what's new; (2) what's similar to the previous editions (but greatly improved); and (3) what satisfied readers the most about *UHB-2* and hence is relatively unchanged in this edition.

What's New

1. The "vignettes," or "stories," that begin and end each major chapter help set *UHB* apart from most other introductory textbooks. They serve many functions: They introduce the student to the topics to be covered within the chapter, they are rewarding experiences for many readers, and they "humanize" psychology in ways that tables of data and descriptions of experiments never can hope to. I have written 10 new stories for this edition, mostly to replace ones that either seemed out of date or that pleased only a limited sample of readers.

2. One of the most exciting and rapidly-developing areas of psychology has to do with the discovery that the two hemispheres of the human brain appear to have rather different functions. Five years ago the prevailing view was that the left (dominant) hemisphere was "logical," while the right hemisphere was "creative." Now we know that both logical thinking and creative problem solving occur when the two halves of the brain *cooperate*.

Recent evidence suggests that patients we label as schizophrenic tend to process information primarily with their left hemispheres, while patients we label as autistic tend to process information primarily with their right hemispheres. As I note in Chapters 1–5, recent *physiological* studies have called into question some of our long-standing assumptions about the causes of (and cures for) a variety of personality problems, and have given us new notions of how our brains process information.

3. Chapter 1 is entirely new. It represents my belief in the necessity for *integrating* all aspects of psychology if we are to achieve any real understanding of what people are like. While the chapter draws heavily on my own experiences and insights, it is actually an attempt to help students see that what goes on inside their brains influences their social responses—and vice versa. I might add, incidentally, that several hundred students who read the chapter in manuscript form gave it exceptionally high ratings.

4. Ten years ago most people assumed that there were but one or two neurotransmitters. Recent evidence suggests that there are, in fact, hundreds of quite different transmitter molecules. Five years ago most people believed that a given neuron secreted only one transmitter substance. Now it seems barely possible that each neuron can secrete a wide range of different transmitters. These new data give us insights into the effects of drugs on behavior (mentioned in Chapter 3) that we never had before.

4. While we have known for some time that violence on television can induce aggressive responses in viewers, only recently have we learned what types of viewers are most affected. And, as noted in Chapter 4, we now have evidence that certain types of television shows can increase positive (pro-social) behaviors in many people.

5. The important role that olfaction plays in influencing both perceptions and behaviors—particularly those involving sexual stimuli—becomes clearer year by year. Some of the latest research findings are covered in Chapter 7.

6. Twenty years ago I suggested that sensory deprivation might be used as a therapeutic tool. Ten years ago scientists in Oklahoma showed that sensory deprivation might help autistic children who suffer from "input overload." And in the last three to four years, a number of researchers have used sensory isolation to help people stop smoking, reduce alcohol consumption, and lose weight. These developments are discussed in Chapter 9.

7. Much in the section on motivation (Chapters 12–14) is new, but I have put particular emphasis on the effects of stress and on strategies for coping with conflict.

8. There is a rapidly-developing conflict in the field of hypnosis, mostly having to do with whether hypnosis is *really* an altered state of consciousness. Chapter 18 presents Ernest Hilgard's latest findings along with T. X. Barber's criticisms of Hilgard's work.

9. Despite Freud's belief that personality development more or less ends during adolescence, we now know that people are capable of psychological growth throughout their lives. Many of the myths we have about the capabilities and attributes of older individuals have recently been exploded. The chapters on human development (19–21) and personality (22–24) cover this new material on life-long development and aging.

10. About the time that *UHB-3* appears in print, the American Psychiatric Association will publish its *Diagnostic and Statistical Manual-III*, which will cause a complete re-evaluation of diagnostic techniques and will bring about even more hostility between psychiatry and psychology than presently exists. *DSM-III* is described in detail in Chapter 24 and is compared with previous viewpoints in the field; the material on abnormal behavior patterns is then related directly to this new diagnostic tool. Any textbook that does not present and evaluate *DSM-III* is woefully out of date (including *UHB-1* and *-2*).

11. *DSM-III* will also bring about many changes in the way that we practice (and evaluate) psychotherapy. Chapter 25 has been rewritten to

take this fact into account. But since *DSM-III* appears to lean more toward "curing symptoms" than "curing underlying causes," I have also updated the long-standing conflict between traditional therapists and the practitioners of behavior modification and social learning theory.

12. In the past two or three years, it has become apparent that Attribution Theory has gained dominance in the field of social psychology. Chapters 26–28 reflect this bias and present the latest applications of Heider's and Kelley's insights into social processes.

13. In 1978 and 1979, the "Scared Straight" program—aimed at trying to frighten juvenile offenders into behaving lawfully by exposing them to prison environments—gained considerable prominence. Unfortunately, as I note in Chapter 28, the data simply don't give much credence to this "scare" approach to solving the problems associated with juvenile delinquency. I have also included in Chapter 28 research published in 1979 that *does* give us new ways of helping youthful offenders learn self-control.

14. Several chapters include new material on sex roles and the drive toward sexual equality. Bardwick's most recent notions on gender identity appear in Chapter 28, as well as data (to be published in 1980) concerning the performance of male and female managers in business and industry. And as you will see, successful managers (of either sex) tend to be people who combine humanistic goals with behavior-modification strategies.

What's Revised or Improved

There are many *physical* improvements in *UHB-3*—more and better photographs and diagrams, more graphs and tables, and a more readable type style. But the most significant change is a very subtle one. In the spring of 1978 I purchased a Lanier word processor, which is really a miniature computer. In order to "put the book on the computer," I had to retype every word in the text. While doing so, I kept the criticisms of my reviewers in mind and *greatly simplified* much of the language I had used in the first two editions. The sentences are—on the average—much shorter, the paragraphs more succinct, and the logical flow of ideas more compelling. Having to rewrite *everything* also allowed me to integrate all the material in the book to a much greater extent than I had in the earlier versions.

This "itch for integration" shows up most clearly, perhaps, in Chapter 5. In *UHB-1* and *-2*, the material on General Systems Theory appeared at the back of the book. Now it is in Chapter 5, where it can best serve its function of giving the student a *holistic* approach to psychology. I have added, as well, new material on "history and systems," in order to give the reader a better feel for psychology's roots.

In Chapter 3, I have cut down on the descriptions of the various "drugs" that alter consciousness, but have increased the coverage of sleep and dreaming. There is more material on those "natural" pain-killers, the enkephalins (which include the endorphins). And there are better graphic representations of the four stages of sleep (including REM sleep and dreaming).

There is a growing emphasis in psychology on change and on personal achievement. This emphasis is reflected in many parts of the new edition, but particularly in the sections on learning applications (Chapters 15–17), on language learning (including Bruner's recent studies, covered in Chapters 20 and 21), and on the importance of social learning theory (Chapters 25–28 and the concluding chapter). These final chapters also point out our growing awareness of the important influence of the social environment on human thoughts and actions. We no longer can assume that there is a strong correlation between attitudes and behaviors, and we now realize that "changing attitudes" isn't quite the same thing as "changing behavioral outputs."

Last but not least, I have reworked the material in the Statistical Appendix so that it is much simpler for most students to understand.

But the important question remains: How do you change the behavioral outputs—and the attitudes and feelings—of students who read this book? Not by the text alone, of course. The classroom teacher is of paramount importance, but teachers often need more help than textbook authors give them. I'm pleased to say that—just as we did with the first two editions—the *UHB* "team" has prepared a number of instructional aids to make the teaching task more manageable. Al Siebert and Tim Walter have greatly revised their outstanding *Student Manual*, while Ray Shrader and Reid Jones have added new elements to their *Unit Mastery/PSI Workbook*. Robert Johnson has prepared an *Instructor's Manual* that new teachers, in particular, will find of considerable value. R. W. Kenny, Dwain Boelter, and Richard Davis have created a helpful set of slide materials for classroom use. The test bank is a near-miracle: A computerized bank of test questions that *really* works! I hope that all instructors will make effective use of these first-rate ancillary materials.

What's Much the Same

We have kept in *UHB-3* the good things that have pleased more than a half million readers of *UHB-1* and *-2*. The "stories" that begin and end each major chapter are still there (though much improved and, generally speaking, somewhat shorter). There are more glossary items than ever before, but they still grace the margins of the book rather than appearing at the end (where few students look). The stories, the "running glossary," the simple language, and the integrated approach to psychology are the four features of *UHB-1* and *-2* that students found particularly useful in their attempts to master the field of psychology.

There is no doubt that *UHB-3* is as different from other introductory psychology textbooks as were the first two editions. If you read *Teaching of Psychology*—the journal published by Division Two of the American Psychological Association—you know that research performed in both the US and Canada suggests that students tend to rate *UHB higher than any other text*. I take great pride in this fact, because I have tried to write the book so that it will both *please and teach* the introductory student. To me, these are two of the most important goals of any psychology text—that readers enjoy what they read and that they understand and remember the material *for a long time*. As best we can tell, *UHB* both "pleases and teaches" better than almost any other book that we have been able to test.

I have tried, as well, to present psychology in such a way that most young readers will give at least passing consideration to making it their undergraduate major. As I have noted elsewhere, none of us gain if our classes (and texts) are so boring that most of our students can't wait to finish the introductory class so that they can take something more interesting.

The question remains: What should a student get out of the introductory psychology course? Facts? an understanding of what psychology is all about? Many of the so-called encyclopedic texts contain a lot of facts, true. But how many students who read them can appreciate or recall those facts a month after the final exam? It seems to me that these texts miss the real point of what a college course should do—to encourage *long-term changes* in human thoughts, feelings, and actions. *UHB-3* surely cites at least 90 percent of the facts and research studies that most other texts do, but explains them in such a way that the facts come to life and thus are important and real enough to be memorable and useful to the reader.

Finally, *UHB-3* is as personal a book as the previous two editions were. Our research shows that most students are put off by a very formal, academic approach to their first psychology course. The students are interested in *people*—themselves and others—and not in esoteric data, statistical equations, and the fine points of experimental design. We sometimes forget that 95 percent of the students who take the introductory course are *not* psychology majors. And probably 90 percent of them will *never* perform a real psychological experiment. Why they should we rub their noses in scientific esoterica when that's the last thing that will "turn them on" to psychology? *UHB-3* is a practical, people-oriented textbook that deals in real-life issues and gives students material that they can put to practical use immediately. Is there any better way to make science understandable to students than by exciting their interest and giving them practical rewards for learning?

Perhaps that's the most important thing I learned from working with my new Lanier word processor. This mini-brain will do what I tell it to do—if I give it the right inputs. I don't need to "motivate" it to respond, other than punching keys. The human brain must be programmed in much the same way, but humans have hearts that "pump emotions" as well as blood. Ordering a student to learn usually doesn't work very well, and no one has yet found a set of simple "brain buttons" to press that will ensure that freshmen "memorize" a textbook as readily and as rapidly as my word processor memorizes data on magnetic disks. Thus teaching and writing remain as much a psychological art as they are a psychological science.

If you are evaluating textbooks, don't just look at the pretty pictures, or at the number of literature citations, or at the names and concepts listed in the index. Instead, judge a text *by the results that it gets.* That is, judge a book by how much the reader actually understands and remembers. If you do, you probably will learn as much about people, and how they differ from computers, as I have learned by working with my word processor.

In brief, I'm all for using computers if and when they will help me achieve my personal goals. But my chief aim remains that of helping *people*—helping teachers teach, and helping students learn to love and appreciate psychology as much as I do.

My sincere hope is that *UHB-3* will bring us all just a bit closer to achieving those goals than did *UHB-1* and *-2.* And what better reason could one have for revising any textbook?

James V. McConnell

Acknowledgments

According to the title page, this is "my" book. Nothing could be farther from the truth. It takes the combined efforts of hundreds of people to produce a good introductory psychology text. The author gets most of the credit, yet the others do much of the real work; without their contributions, the book would never see final publication. Let me acknowledge my great indebtedness to many individuals.

To begin with, there is Louise Waller, the editor of the first edition, who helped *Understanding Human Behavior* through its considerable birth pangs. It was she who fought so hard to help me realize the dream we both had of what a textbook could be like.

Then there is Johnna Barto, who guided me through the editorial anxieties and uncertainties of the second and third editions. It was from Johnna's fertile mind that many of the improvements in the later editions sprang. I owe Johnna great gratitude not only for her creative suggestions, but also for her ability to tolerate and work around my many idiosyncrasies.

Françoise D. Bartlett held the editorial reins, coordinating and executing all of the activities necessary to turn a manuscript into a bound book. To Fran, a warm and hearty vote of thanks.

I am also grateful to Charlyce Jones, who expertly guided the development and production of the ancillary materials.

My special appreciation too to Jeanette Johnson, managing editor, and Ray Ashton and Dick Owen, my publishers, for their bright ideas, their concern, and their continued support. They helped plan the third edition, oversaw its execution, and always put pride and educational accomplishment before mere profit.

I would also like to thank John D. Backe, Stanley D. Frank, and James Mirrielees for their many kindnesses.

Robert Kopelman supervised the art and design program. Susan Yount secured the many photographs that enhance the text. Victor Calderon guided the production process wisely and well. My special thanks to Vic for his continued assistance in matters large and small. Patrick Powers and Daniel Loch rate several pats on the back for their help in marketing and promotion. Pat and Dan are special friends and colleagues. Roseanne Jensen, in her usual cooperative fashion, handled the myriad details connected with the book.

In final analysis, a good share of the success of the first edition was due to the enthusiastic reception given *Understanding Human Behavior* by many Holt, Rinehart and Winston marketing and sales people. I cannot begin to name them all, but would like to extend thanks particularly to Harry McQuillen, Jack Fox, Ted Shields, Jay Plourde, Feeney Lipscomb, and Lyn Peters. A round of applause should go to the following members of the sales staff for their support of the text over the years: Tim Baughman, Fran Beaumont, Russell Boersma, Bill Brisick, Ken Crabb, Paul Davidson, Jack Edmonds, John Lannefeld, Lewis Lembeck, Jim Lizotte, Howard Lockwood, Roger MacQuarrie, Shirley Mason, Mike McCarthy, Page Mead,

Ingrid Nettleship, Chuck Pensinger, Joan Rainer, Alan Resnick, Jerry Riley, Marie Schappert, Alan Steinharter, Marilyn Swank, Randy Terry, Dennis Thetford, Don Welch, Floyd Westervelt, and David Yelton.

Many of my professional colleagues gave generously of their time in reading all or parts of the manuscript and offering their thoughtful comments. Without their collective wisdom, I would have made even more silly errors in the third edition than appeared in the first two. Let me then thank William Uttal, Leslie Purdy, Brian Bate, Anita Haviland, Tim Walter, Al Siebert, E. Roy John, Irwin Pollack, Richard A. Block, Jon Gosser, Reid Jones, and Raymond Shrader for their many useful criticisms. Siebert and Walter are also the authors of the excellent *Student Manual* that accompanies this book, while Shrader and Jones are the authors of the *Personalized Instruction* materials that many students use.

I would also like to thank the following people for their letters, reviews, criticisms, and most useful comments: Michael Biderman, Gary Bothe, Wilbur A. Castellow, Roland Calhoun, Sister Francelle Clarke, Daniel J. Cohen, Sister Mary Corda, Perry Duncan, David Fisher, Beverly Fridley, Carl R. Gaetano, Yaakov M. Getz, Roland Golemba, Peter Clark Gram, Kenneth F. Green, Jane R. Harris, Glenn Hawkes, Austin Herschberger, William A. Johnston, Gary King, John Lakey, Dan Landis, Frank J. Landy, Robert Levy, Gary Lovejoy, John Marr, Gary Oliver, Robert Opaluch, Joan Quartararo, Rebecca Reviere, Dewey Rundus, Ray Saenz, Linda Shadburne, Joan Sieber, Leo Spindel, Larry R. Vandervert, and Clarke Stewart Worthington.

Thanks too to my many friends in Ann Arbor and elsewhere, comrades all, who gave me most of my ideas and whose names I have taken in vain in some of the short stories. To my poker-playing cronies—Brian Healy, W. Robert Dixon, Warren Norman, John Holland, Peter Steiner, Dan Rubinfeld, and Ralph Heine—my thanks for keeping me amused (and broke) during the book's gestation period.

Without the continued and perceptive assistance of Joan McClain, my chief assistant at The University of Michigan, the book would never have been completed on time. My sincere thanks to Joan for all her help.

Last, but most assuredly not least, it is my students—past and present—who deserve my thanks. They taught me how to write; they shaped me into learning more about psychology and about people than I had any intention of learning. Whatever is best in this book is their doing, not mine.

Bless 'em all.

—J. V. McC.

October 1979
Ann Arbor, Michigan

Contents

MOTIVATION

LEARNING AND MEMORY

MATURATION AND DEVELOPMENT

Understanding Human Behavior

3rd edition

Introduction

"Getting It All Together"

It was a blustery spring afternoon when I first met Joe—one of those wild days when the sun shines warmly for a few minutes, and then a cloud blows across the sky and dumps an ocean of cold water on the world below. I came back after my class—dodging the chilly raindrops as best I could—to find Joe sitting in my office. We shook hands, then I asked him to wait a moment while I returned an urgent phone call that had come in while I had been teaching.

As I was talking on the phone, I inspected Joe carefully out of the corner of my eye. He was a relatively plain-looking, dark-haired young man who seemed to be in his mid-twenties. His clothes were inexpensive but relatively well cared for. I got the impression that he was quite nervous, for his dark brown eyes were constantly darting about the room and his hands trembled a bit as he lit a cigarette. I wondered what his problem was, and why he had brought it to me since I couldn't recall ever having seen him before. As soon as I finished talking, Joe answered both questions.

"Dr. McConnell, I need help," he said rather loudly the instant I put down the phone. "I'm sorry to bother you with it, because you're not my teacher or anything. But, well, several of my friends have taken your courses and . . ." Joe shrugged his shoulders and leaned forward a bit in his chair. "And I've read your introductory psych book, you know, and I liked it a lot. It helped me a lot because, well, one of my friends brought it to me while I was incarcerated in the mental hospital. Uh, yes, the book. You see, it was the only thing I had to read while I was incarcerated."

At this point Joe broke into nervous laughter. "Can you believe that I read a psych book about crazy people when I was locked up like a criminal on the ward of a mental hospital? Oh, my. I had to do something to keep from going crazy, uh, so I read your book from cover to cover. I need, yes, I really do need your help because, uh, it wasn't fair what they did to me, and now they want to put me back in the hospital."

The Puzzle of Human Behavior

When someone like Joe asks for your help, how do you view that person? I tend to see the person as a mystery begging to be solved—a human "jigsaw puzzle" whose pieces I must help the person put together so that we both get a truer picture of what the person is really like. We usually begin with small details, fitting this little piece together with the next. Eventually, when we get enough of the small details in place, we begin to get glimmerings of what the "big picture" is. And then, once we know what the person is like at the moment—and what experiences the person has had in the past—we can begin to make plans about how the person would like to grow, change, or solve her or his problems.

So, at this point in my conversation with Joe, I sat back to think things over for a moment or two. What clues did I have so far about this puzzling young man named Joe?

To begin with, he was a middle-class male who either was a college student now, or (more likely, given his age) had been one in the recent past. He was neatly dressed, but in old clothes. I presumed, therefore, that he had little money but that he was still interested in "looking good" when he appeared in public. He had a good vocabulary, but his speech was a bit disjointed and broken up—a most important clue to his problems, as you will soon learn. He was nervous and frightened because "they" had put him in a mental hospital and wanted him to go back.

Most important, *he wanted to make some changes in his life.* Otherwise, he never would have come to me asking for help.

As we talked further, Joe gave me many more clues as to what he was really like. Some of these "pieces of the jigsaw puzzle" I was able to fit into place right away. Other clues I simply missed, or I failed to recognize how important they were when they first surfaced.

If you would like to learn some of the skills involved in understanding human behavior, why don't you follow along as Joe and I continue our conversation? Try to see Joe as I saw him that blustery spring day when he first walked into my life. And as Joe and I put the pieces of his own unique "jigsaw puzzle" together, perhaps you will discover some things about yourself that you never really knew before.

Dead as a Brass Doorknob

It takes guts to admit that you've been "put away" in a mental hospital, and I respect people who are not ashamed to talk about it. So I smiled at Joe and said, "I'm sorry to hear that you've had problems, and I don't blame you for wanting to make sure that 'they' don't send you back. But who are 'they?' And come to think of it, who are you?"

Joe's laugh was high and tightly pitched, almost a giggle. "I'm Joe _____," he said, telling me his whole name. As it happened, although he lived some 60 miles from the University, I had heard of his family because his father was a prominent person often quoted in the Detroit newspapers. (I have changed Joe's name and some other details in order to protect his privacy, but the rest of the story is true.)

"So, you're Joe," I said, reaching over the desk to shake his hand again. "I'm glad to meet you. And I'm delighted that you liked my textbook *Understanding Human Behavior,* even if you did read it under rather unusual circumstances. But you still haven't said who 'they' are."

Joe hung his head in apparent embarrassment. "They're my parents. What can you do when your own mother and father have you locked away in a mental hospital because they say you're crazy?" He shook his head in dismay. "Oh, uh, I still love them, I guess. But, uh, well, it's hard to live with." He looked up at me quickly, waving his hands in a circle in front of his chest. "It's like this, you know," he said, waving his hands some more as if he were trying to show me the *shape* of his own despair.

"Why do you think your parents had you committed, Joe?"

"Because I died," he said in a flat tone of voice.

I'm sure I frowned noticeably. "You died?"

"Dead as a doorknob. I lay there on the ground for maybe ten minutes, dead as a brass doorknob. Uh, brass, you know, it conducts electricity. Uh, like I did, I guess."

Curiouser and curiouser. "You conducted electricity?"

"Like a brass doorknob. Um, the psychiatrist my parents send me to said that the 'death trauma' drove me crazy. Not everybody who dies comes back, you know. Uh, well, he says I haven't resolved my fears and anxieties about being dead and coming back and all that sort of thing."

Joe paused and lit another cigarette. His hands were shaking even more violently now than when he first sat down. And no wonder.

"Joe, how did it happen? When did you die, and how did you manage to come back?"

The young man nodded, then shrugged his shoulders. "Oh, it was years ago. Uh, maybe eight years ago this month. I was, you know, out there flying a kite, that was the crazy part of it. Uh, you shouldn't fly a kite on a rainy day, not near the power lines anyhow. Er, at least that's what they told me after I died and came back."

Joe stopped for a moment again, frowning. "The psychiatrist always wants me to talk about my feelings when I died. He says I have to re-live the experience until all the feelings I had when I was dead come out into the open. Um, but that's ridiculous. I didn't have any feelings when I died, only when I came back. Uh, I mean, do you want me to talk about my feelings too?"

I smiled. "Joe, you can talk about anything you want to talk about. But frankly, I'd rather hear the facts first, and the feelings second. I gather you were flying a kite on a rainy day, and the kite struck some power lines. I would imagine that the electricity came down the kite string and knocked you out."

"Killed me. Fifteen thousand volts, they said. I mean, I wasn't even breathing for five or ten minutes. Uh, I guess I would have stayed dead, lying there on the ground, but my brother saw it happen and he called for help. Uh, there was this doctor living next door, you see, and my brother yelled for him, and the doctor came and, oh, you know, he did that thing . . ." Again Joe's hands fluttered in front of his chest. "He breathed air back into my lungs, and resuscitated me. But, but my brain was killed, you know what I mean?"

Some "Shocking Facts" about Brain Damage

I knew what Joe meant. The jolt of electricity had stopped his heart from beating, and Joe's brain had been without blood and oxygen for several minutes. Some of the nerve cells in Joe's brain had surely died. Pumping air into Joe's lungs might have brought his heart and the rest of his body back to life, but brain cells are among the most sensitive bits of tissue in the body. Once Joe's nerve cells had been damaged, no medicine known to modern science could repair or replace them.

The fact that Joe had "died" and returned to life was, of course, the single most important clue to understanding his present predicament. As Joe's psychiatrist had known full well, such an experience leaves many scars on an individual's personality. But Joe's *psychological* problems were complicated by the *physical damage* that had occurred to his brain cells—as well as by the way his parents and friends had reacted to his death. In order to put the pieces of Joe's jigsaw puzzle together, I first had to learn something about the *interactions* among his body, his mind, and his social environment.

As you probably know, certain parts of your brain influence rather specific aspects of your thoughts, feelings, and behaviors. For example, nerve cells in the front part of your brain have control over the muscles in your arms and legs. If these brain cells were damaged, you might spend the rest of your life in a wheelchair. Your mind might still be capable of "willing" your arms and legs to move; but if your brain cells were so damaged that they couldn't carry out your mental orders, your body would remain permanently paralyzed.

Other parts of your brain control your ability to speak. If these cells were injured, you might lose some or all of your ability to speak. Your mind might still be able to "think" words, but your lips and vocal cords couldn't respond by saying precisely what you were thinking.

Still other regions of your brain act as your "memory storehouse." Damage to these nerve cells might cause you to forget some of your past experiences. In rare cases, you might be able to remember what had happened years earlier, but you would have problems recalling what you had eaten at lunch just a few minutes ago.

If you were unfortunate enough to suffer damage to your brain, you might behave in ways that the people around you would consider unusual or abnormal. If you got the right kind of professional help, you probably could train the undamaged parts of your brain to "take over" the psychological functions you lost when your nerve cells were injured. But if you *didn't* get proper assistance, you might very well become depressed and disturbed because the people around you considered you "insane" or "mentally disturbed."

Joe had suffered considerable brain damage when he "died." That much was certain. It also seemed clear that he hadn't been entirely successful in retraining himself to act or respond in ways that his parents and friends considered completely "normal." The question now was, could I help him find new ways of doing the things he really wanted to do?

Before I could answer that question, I needed a great many more clues about what he was presently doing that disturbed people and, just as important, what he was capable of doing that most people would consider "sane" or "normal."

So I continued to talk, listen, and observe.

"That's a remarkable story, Joe. I've never known anybody who's died and come back to life. You're a pretty special person, aren't you?"

Joe smiled at the compliment. "Oh, I don't know that I'm special. Uh, maybe 'special crazy,' or something like that." His hands fluttered a bit. "Oh, say, you want to know how it felt to be dead?"

"Of course, Joe. How did it feel?"

Joe giggled loudly. "I can't remember. I just can't remember! Isn't that crazy? The most important thing in my life, and I can't remember anything at all about what it was like to be dead. Uh, the doctor said that the damage to my brain probably caused me to forget. 'Amnesia,' he called it. Well, um, but you know, the funny thing is that I can recall everything that happened afterward, and what happened earlier that day up to a few minutes before I got electrocuted, but I can't remember anything, oh, you know, any special feeling at all about being dead."

He rubbed his hands together, and then held them to his chest. "It was, I mean, it was just being dead, like when you're asleep and you don't dream and you don't recall being asleep but the time is gone when you wake up. Um, I guess I was scared about the whole thing, and my parents were awfully upset, and yes, yes, they took me to the hospital in the ambulance. I remember that. And, well, of course my mother kept crying about how God had given me back from the realm of the dead, and uh, it was a sign my life wasn't complete and I had work to do yet. I've told it all to the psychiatrist a hundred times now, and um, he says someday I might remember if I can relive the experience enough times and release the blocked-up fears and anxieties. But, why can't I remember it? Do you know?"

I thought I did. "Joe, as I point out in my book, there are a lot of studies showing that if something shocks or damages your brain, you lose your memory for everything that happened for 30 minutes or so *before* the accident. Oddly enough, you usually can remember what happened immediately *afterward*—but not what had happened to you just prior to the shock. That's what the phrase "retrograde amnesia" really means—a memory loss that extends back in time from the moment of the accident."

"Yeah, but what puzzles me is that I died immediately *after* the shock, not before it. So, er, why don't I remember what came afterward?"

"Joe, the electricity was just the first shock you got. When you died, your brain stopped operating for a period of a few minutes. And then just as suddenly, it came back to life and started working again. Don't you think all that stopping and starting up was something of a shock to your brain too?"

Joe nodded, "Oh, yes. Nobody ever explained it to me that way. Uh, but if I can't remember it, why did it drive me crazy?"

What Is Insanity?

I looked at Joe very, very carefully. He seemed determined to convince me that he was "off his rocker." Yet his behavior so far had been fairly normal. True, his speech seemed a little disturbed, and from time to time his hands "fluttered" in an odd way—but I didn't really understand the significance of those facts until much later on. Despite his relatively normal behavior, however, Joe had been seeing a psychiatrist for years, had spent time in a mental hospital, and was very worried about being hospitalized again. Little wonder he was convinced he was "crazy." My problem now was to find out who and what had done the convincing.

"Who decided you were insane, Joe?"

The young man gave me a puzzled look. "Uh, my parents, I guess. Like, you see, they sent me to see the psychiatrist in the first place."

"What made them do that?"

"I guess I screwed up, or something. I, well, maybe I did. You see, after I died, things didn't go so good for a while."

"What do you mean?"

Joe's hands flew about wildly for a moment. "It's like that, you know. It just didn't go very well. Oh, uh, I did okay in school. I finished high school, and came here to the University. Uh, I never did take one of your courses, because I was majoring in sociology. And then I got a job for a while, too—in Chicago. But they didn't like me there, so I, uh, came back home. And, then the problems with my parents got worse, um, so they made me go see the psychiatrist, you know?"

"No, Joe, I don't know about the problems with your parents, because you haven't told me about them. Why don't you do that now?"

He shook his head forlornly. He sighed. He lit another cigarette. It seemed to me that we were, at last, getting down to the real facts about his present situation.

"Well," he said, puffing nervously on the cigarette, "I can't figure my mother out. Oh, you know. She says she loves me, and she says I'm blessed by God because He sent me back from the grave. Uh, right after I died, and I was in the hospital, she used to hold me in her arms and sing hymns to me. Er, she wanted me to be a preacher, I think. But my daddy wanted me to go to college and become a lawyer. Um, they both were pretty angry when I went into sociology instead. Not much money in being a sociologist, or so they said. And I used to have these spells, you know, when I just couldn't get it together. Uh, uh, that's bad, you know. I, er, argued with them a lot, I guess, and I ran off a couple of times, and uh, I used to get headaches and couldn't go to school all the time. So they sent me to the doctor."

"The psychiatrist?" I asked.

"No, the brain doctor, the neurologist. Oh, man, he did brain scans and electroencephalograms where he measured my brain waves and things like that. Er, he said I had irreversible brain damage from dying and I'd never be normal."

"So?"

Joe gave me an eloquent shrug, then he stamped out his cigarette. "So he gave me some pills to take, to calm down my brain. They helped some, I guess, but mostly those pills just made me sleepy. Uh, I still had headaches and couldn't always get it together. Uh, so mother insisted that I go see this psychiatrist, um, and he kept asking me about how it felt to be dead and come back, and was I anxious about maybe dying again. And, uh, he wanted me to tell him about all my impulses and angers and bad feelings. And, er, I told him all that, but I just felt worse, and some days I just stayed in bed, and my parents kept picking on me to get up and get things done."

Joe shook his head sadly. After a moment I said, "Why do you think your parents responded that way, Joe?"

"I guess they wanted me to be a success, or something, and here I was a big disappointment to them. They just couldn't see inside me, you know, see what I was thinking and feeling, and how hard it was to act the way

A typical large state mental hospital.

they wanted me to. And, uh, they just kept telling me my brain was damaged and I had to strive to overcome it and be like everybody else. Nothing I did seemed to be what they wanted, uh, and one day I got very angry and upset and we had a big argument about it all, and, and, mother called the psychiatrist and they decided I was crazy, and oh, God, they said I needed complete rest and I felt so bad and my head hurt so much that I agreed. Uh, so they sent me to the mental hospital."

Joe paused for a very long time. Tears came to his eyes momentarily, and he opened his hands in resignation. Then he said, "I hated the hospital, and I didn't know why I was there, really, except it was what my parents wanted, and, er, I guess I figured they knew what they were doing. My social worker at the hospital said it was mostly my parents' fault, uh, that they didn't know how to give me the right environmental support. Oh, my. I don't know if I believe that, uh, but I know I don't want to go back to that hospital, Dr. McConnell. That place is hell on wheels. But if you can't work and support yourself, and you can't stand living with your parents, and you feel bad lots of the time, and you have brain damage, uh, doesn't that mean you're insane?"

Insanity versus Mental Illness

Insanity is a legal term, not one that psychologists use very much. If a judge decides that you cannot tell the difference between right and wrong, or that you are not able to resist criminal impulses, you may be certified as being "insane" by that judge. You then will lose certain of your legal rights, and you may be sent to an institution. Thus, technically speaking, you are legally *sane* unless and until a judge signs papers saying that you are legally *insane*.

Psychologists and psychiatrists prefer to use the terms "mental illness" and "unable to cope" rather than "insane"—mostly because we are concerned about helping unhappy people get well. Judges usually are more concerned about protecting the public and determining legal rights and wrongs.

So, to me, Joe wasn't "insane," although by now it was clear that he was very unhappy and very disturbed about a lot of things. But it was just as clear that he had many strengths and many good points. I was as interested in what Joe could do, and *do well*, as I was in what things in life troubled him.

Calling someone "mentally ill" doesn't usually tell you much about how to help the person get well. As we will see in later chapters, there is no universally agreed upon treatment for most types of mental illness—mostly because there is no universal agreement as to what causes people to become mentally disturbed.

But we do know of several things that can give you difficulties. (1) Some psychological problems are primarily caused by physical or chemical damage to the nervous system. (2) Other problems seem mostly to be a result of how your mind reacts to (and copes with) various sorts of highly emotional and stressful experiences. (3) Still other so-called "mental difficulties" are actually due to the person's having learned inappropriate or unhealthy behavior patterns.

What we call "mental illness," then, can be the result of biological problems. Or psychological problems. Or problems having to do with the person's behavior or social environment. Or, more likely, what we call "mental illness" occurs *because an individual has all three types of problems at once.*

Usually we couldn't do a very good job of helping you recover from any type of "mental illness" unless we could view you from a biological perspective, *and* from a psychological perspective, *and* from a social or behavioral perspective *all at the same time.* That is to say, we would need to be able to *perceive* you as being an incredibly complex person who has a body, a mind, and who lives among and reacts to other people. If we looked at *just* your physical reactions, or *just* your mental processes, or *just* your social behaviors, we probably wouldn't be able to help you solve your problems.

My problem as I spoke to Joe was that I couldn't see where his own problems really were. Although he said he was "brain damaged," his actions seemed pretty normal (under the circumstances). He had finished college, and he used complex language rather well. Therefore, the damage to his brain hadn't affected his intelligence in any obvious way. Nor did his thought processes seem disturbed or unusual to me. He behaved politely, he responded to what I said in a logical way, he maintained good eye contact as he spoke to me, and he seemed to have his emotions under control.

And yet . . . And yet there *was* something unusual about Joe that I couldn't quite put my finger on.

Science as a "Detective Story"

Science is, to a great extent, the fine art of solving mysteries. Nature gives us a puzzle—human or otherwise. For some reason, perhaps due to our own peculiar nature as human beings, we are motivated to solve the puzzle. We can either use our "hunches," and make wild guesses about the answer—which is what we did for most of the history of civilization—or we can adopt a logical process of some kind in trying to find out what the solution to the puzzle is.

Even today, most people in the world seem to prefer to use their guesses and their subjective inner feelings when trying to unravel any mystery that they encounter. And that's fine, as a starting point. But ever since the Middle Ages—when the scientific method was first developed—a growing number of individuals have tried to apply a logical, objective approach to the solution of human problems.

This objective approach is called the *scientific method*, and it is based on the belief that most mysteries have *natural* or *measurable causes*. To use the scientific method properly, you must follow several steps:

First, you have to recognize that a mystery of some kind exists that needs to be solved, and that the mystery probably has a natural cause. We might call this step *perceiving the problem*.

Second, you make as many *initial observations* about the mysterious circumstances as you can. Hopefully, your observations will be as exact and as complete as possible.

Third, you use the results of your initial observations to come up with a *tentative solution* or "first guess" as to what the answer is. Scientists often call this step "making an hypothesis." The solution you pick, however, will very likely be determined by how you view the problem—and the world. If you think that the world is affected primarily by *supernatural powers*, then the scientific method won't help you much. But if you believe that the mysterious event might have a *natural cause*, then perhaps you can state your "tentative solution" in a way that will help you determine what that cause is.

Fourth, you draw up a plan for *testing objectively* whether or not your first hunch about the solution was correct. This test may merely involve your making further observations about the puzzling affair. Or it may involve your performing an experiment in which you "do something" to the puzzle in order to get a reaction of some kind.

Fifth—whether you merely observe things, or whether you undertake an experiment of some kind—you will decide as unemotionally as possible whether your "tentative solution" to the problem was right or wrong. If your initial hypothesis was wrong, you will surely want to revise it and make some more observations. But if your first hunch was correct, you will probably want to refine your solution to the mystery by *testing it again and again*. And to do so, you will most likely need to make further predictions about future events.

Sixth, if these further predictions turn out to be accurate, you will have some right to believe that your solution to the puzzle was a *correct* one. But if your predictions were incorrect, you should realize that you goofed up somewhere along the way. And you will have to start the problem-solving process all over again.

The Importance of Objectivity

The key concept in any definition of the scientific method is *objectivity*. And "being objective" means that you must stand back and look at the puzzle as unemotionally and impersonally as you can.

True, your subjective, personal feelings are very useful in *motivating* you to want to solve problems, but your emotions can cloud your judgment if you don't know how to control them when necessary.

For example, Joe's parents loved him and hence were motivated to help him. But they became so upset that they simply couldn't view their family situation as a problem to be understood and perhaps solved. Had they done so, they might have guessed somewhere along the line that part of Joe's difficulties lay in the way that *they treated him*. Then they could have altered their own behaviors to see if Joe changed in return. Had Joe gotten better—and he probably would have—their "tentative solution" to the mystery of Joe's "craziness" would have proved out and they could have gone on to help him more.

As it was, their emotions got in the way. Because they couldn't shoulder part of the blame themselves, they preferred to see Joe's "craziness" as being entirely *inside Joe*. They could not perceive Joe as being a "psychological object" whose actions were as influenced by his environment as by his brain damage. Thus when the social worker at the mental hospital suggested that they might be partially responsible for the way Joe acted, his parents rejected her hypothesis, without ever testing it scientifically.

The history of science is, to a great extent, the history of our ability to perceive the world, and ourselves, as natural objects rather than subjective "spirits." For many centuries, humans believed that each stick and stone had a supernatural spirit inside it. Physics first became a science when we learned to look at rocks and rivers and clouds as *physical objects* whose actions were governed by natural laws rather than by supernatural "spirits." Biology became a science when we first were able to view plants and animals objectively—as being *living organisms* whose physiological processes were predictable and hence understandable.

Psychology became something of a science when we first learned to see ourselves as others see us—that is, when we learned to view people as *highly complex systems* whose feelings, thoughts, and actions are often influenced by our biological inheritance, our personal past experiences, and the people and things presently around us.

Psychology is thus that junction point at which biology and sociology interact to influence the development of our minds and bodies.

We will have more to say about what psychology is—and how it developed—in the next few chapters. For the moment, let's see how we might apply the scientific method to Joe's problem.

The "Mystery" of Joe

I could see and measure Joe's body objectively. However, his mind was hidden to me. He *told* me his thoughts and feelings, and he *behaved* in certain ways that also suggested what might be going on inside him. But I couldn't *directly see* his mental activities.

If there is one fact that almost all psychologists agree upon, it's this one: What goes on inside your mind is a *private set of events* we can never inspect directly. But by being objective—by talking with you and observing your reactions, by giving you "mental tests," by watching how you interact with other people, and by drawing on the results of thousands of scientific studies—we can often gain a pretty good notion of what you are like "inside." (Just as you can come to understand yourself and others better once you learn more about psychology.)

So, I couldn't see directly if Joe was "mentally ill" or "legally insane." But I had observed his actions and reactions as objectively as I could and, frankly, I was still rather puzzled. Which is to say that I didn't yet have enough data about Joe even to be able to guess at a tentative solution to the mystery of his present existence.

And just as frankly, I don't know that I ever would have gained much insight into Joe's problems had fate not happily intervened.

There came a knock at my office door, and a student stuck her head in to remind me I had promised to discuss her research with her—at length.

Joe seemed to panic. He wrung his hands almost violently. "Uh, oh my, I don't mean to intrude. You've got to see this girl, okay, but, listen, I really need your help, you know? I mean, I don't want to go back to that, that *place*, and I know you can help me, uh, if you really want to." He stopped momentarily, and tears seemed to cloud his eyes. "But maybe you don't want to . . ."

"Yes, Joe, I really want to help you if I can." I smiled. "Anybody who read my book in a mental hospital obviously needs help, right?"

Joe smiled too. "Uh, could I buy you a beer after you see this person? I mean, that way we could converse in private for a while."

Mind Talk, Body Talk

An hour or so later, I met Joe at a nearby campus hangout. As I slipped into my seat, I noticed he had a rather large pitcher of beer in front of him. The pitcher was about two-thirds full. When the waitress came up, I ordered a Coke. (If you're going to engage in scientific problem-solving, it helps to remain sober.)

"Gee, Dr. McConnell, I'm glad I came to see you today. Gee. I mean, I feel better already," Joe said, finishing his glass of beer and pouring himself another one.

"I'm glad you came to the office today, too. Been waiting long?"

Joe laughed. "I drank a couple of bottles, you know, and then, and then I ordered up this, this . . ." He pointed at the pitcher. "Oh, you know, the beer. The beer, uh, pitcher." He took a big swallow from his glass and refilled it.

"You seem to be enjoying yourself."

"I guess I am, really. Uh, I feel more 'together' now, you know what I mean? Like this!" He swirled his hands around in a circle.

As I realized later, Joe had just given me several important clues to his problems:

First, he was apparently under considerable tension and, as I soon discovered, often used alcohol to relieve his feelings of stress.

Second, he probably suffered from some slight damage to the speech centers in his brain. All of us resort to using our hands to describe things now and again. But Joe had been doing this a bit too often. I didn't know precisely what his speech problem was, but I was reasonably sure he had one and that it was related to what had happened to his brain when Joe temporarily "died."

Third, "getting it together" was easier for Joe when he was a bit intoxicated. As we will see in the next chapter, your ability to speak is typically controlled by one half of your brain, while your ability to think creatively seems to be controlled by the other half. The "talking half" of your brain is usually *dominant*—which is to say that it is the conscious, thinking side of your brain which expresses itself in language and logical actions. All of your conscious thoughts, then, are "mind talk" that originate in your dominant hemisphere.

The conscious half of your brain is not directly aware of what goes on inside the "silent half" of your brain. But it does appear that your "silent half" monitors, perceives, and responds emotionally to whatever your "talking half" does. What we often call "body talk" or "body language" is actually a set of responses that appear to be controlled by the "silent half" of your brain.

As we will see in Chapter 3, drugs such as alcohol can disrupt the dominance of the "talking half" and thus let the "creative half" of your brain express itself more freely (or wander off on its own). What Joe had just said and done gave me the hunch that—when he was a trifle intoxicated—the dominant or conscious half of his brain didn't cooperate very well with the monitoring, perceptual half of his brain.

Of course, I didn't line up all of these hunches in logical order the very instant Joe had said, "Uh, I feel more 'together' now, you know what I mean?" But I did realize that Joe was decidedly more 'different' in the bar than he had been in my office—and that helping Joe to "get it all together" might end up being more difficult than I had previously imagined.

I took a swig of my Coke. "Now that you're more 'together,' Joe, why don't you tell me something about yourself?"

Joe finished off his glass of beer and poured himself yet another. "Uh, oh, I guess I'm really just like everybody else, you know. Uh, um, well, what else did you care to have me talk about?"

"Tell me where you live. Tell me about your parents. Tell me anything you think is important."

Joe nodded seriously. "You don't know my parents, do you? Uh, my mother, oh, did I tell you sometimes I hate her? Um, oh, did you know that hate is dark green? Dark green hatred. I always thought it was red, uh, like red roses, you know?" Joe giggled. "Or like cheap red wine."

"You were talking about your mother, Joe."

"Oh, yes. Er, she cried a lot after I died, uh, but I told you that, didn't I? Yes, well, what didn't I tell you about my parents? Uh, my parents, well, I guess I really love them, uh, mostly, anyway, but, uh, I wish my parents hadn't put me away in that mental hospital." Joe reached over and grabbed my arm, as if to emphasize his sincerity. "Don't let them put me back in that hospital, please!"

I tried to reassure Joe that I would do the best I could. His talk was becoming more and more disjointed, and his emotions weren't under the firm control he had shown while sitting in my office. It seemed to me that we were getting much closer to the "real Joe," and I wanted to give him a chance to show me anything about himself that he thought was important. I prompted him again.

"About your mother, Joe. Is she a very religious person?"

Joe shook his head in vigorous assent. "Oh, yes, very, very religious, my mother. Uh, mother, yes, she has a lot of free time, uh, and she spends most of it down at the church. Uh, oh yes, that church is something else, big and beautiful, and it's located just off Woodward Avenue. Uh, uh, er, varoom, you know?"

"Varoom?"

"Sure, varoom, varoom, VAROOM! The cars racing down Woodward Avenue."

Woodward Avenue runs right through the heart of Detroit. For decades, hot-rodders have raced their souped-up cars down the Avenue trying both to out-accelerate everyone else and to avoid getting a speeding ticket.

"You raced your car down Woodward when you were young?"

"Uh, yes, particularly right after I died. Um, er, dying is pretty scary, you know. Um, well, I get scared by lots of things, mostly spiders and snakes. Uh, oh, uh, I almost got bitten by a snake, once, in Florida. A funny little coral snake, you know, with big long fangs." Joe made a funny face as he stuck his teeth out like fangs. "Uh, I didn't tell you about that, did I? You want me to talk about the snake?"

I suppose I stared at Joe silently for several seconds. He simply wasn't making much sense. He was jumping from one subject to another like a jackrabbit skipping across hot concrete. This is the sort of jumbled up, "word salad" pattern of speech you might sometimes observe in mental patients diagnosed as being *schizophrenic*. And yet he surely hadn't seemed schizophrenic when he sat in my office.

"Joe, you were talking about your mother, and I do wish . . ."

"RIGHT!" Joe said very, very loudly.

I frowned. I don't like being interrupted.

". . . and I do wish you'd continue on the subject."

Joe smiled. "What subject?"

"Your mother, Joe. Your mother. You said she spent a lot of her time in church."

Joe nodded his head. "Um, yes, she goes to church a lot, particularly on Sundays. Uh, uh, oh, last Sunday I went over to visit a friend of mine, the one who gave me your book to read in the mental hospital. Uh, oh, yes, that hospital was gruesome, terrible, with all those crazy people in it."

Joe paused for a moment, wringing his hands again. "Do you think that dying, uh, like I did was what made me crazy?"

"I don't think you're 'crazy,' Joe, although . . ."

"GOOD!" he shouted.

Another interruption. I was trying to be objective and "cool" about Joe's unusual verbal behavior, but for the moment I reacted very subjectively. That is, I *presumed* that Joe knew that he wasn't supposed to interrupt someone who's talking—particularly not a professor who's trying to help you. Had I maintained an objective viewpoint of Joe, I would have accepted *whatever he did*—and then, standing back at arm's length—I would have tried to figure out what caused his unusual behavior, and how we might help him gain better control over what he did.

But instead of looking at him objectively as "Joe-whose-mystery-needs-solving," I looked at him subjectively and emotionally as "Joe-who-ought-to-know-better." So I got a little bit angry at his rudeness—and for the moment missed the most telling clue of all as to what was wrong with him.

"Look, Joe, you want me to help you stay out of the mental hospital, right? Well, you can't go around interrupting people without annoying them. They think you ought to know better. And if you don't know better, then maybe there's something wrong with you, if you know what I mean."

Joe nodded that he understood.

"I'd guess that part of your problem is that you bother people because you don't do the things they expect you to do. Or say the things they expect you to say. Joe, most of us don't like things that are highly unpredictable, because we fear they may be out of control. When people don't do what we would do under the same circumstances, we often figure they're 'mentally ill,' and we lock them up in mental hospitals because we're afraid of what they might do next. Just as you were afraid of that coral snake down in, in, in . . ."

"In Florida. I told you that."

"Well, yes, Florida," I stammered, and then regained a bit of my own self-control. Joe might be 'crazy,' but he certainly wasn't dumb. He didn't seem to know where he might be going verbally, but he certainly remembered where he had been. Whatever else was wrong with him, his Long-term Memory seemed to be functioning well.

"Uh, there was a guy I knew who saw snakes all the time," Joe said, moving his left arm across the checkered tablecloth as if it were a snake about to strike at me. "Snakes, crawling all over his bed at night in the hospital. Uh, er, my hospital social worker said I came from a disturbed family milieu and needed 'family therapy' so my folks and I could get along better. Uh, um, er, it is a far, far better thing I do than I have ever done before."

I pulled him gently back on target. "What did your psychiatrist say was wrong with you, Joe?"

"He said I lacked impulse control, and I suffered from anxiety and confused thought patterns. Um, yes, oh, oh! Patterns. Look at the patterns on this tablecloth, they're, you know . . ." Joe crossed and uncrossed his arms rapidly.

"What did your psychiatrist say ought to be done about your impulse control and your anxiety?"

"He said I needed to work through my death fears so I could get my psychosexual development back on track. Uh, my, do you think you can track down what's wrong with me?"

"Perhaps. With your help. Why did your psychiatrist send you to the mental hospital, Joe?"

"He said I wasn't responding to treatment because I was brain-damaged, hopelessly so. Uh, oh, really, I cross my heart and hope to die. Uh, er . . ."

Again I reached out verbally and pulled Joe down to reality. "Who told your psychiatrist your brain damage was hopeless?"

"The neurologist who examined me after the accident read my brain waves, I told you that, uh, and he said I suffered extensive brain damage when I died. Oh, uh, oh, I only died that one time, you know."

"I know, Joe. And you came back. But what did the neurologist suggest should be done to help you?"

Joe giggled. "He prescribed a whole bunch of pills, but then he said it was hopeless because the pills didn't help. Uh, yes, help, beer certainly helps me get it all together." He lifted his glass, took a swig, and then saluted me. "Do you think I can get it all together so I don't have to go back to the hospital, or am I hopelessly crazy like the doctors said?"

Three Explanatory Views of Human Behavior

What would you have thought had you been in my place? Was Joe crazy, or mentally ill, or hopelessly brain damaged, or schizophrenic, or merely the product of a disturbed family environment? Or was he all of these things, and perhaps a lot more?

What did the experts say? As Joe talked, I realized that in his quest for understanding himself, he had encountered three different people with three quite different views of what his problem really was.

The Physiological Viewpoint

First, immediately after his accident, Joe had seen a neurologist who had made a thorough examination of his brain. By recording Joe's brain waves on an EEG machine (and by testing Joe in many other ways), this physician had been able to spot various areas of nerve cells that were behaving abnormally. The neurologist then made a *biological* diagnosis of Joe's problems.

Like most physicians, the neurologist took a *physiological viewpoint* toward Joe. That is to say, the neurologist *perceived* Joe as being primarily a complex biological machine. Joe's brain-wave record was abnormal, therefore he had lost some neural tissue when he died. Some of the nerve cells that remained intact were now behaving abnormally. From the physiological point of view, it is the actions of your nerve cells that control the thoughts and reactions of your mind. Joe's nerve cells were acting up, hence (to the neurologist) Joe was acting up.

Unfortunately, the neurologist could not bring those lost nerve cells back to life. All he could do—or thought he could do—was to give Joe medicine that might reduce the abnormal responses his nerve cells were making. If the neurologist could force Joe's nerve cells to act in a normal fashion, wouldn't that force Joe's mind to react in a normal fashion as well?

Well, what do you think? Obviously there is a connection between what goes on inside your brain and what goes on inside your mind. Can we explain everything about your consciousness, your personality, your feelings and emotions *solely* in terms of the flow of electricity through your nervous system? Or should we take a broader view of what makes you tick?

The Intra-Psychic Viewpoint

When Joe's parents were disturbed by his actions, they had sent him to see a psychiatrist. Psychiatrists are medical doctors who have been trained in psychology as well as in brain physiology. Like most psychiatrists—and like most psychologists, for that matter—this man took an *intra-psychic* view of Joe.

That is to say, most psychologists and psychiatrists believe that everything that goes wrong (or right) about a person's psyche or mind or behavior cannot be explained in simple, physiological terms.

Look at it this way. Scientists estimate that your brain has some 15 *billion* nerve cells in it. Each of these nerve cells is connected up to as many as 5,000 other nerve cells. In our present state of physiological ignorance, we cannot measure even 1 percent of what your nerve cells do. How then can we hope to explain the workings of your mind in terms of the workings of 15 billion nerve cells whose actions we can really only begin to guess at?

Another point: Even if our knowledge of neurophysiology were a thousand times more advanced than it presently is, how much would that help us in dealing with someone with complex mental problems?

For example, suppose through some magic I could have restored Joe's brain to its pre-accident state while we sat talking in the bar. Would putting Joe's nerve cells back in order have *immediately* solved all his problems? With his suddenly intact brain, would Joe instantly have gained the impulse control he presently lacked? Would he immediately have been able to find a good job, stop drinking, and relate warmly and lovingly to his parents? Or, in the decade since his accident, had Joe experienced so much grief and pain and anger—and lost so much self-esteem—that he would still have needed *psychological* help in getting his thoughts, emotions, and behaviors back on track?

When I looked at Joe physiologically, I saw him as a "biological machine" with abnormal brain activity that no surgeon could ever hope to repair. But when I looked at Joe from the intra-psychic viewpoint, I saw him as a self-directed, conscious human being with his own unique set of goals and values. True, he had to "make do" with a damaged brain, but human beings (and their bodies) are incredibly flexible. Surely, if Joe got the proper help, he should be able to compensate for those lost nerve cells by finding new ways to achieve his personal goals.

From the physiological viewpoint, your body exercises almost complete control over your mind. From the intra-psychic standpoint, however, your mind dominates your bodily activities.

Both viewpoints are necessary and can be very useful in helping you to understand yourself (and others). But both viewpoints are, in and of themselves, terribly incomplete.

The Social/Behavioral Viewpoint

Joe was not just a biological machine whose behavior was as predictable as a robot's. Nor was Joe just a disembodied mind floating freely in space like a lonely star. Joe was a *social being*, whose thoughts and behaviors were strongly influenced by the people and things around him, and whose thoughts and behaviors strongly influenced the people he was around. Joe had a mother and father; he had friends and lovers; in the past he had had classmates, playmates, teachers, supervisors, bosses, doctors, social workers, and psychiatrists. At the moment, he was talking with a psychologist, smiling frequently at the waitress who served him beer, and looking occasionally at all the other people in the bar. In his brief lifetime he had met and interacted with thousands of other individuals, all of whom had played their parts in helping make Joe what he was today.

Joe had learned to talk (and think) in English because that's the language his parents and friends taught him. He picked his own clothes, but since he looked like most other young men from his particular social class, Joe's choices were obviously affected by the people around him. His values were, for the most part, identical to the values held by almost everyone he knew. Indeed, from the *social/behavioral viewpoint*, there was little about Joe's actions and emotions that couldn't be explained in terms of what he had learned from his social environment.

Joe's social worker at the mental hospital had diagnosed Joe's difficulties as stemming chiefly from "a disturbed family atmosphere." Which is to say that the social worker believed that most of Joe's abnormal thoughts and actions were the result of the way that his parents (and perhaps other people) had treated Joe both before and after his accident.

And surely there was some truth to the social worker's diagnosis. As I discovered later on, Joe's mother was too protective of him immediately after he "died." She fussed over him and gave him everything he asked for. In effect, she rewarded him for "staying sick," rather than encouraging him to learn how to cope with his physical disability. She paid close attention to his every mistake, blaming his failures on his "poor, damaged brain." And with an excess of maternal affection, she overwhelmed his attempts to stand on his own two feet.

But after a while, when Joe became too dependent on her, she started to demand that he "shape up." A young man with a healthy brain might well have done so. Joe didn't—because he hadn't gotten the special training he needed in order to bring his damaged nerve cells and his thoughts under his voluntary control.

Both his parents probably would have been happy to have helped him—had they known what to do. But because they perceived the problem as being "inside his head," they didn't realize that *they* had to change their behaviors toward Joe in order to help *him* learn how to change his behaviors toward them. So they sent him first to the neurologist, second to the psychiatrist, and third to the mental hospital.

By the time that the social worker suggested "family therapy," Joe's parents were convinced that his case was hopeless. And since he couldn't take care of himself, and because his "crazy talk" and "strange actions" were unpredictable and frightening to them, Joe's parents decided that the safest place for him was in a mental institution.

The Holistic Approach

Which of the three viewpoints—the physiological, the intra-psychic, or the social/behavioral—gives you the greatest understanding of Joe and his problems?

The answer is, *all three of them taken together*. Like Joe, you are an incredibly complex living system. There is a biological side to your nature, a mental side, and a social side. You cannot hope to understand yourself—or Joe or anyone else—unless you are willing to view human beings from at least these three different perspectives. And then put all the facts together so that they form *a unified whole* (see Fig. 1.1).

Psychology stands at that scientific crossroads where genetics, biochemistry, physiology, sociology, and anthropology meet to form that unique organism we call the individual human being. Although some people tend to emphasize one or two of the three major viewpoints, most psychologists tend to take a *holistic approach* toward understanding and solving human problems. That is, we know full well that your bodily processes influence how you think and feel, that what goes on inside your psyche or mind can change the way in which your bodily processes operate, and that both your mind and your body are strongly influenced by your social environment.

In brief, we must learn as much as we can about your physiological, intra-psychic, and social "parts" in order to be able to perceive you *as a*

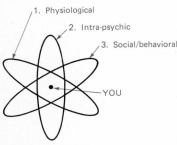

O.K. — Now Just What Is Psychology?

1. Physiological
2. Intra-psychic
3. Social/behavioral

YOU

Fig. 1.1. Three views of human nature make up the holistic approach to psychology.

Chapter 1 Introduction

whole. If we ignore any part of you, we are likely to end up with an incomplete perception of your whole being.

And if you are to learn to understand yourself better—or to understand Joe, your parents, your friends, and your loved ones—you too must learn to see people as being complex organisms made up of interacting parts. Indeed, if I had to guess, I would bet that the ability to see yourself *both* as "interacting parts" and as a fully functioning "whole" is the most important thing you can learn from studying psychology.

Several specialists had looked at parts of Joe from their own restricted viewpoints. They had sincerely done their best, but they had failed to help him very much. What Joe needed most, it seemed to me, was someone who could help him put all his parts together to form an integrated whole. Since I believe in "holistic psychology," I tried to do just that. As it happened, I was lucky, for Joe soon gave me the final clue I needed in order to put a number of pieces of his jigsaw puzzle together.

Joe and the Three Viewpoints

What had I learned about Joe so far?

From a physiological viewpoint, I knew that he had suffered brain damage when he had "died" and come back to life.

From an intra-psychic view I knew that he still had strong emotions connected with that death episode, that he had even stronger fears he would be sent back to the mental hospital, and that he seemed highly motivated "to get well."

From a social/behavioral point of view, I knew that he couldn't support himself, that he had problems getting along with his parents, and that many of his behaviors were so unusual that he disturbed the people around him.

Joe also had a "memory problem," but I wasn't sure what it was. He seemed to be able to remember what he had said five minutes ago, but not what he had said 15 seconds ago. When I asked him a question, his first sentence would be "on target," but then he would seem to lose his sense of direction and would wander aimlessly from one topic to another. Yet if I gave him a cue as to what he was supposed to be talking about, he would pick up right where he had left off. He would complete one or two sentences, and then off he would drift again.

Odd, to say the least. Why couldn't Joe "talk in a straight line?" Was this the sort of behavior that had led his psychiatrist to say that Joe lacked "impulse control"?

I looked him carefully in the eyes and said, "Joe, I'm going to ask you a question, and I want you to try very hard to give me a complete answer. Please keep your mind on the answer and don't go drifting off. Okay?"

Joe nodded his head vigorously.

"Okay, Joe, tell me about the time you died, just like you told me this afternoon in my office."

A normal American family at dinner. Psychologists are interested in studying both normal and abnormal patterns of social interactions.

Joe nodded again. "Well, I was out flying this kite of mine one windy spring day . . ."

I nodded to show I was listening.

". . . and it had rained, you know?" Joe looked directly at me, but I didn't respond. "Uh, yes, er, the rain in Spain falls mainly on the plain, uh."

"Kite, Joe."

"Oh, yes. I was running along trying to get the kite to catch the wind and go up in the air. Um, er, well, I caught an airplane once and flew all the way to the coast. Yes, oh, uh, I just coast along when I have something to drink, don't you like to do that too?"

I was beginning to get angry. "Listen, Joe, you just aren't concentrating. You were talking about the day that your kite string hit the power line and . . ."

"RIGHT!" Joe screamed.

And then the lightning bolt hit.

The Miracle of Normal Speech

For just an instant after Joe interrupted me again, my anger almost got out of control. Indeed, I really wanted to smack him because his impoliteness and his inability to concentrate frustrated me so much.

And then suddenly, some part of my mind took hold, throttled my anger, made me question my angry response, and gave me what I can only call an objective flash of insight.

Joe was basically a very polite person, and yet here he was interrupting me. Polite people don't interrupt you unless they have a reason for doing so. What was Joe's reason? What was he trying to tell me?

Looking at Joe subjectively—seeing him as *Joe*—I had projected my own values and expectations on him. He had said he wanted my help, but when he cut me off in mid-sentence, I immediately presumed that he was being deliberately rude.

Rudeness is a subjective, value-laden term that we use to explain certain types of behavior. Viewed objectively, the term tells us very little about the so-called rude person, but a great deal about our personal expectations.

Standing back and looking at the situation from a psychological distance, I realized that Joe must have some other reason for continually interrupting me. The bolt of mental lightning hit when I realized what it was.

Joe was giving me the kind of verbal reassurance and feedback he needed in order to concentrate.

We take it for granted that if you are "normal," you can answer a question that requires you to string several thoughts or sentences together in logical A-B-C sequence. But in order to get sentence "B" in its right place—after "A," and in front of "C"—you have to remember both "A" and "C" while you are saying "B." And to perform this miracle of logic, one part of your mind must *remember* what the A-B-C sequence is supposed to be, *monitor* or keep track of what you are saying, and then provide your speaking mind with *feedback* to keep it "on target." Talking without paying attention to what you're saying is rather like trying to drive home from a party when you're blindfolded—how can you know where to go next if you don't know where you are or where you've just been?

If the "monitoring" part of your mind wanders off on its own while you are trying to hold a conversation, or if the talking part doesn't pay attention to the feedback it gets from the "monitoring" part, you will probably lose track of what it was you were trying to say.

Since each sentence Joe said was complete in and of itself, I presumed that the talking part of his mind (or brain) was working quite well. But the "monitoring" part seemed easily distracted. Joe could get out the first sentence in a sequence, but by the time he reached the final words in the sentence, he had forgotten what it was he had just said or where he was trying to go.

Joe covered up his forgetfulness very cleverly—he simply began a second sentence using the last word or two he had just said. The fact that this second sentence had no relationship to the first didn't appear to bother him—perhaps because the "monitoring" part of his brain wasn't all that interested in being logical anyhow.

But Joe *could* concentrate if I helped him listen to himself. That's what some part of his mind/brain was trying to tell me by shouting "GOOD," and "RIGHT" at me. I had a hunch that if I would just do the same thing for him, perhaps he could speak and think as logically as I could.

The Scientific Method

A hunch, no matter how good, is little more than an unproved explanation of something. Once I had my flash of insight, I could have told Joe what I thought, and then left the proving up to him. But most psychologists are simply not built that way. Once we perceive a "tentative solution" to a problem, we have an urge to put the solution to the test—either in the real world, or in a scientific laboratory.

My hunch led me to predict that if I nodded my head continuously and shouted encouraging feedback to Joe—as he had done when he interrupted me—he would be able to string several sentences together in logical order. And so I tried it.

Looking squarely at Joe to catch his gaze, I said, "Joe, you were talking about the kite, remember. Tell me about the kite, Joe."

"I was running along . . ."

"YES," I said loudly, nodding my head.

". . . trying to get the kite to catch the wind . . ."

"YES!"

". . . when the kite got caught on a power line . . ."

"GOOD!"

". . . and 15,000 volts came down the kite string . . ."

"RIGHT!"

". . . and killed me deader than a doorknob . . ."

"YES!"

". . . but my brother called the doctor who lived next door . . ."

"RIGHT!!"

". . . and he resuscitated me . . ."

"GOOD!"

". . . and the ambulance came and took me to the hospital . . ."

"YES! YES!"

". . . and I lived happily ever after." Joe giggled, and poured himself some more beer.

I sat back in amazement. It had worked all right, but frankly I felt like a fool. Here I was, sitting in a public place, shouting and nodding my head violently at a man as if I were the crazy one.

And in a sense, I was. Other people Joe knew—seeing Joe either from a very subjective or a very narrow point of view—behaved "sanely" toward him by giving him "polite" feedback when he tried to talk. And that drove Joe crazy. I gave him "crazy" feedback, and that seemed to help Joe think and talk relatively sanely.

Independent, Dependent, and Intervening Variables

When psychologists perform experiments to test their hypotheses, they typically "do something new or unusual" to some organism or group. Then they sit back to see how the thoughts or actions of the person or persons change.

When you "do something new or unusual" to an individual, you decide on the ways that you are going to *vary* that person's environment. Since you make the choice, this *variable* in the experiment is "independent" of the subject's wishes. Psychologists call "what you do to a subject" in a scientific study the *independent variable* because it is under the experimenter's control.

When you act, people react. The subject's reaction is called the *dependent variable* because the response the person makes obviously depends on what you've done to the individual.

Why do subjects react as they do? We aren't always sure. But when we find that a certain act of ours almost always evokes the same response in someone else, we can sometimes "make hunches." These hunches or hypotheses are our ways of explaining what goes on inside the person's mind or brain that *connects* the act with the reaction. Put another way, we guess at what processes inside the person "intervene" between the independent and dependent variable. Psychologists call these internal processes *intervening variables.*

Suppose you show a young girl a kitten because you want to see how she will react to it. She smiles and pets the animal. "Ah, ha!" you say. "She petted the kitten because she loves cats." Showing the girl the kitten is the *independent variable* because you could have shown her a snake. Smiling and petting are *dependent variables* because her response depended on what you showed her. If you'd shown her a snake, she might have run away. "Love" is an *intervening variable* because it's your explanation of why she responded as she did.

You can *see* kittens and petting behaviors. You *can't see* "love" or "fear" or "insanity." Independent and dependent variables can usually be measured directly and objectively. Intervening variables are "tentative solutions" to the scientific mysteries we try to solve.

In Joe's case, I varied the type of feedback I gave him, which makes that the independent variable in the study. Based on my hunch that his "monitoring" hemisphere wasn't paying sufficient attention to what his "speaking hemisphere" was saying, I predicted what would happen when I varied my actions. That is, I guessed that Joe would be able to speak logically when I gave him strong and constant feedback, but would drift off when I didn't. Joe's response (the dependent variable) was precisely what I had predicted it would be. Thus my hypothesis about what really was going on inside Joe—the intervening variable that explained his reactions—had stood the first test.

Experimental Groups versus Control Groups

But is one such test ever enough? Certainly not! You and I both know that Joe's behavior could have changed for a great many reasons—none of which had anything to do with giving him better feedback.

Surely it would help to make more observations. But what kinds of additional data would we need?

Suppose you and I had been working together as a team. Having gotten this initial success in testing our "hunch," what would we do next? If we had been studying the general subject of "the importance of feedback in maintaining mental concentration," would you be satisfied that we had used just one subject—a young man named Joe? After all, Joe might be a particularly exceptional person and not "representative" of other people at all. So, just to make sure of the *generality* of our hypothesis about feedback, we'd want to find a hundred other Joes with exactly the same problem and try the same thing on them. We would call these 100 Joes our *experimental group,* because we were experimenting (trying something new) on them.

Suppose again that all 100 of our experimental subjects changed the same way that Joe did. Could we now be sure that our hunch was correct?

No, we'd need to find another 100 Joes and study how they reacted when we *didn't* give them appropriate feedback. These subjects would be called our *control group,* or *comparison group,* because we would want to compare their results with those of our experimental group.

To put the matter another way, we would want to give different *inde-*

pendent variables to two groups, hoping that their responses would vary in predictable and *dependable* ways.

Our initial hunch had led us to hypothesize that the "experimental Joes" would almost all be able to concentrate, while the "control Joes" would not. If the behaviors of the two groups differed as we had predicted, then we could place some faith in the *validity* or "realness" of our hunch. (As we will see in many later chapters, the use of control groups is one of the most important features of the scientific method.)

Whenever possible, psychologists like to test their theories or hunches on large numbers of experimental and control subjects—simply because the more subjects we use, the more faith we can have in the "generality" of our results.

Unfortunately, in this case—as with most types of therapy—we have but one Joe to work with.

The A-B-A-B Technique

When psychologists are forced to test their theories on just one subject whose problem may be unique, they often try a technique called "using a subject as her/his own control." Making use of the *own-control method*, we first observe the subject without trying to change the person's behavior (Condition A). Then we do something to the subject (such as giving the person more appropriate feedback) to see how the subject's behavior alters. We call this Condition B.

Since Condition A differs markedly from Condition B, we have the same two independent variables as when we used an experimental group and a control group. But in this case, one person acts as both groups *at different times*.

Next, to make sure that it was the variation in conditions that *caused* the change in the subject's response, we revert back to Condition A in which we observe but don't intervene or interfere. In this case, we'd stop giving the person feedback. If the subject shifts back to the same response the person had previously made in Condition A, then we can be reasonably sure that it was *what we did* that *caused the change*.

However, just to make sure, we often switch back to Condition B for a second time. In dealing with Joe, for instance, we would again nod our heads vigorously and shout "GOOD!" while he was talking. If Joe once more showed increased concentration, we could now be fairly certain that it was the feedback that did the trick—because we had shown that his response *depended* on how we varied what we did. In a very predictable fashion, we could turn his concentration on and off—we merely had to switch from Condition A to Condition B, or from B to A.

Naturally, during therapy, we would shift at once to giving Joe the type of feedback that helped him most. More than this, we would probably want to teach him ways of giving that feedback to himself—and getting it from others.

For obvious reasons, the method of using a subject as his/her own control is often referred to as the *A-B-A-B* technique.

Using Joe as His Own Control

The first time that my giving feedback to Joe helped him to increase his concentration, I really couldn't believe that it had worked so well. So I asked him another question and sat passively while he tried to answer. Joe got the first sentence out beautifully. Then he said, "Uh, er, well . . ." for about 15 seconds, his hands pumping away as if he were trying to force the monitoring half of his brain to behave. Then his mind "jackrabbited," he picked up on the last word in his first sentence, and his second sentence darted off in an entirely different direction from the one I had pointed him toward.

When Joe came to the end of this second sentence, he stammered for a few seconds, his hands chopped the air, and once more he flew off on a tangent.

So I switched again to Condition B. I pulled him back on target and began nodding and shouting "RIGHT" at him loudly every 3 or 4 seconds.

Again he responded by speaking as normally and as sensibly as you and I might speak.

Once more I switched back to Condition A and failed to give Joe strong feedback when I asked him a question. And once more he jumped all over the place verbally as he tried to answer. But as soon as I started responding vigorously, he regained his concentration.

So far, so good. But there was one more hunch I wanted to test, so I asked Joe yet another question. But this time, instead of nodding my head and shouting encouragement, I leaned across the table and tapped Joe rhythmically on his right arm. Each time he said a word or two, I struck his arm lightly with my finger. He spoke quite logically and coherently—as long as I tapped. As soon as I stopped, he drifted off almost immediately.

By now I was reasonably convinced that—particularly when he was a little intoxicated—Joe's "monitoring brain" simply wasn't able to do its normal job. Perhaps Joe's brain damage got in the way. Or perhaps his "monitoring hemisphere" simply hadn't learned to shout loudly enough to get through to the talking half of his brain. Whatever the case, the conscious part of Joe's mind wasn't getting the *internal* feedback it needed in order to talk logically. Thus at the moment, Joe needed very strong *external* feedback in order to think and speak normally.

What You Can Learn from Joe— and from This Book

Sigmund Freud is perhaps the most influential psychologist who ever lived. Freud was primarily a therapist—he conducted few laboratory studies on humans in which he used an "experimental group" and a "control group." But he performed hundreds of "clinical studies" in which he noted how his patients reacted when he presented them with new ideas and insights. Freud built his famous Theory of Psycho-Analysis from his studies of his patients, and he often said that we learn about the normal from studying the abnormal. As I sat watching Joe's behavior flip-flop so predictably when I switched from Condition A to Condition B, I realized how insightful Freud's comment was.

Most of us take it for granted that we can think and speak logically. Because we are so accustomed to this behavior, we seldom stop to see it for the miracle it is. Thus we miss the fact that *all of us* surely need some kind of internal or external feedback in order to make sure that we are saying what we ought to say (or behaving the way that people think we ought to behave). It is only when someone as unusual as Joe comes along that we are forced to see ourselves in a new light.

You will find few "great insights" in this book. That is to say, learning about psychology is not generally a matter of finding a set of magic keys that will unlock the "secrets of your mind."

Rather, learning about psychology is a matter of discovering thousands of things that you've been doing and thinking and feeling all your life, but were never really aware of. For example, in the section on social behavior, you will learn that your flow of conversation is often strongly influenced by the responses made by the person you're talking to. In Chapter 4 you will find out something about the many kinds of feedback you need in order to achieve your personal goals. In Chapter 5 you will discover that in order to understand yourself better, you must be able to see yourself from a biological, an intra-psychic, and a social/behavioral viewpoint—*all at the same time*. This is the "holism" we are in search of.

And throughout the book you will encounter many facts suggesting that, whether you're trying to understand one person, like Joe, or studying a hundred Joes in an experimental group—being objective about people and using the scientific method in order to help solve their problems is often a very useful approach.

The Author's Biases

One other thing that you will find in this book is that, like all other teachers, I have my own set of biases or subjective viewpoints about people and psychology. I've mentioned some of these prejudices already. But there are others you should be aware of too, if you are to be able to read this book both with subjective enjoyment, and with objective understanding.

James V. McConnell.

1. To begin with, I believe the study of human behavior is the most fascinating, most awe-inspiring, most important occupation imaginable. I hope that some of my enthusiasm for psychology rubs off on you by the time you finish the book, for it is the greatest gift I can give you.

2. I believe that learning should be made as rewarding as possible; indeed, that learning should be both challenging and fun. One way I can make reading this book a pleasant experience is by making it as interesting as possible. My way of doing that is to focus on the life experiences of real people (such as Joe), and to use these real people as examples. I teach by analogy, by telling stories. To quote again from Sigmund Freud, "Analogies prove nothing, but they do make us feel at home." Freud might have added that analogies or examples also make a marvelous instructional technique.

Psychologists have long known that students remember best that part of a course which is most dramatic, most stimulating. So I have begun and ended each chapter with a story or a case history built around the lives of real or imagined human beings. Some of the stories actually happened; a few are pure fiction; most of them are mixtures of fact and imagination. You may find that you can *understand* the people in the stories much better after you have read the scientific material that comes between the opening and closing fiction. But understanding is of little value if you don't remember what you've learned. So one of my purposes in printing the stories is to reward you for trying to remember the factual material.

However, as we will see in Chapter 12, what is motivating and rewarding to one person may be punishing to another. If you are not fond of fiction, you might ask your teacher if you could skip some of the stories.

3. Some of us like to be coaxed into learning, while some of us prefer to be confronted and challenged. At various points, I have included "thought questions" that often are not answered directly in the text. The purpose of these questions is to push your mind beyond the facts on the printed page. I can't imagine a better intellectual challenge than that. However, if you find these questions a bore, or if the answers don't come easily, either pass the questions by or ask your instructor to help you.

4. As you will see as you read along, I place a great deal more faith in facts than I do in theories and opinions. Most arguments in science revolve around speculations and interpretations of data—not around the data themselves.

It often happens that the objective, repeatable facts discovered by one scientist come into collision with subjective viewpoints and theories held by another scientist. In almost all such cases, the facts will eventually triumph over the theories. Why? Because, in the long run, the facts give us the power to understand ourselves and the world better. In brief, you usually must gather data first, then try to understand the meaning of those data. If you try to understand before you have enough facts, you run the danger of seeing what you want to see—instead of seeing what is objectively *there*.

Here's another reason why facts are important. They give us the power to change ourselves and our environments. Often we find things that "work" long before we understand *why* they work as they do. For instance, we knew that aspirin helped reduce headaches for a century before we had even the foggiest notion of why aspirin was a pain-killer. For another

Clinical psychologists often perform experimental studies based on just one person.

instance, in talking with Joe I found that feedback "worked" to help him concentrate—but I still haven't the vaguest idea of what the damage in his brain was really like.

5. There are two ways of gathering facts—*actively* and *passively*. Sometimes you simply look at the world passively and record what you see as objectively as you can. But since you can't control the events you're watching, you simply have to take whatever data the world gives you.

The active way of gathering data involves making some predictable change in the way the world operates. This active or "experimental" method gives you much more control over what happens, and therefore in the long run gives you much more data to work with.

I will describe many types of active experimentation in this book. Some of these interventions—such as the techniques I tried on Joe—are informal or "clinical" studies which occur in real-life settings. Other experiments— such as those conducted in scientific laboratories or field settings, or which involve giving tests or questionnaires to large numbers of subjects—are very formal and follow well-known sets of rules.

Both clinical and experimental studies are necessary, because they give us different types of facts. And both types of studies are really attempts at "solving psychological mysteries." Clinical studies tell us a lot about a single person or subject, but don't necessarily give us data that are true of people in general. Experimental studies typically tell us something about people in general, but we cannot always apply these data meaningfully to one particular individual whom we happen to be interested in.

6. The scientific method is one of humanity's most glorious achievements. It is surely the most powerful way we have of determining objective facts and of testing our theoretical notions about why people act and think and feel as they do.

You have theories about human behavior, just as I do. Unless you have studied psychology before, the chances are very good that your present theories are based more on your subjective impressions than on objective data. Thus you may find that many of your feelings or theories about yourself and others are challenged or contradicted by the facts presented in this textbook. I do not ask that you give up your present views, merely that you try to examine afresh your notions about people in the light of what new information this book gives you. When I met Joe, his behaviors forced me to re-examine many of my own notions about what controls "logical thought patterns" and "mental concentration" in normal people. I would hope that, when you meet people like Joe in this book, you too will be willing to look at them with as little bias and prejudice as possible.

But a steady diet of objectivity lacks both spice and nourishment, and science is but *one part of human experience*. I looked at Joe objectively, true; but I wouldn't have bothered trying to understand and help him if I had not liked him subjectively as a human being. When I wear the white lab coat of a behavioral scientist, I prefer to study organisms (including people like Joe) through unclouded eyes rather than through rose-colored glasses. But most of the time I put my starched white laboratory coat aside and play the role of teacher, friend, poet, lover, or merely that of an ordinary citizen with the usual quota of virtues and vices.

It seems to me that one major benefit of studying psychology is that it gives you greater freedom and choice in how you behave. Most of the time you will see yourself and others from a subjective, value-laden point of view. But if you've learned your psychology lessons well, you can do something most others can't—namely, you can stand back and look at things objectively *if and when* doing so will be of some benefit to you and the people around you.

7. In my subjective life, I am an incurable optimist. I believe that, through the wise and humane application of the *holistic approach*, we can all come closer to achieving our personal goals in life. And with luck we can also help make the world a more rewarding and less desperate place in which to live. (This moral viewpoint, like most others, rests on faith as well as on science; but it is a faith that is shared by most psychologists or they wouldn't *be* psychologists.)

I also believe in personal responsibility and in the notion that you must pay for what you get in life—that we all suffer the consequences of our actions. A psychologist can tell you how to get good grades in school, how to get along better with your parents and friends, how to achieve a greater degree of self-actualization and personal happiness, and perhaps even help you be more successful in business if you're interested. But advice is the smallest coin in circulation. You won't get A's, or happiness, or money, or maturity unless you are willing to put forth the effort to do so on your own, to make the most of what you have and what you know.

All of which brings us back to Joe again.

Getting It All Together

Joe wanted desperately to get better, so that he wouldn't have to return to the mental hospital. Once we learned about the problems he had in paying attention to his own behavior, I could give him some suggestions about what he had to do to solve his problems. I could help him plan his goals, plot his progress, and I could give him encouragement.

But Joe—and only Joe—was the one who had to put it all together. That is, it was his personal responsibility to make the necessary changes in his thoughts and actions.

We started simply. I told him what I had been doing while we talked— that is, I showed him how I had been giving him "strong feedback" to help him keep his thoughts on target. I suggested that, when he had "died," he might have lost the neural circuits that let the "speaking half" and the "monitoring half" of his brain work together most effectively. But I was confident that, if he tried hard enough, he could learn how to use other (undamaged) parts of his brain to generate the internal feedback that he needed in order to concentrate. And after he "got it all together" inside his own head, he could then go on to the even more challenging task of learning how to get along better with other people.

Teaching Joe to listen to himself while talking turned out to be fairly easy. The next time we met, I recorded our conversation on tape. After he tried to answer a question, or tell a story, I played back what he had said so he could hear his own voice. I suggested that he use his left hand to tap on his right arm while he talked (you'll understand why I did this after you read Chapter 2).

Although he found it a tiring experience at first, Joe soon acquired some of the self-monitoring skills he needed. At the start, he had to pound on his right arm rather vigorously to keep himself on track. Later, he began to "fade out" the arm-tapping. Eventually just nodding his head or gently clenching one of his fists was enough to get him through a long sequence of sentences—even when he was a trifle intoxicated.

Then, without any help from me, Joe began to make some significant changes in the way he lived. He started getting up early every day so that he could look for work. When he did find temporary employment, he set goals for himself daily and tried to keep to them by drawing a graph showing his progress.

However, helping Joe learn how to get along with other people turned out to be fairly difficult. He could still get almost anything he wanted from his parents by "acting crazy" or by throwing a temper tantrum. More than this, even when he did try to act differently toward his parents, they continued to treat him as if he were hopelessly brain-damaged and incapable of showing much improvement (outside of being hospitalized).

Finally, without telling me, he simply packed up his bags and headed for the Coast. He called me a few days after he got there.

"I wanted to do it on my own," he said over the phone. "And my parents just wouldn't let me. So I came out here. Uh, I think it's bound to work, because out here, they don't know me as 'crazy Joey,' I'm just plain Joe."

"You're not plain at all, Joe. You're rather special."

"Yeah, but I want to be special-good, not special-crazy, if you know what I mean."

I did. And he is. You can spend your whole professional life as a psychologist without finding anyone who teaches you as much about human behavior as Joe taught me. Surely I owe him a great deal more than he ever owed me.

Joe told me that he had called his parents when he arrived on the Coast. They were relieved to find out that he was all right, and promised to help him financially if he got a job. So he did that too. The last time I heard from him he was doing pretty well. He told me that he hoped to come back home some day—but not until he was sure he could prove to his parents that he really had "gotten it all together."

Just before we finished our last conversation, I asked him what he liked most about life now.

"Being in control," he responded. "Even if I have to clench my fist now and then to keep things going straight, I'm doing what I want to do because I know what I'm doing. I know what my body is doing, I know what my head is doing, and I pay attention to what other people are doing to me and what I'm doing to them. Um, knowing about yourself, it's a great feeling. I really enjoy it lot."

And, at a very practical and personal level, that's what understanding human behavior is all about.

I hope you enjoy it too.

Recommended Readings

At the end of each chapter, I will list several books or articles that you might wish to read if you want to go into the content of that chapter more deeply. A more detailed list of readings (chapter by chapter) appears at the end of the book.

You may also wish to look over the references that are mentioned in the *Student Manual to Understanding Human Behavior*, by Al Siebert and Tim Walter, that accompanies this textbook. The *Student Manual* also contains many helpful hints on how to study for examinations, how to organize your time, and how to get involved in psychology by doing studies and experiments on your own. If you are having difficulties with any of the courses you are taking, or if you aren't getting as good grades as you think you ought to be getting, you might find the *Student Manual* of practical value. There is a separate manual for those of you taking the course on television or as a personalized course of instruction.

There are also several general source materials that you might wish to investigate. One of the most useful I know of is *The Encyclopedia of Human Behavior* by Robert M. Goldenson (Garden City, N.Y.: Doubleday & Company, 1970). General references, such as the *Encyclopedia Britannica*, contain a surprisingly large number of articles on psychological topics, most of which are written by acknowledged experts.

Psychology Today and *Behavior Today* are far and away the best popular magazines dealing with behavioral topics. There are also dozens of scientific journals, most of which focus on one particular aspect of human or animal behavior. Any psychology teacher or librarian will surely be happy to help you find the journal most interesting to you.

1

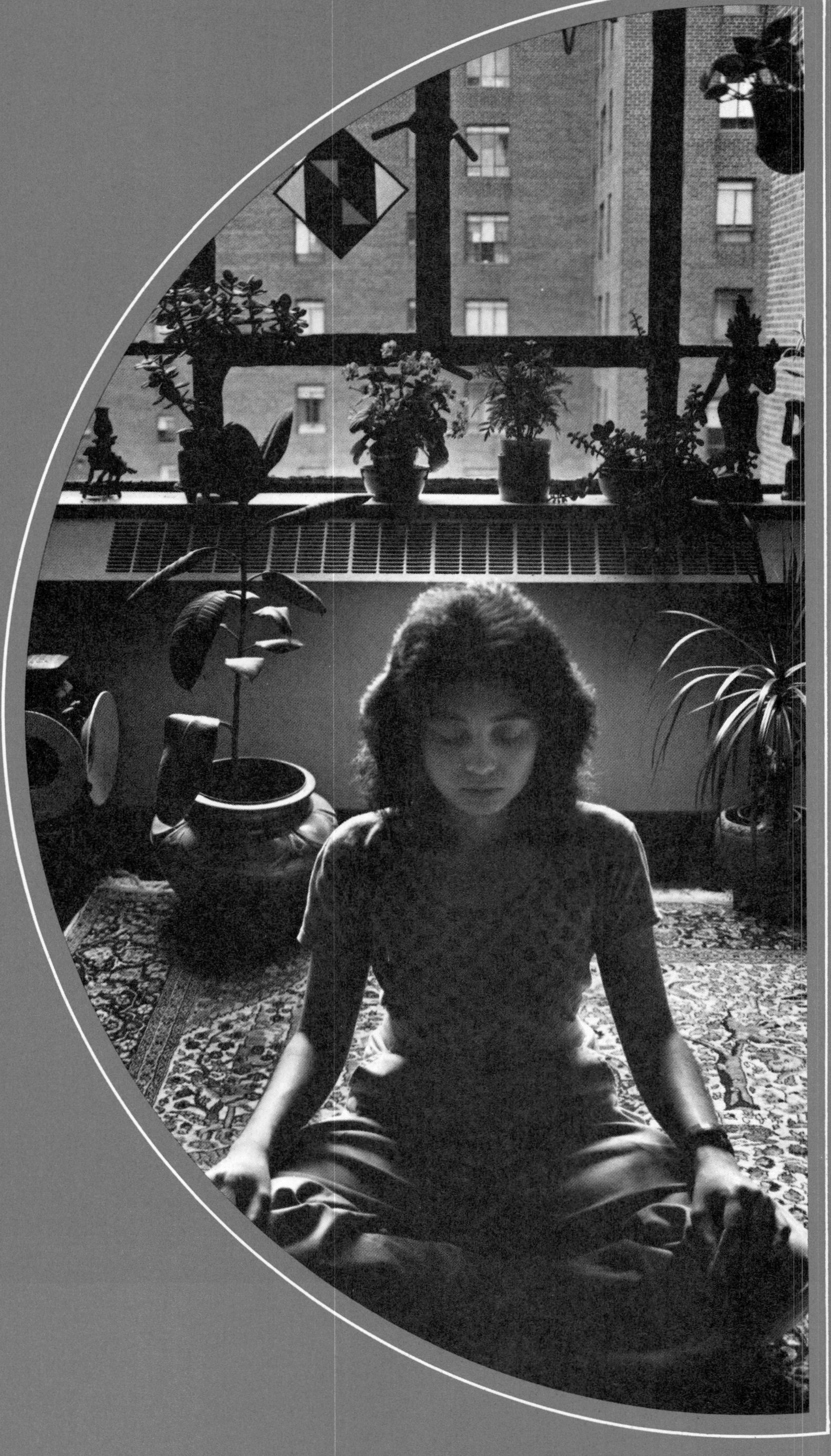

Biological
Bases of
Behavior

The
Brain

Did You Know That . . .

Your brain looks something like a wrinkled mushroom?

Your brain contains at least 15 billion nerve cells (neurons)?

The cortex, or outer layer of your brain, contains most of the "decision-making centers" that influence what you do, feel, and think?

The major psychological function of your brain is to process information?

Some four million people in the United States suffer from epilepsy?

When a nerve cell (neuron) in your brain is excited, a wave of electrical energy sweeps down the neuron from one end to another?

Brain waves are the result of the electrical excitation occurring in thousands or even millions of your brain cells?

The left half of your brain is a mirror image of the right half in most respects?

If you are right-handed, the left half or hemisphere of your brain is usually dominant and controls the right half of your body?

If you are right-handed, your left hemisphere contains your "speech center," and seems responsible for most language and "logical thinking?"

If you are right-handed, your right hemisphere seems primarily responsible for "creative thinking" and for some aspects of your emotional reactions?

If a surgeon separated the two hemispheres of your brain, you might end up with two quite separate and distinct "minds" or "personalities" inside your skull?

Patients suffering from schizophrenia process information primarily with their left hemispheres and block out inputs from their right (emotional) hemispheres?

"On the Other Hand"

"Young man, you are an epileptic?"

Patrick looked the woman over carefully. Her closely cropped white hair was peppered with black, rather like ashes sprinkled on fresh snow. She was wearing a colonel's uniform with lots of gold braid on it. The other soldiers seemed to be a little afraid of her, so Pat guessed she was a pretty important person. But Dr. Tavela had told him not to fear people just because they wore fancy uniforms. So Pat looked straight at the woman and said, "I used to be."

Colonel Garcia picked up a yellow pencil and began tapping it slowly on her desk. She looked squarely at the teenaged youth sitting in front of her for a moment, then said, "Before Dr. Tavela operated on you, then, you were subject to epileptic attacks?"

"Yes."

"These attacks occurred frequently?"

Pat shivered a bit, then ran his fingers nervously over the plaster cast on his left hand. It had been six weeks now since he had last felt the "aura," that strange feeling of impending doom which hit him each time just before he had a seizure. He had gone six weeks now without the headaches—without once losing consciousness, falling to the floor, and embarrassing himself by "having a fit." Despite the bandages on his head and all the terrible things that had happened since his operation, Pat felt so different now that he tried not to think of what the seizures had been like. But since she asked, Pat answered truthfully. "The attacks came several times a day, sometimes."

Colonel Garcia turned to the officer sitting beside Patrick in front of her desk. "Captain Hartman, this has been confirmed?"

The blond-haired man nodded quickly. "Yes, Colonel. When Patrick was three, he contracted a severe fever, which caused considerable damage to his cortex. We have tested him on the EEG machine. Abnormal, spike-shaped brain waves show up in the motor areas of his right hemisphere. *Grand mal* epileptic seizures are almost always associated with 'spikes' in the motor cortex."

"Yes, of course," the woman responded, gazing back at Patrick. "And after the operation, you have been free of these attacks?"

Pat tried to smile politely. "Yes, ma'am."

"Then how did you hurt your left hand?"

Pat rubbed his right hand over the plaster cast covering his entire left forearm. Only the tips of his fingers were free of the plaster. "After the operation, I couldn't walk very well at first. I fell and broke my hand."

Colonel Garcia looked back at Captain Hartman. "This too is confirmed?"

"Yes, Colonel. The X-rays show a compound fracture of the metacarpal bone. The wound is about three weeks old. Patrick will not be able to use his left hand freely for another month or so—except to scratch his nose."

Patrick gently rubbed a finger along the side of his nose.

"Was Dr. Tavela angry with you for breaking your hand?" the woman asked.

Patrick frowned. "He was angry because he said I might have hurt my head. But then, just before he left, he smiled and said it was a good sign."

"A sign of your recovery?"

Pat thought about it a moment. "He really didn't say."

"I wish he had," Colonel Garcia said, and then breathed a deep sigh. "Patrick, although Dr. Tavela lived in a foreign country, he was our friend."

Pat interrupted. "You mean he was your spy. Anyhow, that's what the secret police said when they questioned me."

Colonel Garcia glanced uneasily at Captain Hartman, then back at the boy. "You know Dr. Tavela was a good man, and he would want you to

PART ONE Biological Bases of Behavior

cooperate with us. I know you have told your story many times, Patrick. But I would like to hear it again. Tell me everything that happened, if you don't mind."

The young man shrugged his shoulders. "I don't mind."

"First, why were you sent to see a surgeon in a foreign country? Are there no good physicians here?"

"Because they said that Dr. Tavela was the only doctor in the world who did the sort of operation I needed."

"Dr. Tavela was a brilliant neurosurgeon," Colonel Garcia said, a wan smile on her face. "It's likely he knew as much about the workings of the brain as any man did. Before he died, of course."

Pat nodded. "Anyhow, after I got to his clinic, he gave me a lot of tests for a week or so, and then my seizures got real bad. He said it was the stress that made them worse. Anyhow, they shaved my head and put me to sleep and he cut out the tissue that made me sick."

"How soon afterward could you get up out of bed?"

"After a few days. Just to go to the bathroom. I guess it was a week or so before I could really walk much."

Colonel Garcia nodded and then continued. "You said Dr. Tavela gave you some tests before the operation. Did he test you afterward?"

"Yeah. He had this sort of mask that I looked into. It blocked off part of what I could see. Then he showed me things and asked what they were."

The woman smiled with growing excitement. "What sort of things did he show you?"

"Oh, pictures of cows and horses. Circles and squares. Things like that. Sometimes he showed me printed words and asked me to read them. Sometimes he put earphones on my ears and asked me to do things or say things."

"What kind of things?"

"Oh, point at a circle, or say words like 'cat' and 'dog.'"

Colonel Garcia leaned forward eagerly. "And perhaps he showed you some letters and numbers, perhaps he talked about a chemical formula?"

Pat laughed. "That's what the secret police asked, too. Did I know anything about chemistry? And did Dr. Tavela read me the name of a formula, or anything like that?"

"And you said . . ."

"I said that he never read anything to me except the Bible. Mostly Proverbs."

"Why Proverbs?"

Patrick had never thought to question the actions of the adults around him. "I don't know. He seemed to like them. He said they contained all the wisdom of Solomon."

A startled look appeared on Captain Hartman's face. "Colonel . . ."

The woman interrupted. "Yes, Captain, I know. Tavela's first name was Solomon. You will please get a copy of the Bible from the library."

Captain Hartman rose and left the room.

Putting the pencil carefully down on her desk, Colonel Garcia continued. "Patrick, just before Dr. Tavela was killed by the secret police, someone brought him a copy of a very important secret formula."

"That would be the funny little man in the dark overcoat, I suppose," Patrick said, trying to be helpful.

"Perhaps so, Patrick. Tell me about him."

Pat rubbed the cast on his left hand against his stomach, then picked at one of the bandages on his head with his right hand. "It was that last day, you know, the day the secret police came and . . . and . . ."

"I know. Go on, please."

"Well, I had the earphones on and was looking into the mask. Dr. Tavela was showing me some pictures and asking me questions over the earphones. Sometimes it hurt a little."

"Hurt?"

"Yeah. My ears. Sometimes he would whisper in one ear while he was making a very loud noise in the other. The noise hurt sometimes."

"What did he whisper to you, Patrick?"

Pat sighed. "I couldn't hear most of the time because of the noise. I guess he asked me to point to something, sometimes with my left hand, sometimes with my right."

"But your left hand is in a cast."

"I can point with my fingers," Pat said, poking his left index finger at the pencil on the woman's desk to demonstrate his abilities. "That wasn't the problem."

"What was the problem, Patrick?"

"You're going to think this is pretty funny. I could *do* what he told me to do over the earphones. I pointed my left fingers at the thing he wanted me to touch. But I never was sure what it was he had asked me to do, even when I did it just like he said to do it." The young man stopped, a puzzled look on his face. "I mean, how can you *do* something when you don't know what it is you're supposed to be doing?"

Colonel Garcia frowned, as if she wasn't sure what to make of this. Then she said, "Tell me about the man in the overcoat, please."

"Well, Dr. Tavela was testing me when this man came into the lab. He looked nervous and excited, I guess. He pulled on Dr. Tavela's arm, and they went out of the room for a while. Then, when Dr. Tavela came back, he was awfully excited too. He said that something good had happened, that he had been waiting a long time for it, and now it had happened." Patrick's left hand reached out and touched the pencil again, almost unconsciously.

"And then . . ."

"And then he said we had some work to do. So he whispered to me for a long time, maybe half an hour or so, and had me point to things again and again."

Colonel Garcia leaned forward. "What sort of things, Patrick? Numbers and letters?"

"That's what the secret police asked, but I don't know. I really don't!" Patrick's voice cracked with emotion. "I couldn't see the things, I just pointed to them with my left hand. The usual cat and dog pictures, I guess. That's what we usually worked on."

"You told the secret police about this?"

"Of course, but they didn't believe me at first. So they hooked me up to a polly . . . a polly . . ."

"A polygraph, Patrick. That's what you would call a 'lie detector.'"

"Yeah, well, they stuck this wet, metal thing on the palm of my right hand. It was connected with wires to a machine that made squiggles on a sheet of paper. And they asked me questions and looked at the squiggles." Patrick sighed deeply. "They did it for hours and hours and hours. One man kept insisting that I was lying and said they ought to give me a whipping for lying so much."

"Did they punish you?"

Patrick shook his head. "No, the other man kept saying that the squiggles showed I was telling the truth. And I was!"

Colonel Garcia nodded sympathetically. "I believe you, Patrick. You see, the secret police thought that Dr. Tavela had given you the formula. We put a lot of pressure on them to get you back home, but they wouldn't release you until they made sure that you didn't know what it was."

The woman picked up the pencil again and tapped it nervously. "But he must have known they would arrest him shortly, and I'll bet a million dollars he told you something. He must have hidden some clue deep within your brain, where the secret police couldn't find it, but we could."

"He didn't tell me anything, ma'am." Patrick started to cry a little. "Except, when the police came to the door to get him, he told me to be brave, and tell the truth. He said he was glad I had broken my hand, and that whenever I was troubled, I should read the Bible and seek out understanding."

Captain Hartman entered the Colonel's office bearing a tattered book. "You'd be surprised how difficult it was to find a copy of the Bible around this place," he said, handing the book to the woman.

Colonel Garcia gave the man a bemused look, then turned to Patrick. "What part of Proverbs did Dr. Tavela read to you the most?"

"The third chapter, I think it was."

The woman leafed through the book, found a place, then began to read. "'Happy is the man that findeth wisdom, and the man that getteth understanding.'" The woman looked at the boy. "Is that the part?"

"Further on, I think."

"'Understanding is more precious than rubies: And all the things thou canst desire are not to be compared unto her. Length of days is in her right hand; and in her left hand riches and honor.'"

Patrick became excited. "Yes, that's it. He read that verse to me several times."

Colonel Garcia put the Bible face down on the desk, and picked up the pencil in her right hand. She tapped it gently on the desk, again and again. After a moment she stared at Patrick's left hand, encased as it was in the plaster cast. She gazed intently at the bandages on his shaven head. Next she looked at the innocent smile on the young man's face.

Then she laughed warmly, jubilantly. "Of course!" she said loudly.

Captain Hartman was startled. "Have you found the secret, Colonel?"

"Of course I have, Captain. Where the secret police failed, I have succeeded. Thanks to Dr. Tavela's clue from the Bible, and my knowledge of Patrick's problems, I know the truth." She got up and walked around the desk, pulling up a chair to sit by Patrick. She hugged him in her arms momentarily, then gently touched his head.

"What an appropriate place to hide a secret," she said.

(Continued on page 56.)

Most texts have word lists or glossaries at the end of the book that give definitions of technical terms. Such glossaries are often difficult to use, and few of them tell you how to say the word aloud. The outer margin of each page in this book is reserved for definitions and explanations of the sometimes complicated words or phrases you may encounter in each chapter. Every time you see a **boldfaced** word on a page, you will know that the word is defined (and often a pronunciation given) in the margin.

If you already understand the boldfaced word, don't bother checking it out immediately in the "margin glossary." However, if you have any doubts about the meaning of the word, or about how to pronounce it—or if you are interested in the Latin or Greek derivation of the term—you may wish to check the item at once, without having to lose your place by turning to the back of the book.

Also, when you study for an examination, you may find it helpful to check all the terms in the margins, since many of the key words or thoughts will be defined in this "continuous glossary." Many of these same key words will also be **boldfaced** in the summary that appears at the end of most chapters.

If you encounter a word you don't understand that is *not* defined in the margins, please check the index at the end of the book to see if the word is defined elsewhere in the text. You might note that there is *both* an index of people's names and an index of subjects at the end of the book.

Any dictionary contains thousands of words that you know, as well as thousands that you don't know. I hope you will use the continuous glossary in the margins as you would a dictionary, and that you won't be upset if terms are defined that you think every student ought to be familiar with. Both the first and second editions of this text were read by several hundred students who were asked to circle every word they didn't understand. The words I have selected for defini-

Your Brain

Your brain is the master organ of your body. During open heart surgery, a machine can take over for your heart, as a machine can act in place of your kidneys. But even with mechanical methods of cleaning and pumping your blood, you remain YOU—which is to say that your thoughts, dreams, hopes, and general behavior patterns aren't much affected by mechanical substitutes for most of your bodily functions.

However, even the most *tiny damage* to certain critical parts of your brain can cause you to lose consciousness for the rest of your life. More extensive damage may even turn you from a peaceful, normal, intelligent human being into a mentally abnormal or violent individual. For your brain controls most of the rest of your body: It is the seat of your consciousness—the locus of your intelligence, your compassion, your creativity—and their ugly opposites. Every thought you have, every emotion, every feeling, every movement of your body is affected by the functioning of your brain.

In a very real sense, then, your brain is YOU. But what is this all-important, master organ like?

Inputs, Internal Processes, Outputs

If you like analogies, consider this one for a moment. In a very limited sense, your brain is like a wrinkled mushroom that is packed tightly inside a bony shell we call the skull (see Fig. 2.1). Not counting the skull, your brain weighs about 1.3 kilograms (3 pounds). It is made up of more than 15 billion (15,000,000,000) nerve cells. The physiological activities of these nerve cells help determine what you think and feel and learn and do. But these nerve cells—or **neurons,** as they are called—do not all have the same tasks to perform. Your neurons can function independently, or they can cooperate to achieve some common goal, rather like the employees of a large corporation.

As we will see in Chapter 5, psychologists often consider business organizations to be "complex social systems," much as your brain and heart are "complex living systems." All living systems have three types of functions—**inputs, internal activities,** and **outputs.**

A large manufacturing company, such as Ford, takes in orders from customers and purchases raw materials. These are its inputs. The cars that Ford produces are its outputs. But as you know, it takes more than internal processes and muscular reactions to turn orders and raw materials into the shiny Mustangs and Mercuries that Ford turns out by the millions. It also takes "brainy" decision making. The management at Ford must decide what kinds of automobiles to produce, hire the right number of skilled workers, advertise its products, pay taxes, undertake research of various kinds, and worry about solving pollution problems. Decision making is an "internal activity" in a social organization just as it is an "internal process" in your brain.

tion are those that *at least* 10 percent of these students weren't sure of—including some terms that have no direct connection with the science of psychology. This book is for everybody—for people with large vocabularies and for people with limited knowledge but a large desire to learn. If you know most of the words defined in the margins, congratulations! However, you should remember that the person sitting next to you in class may not be as fortunate, and may need all the help any of us can give.

The pronunciations given with the definitions are in the "Midwest dialect" that is used by many radio and television announcers and newscasters. Pronunciations of many words vary from one part of the country to another. If you have doubts about how to say a word, please ask your teacher about it.

Neuron (pronounced NEW-ron). A single nerve cell.

Inputs, internal activities, and outputs. The three functions of all living systems. Food is a type of input that your stomach digests (internal activity) and converts into energy so that you can think and behave (outputs). The remains of the food are also released as waste products (outputs).

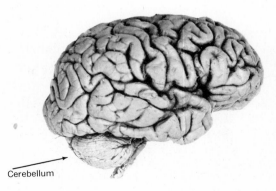

Cerebellum

Fig. 2.1. The human brain, viewed from the right. The *cerebellum* (a Latin word meaning "little brain") at the bottom of the photograph is not a part of the cerebrum, but rather is one of the "lower centers." The cerebellum is involved in coordinating such complex movements as walking, playing the piano, driving a car, and so on.

Internal Processing and Decision Making   Ford could not survive unless its management team was organized into various levels or types of decision making. At the top of the pecking order sit the executive officers, who issue orders to "middle-level management." The men and women in middle-level management supervise the various internal functions that keep the organization alive and carry out the orders they receive from top management. Middle-level managers also send messages up to the executive officers to let them know how things in the factories are going.

At the bottom of the management pecking order are the front-line supervisors and workers who actually receive messages from the outside world, process them, and send them up the chain of command. Inputs to the Ford corporation, then, typically are screened by lower-level people before being sent up the management chain for action. For instance, the president of Ford doesn't usually answer his own phone or open his own mail—these tasks are performed by people much lower on the management ladder.

Other front-line workers produce most of the actual "outputs" of the car company, although, for the most part, they work and produce according to instructions they receive from higher management.

Your Cortex   Your brain is a living system too, which is organized in "levels" much as is Ford. It has its own unique kinds of inputs, internal activities, and outputs. For instance, a large collection of neurons (nerve cells) gathered together at the very top of your brain acts very much as do the top managers in any large corporation. These neurons make up what is called the **cortex** of your brain. (Since we will use this term often, perhaps you should know that *cortex* is the Latin word for the "bark" of a tree or the "peel" or "skin" of a mushroom.)

The outer skin of a mushroom is often darker and tougher than the tissue inside, just as the cortex, or outer layer of your brain, is different from the neurons inside. Your cortex contains millions of very special neurons that seem to be intimately related to your "stream of consciousness," or your moment-to-moment thoughts. It is mostly in your cortex that conscious decisions are made about what your own "corporation" (the Latin word *corpus* actually means "body") is going to do.

It is sometimes said that top management is the "brains" of any corporation. In the same sense we may say that your cortex is the "top management" of your brain.

Sensory and Motor Pathways   Information about the outside world flows into your cortex along a number of routes called **sensory pathways.** Your eyes, ears, nose, tongue, and skin all send messages to your cortex about what is happening around you—and inside you. These inputs go first to the lower parts of your brain, and then to your cortex. Your cortex pays attention to this incoming sensory information, checks its memory files, and then decides what you should do or think or feel in a given situation. *Attending, checking memory files,* and *making decisions* are your cortex's way of *processing* sensory information.

Once your cortical "top management" has processed an input and decided on a response, it sends command messages along **motor pathways** to your body's muscles and glands, which tells them how to react. And just as Ford's top management has the means of checking up on the activities of its employees, so your body has ways of feeding back information to your cortex on what your muscles and glands are doing.

Lying beneath your cortex are a large number of "middle-management" **neural sub-centers** that are quite capable of controlling most of the biological functions of your body on their own if need be, as when you are asleep or lost in heavy thought. For example, when you decide to walk to class, are you conscious of each tiny movement that the muscles in your legs and feet must make to get you there? Surely not, for you would be hard-pressed to keep up with the millions of different neural commands that the lower centers in your brain must issue to your muscles each time

Cortex (CORE-tex). The thin outer layer of the brain, about 0.6 centimeters (¼ inch) thick. The millions of nerve cells (neurons) in your cortex influence most of what you think, feel, and do.

Sensory pathways. Bundles of nerves rather like telephone cables that feed information about the outside world (inputs) into your brain for processing.

Motor pathways. In physiological or biological terms, the word "motor" means "muscular," or "having to do with movement." The motor pathways are bundles of nerves rather like telephone cables that run from your brain out to your muscles (also called "output pathways").

Neural sub-centers. The word "neural" (NEW-ral) means "having to do with neurons or nerve cells." Certain groups or "centers" of neurons in your brain have highly specific functions, unlike those of any other part of your brain. For instance, one neural sub-center called the "thalamus" acts as a sort of "switchboard" through which most input messages pass before reaching your cortex. The thalamus is called a *sub*-center because it is "lower" than your cortex, which is the "highest" part of your brain.

you take a simple stroll. However, these sub-units or "lower" brain centers do send "memos" to your cortex telling it what is going on. And in emergency situations, your cortex may assume direct and voluntary control of what you are doing.

But for the most part, your cortical "top management" (your conscious mind) is free to dream and scheme as it wishes, leaving most of your physical behavior to be directly controlled and monitored by the lower parts of your brain.

Question: If your cortex had to consciously think about keeping your heart pumping and your lungs breathing, what would happen when you went to sleep at night?

Physical Structure of Your Brain   Most of us dislike or are "put off" by having to learn about our bodies—perhaps because we never realize that the *structure* of our brains greatly influences the *shape* of our thoughts, feelings, and actions.

If you would like to get a better feel for the physical structure of your brain, you might try this little **demonstration.** Pause for a moment and go look at yourself in a mirror. Draw an imaginary line across the front of your face running from your left ear through both your eyebrows to your right ear (see Fig. 2.2). The bulk of your brain is located above this line.

If by some magic the flesh and bone of your head could be made invisible, you would see the front part of your brain as you stared into the mirror. Viewed this way, your brain would look much like the mountain ranges along the California coast as seen from an airplane. That is, your brain would appear to be a series of rounded hills with deep valleys in between.

The outer crust of this brainy landscape is, as we said, the *cortex.* It is about 0.65 centimeters (¼ inch) thick. This cortical rind or peel covers the biggest part of your brain, which is called the **cerebrum** (from the Latin word for "brain").

Your cerebrum sits on top of the rest of your brain much as the huge cap of a mushroom sits on top of its skinny stem. Sensory inputs flow up the narrow stem of your brain to your cerebrum. Your lower brain centers do the "preliminary processing" of this incoming information, acting on some inputs but sending most of them to your cortex for final decision making. Output commands from your cortex flow down the stem again to your muscles and glands (see Fig. 2.3). If you could look at your brain from the top, all you would see would be the cortical covering, or the cap of the cerebral mushroom—the lower centers, or sub-units, are all buried deep in your cerebrum or in the stem itself.

In evolutionary terms, the cerebrum has been the last part of the brain to develop. If you inspected the brains of lower animals, you would find that a human has a better-developed cerebrum than a monkey, that a

Fig. 2.2. Your brain viewed in an imaginary mirror.

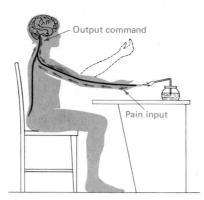

Fig. 2.3. When a child's finger touches a hot object, a "pain input" is flashed up the nerves in the child's arm, to the spinal cord, and thence to the brain. The brain "processes" this input immediately, and sends an "output message" down the spinal cord ordering the muscles in the child's arm to move away from the object.

monkey has more cerebral tissue than a dog, a dog more than a rat, a rat more than a pigeon, and a pigeon more than a goldfish (see Fig. 2.4). Most psychologists believe that, in general terms, the better developed an animal's cerebrum is, the more complex its behavior patterns are likely to be.

Very simple animals, such as worms and insects, have brains made up of just "the stem of the mushroom." Lacking cerebrums, they must make do with what in humans are called "the lower centers." The simplest forms of life, such as single-celled organisms, don't even have brains at all.

Complex intellectual functions, such as writing poems and performing scientific experiments, are controlled by your cerebrum and its cortex. Perhaps this fact helps explain why countless biology students are able to study the earthworm, but no one has ever noticed a cerebrumless worm studying humans. It takes a very large corporate structure indeed to produce such a complex product as a poem—or a Pinto.

The Brain and Behavior

Most companies manufacture a specific product or a series of products that keeps them in business. From a biological point of view, your brain *manufactures thoughts and behaviors.*

The primary purpose of your brain is to create muscular and glandular reactions, just as Ford's primary purpose is to produce cars and profits. The "employees" that make up your corporate brain and produce your behavior are your individual nerve cells, or neurons. When your neurons are

Fig. 2.4. The brains of lower animals are made up chiefly of sensory-input areas and motor-output areas (such as the cerebellum). The larger the cerebrum is in relation to the rest of the brain, the more complex the behavior the organism is typically capable of. Your cerebrum makes up the major part of your brain and is more than 100 times larger than the cerebrum of the rabbit.

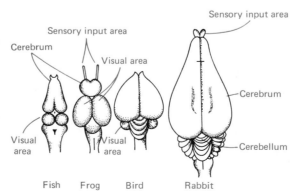

Glossary

Hallucinations (hal-LOO-see-NAY-shuns). Seeing or hearing things that aren't really there. If you attend a horror movie, and see a "ghost" on the way home, the ghost is probably an hallucination manufactured by your fear, rather than being a true sensory input.

Coma (KO-mah). An unusual form of deep sleep from which the person usually cannot be easily awakened. Often caused by drugs, fever, or brain injury.

Motor epilepsy (EP-ee-LEP-see). A type of muscular seizure or attack.

Grand mal seizure (grahn mahl). Perhaps the most dramatic, terrifying type of motor epilepsy. The French words *grand mal* mean "big sickness" (the final "d" in "grand" is not pronounced).

Epilepsy (EP-ee-LEP-see). A "fire storm in the brain" or "attack" in which the nerve cells become abnormally excited.

functioning well, they take in messages properly; they make the right "corporate decisions"; and your reactions flow off this neural assembly line in satisfactory fashion. When your neurons become sick or disturbed, various parts of this input–output process are badly upset.

If your *input* neurons were damaged or drugged, you might suffer from various kinds of **hallucinations.** That is, you might see things that weren't there; hear voices when no one was speaking; or fail to detect important changes in your sensory environment. We will discuss these problems in the next chapter, when we investigate the effects that various drugs can have on your brain.

Drugs such as opium that affect the "processing" neurons in your brain can cause hallucinations.

If your *processing* neurons are disturbed, several things may happen to you. (1) You may suffer a memory loss. (2) You may under-react or over-react to emotional situations. (3) Your judgment may become clouded. (4) You may faint or fall into an abnormal sleep called a **coma.** (5) Your cortex may become so confused that it issues orders which lead other people to think that you are "mentally ill." We will have a great deal more to say about some of these problems in later chapters.

If for any reason your *output* neurons start functioning abnormally, their behavioral product can sometimes be as clumsily put together as would a Lincoln Continental assembled by drunks. Damage to the output systems of your brain can lead to any of the following: (1) a loss of muscular coordination; (2) paralysis of the muscles in your arms, legs, or any other part of your body; or (3) a condition known as **motor epilepsy** or a **grand mal seizure.**

Question: Suppose a young man was hit over the head in a fight, and the doctor treating him suspected brain damage even though the man's skull wasn't broken. How might the doctor get a rough idea of the location of any injury to the man's brain without having to open up his skull and look inside?

Epilepsy

If you were walking down a dark street one night and were suddenly attacked by a stranger, you might very well have to fight for your life. And whenever the neurons in your brain are attacked or stimulated by certain kinds of chemicals, or are physically damaged, your neurons may put on abnormal bursts of activity as if they were defending themselves from invasion. We refer to these unusual bursts of neural energy as **epilepsy,** taking the term from a Greek word meaning "to seize" or "to attack."

Epilepsy is a common but frightening condition that normal people often neither understand nor wish to know much about. Whether you feel this way or not, for just a moment try to imagine what you might experience if you were unfortunate enough to sustain brain damage and have an epileptic attack.

If the site of the damaged nerve cells were in the *input* or *processing* areas of your brain, you might never recognize that you suffered from epilepsy, for seizures in the input and processing areas typically lead to little more than momentary lapses in consciousness. In fact, it was not until very recently that we realized that epilepsy could affect these parts of your nervous system.

If the injured neurons were in your *output* system, however, you would suffer from *motor epilepsy*—a condition that is very hard to overlook. During a full-blown motor seizure, most of the muscles in your body would suddenly contract. As your lungs squeezed shut, the air forced out might cause you to moan or scream. You would lose consciousness and fall to the ground, stiff as a board. For a moment or two, you would stop breathing. Then your arms and legs would begin twitching or jerking rhythmically, and you might lose control of your bladder and bowels.

Your motor seizure would be over and done with in five minutes or less, but you would be confused and sleepy—or have a headache—for some time thereafter. Typically, you would have little or no memory either of what led up to the seizure itself, or of the period of confusion that followed. Within an hour or so, you might be completely back to normal—until the next attack hit.

If the damage to your brain were mild, or if your attack was caused by an overdose of some drug such as alcohol, your seizures might occur infrequently, perhaps no more than once or twice a year. But in rare cases, the damage to the brain is so severe that the attacks may happen several times a day—so frequently that the person does not regain consciousness between seizures. This rare condition must be treated promptly, for it can lead to death.

Why Study Epilepsy? Scientists study brain conditions like epilepsy for several reasons. First, in order to be of help to the person who is suffering from the disease. (More than four million people in the Unites States suffer from some form of epilepsy.) But second, as we noted in Chapter 1, because we often learn a great deal about the *normal* functioning of an organ by trying to find out why it sometimes functions *abnormally*. An epileptic attack is a signal or **symptom** that tells us that something has gone wrong in your brain, just as high blood pressure is a sign that something has gone wrong with your heart or blood vessels.

But just as high blood pressure does not tell us exactly what the difficulty with your circulation is, neither does an epileptic seizure tell us exactly what might be wrong with your brain. In fact, there are many different types of epilepsy and they have many different causes. The scientific study of epilepsy has taught us much about the normal functioning of the brain, so we will mention this **bizarre** and devastating disease several times in these opening chapters. Before we can understand how an epileptic attack affects people psychologically, though, we will first have to look at how the neurons in your brain actually work.

The Neuron

The individual nerve cells in your brain usually function much as you yourself would if you were employed by Ford or some other corporation—which is to say that they work fairly continuously at their own tasks and do their best to cooperate with their neighbors. Although neurons may vary considerably among themselves in size and shape (as do people), neurons are all made up of three main parts—the **dendrites**, the **soma**, or **cell body**, and the **axon**.

Symptom (SIM-tum or SIMP-tum). The visible evidence of a disease or disturbance. Headache, runny nose, and sore throat are often symptoms of a physical illness such as a cold. The unusual speech patterns and behaviors some people show are occasionally symptoms of mental illness.

Bizarre (biz-ARE). Strange, odd, unusual.

Dendrite (DEN-dright). The "feelers" that extend from the cell body of a neuron. The front or "input" end of a neuron.

Soma (SO-mah). The cell body of a neuron.

Cell body. The center or main part of a neuron that "processes" some types of inputs to the cell.

Axon (AX-own). The "tail" or "output" end of a neuron.

The Dendrites   The front end, or *input* side, of a cortical neuron is a network of tiny fibers which reaches out from the cell body like feelers to make contact with surrounding nerve cells. These "feeler" fibers are called *dendrites*. Electrical activity in the dendrites is what causes the *brain waves* that we will discuss later on.

The Soma   The main part, or body, of the cell is called the *soma*. It is inside the soma that most of the complex chemical reactions occur which keep the cell alive and functioning. The soma, then, is (in some ways) the *processing* part of the nerve cell. Many of the drugs that affect human behavior do so because they speed up or slow down the chemical processes that occur naturally and continuously in the soma or cell body of the neuron.

The Axon   The action end, or *output* area, of the neuron is called the *axon*. The axon stretches back from the soma like a telephone cable. At the end of the axon are tiny fibers which connect with the dendrites and cell bodies of nearby neurons, or with the muscles and glands in the rest of the body. The axon is the *output area* of the neuron because the axonic fibers actually pass messages along to other nerve cells, and to the muscles and glands.

Neural Firing

One of the major functions of the neuron is to pass information from one part of the body to another. Each nerve cell contains a certain amount of stored-up electrical energy—the **resting potential**—that it can discharge in short bursts. The battery in your car releases a similar burst of stored-up electrical energy when you turn the ignition key.

These *bursts of neural energy* are the means by which your neurons pass information from one part of your body to another. For example, consider three nerve cells in your brain that are connected together in sequence, in *A-B-C* fashion. As Fig. 2.5 shows, the axon of *A* makes contact with the dendrites of *B*, and the axon of *B* makes contact with the dendrites of *C*.

A, *B*, and *C* all have a certain (and very similar) amount of potential energy to call upon when necessary. When a message is to be passed from *A* to *C*, a chemical change occurs in the axon of *A* that releases a brief burst of stored-up energy in the dendrites of *B*. This burst of electro-chemical energy sweeps the length of the *B* cell, beginning in *B's* dendrites and moving wave-like to the end of *B's* axon. When this wave reaches the tips of *B's* axonic fibers, it causes a chemical change to occur that triggers off a similar burst of electrical energy in neuron *C* (see Fig. 2.6).

Thus, the message passes from *A* to *B* to *C* as each releases its resting potential in an electro-chemical wave which stimulates the next neuron in line.

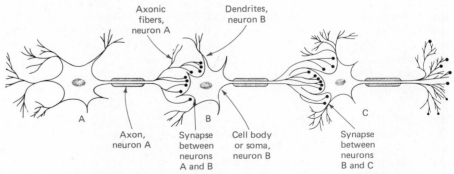

Fig. 2.5. Three neurons in a row. The axonic fibers of A make synapse with the dendrites and cell body of B, and the axonic fibers of B make synapse with the dendrites and cell body of C.

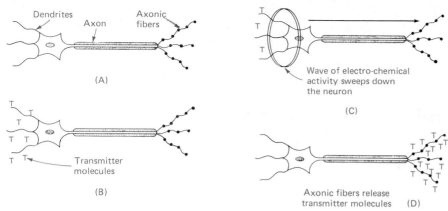

Fig. 2.6. Transmitter molecules (T's) excite the dendrites of a neuron, causing the neuron to fire. During "firing," a wave of electro-chemical activity sweeps down the neuron causing its axonic fibers to release more T's (transmitters) which stimulate the next neuron in line.

Whenever a wave of electrical energy passes from the dendrites to the axonic fibers, we say that a nerve has **fired,** because the action involved is much like the firing of a gun. There is a great deal of potential energy stored in the chemical gunpowder in a bullet. When you pull the trigger on a gun, you translate this *potential* chemical energy into the *mechanical* energy of an explosion, and the bullet is propelled down the barrel of the gun. And when a neuron fires, it translates its resting potential into a burst of electro-chemical energy.

Let's carry the bullet analogy a step further. The neuron behaves in some ways as if it were a machine gun loaded with electro-chemical bullets. If you press the trigger on a machine gun very lightly, you can fire the shells slowly, individually, one by one. But if you press down hard on the trigger, you can fire off whole bursts of bullets in a second or two.

In similar fashion, if you tap very lightly on your arm, the receptor (input) nerve cells in your skin will fire at a very slow rate—a few times a second. If you press very hard on your arm, these same input neurons can fire hundreds or even thousands of times per second.

Every time you move a muscle—or think a thought, or experience an emotion—you do so in part because one group of nerve cells in your brain *fires off messages* like a machine gun to your muscles, glands, or to other groups of neurons.

As long as you are alive, all of the neurons in your brain will be firing at one speed or another. When you are engaged in vigorous mental or physical activity, most of these nerve cells will be responding rapidly, for they will have a great deal of information to process and to pass along to other parts of your body.

As we will see in Chapter 6, your brain is particularly sensitive to changes in your environment. Therefore, much of the activity that goes on inside your brain is initially triggered off by *stimulus inputs from the world around you.* But even when you are resting or fast asleep, your nerve cells will still be active, although many of them will be firing very slowly if you are deeply asleep. We will have more to say about these patterns of nerve cell activity in just a moment.

The Synapse   Now, let us go back to neurons *A, B,* and *C.* The axonic end-fibers of *A* come close to, *but do not actually touch,* the dendrites of cell *B.* The fluid-filled space between *A's* axonic fibers and *B's* dendrites is called the **synapse.** This synapse (or fluid-filled gap) is so tiny that you would have trouble seeing it even with the most powerful microscope.

When two neurons make contact with each other, as do *A* and *B* in our example, we say that they "make *synapse* with each other." The synaptic space between two nerve cells is really a *small canal*—a canal filled with

Fired. When a neuron releases its resting potential in a burst of energy, we say that the nerve cell has "fired."

Synapse (SIN-aps). The extremely narrow, fluid-filled space between two nerve cells. When the axonic fibers of one neuron come close to the dendrites or cell body of a second neuron, the first can cause the second to fire. Therefore, the two neurons "make synapse with each other."

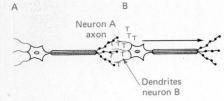

Fig. 2.7. When neuron A fires, its axonic fibers release transmitter (T) molecules into the synapse with neuron B. These molecules bind to receptor sites on the dendrites and cell body of B, causing B to fire.

Packets. Bundles or "drops" of transmitter chemicals released by the axonic fibers of a neuron.

Transmitter chemicals (TRANS-mitt-er). Chemicals released into the synapse by the axonic fibers of one neuron that cause the second neuron to fire. Chemicals that thus "transmit a message" from one neuron to the next.

Receptor cells. Nerve cells in your eyes, ears, skin, and the rest of your body that receive information about your own body and the world around you. Input neurons.

Processing cells. Nerve cells in your brain that respond to information coming from the receptor cells.

Motor neurons. Output neurons. Nerve cells with very long axons. The dendrites and cell body of your motor neurons are usually in a motor center in your brain. The axon stretches out like a telephone cable from the brain to make synapse with other neurons and from thence to individual muscles somewhere in your body.

Neuro-muscular synapse (NEW-ro). The synapse or connection point between a motor neuron and a muscle.

fluid that contains many different types of chemical substances. These chemicals all have a definite, and, as in the case of epilepsy, sometimes devastating effect on your behavior.

The message that one neuron passes along to another is a series of bursts of energy—like a stream of bullets fired from one nerve cell and hitting the bull's eye on the next nerve cell. When a neuron fires, a wave of electrical energy shoots along the length of the cell and reaches the tiny fibers at the end of the axon. This "firing" causes the tiny axonic fibers to release tiny drops of chemicals (called **packets**) into the synaptic gap or canal.

As we will see in the next chapter, these chemical *packets* move across the synaptic canal and stimulate the dendrites of the next cell. Thus when the axonic fibers of *A* release chemical packets into the synapse with *B*, this chemical stimulation to *B*'s dendrites causes *B* to fire too (see Fig. 2.7).

These packets of chemicals serve to *transmit* information from one cell to another. The more **transmitter chemicals** that *A*'s axonic end-fibers release into the synaptic fluid between *A* and *B*, the more often cell *B* will be triggered into firing.

Nerve cells have many functions. There are neurons in your eyes and ears—called **receptor cells** or input neurons—that sense or detect changes in the world around you and relay information about those changes to your brain. Specialized **processing cells** react to this incoming information by checking your memories to determine the input's importance and emotional value, and then decide how your body should react.

Output or **motor neurons** relay the "command decision" to your muscles and glands, thus causing your body to go into action. These motor neurons actually "make synapse" with the muscles much as your cortical neurons make synapse with each other.

The more vigorous the activity, the faster your neurons fire.

When a motor neuron fires, it releases *transmitters* into the synaptic canal between its own axon and the muscle it connects to. These packets of chemicals cross the synaptic gap and cause the muscle to twitch or contract. Even the most complex muscular reactions—a rock musician playing a crashing chord on a guitar, or a secretary typing 100 words a minute on a typewriter—are made up of *orderly patterns of individual muscle contractions*. And all these reactions are brought about by the *orderly firing of motor neurons* and the release of transmitter chemicals at the **neuro-muscular** (nerve–muscle) **synapse**.

If all your neurons were connected in simple *A-B-C* fashion, your behavioral potentialities would be even simpler than those of an earthworm. In fact, in the decision-making centers of your brain, the dendrites of any nerve cell *B* are likely to make synapse with (and hence receive messages from) axonic fibers from a thousand or more different *A*s. And *B*'s own axonic end-fibers are likely to make synapse with (and hence pass messages along to) the dendrites of a thousand or more *C*s. We will describe these complex inter-connections in more detail later. For the moment, it is enough to realize that any given neuron in your brain is likely to be hooked up to *thousands* of its neighboring neurons.

How does epilepsy occur? Under normal conditions, the nerve cells in your brain act as independent agents, each performing its individual tasks as necessary. That is, at any given moment, most of the 15 billion neurons in your brain will be doing quite different things. Yet each would be busy working toward the common goal of keeping you alive and functioning well.

If a nerve doctor, often called a **neurologist** or a **neuro-physiologist,** wanted to get an idea of how your brain was performing, she or he might place a small piece of metal called an **electrode** on the outside of your head. The electrode would be connected by wires to a machine called an **elec-tro-encephalo-graph** (EEG; see Figs. 2.8 and 2.9).

This EEG machine, as it is called, translates electrical energy from your brain into *visual patterns on a screen,* much as a television set translates electrical energy into patterns you can see on the picture tube. Each time a nerve cell close to the electrode fires, the electrode sends an electrical impulse to the EEG machine. This impulse is displayed visually on the EEG's picture tube (or perhaps printed out on a sheet of paper).

If, by some chance, all the cells in your brain near the electrode were silent for a second or two, the picture tube would show a flat, horizontal line. If one or two cells fired at exactly the same time, the line would have a tiny pip or bump in it. If 1,000 cells fired at exactly the same time, the peak would be very high indeed. And if, half a second later, 500 of these cells fired again, the screen would show a second peak about half the size of the previous one.

In a sense, the EEG gives you the same sort of fuzzy, imprecise picture of what is going on inside the skull that you would get if you stood outside a huge football stadium and tried to guess what was happening inside by listening to the roar of the crowd. Standing outside the stadium, you could tell whether the football game was exciting, and when an important play had been made. But you couldn't always tell which team had the ball, or what the score was (much less what individual members of the crowd were doing or experiencing).

The EEG electrode "listens" outside the skull to the electrical noise made inside by thousands of individual neurons, but all it can tell you is how active the *bulk* of the nerve cells are, not the precise behavior patterns of each *single* neuron.

When you are actively engaged in thought—as when you are mentally

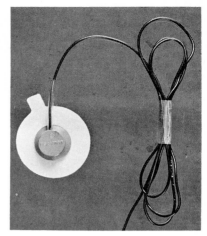

Fig. 2.8. An electrode.

Neurologist (new-RAH-low-jist). A medical doctor who treats nerve diseases.

Neuro-physiologist (NEW-ro FIZZ-ee-OLL-oh-jist). A scientist who studies the functioning of neurons.

Electrode (ee-LEK-trode). A device used to detect electrical activity in the brain. Disk-electrodes are coin-shaped pieces of metal that can be placed against the head to read brain waves. Needle-electrodes are thin wires inserted through holes in the skull directly into the brain.

Electro-encephalo-graph (ee-LEK-tro en-SEF-uh-low graf). An electric machine that makes a graphic record of brain waves. *Cephalo* is the Greek word for "head."

Fig. 2.9. A patient hooked up to an EEG machine.

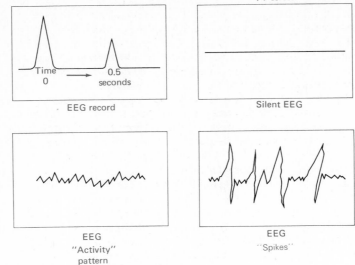

Fig. 2.10. Examples of EEG records.

trying to work through a difficult problem—electrodes on your skull would detect and display on the EEG machine a rapid pattern of electrical activity. This rapid pattern is a sign that each of the nerve cells near the electrode is operating normally, taking care of its own business. We call such an electrical output the **activity pattern** (see Fig. 2.10), since it usually means that your brain is actively engaged in some kind of work.

Under certain conditions, however, the nerve cells in a given part of your brain can begin to fire more and more together, in unison or **synchrony.** When this *firing in synchrony* occurs, waves of electrical activity can sweep across the surface of your brain like ocean waves sweeping up on a beach. The electrode on your skull would translate these synchronous brain waves into wavy lines on the EEG machine. And just as you can tell something about the wind and weather by measuring the size and shape and rhythm of ocean waves, so you can tell something about the weather inside your brain by looking at your own EEG record as it appears on the screen.

The visual parts of your cortex are located primarily on the rear surface of your brain. When you relax and close your eyes, these visual parts of your brain will show rather fast waves called alpha waves or the **alpha rhythm** (see Fig. 2.11).

When you go to sleep, your brain-wave activity generally slows down and becomes more synchronous. The large, slow *sleep waves* that occur in your brain when you are deeply asleep are called *delta waves* or the **delta rhythm.**

The Chemical Causes of Epilepsy If your EEG record showed the activity pattern of the alpha or delta rhythms, it would mean that things are probably rather normal in your brain. In the brain of an epileptic, however, things are often quite different.

When a part of a person's brain is badly damaged, scar tissue often develops. The chemicals that ooze from this scar tissue can build up in nearby synapses and act as *transmitters.* If this build-up gets out of hand—as it occasionally does in epilepsy—so much of this "scar-tissue transmitter" is produced that the neurons nearby begin to fire very, very rapidly and too much in unison. Pulsing waves of electrical activity rapidly spread over the brain, much as ocean waves can pound frantically at a beach during a storm.

These abnormal, *hyper-synchronous bursts* of electrical activity show up on the EEG screen as **spikes.** If the hyper-synchrony is limited to a small area of the brain—and particularly if the damage is in the input areas of the

ALPHA

DELTA

Fig. 2.11. Alpha rhythm in the brain is made up of electrical waves that have a frequency of 10 or so cycles per second. The delta rhythm registers on an EEG machine as large, slow waves that have a frequency of about 1–3 cycles per second.

brain—the affected person may experience little more than a queasy feeling or a quick hallucination that is soon forgotten. Indeed, the person may not realize that anything abnormal has happened in her or his brain.

If the seizure affects the processing areas of the brain that are associated with consciousness, the person may black out for a second or two, and then continue as if nothing had happened. Such a seizure is called the **petit mal** attack, from the French term that means "small illness."

If the hyper-synchrony reaches the motor or output parts of the brain, however, a motor epilepsy or **grand mal** ("large illness") attack occurs. During the *grand mal* seizure, the motor neurons begin firing in rapid pulses; the muscles start contracting in rapid rhythm, and convulsions typically occur.

If you have ever seen anyone suffer an epileptic seizure, you know what a distressing event it can be. The person affected appears to be seized by some external force or agency that takes over control of his or her body. It is little wonder, then, that until very recently most people believed that the epileptic person was being *possessed* or "seized" by a devil or evil spirit.

However, as we have seen, epileptic attacks are triggered by complex chemical changes within the brain and usually are the result of some kind of *injury to the neurons*—a blow to the head, brain damage during birth, a high fever, a disease, or a **tumor.** Eating or drinking certain chemicals (including an excess of alcohol) can also bring on a seizure.

During a grand mal attack, the scar-transmitter chemicals are used up, and it typically takes a while for enough of these chemicals to build up to trigger off another seizure that involves the whole brain. However, the neurons right next to the scar tissue are continuously affected, and they may show *spikes* every few seconds, even when the person is feeling normal and hasn't had an attack for weeks.

Medical doctors can often track down the exact location of the scar tissue by putting electrodes all over a person's skull and noting where the spike activity is greatest. If the scar is on the surface of the brain, a surgeon can sometimes cure the problem by cutting out the damaged tissue. (Surgery usually produces a much "cleaner" scar than does injury or disease.)

However, the site of the scar tissue is often deep down inside the brain, or the injury is so widespread or so subtle that it cannot be located precisely with the EEG machine. In such cases, treatment usually consists of giving the patient an anti-transmitter drug such as **Dilantin.** In fact, any drug that makes it more difficult for the neurons to fire in hyper-synchrony will help prevent epileptic attacks—as will teaching epileptic patients to relax when the **aura** occurs and they feel a seizure coming on.

Occasionally the damage to a patient's brain is so extensive that neither surgery nor drugs can control the seizures. These patients, though small in number, were rather pitiful cases for whom medical science offered little hope, until recently. Then, in the 1950's, a number of "animal" psychologists began studying what happened to rats and cats when their brains were "split in half" surgically.

At the beginning of their research, these animal psychologists had no real thought that their work might be of rather immediate help to epileptic patients. The scientists were merely trying to discover some of the basic facts about the way that animal brains function. As it turned out, their findings were not only fascinating from a scientific point of view, but were of some practical value as well.

The Split Brain

A few pages back, we left you standing in front of a mirror trying to look at the mountains and valleys of your cerebrum. For just a moment, let's go back to that magic mirror.

The biggest "valley of the brain" is a deep groove that runs down the center from front to back. It is called the **central fissure,** and it divides your

---

Petit mal (PET-tee mahl). A brief epileptic attack in which the person typically loses consciousness for a few seconds. (The final "t" in *petit* is silent.)

Grand mal. A full-blown epileptic attack involving the motor centers.

Tumor (TOO-more). An abnormal and often cancerous growth anywhere on or in the body.

Dilantin (die-LAN-tin or dee-LAN-tin). A drug used to help control epileptic seizures. The effect of the drug is to make neural firing more difficult.

Central fissure (FISH-sure). The "valley" that separates the left half of your brain from the right.

Aura (AW-rah). The strange "prickling" sensation that often marks the onset of an epileptic attack.

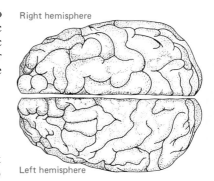
Right hemisphere

Left hemisphere

Fig. 2.12. A top view of the human brain showing the left and right hemispheres.

brain into two sphere-shaped parts called the **cerebral hemispheres** (see Fig. 2.12). These hemispheres are *mirror images* of each other, just as the left half of your face is a mirror image of your right half, and your left hand is a mirror image of your right hand. In scientific terms, your whole body is **bilaterally symmetrical.** All of the higher animals—including humans—are bilaterally symmetrical, which is to say that if you split any of these animals in half from top to bottom, the right and left halves of their bodies would be symmetrical, mirror images.

Despite the fact that your two cerebral hemispheres are reversed images of each other, however, there are major differences between them—just as there are functional differences between your right and left hands. Many things that you can do easily with one hand are very difficult for you to perform with the other. If you are **right-handed**—as about 93 percent of the people in the world are—you write with your right hand but probably have trouble doing so with your left. If you are left-handed, then you will typically write better with your left hand than you do with your right.

Now, ask yourself this question: If you are right-handed, why can't you write with your left hand since it is a mirror image of your right? The answer seems to lie in your *brain*, not in your *hands*.

As confusing as it may seem to you at first, your *right* cerebral hemisphere mainly controls the *left* side of your body, and your *left* cerebral hemisphere mainly controls the *right* side of your body.

If you are right-handed, your left hemisphere is your **dominant hemisphere.** When you speak or write, you do so with your dominant left hemisphere. When you think or scheme about something by "talking to yourself," you probably do so as well with this same dominant left hemisphere.

Your right hemisphere is called by many names—**minor hemisphere,** "perceptual" hemisphere, "emotional" hemisphere, or "monitoring" hemisphere. It understands language, but all on its own can neither talk nor write very well.

If you damaged certain language areas in your major (left) hemisphere, you might lose the ability to speak or to write. You might even forget the meaning of words. This inability to communicate through written or spoken language is called **aphasia,** and its primary cause is damage to the major or "talking" hemisphere of the cerebrum.

If you are left-handed, your situation is much more confused. It may be that, like many left-handers, the right half of your cerebrum is the "talking hemisphere" and produces most of your spoken and written language. However, in some "southpaws," both hemispheres share the ability to speak and write, and neither of them is really "dominant." Interestingly enough, these left-handed people who lack a major hemisphere often show a slight imprecision in their speech patterns. That is, they can communicate almost any thought they wish to, but they often speak in a sloppy or involved fashion and frequently misuse words ever so slightly.

The Corpus Callosum

As we said, the two cerebral hemispheres of your brain are separate and distinct from each other, but they are joined together in the center by a bridge of very special tissue—much as the north American hemisphere is joined to the south American hemisphere by a narrow bridge of land we call Central America.

The slim bridge of tissue connecting the two hemispheres of your brain is called the **corpus callosum,** two Latin words meaning "thick or hardened body" (see Fig. 2.13). The corpus callosum contains a large number of axonic fibers that act like telephone cables running from one side of your brain to the other. Your dominant "talking" hemisphere and your "monitoring" or "perceiving" hemisphere keep in touch with each other *primarily* through your corpus callosum.

Cerebral hemispheres (ser-REE-bral HEM-ee-spheres). The two halves of the globe-shaped or spherical cerebrum. The two hemispheres are separated by the central fissure.

Bilaterally symmetrical (buy-LATT-er-al-lee sim-METT-tree-cal). Any object whose left side is a mirror image of the right is said to be bilaterally symmetrical. *Lateralis* is the Latin word for "side."

Right-handed. Recent studies of cave drawings thousands of years old—and of art from all cultures and times—suggest that about 90–93 percent of all human beings have been right-handed since people first started drawing on the walls of caves. Why the ratio of right- and left-handed people should remain so constant over the years is still something of a mystery.

Dominant hemisphere. The half of the cerebrum that dominates or controls such activities as speech. Also called the "talking" hemisphere and the "major" hemisphere.

Minor hemisphere. The non-dominant half of the cerebrum which is a "silent partner" to the dominant or major hemisphere. Also called the "perceptual" hemisphere and the "emotional" hemisphere.

Aphasia (uh-FAZE-ya). The inability to recognize the meaning of words, or to speak or write in meaningful terms. Aphasia is usually a symptom of some kind of brain damage.

Corpus callosum (KOR-pus kah-LOW-sum). The bridge of nervous tissue that connects the major and the minor hemispheres.

PART ONE Biological Bases of Behavior

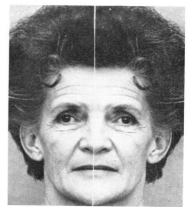

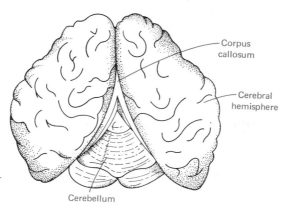

Fig. 2.13. The two cerebral hemispheres of the brain connected by the corpus callosum.

When your corpus callosum is intact and healthy—as it is in most people—sensory inputs that reach one hemisphere are almost automatically flashed to the other. Thus, on the *input side* of your brain, if one of your hemispheres learns something, it shares the information with the other hemisphere almost immediately.

The situation is similar on the *output side* of your brain. Suppose, for instance, your left hemisphere sends a message to the muscles in your right hand telling them to write the word *dog* with a pencil. Your dominant hemisphere would immediately send an "information copy" of the command message to your right hemisphere as well, so that your "minor" hemisphere can monitor what is going on in the other half of your brain.

Should your right hemisphere order your left hand to scratch your nose, it would also let your left hemisphere know what it is doing by sending a message across the corpus callosum. As far as your body movements are concerned, however, your "monitoring" or "perceptual" hemisphere probably takes directions from your dominant hemisphere most of the time.

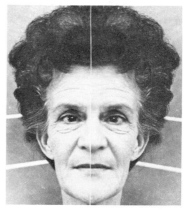

Why a Dominant Hemisphere? Why should one hemisphere dominate the other? Well, consider for a moment the movements your body makes when you perform a simple task like walking down a street. Your left leg moves in perfect sequence with your right, and your right arm swings in rhythm with your left. But your right leg and arm are controlled by your left hemisphere, while your left arm and leg are directly under the control of your right hemisphere. Surely one part of your brain must coordinate or dominate these activities, or you'd never get anywhere. For instance, can you imagine what would happen if your left hemisphere ordered its arm and leg to *stop*, while your right hemisphere told its arm and leg to *go*?

At birth (or shortly thereafter), one hemisphere starts to gain the lead over the other and eventually takes over major control of the whole body. By the time an infant is old enough to talk, the major hemisphere is the only one that needs to learn how to talk—*since it has major control over the movements of your lips and tongue anyhow*. Having one hemisphere "do the work," while the other monitors your activities and thoughts, probably gives you a great deal more flexibility than if each of your hemispheres had to be able to do *everything* the other was capable of doing.

The *tendency* to be right- or left-handed seems to be inherited. However, our society is built primarily for "right-handed" people, and thus many parents attempt to impose right-handedness on their children even if the child is naturally left-handed. Unfortunately, if the child is punished for trying to do things with its left hand, the child may become confused and afraid. And since its naturally dominant hemisphere won't develop language skills as it normally would, the child may end up stuttering or having other speech or emotional problems.

The top photo is a composite made up of the left half of a woman's face joined to its mirror image. The bottom photo shows the right half of the woman's face joined to its mirror image. The "normal" view of the woman is in the middle. The left half of the face is controlled by the right (emotional) hemisphere. When photos such as these were shown to subjects, most of them selected the "left" composite photos as displaying the most emotional expression. Notice too that the right half of the face (controlled by the dominant left hemisphere) is larger, as is customary in most right-handed individuals.

Indirect Cortical Pathways   Your major hemisphere controls its side of your body *directly*. It controls the other side of you by "long distance"—that is, by sending orders across the corpus callosum to neural centers in the minor hemisphere.

However, there are also *indirect* output pathways from each hemisphere to *both sides of your body*. These indirect pathways bypass the corpus callosum by running through the lower centers of your brain. Theoretically, either hemisphere could control the movements of both sides of your body by sending output orders through these indirect motor pathways—but the other hemisphere wouldn't know what was happening because it wouldn't receive an "information copy" of the command via the corpus callosum.

Under normal conditions, however, these indirect control routes seem not to be used very much, perhaps for two reasons. First, the corpus callosum bridge is a much more efficient way for the dominant side of your brain to coordinate movements. Second, it is likely that your dominant or conscious hemisphere would resist having the "monitoring" hemisphere send out orders that the major hemisphere wasn't aware of, and hence couldn't control.

Whatever the case, your "monitoring" hemisphere seems mostly to follow orders that come to it across the corpus callosum, although it is technically capable of thinking and acting on its own. Even in the case of **ambidextrous** people, who can write with both hands, one hemisphere appears to be dominant and to handle language functions much better than the other.

Now, with all these facts in mind, can you guess what would happen to you if your corpus callosum were cut, and the two hemispheres of your brain were suddenly disconnected?

This is precisely the question that psychologists R.W. Sperry and R.E. Myers were trying to answer when, in 1953, they performed their first split-brain operation on cats—and ended up making one of the most exciting discoveries in modern psychology.

Two Minds in the Same Body

The surgical technique used by Sperry and Myers involved opening up the cat's skull, then slicing the animal's corpus callosum and a few of the sensory input pathways to both hemispheres.

Normally, sensory input from *each* eye goes to *both* cerebral hemispheres. The split-brain surgery, however, left the cat's eyes as isolated from each other as were the two halves of its cerebrum. Now, whatever the animal's left eye saw was recorded only in the left hemisphere; and whatever the animal's right eye saw was recorded only in the cat's right hemisphere.

Immediately after the operation the cats had difficulty coordinating their movements. But after a while their behavior became fairly normal again. Either the two hemispheres had learned to cooperate with each other, or both sides of the brain took turns in controlling the entire body using the *indirect* pathways we've already mentioned.

Once a cat seemed recovered from the surgery, Sperry and Myers tested it in various ways. First they blindfolded its left eye and taught the cat to solve a visual problem using just its right eye (and, of course, just the right hemisphere of its brain). The cat learned this lesson very well.

Next, they switched the blindfold to the trained right eye and tested the cat with its untrained left eye (and left hemisphere). The question was, would any information about the problem have "leaked" from the right half of the cat's brain to the left?

The answer was a resounding *no*. Using just its untrained left eye, the cat appeared to be entirely ignorant of what it had just learned with its right eye. When Sperry and Myers trained the left eye in similar fashion, the right eye (and hemisphere) seemed unaware of what the left part of the brain had learned.

PART ONE   Biological Bases of Behavior

Sperry and Myers concluded that the cat now had two "minds," either of which was capable of *learning on its own*—and of responding intelligently to changes in the world around it on its own.

Subsequent experiments with rats and monkeys gave similar results. However, the animals recovered so nicely that if you hadn't known about their operation, you probably wouldn't have guessed that there were two more-or-less independent "entities" inside each animal's body.

The split-brain surgery was seemingly safe and relatively easy to perform in animals. But what would the operation do to a human, and why would anyone want to find out?

Epilepsy and the Corpus Callosum

The application of electricity was once used as a treatment for epilepsy. In this engraving the boy is suspended on silk lines and electrified by the excited glass tube held by the lecturer.

Epilepsy is an odd and unfortunate disease. The scar tissue that causes a seizure usually has a specific **locus** or location on *one side of the brain*. If you took an EEG record from this damaged area, you would see continual "spike" responses.

But remember that the two hemispheres are "mirror images." What would happen if you took an EEG record at the same point in the undamaged hemisphere? In fact, the EEG record from the unscarred hemisphere would usually look pretty normal. However, at the onset of an epileptic attack, you would detect spikes on *both sides of the brain*.

How could there be spike responses coming from apparently healthy tissue?

Almost every neuron in your *left* hemisphere has a nerve cell in your *right* hemisphere that is its "identical twin," or mirror image. Many of these nerve cells are tied together by axonic fibers that pass through the corpus callosum. Whenever a neuron in your dominant hemisphere fires, it may send a "command message" telling its mirror-image cell in the minor hemisphere to fire too. And whenever the mirror-image neuron fires, it sends a message back to the dominant hemisphere saying that it *has* fired.

These command messages are the primary way in which your dominant hemisphere coordinates activities in both sides of your brain.

Whenever an epileptic seizure begins at a point in one hemisphere, the mirror-image neurons in the other hemisphere receive a "seizure message" via the corpus callosum. This "seizure message" causes the mirror-image

Locus (LOW-cuss). From the Latin word meaning "place" or "site."

neurons to fire very, very rapidly themselves. The cells may even start showing spike activity on their own as they "catch fire" from all the stimulation they are receiving from the other hemisphere. So the spike activity begins to build up simultaneously at the *same spot in both hemispheres.*

Worse than this, the mirror-image neurons may send seizure messages back to the original site of the trouble. This return message from the undamaged hemisphere sets off even more spiking in the damaged area, which then sends even wilder messages back to the mirror-image cells, which causes them to fire even more rapidly.

Each time the seizure message flashes back and forth across the corpus callosum, a few more cells in each hemisphere get caught up in the spiking. Within a few seconds, the whole brain can become involved, and a grand mal attack occurs.

Epilepsy-Positive Feedback Loop

An epileptic seizure is a good example of what is called a **positive feedback loop** (see Fig. 2.14). Suppose you are talking on the phone to a friend. He says something mildly critical to you that you don't particularly appreciate, so you take a verbal swipe at him in return. Your response annoys him, for he thinks it is uncalled for, and he feeds back to you an even cruder remark, which makes you rather angry, so you call him a very dirty name, which infuriates him. Rapidly the matter builds into a fight, and an emotional explosion takes place.

Explosions are almost always the result of a positive feedback loop, whether they occur in a stick of dynamite, on the telephone, or in the brain. If we could cut the telephone wire between you and your friend before things got out of hand, we could sever the loop, stop the increasingly critical feedback, and prevent the emotional explosion from taking place. (But, of course, we'd also cut off all communication between you and your friend as a result of cutting the connecting wire.)

When medical doctors learned of the Sperry–Myers split-brain operation, they reasoned that if they cut the corpus callosum and separated the two hemispheres of the brain, they might prevent full-blown epileptic seizures from occurring in patients for whom Dilantin and ordinary surgery just didn't work.

And the doctors were right. They tried the operation on a middle-aged man whom we shall call John Doe. During the Korean War, John Doe had served in the armed forces. He had parachuted behind enemy lines, had been captured, and was struck on the head several times with a rifle butt while in an enemy concentration camp.

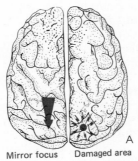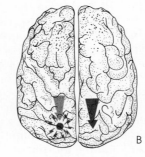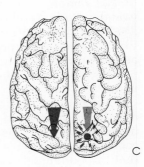

Mirror focus   Damaged area

Fig. 2.14. A. Damaged cells in the left hemisphere cause abnormal electrical activity in nearby cells—and send an "excited" message to their "mirror image" cells in the right hemisphere. B. The "mirror image" cells are stimulated to fire by this abnormal input, and feed an "excited" message back to the right hemisphere. C. Soon the whole brain is "on fire" with neural excitation, and an epileptic seizure results. Cutting the corpus callosum "cuts the feedback loop" and reduces the likelihood of a seizure.

Shortly thereafter, John Doe's epileptic seizures began. By the time he was released from the prison camp, his brain was in such bad physical shape that neither surgery nor drugs could help much. His seizures increased in frequency and intensity until they were occurring a dozen or more times a day. Without the split-brain operation, John Doe would probably have died, or committed suicide, as had many other epileptic patients with similar problems.

After the surgeons cut John Doe's corpus callosum, his seizures stopped almost completely—just as the surgeons had expected. And although the doctors had assumed that both sides of John Doe's brain would be able to function independently, they weren't totally prepared for what actually happened. For, when the doctors split John Doe's brain, they also cut his "mind" into two separate but similar personalities—each of which existed more-or-less independently of the other, and each of which had its *own unique claim on his body*. As far as his mind was concerned, John Doe had suddenly become Siamese twins!

John-Doe-Left and John-Doe-Right

Immediately after the operation, John Doe was able to communicate in almost normal fashion. Some of his speech was slurred, as if he didn't have complete control over the muscles in his tongue (or wasn't getting the proper feedback), but his thinking seemed clear and logical, and he suffered no noticeable loss in intelligence.

But John Doe did have moments of confusion, and he was often unable to coordinate his body movements and his emotional reactions. Every now and then, he reported, the left half of his body "did odd things," as if it had a will of its own.

John Doe was right-handed, so his "talking hemisphere" controlled his right hand and leg. Occasionally, when John was dressing, his right hand would zip up his pants (as it normally did) and John would start to go about his business. Moments later, however, his left hand (controlled by his silent or "monitoring" hemisphere), would casually reach down and unzip his pants—or even perform more **obscene** actions. Usually these odd behaviors would occur in fairly emotional situations. They almost always embarrassed John Doe's dominant hemisphere, because he could offer no logical (verbal) explanation for why his left hand was behaving so peculiarly.

The doctors soon began to suspect that when John Doe answered their questions and reported his feelings and thoughts, it was only his dominant (left) hemisphere that was doing the talking. Since his silent or "monitoring" hemisphere couldn't communicate it own feelings via the corpus callosum (now cut), it offered its comments behaviorally—by occasionally doing odd things that would *disrupt* the ongoing flow of behavior controlled by John Doe's dominant hemisphere.

As we mentioned earlier, the input pathways to each hemisphere of the brain can sometimes be **functionally isolated.** Using this fact as a guide, psychologists working with John Doe were able to find ways of communicating with either side of his brain without the other side's knowing what was going on. Talking with the dominant left hemisphere (John-Doe-Left) was no problem, since this hemisphere possessed full language control. But John-Doe-Right could not talk, although he could point to things (with the left hand) in response to questions that John-Doe-Left couldn't hear. Given the appropriate sensory inputs, either of the John Does could learn things that the other wasn't aware of.

Similar Personalities

Psychological tests showed that both John Does had remarkably similar personalities: Except for language ability, they were about as much alike as identical twins. Their attitudes and opinions seemed to be the same; their

Obscene (obs-SEEN). Anything repulsive to the senses or to common morality is considered obscene. Hard-core, X-rated movies are often said to be obscene.

Functionally isolated. A person put into solitary confinement in jail is "functionally isolated" from all other people. The person still exists, but cannot communicate with others. Cutting the corpus callosum "functionally isolates" one hemisphere from the other, but both continue to operate independently.

perceptions of the world were the same; and they woke up and went to sleep at almost the same times.

There was one area of difference, however. Perhaps because John-Doe-Left could express himself in language, the dominant hemisphere appeared to be somewhat more logical and better at orderly planning than was John-Doe-Right. On the other hand, the minor or "monitoring" hemisphere tended to be somewhat more aggressive, impulsive, and emotional—perhaps out of frustration that it could not talk, or perhaps because it could no longer influence the dominant hemisphere by giving it feedback across the corpus callosum.

The split-brain operation was so successful in reducing epileptic attacks that it was tried with more than a dozen patients who might otherwise have died from the severity of their uncontrollable seizures. In many of these patients, one hemisphere (usually the dominant one) was able to gain control of both sides of the body, presumably by somehow suppressing the powers of the other hemisphere. Usually the two halves learned to cooperate and share control, but the dominant hemisphere was in the driver's seat most of the time. In some cases, however, neither half of the brain ever gained the ability to coordinate all bodily movements.

Generally speaking, the younger the patient was when the corpus callosum was cut, the better the person's recovery. Because of the problems older patients such as John Doe experienced, and because new types of treatment can now help control epilepsy without the necessity for splitting the brain, the operation is seldom used anymore.

Logic, Creativity, and Feedback

Until the split-brain studies of Sperry and his associates, most people had assumed that the "mind" was a unitary system. That is to say, you think and feel and act as if you were a *single* individual, not a pair of mental "Siamese Twins" that happen to inhabit the same body. When you refer to yourself, you say "I," not "we."

Little wonder, then, that the split-brain experiments turned psychology on its ear, for these studies indicate that *all of us* have two similar but different "minds," and that these two "minds" have control over quite different parts of our daily existence.

If it seems highly unlikely to you that *you* have two minds locked away inside your skull, you might consider this fact: Sperry's split-brain patients simply had no conscious awareness that "anything was missing" after their operations. Although their left (conscious) hemispheres had lost most of what we call **depth perception,** and could no longer hear music in "full stereophonic sound," the patients typically did not become conscious of this loss until it was demonstrated to them in the laboratory.

More than this, the patients often verbally rejected those few responses that clearly came from the "silent" hemisphere. For instance, Sperry (and others) soon developed ways of presenting both visual and **auditory** (sound) stimuli to just one of the hemispheres. Using this special apparatus, Sperry could show a series of pictures just to a patient's right hemisphere. Sperry would then ask the right hemisphere to respond to questions by pointing at various objects with the left hand which, of course, is under the control of the "silent" hemisphere. Occasionally, when the patient would make a **left-handed response,** the person would say something like, "Now, I know it wasn't me who did that!"

From these (and many other) studies, Sperry concluded that the "silent" hemisphere is particularly good at *spatial* and *visual perceptions.* For instance, in one film Sperry made of his studies, a split-brain patient is shown trying to put together colored blocks to form a complex design using just one hand at a time. The man first looks at a printed design, then attempts to duplicate it with the blocks. When the man's left hand ("silent" hemisphere) attempts the task, it performs swiftly and correctly. But when the patient's right hand ("conscious" hemisphere) tries to duplicate the

Depth perception. The ability to see the world in three dimensions. The ability to judge how far away objects are.

Auditory (AW-ditt-tor-ee). Having to do with hearing. From the Latin word meaning "to hear."

Left-handed response. When the right hemisphere is functionally isolated from the left, the right ("silent") hemisphere can usually express itself only by moving the person's left hand (or foot). Since the left ("dominant") hemisphere is not consciously aware of what caused the response, the person often denies that she or he "made" the response.

PART ONE Biological Bases of Behavior

feat, it proceeds slowly, clumsily, and makes many mistakes. (In fact, in the film, the man's left hand occasionally "corrects" the right hand's mistakes, much to both Sperry's and the patient's annoyance.)

I Remember Your Face, But . . .

In 1978, Ruben Gur, Martin Reivich, and Jesse Weinberger of the University of Pennsylvania confirmed some of Sperry's findings using people with normal brains. Gur and his colleagues gave 13 right-handed males various tasks to solve. Half of these tasks involved the use of complex language, while the other half were problems having to do with the visual perception of incomplete patterns. When the subjects were working on the verbal problems, the blood flow through their *left* hemispheres increased markedly, but the blood flow through their *right* hemispheres did not increase at all. And those subjects who did best at solving the visual problems showed an increased blood flow through their *right* hemispheres, but not through the *left* half of their brains.

In a similar set of experiments, David Galin and his associates at the Langley Porter Neuropsychiatric Institute in San Francisco found that normal subjects show increased electrical activity in their "speaking" hemispheres when attempting to solve verbal tasks, but increased activity in their "silent" hemispheres when solving tasks of **spatial ability.**

Further studies from many laboratories indicate that most *logical functions* (such as mathematics and verbal problem solving) are controlled by the left hemisphere, while visual and musical perception seem to be controlled by the right hemisphere.

Galin believes that "each hemisphere is specialized for a different **cognitive** style; the left for an analytical, logical mode for which words are an excellent tool, and the right for a holistic **Gestalt** mode, which happens to be particularly suitable for spatial relations."

Question: Given what you know about the functions of the two hemispheres, how might you explain the fact that most of us seldom forget a face, but we so frequently forget the name associated with that face?

Emotions and the Two Hemispheres

It might be tempting at this point to assume that your "speaking" brain is a logical, plodding sort that "runs" your daily activities most of the time, while your "silent" hemisphere is the perceptual or creative side of your

If you are right-handed, as this young man is, your right hemisphere takes the lead in creative activities such as writing poetry.

Spatial ability (SPAY-shull). The ability to perceive or deal with objects in three-dimensional space. Also the ability to perceive three-dimensional patterns.

Cognitive (COG-nih-tiv or COG-nuh-tiv). Cognitive processes are those that go on inside your mind. From the Latin word meaning "to think."

Gestalt (guess-TALT). A mental or perceptual pattern. From the German word meaning "figure," "pattern," or "good form." The ability to see something "as a whole"—rather than just see its parts—is the ability to "form a Gestalt."

personality. But the situation is actually much more complex, for we haven't yet discussed how the two hemispheres react to emotional situations.

Schizophrenia is a form of "mental illness" which typically involves two abnormal types of behaviors. First, the schizophrenic person usually shows "disturbed thought patterns," which is to say that the person uses inappropriate language and cannot "think straight" in all situations. Second, the schizophrenic individual often shows "flattened **affect**," which is to say that the person often shows little emotional involvement in life and seems indifferent to his or her fate.

Could schizophrenia be related to a breakdown in communications between the two hemispheres? Perhaps so. In 1978, psychiatrists Laurence Schweitzer, Eugene Becker, and Howard Welsh reported on experiments they had performed on schizophrenic patients at the Downstate Medical Center in Brooklyn, New York. When normal subjects were asked to deal with emotional material, it was usually their "silent" right hemispheres that took the lead. However, when schizophrenic patients were asked to "process" the same information, they tended to use their left "talking" hemispheres almost entirely. Schweitzer and his colleagues believe that schizophrenia may be a mental disorder in which the person's left hemisphere *blocks out* emotional or motivational feedback from the right hemisphere.

In 1978, too, British researchers reported that schizophrenic patients had trouble identifying objects held in their left hands. While blindfolded, the patients could fairly readily describe an object held in the right hand—but comparing this object to a similar one held in the left hand gave them problems. Normal subjects had no difficulty at all with this task.

In an earlier set of experiments, G. Alema, G. Rosadini, and G.F. Rossi reported a rather strange set of findings using normal subjects. They injected a drug into the arteries leading to either the right or the left hemisphere. This drug would momentarily paralyze one hemisphere, but not the other. When their subjects recovered from left-hemisphere paralysis, most of these people became extremely depressed. They expressed a strong sense of guilt, of worthlessness, and great fears for the future. But when the subjects recovered from right-hemisphere paralysis, almost all of them showed great happiness and pleasure, and expressed a strong sense of well-being and joy.

In many other studies of human brain damage, experimenters have reported that patients with damage to their left hemispheres tend to be depressive, while patients who suffer damage to their right hemispheres tend to be somewhat **manic** or **euphoric.**

We will have more to say about these findings in the next three chapters. However, it does seem that your "talking" or dominant hemisphere does need appropriate input and feedback from your perceptual/emotional hemisphere in order for you to maintain a balanced and mentally healthy approach to life.

The "Two Cultures"

What parts of your mental and behavioral life are controlled by which parts of your brain? Although current research does give us a partial answer to this question, we should realize two things.

First, almost all of the theories we have today are "subject to being recalled," which is to say that they may be drastically changed by new data as they come from the laboratory. For example, in 1783 the noted British poet William Cowper wrote, "If man had been intended to fly, God would have provided him with wings." What would Cowper have thought of today's jet airplanes? (And do you *really* believe you have two minds?)

Second, long before people had electrodes or EEG machines, they knew quite well that the "unconscious" part of the mind was often more creative than the "conscious" part. For example, the great physicist Albert Einstein once remarked that he usually thought in logical, orderly fashion—just like everybody else. That is, his thoughts were usually formed in words, in sentences. But during a few periods of great creativity, Einstein seemed to relax and "let his mind wander." At these moments, Einstein could think in concepts, in symbols, in non-verbal and often non-logical patterns. Perhaps language imposes a rigid logic to the thought processes of the dominant hemisphere, while the minor hemisphere (being less verbal) is spared this verbal straight-jacket.

Opium (OH-pee-um). A drug that can cause euphoria. See Chapter 3.

We have known for centuries that certain drugs seem to enhance artistic creativity. For instance, the noted British poet Samuel Taylor Coleridge was addicted to **opium.** Coleridge often claimed that he wrote his imaginative poetry while "high" on opium. Perhaps this dangerous drug somehow weakened the dominance of his major hemisphere just enough so that the non-logical dreams and imaginings of his "silent" hemisphere could leak through to consciousness. When Coleridge "hunted for words" to express his fanciful thoughts, perhaps his dominant hemisphere was merely searching for ways of translating the symbolic thoughts of his minor hemisphere into verbal terms. (As we will see in the next chapter, there are better ways of opening up channels of communication between your two hemispheres than by taking drugs.)

The noted British scientist and writer, Lord Snow, wrote several books about what he called "the two cultures"—the often opposing worlds of logical science and creative art. He was dismayed that poets and physicists were frequently intolerant of each other's activities. Lord Snow looked to education to bridge this cultural gap. Perhaps he should have looked at that neural bridge, the corpus callosum, as well.

Summary

1.   The **brain** is the master organ of your body that, in many ways, coordinates or controls many of the functions of the other organs.

2.   The biggest parts of your brain are the two **cerebral hemispheres** that sit atop the stem of your brain like the cap on a mushroom.

3.   The thin outer covering of the cerebral hemispheres is called the **cortex.** Most of the functions of the brain that relate to conscious decision making are located in the cortex.

4.   Your brain contains at least 15 billion nerve cells or **neurons.**

5.   Most cortical neurons have three main parts—the **dendrites,** the cell body or **soma,** and the **axon.**

6.   The main purpose of most neurons is to pass messages from one part of the body to another. These messages are really waves of electro-chemical energy.

7.   When the dendrites are stimulated by **transmitter** chemicals, a wave of electrical activity sweeps down the neuron like a bullet speeding down the barrel of a gun.

8.   As this electrical wave reaches the end of the axon, it causes the axon to release chemical transmitters into the **synapse**—the fluid-filled space between the axon of one neuron and the dendrites of a second neuron.

9.   Transmitter chemicals released into the synapse excite the dendrites of the second neuron; it responds by "**firing** off" a wave of electrical energy on its own. The first neuron thus transmits a message to the second chemically.

10.   **Sensory input neurons** receive information from the outside world and transmit this information to **cortical processing neurons** which "make decisions" about how to respond.

11.   **Command messages** telling your muscles to respond go out from the brain via **motor neurons.**

12.   Damage to various parts of the brain can cause a condition known as **epilepsy.** Epileptic **seizures** show up on an **EEG** machine as **spike-shaped brain waves.**

13.   If epileptic seizures become too frequent or severe—and cannot be controlled by the use of drugs—a surgeon may cut the tissue con-

necting the two hemispheres. This **split-brain operation** may leave the patient with "two minds in the same body."

14. In normal people, the **dominant cerebral hemisphere** has the power of speech and usually thinks and controls the body in a logical fashion.

15. The minor or **monitoring hemisphere** can understand most language, but cannot usually speak. It seems more specialized to handle **perceptual** and **emotional processing** than is the dominant hemisphere.

16. In split-brain patients, the minor hemisphere can communicate with the outside world by moving the left hand.

17. Patients with damage to the dominant hemisphere often are **depressive.** Patients with damage to the perceptual/emotional hemisphere tend to be **euphoric.**

18. **Schizophrenic** patients appear to process most incoming sensory inputs just with their left hemispheres. They seem also to block out or **repress** emotional and informational messages coming from their right hemispheres.

19. What we call **"conscious awareness"** seems a function of the talking hemisphere, while **"unconscious"** creativity and artistic ability seem more a function of the perceptual/emotional half of the brain.

(Continued from page 33.)

"What an appropriate place to hide a secret," Colonel Garcia said, caressing Patrick's head again.

"I do not understand," said Captain Hartman. "How can the boy have a secret in his brain that the secret police over *there* could not discover?"

Colonel Garcia beamed. "Because Tavela knew more than they did, for one thing. Because they are atheists and God-haters, for another."

"Are you trying to tell me that Tavela hid the secret in Patrick's *soul?*" Captain Hartman said, a touch of sarcasm in his voice.

"Not quite, Captain, but perhaps you are closer than you know." The woman turned to the young man sitting beside her. "Tell me, Patrick, did you mention the Bible to the secret police when they questioned you?"

"Yes."

"And I'll bet they laughed, didn't they? And spoke of fairy tales and capitalist fantasies, didn't they?"

Patrick nodded his agreement.

"But 'understanding is more precious than rubies,' Patrick. Don't ever forget that. Tavela knew we would not reject his clue, that we would understand. And we do."

"I don't understand at all," said Captain Hartman.

Colonel Garcia grew serious. "It is simple, when you know something of how neurons and cerebral hemispheres actually work. Patrick, when Dr. Tavela operated on you, he cut your corpus callosum, didn't he?"

"Yes, I think that was it. He said it would stop the seizures."

Nodding, Colonel Garcia continued. "And then he tested the two hemispheres of your brain to determine what each could see and hear and respond to."

"What has that got to do with the formula?" asked the Captain.

"Everything—if you understand the third chapter of Proverbs. You see, Captain, the 'mask' that Patrick looked into was a device which presented stimuli to just one half of his brain. If Dr. Tavela showed something to the left hemisphere, Patrick would be conscious of it and could answer questions about it verbally." She looked at the young man. "Is that not so? Didn't he ask you what you could see?"

"All the time," replied Patrick. "Sometimes I could tell him, and sometimes I couldn't. I sort of *knew* he had showed me something, but I couldn't tell him what it was."

"But you could point to it with your left hand, couldn't you? Not your right hand, but your left hand?"

Patrick considered the matter. "I guess you're right. When I couldn't tell him what it was, I could almost always point it out with my left hand. But I still didn't *recognize* it, if you know what I mean. I *knew* it was right, but I still didn't know what it was."

"All right," said the Captain. "I think I see what you mean. 'And in her left hand is riches and honor.' When Tavela knew the police were coming for him, he had at most half an hour to hide the secret formula where we could find it later. Not in the cast or in the bandages, because the police would check them."

Patrick nodded excitedly. "Yes, they took off my cast and changed my bandages. And they took lots of X-rays."

"And they didn't find anything, because they rejected the clue to the Bible," continued the Colonel.

Hartman smiled. "Because Dr. Tavela had spent thirty minutes of freedom presenting the formula to the right half of Patrick's brain. But how did he do that?" asked the Captain.

"He wouldn't have dared write it down," replied Colonel Garcia. "He must have whispered it in Patrick's left ear." She turned to the young man sitting beside her. "You see, Patrick, when I talk into your left ear, the right half of your brain will hear me clearly. But your left hemisphere will hear what I say very weakly. So I can talk to the silent half of your brain . . . over here . . ." She touched the right side of Patrick's head. " . . . and your talking hemisphere will just barely hear me."

Hartman seemed confused. "But his left hemisphere doesn't *know* what the formula is at all!"

"That's what the loud noise was for, Captain. To block out the very weak whispering. Patrick's left hemisphere heard loud noises and missed the whispering. Patrick's right hemisphere heard very weak noises and loud whispering. So it knows, but Patrick doesn't, eh?" She smiled at the young man. "You still don't know what the formula is, do you?"

"No," he said, a puzzled look on his face.

Hartman's confusion continued. "But the secret police gave Patrick extensive polygraph tests. Surely his right hemisphere would give the show away, for the so-called 'lie detector' actually detects emotions. And the right hemisphere is the emotional/feedback half of the brain."

The Colonel laughed. "You missed another clue, Captain. Tell me, why do you think Dr. Tavela said it was lucky that Patrick broke a bone in his *left* hand?"

"Oh, of course," replied Hartman. "Because of the cast on Patrick's left hand, the police had to put the polygraph electrodes on the palm of his right hand."

"Which is controlled by the left half of Patrick's brain . . ." said the Colonel.

"Which *wasn't* conscious of the secret and hence couldn't give it away."

"Exactly," said the woman, nodding slowly. She picked up the pencil from her desk and wrote "Yes" and "No" on a sheet of paper. Then she put the paper close to Patrick's left hand. "Now, Patrick, I'm going to ask you some questions, but I don't want you to answer out loud. Instead, I want you to answer them by pointing to 'Yes' or 'No' on the paper—with your left hand. All right?"

"All right," he responded, his left hand moving toward the paper.

"Patrick," the Colonel continued, "I want to talk to your right hemisphere. If you hear what I am saying, please point to 'Yes.'"

Patrick's fingers touched "Yes."

"Patrick, did Dr. Tavela tell you the secret formula?"

"No," said Patrick out loud. But his left hand pointed to "Yes."

"Weird," muttered Captain Hartman.

Patrick stared at his left hand in amazement. "I don't understand what I'm doing."

Colonel Garcial reached over and hugged him tightly. "Patrick, dear. You are a very special person. You are special to us, because you are different. You must face that fact, Patrick, and be proud of it. We all have two minds, you see, one in each half of our brains. But most of us never know it, never have a chance to experience the world as you do. When you lost your corpus callosum, Patrick, you gained freedom for the right half of your brain. It is your twin brother, and you can talk to him, and he can respond by pointing with your left hand. So you always have someone with you, someone slightly different from you, but someone just as special as you are. If you learn to listen carefully, you'll never be alone again, all the rest of your life."

"Incredible," said Captain Hartman. "But on the other hand . . ."

Colonel Garcia silenced the man with a wave of her fingers. "Patrick, in the world of espionage and spying, we are constantly told, 'Never let your right hand know what your left is doing.' You are the only person I know of who can actually follow that advice. Because of your special brain, you have helped us, and Dr. Tavela, and even yourself. Be proud of that too."

She gave him a final hug, then stood up and reached out to him. "Come, Patrick. It is time that your left hand had a long talk with one of our chemists."

Patrick's left hand pointed to "Yes."

Recommended Readings

Galin, David. "Implications for psychiatry of left and right cerebral specialization," *Archives of General Psychiatry.* 31 (1974), pp. 572–583.

Gazzaniga, Michael S. *The Bisected Brain* (New York: Appleton, 1970).

Ornstein, Robert. "The split and whole brain," *Human Nature,* Vol. 1, no. 5 (1978), pp. 76–83.

Sagan, Carl. *The Dragons of Eden: Speculations on the Evolution of Human Intelligence* (New York: Ballantine, 1978).

Sperry, R.W. "Hemisphere deconnection and unity in conscious awareness," *American Psychologist,* 23 (1968), pp. 723–733.

Sterman, M.B. "Biofeedback and epilepsy," *Human Nature,* Vol. 1, no. 5 (1978), pp. 50–57.

Sleep, Drugs, and Altered States of Consciousness

Did You Know That . . .

"Consciousness" is a "primitive term" that is almost impossible to define?

You can alter your normal state of consciousness by speeding up or slowing down your brain's activity level?

Your body has regular physiological rhythms that vary according to the time of day?

You go through several 90-minute sleep cycles nightly?

You dream more just before you awaken?

"Short sleepers" are often active, ambitious, and conformist, while "long sleepers" are often shy, passive, and sexually inhibited?

Dreaming may help you store the day's experiences away in memory?

Nightmares frequently occur a day or so after you've stopped taking sleeping pills?

Drugs affect you chiefly by speeding up or slowing down your bodily processes?

Your neurons can secrete both transmitters and inhibitors?

"Uppers" act like neural transmitters, while "downers" act like neural inhibitors?

Hallucinogens may have their odd effects because they disrupt the delicate functional balance between the two hemispheres?

Marijuana apparently does less damage to the body than does alcohol?

You can learn to control your brain waves using a biofeedback machine?

"Nightmares and Nirvanas"

The Washington Bureaucrat leaned back in his overstuffed chair, puffed on his pipe, and meditated quietly as he looked at the man and woman sitting in front of his desk. They were nice people, really—bright, eager academics—and he did want to help them. They needed research funds to study some savages living in a jungle in South America, but they hadn't the foggiest notion of how to survive in that "jungle by the Potomac" called Washington, D.C.

"Look," the Bureaucrat said, putting down his pipe. "It's a simple trade-off, really. You, Dr. Ogdon, and your husband are both psychologists. You want to go study language development in some very primitive people who live near the Amazon. Right?"

Susan Ogdon looked at her husband and then nodded assent.

"Well," continued the Bureaucrat, "Our department wants someone to study marijuana use, and in just the same sort of backwoods people. We don't care what language these people speak or how they learn to speak it. But we do want to find out how pot-smoking affects their lives, their health, and their ability to get along in the world. You make our study for us, and we'll pay for the research." The Bureaucrat picked up his pipe again and leaned back in his chair. "What you choose to do in your spare time is your own affair, naturally. If you want to study language development on the side, we couldn't care less."

The woman cleared her throat. "What do you wish us to prove for you?"

The Bureaucrat sat bolt upright. "Nothing! Nothing at all! We have no preconceived notions of what your findings will be." The man paused, remembering how upset the Deputy Assistant Secretary of the department got at the mere mention of marijuana. "Well, no *official* preconceived notions, you understand. But truthfully, we'll accept and let you publish whatever results you get."

"Why us?" asked Roger Ogdon.

"Because you've been there, and you know the people. Otherwise you wouldn't want to do your own research there." The Bureaucrat's voice softened and he put on his warmest smile. "Speaking personally, I do happen to be quite interested in language development. But the department simply is not able to fund such projects these days. So, when I read the proposal you sent us on language development in primitives, I thought . . ." He let his words drift slowly toward the ceiling like verbal pipe smoke.

The woman's face brightened when the Bureaucrat gave his personal approval of their project. "Roger," she said, turning to her husband, "I do think we ought to consider it. But we'd surely have to think a while about how to measure the effects of long-term marijuana smoking on *anybody,* much less on the natives."

"You're right, Sue," Roger Ogdon said. He turned in his chair and looked straight at the Bureaucrat. "Why do you want us to study Amazon primitives? If you want to know the effects of pot-smoking on American citizens—and I suspect you do—why not do your research right here in Washington? Surely there are enough people in government who . . ."

"You're thinking of the Previous Administration," said the Bureaucrat quickly. "But really, you two, you know perfectly well we can't fund any research on marijuana consumption in the US because it's illegal to smoke the stuff here. We'd have to arrest anyone who dared to be a subject in such research. Besides, I suspect those natives have been smoking pot for many generations. You can look for long-term genetic effects as well as measuring the problems it gives them today."

Sue Ogdon frowned. "I thought you said you had no preconceived notions of what we'd find. What if there aren't any long-term genetic effects, or any real problems today?"

Now it was the Bureaucrat's turn to frown. These people were giving him a mild headache. Surely they saw that he was trying to help them. Why didn't they just take the money, and do what they were told? He reached in a desk drawer and took out an aspirin. Taking a sip of water, he swallowed the tablet quickly.

"Look, Dr. Ogdon," he said. "I will be frank with you. It would greatly please certain people upstairs if you found that marijuana had bad effects on the natives. Maybe that's what you'll find, and maybe not. But let's get things straight. I don't care what you find. Just plan the best

PART ONE Biological Bases of Behavior

study possible, use as many controls as you can, and get the facts. We'll pay the bills, no matter what."

"Haven't you supported similar studies before?" asked the woman.

The Bureaucrat's face went slightly white. "Er, yes, I believe so. A couple, perhaps. But the more data are repeated or replicated, the more firmly we can believe the data. As my senior professor said in graduate school, 'Replication is good for the soul.'"

Susan Ogdon persisted. "What did the other investigators find?"

"Now, now," said the Bureaucrat in a soothing tone of voice. "I'd rather you approached this problem with fresh minds. Just make sure that you measure the biological, psychological, and social effects of marijuana use, and do so as objectively as you can. That's the important thing."

Roger Ogdon was puzzled. "I don't think I've read the results of those 'couple of studies' you've already funded."

"Well," said the Bureaucrat, reaching for another aspirin. "I don't believe we've published the results yet. Later this year, perhaps . . ." He let his words drift off again.

Susan Ogdon became quite angry. "You mean, you suppressed the results because the data didn't come out the way you expected them to!"

The Bureaucrat sighed. "The results were certainly not surprising to anyone who had bothered to read the scientific literature on the subject."

"Then why do you want to pay for still another study whose results you may have to suppress?" the woman continued.

The Bureaucrat put down his pipe in an angry gesture. "Listen to me. You are both psychologists, and you're supposed to be able to understand why people and organizations act the way they do. You know perfectly well that it takes a long time for an organization to change its mind on a subject. It takes a lot of data to accomplish that miracle, and a lot of gentle pushing from inside. The people upstairs have come a long way in the past decade, but they still have a couple of miles to go. Your data could be the straw that broke the camel's back, if you see what I mean."

The Bureaucrat's voice became impassioned as he continued. "I want good data, and I need your help. You go do the study, and report anything you find. Repeat, *anything.* Do your own work on the side, if you wish. And leave it up to me to see that your findings have the maximum impact upstairs. Okay?"

The man and woman exchanged glances. Then the man said, "Well, I think we understand each other. We'll go plan a study, and submit a proposal to you. If we agree on the details, you'll get us the funding. And, as you said, any other research we do 'on the side' is our business."

The Bureaucrat beamed. "Marvelous! I hoped you'd see it that way. Now, let's go find a drink somewhere and celebrate!"

(Continued on page 90.)

Consciousness

This chapter is about drugs—how they affect your body and brain, how they influence the workings of your mind, and how they alter your behavior and relationships with other people.

Nirvana (near-VAHN-ah). From an ancient Indian word meaning "blowing out." In modern usage, Nirvana means a state of freedom characterized by the extinction of desire, passion, illusion, and the attainment of rest, truth, and unchanging being. It also refers to any mental condition that we might call "heavenly pleasure" or paradise.

Consciousness (KON-shuss-nuss). The act or process of being aware, particularly of one's surroundings and bodily condition. Also, being alert, understanding what is happening.

Primitive terms. Concepts or ideas that are basic to a particular science—so basic that the science cannot exist without these concepts. Because the terms are so fundamental, they cannot be readily defined except in their own terms.

Tautology (taw-TOLL-oh-gee). A useless and repetitive way of speaking, or defining words in terms of themselves. For instance, "consciousness is being conscious of something."

This chapter also makes brief mention of sexual orgasm, and touches on a heavenly experience that some people call **Nirvana.**

But most of all, this chapter deals with what we shall shortly define as "altered states of consciousness," such as sleep and dreaming.

However, if you wish to find out some new things about drugs, sex, Nirvana, and dreams, you will have to pay a small price for that pleasure. That is, you will have to understand a bit more about the *systematic interactions* among your brain, your mind, and your social environment. For unless you know something about what goes on inside your brain, the new information about your states of mind may not make much sense to you.

So let us begin with what may seem a dumb question. What do we mean by the term **consciousness?** After all, if the main theme of this chapter is *altered* states of consciousness, perhaps we had better first make sure that we know what it is we're altering.

Primitive Terms

Every science has what are called **primitive terms.** That is, every science has ideas or concepts which are so elemental that they are exceptionally difficult to define.

For instance, if you want to make a physicist sweat just a little, ask that person what "energy" and "matter" are. You must have a rough notion of what these words mean, but you may also realize that great philosophical battles have been fought over their exact definitions.

Or ask a biologist what he or she means by the term "life." Now, there's a lively way to start a deadly discussion! Biologists have spent many centuries trying to pin down just what "life" is—and isn't. But in truth, there is no one definition for "energy" or "matter" or "life" that all scientists will agree is completely accurate.

Psychology has its primitive terms too. One of these is *consciousness.* (Another, in case you're wondering, is *mind.*) The dictionary gives many definitions of "consciousness," most of which have to do with awareness, awakeness, understanding, being alert, or even being alive. Some of the dictionary meanings have to do with *self*-awareness, or the experience of knowing that you are having the experience of knowing.

And although you surely have some conscious awareness of what consciousness is all about, you too might find it hard to describe *consciousness* without slipping into **tautology**—that is, without defining the word in terms of itself.

One reason that primitive terms give us fits is that they often refer to processes or conditions, rather than referring to things or objects. For instance, it is much easier to define a track shoe than it is the act of running. Objects such as track shoes usually have a location in space, and can be measured accurately. Processes often have no clear-cut beginning or end, and there are very few processes that you can hold a ruler to or weigh on a scale.

Conscious awareness is even more difficult to talk about than running or jumping. For self-awareness is something that occurs inside your head and can't be seen or observed directly. Anyone with eyes can tell whether you are running or standing still, but not even a psychologist can read your mind. However, if we begin with the thought that consciousness refers to a process—*a sequence of events*—rather than referring to a "thing" we can touch or smell or see, then we're off to a good start in defining this primitive term.

And define it we must, for *consciousness* is one of the most controversial yet important concepts in all of psychology.

The Process of Consciousness

Perhaps the following five points are as close as we can come (at the moment) to defining the process of consciousness scientifically:

PART ONE Biological Bases of Behavior

1. You take in information from the world around you (and from your own body).

2. You recognize that you have (or haven't) experienced these inputs before.

3. You make decisions about what these sensory inputs mean, and what their emotional value might be to you.

4. You respond to the inputs.

5. You then notice what the consequences of your actions and feelings are.

This definition surely gives us a better "handle" to study and discuss consciousness than we had before, since we know that inputs, internal processes, outputs, and feedback are necessary to the experience of self-awareness. And even if we cannot inspect your consciousness directly, we can at least measure the inputs, outputs, and feedback that so strongly influence what you think and feel.

If consciousness is a process, then it *exists in time*. That means that some aspects of consciousness can be changed if we alter either your environment or what's going on inside your body. Here are three examples of how this might be done.

First, if we shut you off from your environment, your consciousness in fact slows down and may stop altogether for long periods of time (*see* Chapter 9).

Second, as we will see later in this chapter, if we give you certain drugs that alter the speed with which your brain reacts to incoming sensory stimulation, then we probably will alter your conscious response to those inputs.

Third, if we reduce the amount of feedback that you get from your body and from the outside world—or if we greatly enhance the pleasurable or painful aspects of the feedback—we can sometimes have profound effects on your awareness of yourself and of your environment.

Thus, by varying the inputs that we give to people (the *independent variables* in most experiments), we can change both their biological and their intra-psychic processes. And because we can alter what goes on inside people by changing their inputs, we can often affect the verbal reports or behaviors (*dependent variables*) that people use to tell us what state of consciousness they are experiencing at the moment.

States of consciousness can usually be altered in just two ways—**quantitatively** and **qualitatively.** Much of the time, both types of changes occur almost simultaneously, but many psychologists believe that quantitative changes are by far the most frequent. Certainly quantitative changes are easier to measure and to discuss, and it is a fact that most of the drugs that people commonly use primarily affect the *speed* at which their minds and bodies operate.

So let us begin our exploration into this wild and wonderful area of human experience by talking about two quantitatively altered states of consciousness that all of us experience almost every day—sleeping and dreaming.

Sleep and Dreams

Although you may not be consciously aware of it, your body goes through rather regular **physiological cycles** every day. Your temperature, for instance, is usually lowest in the middle of the night (if that is when you normally sleep), begins to rise about the time you get up in the morning, continues to rise slightly for the first three hours you are awake, and then remains relatively constant until you go to bed again at night. This **diurnal** temperature change is very slight—usually no more than a degree or so—but it does seem to occur in just about everybody. *Why* this diurnal rhythm occurs, no one is really sure. But we do know that it takes place even in people who are totally inactive throughout the day.

Quantitative (KWAN-tee-tate-tiv). The act of measuring something which exists in the outside world, such as a pound of potatoes, or how long it takes to fly from Los Angeles to New York City.

Qualitative (KWAL-lih-tate-tiv). The act of measuring some inner characteristic, or placing a value judgment on some object or experience. For instance, measuring (or estimating) how hungry you are for mashed potatoes, or how afraid you are of flying. Quantities exist "out there" and generally are independent of the observer. Qualities, however, are the "mental labels" you assign to things or experiences and thus are not independent of your own observations. The sciences generally deal with quantities; the humanities with qualities.

Physiological cycles (FIZZ-see-oh-LODGE-uh-kal). Changes in bodily activities that occur regularly and dependably, and that usually are strongly influenced by the outside world, or that are inherited, or both. The mating cycle in animals is greatly affected by the seasons of the year, by how long the days are, by the temperature, by the amount of hormones present, and (sometimes) by the animal's previous experiences. The menstrual period in women is an example of a human physiological cycle that repeats itself about every 28 days.

Diurnal (dye-YOURN-ull). Anything that occurs every day. A physiological cycle with a "period" of 24 hours.

Your ability to taste, smell, and hear also varies during the day, reaching its peak (in most people) at the very odd hour of 3 A.M. A second peak in your sensory ability usually occurs between 5 and 7 P.M., which may account for the fact that you are likely to prefer your largest meal of the day about then—when food should taste and smell best. Also, your **alpha rhythm** is typically a little faster around 5 P.M. than at any other time of the day—although again, no one really knows why this should be.

The most noticeable diurnal or daily rhythm you have, however, is that of sleep and wakefulness. Sleep is obviously an interruption in your stream of consciousness—that much is clear. But scientists are still uncertain as to what sleep actually is or what functions it serves. True, we all need to rest now and again to recover from the day's activities. But does unconscious sleep help your body recover more than would "deep rest" in which you stayed peacefully awake?

To put the matter another way, if the main function of sleep is to let your body repair itself *physiologically,* why do you have to be unconscious for the repair to occur? We don't know the answer to that one. But there is growing evidence that sleep is important *psychologically* because it allows us to dream. And, as we will see, if sleep refreshes the body, dreams may be necessary for us to store the day's memories away and refresh our minds.

Sleep Cycles

Sleep is part of your daily activity cycle, but there are several different types or stages of sleep, and they too occur in cycles.

If you are an average sleeper, your sleep cycle will go something like this (see Figs. 3.1A through 3.1D):

1. When you first drift off into slumber, your eyes will roll about a bit, your temperature will drop slightly, your muscles will relax, and your breathing will slow and become quite regular. Your brain waves slow down a bit too, with the alpha rhythm predominating for the first few minutes. This is called *Stage 1 sleep*.

2. For the next half hour or so, as you relax more and more, you will drift down through *Stage 2* and *Stage 3* sleep. The lower your stage of sleep, the slower your brain waves will be.

3. Then, about 40–60 minutes after you lose consciousness, you will have reached the deepest sleep of all. Your brain waves will show the **delta rhythm.** This is *Stage 4* sleep.

4. You may think that you stay at this deep fourth stage all the rest of the night, but that turns out not to be the case. Instead, about 80 minutes after you fall into slumber, your activity cycle will increase slightly. The delta rhythm will disappear, to be replaced by the *activity pattern* of brain waves. Your eyes will begin to dart around under your closed eyelids as if you were looking at something occurring in front of you. This period of *Rapid Eye Movements* lasts for some 8–15 minutes and is called **REM** sleep (Fig. 3.1E).

It is during REM sleep that most dreams seem to occur. It is also during this period that most males (whatever age) experience an erection of the penis, and most females experience vaginal swelling and sometimes a hardening of their nipples.

During both light and deep sleep, the muscles in your body are relaxed but capable of movement. However, as you slip into REM sleep, a very odd thing occurs—most of the **voluntary muscles** in your body become *paralyzed.* Although your brain shows very rapid bursts of neural activity during REM sleep, your body is incapable of moving. In more technical terms—as we will see later in this chapter—we can say that REM sleep is accompanied by extensive *muscular inhibition.*

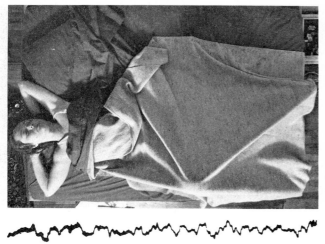

Fig. 3.1A. In first of normal sleep's four stages, small, fast brain waves appear on EEG record (below sleeper).

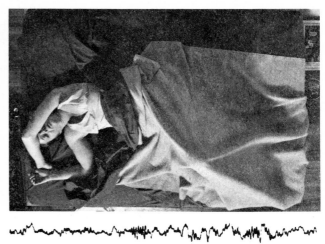

Fig. 3.1B. In second stage, brain shows short bursts of activity (resembling spindles) as light sleep begins to deepen.

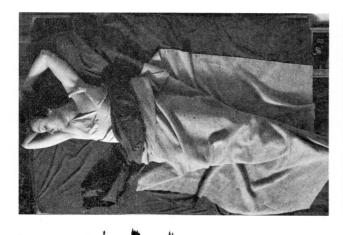

Fig. 3.1C. In the third stage, larger, slower brain waves appear as the half-hour descent to deep sleep continues.

Fig. 3.1D. Fourth stage, with large delta waves, is followed by ascent to lighter sleep, then to dreaming (REM sleep).

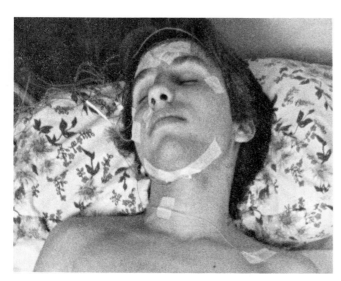

Asleep

EEG
Awake-like activation

EOG
Rapid eye movements

EMG
Muscle tone absent

Fig. 3.1E. In REM sleep, when dreams take place, a volunteer's polygraph shows brain waves similar to waking state (top row), intense rapid eye movement (middle), and virtually no activity of chin muscles (bottom).

Question: When would you be more likely to sleepwalk, during Stage 4 sleep, or during REM sleep?

No one knows why this muscular inhibition takes place during REM sleep, but many scientists speculate that it serves to keep you from acting out your dreams.

One other odd thing that we have learned recently is that dreaming seems to be a function of the right "silent" hemisphere, not of the left "talking" hemisphere. Scientists from several laboratories have found that the right hemisphere is much more active electrically during dreaming than is the left. And Sperry notes that while many of his split-brain patients reported having vivid dreams prior to the surgery, they reported no dreams at all after the operation. Either their dreams had stopped occurring, or their "talking" hemisphere was no longer aware of all the fun the right hemisphere was having.

Question: Why might you have trouble remembering your dreams unless you "say the dream out loud" as soon as you awaken?

Provided that you don't wake up during the first REM sleep period, your body will soon relax again, your breathing will grow slow and regular once more, and you will slip gently back from Stage 1 to Stage 4 sleep again—only to rise to the surface of near-consciousness some 80 minutes later.

Most people experience four to five such sleep cycles per night, although both the quality and the intensity of the experience change slightly the longer the person sleeps. Your first cycle usually yields the deepest sleep, and your first REM period is typically the shortest. But no matter how many sleep cycles you experience during the night, you are more likely to awaken during a REM period than at any other time.

Question: Why is it that human males so frequently awaken with an erection?

Effects of Sleep Deprivation The length of the sleep cycle varies considerably from one species to another, and within a species it varies according to the age of the organism. Rats typically go through a full cycle in 10–13 minutes; children do so in 50–60 minutes; adult humans take 85–110 minutes; and adult elephants require about 120 minutes. (As we will see, however, there is considerable variation even among adult humans as to the number of cycles per night an individual needs or wants.)

If you are an average person, you can tolerate up to 40 hours or so of sleeplessness without suffering ill effects. If you are kept awake much past 40 hours, however, you will probably begin to show an increased irritability and impulsiveness. Your decision-making processes will be affected, and you will react more slowly and make poorer intellectual judgments than you would when rested.

If you are deprived of sleep for 100 hours or more, you will very likely show considerable stress and even signs of mental disturbance. Which is to say that you will become almost as hostile and suspicious as are people who suffer from a "mental illness" called **paranoid schizophrenia.**

Whenever you are allowed to sleep after being severely deprived, your cycles may change to include much *more* Stage 4 (deep) sleep than usual, and a good deal *less* REM sleep than usual.

How much sleep do you normally get each night—when you've not been particularly deprived? According to researchers Frederick Baekeland and Ernest Hartmann, if you are average in your sleep habits, you will get about 7.5 hours per day. About 5 percent of the population regularly chooses to

Paranoid schizophrenia (PAIR-uh-noid skits-zoh-FREE-knee-uh). The major symptoms of this type of "mental illness" are illogical thought patterns, changeable delusions, and sometimes vivid hallucinations. Delusions of persecution ("they're controlling my mind by radio waves") are most common.

PART ONE Biological Bases of Behavior

sleep less than 6 hours a night, while another 5 percent will sleep more than 9 hours if given the chance. Baekeland and Hartmann call these people "short sleepers" and "long sleepers," and they make a fascinating study.

"Long" and "Short Sleepers"

Baekeland and Hartmann brought 20 young men who were identified as "short sleepers" and another 20 men who were "long sleepers" into the laboratory and studied their sleep patterns using **EEG machines** attached to the men while they slept. The subjects, who averaged about 25 years of age, were given two nights to adapt to bedding down in the laboratory situation. Then the scientists collected data for several nights while the subjects slept at the laboratory. Baekeland and Hartmann report that there were differences not only in the type of sleep patterns the men showed, but also in the personalities of the men themselves.

To begin with, after the first two nights of adjustment, the men seemed to sleep in the laboratory pretty much the same way that they slept in their own beds. The "short sleepers" dozed off almost immediately and got but 330 minutes of sleep. The "long sleepers" took much longer to get to sleep, but totaled about 527 minutes of "sleep time."

Both groups averaged some 75 minutes of Stage 4 (deep) sleep per night, a fact that led Baekeland and Hartmann to conclude that we get most of our really profound sleep during the first few hours we are in bed. However, the "long sleepers" averaged almost twice as much REM sleep per night as did the "short sleepers." Some people obviously need more dream time than do others. And this need for lengthier dreams seems to stem from the personality characteristics of the men themselves.

"Short Sleepers"   Baekeland and Hartmann report that the "short sleepers" had been more or less average in their sleep needs until the men were in their teens. But at about age 15 or so, the men voluntarily began cutting down their nightly sleep time because of pressures from school, work, and other activities. These men tended to view their nightly periods of unconsciousness as bothersome interruptions in their daily routines.

In general, these "short sleepers" appeared ambitious, active, energetic, cheerful, conformist in their opinions, and very sure about their career choices. They often held several jobs at once, or worked full- or part-time while going to school. And many of them had a strong urge to appear "normal" or "acceptable" to their friends and associates.

When asked to recall their dreams, the "short sleepers" did poorly. More than this, they seemed to prefer *not* remembering. In similar fashion, their usual way of dealing with psychological problems was to deny that the problem existed, and then to keep busy in the hope that the trouble would go away.

The sleep patterns of the "short sleepers" were similar to, but less extreme than, sleep patterns shown by many mental patients categorized as **manic** (see Table 3.1).

"Long Sleepers"   The "long sleepers" were quite different indeed. Baekeland and Hartmann report that these young men had been lengthy sleepers since childhood. They seemed to enjoy their sleep, protected it, and were quite concerned when they were occasionally deprived of their desired 9 hours of nightly bed rest. They tended to recall their dreams much better than did the "short sleepers."

Many of the "long sleepers" were shy, anxious, **introverted,** inhibited, passive, mildly depressed, and unsure of themselves (particularly in social situations). A number of them, for instance, were still virgins at age 25–30. Several openly stated that sleep was an escape from their daily problems.

EEG machines. Electro-encephalo-graphs. These devices measure brain waves and other forms of electrical activity in the nervous system. The brain-wave pattern is usually displayed graphically on a sheet of paper, or flashed on a picture tube similar to the one used in television sets. See Chapter 2.

Manic (MANN-ick). From the Greek word *mania,* meaning "insanity." A manic person is someone terribly excited, almost to the point of madness. The opposite of depression.

Introverted (INN-trow-ver-ted). A term made famous by the Swiss psychiatrist, Carl Jung. Introverted people spend much of their time looking inward, inspecting their own thoughts, feelings, and values.

Table 3.1

A Comparison of Baekeland and Hartmann's "Short Sleepers" and "Long Sleepers."

	Average Length of Sleep	Amount of Stage 4 Sleep	Amount of REM Sleep	Personality Characteristics
"Short sleepers"	330 minutes	75 minutes	About 50 minutes	Active, cheerful, conformist; dislikes sleep and dreaming
"Long sleepers"	527 minutes	75 minutes	About 100 minutes	Shy, anxious, inhibited, loves sleep and dreaming

Data based on Baekeland and Hartmann, 1977.

Question: As you know, the left hemisphere seems to be the logical one, while the right hemisphere seems to be the creative side of the brain. Which hemisphere seems to predominate in "short sleepers?" In "long sleepers?"

Baekeland and Hartmann suggest that "short sleepers" might be afraid of the subjective experiences that accompany dreaming and that they deliberately curtail their bed time in order to escape any fantasies that might force them to inspect their own thoughts and feelings more carefully. By contrast, "long sleepers" seem to need lengthy REM times in order to work out their personal uncertainties, fears, and conflicts during that altered state of consciousness we call dreaming.

The young men studied by Baekeland and Hartmann were, by definition, extremes. Most of us need both deep sleep and ample REM sleep each night. But as we will see in a moment, there is evidence that we all need more dream time when we are worried, or when we have been exposed to new and challenging situations during the day.

Dreams

People have studied dreams and dreaming since the dawn of time, but it has only been in the last century that we have had the tools to investigate the subject scientifically.

The presence of "brain waves" in animals was discovered by Richard Caton in 1875, but few scientists a century ago realized that Caton's work had much relevance for the human race. However, beginning about 1902, a German neuro-physiologist named Hans Berger began recording electrical changes in brain activity in humans using large electrodes placed on the scalp. By 1930, Berger had developed the first practical EEG machine and noted many of the changes in brain waves that occur during waking and sleep periods. (The alpha rhythm is still sometimes called the *Berger rhythm* in his honor.) Thus it was not until the EEG was available that we had a precise physiological index of when a person was deeply asleep.

Before Berger's discoveries, about all we could do was to *ask people* to tell us about their sleep experiences. But asking people to be conscious of what happens to them when they are unconscious is not necessarily the best way to study sleep. For in such situations, their *subjective* reports usually tell us more about the people's attitudes and prejudices than it does about what really happened to them. Thanks to the *objective* data we have gotten from EEG records, we have learned more about sleep in the past 50 years than we did in the previous 50,000.

The Dream Cycle

Sleeping people also dream, but we really didn't know much about the frequency of dreaming until the early 1950's. Prior to that time, scientists could do little more than record what people remembered about their dreams. Some people insisted they never dreamed at all; other individuals were confident that they dreamed the whole night long. We now know, however, that everyone dreams several times a night, during each sleep cycle. For in 1953 Nathaniel Kleitman and E. Aserinski discovered the connection between REM sleep and dreaming.

Kleitman and Aserinski performed their experiment by waking up their subjects at various times during the sleep cycle. If the subjects were awakened during deep sleep, they seldom reported they were having a dream. However, if the subjects were awakened during initial light sleep, or particularly during REM sleep, the subjects frequently stated they had been dreaming. Furthermore, the dreams seemed very fresh in their memories, for the subjects could almost always give rather vivid descriptions of what they had just dreamed. (If they were asked about their dreams later on, however, the subjects seldom could remember.)

It now seems fairly clear that, when you are in Stage 4 (deep) sleep, your sensory inputs are almost entirely cut off, your cortex does little or no "processing" of incoming information, and only the lower centers of your brain are really functional. As each of your sleep cycles concludes, however, your cortex becomes active, your eyes frequently begin to dart about under your eyelids, the activity pattern appears on your EEG record, and you rise gently but quickly from complete unconsciousness into the twilight zone of dreaming.

Dream Frequency

According to Kleitman (and most other authorities), you probably have several dreams a night. In fact, you usually have several dreams within each REM period. Each dream probably runs from a few seconds to several minutes in length. And since REM periods at the beginning of your sleep tend to be the shortest, you most likely dream less in the early evening than later on.

Question: If you wanted to determine whether animals have dreams, what kinds of observations would you want to make?

Dream Deprivation

Since all humans seem to dream nightly, we may assume that dreaming serves some necessary function. Although we are still not entirely sure what that function is, we now know that depriving people (or animals) of REM sleep can have fairly unpleasant effects. For in 1960, Stanford University scientist William C. Dement reported data suggesting that dream time is necessary to many people's mental health.

Dement had subjects sleep in his laboratory. As long as the subjects were showing light or deep sleep, he let them alone. Once a REM period began, however, Dement would wake them up immediately. When the subjects would go back to sleep, their cycles would (as is almost always the case) begin at Stage 1, proceed through Stage 4, and from thence to REM, at which point Dement would wake them up again. His subjects therefore got all the *deep sleep* they normally would, but they got in very little *dreaming* because dreams are associated almost entirely with REM periods.

Many of Dement's subjects became cranky, annoyed, impulsive, and hostile when deprived of dreaming for several nights. They seemed to have considerable difficulty remembering things they had learned the day before

William C. Dement.

(animals deprived of REM sleep also show poor memory for tasks unless given adequate REM sleep). When Dement's subjects were later allowed to sleep without having their dreams interrupted, most of the subjects showed greatly increased REM periods—as if they were trying to "catch up" on all the dreaming he had deprived them of.

Further experiments by Dement and other scientists have shown that not all people respond to REM deprivation in the way that Dement's first subjects did. In fact, some people can tolerate a week of deprivation without showing too many ill effects. However a few people—perhaps of the "long sleeper" personality type described by Baekeland and Hartmann—are apparently pushed near the edge of insanity if they are not allowed to dream for several nights.

Dream Content

If you are like most people, your first dreams of the night will tend to be rather dull and trivial, mostly having to do with things that you have done during the day. In later REM periods, however, your dreams will probably become more unusual, more vivid, more colorful, easier to remember, and sometimes more anxiety-provoking.

During any one REM period, you are likely to experience a *sequence of related dreams*, or to run through the *same dream two or three times*. Mostly, though, you will dream about things that are of some interest or importance to you.

For instance, C. Hall and R. Van de Castle reported in 1966 that 30 percent of the 50 laboratory dreams of a young man who loved sports cars were related to driving and to automobiles, while another man who had a strong emotional tie to football dreamed about that sport 36 percent of the time.

The connection between dream content and the rapid movements your eyes make while you dream is not entirely understood. But there does seem to be a close relationship between the *direction* in which your eyes move and what you are dreaming about. For instance, if you dream you are watching someone walk up a hill, your REMs will be predominantly up and down. But if you dream you are observing a tennis match, your eyes will mostly dart back and forth from right to left.

Question: If dreams are primarily a "right hemisphere" activity, would you expect to carry on lengthy conversations (or write a book) in most of your dreams?

With the exception of nightmares, most of our dreams are rather ordinary. Sigmund Freud, one of the first modern scientists to pay special attention to the content of dreams, suggested that we use the dream state as a time of working through the day's events and of acting out in fantasy some of our unfulfilled desires.

Ramon Greenberg, director of sleep research at the Boston Veterans Hospital, goes a step farther. Greenberg believes that dreams are the brain's way of *storing memories*. According to Greenberg, while you dream you may be transferring memories of the day's events from the perceptual input areas of your brain to those parts of your cerebrum that are involved in memory storage. We will have more to say about this intriguing notion in Chapter 17.

But now it is time for us to delve into the murky, even frightening subject of the most memorable dreams of all, *nightmares*.

Nightmares

Imagine yourself comfortably sleeping in your bed, **oblivious** to everything around you. Then you begin to sense—deep down inside you—that some-

Oblivious (ob-BLIV-ee-us). From the Latin word meaning "to smooth over," or "to forget." If you are oblivious to the rattlesnake crawling at your feet, you simply pay no attention to it or forget that it is there.

PART ONE *Biological Bases of Behavior*

thing has changed, that something has gone very wrong. Slowly, almost dimly, you regain enough consciousness to realize that you are suffocating, that some heavy weight is lying on your chest crushing your lungs. Suddenly you realize that your breathing has almost stopped, and you are dying for air.

Terrified, you scream! At once, you seem to awaken. You see this *thing*—this big, black, furry, cat-like beast crouched on your chest. The beast's burning eyes are peering straight into your face, its saliva-drenched lips hovering over your mouth as if it were sucking the very life out of your lungs.

You try desperately to move, but you are paralyzed by the oppressive weight of the cat-being on your chest. A feeling of doom falls on you like a net, wrapping you tightly in the cat-creature's web of death.

Suddenly you start to resist. Your pulse begins to race, your breathing becomes rapid, and you push futilely at the thing that is choking you to death. Your legs tremble, then begin to thrash about under the covers. You sweep the bedclothes from your body, stumble to your feet, and flee as fast as you can in the darkness. You hear strange noises behind you, as if terror were following you like a hungry tiger. You run clumsily through the house, your arms outstretched blindly in front of you, the cat-like animal in hot pursuit.

And then, all at once, you find yourself in your living room. The lights come on, the cat-beast retreats to the shadows of your mind, and you are awake. You are safe now, but you are intensely wrought up and disturbed. You shake your head, wondering what has happened to you.

Incubus Nightmare   What I've just described is a classic example of the **incubus** nightmare. You may have read about this awful experience, but chances are that you've never experienced it yourself. For as **harrowing** as an incubus attack is, it occurs to but one person in several hundred. A few individuals do seem to be particularly prone to incubus dreams, however, and in these people the attacks may occur fairly frequently.

Unlike most other dreams, the incubus nightmare *begins* during Stage 4 (deep) sleep and *not* during a REM period. As you now know, your pulse and respiration rate normally slow down considerably during deep sleep. In someone about to have an incubus attack, however, the pulse and breathing rate become abnormally slow. The person seemingly moves too close to physiological death, and one or more centers of the brain "panic" as if the body were being suffocated. The longer this severely depressed Stage 4 sleep goes on, the greater the probability that the person will have an incubus nightmare (and the more terrifying it will be). Incubus episodes happen most frequently during the first or second sleep cycle of the night, when body functions always slow down the most (see Table 3.2).

If you ever experience an incubus nightmare, the "dream" part of your attack will usually begin with a scream. Your body's defenses are mobilized,

Incubus (INN-cue-buss). From the same Latin word that gives us incubate," meaning "to sit" or "to lie" on something. The incubus is an evil spirit said to lie on people while they sleep, and often to have sexual intercourse with women at night.

Harrowing (HAIR-oh-ing). Anything that is distressingly or acutely painful.

Table 3.2
A Comparison of Incubus and Anxiety Nightmares

	Frequency in Average Person	Occurs in Cycle	Stage of Sleep	Conditions Favoring Occurrence	Vocalizations and Movement	Content of Dream
Incubus Nightmare	Extremely rare	1,2	Stage 4	Sleep deprivation	Scream, sleepwalking	Cat-Animal suffocating dreamer
Anxiety Nightmare	Not uncommon	5,6,7	REM Sleep	Dream deprivation	None, usually	Falling, fleeing, mild fear

and your pulse rate may double or nearly triple. You will start breathing deeply and rapidly. Immediately after your scream, you are likely to hallucinate. You may see an animal of some kind squatting on your chest, leaning over your face, sucking your life away. You may even become so frightened that you *sleepwalk* in order to escape this terrifying beast.

While you are sleepwalking, you will be very unresponsive to your environment. You will resist waking up if someone tries to arouse you. In fact, to an objective observer, it will seem as if your dream must run its course before it can be interrupted and you can regain full consciousness.

Anxiety REM Nightmare By far more common than the incubus attack is the **anxiety nightmare,** which typically occurs late in the sleep cycle at the end of a very long REM period. If you have an anxiety nightmare, your body will seldom be aroused to a panic state. In fact, there will really be little change in your body's *physiological responses* during the nightmare. It is, therefore, the *psychological content* of the dream itself (being chased, falling, witnessing frightening events) that leads to the anxiety attack.

If you experience this sort of dream, you will usually awaken from it rather readily. You will seldom sleepwalk during this type of nightmare, and while you may talk or mumble a bit, you are not likely to scream. And as distressing as this type of dream might seem to you, anxiety attacks are fairly mild events compared to the stark terror of the incubus nightmare.

Incubus attacks are most frequent when your *physiological need for deep sleep is greatest.* Anxiety nightmares, however, occur when you are physically rested but when your *psychological need for dreaming and REM sleep is greatest.*

Various illnesses—particularly those accompanied by high fevers—often reduce the amount of REM sleep you experience. Sleeping pills also reduce REM sleep. Knowing these facts, you can understand that anxiety nightmares happen very often when a person is recovering from sickness, or just after a person has stopped taking sleeping pills of any kind. These facts may also explain one of the real dangers of taking drugs even temporarily to help you sleep. The pills may indeed make it easier for you to doze off, or to stay asleep during the night. But once you stop using the drug, your REM sleep increases tremendously, and you may have almost constant anxiety nightmares for several nights in a row. Some people then return to the pills—not to put themselves to sleep—but to reduce their REM periods and hence get rid of all those disturbing nightmares.

Question: One of the most common anxiety nightmares is that of "running through molasses"—trying to escape something terrible, but not being able to move. What happens to your muscles during REM sleep that might help explain the commonness of this anxiety nightmare?

Altered States of Consciousness

Psychologists generally assume that everything you feel or experience is reflected by the functioning of your body—particularly by the way in which your nervous system reacts. When your brain is alert (activity pattern), *you* are consciously alert. When your brain sleeps (delta rhythm), *you* become almost totally unconscious. And when your brain waves speed up a little during sleep, *you* quite frequently dream.

If your nerve cells fire at a faster-than-normal rate, you may experience great anxiety, fear, pain—or great pleasure. If your neurons fire more slowly than usual, you may feel relaxed, peaceful, dreamy—or you may fall into a black depression.

In short, almost any change in the *speed* at which your brain takes in sensory information and processes it will usually be accompanied by a change in the way you think and feel about yourself and your personal world, as well as by a change in how pleasant or unpleasant you perceive that world to be.

Nirvana

To some people, the most heavenly pleasure imaginable is that of *immense sensory excitation*—a blinding light, a crashing sound, or sexual stimulation that drives their brains and minds to the limits of human endurance. But to a great many other individuals, heaven comes from *reducing sensory inputs* so that they can shut off the outside world and turn their minds inward. This "looking inward" helps these people achieve *Nirvana*—an almost indescribable condition characterized by such things as freedom from all earthly passions, problems, wants, desires; a feeling of floating gently in black nothingness; a peaceful union with all the universe; a quiet resting in the arms of God.

Individuals who have achieved Nirvana often describe it as being the greatest of human pleasures, the ultimate goal toward which all other joys are mere stepping stones. But to the **jaundiced** eyes of many psychologists, Nirvana and all other heavens (and hells) are but states of mind. Or, to put the matter in biological terms, they are mental experiences greatly influenced by *conditions of the brain*.

Consider, for a moment, the very earthly pleasure of sexual climax. From a biological point of view, each time you experience this sexually-induced altered state of consciousness, many of your nerve cells respond in more or less the same way. The *psychological* aspects of the response will surely vary from one sexual encounter to the next. But at a *biological* level, orgasm almost always involves the same type of neural response pattern in your brain. Unless this unique pattern of neural firing occurs, you simply will not achieve orgasm.

You may attempt to bring about the orgasmic firing pattern indirectly (or psychologically) by altering your thoughts, feelings, and emotions. Or you may attempt to bring about this firing pattern directly and biologically by controlling the sensory input to the sexual centers of your brain. Or you may do both at once. But the important point is this: Anything you do that brings about the *neural firing pattern* associated with sexual climax will almost always lead to the *psychological experience* of orgasm.

What is true of sexual climax is true of all other altered states of consciousness. Any time you wish to achieve a Nirvana-like experience, for example, you must either find some way to change the functioning of your *mind*—hoping that your body will follow along—or you must discover a physiological means of shifting your *brain* directly from its normal state to that associated with Nirvana—hoping that your mind will respond appropriately.

Drugs are a *direct* method of speeding up or slowing down neural firing—a quick if sometimes deadly way that people have chosen for a great many centuries. When we look at the effects of drugs on human behavior in just a moment, we will find that there is a chemical compound that can affect your brain almost any way that you wish—but usually at a cost of some kind.

In the past, religion, philosophy, and mental discipline offered the only non-drug or *indirect* ways to alter the state of your brains—but usually these methods are effective only after you have undergone long training and practice. Today we have much more efficient ways of educating or conditioning our brains, including the use of highly sophisticated electronic gadgets to help guide anyone to a gentle kind of Nirvana. We will see later in this chapter that there is a fairly easy way to alter your brain waves (neural firing patterns) merely by willing them to change.

Before we can sensibly discuss the rather abnormal brain states that drugs and discipline can bring about, though, we first must delve a little more deeply into the manner in which your brain functions under more normal conditions.

Jaundiced (JAWN-dist). From the French word meaning "yellow." Certain diseases of the liver turn the skin yellow—and leave their colorful mark on the skin even after the disease is cured. In more popular usage, the word means to be embittered or prejudiced by unpleasant experiences. Someone with a jaundiced eye is supposed to see only too clearly how foolish or unbelievable other points of view may be.

Secrete (see-KREET). The cells in your body manufacture many types of chemicals that are released or secreted into the blood or onto your skin. Cells in glands at the corners of your eyes secrete tears onto the surface of your eyes.

Synaptic space. The synapse is the incredibly narrow gap or space between the axonic end-fibers of one nerve cell and the dendrites or soma of the next neuron in line. For further discussion, see Chapter 2.

Transmitters. Chemicals released by axonic end-fibers that cross the synaptic space and excite or stimulate the dendrites or soma of the next neuron.

Receptor sites (re-SEPT-er sights). Only certain small spots or sites on the dendrites or soma seem to be sensitive to the transmitter chemicals. If nerve cell *B* is to be stimulated into firing by nerve cell *A*, the transmitter molecules must cross the synaptic space and reach one of these receptor sites.

From a biochemical standpoint, your whole body is little more than a bag of complex molecules kept in place by your skin and skeleton. You take in molecules (oxygen, water, food), make use of them (digestion, respiration), and return them in altered form back to the environment (carbon dioxide, urine, feces). If you don't get enough of the right kinds of chemical inputs, or get too much of the wrong kinds, you die.

The cells in your body are bags of chemicals too, kept together by a cellular "skin" or membrane. The cells take in oxygen and food from your blood and excrete waste products back into the blood. The neurons in your brain are highly specialized in the way that they function, but primarily they are *cells* that keep alive by maintaining a delicate balance between the chemicals inside the membrane and the chemicals that must remain outside if the neuron is to survive.

But neurons do more than excrete waste products—they **secrete** very complex substances which affect everything that happens in your brain.

As you know from reading Chapter 2, when a neuron fires, a wave of electrical energy sweeps down the length of the cell. This wave begins at the front end of the neuron (the dendrites), then moves past the cell body to the rear end of the cell (axon). The wave does little in and of itself, except to cause the neuron to *secrete more molecules*.

Nerve cell *A* cannot stimulate nerve cell *B* by shocking it *electrically*. Rather *A* must stimulate *B* chemically, by releasing one or more complex molecules into the tiny **synaptic space** between the axonic end-fibers of *A* and the dendritic beginning-fibers of *B*. Since these synaptic chemicals actually transmit the neural message from *A* to *B*, they are called **transmitters.**

The more frequently that neuron *A* fires, the more transmitter molecules it launches into the synaptic space, and the greater the likelihood that *A* will cause *B* to fire (see Fig. 3.2).

The dendrites of all neurons seem to have certain tiny "gaps" or **receptor sites** that are particularly open or sensitive to transmitters. If a transmitter molecule lands on one of these receptor sites, it triggers off a chemical reaction in the dendrite that causes neuron *B* to fire. A wave of electrical energy then pulses down the length of neuron *B*, causing another batch of transmitter chemicals to be released at the synapse between *B* and *C*.

If a transmitter molecule doesn't land on a receptor site—*or if the sites are already filled by other molecules*—the transmitter will rapidly break down chemically and lose its effectiveness. And even if the transmitter molecule does find a receptor site, it will usually break down quickly and wash away, so that another transmitter molecule can take its place and cause yet another neural firing (see Fig. 3.2).

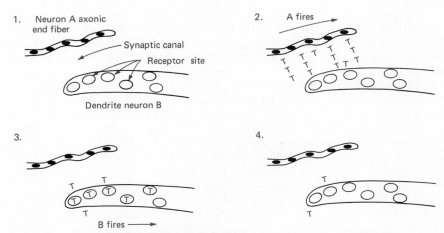

Fig. 3.2. Diagram showing transmitters released by neuron A cause B to fire.

Of course, you are not directly aware of all the chemical activity that goes on inside your brain. Yet it is true that you cannot lift a finger, see a sunset, solve a problem, or even remember your own name unless you can somehow control the transmitter substances in your brain.

Drugs such as marijuana, alcohol, heroin, and LSD either *act like transmitters* themselves, or subtly *change the transmitters* your brain produces. Generally speaking, all these drugs act by speeding up or slowing down the firing of the neurons in various parts of your nervous system. As surprising as it may seem, then, a drug-induced change in the *speed* at which the brain operates may cause a profound change in the *quality* of your conscious experience.

To appreciate why a *quantitative* change in neural firing can bring about a *qualitative* change in your conscious experience, you need to know a little more about neural **excitation** and **inhibition**.

Excitation and Inhibition

Suppose that, later on today, you are sitting quietly in your chair, reading. Suddenly you get an urge to eat an apple lying on the table beside you. You decide to reach out and take the apple in your hand. Both the "urge" and the "decision" are communicated from one part of your brain to another by electro-chemical means.

The motor output centers in your cortex transmit the order "reach for the apple" by sending a signal down to the muscles in your arm telling them to get to work. The motor nerves that make synapse with your arm muscles respond by dumping transmitter chemicals into those synapses. These transmitters cause a *chemical reaction* in your muscles so that they extend and contract in just the right way for your arm to be guided toward the apple.

Now, let's add some complications. Suppppose that, just as your hand nears that beautiful apple, you notice something terrible. Crouched just behind the big red fruit is a huge, hairy, black spider that you recognize as a tarantula! Suddenly a great many nerve cells in your brain that were sitting back resting will shift into emergency gear. These neurons will begin dumping a great many transmitter chemicals into a great many synapses all over your nervous system!

Your first impulse may be to jerk back your hand as quickly as you can. But a tarantula can jump 5 meters (16 feet), and any quick movement on your part might disturb the spider and make it leap to the attack. So what you really should do is to *freeze* for a moment before you slowly retract your hand. (And then maybe you should exit from the scene as gracefully but as quickly as possible.)

At the instant you spotted the spider, your hand was in the process of *reaching out* for the apple. How do you go about explaining to your hand that you've suddenly changed your mind, and that it should *freeze?* The problem is that your motor nerves have already dumped a rather large supply of transmitter molecules into their synapses. So how do you recall those molecules once they've been launched into the synaptic space?

Actually, you will do three things at once. For each muscle that (when chemically stimulated) will cause your hand to reach out, there is another muscle that will make your hand pull back. So the first thing you will surely do is to order the "pull-back" muscles to get *excited* and rescue you. Your brain will obey this first order by releasing transmitters into the synapses that control the "pull-back" muscles.

Second, the motor centers in your cortex will *stop* sending output messages to the "stretch-out" muscles, so that no further transmitters are released into those synaptic canals.

But third, since there are still a lot of surplus molecules floating around in the "stretch-out" synapses, your brain goes one step farther. It causes certain *anti-transmitter* molecules to be released into these synapses. Since the function of these anti-transmitter chemicals is to block or inhibit synaptic transmission, they are called **inhibitors.**

Inhibitor chemicals act in one of two ways. Some inhibitors *destroy excitatory transmitters.* Other inhibitors seem to *block the receptor sites* so that the transmitters can't get through to excite the dendrites.

Excitation and inhibition are not just chemical events, however. They also exist at the intra-psychic and the social/behavioral level. To show you how changes in your body chemistry can affect both your mind and your behavior, let us explore the subject of *drugs.*

Drugs

A **drug** is usually defined as any substance that can affect the structure or functioning of your body. Actually, that definition doesn't mean very much because almost any chemical will have some kind of effect on you—if you take a large enough dose, or take it the wrong way. For instance, water is not usually considered a drug, but if you get too much of it in your lungs, you may drown.

A more useful definition is the one we will use in this book. A drug is any chemical which, when taken in relatively small amounts, *significantly increases or decreases activities somewhere in your body.*

Most of the drugs we will discuss in this chapter have their main effects on neural firing, usually by altering the *speed* at which your nervous system handles sensory inputs, cortical processing, and motor outputs. Some drugs (such as aspirin) primarily affect sensory inputs. Others (such as alcohol) can affect cortical processing and motor outputs as well, depending on how much of the drug you take.

However, the actual effects of a particular drug on a particular person are often complex and hard to predict. For to predict how a drug will influence a specific individual, you must know as much about the person's genetic background, past history, and present social environment as you know about the chemical composition of the drug itself. We can, however, categorize drugs according to whether their **neurological** effects are fairly specific or rather general. That is, does the chemical speed up or slow down just *inputs,* just *cortical processes,* or just *outputs*—or does the chemical stimulate or inhibit neural firing throughout your body?

Let us begin by looking at drugs that influence almost every one of your 15 billion nerve cells.

Drugs Affecting General Activity Levels

One of the most common effects a drug can have is to change your activity level. You normally walk at a certain pace, talk at a certain speed, sleep a

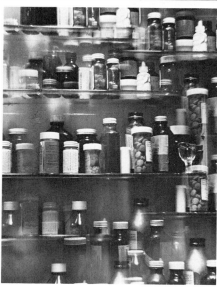
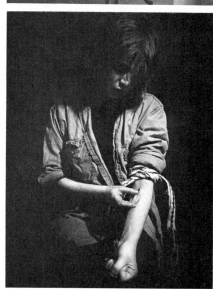

More people in the United States die from an overdose of ordinary drugs or from physiological problems associated with coffee, smoking, and aspirin than die from the use of illegal drugs such as heroin.

certain amount each 24 hours. If you cared to make precise physical measurements of your own behavior, you could fairly readily determine what your own general level of activity would be in most situations.

When you swim, ski, play tennis, jog, or dance, this level increases. The more active you are physically, the more rapidly your neurons must fire. Anything that increases your activity level also causes more transmitters to be dumped into the synaptic canals between the nerve cells in your brain and also in the synapses between your motor nerves and your muscles.

"Uppers" "Uppers," or **psychological energizers,** are drugs that facilitate or increase synaptic transmission. "Uppers" thereby usually make you physically and mentally more active. Often, but not always, psychic energizers affect every synapse in your brain about the same way. That is, they speed up almost *all bodily processes* controlled by synaptic transmission.

"Uppers" are also called **stimulants,** because they chemically stimulate your neurons into firing more often. As your nerve cells are stimulated to fire faster, they release more transmitters into the synaptic canals, and your

Psychological energizers.
Drugs that speed up neural firing, that "turn on" the nerve cells by acting as super-transmitters, that make you use up your energy resources at a faster speed. Also called "stimulants" and "uppers," because they often elevate or "turn up" both your neural firing and your mood—at the price of using up more energy per minute.
Stimulants (STIM-you-lants). Another term for "psychological energizer" or "upper." Any drug that stimulates neural firing.

Chapter 3 Sleep, Drugs, and Altered States of Consciousness

Amphetamines (am-FETT-uh-meens). A type of stimulant or "upper." Also called "speed."

Speed. Any powerful neural excitant, stimulant, or "upper." In moderate doses, speed can pep you up, and make you feel good if you are depressed. After a while, you may begin to feel "jangly" and nervous, and you can't relax or go to sleep.

Barbiturates (bar-BITT-your-ates). Neural inhibitors that come from barbituric acid, often used as sleeping pills. Not to be confused with narcotics (from the Greek word *nark*, meaning "to benumb" or "to paralyze"), most of which come from opium or alcohol. Narcotics are more effective as pain-killers than are barbiturates, but both types are habit-forming.

Tranquilizers (TRAN-quill-eye-zers). Drugs that help people relax and become less afraid of things.

Phenobarbital (FEEN-oh-BARB-it-tall). A barbiturate, or sleeping pill, made from barbituric acid. Chemically very similar to all the other barbitals—amobarbital, secobarbital, and pentobarbital.

Analgesic (an-al-GEE-sick). From the Greek words meaning "no pain." Technically speaking, any drug that reduces pain without causing a loss of consciousness.

whole body speeds up its tempo. As a result, any or all of the following responses may occur: (1) Your heart beats more quickly; (2) your mouth becomes dry; (3) blood rushes to the surface of your skin; (4) the pupils in your eyes open or dilate; (5) you breathe more rapidly; your hair stands on end; (6) your digestion is shut down; (7) your appetite vanishes; (8) your urine flow and bowel movements are inhibited; (9) you may become sexually excited if the environment or your own thought processes encourage you to do so; (10) your muscles become tense, and your reaction times are speeded up; and (11) you typically wake up and become alert, but often find it difficult to concentrate. (The exact pattern of your responses will vary according to your health, personality, and past experience.)

Caffeine is perhaps the most common "upper" in our society. Less common—and considerably more dangerous—is a class of drugs called by such names as **amphetamines,** pep pills, or **speed.** Amphetamine itself is often referred to as Benzedrine. Two other similar, but more powerful, drugs are Dexedrine and Methedrine. The street names for these drugs are "bennies," "dex," and "meth." Since they all speed up neural activity, any or all of them can be referred to as *speed.*

"Downers" Drugs that slow down or inhibit neural activity go by the general name of "downers." The strongest "downers" in general use are the **barbiturates,** which are sometimes called "sleeping pills," because they depress neural activity so much that they often put a person to sleep.

The **tranquilizers** are both more specific in their effects and usually less powerful than the barbiturates. Tranquilizers affect the nervous system in several different ways, but many of them act either by stimulating inhibitory neurons or by inhibiting excitatory neurons.

The general effects of "downers" are the opposite of those produced by "uppers." That is, "downers" slow the beating of your heart, take blood away from the surface of your body, retard the rate at which you breathe, cause your pupils to constrict, and generally make it more difficult for you to react quickly to any emergency. Some "downers" are relaxing because they make it more difficult for you to move your muscles: It is hard for you to experience blind panic and the urge to flee when you are so relaxed that you can barely move.

The first of the modern barbiturates was *barbital,* or Veronal, which was produced in 1903. More recent types include the long-acting **phenobarbital,** as well as Amytal, Seconal, and Nembutal—all of which affect your body for shorter lengths of time than does "pheno-barb."

The most common types of tranquilizers go by such exotic names as Valium, Librium, Mellaril, reserpine, chlorpromazine (Thorazine), and methaqualone (Quaalude, or "quads").

All of the "uppers" and "downers" have physical and psychological side effects that range from mildly unpleasant to downright deadly. Wisely used, these drugs can be of considerable medical help; when taken in excess, they can be fatal.

Drugs Affecting Sensory Input

Information about the world around you comes to you through your sensory receptors. As we will see in later chapters, if you were totally cut off from the outside world, you would rapidly stop being a normal human being. But not all of the sensory messages that reach your brain bring you pleasant news—some involve the experience of *pain,* a rather complex topic that we will discuss more fully in Chapter 18.

Pain is a *neural signal* that something has gone wrong with the functioning of your body. Pain commands your attention because "it hurts." Since the dawn of recorded time, the human race has made use of various chemicals in order to soothe the pain that our bodies often give us. Some of these drugs, such as aspirin, have their **analgesic** or pain-killing effects by *blocking out* the neural messages before they can reach the brain and thus before they can be perceived as "hurting." Other drugs—such as morphine, heroin, ether, chloroform, and marijuana—are analgesic because they affect the way that your brain *processes* painful inputs.

Aspirin is perhaps the most common pain-killing drug known to humans. It is probably the only drug that everyone reading this book will have tried at least once. Aspirin occurs naturally in the bark of the willow tree and was first **synthesized** in 1860. Some 12 million kilograms (27 million pounds) of aspirin are consumed annually in the United States—enough to treat 17 *billion* headaches. As potent a pain-killer as aspirin is, though, it is also a deadly poison that must be treated with respect. Perhaps 20 percent of the deaths by poisoning that occur in the United States each year are due to an overdose of aspirin. When taken in large doses by a pregnant woman, aspirin may either kill the unborn child or cause it to be badly deformed.

Aspirin is a mild pain-killer. In case of severe pain, a more potent medicine—such as an **opiate**—is needed. *Opiates* are derived from opium, a drug widely used for centuries as an analgesic in the Near and Far East. When the seed pods of the opium poppy are slashed, a sticky **resin** oozes out. This resin is collected by hand, heated, and then smoked in tiny pipes as opium.

In 1806, **morphine** was first synthesized from opium. Since morphine can be injected directly into the body in controlled amounts, and since it lacks some of the side effects of opium, morphine rapidly gained wide use in medical circles.

No one really knows why the opiates reduce or kill the experience of pain. It seems likely, however, that these drugs *block the receptor sites* on those neurons whose firing leads to our feeling pain—or feeling the unpleasant qualities of pain.

As an example of how this blocking effect might work, consider what happens when you cut your finger. Receptor cells in your skin are affected, and pain signals rush down the axons of these sensory input neurons. These axons "make synapse" with input neurons in your spinal cord, which relay the message to the "pain centers" of your brain. When a pain signal shoots up from your wounded finger, the spinal input neurons dump a large number of transmitter molecules into the synapse they make with the "pain center" neurons. You then experience pain—and keep on feeling it as long as the transmitters can get across the synapse and find receptor sites.

When you take an opiate, however, the opiate molecules grab up most of the receptor sites on the "pain center" neurons. The opiate molecules don't stimulate these "pain center" neurons—they simply block the receptor sites and keep the usual transmitters from doing their job. Opiate molecules are much longer lasting than are transmitter molecules. Thus as long as the opiates block the receptor sites on the "pain center" neurons, the "pain message" coming from your cut finger simply can't get through to your brain.

Opiate Addiction Morphine has one terrible side effect: It is very *addictive*. The exact biological mechanism underlying addiction is still not fully understood. However, there is a growing body of evidence suggesting that the body itself produces a complex chemical—somewhat similar to morphine—that acts as a "natural pain-killer." Scientists both in Great Britain and in the United States have recently isolated this chemical, which they call **enkephalin**, in the brains of both rats and human beings. When enkephalin is injected into the bodies of rats, it appears to reduce pain at least as much as does morphine. However, enkephalin does not seem to have quite this same strong "pain-killing" effect in humans.

Dr. Solomon Snyder and his associates at Johns Hopkins University were among the first to identify enkephalin. Dr. Snyder believes that all of us have a certain amount of this analgesic chemical present in our bodies at all times. Enkephalin seems to act as a *neural blocking agent*. That is to say, enkephalin binds to (or fills up) many of the receptor sites on neurons in your "pain centers" just as the opiates do. By binding to the receptor sites, enkephalin blocks out the transmitter molecules that would normally bind

Synthesized (SIN-the-sized). Complex drugs like aspirin are often "manufactured" by plants or animals as part of a natural process. But all drugs are chemical molecules that can be made artificially or synthetically in a laboratory (if we are smart enough to figure out how to do so). It is much cheaper to make drugs like aspirin synthetically than to grow the millions of willow trees we would need to yield enough "natural" aspirin to drive away our headaches.

Opiate (OH-pee-ate or OH-pee-at). Any of the narcotic drugs that come from the opium poppy. Almost all opiates are habit-forming.

Resin (REZ-in, or sometimes ROZ-in). Soft, usually clear, sticky substances manufactured naturally by plants. Many resins, like the "tar" that oozes out of pine trees, smell good when burned and are used as incense. Most resins will not dissolve in water.

Morphine (MORE-feen). A product of opium. The Latin god Morpheus was supposed to cause dreams in which a human being appeared. Hence, morphine is a dream- or sleep-inducing drug. Like all opiates, morphine is a powerful pain-killer.

Enkephalin (enn-KEFF-uh-linn). A natural pain-killer discovered in the brain by scientists in the United States and Great Britain. Recent evidence suggests that there are several different types of enkephalin.

to these receptor sites. When the transmitters are blocked out, they can't stimulate your "pain center" neurons very effectively. So the "pain center" neurons fire less, and you experience less discomfort. Enkephalin thus *blocks out* whatever painful inputs your body might be sending to your brain (see Fig. 3.3).

The amount of enkephalin your body normally produces is sufficient to protect you from many of the ordinary aches and pains of life. When you experience severe pain, however, you are likely to turn to stronger medicine, and morphine is one of the strongest yet available.

If, for medical reasons, you were to take morphine, it would act much as enkephalin does. That is morphine also binds to the receptor sites on the neurons in the "pain centers" in your brain. And since it has a much stronger blocking effect than does enkephalin, it is a much stronger pain-killer.

The trouble comes when you take morphine for any length of time. Morphine apparently has a marked effect on how much enkephalin your body produces. It does such a fine job of binding to neural receptor sites that it leaves a lot of enkephalin molecules "just floating around" in your body. Your body seems to sense this excess enkephalin, and gradually stops manufacturing this natural pain-killer. If you take morphine long enough to become *addicted*, your body will probably stop making enkephalin altogether.

Now, can you guess what happens when you try to give up morphine? Surely it will take some time for your body to start producing enkephalin again. During this period of time, you will have no protection at all from even minor pains! Thus you may experience even the slightest ache as being *terribly painful* because you have no natural pain-killer left. And you may then feel a strong craving to return to the morphine because you feel so miserable.

Snyder believes that one of the main reasons morphine is addictive is this: If you take morphine long enough, it will "turn off" your body's normal pain-protection mechanism (the production of enkephalin). And to break the addiction, you have to give up morphine and leave yourself vulnerable to great pain until your body recovers. Little wonder, then, that so few addicts withdraw from using the drug voluntarily.

When enkephalin was first discovered, Dr. Snyder hoped that it might be useful in treating morphine addiction. After all, if we could find some way to get the body to manufacture large amounts of enkephalin, we could probably reduce the terrible **withdrawal symptoms** that occur when an addict is cut off from morphine.

However, we must wait for further research before we can be entirely sure that enkephalin will help cure opiate addiction. Late in the 1800's, scientists hunting for a non-addictive opiate (to replace morphine)

Withdrawal symptoms.
Those physical and psychological changes that accompany giving up a drug after you have become addicted to it. Vomiting, fever, loss of appetite, compulsive shivering, and even hallucinations often accompany withdrawal from narcotics such as heroin.

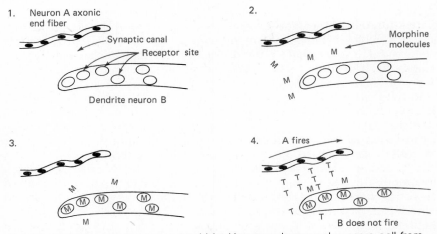

Fig. 3.3. Diagram showing how neural blocking agents prevent a nerve cell from firing.

stumbled upon **heroin,** which is also made from opium. Heroin is several times more powerful than morphine as a pain-killer, and at first heroin was thought to be the salvation of the human race. So, in the early 1900's, morphine addicts were given heroin instead. Unfortunately, heroin soon proved to be even more addictive and dangerous than morphine. Because of its addictive qualities, heroin is seldom used as an analgesic in the United States today—except by the million or so drug addicts who take it as regularly as their funds allow them to.

Local Anesthetics   Laughing gas, or nitrous oxide, is another example of a pain-killer that once enjoyed great medical popularity, but which is not used much today.

First discovered in 1799, nitrous oxide was often employed by dentists and surgeons as an analgesic because it made their patients so "happy" that tooth-pulling and minor surgery didn't seem to hurt very much.

The effects of laughing gas were often unpredictable, however, and it eventually gave way to morphine, **procaine,** or Novocain. Both procaine and Novocain are synthetic forms of **cocaine** that kill pain by *blocking neural activity* wherever they are injected into the body.

Cocaine, or "coke," is a strong drug made from the leaves of the coca plant. It is notorious for the rush of pleasure or **euphoria** that it gives almost immediately after a person takes it (usually by sniffing).

Cocaine was first used as a local anesthetic by a Viennese doctor named Carl Koller. Sigmund Freud, who also lived in Vienna, soon learned of Koller's work and began experimenting with the drug. Freud found it such a pleasurable medication that he recommended it to his patients as a substitute for aspirin. Later, the terribly addictive properties of cocaine were discovered, and experiments showed that it could cause severe damage to the body if overused. At this point, Freud faced the embarrassing problem of "de-addicting" a large number of solid Viennese citizens who had become "hooked on coke."

Drugs Affecting Cortical Processing: Hallucinogens

Analgesics reduce pain by acting like *super-inhibitors*. That is to say, they either prevent painful inputs from occurring, or they keep the inputs from stimulating the "pain centers" in your brain by blocking receptor sites. In other words, analgesics "work" because they prevent you from experiencing the world (and your body) as it really exists.

Hallucinogens are a class of drug that have the opposite effect. By acting like *super-transmitters*, hallucinogens make you experience or perceive the world as it actually isn't.

A drug that caused you to see something that really wasn't physically present in front of your eyes would cause you to *hallucinate*. This hallucination could be pleasant and amusing—or incredibly frightening—depending on your state of mind (and your social environment) when you took the drug.

LSD, mescaline, psilocybin, and **PCP** are perhaps the best-known hallucinogens in our society, although a wide variety of other drugs also fall into this category.

LSD   The technical name for LSD is d-lysergic acid di-ethyl-amide. Its common name is *acid.* LSD is an artificial or synthetic chemical not found in nature. It was first made or synthesized in a Swiss laboratory in 1938. Its rather profound effects on human behavior were not appreciated until five years later, when one of the scientists who discovered it accidentally licked some of the drug off his fingers. LSD was subsequently tested in a psychiatric clinic. Because LSD made the patients see things that weren't there, it was said to produce "temporary insanity."

Actually, LSD is similar to a chemical produced by **ergot,** a fungus or "rust" that grows on such grain products as rye and wheat. The nasty

Heroin (HAIR-oh-in). An opiate derived from morphine. Very addictive, or habit-forming.

Procaine (PRO-cane). Like Novocain (NO-voh-cane), a synthetic form of cocaine.

Cocaine (KO-cane). A very powerful "local" pain-killer made from leaves of the coca plant. Usually taken by "sniffing" the drug in powder form. Continued use of the drug leads not only to addiction, but to considerable damage of tissues in the nose and throat.

Euphoria (you-FOR-ee-ah). From the Greek word meaning "good feeling," hence a rush of pleasure.

Hallucinogens (hal-LEW-sin-oh-jens). Drugs that affect sensory input neurons, or "processing" neurons, and hence "trick" you into seeing or hearing or feeling things that really aren't there. See Chapter 2.

LSD. Common name for d-lysergic acid di-ethyl-amide (dee-lie-SIR-gick A-sid die-ETH-ill-A-midd). Also called "acid." Synthetic hallucinogen first synthesized in Switzerland.

Mescaline (MESS-ka-lin). An hallucinogen found in the peyote (pay-YO-tee) cactus.

Psilocybin (SILL-oh-SIGH-bin). An hallucinogenic drug that comes from a wild mushroom.

PCP. Common name for phencycli-dine (fenn-SIGH-kli-deen). Also called "Angel dust."

Ergot (UR-got). A disease or fungus that grows on various types of grain plants. Produces a poisonous chemical similar to LSD.

Angel dust. Street name for PCP. Rated by the National Institute on Drug Abuse as being the most dangerous hallucinogen presently available "on the street." Also known as goon, busy bee, crystal, hog, elephant tranquilizer, and superjoint.

Coma (KO-mah). An abnormal form of sleep usually caused by accident or disease.

Psychosis (sigh-KO-sis). A very severe form of "mental illness" which often requires hospitalization.

effects of ergot were perhaps first discovered about a thousand years ago in France. In A.D. 994, weather conditions were such that ergot infected much of the wheat and rye that was used to make flour for bread. More than 40,000 French men and women died from eating bread poisoned with ergot. An even larger number suffered from convulsions and hallucinations.

Because LSD is a slightly different chemical than ergot, it usually produces hallucinations but not convulsions or death. Black market acid, however, occasionally is more like ergot than is pure LSD; thus it should be approached with considerable caution (as should all drugs purchased "on the street").

Mescaline and Psilocybin *Mescaline* is a chemical found in buttons on the peyote cactus. It can also be produced in synthetic form in a laboratory. The hallucinogenic effects of mescaline have been known for centuries to American Indians, who at times have eaten peyote buttons as part of their religious ceremonies.

Less well known is a drug called *psilocybin*, which is found in a mushroom that grows wild in certain parts of the world. Psilocybin also produces hallucinations and has been used in religious ceremonies.

PCP *PCP*, also known as **Angel Dust,** has to some extent replaced LSD and mescaline as the hallucinogen most readily available "on the street." Developed in the 1950's as an anesthetic, PCP was banned for human use after tests showed it produced hallucinations, convulsions, uncontrollable rage, **coma,** and death.

One of the greatest dangers of PCP seems to be the unpredictability of its effects—sometimes it causes euphoria, sometimes fear, sometimes rage, sometimes severe depression, and sometimes a complete loss of reality. According to a recent report by the National Institute of Drug Abuse (NIDA), about one-fifth of the younger patients requesting help from drug-treatment centers admitted that they use PCP regularly. The NIDA report notes as well that up to 50 percent of the patients admitted to mental hospitals for drug-related problems suffer from PCP **psychosis.**

Effects of Hallucinogens No one really knows how the various hallucinogens achieve their effects, but it seems that they either act like transmitters themselves, or cause the neurons in the cortical processing regions of the brain to release more transmitters (or fewer inhibitors) than these neurons normally would release. In small doses, LSD and mescaline act as mild "uppers," as well as cause hallucinations. In larger doses they can so disorganize the normal processing of your brain that you lose awareness of where you are and what you are doing.

As we will see in later chapters, you typically make sense out of incoming sensory messages by matching them against your memory of past experiences. If your memory process is either greatly inhibited, or greatly excited, mismatches can occur. You may "recognize" something that you've

The peyote cactus from which mescaline is obtained.

PART ONE Biological Bases of Behavior

never seen before, or fail to recognize a very familiar object or person.

As we suggested in Chapter 2, it may be that some drugs temporarily suppress the dominance of the major hemisphere, letting the usually silent hemisphere break through to consciousness more than it would. Inputs from the silent hemisphere tend to be emotional and non-logical, and thus can be disturbing if you experience them in uncontrollable full force. If you don't realize what is happening, you may "hear voices" that seem to come from God or some outside force, but which are really nothing but the mutterings of your minor hemisphere.

As we will see in Chapter 5, maintaining voluntary control over your thought processes takes great skill—as does thinking logically and predicting what might happen to you next. "Maintaining control" thus calls for constant cooperation between your two hemispheres. Hallucinogens appear to disrupt the delicate balance between the two halves of your brain, mostly by affecting the way in which your hemispheres process incoming information. If these disruptions in your flow of consciousness are not too great, "pulling it all together" or "maintaining control" can be amusing and may occasionally give you some insight into the workings of your brain and personality.

Sometimes, however, your left hemisphere can't maintain enough dominance, and you "lose control" and do things that could hurt or embarrass yourself or others. Even if you realize that the chemical is causing the experience, you may panic when your thought patterns become too outrageous, or when you badly misinterpret the actions of others. The more value you place on being "normal" or conventional, or the more difficulty you have under the best of circumstances in "maintaining control," the greater your panic is likely to be.

The emotional impact that a "trip" has on you is influenced by biological, intra-psychic, and social factors. The smaller the dose of a drug that you take, the less likely it is that you will have a panic response. The healthier your mind and body are, the less likely it is that you will experience a devastating "loss of control." And the more stable your social environment is, and the more emotional support you get from the people around you, the less likely it is that you will have a "bad trip."

Of course, the safest way of all to avoid having a bad trip is to leave LSD, mescaline, psilocybin, and PCP to the 5 percent or so of the people who seem to enjoy seeking an hallucinogenic road to Nirvana.

Marijuana Marijuana is a product of the hemp or **cannabis** plant, a weed found in abundance in many parts of the world. The "active ingredient" in marijuana is a chemical that goes by the complex name of delta-9-trans-tetrahydro-cannabinol—which we can gladly abbreviate as **THC.**

Although THC is most abundant in the flowers and seeds of the female cannabis plant, it is found to some extent in the leaves and branches of both male and female plants. The female flowers exude a sticky substance or resin that is particularly rich in THC. If the resin alone is harvested from

A marijuana plant.

Cannabis (KAN-ah-biss). The common hemp plant, from which come such drugs as marijuana (also spelled marihuana) and hashish. In the Western world, the most widespread species is *cannabis sativa* (SAT-ee-vah), which grows wild in most of the continental US.

THC. An abbreviation for tetra-hydro-cannabinol (TET-trah HIGH-dro kan-NAB-uh-nol). Marijuana contains many chemicals, of which THC seems the main one that induces a "high." Although THC was synthesized in Israel in the 1960's, it is very expensive to make. When exposed to air, THC soon loses its power. The "street drugs" sold as THC are usually some other substance, since THC cannot be kept in pills or powders.

the plant, the product is a brown or blackish cake of material usually called *hashish* or **hash.** If the entire plant is harvested for smoking, the material is commonly called "grass," "pot," or "dope."

As Dr. Solomon Snyder (whom we mentioned earlier in this chapter) points out, cannabis has a long and interesting history. In his book, *Uses of Marijuana,* Snyder states that a century ago cannabis was almost as commonly used for medicinal purposes as aspirin is today. It could be purchased without a prescription in any drug store and was prescribed by physicians for such medical problems as ulcers, headaches, cramps, and even tooth decay.

Cannabis became illegal in the US in 1937, but scientific evidence suggests that it still might be useful as a medicine. It seems particularly effective against diseases caused by tension and high blood pressure, menstrual bleeding, glaucoma (a build-up of pressure within the eyeball)—if the patient can tolerate its euphoric side effects.

Very little is known about how cannabis affects the central nervous system, for it is chemically very different from the opiates, from all other known hallucinogens, and from cocaine. In small doses cannabis can produce a pleasant change of mood. In larger amounts it can produce mild hallucinations similar to those brought about by a small dose of LSD or mescaline. In very large doses it can induce vomiting, chills, and fever—as well as the bad-trip "loss of control" caused by hallucinogens.

Marijuana does have two points in its favor, however. First, it is almost never fatal. Second, it is not physiologically addicting as are alcohol, morphine, and heroin.

Aside from euphoria, the main psychological effect that cannabis seems to have is a *distortion of memory.* Asked a complex question, a person "high" or euphoric on cannabis may begin talking, then break up into laughter because she or he has suddenly forgotten what the question was. This inability to "think in a straight line" is also found in people like Joe (*see* Chapter 1), who suffer from certain types of brain damage. Although the "memory effects" that come from smoking pot tend to disappear a few hours later, we might note that psychologist Elliot Entin at Ohio University has recently found that cannabis can have long-term effects on the smoker's memory as well.

Is marijuana dangerous? Marijuana is, in the United States, as much a social and legal problem as it is a medical one. In recent years, many reports have appeared in the popular press suggesting that cannabis causes brain damage and lowers resistance to disease (particularly cancer), that it causes birth defects and lung damage, that it makes men more "feminine" by causing their bodies to produce female sex **hormones,** and that cannabis makes people sterile and lowers their sex drives.

Writing in the March and April 1975 issues of *Consumer Reports,* Edward M. Brecher casts considerable doubt on almost all these studies. After reviewing all the data he could find, Brecher concludes that most of these experiments were poorly controlled and were conducted by scientists who had a strong personal interest in proving that marijuana was a terrible curse to the human race. Most of the studies yielding negative data simply could not be repeated by other scientists.

Brecher does not feel that marijuana is harmless. To the contrary, he points out that "no drug is safe or harmless to all people at all dosage levels or under all conditions of use." Brecher does believe, however, that the adverse legal and social consequences of misinformation about the health effects of marijuana are worse than the biological effects of the drug itself.

In 1973, the Presidential Commission on Marijuana and Drug Abuse came to the conclusion that:

1. Alcoholism is our worst drug problem.
2. Heroin dependence is our second worst problem.
3. *Legal* use of "downers," particularly by housewives, is our worst "hidden" drug problem.

4. Cannabis use is a minor problem compared with the abuse of alcohol and other drugs.

The commission then reaffirmed its earlier recommendation that we should end all criminal penalties for smoking marijuana.

Drugs Affecting Motor Input

Almost all of the "uppers" and "downers" affect motor outputs as well as sensory inputs and central processing. However, many drugs have their major influence on muscular reactions.

Perhaps the best known of these drugs is **meprobamate,** also called Miltown or Equanil. When meprobamate was first introduced, it was called a "psychic" tranquilizer. Later research indicated it does not affect central processing all that much, but rather increases the output of inhibitory molecules at the neuro-muscular synapses, thus lowering the level of muscular activity.

Curare   Perhaps the most **potent** common drug that affects motor input is **curare.** Actually, though, curare is not just one drug. It is several related chemicals that are found in many types of South American plants. The "class name" for all these drugs, however, is *curare.*

For many centuries, curare has been used by South American Indians who put it on their arrows and blow-gun darts to "poison" the wild animals they hunt. A dart tipped with sticky, tarry curare will paralyze even a fairly large animal if the drug gets into the beast's bloodstream.

When injected into humans, curare-like compounds bring about a profound relaxation of the muscles, chiefly by *blocking the receptor sites* on muscles. By filling up these receptor sites, curare prevents neural transmitters from stimulating these muscles. And if they aren't stimulated, the muscles can't contract and do their normal work.

In small amounts, curare primarily affects the "voluntary" muscles—that is, those muscles under your voluntary control. But because curare only blocks muscles, not neurons, it has little direct influence on your sensory input or cortical processing neurons. Thus if you were given the drug, you would remain conscious—but you wouldn't be able to lift a finger or even blink your eyes because your muscles just wouldn't respond to the neural commands flowing down from your conscious brain. In larger doses, curare can paralyze the "involuntary" muscles that make you breathe and keep your heart in action.

Synthetic forms of curare are widely used in medicine, particularly by surgeons, to make absolutely sure that a patient does not move a muscle during an operation. However, the dosage must be carefully controlled, since too large an amount can quickly lead to respiratory or cardiac arrest (stoppage of the lungs or the pumping of the heart).

Nirvana

People take drugs primarily because certain chemical compounds make them feel better than they do without the drugs—or because people *believe* that the drugs will make them feel better. In either case, the major effect of the drugs is to make the person's nervous system (or parts of it) function *faster or slower* than before the chemical was taken.

But there are often other, non-chemical ways to achieve the same psychological ends. A warm spring day can be as much of an "upper" as a mild dose of Benzedrine, and a love affair can bring about the same euphoria as does cocaine or marijuana. Prolonged starvation can cause hallucinations, as can an overdose of vitamin B-12, hypnotism (*see* Chapter 18), or isolating yourself in a dark room for a few hours (*see* Chapter 9).

Meprobamate (mepp-pro-BAMM-ate). A drug that acts to relax the muscles.

Potent (PO-tent). From the Latin word meaning "powerful." Many oriental kings and emperors were called "potentates" (PO-ten-tates) because they were all-powerful.

Curare (cure-RAR-ee). A paralyzing drug that occurs naturally in many plants native to South America.

And religious experiences can so alter your state of consciousness that you experience *Nirvana*—that is, a "floating, peaceful, pain-free mystical union with the Universe."

Although there is disagreement on the subject, many psychologists consider the Nirvana-like condition to be a **trance state,** and the person experiencing it is said to be *in a trance*.

Yoga

Many Eastern religions have developed methods to train a person to go into a trance state more or less at will. Perhaps the best known of these disciplines is **yoga,** which developed among the Hindus of India many hundreds of years ago.

In its strictest interpretation, yoga refers to a set of beliefs and practices whose aim is to help you attain a union of your conscious self with what is called "the Supreme Reality," or "the Universal Self." Many **yogis** believe that we all have **latent** or hidden powers in our nervous systems. At the base of the spine, for example, lies the "serpent power," which is said to be a feminine power. At the top of the skull is said to be an even greater power center called "the lotus with a thousand petals," which is masculine. Between these two sources of psychic power are six other centers, which some yogis believe lie one above the other along your spine.

Many yogis practice spiritual and bodily exercises in order to raise the feminine serpent power up through each of the six psychic centers of the spine until the serpent unites with the masculine lotus power—at which time full "Union with the Universal Self," or Nirvana, is achieved.

The exercises that lead to this particular altered state of consciousness involve self-control, physical postures such as the Lotus Position (see photograph), breath control, cutting off your sensory inputs by staring at an object (such as a flower) for long periods of time, concentrating on your inner feelings and perceptions instead of focusing on the outside world, and finally a trance state so complete that you become unaware that you actually are concentrating and meditating. This final condition yields the *Nirvana experience* that followers of yoga often wish to achieve.

From a purely physiological point of view, the yogic description of the various "power centers" is highly inaccurate. But perhaps this is only to be expected, since yoga came into being when no one even knew that we had a nervous system as such—much less that it has electrical and chemical activity in it. However, one way or another, the early yogis hit upon crude, if eventually effective, ways of altering both their brain functioning and their subjective states of consciousness.

The lotus position.

Brain Waves

All roads to Nirvana lead through the brain. You cannot alter your own stream of consciousness without somehow achieving a change in the electro-chemical functioning of your brain. Drugs are a "quick and dirty" way to do so, but the cost sometimes outweighs the advantages. For even at their best, drugs are a "chemical crutch," an artificial way of controlling your own natural transmitters and inhibitors. Yoga is a far more natural way of altering your state of consciousness—but not everyone is willing to bother with the extensive training and discipline that yoga requires.

Luckily, within the past few years, scientists may have discovered a much quicker route to one type of Nirvana than yoga appears to offer.

In Chapter 2 we discussed the connection between your brain waves and your state of consciousness. When you are actively engaged in thinking, or are working on some task, most areas of your cortex show the *activity rhythm*. But when you slip into a state of *relaxed alertness,* much of your cortex shows what are called *alpha waves,* an EEG pattern that cycles or repeats itself 10 to 12 times per second.

For example, when you are sitting quietly in a chair with your eyes closed, you have cut off part of your external world—and the visual-input areas of your cortex show the alpha rhythm. If you stare at an object for a long time—as you would in some yogic exercises—your visual areas may again produce the alpha rhythm. But as soon as you look around, or become aware of your environment, the alpha rhythm disappears and the activity rhythm appears again.

Several groups of scientists have recently recorded the brain waves of master yogis, both while the yogis were functioning normally and when they were in trance states. These scientists report a very strong relationship or **correlation** between yogic expertise and brain-wave activity. When yogis are in a deep state of meditation, they show a great deal more alpha activity than does the average person. Additionally, the more experience that the yogi has, the more alpha he shows, and the more likely it is that the yogi will report having achieved Nirvana.

The yogic exercises—worked out over many hundreds of years—seem to be effective at least in part because they lead to *voluntary control* over a person's alpha activity. But it may take a highly motivated yogi 15 to 20 years to master his brain waves. Now, thanks to recent scientific studies on brain waves, we may be able to do the job much more quickly.

Biofeedback and Alpha Control In 1962, Dr. Joe Kamiya and his colleagues at the University of California Medical Center in San Francisco reported that they had been able to train college students to achieve much the same

Correlation (KOR-re-LAY-shun, or KO-re-LAY-shun). Things that "go together," or that are "co-related." The behavior of a couple engaged to be married is usually "correlated." That is, the young man often appears at the same places that the young woman does, and vice versa. The important thing to remember is that correlations don't tell you what *causes* what. The young man doesn't cause the young woman's behavior, for instance—their love causes them to go places together. Most blondes have blue eyes, so eye color and hair color are correlated. However, blue eyes don't *cause* light-colored hair. Rather, they are both determined by related genetic factors.

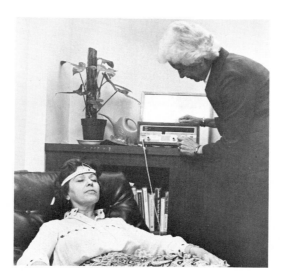

Using a biofeedback machine a scientist measures the brain waves of a woman subject.

sort of *alpha control* as yogis do by using a technique involving **biological feedback.** A full description of *biofeedback* (as it is usually called) must wait until Chapter 16. We can, however, discuss Kamiya's work briefly here.

The major reason that you cannot readily learn to control your own alpha activity is that you are almost never directly aware of what electro-chemical events are going on in your brain. You *are* aware of your feelings, your thoughts, your perceptions, and your emotions—but you are *not* directly aware of the neural activity that underlies these experiences.

By placing large metal electrodes on your scalp, and by connecting these electrodes to an EEG machine (*see* Chapter 2), a scientist such as Kamiya can take a relatively precise reading of the *average activity rates* of the nerve cells lying close to the electrodes. Then, by looking at your EEG record as it appears on the screen, Kamiya knows when your brain is putting out alpha rhythms and when it is not. But *you* still don't know, of course, unless you can see the screen (and interpret its "squiggles" correctly).

Kamiya "closed the feedback loop" by programming a computer to inform his subjects when they were showing alpha and when they weren't. The computer simply turned on a light when the subjects were producing alpha waves. The brighter the light, the more alpha the subjects were producing. Using this information fed back to them by the computer, the students were often able to learn what thoughts to think in order to increase their own alpha activity. Once they had learned the trick, they were often able to turn their alpha rhythms on—or off—simply by thinking the right thoughts. And the students could often do this even when they were no longer connected to the EEG machine.

Many of Kamiya's subjects found the experience so enjoyable that they begged for further training—even when Kamiya could no longer afford to pay them to be subjects in his experiments. The students described this "alpha state" as being very similar to a mild drug "high." A few subjects in studies such as these have apparently achieved Nirvana-like states of consciousness very similar to those reported by master yogis.

Voluntary Control of Conscious States

This area of psychology—that of teaching people to alter their own states of consciousness voluntarily—is still in its infancy. The Hindu yogis took centuries to discover the yogic techniques because they had *no feedback from their brains* except their own, often unreliable, perceptions. Using the kind of biological feedback pioneered by Dr. Kamiya (and others), we now can cut down the training time considerably. But our methods are necessarily crude, because we still do not know what types of neurological activity are associated with what types of conscious experiences.

The Nirvana state appears to come not merely from the *amount* of alpha rhythm a brain puts out, but the strength or **amplitude** of the rhythm as well. And alpha is but one of dozens of electrical patterns that we might want to look at. Until we know what brain activities to measure, we cannot develop the sophisticated electronic gadgets that will be needed to give you the most helpful forms of biofeedback.

There is also the problem of individual differences. As roughly similar as brains are, no two human nervous systems are exactly the same. Kamiya's techniques seem to work better and faster with some subjects than with others. It would appear likely that some people are born with more easily trainable brains than are other people. It is also probable that a person's social environment and past history will affect that person's ability to utilize biofeedback.

In a sense, your nervous system is like a giant computer with billions of electro-chemical parts. You are born with certain "circuit diagrams" that determine the basic set of **instincts** or inborn responses that all infants have. But once you are born, your social/behavioral environment and your own mind begin to reprogram that brain-computer so that it functions closer to your heart's desire. And as is true of all computers, the more that you know about the basic circuitry of the machine, the more effectively you are likely to be able to reprogram it.

If you look upon your mind as some deeply mysterious force that cannot be studied scientifically, then it may take you as long to learn effective ways of developing self-control as it took the Indian yogis. However, if you can see your brain as being an input-processing machine—and if you develop ways of measuring your outputs so that you can gain better control over what goes on inside your head—then you may be able to achieve whatever type of Nirvana you desire rather rapidly, without needing "chemical crutches" of any kind.

Summary

1.   Your ordinary state of mental functioning is defined as being your usual **state of consciousness,** or your usual state of awareness.

2.   Certain experiences—such as falling asleep, dreaming, taking various drugs, achieving sexual orgasm, or concentrating intensely—can lead to unusual or **altered states of consciousness.**

3.   The behavior of the nerve cells in your brain typically changes markedly whenever you achieve an altered state of consciousness. In fact, you cannot alter your consciousness *without* altering the electro-chemical "activity patterns" in your brain.

4.   When you relax, or fall asleep, most of your nerve cells fire at much slower rates than normal. Whenever you are extra-alert, or extremely excited, many of your neurons fire at much faster rates than normal.

5.   Your body has certain **diurnal rhythms** that involve altered states of consciousness, the most obvious one being the **sleep–waking cycle.**

6.   The four stages of sleep run from light sleep **(Stage 1)** to deep sleep **(Stage 4).** Following Stage 4 sleep, you typically experience an **REM period** during which you will have one or more dreams.

7.   Each sleep cycle is about 90 minutes long, including an REM period of about 10 minutes. Stage 4 (deep) sleep predominates during the first and second sleep cycles of the night. REM periods and **dreaming** increase during later cycles.

8.   During REM sleep, most of the **voluntary muscles** in your body are inhibited—except for those that control eye movements.

9.   Dreaming seems to be primarily a function of the right "silent" hemisphere.

10.   There are two main types of nightmares: **anxiety dreams** and **incubus attacks.** Anxiety dreams take place during REM sleep and do not usually involve bodily movements. Incubus attacks take place during Stage 4 sleep and occasionally are followed by sleepwalking.

11.   **Nirvana** is a term many people apply to a mental state that involves great inner peace, freedom from anxiety and need, and intense feelings of well-being and pleasure.

12.   To attain Nirvana, you must somehow induce a change in your bodily reactions, particularly in the way that your brain processes incoming sensory information. **Drugs** are a direct way of inducing these neurological changes, for drugs can excite (speed up) neural firing rates or inhibit them (slow them down).

13.   **Neural excitants** ("uppers") act as **super-transmitters**—that is, they make it more likely that certain brain cells will fire. **Neural inhibitors** ("downers") act as **anti-transmitters** that prevent certain brain cells from firing.

14.   Drugs that inhibit sensory inputs can sometimes reduce the intensity of painful stimulation.

15.   Drugs that affect cortical processing can also alter the experience of pain, change moods, and cause you to hallucinate or misinterpret your sensory inputs by disrupting your memories of what the world is really like.

16. Drugs that affect motor outputs can cause relaxation or muscular paralysis.

17. Various forms of mental discipline, such as **yoga,** are indirect ways of altering your state of consciousness.

18. Perhaps the most effective indirect way of markedly changing your level of consciousness is through **biological feedback**—that is, feeding back to your mind information on the performance of some part of your body.

19. EEG machines can be used to induce Nirvana-like states of consciousness because the apparatus shows you (feeds back to you) an exact measure of the firing rates of many of the neurons in your cortex.

20. Using this fed-back information, you can learn to "will" your brain to function in altered ways—without needing the "chemical crutch" offered by various drugs.

(Continued from page 61.)

"Well," said the Bureaucrat, puffing nervously on his pipe. "Back from the Amazon so soon?"

"It's been 18 months," said Dr. Susan Ogdon.

"Ah, yes. Well, time certainly flies, doesn't it?" The Bureaucrat carefully inspected the faces of the two psychologists sitting in his office. They seemed tanned and relaxed. He wished that he could go buzzing off to tropical climes any time he wished. "And how were the pot-smoking natives? Still lost in the 'Stoned Age,' I suppose?" He chuckled over his little joke.

Roger Ogdon smiled wanly. "The natives are decent human beings, just like you and me. Some of them do smoke marijuana, of course, but I doubt theirs is any more of a 'Stoned Age' than ours."

"Um, yes," said the Bureaucrat. "And what were the results of your study?" In fact, he had a copy of the Ogdons' report lying on his desk in front of him. But he had only found time to skim the first page or so. Besides, he preferred to hear such things first-hand. "I trust you didn't come up with anything too radical?"

Susan Ogdon sighed. "No, our results were about the same as those that Vera Rubin and Lambros Comitas found in their study of marijuana use in Jamaica, and that Paul Doughty and his colleagues at the University of Florida found in their work in Costa Rica."

The Bureaucrat frowned. "Oh, you read those studies, did you?" He wondered why scientists were always checking out the literature when it seemed that tackling a problem with a fresh mind might be so rewarding. He stirred his cup of coffee and took a small sip to perk him up a bit.

"Well," said the woman, "we began by looking at the various ways in which our natives used marijuana. They chew it, smoke it, brew it as tea, and use it in their cooking."

"Oh, my," said the Bureaucrat. "That much, eh?"

"Yes," Roger Odgon responded. "They give it to their children as a medicine, so they start using cannabis at a very early age. But, of course, not all of the natives use it."

"Good," the Bureaucrat said. "That means that you could find a control group of non-users, I presume?"

"Yes," said Susan Ogdon. "We found 30 men who were long-time, heavy pot smokers, and 30 who had never used it at all. The users smoked an average of 8 'joints' a day, except that they call them 'spliffs' instead of joints. And, as we note in our report, they refer to pot as 'ganja,' just as the Jamaicans do. It has much more THC in it than does the pot that usually finds its way to the US."

"Excellent!" said the Bureaucrat, reaching for his pipe. "And the non-users were similar to the users in all respects other than the use of this 'ganja'?"

Roger Ogdon nodded. "They were of about the same height, age, occupation, and educational background. And the men in both the experimental and control groups were heavy smokers of tobacco."

The Bureaucrat refilled his pipe and lit it. "Well, if the groups were that similar, then any differences in their mental or physical health most probably was due to the fact that one group smoked marijuana and the other didn't, right?"

"That's what we presume," said the woman.

"And what was the major difference?" asked the Bureaucrat. "Something startling, I presume?"

Susan Ogdon laughed softly. "Very startling. The ganja smokers weighed, on the average, seven pounds less than did the non-smokers."

The Bureaucrat frowned. "Seven pounds?" he asked. He rubbed his stomach and wondered if he shouldn't lose a little weight. Perhaps those diet pills his wife was taking would help. Then a stray thought popped into his mind. "Wait a minute," he said. "Here in the States, pot smoking is supposed to give you what my grown son calls 'the blind munchies.' How come the ganja smokers weighed less, not more, than the natives in your control group?"

Roger Ogdon answered. "It's a cultural thing, I suppose. Here the myth is that pot makes you hungry. In the Amazon, they believe it calms your stomach. As I'm sure you know, our feelings and behaviors often reflect our cultural backgrounds and biases."

"Everyone knows that," responded the Bureaucrat. "But stop teasing me. What else did you find? Surely that ganja smokers had poorer health. . ."

"No," said Susan Ogdon. "Not at all. We took X-rays of their lungs. Both groups showed fairly normal tissue, except that the men who *didn't* smoke ganja had a bit more scarring of the lungs. But then, as we said, both groups were heavy tobacco smokers as well."

The Bureaucrat put down his pipe. "Well, imagine that. But what about genetic damage?"

Susan Ogdon responded. "The ganja smokers all had parents and grandparents who had been heavy smokers. You'd expect some genetic problems from that, wouldn't you? Yet the ganja smokers actually showed slightly fewer genetic abnormalities than did the men in our control group."

"Oh, my," replied the Bureaucrat, as he poked a nasal inhaler up one of his nostrils, inhaling deeply. "I don't think the Deputy Assistant Secretary is going to like your data at all. But that's his problem, now isn't it?" He put the inhaler back in his desk before continuing. "Well, what about personality differences between your experimental and control group subjects?"

"None," said the woman. "We found no significant differences in personality, intelligence, tendency toward mental illness, or brain-wave recordings between the two groups."

The Bureaucrat reached in a desk drawer and extracted a small, white capsule. He had spent the morning in a conference with the Deputy Assistant Secretary, and the meeting had not been particularly pleasant. A mild "downer" might help soothe his nerves, he told himself. He swallowed the pill and then picked up the thread of the conversation. "But what of the social consequences? What of motivation? It is the firm belief of certain people in this department that pot-smoking decreases the desire to work and to get along in society. Did you find that was true in the Amazon?"

"Of course not," Roger Ogdon replied. "The smokers had no more trouble getting or holding a job than did the non-smokers."

"But how long had the pot smokers been puffing on this 'ganja'?" asked the Bureaucrat.

"On the average, about 18 years," said Susan Ogdon.

"And all that ganja didn't even affect their sex lives?" the Bureaucrat said with a gasp.

Roger Ogdon laughed. "Not that we could tell. Or at least not that their wives or girl friends noticed. More objectively, the men in both groups had normal amounts of male hormone."

"Oh, my," said the Bureaucrat. The Deputy Assistant Secretary wasn't going to care for this at all. His stomach rumbled. He patted it gently, then helped himself to an antacid tablet he found in a drawer.

"You aren't going to object to our publishing the results of our study, are you?" Susan Ogdon asked.

The Bureaucrat smiled. "No, surely not. As you obviously know, your findings really aren't all that surprising, given the results of the Jamaica and Costa Rica studies."

"But what about your Deputy Assistant Secretary?" she questioned.

"Well," responded the Bureaucrat, "I take my cue from Winston Churchill. He once said, 'The truth is incontrovertible. Panic may resent it; ignorance may deride it; malice may distort it; but there it is.'" The man chuckled for a moment. "Leave the Deputy Assistant Secretary to me. Besides, rumor has it that he will be leaving for another position shortly. So let the truth prevail."

"'And the truth will set you free,'" replied Roger Ogdon, smiling.

"Let's hope so," said the other man. "But the truth is, I still don't understand why some of the natives smoke ganja, and others don't."

"Individual choice, we presume," Roger Ogdon replied.

The woman nodded. "Yes, and perhaps some difference in their sensitivity to pain."

"Pain?"

"Look," Roger Ogdon continued. "Those men work 10 hours a day or more in the fields, doing very difficult manual labor. They use cannabis as a pain-killer. They probably produce less per hour when they're stoned, but they seem to be able to work longer."

"Then what do they do at night, when they want to relax?" asked the Bureaucrat?

Roger Ogdon laughed. "They drink alcohol."

"No kidding?" responded the Bureaucrat. "Perhaps they're not so different from us after all. But that's what we wanted to know, and that's why we supported your research. Please do publish it, wherever you wish, and let me worry about the consequences here, if any. And in conclusion, let me say that it's been a real pleasure to work with you."

The Bureaucrat shook their hands and walked the two psychologists to the door. Then he returned to his desk, gathered up his papers, and put them in his briefcase. He tossed in a box of aspirin, and then glanced briefly at his watch. It had been a long, hard day, and he hoped that his wife would have a martini waiting for him at home.

Then a sad thought crossed his mind. "Pity about those natives having to work so long and hard in the fields," he said aloud. "I suppose they need a little something too, just to get them through the day." He picked up his pipe and tucked it into his briefcase. "Ah, well, different smokes for different folks."

Recommended Readings

Blakemore, Colin. *Mechanics of the Mind* (Cambridge and New York: Cambridge University Press, 1977).

Brecher, Edward M., *et al.*, eds. *Licit and Illicit Drugs: The Consumer's Union Report on Narcotics, Stimulants, Depressants, Inhalants, Hallucinogens, and Marijuana—Including Caffeine, Nicotine, and Alcohol* (Boston: Little, Brown, 1972).

Bullock, T.H., Richard Orkand, and Alan Grinnell. *Introduction to Nervous Systems* (San Francisco: Freeman, 1977).

Dement, William C. *Some Must Sleep While Some Must Watch* (San Francisco: Freeman, 1974).

Schwartz, Gary E., and David Shapiro, eds. *Consciousness and Self-Regulation: Advances in Research, Vol. 1* (New York: Plenum, 1976).

Snyder, Solomon H. *Uses of Marijuana* (New York: Oxford University Press, 1971).

Weinswig, Melvin H. *Use and Misuse of Drugs Subject to Abuse* (New York: Pegasus, 1973).

Localization of Function in the Brain

Did You Know That . . .

Many early Greeks believed the mind was located in the heart?

Many European and US doctors once believed you could read someone's personality by studying the bumps on the person's head?

There are four main sections or lobes in each of your cerebral hemispheres, and each lobe has quite different functions?

If you electrically stimulate certain parts of your frontal lobes, your arms and legs will twitch and move about whether you want them to or not?

About 90 percent of the murders committed each year involve people related to or friendly with each other?

Most murderers and their victims are under 30 years of age?

British studies suggest that young boys who commit violent acts are very likely to be "heavy" TV watchers?

Studies in the US suggest that the program content of TV shows can have either a good or an anti-social effect on people who watch them?

A mouse shocked in a confined space will sometimes attack a large cat?

Electrical stimulation to certain parts of your own brain will cause you to fly into a rage and attack people near you?

Removal of a small part of a monkey's brain can cause it to become hyper-sexual in its behavior?

Some scientists believe that much human violence is due to hidden brain damage?

There apparently is no simple cure for the violence we find in the world?

"The Riddle of Rage"

TO: Senior-Robot-in-Charge, Space Exploration Program

FROM: Leader Robot, Scout Ship XJ–12

SUBJECT: Planetary System MB–450–SEL 6.9

SenRo, may it please your circuits, we think we have found it! For thousands of years now, since we became space-borne, our scout ships have roamed the vacant reaches of the universe, hunting for intelligent metallic life. We have touched down on a million planets sprawling with softflesh species—but never once have we found even the rusty remnants of another hardflesh race. But now, SenRo, may your wheels never spin, we have discovered a planet filled to overflowing with mechanical marvels!

We were still billions of miles from solar system MB–450–SEL 6.9 when our navigator, MT/POR 928, first detected signs of electronic life, namely, very faint radio waves. Our ship's computer soon informed us that these signals probably constituted a language of some sort. To date, the computer has not been able to decode the signals, but it was clear from the start that we were listening to signals, to communications, and not to random radio noise.

So we approached the planetary site of these signals slowly, quietly, stealthily, but with our emotionality circuits pulsating at top speed. Were these creators of intelligent radio signals hardflesh like us, or were they some particularly advanced form of softflesh? Either way, of course, we had a discovery of prime importance, but our expectation circuits were glowing with the hope that we had at last come upon a race of robotic brothers.

Our space exploration rules, as you well know, SenRo, demand that we not approach any closer than 40,000 kilometers to any planet that might contain intelligent life. So we put the scout ship into an orbit that held us stationary right above one of the major continents on this world. We picked this particular continent because from it seemed to come an incredible number of radio signals, both day and night.

As we discovered later, our choice was an excellent one, for much of the mechanical life on this planet is concentrated in the mid-section of this particular continent. But you can imagine the thrill that ran through our pleasure circuits when first we focused our viewer on the surface of this amazing planet.

As leader of the ship I, CD/RR 6.7, had the opportunity for first glance through the viewer. Navigator MT/POR 928 fiddled with the apparatus until it gave us clearest sight, and then I peered into the vision hole. I scanned the land rapidly, noting mountains and rivers, green fields, and bare brown deserts. And then, pushing the viewer to its limit, I noticed what at first seemed to be a series of canals running the length and breadth of the continent. Canals we have seen before, of course. But, praise be to the Prime Robot, these were not canals—they were roads!

I narrowed the focus on the viewer down for an even better look. And I could not believe my vision circuits! For there was life—mechanical life!—rushing along the roads in all directions. Bright metal beasts, of various sizes and colors, racing along those narrow ribbons of concrete. I let navigator MT/POR 928 and engineer RT/HEMI 454 both have a look, and they too were as stunned with the magnitude of our discovery as was I.

Our circuits were overloaded. We paused, broke out a bottle of high-quality oil we had saved for a special occasion, and drank a small cocktail. (Only one, you understand!) Never before in the history of our race had three robots so much to celebrate! And then, when our relays had snapped back into place, we took another look through the viewer.

How I wish, SenRo, that you could be here to share with us this discovery. For the life on this planet is a veritable marvel! Primitive, of course—they are just on the verge of space exploration and hence thousands of years behind us in their development. But what a charmingly diverse set of species we found.

By far the major form of life is a four-wheeled, self-propelled machine shaped much like us. It ranges from about 3 to 6 meters in length. These are the robots that amble along the roads so frequently day and night. We call them Compact Ambulatory Robots, or CARs, because they are so small that our viewer can barely discern them as individuals. Later, we will move in closer so that we can get a clearer picture of what these CARs are like. But we have spent the past hours studying them as best we can from this distance.

A quick census suggests that there are about 200 million CARs on the planet, but more than half of them are found on this one continent that we have studied most closely. At first glance they all look more or less alike, but on closer inspection we have found subtle but important differences.

Some of the CARs are very large and seem to be hollow, as if designed for carrying materials. Most run independently on concrete roads, but there are some that appear confined to metal tracks. These latter are obviously transportation robots of a low intellectual development, for they enjoy none of the freedom of movement that the CARs do. A small number are aquatic, but these too seem specialized for transport.

There are even a few winged species that travel great distances at high speed, but the smallness of their numbers suggests that these flying robots are of a lower order of development than are the CARs. (If wings were all that important, wouldn't the Prime Robot have given them to us instead of the wheels that we run on?) There are also very specialized forms of life for roadbuilding, and for herding and taking care of the softlife.

Yes, SenRo, there is indeed softlife on this planet! There are very large forms that float in the seas, and smaller types that roam the empty landspaces. Our viewer is not powerful enough to detect the smaller forms, but they seem to exist in abundance. But then, softlife is cheap and easily formed, so we would expect that softflesh species would outnumber the more highly evolved hardflesh CARs.

The relationship between the CARs and their softflesh companions is

A photograph of Earth as seen from outer space.

PART ONE Biological Bases of Behavior

indeed a fascinating one to speculate on. Of course, the CARs are the dominant species—their size, strength, and speed prove that beyond a shadow of a doubt. Why then so many softfleshers? At the moment, the three of us aboard this scoutship have quite different theories.

Engineer RT/HEMI 454 believes that robot and softflesh evolved independently, but that the CARs eventually succeeded in domesticating the softies as slaves. The engineer believes that the slaves are used to handle the more menial, repetitive, and humdrum aspects of life that no robot would wish to bother his intellectual circuits with. A fascinating idea, no? The Prime Robot knows that all of us could use a softflesh slave now and again to polish up our shiny parts, and to run and fetch for us when our energy levels are low. The engineer points out that some of the land seems to be cultivated, and that there are a number of CARs that appear to do little more than dig in the earth, as if plants of various kinds were grown deliberately. Since it is difficult to imagine what need a robot might have for plant life, perhaps the plants serve as fuel for the softflesh slaves.

Navigator MT/POR 928 disputes part of this view—he believes that the softflesh species are kept as pets for the amusement of the CARs, much as we have bred a few highly energetic and cuddlesome species from other planets to delight us with their antics when our current flow is depressed. The navigator points out that the CARs have built huge pens or corrals to house the softies in. No sane robot would waste so much energy taking care of mere slaves, although, as we know from our own experience, even our race will expend great amounts of our limited resources to make its softie pets comfortable.

For myself, I have quite a different theory, but it is too radical even to discuss with my fellow scouts. I can do no more at the moment than hint that it involves the "missing mechanical linkage" hypothesis put forth by some of our early scientists.

Did our hardfleshed mechanical beauty spring straight from the creative electronic circuits of a Prime Robot at the start of time? Or did we evolve from some simple, toylike mechanisms through some accident of mechanical mutation? Or were we created, as some of the more daring theorists claim in secret, by some particularly intelligent species of softfleshed creatures, all of whose traces are now lost to our historians?

If we were the offspring of softlife, then there must be somewhere in the universe some metallic species that stands halfway between soft- and hardflesh. And I tell you in confidence that I hope it is this "missing mechanical linkage" that we have discovered here on this petty planet so far from the center of the galaxy. I realize this theory is now officially discredited in many quarters, and I will not mention it again unless this wonderful new world yields up fresh evidence. But I dare to raise the matter because I know that you, SenRo, have often speculated on this matter yourself, and that I have come to share your own unique views on the evolution of our species.

But such intellectual curiosity must wait. Now we must observe, observe, and then observe some more. Discovery is one thing, and we are pleased that the Prime Robot has given to the three of us such an electrifying opportunity. Now we must turn our analytical circuits up to full volume as we attempt to answer the question of the century: "What makes these CARs tick?"

(Continued on page 121.)

What makes you tick?

A simple-sounding question, perhaps, but one that humans have debated (sometimes violently) for a great many centuries. Most of the time, when people raise this question, they are asking, "Who are you?" That is, what biological, psychological, and social events have made you into the person you are today. (To anticipate a bit, we will spend most of the rest of this book trying to answer *that* particular question.)

But there is an even more basic problem hiding behind the innocent-appearing words, "What makes you tick?" Namely, what do we really mean when we use the pronoun YOU? At this deeper level of analysis, the question becomes not "WHO are YOU?" but "WHAT are YOU?"

Are you merely a biological machine, a body full of complex clockwork run by a motor called the brain? Or are you a unique psychological or spiritual identity that happens to inhabit a certain body the way that you also happen to inhabit a certain house, apartment, or dorm room?

Put this way, the original question becomes, "Does your mind run your body, or does your body run your mind?" (Or, to raise a more disturbing thought, are they both perhaps controlled by outside forces that neither your mind nor your body is aware of?).

This kind of questioning may seem odd to you, or even downright stupid, if you've never encountered it before. For most people act as if they *presumed* their minds controlled their bodies. YOU make up your mind to go to the store, so your legs carry you there. YOU decide to have dinner, so your hands get the food and your mouth eats it. From this viewpoint, what your "psychological" mind orders is what your "biological" body does.

But consider the following troublesome facts: First, you spend about one-third of your life asleep, yet your body continues to function beautifully even when your mind is unconscious. Who runs your body when your cortex takes a nap?

Second, if you take a couple of drinks, or smoke some pot, YOU become **intoxicated.** It is easy to understand how the chemicals in alcohol and cannabis can affect the ticking of your nerve cells, but how can *physical* reactions in your brain cause the *psychological* or *spiritual* YOU to get high?

And third, if your mind controls your body, *how does it do so?* When you drive a car, you sit in the driver's seat, push on the pedals with your feet, and turn the wheel with your hands. If you consider your body to be a biological machine "driven" by your mind, where does the driver "sit," and how does your purely spiritual or psychological "mind" pull the biological strings that make your neurons fire and your muscles move?

The Mind–Body Problem

The question, "What and where is the mind?" has puzzled people at least since the time of the early Greek philosopher **Plato.** Yet we still do not have

Intoxicated (in-TOCKS-uh-kay-ted). From the Latin word *toxicum,* meaning "poison." A toxic substance is one that is dangerous or harmful to life. In everyday speech, to be intoxicated is to be drunk, stoned, or "high" from drinking or smoking a toxic chemical such as alcohol or marijuana.

Plato (PLAY-toe). A Greek philosopher-psychologist who founded one of the Western world's first colleges or academies in Athens about 400 years before Christ. Plato believed that spiritual affection was the highest form of friendship. A platonic love is one that involves no sexuality (or, as one humorist put it, "not much play for the man, not much tonic for the woman").

When you drive a car your body responds to your mind's commands.

PART ONE Biological Bases of Behavior

one simple, agreed-upon answer as to how the mind and the body interact with each other. For buried away within the question "What is the mind?" is a psychological **nettle** that stings almost everyone who attempts to grasp it. Philosophers call this nettle the **mind-body problem,** and it has to do with the relationship between your mental and physical activity—and where inside your body this mental activity takes place.

If you are like most Americans, you probably feel that your mind—the essential, psychological YOU—is located somewhere in your head. But ancient humans were not quite so wise and **sophisticated.** Aristotle, a Greek scholar who lived long before the birth of Christ, believed that our minds (or souls) reside in our hearts. From his observations of animals being slaughtered and of humans wounded in battle, Aristotle knew that the heart was in constant motion—beating, beating, beating. If you pierced a man's heart with a sword or arrow, the man almost always died. The brain, on the other hand, was quiet. No matter how much you poked or prodded it with an arrow, the brain *simply did not respond.* Many early Greeks considered the brain to be little more than a radiator where blood was pumped to be cooled off when a woman or man flew into a "hot rage."

Another view, supposedly held by the early Egyptians, was that a "little man" lived inside each person's skull. This **homunculus** (to use the Latin word for "little man") supposedly peered out through your eyes and listened through your ears. Once the "little man" decided how to *process* or react to incoming sensory information, he pulled the strings that operated your muscles much as a puppeteer pulls the strings that make marionettes behave.

Nor was this *homunculus theory* as ridiculous as it may seem at first. Ancient people knew that if you bent over and looked directly into a friend's eyes, you would see a "little man" or "little woman" looking out at you (try it—it works!).

Furthermore, the theory established our superiority over lower animals. If you stare into a dog's eyes, you will see a human face looking out at you, not a dog's. So "little men" obviously pulled the strings for animals as well as for humans. (What the dog sees when it looks into your eyes is a question the early theorists apparently forgot to ask themselves.)

Even today, the homunculus theory has its believers. How many TV commercials have you seen in which "little men" or "little women" chase about the human body causing headaches or stomach upsets?

Question: If a "little man" pulls the strings that move your muscles, who pulls the little man's strings?

Three centuries ago the French philosopher **René Descartes** offered one of the first modern solutions to the mind–body problem. Descartes believed that mind and body were made of *separate substances.*

According to Descartes, your body—whose actions are purely mechanical—is composed of *physically measurable* objects such as blood and guts. Your mind is supposedly a ghostly something that exists *spiritually* or *psychologically,* but has no physical existence.

Descartes thought that mind and body were *coupled,* like husband and wife. The mind did not control the body directly, nor did the body control the mind. But, like a married couple, mind and body were very closely related and they did *interact* with each other. The brain (which was physical) was the most important part of the body because it was the "marriage bed"—that is, *the point of maximum interaction between mind and body.*

René Descartes had little or no idea about the biological functioning of the brain, for modern biology didn't exist at the time that Descartes lived. But he was one of the first scientists to insist that the seat of consciousness (YOU) lay within the skull, and thus he turned the mind–body problem into the mind–brain problem.

Nettle (rhymes with "kettle"). Any plant that stings you when you touch it. The phrase "to grasp a nettle" means to deal with a very painful or difficult problem.

Mind-body problem. The foremost problem in psychology. Namely, where and what is the mind, and how does it function? How does it affect the behavior of the body, and how does the body affect the behavior of the mind? (See Chapter 5.)

Sophisticated (so-FISS-tic-kay-ted). A group of philosophers called Sophists lived in Greece several hundred years before Christ was born. The sophists were very good at winning arguments, more through their ability to "shoot the bull" effectively than through logical thinking. Our English words "sophomore" and "sophisticated" come from "Sophist." A sophisticated person is someone who has experienced a lot; someone who has seen a great deal of the world; hence supposedly knows what wines, foods, musical compositions, and intellectual ideas are "best."

Homunculus (ho-MUN-cue lus). The Latin word *homo* means "man." A homunculus is a "small man," such as a dwarf or midget.

René Descartes (ren-nay day-cart). Usually considered the greatest French philosopher. He was born in 1596 and lived until 1650. A world-famous scholar who made many great contribu-

Franz Joseph Gall.

tions to physics, mathematics, psychology, and philosophy. Close to the end of his life, Queen Christina of Sweden invited him to come to Stockholm to be her personal teacher. She then insisted that her "lessons" in philosophy take place at 5 A.M. daily, in an unheated room of her castle. One bitter cold morning in 1650, Descartes caught a chill and died shortly thereafter. Little wonder, then, that few professors

Phrenology

By the year 1800 medical doctors were convinced of the psychological importance of the brain, but they could not begin to unlock its secrets because they knew so little about chemistry and electricity. So the medical profession studied the brain as best it could—by poking and cutting at this magnificent organ as if it were a lump of muscle tissue.

As we said in Chapter 2, most of us are right-handed (and left-brained). Because we do most of our heavy labor with our right hands, the muscles in our right arms are slightly larger and better developed than are the muscles in our left arms. Any time you exercise a particular muscle, it swells a bit. And if your brain reacted like muscle tissue, then the more you used it, the larger it should grow. Right?

Well, that's what a European medical doctor named Franz Joseph Gall said around the year 1800. After Gall had studied anatomy at the University of Vienna, he spent considerable time studying people in jails and insane asylums. Gall found (or so he thought) that most pickpockets and thieves had a "bump" on their skulls just above their ears. Thieves differ from honest people because thieves continually exercise the psychological habit of "acquiring" other people's property illegally. Therefore, Gall reasoned, that part of their brains associated with "acquisitiveness" would surely be largest because it got the most exercise!

And as this "acquisitiveness center" of the brain swelled and grew from all that use, it would presumably *push outward on the skull*, causing a bump. Since these thieves had bumps just over their ears, then shouldn't it be true that the brain tissue immediately under this bump was the location of the "acquisitiveness center"?

Now, if you adopted Gall's rather odd viewpoint, how would you go about determining anybody's personality? Obviously, all you would have to do would be to "read the bumps" on a person's skull!

Gall gave the practice of bump-reading a very fancy name, **phrenology,** which he made up from the Greek words meaning "to study the mind" (see Fig. 4.1). He went around Europe hunting for people with special talents or

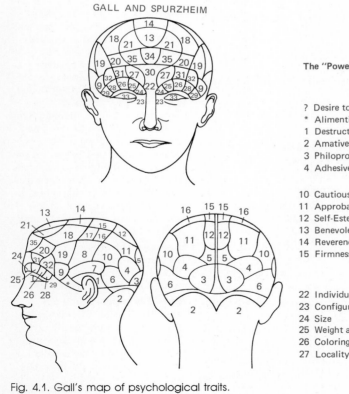

Fig. 4.1. Gall's map of psychological traits.

The "Powers and Organs of the Mind" according to Spurzheim.

AFFECTIVE FACULTIES
Propensities

? Desire to live	5 Inhabitiveness
* Alimentiveness	6 Combativeness
1 Destructiveness	7 Secretiveness
2 Amativeness	8 Acquisitiveness
3 Philoprogenitiveness	9 Constructiveness
4 Adhesiveness	

Sentiments

10 Cautiousness	16 Conscientiousness
11 Approbativeness	17 Hope
12 Self-Esteem	18 Marvelousness
13 Benevolence	19 Ideality
14 Reverence	20 Mirthfulness
15 Firmness	21 Imitation

INTELLECTUAL FACULTIES
Perceptive

22 Individuality	28 Order
23 Configuration	29 Calculation
24 Size	30 Eventuality
25 Weight and Resistance	31 Time
26 Coloring	32 Tune
27 Locality	

Reflective

34 Comparison
35 Causality

PART ONE Biological Bases of Behavior

psychological traits, and then tried to find a bump that matched each trait. For instance, Gall placed the trait of "destructiveness" just behind the ear because he found bumps there in: (1) a medical student who was "so fond of torturing animals that he later became a surgeon"; and (2) a man who enjoyed his work as an executioner.

Question: How many reasons can you think of why Gall's conclusions were unsound?

Phrenology became very popular in the United States during the early 1800's since it seemed to offer practical-minded Americans an easy way to improve themselves. They would see a phrenologist and have this person read their bumps to tell them what their personalities were like. If their "bump of destructiveness" was too large, they would work very hard to be more friendly and less hostile toward others. But the phrenology fad didn't last very long—perhaps because Gall never could give his clients a workable set of "mental exercises" to reshape their personalities, and because the bumps didn't seem to change no matter what the client did.

Pierre Jean Marie Flourens.

Science versus Phrenology

In the long run, however, it was the scientific method that effectively bashed phrenology over the head. **Pierre Flourens,** the great French physiologist, demolished most of Gall's claims in the 1820's by performing actual experiments on brains instead of merely reading bumps on people's skulls.

Gall had located the "bump of amativeness" (or sexuality) on the back part of the head, in areas we now know are associated with visual sensory inputs. What would happen, Flourens asked, if this part of the brain were destroyed? Presumably, the person's sex life would also be destroyed—or at least greatly changed. As a surgeon, Flourens was occasionally called upon to remove this part of a patient's brain in order to save the person's life. But on recovery from the operation, such patients seldom showed a decreased sex life. They might be partially blinded, but they could still make love (and did)! In fact, large areas of the cortex could be removed from badly wounded patients without destroying the psychological traits that Gall said were lodged in those areas of the brain.

Since Flourens knew little or nothing about electricity and chemistry, his primary means of studying the brain was by removing parts of it to see what effects this **extirpation** would have on people's behaviors. Since patients with brain damage had trouble taking care of themselves, Flourens decided that the cerebral hemispheres were the seat of perception, intelligence, and all *voluntary activity*—which is to say that Flourens believed that the hemispheres were "the seat of the mind." And perhaps in reaction against Gall's wildly incorrect ideas, Flourens decided that psychological traits or abilities had no *specific locus* or homesite within the brain.

It took a lunatic to prove Flourens wrong.

The Speech Center

In 1831 there came to an insane asylum near Paris a young Frenchman whose only mark of madness was that he wouldn't talk. He could communicate by making signs, but he refused to write or to use his vocal cords. Athough he appeared to be normal in all other aspects, he was put into the insane asylum because the authorities decided that no sane man would refuse to talk to his fellow beings. The doctors could find no cure for his silence, so the man remained in the hospital for 30 years.

since Descartes' time have shown much interest in teaching early morning classes.

Phrenology (free-NOLL-oh-gee). Reading the bumps or despressions on a person's skull in order to make guesses about the person's psychological abilities. Phrenology, which was invented by Franz Joseph Gall, doesn't work very well.

Psychological traits. Distinguishing qualities of character. A trait is a particular mental ability or skill, or a psychological peculiarity of some kind. Intelligence is a mental trait.

Pierre Flourens (pee-air flurans). A noted French medical scientist who, in the early 1800's, made many brilliant discoveries about how the brain works.

Extirpation (ex-teer-PAY-shun). From a Latin word meaning "to pull up by the roots." To extirpate thus means to destroy, usually by taking something out or cutting something away. In medical terms, to extirpate is to remove a part of the body or brain by surgery.

Paul Broca.

In April of 1861 the man caught an infection and was put under the care of Paul Broca, a noted French surgeon. Broca examined the man carefully, determined that the man's vocal cords were perfectly sound, and that the patient was intelligent enough to be able to speak. Five days later—unfortunately for the man, but perhaps fortunately for millions of other patients—the man died of the infection.

Broca put the man's body to **autopsy** at once and discovered a mass of scar tissue in the *left hemisphere* just about where the man's temple would have been. Broca assumed, rightly, that this part of the brain must contain the neural tissue responsible for speech.

Gall had assumed that *each part of the brain* had a highly specific function; he was proven wrong by Flourens. Flourens had assumed that there was *no specific locus within the brain* for specific psychological functions or traits, and he was proven wrong by Broca, who correctly located the speech center in the left half of his patient's brain.

And for the next century, the battle seesawed between these two viewpoints. On the one hand, there were many scientists who believed that there must be thousands of specific centers or sites in the brain—one for each type of behavior you are capable of. And on the other hand, there were many other scientists who were convinced that almost every part of your brain participated in producing each thought or action that you experience.

As is usually the case in such scientific free-for-alls, the truth is somewhere in between these two extreme viewpoints.

Question: Given the fact that the speech center in Broca's patient was in the man's left hemisphere, was the patient right- or left-handed?

The Lobes of the Brain

Let us return once more to that magic mirror that allows you to inspect your own brain. If you could look into that mirror, you would probably first notice the **central fissure**—that huge, deep valley between the left and right hemispheres of your brain. But if you inspected your brain a little more closely, you would see that each hemisphere is actually divided into *sections* (see Fig. 4.2).

Viewed from the top, as we mentioned earlier, your hemispheres look much like a mountainous landscape—there are dozens of smoothly rolling hills which are separated by steep-sided valleys. Some of the valleys are so large that they seem to separate the cerebrum into definite areas or sections, which we call **lobes**.

Autopsy (AW-top-see). A careful inspection of a dead body to determine why the person died.

Central fissure. The large "valley" that lies between your right and left hemispheres (see Chapter 2).

Lobes. Rounded bumps that typically project out from the organs of the body. Each half of your cerebrum has four main lobes or projections.

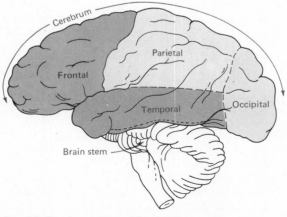

Fig. 4.2. The four lobes of the brain.

PART ONE Biological Bases of Behavior

There are four main sections or lobes in *each* cerebral hemisphere.

1. The **frontal lobe,** which lies just under the skull in the region of the forehead.

2. The **temporal lobe,** which lies under the skull just above each ear, in the general region of your temple.

3. The **parietal lobe,** which lies under the top center of your skull.

4. The **occipital lobe,** which lies at the back of your head, just above your ear.

It was tempting to Broca to assign highly specific psychological traits or functions to each of these lobes and, as we will see, Broca was partially correct in doing so.

But as much as he learned about the brain from his surgery and his autopsies, Paul Broca didn't know enough to help hundreds of his patients who were sick or dying from brain disease. For, like all of his colleagues at that time, Broca did not understand that the nerve cells work electrochemically.

What the scientists of the 1860's obviously needed was an *electrical* method of investigating brain reactions. And in 1870 they got just that—but it took the violence of a major war to give it to them.

The Electrical Probe

The Franco-Prussian War between Germany and France reached its climax late in the summer of 1870 near the small French town of Sedan. The immediate political consequences of that war have long since been forgotten—even by most Germans and Frenchmen. But a discovery that two German doctors made on the battlefields outside the sleepy little village of Sedan changed the course of modern medicine.

G. Fritsch and E. Hitzig were trained as medical doctors. When the Franco-Prussian War broke out, Fritsch and Hitzig both entered the armed forces of Germany. But these two men were basically scientists rather than practitioners, and thus they were as interested in gaining new knowledge as they were in applying what facts they already knew.

During the battle of Sedan, Fritsch and Hitzig wandered among the wounded men, helping those they could. However, some of these soldiers were simply beyond help; many of them had had their skulls blown open by cannon fire. They were unconscious and dying, and nothing could be done to save them. But perhaps, thought Fritsch and Hitzig, these men could contribute priceless medical information to the world in their dying moments.

In 1870, biologists were already speculating that electrical currents might flow through the brain. What would happen, Fritsch and Hitzig asked themselves, if they provided *electrical stimulation* to the brains of the dying soldiers? So they did just that.

As inhumane as their actions might seem after the fact, the truth is that the experiments performed by Fritsch and Hitzig on the battlefield led to important insights on brain functions. And, in the final analysis, their work has probably helped millions of brain-damaged patients.

Fritsch and Hitzig soon found that if they applied electrical stimulation to an area at the top rear of the *frontal lobe,* just where it joins with the parietal lobe, the arms and legs of their human subjects would show repeated, jerky movements. Once the war was over, Fritsch and Hitzig continued their experiments (using animals) and reported they had discovered what seemed to be a "motor output center" in the cortex of both frontal lobes.

Fritsch and Hitzig had also pioneered a new tool for investigating the functioning of the brain and for curing some of its ills—the *electrical probe.*

Frontal lobe. The part of your cerebrum which lies just above your eyes. Experiments suggest this part of your brain may be involved in decision-making, among many other things. The motor cortex is part of the frontal lobe.

Temporal lobe (TEM-por-ull). Part of your cerebrum that lies just above your ears. It seems to be involved in hearing, in speech production, and in emotional behavior, among many other things.

Parietal lobe (pair-EYE-uh-tull, or puh-RYE-uh-tull). Part of your cerebrum at the very top of your brain. Sensory input from your skin receptors and muscles comes to this part of your cerebrum.

Occipital lobe (ox-SIP-it-tull). The lower, rear part of your cerebrum just above the back of your neck. The visual input area of your brain, among other things.

Mapping the Cortex Electrically

Motor cortex. The "output" area of your cortex. Located on the rear edge of each of your frontal lobes.

Association areas. Those parts of your cortex which, when stimulated electrically, do not yield any sensory experiences. Although the full functions of these "silent areas" of your cortex are not fully understood, we assume that they are involved in cortical processing—that is, in evaluating incoming sensory information. (See Chapter 5.)

If someone stuck a pin in your arm, you would experience pain. Surprisingly enough, however, if someone stuck a pin directly into your exposed cortex, you probably wouldn't *consciously* experience any pain at all.

With certain minor exceptions, there simply are no "pain receptors" in the brain. For this reason, patients undergoing brain surgery are often conscious, so that they can help the doctor locate whatever damaged section might need to be removed or treated. During such surgery, the doctor may stimulate various parts of the patient's cortex electrically and ask what the patient feels the moment the current is turned on.

What would you experience if you were willing to let a scientist "map" your *entire cortex* with an electrical stimulator? Well, the most dramatic results of all would surely come if the scientist touched the probe to the motor output area **(motor cortex)**, which lies at the rear of each frontal lobe (see Fig. 4.2). Stimulation of the nerve cells in the motor cortex in your left hemisphere would cause the muscles on the right side of your body to twitch or jerk—even though you didn't *consciously will* these muscles to move. Stimulation of the motor cortex in your right hemisphere would, of course, make the muscles on the left side of your body move involuntarily.

When the probe was applied to the *occipital* lobe at the back of your head, you would see brief flashes of light or "shooting stars."

If the scientist stimulated parts of your *temporal* lobe, you would hear brief bursts of sounds.

And if the probe were touched to parts of the *parietal* lobe at the top of your head, you would feel odd "prickly" sensations in your skin.

Strangely enough, however, the scientist could apply the probe to large areas of all four lobes without your experiencing *anything at all!*

Sensory, Motor, and "Silent" Areas   The physiologists who first mapped the brain electrically concluded that your cerebral cortex has three general types of areas:

1.   *Sensory input areas,* where nerve axons carrying messages from your sense organs make contact or synapse with dendrites of cortical neurons. We will discuss these areas in detail in later chapters.

2.   *Motor output areas,* which contain nerve cells whose axons reach out to make contact with the muscles and glands of your body.

3.   *"Silent" areas,* which have no function that can be determined directly from electrical stimulation.

The early physiologists were surprised to find that *most of the surface area of the cortex is "silent"* to an electrical probe. At first, these early scientists assumed that the silent areas were where memories—or *associations* between sensory inputs and motor outputs—were located. So these silent parts of the cortex were nicknamed the **association areas.** But many lines of evidence now suggest that these should be called the cortical *processing areas,* for it is in these regions that incoming sensory information is processed and evaluated, and where "command decisions" seem to be made.

When electrical probing of the brain first began, many early physiologists were convinced that they were about to resolve the mind–body problem in favor of the body. These scientists presumed that they would be able to find a specific point in your brain that was associated with each unique hope, fear, dream, thought, love, hatred, and desire that you might ever experience. (Had they been able to find such specific brain sites, then biology would have swallowed up psychology, and you would be reading a book quite different from this one.)

Imagine the frustration of these physiologists, then, when electrical stimulation of much of the brain failed to elicit any "mental" responses at all. The physiologists were convinced that "the mind" was lurking somewhere in that 1.3 kilogram (3 pound) mass of neural tissue inside the skull, but somehow the most important parts of human experience kept eluding (and still elude) their needle-like probes.

In a sense, intra-psychic and behavioral psychology grew out of both the successes and failures of the early physiologists. Although these scientists had failed to solve the mind-body problem to everyone's satisfaction, they had demonstrated that the *scientific method* could be usefully applied to the study of human behavior.

Around 1900, then, a group of scholars who called themselves *psychologists* started applying the scientific approach to the study of what humans thought and did. Some psychologists began to develop "mental probes" to map out the mind as the physiologists had mapped out the brain. Other psychologists tried to measure and record the visible behavior of the human organism as precisely as the physiologists had measured and recorded the electro-chemical behavior of cortical neurons.

Out of this sudden burst of scientific activity, there emerged three quite different ways of answering the question, "What makes you tick?" These three are the *biological*, the *intra-psychic*, and the *social/behavioral* approaches to psychology. Each of the three has its own strengths and weaknesses, and its own contributions to make to resolving the mind-body issue.

To help us put all three approaches in perspective, let us first look at them briefly, then discover how each attempts to explain a pressing human problem—the occurrence of such violent behaviors as war, rape, and murder.

The Mind–Body Problem: Three Theoretical Viewpoints

The Biological Viewpoint

As we have noted, psychology partially grew out of the sciences of medicine and physiology. That area of psychology concerned with studying how functions of the brain affect behavior is called **physiological psychology.** This old and highly respected field is now sometimes referred to by such newer names as *biological psychology, psychobiology,* or *biopsychology.* Some physiological psychologists work primarily with **animal subjects,** while others usually work with human subjects.

For the most part, physiological psychologists are interested in the *interactions* between physiological processes and behavior. That is, they study how changes in your biology are related to changes in your behavior.

At times, a biopsychologist may induce a change in an organism's behavior—for instance, by teaching a dog to perform a trick—and then study what happens in the dog's brain as a result of the change in its performance. For the most part, however, the physiological psychologist is likely to alter the functioning of the brain in some way to see how the organism's behavior changes *thereafter.* For example, if you stimulate parts of a cat's motor cortex, the animal's legs will move. If you stimulate other parts of the cat's brain electrically, the animal will fly into a rage.

Perhaps because biopsychologists tend to "do something physical" to an animal and then note its behavioral changes, these scientists occasionally talk as if biology *causes* psychology. Not all physiological psychologists take this restricted, biological view toward the mind–body problem, of course. But many of them do occasionally speak as if they believed the interaction between brain and mind was a one-way affair, as if physical events in your nervous system were the *major cause* for all the subjective experiences in your mind.

The Intra-Psychic Viewpoint

At the beginning of this chapter, when we asked where the "essential, psychological YOU" resided, we were speaking in intra-psychic terms. That

Physiological psychology (fizz-ee-oh-LODGE-uh-cal). That part of psychology which looks upon humans primarily as biological organisms. Physiology is that division of biology dealing with the activities and processes of living systems.

Animal subjects. As you will see in Chapter 5, scientists assume there is a continuity or relatedness to life. The bodies of animals are very similar to the bodies of humans. Therefore, many of the facts discovered about animal physiology should also hold for human physiology. Psychologists often assume that there is, as well, a continuity between animal and human minds. Therefore, studying how rats, cats, and monkeys solve problems might give useful information on how human beings solve similar problems. The similarities between humans and the rest of the animal kingdom are very important and worthy of scientific study—but so are the differences between humans and other animals.

Biological inheritance. You inherit from your parents a "genetic blueprint" that helps determine the shape and size of your body, including your brain. You also inherit from this blueprint certain behavioral tendencies called "instincts." However, your inheritance is always influenced by the environment in which you grew up. Everything you do is affected both by your biological inheritance and your past experiences. (See Chapter 19.)

Attitude. A characteristic and usually long-lasting way of thinking, feeling, or behaving toward an object, person, idea, or group of persons. See particularly Chapters 26–28.

is, we were asking the location of your own subjective world, of your own stream of consciousness, or of your *mind*. Traditionally, the intra-psychic or mental viewpoint has dominated the psychological sciences, just as it dominates most of the material in this book.

From an intra-psychic standpoint, YOU determine almost everything you think and feel and do. Our legal system takes this intra-psychic point of view, for the laws of the land hold you responsible for your actions.

Likewise, the people around you typically assume that what you say to them (and the ways that you react to what they say) are products of your conscious, mental functioning. From this viewpoint, your mind has *voluntary control* over your body (brain), and not the other way around—just as your mind is presumed to control your behavior.

Scientists who study what the "inner woman" or "inner man" is really like will usually admit that your **biological inheritance** helps determine what your mind is like. For example, a brain-damaged person such as Joe (whom you met in Chapter 1) cannot be expected to act and think exactly as normal people do. But from a strictly "mentalistic" viewpoint, the condition of your body merely *sets limits* to what your mind can accomplish. Within these biological limitations, YOU are presumed to become whatever YOU decide you should be.

The Social/Behavioral Viewpoint

As the poet John Donne said, you are not an island unto yourself. Rather, you grow up around other people who help determine your ideas, your values, your joys, your disappointments, your speech, and your behaviors.

Because the intra-psychic viewpoint has dominated our thinking for so many centuries, it has taken us a very long time to realize the importance of the environments we live in. Those psychologists who emphasize the strong influence that the outside (social) world has on what we think and do typically have adopted the social/behavioral viewpoint as their solution to the mind–body problem.

The *social psychologist* (see Chapters 26–28) is perhaps most interested in how our attitudes and behaviors are affected by the actions of the *groups* we belong to (for instance, our family and friends).

An **attitude** is usually defined as a characteristic way of thinking, feeling, or behaving toward an object, person, or group of persons. Although the social psychologist admits that your attitudes exist "inside your mind," and that these attitudes are determined partly by your biological inheritance, it is *the environment you were reared in* that the social psychologist deems most important.

From the strict *social viewpoint*, your body creates your mind at birth and has a minor influence on it thereafter—but the outside world creates all your important attitudes and behavioral reactions while you are growing up. From this social viewpoint, therefore, if you want to change your mind, you must first change your environment (or the way that it treats you).

The *behavioral psychologist* goes a step farther. To a behaviorist, your own thoughts, feelings, and emotions are *subjective* events. Because they take place inside the privacy of your own mind, these events cannot be seen or measured directly by a scientist. You may tell a behaviorist what you are thinking, or state that you feel sad or happy at the moment, but the behaviorist cannot peer straight into your mind to see how accurately you are reporting these inner experiences of yours.

However, your *behavior* is something that most certainly can be seen and recorded by a scientific observer. *What* you do—the movements you make and the things you say—are non-mental events. Your behavior therefore can be treated like an *object* and measured "objectively," just as one can measure the "behavior" of such other objects as a falling stone, an ocean wave, or a neuron firing.

If you press most behaviorists hard enough, they will admit that you do indeed have a mind. But your mental functioning is extremely difficult to measure or to talk about in objective terms. Therefore, the behaviorist tends to ignore your personal conscious experience as much as possible.

To a behaviorist, your actions are determined partly by your biological inheritance. But one of the main ways that your genes influence your behavior is by making you particularly sensitive to your environment. Many behavior studies suggest that your actions are strongly affected by the *consequences* of those actions. For example, if something you do brings you pleasure or reward, you will tend to repeat that behavior. Why? Because that's the way your genes make you behave. If a response you make is punished or brings you pain, you will tend not to do that same thing as frequently in the future. Why? Again, because pain is "nature's no-no."

To put the matter another way, you seem to be "biologically programmed" to seek pleasurable inputs and avoid painful inputs. And since these pleasures and pains come to you primarily from outside your body, the behaviorist believes that all of your mental and physical reactions are the *consequences* of external inputs. A behaviorist believes, therefore, that if you want to change your own behavior, you typically must first change your input—that is, the behavior of the people in the world around you.

Which View Is Correct?

Despite occasional arguments on the subject, very few psychologists hold rigidly to one of the three viewpoints we have just described. Instead, psychologists use whatever view seems most appropriate or useful in solving whatever human problem they happen to face at the moment. Different psychologists may *emphasize* the value of one viewpoint or another, but almost all psychological theories make reference to biological, intra-psychic, and environmental influences.

We need to learn as much as we can about all three points of view, for none of them, *all by itself,* can explain the rich complexity of human experience. To demonstrate this point as vividly as possible, let us now study one aspect of human behavior—*violence*—as seen from the social/behavioral, the intra-psychic, and the biological points of view.

Violence: Three Theoretical Viewpoints

To many people, surely the most terrifying form of violence is murder. Few of us who have walked the near-deserted streets of a big city late at night have not feared that some madman would leap out of the shadows and brutalize or kill us. If we read in the newspaper (or see on TV) the results of some particularly bloody massacre, we are likely to shiver in our boots and demand that the police give us greater protection from such **depraved** lunatics. But as Donald T. Lunde points out in his fascinating book *Murder and Madness,* the facts about violent death are somewhat different from our fantasies and fears.

To begin with, we are quite right to worry about violent death, for at least 15,000 Americans are murdered annually. In fact, more of us in the United States were killed by other Americans in the last four years than were killed in Vietnam during the entire war there. According to US government statistics, in any given year there are about 15,000 murders, at least 30,000 rapes, and some 300,000 cases of violent assault.

However, you really are much safer on the streets than in your own home, and probably better off with strangers than with people you know and love. For almost 90 percent of the murders committed each year involve people related to or friendly with each other, and about 40 percent of the killings occur in homes or apartments.

Daytime is safer than night; few murders take place during business hours. In Philadelphia, as Lunde reports, two-thirds of the killings occur on weekends, most of them on Saturday night between 8 P.M. and 2 A.M.

Donald T. Lunde.

Perhaps because we're around friends and family more during summer holidays and at Christmas, the murder rate peaks in July and in December. And the South is more dangerous than the North. Some 44 percent of all recent murders occurred in the southern states, while the lowest murder rate **per capita** is found in New England.

Young people are much more dangerous than are people past 40. Less than one victim in 10 is murdered by someone over 50. In fact, the average murderer is about *20 years of age*. It is also true that older people get killed a lot less than do younger ones, for most murder *victims* are under 30 years of age.

As you might suspect, men are three times as likely to kill someone as are women. But women are frequent victims. One-fifth of all the people killed in the US are women murdered in their own bedrooms (usually shot to death by husbands or lovers). When a woman murders, she is most likely to kill a husband or lover by stabbing him to death or shooting him in the kitchen.

According to Lunde, race plays an important part in murder. In some 90 percent of all killings, the victim and the murderer are of the same race. However, black men are 10 times as likely to be victims as are white women. When cross-racial murders do occur, whites are much more likely to kill blacks than vice-versa. Blacks are more likely to use knives as murder weapons than whites, while whites are more likely to use guns.

No matter what their race, however, murderers under 15 and over 50 use guns almost exclusively. And in at least one-third of the cases, the victim seems to have *precipitated the killing*—either by taunting or goading the murderer, or by pulling out a weapon first.

Surprisingly enough, there is only the slimmest connection between murder and mental illness. Less than 4 percent of convicted murderers in recent years were judged criminally insane in courts of law. A patient released from a mental hospital is no more likely to commit a murder than is the average person (*unless* the patient was hospitalized for being violent, and then the patient is only slightly more likely to commit a crime than is anyone else).

Murderers seldom repeat their crimes. The state of Michigan has given early parole to hundreds of convicted murderers in the past 23 years. None of these people ever killed again. And in England, in a 50-year study of 7,000 convicted murderers, only two killed again after being released from jail.

If, then, we cannot blame most acts of violence on insanity, what is it that causes people to kill each other? Probably each of us has her or his own answer to this question, but most of the explanations will fall within the social/behavioral, intra-psychic, or biological viewpoints.

Question: Knowing these statistics on murder, what things could you do to decrease the likelihood that you would either commit a murder or be a murder victim?

Environmental Determinants of Violence

Does the society you grow up in affect the probability that you will strike or otherwise harm another individual? Do some cultures repress violent behaviors, while other cultures reward or encourage rape, assault, and murder? There are a great many data suggesting that the attitudes held by the majority of people within a given society have a marked effect on the level and type of violence found within that society.

In the United States, as we just mentioned, there are at least 15,000 murders a year. The majority of these deaths stem from gunshot wounds. About 51 percent of all American murders are committed with pistols or hand guns, while rifles and shotguns account for another 15 percent or so of the recorded **homicides.**

PART ONE Biological Bases of Behavior

The city of Detroit has about two million people who, according to police estimates, own about two million guns. In 1978, there were some 700 murders in Detroit, the majority of these being deaths from firearms. By contrast, during the same year, there were fewer than 150 murders in *all* of Great Britain—a land of some 50 million people. Americans, in general, take a fairly positive attitude toward the private ownership of hand guns, and almost all of our police are armed. In Great Britain, hand guns are illegal; not even the police wear pistols, except on rare and very special occasions.

Does the fact that British society takes quite a different attitude toward guns (and violent behavior in general) in any way help explain the fact that there are 100 times as many murders in the United States each year as in Great Britain? Or should we point the finger of shame at television and other cultural influences instead?

Effects of TV on Violence   In 1969 the US Senate, worried about the impact of television violence on the personality development of young children, asked the Surgeon General to undertake an extensive study on this subject. In 1972, after an expenditure of one million dollars in research funds, Dr. Jesse Steinfeld (the Surgeon General) reported some interesting findings.

Is there violence on television? Yes, indeed. In 1967, according to the National Commission on the Causes and Prevention of Violence, a staggering 94.3 percent of cartoon shows contained violent episodes. That same year, 81.6 percent of all prime-time entertainment shows on TV contained violence. The Commission estimated that a normal child, growing up during the 60's and 70's, would have watched at least 20,000 incidents of violence on television by the time he or she was 19. By the late 1970's, the amount of violence on TV had declined somewhat, but more than two-thirds of *all* programs still featured episodes of violence.

So television certainly does expose us to violence, but how does this exposure affect us? According to Dr. Robert M. Liebert, a psychologist who helped prepare the Surgeon General's report, "The more violence and aggression a youngster sees on television, regardless of his age, sex, or social background, the more aggressive he is likely to be in his own attitudes and behaviors." Dr. Liebert came to this conclusion after reviewing more than 50 scientific studies covering the behavior of 10,000 children between the ages of 3 and 19.

Belson's London study.   By 1980, many other scientists had published experiments whose results tended to confirm some, but not all, of Liebert's

Research in England suggests that children who regularly see violence on TV are more likely to exhibit aggressiveness in their own behavior.

conclusions. For example, in 1978 William Belson published a book describing his study of TV-watching and violence among young British men. According to Belson, who works at the Survey Research Centre of the London School of Economics, boys who are "heavy" watchers of TV violence are much more likely to commit violent acts themselves than are boys who view such violence only occasionally.

The several hundred young men in Belson's study were from 12 to 17 years old when tested. They were selected by **random sample** from all parts of London. Belson then interviewed and observed the boys for some 10 hours to determine how many violent TV programs they had viewed in recent years. As you might guess, some of the young men were "heavy" viewers, while others saw violent programs only now and then. Belson then divided the boys into two groups—the "heavy watchers" and the "occasionals"—and studied them further.

Surprisingly enough, there were no obvious social, physical, or educational differences between the boys in the two groups. But when Belson asked the boys to report secretly how many acts of violence they had actually engaged in during the six months prior to their interviews, he found rather shocking results. The "heavy watchers" reported having performed a much larger number of violent acts than did the "occasionals." (Some of the acts reported, incidentally, were dropping lighted matches into a shopper's bag, busting open pay telephones, kicking other boys in the crotch, and beating on automobiles with hammers.)

We should note two important things about Belson's work. To begin with, some 50 percent of the boys in the study did not report *any violent acts at all.* A mere 12 percent of the boys were the "active" aggressors—and most of them were "heavy" watchers of violence on television. But each of these "actively" violent young men reported having performed *at least 10 acts of serious violence* in the six months before being interviewed.

Based on his evidence, Belson reports that some forms of violence on TV produce more real-life violence than others. Among the worst offenders are the following:

1. Programs that feature physical and verbal violence between people who have close personal relationships.
2. Stories that present violence in a very realistic fashion.
3. Violence committed by "good guys" in pursuit of "good causes."
4. Violence that seems to be "just thrown in for its own sake," and does not grow out of dramatic needs of the program.
5. Westerns.

In contrast, Belson finds that some types of television violence do not seem to promote "imitative violence" in young viewers. Among the examples that Belson offers are these:

1. Comedies that feature slapstick violence, verbal or physical.
2. Violent cartoons. (Belson states that this type of violence is unrealistic and next to impossible to imitate.)
3. Sports other than boxing or wrestling.
4. Science fiction programs which include violence (again, Belson says that this type of show is usually "unrealistic").

Belson, like many other scientists and educators, is worried primarily that television programs which feature violence as a "natural or acceptable thing" may serve as *models* of what "acceptable social behavior" should be. Thus children who watch violence on TV may end up imitating a poor set of models indeed.

How Does TV Affect Adults? Most of the well-controlled studies suggest that TV can influence the aggressive behaviors of young people. But what of the effects of TV violence on adults? After we have grown up and settled down, how does television affect our moods and behaviors? To answer this question, UCLA psychiatrist Roderic Gorney and his associates recruited 183 couples in Los Angeles to be their subjects for a one-week study. The 183 men were divided into five groups:

1. Those who were asked to view only programs high in violence or what Gorney calls "hurtful" content for seven days.

2. Those who were asked to view only programs high in **prosocial** or "helpful" content.

3. Those who were asked to look only at programs with a "neutral" content that was neither "violent" nor "prosocial" (such as light comedy).

4. Those who were asked to watch an equal number of "hurtful" and "helpful" programs.

5. Those who were free to watch any program they wished.

The men were asked as well to record their feelings and moods both before and after watching each of the programs.

The men's wives participated in the UCLA study by watching their husbands while the husbands watched the tube. The wives then recorded the actual programs the men viewed, to make sure that the men had "followed instructions." The wives also recorded the number of "helpful" and "hurtful" behaviors that their husbands engaged in during the week of TV viewing.

Gorney and his colleagues report that the men in Group 2—who watched "helpful" programs during the week—showed a marked *decrease* in aggressive feelings and moods over the seven days. The other groups showed no such change. There was also a marked *increase* in the number of "helpful" behaviors these men engaged in with their families.

The men in Group 1—who watched violent programs—did not show an increase in their aggressive *feelings* or *attitudes*, but they did show a significant increase in the number of "hurtful" behaviors they engaged in with their families. (The men in the other three groups were, generally speaking, somewhere in between these two extremes.)

Gorney and his associates conclude that television can have *either* a good *or* a harmful effect on adults—depending on what types of programs the adults choose to watch.

Parents as "Role Models"   Not all people—young or old—who watch violence on television become violent. Indeed, only a small percent of "people in general" engage in behaviors sufficiently violent to get them into trouble with the law. For example, psychologist Sarnoff Mednick found, in his study of 30,000 men in Denmark, that 1 percent of the men accounted for some 50 percent of the violent crimes committed by the group. What is

Prosocial (pro-so-shull). The Latin term *pro* means "in favor of." Prosocial behaviors are actions that society favors or approves of. Prosocial is the opposite of "anti-social."

A variety of factors in US culture contribute to the development of aggressive behavior.

there about this handful of violent individuals that makes them so easily influenced?

Dr. Murray Straus, a sociologist at the University of New Hampshire, believes that *parents* are the real cause of later violence. According to Straus, the family is not only "the most violent institution in our society," but the family is also where "most of us *learn* to be violent."

Straus states that many children receive "basic training in violence" from the physical punishment they receive from other members of the family, from watching violent behavior in **siblings** (their brothers and sisters), and by being told verbally that "it's all right to hit somebody when they're wrong." Straus notes that adults arrested for violent crimes typically come from a family in which fights among family members were considered "just a part of life." Their parents also tended to allow the children to punish each other when the offending child had "done something wrong" or "wouldn't listen to reason."

If we put together the various studies on violence, it seems reasonable that the most likely "candidate" for aggressive behaviors would be a young person who grew up in a family that approved of violence, whose parents watched violent TV shows and encouraged the young person to do so too, and who lived among neighbors who behaved and thought likewise.

But are social factors the only, or even the major, determinants of violent actions? Is all aggression learned by "imitation," or is the situation much more complex than that?

Bowling Green University psychologist J.P. Scott has studied aggression in man and animals for a great many years. Scott believes that violence is usually **multi-determined.** That is, aggressive attacks almost always have biological, intra-psychic, and social/behavioral causes.

Scott says that, at the human level, societal factors are usually the most important of all. He points out that males in our culture are encouraged to leave home when they reach sexual maturity, but typically do not form new family ties until several years afterward. Perhaps this is why, in the United States, violent crimes are most likely to be committed by single or divorced males between the ages of 16 and 25.

It is likewise true that these men commonly come from a poverty-stricken background and from homes broken by desertion, divorce, or death. Furthermore, as Scott notes, unmarried young men frequently organize into groups whose main purpose is that of making war or terrorizing others.

Scott believes that we will not do away with such violence until we create societies that promote peace, stability, and positive interpersonal relationships—particularly among disadvantaged young people in all cultures.

But do we need to teach "peaceful thoughts and behaviors" to *all* people, or are there some individuals whose "inborn personalities" are such that they are likely to become violent no matter what social environment they grow up in?

Intra-Psychic Determinants of Violence

In the later chapters of this book, when we discuss a topic called *personality theory*, we will find that many psychologists view violence as a mental trait or characteristic that is determined by a person's subjective outlook on life. From this intra-psychic position, **personality traits** are produced both by one's biological inheritance and by what happens during certain critical stages in a person's early development.

We are born with certain innate response patterns—called **instincts**—that are passed along to us genetically by our parents. Our childhood environments, particularly our interactions with our mothers and fathers, shape or mold these instinctual thoughts and behaviors into what we call our *minds*.

As we mature, our minds become more and more capable of acting on their own, and we become more and more capable of achieving our

PART ONE Biological Bases of Behavior

personal, subjective goals—within the limits set by our bodies and our cultures.

Many social/behavioral psychologists theorize that we are born without any strong tendency either to be violent or non-violent: We thus become what our environment *teaches* us to become. But according to many intra-psychic theorists, we are born with an aggressive instinct that we must somehow *learn to control*. Thus one of the major functions of civilization is that, at its best, a civilized society trains us to **repress** our aggressive instincts.

As evidence to support their view, intra-psychic theorists often point to the research of **Konrad Lorenz,** a German scientist who got his ideas about human aggression after spending many years studying the behavior patterns of wild animals. Lorenz believes that while aggressive instincts first evolved in lower animals, the tendency toward senseless violence has reached its peak in human beings. Lorenz notes that animals of one species will often kill members of another species for food, or if threatened, but they seldom kill out of hatred, prejudice, politics, or "just for fun." During mating season, males will occasionally battle other males for possession of females, but the males rarely do each other lasting physical harm.

Despite Lorenz's very creative research on aggression in animals, however, it is still an open question whether or not human beings are born with an aggressive instinct that we must learn to control. But in seeking further data on this matter, it might help if we asked the following question: Do animals ever show the kind of "vindictive nastiness" that we see too often in humans—both on television and in real life?

Pain and Aggression   Pyschologist Nathan Azrin and his colleagues, working at the Anna State Hospital in Illinois, fell into the study of violence quite by accident. Azrin is a behavioral psychologist who believes in the importance of rewards and punishments in determining behavior, and he wanted to see if he could train two rats to become "more social" by "moving toward each other." Azrin presumed that the more he could reward them for "seeking each other's company,"the more social behavior they would show.

Azrin and his group began by putting the two rats in a "shock box" (see Figs. 4.3 and 4.4). They planned to turn on the shock, hoping that they could reward the rats by turning off the shock when they made the first tiny movement toward one another. To the great surprise of Azrin and his group, they never got the chance to reward the rats for "social behavior." For the moment the shock went on, the two animals turned on each other and attacked each other violently.

Wisely enough, Azrin *et al.* (a Latin term meaning "and colleagues") abandoned their original objective and began to study aggression.

First, they had to make sure they knew what they were studying. Think about it for a moment. How would you go about defining **aggression** in a rat? Azrin *et al.* found that the animals had a characteristic posture: As soon as a rat was shocked, it would stand up on its hind legs, face another rat, open its mouth, bare its front teeth, and then strike out at the other animal with its forepaws. Oddly enough, if another rat (or some similar object) was not present, the shocked animal would show none of this behavior, but would keep its mouth closed and would cling with all four paws to the metal grid on which it stood.

Second, Azrin *et al.* had to determine whether it was really the *shock* which was causing the aggression, and not some incidental factor they had overlooked. The psychologists tested the relationship between shock and violent behavior by varying the strength or *intensity* of the electrical current to see what this would do. They found that: (1) the stronger the shock, the longer the aggression lasted; and (2) the more frequently the shock was given, the more vigorous and vicious the animal's attack was. Furthermore, the rats did not ever seem to get used to or **habituate** to the shock. The animals would display the attack behavior several thousand times a day if the experimenters shocked them that often.

Konrad Lorenz.

Repress. To block out or to forget something deliberately.

Konrad Lorenz (CONE-raht LOR-rents). A noted German biologist who became famous for his studies of animal instincts. Lorenz believes that humans have stronger killer instincts than any other animals, but not all psychologists agree with Lorenz. Technically speaking, Lorenz should be called an *ethologist* (ee-THOL-oh-gist)—that is, a scientist who is interested in the biological basis of behavior. Lorenz received the Nobel Prize in 1973 for his ethological research.

Fig. 4.3. A raccoon and a hooded rat remain far apart in cage before shock.

Fig. 4.4. Two seconds after receiving a shock, the animals move toward each other.

Et al. (ett-all). From the Latin term *et alia,* meaning "and allies." Scientists like to give each other credit. If an experiment was performed by Smith and Jones, it is usually referred to as "the study by Smith and Jones." But some experiments are performed jointly by a dozen or more scientists. Rather than writing Smith, Jones, Johnson, Ginsburg, Washington, Lee, Brodsky, Blanc, and Negra each time we speak of the study, we usually say "Smith *et al.*" Usually—but not always—the first name listed is that of the "senior scientist" who had the greatest responsibility for the research.

Aggression (ag-GRESS-shun). From the Latin word meaning "to attack." An aggressive behavior is an unprovoked act of force against someone else. The aggressor in a war is usually the nation that starts the fighting first.

Habituate (hab-BITT-you-ate). To become accustomed to a place or to a given stimulus. The first time you handle a snake, you may be very frightened. But if snake-handling becomes a habit, your fears may habituate.

Syndrome (SIN-drome; rhymes with "BEEN home"). A group of symptoms or signs typical of a particular disease or reaction pattern. The aggressive syndrome varies from one animal to another. In cats, for instance, it usually includes spitting, scratching, biting, arching of the back, flattening of the ears, baring of the teeth, twitching of the tail, and so forth.

Azrin *et al.* also showed that this aggressive response was instinctual and not learned, for animals raised from birth in complete isolation from other rats still demonstrated the violent attack pattern when they were first shocked. Rats that lived together from birth attacked one another just as often as they attacked animals that were complete strangers. And since both males and females attacked members of either sex, Azrin *et al.* concluded that neither sexual competition nor attraction was responsible for this reaction.

Azrin believes that it was the *pain* of the shock that triggered off an instinctual behavior pattern, which was relatively independent of the animal's prior experience.

Next, Azrin and his colleagues set out to discover whether shock would make animals of one species attack members of a different species. For example, would a shocked mouse attack a cat or a snake? The answer was yes, indeed—although the mouse seldom survived the encounter! In fact, the shocked animal would attack almost anything, even something like a tennis ball, if given the opportunity.

Violence Induced by Frustration   Is there something special about the *physical* pain caused by electrical shock that triggers off aggressive behavior, or would a *psychologically* painful stimulus do just as well?

In their next series of experiments, Azrin *et al.* found that almost any situation which caused the animal psychological discomfort or *frustration* would set off an attack. If a hungry pigeon is rewarded with a piece of grain each time it pecks at a button, it will soon learn to peck the button vigorously. If, after it has been pecking away for some time and earning its corn, the reward is suddenly stopped, the pigeon will typically first attack the button—and then any other object (such as another pigeon) that happens to be handy. Obviously, "psychological pain" or frustration can lead to violence as readily as can electric shock.

An animal can be taught to repeat almost any behavior pattern if it is *immediately rewarded* each time it makes that response. Even a cowardly pigeon can be turned into an aggressive terror if it is kept very hungry and is given food each time it attacks a fellow pigeon. In short, although the *tendency* to attack is present in the animals at birth, rewards can surely strengthen the tendency (and lack of reward or punishment weaken it).

But what about the animal that is the object of the aggression? Suppose we have two pigeons close to each other, and we shock Pigeon *A,* but don't shock pigeon *B?* What will happen? *A* attacks *B,* as you might guess, but the attack inflicts pain on *B.* The pain apparently annoys or frustrates *B,* who then retaliates by striking back at pigeon *A.* This counter-attack causes *A* further frustration, so *A* repeats its aggression against *B* even more vigorously. Pigeon *B* then hits back even harder, and the battle is on.

Question: What similarities do you see between the battling pigeons and the positive feedback loop that builds up between the two cerebral hemispheres at the start of an epileptic attack?

Is there no way out of this explosive situation? Luckily, as Azrin and his associates found, there is. The aggressive **syndrome** usually does not occur if the frustrated animal is given the alternative of *escaping* rather than *attacking.* A rat cooped up in a small box with another animal will attack because it apparently has no alternative. The same rat, if shocked in an open field, will flee from the pain rather than take out its frustration on nearby objects.

The attack behavior will also not occur if the animal is given the

Frustration often leads to emotional responses such as crying or aggression.

opportunity to *avoid* the pain in the first place, or if the animal can end or *terminate* the pain through a peaceful gesture.

Question: From an intra-psychic viewpoint, why might violence be expected to occur more frequently in crowded ghettos than in surburban areas?

Frustration–Aggression Hypothesis Perhaps the greatest modern contributor to the intra-psychic viewpoint was Sigmund Freud, the Viennese psychiatrist who developed an intra-psychic theory of personality called Psycho-Analysis. As we will see in later chapters, Freud believed that there is a childish part of our personalities which demands immediate gratification of all its wishes. Whenever this "child" in our minds is frustrated, it may either throw a temper tantrum or display other immature forms of emotion.

Using Freud's basic idea, psychologists John Dollard and Neal Miller derived what they call the **frustration–aggression hypothesis.** According to this hypothesis or theory, frustration occurs whenever a highly motivated individual encounters a barrier of some kind that prevents the person from reaching a much-desired goal. The barrier may be physical, psychological, or symbolic. If the individual cannot get around the barrier, frustration develops, and the person's behavior typically becomes less logical and more strongly emotional than would usually be the case. According to Dollard and Miller, aggression is *always* caused by frustration, but a frustrated person may do many things other than strike out against other people.

But are Dollard and Miller right? Is violence *always* a product of frustration? Well, what about people like Joe who suffer brain damage in an accident? For the most part, Joe was a **placid** and unemotional individual. But at times he did throw rather violent temper tantrums. Did the damage to Joe's neurons merely cause him to be more easily frustrated than you and I, or did the damage somehow set off "rage attacks" in Joe's brain much like the *grand mal* seizures experienced by people with epilepsy?

To answer that question, we must turn to the "third viewpoint" to discover what scientists know about violence and the brain.

Biological Determinants of Violence

What goes on in the brain of an animal—or a human—that might lead it to attack its neighbors when it is shocked or suddenly frustrated? Well, there is one thing we know for certain. The *motor output centers* of the cortex

Frustration-aggression hypothesis. A theory put forth by John Dollard and Neal Miller that aggression is always the direct result of some kind of frustration. Although aggressive behavior obviously does result from some types of frustration, aggressive reactions apparently have other causes as well.

Placid (rhymes with "acid"). From the Latin word meaning "to please." A placid person is someone with a pleasant, calm appearance. As we will see in Chapter 19, our term "placebo" (plah-SEE-bo), or "sugar pill," comes from the same Latin root.

must be involved in violent attacks, since the shocked animal makes aggressive *movements*.

But, as we said earlier, your cortex is merely the thin outer covering of your cerebral "mushroom." Buried away in the "flesh" of the two hemispheres are a number of neural centers that have rather specialized functions. These centers are located underneath the cortical covering, but they are still a part of your cerebrum itself. Although activity in these centers is typically under the control of your cortex, the centers can act independently if need be. In a sense, these centers are much like the "middle managers" in a large corporation. Much of the time they go about their appointed tasks on their own, with little supervision from "top management" (that is, your conscious cortex). But in emergency situations, you can usually gain direct control over these centers via cortical commands.

Your *limbic system* is a good example of the "lower centers" in your brain that influence your thoughts and actions even though you are not consciously aware of what these centers are doing.

The Limbic System   Your emotional behavior is, to a great extent, controlled by a section of your brain called the **limbic system.** The Latin word *limbus* means "border," and the limbic system is so named because it makes up the "border" or inner surface of both your cerebral hemispheres. This inner border is the part of the cerebrum you would see if you could turn a human brain upside down and look at the "mushroom cap" from the bottom (see Fig. 4.5).

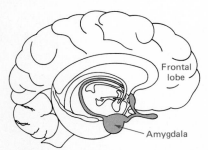

Fig. 4.5. The limbic system in color, showing the amygdala.

There are identical limbic systems in both your hemispheres, but since they are usually in close touch with each other (via the corpus callosal bridge), we can consider them as one unit.

Just as each of your cerebral hemispheres is divided into sections—the four lobes—so your limbic system has several parts or structures to it. One of these structures is the **amygdala,** which is buried deep within the mountains of the temporal lobe on each side of your head. The amygdala is a nut-shaped group of neurons that gets its name from the Latin word for "almond." Since the amygdala in each of your temporal lobes has a decided influence on how violent you are, and on your sex life, it is well worth studying.

Cortex versus limbic system.   Under normal circumstances, your cortex maintains control over the primitive and emotional reactions that are set off by activity in your limbic system. But what happens when a person gets drunk? A number of studies suggest that alcohol appears to affect the *inhibitory centers* in the cortex sooner than it affects the *emotional centers* in the limbic system. We might assume, then, that intoxicated people sometimes behave in childish, aggressive ways because the alcohol effectively removes or knocks out cortical control of the limbic system.

Further support for this assumption comes from experiments on cats, in which the cortex is removed surgically but the limbic system is left intact. How do you think a cat would react if we used a surgical knife rather than a drug to free the limbic system from cortical inhibition?

To begin with, this "de-cortex-ed," or **decorticate,** animal gets along surprisingly well, considering that it has been deprived of a goodly portion of its brain. There seems to be no basic change in the animal's personality—friendly cats remain friendly, and aggressive felines remain aggressive. However, even *very slight pain or frustration* is enough to set these animals into an explosive, violent rage.

Next, what do you think would happen if we "reversed" the kind of operation just described? That is, what would happen if we removed parts of the limbic system in animals but left most of the cortex intact?

Heinrich Kluever and Paul Bucy were probably the first scientists to perform this operation. Their experimental animals were rhesus monkeys, a species of **primate** noted for its vile temper and its readiness to aggress. Kluever and Bucy removed the temporal lobes from both hemispheres in their animals—thus taking out the amygdalas and other parts of the limbic system.

After the monkeys had recovered, their personalities appeared to have changed rather profoundly. They were gentle and placid in almost all circumstances, even when attacked by another animal. They also became markedly *oversexed*. The males would attempt to mount anything handy, including inanimate objects. The females would attempt to have sex even with such strange "partners" as water faucets.

The Kluever and Bucy monkeys also showed rather bizarre eating behavior. Not only did they over-indulge, but they also "tested" all small objects in their environment by putting them in their mouths. If given a bowl full of peanuts mixed with small metal bolts, a normal monkey will rapidly learn to pick out the edible nuts from the inedible bolts either by look or by feel. Kluever and Bucy's monkeys couldn't make this judgment. They had to *bite* the objects first, and then discarded the bolts only when they couldn't be chewed.

Later studies confirmed the Kluever and Bucy experiment by showing that removal of the amygdala in ferocious animals like the lynx or the wolverine makes them relatively tame.

Knowing all this, what do you think would happen if you could somehow *stimulate* the amygdala in a normal cat electrically? When Fritsch and Hitzig performed the first research on brain stimulation in 1870, they touched a piece of metal *directly* to the surface of their wounded soldiers. But the amygdala lies far beneath the cortical surface. To reach the amygdala, you need a long, thin instrument called a **needle electrode.**

This needle electrode is so thin that it can be inserted with little damage deep into the brain of a living organism. Since the tip of the electrode is metallic, it can be used to *record* the firing of nerve cells far below the brain's surface. However, this type of electrode may also be used to probe or to electrically *stimulate* the brain cells lying very close to its tip. Thus the needle electrode can either measure outputs from the brain, or deliver stimulating inputs to it.

If electrodes implanted within the amygdala or other areas of the limbic system are used to stimulate an otherwise normal cat, the animal goes into a rage as soon as the current is turned on. The cat's hair stands on end, its back arches, it spits and screams, and it will usually attack anything nearby (including the experimenter).

(We don't as yet know whether the electrical stimulation of the cat's limbic system causes the cat to *experience* intense pain which leads the cat to react emotionally, or whether the stimulation simply triggers off an unconscious *aggressive reflex* which may or may not cause the animal to feel pain. But we do know, from many recent studies, that pain-killing drugs such as morphine and enkephalin seem to have a *blocking effect* on neural activity in various parts of the limbic system.)

The "Stimoceiver" When needle electrodes were first used for both recording and stimulating purposes (about 1930), they had to be connected to complicated electrical equipment by means of long wires that carried the current either to or from the brain. Recently, however, physiologist Jose Delgado has devised a tiny radio transmitter/receiver that can substitute for the wires. The electrodes are connected directly to this **stimoceiver,** which weighs less than 100 grams (3 ounces) and can easily be taped directly to the cat's head. An experimenter 30 meters (100 feet) away can record the activity of several electrodes at the same time. Or, if the scientist wishes, he or she can stimulate whichever centers in the animal's brain contain needle electrodes—and perform this stimulation without having to go near the animal.

Delgado has implanted "stimoceivers" in the brains of many different kinds of animals. By stimulating various parts of the limbic system, Delgado has been able to induce ferociously aggressive behavior in a variety of monkeys and apes. Stimulation to certain other parts of the brain makes these same animals passive and unresponsive to attack. Using the "stimoceiver," Delgado has been able to turn dominant monkey "leaders" into

Needle electrode. A thin, needle-shaped piece of metallic wire that can be inserted into the brain to measure the electrical activity of small groups of neurons, or to stimulate nerve cells close to the electrode's tip.

Stimoceiver (STIM-oh-SEE-ver). An electrical apparatus connected to needle electrodes implanted in an animal's brain. When the stimoceiver receives radio commands from a nearby transmitter, it stimulates the brain with weak electrical currents.

"followers," while the most submissive monkeys have been stimulated into becoming dominant "leaders" of monkey troops.

The "stimoceiver" obviously has told us a great deal about the *physiology of aggression* in animals, but what can it tell us about rage and violence in human beings? Are your passions so mechanical that they too can be induced by electrical stimulation? The answers to these questions seem to come from a series of studies first performed in Boston.

The Case of Julia

Drs. Vernon Mark, Frank Ervin, and their colleagues in Boston were among the first scientists to use the "stimoceiver" to diagnose damage in the limbic systems of the brains of human patients. One of their first patients was a young girl named Julia, who had a long history of violent assaults on other people.

At the age of two Julia had suffered from a rare form of brain infection that gave her a very high fever. At first it seemed as if she had recovered from the sickness entirely. But about the time she was 10, she began having "spells" that suggested the illness had left her with a damaged brain. The "spells" were not the *grand mal* type of seizure. Rather, Julia would suddenly become terribly frightened even though there usually wasn't anything for her to be frightened of.

If the "spell" took place when Julia was at school, she would sometimes attack her schoolmates. More often, she would begin running as if she feared for her life. Often she would run for miles and miles before the "spell" wore off. Since she frequently ended up in a strange part of her home town, Julia began carrying a little pocketknife with her "for protection."

One evening when Julia was about 16, she went to the movies with her parents. During the film, she began to feel sick, and went to the restroom. The lounge was empty when she arrived. She glanced at herself in the mirror and was horrified. It seemed to her that *the whole left side of her body* had become shriveled up, evil, and distorted.

Julia was terrified by what she saw in the mirror, and couldn't believe that it was really she. At just this moment, unfortunately, another young woman came into the lounge. In trying to pass, the other woman touched Julia on her *left* arm. Julia grabbed for her knife and stabbed the other woman several times. Then Julia began screaming at the top of her voice. Fortunately for all concerned, the injured girl was rushed to the hospital, and her life was saved.

Question: Since the left side of Julia's body seemed to be the one most affected, on which side of Julia's brain was the damage apparently most severe?

After this attack, Julia's parents had her committed to a hospital. Julia was given many different types of treatment or therapy, but became worse rather than better. If not watched continuously, she would assault the other patients. Once she even stole a pair of scissors and stabbed a nurse who angered her. In desperation, her parents took her to Boston for the new type of treatment that Drs. Mark and Ervin were developing.

The first EEG records that Mark and Ervin made of Julia's brain showed abnormal, epileptic "spike" waves in the regions of both her temporal lobes, but an X-ray photograph suggested that her *right* temporal lobe was slightly shrunken. Since Julia's violent episodes were continuing, Mark and Ervin decided that they were justified in taking certain risks. They implanted temporary needle electrodes in both of Julia's temporal lobes (which were safely removed later on). After Julia had recovered from this relatively minor operation, Mark and Ervin were able to record directly from both her right and left amygdalas. They found epileptic electrical activity in both.

When Mark and Ervin used the implanted electrodes to *stimulate* Julia's amygdalas rather than just for recording, they discovered they could trigger off episodes of violence much like the ones she usually had. Mark and Ervin were convinced that tiny bits of scar tissue in her amygdalas were causing Julia's difficulties, but the scars were too small and buried too deeply in her brain to be removed by normal surgical methods.

So Mark and Ervin decided to try something rather new in brain surgery. First, they would move their electrodes around until they had located the exact *center* of the scar tissue in each amygdala. Then, they would pass a very brief but strong electrical current through the electrodes, a technique that would "burn out" the scar tissue.

Before Mark and Ervin could undertake the operation, however, Jose Delgado made his "stimoceiver" available to the Boston doctors. They were then able to implant electrodes in various parts of Julia's amygdala, connect the electrodes to the "stimoceiver," and record from (and stimulate) Julia's brain while she was moving freely about her hospital ward. They could also make movies of her—and then match this film recording of her behavior with EEG records coming from the "stimoceiver."

During one of their first recording sessions, a "natural" seizure occurred in Julia's limbic system. She was sitting down and in a fairly pleasant mood when the EEG began to show "spiking" in her *right* amygdala. Moments later, Julia jumped up and ran over to the wall of her bedroom. Once she reached the wall, her eyes narrowed. She clenched her fists and bared her teeth as if she were about to attack the wall. The spike-like seizure activity in her right amygdala slowly subsided at this point, and Julia's behavior rapidly returned to normal.

Shortly thereafter, Mark and Ervin *stimulated* Julia's brain directly. Although Julia had given her permission for them to do so, she was not told exactly when the stimulation was to occur. Mark and Ervin waited until Julia was sitting in her room, peacefully singing, playing a guitar, and talking to a doctor who was in her room to help if needed. Mark and Ervin turned the current on for a very brief moment, then turned it off.

A few seconds after the stimulating current had stopped, a blank stare slipped over Julia's face and she stopped singing. The doctor began asking her questions about how she felt, but she was unable to answer. The recording electrode now showed a full-blown epileptic seizure was occurring in her right amygdala—triggered off, of course, by the brief burst of direct electrical stimulation. Suddenly Julia grabbed the guitar by its neck and swung it at the doctor. She narrowly missed the man's head, smashing the guitar against the wall instead.

Julia's behavior suggested that Mark and Ervin had indeed located the scar tissue that was causing the seizures. Shortly thereafter, the doctors used their electrodes to destroy the scar tissue in her amygdala and then removed all the electrodes from the girl's brain. In the first year after the operation, Julia suffered but two rather mild attacks of rage behavior. She had no attacks at all after that first year.

Julia was lucky. Many other patients given similar surgery have not fared as well.

Violence and "Psychosurgery"

Physicians call operations such as the one performed on Julia **psychosurgery,** because the purpose of the surgery is to "cure" patients of inappropriate *thoughts or behaviors* that seemingly cannot be "cured" by pills or medication.

But before we go around chopping up people's brains in order to "make them behave," there are several dangers we should note. First, Mark and Ervin have been able to demonstrate clear-cut brain damage in but *a small fraction* of the patients they have studied. Many of their patients (after Julia) have shown little or no lasting improvement after removal of their amygdalas, and not all scientists have been successful in their attempts to repeat the Mark and Ervin research in this area.

Psychosurgery (SIGH-ko-SIR-jurr-ree). Operations performed on the brains of people or animals in order to get them to change their thoughts or behaviors. Biological surgery in order to achieve a psychological "cure" of some kind.

Karl Pribram, a noted neurosurgeon at Stanford, has pointed out that there is no doubt at all that a damaged amygdala can lead to episodes of violent rage in human beings. But, according to Pribram, we would be very wrong to assume that the reverse is true—*that episodes of violence are a universal sign of scar tissue in the amygdala.* In fact, *most* assaults and aggressive behaviors seem to be caused by psychological and social factors, not by brain damage.

Psycho-surgery, then, not only doesn't work very well in most cases, but seems to be aimed at the wrong goal—that of changing the *brain*, rather than changing the violent person's *mental processing* or *social environment*. Furthermore, the moral questions raised by such operations are complex and often frightening. Pribram reminds us too of another factor that we must always consider in evaluating research such as that performed by Mark and Ervin. Even if a patient does cease being violent after psycho-surgery, we cannot be certain that it is the *surgery* that was responsible for the behavioral change. It may be that the changed *attitudes* of the patient's family, friends, and the medical staff after the operation caused the decrease in aggression. If we *expect* psycho-surgery patients to behave more maturely after parts of their brains are removed, the patients may *respond* to our expectations even if the surgery itself was not particularly successful.

Violence and the Mind–Body Problem

What Causes Violence?

By now, you will understand that your answer to that question depends on your solution to the mind–body problem.

If you take the social/behavioral viewpoint, you will see violence as stemming primarily from the "models" we see in our own family settings and on TV, as well as from the effects that environmental rewards and punishments have on our attitudes and behaviors.

If you take the intra-psychic viewpoint, you will think of violence as a personality trait, an instinctual emotional response to a frustrating or painful situation.

If you take the biological viewpoint, you will look upon violence as caused primarily by electrical activity in the limbic system and other parts of the brain.

If you take an even broader view, however, you will see that there really is *no single cause for violence.*

Behavior is always *multi-determined.* Your thoughts and actions are always affected by your biological inheritance, your past experience, and what is going on in your present environment. To give up any of the three main viewpoints toward the mind–body problem would be to short-circuit your understanding of why you think and act as you do.

As we will soon see, however, the major conflict among the three viewpoints comes not so much in explaining "what makes you tick," as it does in suggesting how to repair the human clockwork when it gets violently out of adjustment. Or, to put the matter another way, your *theoretical viewpoint* toward people almost always determines the type of *treatment* that you think they should have in order to "tick" better.

We will begin our discussion of theories and therapies in the next chapter.

Summary

1. The complex interactions among brain, mind, and environment are often referred to as the **"mind–body"** problem.

2. For centuries, philosophers and scientists argued about whether bodily activities *caused* thinking, or whether thoughts *caused* bodily activities. Probably the best solution to this problem is to say that electrical and chemical reactions in your brain are correlated with—but do not really cause—your thoughts, feelings, and behaviors.

3. It was not until the 1800's that we learned much about the structure and function of the human brain. We now know that each cerebral hemisphere is divided into four parts—the **frontal lobe,** the **temporal lobe,** the **occipital lobe,** and the **parietal lobe.**

4. The frontal lobe contains the **motor cortex.**

5. The temporal lobe contains nerve centers that influence speech, hearing, and emotions.

6. The occipital lobe is the visual center of the brain.

7. The parietal lobe receives sensory inputs from the skin and muscles.

8. If the motor cortex in the frontal lobe is stimulated electrically, the person's muscles move or jerk.

9. If the visual input areas of the occipital lobe are stimulated, the person "sees stars."

10. Large areas of the cortex are silent to electrical probing. These so-called **association areas** are presumably the parts of the cortex where information processing and decision making occur.

11. Emotional behavior is highly correlated with electrical activity in the **limbic system,** a related set of neural centers that include the **amygdala** in the temporal lobe.

12. Stimulation of the human or animal amygdala is often followed by aggressive attacks.

13. Removal of the amygdala leads to a marked reduction in **aggressive behavior** in animals, but not necessarily in humans.

14. Pain-killing drugs such as morphine seem to block neural activity in parts of the limbic system.

15. Violence in humans is influenced by psychological and environmental factors as well as by neural activity in the limbic system.

16. Two of the most potent environmental factors may be the behavior of people we see on television, and the behavioral patterns we see in other people close to us in real life.

17. Psychological **frustration** or pain often (but not always) leads to **aggression.**

18. Frustration most often leads to aggression when the organism cannot escape from the painful situation.

19. People and animals can be trained to display violent behavior if they are rewarded for being aggressive. They may also be taught to control their aggressive actions by using rewards and punishments.

20. Behavior is **multi-determined.** There is no one unique solution to the problem of violence in today's world because almost all violence involves biological, psychological, and environmental factors.

(Continued from page 97.)

TO: Senior-Robot-in-Charge, Space Exploration Program

FROM: Leader Robot, Scout Ship XJ–12

SUBJECT: Planetary System MB–450–SEL 6.9

SenRo, may your batteries never run down, it is with dampened circuits and low meter readings that we communicate with you again. How can we tell you of the great disappointment that has crept slowly into our fuse boxes and circuit breakers? How can we make you feel the dismay that has settled over us like a rusting fog?

In our first message, filled with pulsating high expectancy, we described in brief detail our discovery of the CARs on this dismal planet. Were they our brothers? Were they our heirs? Were they even the "missing mechanical linkages" some of our more heretical scientists have speculated about? The strong spark of hope raced through our metal bodies as we began our studies of the CARs. And now we come to you, dragging our wheels behind us, to confess that things are seldom what they seem at first viewing.

It was Engineer RT/HEMI 454 who cast the first doubt on our initial positive impressions. The good engineer was observing the behavior of a cluster of CARs in a large city located close to the center of a string of five large inland lakes. Suddenly the engineer cried, "This is where they are hatched!"

And it was true. To our amazement, we saw through the viewer large buildings that fairly spat forth newborn CARs at fantastic rates! Hundreds upon hundreds per hour!

Navigator MT/POR 928 was incensed, as well one might expect. "Have they no shame? Must they behave like unfeeling softlife, manufacturing their offspring in public?"

We shook our antennae in amazement. Then I looked through the viewer, and I too made a dramatic if terrifying discovery. "Why, they are birthing their youngsters on an assembly line!"

The others would not believe me until they too had looked for themselves.

Can you imagine, SenRo, a race of hardflesh so insensitive to matters of quality control? It is true that their planet is still young, and they have just begun to exhaust their natural resources. But to cast their seed forth into the world so quickly, without the careful, secret, loving attention to detail that marks our own procreative process? Can you believe this?

And the hatcheries themselves! Huge barren steel and concrete boxes, with smoke belching from high chimneys to pollute the landscape and rust those gorgeous metal bodies! And smoke puffing from each CAR's exhaust pipe, as if they couldn't care less how much they poisoned their own air! We dread the necessity of ever having to drive on the surface of this planet and meet these CARs headlight to headlight. What stinking breath they must have!

Bad enough, I can hear you whisper through your voice box, but there is more, much more. For if their birth rites are primitive, their death rites are worse than that. It was Navigator MT/POR 928 who first noticed, near the hatchery, mounds of dead, decaying chassis of expired CARs. There they were, piled in heaps, as if no one cared to pay reverence to his passed-on ancestors. Some of the CARs were missing parts. We dread to say it, SenRo, but we fear we have happened upon a race of cannibals!

What can motivate these CARs to behave as they do? When first we looked, we thought them to be guided by the Electronic Spirits, as we are. But now, we have grave doubts. For as we watched more closely, we began to notice even more terrible things. The CARs rush about, almost aimlessly. Each morning there is a mass migration from the outskirts of the city to its center, and each evening the rolling hordes of CARs migrate outward again. But all they do when they get to their destinations is to sit, meditating, by the hour. Does this make sense?

And as they move, courtesy to other living mechanical things seems almost entirely absent. These CARs weave in and out of lanes as if possessed of demons, charging at each other with blind abandon. And can you imagine the terror that touched our circuit breakers when first we saw two lovely CARs smash head-on into each other! At first we thought these must be accidental encounters, but as we looked and looked and looked, it slowly came to us that "accidents just don't happen."

No, SenRo, there was a pattern to their behavior that we could not ignore. These CARs are actually hostile and aggressive to one another! We pushed the viewer aside wearily, drank several pints of oil, and became well lubricated. For we knew what we must look for next. Yet none of the three of us wished to make the first move.

Finally, hours later, our gallant engineer set the viewer on "Rapid Scan," and watched the dials sadly. When we failed to get any readings on this continent, we moved the scout ship and looked elsewhere. It took us several hours to find what we had feared, but there it was.

How can I put the truth into speech symbols? For there, on the opposite of this accursed globe, we found unmistakable evidence of war-like behavior among these crazy CARs. Rather than share and share alike, they have established territories that they defend with all the passion of softlife.

And they seem to have evolved specialized forms for doing battle— clumsy metal monsters with treads instead of wheels, and with long snouts that sniff out other CARs and then spit forth explosive missiles. We saw winged CARs zoom over cities and drop clutches of bursting eggs (further proof, I think, that the air CARs are a regressed species).

We ground our gears in anguish. These creatures, hardflesh though they be, must exist solely on a primitive, instinctual level. They cannot have discovered reason and still behave as they do. They are pushed by blind passions they surely cannot comprehend themselves. As such, they are scarcely better than softflesh. "Missing mechanical linkage?" I think not!

For hours we sat quietly, wheel to wheel, attempting to find a reason for this sick behavior. Could the CARs be insane? Would mechano-therapy be of help? And are there enough mechano-therapists in the whole universe to help such a diseased world?

It was, perhaps, the word "disease" that prompted us to our final observation, and it was the engineer who first made it. We had moved the scout ship a little closer to ground level and could now resolve images 1 to 3 metres in length.

"Look," the engineer said. "I think the CARs are infested with a strange form of softflesh."

We looked long and hard and very carefully. It was true, SenRo. One had to be quick to notice, but from time to time, just after a CAR would come to a stop, a small panel would open in the CAR's side. And out would slither a funny form of softlife. The panel would then close, and the softlife would disappear. The CAR would sit there, meditating peacefully, sometimes for minutes, sometimes for hours. And then the blurred image of another softlife would approach, the panel would pop open again, and the softlife would ooze into the body of the CAR. Within seconds, the CAR would roar into movement, as if the presence of this softlife in its innards had goaded it into movement.

"Mindworms!" the navigator cried. "The CARs are possessed by mind-worms! Softflesh devils that feed on electrical energy, that gnaw on circuitry and suck off insulation! Mindworms that nibble at the aggressive centers in their computer-brains, that bite and scratch and itch and frustrate and drive a CAR to ruin! No wonder these CARs are hostile, aggressive, and war-like! They are infected with parasites!"

SenRo, we are agreed. There can be no other explanation. We do not need mechano-therapists, we need worm-killers! Therefore, we beg of you, send to us at once a ship filled with the most powerful form of worm poison we have available. Perhaps all is not yet lost! Perhaps, once we have sprayed the whole planet with pesticide, we can cure the CARs of their softflesh demons that drive them to distraction. And then at last, we can welcome the CARs into the metallic brotherhood!

SenRo, may your transmission never whine, we await your wisdom—and the arrival of the pesticide! But please do not let our petition get lost in the cogs of bureaucracy! We do not think the CARs can hold out too long!

Recommended Readings

Belson, William. *Television Violence and the Adolescent Boy* (London: Teakfield, 1978).

Cater, Douglass, and Stephen Strickland. *TV Violence and the Child: The Evolution and Fate of the Surgeon General's Report* (New York: Russell Sage, 1975).

Dollard, John, and Neal E. Miller. *Personality and Psychotherapy: An Analysis in Terms of Learning, Thinking and Culture* (New York: McGraw-Hill, 1950).

Larsen, Knud S. *Aggression: Myths and Models* (Chicago: Nelson-Hall, 1976).

Loye, David. "TV's Impact on Adults," *Psychology Today* (May 1978), pp. 87–94.

Lunde, Donald T. *Murder and Madness* (New York: Scribner; San Francisco: Freeman, 1975).

Mark, Vernon H., and Frank R. Ervin. *Violence and the Brain* (New York: Harper & Row, 1970).

Valenstein, Elliot S. *Brain Control: A Critical Examination of Brain Stimulation and Psychosurgery* (New York: Wiley, 1973).

Psychology: A Holistic Approach

Did You Know That . . .

The better the predictions that a scientific theory makes about future events, the more accurate it probably is?

The most important reason for accepting or rejecting a scientific theory is usually its usefulness?

According to General Systems Theory, you are a "living system?"

All living systems are capable of learning how to alter their behaviors in order to get the inputs they want?

When you "decide" to do something, you typically make use of "feed-forward" and "feedback?"

The "mind/body" problem is one of the oldest and most important in the whole field of psychology?

Early in this century, the behaviorists denied that "mind" existed?

Mental problem solving and creativity may involve a "dialogue" between the two hemispheres of the brain?

Schizophrenic patients may have difficulties "thinking straight" because they block off inputs to and from their right hemispheres?

Learning to help others often means learning to change yourself first?

"The System Is the Solution"

"Well, do you think you can do it?" Dr. Severeid asked as he and his graduate student, Tom Watson, walked down the quiet street.

"How can you help a child who's so badly retarded?" Tom replied, a certain amount of frustration audible in his voice. "Patti has such a damaged brain that it would take a miracle to make her normal. Look, she's four years old, but she acts like a spoiled two-year-old. She's fat, she can't talk very well, she has little or no self-discipline, and she's got a mean streak in her that's a mile wide. She eats like a pig, and she pinches you every chance she gets." Tom rubbed his right arm, which still hurt a bit from the pinches he had received. "I don't think we can do very much for Patti. She just doesn't have much going for her, and you can't make a silk purse out of a sow's ear, you know."

Dr. Severeid grinned. "That old saying about sow's ears was popular before scientists developed synthetic fibers, Tom. And if Du Pont's chemical technology can produce the miracles of Nylon and Qiana, why can't our psychological technology come up with an equally miraculous way of helping severely retarded children develop into something much better than they've been before?"

"But Nylon isn't silk, you know," Tom responded quickly, as the two men turned a corner and headed for Dr. Severeid's office on campus.

"No, Nylon isn't silk, and doesn't pretend to be. But Du Pont makes Nylon cheaper, more durable, washable, and useful in lots of things where silk won't work. Tom, we can't make Patti into a normal child because the disease she had when she was an infant tore up too much of her brain. But we can help her develop to the maximum that her beat-up brain cells will allow. If we can't make her into a silk purse, we can at least try for a high-grade Nylon handbag."

"Nice family," Tom said. "Too bad it had to happen to them."

Dr. Severeid shook his head in sad agreement, thinking of the people in the pleasant faculty home they had just left. "They will be more than willing to cooperate, Tom. They've done everything they can on their own, but they know that they lack professional skills. So they asked us to help. I can give you some ideas on what's needed, but the real work will be up to you. So the most important question is the one I asked earlier. Do you think you can do anything to help Patti learn new ways of coping with her problems?"

Tom sighed deeply. He had always loved working with children, but all of his experience was with normal children. He loved normal children. He didn't love Patti much at all, particularly when she spat at him and pinched his arm. But Tom was taking Dr. Severeid's course on the psychology of exceptional children, and Patti certainly was exceptional. So perhaps he ought to try . . .

"What should we do first?" Tom asked, getting back to business.

"What do *you* think should be done first?" Dr. Severeid asked, turning the problem back to Tom.

"Well, I could smack her behind every time she pinches me," Tom said, a gleeful look in his eye.

"Tom, be serious. Her parents have tried that, and it just hasn't worked."

"I know," Tom said, laughing. "But I sure do get the urge, now and then, to dust her pants for her. Well, let's see. First off, she's a pig. Maybe she's fixated at the oral stage of development."

A puzzled look spread quickly over Dr. Severeid's distinguished face. "Yes, if you take the Freudian approach, you could say that. But surely you wish to consider other approaches as well. You're not trained in psychoanalysis, Tom. So there would be little or nothing practical you could do if you insisted on viewing Patti from just that one intra-psychic approach. For instance, what would a neuro-physiologist say about the girl?"

"Maybe she has a damaged limbic system," Tom replied.

Dr. Severeid nodded. "Quite possibly so. But where does that leave us? She's seen a neuro-physiologist, and he says there's no surgery that will help. Are you going to invent a new kind of brain operation?"

Tom laughed. "Of course not. I don't know beans about neuro-physiology."

"Then look at the girl from a behavioral or social point of view. Now how do you explain Patti's problems?"

Tom thought a moment. "Well, from *that* viewpoint, we could say that maybe she just hasn't learned how to eat properly."

Dr. Severeid's face brightened into a smile. "Why might she not have learned the proper eating habits?"

Tom snapped his fingers loudly. "Of course! She can't talk very well, so she can't ask for food. You saw how she just goes to the fridge and grabs whatever's inside. And her parents reward her piggishness by fussing at her. So she gets a lot of attention for misbehaving."

Dr. Severeid positively beamed. "Good thinking! So what could you do about it?"

Tom, very serious now, continued. "Well, I could teach her the names for the things she likes to eat. Then I could teach her to say 'please' and 'thank you,' so she'd have a way to get what she wanted politely instead of having to grub in the fridge on her own. If I could get her parents to cooperate . . ."

"They will, Tom, they will."

". . . then we could help her learn how to control her piggishness. She'd have to ask politely for what she wanted in order to get it. After she learned that, we could delay giving her the food reward for a few seconds. We could coax her into waiting longer and longer periods of time, because she'd know she would eventually get the food. She'd learn self-control, and her parents would learn more positive ways of influencing her development than by spanking her when she misbehaves."

"Good, good," said Dr. Severeid as they reached the psychology building and started up toward his office. "But how are you going to start?"

Tom walked briskly up the stairs, a new confidence in his step. "The first thing is to make friends with Patti. If she likes me, she'll learn because I want her to learn. I ought to make friends with her parents, too, and try to find out everything about Patti and the family that I can."

"Wouldn't hurt to read up on the oral stage of development, plus the physiology of brain-damaged children, now would it?" Dr. Severeid said as they arrived at the door to his office.

Tom groaned. "I knew there'd be a catch somewhere. I know a little about Freud, but I just don't get along very well with all that physiological stuff."

"If Patti with her damaged brain can learn how to control her piggishness, as you call it, aren't you bright enough to learn a few things about the physical growth and mental development of children?"

"Of course I am," Tom said in an annoyed tone of voice. He knew that Dr. Severeid was conning him into something, but maybe the professor was right after all. "I'll hit the books tonight."

"I'm sure you can do it, Tom, or I wouldn't have asked you. Just treat Patti wisely, objectively, but with a great deal of love and understanding. Treat her the way you'd want to be treated if you were in her place. And when you succeed—and I know you will—you can give a report to my class on what you've done. Okay?"

"Okay, Dr. Severeid. But I warn you, if she pinches me one more time . . ."

"Tom, you are allowed to pinch her back once. Only once. And then only if you're making progress."

Tom grinned. "Dr. Severeid, you've got a deal."

And what a "deal" it turned out to be! Tom spent many hours reading about the course of physical and intellectual development in young children. He learned about "fine motor coordination" (the ability to make delicate and precise movements, such as picking up small objects with one's fingers). And he learned about "gross motor coordination" (the ability to walk and run). Patti had no difficulties at all in picking up the tiniest bit of food on a plate, but even with physical therapy she had problems in getting from the refrigerator to the kitchen table. The fact that she had better control over small muscle movements than large muscle movements told Tom something about where in Patti's brain the damage might be worst.

Not that Patti didn't have ways of getting what she wanted, and of going where she wanted to go. When Tom would take the little girl walking, holding on to her tightly to give her support, Patti would point out the direction she wished to head in next. If Tom wouldn't take her there, she would begin to scream at the top of her voice.

"Pity her brain damage didn't affect her vocal cords," Tom said sarcastically to Dr. Severeid one day. "There I was, in the middle of a supermarket, trying to teach her the names of various foods, when we had a slight disagreement about where to go next. I wanted to go home; Patti wanted to stay. I started pulling, and she started screaming. Three women came over and bawled me out for hurting the little darling." Tom smiled. "Patti pinched all three of them. I think they got the message."

"How did you handle the screaming response, Tom?" Dr. Severeid asked.

"One day when we were heading home from a walk, we took a shortcut across the football field. Not a soul in sight. Patti decided she didn't want to go home, so she started yelling. I just sat down, covered my ears, and let her scream. Every once in a while, when she was catching her breath, I'd tell her quietly that we'd go home when she stopped the noise. It took 20 minutes or so before she calmed down, and she almost ruptured my eardrums, but finally she gave in and let me take her home. Funny thing, she hasn't screamed at me much at all lately."

Professor Severeid nodded. "Extinction of a learned response. If you don't reward her for screaming, she eventually stops it. A bit wearing on the nervous system, but it works. Have you tried extinguishing any of her other inappropriate behaviors?"

"A couple of them," Tom said. "Mostly having to do with soiling her pants. You know, her neuro-physiologist said that she might be too retarded to learn how to control her bowels, but that's not her problem at all. She's got too much control! When she gets tired of working on food-names, she begins to whine. If you don't stop right away, she cries, 'Oh, oh! B.M.!' And then she dumps. Takes about half an hour to clean her up, and by then I don't feel like doing much of anything except go home."

"How are you handling the soiling response?" the professor asked gently.

"I asked her doctor if I could put her back in training pants. He agreed. Now when she cries, 'Oh, oh! B.M.!' I just let her sit in her own mess for a while and continue the lesson. She hasn't tried that little trick on me now for a couple of weeks."

Dr. Severeid nodded soberly. "Well, Tom, it sounds like you're making real progress. I wonder if you wouldn't like to bring Patti over to show to the class. You might talk with her parents and, if they approve, you can give her a lesson in that demonstration room with the one-way mirror. The class can watch what you're doing without Patti's seeing them. And afterward, they can ask you questions about your work.''

A week or so later, Tom escorted little Patti into the demonstration room. As the door clicked shut solidly behind them, Tom led her over to the table and dumped a bag of goodies on the table.

"Food,'' Patti said, pointing at the bag.

"Yes, food,'' Tom responded, pulling two chairs up to the table. He looked at the mirror-like window set in one wall. The other graduate students in Dr. Severeid's class supposedly were standing behind the glass, watching. They could hear his voice—and Patti's—through a loudspeaker. Tom waved a big "hello'' to his comrades and then turned his attention to the little girl.

Holding up a piece of sweet cereal so that Patti could see it, Tom asked, "Patti, would you like this?''

"Oh, yes,'' Patti squealed delightedly.

"Ask for it politely, by name, and you can have it.''

Patti frowned. "Froot Loop,'' she said, and reached for the sweet.

"No, ask for it politely, and I'll be happy to give it to you.''

"Please, Tom, can I have the Froot Loop?'' she said, working hard to get the words right.

"Patti, you can have anything at all if you ask for it nicely,'' Tom said, giving her the piece of cereal.

Patti devoured the sweet greedily. "More!'' she cried.

Tom ignored her and pulled a fresh green grape from the bag of goodies. "What is this, Patti?''

"I want it,'' was the eager reply.

"Tell me what it is, and ask for it politely, and you can have it. Now, what is it, Patti?''

"Groop,'' said Patti.

"That's good, very good. You said it almost right. Grape, Patti, grape. Now you say it.''

"Grape,'' she squealed, and grabbed for the piece of fruit.

"Say please, Patti.''

"Please give me the groop.''

Tom could hear some muffled giggles from the other side of the one-way mirror. He tried a little harder. "Please give me the *grape*.''

"I want it!'' Patti wailed.

"I'll give it to you when you ask politely,'' Tom said, fearing that the students wouldn't appreciate what a great advance even this behavior was over the way she had acted when he first started working with her.

"Please give me the grape, Tom,'' Patti said, all sweetness and smiles.

Tom handed her the grape. "You're doing beautifully, Patti. Just keep it up and I'll get an A in this course, for sure.'' He reached in the bag again and pulled out a bit of cookie, knowing it was one of her favorites.

"What is this, Patti?''

"Cookie!'' Patti squealed with delight. "Gimme.''

"Yes, you're right. It's a cookie. But you have to ask for it, and then when I give it to you, you have to wait until I say "Go" before you eat it. Okay? If you can wait until then, you can eat that cookie, and another one too!" He pulled another cookie out of the bag. "Now ask for it politely . . ."

"Please, please, can I have the cookie?" She held out her hand.

"Okay," Tom said, placing the bit of cookie on her open palm. "Now just hold it there safely until I say 'Go.'" He started to count off 30 seconds. "Thirty, twenty-nine . . . that's marvelous, Patti. You're really doing beautifully . . . twenty-one, twenty . . . You're a good girl, Patti. You're really learning self-control. Now just a little longer . . . six, five, four, three, two, one. EAT."

Patti gobbled the cookie down at once. Tom smiled and gave her the second cookie, which she pushed into her mouth even before she had finished the first.

"Good girl, Patti," Tom said, bowing low in the direction of the one-way mirror. "You did just beautifully. I bet you could wait even a bit longer next time, couldn't you?"

Patti nodded, still munching on the cookies.

"Okay, now it's time to learn a new word." Again Tom reached into the bag and pulled something out. It was a tiny sweet pickle. "Do you want this, Patti?"

Patti turned up her nose. "Don't like. Wanna go home."

Tom panicked. "No you don't. You want to learn some new names today, don't you? This is a pickle, Patti. A sweet pickle. Say 'sweet pickle' and I'll give you a bite."

Patti turned away from him. "Don't like."

"You'll get us both in a pickle if you don't behave, Patti. Tell you what, if you try to say 'sweet pickle,' I'll give you another cookie? Okay?"

"Wanna go home!" Patti shrilled.

"Not yet, darn it. We've got a lot of work to do, and . . ."

"Oh, oh! B.M.!" Patti screamed.

There was a funny noise, and a strangely contented look came over the little girl's face.

Tom ignored the whole episode. "Okay, Patti, just a little longer, and then we'll go home, okay? Now, please try to say 'sweet pickle.' Please?"

Patti squirmed uncomfortably in her chair. A peculiar and rather upsetting smell arose from her vicinity.

"Don't like. Wanna go home," she said, rather softly.

"I know. I'll take you home just as soon as you try to say 'sweet pickle.' So please, Patti, try to say it and make us both look good."

The smell got worse.

"Sweat puckle."

"That's close. Very close." He patted her on the back. She squirmed again, and the odor became more intense. "Sweet pickle. Just say it right once, and we can go home."

"Sweet buckle."

The stench was now so bad that Tom was feeling a bit sick. In fact, he felt that if this went on much longer, he might end up being extinguished himself. But then he remembered the graduate students watching him. Since they couldn't smell anything through the mirror, they didn't know what he was putting up with. So he tried again.

"One more time, Patti. You're doing really good. Just say 'sweet pickle,' and we'll go home right now. And I do mean now."

"Sweet pickle," Patti said, smiling brightly.

"Beautiful, Patti. I knew you could do it. Here's the cookie." He gave her the reward, and gathered up what was on the table and stuffed it into his bag. "And now let's get out of here," he said, gagging a bit as he talked.

Grabbing the little girl by the hand, he led her to the door. He reached for the knob and started to pull. The door wouldn't budge. Tom tried again. And again. The knob wouldn't turn even a fraction of an inch. It was obviously locked from the outside.

Tom turned toward the mirror. "Hey, you guys. The door is locked. Somebody come open it before I die of asphyxiation."

There were noises from the other room, and soon other noises outside the door. Patti began to cry softly, and the odor became unbearable.

Moments later, Tom heard a muffled voice outside the room. "The door is locked, Tom, and we haven't got a key. You'll just have to stay there until we can find the janitor."

"Well, hurry up!" Tom yelled.

"Okay," came the indistinct voice on the other side of the locked door. "But it's after four, and I think the janitor's gone home. We'll do the best we can."

"I wanna go home," Patti wailed, and pinched Tom's arm.

"Listen," Tom said angrily. "You do that once more and I'll pinch you back right where it will hurt the most." He reached down, his fingers threatening painful revenge.

Patti screamed in terror. "Oh, oh! B.M.!"

"Oh, oh," Tom moaned. "Sweet pickle!"

(Continued on page 156.)

How To "Tick Better"

In the last chapter, we asked you, "What makes you tick?" And we found that "ticking" is *multi-determined*—that your speech, your attitudes, your feelings, and your actions are influenced by physiological, mental, and environmental variables. In this chapter, we ask you, "What do you have to know or do in order to tick *better?*"

The answer to that question turns out to be surprisingly complex. For in order to help yourself, you often must learn how to understand, deal with, and help other people. And in order to deal successfully with others, you typically must have some understanding of—and control over—your own thoughts and actions.

It is at this very practical level of trying to help ourselves (and others) that most of us run into difficulty. For most of us have never been trained to look at human behavior *systematically,* much less *objectively.* That is, most of us have not learned how to identify and deal with the biological, intra-psychic, and social influences on our thoughts, feelings, and actions. Which is to say, most of us have never acquired a **holistic** or unified "theory of human nature."

Holistic (ho-LISS-tick). From the old English word *hool,* meaning "whole." A holistic theory is one that assumes that "the whole is greater than the sum of its parts." Put another way, you are more than a collection of organs and cells, for you have properties (such as consciousness) that cannot be explained in terms of the actions of your parts.

The major purpose of this chapter, then, is to give you a *theoretical perspective* that may enable you to see yourself and others in a more unified way. And once you learn to *perceive* the world differently, you may find new ways to *reshape* that world to bring it closer to your heart's desire.

Scientific Theories

All sciences, including psychology, are built on **theories.** Theories are extremely handy things to have around, since they give you a framework for understanding yourself and the world around you. But as necessary as these theoretical explanations may be, they can mislead you if you don't remember one fact—theories are merely *approximations to the truth.*

To put the matter another way, even our best scientific explanations are *limited in their usefulness.* For theories are merely verbal or mathematical descriptions of the world, and the world is far too complicated for the simple words and mathematical symbols we presently have available to us. Thus all theoretical frameworks are "somewhat wrong" because they are *incomplete* and somewhat *inaccurate* descriptions of real-world systems.

But we cannot live without theories because they are summaries of what we know (and don't know) about ourselves and the rest of the world. The question then becomes, how should we pick and choose among the many psychological explanations of human behavior available to us?

Judging a Scientific Theory

Scientists have many different **criteria** by which they judge theories. Four of these criteria are as follows:

1. How accurate is the theory?
2. How complete is the theory?
3. How impressive is the theory?
4. How useful is the theory?

Let us look at these four criteria one by one.

1. All theories are somewhat inaccurate, but one theory is usually "less wrong" than a second. In order to test the accuracy of a theory, we usually follow the *scientific method.* That is, we use the theory to *make a prediction* about something, and then we run experiments to see how accurate the prediction was. If the theory does a good job of predicting, we tend to accept or believe in the theory. If it does a poor job of predicting, we probably should either revise the theory, or switch to another one.

2. Some theories give us detailed descriptions of one limited part of the world, while other theories give us broad descriptions of "the whole big ball of wax." Psychology is made up of both types of theories.

For example, *perceptual theories* are an attempt to describe one small part of your life—how you take in information about your world and process it so that it makes sense (see Chapters 6–11).

Motivational theories are a way of describing another limited aspect of your life—your goals and how you attempt to reach them (see Chapters 12–14).

Learning theories treat yet another **circumscribed** part of your psychological world—how you acquire new thoughts, attitudes, and behaviors, and how you remember them (see Chapters 15–18).

Developmental theories are a bit more complex, for they attempt to describe where all your perceptions, motives, habits, and memories come from—and how they develop over the span of your life (see Chapters 19–21).

Personality theories are even more complicated, for they try to lay out in systematic terms not only how you became the person you are, but also how you might go about changing yourself (see Chapters 22–25).

Social theories are ultimately the broadest of all, for they try to tell us not only how individuals interact with each other, but also how social systems (such as groups and organizations) grow and develop (see Chapters 26–28).

Theories (THEE-or-rees). From the Latin word meaning "to behold, or view." A "theorem" (THEE-or-em) is a scientific or mathematical statement whose truth has been proven, or at least assumed. A theory is a set of related theorems, thus a collection of statements about some aspect of science. Generally speaking, a theory is a set of assumptions about the way the world (or a part of it) works. A theory is thus a *viewpoint* that is capable of being disproved by factual evidence. A theory that is incapable of being *disproved* is, scientifically speaking, not worth the paper it's written on. Never forget that the word "theater" comes from the same Latin word as does "theory," and a theory presents the same condensed view of things that a play or movie does.

Criteria (cry-TEER-ee-uh). Plural of *criterion* (cry-teer-ee-ON). From a Latin word meaning "to judge, or decide." The criteria for success in school usually include good grades, the ability to read and write effectively, to think logically, and so forth.

Circumscribed (SIR-cum-scribed). From the Latin words meaning "circle" and "to write." Anything that is circumscribed is something that you can draw a circle around, something contained within a given set of boundaries. Circumscribed behaviors are those that fall within the boundaries of normal or expected social actions.

PART ONE Biological Bases of Behavior

In psychology, then, our theories run from the simple to the complex. But what we need in addition is a sort of "master viewpoint" that would let us put all these individual theories together into one comprehensive whole. By far the most holistic or unified of the "master viewpoints" is *General Systems Theory*. We will talk more about this approach in just a moment.

3. Some scientific theories may impress you because they are particularly simple or **elegant.** Other theories may impress you because they fit the world as you see it. For example, if you stand on the beach and look out at the ocean, the world surely *looks* flat. We now know that "looks are deceiving." But up until 1520, when Ferdinand Magellan and Juan del Cano sailed around the world, most people refused to question the "flat earth" theory because it fit what they saw.

Other viewpoints are impressive because they tell us what we want to hear. For instance, consider the very strange theory of intelligence dreamed up 100 years ago by Paul Broca, the noted French scientist who discovered the "speech center" in the brain. Broca began with an incorrect assumption, namely, "the bigger the brain, the brighter the person." He then performed a rather sloppy study of the *size* of human brains. Broca concluded, incorrectly, that males had larger brains than females, and that whites had larger brains than blacks. Broca then announced that he had *proven* that men were more intelligent than women, and that whites are innately smarter than blacks.

Actually, there is no known relationship between "brain size" and "intelligence." But because Broca's poorly done research tended to confirm what many French citizens believed anyhow, his work was accepted as "fact" rather than "theory."

If you are like most people, you will tend to prefer beautiful, elegant, simple theories that reinforce your own observations and prior beliefs. And once you have accepted a theory because it impresses you favorably, you may find yourself reluctant to give it up even when newly discovered facts show that it is less accurate or complete than another theory.

4. By far the most important criterion by which a theory is judged is this—how useful is it to you?

The *usefulness* of a theory can be measured in many ways. If the theory pleases you intellectually or emotionally, if it gives you an appreciation of things that you wouldn't have appreciated otherwise, then it is useful to you at a very deep psychological level. The ultimate pleasure for most of us, however, is that of reaching our own personal goals. In the long run, therefore, you will most likely adopt the theory that gives you the best predictions about yourself and others, and thus gives you sufficient control over yourself and your environment so that you can reach your goals.

One of the major purposes of this book is to make you aware of *the theories you already have*—and to try to impress you with the usefulness of other viewpoints that *you might wish to consider adopting.*

Of all the psychological theories available to us, **General Systems Theory** is one of the most comprehensive and elegant. Even more important, the General Systems approach is one of the most useful in helping us change ourselves—and others. So let us spend a few pages describing General Systems Theory, and then discuss both its good points and its failures.

General Systems Theory

If you are like most people, you will marry and raise a family sometime in your future life, or you are already doing so. And if you are like most parents, at some point after the birth of your first child, you will give considerable thought to what your child's future might be.

So, imagine that you are sitting beside a crib, in which your own first child is lying. The infant is now a healthy six weeks old. Chances are good that, as you look as this marvelous youngster, you will perceive it (theorize about it) in several ways. First, you will see it as being *your* child—that is,

Elegant (EL-ee-gant). From a Latin word meaning "to select, or elect." To be elegant is to be graceful and dignified in appearance or manner. An elegant theory is one that is a neat, simple way of defining and solving scientific problems. Given a choice between two competing theories, most scientists will prefer the one that has the fewer loose ends hanging about, or that is the shorter or more "refined."

General Systems Theory. A holistic view of the biological, psychological, and sociological sciences. According to General Systems Theory, humans are living systems made up of sub-systems (cells, organs). But humans are themselves sub-systems of such larger social systems as groups, organizations, and societies. In order to understand yourself, then, you must learn how your own sub-systems affect you, and how you affect (and are affected by) the groups, organizations, and societies to which you belong.

you will *assume* the infant is an extension of your own mind and body. Second, you will perceive it as being a normal *human being* which, according to most theoretical viewpoints, you ought to love and help as best you can.

But just for a moment, stand back and—like a physician judging your infant's state of health—look upon this child of yours as being a **living system.** This child has biological needs that must be met if it is to survive. No matter how much you may love the child, if you do not give it food, air, and water, and if you do not protect it from germs and other physical dangers, the child will die before it can reach maturity.

First and foremost, then, your infant is a *biological system* that requires certain inputs from its environment in order to maintain that miraculous internal process we call "life." But infants are more than mere biological machines. Each person is a unique *psychological system* as well, and each of us is a part of such larger *social systems* as groups, organizations, and societies.

Thus, in order for you to best meet all the needs of your infant, you may have to *perceive* this tiny child as being much, much more complicated than you had ever dreamed it was. And to help it survive, you must come to *understand* how the child interacts with you and the rest of its environment.

Question: In some present-day cultures with very high rates of infant mortality, parents understand very little about germs and disease. The parents thus see no reason for boiling their drinking water or keeping their children clean. Could you reduce the number of infant deaths in these cultures without first changing the parents' "theoretical viewpoint" toward dirt and germs?

What Is Life?

A Pattern of Interactions What does it mean—in practical terms—to view your infant as a *living system?* Before we can answer that question, we must first define a few terms.

As we noted earlier, **primitive terms** such as "life" are terribly slippery things to define. Life is a *process,* not a piece of concrete reality. The instant after you die, much of your body will still be *physically* what it was the moment before. But because most of your organs would no longer be actively interacting with each other, you would be dead rather than alive. Life, then, is determined by a *pattern of interactions* among the various parts of your body.

This pattern of interactions *among* your body parts is so incredibly complex that we understand very little about how the miracle of life occurs. Indeed, we don't really know all that much about how any *one* part of your body takes care of itself, much less how it communicates with other parts. But at least we have learned some of the *biological characteristics* that all living things seem to possess. We know, for example, that biological systems function as if their *major purpose* in life was that of *survival.*

Goal-Oriented Behaviors Oddly enough, as soon as we use the word "purpose," we have switched from a biological to a psychological viewpoint. For "purposes" imply actions and behaviors, and it is difficult to discuss *behavior* in purely physiological terms.

So we might note that, *psychologically speaking,* all living systems possess certain specific characteristics too. For instance, from the tiniest cell to the largest animal, all living things behave as if they were *goal oriented,* which is to say that all living systems have ways of achieving the inputs (or goals) that they require to sustain life.

Motivation and Emotion If you observe your child carefully, you will soon note an interesting fact. The infant cries when it is hungry, and it stops crying when it is full. Why? The child cries because it experiences hunger

---

Living systems. The cell, organ, organism, group, organization, and society are all examples of living systems. All systems are made up of related parts (sub-systems), are open to the environment (have inputs and outputs), act as if they were motivated to achieve goals, are controlled by feed-forward and feedback, and are capable of a certain amount of self-control.

Primitive terms. For just a moment, think of a theory as being a house built of bricks. The arrangement of the bricks *defines* the shape and function of the house, but the house does *not* define the bricks themselves. Primitive terms are the "bricks" (building blocks or fundamental ideas) that a theory is constructed from. The theory therefore cannot define the primitive terms from which it is shaped. Terms such as "God," "matter," "energy," and "time" are all primitive terms that are almost impossible to define.

A baby learns to give cues to its parents when it needs food.

Motivation (mo-tee-VAY-shun). From the Latin word meaning "to move." Thus your "motivation" is whatever internal processes that *move* or energize you to seek various goals.

Emotion (EE-mo-shun). From the same Latin word meaning "to move," but usually means "to move in an excited or agitated way." As used in psychology, the term includes both movements (behaviors) and inner *feelings* that presumably cause the excited actions.

Systems. From the Latin word meaning "to bring together, or combine." A system is a set of parts that are related to each other in some way, that are in communication with each other, or that have ways of affecting each other. The system itself is *always* greater than the sum of its sub-systems. Living systems are open to the environment—that is, they take in energy and information from the world, and give energy and information back to the environment.

and is motivated to reduce its hunger pangs. It stops crying when the food it has eaten reduces its hunger and thus its motivation.

The term **motivation** almost always refers to goal-oriented behavior, and *motivation* is one of the key psychological characteristics of all living things. Hunger is a type of motivation that the infant experiences as a painful event. The child cries because of the pain: Crying is the child's way of expressing its *emotional feelings* about its need for food.

When deprived of something needed for life—or when kept from achieving a goal—almost all living systems show *agitated movements* that we typically call "emotional behavior." **Emotion,** then, is another psychological characteristic of all living systems.

Learning The first time a newborn infant cries for food, it usually does not stop its agitated actions until long after it has begun to eat. After a few days or weeks, however, the newborn child will often cease its crying as soon as its mother or father appears, for it has *learned* that the arrival of a parent (or whomever feeds the child regularly) means that food is at hand. Eventually, the infant learns to cry in one way when it is hungry, but cries another way when it is wet or cold or wants to be played with.

Of all the psychological characteristics of life, *learning* is probably the most important. Without the ability to change, to adjust, and to grow, we surely wouldn't survive for a very long time.

Life, then, is a process with many different biological and behavioral aspects to it. But this process of life occurs only in **systems,** so before we can appreciate fully what life is, we must define the second word in the term "living systems."

Question: How does the infant's ability to learn to cry in "different tones of voice" aid its survival? What would happen if the parents responded the same way no matter how the infant cried?

What Is a System?

An Organization of Related Parts What do you think of when a person says, "I have a system"? Probably you will imagine some technique or series of steps that the person has in mind for achieving a particular goal. But what do you think of when a friend of yours says, "I want to beat the system!" Now you will probably see "the system" as being a social organization of some sort.

The key word in defining the term "system" is *organization.* Technically speaking, a system is *an organization of related parts.* For the parts of a living system (such as you or your infant) to be "related to each other," these parts must be in some kind of *communication* with each other. As an example, the organs in your body communicate with each other in many

Fig. 5.1. The interconnection of input, output, and feedback.

Feed-forward. A series of commands or orders that you issue (usually all at once) that are to be executed in sequence at some time in the future. Any time you get information about what your future behaviors are *expected* to be, you have gotten psychological feed-forward. The "rules and regulations" issued by any group or organization are feed-forward in that the rules tell the members of the group or organization what behaviors are allowed, what behaviors are forbidden, and what the *consequences* of obeying or disobeying the rules will be. Your own personal "code of ethics" (conscience) is also a type of feed-forward in that this code tells you what sequences of actions to perform in certain situations in the future.

---

different ways. Your heart pumps food and oxygen to your brain; your brain sends neural messages to your heart telling it when it should become excited and pump blood faster, and when it should relax and pump slower. Your heart thus communicates *energy* to your brain, while your brain communicates *information* to your heart.

Inputs, Processes, Outputs   In order to survive, each living system must take in such things as food and water from its environment. The system then uses (or *processes*) what it gets, and releases its wastes back out into the environment. One of the major characteristics of living systems, then, is that they have *inputs, internal processes, and outputs* (see Fig. 5.1).

Information vs. Energy   Generally speaking, there are two major types of inputs, internal processes, and outputs: those having to do with *energy,* and those having to do with *information.* When you eat supper, your body takes in food, which it then digests or processes internally. Later, your body will release energy (and matter) back into the environment—in part through waste products, in part through behavior.

As you read this book, you are "inputting" information of one kind or another. You process this information as you evaluate it, try to understand it, and as you file the material away in your memory.

Most inputs, internal processes, and outputs involve *both* energy and information. You learn what to eat, and what not to eat. And you need food in order to learn new habits that will help you survive.

Controlling Your Inputs   Think back again to your infant lying in its crib. We have already said that it is strongly goal oriented, and that its major goal is that of survival. But how does an infant survive? By now, perhaps you can see that no living system (including both you and your infant) can survive unless that system can somehow *control its environmental inputs.*

Almost all of your goals in life can be expressed in terms of getting the inputs that you need in order to thrive and survive. That's what motivation and emotion are really all about. When you need something from your environment, you typically experience a painful emotion. When you satisfy that need, you typically experience a pleasurable emotion. Motivation and emotion thus are internal, psychobiological processes that *direct* your behaviors toward satisfying your input needs.

Now think a little bit further. In order to control your *inputs,* you usually must control your *outputs.* That infant of yours needs food in order to survive. It soon learns that it is more likely to get food (rather than a fresh diaper) if it cries in one tone of voice when it is hungry, but in another tone of voice when it is wet. Crying is thus *information* about its internal energy needs that the infant *outputs* to its environment. By controlling its crying, your newborn child influences what sorts of inputs it gets from you and from other people in its world.

Question: How does an infant reward its parents when they help satisfy the child's needs?

Feed-Forward and Feedback   Generally speaking, systems are controlled by their inputs. For example, how do you get a computer to solve an equation for you? The first thing you do is to feed the machine information about the *sequence* of steps it should follow in order to generate a solution to the equation. The computer then carries out your commands "one step at a time" until it completes the task you have given it. The "programming" input that you initially give the machine is called **feed-forward** because you tell the computer *now* what you want it to accomplish during some *future* (forward) time period.

Living systems too make use of "feed-forward" in order to plan and execute a series of responses that will lead them toward some goal. Suppose you are reading a book when you suddenly "feel hungry," so you decide to go get an apple from the refrigerator. Your "mind" can't accomplish this goal on its own—your body must do the actual moving (and eating). Thus when you "make up your mind" to get the apple, parts of your cortex map out a *sequence of movements* that will get your body up from the chair and moving toward the refrigerator in the kitchen. Your cortex next "feeds the sequence forward" to the lower centers of your brain. These lower centers then execute the movements without any conscious effort on your part.

This fed-forward *sequence of actions* is but half of the process, however. For as you move, you interact with the outside world, and you must be ready to adjust your movements to take account of any unexpected *consequences of your actions*. What if you stumble on the rug? What if the kitchen door is locked? What if the refrigerator is bare?

As you move toward a goal, your body gives you **feedback** information that tells you how you are performing. If you stray too far off track, your brain uses this information to keep your body "on target."

Feed-forward is thus an informational input that tells a system what its actions should be at some time in the near future. *Feedback* is an informational input that tells a system about its past or present performance. You need both kinds of inputs in order to achieve most of your goals in life.

Question: Blind people are perfectly capable of planning and executing the complex motor movements involved in playing golf. Thus there is nothing wrong with their ability to utilize "feed-forward." Why, then, don't blind people usually become good golfers?

Self-Control   At first glance, it may seem that General Systems Theory views human beings as being little more than computers. Not so, for even the most complex of machines lacks one critical ability shared by all living systems—the ability to choose among various goals and *voluntarily* change your actions in order to achieve whatever goal you pick.

To put the matter another way, you are capable of exercising voluntary **self-control,** but machines aren't.

Like all other human beings, you weren't born with very much innate self-discipline—but you were born with the capacity to *learn it.* That is to say, you inherited the ability to see that the best way to satisfy your biological, psychological, and social needs is to control your biological, psychological, and social outputs. And to do that, you need informational inputs that will tell you what your actions should be in the future (feed-forward) and what you have been doing right and wrong in the past (feedback).

To a great extent, what we call *personal development* is little more than the study of how people learn self-control. That is, much of what you will do as a parent is to give your child informational inputs about what it should do, what it could do, and what it is presently doing. Your child can then make use of this feed-forward and feedback to satisfy its own unique needs. But the key to meeting its needs is self-control, for as your offspring learns to control its own thoughts and actions, it learns how to get what it wants from you, and from the rest of its environment, as well.

From a General Systems Theory viewpoint, then, one of the *main tasks of a parent* is to discover what inputs a child needs in order to learn how to control and change its own thoughts, values, and actions. For it is only in this way that the child can achieve what humanists call **self-actualization.**

Let us pause for a moment to summarize what we have learned about "living systems," and then finish our study of General Systems Theory.

The Living System: A Summary   Living systems have the following characteristics:

Feedback. Information about a system's present or past performance which is fed back into the system to control the system's present or future actions. If you ask a friend, "How do I look?" you are asking for feedback on your present appearance. If your friend says, "You look great!" you are likely to continue to dress as you have been doing. If your friend says, "Terrible," you may use this feedback to correct the way you dress in the future—or to find a new set of friends!

Self-control. Living systems have the ability to make use of feed-forward and feedback in order to grow, mature, change, learn, and hence achieve their goals more effectively. Self-control is the ability voluntarily to change your outputs so that you can gain the present or future inputs you desire. Children learn self-control when they discover that reducing their temper tantrums and impulsive actions will yield them rewards they can't otherwise get.

Self-actualization. A term from *humanistic psychology* that means "the act of becoming the best person you possibly can become." The process of actualizing, or achieving, your own goals or your own ideal state of personal development—usually by learning that you must help others achieve their own goals so they can help you achieve yours too.

1. Living systems behave as if they were goal-oriented.

2. They frequently show emotional reactions associated with achieving (or not achieving) their goals.

3. Living systems are capable of learning.

4. They are made up of organized parts that are in some kind of communication with each other.

5. They have inputs, internal processes, and outputs. Some of these inputs, internal processes, and outputs are informational. Others have to do with energy.

6. Living systems are capable of self-control—that is, of learning to control their internal processes and outputs in order to achieve the inputs (goals) they need.

7. They learn self-control by learning how to make effective use of feed-forward and feedback.

Systems within Systems

Now that we have gotten the definitions out of the way, let us view you through the eyes of General Systems Theory—both to add to your understanding of yourself, and to demonstrate why you must learn as much about relationships *among* systems as you do about individual systems themselves.

Biological Systems

The Cell Every cell in your body is a living system. Cells are made up of complex molecules, but these molecules do not exhibit the property of *life.* Only when these molecules interact with each other in very complicated ways does the property of life *emerge* in the living cells.

A muscle cell in your heart takes in food from its environment (your bloodstream), converts the food internally into energy, and excretes waste products back into the bloodstream. Muscle cells also have information inputs—neural messages that come from your brain (and chemicals in your blood) that speed up or slow down the cell's activities. The contracting and expanding of the muscle—its *behavior*—is its "informational output," as well as its "energy output."

Like other biological systems, the cell is affected by its genetic inheritance and by any damage that it may have sustained in its past history. In a sense, then, each muscle cell in your heart is as much a unique, individual living system as you are yourself.

The Organ But one cell isn't enough to keep a heart going—any more than one person is enough to keep a group going. The various types of cells in your heart play quite different biological roles. But, working together, they manage to keep the blood pumping through your body.

Your heart itself is an **organ**—that is, an organized group of individual cells—but it is also a system in and of itself. You can learn a great deal about hearts by studying the behavior of individual cells, but if you want to view the heart as an *organ*, you must also look at the way these cells cooperate. That is, you must study the *relationships among cells.* For if the cells did not relate to each other in some way, they would not be organized enough to form a system as complex as your heart.

The cell is the simplest form of living system. As we noted, it is made up of non-living molecules that combine to produce something new—*life itself.* Cells make up organs, but your heart is more than a random collection of different types of cellular systems. For when we shift our level of analysis from the cell to the heart, we find that the heart has properties that we could not have predicted no matter how thoroughly we understood the functioning of its individual cells.

The major **emergent properties** at the organ level seems to be those of

Organ. From the Greek word meaning "tool, instrument, or parts that work together." An organ is thus a means of accomplishing something. Your heart is an instrument for pumping blood. Your brain is a tool for processing informational inputs.

Emergent properties (ee-MER-jent). From a Latin word meaning "to rise, or come out of concealment." When you put the pieces of a jigsaw puzzle together, the "picture" emerges. But you cannot usually predict what the *whole* picture will look like just by looking at a single piece or two. Thus the visual properties of the picture emerge from concealment only when the pieces are put together in a *systematic* way.

PART ONE Biological Bases of Behavior

cooperation and what we might call *role specialization*. A single-celled organism—such as the **amoeba**—lives and dies in solitary splendor. It reproduces by splitting in two, but these two offspring don't cooperate or even associate with each other as two human brothers or sisters might. Rather, each amoeba does almost everything on its own.

Any system that acts entirely on its own must play many roles—such as food gatherer, warrior, and reproductive agent. Heart cells, however, *specialize*. Some of them are built for working, others for support and protection, still others for circulating food and oxygen. A few nerve cells inside the heart act as "organ regulators" by controlling the rate at which the organ beats. And because each of these many types of cells is specialized for a single task, the heart cells must *cooperate* with each other—or die.

It is this *cooperation* (born of *specialization*) that allows the heart cells to create a more complex system—the organ. As you might suspect, the heart (as an organ) functions best when its actions help its individual cells meet their own unique needs. And since the cells could not long survive without the heart itself, heart cells are most likely to thrive when their own outputs help satisfy the needs of the larger system.

Question: Your brain is an organ. Can you list the various "roles" played by your left hemisphere? By your right hemisphere?

Psychological and Social Systems

The Organism Each organ in your body is a complex living system with its own types of inputs, internal processes, and outputs. Indeed, your organs are so complicated that medical doctors often specialize in treating the diseases of just *one* organ system.

But your body itself is an **organism,** a much more complex living system than any one of its component organs. A "family physician"—someone who usually practices **holistic medicine**—must not only understand the behavior of your heart and liver and brain, but the *relationships among them as well.*

You, as a living organism, are surely something more than a heart, a liver, a brain, and a few other organs loosely thrown together inside your skin. For you have properties (such as perceptions, thoughts, memories, and attitudes) that your individual organs simply do not possess. Your heart is not "conscious," and never will be, because *consciousness* is a characteristic that emerges only at the level of the organism.

As you know only too well, you function best when the needs of all your organs and cells are best met. And since your "biological systems" cannot live for long without the "conscious you," they survive best by keeping you happy and healthy.

Question: How long would a "General Hospital" survive if its staff was made up just of kidney specialists? What other "medical roles" are needed in order to keep the hospital functioning smoothly?

The Group You do not live your life in social isolation, as does the amoeba. Rather, you share your existence with, and are dependent upon, other human beings. To put the matter into more technical terms, organisms form **groups** in much the same way that your individual organs unite to form organisms such as yourself.

From the standpoint of General Systems Theory, the group is a kind of *super-organism* with emergent properties that are unique unto it. Sexual reproduction is one such property. It takes two people to tango, and it takes both a male and female human being to produce that new living system we call an infant.

Spoken **language** is another property that emerges at the level of the

Amoeba (ah-ME-bah). A very primitive, simple, single-celled organism that looks more like a moving blob of gelatin than it does a "real" animal.

Organism (OR-gan-ism). A living system capable of getting along on its own. You are an organism. Your heart is a living system, but it is not an organism because it can't ordinarily function on its own without the rest of your body (or some artificial support system).

Holistic medicine. The act of treating patients as complex living systems, of considering them in terms of their psychological needs and social backgrounds as well as in terms of their physiological problems and processes. A physician who orders you to stop smoking (or lose weight) but doesn't help you learn the habits involved in changing your life style is *not* practicing holistic medicine.

Groups. Sets of individuals considered as single entities. A group is a *super-organism* in much the same way that your body is a sort of *super-organ*.

Language. A way of exchanging information in symbolic terms.

group. Cells and organs communicate with each other chemically and electrically. Members of family groups communicate with each other using verbal and non-verbal signals. *Speech*, then, is a system of informational inputs and outputs that emerges at the level of the group.

Newborn children cannot survive physically without the support of a social system such as the family group, but it is likewise true that groups cannot get along without the willing assistance of individual family members. The better the group helps satisfy the infant's biological, psychological, and social needs, the more likely it is that the infant will grow up willing to help the group survive.

Question: How many different "roles" would you like your own child to learn as it grows up? How do you plan to help the child learn these roles?

The Social Organization   You started life as a single cell that divided billions of times to form new cells. In a sense, then, you began your life as the simplest form of living system, but grew in complexity until you developed into the adult organism that you presently are.

Now, did you ever stop to ask yourself how all those billions of cells in your body managed to form the highly structured body you now inhabit? Why didn't you turn out to be a sack full of individual cells—each striving to go its own way, and do its own thing?

The answer seems to lie in the fact that living systems are made up of *organized* parts. The first few cells you started life with were bound together in a tight little ball of tissue (see Chapter 20). As these cells began to multiply, they also began to specialize. That is to say, they began to take on *different roles*. Some of the cells grew together to form your brain; other cells organized themselves to form your heart, your skin, your stomach, and your blood vessels.

A heart cell does not have the freedom to behave like a liver cell, nor can your liver start acting like your brain if you are going to survive for very long. Your **genes** keep your cells and organs from "misbehaving" by specifying what role each should play. That is, your genes *specify in advance* what inputs each of your cells and organs will be sensitive to, and what kind of output they will give to each type of input received. Your genes thus provide your cells and organs with *biological feed-forward*—a set of genetic "rules and regulations" designed to keep all the parts of your body in touch with each other, and striving toward the common goal of keeping you intact and healthy.

Social organizations are much like your body. They typically start small and develop slowly into highly complex systems. And since social organizations don't have "genes" to guide them, they must have *formal* rules and regulations to guide their functioning. Being able to write these "rules and regulations" down in some formal language can aid an organization in many ways. Thus *written language* is a property that probably first emerged when people began to form large organizations.

It is also at the level of the organization that formal **social roles** first appear, including those of "teacher," "student," "parent," "worker," "manager," and "police officer" (see Chapter 26). As perhaps you can guess from the titles we usually assign them, these roles are actually a set of *expected behaviors, attitudes, and outputs*. Thus knowing a person's social role also tells you something about the response (feedback) you can expect from the individual when you behave in a certain way.

Individual organisms who play the role of "teacher" are expected to act and think in one way, while organisms who play the role of "student" are expected to produce quite a different set of behavioral outputs. From an *organizational* point of view, however, it often doesn't matter which organism fills which role, any more than it matters to you which of your cells becomes a part of your liver and which becomes brain tissue. All you care about—and all the system cares about—is that all the roles are filled, and all the goals are met, so that you (and the organization) can survive.

Genes (pronounced as "jeans"). A single "word" in the genetic code that determines the structure and function of your body. When you were conceived, a set of genes from both your mother and father combined to form your own unique "biological language" that described the body you would be born with.

Social roles. A role is a stereotyped or systematic way of behaving or thinking about something. When you say, "The good guys always wear white hats," you are describing a social role both in terms of the actors' behaviors and style of dress. A social role is thus a set of feed-forward instructions telling you how to act if you wish to play a certain part or role in society.

PART ONE   **Biological Bases of Behavior**

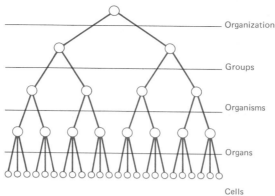

Fig. 5.2. Individual parts build up into an organism.

Question: Does an organization have the ability to control its outputs voluntarily?

Metaphors (MET-ah-fors). From the Greek word meaning "to transfer, or change." A metaphor is a figure of speech in which one object takes on the properties of something else, or in which one object is compared with something else. To say that "Freedom of speech is the most precious diamond in Liberty's crown" is to transfer (metaphorically) the value of a jewel onto the ability to say what you think. A mixed metaphor is an inappropriate or contradictory comparison, such as "Freedom of speech is a pig in a poke floating like a cloud on the blue American sky."

Esoteric (ee-so-TAIR-ick). Anything that demands special training in order to be understood or appreciated is esoteric, such as psychology, calculus, chess, or rock music.

Societies and Cultures   You are a complex system composed of cells and organs, but you are also a member of groups, organizations, and societies. That is to say, you are made up of living systems, and you help make up complex social systems.

A group is a simple social system composed of organisms like you (and hence of cells and organs). An organization is a fairly complex social system made up of groups and individuals. A society or culture is an extremely complex social system that is composed of formal organizations, each of which plays its role in supporting the society (see Fig. 5.2).

Although organizations sometimes act as if they should be free to work toward any goals their members wished, the fact is that no complex social organization can long endure without the strong support of the rest of society. Thus, the better that an organization fulfills its cultural expectations, the better off will be the society, the organization, and each individual member thereof.

Question: A scientific experiment usually consists of changing the inputs to a system and then noting what changes occur in the system's outputs. What would be the easiest system to study scientifically—a cell, an organ, an organism, a group, an organization, or a society? Which science seems most advanced these days—biology, psychology, or sociology?

The Mind/Body Problem: A Systems Approach

In a recent article in *Science,* George L. Engel points up a difficult problem that confronts psychiatrists today: Until theorists find some workable solution to the "mind/body" problem that we discussed briefly in Chapter 4, psychiatry will remain "a hodgepodge of unscientific opinions, assorted philosophies and 'schools of thought,' mixed **metaphors,** role diffusion, propaganda, and politicking for 'mental health' and other **esoteric** goals."

On the one hand, there are those psychiatrists who emphasize mental processes to the near exclusion of the body—or of the social environment. These psychiatrists tend to focus on "what goes on inside your head," not on the ways in which inputs from your body (and the people around you) influence your thoughts and feelings. On the other hand, there are those psychiatrists who try to reduce all mental activity to biochemical and electrical events inside your brain, without taking into account the strong influence that your mind has on your body—and on your environment.

Dr. Engel—who is a professor of psychiatry at the University of Rochester—believes that General Systems Theory may offer a new approach to solving the mind/body problem.

George L. Engel.

Introspectionism

As we noted in an earlier chapter, the conflict between "mentalists" and "physiologists" has a long history in the behavioral and social sciences. At the turn of the century, psychology was defined as "the science of mind" by most scholars. The dominant approach to studying people was to get them to **introspect**—that is, to look inside their minds to analyze their own mental experiences.

The **structuralists** were probably the first "mentalists" in psychology. Taking their cue from physics, the *structuralists* assumed that the "mind" was constructed of "mental atoms" just as a lump of coal is made up of carbon atoms. By "introspecting" their own inner experiences, the structuralists assumed they would be able to identify what this "atom" of the mind actually was. But because "looking inward" is a technique with many flaws to it, the structuralists never succeeded in describing the "structure of the mind" in any meaningful way. They did, however, interest many psychologists in looking for more-or-less permanent "psychological structures." As we will see in Chapter 24, such devices as the IQ test and the personality inventory are, in their way, more efficient attempts at getting at "the structures of the mind" than one can achieve merely by asking subjects to introspect.

Next in line were the **functionalists,** who also believed in "introspecting," but who thought it equally important to measure behavioral responses. William James, who founded the first psychological laboratory in the United States some one hundred years ago, was the first American functionalist. According to James, the purpose or *function* of both your mental processes and your behaviors was to help you adapt to your environment. Because they were more interested in "process" than in "structures," the functionalists had a great impact on psychology—particularly in the field of education. Many of the contributions that James and other functionalists made are still valid and useful. However, as a *theoretical approach*, functionalsm fell out of favor when psychologists began searching for more objective ways of studying human behavior than by asking people to describe their conscious experiences.

Introspectionism ultimately failed for two reasons: First, because your "conscious experiences" are private events and thus cannot be measured directly by an outside observer. You can *tell* a psychologist about the things you are conscious of, but you cannot *show* the psychologist what you are experiencing.

Second, introspectionism failed because you are not directly "conscious" of most of the activities that go on inside your head. As you learned in Chapter 2, consciousness is a property of your left hemisphere—not of your right hemisphere or of the lower centers of your brain. Therefore, your "conscious" left hemisphere is not *directly aware* of the processes occurring in the "unconscious" parts of your brain (such as your right hemisphere).

To put the matter another way, when you introspect, your left hemisphere tries to look at its own internal activities. And your left hemisphere can no more introspect on the mental processes occurring inside your *right* hemisphere than a person standing beside you could observe what goes on inside your "conscious" *left* hemisphere. Therefore, "introspecting" is at best a very limited tool for discovering either the structures or the functions of the mind because it deals primarily with left-hemisphere, conscious activities.

Watson's Behaviorist Revolution

In 1913, John B. Watson began the behaviorist revolution by throwing out the concept of "mind" entirely. To Watson, people were like simple adding machines—a stimulus input came along, pressed a button in our brains, and out popped a response of some kind. Since psychologists could study

John B. Watson

PART ONE Biological Bases of Behavior

stimuli and responses objectively, why should they bother looking at the "mental processes" that came in between?

This very mechanistic approach to psychology probably disturbed more people than it pleased, particularly the **humanists** and the **psychoanalysts** we will discuss in later chapters. But Watson's approach did tend to force the "mentalists" to pay a bit more attention to environmental stimulation.

The major problem with Watson's brand of behaviorism is this—you know full well you have a mind, even if Watson couldn't inspect it or measure its processes directly. You know too that "what goes on inside your head" does have a meaningful relationship to how you behave. Thus, you may ask, how could Watson explain thinking, problem-solving, and creative activities if he denied the existence of the mind?

Watson's solution was a clever one. He viewed thinking as a series of **implicit** responses run off in *sequence*—much as "feed-forward" is a sequence of **explicit** responses. You don't think "in your head," he said. Rather, you "speak silently" by moving your lips and vocal cords *very slightly* (implicitly) in response to some environmental input. Watson thus made cognitive activities *measurable* because they boiled down to being muscle movements of one kind or another.

Watson was both right and wrong in his approach. Studies do show that many people make slight movements of their vocal cords and lips while "thinking." But we also know that you are quite capable of continuing to think even when a drug such as **curare** paralyzes your voluntary muscles. And Watson never could explain the "silent voice" that seems to guide many types of problem solving and creative thought.

Watson had an excellent idea of what "feed-forward" was all about, but he missed the boat by denying the importance of "feedback." As far as Watson was concerned, people (like adding machines) respond to stimulation mechanically—without taking account of the consequences of their actions.

It thus fell to Harvard psychologist B.F. Skinner to take the next step in the behaviorist revolution, that of adding feedback to the human equation.

B. F. Skinner.

Skinner's Contributions

B.F. Skinner took Watson's half-formed ideas on behaviorism and made them work in real-world situations by showing how important feedback is to most types of learning. "Behavior is determined by its consequences," is one of Skinner's best-known sayings. With this slogan as his motto, Skinner went on to develop one of the most impressive *technologies* of behavioral change the world has ever known (see Chapter 16).

Even though Skinner added feedback to Watson's feed-forward sequences—and turned the adding machine into a programmable computer—Skinner still had difficulties explaining how people perform creative mental acts. He solved the problem by saying that, while "mind" exists, its processes are unmeasurable. Skinner therefore focuses entirely on *behaviors*. He does not study "thinking," he studies verbal responses; he does not study "creativity," he investigates creative reactions to external inputs. Thus "thought processes" and "mental creativity" become, for Skinner, *learned behaviors* that are entirely under environmental control.

"You do not *write* a poem," Skinner said in a speech in the mid-70's, "You *have* a poem, much as a woman *has* a baby." A pregnant woman does not create an infant by an act of will—the **procreative** process takes place automatically and without her conscious direction. According to Skinner, the "creative process" occurs in much the same way. The environment stimulates you to put words down on paper, and you have as little control over the shape of a poem as a pregnant woman has over the shape her infant is born with.

Skinner's solution to the mind/body problem pleased neither poets nor cognitive psychologists, both of whom insisted that the creative process is

Humanists. A "school" of psychology that probably started with Alfred Adler (see Chapter 24). Humanists tend to emphasize the *differences* between humans and other members of the animal kingdom, and to believe that people are capable of *self-actualization*, or of achieving their own unique goals.

Psychoanalysts (sigh-ko-ANN-uh-lists). Psychologists or psychiatrists who are followers of Freud's theoretical position (see Chapter 24).

Implicit (IM-pliss-sit or im-PLISS-sit). From the Latin word meaning "to involve, or engage." Something is implicit if it is implied, but not stated openly or readily visible. A person wearing very tight clothing gives you an implicit view of her or his body.

Explicit (EX-pliss-sit or ex-PLISS-sit). From the Latin word meaning "to show openly." A naked person gives you an explicit view of his or her body.

Curare (cure-RAHR-ree). A paralyzing drug obtained from a variety of South American plants.

Procreative (PRO-cree-ate-tive). To procreate something means to make a copy of that thing. When you have children, you procreate yourself.

E. Roy John.

Fig. 5.3. The John and Killam neural studies of problem solving began by teaching a hungry cat to press a lever in order to receive a few sips of milk.

Association areas. As we saw in Chapter 4, those parts of the cortex that are "silent" to an electrical probe. We assume these areas of the brain are involved in processing information, thinking, remembering, or "making associations" between stimulus inputs.

shaped more by *internal processes* than by direct *environmental stimulation.*

The behaviorist tradition has given us highly effective ways of changing ourselves—and of helping others do likewise. But in doing so, it has failed to explain the mental processes we all are aware of—even if we cannot prove their existence to the behaviorist's satisfaction.

As Dr. Engel has suggested, General Systems Theory seems to provide a comfortable middle ground between the warring camps of "mentalism" and "behaviorism." And thus it offers its own *systematic* solution to the mind/body problem.

Let us begin our description of the solution by finding out what goes on inside an animal's brain as it learns how to "think its way" through a problem.

A Neural Study of Problem Solving

Several years ago, E. Roy John and K. F. Killam performed an interesting series of studies on "neural feed-forward" in cats and other animals. To understand what they did, you will have to draw upon all the knowledge of brain processes that you gained from reading the first four chapters. For example, you should remember that visual inputs from your eyes travel up through the lower centers of your brain until they reach the *occipital lobes* at the back of your cortex. These lobes are the "visual input areas" of your brain. The "motor output areas" lie in your *frontal lobes.* Thus when you see something—and respond to it—the input message must somehow travel from the back of your brain to the front. And it must be "processed" or acted upon by various **association areas** of your cortex which lie between the input and output regions of your brain (see Chapter 4).

What John and Killam did was to try to discover what goes on in these "association areas" when a cat learns to respond to a visual signal. That is, they were hunting for *neural patterns* in the processing areas that would show them what the cat was "thinking about" *before* it actually behaved. And, in a sense, John and Killam did just that. But to appreciate the importance of their findings, you will have to keep the conflict between the "mentalists" and the "behaviorists" firmly in mind.

John and Killam began by teaching a hungry cat to press a lever in order to get food (Fig. 5.3). The cat quickly learned that each time it pressed the bar, it would get a few sips of milk. While the cat was learning this task, the experimenters made recordings of the electrical activity occurring in the cat's brain.

Next, they turned on an electric light that flickered at a rate of 10 cycles-per-second. Immediately a recognizable neural pattern (close to 10 cps) began showing up in the *visual input areas* of the cat's cortex (but *not* in the association areas). We can call this the "neural input pattern," and its appearance means that the flickering stimulus was obviously "getting through" to the input areas of the cat's brain—but no further.

Next, John and Killam taught the cat that it would be given milk *only* when it pressed the lever while the light stimulus was flickering. Very rapidly, a recognizable neural pattern (again, close to 10 cps) started showing up in the *association* areas a second or two after the corresponding pattern appeared in the visual *input* areas. We can call this the *approach pattern* since it rapidly became *associated* with the cat's approaching and pressing the bar (and getting its milk reward). The "input pattern" and the "approach pattern" differed from each other in some details, but they both had a frequency of about 10 cps.

At the beginning of a trial, the input pattern would instantly show up in the visual areas—and would continue as long as the cat was looking at the light stimulus. Next the approach pattern would appear momentarily in the association areas, then disappear and reappear several times in a row. John believes that the cat was "thinking through" the problem by testing its "thoughts" against its visual inputs. Then the approach pattern would appear in the processing area almost continuously. Shortly after the pattern "stabilized," the cat would press the bar and drink the milk.

After the cat had learned to press the bar only when the light was on, the *sequence* of events on any single trial went something like this:

1. The cat would sit quietly staring at the light.
2. The light would flicker at 10 cps.
3. The neural "input" pattern (about 10 cps) would show up almost immediately in the visual input areas of the cat's brain. The cat would not respond just yet, however.
4. Moments later, the "approach pattern" (also about 10 cps) would appear in the association or "processing" areas of the cat's cortex. The approach pattern would disappear and reappear several times, then would "stabilize" by appearing almost continuously.
5. Shortly after the approach pattern stabilized, the cat would press the lever, the light would turn off, and milk would appear in the dipper.
6. The "input" pattern would immediately *disappear* from the cat's visual input areas, but the "approach" pattern would *continue to appear* in its association cortex while the cat claimed its reward.

Question: How might this sequence of neural events be explained in terms of the cat's learning to associate a specific stimulus with a specific response?

Neural "feed-forward"   There are several points of interest about the experiment so far. First, the approach pattern which appeared in the central association areas presumably was some sort of *feed-forward* sequence of responses associated with pressing the lever. Why? Because the cat would never press the bar until *after* this pattern had stabilized in its processing areas.

More than this, occasionally the approach pattern would appear in the processing areas *even when the light wasn't turned on* (and hence the 10 cps pattern wasn't appearing in the visual input areas). In these cases, the cat would still press the lever shortly *after* the approach pattern had appeared in its association cortex. In this situation, the animal obviously "called to mind" and reacted to a stimulus pattern that *didn't presently exist in its external environment*—an action the behaviorists would have difficulty explaining in purely "stimulus-response" terms.

The second point of interest lies in the fact that the approach pattern would always *continue to appear* for a second or two in the central "processing" areas after the cat had pressed the lever. Why is this so odd? Because the input pattern *disappeared* from the visual input areas as soon as the cat pressed the bar and the light turned off. Apparently the association areas continued to issue the feed-forward command until the cat could check out the *consequences* of pressing the lever.

Neural Patterning During Discrimination Training   Next, John and Killam forced the cat to **discriminate** between two visual stimuli. That is to say, they continued to reward the cat when it pressed the lever while the 10 cps light was on. But occasionally they presented the animal with a 6 cps light. If the cat pressed the bar while the 6 cps light was on, it didn't receive milk—and the next trial on which it could get food was *delayed* for several seconds. Since the cat was punished for responding when the 6 cps stimulus appeared, the animal had to learn to *discriminate* between the 6 and the 10 cps inputs—and then avoid the bar when the light flickered at 6 cycles per second.

Once this **avoidance learning** had occurred, the sequence of events went something like this:

Discriminate (diss-KRIM-in-ate). From the Latin word meaning "to divide, or distinguish." When you learn to play the piano, you must learn to discriminate one musical note from another. If you think that "all Chinese look alike," you must learn to distinguish their individual features before you can tell them apart.

Avoidance learning. In order to avoid punishment, you must discriminate between lawful and unlawful behaviors. Avoidance learning almost always involves learning to approach some stimuli, while not approaching (or moving away from) other stimuli.

1. When the 6 cps (avoidance) stimulus came on, an "input" pattern of about 6 cps would appear immediately in the visual input areas of the cat's cortex. Shortly thereafter, a recognizable "avoidance" pattern (also about 6 cps) showed up in the central processing areas of the cat's brain. Under these circumstances, the cat would avoid responding.

2. When the 10 cps (approach) stimulus came on, a similar "input" pattern (about 10 cps) would appear at once in the visual input areas, but the *avoidance pattern* (about 6 cps) would momentarily show up in the processing areas. A second or so later, the "approach" pattern (about 10 cps) would begin to appear in the association areas. Once the neural pattern had switched from avoidance to approach, the cat would press the lever and drink the milk. Again the approach pattern continued to persist in the association areas *after* the cat had pressed the lever.

In both these cases, you could predict the cat's behaviors quite accurately if you knew what neural pattern was occurring in its *processing areas*, but not if you merely knew what pattern was present in its *visual input areas* (or in its external environment). Thus taking "neural patterns" into account gives you a much more precise prediction of what the cat will do than would a purely behavioral description of the cat's reactions.

Question: The avoidance pattern (about 6 cps) inhibited movement. Could the fact that this pattern appeared in the "processing" areas even when the 10 cps light was on have helped the cat "think carefully" before it responded?

Neural "Expectations" The neural patterns appearing in the "processing-areas" of the cat's brain seem to be a type of *neural feed-forward*. That is to say, they may specify a precise sequence of behaviors *before* the cat makes them. But this feed-forward also helps determine the animal's expectations of what the *consequences* of its actions will be.

For example, now and again the cat would make a mistake. When the "avoidance signal" came on, the *correct* input (6 cps) pattern would show up in its visual input areas, but the *incorrect* approach (10 cps) pattern would emerge in the cat's "processing" areas. The cat would then press the lever and stare intently at the milk dish. When no food appeared, the cat would react as if it were *disappointed* at this unexpected turn of events—that is, as if it had expected a different consequence. The approach pattern (about 10 cps) would then disappear from its "processing" areas, and the avoidance pattern (about 6 cps) would show up *throughout the animal's brain*.

Seemingly, the cat was using "real world feedback" to correct two things: (1) The sequence of neural commands that its brain had fed forward to its muscles in response to a given stimulus input, and (2) its expectations about what the consequences of its actions would be.

To put the matter another way, "real world feedback" apparently changes *both* parts of the "problem-solving" process—the fed-forward sequence of motor commands, and the pattern of neural expectations that these commands presumably will yield.

How Feed-forward Might Affect You The John and Killam research is controversial for many reasons. First, it hints that external stimuli may have highly-specific "neural representations" in your brain. That is, there may be a specific neural pattern stored in your memory for each stimulus that you encounter in your environment. And "thinking" may thus be a matter of recalling and "processing" these patterns in your association areas.

Second, this work suggests that there is also a one-to-one correspondence between these neural patterns and your own "unmeasurable" mental processes. The fact that the approach and avoidance patterns *alternated* in the cat's association areas before the animal responded is a fascinating

Creative activities seem controlled by the non-verbal hemisphere.

thing to contemplate. It would appear that John and Killam may have provided us with a direct measure of the "thought processes" that occurred in the cat's brain as it attempted to solve a real-life problem—something that the behaviorists had long held was a scientific impossibility.

However, there is something you must understand. Many scientists simply do not agree that these conclusions are presently justified. They note, for example, that while the work has been successfully repeated more than once, some researchers have had problems getting the same results that John and his colleagues have.

Nonetheless, the John and Killam research does give strong support to the General Systems approach. So let's keep the **tentative** nature of their findings in mind as we *theorize* about how feed-forward might work in your own brain as you get the apple from the refrigerator.

As soon as you decide to go to the kitchen, your left hemisphere probably does two things: (1) It feeds forward a pattern of neural "commands" to the lower centers of your brain so that they can get your muscles moving, and (2) it sends your right hemisphere an "information copy" of the neural pattern. Your right hemisphere probably "processes" this pattern to determine the type of feedback you *should receive* as you approach your goal.

Then, as you walk toward the refrigerator, receptor neurons in your skin, muscles, and joints feed back information about your actual movements to your brain. Your right hemisphere probably compares the *actual* neural feedback it receives with the *expected* feedback specified in the neural feed-forward. As long as you are on target, your right hemisphere might encourage you onward. But when you stumble over the rug, the feedback from your receptors would depart seriously from the input your right hemisphere had *anticipated.* It then might sound an emotional alarm so that your left hemisphere would change its commands to get you back on target.

Question: Why couldn't your right hemisphere simply tell your conscious mind "in words" what is wrong when you get off track?

Problem Solving and Creativity   Of the many types of thought processes that psychologists study, two are of particular importance. One is often called *problem solving,* while the other involves artistic or intellectual *creativity.* A variety of studies suggest that both types of "thinking" may consist of some sort of "silent conversation" between the two hemispheres.

Problem solving usually occurs when you are trying to discover a path to a *particular* mental or behavioral goal. Your left hemisphere seems to generate a "trial sequence" of neural commands that might get you to the goal. These neural commands are probably sent to the muscles in your tongue and throat just as if you were going to speak out loud. But your speech muscles apparently are inhibited from moving while you

Tentative (TENN-tah-tive). From a Latin word meaning "to feel, or to attempt." A trial solution to a problem is a "tentative" solution because you're not yet sure that the answer is correct. A tentative action is one that you cannot entirely predict the consequences of.

"think"—presumably because, as a child, you learned to inhibit them in order to "speak silently."

Whether you spoke aloud or not, your right hemisphere presumably would receive an "information copy" of the neural commands. Your "monitoring" hemisphere could then *anticipate* the results of these actions, and "shape" the commands (with emotional feedback) until your left hemisphere came up with a workable scheme.

During *creative* or artistic activities, however, your right hemisphere would take the lead. It presumably would have sensed some perceptual pattern that it wished your left hemisphere to reproduce in word or deed. Your left hemisphere would then generate behavior patterns until it hit upon the one that most closely approached what the right hemisphere was perceiving.

In many situations, of course, you will make use of both "logical problem solving" and "creativity." But theoretically speaking most scientific and artistic *insights* probably begin their lives as "perceptual patterns" in your right hemisphere. And your artistic and scientific *behaviors* may be little more than your attempts to express these patterns in the language of the left hemisphere.

Question: In either problem solving or creative thinking, would your left hemisphere be consciously aware of the "shaping inputs" from your right hemisphere (which is generally non-verbal)?

Schizophrenic Thought Processes   Theories are useful if they give us new insights into old problems. Now that we have offered a tentative explanation for "normal" thought processes in General Systems Theory terms, let us see if this approach can shed new light on our understanding of "abnormal" thinking.

There are many different theories explaining why people become psychotic. No one has yet discovered a biological cause for schizophrenia. But as we noted earlier, people diagnosed as schizophrenic appear to process most of their inputs with their left hemispheres. That is, they block out almost all information coming from their right hemispheres. Since their right hemispheres don't communicate very well with their left hemispheres, you might expect that schizophrenic patients might have problems controlling their own actions.

And they do. Three of the many **symptoms** shown by schizophrenic patients are as follows:

1.   They experience difficulties in planning and executing patterned sequences of responses—that is, they have trouble talking and thinking logically, and their artistic efforts don't always "make sense" to the rest of the world.

2.   They are often unable to perceive the effects that their actions have (or might have) on themselves and others—which is to say that they don't pay much attention to feedback either from their right hemispheres or from other people. Schizophrenic patients often can't take care of themselves very well, in no small part because they don't know how to get along with other people.

3.   Perhaps because they block out inputs from the emotional parts of their brain, these patients also show a decided lack of motivation or "desire to change" when their expectations about life aren't met.

Although schizophrenia is a very complex form of "mental illness," and we still do not know what *causes* this type of psychosis, it would seem that patients suffering from this condition don't use inter-hemispheric feedforward and feedback to guide their thoughts and actions quite as normal individuals do.

Symptoms (SIMM-tums). From the Greek word meaning "a property that goes with something, or two things that fall together." A runny nose is a symptom that "goes with" having a cold. Abnormal behavior patterns are sometimes said to be "symptoms" of an underlying mental illness.

Question: Many schizophrenic patients hear "indistinct voices" that seem to be telling them to do strange or unusual things. The patients often insist that the voices come from some god or devil. Where else could these indistinct verbal inputs be coming from? How might you help train schizophrenic patients to make better use of their right hemispheres?

Solving "Social Problems"   In recent years—as we learned the strong influence that the people around you have on your thinking and behavior—the mind/body problem has become the mind/body/environment problem. As Dr. Engel suggests, one of the strengths of the General Systems approach is that it views people as "sub-systems" within groups and organizations, just as your left and right hemispheres are "sub-systems" within your brain. Thus the concepts we used to explain "mental problem solving" might also help us understand how you solve "social problems."

From a General Systems viewpoint, you usually go through three steps when you work through your relationships with others:

1. Learning a set of behaviors associated with your **role** in a group, organization, or society. A *role* thus is a type of "social feed-forward" in that it specifies in advance a sequence of behaviors you must perform in order to achieve some social goal.

2. Checking the correctness of your *role-behavior* by anticipating the **attitudes** that others will express in response to your own actions and beliefs. An *attitude* is thus a type of "anticipated social feedback."

3. Monitoring the way people *actually* react to you, and using this "social feedback" to shape both your actions and your expectations.

Question: How might you explain organizational "rules and regulations" in terms of "social feed-forward?"

The Mind/Body/Environment System   As you must have gathered by now, the General Systems solution to the mind/body problem is based on the belief that your body is made up of sub-systems which, through their *interactions*, create your total organism, including your mind. In similar fashion, you are a sub-system within groups, organizations, and societies.

Role. A set of feed-forward instructions on how you should behave or think in certain social situations.

Attitudes. A set of behaviors, feelings, and perceptions associated with a given object or role. Your attitude toward sex includes what you do, think, and feel about procreative behaviors.

Members of organizations must learn to perform roles such as those related to their jobs.

And only by viewing yourself from several **perspectives**—the biological, the intra-psychic, and the social/behavioral—can you hope to understand the *whole you.*

Now that we have given you an outline of General Systems Theory, it is time to evaluate it using the criteria we mentioned on p. 132. As you will see, while there are many things to be said in its favor, there are also several problems associated with adopting the "holistic" approach to psychology.

General Systems Theory: An Evaluation

Accuracy

Most psychological theories are *qualitative* rather than being *quantitative*—which is to say that psychologists tend to describe things in words rather than in the sorts of mathematical symbols used by physicists, chemists, and biologists. It was perhaps for this reason that our first great psychologist, William James, described physics as a "hard" science, but called psychology a "soft" science. Hard or soft, theoretical insights about human behavior can certainly be useful. But as James noted, it is not very easy to judge the accuracy of most psychological theories because they are based more on hunches than on **empirical** data.

General Systems Theory grew out of the writings of the great philosopher and mathematician, Alfred North Whitehead. The theory was nurtured first at the University of Chicago, and then at The University of Michigan, by a group of scientists led by James G. Miller. Miller's 1978 book, *Living Systems*, gives both the details of the theory's history and describes the many experimental studies which tend to support its acuracy.

Briefly put, General Systems Theory is probably at least as accurate as any other theory in that "soft" science we call psychology.

Alfred North Whitehead.

Completeness

As Dr. Engel pointed out in 1977, the General Systems approach seems by far the most complete psychological theory presently available. General Systems Theory therefore does not *disprove* or *displace* any of the other theories in psychology—it merely helps pull them together into one **coherent** whole.

Impressiveness

Just how impressive General Systems Theory is to you will depend on your own prior assumptions about what a theory should do. Writing in the June 1979 issue of *Contemporary Psychology*, Harvard psychologist Brendan Maher states that "Those who seek universal, coherent, elegant formulations in the grand manner" will find the systems approach to their liking. Thus if you prefer a simpler view of human nature—or a more complex one—you may not find the General Systems Theory very impressive at all. Whatever the case, it is not important that you *believe* the theory—just that you understand it well enough to translate the material in this book into terms that make sense to you.

Whenever we mention another theory in this book, then, we will attempt to state it both in its own terms, and in General Systems terminology.

James G. Miller.

Usefulness

General Systems Theory may be useful to you in at least three ways: (1) it offers you a more objective ("hard" science) understanding of yourself than most other theories; (2) it can give you a better technology for personal change than most other approaches; and (3) it is indeed a very optimistic theory.

Objective Understanding   You probably know a fair amount about your-self (and others) from a *subjective* or introspective point of view. How, then, might *objective* knowledge of human behavior be of any use to you?

To begin with, objective information picks up where subjective insight leaves off. Thus, being able to perceive yourself as a *living system* may offer you insights about yourself you couldn't gain any other way.

Almost all of the so-called "hard" sciences—physics, astronomy, chemistry, and biology—are based on the knowledge gained from thousands of experiments and objective observations. In most of these studies, scientists presented some physical or biological system with various types of new inputs, and then noted changes in that system's outputs.

The first step in *any* science, including psychology, is almost always that of establishing a clear-cut pattern of input–output relationships in whatever system it is that you are studying. Only then can you go on to the fascinating task of trying to guess what goes on inside the system that *accounts* for the change in input–output relationships. That is to say, until you have measured *what* you have to do to get a system to behave in a particular way, you are in no position to spin out fancy theories about *why* the system behaves as it does.

The so-called "social/behavioral sciences"—psychology, sociology, and anthropology—are not as empirically developed as are physics and chemistry. Little wonder, since people and organizations are surely more complex than are atoms and molecules. Faced with this complexity—and with a pressing need to solve human problems—many social scientists have therefore made tries to guess at what goes on *inside* people without first studying the input-output relationships that "make people tick."

General Systems Theory offers an *objective* understanding of human behavior. That is, the theory is based on a large number of controlled experiments aimed at discovering *how* people change their thoughts and actions when you alter their stimulus inputs. *Subjective* theories about human nature are typically built more from creative insights than they are from empirical data. Thus General Systems Theory may be useful to you because it offers you a different explanation of your thoughts and behaviors than would a theory based primarily on guesses and **speculations.**

Stronger Technology

If "hard" science is primarily a matter of discovering new input–output relationships, then technology is chiefly a matter of using this information either to maintain a system's old outputs or to establish new ones.

From a technological point of view, you don't always have to understand *why* a system changes in order to *get* it to change. Indeed, in many cases, you can help systems acquire new responses without ever knowing for sure "internal processes" **mediated** this learning.

For example, in the past 20 years scientists have discovered that "retarded" children can learn fairly effectively—*if* we plan the learning properly and break the tasks up into extremely small parts, and *if* we give the children immediate and very rewarding feedback for every bit of progress they make (see Chapter 19).

We still don't know *why* these new teaching techniques work, any more than we know for sure what "mental retardation" really is. But we do know that if we give handicapped individuals somewhat different inputs than we give "normal" people, we can often help "retarded" individuals overcome many of their handicaps.

Subjective theories tend to focus on *mental processes*, not on inputs or outputs. Thus these "soft" theories may give you some understanding of the "inner causes" of a psychological problem, but they seldom give you an

Speculations (speck-you-LAY-shuns). To speculate is to guess or gamble. When you "speculate on the stock market," you try to make money by guessing whether a stock will go up or down. When you speculate in science, you try to out-guess Nature.

Mediated (ME-dee-ated). From a Latin word meaning "to take the middle position." If you mediate a dispute, you help the people arguing with each other come to some resolution of their conflict—usually by taking a position that is between the positions held by the parties having the dispute. The *median* of a super-highway is the strip running down the middle between the two outer lanes.

From a General Systems Theory point of view we should look at people's *abilities,* not their *disabilities.*

effective, step-by-step explanation of how to *change* yourself or your relationships with others. General Systems Theory yields a stronger "technology of change" because it focuses on *what works*—that is, it helps you find the inputs you need in order to alter your own outputs (and those of other systems).

At times it may best satisfy your own needs to seek the sort of "deep understanding" of human nature that the more subjective theories give you. But at other times—when you are looking for the most effective way of changing yourself or of working with others—the General Systems approach might prove useful.

Question: If a child of yours turned out to be retarded, which would be of greater value to you—a subjective understanding of the nature of the retardation, or finding the most effective technology for helping the child?

Greater Hope for Change   Perhaps the most important thing that General Systems Theory has going for it is this—it is a very **optimistic** theory indeed.

We are all affected by our social environments, and all cultures have certain biases or prejudices about human conduct built into them. As an example, our society has dozens of "folk sayings" that seem to tell us that people cannot change very much no matter how hard they try.

One such saying is, "You can't change human nature." Another is "You can't teach an old dog new tricks." Still others are, "Leopards never change their spots," "You can lead a horse to water, but you can't make it drink," "You can't fight city hall," and "Like father, like son; like mother, like daughter."

All of these sayings seem designed to convince you that human change is difficult if not impossible. And if you view people as being old dogs, horses, leopards, or even "chips off the old block," you might also assume that there is little you can do to help yourself or others achieve new and exciting goals.

From a General Systems Theory standpoint, however, *change is always possible* (at least theoretically). A system will *always* change its internal processes and its outputs *if* you are bright enough to find the input that will cause the change you desire. If you desire change, then—in yourself, in someone else, or in a group, organization, or society—it is up to you to discover the inputs that will do the job.

In brief, from a General Systems viewpoint, although you may *not* be able to "change human nature," you certainly *can* alter the outputs of any system if you try hard enough and are willing to pay the price for doing so.

Optimistic (opp-tuh-MISS-tick). From a Latin word meaning "power, wealth." To be optimistic is to assume that things will almost always work out for the best—to give you the wealth, power, and other rewards you wish.

Problems with General Systems Theory

As useful as the General Systems Theory viewpoint may be to you, there are many arguments that can be raised against adopting it. After all, the "softer" approaches have told us much about human nature that is valid, useful, and important. And many of the greatest contributors to psychological knowledge have preferred—often with good reason—a more subjective way of explaining the workings of the mind.

In order to evaluate *any* theory, you must know both its strong points and its weaknesses. We have already mentioned some of the benefits involved in taking the systems approach to psychology. But here are some problems you may encounter in trying to look at yourself and others from this new viewpoint:

Some New Insights Are Painful Suppose your child doesn't learn as fast as you wish it to. You try criticizing the child, and correcting its mistakes, but you may find that its progress is still very slow. How will you handle this situation?

If you adopt a process-oriented explanation of the child's slowness, you might blame its retarded behaviors on "fate," "bad genes," or "human nature." And you might well be right. But if you adopt the General Systems viewpoint, you may face a serious **dilemma.** For you will no longer be able to blame all human failures on "bad genes," "human nature," or "fate." Rather, you will have to face the fact that many of the unpleasant things that happen to you, and to the people you love, are a direct result of your not finding the inputs that will help you achieve the outputs you desire from life.

To put the matter in different terms, when you look at yourself (and others) in objective terms, you may grow painfully dissatisfied with your past actions. Under these circumstances, you may be tempted to reject your new insights, since they will force you to make some fundamental changes in the ways you think and behave.

Attitude Change Is Not Always Enough All of us occasionally must face up to a very thorny problem—namely, our attitudes don't always **jibe** with our actual behaviors. For example, the parents of many retarded children will tell you that they prefer to reward their child's progress rather than merely punish the child when it does something wrong. And yet, if you measure the *actual performance* of the parents in real-life settings, you may find that they are more likely to be **punitive** than rewarding.

As we will note in Chapter 27, psychologists have made many scientific studies of what happens when a person's attitudes come in conflict with that person's actual behavioral outputs. For the most part, people tend to reduce this type of conflict by producing complicated **rationalizations** for their actions, and then continue to behave just as they always had. Put another way, our attitudes don't always predict our behaviors very well, and most of us seem to pay more attention to our *intentions* and attitudes than we do to our actions.

Scientific theories that deal primarily with *internal processes* are more likely to change our attitudes and perceptions than to change our actual behaviors. Scientific theories that concentrate on input–output relationships don't always alter our attitudes very much, but they do give us an effective technology for achieving our behavioral goals.

You will not really understand how powerful a tool any theory is until you attempt to put it into practice and monitor the results of your actions. If all you get are attitude changes, or perceptual insights, then the theory was probably "process-oriented." However, if you get *output* changes, then it probably was an "empirically-based" theory that you may find useful in many real-life situations.

Dilemma (dye-LEMM-uh). From a Greek word meaning "involving two assumptions." When you are "caught between the devil and the deep blue sea," you face a dilemma. That is, you must choose between two equally unpleasant alternatives.

Punitive (PEW-nih-tive). To be punishing is to be punitive.

Rationalizations (rah-shun-nall-eye-ZAY-shuns). From the Latin word meaning "to reason, or compute." To explain something in rational terms is to make it seem reasonable. To rationalize, however, is to offer "logical excuses" for what you wanted to do anyhow—to explain your emotional impulses in reasonable terms. Freud considered *rationalization* to be a mechanism by which the ego defended some of its more neurotic actions (see Chapter 24).

Helping Others Means Changing Yourself First From a General Systems viewpoint, people need each other—desperately. For we all require feedback from our environments if we are to change, grow, or achieve the highest level of personal satisfaction. And other people are usually our best source of feedback, since they see our *actual behavioral outputs* rather than our intentions.

According to the systems view, personal growth tends to occur fastest when the feedback you get from others is rewarding or encouraging. But what can you do if most of the feedback you receive is critical or punishing rather than **positively reinforcing?** How can you get the important people in your life to treat you in a more encouraging and rewarding manner?

The answer is that first you must learn how to give positive reinforcement to the people around you! If you do not "reflect back" to others information about the good things they are doing, can you really expect them to give you the sort of encouragement that you need from them? For example, in their 1977 book *Child Effects on Adults*, Richard Bell and Lawrence Harper note that "problem children" in school often improve remarkably if they are taught how to *reward their teachers* whenever the teachers are particularly helpful. Put more bluntly, these students had to learn to change their own behaviors before they could change the way their teachers treated them. Bell and Harper report similar findings with children and their parents—the child often can aid its own development by learning to respond positively toward its mother and father whenever they give the child the loving support it needs.

This then is perhaps the major stumbling block in adopting the General Systems approach: To help others learn the most effective use of feedback, you must first learn how to use it yourself.

Learning Is Time-Consuming Before you can begin to make use of *any* psychological theory, you must first learn as much as you can about the "nuts and bolts" which hold the theory together. This is to say that you must learn facts and techniques first, and applications later.

For example, many "mental process" theories do not demand that you know much about neurophysiology, and it is just barely conceivable that you might dislike having to learn how neurons function because you are more interested in "the mind" than in "the brain." Yet how can you hope to comprehend the workings of your own mind unless you have some notion of how your brain "inputs" the information that your mind then "processes?"

In similar fashion, suppose you wish to help a retarded child change its input–output relationships so that it can attain better self-control. Wouldn't the sensible approach be first to learn some simple facts about what the child's inputs and outputs actually are, and how they are measured, before you attempt to change them?

By now you probably understand that, from a General Systems Theory point of view, all psychological processes begin with inputs. If you want to "make sense" out of what goes on inside your head, therefore, you may find the most sensible approach is to start by learning some of the "nuts and bolts" facts about what your senses actually do for you.

Now that we have described and evaluated General Systems Theory, let us next turn our attention to the study of *sensory psychology*.

Summary

1. Science is a mixture of facts and theories. The facts describe the world in very concrete or **empirical** terms. A **theory** makes use of the facts in order to describe the world in words or mathematical **symbols.**

2. Scientists judge theories by at least four **criteria:** Accuracy, completeness, impressiveness, and usefulness.

3. The better the predictions that a theory makes about future events, the more accurate it probably is.

4. Some theories describe in detail a limited part of the world. Other more **holistic** theories can sometimes tie several simple theories together to give us a more complete picture of the world.

5. Impressive theories tend to be both elegant and simple.

6. By far the most important criterion for accepting or rejecting a scientific theory is its usefulness.

7. **General Systems Theory** is an attempt to analyze the world in terms of the **living systems** that inhabit the world.

8. Living Systems:

a. Are goal-oriented, their major goal being that of survival.

b. Show emotional reactions associated with achieving or not achieving their goals.

c. Are capable of learning and adapting.

d. Are made up of organized parts that are in some kind of communication with each other.

e. Have **inputs, internal processes, and outputs.**

f. Are capable of **self-control**—which is to say they can alter their inputs in order to achieve the outputs they desire.

9. In order to achieve self-control, systems make use of **feed-forward** and **feedback.**

10. Feed-forward is a **sequence of responses** the system can make at some future time.

11. Feedback is information about the system's past or present performance.

12. The cell is the smallest living system, which is made up of non-living **molecules.** It is the organization of these molecules which gives the **emergent property** of "life" to the cell.

13. When cells cooperate with each other—and take on different **role specializations**—they can combine to form **organs.**

14. The **organism** is a collection of specialized organs which cooperate to produce the emergent property of **consciousness.**

15. Organisms form **groups** by learning how to communicate and cooperate with each other.

16. Groups form **social organizations** in which **formal** rules and written language typically emerge.

17. Social organizations can combine to form such complex **social systems** as societies and cultures.

18. The **mind/body problem** is one of the oldest problems in psychology—and one of the most important.

19. Early in this century, the **structuralists** and the **functionalists** tried to describe "the mind" by using **introspection**—the act of looking inward at your own mental processes.

20. Introspectionism failed because mental events are not objectively measurable, and because you cannot "introspect" your unconscious processes.

21. The behaviorists deny the importance of mental processes, and tend to focus on measuring behaviors instead.

22. By emphasizing the great influence feedback has on behavior, the behaviorists developed a most impressive **technology** of personal change. However, the behaviorists have problems explaining how people "think" their way through problems.

23. When a cat learns to solve a problem, **patterns of neural expectancies** seem to develop in its brain. The cat responds not to stimuli themselves, but to their representations in its brain.

24. From a General Systems Theory point of view, both **problem solving** and **creative thinking** may involve a **dialogue between the hemispheres.**

25. Some of the mental problems that **schizophrenic** patients show may stem from their tendency to process inputs primarily with their left hemispheres.

26. Social systems tend to solve problems as do organisms—by using feed-forward, expectancies, and feedback.

27. General Systems Theory seems to be a reasonably accurate and complete theory.

28. General Systems Theory may be useful in three ways—it offers an objective viewpoint of the world, it yields a strong technology of personal change, and it is optimistic.

29. The following problems are associated with adopting General Systems Theory:

    a. Some new insights are painful.

    b. It requires you to change both your attitudes and your behaviors.

    c. Helping others often means changing yourself first.

    d. You must learn many facts before you can use the theory.

(Continued from page 131.)

The party was marvelously noisy. There were a great many people on hand, all to help Patti's parents celebrate their "lucky seventh" wedding anniversary. Dr. Severeid and Tom Watson sat quietly in a corner, ignoring the turmoil. They knew very few of the people at the party.

"I still don't believe that you took Patti back to the table and continued her lesson after you found out the door was stuck," Dr. Severeid said, taking a sip from his glass. "Surely that was above and beyond the call of duty, Tom."

Tom Watson gave a bemused groan. "It was either that, or sit down on the floor and cry. Especially since it took them 45 minutes to find the janitor."

"Has she stopped the voluntary 'soiling' behavior now?"

"It was a case of 'one-trial learning' on both our parts," Tom responded. "I never threatened to pinch Patti again, and she never soiled her pants to try to control me."

Dr. Severeid nodded "Hello" to Patti's mother as the woman walked through the room headed for the kitchen. "What about her self-control with food? Can she really hold a cookie in her hand for several minutes without eating it?"

"You won't believe this, Dr. Severeid, but we've timed her at 30 minutes by the clock. Of course, she did sort of grind it up a bit with her fingers by then, but she didn't eat a bite of it before I told her to. That's why I asked Patti's parents to invite you to the party tonight. It's their wedding anniversary, but it's final exam time for Patti and me."

"How so?"

Tom leaned back in his chair, confident he had the professor's attention. "Well, it used to be that her parents could either have a party, or Patti, but not both. Once the food was put out, she'd run screaming from plate to plate, grabbing everything in sight, and stuffing it into her rosebud mouth. She'd even snatch food from the guests. But she's learned so much self-control that tonight she's going to be allowed to show off."

"For both of you, I assume?" Professor Severeid said amusedly.

Tom frowned. He didn't think his eagerness to impress his teacher had been that obvious. "Well, I suppose you could put it that way. What she's going to do is to pass a tray of goodies among the guests. If she doesn't snitch any along the way, after half an hour she gets to eat whatever she wants. We've been practicing with her for several days now, and I'm sure she'll make it."

Dr. Severeid cleared his throat, as if in polite disbelief. "Well, if she does, you've surely earned an A in my course, Tom."

"She'll make it. Just you wait and see," the young man said as he squirmed nervously in his seat.

At that moment, Patti's mother came into the room. "Listen, everybody," she said loudly. "Patti is going to serve you some food. Please help yourself to anything you want." The little girl came into view holding a large platter heaped high with delicacies. "But please don't encourage Patti to eat anything, because she has promised to wait until you've all been served before she eats."

Patti smiled and, with her mother's assistance, walked up to an elderly woman and offered the plate to her. The woman beamed, took a little sandwich, and patted the girl on her cheek. Patti limped to the next guests, a young couple, and presented the plate to them. Both the man and the woman took something to eat from the platter and thanked Patti warmly.

Then she was in front of Tom. "Can you have a cookie, please?" she said, giggling just the smallest amount.

"Thank you very much, Patti. You're doing beautifully."

Patti offered Dr. Severeid the plate and, after he thanked her, moved to the next bunch of guests. Watching her actions carefully, the Professor sighed softly. "Absolutely amazing progress for a little girl we all thought was too badly retarded to learn very much."

Tom smiled paternally. "She's an amazing person. I suspect we were the ones who retarded her, really. As long as we viewed her as being 'hopelessly brain-damaged,' or 'fixated at the oral stage,' there wasn't much we could do to help. But when we took a broader view . . ."

"When you saw her as a living organism, imbedded in a social system . . ."

"Then we realized that we had to change the way the social system treated her first, in order to get her to grow and develop as she always could have. Patti can learn anything we're smart enough to teach her."

Professor Severeid nodded in agreement. "It's as the telephone company likes to say, Tom. Sometimes 'the system is the solution.'" The man thought for a moment, then continued. "Her parents are the most important part of the system, of course, and they've obviously changed considerably. They owe you a lot, Tom. I hope they're properly grateful."

"Oh, they are. I think they understand that, for the most part, Patti just responds to the way they treat her. So they're trying hard to change themselves. They helped Patti rehearse for tonight, and they give her lots of love and encouragement. And they're making a big sacrifice for me tonight."

The professor looked puzzled. "What do you mean?"

"Although it's Patti's mother's favorite food, there's one item she promised me wouldn't be on the menu tonight."

"What's that?" the older man asked.

Tom grinned. "Sweet pickles."

Recommended Readings

Engel, George L. "The Need for a New Medical Model: A Challenge for Biomedicine," *Science,* 196 (1977) pp. 129–136.

John, E. Roy. *Mechanisms of Memory* (New York: Academic Press, 1967).

Miller, James G. *Living Systems* (New York: McGraw-Hill, 1978).

2

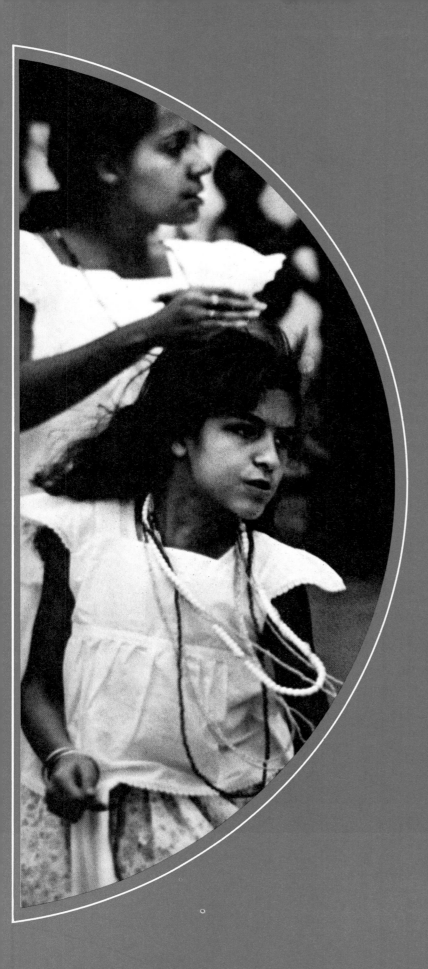

Sensation
and
Perception

Introduction to Sensory Psychology

Did You Know That . . .

Your skin is sensitive only to warm, cold, pressure, and, in a complex way, to pain?

Some 95 percent of your skin is hairy?

Each hair on your skin has a pressure receptor called a "basket cell" wrapped around its base?

Almost every muscle in your body has a receptor neuron attached to it?

Muscle receptors tell your brain where your arms and legs are, and what they are doing?

The skin on your lips and fingertips is the most sensitive skin of all?

Special receptor cells in your inner ear help you detect "up" from "down?"

Your sense receptors primarily detect *changes* in your environment?

You can learn to communicate with others using your skin even if you are deaf and blind?

"How To Build a Better Robot"

The big chunk of rock hung suspended in the dark of outer space like a frayed cigar floating motionless on the surface of a black lagoon. The little NASA space ship circled the asteroid-rock twice, and then dropped toward it slowly for a landing. The ship's directional jets hissed like nervous dragons as it twisted this way and that, now slowing its speed a bit, now correcting its slippery course through space with just the briefest puff of gas from one of the many jet nozzles protruding from its sides.

The space ship was millions of kilometers from earth, probing the ring of asteroids that girdled the sun like the belt in a fat man's pants. But this belt was a circle of rocks flung far out in space, sandwiched somewhere between the orbits of the planets Mars and Jupiter. A few of the asteroids were large enough to be seen by telescope from earth, but most of them were so small that you had to be right on top of them to detect them.

No one knew where the asteroid belt had come from—probably from some planet that had blown up a billion years ago—and only a few dedicated scientists really cared one way or another. But everybody knew and cared that some of these hunks of celestial garbage were loaded with valuable metals. At least the National Aeronautics and Space Administration knew, and NASA cared a great deal about metals. And that's what the little NASA space ship was out there for, to hunt for such rare earth metals as radium, uranium, and plutonium.

Major Jack Amundsen watched the dials and displays on the ship's control panel cautiously. The asteroid toward which he was guiding his craft was less than a mile in length and shaped rather like a stubby cigar. But if the space ship's detector circuits were right, it contained a chunk of uranium big enough to make the NASA brass back in Houston very happy indeed, and to earn him a very accelerated promotion. And Amundsen was the sort of man who found promotions very accelerating indeed.

As the ship inched in for a landing on the cigar-shaped rock, Amundsen switched on the landing lights. That close, the asteroid loomed huge in the ship's vision screens. For the most part, its surface seemed pitted with cracks and craters. But almost in the center, where its equator would be if it had one, was a shallow groove that appeared to have a reasonably flat bottom. Amundsen dropped the little ship down into the depression so carefully that it brushed the surface as gently as a good-morning kiss. Immediately, high-speed drills in the ship's legs chewed their way into the hard rock underneath and effectively bolted the ship to the asteroid. Only then did Major Amundsen lean back in his command chair and relax.

"Pretty good piloting, don't you think, Mark? Bet you couldn't do half that good."

Robot XSR 5 Mark III/21, sitting next to the Major, turned its head from the control panel. Its electronic eyes sparkled as if in amusement.

"You know, Major, that I am not programmed for landings except in emergency conditions. I am an exploratory space robot, not a pilot robot." The robot's voice was so musical that it almost sounded human.

"Then go explore. And don't let any meteorites puncture your space suit." The Major smiled at his little joke, for the robot wore no space suit at all.

Raw space was dangerous to man, as the deaths of many US and Russian astronauts had proved only too dramatically. The NASA brass had split down the middle on how to overcome the dangers. Some administrators wanted all exploration done by machines. But some space experts insisted that machines were not flexible enough to meet the challenge of unknown conditions.

So a compromise was worked out. Humans would go into space, but would be mostly confined to the ship. As their companions, the astronauts would have advanced and highly complex robots to perform all the very dangerous work outside the ship.

At first, Amundsen resented the robot, wishing it were flesh and blood rather than metal and plastic. But during the long trip out, Amundsen had grown to accept Mark as being "almost human."

Mark entered the space lock, evacuated the precious air back into the ship, then moved slowly down a ladder onto the surface of the asteroid. Being a robot, Mark did not need much protection from the vacuum and cold of space. But Mark did need a searchlight and various other tools. As the robot moved away from the ship, the needle on its portable detector hinted that the lode of uranium should be a few hundred meters ahead and very close to the surface. The robot moved cautiously, testing each step, the balance sensors in its head working overtime as it attempted to remain upright while walking weightlessly up the side of the small depression into which the ship had settled.

"How are you doing?" came the Major's gruff voice over the radio.

"Major, all is well. The stick-tite shoes grip the surface of the asteroid tightly, my walking reflexes function well; I have not stumbled once." The robot rounded a boulder and stopped, directing the light fastened to its head toward the mouth of a cavern near where it was standing.

"Major, the uranium appears to be buried inside a cave. May I descend?"

All hazardous procedures had to be approved by the human pilot.

"You may descend," came the Major's quick response.

Mark III/21 moved slowly into the mouth of the cave, stopping each few feet to mark a spot of fluorescent paint on the rocks. The paint marks would help guide the robot back to the surface, should it lose its way inside the cave. The deeper underground Mark went, the more wildly the needle on the electronic detector danced. When the robot had pushed its way more than 300 meters into the ground, it came to the top of a large, hollow chamber in the cave.

As the robot crawled to the bottom of the chamber, the detector needle jumped off the dial. Mark stopped and swung around, the light on its head flooding the chamber with brightness. Then the robot knelt, put its tools down beside it, and picked up a handful of black, soft, somewhat sticky material. Under the light, the soft stuff looked like pitchblend, one of the most common ores that contains uranium.

"Major, we have apparently struck paydirt, if I may use that phrase."

Back at the space ship, Amundsen was standing beside the control console waiting for news. When he heard what Mark said, he grinned.

"That's great, Mark, super great. Just gather up a sample in your bag and then . . ."

And then their world nearly ended.

Coming up from their blind side at a high speed, one of the asteroid's smaller brothers plowed into it smack in the asteroid's mid-section, just a few hundred meters from the ship. The asteroid shuddered like a punching bag hit by a world heavyweight. The smaller rock then bounced off into space again, leaving its devastation behind for the Major and the robot to handle as best they could.

Amundsen had been knocked off his seat when the crash occurred, but he came up fighting. A quick glance at the dials and lights on the control console assured him that the ship was intact and safe. But the robot?

"Mark!" he called into the microphone. "What happened? Are you all right?"

The answer was slow in coming, and the robot's voice seemed distorted, fluttery, and very unmusical.

"Major, I survive, but barely. A rock hit my head. My light is gone. My vision circuits are inoperative. I am blind. I have lost contact with the bottom surface of the large chamber I was in. I float. What am I to do?"

The Major thought a while, picturing the robot tumbling about in the hollow underground bubble like a piece of meat in a bowl of stew.

"Reach out your arms and legs and wait until you make contact with one of the chamber walls."

"I obey, Major," the robot said, but it was minutes later before it reported success.

"Now what do I do, Major? I cannot see. I cannot find the trail markers. I cannot find the tiny entrance to this large chamber. I have but three hours of current left in my batteries. How do I find my way back to the ship, Major?"

The problem was serious. Amundsen was under strict orders not to leave the ship even if the robot became endangered. He could return to earth safely without Mark, but when the robot's batteries were exhausted, its heater would no longer function. Then its delicate "brain" circuits would freeze and warp. For all practical purposes, the robot would be "dead." NASA would be furious at the loss of a multi-million dollar piece of equipment, and Amundsen would have lost a . . . friend?

Amundsen retraced the robot's path in his mind's eye. Always Mark had reported going down, down, deeper into the ground. Suddenly the solution seemed obvious.

"Mark, just keep moving upward. If you move upward, you'll get to the surface eventually and I can pick you up then with the ship. No sweat at all, really, Mark. Just keep moving upward."

"Major," said the robot after a while. "There is no gravity here and I do not know in which direction I am pointed. Major, which way is up?"

(Continued on page 177.)

The Skin

Earth is the third planet out from the sun. Mercury is the closest, Venus next, then earth. Then come the outer planets: Mars, Jupiter, Saturn, Uranus, Neptune, and Pluto.

A few years from now, our first real inter-planetary space ships will blast off from earth and take people out to Mars—and perhaps beyond. Venus is closer to earth than is Mars, but both Venus and Mercury are too hot and too close to the sun for us to explore "in person" at the moment. The outer worlds are very cold and very far away.

Some of the planets, such as Jupiter and Venus, have such heavy atmospheres that we would be crushed to death on their surfaces. Others have little or no atmosphere at all. And none of them has the right kind of air for us to breathe. Naked and unprotected, humans cannot exist unaided on any of the planets except Earth.

As you know, the US space program is directed by the National Aeronautics and Space Administration. Let us suppose that, some time in the future, NASA decides that the environments that exist on the eight other planets are so hostile that robots should be sent out first to investigate—to test things out to make sure that human beings can survive in space suits if and when we do arrive.

For many reasons, NASA further concludes that the robot ought to be man-sized. And indeed, if the robot is going to tell us what we need to know, it should have many human-like characteristics. It should be mobile, and it should carry its own protection against the elements. The robot should also have a means of sensing and measuring its environment, and a way of sending messages back to its home base to report the data it gathers.

Now, let us further assume that you are hired by NASA to help with "Project Robot." Your first assignment is to worry about what kind of covering the robot is going to have, so you begin by asking yourself: *What purpose does your own skin serve?*

A little thought convinces you that your skin answers many needs. It keeps your vital organs inside where they belong, and keeps the outside world outside where it belongs. Your skin has several layers to it, layers that help it insulate you against the cold. When you get too hot, your skin has sweat glands that release water which cools you by evaporation. Your skin stretches as you gain weight and shrinks when you lose weight. And most important, your skin is filled with *receptors* that let you know what the world around you is like.

But would your skin serve a robot's specialized needs?

After due consideration, you conclude that you can't tell what type of covering the robot ought to have until you know more about what this robot is going to have to do. So you begin to think about what types of *sense organs* the robot is going to need in whatever skin it gets.

Contours (KONN-tours). From the Latin word meaning "to round off" or "to smooth the edges." Contours are the outside edges of a figure.

The Skin Receptors

If you like to experiment on yourself, please go find several small objects—things like a pencil, a glass, a rubber band, a ring, a key, a piece of cloth—and put them on a table near you. Now, close your eyes and *feel* each object. Begin by just pressing the palm of your hand down on the objects.

What can you tell about these small objects without fingering them? That they are hard or soft, large or small, that they have points or sharp edges or rounded **contours**—and that is about all you can tell. A pencil or key is hard, a rubber band or an eraser yields when you press on it and hence feels soft.

But to ask what may at first seem a stupid question, *how do you know what is hard and soft?*

The Pressure Receptors

When you touch an object gently, you depress or deform your skin. Very sensitive nerve cells detect this *deformation of your skin* and fire off a message to your cortex. This input message moves down the axons of the

What do you feel if you "palm" these objects?

Chapter 6 Introduction to Sensory Psychology

Corpuscles (KOR-pus-sulls). The Latin word *corpus* means "body." We get our English words "corpse" (a dead body), "corps" (the Marine Corps), and "corporation" (a body of people) from this Latin term. A corpuscle is a "little body" or "little cell," particularly one that is isolated from others like it. The red blood cells, for instance, are called the "red corpuscles."

Dendrites. The "feelers" or input area at the front end of a neuron. See Chapters 2 and 4.

Basket cells. Sensory-input neurons or receptors cells found at the bottom of each hair cell on the skin. The dendrites of the basket cells are woven around the base of the stalk of hair. Any sort of movement of the stalk causes the basket cell to fire off a message to the cortex indicating that something has made contact with the hair.

Free nerve endings. Simple receptor cells found widely distributed through both hairy and hairless skin. If you "unwove" the dendrites of a basket cell and spread them throughout the skin, they would look something like free nerve endings.

---

receptor cells until it reaches your spinal cord, then moves up the cord to the stem of your brain. From your brain stem, the message flows through several "lower centers" and finally works its way up to your cortex. Only when the input arrives at your *cortex* do you realize consciously that your skin has encountered a foreign object of some sort.

Now, with the fingers of one hand, gently pinch the palm of your other hand. You will notice that the skin on your palm feels fairly thick. Next, gently pinch the skin on your forearm. The skin is much thinner there. But the major *physiological* difference is that the skin on your forearm has hairs on it, while the skin on your palm does not. Some 95 percent of the skin on your body (whether you are male or female) is *hairy* skin—only the palms of your hands, the soles of your feet, your lips and mouth, your eyeballs, some parts of your sex organs, and a few other scattered areas are made up of *hairless* skin.

Now, pick a single hair on your arm and pull it gently. You will experience a soft, "pressury" feeling. Tap the hair gently (without touching your skin). You will experience much the same sensation of *pressure* as when you pulled on the hair.

In the *hairless* regions of your body, the skin contains tiny receptor nerve cells that look, under a microscope, much like small onions. These hairless skin receptors are called **corpuscles.** They are more-or-less round in shape and, as you would find if you were to cut one open, these "onion-shaped" corpuscles have many layers to them (see Fig. 6.1).

Hairy skin does not have corpuscles, but it does have a unique type of touch-receptor neuron buried at the base of each hair. The **dendrites,** or front-end fibers of these nerve cells, are woven around the bottom of the stalk of hair. Whenever the hair is pushed or pulled in any direction, the dendrites are squeezed so that they fire off a "pressure" message to your brain. These hairy skin receptors are called **basket cells** because they look like a wicker basket wrapped around the bottom of the hair stalk.

Both hairy and hairless skin also contain receptor neurons called **free nerve endings**—"free" meaning that they are not attached to any particular place. The free nerve endings are very simple nerve cells whose dendrites spread out freely like the branches of a vine just under the outer layers of your skin. Since they are found everywhere on the surface of your body, free nerve endings are by far the most common sort of skin receptor that you have.

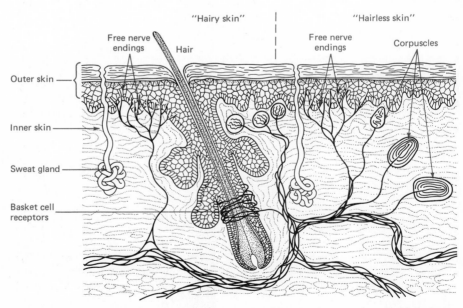

Fig. 6.1. A schematic diagram of the skin. Basket cell receptors are found only in hairy skin. Corpuscles are found only in hairless skin. Free nerve endings are found in both hairy and hairless regions.

PART TWO   Sensation and Perception

All three types of receptors—the corpuscles, the basket cells, and the free nerve endings—yield a simple "pressure sensation" when they are stimulated. (As we will see, however, some of the free nerve endings manage to do a bit more than that.)

Complex Pressure Sensations   Now, go back to the objects that you were feeling on the table near you. Close your eyes and have someone place first a wooden object and then a metal object in your hands. You can tell wood from metal in two ways: (1) the wood is usually softer than the metal; and (2) the wood will feel warm while the metal feels cold.

Your skin receptors can give rise to different sorts of sensory experience that are *qualitatively* different to you. One experience is *pressure*, the other is *temperature*. Your *pressure detectors* tell you when you come in contact with some foreign object or with parts of your own body. Your *temperature receptors* tell you whether the object is hot or cold.

The corpuscles in the hairless regions and the basket cells around each hair are primarily *pressure receptors*. The free nerve endings detect *both pressure and temperature*.

It may come as a surprise to you that these two sensations (plus pain, which we will discuss later) are the *only two sensory qualities* that your skin can tell you about. All the information you get from your skin about the world around you is a *combination* of pressure sensations plus temperature sensations—plus, occasionally, the experience of pain (*see* Chapter 18).

Next, rub the palm of your hand over your clothes, the surface of the table, the cover of this book, the upholstery of a chair, or the top of a rug. Some objects feel smooth to your touch, others feel rough. How does your skin tell you which is which if it can only experience pressure and temperature?

The answer comes from this fact—when you move your hand across a surface, you stimulate many receptors at once. The harder you press against something with your fingers, the more you *deform the skin* and the more frequently the pressure receptors *fire*. Your brain makes good use of this *quantitative* information (that is, the frequency with which the receptors fire) to help it identify an object that your skin is in contact with.

If the surface of an object is rough, parts of your skin "stick" as you rub your palm across the object. This "sticking" causes your skin to wrinkle a bit as it rubs across the object. Where the skin is wrinkled the most, the receptors fire vigorously. But where the skin is unwrinkled and smooth, the receptors fire hardly at all. Your brain interprets this *pattern of incoming sensory information* as "roughness" or "smoothness."

If the robot you are helping build for NASA is going to stroll about the surface of some distant planet, you will want it to be able to bend over, pick something interesting off the ground, and examine it. If you put pressure receptors of some kind in the robot's fingers, you will be able to tell if the object is hard or soft, or rough or smooth, simply by decoding the *pattern of signals* from the robot's receptors.

You could also put temperature detectors in the robot's fingers to learn whether the object was hot or cold.

But hot or cold in relation to what?

The Temperature Receptors

When you first crawl into a bathtub of hot water, it may seem that you are going to be boiled alive before the bath is over. The water feels intensely hot, and your skin turns lobster red as your brain orders an increase in the flow of blood through your skin to help cool things off. If you stay in the tub for a while, the water feels cooler and cooler (even if you manage to keep the temperature of the water as hot as when you first crawled into the tub). When you get out, the air in the bathroom may seem surprisingly cool to your naked skin.

If, on a hot summer day, you leap into a cold swimming pool, you will get the opposite effect. First you think you will freeze, then you adjust. And when you get out of the pool, the rest of the sun-drenched world seems even hotter than before.

"Hot" and "cold" are *relative* terms that, in your body's case, are always related to *whatever your skin temperature is.* Anything you touch that is *colder* than your skin will seem cool to you. Anything you touch that is *hotter* than your skin will seem *warm.*

Question: How do you think your skin receptors respond to constant stimulation if hot water seems cooler to you after you have been soaking in it for a while?

When you get into that steaming tub of water, the temperature *deep inside* your body remains more or less the same, but the skin temperature at your fingertips may rise above 38° **Celsius** (100° **Fahrenheit**). If just before you entered the water you touched an object that was 45° C, it would be 5° above your skin temperature. The "warmth" receptor organs in your fingers would fire a message off to your cortex telling it that they had encountered something warm. Just after you got out of the tub the same object might be 5° *below* your skin temperature and would seem cool to your touch.

As you might surmise, your "cold" detector cells will fire more vigorously if you touch an object that is 30° below skin temperature than if you touch an object that is merely 5° below skin temperature. And the "warmth" detector cells will fire more vigorously if you come in contact with an object that is 25° above skin temperature than they would if you touched an object that is merely 15° above the temperature of your skin.

The Somatic Cortex

The message that the skin receptors send to your brain tells you three things: First, the *quality* of the experience (that is, pressure or temperature). Second, the *quantity* or intensity or strength of the experience (strong pressure or weak, slightly warm or very cold). But third, and very important, sensory inputs from your skin tell you *location*—that is, what part of your body is detecting the sensations.

If you are walking barefooted and step on a tack, your brain knows almost instantly what part of which foot has been punctured. How does it know this fact so quickly?

To answer that question, think for a moment about the NASA robot that you were helping design. If you wanted the robot to *localize* its skin sensations, how would you hook its skin receptors up to the robot's brain?

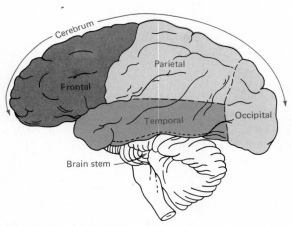

Fig. 6.2. The lobes of the brain.

Probably you would want to put in a direct "telephone line" between each receptor and a *specific* part of the "brain." Each receptor would, in effect, have its own "telephone number." The robot could tell where the stimulation was coming from simply by checking to see which telephone line the message was coming over.

In a sense, your brain acts much the same way. Each receptor cell in your skin is connected to a specific region in the *sensory input areas* in your **parietal lobes.**

You may recall from Chapter 4 that the parietal lobe in each of your cerebral hemispheres is located at the very top center of your brain (see Fig. 6.2). The front edge of the parietal lobe is immediately adjacent to the *motor output areas* at the rear of the frontal lobe. The cortex at this front edge of the parietal lobe is often called the **somatic cortex.**

"Soma" is the Greek word for "body," and it is to this part of your cortex that all of your body or *somatic receptors* send their sensory messages. Receptors in the left side of your body send their inputs primarily to the somatic cortex in the right half of your brain. The receptors in the right side of your body send their messages to your left somatic cortex.

You will recall that in Chapter 4 we discussed the layout of the motor output cortex in each of your frontal lobes. We said then that each point on the motor cortex seemed to have dominant control over a specific set of muscles. The muscles in your toes are controlled by neurons near the **corpus callosum** in the middle of your brain, while the muscles in your neck and head are controlled by neurons lying on the outer edge of your brain, just above your ear (see Fig. 6.3).

The somatic cortex is laid out in exactly the same fashion as the motor cortex. Messages from skin receptors in your toes travel up your spinal cord to your lower brain centers. Axons from these centers connect or make synapse with parietal neurons near your corpus callosum. Messages coming from your lips and tongue, however, reach parietal neurons lying on the outer edge of your brain, just above your ear.

For every somatic input area in your parietal lobe, there is a corresponding motor output area in your frontal lobe. The "little man" in your motor output area thus has an identical twin living right next door in the somatic input area.

Parietal lobes (pair-EYE-uh-tull, or puh-RYE-uh-tull). That part of each cerebral hemisphere located at the very top of the brain. Sensory input from the skin receptors and the muscles comes to this part of your cerebrum. See Chapter 4.

Somatic cortex (so-MAT-ick KOR-tecks). The outer layer of the parietal lobe is called the "parietal cortex." The front section of the parietal cortex receives sensory-input messages from the skin and muscle receptors. This front section is called the "somatic cortex."

Corpus callosum (KOR-pus kah-LOW-sum). The "hardened body" of axonic fibers that acts as a bridge connecting the two hemispheres of your cerebrum. See Chapter 2.

Question: Why might it be important to your survival and well-being to have your somatic cortex so closely connected to your motor cortex?

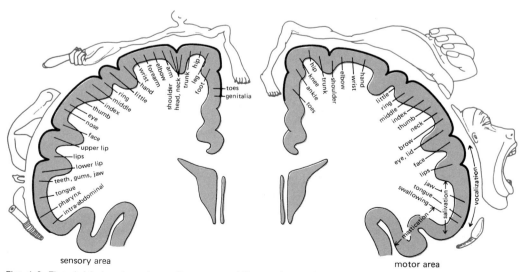

Fig. 6.3. The right drawing shows the areas of the motor cortex that control various muscles in your body. The left drawing indicates the corresponding sensory-input areas in the parietal lobel.

The Deep Receptors

Deep receptors. Your brain must have some means of determining the movement, position, and condition of the various parts of your body. Each of the muscles, joints, tendons, and bones of your body has special receptor cells that fire whenever the muscle (joint, tendon, or bone) moves or is damaged in any way. Your brain sends out command messages (feed-forward) telling your muscles to move, for instance. The deep receptors provide informational feedback to your brain as to whether the movement has actually occurred.

If you made the NASA robot much like yourself, it could tell the hardness, smoothness, and temperature of an object it had picked up just by noting what its "skin" receptors were signaling. But what about the object's size, shape, and weight?

Pick up a pencil, close your eyes, and roll the pencil around in your hand. You can tell at once what size, shape, and weight the pencil has. But it is *not* the surface or skin receptors that give you this information; we could anesthetize all the nerves in the skin of your hand and you would still be able to tell the size, shape, and weight of the pencil. For the muscles, joints, tendons, and bones in your hand (and in much of the rest of your body, too) all have sensory receptors in them. These are called **deep receptors,** to distinguish them from the *surface receptors* in your skin.

Whenever you contract a muscle in your hand, a tiny nerve cell buried in that muscle sends a feedback signal to your somatic cortex saying that the muscle is in operation. The heavier an object is, the harder your muscle must work to lift the object and hold it steady. The harder the muscle pulls or contracts, the more vigorously the tiny receptor neuron buried in the muscle fires—and the more intense feedback you get.

Your cortex keeps track continuously of where your fingers are and how far apart they are. Your cortex also notes continuously what each of your muscles, tendons, and joints is doing. By adding this information to the inputs it gets from your skin, your brain is usually able to gain a very clear *sensory* picture of what you're holding in your hand. But this sensory picture has no *meaning* until your brain *processes* the incoming information—by checking your memory files to determine whether the object in your hand is a pencil and not a book, an apple, or a rattlesnake.

Distribution of Receptors If you were building a robot, you would surely want its *fingers* to be more sensitive to pressure and temperature than, say, the middle of its *back*. For robots (like people) would seldom be called upon to make fine discriminations or judgments about objects with the "skin" on their backs. So you would probably want to put *more* sensory receptors in the robot's fingers than on its back.

There are more receptors in your fingertips, your lips, and the tip of your tongue than anywhere else on your body. The skin on your back and buttocks contains but a fraction of the number of receptors per square centimeter of tissue that the skin on your lips contains.

Generally speaking, the distribution of the sense receptors in your body is just about the same as you would logically decide should be the case for your robot. Those parts of your body that you use most to make sensory discriminations have the most receptors, while those parts that you use least have fewer receptor neurons.

Motion Detectors

By working out electronic circuits that would operate, much the way the neural circuits in your body operate, you could fairly easily design a robot that would be able to pick things up, measure them with its fingers, and keep track of where all its arms and legs were in the process. But what if your robot fell over and ruined its vision tubes? How would you get it upright and walking again? How would it know which way was up?

Contact receptors in the soles of your robot's feet might be helpful, but they would not tell the robot whether its head was bent over or upright. You could add movement detectors in the robot's "muscular" system that could monitor the position of all its limbs and its head. But even these receptors would not be enough, for the robot still could not tell "up" from "down" just by getting feedback about where its arms and legs were.

Your own body solves this problem of location and movement in space with a special set of detectors inside your ears. To understand how these receptors work, however, you need to remember what Newton's *law of inertia* is all about.

In brief, the law of inertia states that a body at rest tends to remain at rest, while a body in motion tends to continue to move. When you are riding in an automobile, your body is only loosely connected to the car. Unless you wear a seat belt, you are free to move about inside the automobile even when it is in motion.

For instance, imagine that you are sitting in the front passenger seat of a car that is stopped at a red light. When the light turns green, the driver really hits the gas pedal, and the car leaps forward rapidly. But your body will "tend to remain at rest," so you are pushed back rather roughly into the seat cushions and you feel a great surge of acceleration as the car picks up speed. If the car stops suddenly, your body "tends to continue to move" and, if you forgot to buckle your seat belt, you are thrown into the dashboard or the windshield. It is the law of inertia, then, which makes it important that you wear some kind of restraint when riding in an automobile or airplane.

Whether you are considering cars or robots, basically there are but two types of motion: (1) straight-line or linear movements; and (2) rotary or circular movements. Buried away inside each of your ears are two types of receptor organs that detect changes in the motion of your body (see Fig. 6.4). One type of receptor responds to changes in *straight-line motion*. The other type responds to changes in *circular* motion. Both types of receptor organs function by obeying Newton's law of inertia.

Linear Motion Detectors

The "flip-flop" movements that your body makes when an automobile speeds up or slows down are usually straight-line or *linear* movements. The linear motion detectors in your ear are two small organs called the **saccule** and the **utricle.**

Both the saccule and the utricle are made up of jello-like or gelatinous tissue filled with tiny stone-like particles—rather as if someone had made a bowl of cherry jello and put in just the pits instead of the cherries. When your head begins to move in a straight line, the saccule and utricle flip-flop in your inner ear the same way that your body flip-flops in an automobile. The "rocks in your head"—that is, the bits of stone in the saccule and utricle—increase the quivering of jello-like material. Hair cells buried in this gelatinous tissue are pushed or pulled this way and that by the quivering.

Saccule (SACK-you'll). One of the two small organs in your inner ear that detects straight-line movements of your head (and hence of your body). The Greek word *sakkos* means "bag" or "sack." The saccule is thus a "little bag."

Utricle (YOU-trick-ull). From the Latin word meaning (you guessed it!) "little bag." The second of the small organs in your inner ear that detect linear motion.

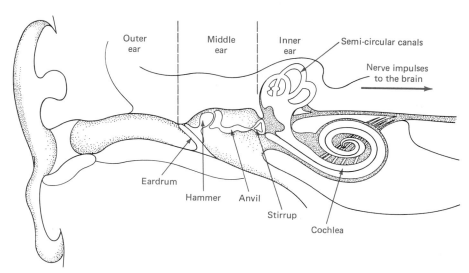

Fig. 6.4. The major structures of the ear.

The *basket nerve cells* at the base of each hair cell are stimulated by the flip-flop quivering and signal your somatic cortex that your body is starting or stopping a movement.

Rotary Motion Detectors

When you were younger, did you ever sit in a swing and twist the rope around and around until it was wound up tightly, then let go? You would spin quite rapidly until the rope had unwound. If you got off the swing and tried to walk, you would still seem to be spinning.

Rotary motion of your body is detected by the **semi-circular canals** in your ear. These three canals are positioned at right angles to each other inside your ear so that they can detect circular motion in any of the three dimensions of space.

When you turn your head, the fluid in the canals accelerates more slowly than does the rest of your head. This fluid presses against a small mound of gelatinous tissue at the base of each canal. When this jello-like tissue is pushed one way or the other, hair cells in the gelatin are twisted or pulled. The basket nerve cells at the base of each hair then signal your somatic cortex that your head has either stopped or started some kind of rotary motion.

Motion Sickness

For reasons no one really understands, the motion detectors in your ears have direct connections with those parts of your brain that control the vomit reflex. If you have a rough airplane ride, you may stagger off the plane feeling very dizzy and with a queasy stomach. But it is not your *stomach* that is upset—it is your *inner ear* that is complaining.

Motion sickness does not come entirely from such physiological causes as over-stimulation of the motion detectors, however. Intra-psychic factors—such as fear and tension—can make it much more likely that you will become ill when riding in a car, ship, or airplane. You can sometimes reduce this tension and fear by using a procedure called **progressive deep muscle relaxation.** We will discuss this technique in detail in Chapter 15, but basically it involves gaining voluntary control over your muscles so that you can make them relax "on command." The more relaxed you are psychologically, the less likely it is that you will get sick while riding in a plane or auto.

People who are prone to motion sickness often find a drug called Dramamine helpful in reducing their discomfort. Dramamine does not affect the stomach directly; rather, it causes certain nerve cells in the brain to fire more slowly.

Neither Dramamine nor muscular relaxation changes the sensory inputs from your motion detectors, however—they merely alter the way in which your brain *processes* or reacts to the inputs.

Centrifugal Force

If you have ever been to a carnival or amusement park, you may have ridden on a "loop-the-loop" roller coaster. If you have taken one of these thrilling yet frightening rides, you may have asked yourself why you didn't fall out of the car when it turned you upside down at the top of the "loop."

The answer is, **centrifugal force.** Centrifugal force tends to throw any object in the roller coaster car *away* from the center of the rotation. As the car makes the loop, therefore, centrifugal force plasters you firmly against your seat cushion.

Centrifugal force is actually an example of Newton's law of inertia, and your motion detectors respond to centrifugal force just as they do to any other form of movement. If you stand up in the roller coaster car just as

---

Semi-circular canals. In each inner ear you have three fluid-filled tubes or canals that detect rotary motion of your head. These tubes, called the "semi-circular canals," are positioned at right angles to each other. Since there are three canals in each ear, they can sense rotary motion in all three dimensions.

Motion sickness. The dizziness you feel from twirling around, or from "feeling unsupported," is caused by over-excitation of the semi-circular canals, not by over-excitation of your stomach. The semi-circular canals are connected to the "vomit reflex," which when triggered off causes you to "feel sick to your stomach."

Progressive deep muscle relaxation. A technique for learning how to control your muscles voluntarily. Once you have acquired the skill, you can make your muscles relax (rather than feel tensed up) anytime you wish. As you will see in Chapter 15, the technique is quite useful in overcoming a variety of fears and upsets, including those associated with motion sickness.

Centrifugal force (sen-TRIFF-few-gull). From the Latin words meaning "center" and "fugitive." Centrifugal force is that which causes an object to "flee" from the center of rotation.

PART TWO Sensation and Perception

A "Lightnin' Loop" at an amusement park.

you reached the top of the "loop," your head would be pointed straight at the earth. Yet the bottom of the car would seem "down" to you, while the earth itself would seem to be "up."

Some of the more creative thinkers at NASA have designed wheel-like space ships that we might use to visit the planets. During the journey, the

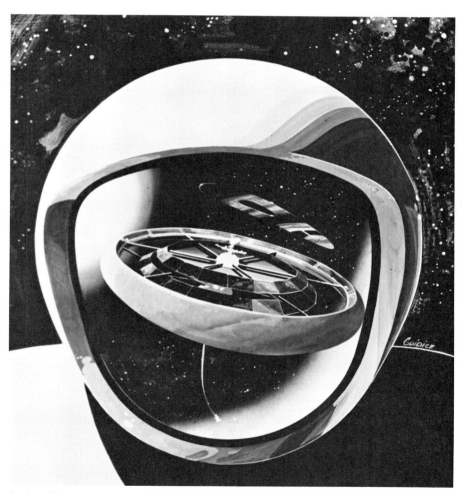

A wheel-like space colony of the twenty-first century.

wheel would turn just rapidly enough to create an artificial gravity so that the men and women on board could walk comfortably around the inside wall of the wheel—with their heads pointed to the center of the wheel. Since the motion detectors in the travelers' ears couldn't tell the difference, centrifugal force presumably could make a pleasant substitute for gravity.

Adaptation and Habituation

Your brain is your main organ of survival. And if you are to survive, you must usually pay more attention to *changes* in your environment than to stimuli that *remain constant* for a period of time.

There are at least two ways in which your nervous system adjusts to constant inputs: first, by what we will call **receptor adaptation;** and second, by what we will refer to as **central habituation** to a stimulus input. Receptor adaptation occurs in the receptor neurons themselves, while central habituation occurs in your brain.

As an example of receptor adaptation, consider how the motion detectors in your inner ear let you know that you are moving. Strictly speaking, your inner ear does not detect motion at all. Rather, it senses *changes in motion.* When you are riding in a jet plane that accelerates for a takeoff, your saccule and utricle notice the increase in speed. But when the plane is flying smoothly at 1000 kilometers per hour (about 625 miles per hour), the gelatinous tissue in your inner ear comes to rest and you cannot tell that you are moving that fast without looking out the window.

In similar fashion, when you first sink into a tub of water that is 20° warmer than your skin, your temperature receptors fire vigorously. But as you remain lying in the tub, your skin temperature itself warms up. After a short period of time, your free nerve endings will fire less vigorously because the temperature of your skin is now much closer to that of the water. Because your skin and your free nerve endings have *adapted* to the heat, the water will now seem much less hot to you.

As we will see in later chapters, your brain also has ways of changing its response to stimulus inputs even when your receptor cells continue to fire at rapid rates. When you are flying along in a jet, the sound of the engines may seem particularly loud to you at first. But as you settle down and relax, the noise of the jets may soon become a faint, background drone because your cortex is no longer particularly interested in this sound.

Does this fact mean that your ears *adapt* to the noisy sound of the jet engines? No, for your hearing receptors are rather special. They *seldom, if ever, adapt* to noisy inputs from the world around you. Almost all the rest of your receptor neurons do adapt—but not those in your ears.

So when you are flying in a plane your hearing receptors *continue to fire rapidly,* but your brain *habituates* to this noise by inhibiting, blocking off, or even just ignoring the input messages that your ears are sending to your cortex. However, if the engines slow down or speed up, you are likely to notice this *change* almost immediately—because your brain pays instant attention to changes in the world around you.

In general, we use the term *adaptation* whenever your receptor cells themselves slow down or reduce their firing rates in response to a constant stimulus.

The term *habituation,* however, almost always refers to your brain's tendency to ignore sensory inputs that seem of little interest or importance.

Adaptation and habituation are complex subjects that we will discuss often in this book. For the moment, you should remember that your body has a great ability to adjust to the world around it, but this adjustment hinges on your body's being able to notice and react to what is *changing* in the environment.

Question: Why might you want your robot to be able to adapt to a constant stimulus?

PART TWO   Sensation and Perception

When you are in a noisy environment such as a New York City subway station, the receptor neurons in your ears fire rapidly but your brain blocks out the message your ears are sending it.

A Window of Skin

Your skin senses are among the most important senses that you have, surely as critical to your survival as are vision and hearing. And yet, perhaps because you seldom use them for communication or artistic expression, you may have overlooked their complexity, their beauty, and their incredible usefulness.

As an example of your skin's usefulness, consider the story of Helen Keller. She was born a normal child, but an illness when she was 19 months old left her deaf and blind. Although she had learned to say a few words

Helen Keller, blind and deaf from childhood, met President Dwight D. Eisenhower at the White House in 1954. She "listened" to what the then President was saying by placing her fingers on his lips.

before the illness, she soon stopped speaking. For the next several years of her life, Helen Keller was little more than an animal, trapped in a black and silent cage, completely unable to communicate with those around her.

When she was 6, however, her parents appealed to Alexander Graham Bell for help. Bell, the inventor of the telephone, recommended as a teacher a young woman named Anne Sullivan. Within a month Miss Sullivan had taught Helen to make sense of the myriad sensations her skin receptors poured into her brain. Helen learned how to "talk" using her fingers, and how to "listen" when someone "wrote" on the palm of her hand. Later she learned to "read speech" by placing her fingers on the lips of the person who was speaking.

Helen Keller's skin was her only window to the world, but she "saw" through this window with exceptional clarity. When she would meet someone for the the first time, she would run her hands over the person's face to find out what the person "looked like."

If you would like to learn "skin language," do as Helen Keller did. The next time you are alone with a very good friend or relative, have this person sit quietly while you close your eyes and explore the person's face with your fingers. Do not speak. Simply move your fingers gently around the person's eyes, ears, nose, lips, and hair. What kind of a person is this? What does the person *feel* like?

Every scrap of knowledge you have about the world around you, including the images you have of people you love and hate, first came to you as a pattern of neural inputs that your sense organs sent to your brain for processing. If you understand where your inputs come from—that is, how your receptor neurons react and why they function as they do—you will certainly be able to build a better robot if you ever have to. But, more important, you will also come closer to understanding your own internal psychological processes—and your behavioral outputs—than if you choose to ignore the "input side" of your own body's functioning.

Summary

1. Your skin is your window to a great part of the outside world.

2. **Receptor cells** in your skin provide **sensory inputs** to your **somatic cortex (parietal lobe)** telling your cortex what your body is doing, what your skin is touching, and whether the outside world is warm or cold.

3. The **corpuscles** in the hairless regions of your skin, and the **basket cells** in the hairy regions, detect pressure.

4. The **free nerve endings**—found in all skin—detect both pressure and temperature.

5. Any object warmer than your skin will be sensed as warm. Any object cooler than your skin will be sensed as cold.

6. The **deep receptors** in your muscles, joints, tendons, and bones tell your cortex the position and condition of various parts of your body.

7. Buried away in your inner ear are your motion **detectors**—the **saccule**, the **utricle**, and the **semi-circular canals.**

8. The saccule and utricle sense straight-line or **linear motion.**

9. The semi-circular canals respond to circular or **rotary motion.**

10. Your nervous system is geared to respond primarily to *changes* in your environment, but often adapts or habituates to *constant* stimulation from the outside world.

11. Receptor **adaptation** is a slowing down of the firing rate of your sensory receptors, which occur when the receptors are stimulated at a constant rate.

12. Central **habituation** is a process that occurs in your brain when you no longer pay attention to a constant stimulus input.

13. All your receptor neurons, except those involved in hearing, adapt to constant inputs. When a constant noise seems less intense to you after a time, it is because your brain has habituated to the noise by paying less attention to it.

(Continued from page 164.)

Major Jack Amundsen turned down the volume on the radio link between him and the robot. Mark III/21 was trapped somewhere in the very heart of the asteroid, clinging to the walls of a cave that had no top or bottom as far as the robot could sense. Amundsen could rescue Mark easily, quickly, if he could only find some way to let the robot know in which direction it should move to get out of the cave. But how was he to tell Mark which way was "up" on an asteroid that had no gravity?

But what is gravity, after all, but a force that keeps the human race glued to the earth? Were it not for gravity, the Major reminded himself, the centrifugal force created by the earth's rotation would have flung us all into outer space long ago. Could he perhaps substitute one force for the other?

"Listen, Mark," the Major said on the radio. "I'm going to try something. Our space ship is bolted to this cruddy piece of rock. If I turn on the positioning jets just right, I can probably set the whole asteroid spinning slowly like a top. If it does, your direction detectors will start operating again."

The robot was silent as Amundsen calculated what to do. The ship was parked almost dead center on the asteroid. If the positioning jets could generate enough sideways power—that is, generate enough thrust at right angles to the surface of the asteroid—the asteroid would start to rotate. Amundsen turned on the jets and watched the dials on his control console. Slowly, ever so slowly, the huge piece of cosmic debris started to rotate like a wheel.

"Major, I feel it moving. The loose rocks that were floating around in the cave are falling to the floor of the chamber. Your idea worked." Mark's voice was as unemotional as ever, but Amundsen could swear the robot was smiling electronically.

"Major, my sensors are now functioning. I now know which way is up. I shall return to the ship shortly."

Amundsen suddenly panicked. "Wait a minute, Mark! Which way are you moving?"

"Up, Major, ever upward," came the calm reply.

"Stop, Mark! You're going the wrong way! Your sensors are giving you the right information, but you're interpreting it incorrectly. What seems to be 'up' to you is actually the center of the centrifugal rotation, the center of the asteroid. To get up to the space ship, you've got to move in the opposite direction of what seems up to you right now. It may seem screwy to you, Mark, but you've got to walk *down* in order to get *up*."

"But Major, my reflexes are all wrong. I see the logic of what you say, yet my motion detectors indicate that I would be going in an inappropriate direction if I moved downward. Help me, Major. I cannot decide which way to go."

Major Amundsen grinned. Wait till he told the boys back in Houston about this! There were some things that a robot couldn't handle after all!

Amundsen pressed the button on his microphone and issued a command:

"Robot XSR 5 Mark III/21, this is your superior officer, Major Jack Amundsen, speaking. I hereby order you to continue to move in what seems a downward direction until you reach the surface of this asteroid and can then return to the space ship."

"Yes, Major. I hear and will obey."

Major Jack Amundsen breathed a sigh of relief, and then said gruffly, "Listen, Mark, be careful. The asteroid is whirling around fairly rapidly. So, when you get to the surface, use your stick-tite shoes to keep from flying off into outer space."

Amundsen paused to think of what had happened to him and his robot companion, then laughed out loud. "And Mark, may the centrifugal force be with you!"

Recommended Readings

Boring, E.G. *Sensation and Perception in the History of Experimental Psychology* (New York: Appleton, 1942).

Keller, Helen. *Story of My Life* (New York: Airmont, 1970).

McBurney, Donald H., and Virginia B. Collings. *Introduction to Sensation/Perception* (Englewood Cliffs, N.J.: Prentice-Hall, 1977).

Uttal, William R. *The Psychobiology of Sensory Coding* (New York: Harper & Row, 1973).

Taste, Smell, and Hearing

Did You Know That . . .

What we commonly call "touch" is really several quite different senses?

Even the best steak doesn't *taste* much different from old shoe leather?

Your tongue is covered with tiny nipples called "papillae?"

There are only four basic taste qualities: sweet, sour, salty, and bitter?

Smell is a much richer sense than is taste?

The best way to smell the aroma of wine is to "chew" it with your mouth open?

A woman's sensitivity to tastes and odors varies with her menstrual cycle?

Sex-related odors can change the way many women *perceive* other people?

Taste and smell are "mono" senses, while hearing and vision are "stereo" senses?

You can locate sounds in the left–right dimension better than in the up–down or front–back dimension?

Three little bones in each of your middle ears act like stereo amplifiers?

The two most important attributes of a sound wave are its frequency and its amplitude?

Animals can often hear higher frequency sounds than can humans?

Certain types of deafness cannot be corrected with a hearing aid?

"Membranes and Molecules"

"Okay, dear, which kid do you want?"

Judy Jones looked around the room. There were children of all ages, all sizes, all colors. Some were playing together, some were fighting, some were sitting quietly in corners minding their own business. Judy glanced quickly at Mrs. Dobson, the woman who had asked the question, and then gazed back at the dozens of children packed into the room.

"How about that little girl over there, in the pink dress?" Judy asked, pointing her finger at a dark-skinned, handsome girl who was playing with several other youngsters. "She looks adorable."

Mrs. Dobson turned to see which child Judy was pointing to. "Oh, Arabella. Sorry, dear, but somebody's already working with her. The pretty ones are always picked first, you know. Pick an ugly one instead, if you want my opinion. They're starved for love, and they need your help just as much as the cute ones do."

Judy was shocked at Mrs. Dobson's bluntness, but guessed the woman might be right. Judy inspected the room carefully, then spotted a little boy with red hair sitting by the window, looking at a magazine. He was by far the most unattractive child in the room. His eyes were watery, his hair uncombed, his skin covered with brown blotches and blemishes. His face was lopsided, and his head seemed too large for his body. Not only that, but he was white. Judy, a black student at a college near the Children's Home, had hoped to work with someone of her own race.

"What about him?" Judy said, pointing again.

"Oh, that's Woodrow Wilson Thomas. Ten years old. Nice little fella, but ugly as home-made sin."

"Home-made sin?" Judy asked.

"Sorry, dear. It's a saying I got from my mother," Mrs. Dobson replied. "Appropriate enough in his case. Woodrow is a bastard, you see."

Judy was shocked. "You mean, he's nasty?"

"No, dear," came the calm response. "I mean bastard in a technical sense. A love child, a natural-born child, the offspring of an unwed mother. I read his record a couple of years back. His mother was 16 when she got pregnant, and she didn't quite remember who the father was. Maybe somebody in the family, for all we know. Anyhow, the mother got rubella—that's the German measles—while she was carrying poor little Woodrow, and he just didn't turn out right. They thought of putting him up for adoption when he was born. But he was so ugly, they figured nobody would take him. So they kept him for a while."

"For a while?" Judy asked, beginning to sympathize with the little boy more and more.

"For a while. Woodrow got off to a bad start in life, and he didn't grow up very well either. The record says he crawled and walked at a normal age, but his speech was very retarded. Made animal noises and grunts instead of talking words. Still does, poor little fella. Doesn't understand much when you talk to him, and he won't do what you tell him to do. When you try to get through to him, he just stares at you with those watery eyes, and then he looks out of the window while you're trying to say something. No wonder his folks put him in the Home here so the state could take care of him. Retarded, that's what Woodrow Wilson Thomas is."

Judy turned the matter over in her mind. "Do you think there's anything I can do for him? I mean, it's part of an assignment for my psych class. We're supposed to show that we can help a retarded or emotionally disturbed child. Can I help Woodrow?"

Mrs. Dobson sighed. "I don't see why not. There must be something you can do. We're so overcrowded here, and we've got such a small staff, I reckon nobody's worked with that child for two or three years. He's no trouble, you see. Doesn't have temper tantrums or act up. Never plays with the other kids, or gets into difficulties. He just sits by the window and looks at his books and magazines all day long."

"Well, if he can read magazines at his age, he can't be all that retarded."

Mrs. Dobson laughed. "Read? Don't be foolish, dear. He just looks at the pretty pictures, and smiles. One day, a year or so ago, I saw him puzzling over a picture like he was trying to figure out what it was. So I asked him what he saw. He just ignored me. Maybe you can get through to him, but I don't promise. But you should learn a lot, and he won't give you any trouble."

Judy accepted the challenge. She went over to the window and tried to talk to Woodrow, but he didn't seem to want to listen. Finally, in desperation, she tugged on his shirt and pulled him over to a nearby table. Woodrow seemed happy to come along with her.

"Now, Woodrow, we're going to draw some pictures. You like pictures, don't you?"

The boy's watery blue eyes drifted toward the window.

Judy pulled on his shirt again until he looked back at her, then she picked up a crayon. She drew a crude picture of a cow while Woodrow watched, seemingly interested. She gave him the crayon and motioned to him that she wanted him to draw. Woodrow took the crayon carefully in his right hand, then looked up at Judy, a puzzled stare on his face.

"Draw a cow, please, Woodrow," Judy said, making scribbling motions with her hand and pointing to the drawing she had just made.

Woodrow smiled serenely as he touched the crayon to the paper. Within three minutes, he handed back to her a crude but recognizable picture of a cow. Judy was so pleased that she wrote the letters C-O-W beneath the drawing. Woodrow took the scratch paper back and copied his own version of the letters underneath those Judy had written.

Judy was thrilled by his response. She got out some of the textbooks she had brought along and hunted through them until she found other pictures for Woodrow to draw. He made a horse, and an auto, and a house. When Judy wrote their names on the scratch paper, Woodrow copied the letters as carefully as he could.

When her time with Woodrow was up, and she had to catch the bus back to the college, Judy kissed Woodrow on the forehead.

"I don't care if you are retarded, young man. You're going to learn to read. I just know you are!"

Then she gathered up her textbooks and rushed off.

In her excitement at wanting to tell the other students how well things had gone, Judy failed to notice that she had left her algebra textbook behind. Woodrow picked it up and began to look through it. Although it didn't have any real pictures in it, he found the book utterly fascinating.

The next week, when Judy came back to the State Home for the Retarded to be with Woodrow again, he solemnly presented her with a sheet of scratch paper. On one side were childish drawings of a cow, a tree, a car, and a house, each correctly labeled several times over. On the other side, in very poor but legible script, were written out the first two review problems at the end of the introductory chapter of the algebra textbook.

"My God," said Judy when she saw them, "You've done the algebra correctly!"

(Continued on page 195.)

According to popular opinion, there are but five senses—vision, hearing, taste, smell, and touch. But there is also "common sense," which is unfortunately rare; "non-sense," which is unfortunately common; and the "sixth sense," which some people claim warns them of impending disaster (and which may be ordinary "horse sense").

In the last chapter, we discovered that touch is not one sense but several—pressure, temperature, feedback from your muscles that lets you know where your arms and legs are, and motion detection. In this and the

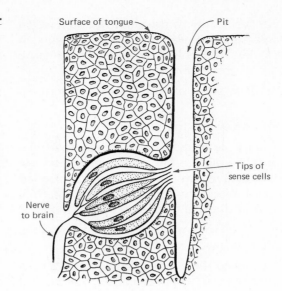
Fig. 7.1. A single taste bud.

next chapter we will study taste, smell, hearing, and vision. And in case you have any doubts, some of the facts are guaranteed to be sensational!

Taste

Imagine that you have been hiking in the woods all day long. You return home, clean up, and go to dinner at the fanciest restaurant in town. Since you are **ravenously** hungry—and since someone else is paying the bill—you decide to order everything on the menu that you like. What would taste best? A shrimp cocktail, caviar, a juicy steak, a large green salad, mock turtle soup, broccoli in hollandaise sauce?

Pick your favorite food and imagine it in your mind's eye. Let's say that you picked a steak—a sirloin strip 2 inches thick, wrapped in bacon, and cooked just the way you like it.

Now, why does the steak *taste* good to you?

Whatever reasons you come up with, chances are that they're partly wrong. For even the best of steaks has almost no *taste* at all—at least if we speak technically and we restrict "taste" to the sensory qualities that come from your tongue. Steak *smells* good; it *looks* good; it has a fine *texture* to it that you enjoy chewing; and if it comes to your table sizzling hot, it both *sounds* good and has just the right *temperature*.

But none of these sensory qualities has anything to do with the *taste* of steak. In fact, if we could block out all the other sensory qualities except those that come from your taste receptors, you'd find that you could hardly tell the difference between the taste of steak and that of old shoe leather.

The Taste Receptors

The **taste buds,** which are your taste receptors, are your body's "poor relations" (see Fig. 7.1). Impoverished in almost every sense of the word, your taste buds are scattered in nooks and crannies all across the surface and sides of your tongue. Mostly, however, they are found clumped together in bumps on your tongue called **papillae** (from the Latin word meaning "nipples"). If you go back to the mirror you were using in Chapter 2 and stick out your tongue and look at it, you will see the papillae very clearly.

Most of the papillae have grooves around their sides, like the moats or canals that circled old European castles. The taste buds line the sides of the papillae, like windows in the outer wall of a castle (see Fig. 7.2).

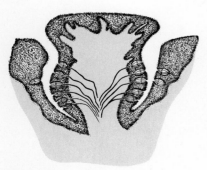
Fig. 7.2 A papilla in the tongue.

Taste buds are made up of receptor cells, each of which has a hair sticking out of one end. These hairs poke out into the "moat" around the papillae like the **dendrites** at the front end of a neuron. When you eat or drink something, the liquids in your mouth filled up the moats, and various molecules in the food stimulate the hair cells chemically. The cells then fire off their sensory input message to your brain, and you experience the sensation of taste.

The chemical processes that lead to the experience of taste are not entirely known. But it appears that the food molecules fill in specific **receptor sites** on the hairs and receptor cells, much as the transmitter molecules in the **synaptic canals** find receptor sites on the dendrites and cell bodies of your neurons.

Certain types of food molecules fit into one receptor site but won't fit into others, much as a key will fit some locks but not others. When a molecule fits into a taste receptor site, it causes the receptor cell to fire. Your brain then figures out what kinds of chemicals are present in your mouth by noting which receptors have been "unlocked," or stimulated.

Taste Qualities

There are only four basic taste qualities: **sweet, sour, bitter,** and **salty**—a paltry few qualities compared to the richness of the sensory experiences you get from vision, hearing, and smell. The number of your taste receptors is limited, too—a fraction of the number of receptor cells to be found in your eyes, ears, or nose. And yet your tongue plays a very important role in your life for, along with your nose, it acts as *guardian of your stomach*.

Newborn infants will typically spit out sour or bitter substances, but usually will accept sweet or slightly salty food. The liking for beer or for "gin and tonic" that some people have, therefore, seems a learned or acquired taste since sour and bitter tastes are not innately pleasing.

Some people are very insensitive to the taste of certain foods—you must really **saturate** their tongues with these foods for these people to get any taste at all. This **taste blindness** is far from rare, and seems to be caused by some inherited deficiency in the chemical composition of the person's saliva. However, the taste-blind individual can usually taste the food easily if you first dissolve the food in the saliva of a person with normal taste sensitivity.

Many types of chemicals can change your own **gustatory** sensitivity. Smoking a cigarette will temporarily dull your sensitivity to sweet and salty substances, but not to sour and bitter tastes. Monosodium glutamate (MSG), used frequently in oriental foods, improves some flavors since it makes the tongue more sensitive to sour and bitter tastes. MSG has such a strong effect on sensitivity to bitter substances that if you use MSG on your food at lunch, a cigarette that you smoke that evening will seem much more bitter than usual—a fact smokers might remember if they ever decide to kick the nicotine habit.

Taste is a necessary but not particularly rich "sense." For the truth is, most of the food qualities that you ascribe to your tongue really should be credited to your nose.

Question: When you catch a cold, and your **nose** *is clogged but your* **tongue** *is not affected, why does food suddenly lose its "taste?"*

Smell

Your nose has two cavities or open spaces inside it (see Fig. 7.3). The roof of each of these nasal cavities is lined with a thick covering called the **olfactory membrane.** Embedded in this membrane are millions of olfactory receptor cells. At the base end of each of these receptor cells is an axon that

Dendrites. The input "feelers" at the front end of a neuron. See Chapters 2 and 4.

Receptor sites. Points on a neuron (or a hair cell) that are sensitive to sensory inputs. See Chapter 3.

Synaptic canals. The fluid-filled spaces between two connected nerve cells. See Chapters 2 and 4.

Sweet, sour, bitter, and **salty.** The four basic taste qualities. All the thousands of different tastes of food are combinations or mixtures of these four simple tastes.

Saturate (SAT-your-ate). To fill completely. A sponge that is as full of water as it can possibly get is said to be saturated with liquid.

Taste blindness. The inability to taste one or more of the four basic taste qualities. Actually should be called "tastelessness," since "blindness" ordinarily refers to vision and not to taste. However, "lack of taste" is a term we use to refer to someone whose attitudes or opinions don't agree with ours; thus we use "taste blindness" to refer to those individuals whose tongues don't function as ours do.

Gustatory (GUSS-tah-torr-ee). Vision is the process of seeing. Gustation (guss-TAY-shun) is the process of tasting. From the Latin word meaning "to taste." We get our word *gusto* from this same Latin word.

Olfactory membrane (oal-FACK-torr-ee). "Olfaction" (oal-FACK-shun) is the process of smelling. The olfactory membrane is a layer of tissue at the top of each nasal cavity that contains the receptors for smell. There are two olfactory membranes in your nose—one inside each nostril.

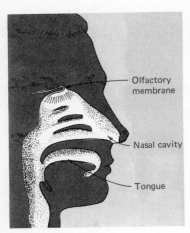

Fig. 7.3. The nasal cavity in cross section.

runs directly to your brain. At the front end—as is the case with the taste receptor cells—is a hair-like object that sticks out of your olfactory membrane to make contact with the air as it passes through your nasal cavity en route to your throat and lungs.

The stimuli that excite your olfactory cells are complex chemicals in *gaseous form* that are suspended in the air you breathe. These gaseous molecules appear to lock onto specific receptor sites on the receptor cell hairs. This "locking on" stimulates the receptor cell to fire off an input message to your brain.

To be truthful, no one yet knows exactly how these chemicals cause your receptor cells to fire. We are sure, however, that most of the odors your nose detects come from gaseous molecules that are heavier than air. Unless the air is stirred up, these heavy molecules tend to collect at ground level. If you want to "smell better," then, you might try putting your nose down close to the floor—where the majority of the odors around you actually congregate!

Smell Sensitivity

If you were to ask a number of your friends whether dogs or humans have the keener sense of smell, most of them would surely say that the dog's nose is much more sensitive than yours. After all, bloodhounds are used to track down fugitives, and the police sometimes use dogs to sniff out marijuana.

But the truth is that your nose is probably just as sensitive as any dog's—if you were trained to use it properly. However, if you wanted to follow someone's trail, you would have to crawl about on your hands and knees with your nose to the ground as the dog does, which is probably why we will continue to use bloodhounds for such tasks. In its own way, though, your nose is as sensitive to faint odors as your eye is to the dimmest of lights, and your ear is to the softest of sounds.

As we mentioned, your nose has two nasal cavities—one for each nostril. These cavities are separated by a very thin wall of tissue. When you breathe through your nose, air is forced past the small bones in the nasal cavity, but only a small portion of this air reaches your olfactory membrane at the top of each nasal cavity. When the current of air stops suddenly or reverses

Wine tasting at a German winery.

PART TWO   Sensation and Perception

itself rapidly—as it does when you chew and swallow your food, or when you sniff the air—the current of air is pushed up to the top of each cavity and stimulates your olfactory receptor cells. You sniff a flower because this action forces the "smelly" molecules in the blossom up to the olfactory membrane where you can best detect these chemicals.

Most whiskey companies employ professional tasters who judge the quality of their products. These tasters take small sips of the alcohol and roll it around in their mouths while making chewing motions. This "mouthing" of the liquid can force the odor-laden air up the back entrance to the nasal cavity toward the olfactory membrane.

If you order a bottle of wine at a good restaurant, the wine steward will open the bottle and give you the cork to sniff. If the cork smells "sweet" and fresh, the wine is probably good. But if the cork smells "sour" or "putrid," it may indicate that the wine has turned to vinegar. Presuming the cork smells fine, the steward will pour a little of the wine into your glass. If you swirl this sample of wine around in your glass, you will release the odor molecules into the air inside the glass. You may then stick your nose into the glass and sniff the wine to make sure that it too smells good.

The next stage in this pleasant ritual comes when you sip a bit of the wine sample in order to "taste" it. Actually, you should "chew" the wine and roll it around in your mouth the way that professional whiskey tasters do before you swallow it. If the wine suits your taste (actually, if it suits your smell), you may nod approvingly to the wine steward, who will follow the ritual of filling your guests' glasses before he fills yours.

Hormones and Sensory Acuity Speaking olfactorily, some people smell better all the time, and you smell better some days than others. Which is to say that olfactory sensitivity varies considerably from one individual to another, presumably because of inheritance. Loss of the capacity to smell occasionally occurs in older persons. And recent experiments suggest that your olfactory thresholds are influenced by the amount of sex hormones present in your body.

Hormones are chemicals secreted by various glands in your body that have a profound influence on your growth and behavior. As we will see in Chapter 13, the sex hormones are created primarily in the sex organs and serve to regulate sexual development and behavior.

Berkeley psychologist Frank Beach reports that before and during menstrual bleeding, a woman's body is almost totally deprived of sex hormones. As a consequence, during menstruation most women become less sensitive to inputs in *all* their sensory **modalities.** In fact, only in the middle of their menstrual cycle are women usually as sensitive to sensory inputs as men are all the time. However, women who are "on the pill" maintain a continuously high hormone level. Hence their sensory **acuity** also remains high.

Beach and many other psychologists have noted as well that men are more sensitive to some odors just after receiving injections of the male sex hormone **testosterone.**

Question: Whiskey makers have long contended that men have "better noses" for judging smells than do women. Can you see why this might be so, and how a woman might overcome the problem?

Smells and the Menstrual Cycle The relationship between smells and sexual behavior is a complex but very interesting one. To begin with, the menstrual cycle itself seems to be sensitive to olfactory inputs. The sexual cycle of female mice, for instance, seems to be primarily controlled by smells. When both male and female mice are housed together in a laboratory, the females tend to go through their cycles every four to five days. When the two sexes are separated, however, the female cycles become very irregular and often disappear entirely. As recent studies from both Holland

Hormones (HOR-moans). Chemicals from various body glands that affect both growth and behavior.

Modalities (moh-DALL-it-tees). From the Latin word meaning "measures" or "manners." A modality is a way of doing or arranging something, or a type of sensory experience. Vision is one sensory modality; taste is another.

Acuity (ack-CUE-it-tee). The ability to detect very weak stimulus inputs, or to make fine sensory discriminations—that is, to judge very small differences among quite similar stimuli.

Testosterone (tess-TOSS-tur-own). One of the male sex hormones, secreted primarily by the testes (TESS-tees) or testicles (TESS-tickles) of the male. Masculine behavior patterns are strongly influenced by the presence of testosterone in the body.

Synchronous (SIN-kro-nuss). Things that are "synchronous" are things that run together, or operate in parallel. When you "synchronize" your watch with someone else's, you set the watches operating in parallel.

Apocrine glands (AP-poh-krin). Glands in your armpits that, when stimulated by sex hormones, release a "smelly" type of sweat.

Copulins (KOPP-you-lins). Chemicals released by female animals (including women) that act as sexual attractants for many males. Thus chemicals that stimulate organisms to copulate, or engage in sexual activity.

Aphrodisiacs (AFF-roh-DEE-see-acks). Sexual stimulants. The Greek goddess of sexual love and beauty was Aphrodite (AFF-roh-DIH-tee). The Romans called her Venus. According to the famous Greek poet Homer, Aphrodite "overcomes all mortal men and immortal gods with desire." Thus anything to eat, drink, or be merry with that raises the passions—among other things.

Attractant. Chemicals that cause one organism to approach, or to be sexually interested in another organism. Perfume is a good example of a sexual attractant used by many men and women.

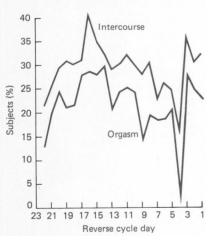

Fig. 7.4. This graph shows the percentage of married women in the Udry and Morris experiment who reported having intercourse and orgasm. Hormone levels are lowest about day 4 in the menstrual cycle and highest about day 15. Sensory acuity follows almost the exact same pattern.

and Australia have shown, though, if the females are allowed to smell urine from male mice, their sexual cycles almost immediately return to normal.

There are many "old wives' tales" suggesting that women who live together tend to have menstrual periods that are "in synch" with each other. In 1971, Martha McClintock tested this folk belief by studying the menstrual cycles of 135 women living in a dormitory at Wellesley College. McClintock found that, as the college year progressed, the menstrual cycles of good friends and roommates did in fact become more similar.

An explanation for this **synchronous** effect may come from research reported in 1977 by California psychologist Michael Russell and his colleagues. Russell believes that when we sweat, the **apocrine glands** under our arms release sexual substances. To test this notion, Russell and his group asked a woman with a very regular menstrual cycle to wear cotton pads under her arms daily. They then rubbed portions of these pads on the upper lips of female volunteers who agreed not to wash their faces for several hours afterward. (A second or "control" group of volunteers was treated with pads not containing human sweat.) The women in the control group maintained their normal menstrual cycle. However, the menstrual cycles of the women treated with the sweat became strikingly similar to that of the woman who had donated the sweat.

It would seem, then, that the mere *smell* of certain natural sexual substances is enough to strongly influence the menstrual cycle.

The Sweet Smell of Sex It has long been known that both male and female animals secrete chemicals that attract the opposite sex. But what about humans?

Naomi Morris and Richard Udry have studied the relationship between smells and sexual intercourse for more than a decade in various groups of married women. In 1968, Udry and Morris reported that many of the subjects in their first study were more likely to engage in intercourse—and to achieve orgasm—during the middle of their menstrual cycles than at any other time (see Fig. 7.4). The women's hormone production (and hence smell sensitivity) is, of course, greatest in mid-cycle. But how could an increase in olfactory acuity account for an increase in sexual behavior?

In 1974, Richard Michael and his colleagues at Emory University reported that female monkeys secrete chemicals called **copulins** that smell sexually attractive to males. More recently, Michael has discovered that these same copulins are produced by human females. Michael believes that the peak production of copulins occurs in the middle of the menstrual cycle.

Although some scientists have criticized Michael's work, a study reported in 1978 by Morris and Udry does seem to support the belief that human females release chemicals that act as **aphrodisiacs.** Morris and Udry asked 62 married women to rub one of four different perfumes on their chests before going to bed at night. Only one of the four perfumes contained copulins, and the women were not told which perfume was which. The women used a different perfume each night, and kept records of their sexual activities and of their menstrual cycles.

Morris and Udry report that only 12 of the 62 couples showed the expected "peak sexual activity" at the middle of the woman's menstrual cycle. These same 12 couples were, in addition, the only ones that seemed affected by the copulins in the perfume. It would seem, then, that while human females do secrete copulins, these sexual **attractants** do not affect all men in the same way.

But what about males? Do men secrete copulin-like substances too? The answer seems to be a qualified "yes." In 1952, a French scientist named J. Le Magnen reported that women seem to be particularly sensitive to the odor of a chemical named **exaltolide.** This musky fragrance—which is found in many well-known perfumes—is excreted in human urine, but men produce about twice as much of it as do women.

Sexually mature women can detect the smell of exaltolide readily, particularly in the middle of their menstrual cycle when their hormone levels are highest. Men are relatively insensitive to the odor. Women who have had their ovaries removed—and hence are no longer producing female sex hormones—are as insensitive as are males. But even a woman without ovaries becomes highly sensitive to the smell shortly after receiving an injection of female sex hormone.

Although J. Le Magnen believes that the smell of exaltolide is sexually attractive to women, the matter has not as yet been proven scientifically. It does seem clear, however, that sex-related odors can change the way in which women perceive and feel about other human beings.

In the late 1970's, J.J. Cowley and his colleagues at Hatfield Polytechnic in England reported they had been able to influence the judgments that women students made about political candidates. Cowley and his group presented a large class of psychology students with printed information about six people who were competing for a student government position. Three of the candidates were men, three were women. The psychology students were asked to judge each candidate in terms of her/his personality and fitness for office.

While the members of the class were making their judgments, they were asked to wear paper masks—supposedly to keep their classmates from noticing their facial expressions. In truth, some of the masks had been coated with small amounts of sexual attractants. One-third of the masks contained exaltolide, and one-third contained copulin-like chemicals. The final third contained no attractants at all, and the students who wore these masks made up the "control group" in this experiment.

Crowley reports that the male psychology students were seemingly not affected at all by the "smelly" masks. The sex-related odors did alter the judgments of the women students, however. Those women exposed to exaltolide tended to favor the more assertive and aggressive of the six candidates for office. Those women exposed to copulins, however, preferred the shy and unaggressive candidates. The odor inputs thus apparently affected the *feelings* that the women students had concerning the office-seekers.

Olfactory Habituation

Not all the odors in our world are sexually exciting or even particularly pleasant, but many of them are fairly *persistent.* Anyone who has passed by a petroleum refinery, a glue factory, or a cattle barn knows that many smells are pervasive and lingering.

If your nose were continually sensitive to the odors around it, however, the world would seem a smelly place indeed—and few people would willingly work in cheese factories and chemical plants. But your nose has superb powers of **adaptation,** for it can adjust to almost any smell at all.

For example, chances are that your own home has an odor characteristic of the food your family eats. Normally you don't notice it at all, but if you are gone for a few days, you will smell this unique scent the moment you walk through the front door.

How does your olfactory apparatus adjust to the stimuli around it? As we pointed out in Chapter 6, your sense receptors are geared to detect *changes* in your sensory world. When a new stimulus comes along, the receptor typically begins firing rapidly, putting out a burst of neural impulses rather like the bullets from a machine gun. However, if the stimulus remains fairly constant (as when you plunk yourself down in a tub of hot water, or when you remain for a time in a room with a characteristic odor), your receptor cells fire less rapidly, and your cortex can more easily ignore this particular stimulus input.

The Chemical Senses

Smell and taste are often called **chemical senses** because the stimulus that excites the receptors in your tongue and nose are *complex chemical molecules.*

Exaltolide (ex-ALL-toe-lide). A chemical compound released in urine. Men secrete twice as much exaltolide, on the average, as do women. Supposedly an aphrodisiac for women, but not for men (who cannot detect its smell).

Adaptation. When an odor first stimulates your olfactory receptors, they fire rapidly. Within seconds, however—even though the odor is still strongly present—your olfactory receptors will "adapt" by firing less and less frequently. Adaptation is a process that occurs in receptor neurons. Habituation, on the other hand, is the process by which your brain adjusts to or ignores stimulus inputs coming from your receptor neurons.

Chemical senses. Taste and smell are called the "chemical senses" because the stimulus input that sets them off is a chemical molecule of some kind.

Most of the delights of eating come from smell and skin sensations, not taste.

But there is a very important difference between taste and smell—whatever your tongue tastes must ordinarily be brought to your mouth, while your nose can detect stimuli that are some distance away.

The skin senses, including taste, are *local* receptors—that is, they give your brain information about the exact point on your body that is being stimulated. Olfaction, hearing, and vision are *distance* receptors—that is, they typically tell your brain what is going on some distance away from the surface of your body.

However, to borrow a phrase from the world of high-fidelity music, taste and smell are essentially **monaural** or "mono" senses. It may take you some time to locate the body of a mouse that had the misfortune to die in some out-of-the-way corner of your home, or to find in July an egg that was hidden too well at Easter. Your ears, on the other hand, are strictly "stereo." Standing quite still in the middle of a strange room with your eyes closed, you can point out rather precisely the location of some noisy object like a ticking clock.

If you wish to find out why, just "lend an ear" as we discuss hearing.

Hearing

What do your ears have that your nose and tongue lack? The answer is—*separation.*

If you block one of your ears with cotton, your ability to localize the position of sounds diminishes considerably. But if just one of your nostrils is stopped up when you have a cold, you could locate a rotten egg just about as rapidly as if both your nasal chambers were operating unimpaired.

The important difference between hearing and the chemical senses, then, is this: Your ears are some 15 centimeters apart; your nasal chambers are separated by less than a single centimeter.

If you would like to demonstrate to yourself the importance of the "space between your ears," you might try a musical experiment. Find a stereo set with two *movable* speakers. Put the speakers as far apart in the room as you can. Now put on your favorite stereo record and sit between the two speakers with your eyes closed. You will hear music coming at you from all directions, but some sounds will seem to be on your left, while others will seem to be on your right.

Next, put the two speakers right next to each other and repeat the experiment. Now, the music is compressed, pushed together, cut down in size to a *point source of sound*. In short, the stereo music will now sound monaural or "mono."

Your ears are like the two speakers spread far apart. Your nose and tongue are like the two speakers put close together.

Localizing Sounds

In a sense, your ears are similar to the microphones used to record music. To get a stereo effect, the record company must use at least two mikes that are some distance apart. When a band performs, each mike "hears" a slightly different version of the music.

Suppose the lead guitarist in the band is on the left. The mike on the left would then "hear" the guitarist much more loudly than would the mike on the right. If the drummer is on the right, then the right microphone would pick up the sounds of the drum more loudly than would the mike on the left.

Record companies typically make a completely separate recording of what the left mike "hears" and what the right mike "hears." These two different records make up the two channels of stereophonic music that are pressed on stereo discs or dubbed on tapes.

By keeping the two channels separate during both recording and

Monaural (mon-R-al). Sound produced by a single source, as through just one loudspeaker.

PART TWO   Sensation and Perception

A musical experiment begins with a stereo outfit.

The experiment continued.

playback, you can maintain left–right relationships. That is, when you hear the record, the sounds made by the lead guitarist come primarily from the left speaker. The drummer's beat, however, will come to you mostly from the right speaker.

Your ears are just far enough apart so that you can readily detect left–right differences in sound sources. Sound waves travel at about 1,200 kilometers an hour (750 miles/hour). If a cricket chirps 2 meters away from your left ear, the noise will reach your left ear a fraction of a second before it reaches your right ear. And since the insect is closer to your left ear than to your right, the noise will be louder when it reaches your left ear than when it finally gets around your head and reaches your right ear.

Your brain *interprets* the difference in the auditory inputs from your left and right ears to *mean* that the cricket is to your left. But, as we will soon see, your brain can be fooled in such matters if you know how to go about it.

The farther apart your ears are, the more precisely you can detect the location of a sound—because there is a greater difference in what your two ears would hear. When a recording company sets its microphones 3 meters (10 feet) apart, they are effectively increasing the *apparent* distance between your ears to 3 meters—particularly if you listen to the music with stereo headphones.

Now go back to your stereo set and put one speaker on the floor and the other as high up in the air as you can directly above the first (see photograph). Sit with your head upright between the two speakers. When you play music now, it will seem strangely monaural, for each of your ears is the *same distance from both speakers.* In fact, you may find that you tilt your head to one side without realizing it, as your brain attempts to turn monaural music into a stereo message that carries much more interest and information.

Your ears can detect the location of sounds spread out in the *left–right* dimension rather well. But your ears do very poorly in locating sounds in the *up–down* dimension.

Question: Why might it help to "cock your head to one side" when trying to locate the source of a sound over your head?

The Auditory Stimulus

Hearing is a *vibratory sense*—which is to say that the stimulus for **audition** is a sound wave. (Words such as "audition," "audio," and "auditorium" all come from the Latin word *audire,* meaning "to hear.")

Imagine yourself seated on a rock a couple of feet above a very quiet pool in a forest. You take a stone and toss it in the center of the pond, and what happens? Wave after wave of ripples circle out from the center until they strike the edges of the pool. If you looked closely, you would see that

Audition (aw-DIH-shun). To hear, or to be heard. The sense of hearing.

when one of the waves reached the shore, it "bounced back" in a kind of watery echo.

The sound waves that stimulate the *auditory receptors* in your ear are not very different from the ripples that you set up by dropping the stone in the pond. Whenever any fairly rigid object is struck forcibly, it tends to *vibrate*. As this object vibrates back and forth, it pushes the molecules of air around it—pushes these molecules away from the object, just as the stone pushed water molecules away from it when you dropped the rock in the pond.

If you dropped several pebbles into the water in rapid succession, you would set up a whole series of waves on the surface of the water. When an object vibrates, it sets up a continuing series of *waves of energy* that ride the molecules in the air just as the waves in the pond ride the surface of the water. When these *sound waves* reach your ear, they set your eardrum to moving back and forth in rhythm with the vibrating object. Other parts of your ear then translate the vibrations of the eardrum into patterns or *waves of neural energy* that are sent to your brain so that you can "hear."

Parts of the Ear

Your ear has three main divisions: (1) the outer ear; (2) the middle ear; and (3) the inner ear.

1. The **outer ear** is that flesh flap of skin and other tissue you see when you look at yourself in the mirror. Sound waves enter your outer ear and move into a little "hole in your head" called the **auditory canal.** At the inner end of this auditory canal is your eardrum, a thin membrane stretched tautly across the auditory canal like the skin on a drum. The eardrum separates your outer ear from your middle ear.

2. The **middle ear** is a hollow cavity in your skull which contains three little bones called the **hammer,** the **anvil,** and the **stirrup** (see Fig. 7.5). If you looked at these three little bones under a microscope, you would see that they look much like the real-world objects they are named after. One end of the hammer is connected to the eardrum, so that when your eardrum moves, it pulls the hammer back and forth rhythmically.

The hammer transmits this "wave" of sound energy to the anvil, making the anvil move back and forth. The anvil pulls the stirrup back and forth in similar fashion.

The stirrup is connected to another membrane stretched across an

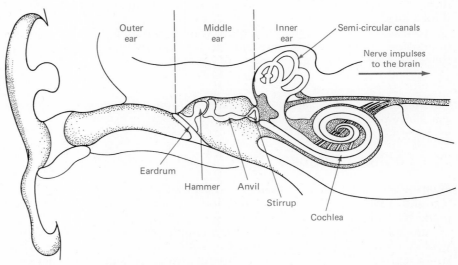

Fig. 7.5. Structure of the human ear.

PART TWO   Sensation and Perception

opening called the **oval window.** As the stirrup moves, it forces the membrane on your oval window to wiggle back and forth in rhythm too.

The purpose of this complex arrangement is easy to understand. The three little bones and the two membranes act as the *amplifiers* in your own biological stereo system. By the time the sound stimulus has reached your oval window, it is many times louder or stronger than it was when it first struck your eardrum.

3. The oval window separates the middle ear from the **inner ear.** Your inner ear is a fluid-filled cavity that runs through your skull bone like a tunnel coiling through a mountain. This inner ear of yours has two main parts: the **cochlea** and the motion detectors we discussed in Chapter 6 (the saccule, the utricle, and the semi-circular canals).

Your auditory receptors lie on your cochlea, which gets its name from the Latin word for "small shell." And, from the outside, the cochlea does look much like a shell you might pick up on a beach somewhere.

The receptor neurons for hearing are hair cells similar to those found in your skin, nose, and tongue. These hair cells lie on the **basilar membrane** that runs the length of the spirals in the cochlea.

Frequency and Amplitude

Sound waves (see Fig. 7.6) have two important aspects: their **frequency** and their **amplitude.** The frequency of a musical tone is related to how *high or low* the tone sounds to your ear. The amplitude of a musical tone is related to how *loud or soft* the tone appears to be.

If you drop a stone in a deep pond, you set up just one big wave that moves out from the point at which the stone hits the water. But if you drop several pebbles in, one after the other, you set up a *series of waves.* If you dropped in 10 pebbles each second, you would set up 10 waves a second (under perfect conditions). The *frequency* of the waves would then be 10 per second.

When you pluck a string on a guitar, you are doing the same thing as dropping a rock in a pond (see Fig. 7.7). For the string creates sound waves that have *exactly the same frequency* as the number of vibrations that the

Oval window. The thin membrane lying between your middle and inner ears. The stirrup is connected to one side of the oval window, the basilar membrane to the other.

Inner ear. A fluid-filled "worm hole" in your skull that contains both the motion detectors (the saccule, utricle, and semi-circular canals) and your receptor neurons for hearing.

Cochlea (COCK-lee-uh). The snail-shaped portion of your inner ear that contains the basilar membrane.

Basilar membrane (BASS-il-lar). The thin, skin-like membrane on which lie the hair cells that detect sounds.

Frequency. In auditory terms, the number of times a sound source vibrates each second. The frequency of a musical tone is measured in Hertz.

Amplitude (AM-plee-tood). From the Latin word meaning "muchness." We get our word "ample" from the same Latin source. Amplitude is the amount of sound present, or the strength of a musical tone. Literally, the "height" of a sound wave.

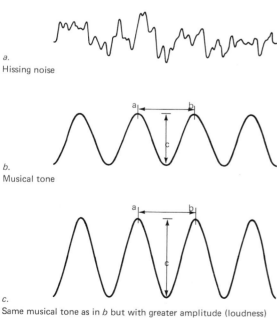

a.
Hissing noise

b.
Musical tone

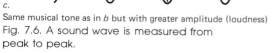

c.
Same musical tone as in *b* but with greater amplitude (loudness)
Fig. 7.6. A sound wave is measured from peak to peak.

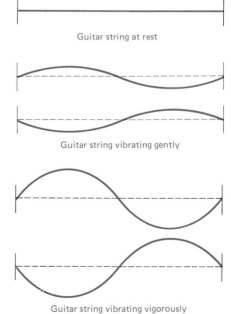

Guitar string at rest

Guitar string vibrating gently

Guitar string vibrating vigorously
Fig. 7.7. A vibrating guitar string.

string makes per second. Your ear detects these sound waves, and your brain turns them into musical tones. The *faster* a particular string vibrates, the *more* "waves per second" it creates—and the *higher* the tone sounds to you.

If you plucked the "A" string on a guitar, it would vibrate 440 times per second. This number is called the *frequency* of the musical tone "A." Each single vibration of the string is called one **Hertz,** abbreviated Hz—the name coming from the German physicist Heinrich Hertz who made the first definitive studies of energy waves. Since the "A" string vibrates 440 times per second, we say the "A" has a frequency of 440 Hz. In general, the thinner and shorter a string is, the higher the frequency at which it vibrates—and the higher the tone that it makes.

Amplitude has to do with the *loudness* of a tone, but not with the frequency. If you happen to pluck the "A" string of the guitar *very gently*, it vibrates 440 times per second; and if you plucked the string *as hard as you could*, it would still vibrate at about 440 Hz. If it didn't, you wouldn't hear the note as being an "A."

But surely something different happens, for the more energetically you pluck a string, the louder the note sounds. The answer is that the string moves *further up and down* during each vibration—but it still vibrates at about 440 times per second. In similar fashion, if you gently drop 10 pebbles per second into a pond, you create 10 very small waves. But if you throw 10 pebbles per second into a pond as hard as you can, you create 10 very large waves. In either case, however, there are still just *10 waves per second.*

In technical terms, the "bigger the wave," the greater the *amplitude.* And the greater the amplitude that a sound wave has, the louder it will sound to your ear.

The Range of Hearing

What kinds of musical tones can your ear hear?

Your range of hearing is, roughly speaking, from *20 Hz to about 20,000 Hz.* Actually, the size of your cochlea determines to some extent what your range of hearing will be. The larger your cochlea, the better it can hear at the *lower* end of the auditory scale. The smaller your cochlea, the better it can hear at the *upper* end of the auditory scale.

The size of your cochlea depends primarily on the size of your head. People with "big heads" (and hence large inner ears) can occasionally hear as low as 16 Hz—lower than any musical instrument usually plays. But people with large cochleas usually have difficulties hearing much above 14,000–16,000 Hz. People with smaller cochleas usually cannot hear much below 25 or 30 Hz, but may hear notes as high as 18,000 to 20,000 Hz.

As you may deduce from these facts, since men are generally physically larger than women, men do better at the "bottom" of the musical scale than do women. Women, however, can generally hear high notes better than men.

Question: Why do you suppose that men generally have lower sounding voices than do women?

Small animals generally have smaller cochleas than do humans, and hence can hear much higher notes than we can. The dog can hear notes at least as high as 25,000 Hz. The bat can hear tones as high as 100,000 Hz.

Question: If you wanted to design a whistle that could be used for calling dogs but that couldn't be heard by human beings, what frequency range would you want to investigate?

Deafness

What difference would it make to your life if you became deaf?

Hearing is the major *social sense*, the ears being the main avenue of human communication. Our customs, social graces, and moral beliefs are still passed down from one generation to another primarily by word of mouth rather than in writing. And most of us (textbook writers included!) prefer the informal transmission of knowledge that comes from talking to the formal, stilted **phraseology** of the written word.

The person who loses her or his hearing often feels more cut off from the world, and hence makes a poorer adjustment to these changed circumstances, than does the person who loses his or her vision. For when we talk to someone, our listener usually responds to what it is we have just said.

If you are telling someone a story or teaching someone a lesson, you typically will watch your listener's face and can tell at once if the person has understood what you said. This *feedback* from your listener is of critical importance in shaping your own verbal behavior. For communication is best when it is a two-way street. You give out a message; it is received by a listener who, in turn, sends you back a message evaluating or responding to what you have said. What would it be like if, when you talked, no one ever answered?

Question: Do you give as much special consideration to a person you know is deaf as you do to someone you know is blind?

Learning to sing, dance, play the guitar, or drive a car—all these complex motor tasks—require *feedback*. A boy who is born deaf, or partially deaf, has trouble learning to *talk* because he cannot *hear* what noises his voice is making. Without the auditory feedback from his vocal cords, the boy can never learn to shape his spoken words properly, because he simply does not know *what his own voice sounds like.*

If you have ever tried to talk to someone who was wearing earphones and listening to music, you know how important auditory feedback is in controlling your voice. For when the person wearing the phones attempts to speak, she or he cannot hear her or his own voice very well and hence starts to shout. The louder the music pouring out from the earphones, the louder the person shouts.

When people grow older, the three small bones in the middle ear often become brittle and hard and hence do not work properly. Since the hammer, anvil, and stirrup serve to *amplify* the sound waves as they come into the ear, the person becomes deaf when these bones malfunction. This type of *bone deafness* can usually be corrected if the person is fitted for a hearing aid, a device that acts like a miniature hi-fi set and "turns up the volume" electronically (see Fig. 7.8).

Many types of infection can attack the hair cells on the basilar membrane or the axons that run from these cells toward the brain. If the receptor cells (or their axonic fibers) are permanently damaged, the person suffers from **nerve deafness.** If only a small section of the basilar membrane is affected, the person may lose the ability to hear just high notes, or low notes, or even notes in the middle of the auditory **spectrum.** If the damage to the nerves is widespread, however, the person may become totally deaf for *all frequencies.* Nerve deafness usually cannot be helped much, if at all, by a hearing aid.

Children who are born *partially deaf* are often in worse shape psychologically than is a child born completely without hearing. Why? Well, it is easy for you to detect the fact that a child simply cannot hear at all. But if the child can hear some things—sometimes—you may think the child's slowness in learning to talk and the indistinctness of its words are indications of *mental retardation* rather than of deafness.

Phraseology (fray-zee-OLL-oh-gee). From the Greek word meaning "to tell." Your own phraseology is your unique manner of expression, your way of phrasing words, your style of writing or speaking.

Nerve deafness. A form of hearing loss caused by damage to the hearing receptors or to the auditory nerve. Nerve deafness can seldom be helped either by surgery or by use of a hearing aid.

Spectrum (SPECK-trum). From the Latin word meaning "to look," from which we also get the words "specter" (ghost) and "spectacle." As we will see in the next chapter, the word "spectrum" means a set or array of related objects or events, usually a set of sights or sounds.

Fig. 7.8. Some kinds of deafness can be helped with hearing aids.

Until scientists discovered how necessary some kind of feedback is in learning to talk, we often thought that partially deaf children were dumb or stupid. Occasionally we mistakenly confined these children to homes for the mentally retarded—although many of them were really very bright.

Fortunately, now that hearing tests for young children are much more common than they used to be, and now that we know what the effects of partial deafness are, we don't make that particular mistake too often any more.

Summary

1. Taste and smell are called **chemical senses** since the receptors in the nose and tongue are stimulated primarily by complex chemical molecules.

2. The primary receptors for taste are the **taste buds,** which are located in mushroom-shaped bumps (called "**papillae**") on the surface of the tongue.

3. The four basic taste qualities are **sweet, sour, bitter,** and **salty.**

4. The smell receptors lie on the **olfactory membrane** inside each of the two nostrils. Whenever you breathe in air containing certain types of molecules, these chemicals stimulate the olfactory receptors and you experience the sensation of smell.

5. Taste is a very simple sense, with but four basic qualities. Smell is much more complex. Most of the "taste" of food is really the smell of the food rather than its taste.

6. Smells affect many types of behaviors, including sexual responses.

7. Women are more sensitive to all types of sensory inputs in the middle of their menstrual cycles—when their **hormone** level is high—than at any other point in the cycle.

8. The sensory **acuity** of males is not cyclical as it is in women. However, men do become more sensitive to sensory inputs immediately after an injection of male sex hormone.

9. Women who are housed together tend to experience similar menstrual cycles. This menstrual **synchrony** seems to be caused by chemicals that the women release in their sweat.

10. Women (and many female animals) release chemicals called **copulins** that can be sexually attractive to many males.

11. Both men and women release a chemical called **exaltolide** in their urine, but men produce twice as much of it as do women.

12. Exaltolide has a musky odor and is used in many perfumes and **aphrodisiacs.** Men are generally insensitive to the smell of exaltolide, but women are fairly sensitive to its odor—particularly in the middle of their menstrual cycle. Women without ovaries can smell exaltolide only if given injections of female hormones. The odor of exaltolide can affect the way women perceive or feel about other humans.

14. Your nose **adapts** fairly readily to most constant olfactory inputs.

15. Smell and taste are both **monaural** (single) senses in that they seldom help you locate objects in space very well.

16. Hearing is a **stereo** sense. Because your two ears are several centimeters apart, sounds reach each of your ears at slightly different times and at slightly different loudnesses. Your brain analyzes these differences and converts them into an understanding of whether the source of the sound is to the left or right.

17. While your ears discriminate left–right differences in sounds very well, they do not discriminate up–down differences at all well.

18. When sound from any source arrives at your ear, the sound passes through the **outer and middle ear** until it reaches the hair cells in

your **inner ear.** These inner-ear hair cells are your true auditory receptors.

19. Sound waves have both **frequency** and **amplitude.** Frequency is measured in **Hertz,** or Hz.

20. The greater the frequency of a musical tone, the higher it generally sounds.

21. The larger the amplitude of a sound wave, the louder it will usually seem to be.

22. **Bone deafness** is a hearing loss caused by improper functioning of the three little bones in your middle ear—the **hammer,** the **anvil,** and the **stirrup.** Bone deafness can usually be corrected with a properly fitted hearing aid.

23. **Nerve deafness** results from damage to the hair cell receptors. This form of deafness can seldom be corrected.

24. Children born deaf have problems learning to speak because they cannot hear the sound of their own voice.

25. Children born partially deaf are slow to speak and to respond to their social world. Until hearing tests were routinely given to small children, partially deaf youngsters were often mis-diagnosed as being mentally retarded.

(Continued on page 181.)

Dear Judy Jones:

I was going through some of my stuff today, packing it all up, when I found this old sheet of scratch paper. It had a cow on it, and a horse, and an automobile. On the back was a couple of algebra problems, written out in long hand. My ticket to the world, I always used to call it. Reminded me that I hadn't written you a letter in some time, so maybe you ought to get caught up on the news.

I'm going to college! Can you believe it! That's what I was packing for, when I found the scratch paper. Bet you never thought, the first time you saw this ugly boy, Woodrow Wilson Thomas, that he'd be going off to college someday. I don't remember that first day you came to the Home too well, maybe because I didn't know the words to remember things with back then. But the algebra book, that is something I sure won't ever forget. I guess I learned how to read with that book. And your help too, and then Mrs. Dobson's. She told me later you had a real argument with her. She thought I was retarded, but you insisted I must just be deaf. Then there was a doctor checking me out, and the hearing aid that the State bought me. Did I ever tell you, the first day I had the hearing aid, I just sat and listened to the birds all day long? Can you imagine not knowing what a bird sounds like until you're 10 years old?

Anyhow, as you know, it took me a couple of years to learn how to talk like normal people do. Still not too good at it, I guess. But I went to school, and I caught up, and now I'm going to college. I still can't believe it. I guess I did pretty good in high school, except maybe in English. But real good in math. Good enough to get a scholarship. How about that? I'm going to study math in college. Hope to be a teacher some day. My complexion has cleared up a lot since you saw me last, and maybe I'm not so ugly any more. Anyhow, I've got me a girl friend. Sort of.

It's been so long, maybe you're married now and have kids of your own. If you do, I bet you'll have their ears checked out early, won't you?

Anyhow, I just wanted to let you know how things are going, and about the college bit. I guess if it hadn't been for you, I'd still be at the Home, sitting in the window, looking at the pretty pictures in the magazines. I guess I really owe the world to you, Judy Jones. So I thought I'd write and say thank you.

Peace,
Woody

Recommended Readings

Braginsky, Dorothea D., and Benjamin M. Braginsky. *Hansels and Gretels: Study of Children in Institutions for the Mentally Retarded* (New York: Holt, Rinehart and Winston, 1971).

Dethier, Vincent. "Other Tastes, Other Worlds," *Science*, 201, 224–228, 1978.

Hassett, James. "Sex and Smell," *Psychology Today*, vol. 12, no. 3 (1978), pp. 40–45.

Hopson, Janet. *Scent Signals: The Silent Language of Sex* (New York: Morrow, 1979).

Kling, J.W., and L.A. Riggs. *Experimental Psychology*, 3rd ed. (New York: Holt, Rinehart and Winston, combined ed., 1971, Vol. 1, 1972).

Montagne, Prosper. *Larousse Gastronomique: The Encyclopedia of Food, Wine & Cookery* (New York: Crown, 1961).

Vision

Did You Know That. . . .

The smallest unit of light is the photon?

Light travels at a speed of 300,000 kilometers per second (186,000 miles/second)?

The color of a light is determined primarily by its wave-length?

The colors of the rainbow make up the visible spectrum?

The most sensitive part of your eye is called the "fovea?"

Each of your eyes has a blind spot almost in the middle of your visual field?

The receptor organs for vision are the rods and cones?

The rods are totally color-blind?

The retina of the eye is sometimes considered to be an extension of the brain?

Far-sightedness and near-sightedness are visual problems caused by the shape of the eyeball?

Far-sighted people get more headaches than do near-sighted people?

You can have better than 20/20 vision?

Eating carrots could help improve your night vision?

Most people can reproduce all the colors of the rainbow by mixing just three primary colors?

About 1 person in 20 is markedly color-blind?

"The Eyes Have It"

"What is the first thing you do when a sixth-grade boy comes to your office and wants an appointment for counseling?" Mrs. Carson asked her graduate class in educational psychology.

The class members looked at each other quizzically, then a young woman named Martha raised her hand. "Look over his records first, so you know what his test scores are."

Mrs. Carson nodded. "If you have time, yes, that can be helpful. But suppose the boy is right there, tears in his eyes, begging to see you immediately. Then what?"

"Find out what his name is," a young man named Bill said.

"Ask him what's wrong," said John.

Mrs. Carson smiled warmly. "Yes, of course, ask him his name and what's gone wrong. And suppose he tells you that the other boys have been picking on him, teasing him. Now what do you do?"

"Try to get to know him better, so you can understand his problem," said Martha.

"Yeah, try to relate to the kid," added John.

"True," said Mrs. Carson. "At some point you will want to understand his personality so well that you can look at the world through his eyes. That's the intra-psychic approach. And surely you will want to consider his biological inheritance and his social environment. But how do you find out these things about him?"

"Encourage him to talk," said Bill.

"Ask him what his life is like," said Alice. "What his parents do, where he lives, what he's interested in—things like that."

Mrs. Carson agreed with a nod of her head. "All good points. You sense the need to establish a warm, friendly relationship with the boy. But in order to do all these things—to become friends, to see the world through his eyes, and to learn about his environment—there is something very important that you must do. Can you guess what it is?"

The class was silent.

"First you must see the boy through your own eyes," Mrs. Carson said. "Most of you want to leap right inside his mind to see what's going on there. However, you must learn to see what he's like on the outside before you can discover what he's like on the inside."

"What do you mean?" John asked.

"As simple-minded as it may seem to you, the first step should be to look at his clothes: Are they cheap or expensive? Do they fit him or not? Are they clean and in good repair, or are they filthy and in rags? Is his hair combed? Are his teeth brushed? Is he wearing jewelry or a watch? Are there nicotine stains on his fingers? Is he thin, fat, or muscular?"

"Oh, come on now," said Bill. "Never judge a book by its cover."

Mrs. Carson leaned against her desk. "True. These are superficial things, and you will eventually learn to take them into account rather rapidly. That is, you will learn to size up the child with but a few shrewd glances. But when you're just beginning your work as a counselor, you must take the time to train your eye so that you don't miss the simple things— things that can tell you so much about a child. You must be detectives. Only after you comprehend the significance of simple clues about the child can you safely go on to solving the complexities of his mind."

"Yeah, but can you learn anything really important about a sixth-grade boy just from looking at his clothes?" Martha asked.

"Class, let me tell you a detective story. I'll give you all the clues and let's see if you come up with the right solution. Let me tell you about the Case of Johnny W."

Mrs. Carson closed her eyes for a moment, then opened them wide. "Johnny W. was 12 years old when he first came to my office. He was a nice looking boy with hair the color of cotton and skin so pale it was almost chalk white. He was wearing dark green pants, a light blue shirt, a red jacket with yellow trim, and tan shoes. His clothes were slightly mussed, but of excellent quality. When he sat in the chair by my desk, I noticed one of his socks was bright red, the other coal black. Now, what do you know about him already?"

"Nothing important," said John.

"No," said Alice, "you know something about his home life. I'll bet he dressed himself for school."

"Beautiful," said Mrs. Carson enthusiastically. "Good detective work. I asked him about that right away. He said his mother and father both worked. They woke him up before they left, so he dressed himself and made his own breakfast. So you were right about his home life. But his clothes tell you something else, something much more important. Think of Johnny W. as a living system, with a biological side, a mental side, and a social or behavioral side to him. Now, what do his clothes tell you about him that you couldn't guess otherwise?"

When no one in the class responded, Mrs. Carson continued. "All right, some more clues. I assumed from the fact that he dressed himself and got to school on time that he was mature for his age and apparently dependable. While he was telling me about his home life, I scanned his school records. His mental test scores were well above average. He was behind his class in reading ability, but otherwise Johnny seemed to be doing well."

Mrs. Carson sighed. "One thing I noticed right away. Johnny W. seemed very nervous. As he talked to me, his eyes darted back and forth quickly, and he kept putting one hand up to shield them from the glare of the window. I lowered the shade, and then asked him what was wrong. Can you guess yet?"

No one could.

The woman spoke again. "More clues. Johnny said, 'I'm no good at all. The kids laugh at me. They call me Bunny Rabbit. They don't like me. They won't let me play ball with them. Why won't they let me play ball with them?'"

Mrs. Carson surveyed her class in educational psychology. "Now what do you think was making him so unhappy?"

Martha said, "He didn't know how to get along with the other kids. He needed training in social skills."

"His father never taught him to play ball. Bad father–son relationship," said Bill.

"Good points," replied Mrs. Carson. "But you're still missing most of the clues. Part of his problem came to Johnny from his father, true. But his mother was at fault as well." Mrs. Carson looked the class over, but since none of the students raised a hand or offered a comment, she continued. "Next Johnny said, 'I practice hitting the ball and catching the ball hours and hours. Even when the light hurts my eyes. I practice hard. But I have to wear my dark glasses outside, and when they throw the ball to me, it just disappears. It just disappears! I swing the bat, but I miss. And sometimes the ball hits me, and it really hurts. I know I'm not like the rest of the kids. I can't help that. But why can't I even see the ball when they throw it to me?'"

Mrs. Carson paused. "All right, class. What was Johnny W.'s problem?"

Bill stuck up a muscular hand and waved it energetically to get her attention. "He was a sissy," Bill said gruffly.

"No, he just needed new glasses," said John.

"No, he was emotionally insecure," said Alice. "He needed more love."

"No, he just needed psychological counseling," said Martha.

Mrs. Carson shook her head. "Those are good guesses, but you're really not using the clues I've given you. Johnny's glasses were as good as they could be. He was very insecure all right, but not because he was a sissy or because his parents didn't give him enough love. He needed psychological help, but you'd go off entirely in the wrong direction if you didn't pay attention to the descriptive things about Johnny that I've mentioned. Before you can solve his emotional problems, you have to solve a mystery about Johnny that even his parents didn't fully understand.

"Think, class, think. Why couldn't Johnny W. see the ball when the other children threw it at him?"

(Continued on page 213.)

Vision

Of all the senses, *vision* is the richest and most stimulating. Although there is no way to prove such matters experimentally, some psychologists estimate that two-thirds of your informational inputs come to you through your eyes. Perhaps that estimate is a little high, but we do know one thing for certain. Although your visual system makes up far less than 10 percent of your brain, it consumes about a quarter of the energy inputs available to your nervous system.

If you would like to learn something about your own eyesight, just imagine trying to describe the following scenes to a blind person: The Rose Bowl parade, a painting by Picasso, the riotous colors of a spring landscape, and the sort of "light show" that occurs at a rock concert or a disco dance hall. Could you really make the blind person "see" these sights merely by painting word pictures?

Because vision dominates most of our lives, psychologists have studied it in much greater detail than they have the other senses. As a result, we know more about how and why we see than we do about how we experience the rest of our sensory world.

Vision has often been called "the sense of wonder." To appreciate how your ability to see influences your thoughts and behaviors, however, you need to understand at least three things: (1) what the visual stimulus (light) is like; (2) how your eye converts light into a sensory input to send to your brain; and (3) how your brain interprets this incoming sensory information.

The Visual Stimulus

The stimulus for vision is *light*. The smallest, most elementary unit of light is called the **photon,** which gets its name from the Greek word meaning "light." The flame from one match releases millions of photons. A flashlight releases a great many more photons than does a match. Thus, in general, the *brighter* the light source, the *more* photons it produces in a given unit of time (such as a second).

When you turn on a flashlight, photons stream out from the bulb at an incredible speed or **velocity.** To give you a better "feel" for this speed, consider the fact that the velocity of sound waves is about 1,200 kilometers per *hour* (750 mph). The speed of light, on the other hand, is about 300,000 kilometers per *second* (186,000 mps).

If you could travel as fast as a photon, you could zoom all the way around the world *seven times* in just a second, and you could go to the moon and back in less than three seconds.

Wave-lengths of Visual Inputs

The bulb of a flashlight produces photons in pulses or *waves*—much as the string on a guitar produces sound waves when the string vibrates, or the

Photon (FO-tahn). A tiny packet of energy which is the smallest unit of light. A burning match will release millions of photons. Under ideal circumstances, your eye is so incredibly sensitive that it can detect as few as 10 photons if they strike your eye at the same time.

Velocity (vee-LOSS-sit-tee). The speed at which an object or wave moves. From the Latin word meaning "to be quick." The velocity of natural objects such as photons tends to be *constant* under normal conditions.

wind produces waves on the surface of the ocean. If you wanted to, you could take a boat out on the ocean and actually measure the distance *between* one wave and another. And if you did so, you would find the distance between the crests of the waves was remarkably consistent.

On a calm, peaceful day, as the ocean waves move slowly and majestically, the distance between waves would be rather large. But on windy, choppy days, this wave-length would be rather small. Thus if you knew the strength of the wind, even without going out on the water, you would have some notion of what the length between the crests of the ocean waves would be.

Much the same sort of consistency holds for the wave-length of light and what color it appears to be. If you will turn to color Plate 1, you will see a rainbow-like display called the **visible spectrum.** The blue colors have very short wave-lengths. The reds, at the other end of the spectrum, have much longer wave-lengths. The colors between red and blue have wave-lengths that fall between these two extremes. Thus if you know what the *length* of the light wave is, you will know what *color* it will ordinarily appear to be.

However, the distance between the crests of light waves is much, much smaller than the distance between any two ocean waves. The wave-length for red is so short that it takes about 38,000 "red waves" to make an inch (2.5 centimeters). The wave-length for blue is much shorter—it takes about 70,000 "blue waves" to make an inch.

Scientists seldom measure the wave-length of light in fractions of an inch, because the figures are just too clumsy to use. Instead, scientists measure wave-lengths in **nanometers.** The Greek word for "dwarf" is *nanos.* From this fact, you can perhaps guess that the nanometer is a "dwarf" or fraction of a meter. In fact, there are one billion nanometers in each meter (39.37 inches).

Amplitude of Visual Inputs

Wave-length specifies the color of a visual stimulus, such as a blue or red light. But some lights are bright, while others are dim. The *intensity* or brightness of a light can be specified in terms of the height or **amplitude** of the wave (see Fig. 8.1).

If you measured the *length* between crests of ocean waves on a calm day, you might find that the wave-length was about 6 meters (20 feet). The *height* of each wave, however, might be no more than 1 meter (3.28 feet). During a storm, the wave-length might still be 20 feet, but the height of each ocean wave might now be 3 to 4 meters (10 to 13 feet).

In similar fashion, a dim blue light might have a wave-length of 423 nanometers. If you "turned up the intensity" of this blue light until it was so bright it almost blinded you, it would still have a *wave-length* of 423 nanometers—but the *amplitude* of each wave would be many times greater.

When you make a light brighter, you *amplify* the height of each light wave, just as when you turn up the volume on your stereo set you *amplify* the height of each sound wave the machine puts out.

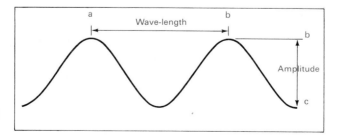

Fig. 8.1. Amplitude and wavelength.

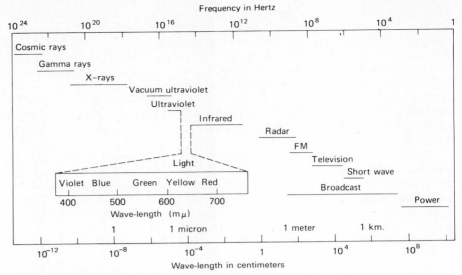

Fig. 8.2. The visible spectrum.

The Visible Spectrum

In a manner of speaking, light waves are much like X-rays and radio waves, except that X-rays have such a short wave-length that they are invisible to your eye, and radio waves have such a long wave-length that you can't see them. As Fig. 8.2 suggests, the only waves you *see* lie between 400 and 760 nanometers. We call this range of waves the *visible spectrum*.

Below 400 nanometers lie the ultra-violet rays that are used in "black lights" and in sun lamps. These rays have a very damaging effect on the complex chemicals in your eye that help you see, which is why you shouldn't look directly at "black lights" for very long—and why you should wear dark glasses when you sit under a sun lamp.

Beyond the red end of the visible spectrum (760 nanometers) lie the *heat rays*. If you stare at a heat lamp for too long, you may not only warm up your face but "cook" parts of your eyes as well.

Why does a psychologist interested in human behavior bother with such technical measures as wave-length and amplitude? For two reasons, really.

First, because visual inputs *stimulate* people to act and respond, and the more precisely we can specify the *stimulus* that evokes a certain reaction, the better we can understand the *behavior* itself.

Second, because we are often interested in individual differences. If we show *exactly the same* visual stimulus to two people, and they report *different* psychological experiences, we know that these differences are due to the people and not due to some variability in the physical stimulus itself.

The Eye

What physiological processes occur when you see? These processes are so complex that we still understand them only vaguely.

In some ways your eye is like a color TV camera (see Fig. 8.3). Both are essentially "containers" which have a small hole at one end that admits light. The light then passes through a lens which focuses an image on a **photo-sensitive surface.** In both your eye and in the color TV camera, the "hole" can be opened to let in more light, or closed to keep light out. And in both, the lens can be adjusted to bring near or far objects into focus.

In the case of the color television camera, the light coming through the lens falls on an electronic tube that contains three complex chemicals. These chemicals are photo-sensitive—that is, they react chemically when struck by photons. (The older TV cameras had a tube with only one such

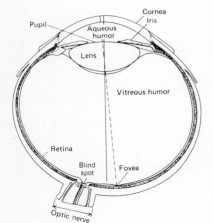

Fig. 8.3. A diagram of the eye.

PART TWO   Sensation and Perception

In a sense your eye works much like a TV camera does, except that your eye typically sees more of a given scene.

chemical, hence the camera could record the scene only in blacks and whites.)

In the case of your eye, the "hole" or opening through which light passes is called the **pupil.** The **iris** is the colored part of your eye which, by expanding and contracting around the pupil, controls the amount of light admitted inside your eye.

Before the light passes through your pupil, however, it must first pass through both the **cornea** and the **aqueous humor.** "Cornea" comes from the Latin word meaning "tough" or "horny," so you can guess that the cornea is the tough tissue at the front of your eye. The Latin word for water is *aqua;* hence the aqueous humor is a watery substance between your iris and your cornea that helps keep your eyeball filled out in its proper shape.

Once a ray of light has entered your inner eye through the pupil, it passes through the lens. The purpose of the lens in your eye—like the lens in a camera—is to allow you to focus clearly whether you are looking at something close or far away. As you change your point of focus from a near object to something several feet away, muscles inside your eye pull on the lens to change its shape and thus refocus the light.

The lens *focuses* the image of what you are looking at and projects this image on the *inner surface of your eyeball,* just as the lens in a camera focuses the image or picture and projects it on the film in the back of the camera.

The inner surface of your eyeball is called the **retina,** from the Latin word meaning "net" or "network." Your retina is a network of millions of cells that—like the picture tube in the TV camera—contains several photosensitive chemicals.

The Retina

In a sense, your eyeball is a hollow sphere whose outer shell has three layers. The outer layer—which contains the cornea—is the "skin" of your eyeball. Like most other skin tissue, this outer layer contains *free nerve endings* that are sensitive to pressure, temperature, and pain. The middle layer of the "shell" of your eye is a dark lining that, like a window shade with a small hole in it, blocks out all the light except that entering through the pupil. The third layer is the *retina,* which is really the inner surface of your eyeball.

The hollow cavity in the center of your eyeball is filled with a transparent, Jello-like substance called the **vitreous humor.** Like the aqueous humor, the vitreous humor acts to keep your eyeball "inflated" in its proper, rounded shape.

Pupil (PEW-pill). The opening in the iris through which light passes into the eye.

Iris (EYE-riss). The colored or pigmented area of the eye. When you say that someone has brown eyes, you really mean the person has brown irises. The Greek word for "rainbow" is *iris.*

Cornea (CORN-ee-ah). From the Latin word meaning "horn-like." We get our words "horn" and "corn" (the kind of blister you get on your foot) from this same Latin source. The cornea is the tough, transparent tissue in front of the aqueous humor.

Aqueous humor (A-kwi-us). The watery substance between the iris and the cornea that keeps the front of your eyeball inflated to its proper size and shape.

Retina (RETT-tin-ah). The photo-sensitive inner surface of your eye. Contains the visual receptor organs.

Vitreous humor (VITT-tree-us). From the Latin word meaning "glass." The vitreous humor is a clear, glass-like substance in the center of the eyeball that keeps your eye in its proper rounded shape. Light must pass through the vitreous humor before it strikes your retina.

The Fovea Your retina contains the *receptor cells* that translate the physical energy of a light wave into the patterns of neural energy that your brain interprets as "seeing." There are two special parts of your retina that you should know about. The first is called the **fovea.** The second is your **blind spot.**

Fovea is the Latin word for "small pit." The fovea in your eye is a tiny, yellow-colored pit in the center of your retina where your vision is at its sharpest. The *blind spot* is a small area of your retina near the fovea which is, for all practical purposes, totally blind. We will discuss the blind spot in greater detail later in this chapter. The reason that this part of your eye is "blind," however, is that it has *no receptor neurons* in it. (See color Plate 15.)

While your eye is like a TV camera in some ways, there are many differences between the two. The camera is large, bulky, clumsy to operate, and requires an external power source of some kind. Your eye is small and, in a sense, self-powered. The photo-sensitive plate or picture tube in a camera is flat, while the retina in your eye is *curved* to cover almost the entire inner surface of the eyeball.

But perhaps the major difference between your eye and a TV camera is the way that each mechanism *translates* light waves into patterns of electrical energy. The picture tube in a black-and-white TV camera contains just one kind of photo-sensitive chemical, while the tube in a color camera has three such chemicals. Your eye is something like a combination of the two, for it has both black-and-white detectors and a separate set of color detectors.

The Rods and Cones The receptor neurons for vision are the **rods** and **cones.** Their names are fairly descriptive of their shapes. In the human eye, the rods are slim, pencil-shaped nerve cells. The cones are thicker and have a cone-shaped tip at their "business" end. (See color Plate 14.)

Both the rods and cones contain chemicals that are very sensitive to light. When a beam of light strikes a rod, it causes the *bleaching* or breakdown of a chemical called **rhodopsin,** or visual purple (the Greek word *rhod* means "rose-colored"). In ways that we still don't entirely understand, this bleaching action sets the rod to firing as it signals your brain that it has been stimulated. The cones contain other types of photo-sensitive chemicals which break down when struck by light waves. This chemical reaction triggers off a wave of neural firing in your cones.

Your rods are *color-blind.* Like the old-fashioned TV cameras, they "see" the world in blacks and whites no matter how colorful the world actually is. For the most part, the rods are located in the outer reaches or **periphery** of the retina. There are about 120 million rods in each of your eyes.

The cones are your *color receptors.* For the most part, your cones are bunched together in the center of your eye near the fovea. The fovea contains no rods at all, *only cones.* There are between six and seven million cones in each of your eyes.

Since your cones are located primarily in the center of your retina, this is the part of your eye that is *most sensitive to color.*

When you look at something straight on, the light waves coming from that object strike your fovea and stimulate the cones, giving you clear color vision. When the same object is at the outer edges (periphery) of your vision, the light waves from the object strike primarily the rods in the periphery of the retina. Since the rods are color-blind, you will see anything that appears at the edges of your visual world as lacking in color.

Structure of the Retina If you were called upon to design the eyes for a NASA robot, the odds are that you would never think of making the robot's retina like yours. To begin with, your retina has *ten distinct layers,* with the rods and cones making up the layer at the *bottom.* The tips of your rods and cones—which contain the photo-sensitive chemicals that react to light—are actually pointed *away* from the outside world. For light to strike your rods and cones, it must first pass through *all nine other layers of your retina.* (See color Plate 16.)

The receptor cells in your skin are a part of your **peripheral nervous system.** That is, they are nerve cells which lie outside your brain and spinal cord. Your spinal cord and brain make up your **central nervous system.** The retina evolved directly from the brain, however, and is considered by some authorities to be almost a part of the central nervous system.

The middle layers of your retina contain a great many "large neurons" that are very similar in structure to those found in your cortex. These "large neurons" begin processing visual information right in the retina, before sending messages along to your visual cortex (in the occipital lobes at the back of your brain).

The middle layers of your retina also contain the blood vessels that serve the retina. Surprisingly enough, light must pass through these "large neurons" and the blood vessels before it can stimulate the rods and cones. Fortunately, these neurons and blood vessels are almost totally transparent, so they seldom interfere with your vision.

The Blind Spot   It is probably hard for you to imagine that each of your eyes has a spot that is, for all practical purposes, *totally blind.* This fact means that there is actually a "hole" in your visual field where you see nothing at all.

Why this hole in your visual field? Well, your eyeball is hollow like a balloon, and your retina is *inside* the eyeball. The blood vessels that feed your rods and cones must somehow get into this balloon, and out again. And the axonic end-fibers from the "large neurons" must somehow get through the walls of the eyeball if they are to reach their destinations in your brain.

All these axons meet at a point near the fovea to form the **optic nerve,** which exits from your eye at the *blind spot.* There are no receptors at this point in your retina—only axonic fibers and blood vessels—and so the part of your visual world that falls on the blind spot is not recorded in your brain.

You are usually unaware of the blind spot because your brain "cheats." That is, it fills in the hole by making the empty spot in your visual world look like whatever surrounds it. You can prove this to yourself by following the instructions given in Figure 8.4. If you look at the picture from just the right position, the man's face disappears. But notice too that the spot where the man's face should be is filled in by your brain with the lines that surround the man's picture.

Your brain is constantly *making assumptions* about the world around you and filling in details which are not actually there. That is to say, sometimes your brain creates imaginary inputs where real ones don't actually exist, and sometimes it blocks out real inputs it doesn't wish to deal with. Thus we all have *psychological* blind spots which can greatly affect our perception of the world.

Visual Skills and Eye Structure   That complex process we call "seeing" actually begins in the retina, and the way in which you respond to visual inputs depends not merely on the structure of your brain, but on the structure of your eye as well.

Dan Landers is a professor at the Motor Behavior Laboratory at Pennsylvania State University. In 1978, Landers announced that he had found a **correlation** or connection between *eye color* and *reaction times.* According to Landers, brown-eyed people tend to react faster to visual inputs than do

Peripheral nervous system (pair-IF-er-al, or purr-RIF-er-al). Those neurons that lie at the outer edge of your body, such as your skin receptors.

Central nervous system (often abbreviated CNS). Technically, the entire brain (the cerebrum and the brain stem) and the spinal cord. Contains more than 90 percent of the nerve tissue in the body.

Optic nerve (OP-tick). The bundle of axonic "telephone cables" running from the eye to the brain.

Correlation (kor-re-LAY-shun). Things that are "co-related" are things that "go together." Two events that are correlated, however, don't necessarily *cause* each other to occur. For instance, birds fly north when springtime arrives, so spring and bird migrations are *correlated* events. However, bird migrations don't *cause* spring to occur.

Fig. 8.4. Close your left eye and stare at the crossed dot with the book held about 6 inches away. The face should disappear.

Near-sightedness. If your eyeball is too long, your lens may focus the visual image so that you see near objects clearly, but see distant objects as being fuzzy. Near-sightedness can usually be corrected with glasses.

Far-sightedness. If your eyeball is too short, your lens may focus the visual image so that near objects seem fuzzy to you, but distant objects are clear. Can usually be corrected with glasses.

About one person in four wears or should wear corrective lenses.

blue-eyed people. Furthermore, individuals with dark brown irises tend to be quicker than are individuals with light brown eyes.

In one study, Landers compared the reaction times of players on the Penn State football team. Landers reports that linebackers had the darkest irises of all the team members. The linebackers also were quickest at reacting to many types of visual inputs.

Landers is not certain why this correlation exists. One possible explanation is that the color of your eye is determined by the amount of *pigment* in your iris. But the *neurons* in your retina also contain this same sort of pigment. According to Landers, there is some evidence that the function of this pigment is to *increase* the speed of neural impulses.

Blue-eyed people have their own advantages, however. In 1978, *Sports Illustrated* reported that the best quarterbacks in professional football tend to have light-colored irises. Perhaps this finding is not so strange, since people with light-colored irises tend to have better *peripheral vision* than do people with dark-colored eyes.

It would seem that for quarterbacks—who must rapidly scan the entire football field the instant a play begins—peripheral vision is a decided plus. But for defensive linebackers—who must respond instantly to whatever the quarterback does—speed of reaction is of greater importance than is good peripheral vision.

Thus *visual skills* may be as important in sports as are intelligence and muscular strength. And these skills are determined in no small part by what visual stimuli actually reach your retina, and by the speed with which the neurons in your retina process these inputs.

Optical Defects

Near-Sightedness and Far-Sightedness

Many distortions of your visual world are caused by misinterpretations made by your brain, but quite a few distortions stem from physiological problems with the eye itself. For example, the chances are one in four that you either wear glasses or should wear them to help you overcome correctable visual difficulties. For the most part, these problems come from slight abnormalities in the *shape* of your eyeball.

If your eyeball is *too long*, the lens tends to focus the visual image a little *in front* of your retina rather than clearly on it. You then see *near* objects rather clearly, but distant objects would appear fuzzy and blurred to you. We call this condition **near-sightedness** (see Fig. 8.5).

If your eyeball is *too short*, the lens tends to focus the visual image *behind* the retina rather than directly on it. Close objects are therefore indistinct to you, but *far* or distant objects are usually in clear focus. We call this condition **far-sightedness.**

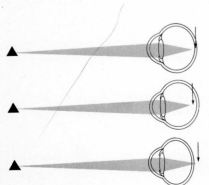

Fig. 8.5. A normal, near-sighted, and far-sighted eye. Notice where the image ends at the arrow in each case.

If you watch carefully in the next movie you attend, you may notice something like the following: A woman standing close to the camera is talking with a man several feet away. When the woman is speaking, the camera focuses on her face, which you see clearly, but the image of the distant man is blurred and fuzzy. *This is the way that the near-sighted person typically sees the world* (see left photo below).

Now, as the dialogue in the movie continues and the man begins to speak, the camera shifts focus (but not position). Suddenly the woman's face, which is close to the camera, becomes blurred—but the distant image of the man sharpens and becomes distinct. *This is the way the far-sighted person typically sees things in the world* (see right photo below).

Old-Sightedness

The lens in your eye operates much the same as does a camera lens, changing the focus from far to near as the occasion demands. As you grow older, however, your lenses become brittle, and you cannot focus as readily on *near* objects. This condition is called **old-sightedness,** or *presbyopia.* (The Greek word *presby* means "old," or "old man"; the Presbyterian Church is governed by a Council of Elders, or presbys.)

Since everyone becomes more far-sighted as she or he grows older, the near-sighted individual may actually find his or her vision apparently improving with age. Far-sighted people have by far the worst of the lot, since their vision *deteriorates* with age. Far-sighted people are also subject to severe headaches if they strain their eyes trying to read or see other things up close to them. The near-sighted person generally does not suffer as much from headaches induced by eyestrain since the person usually sees things "up close" fairly well.

Visual Discrimination

When you go to an eye doctor to be tested for glasses, or when you apply for a driver's license, you will be given one of several tests to determine how accurately your eyes *discriminate* small objects. One very common visual test is the **Snellen chart** (see Fig. 8.6), which presents letters of different sizes for you to read. A person with normal vision can barely read the largest letter on this chart at a distance of 200 feet (60 meters), and can just make out the next largest letters standing 100 feet away. There is one line of letters that the person with normal sight can just barely discriminate when standing 20 feet (6 meters) from the chart.

If you took this test yourself, you probably would be asked to stand 20 feet away from the Snellen chart. If you could read the "normal" line of letters at this distance, we would say that you can "see at 20 feet what the normal person can see at 20 feet." Hence, you would have 20/20 vision.

If you stood 20 feet away from the chart and could only read what the normal person can easily see at 100 feet, your vision would be 20/100, which is fairly poor. But if you could make out the very small letters on the bottom line when you were standing 20 feet away, you would be able to read letters that normal people can discriminate only when they are *10* feet away from the chart. In this case, you have 20/10 or very superior visual acuity.

Old-sightedness. A type of far-sightedness associated with aging. Older people often hold books or newspapers far away from them because they cannot see near objects as clearly as can most young people. Also called *presbyopia* (prez-bee-OH-pee-ah).

Snellen chart (SNELL-en). A visual test devised by a Dutch eye doctor named Herman Snellen. The chart usually has a big "E" at the top, with lines of progressively smaller letters underneath.

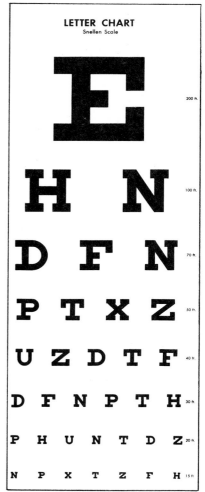

Fig. 8.6. The Snellen chart.

(*Left*) A view of a scene as a near-sighted person might see it. (*Right*) The same scene as viewed by a far-sighted person.

Visual Sensitivity

In order to *discriminate* objects in your visual world, you typically depend on your cone vision.

The reflexes of your eye are so arranged that the visual image of anything you want to inspect closely will fall on your fovea, where there are millions of tiny cones packed together in an area about the size of the head of a pin. During daylight hours, when there is plenty of illumination, your color vision dominates and you can easily make out the details of objects in your visual world.

But at night (or in any dim illumination)—when you are often more interested in *detecting* faint sources of light than in *discriminating* fine details—your rods come into play. Your rods are much more sensitive to light than are your cones, which is to say that the rods are better light detectors than the cones are.

Visual Adaptation

When light strikes one of your rods or cones, the light causes the photo-sensitive chemicals in your receptors to *bleach*. Bleaching is a chemical reaction in which molecules *break apart* because they have been struck by a beam of light. It is this "breaking up" of the photo-sensitive molecules which causes your rods and cones to fire off input messages to your brain.

Your eye replaces the "broken down" photo-sensitive molecules fairly rapidly. If it didn't, you'd only "see" until all the light-sensitive chemicals in your eye were exhausted.

As you might guess, your eye can replace these "visual chemicals" more rapidly in the dark than in bright illumination. And the larger your supply of these photo-sensitive molecules, the more sensitive your vision becomes. Thus after you have "adapted" to the darkness for a while, your ability to detect faint light sources is much better than when you've been sitting in bright sunlight. This **dark adaptation** is caused by your having a surplus of rhodopsin (visual purple) in your rods and a surplus of various other photo-sensitive chemicals in your cones.

As an example of dark adaptation, consider what happens when you walk into a darkened theater. For the first few minutes, you can barely make out the shapes of the people sitting around you. But after your eyes have "adapted" to the dim illumination—and hence have built up a large store of photo-sensitive chemicals—you may notice that you can see quite well.

Your cones adapt more quickly in darkness than do your rods. Your cones become almost as sensitive as they are ever going to get in a matter of 10 minutes or so. Your rods continue to adapt for 30 minutes or more. Because they build up a larger "surplus" of photo-sensitive chemicals, your rods are a thousand times more sensitive than your cones when fully adapted to the dark.

When your eyes are dark-adapted a bright light can be blinding.

Night-Blindness

Some people do not see at all well at night. Usually this defect is caused by some disability of the rods. Night-blindness may have many causes, but a lack of Vitamin A is perhaps the most common one. Vitamin A is necessary for the build-up of rhodopsin (visual purple) in the rods. Since yellow vegetables, such as carrots, often contain large amounts of Vitamin A, these vegetables are often recommended to night-blind persons.

Even if your vision is perfectly normal, however, you may have difficulties seeing at night unless you've received special training. For under very dim illumination, your cones don't function very well. And when you try to stare at something in the dark, your visual reflexes work against you.

In daylight, your eyes automatically focus the image of an object on your fovea—where your vision is clearest in good illumination. But your fovea contains only cones, hence it is "blind" at night. So when you stare directly at an object in dim light, the object may "disappear" because you're trying to see it with your cones. And the harder you try to focus the image of the object on your fovea, the less you will be able to see it!

If you want to see something at night, don't try to look directly at it. Instead, remember that your rods are most numerous in the *periphery* of your retina, so you should try to stare at the object "out of the corner of your eye." The object's visual image will then fall on the periphery of your retina, and thus you will be able to look at the object with your rods, not your cones. And that way, you can actually see better in dim illumination.

Question: If someone threw a baseball at you at night, why might you not be able to see it if you stared directly at it?

Color Vision

Hue

When you speak of the color of something, you are really talking about that object's **hue.**

The reds, greens, blues, and yellows—and all the shades in between—are the *hues* that your cones detect. That is, these hues do not seem to be a *mixture* of any other two colors.

But some colors are obviously mixtures—orange seems a combination of red and yellow, chartreuse a combination of yellow and green, and purple seems to have both red and blue components in it. Most of the colors of the rainbow (the visual spectrum) are mixtures of two or more of the *psychologically pure hues*—red, green, blue, and yellow.

But where does purple appear in a rainbow? Or brown, for that matter? Because the rainbow lacks many of the red–blue mixture colors, psychologists prefer to work with a color circle made by joining the ends of the rainbow. Arranged around the outer edge of this circle are all of the spectral colors that we can see, and any color found on the circle can be made by *mixing* two or more of the four pure hues (see color Plate 3).

Saturation

Hue alone is not enough to explain all of the color visual experiences that you have. For example, what two hues mixed together make pink? Red and blue? Red and yellow? No, pink is not a mix of any two hues, but rather is

Hue (rhymes with "few"). The colors of the rainbow, or of the visible spectrum. Technically speaking, "color" includes not only the hues of the rainbow, but all the mixtures of hues plus blacks, whites, and grays. Black and white are not considered hues, although technically they are "colors." Pink (red + white) is a color; its hue, however, is red.

a weak or *diluted* red. The vividness or richness of a color is what we call **saturation.**

Saturated colors are strong and bright. Desaturated colors are weak and diluted. For example, suppose that you poured red food coloring into a fishbowl filled with tap water. The water would become deep red—a highly saturated color. Now suppose you pour in a lot more tap water. What happens? The ruby red soon becomes a pale, *desaturated* pink.

The hues around the outer edge of the color circle were carefully picked to be the most saturated possible. As you move inward toward the center of the circle, the colors become less and less saturated until you reach gray, which has *no hue at all*. By definition, black, white, and gray are considered to be *completely desaturated*.

Color Mixtures

If your color vision is normal, you can take any three fairly widely spaced hues from the color circle and, by mixing various amounts of *just these three hues*, reproduce all the colors of the rainbow.

The people who design color television sets take advantage of this fact by putting three different photo-sensitive pigments in their picture tubes. Color TV cameras are actually triplets—that is, they usually have three separate TV systems inside them.

When a color camera "shoots" a TV picture of your face, one system records all the red coloring in your face, a second system records all the blue coloring, and a third system records your face in terms of green-yellow. The TV system then mixes these colors *electronically* in just the right proportions to give the precise tint of your skin color (and your eyes, hair, teeth, and so on).

Although your eye works quite differently, your cones also appear to record the world in terms of the three primary colors (plus the black-and-white version recorded by your rods). The various sensory centers in your brain—primarily the visual cortex in your occipital lobes—then "mix" these colors *neurophysiologically* to give you the perception of "living color."

Color-Blindness

When tested in a psychological laboratory, many people appear to need abnormally large amounts of one of the three "mix" colors in order to reproduce all the hues of the rainbow. These people appear to be **color weak,** although they can indeed see every color that a normal individual can see.

For instance, a person with normal color vision might mix equal amounts of red and blue to get a particular purple. A man who was "red weak" might need twice as much red to get the same visual experience. To the normal person, of course, the mix would seem very reddish—but the red-weak person would see it as being an "equal" mix of red and blue.

Most *color-weak* individuals show a deficiency either in their response to red, or to green, or to both these hues.

About 5 percent of the people in the world are almost totally blind to one or more hues on the color circle, although they can see most of the other hues perfectly well. The majority of these **partially color-blind** people are men for, as we will see in a later chapter, color-blindness is an inherited deficiency that seldom affects women.

The partially color-blind individual can reproduce all of the colors she or he can see by mixng just *two* basic hues. The main types of partial color-blindness involve a red-green deficiency or a blue-yellow deficiency.

Although there are several kinds of red-green blindness, a person who suffers from any one of them will see the world almost entirely in blues and yellows (plus black and white). A bright red fire engine will look dull yellow to such a person, while grass would appear to be a desaturated blue.

The rare person who is blue-yellow blind sees the world entirely in reds and greens (plus black and white).

Although the exact mechanism for partial color-blindness is not fully understood, psychologists assume that the cones are somehow responsible. There appear to be several different types of cones, each of which may be responsive to different wave-lengths. The person who is partially or totally blind to red stimuli, for instance, may have been born with few if any of the cones that respond to wave-lengths greater than 600 nanometers.

There are many different theories of color vision that attempt to explain why some people see colors normally, while other people don't see colors as they should. To date, none of the theories has proved itself fully acceptable to all psychologists.

Color-Blindness Tests

Odd as it may seem, many partially color-blind individuals reach maturity without knowing that they have a visual defect. For instance, Karl Dallenbach, a psychologist who spent his professional life studying sensory processes, learned of his red–green blindness in an introductory psychology class.

Karl M. Dallenbach.

Students in this particular class were seated alphabetically to make checking attendance easier for the teacher. Dallenbach was in the front row. During a lecture on vision the professor wished to demonstrate an old color-blindness test called the **Holmgren wools.** The test consists of a large number of strands of colored wool that the subject is asked to sort into various piles according to their hues. Dallenbach was tapped for the honor of being a subject simply because he was right under the teacher's nose.

When asked to sort all the reds into one pile, Dallenbach included all the wools with a greenish hue as well as those that were clearly red. When asked to sort all the greens, he included the reds.

At first the teacher thought that Dallenbach was playing a joke, but subsequent tests proved that he was red–green blind. Like most partially color-blind people, Dallenbach had learned to compensate for his handicap while growing up. Since everyone said that grass was green, he saw it as being somehow different from red roses—although, under controlled conditions, Dallenbach could not tell the color of grass from that of most red roses.

Despite this visual problem, however, Dallenbach went on to become a noted psychologist. But perhaps because of his red–green color-blindness, Dallenbach specialized in the study of taste and smell—not of vision.

The Holmgren wools are but one (and perhaps the least accurate) of many different tests for color deficiencies. Most of the other tests contain hundreds of tiny dots of colors. These dots are so arranged that a person with normal vision sees letters, numbers, or geometric figures in the dots. A person with partial color-blindness, however, sees only a random jumble of dots or a different number than would the normal person. An example of this sort of color-blindness test is shown in color Plate 4.

Question: Red and green were picked as the colors for our traffic signal lights before we realized that millions of drivers are "blind" or "weak" to these two hues. How might we slightly alter the "pure red" and "pure green" colors to make them more visible to drivers with red–green deficiencies? (Remember, these drivers can see blue and yellow quite well.)

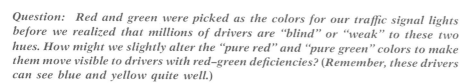

Holmgren wools (HOLM-grin). A color-vision test devised by a Swedish scientist named Alarick F. Holmgren. The test consists of strands of colored wool yarns that the subject must sort according to their hues. The test is seldom used these days.

Total Color-Blindness

Only about one person in 40,000 is totally color-blind. A few of these totally color-blind individuals were born with normal vision, but lost the ability to see hues as a result of disease. Others became totally color-blind because their cones were poisoned by such pollutants as lead or carbon disulfide. Many of these people can recover at least some of their color vision if given proper therapy—including large doses of Vitamin A.

Most totally color-blind people, however, suffer from **albinism**—an inherited condition involving a lack of pigment throughout their bodies. Like the albino rabbits and rats, these people have colorless hair, dead white skin, and pinkish eyes. Since the photo-sensitive chemicals in the cones are, in fact, *pigments*, albino individuals lack functional cones and *cannot see color at all.*

All albino humans have foveas that are *totally blind,* so the albino must learn to defeat the usual instinctive reflexes that tend to focus images in the area of the fovea. Most albinos develop rather jerky eye movements that prevent their visual images from focusing in on the fovea. But even so, their visual acuity is well below average. For if they look straight at something, it disappears from their sight.

Since albino individuals have only rod (or night) vision, they find normal day illumination blindingly bright. They usually compensate by learning to keep their eyelids half-closed, or by wearing dark glasses even when they are indoors.

There is no cure for albinism, but most albino individuals learn to live with their problem and can enjoy reasonably normal lives in spite of their visual handicap.

Summary

1.   The stimulus input for vision is light.

2.   Light is made up of waves of very tiny energy particles called **photons.** Whenever you strike a match or turn on a lamp, you produce millions and millions of photons.

3.   The **frequency** of a light wave helps determine the color the light will appear to be. The **amplitude** (strength) of the light wave generally determines how bright it will seem.

4.   The **visible spectrum** (or rainbow of colors) runs from blue through green, yellow, and orange to red.

5.   The **wave-lengths** for the visible spectrum run from 400 **nanometers** (blue) through 760 nanometers (red).

6.   Beyond the blue end of the spectrum lie the **ultra-violet** ("black light") rays and the X-rays. The wave-lengths of these waves are less than 400 nanometers.

7.   Beyond the red end of the rainbow lie the heat waves. The wave-lengths of these waves are more than 760 nanometers.

8.   Your eye is something like a color TV camera. Light enters your eye through the **cornea** and **aqueous humor,** then passes through the **pupil,** the **lens,** and the **vitreous humor.** The light then strikes your **retina,** which is where sight actually begins.

9.   Muscles attached to your lens help focus the visual input so that it falls squarely on your retina.

10.   The retina is the inner surface of the hollow eyeball.

11.   The retina contains your **visual receptors** the **rods** and **cones**—which have within them photo-sensitive chemicals that respond to light by firing off a message to the **visual centers** of your brain.

12.   The cones are sensitive to all the colors, including whites and grays. The rods see the world only in shades of gray.

13.   In the center of your retina is a small pit called the **fovea** that contains only cones. Your vision is at its sharpest when the visual image falls on the fovea.

14.   Near the fovea is the **blind spot,** which contains no visual receptors. The optic nerve, which runs from your retina to your brain, exits from the eyeball at the blind spot.

15.   What you see, and the speed with which you react to visual inputs, is affected by the amount of **pigment** in your irises. Blue-eyed

people tend to have excellent **peripheral vision,** while dark-eyed people tend to respond more rapidly to visual stimulation.

16. Near-sighted people typically see close objects more clearly than they do far objects.

17. Far-sighted people typically see distant objects more clearly than they do objects that are close to their eyes.

18. We all tend to become more far-sighted as we age.

19. A person with normal **visual acuity** (keenness of vision) is said to have **20/20 vision.** This means that the person can see at a distance of 20 feet (6 meters) what the average person can see at a distance of 20 feet.

20. The eye has a tremendous ability to adjust to the amount of light available to it. When you sit in the dark, your rods and cones adapt to this decrease in light intensity. **Dark adaptation** is mostly complete in about 30 minutes or so.

21. Your rods are more sensitive at night (or in dim illumination) than are your cones. If your rods don't function as they should, you are likely to have more trouble seeing in the dark than the normal person—a condition known as **night-blindness.**

22. Because your rods are **color-blind,** you will have difficulties seeing colors accurately in dim illumination or at night.

23. Colors have both **hue** (red, green, blue, yellow) and **saturation.**

24. The more intense or rich a color is, the more saturated it is. Black, white, and gray are completely **desaturated colors.**

25. If a person can see a color, but only when it is very intense, the person is said to be **color-weak.**

26. If a person cannot see a particular color no matter how intense it is, that person is said to be **partially color-blind.**

27. Men tend to be "color-weak" and "partially color-blind" more frequently than women.

28. The most common form of partial color-blindness is the failure to see reds and/or greens as people with normal color vision do.

29. Albino humans and animals lack the pigments necessary for normal color vision. They therefore see only with their rods and are **totally color-blind.** They are also totally blind in their foveas.

(Continued from page 200.)

(Continued from page 200.)

"All right, class. Why do you think Johnny W. couldn't see the ball when it was thrown to him?" Mrs. Carson asked her students.

After a pause, Martha held up her hand. "Let's see if we can review the clues you gave us. You said the light hurt his eyes, that he had to wear sunglasses outdoors, and that he was behind in his reading scores. Sounds like he had a visual problem of some kind."

"Beautiful," Mrs. Carson said, smiling in agreement. "Go on. What else?"

Bill stuck up his hand. "The kids called him Bunny Rabbit because he looked so pale. And you mentioned that his hair was cotton white. Mrs. Carson, could Johnny W. be an albino?"

"Good thinking! Yes, Johnny W. was an albino."

Alice became furious. "But you could have told us that! Anybody with their eyes open would have noticed that right away!"

"Perhaps. Perhaps not. When he wore his dark glasses, you couldn't see the pink color of his irises. With his glasses on, Johnny appeared to be a very pale but very normal blond child."

Alice persisted. "But it wasn't fair not to tell us. That was his whole problem!"

Mrs. Carson shook her head. "No, I don't think so. His problem was that people don't understand the visual difficulties that an albino has. His parents didn't understand; Johnny didn't understand; and neither did the other children in school."

"But . . ." said Alice angrily.

"But what if he hadn't been an albino?" Mrs. Carson continued, over-riding Alice's protest. "What if a normal-looking boy with brown eyes and dark hair came to you in tears? What if he complained that his art teacher had thrown him out of class insisting that the boy had no talent? What might his mismatched clothes have told you about him then?"

"Of course," said John. "He was color-blind!"

Mrs. Carson smiled her approval. "At least one boy in 20 has problems identifying colors correctly, and most of them don't realize their handi-cap when they're in elementary school. Would you expect a color-blind boy to do well in art class? And shouldn't you keep your eyes open for such clues?"

Bill frowned. "I still don't see why he couldn't see the ball. Was it a funny color or something?"

"Anyone who is totally color-blind has frightful visual problems. The entire center of Johnny's visual world was blank, because the color receptors are located in the center of the retina. When Johnny tried to look straight ahead, he was functionally blind. He could only see things out of the corner of his eye. If you threw a ball to him, it would simply disappear when he tried to focus on it."

The class thought about that for a moment.

Then Martha asked, "What did you tell him to do?"

Mrs. Carson leaned back against the desk again. "What would you have told him to do? You're the ones learning to be counselors."

Martha considered the matter, then continued. "I would have told him to get the hell out of baseball. Find something else that he could do that would make him popular with the other kids."

"Something he could do indoors or at night, so his eyes wouldn't hurt," said Bill.

"A musician! He could learn to play the guitar, and then perform at dances and parties and things like that," said Alice, recovering nicely from her anger.

" Yeah, that way he could wear his shades even when he was inside," said John. "If anybody asked him about it, he could just say that he was practicing to be a musician, because they sometimes wear dark glasses even in the middle of the night."

"And lots of rock stars wear wild-colored clothes anyhow, so he wouldn't have to worry if his socks didn't match," said Martha.

Mrs. Carson closed her eyes as if to picture the scene in her mind. "I see what you mean," she said. "A colorful solution to a case of black-and-white vision!"

Recommended Readings

Carterette, Edward C., and Morton P. Friedman, eds. *Handbook of Perception, Vol. 5* (New York: Academic Press, 1975).

Geldard, R. Frank. *The Human Senses,* 2nd ed. (New York: Wiley, 1972).

Teevan, Richard C., and Robert C. Birney, eds. *Color Vision* (Princeton, N.J.: Van Nostrand, 1961).

PART TWO Sensation and Perception

Sensory Deprivation and Cortical Arousal

Did You Know That . . .

When you are deprived of your normal sensory inputs, you may lose voluntary control of your thoughts and actions?

A person who gains complete control of your sensory inputs can brainwash you into making profound changes in your personality?

A person who gains even partial control over your inputs can often indoctrinate you into accepting new beliefs and attitudes?

Human subjects who underwent sensory deprivation experienced hallucinations, distortions in their body images, and long "blank periods" in which they couldn't really think at all?

One scientist who immersed himself in a tank of warm water for several hours believed that he had returned to the womb?

Sensory inputs reach your brain by two pathways, the straight-line system and the reticular activating system?

The reticular activating system keeps the rest of your brain alert?

Sensory deprivation can be used as a type of therapy to help normal people lose such bad habits as smoking and overeating, and can help autistic children learn to adjust to their social environments?

"Black Boxes and Womb Tanks"

Philip Cassone laughed when they shut the door. This was going to be a cinch, no doubt about it. Imagine those crazy psychologists wanting to pay him 20 dollars a day for just doing nothing!

Plus room and board!

He just might stay here for weeks, maybe for months. Let them go bankrupt, as far as he was concerned.

The bed Phil was lying on was narrow but comfortable. The long cardboard tubes into which his arms were stuck were annoying, but Phil was sure he could adjust to them with little difficulty.

The goggles that he wore let in some light, but the glass was milky and translucent and he couldn't make out any details of the room he was in, except that the walls were painted black. He knew the room was small, though—maybe 2 meters wide by 3 or 4 meters long. Big enough to live

in if you didn't move around very much, and the crazy psychologists were paying him for not moving.

All Phil could hear was the quiet, gentle, soothing whirr of an air-conditioning unit. Black and quiet, that's what the room was.

Phil yawned, stretched a little on the narrow bed, and relaxed. A lead-pipe cinch, that's what it was going to be. He drifted off to sleep.

Some time later, Phil awoke. He had a moment of panic when he couldn't remember just where he was. But then he smiled and relaxed.

"Inside the little black box," he said to himself. That's where he was. He must have slept for, oh, maybe 3 hours. Or was it more like 4 or 5? Phil couldn't tell exactly, and that bothered him a bit.

How long had he been in the room so far? Maybe 6 hours? How much had he earned? Maybe 5 dollars? Not bad for just sleeping.

A few minutes later, Phil decided that he needed to go to the bathroom, so he yelled out, "I want to go to the john." There was a microphone in the room that carried his voice to the crazy psychologists in the next room. If they were still there, like they said they would be. They could talk to him too, over a loudspeaker hanging on the wall, but so far they hadn't said anything at all.

The door opened and someone came in and touched him on the shoulder. Phil hopped out of bed and almost fell flat on his face. Funny he should be so clumsy. Maybe he was still half asleep. He spoke several times to the person leading him, but got no answer. After he had urinated, he was led back to the little black room by his silent escort. Strange the man wouldn't talk to him . . . if it was a man.

Phil lay down on the bed again and started to think. He thought about his school work; he thought about his family; he gave serious attention to several girls he had encountered in recent weeks. And then, when he ran out of things to think about, he started over again.

It was all getting pretty boring. Maybe he'd only stay in the room for a few weeks after all, until he had earned enough money to make a down payment on that car he had seen in the showroom. What did that car look like anyway? He could barely remember . . .

"Phil, are you awake?"

The voice sounded remote and at first he couldn't be sure that he wasn't imagining it.

"Hello, Phil, are you awake?"

He told the crazy psychologist he was, but his voice sounded odd and hollow to him.

"Okay, Phil, I want to give you some tests. Are you ready?"

Phil said he was.

The psychologist's voice came out of the black haze again. "All right, let's start with the letter H. How many words can you think of that begin with the letter H? Don't use verbs and don't use proper names. Go ahead and start now."

H? What begins with H? Hell, for one thing. And Horse and House and Heart and Hurt and Help. And Hungry. Am I hungry? Maybe that was what was wrong. What will they give me for dinner? Maybe a hamburger. Oh, yes. Hamburger begins with H. And Horse. No, I said that. Horse-meat in the Hamburger . . .

PART TWO Sensation and Perception

What else? Celery? No that doesn't begin with an H. Helpless? Honda. No, that's a proper name. Hello out there. Funny, there must be more words in the English language that begin with H. Happy? No, that isn't a word, is it? More a state of mind, really. Head! Yes, Head would do.

Then Phil thought and thought, but nothing else popped into his head. Finally he asked, "Is that enough?"

"If that's all you can think of, that's fine, Phil."

He smiled and relaxed. That ought to show them.

My God, it's quiet, he said to himself a few moments later. The silence seemed to stab at his eardrums like an ice pick. How could silence be so loud, so overwhelmingly bright?

And the colors, the sparks of colors. Banners of different colors waving back and forth. The wallpaper was wiggling, writhing, pulsating, just the way it did that time he had foolishly taken that drug his friend Vin had given him.

Oh! What in the world was that sound? A dark green clunking noise. Could it be in the air conditioner? Sounded more like an elephant stomping around. Clunk, clunk, clunk. My God, it was a herd of elephants!

The elephants changed color. Now they were sort of black, with pink and blue and purple . . . elephants moving . . .

No, the elephants are standing still, aren't they? It's the picture that's moving, and the elephants are like cutouts in a moving picture. There they go, over the hill . . .

"Hey. You people listening in. Do you know there's a herd of elephants marching around in here?"

Why didn't the crazy psychologists answer?

And the quiet again. How long has it . . .

"Now, Phil, we have a series of records you can listen to if you wish. Would you like to hear them?"

Records? Why not? Maybe some good rock . . .

But no, it's a voice talking about ghosts. Who the hell cares about ghosts? Dullsville. But at least it's a voice, talking . . .

Yes, play it over one more time. This is getting interesting. Yes, play it again, Sam . . . It sure sounds more sensible this time round. Yes, ghosts are for real. Why hadn't he realized that before? Yes, play it just one more time . . .

"Hey, you people. What time is it? Why don't you answer? Don't you know I can't stay in here too long? Why don't you say something? It's been at least 24 hours, hasn't it? I've earned my 20 bucks, now tell me what time it is . . .

Floating . . . looking down . . . Who was that strange person lying on that little bed down there with the cardboard tubes on his arms? Maybe he was dead and nobody knew it . . .

. . . There's that dark green clunking sound again. They must be letting something else into the room. Last time it was elephants. Wonder what it is . . .

My God, it's a space ship! It's only 6 inches long, but it's a real space ship. How did they manage that? It's buzzing around the room like a Battle Star chasing a . . .

"Hey, you crazy psychologists, what are you trying to pull? Get that space ship out of here! Shooting at me, that's what it's doing. It's shooting laser beams at me!

"Ouch! Oh, my God, I'm hit! Hey, you stupid people, stop that! If you don't stop that, I'll have to come out right away. You know that. What are you trying to do, make me quit? I can't take this much longer. That Battle Star is going to kill me with its laser beams . . .

"Why won't you help me? If you don't do something right now, I'm coming out. Don't you understand, it's your fault!"

Philip Cassone angrily stripped the tubes from his arms and jumped off the bed. He jerked the door open and marched into the room next door where two startled psychologists sat working at a table containing recording equipment.

"You bastards ruined the experiment. You made me come out. Now aren't you sorry you let those elephants and that space ship get at me?"

And then Phil started to cry.

(Continued on page 233.)

Sensory Isolation

Whether you realize it or not, you spend much of your time and energy trying to *predict and control your sensory inputs*. Little wonder that you do, since you can't survive unless you can gain some measure of control over what your environment gives to you. For most of your biological needs can only be satisfied by energy inputs, and most of your intellectual and social needs can only be satisfied by informational inputs.

Even the "joys of doing" can be considered inputs, since it is usually the feedback from your muscle movements (or the effects your actions have on your environment) that you find rewarding. Sensory psychology is primarily the study of *inputs*. Sensory psychology thus tells you a great deal about such "internal processes" as perception, learning, motivation, attitudes, and personality. For you can't begin to grasp what goes on inside your head—what makes you tick—unless you can identify, measure, and, to some extent, control the stimulus inputs that prompt your head to tick the way it does.

If you still doubt that your senses are the window to your mind, ask yourself this question: What would happen to you if, as you were reading these lines, you suddenly lost *all* your sensory inputs?

What would you experience if something unexpectedly blocked off all incoming information from both your body and the outside world? What if you couldn't hear, see, smell, taste, or feel anything at all? How would you know where your arms or legs were? How would you discover whether you were wearing clothes or not, or whether it was hot or cold where you were? How would you react if you couldn't determine whether any parts of your body were moving, or whether you were standing up or lying down?

Cut off from all sensory inputs, you would probably find yourself lost in an empty, senseless space. How do you think you would react to this frightful disaster? Would you panic? And if you did, what would the panic "feel like" since you would be cut off from all the usual reactions your body makes when you experience great fear and anxiety?

"To Wash the Brain"

Now, let's push the nightmare one step further. Suppose that, after you had been floating in a dark, soundless, bodiless **void** for many hours, you

Void. From the Latin word meaning "vacuum." A void is empty space, or a complete absence of something (such as stimulation).

PART TWO   Sensation and Perception

suddenly heard a voice talking to you. If this voice represented your *only* contact with the outside world, and if it spoke in soothing and reassuring tones, what would your emotions be?

And if this voice told you that many of your previous attitudes and beliefs had been "improper" and "incorrect," would you believe the voice?

And if the voice said that you had to clean a great many evil thoughts out of your mind, would you agree to do so?

And if you did all this, would you say that you had been *brainwashed?*

The term **brainwashing** seems first to have been used in print by journalist Edward Hunter in his book *Brain-Washing in Red China,* published by Vanguard Press in 1951. Hunter took the term from the Chinese words *hsi nao,* which literally mean "to wash the brain."

As we will see, the technique the Chinese used to "scrub people's minds" involved isolating the individual from almost all the person's normal sensory inputs. But before we can discuss brainwashing sensibly, we must first gain a better knowledge of the effects of reducing your sensory inputs.

The Consequences of Sensory Deprivation

Whenever you are deprived of the inputs you want or need in life, several things happen to your body and mind. To begin with, your motivational systems are aroused. If you get no food, you become hungry. If you are deprived of **cognitive** inputs, you will hunger for intellectual stimulation. If you are cut off from other people, you will surely yearn for the sight of a familiar face.

The second important consequence of deprivation has to do with your values. The hungrier you become, the more important food becomes to you, the better the food will taste when you finally get it, the more likely it is that you will be willing to work for food, and the more probable it becomes that you will eat new or unusual items. As we know from occasional stories in the newspapers, a starving person will sometimes resort to *cannibalism*—although under normal conditions the mere thought of eating human flesh might make the person violently ill. In short, the greater your need, the more flexible and changeable you are likely to become in your attempts to satisfy that need.

The third consequence of deprivation, highly related to the first two, has to do with the voluntary control you have over your thoughts and actions. Although you may not realize it, your mind and body are so constructed that they *cannot operate normally if you are cut off from your environment.*

You can't make hamburger if you don't have meat to grind, you can't digest food until you've swallowed it, and you can't think about things for very long if you don't have sensory inputs to process.

Deprivation and Personal Change

We are all much more sensitive to the world around us than we usually like to imagine ourselves as being. If another person ever gained *complete* control over your sensory inputs, that person would also gain extensive control over your mind and your bodily reactions—whether you liked it or not. The more the person deprived you of the stimulation you needed, the more eager you would probably become to do whatever was necessary to satisfy your biological, intra-psychic, and social needs. Thus if someone could isolate you completely from your environment, you might indeed be brainwashed into doing or becoming whatever that person demanded.

Technically speaking, you should use the term *brainwashing* only in reference to situations in which the following events occur:

1. An individual is put under almost complete **sensory deprivation** for a period of time.

Even when you can see the world outside, you may still suffer from social isolation.

2. The individual is rewarded with sensory inputs for changing his or her actions and ideas.

3. The individual is punished for misbehavior by having sensory inputs withdrawn.

The term "brainwashing" does *not* apply to any situation in which long-term sensory isolation is not employed. Since it is very unlikely that anyone would be able to isolate you from all your sensory inputs, it is also unlikely that anyone will ever "brainwash" you. However, as we will see, even mild states of social, intellectual, or biological deprivation can make you more amenable to change.

Question: The leaders of many of the "wilder" religious cults often demand that their followers have little or no contact with people who do not belong to the cult. How might this social isolation make it easier for the cult leaders to control the behavior of their followers?

Communist Brainwashing Techniques

US psychologists first became interested in brainwashing in the 1930's, when strange happenings in Russia began filtering into the newspapers. Joseph Stalin was then dictator of the Soviet Union, and during his **reign,** the Russians staged many rather odd political trials. During these trials, some of the most powerful men in the USSR openly confessed that they had been traitors to the Communist cause.

It was commonly thought in the 1930's that the Russian secret police must have used torture, drugs, and hypnotism to get these politicians to degrade themselves in public. But, as it turned out, the Stalinists' primary weapon was *isolating* a man for a long period of time until he had lost all of his personal bearings. Then the man was told again and again that he had to think of himself as a criminal because the Russian government said he was one—and the government was never wrong.

The Chinese Communists did things slightly differently. Beginning in the 1940's, they started locking their political **deviants** into isolated rooms for weeks on end. They gave these prisoners little or nothing to eat or drink and no human contact. A person treated this way was usually told that she or he could escape from isolation after "washing the mind" of unacceptable thoughts. Only when the person's brain had been "cleansed" could the individual hope to be worthy of again returning to Chinese society.

Oddly enough, the Chinese authorities did not consider brainwashing to be *punishment* at all! Rather, they saw it as a kind of "helpful **psycho-therapy**" that could bring a *politically* insane person back to "social health." The Chinese did not restrict their "political psycho-therapy" to their own citizens, however. In the early 1950's, during the Korean War, the Chinese and North Koreans took more than 7,000 US soldiers as prisoners. Of these, some 3,000 men died while in captivity. The remaining 4,000 were kept chiefly in prison camps near the Korean–Chinese border. Many of these men came under strong pressure to "convert" to Communism.

While they were held captive, the US soldiers underwent rather severe *physiological deprivation*—they had little food and little in the way of medical attention. The soldiers also underwent *psychological deprivation*, in that they heard and saw only what the Chinese wanted them to see and hear. The men were allowed to read only books and magazines that praised the Chinese way of life. Mail from home was almost always censored, and the letters were given out to the prisoners only as "rewards" for cooperation—or for spouting back the political **propaganda** that the Chinese tried to teach them.

Brainwashing of US soldiers by Chinese, as depicted in the film "The Manchurian Candidate."

Sidebar (left column):

Reign (rhymes with "pain"). From the Latin word meaning "to rule." Our words "Rex," "ruler," and "royal" come from the same general source.

Deviants (DEE-vee-ants). To deviate is to move away from the "straight and narrow path," or from the accepted way of thinking and acting. When you fight against the government, you are often considered to be a "political deviant." When your sexual behavior departs from the norm, you are often considered to be a sexual deviant—at least within your present culture or society.

Psycho-therapy. "Therapy" means *treatment.* Psycho-therapy is therefore the act or process of treating someone psychologically instead of medically.

Propaganda (prop-uh-GANN-dah). "To propagate" means to spread. When you have children, you propagate the human race. When you give someone a political lecture, you are spreading political propaganda.

The US prisoners were not truly *socially deprived*, however, since they were housed in groups. But the intellectual and physical deprivations were enough so that many of the soldiers did go along with what the Chinese asked them to do—even to the extent of "squealing" on their fellow captives who refused to accept the Communist viewpoint.

Because the soldiers were not *completely isolated* from all inputs, we cannot say that they were *brainwashed*. Nor did the Chinese actually succeed in making many converts to Communism. Of the 4,000 men captured, only 21 chose to remain in China, and several of them changed their minds later on. Careful studies by the US government showed that, once the prisoners were back in their normal environments, almost all of them gave up the beliefs that the Chinese had forced on them during captivity.

Question: Young people who run away to join off-beat religious cults often revert back to their prior beliefs if they are reunited with their families. Can you think of at least one reason why this might be so?

Indoctrination and Re-education

Psychologists often used the term **indoctrination** to refer to attitudinal or behavioral changes brought about in situations involving *partial* isolation. What the Chinese practiced against US prisoners in Korea, therefore, was *indoctrination*—that is, the same sorts of physical, psychological, and social pressures toward **conformity** that are commonplace in Marine and Army camps, in Boy and Girl Scout training, in fraternity and sorority groups, in jails, in radical movements, and in many religious institutions (*see* Chapter 27).

Indoctrination always seems frightening when performed by groups whose beliefs we do not share. When "our side" uses the same persuasive devices, we call it "re-education," and often feel much better about its use.

Sensory Deprivation

The Stalinist political trials, the reports of brainwashing in China, and the indoctrination of US prisoners in Korea had one fairly immediate effect—Western governments became worried that the Communists had discovered some kind of psychological magic.

The Canadians were perhaps the first to react. As early as 1951, the Canadian government commissioned a group of psychologists at Donald Hebb's laboratory at McGill University to investigate the effects of sensory isolation on *attitude change*. While the experiments were supervised by Hebb, the actual work and planning were done by W. Heron, W.H. Bexton, T.H. Scott, and B.K. Doane.

Although this research itself was not classified as secret, the first explanation given was that the Canadians were interested in studying the effects of monotony and isolation on watch-keeping and other such tasks. In fact, this "pretend" reason for the research is fascinating in and of itself.

For centuries, people have often reported undergoing very peculiar psychological experiences when they were accidentally caught in isolation situations. Shipwrecked sailors would, upon rescue, often describe the weird and wonderful hallucinations they had while adrift in the middle of the ocean. Pilots flying thousands of feet above the earth reported what was called a "break-away" effect. After they had been cruising along for several hours, they seemed to lose contact with the earth—and with reality. Sometimes they would break out in cold sweats. At times they would feel that they could no longer trust their eyes or their instruments. And they often reported seeing strange objects flying around them. Many such episodes

Indoctrination (in-dock-tree-NAY-shun). Literally, "to teach" or "to educate." The word often has a negative tone to it, however—implying that the teaching is by discipline, drill, repetition, and punishment for incorrect responses. Psychologists sometimes use the term to refer to situations in which partial sensory deprivation (usually of intra-psychic inputs) is used to motivate a person to change his or her beliefs or attitudes.

Conformity (con-FORM-mitt-tee). From the Latin word meaning "to make into the same shape." When you conform to other people's opinions, you learn to form your thoughts as they do.

ended in crashes, and if the pilot did succeed in landing his plane, he was often psychologically unfit to fly again.

At a more earthbound level, truck drivers rumbling along deserted highways late at night sometimes reported seeing jackrabbits larger than their trucks.

In all of these **bizarre** situations, the person affected was obviously *deprived* of the normal amount of sensory information she or he had come to depend on in everyday life.

The McGill Experiments

When Heron and his colleagues at McGill decided to study sensory deprivation, they began by building a small **isolation chamber** (see Fig. 9.1). They then paid students 20 dollars a day to lie on a small bed, with their arms inside cardboard mailing tubes. The students' eyes were covered by translucent goggles, and their hearing was masked by a noisy air conditioner. The students were fed and watered when necessary, but were asked to remain as motionless as possible during the entire experiment.

Prior to undergoing the sensory deprivation, the student subjects were given a battery of tests and questionnaires. The subjects received similar tests while in the isolation chamber, as well as after the deprivation experience had ended.

While they were in the chamber, the students were exposed to a series of propaganda messages read in a rather boring monotone. These messages concerned such supernatural events as mental telepathy, ghosts, and those noisy spirits called **poltergeists.**

In order to make sure that any changes in the students' attitudes or behavior was due to the isolation, and not merely to exposure to the propaganda, Heron and his colleagues hired a separate group of students to serve as a *control group*. These students simply sat in a quiet room and listened to the propaganda speeches through earphones without undergoing any real sensory isolation.

The results of the McGill experiments were somewhat surprising. To begin with, Heron and his colleagues had expected that most of the subjects would be able to withstand the isolation for several days. In fact, almost half of the students quit during the first 48 hours.

Those who stayed showed considerable intellectual impairment during the sensory deprivation itself and for some hours afterward. Simple prob-

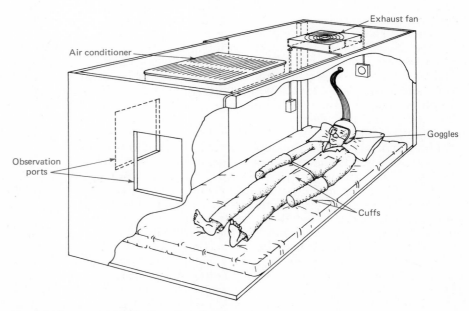

Fig. 9.1. A sensory-deprivation chamber.

lem-solving exercises often seemed beyond the students' mental capacities. Furthermore, they had difficulties with motor coordination, and they did not adapt well to new situations.

Not all of the isolated subjects lasted long enough to be exposed to the dull and repetitious propaganda messages. But those who did asked to hear the speeches again and again and again. These subjects were also much more profoundly affected by what they heard than were the members of the control group.

Of equal interest were the subjective reports the students gave of their experiences while in the "black box." At first, they thought a great deal about their various personal problems. But as time went on, they found such organized thinking more and more difficult. They could no longer concentrate on much of anything, so they just relaxed and let their minds drift.

Eventually most of these subjects experienced "blank periods" during which they simply could not *think* at all. They were conscious—which is to say that they were not asleep—but their minds simply were not functioning in a logical fashion. During these periods, their emotions often ran wild.

All of the students found the sensory deprivation very stressful and even very frightening.

Hallucinations

About 80 percent of the McGill subjects reported some form of *visual hallucination*. Often the first symptom the students experienced was a lightening or brightening of their visual fields, followed by the appearance of dots or lines all around them.

Next, the students would "see" geometric figures that duplicated themselves like wild patterns of wallpaper. Very vivid, cartoon-like scenes were usually next in the hallucinatory sequence. Often these scenes looked like something out of a Walt Disney movie. For instance, one student reported seeing a line of squirrel-like animals with sacks over their backs marching "purposefully" over a hill.

For reasons no one yet understands, the *content* of these hallucinations seemed beyond the control of the subjects. One student, for example, could see nothing but eyeglasses, no matter how hard he tried to think of something else. Presumably some unconscious part of his mind—perhaps the right hemisphere—was producing these vivid scenes. (As we noted earlier, the left hemisphere does not have voluntary control over the thoughts of the right.)

Many subjects reported disturbances in what might be called their *body images*. One student had the impression that his body had turned into *twins*. That is, he was convinced that there was another body lying on the bed with him, and that his own body partially overlapped this "twin."

A second student stated that his mind seemed to leave his body and roam around the cubicle. Occasionally this "free mind" would look back at the "body" lying quietly on the bed to see what it was doing.

Still other students had "floating" feelings, as if their bodies had somehow overcome gravity and were hanging suspended in midair.

The students' abilities to judge distances and to see the world in three-dimensional depth were markedly disturbed both during and after the isolation experience. According to one unpublished account, a rash of minor driving accidents occurred among the students soon after they had left the deprivation chamber. Most of these accidents involved parallel parking. When backing into an empty parking space, the students apparently could not judge where their cars were in relation to other objects.

Once this problem became known, the experimenters warned the students not to drive a car for a period of several days after their isolation period was over. Most of them complied, but one subject reportedly took the warning about *cars* too literally. This man was learning to be a pilot and wanted to get some flying time in, so he asked a friend to drive him to the airport, where he then took off in a light plane. To his dismay, once he was airborne, he found he simply could not perceive up from down. Fortunately, the control tower was able to talk to him by radio and brought him down safely.

Other Deprivation Studies

When the results of the McGill experiments were made public, psychologists in many laboratories in the United States began paying students to stay inside "black rooms" too. The results of these studies soon showed a common trend—the reactions a subject showed to sensory deprivation were mostly a function of what the subject's personality was like prior to entering the isolation chamber.

For example, students judged as being "normal and healthy" tended to *underestimate* the length of time they had been isolated. As one subject put it, "I think I've been here about 36 hours, but I'll say I've only been here for 24. That way, I won't really be disappointed no matter what the time has been." A second student kept track of the time by humming Beethoven's Fifth Symphony over and over again, because he knew it took him exactly 37 minutes to do so. Yet a third student—one with medical training—counted the number of times he breathed and used that figure as a rough index of the passage of time.

However, subjects who were judged as being "somewhat psychologically disturbed" before isolation often *overestimated* the length of time they had been in the cubicle. These subjects also broke off the experiment more readily than did subjects with apparently stronger or more mature personalities. Those subjects who quit in a state of panic often accused the experimenters of using some trick to "force" them to flee the isolation chamber.

Almost everyone who underwent sensory deprivation reported wild flights of fancy, at least during the first stages of isolation. Although the content of these fancies varied widely from one person to another, they were all similar to "tripping" on LSD or mescaline. However, the subjects seldom reported having sexual daydreams. As one subject put it, "I was surprised I couldn't **conjure** up more than I did."

In general, the greater the state of deprivation, the less the subjects were able to tolerate the isolation. If the subjects were allowed to move around freely (in a totally dark room), they could often stand the experience for several days. But if they were forced to remain lying on a bed, the subjects quit much sooner.

The shortest stays of all were reported by a group of scientists who asked their subjects to lie inside an iron lung—that is, a small tank-type **respirator** used by some victims of polio (see Fig. 9.2). Most of the subjects were terrified at being trapped inside such a narrow space and demanded to be released after spending but a few hours in the iron lung.

Lilly's Womb Tank

The man who put himself through the most complete sensory deprivation of all was probably John C. Lilly, a psychiatrist who immersed himself in a tank of water for many hours at a time. Before entering the tank, Lilly donned a diving helmet so that he could breathe under water. Then he submerged himself, hanging absolutely motionless between the surface of the water and the bottom of the tank. Since Lilly kept the water at his body temperature, he had little or no sensory input from his skin receptors. Since he didn't move, he received no feedback from his muscles. And since the diving mask blocked out vision and hearing, Lilly was almost completely isolated from *all* types of sensory stimulation.

Lilly has only recently commented in any detail on what he experienced during his stay in this "womb tank." He does note that after he had been in

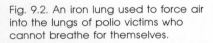

Fig. 9.2. An iron lung used to force air into the lungs of polio victims who cannot breathe for themselves.

the water for an hour or so, he had tremendous urges to move—to twiddle his fingers or twitch his nose. He had to exercise tremendous willpower to resist the desire to move. After two or three hours, however, the urges left him. Then he seemed to slip down into a "warm, dark cave." The cave soon became a "black tunnel with a strange blue light dimly visible in the distance."

When Lilly finally came out of the water, a few hours later, he felt that he had been "born again."

John C. Lilly.

Arousal

As we will see in a moment, by the mid-1970's psychologists had figured out how to use isolation experiences as *therapy*. Nonetheless, the early studies of sensory deprivation might well have remained little more than a scientific curiosity were it not for H.W. Magoun and his colleagues at UCLA.

Magoun was interested in the problem of **arousal**—that is, the physiological and psychological mechanisms that wake us up and keep us functioning at a level of peak performance. At first it seemed that Magoun and his associates were working on quite a different problem than the one that Hebb, Heron, and Lilly were investigating. However, it soon became clear that Magoun's arousal research offered an explanation for what might be going on *inside the nervous system* of humans subjected to sensory isolation.

Arousal. Certain parts of the brain seem particularly involved in waking an organism up or in increasing an organism's activity level. Magoun (mah-GOON) and his colleagues discovered that electrical stimulation delivered to a part of the brain stem called the reticular system greatly increased the arousal level of their animal subjects.

Impinged (rhymes with "infringed"). From the Latin word meaning "to drive things into." To impinge on something is to make an impact on something. Stimulus inputs impinge on your consciousness when you become aware of them as inputs.

Two Important Sensory Pathways

Prior to Magoun's work, scientists generally assumed that sensory information reached your brain in only one fashion. First, external stimuli **impinged** on sensory receptors such as the free nerve endings in your skin. The receptor neurons were excited by this external energy and fired off a message up your spinal cord to the somatic sensory cortex in your parietal lobe. This informational input lets your brain know which receptors had been stimulated. Your brain then processed this information and, if you needed to respond, the motor centers in your frontal lobes caused your muscles to move.

This view of sensory functioning was correct as far as it went, but it pictured the sensory pathways as being "one-way streets." That is, it assumed that information flowed in *one direction only*—from receptors to the brain and then to the muscles (see Fig. 9.3).

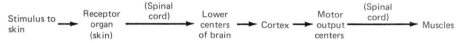

Fig. 9.3. Until recently, scientists believed a stimulus input passed up your spinal cord to your cortex, which processed the input and sent command messages to your muscles. This is the "straight-line sensory system."

What Magoun (and later, many other scientists) showed was that incoming information actually reaches your cortex through *two* quite different pathways. Magoun also proved that your brain exercises considerable *control* over what information gets through it, and over what messages are blocked out in lower centers and never reach your cortex.

Magoun proved that the sensory routes to your brain are not "one-way streets." Rather, they are "superhighways" where messages flow in *both* directions (see Fig. 9.4). These sensory routes also have "toll booths" spotted here and there to keep out unwanted travelers. The road map for this maze of interconnected pathways is far from being completely drawn, but we can at least sketch in some of the landmarks.

When a receptor cell, such as a free nerve ending, fires, a patterned burst of electrical energy passes up your spinal cord to the brain stem (the

H.W. Magoun.

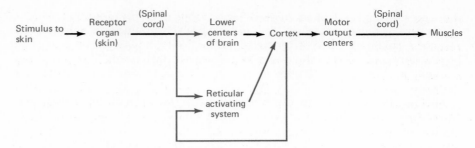

Fig. 9.4. We now know that sensory input messages "split" at the top of the spinal cord. Unless activated by the reticular system, the cortex does not respond to the message coming through on the "straight-line" system. But activity in the cortex can inhibit or enhance activity in the reticular system as well.

Straight-line sensory system. The sensory input pathways that lead from the body's receptor neurons directly to the sensory regions of the cortex.

Reticular activating system (ree-TICK-you-lar). The information contained in sound waves goes from your ear to your temporal lobe by way of the auditory nerve (a straight-line sensory system). The *meaning* of the sound is carried by the auditory nerve. However, auditory inputs are also passed along to the reticular activating system in your brain stem. If the auditory stimulus seems important enough, your reticular system turns on or "activates" your cortex so that you pay conscious attention to the message coming in on the auditory nerve.

RAS. Abbreviation for "reticular activating system." When Magoun and his associates made their first discoveries, they spoke of the "ascending reticular system," which they abbreviated ARS. The name was changed for perhaps two reasons. (1) Most important, it was later found that the reticular system "descends" as well as "ascends"—that is, it sends neural commands down toward the receptor neurons, in addition to sending messages up to the cortex. (2) Amusingly enough, ARS is close to the British word "arse," meaning "ass." For a time, the reticular system was referred to as "Magoun's ARSe."

"stem" of the cerebral mushroom). In your brain stem, however, the road to your cortex "splits" into two pathways.

One road leads directly to the somatic sensory cortex in your parietal lobe. This route is called the **straight-line sensory system,** and it lets your brain know what part of your body has been stimulated and how strong the stimulation is.

A second road leads into the **reticular system,** which gets its name (like the retina) from the Latin word for net or network. The reticular system is a network of cells that begins at the top of your spinal cord and runs up through the brain stem to the lower parts of your cerebrum.

The reticular system acts as an *alerting system* for the rest of your brain—rather like the bell on your telephone. When the reticular system is activated, it rings up your cortex to let it know that an important message is coming through on the straight-line sensory "telephone."

The message from the free nerve endings in your skin will usually reach your somatic sensory cortex *whether or not* your reticular system is aroused. However, unless the reticular system "rings the bell" and activates your cortex, your brain appears to *ignore* any information that comes through on the straight-line system.

The Reticular Activating System (RAS) Magoun's experiments, which demonstrated the function of the **RAS** (reticular activating system), actually involved animal subjects rather than humans. So let us talk about cats first, and people second.

Suppose we implant an electrode in the RAS of a cat. Then we let the animal continue its daily life but, occasionally, we deliver a small amount of electrical current to the cat's RAS. What happens?

If we stimulate the cat's RAS when it is awake and moving about, it reacts as if it had "heard something." That is, the animal suddenly becomes tense and alert, as if its environment had suddenly *changed* dramatically and it ought to pay attention to what was going on around it.

If we wait until the cat goes to sleep, a short burst of electrical energy delivered to the RAS causes the cat to open its eyes and jump up, rather as if someone had stepped on its tail.

If we cut or surgically remove the cat's RAS, it lapses into deep sleep from which it seldom, if ever, recovers. If you shook the cat violently, it would wake up momentarily and move around for a minute or two, but even if it were starving to death it would soon lie down and drift off to sleep.

Next, suppose we put a recording electrode in the somatic sensory cortex of the cat whose RAS we had removed. Then we pinch the animal's tail. The EEG record coming from the electrode would show that the message from the receptors in the cat's tail does in fact reach the animal's brain. So the animal's straight-line sensory system is still functioning properly. However, since there is nothing to *arouse* the animal's brain—to *alert* it that information is coming through that needs to be acted on—the cat remains asleep.

Your own RAS functions much as does a cat's. As you know, we can record the electrical activity that occurs in your brain while you are asleep. Recordings taken from human volunteers suggest that information from almost all your sensory receptors does indeed *reach your cortex* while you are unconscious. But falling asleep involves "turning off" the alarms of the outside world—that is, slowing down the neural activity in your RAS, but not in your straight-line sensory system.

As you drop off to sleep, then, some part of your brain *inhibits* the firing rates of the neurons in your RAS so that the RAS won't bother you except (as we will see) in cases of real emergency.

Anything that affects neural activity in your RAS also affects your consciousness. Many of the sleep-inducing drugs have their anti-transmitter effects on the synapses in the RAS (*see* Chapter 3). And if an accident of some kind damaged your RAS, you would lapse into a **coma** from which you might never awaken—despite the fact that the rest of your brain was in perfect condition.

Coma (ко-mah). An unusual form of deep sleep from which the person usually cannot be easily awakened. Usually caused by drugs, fever, or brain injury.

Attention and Habituation

Since it sits atop your spinal cord—and extends up into your lower brain centers—your RAS is in a perfect position to act as a toll booth or *gate* through which incoming sensory information must pass if it is to have an effect on your cortex (see Fig. 9.5). If the incoming message is trivial or routine, the RAS will allow your cortex to ignore the input. But if the message seems important, the RAS *alerts* the higher centers of your brain and they pay attention to what is coming through on your straight-line sensory system.

What do we mean by *important* messages? Experiments with animals suggest that your RAS can *learn* which stimuli need your instant attention—and which stimuli are unlikely to be threatening or to require a response.

As you read this book, your receptor cells are sending millions of messages per minute through to your brain on the straight-line sensory system. But your RAS is (presumably) telling your cortex that it needn't bother with most of this sensory input. For instance, until you read this

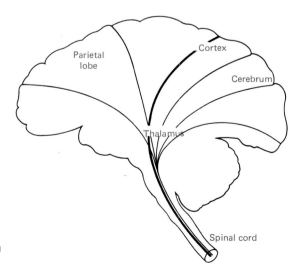

Fig. 9.5. The reticular activating system.

sentence, you probably were not consciously aware that your shoes (or socks) are full of feet, or that your clothes are pressing in on various parts of your skin. Your RAS has *learned* that these signals don't need your **attention** while you read.

But a sudden *change* in the pattern of incoming stimulation (as when a friend shouts at you) is recognized by the RAS as being important information, and it alerts your cortex that an *emergency message* is coming through. Your attention then shifts from vision (reading) to hearing (listening). The words your friend shouts at you are immediately processed by your cortex, and you respond appropriately to the emergency input.

People who live next to a railroad track—or to an airport or freeway—soon *habituate* to the sounds of the passing traffic. But friends who come to visit are often kept awake at night by these noises until their own RAS's learn to ignore them. And if, in a given family, it is the wife's job to take care of the children, she will awaken at night to a child's whimpering while the husband's RAS screens out these stimuli and lets him continue to sleep soundly.

Question: Suppose you are reading something interesting when a friend says something to you. Why do you often have to ask your friend to repeat what was said, even though you know that your friend did in fact say something important?

Cortical Influence on the RAS   The road between the cortex and the RAS is, as we suggested earlier, a two-way street. Early studies on the RAS showed that it had a marked influence on activity in the cortex, but later experiments showed that the cortex has ways of affecting what goes on in the RAS as well.

Whenever you choose to concentrate or focus your attention on something, your cortex tells your RAS not to bother it for a while. Your cortex exerts this control directly by *inhibiting* neural activity in the RAS.

On the other hand, if you decide to cram for an exam by studying all night, your cortex is usually able to keep itself awake by continuing to *stimulate* the RAS—which feeds this stimulation back to the cortex itself.

Stimulus Hunger

Your body has certain physiological needs that you are often only too painfully aware of—a need for food, air, water, sleep, and for a certain range of comfortable temperatures. Thanks to the sensory deprivation experiments, and the research on the RAS, we now know that your nervous system also "needs" a certain constant level of *incoming sensory stimulation* in order to function properly. Psychologists often refer to this need as a **stimulus hunger.**

If you were to take part in a sensory isolation experiment, you would be putting your cortex in as deprived a situation as your body would be if you went without food and water for a long period of time. For without continual alerting from the RAS, your brain simply does not behave as it should. And your RAS is activated primarily by the flow of sensory information along the straight-line sensory system.

At the beginning of a period of sensory deprivation, your RAS would slow down and, if you needed sleep, you would probably drift off into unconsciousness. But once your body rested, you would awaken, only to find that you had absolutely nothing to do. Your cortex could keep things going for a while by engaging in thought or daydreams—*but even thinking is dependent on activity in the RAS.* When you are in isolation, not many messages come through on your straight-line sensory system. Hence your RAS simply cannot do its job of keeping your cortex stimulated into alertness.

Your cortex appears to have built-in mechanisms that force it to take action when it needs sensory stimulation—just as your brain has built-in mechanisms that motivate it when your body needs food or air. For example, when your brain finds itself deprived of stimulation, it tends to "turn up the volume" on whatever inputs it does have available to it. That is, your brain *greatly magnifies* weak incoming sensory signals. And it pays attention to faint stimuli that it might never notice if you were in a stimulating environment.

If these faint incoming signals are vaguely pleasureable, you might experience overwhelming joy. But if the signals are slightly painful, you might experience incredible pain.

As an illustration of the way in which your brain can *intensify* faint sensory inputs, consider the following story told by John C. Lilly. Once when he was floating in his womb tank, the air hose connected to his diving helmet sprang a leak. Very slowly, air began bubbling into the water. Each individual bubble was no larger than those in a glass of beer, and the leak was so small that only one bubble popped out every 15 seconds or so.

Once the bubble was released into the water at the bottom of the tank, this tiny bubble of air drifted upward and struck Lilly on his naked thigh. Lilly reports that when each bubble hit his skin, it gave him a feeling of intense sexual ecstasy much like an orgasm. For several minutes, these bubble-induced orgasms occurred every 15 seconds—one after another after another.

But all good things must come to an end. Eventually the bubbles speeded up to a frequency of one every 5 seconds or so. At this point, the pleasure turned to intense pain—such devastating pain that Lilly had to discontinue that session and get out of the tank. Under normal circumstances, of course, Lilly would probably not have noticed the bubbles at all. (Lilly has recently admitted he was under the influence of LSD at the time, in an attempt to "get his mind to leave his body." Thus we cannot be entirely sure if it was the drug, the deprivation, or—more likely—the combination of the two that caused his intense reaction to such weak stimulus inputs.)

Isolation as a Therapeutic Tool

Because your brain needs a certain level of inputs in order to function effectively, you might well consider a "womb tank" or "deprivation cubicle" something to be avoided at all costs. And you might also assume that the sorts of brainwashing techniques used by the Communists could only be used to harm people.

But most scientific techniques can be used for good purposes as well as for negative ones. Beginning in the 1960's, many psychologists started employing "reduced sensory stimulation" as a type of *therapy* with certain groups of people who needed rather special help.

Drinkers, Smokers, and Over-Eaters

One group of individuals for whom sensory isolation has proved useful are those individuals who need "extra motivation" to change their personal habits. Canadian psychologist Peter Suedfeld has performed a series of experiments in which he has put clients in very restricted environments. Some of these people were overweight and simply could not keep to a diet. Others were heavy smokers who found it almost impossible to give up cigarettes no matter what kind of therapy they tried.

Suedfeld's clients typically remained in a sensory deprivation chamber for 24 hours or so. During this period of time, Suedfeld played them recorded messages aimed at convincing them either to lose weight or to stop smoking. The clients were then given "booster sessions" two months later in which they again spent some time in the chamber. Suedfeld reports considerable success. For example, all of the smokers on which he tried the

Peter Suedfeld.

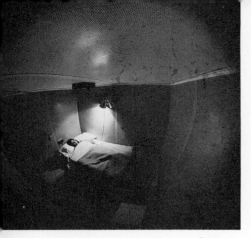

A subject of psychologist Peter Suedfeld in a sensory deprivation chamber.

technique reported a significant reduction in their "craving" for cigarettes, and the majority were able to give up smoking for at least a period of several months.

In another set of studies, psychologists G. David Cooper and Henry Adams worked with a group of 60 people who were heavy social drinkers. Half of the group were men, half were women. The drinkers voluntarily spent some three hours in a sensory deprivation chamber similar to the one used in the McGill studies mentioned earlier in this chapter.

After the subjects had been in the cubicle for 90 minutes, they heard an anti-alcohol message. For half the subjects, this message was *confrontational*. The subjects were told, "If you need alcohol to feel sociable, you're in trouble." The other heard a supportive message that said, "You don't really need to use alcohol as a routine part of your life-style."

Cooper and Adams used several *control groups* of people who had similar drinking problems. One control group heard the messages, but not while in sensory deprivation. A second control group spent time in the deprivation cubicle, but heard no messages. Yet a third control group was given no treatment at all.

According to a report Cooper and Adams made in 1977, the experimental subjects who heard the confrontational message while in the cubicle cut their subsequent drinking by about 30 percent. The subjects who heard the supportive message reduced their alcohol consumption by about 20 percent. The subjects in the three control groups, however, continued to drink about as much as they did prior to the study.

It seems likely that sensory deprivation increases (1) the *attention* that a subject pays to a propaganda message; and (2) the *acceptability* or social value of that message.

Autistic Children

Of all the types of children diagnosed as being "mentally ill," it is likely that the **autistic** child is the most difficult to work with. As we will see in later chapters, these young people act as if they are totally unable to deal with normal society. They are frequently non-verbal, they tend to avoid contact with others, and they usually avert their eyes when you attempt to speak to them.

Autistic (aw-TISS-tic). Autism (AW-tism) is a type of mental disorder found chiefly in children. The autistic child avoids sensory inputs, particularly social inputs, and usually is non-verbal. The autistic child processes inputs chiefly with its right hemisphere.

After spending time in sensory isolation autistic children often are more willing to learn new skills.

Until fairly recently, autistic children were generally thought to suffer from severe emotional disturbances. In the past decade, however, psychologists have begun to suspect that these young people simply cannot "process" incoming information in the same way that normal children do. Recent studies, for instance, suggest that autistic children tend to block out inputs to their left (verbal/logical) hemispheres, relying instead on their right (emotional/perceptual/creative) hemispheres to handle most of their sensory inputs. They often do quite well, however, at right-hemisphere tasks: Psychiatrist Bernard Rimland reports that at least 10 percent of these children show amazing mathematical, artistic, or musical talents. It seems likely, therefore, that much of the autistic child's "withdrawal from society" can be seen as the child's way of *reducing stimulus inputs* so that its brain isn't overloaded with sensory inputs.

Marshall Schechter.

What the normal child views as a stimulating environment, then, the autistic child may experience as **input overload.**

In 1969, psychiatrist Marshall Schechter and his colleagues at the University of Oklahoma Medical Center reported that they had successfully used long periods of sensory isolation as a form of treatment for three autistic boys. Their isolation chamber was a small room with an adjoining toilet. The room was almost entirely bare, but did have a mattress on the floor for the child to sleep on. Both the chamber and the toilet were kept almost in darkness.

Each boy remained in the room by himself for a period of some 40 days. The child was given three meals daily and was cleaned up after each meal. But the staff members did not speak to the child during feeding and cleaning periods.

The Medical Center staff observed each boy almost continuously through observation windows and listened to each of them over a P.A. system. The only social contact the child had was with his therapist, who entered the room twice a day to talk to the boy. Otherwise, the boy spent all his time in a dimly illuminated and very quiet environment.

At the beginning of the study, many of the staff members were highly concerned about the bad effects the sensory isolation might have on the boys. To their great relief, there seemed to be none. Indeed, the boys seemed to relish the experience. Schechter and his colleagues note that, "Each of the boys appeared comfortable and pleased in the experimental room." Each boy spent a fair amount of time laughing and babbling to himself.

During the early part of the experiment, the boys simply refused to leave the room when the door was left open. Later, they seemed to "hunger" for human companionship in ways they seldom had before. They dropped their "defensiveness" toward other people, showed considerably more eye contact, and for the first time in years began to play with and talk to other individuals.

Schechter and his associates believe that the sensory isolation helped these autistic children in two ways. First, it gave them an environment that did not *overload* them with sensory inputs. Thus they could relax and feel comfortable for perhaps the first time in their young lives. Second, once they had dropped their defensiveness toward others, Schechter was able to increase their social inputs *bit by bit*. The boys thus had more than sufficient time to adjust to the increased stimulation.

Since the research of Schechter and his group was reported, sensory isolation had been used successfully to treat autistic children in many other hospital settings.

Isolation Versus Stimulation

At times you may well need a stimulating environment to keep you on your toes. But at other times, when the world threatens to overload your neural circuits, you might wish for a **sanctuary** where you could cut off most sensory inputs.

Input overload. A General Systems term meaning that you are experiencing so many inputs that you cannot handle or process them all. Input overload leads to stress. Sensory deprivation is the opposite sort of stress-inducing—input *underload.*

Sanctuary (SANK-tchew-ar-re). From the Latin word meaning "church" or "holy place." In the old days, anyone escaping from the wrath of the king could save her or his life by taking refuge in a church or holy place, since it was forbidden to arrest or kill someone in "God's Place." Thus "to take sanctuary" means to find some place where you will be safe from stress and various kinds of input overload.

Perhaps the important thing is that you should be able to *choose* which sort of environment suits you at a given moment. That is, you shouldn't be forced to undergo either too much or too little stimulation. And if you choose to isolate yourself for a period of time, you should surely have control over any "propaganda messages" that were piped into your sanctuary.

Sensory deprivation is a useful scientific tool that has taught us much about the functioning of the human nervous system. It is also part of a "mind-change" technique that has been humanely used to help autistic children, and inhumanely used to "brainwash" people into accepting various political or moral viewpoints.

The technique itself is thus *morally neutral.* It is the ways in which we employ the technique that are *ethical* or *unethical.* However, as is usually the case with scientific knowledge, we cannot hope to make moral judgments about the potential value or dangers of the technique unless we first take time to view the scientific data objectively and dispassionately.

Now that we have learned something about how your brain takes in some information, and blocks out other inputs, perhaps it is time to find out how your brain processes or *perceives* these inputs after they reach your cortex.

Summary

1.   Humans separated from their usual social environments soon stop functioning normally. Both the Chinese and Russian governments have, in the past, made use of this fact to **brainwash** or **indoctrinate** people into changing their attitudes and behaviors.

2.   Brainwashing consists of putting a person into total isolation **(sensory deprivation; sensory isolation)** for a period of weeks or months until the person is so desperate for inputs that he or she will often admit to past "mistakes" and promise to behave differently in the future.

3.   In contrast to brainwashing, indoctrination often involves isolating groups of people (rather than individuals) from their usual environment, lecturing them about what they should become, and then rewarding any movement toward the indoctrinator's desired goal.

4.   Worried by these Communist techniques, Western scientists began in the early 1950's to study the effects of isolating normal people from most incoming **sensory stimulation.**

5.   At McGill University, researchers paid male student volunteers to lie blindfolded in a tiny room or **isolation chamber** for as long as they would stay. The results of these experiments were as follows:

   a.   The subjects soon lost much of their ability to "think straight."

   b.   They began having **hallucinations,** or feeling they were floating in air looking down at their bodies on the bed below **(body images).**

   c.   The longer and more severe the deprivation, the worse the subjects performed.

   d.   The subjects became so desperate for inputs that they accepted uncritically much of what they were told by the experimenters.

6.   In an attempt to get complete sensory isolation, John C. Lilly immersed himself in a tank of warm water **(womb tank)** and floated there for hours on end. While in the water, Lilly felt as if he had returned to the womb, and that getting out of the tank was like being born again.

7.   The sensory isolation experiments suggest that your cortex cannot function properly without continual input from your sensory receptors.

8.   Sensory signals reach your cortex by two separate pathways. The **straight-line sensory system** carries messages directly from the receptor neurons to your cortex. The **reticular activating system (RAS)** evaluates

these messages before they reach the cortex. If the message is important, the RAS "activates" your cortex by sending it "alarm messages."

9. If an organism's RAS is surgically removed, the organism lapses into a **coma** from which it never recovers.

10. Your RAS both arouses your cortex and directs its **attention** to certain stimulus inputs.

11. When you are isolated from environmental changes, your RAS slows down, and so does your cortex. When isolated from inputs, your brain either goes to sleep or intensifies whatever incoming messages are available to it.

12. Sensory deprivation has been used successfully to help people stop smoking, lose weight, and reduce their drinking.

13. **Autistic children** seem to process incoming information primarily with their right hemispheres. They are often creative, but lack normal emotional control. Their "withdrawal from society" and speech problems suggest they may suffer from **input overload** to their left (speaking) hemisphere.

(Continued from page 218.)

A few hours after he got out of the "black room," Philip Cassone returned to the laboratory to take some more tests. The psychologists explained that they were giving him the tests to find out how soon he had recovered from the effects of the sensory deprivation.

When he took the tests again, Phil did much better than when he had taken them in isolation. Although, to be truthful, he still didn't seem to be as sharp as he usually was. Obviously some of the effects were still lingering on. But the psychologists assured him that within a few days he would be as good as ever.

"How did I do as a subject?" Phil asked the man in charge, when the tests were done.

"Let's see," the man said, putting down his pipe and checking the records. "You stayed in for about 26 hours. That's about average. Not bad at all."

Phil was annoyed. He had hoped to do much better than average. He turned to leave in disgust, when he spotted a tape recorder sitting on one of the tables.

"Did you record my voice?" Phil asked.

The psychologist put his pipe in his mouth and nodded gravely.

"Could I listen to some of it?"

The man picked a tape up off the table, put it on the machine, and started the tape in motion.

Phil was shocked to hear the way his voice came out. "Do I really sound like that?"

When the psychologist again nodded soberly, Phil paid even closer attention to the tape. He heard himself demand to know what time it was, heard himself insist that the psychologists talk to him, listened to his scream that if they didn't say something right away he was coming out.

And then he heard a door open and his voice come faintly from a distance . . . "You bastards ruined the experiment. You made me come out."

Phil blushed. "Did I really call you guys bastards?"

Again the psychologist nodded his head slowly in agreement.

Phil groaned. It was the first time he had ever called a professor such a name—at least to his face. "I must have been deprived of my senses to have done something like that," Phil said.

The psychologist just puffed on his pipe and smiled.

Recommended Readings

Burgess, Anthony. *A Clockwork Orange* (New York: Ballantine, 1965).

Koestler, Arthur. *Darkness at Noon* (New York: Modern Library, Inc., 1946).

Solomon, Philip, ed. *Sensory Deprivation* (Cambridge, Mass.: Harvard University Press, 1961).

Suedfeld, Peter. *The REST Cure: Restricted Environment Stimulation Therapy* (New York: Wiley-Interscience, in prep.).

Vernon, Jack. *Inside the Black Room* (New York: Clarkson N. Potter, Inc., 1963).

Visual Perception

Did You Know That . . .

Perceptions are made up of sensory inputs plus the meanings your brain assigns to these inputs?

A person born blind who recovers sight as an adult has great difficulty in recognizing people's faces?

You probably learn to judge distances by moving about?

If you look at two unfamiliar objects that are the same distance from you, the larger will usually appear closer?

You tend to see all objects as appearing on a background of some kind?

You typically group objects together according to such principles as proximity, closure, and continuity?

Infants usually prefer to look at human faces rather than at random visual patterns?

Infants seem innately able to recognize the dangers of approaching cliffs or sharp drop-offs?

Blind children are slow to build up an adequate concept of themselves?

The pupils of your eyes often open wider when you are staring at something of interest to you?

Your brain may suppress inputs that disturb or annoy it?

Since you "see" what you expect to see, you view the world through very biased eyes and seldom perceive things as they actually are?

"Great Expectations"

The Professor was sitting on a large box, cursing like a trooper and sweating like a stallion. There was several other boxes stacked nearby, all of them covered with address labels. On the smallest label of all there was just room for

> Dr. M.E. Mann
> Dept. of Psych.
> Univ. of the Mid-West, USA

Moments before, a group of porters had unloaded the boxes from an ancient pickup truck and trundled the cartons inside the airport, dumping them near the Customs office.

Outside the airport the African sun shone fiercely, roasting any man or beast foolish enough to venture forth unprotected. Even inside the airport building the temperature was nearly 40°C, reason enough for the Professor's clothing to be soaked with sweat. The cursing was no doubt due to the fact the Professor Mann was going home royally frustrated.

 A small, dark man walked briskly out of the Customs office and headed toward Mann. Despite the heat, the little man's expensive suit and his silk shirt and tie looked as crisp and elegant as if he were ready to pose for a fashion ad.

"Ah, my dear Professor, all is in order, all is in readiness," the man said in an elegant tone of voice. "I assure you that we will tuck your boxes of scientific equipment on the plane as gently as a mother tucks a child into bed. Let no one say that the Republic of Lafora treats visiting scientists shabbily. Now, perhaps we might repair to what passes for a cocktail lounge in this ancient airport. I am certain that the limited budget of the Ministry of Science and Technology can be stretched to provide us with a glass or two of cheer while we await the arrival of your jet."

Mann's response was sharp and unprintable.

"Ah," the small man replied. "You are still angry with us because we cannot approve your venturing into our back country to complete your research. But surely, my dear Professor, we have argued this out at length before, and you understand my country's position. We are responsible for your safety. Our nation is large, poor, and only recently liberated from colonial rule. We have not yet found the resources to bring the benefits of civilization to all our people, and the tribes that you wish to study are still little more than savages."

The Professor made a savage remark.

"No, no," the small man continued hastily. "We could not in good conscience let you go among those tribes unprotected, for they would surely murder you. Your research grant is not of sufficient magnitude to allow you to hire a private troop of soldiers to protect you. And, as you know, all of our military personnel are required at our borders at this dangerous time in our nation's existence. Now, come and have a drink and soothe yourself while we wait . . ."

Mann interrupted. "Oh, come off it, Freddie. All this formality and politeness is just a cover up for the truth. It's prejudice. Pure and simple prejudice. You're a city-born, Oxford-educated, wealthy, sophisticated man. You hold two cabinet posts in the Laforan government. You've been wined and dined in half the capitals of the world, but I'll bet a year's pay that you've never broken bread with one of your backland natives. If they occasionally do away with one of your tax collectors or military types, I don't doubt they've been provoked into doing so. But *murderers*? No, that's pure, superstitious prejudice on your part. I've talked to those natives, and many of my anthropologist friends have been out there. You don't understand the backlanders, so you perceive them as savages. The truth is that they're frightened to death of you city people."

The sharply dressed Minister of Science and Technology began to sweat a little. "My dear Professor, I took your case to the highest authorities in my government, and the answer was no. Absolutely not. What more can I do?"

"You could have pleaded my case with the President himself, that's what," the irate American continued.

"Our great leader is too busy to concern himself with such trivial matters. As you no doubt are aware, we are threatened by enemies on all sides. The President must plan strategy, he must alert our populace to the constant dangers around us. Even though you are a noted scientist from a country that has long supported our freedom and independence, I would not dare bother the President with such minor problems at this time."

Mann laughed sharply. "That's hogwash! You still see the world in terms of absolutes, in blacks and whites. You wouldn't dare turn down my request if your native prejudice wasn't so great that . . ."

The scream of a shrill siren interrupted them. A large black automobile screeched to a halt in front of the airport, and out popped a huge man dressed in the uniform of a Laforan general. The big man came striding into the building at top speed. Then, catching sight of the Minister and Mann, the General rushed up to them.

"Ah, Freddie," said the General, "it's good to see you. We have a terrible emergency on our hands. Perhaps you can help." Freddie quickly introduced General Chambro, head of security for the Republic of Lafora, to Professor Mann.

"Charmed, I'm sure," the General said, bowing slightly to acknowledge the American's presence. Then he continued in an excited tone of voice, "Freddie, the Snake is coming!"

Freddie looked puzzled. "The Snake?"

"Yes, on the next airplane. We just got the message from our agents in Paris. They're sure he's coming to kill the President! You must help us figure out what to do!"

"Well, why don't you just arrest this 'Snake' as soon as he gets off the airplane?" asked the American in a matter-of-fact tone of voice.

"I'm afraid you don't understand," the General said, giving Dr. Mann a withering look of contempt. "The Snake is the best-known killer in the world, responsible for dozens of the foulest political assassinations you could imagine. He's been hired by one of the enemy states on our borders, because they know our beloved leader is all that holds this poor country together." The General took out a large, white handkerchief and began mopping his face.

Freddie began to fret. "Yes, but Chambro, why don't you follow the good Professor's advice and merely arrest the Snake as soon as he lands?"

The General shook his head. "You don't understand either, Freddie. The problem is, we simply don't know what the Snake looks like! Not a jot or tittle of information about this assassin do we have. Is he young, old, tall, short, fat, skinny? He's done his murders all over the world, but no one has ever seen him. All we know is that he usually kills his victims by injecting snake venom into them with a fang-shaped needle. The victim dies in horrible convulsions. And to arrange to arrive on this plane! No wonder they call him the Snake!"

Freddie paled visibly during the General's speech. Turning to the American, he said quietly, "There is something you don't understand, Dr. Mann. This particular flight brings to Lafora almost a hundred of the biggest munitions dealers in the world. They are wormy characters, all of them. But we need their wares badly since we refuse to accept military supplies from any of the major powers. So we spread the word that we wished to buy guns, and chartered a special plane to bring in from Europe anyone interested in selling us weapons. That is one of the reasons I am at the airport now. To greet these men and make them welcome. If we treat them badly . . ."

The General interrupted. "And we cannot check out their passports because most of them travel incognito anyhow—and probably on forged or illegal identification."

"What about giving them a lie detector test?" Freddie asked.

"They wouldn't submit to such a test, of course," said the General contemptuously.

"And the lie detector isn't that accurate anyhow," the American added. "It measures emotionality, not truthfulness. And I'd guess that your 'Snake' isn't exactly the sort who would lose his cool very readily."

"Too true," said the General, and mopped his face again. "But we must find some way of separating the Snake from—er, the worms, or we are in grave danger."

For several seconds the three of them stood silently, lost in thought. Then Freddie cleared his throat and ventured a question. "Professor Mann, you are an expert in the field of perceptual responses. You told me once you are wished to give certain tests to our backland natives that would tell you a great deal about their minds, even if they did not understand the purpose of the tests, and even though you could not speak their language. I don't suppose that now . . ."

Professor Mann was suddenly all business. "Yes, Freddie, it might work. We could set up my equipment right here in the airport and test each person as he or she gets off the plane. I would have to draw up some new stimulus cards, but that shouldn't take long. Of course, I don't guarantee anything. The error rate is really very high, you know, and I could easily make a dreadful mistake. But if you're really desperate, perhaps it's better than nothing."

The General looked confused. "I don't understand . . ."

Freddie turned to the military man and said, "You aren't expected to understand—this is a matter for scientists such as Dr. Mann and myself. We will screen the men on the plane with the Professor's equipment. You have your soldiers standing by, looking as innocent as possible. When we detect the Snake, we will give you a signal and you must move in for the arrest at once. More than that, you need not know."

"But what will we tell the arms dealers?" the General wailed. "They will want an explanation . . ."

"We will say that Paris has reported an outbreak of a highly infectious eye disease, and we must check each person on the flight to make sure they are not carrying the illness," Dr. Mann said brusquely. "I will put on a white uniform and be very efficient about it all."

At this final comment, Freddie smiled broadly. "You are a positive genius, my dear Professor. We will do just what you say!" And then he turned to some porters standing idly by. "Here, you men! Help us open these crates and set up this equipment!"

(Continued on page 259.)

Perceiving the World

As we noted in Chapter 7, when it comes to perception, the eyes have it. But your eyes are more than "the windows to your soul." They are also the main sensory route by which you acquire information about the world around you.

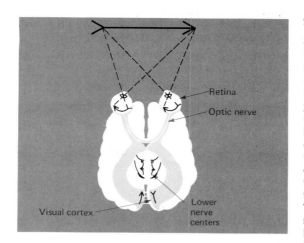

Fig. 10.1. The pathways of vision. Note that part of each path crosses over from one eye to the opposite part of the brain.

Sensations (sen-SAY-shuns). Neural messages from your sense receptors that are triggered off by changes in your external or internal (bodily) environment. When you hear a sound, for instance, the sound waves act as a stimulus to the hair cells in your inner ear. Your hair cells respond to this external stimulation by firing off a message that goes along the auditory nerve until it reaches the temporal lobe of your brain. The message remains a relatively meaningless sensation until it has been "processed" by your brain. Sensations are thus the "raw stuff" from which perceptions are formed. Also called "sensory inputs."

Scanned (rhymes with "canned"). From a Greek word meaning "to trap." As used today, "to scan" means to inspect closely.

Images. As used in this chapter, the term "images" means memories of past experiences. If you close your eyes and imagine what your family pet looks like, you have called to mind an image or memory of the animal.

Perception (per-SEP-shun). The process of matching sensations with images. "To perceive" usually means to experience something in a meaningful way, or to recognize something.

Percept (PER-sept). The end product of the process of perception. Anything that you recognize, experience, or understand—or something whose future behavior you can predict.

When light strikes the retina in your eye, it triggers off a wave of neural activity that passes along the optic nerve to your brain. Sensory inputs from your eyes—or from any of your sense receptors—are called **sensations.** These sensations have little *meaning* in and of themselves, however, until they have been *processed* by your brain—just as radio waves have little meaning until they have been processed by a radio and converted into meaningful sound waves.

When these sensory inputs arrive in your central nervous system, they set in motion a complex chain of neural events. First, the sensations are **scanned** or looked over in your lower brain centers (such as your reticular activating system) to see if they are *important* enough to bother your cortex with. Some processing of information actually occurs in these lower centers (see Fig. 10.1).

Visual Inputs

When a sensory message reaches your cortex, it arrives first at one of the *sensory input areas.* Your visual input areas are in your occipital lobes (see Fig. 10.2). From the visual-input area, the message is next sent to your "association cortex" for handling. It is here, presumably, that many of your *memory circuits* are located—that is, where neural traces or **images** of your past experiences are found. When these image circuits fire, they give a sort of "instant replay" of what you have seen and heard and felt in the past.

Your cortex scans or compares both the past image and the present incoming sensation. If the two are similar enough, your brain "recognizes" what you are looking at as something it has encountered in the past.

If no memory image exists that matches the incoming sensation, your brain "recognizes" that what you are "seeing" is new, different, and has no identifiable name or verbal label.

Perception Begins with Recognition This process of *meaningful recognition* is a large part of what is called **perception.** The thing that you recognize (or realize that you've not seen before) is called a **percept.** We use the term "percept" to refer both to objects in your visual world and to relationships between two or more objects.

Technically speaking, a percept is defined as a set of sensations *plus* the images that the sensory input evokes. At a more practical level, a percept is anything that you recognize, know anything about, experience, or appreciate.

Thus when you say that you *perceive* something, you really mean that: (1) you can remember the past contexts in which this thing appeared; and/or (2) you are experiencing something which is meaningful to you; and/or (3) you have certain expectations about what the thing will be like in the future.

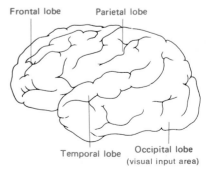

Fig. 10.2. Visual input area.

Perception begins with recognition. After you recognize this as a photo of a boy standing on some steps, you perceive it quite differently.

Perception, then, is your brain's way of coming to grips with the world around it. And, because much of the data about your world came to you through your eyes, perception is primarily a *visual* process. Indeed, when you say that you "see" something, you usually mean that you perceive or understand it.

But perception is also a very *active process*. You do not simply sit at home waiting for the world to come to you. Instead, you go out into the world. You challenge it, and you attempt to find out what it and you are all about.

And one of the main reasons that you engage in all this activity is that your eyes *lie* to you constantly, and your brain knows it. Perhaps an illustration about flying will help you "see" the point about your "lying" eyes.

Plane and Fancy Vision

Suppose it is a beautiful spring day, far too nice to work or to sit in class. While you are trying to decide how best to enjoy this gorgeous gift of nature, the phone rings. A friend of yours has somehow come up with an invitation to go flying, and you're invited too.

An hour or so later you find yourself standing beside a plane not much bigger than a delivery van. Rather small, you think, but then you're comparing it in your mind's eye with the huge jetliners at the other end of the airport.

Moments later you are inside, comfortably strapped into a very large seat. The pilot starts the engine, and the plane moves smartly away from the hanger. It then bumps along a taxi strip heading toward the end of the runway.

You pass very close to a firetruck parked by the edge of the taxi strip. The truck is large and red and shiny. The pilot calls the control tower on the radio, gets permission to take off, checks the engines, and turns the plane onto the end of the runway.

For just a moment you sit there, the plane shaking eagerly as if anticipating its chance to go roaring down the narrow ribbon of concrete that stretches for a mile in front of you. The number "25" has been painted in large numerals on the runway, obviously an identification of some kind. Oddly enough, the tops of the numbers seem compressed and small from where you are sitting in the plane, yet you know that this can't be so.

And then the pilot releases the brake, guns the engine, and you are rolling faster and faster down the runway. As you pass the numbers painted on the concrete, you see that they were normal size after all. Your eyes were just playing tricks on you (see Fig. 10.3). A second or two later the pilot pulls back on the control wheel and the plane leaps eagerly skyward.

Airborne . . .

You climb steadily upward for a few minutes, then the pilot dips one of the wings and turns around in a slow, lazy circle over the airport. Down below you see the firetruck. Why does it now look so tiny and artificial, like a toy that a loving parent would hide under a Christmas tree? And the people—they look more like bugs crawling on the ground than like human beings.

The pilot flies over a nearby town. You see a traffic circle below, the streets radiating out from the center like spokes from the hub of a wheel. A small lake is nestled close to the traffic circle. You happen to know that the lake is almost perfectly round, but from the plane it looks oddly distorted. Maybe it's the height that makes it look so funny.

Fig. 10.3. The same numbers seen from the ground and from the air. The numbers do not change, but your perception of them does.

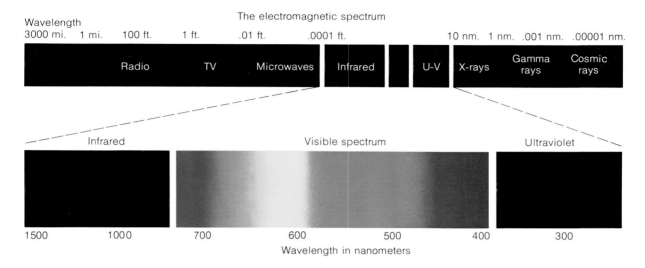

The electromagnetic spectrum

Wavelength
3000 mi.   1 mi.   100 ft.   1 ft.   .01 ft.   .0001 ft.   10 nm. 1 nm. .001 nm. .00001 nm.

| Radio | TV | Microwaves | Infrared | | U-V | X-rays | Gamma rays | Cosmic rays |

Infrared   Visible spectrum   Ultraviolet

1500   1000   700   600   500   400   300

Wavelength in nanometers

PLATE 1 The full spectrum of electromagnetic radiation. The human eye can see only the narrow band extending from 400 to 700 nanometers in wavelength. A nanometer is the equivalent to one-billionth of a meter (one meter=39.37 inches). (From Bourne and Ekstrand, 1976)

PLATE 2 The purple-blue to yellow color solid on the left is viewed from the green side. The yellow to purple-blue range on the right is viewed form the red side. (Munsell Color, Macbeth Division of Kollmorgen Corporation)

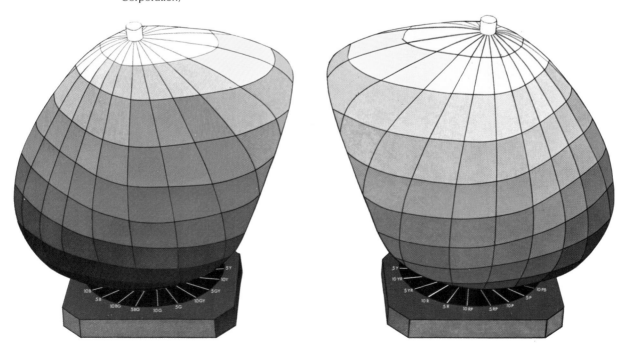

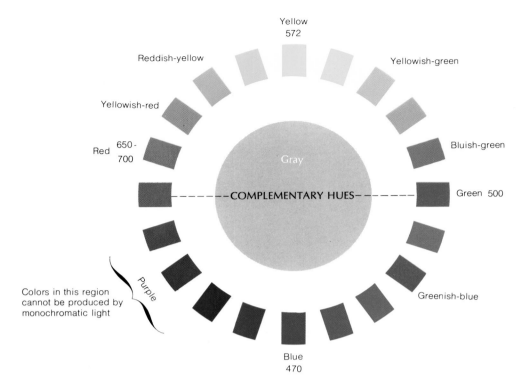

PLATE 3 The color circle illustrates the facts of color and color light mixture. The color names and their corresponding wavelengths (in nanometers) are given along the outside of the circle. Complementary colors are those colors opposite each other in the circle (such as reddish-yellow and greenish-blue); they will result in gray when mixed. The mixing of any two other wavelengths gives us an intermediate color. For example, equal amounts of reddish-yellow and green yield yellow. Some colors such as purple (a mixture of yellowish-red and blue) cannot be produced by a single wavelength, or monochromatic light. By proper mixing of three wavelengths equidistant in the circle (such as blue, green, and reddish-yellow), we can produce all color sensations. (From Bourne and Ekstrand, 1976)

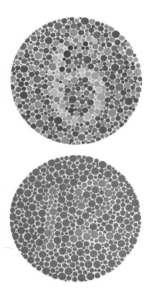

PLATE 4 These two illustrations are from a series of color-blindness tests. In the top plate, people with normal vision see a number 6, while those with red-green color-blindness do not. Those with normal vision see a number 12 in the bottom plate; red-green blind people may see one number or none. These reproductions of color recognition tests cannot be used for actual testing. The examples are only representative of the total of 15 charts necessary for a complete color recognition examination. (American Optical Corporation from their AO Pseudo-Isochromatic Color Tests)

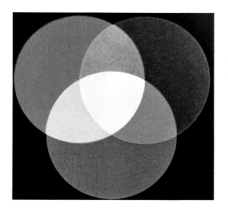

PLATE 5 Look at the design on the cover of this book. A person with normal color vision would see all the colors. At the top left of the page the cover design is reproduced as it might look to someone with red-green color-blindness; and at the top right as a person with yellow-blue color-blindness might see it. At right is a black-and-white reproduction of the cover design as a totally color-blind person might see it.

PLATE 6A Additive color mixture. By shining a light of a single wavelength onto a white surface, we will see the color that corresponds to that wavelength because the surface reflects only that wavelength to our eyes. However, if two lights of different wavelengths are shined on the surface together, the surface reflects both wavelengths which add together to produce an additive mixture. In fact, the complete color spectrum can be produced by mixing three properly chosen wavelengths in correct proportions. (Inmont Corporation)

PLATE 6B Subtractive color mixture. Now if we mix paints (instead of colors) the color we see is produced by subtraction. For example, when yellow paint is mixed with blue paint, the yellow paint absorbs or subtracts non-yellow wavelengths from the blue paint, leaving the wavelengths between yellow and blue—resulting in green. As this plate shows, we can produce a variety of colors by subtractive mixtures of three properly selected paints. (Inmont Corporation)

PLATE 7 Vincent van Gogh's "The Starry Night" (1889) illustrates the painter's imperfect sensory perception. Look at the concentric rings of color around the "starry lights." (Oil on canvas, 29x36¼". Collection, The Museum of Modern Art, New York. Acquired through the Lillie P. Bliss Bequest)

PLATE 9 A sixteenth-century Persian miniature from the manuscript of *A King's Book of King's*, "Zal receives Mihrab's homage at Kabul." The artist's work illustrates the flat perspective often used by Eastern painters. Look especially at the canopy over Zal's head. (From the Collection of Arthur A. Houghton, Jr., 1970; The Metropolitan Museum of Art)

PLATE 8 Jan van Eyck's "The Madonna of Chancellor Rolin," a fifteenth-century painting showing the property of linear perspective. (Shostal Associates, Inc.)

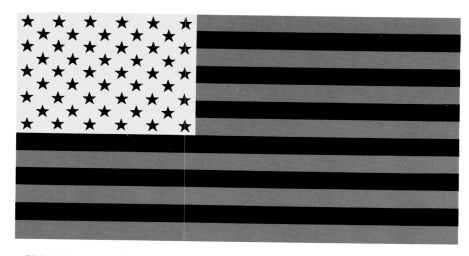

PLATE 10   Stare at the center of this flag for about 30 seconds. Then look at a white wall or sheet of paper. You will see a negative after-image in the colors complementary to those shown here.

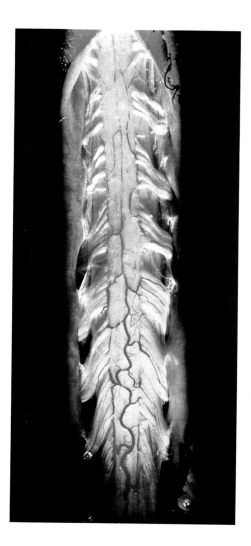

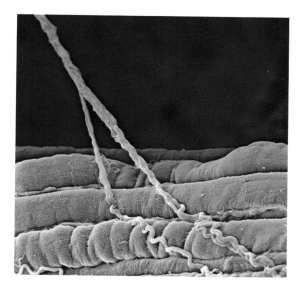

PLATE 11   Photograph of the nerve-muscle synapse. Axonic fibers (upper left) reach down to make a synapse with thick muscle fibers. (Photograph by Lennart Nilsson from *Behold Man*. ©1973 by Albert Bonniers Förlag, Stockholm, published by Little, Brown & Company, Boston, 1974.)

PLATE 12   The spinal cord viewed from the rear, shown with the backbone removed. (Photograph by Lennart Nilsson from *Behold Man*. ©1973 by Albert Bonniers Förlag, Stockholm, published by Little, Brown & Company, Boston, 1974.)

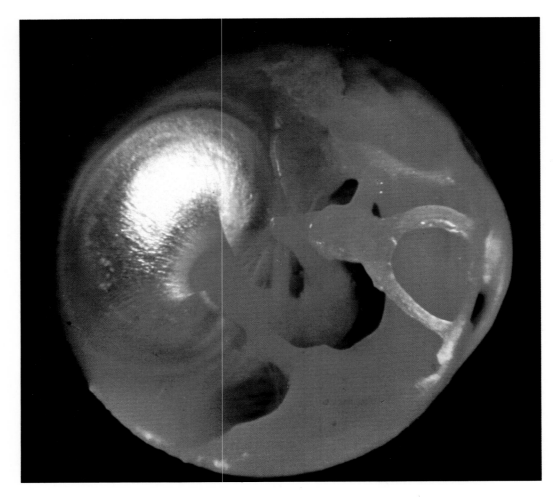

PLATE 13 A cross section of the middle ear. The hammer is connected to the eardrum which is the bright spot in the middle of the photograph. The stirrup, seen on the right, is connected to the oval window. The anvil connects the hammer to the stirrup. (Photograph by Lennart Nilsson from *Behold Man*. ©1973 by Albert Bonniers Förlag, Stockholm, published by Little, Brown & Company, Boston, 1974.)

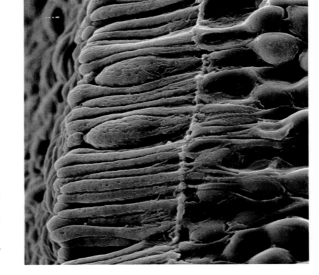

PLATE 14 The rods are the slim, pencil-shaped cells on the left of the photograph; the cones are the two fat cells squeezed in between the rods. Light enters the retina from the right; the back of the eye is to the left in this photograph. (Photograph by Lennart Nilsson from *Behold Man*. ©1973 by Albert Bonniers Förlag, Stockholm, Published by Little, Brown & Company, Boston, 1974.)

PLATE 15   A cross section of the fovea, which is a pit in the center of the retina where vision is clearest. The two black bands to the left are supporting cells that help process visual inputs. The third band of cells from the left is made up of rods and cones. Light enters from the left; the back of the eye is to the right. (Photograph by Lennart Nilsson from *Behold Man*. ©1973 by Albert Bonniers Förlag, Stockholm, published by Little, Brown & Company, Boston, 1974.)

PLATE 16   A cross section of the retina showing all ten layers. The rods and cones are at the bottom. (Photograph by Lennart Nilsson from *Behold Man*. ©1973 by Albert Bonniers Förlag, Stockholm, published by Little, Brown & Company, Boston, 1974.)

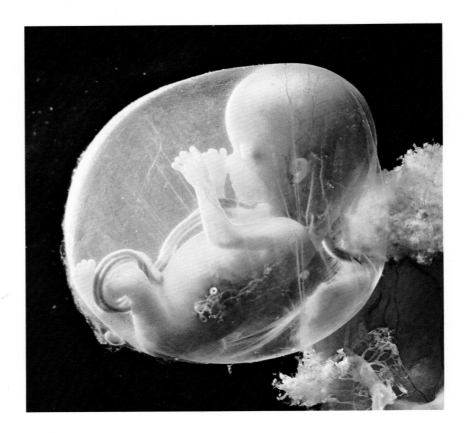

PLATE 17 The human fetus, three months old. It is about three inches (7.6 centimeters) long and weighs about an ounce (28 grams). (Photograph by Lennart Nilsson from *Behold Man.* ©1973 by Albert Bonniers Förlag, Stockholm, published by Little, Brown & Company, Boston, 1974.)

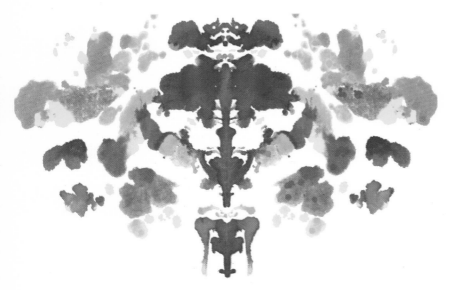

PLATE 18 This water color is similar to the colorful inkblots used in the Rorschach test. A psychologist can gather data about an individual's personality by asking that person to report what he or she sees in the inkblots.

The plane remains the same size, even though if looks tiny from the air.

Next you pass a large warehouse with a name written on top of it in very large letters. Surprisingly enough, you can't read the name very easily because, from where you sit, the letters are upside down.

ŻNMOꓷ ƎꓷISꓷ∩ Ǝ⊃NƎꓕNƎS SIHꓕ
ꓷⱯƎꓤ Oꓕ ꓷꓤⱯH OS ꓕI SI ⅄HM

A few miles farther on, the plane encounters a bank of thick, fleecy clouds. Although you feel rather uneasy about this turn of events, the pilot plunges the plane into the clouds apparently without a second thought.

Suddenly the world around you goes gray, and you can't see a thing. You look straight down, hoping for some glimpse of the ground below, but the swirling gray is featureless. The harder you stare at it, the vaguer and more fog-like the cloud becomes. After a few seconds your eyes begin to hurt from the strain of trying to focus on pure nothingness. But you keep on looking down because you feel safer when you can see the land below.

Then the cloud begins to break up a little, and just for a second you see a patch of ground through a hole in the cloud. Is that a big hill you're looking at? But there aren't any hills like that around this area. Then the hole in the cloud gets larger, and you see that the "hill" was really a huge gravel pit dug deep into the ground. Odd that it should look like a mountain the first time you saw it.

Perhaps sensing your uneasiness, the pilot lets down below the cloud and heads back to the airport. The tower gives you permission to land, and the pilot circles the airport, then lines the little plane up for a straight-in approach to the runway. As the plane glides down closer and closer to the ground, you notice again that the numbers on the runway seem bigger at the bottom than at the top.

A bit of dirt blows into your left eye, so you close it and begin rubbing it. And you suddenly realize that with one of your eyes shut, you have a very difficult time deciding exactly how near you are to the ground. For some reason, with one eye shut, the wide **panorama** ahead of you seems flat, almost like a painting.

But you are rather puzzled by the way your eyes have been acting. Did the altitude somehow affect your vision?

The answer is no—it wasn't the altitude at all. Sometimes it takes an unusual or abnormal situation to help you understand what your eyes are doing *all the time*. Let's see what was going on.

Illusions

When Philip Cassone (see Chapter 9) insisted that he saw a herd of elephants lumbering around the tiny "black room" he was lying in, Phil was suffering from an *hallucination*. As real as the elephants seemed to him at

Panorama (pan-or-RAH-mah). From the Greek words *pan*, meaning "all," and *horama*, meaning "view." A panorama is thus a "view of everything," such as you get from the top of a mountain on a very clear day.

the time, they existed only in his imagination. In more technical terms, Phil's experience was not triggered off by visual inputs—his eyes did not *see* elephants at all, but his brain saw *memory images* that it confused with sensations.

As we said in Chapter 9, your stream of consciousness is greatly influenced by inputs from the world around you. In conditions of sensory deprivation—as well as when drugs upset your neural functioning—the image circuits of your brain are somehow freed from their usual sensory control. Under these conditions, your mind can bring up from its memory files any combination of images that it wishes to recall, and you will often accept the image as the real thing.

A true hallucination, then, is *not* dependent on stimulation from the external world. But this *imagined reality* may appear to be so striking that you accept the hallucination as if it were a *percept* instead of being an *image.*

On the other hand, sometimes the neural circuitry in your brain so distorts the incoming sensory message that you *misperceive* something in the world around you. Such faulty perceptions are called **illusions.**

Some illusions are due to our expectations. For example, suppose you see a spider crawling on the wall just before you get into bed. As you lie awake trying to sleep, a loose thread from the pillow case gently touches your cheek. You may sit up instantly, sure that you have "felt" a spider crawling on your face.

Other illusions are apparently caused by odd imperfections in our sensory apparatus. As the famous painter Vincent van Gogh reached the end of his life, he began depicting shining objects (such as the sun) as if they were surrounded by concentric rings of color. For a long time, art critics were convinced that van Gogh had "broken through to a new level of reality" by letting his imagination run free. If this were the case, then we might say that van Gogh was *hallucinating* the circles around the sun that he so often painted.

But we now suspect that van Gogh suffered from a dreadful disease that was systematically destroying his nervous system. One of the symptoms of this particular illness is that the person's vision becomes cloudy and all bright lights have halos around them. It is likely, then, that van Gogh was suffering from the same kind of illusion that you can experience if you look at a street light on a foggy night, or watch a full moon through a thin layer of clouds. (See color Plate 7.)

Size Constancy

For the most part, your brain does an excellent job of sorting out illusion from reality. As you might guess, though, it takes considerable time and experience for your cortex to build up the necessary neural circuitry so that you can interpret incoming sensory information accurately.

When you were a baby, lying in your crib, your parents dangled toys in front of you. As you reached out a tiny hand to grasp the brightly colored objects, you began learning about distances.

When someone gave you a teddy bear to cuddle, it was so large that it filled all of your visual world. A day or so later you saw the teddy bear far across the room, and now it occupied only a small fraction of your visual world. It looked so much smaller over there—perhaps it had shrunk in size. But no, when you crawled over to it, the bear seemed to grow and grow in size until, when you reached it, the bear was as large as ever. Was this some kind of magic?

When your mother was far away from you, she seemed to be smaller in size than the teddy bear when it was sitting next to you. Yet when your mother handed you the bear, it was obvious that she was much larger than the bear.

Without ever sitting down to think about such things, you eventually learned that *objects remain constant in size whether they are near to you or*

A demonstration of size constancy. Most people see the car as coming closer rather than as changing in size.

Size constancy (KON-stan-see). Your brain gets a rough idea of the physical size of an object by noting how large a visual image the object casts on your retina. Generally speaking, the larger the visual image, the larger the object will be. However, an object very close to you will cast a much larger image on your retina than will the same object if it is far away from you. If the object is very familiar, your brain will interpret any change in the size of the retinal image as a change in the distance the object is from you. This is the principle of size constancy. If the object is unfamiliar, you may overestimate its size if it is close to you and underestimate its size if it is far away.

Depth perception. The ability to see the world in three dimensions. The ability to judge visually how distant an object is from you.

Cornea (CORN-ee-ah). The tough, transparent tissue at the front of the eyeball (see Chapter 8).

far away. It probably seems so obvious to you now that you can't remember having learned that lesson.

And yet, if somewhere along the way you hadn't worked out the principle of **size constancy,** how could you cross a busy street? For instead of seeing cars rushing down on you from all directions, the automobiles might seem to be stationary. And instead of seeing them as moving, you might perceive them as ballooning up in size as they "approached you," and dwindling in size as they sped into the distance.

In short, during your early years you learned that, in many ways, visual size and distance are closely related. When you look at a fire engine a block or so away, the *amount of space* that its image occupies on your retina is smaller than that of a toy fire engine up close to you. But you see the distant firetruck as being large and far away, while you perceive the toy as being small and close up.

The principle of size constancy breaks down in extreme cases, primarily because you haven't had the proper sorts of experiences. When you look down at people and cars from a great height—either from the top of a tall building or from an airplane—the objects below often lose reality. People seem like cardboard cut-outs and automobiles seem like toys.

Construction workers who put up tall buildings are often exceptions, however. It takes a lot of time to construct a skyscraper that is 100 stories high, and the workers move up and down the building daily. So first the workers see the people below from 3 meters (10 feet) or so above ground level. Then, as they add more and more stories to the building, they progressively see the world below from higher and higher elevations—6 meters (20 feet), 15 meters, 50 meters, 300 meters. These construction workers usually report that even from 300 or more meters above the ground, people still look like people to them—and not like the tiny crawling insects that you may see them as being when you look down at them from an airplane.

Visual Depth and Distance

Your visual receptors are located in the retinas of your eyes. The retina is, for all practical purposes, little more than a flat, two-dimensional movie screen on which the lens in your eye projects images of the world around you.

Yet when you look at the world, it doesn't seem to be flat and two-dimensional to you. The world is *three-dimensional.* It has *depth* to it. A blank movie screen has but two dimensions—left/right and up/down. But when you project a first-rate movie on the screen, suddenly a third dimension appears in the picture—depth. How does this near-miracle occur?

The Case of S.B.

Depth perception, like most psychological experiences, is partially learned and partially due to innate factors. Obviously you wouldn't see *anything* unless you were born with sound eyes and visual cortex, but what would your world be like if you had been born blind and only now opened your eyes? The answer may surprise you.

British psychologist Richard L. Gregory reported the case of a man who had been blind from infancy, but whose vision was restored at age 52. This patient—whom Dr. Gregory calls S.B.—was an intelligent person whose vision had been normal at birth. At age 10 months, S.B. developed a severe infection of the eyes that left his **corneas** so badly scarred that he could not see objects at all.

Enough light leaked through his damaged corneas that S.B. could just tell day from night, but he saw the world much as you would if someone cut a ping pong ball in two and placed one of the halves over each of your eyes. S.B.'s corneal scars were so bad, in fact, that for most of his life no doctor would operate on him. Nonetheless, S.B. led a pleasant and very active life. He went places by himself, waving his white cane in front of him to let people know he was blind. He often went for rides on a bicycle, with a friend holding his shoulder and guiding him.

S.B. spent considerable time making wooden objects with rather simple tools. He had an open-faced watch that let him tell time by feeling the positions of the hands. He took care of animals and knew them all by touch and smell. And he always tried to imagine what things looked like. When he washed his brother's car, he would vividly try to picture what color and shape it really was. When S.B. visited the zoo, he would get his friends to describe the **exotic** animals there in terms of how different they were from dogs and cats in his home.

S.B. had always hoped to be able to see. Finally, when he was well past his fiftieth year, he prevailed upon a surgeon to attempt an operation in which his corneas were removed and new ones were **grafted** on in their place.

The operation was a great success but, as Dr. Gregory reports, S.B. was anything but happy with the results. When the doctor first removed the bandages, S.B. looked straight into the doctor's face—and saw nothing but a blur. He knew that what he saw had to be the doctor's face, because he recognized the man's voice. But it was several days before he could begin to tell one person from another merely by looking at them, and he never became very good at identifying people visually.

Nonetheless, his progress in some areas was rapid. Within a few days S.B. could successfully navigate the halls of the hospital without running into things. He could tell time by looking at the face of a very large clock. And he dearly loved to get up early in the morning and sit at his window watching the traffic rumble by on the street far below his hospital room.

But there were problems. S.B. rapidly learned the names of the colors red, black, and white, but he had difficulty identifying most other colors. He could judge horizontal distances fairly well when looking at objects whose size he was familiar with. But vertical distances—heights of any kind— always bothered him. One day they found him crawling out the window of his fourth-floor hospital room, presumably because he wanted to inspect more closely the automobile traffic in the street below. He looked at the ground 12 meters (40 feet) beneath him and thought it to be no more than 2 meters (6 feet) away.

Prior to the operation, S.B. had crossed even the busiest intersection alone without the faintest fear. He would plunge into traffic waving his white stick in front of him, and somehow the sea of cars and trucks would part for him much as the waters of the Red Sea parted for Moses in Old Testament times. After S.B. got his vision back, he was absolutely terrified of crossing a street. Dr. Gregory states that it usually took two people holding his arms to force him across an intersection.

Often when S.B. saw a fairly familiar object for the first time, he would be unable to identify it until he closed his eyes and felt it. Then he knew it by touch. And once he "had the picture in his mind," he could recognize it visually after he had looked at it a few times.

But objects that he hadn't (or couldn't) run his hands over before regaining his sight always gave him problems. The moon, for instance, puzzled him greatly. The full moon he could make out, but the quarter moon he had expected to be wedge-shaped, rather like a large slice of pumpkin pie. And when S.B. looked at the two long lines in Fig. 10.4, he saw them as being the same length. How do they look to you?

Immediately after his operation, S.B. was very enthusiastic and happy. He loved bright colors (although he couldn't always give their right names), and he enjoyed being able to see the faces of people he knew.

But then he began to get depressed. He complained bitterly about the ugliness in the world around him—houses with the paint coming off, buildings with dirty walls, people with blemishes on their faces. He would spend hours sitting in his local tavern watching people in the mirror. Somehow their reflections seemed more interesting to him than their real-life images.

Exotic. (x-OTT-ic). From the Greek word meaning "outside." Anything that is strange, foreign, or introduced from some other country is considered exotic.

Grafted. Joining parts of one organism to another is called "grafting." You can sometimes graft a branch from one tree onto another. If the graft "takes," the new branch will take its food and water from the sap of the "host" tree and grow normally. In corneal grafts, part of the donor's cornea just in front of the pupil is surgically removed and transplanted to the eye of the recipient ("host"). If the corneal graft "takes," the grafted tissue will connect up to the recipient's bloodstream and function more or less normally.

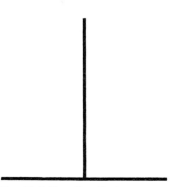

Fig. 10.4. Bisection illusion.

Often S.B. would withdraw from human contact and spend most of the day sitting in darkness, claiming that he could "see" better when there was no light.

There have been no more than a half dozen confirmed cases of people who have gained sight as adults. According to Gregory, depression and unhappiness are common consequences of their getting back their vision.

For instance, in 1777, Anton Mesmer (an unusual scientist whom we will meet again in Chapter 18) studied a French girl who regained her sight at age 17. After being able to see for a few months, this young woman complained angrily that the world was so ugly and tiresome that she wished she were blind again.

In part, the unhappiness and depression come from the discovery of how hard it really is "to see," and in part they stem from the slow realization of how much life the person has missed.

Mueller-Lyer Illusion

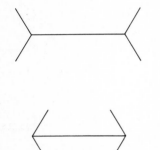

Fig. 10.5. The Mueller-Lyer illusion.

Cases such as that of S.B. demonstrate the critical influence that your early life experiences have on shaping how you will see the world when you have grown up. For during your childhood years, you learn the "rules of visual perception" even though you are far too young to know what words like "visual" and "perception" really mean.

Look at Fig. 10.5. Doesn't the bottom line with the arrowheads seem much shorter than the upper line with the "V's" on each end? Yet if you measure these two lines, you'll see they are exactly the same length.

Why does one line look longer than the other? Richard Gregory believes that this illusion is based on our perception of corners. If you are reading this book indoors, look at one of the corners of the room you're in. Notice that the angles the wall makes with the floor or the ceiling form lines much like those in the "V" figure. If you are sitting outdoors, look at the corner of a building. You will see that the angles made by the roof and the ground are close to the same lines in the "arrowhead" figure (see Figs. 10.6 and 10.7A and B.).

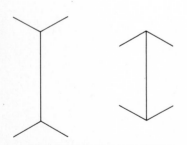

Fig. 10.6. The Mueller-Lyer illusion.

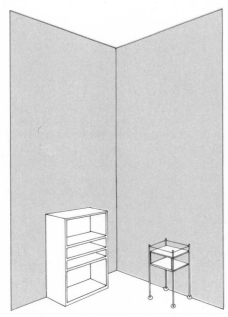

Fig. 10.7A. The corner where the walls meet is actually the same height as the edges of the walls shown.

Fig. 10.7B. The outside corner of this building is the same height as the other edges. With the illustration on the left the Mueller-Lyer illusion is formed.

PART TWO   Sensation and Perception

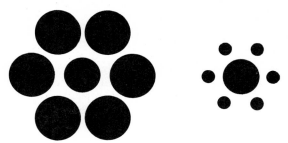

Fig. 10.8. Are the center dots in both figures the same?

Diagonal (die-AG-oh-null). If you were standing straight up, then leaned over at an angle, your body would be diagonal to the floor. The "slant mark" (/) on the typewriter is a diagonal line.

Question: It is rather simple to train a pigeon in a laboratory to peck at the shorter of two lines in order to be rewarded by food. How would you set up a demonstration that pigeons are as fooled by the Mueller-Lyer illusion as humans are?

Circles and Straight Lines

The Mueller-Lyer illusion points up an interesting fact—you seldom see an object all by itself. Instead, you almost always see an object *in context*, or in relationship to the other objects around it. In the Mueller-Lyer illusion, the two horizontal lines have "tails" at either end that affect your perception of the lines themselves.

Now look at Fig. 10.8. The two center dots are exactly the same size, but they surely don't look the same!

Look also at the "top hat" drawing (Fig. 10.9). Is the hat taller than it is wide? If you think so, take out a ruler and measure the distances. The "bisected line" drawing shows the same sort of illusion.

The apparent straightness of a line can easily be affected by whatever objects the lines seem to penetrate. In Fig. 10.10, the **diagonal** line crossing the two bars seems to be three disconnected lines. In fact, as you can determine by using a ruler, the line is absolutely straight. Oddly enough, the illusion disappears for most people if they turn the drawing around so that the line is straight up and down.

A circle drawn in the middle of a "wheel," such as that in Fig. 10.11, somehow looks lopsided. A square drawn in the middle of concentric circles looks warped (see Fig. 10.12). These figures—like the lake you

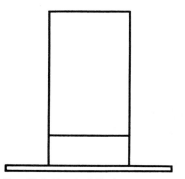

Fig. 10.9. Top hat illusion.

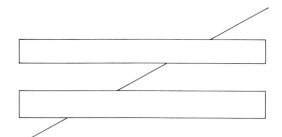

Fig. 10.10. Is the diagonal line straight?

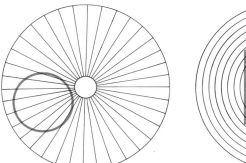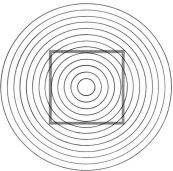

Figs. 10.11 (left) and 10.12 (right). The backgrounds in these two figures distort the colored circle and square.

observed from the air earlier in this chapter—are good illustrations of how difficult it is for your eye to follow a line when the line is interrupted by other lines.

A "straight line" and a "circle" are not things that you simply "see." Rather, they are *concepts* that your cortex *perceives* after taking many things into account. Straightness and circularity are *percepts* that are affected by feedback from your eye muscles as much as by input messages from your retina.

As you will see momentarily, some aspects of visual perception are determined by the genetic blueprint you inherited. For the most part, however, your past experiences determine what you see in the world around you.

We grow up in a world of straight lines, corners, and sharp angles. But what of someone who matured in an environment where straight lines were **taboo,** someone who saw only curves and wavy lines as a child? How would this person see the Mueller-Lyer illusion?

The answer is—the person probably wouldn't see the illusion at all. The Zulus, a tribe of primitive people living in South Africa, live in what Gregory calls a "circular culture." The huts they live in are round mounds with circular doors. They plow their fields in curved lines, and even their toys and tools lack straight edges. When shown the Mueller-Lyer illusion, the typical Zulu native sees one line as being only very slightly longer than the other. Some illusions, such as that shown in Fig. 10.12, affect the Zulu hardly at all.

Clues to Visual Distance

Your eye inspects the world in front of you and reports to your brain what it sees. Your brain takes into account not only the visual sensations coming from your retinas, but also the way that your eyes move in their sockets, the sounds your ears report, the smells around you, your bodily posture, and all the memories it can dredge up. Then, and only then, does your cortex decide what you are looking at.

An automobile passes you on the street. You know that it is about 9 meters (30 feet) away from you because you remember what size cars ought to be, how long it takes you to walk 9 meters, and how the visual image of the car will change as you walk toward it.

The *apparent size* of an object gives you a good notion of how far away the object is. But there are other clues that your brain uses, even though you are often unaware of what these clues are.

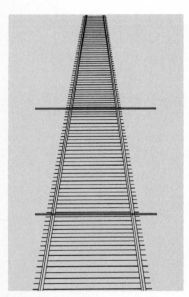

Fig. 10.13. The railway line illusion. The wooden ties are all the same size; do they look that way to you?

Perspective If you stood in the middle of a railroad track and looked down the roadbed, the rails would seem to come together in the distance. Your mind tells you that the rails don't actually converge or meet on the horizon, but your eye insists that they do. And if you draw two identical lines between the tracks, the top line seems to be longer (see Fig. 10.13). Can you figure out why?

And when you stand at the end of a runway at an airport, looking down toward the other end, can you understand why the tops of the numbers painted on the runway look "scrunched up?"

This apparent *convergence* of parallel lines as they approach the horizon is called **linear perspective,** and is one of the cues that your brain uses to judge distance. And, as the "area illusion" (Fig. 10.14) shows, linear perspective also affects your judgment of the *size* of objects in the distance.

Oddly enough, it took artists a long time to realize that they had to make use of linear perspective in their paintings if they wanted to reproduce distances effectively. In some paintings, such as those by Persian artists in the sixteenth and seventeenth centuries, the almost complete lack of linear perspective gives the painting a curiously flat, distorted, and unreal appearance (see color Plate 9).

Fig. 10.14. We know the man and building are not the same height, so we assume the building is far away from us and the man close.

Fig. 10.15. Seen in a haze, buildings and other objects seem to be further away.

Aerial perspective (AIR-ee-ull). Literally, the "way you see an object through the air." Fuzzy objects seem distant; clear (distinct) objects seem close.

Question: If an artist paints a scene that lacks linear perspective, does this mean that the artist actually does not **see** *perspective in his or her own visual world? How could you* **prove** *experimentally that your answer is correct?*

Anyone who has grown up in a smog-ridden city knows that there are often days when you can't see more than a block or two away. But there are parts of the world still blessedly free from this aerial pollution. In some of our deserts, for instance, the air is often so clear that visibility is practically unlimited. The city dweller who first visits these regions is sometimes shocked at how badly she or he actually judges distances in clean, fresh air. A mountain peak that appears to be no more than 5 or 10 kilometers away may actually be more than 80 kilometers down the road.

The more hazy and indistinct a remote object seems to you, the further away it appears to be—a fact that psychologists refer to as the **aerial perspective** of an object (See Fig. 10.15).

Often we use the *color* of an object to give us some notion of its size or distance from us. For reasons we still don't understand, dark-colored objects often appear to be smaller than light-colored objects. For example, look at the seven dots in Fig. 10.16. Although it doesn't look like it at first glance, the distance *between* the dots is exactly the same as the size of the dots themselves.

Sometimes we make judgments about the visual world from what we *don't* see, instead of from what we *do* see. Look at the illustration in Fig. 10.17, which is a simple representation of the word "shadow." Notice that each of the six letters in this word is printed in full. Now look at the next word. Here there are no letters, just the shadows themselves. But look carefully. Doesn't your eye actually *see* the forms of the letters as if they were really there? And what about the five black figures in Fig. 10.18? Can you see the word "fly" spaced between the figures?

How does your brain manage to see letters where only empty spaces exist? Well, as we pointed out in Chapter 8, your brain has the happy habit of filling in details of objects it *assumes* ought to be there. For instance, we often make use of shadows in judging whether we are looking at a mountain or at the hole left in the ground when somebody dug up the mountain and carted it away. Photographs of the craters and hills on the moon and

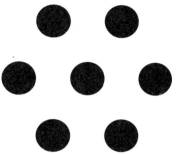

Fig. 10.16. Irradiation illusion.

Is this a hill or a crater in the surface of the moon? Now turn the page upside down and look again.

SHADOW SHADOW

Fig. 10.18. A perception illusion.

Fig. 10.17. If you look closely you will see that the letters on the right are not round letters casting a shadow, but only shadows. Look at the illustration at the left.

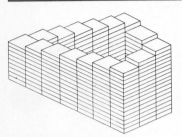

Fig. 10.19. The magic stairs.

Fig. 10.20. Do you see two profile faces? Or a wine glass?

on Mars are fairly commonplace now. When you look at one of these photographs, you automatically make an assumption about how the sunlight is falling on the landscape. If you make the *wrong assumption*, then your brain will show you a hill instead of a crater.

Question: S.B. often mistook shadows for real objects. Why do you think this was the case?

Convergence Humans are essentially two-dimensional animals, bound to those parts of the surface of the earth that our two feet can walk on. The bird soaring into the air, the porpoise diving to the bottom of a shallow bay—these are animals that live in all three dimensions.

We judge distances rather well—if the distance is no greater than we can walk or run or ride. But we judge heights rather poorly, at least in comparison to most birds and fish.

When you look at something in the distance, both your eyes point straight ahead. When you look at something up close, however, both of your eyes turn inward, toward your nose. The amount of strain that this **convergence,** or "turning inward," causes on the muscles is noticed by your brain, which uses this cue as an index of how far away the object is.

To judge how far away from you another person is, you have merely to let your eyes converge and notice the strain on your eye muscles. But to judge height, you usually have to move your head up and down or crane your neck. For all but the most experienced airplane pilots, the neck muscles are poorer judges of distance than are the eye muscles.

Often our eyes trick us when we try to judge perspective, however. Look at the "impossible figure" in Fig. 10.19. Do the stairs go up or down, or both ways? What is there about the perspective of this figure that "fools" your eyes?

Figure–Ground Relationships

The perception of a single object in visual space is fairly well understood by psychologists. You seldom get the chance to look at just one object, however, for usually your visual world is crowded with all manner of things to look at and admire.

And you typically see all the things in the world as having some kind of *relationship* with each other. The simplest form of this relationship is that of **figure–ground.** Even such a simple percept as that of a fluffy white cloud dancing alone in the clear blue sky is usually seen as a *something on a something*, a figure or object on a background.

Whatever you focus on or pay most attention to is usually said to be the *figure*, for it appears to stand out in your visual world. Psychologists call anything that stands out from its background a **salient** figure. As the object becomes more complex, however, you may have difficulty telling figure from background.

Look at Fig. 10.20, for instance. Which do you see, two shadow-faces looking at each other, or a fancy wine glass? These two stimulus patterns are so related to each other that either one can be figure *or* ground. If you stare at the illustration for a few seconds, you will find that it is almost impossible to see *both* patterns at once—rather, first you see one, then the other. And the percepts alternate rather rapidly.

This same sort of "percept alternation" is true of the famous Necker cube shown in Fig. 10.21. You can see the cube as projecting upward or downward, but not both ways at once.

Question: Why do you think you can't see the cube as projecting up and down at the same time? And second, S.B. saw the cube as being flat instead of having three dimensions. What does this fact tell you about your own depth perception?

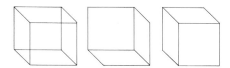

Fig. 10.21. The Necker Cube. It can be seen as projecting up or down in three dimensions in the first cube. In the other two cubes the perspective is stabilized.

Expectancy

As we said earlier, you usually see what you *expect* to see. When a novelist writes a mystery story, the writer will usually give the reader clues or hints as to who did what to whom. But often the clues are so stated that, while entirely factual, the reader gets quite the wrong impression or *expectancy*. For many readers, half the fun of reading a mystery is trying to outguess the author as the story proceeds. The other half comes (once the piece is finished) in going back over the tale trying to discover how the author led the reader astray.

With that thought in mind, look at Fig. 10.22. As you can see, it is a drawing of an *ugly old woman* with her chin buried in a fur coat. Look at it carefully and try to figure out what kind of an old woman she is. Is she happy or sad? And what is this old woman thinking of?

The artist who drew the picture claims she is dreaming of her daughter. And if you look carefully at the picture again, you will see the face of the old woman change into that of the younger woman. The old mother's nose becomes the chin and the jawline of the younger woman's face. The older woman's left eye becomes the daughter's left ear, and the mother's mouth becomes a necklace around the daughter's neck.

Several experimenters have shown this picture to groups of college students. If the students are given the expectancy that they will see a picture of an *old woman*, most of them discover the mother's face before finding the daughter's. But if the students are told they will see a drawing of a *young woman*, they tend to see the daughter's face easily but often have trouble "finding" the picture of the mother.

Visual Grouping

As you look out at the world, your mind makes use of several psychological principles in trying to bring some kind of order to its percepts. As an example of one such principle, you tend to *group things together* according to how close they are to each other. In part *a* of Fig. 10.23, you probably see three "pairs" of lines. You will group *a* and *b* together because they are close to each other.

In part *b* of this figure, however, things have changed. Now *b* and *c* seem to go together—to form a rectangle of some kind. Indeed, if you stare closely at the *b–c* rectangle, you will see rather faint but *imaginary* lines as your brain attempts to fill in or close up the open figure.

Fig. 10.22. Do you see an old lady or a young girl?

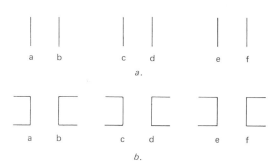

Fig. 10.23. Which lines seem to relate in each of these pairs?

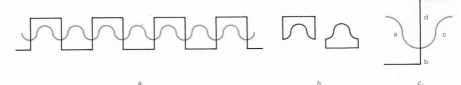

a. b. c.

Fig. 10.24. The Principle of Continuity.

Proximity (procks-IM-it-tee). That which is close. If you live a block from the fire station, you live in the proximity of the fire station. Objects that are proximate (close to each other) tend to be perceived as units.

Closure. "To complete" or "to close." If you glance very quickly at a circle that has a tiny gap in it, you may very well see the circle as being closed, or complete.

Continuity (con-tin-NEW-it-tee). From the word "continue" or "continuous." Things that are connected together in time or space have continuity. Your own stream of consciousness has a certain continuity or connectedness, in that one experience follows the other without a noticeable gap of "blank period of consciousness."

Similarity. Objects that are physically like one another tend to be perceived as units or wholes.

Ambiguous (am-BIG-you-us). Anything that is vague or indefinite. If you ask someone to go on a date and the person says "maybe yes, maybe no," the person has given you an ambiguous answer.

Part *a* illustrates the principle of **proximity,** or physical closeness. Part *b* illustrates the principle of **closure**—that is, your brain's tendency to join broken lines together to make a closed figure of some kind.

A third perceptual principle is that of **continuity,** which is illustrated in part *a* of Fig. 10.24. In this illustration you will probably see a wavy line superimposed on a square-cornered line. If we now break up the pattern somewhat differently, as in part *b,* you see not two lines but two closed figures joined together. Why do you think this is so?

And if you wish, you may even break the figure up into a different set of components, as shown in part *c.*

Once you have learned what the parts of the figure can be, you can perceive it many different ways. But, at the beginning, your eye tends to follow the wavy line because it is *continuous.*

A fourth principle of perceptual grouping is that of **similarity.** Fig. 10.25A shows a series of 25 circles arranged in a square. If you fixate on this figure, you will notice that sometimes you group the circles together in bunches of 4s, or 9s, or 16s. Sometimes you see 5 horizontal rows of circles, sometimes 5 vertical columns. In such **ambiguous** situations your brain tests out various percepts, attempting to see which fits the stimulus pattern best.

When you look out into a cloud from an airplane, your brain is faced with a similar but even more difficult perceptual situation. For a cloud has no firm structure at all—whatever patterns you see in such *ambiguous* situations are those which your brain actually imposes on incoming sensory information.

In Fig. 10.25B, the situation is much less ambiguous. Here, you see a cross formed of Xs, while the circles group themselves into squares of four circles each.

Gestalt Principles

Early in this century a group of German psychologists began a detailed study of the perceptual principles outlined above. These men eventually

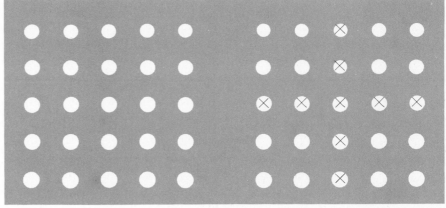

Fig. 10.25A. How do you "group" these circles?

Fig. 10.25B. Why do you "group" the circles in Fig. 10.25A differently than you do those above?

 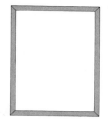

Fig. 10.26. What is the shape of these drawings?

Fig. 10.27. The same picture frame head-on and at an angle of 45 degrees is no longer visually the same.

Gestalt (guess-TALT). A German word that is difficult to translate. Literally, it means "good form" or "good figure." Also means the tendency to see things as "wholes" rather than as jumbled bits and pieces.

Ellipse (ee-LIPS). An oval or somewhat egg-shaped figure.

Shape constancy. The tendency to "see" an object in its correct shape even when you view it from an odd angle. When you look at a coin tilted away from you, most likely you will see the coin as being round—although its visual image is really that of an ellipse.

decided that the brain was so organized that it tended to see **Gestalts,** which is the German word for "good figures."

To these Gestalt psychologists, a circle was a "better" or more natural figure than an **ellipse,** hence (they said) we tend to see the left part of Fig. 10.26 as a round half-dollar turned slightly away from us, rather than as a coin that has somehow been squashed into an elliptical shape.

The Gestalt theorists explained most of **shape constancy** as the brain's desire to force all percepts into better or more natural shapes. For example, imagine what an empty picture frame looks like when you see it head-on. Now, in your mind's eye, rotate the frame away from you about 45 degrees. In its rotated position, the edge of the picture frame nearest you actually looks longer than the edge farthest away from you. But you *still see the picture as being square* (see Fig. 10.27).

Adelbert Ames, a US psychologist who began his professional life as a painter, took advantage of this *shape constancy* to produce a number of very amusing illusions, the best known of which is his "distorted room" (see Figs. 10.28A and 10.28B).

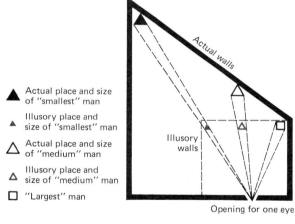

▲ Actual place and size of "smallest" man

▴ Illusory place and size of "smallest" man

△ Actual place and size of "medium" man

△ Illusory place and size of "medium" man

☐ "Largest" man

Fig. 10.28A. A diagram of the Ames "distorted room" as seen from the top.

Fig. 10.28B. The Ames "distorted room" as seen from the front. The man on the left is really the same height as the other two men.

Trapezoid (TRAP-ee-zoid). A four-sided figure with two sides that are parallel. In the drawing of the picture frame "tilted away from you" on page 253, notice that the left and right sides of the frame are parallel, but the top and bottom sides are not. The picture frame—as viewed from this angle—is a trapezoid.

Neonate (KNEE-oh-nate). From the Latin words *neo*, meaning "new," and *natus*, meaning "born." Hence a child less than a month old. Your "natal day" is the day you were born, your birthday.

Genetic blueprint. At the moment of your conception, you inherited a set of genes from your mother and your father. These genes contained a chemical pattern or "blueprint" of what your body would eventually be like. This blueprint specified what form and shape your brain and spinal cord would take. In short, the basic "wiring diagram" of your nervous system was contained in your genes, or genetic blueprint, and at birth you started life with a "prewired brain." See Chapter 19 for a further explanation.

Fig. 10.29. Infants using Fantz's apparatus looked at the simple face longer than they did at the design with facial features.

When looked at head-on, the "distorted" room appears quite normal, until you see three people standing in the room. And then you know that something is very definitely wrong.

The windows in the room look "square," as the Gestalt theorists would predict. But in fact, the windows are really **trapezoids.** But your brain assumes that windows ought to be rectangular, hence your brain "sees" them as being rectangles.

In order to keep the windows looking like rectangles, your brain must produce *distance distortions* that make one of the men in the room look much larger than his smaller companions. Given the choice between preserving "good form" (the shape of the windows) or "size constancy" (the size of the men), your cortex typically votes in favor of good form—just as the Gestalt theorists predicted.

Although not all psychologists agree, the Gestalt position is that all the really important aspects of your visual experience are determined by your genetic inheritance, not by what you have learned.

Innate Aspects of Perception

Almost 100 years ago, the famous US psychologist William James supposedly stated that an infant perceives the world as a "blooming, buzzing confusion." While it is true that the **neonate** probably experiences its environment as a blurred, noisy mess, some aspects of visual perception appear so early in the child's life that they are surely a part of what we might call the **genetic blueprint.**

In a previous chapter, we mentioned the fact that scientists had recently shown that infants only 10 days old will mimic the expressions on the faces of adults around them. This research suggests that there is something rather special about the human face—at least from an infant's point of view.

Look at Fig. 10.29. One drawing is that of a face with the nose, eyes, and other features in their proper places. The other drawing has the same elements, but they are oddly scrambled. Now imagine a very young infant lying comfortably on its back looking up at these figures. Which do you think it would spend more time looking at—the normal face, or the scrambled one?

Psychologist R.L. Fantz photographed the eye movements of young babies using the apparatus shown below. Fantz found that the infants she

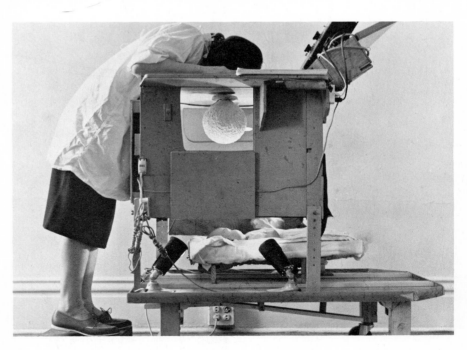

Fantz's equipment for observing infants' eye movements.

studied spent much more time looking at the normal than at the scrambled bled face—a fact which suggests that the child has **innate** response patterns built into its brain which allow it to recognize what the human face looks like.

Fantz also found that babies seem to prefer to look at simple round objects rather than at two-dimensional drawings of the same objects. Fantz believes that infants may have an *innate appreciation of depth*, but points out that her experimental results may also mean that babies learn about faces and depths very early in their lives.

The Visual Cliff

A more intriguing bit of evidence concerning the innate properties of perception comes from a series of experiments pioneered by Eleanor Gibson, one of America's best-known perceptual psychologists. One day several years ago, Gibson found herself eating a picnic meal on the rim of the Grand Canyon. Looking straight down into that deep and awesome **chasm**, she began to worry about the safety of the children around her. Would a very young child be able to perceive the enormous drop-off at the end of the cliff, or would the child go toddling right over the edge if no adult were around to restrain it?

What Gibson was really asking, of course, is this: Are babies born with an innate ability to perceive depth and a built-in fear mechanism that would make them retreat from sharp drop-offs even without having been trained to do so? Once Dr. Gibson had returned to her laboratory at Cornell University, she designed an artificial **visual cliff** on which she could test infants safely (see Fig. 10.30).

Running down the middle of the apparatus was a raised plank of wood painted in a checkerboard pattern. To one side of the plank was a sharp drop-off. To the other side was a normal "floor" an inch or so below the center plank. The entire apparatus was covered with sturdy glass so that the infant could see the cliff but could not fall off it.

When an infant was tested, it was put on the center board and allowed to explore freely. Very few of the infants crawled off onto the "cliff" side, although most of them freely moved onto the "floor" side. Even when the child's mother stood at the side of the apparatus and attempted to coax the child to crawl out over the "cliff," most infants refused to do so. Instead,

Innate (in-EIGHT). Inborn, or present at birth.

Chasm (KAS-em; rhymes with "has 'em"). From the Greek word meaning "to gape or yawn." Thus, a deep or "yawning" hole.

Visual cliff. An apparatus designed by Eleanor Gibson which has an apparent "chasm" on one side that many infants and newborn animals refuse to cross.

Fig. 10.30. The "visual cliff," actually a solid glass surface, which reveals a checked material that cascades to the floor.

they began to cry loudly. If the mother stood on the "floor" side of the box, however, the infant would crawl toward her willingly.

A variety of newborn animals—lambs, kittens, puppies, and rats—have been tested on the visual cliff too. For the most part these animals showed an almost immediate perceptual awareness of the "dangers" of the cliff.

Apparently most higher species have behavioral mechanisms built into their brains at birth that tend to protect them from the dangers of falling from high places.

Developmental Handicaps of the Blind Some innate visual tendencies are so subtle that we tend to overlook them—except when we observe the development of a child who is born blind. In her recent book, *Insights from the Blind*, Selma Fraiberg points out that the blind youngster has two severe problems to overcome: (1) Learning to recognize its parents from sounds alone; and (2) acquiring a healthy *self-concept* or *self-image*.

Fraiberg notes that a normal 8-month-old child will reach out its arms the moment it hears its mother's voice—*anticipating* the sight of the parent even before she appears in the child's view. The blind baby does not show this reaching response until much, much later. The blind infant *hears* and *feels*, but cannot "integrate" these sensory experiences very well to form a unified percept of *mother*. Vision, then, is particularly important to a youngster because sight allows the child to pull the other sensory **modalities** together in its mind.

Blind children are retarded in their speech development too. They talk later and more poorly than do sighted children. Much of this speech retardation seems to be due to their slowness in recognizing the *permanence* of objects in the world around them. Blind children also have problems "imagining" things while young and do not identify readily with a doll or with a character in a story read to them. And they often do not learn the correct use of "I" and "you" until they are five or six.

Fraiberg concludes that blind youngsters cannot *picture* themselves as objects that exist separate from their environments. And since they cannot *visualize* themselves as independent entities, they are slow to develop any real notion of "self." In brief, seeing yourself and others may be a necessary first step in believing in your "self."

Innate or Learned? The question of which aspects of vision are learned and which are innately determined may never be entirely solved. For, in truth, every aspect of your visual life is affected both by your genetic blueprint and by what you have experienced in the past. For example, your pupils have an innate tendency to open when you are aroused, and to close slightly when you are bored or resting.

But what arouses or interests you? Surely the stimulus inputs that lead to emotional arousal are primarily learned. Thus even the way your pupil changes in relation to the world around you is affected both by inborn reflexes and your past experience.

As we will now see, psychologists have learned how to measure the size of your pupil and thus gain some notion of what things you really find interesting.

Pupil Responses

One of the major purposes of your visual system is to gird you for *action*. When you walk out of a darkened movie theater, your pupils decrease in size rapidly to keep you from being blinded by the sudden increase in light. Your cortex doesn't have to tell your pupils to change size under these conditions—the response is an automatic one controlled by neural centers in the lower parts of your brain.

At dusk, when the sunlight dims, your pupils automatically open up or **dilate.** The wider your pupils open, the more light comes through and the better you can see and react to objects in your visual environment. When

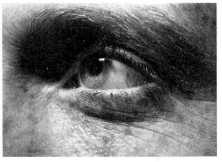

Your pupil usually dilates (opens), as in the photo at the right, when you are looking at something of interest and closes a bit, as at the left, when you are not.

you look closely at some object, your pupils also dilate, even though there is no change in illumination. The harder you stare at the object, the wider your pupils will open.

Psychologist Eckhard Hess made use of this information a decade or so ago to test a hunch of his. Hess reasoned that you would stare more at something you were really interested in than at something you disliked or were bored by. So he showed pictures of many different objects to the college students he used as subjects in his experiments.

Hess found that women typically had much larger pupil openings when he showed them pictures of babies or nude males than when he showed these women pictures of landscapes or nude females. Men, on the other hand, usually had wider pupils when shown pictures of nude females than when they were shown photographs of babies, landscapes, or nude males. Hess' research suggests that you can often discover a person's *real* interests simply by noting when the person becomes "wide-eyed."

Visual Suppression On very rare occasions your cortex is forced to choose between two quite different visual inputs. Imagine a large black box with two eyeholes in one side. There is a wooden partition inside the box that divides it in half. Thus when you look through the holes, your left eye sees quite a different scene than does your right eye. How would your brain handle this odd situation?

Generally speaking, there are two types of responses your brain makes when faced with conflicting visual inputs. Most of the time your brain simply **suppresses** or rejects one of the pictures and *concentrates* on the other. But on rare occasions, your cortex may *combine* the two inputs into one.

Fig. 10.31. The teapot pouring liquid and the teacup can be fused visually so that the tea seems to flow into the cup.

Suppresses (sup-PRESS-es). To inhibit or to put down.

If we show a different scene to your left eye than to your right, which scene will your brain suppress? If your vision is clearer in one eye than in the other, your cortex will almost always pick the scene that it sees best. But if both your eyes are in good shape, your brain faces a **dilemma.**

If your left eye is looking at a teacup, while your right eye is looking at a teapot that is pouring liquid from its spout, your brain may actually fuse or **meld** the two scenes together so that you see a pot pouring tea into a cup (see Fig. 10.31). If one of your eyes sees a baby hanging in mid-air, while the other sees a woman holding out empty arms, your brain may superimpose one scene on the other so that you see the woman holding the child.

But suppose the two pictures are so different that they can't be fused? Then your brain typically concentrates on whichever scene it finds *more interesting,* and suppresses the other scene almost completely. In many cases this suppression takes place so rapidly that you are simply not aware that you are being shown two different objects or photographs.

Research suggests that you are more likely to suppress unpleasant or frightening scenes than you are to block out pleasant or stimulating scenes.

Question: Suppose you need to determine whether a group of workers has unconscious prejudices about female supervisors. How might you use photographs of male and female supervisors—presented in the "black box" apparatus—to help determine the workers' underlying attitudes?

Predicting is Prejudging   You can "see" at birth, but you must learn to make *sense* of what you see. That is, you must learn to *perceive* the meaning and value of the rich variety of visual inputs that come your way. Without either your innate reflexes, or learning how to put them to best use, you simply could not survive.

But learning always carries with it the burden of prejudice. When your brain predicts what will happen to you next, it is *prejudging* the situation more on the basis of its past experience than on the basis of present inputs.

Given the data on how perceptions are built up, we probably should examine our viewpoints constantly to make sure that we aren't being fooled by the thousands of illusions that populate our worlds.

Summary

1.   Much of what you know about the world comes to you through your eyes.

2.   Visual stimuli excite your rods and cones, which fire off input messages **(sensations)** to your cortex. Your brain scans these sensations and compares them to **images** or memories of what it has seen in the past. If the image matches the sensation, your brain recognizes or **perceives** what the stimulus is and what it means to you.

3.   When you mismatch sensation and image, you experience an **illusion** or misperception.

4.   When you mistake an image for a sensation, you experience an **hallucination.**

5.   Visual perception is influenced by many stimulus factors:

a.   Large objects often appear close to us, and close objects appear large.

b.   Small objects often appear far away, and distant objects appear small.

c.   Parallel lines seem to converge at the horizon **(linear perspective).**

d.   "Fuzzy objects" typically seem farther away than do distinct objects **(aerial perspective).**

6.   As you grow up, you learn about **size constancy.** Thus if you

know what an object is, you will probably interpret both its size and its distance correctly.

7. Humans who lose their sight in childhood but regain it as adults often have severe problems adjusting. They must learn to recognize visually objects that they had only touched or heard about. They do not perceive visual illusions in the same way that sighted humans do.

8. While some aspects of visual perception are learned, many are **innately determined:**

    a. You tend to see objects in terms of their **figure-ground relationships.**

    b. You tend to see incomplete or "open" figures as being closed because closed figures make better **Gestalts.**

    c. You tend to group figures together visually so that they make the best possible visual forms (Gestalts).

    d. Infants tend to pay more visual attention to human faces than to random figures.

    e. Children and young animals seem to avoid crawling out over open spaces or **visual cliffs** the first time they experience the cliff.

9. Because vision appears to "tie the other senses together," children born blind have difficulty learning to talk, learning to relate to their parents, and are slow in building up an adequate self-concept.

10. Your **pupil size** is primarily determined by visual reflexes that you had when you were born. However, some aspects of the **pupil reflex** are affected by learning. For example, your pupils automatically open wider when you look at something interesting than when you look at something boring.

11. When your two eyes are shown different scenes, your mind may **suppress** one of the scenes, or it may **fuse** the two together to make a Gestalt. However, you are more likely to suppress threatening scenes than pleasant ones.

12. Your visual mechanisms seem designed to help you predict and control future inputs.

13. The most basic principle of visual perception is that you tend to see what you expect to see.

(Continued from page 238.)

The last of the male passengers came out of the little airport waiting room sweating profusely and shaking his head. "Bunch of dratted nonsense," the man muttered to himself as he passed by the elegant figure of the Laforan Minister of Science and Technology.

Freddie glumly watched the man depart. They had held the passengers of the special Paris jet in a quarantine waiting room, letting them pass one by one through the office where Professor Mann had inspected their eyes. Mann had agreed to signal Freddie if the tests had detected which person was the Snake, but no signal had come.

And now the waiting room was empty, save for a number of very attractive but rather overdressed young women and one rather forlorn-looking matron cradling a baby in her arms. Freddie was confident that the good-looking young women were girl friends of the munitions dealers. The matron was probably a wife of one of the dealers—although why a man would bring a wife and child to Lafora on a business trip, Freddie wasn't sure.

Freddie sighed. It seemed certain that Dr. Mann's tests had failed him—and failed the Republic of Lafora as well. The former fault he could tolerate. The latter came close to treason, and he mentioned this point to the American Professor.

"What have you done, and why didn't it work?" Freddie demanded.

Mann looked annoyed at the Minister's bluntness. "First I showed a series of drawings to each man and measured the size of his pupils while he was watching. One of the drawings was of a snake. I had thought that our friend the assassin would show a larger pupil size to this drawing than to any other. Three of the men did so, but they failed the second test".

"Which was . . . ?"

"A suppression test. I have a variety of drawings—a pile of money, guns, airplanes, a picture of your President, a number of animals, and a snake striking at something with dripping fangs. I had the men look into my little black box that shows one drawing to the person's left eye, another to the right eye. And then I simply asked them to report what they saw. I figured most of the men would suppress the image of the snake, since most people are afraid of snakes."

Freddie snorted inelegantly. "But wouldn't the Snake see through your little tricks?"

"Perhaps, although I figured that, at the very least, he'd hesitate or be a little confused. But every man on the plane suppressed the picture of the snake without a moment's hesitation."

"And so your oh-so-scientific tests have failed," Freddie said glumly.

"No, Freddie, we're not through yet. There are still people in the waiting room."

Freddie looked around. "Just women and children, my dear Professor. We might as well let them go."

"You'll do nothing of the kind. Send them along for the eye checks, or their boy friends are going to be rather suspicious, don't you think?"

Freddie paused to consider the matter. As he did so, the matron approached them hesitantly and spoke to Freddie, "Excuse me, sir, my little boy is not feeling well. I'd like to get some warm milk for him and change his diaper. I wonder if you would allow us to go on through to the ladies' powder room?"

Before Freddie could respond, Professor Mann said loudly, "Right after you have your eyes checked, Madam. Part of the health inspection, you know. Now if you'll just look into this black box and tell me what you see . . ."

"Of course," the matron said, "if you'll promise to hurry."

The woman turned to Freddie and handed him the infant, which immediately set up a lusty bawling. Freddie's nose crinkled at the moist little bundle he had been handed, and he held the child clumsily and with obvious distaste. "Hurry it up, will you?" he said loudly to the Professor.

"Here's the first picture. What do you see?"

The matron leaned back a bit. "It's a gun of some kind," she said. "I don't approve of guns, you know."

"And how about this second picture?"

The matron glanced into the eyeholes in the black box, then leaned forward a bit. "Why, it's a snake—a big, black, ugly snake."

Freddie glanced up immediately. The Professor smiled at him with wide-open eyes.

"And now we'll try another test entirely. When I say 'Now,' I want you to look into the apparatus and tell me as quickly as you can what you see. All right?"

"Certainly," said the matron demurely, as Professor Mann adjusted the slides inside the box.

"Now."

The woman leaned forward to look. She paused for several seconds, then responded. "That's odd, very odd indeed. I seem to see two things at once. First I see that snake again, and then I see a picture of the Laforan President, and then . . . then I see the snake biting the President. Now why would I see something like that?"

Freddie knew perfectly well why. He moved the infant to one arm and signaled vigorously with the other. Two large guards swooped down on them at once.

"Arrest this woman and search her baggage carefully," he told the guards.

General Chambro hurried up to them, a worried look on his big, round face. "Freddie, you've gone mad! This woman can't be the Snake!"

"How do you know?" the Professor asked, as the guards removed the matron from the scene. "You're just prejudiced against women, you two."

"Yes, my dear General," Freddie said, a smile on his face. "I'll bet you a month's pay that Professor Mann has snared the Snake for us. The perceptual tests are positive."

"Perceptual tests be damned," said the General loudly. "Killing is a man's business, and everybody knows that the Snake is a man . . ."

"And that's why nobody ever caught her," replied Professor Mann. "She gave you a beautiful illusion to fool yourselves with. Down through history the snake has always been a symbol of masculine sexual power and ruthlessness. Take the primitive tribe that I had hoped to visit, for instance. The chief warrior has a snake carved on the staff he carries. And if you look closely at those gold buttons that cover your uniform, General, you'll find the snake symbol on them all."

The General inspected his buttons, then frowned.

Professor Mann continued. "But of course the Snake did give you one clue to her identity—isn't poison a woman's weapon? Or was it just your minds she was attempting to poison?"

Freddie grinned, the General sputtered in protest, and Professor added a footnote. "I'll offer one more suggestion. Look through those baby things very closely. What more unlikely place to carry snake venom than in a child's rattle?"

A few moments later the guards reported that they had found a tiny hypodermic needle and a small bottle of white liquid inside the bottle of milk that the woman carried.

General Chambro was beside himself with happiness. He embraced Professor Mann in a huge bear hug, then hurried off to tend to military matters.

"He smells a promotion, I'm sure," said Freddie caustically.

"Helping catch the Snake won't hurt your image any either, now will it, Freddie?"

"My dear Professor Mann, you speak with a forked tongue. But you are right, of course. The President will be very pleased . . ."

"And as for me?"

Freddie frowned. "Whatever do you mean?"

"What about those 'murderous savages' that I want to visit? Are you still afraid that they might do me in? Well, if I can catch a snake for you, can't I manage to handle a few frightened primitives?"

"Well, my dear . . ."

The Professor interrupted. "You're still showing your prejudices, Freddie. When you look at a woman, you see a helpless little creature who couldn't possibly survive unless she had a great big man handy to protect her. You get very, very angry at all the whites in this world who judge a man by his skin color rather than by his true capabilities. Yet your view of women is just as biased and as distorted as their view of skin color. Isn't it about time you saw through some of your own illusions?"

Freddie smiled. "You psychologists! Ah well, I suppose that I might just mention to the President what your part in this afternoon's activities was. And our President is a very generous man indeed."

Freddie looked around and saw a couple of porters lounging near one of the doors.

"Here, you men! Get Professor Mann's equipment packed up again, then take it outside and put it back on the truck. She'll need it in the back country."

The Professor smiled softly. "Thanks, Freddie. I do appreciate your changing your mind. And now, how about that drink you promised me two hours ago?"

They walked off, arm in arm, headed for the cocktail lounge. The porters began to load up the heavy crates with the perceptual apparatus. The boxes were covered with address labels. On the largest label of all, written in scrawling print was:

> Dr. Mary Ellen Mann
> Department of Psychology
> University of the Mid-West
> USA

Recommended Readings

Cornsweet, Tom N. *Visual Perception* (New York: Academic Press, 1971).

Fraiberg, Selma. *Insights from the Blind: Comparative Studies of Blind and Sighted Infants* (New York: Basic Books, 1977).

Gombrich, E.H. *Art and Illusion: A Study in the Psychology of Pictorial Representation* (Princeton, N.J.: Princeton University Press, 1961).

Gregory, Richard L. *The Intelligent Eye* (New York: McGraw-Hill, 1970).

Haber, Ralph Norman, and Maurice Hershenson. *The Psychology of Visual Perception*, 2d ed. (New York: Holt, Rinehart and Winston, 1980).

Locher, J.L., ed. *The World of M.C. Escher* (New York: Abrams, 1971).

Rock, Irwin. *An Introduction to Perception* (New York: Macmillan, 1975).

Dember, William N., and Joel S. Warm. *Psychology of Perception*, 2d ed. (New York: Holt, Rinehart and Winston, 1979).

ESP and Subliminal Perception

Did You Know That . . .

Some people once believed you could control people's minds by flashing "hidden" messages on movie screens?

Many sensory messages get through to the lower centers of your brain and affect your behavior without your being conscious of what these stimuli are?

You are often unaware not only of incoming stimuli themselves, but also of how you react to these stimuli?

For a stimulus to prompt you to make a conscious response, the stimulus must first cross the sensory threshold, then the perceptual threshold, and finally the action threshold?

Some people repress awareness of emotional, sexual, or threatening stimuli, while other people actively seek out such sensory inputs?

Most psychologists do not have a strong belief that mental telepathy and other forms of ESP exist?

When you are highly motivated, you may respond correctly to stimulus inputs you cannot consciously describe?

"It's All in Your Mind"

Mrs. Sarah Wilson
823 Third Street
South Clarion, Missouri

Dear Mother:

Well, here it is another week. Mostly I've just hit the books and written a couple of short papers for my poly sci class. Nothing too energetic. Had a date with Charlie Saturday night—we went to see that new takeoff on Superman because it was the only flick one of us hadn't seen. Charlie grooves on macho-type heroes anyhow. I rated the film S for Silly. Not a good night at all.

In fact, I knew from the moment Charlie picked me up at the dorm that it was going to be one of "those" nights. I swear, I do *like* Charles, but sometimes we just don't communicate, we don't relate.

Sunday, Father Pratt talked about spirits that move us mysteriously from within. I've thought about that a lot, particularly since Tuesday night.

Tuesday was a funny night too. I think I told you that Dr. Tompkins had invited me over to his house for coffee. I'm taking this course of his on the psychology of religion. He doesn't just go into Christianity or Judaism—he covers the Eastern religions too. Zen and Buddhism, and then he spends a lot of time on spiritualism. You know, the *occult.*

Weird stuff, the occult, and I don't always know quite what to make of it. Or of Dr. Tompkins. He *talks* as though he believes in *something,* but secretly I think he's an atheist. I mean, aren't most scientists atheists? And he keeps trying to do *experiments* on things, instead of just trying to read about things and *understand.*

Anyway, he asked me over to have coffee with him and his wife. She's a *living doll.* Sort of quiet and sweet and understanding—reminded me of Mrs. Merriweather back home. I thought maybe there would be several students from his class there, but no, I was the only one. And I'm not that great a student. Well, no complaints. If the Great Professor wants to have me stop by for coffee, it's fine with me.

Incidentally, I wore that pretty green dress that Aunt Debbie gave me for my birthday last year. You might tell Aunt Debbie that Mrs. Tompkins complimented me on it.

Well, I knew it was going to be a weird night from the moment I got in the car. My bones ached, I guess, and I said to myself, it's going to rain tomorrow. And then while I was driving, I had the radio on and the weather forecast was "clear tonight, rain tomorrow." Isn't that queer?

And I almost got killed on the way over, but it wasn't my fault at all. I was cruising down Parker Drive, minding my own business and thinking about how to get Charlie to ask me out on Friday, when I got this *feeling.* You know me and my feelings. It was like a flash of lightning. Like I could see myself dead in a car wreck or something.

Well, it scared me so much that I slammed on the brakes and came to a screeching halt right there in the *middle* of Parker Drive. And then a second later, this guy comes roaring out of a driveway about 10 feet ahead of me, didn't stop, just cut right in front of me and roared off into the distance.

That guy must have been drunk, I'm sure. If I hadn't stopped . . . Well, no need to dwell on bad thoughts, but it really was scary.

When I got to Dr. Tompkins', I told him about it. He smiled that professional smile, and said "very interesting," and asked me if I wanted cream in my coffee. I swear, those teacher types are *too much.* But Mrs. Tompkins gave me a hug and told me how pretty I looked and wasn't it a shame there were so many bad drivers in the world and I should sit down and relax a while.

Their living room is lovely—sort of middle-class modern with lots of bad paintings in bright colors. They asked me all about my family, and I told them about you and Dad and Bud. And then we got to talking about the occult, and Dr. Tompkins said he wanted to show me something, so we moved our coffee into his study.

I swear, I've never seen such a cluttered place. Books piled everywhere, junk of all kinds on his desk, papers and magazines stacked on the floor, vases and photographs and lamps and chairs and souvenirs from all around the world. Just thrown everywhere. I moved some books off a chair and sat down and just *looked* at all the stuff he's got. Then Dr.

Tompkins started pawing through various piles of journals hunting for an article on ESP—that's extra sensory perception.

Well, I sat there for a few minutes, and then the hackles began to rise on the back of my neck. I mean, it was so *strange*. It wasn't at all like the lightning flash I got while driving over there. It was something really *different*. I felt like I had been there before—like I had been in their house before. But I never even knew of Dr. Tompkins before this semester!

Finally the feeling got so intense I had to say something about it. Dr. Tompkins was very nice to me, asked me all about it. Then he said it was called *déjà vu*, which is a fancy French term for "I have seen this before."

Of course we had a little argument. Dr. Tompkins seemed to think that maybe something had *caused* me to have the feeling, but of course it wasn't a *cause* at all. It was an experience, a feeling. How can you *analyze* things like that?

Well, after a while, we went back into the living room and the feeling sort of dribbled away. But isn't that *peculiar*?

Not much else to tell. Oh, yes, thanks much for the extra 20 bucks. I can use it, I assure you. Give my love to everybody and tell Bud that he still owes me a letter. Postcards don't count!

Love,
Barbara

(Continued on page 281.)

Subliminal Advertising

In 1956, a public relations executive named James Vicary held a press conference that set New York City on its ear. Vicary announced to the press that he had discovered a new advertising technique that he was sure would revolutionize America's buying habits. The technique was so powerful, according to Vicary, that almost no one would be able to resist it, and so subtle that most Americans would never realize that their behaviors had been affected.

What Vicary did was to flash "secret messages" on a movie screen so rapidly that the people watching the movie weren't *consciously aware* that the messages were there. The messages said, "Drink Coke," and "Eat Popcorn." According to Vicary, sales of both Coca-Cola and popcorn rose dramatically. Vicary claimed that the advertisements stimulated the *unconscious* portions of the mind. He claimed as well that the people in the audience purchased Coca-Cola and popcorn because their *unconscious minds* told them to do so in terms their conscious minds couldn't resist.

Vicary called his technique **subliminal advertising.** Within a few days after the 1956 press conference, the newspapers and magazines were full of anguished articles denouncing Vicary for having thrust a new and terrible method of "mind control" upon an unwilling world.

In point of fact, *subliminal advertising* was neither new nor particularly effective. As we will see, the technique had been tried many times earlier, and was abandoned because it simply didn't work. And after the press conference, many scientists tried to repeat Vicary's experiment, but failed to get the same results. To tell the awful truth, there has never been a *well-controlled study* demonstrating that "hidden advertisements" of any kind work very well in real-life settings.

Despite the fact that there is no scientific proof that subliminal advertising can affect what people do or buy, Vicary's claims were so startling that they continue to terrify some people—and to motivate others with greed. Thus, as late as 1979, advertisers were still "hiding" emotionally

Subliminal advertising (sub-LIM-in-ull). From the Latin words *sub*, meaning "below," and *limen*, meaning "threshold." A subliminal stimulus is one that is below the threshold of consciousness. Subliminal advertising consists of commercial messages or ads that are flashed on a screen so rapidly that your mind is not conscious of seeing them. First thought to be a dangerous form of "mind control," subliminal advertising turned out to be more of a "flash in the pan."

laden words in their ads, and psychologists were still reporting two or three studies a year showing that the technique has no practical value.

To understand what subliminal advertising is all about, where the idea came from, and why it doesn't work very well, you will need to learn a few things more about how your nervous system "processes" sensory inputs.

Question: James Vicary did not use "control groups" in his study of subliminal advertising. What kinds of control groups do you think he should have used in order to be sure that it was the "hidden messages" that caused the increase in sales?

Thresholds

What does the word "threshold" mean? If you find yourself on the threshold of a dream, you are still awake—but you are just on the *verge* of entering or obtaining your dream. If you stand on the threshold of a room, you are obviously in the doorway—neither entirely *in* the room nor all the way *out* of it. The threshold, then, is a *halfway point* between two places or states of being.

But a threshold is also a *barrier* of sorts that you have to cross in order to get from one place or state into another. Some thresholds are low and hence easy to cross over, while others are higher and more difficult to negotiate.

A sensory input from the outside world must pass over at least two neural "tollgates" before you become conscious of the stimulus, and must negotiate yet a third neural threshold before you respond to the input.

1. The **sensory threshold.** A stimulus must process enough *physical energy* to excite your receptor neurons. If the stimulus is strong enough, it will cause your receptors to fire and hence send a message to the lower centers of your brain. But if the stimulus is not strong enough, your receptors will fail to respond, and the message will never be sent. A whisper may be far too weak to excite the hair cells in your cochlea, but a shout will almost always get through, at least to the lower parts of your brain.

2. The **perceptual threshold.** The mere fact that a stimulus is physically strong enough to reach the lower centers of your brain doesn't mean you will become conscious of the input. For unless the message is *psychologically important* to you, your reticular activating system may block it out. At any given moment, thousands of stimulus inputs reach the lower centers of your brain. If you had to pay conscious attention to all of them, you'd never get anything done. Generally speaking, then, only meaningful stimuli are strong enough to attract your attention and hence cross your *perceptual threshold* into conscious awareness.

3. The **action threshold.** The mere fact that you are aware of an input doesn't mean that you will respond to it in any measurable way. If a stranger shouted a dirty word at you, you might choose to ignore it. If the same stranger shouted "Help," you might decide to take action.

These three thresholds are so inter-related that you might have trouble telling where one begins and the other leaves off. For instance, how cold does a room have to be in winter before you notice the chill? And how much colder does it have to get before you either put on a coat or turn up the heat?

How long must you go without food before you *perceive* that you are hungry? And once you take action, how much food must you eat before you realize that you're "stuffed" and hence stop eating?

How much annoying sensory input do you have to put up with from a friend before you get angry? And how much kindness do you have to receive from someone before you do something in return?

Sensory threshold. A threshold is the dividing line between two places or states of being. A stimulus must have a certain strength to cause your sensory receptors to fire—that is, to cross the sensory threshold.

Perceptual threshold. A very weak light may be strong enough to cause your rods and cones to fire—that is, to cross the visual sensory threshold—but not strong enough to push all the way to consciousness. Any stimulus that you are aware of has crossed the perceptual threshold. Subliminal stimuli are thought to be above the sensory threshold but below the perceptual threshold.

Action threshold. Just because you perceive something doesn't mean that you will necessarily respond to it by moving or taking action. You might ignore the family cat if it strolled into your room. You might do something else if a hungry lion walked in on you. Stimuli strong or important enough to provoke a response are above the action threshold.

Perhaps if you learn how sensory, perceptual, and action thresholds are actually *measured*, you will better understand how to tell them apart.

Action Thresholds Probably the most famous "action" threshold in history is described in the old story about "the straw that broke the camel's back." Suppose that you decided to run a scientific test to see if, indeed, adding one more straw to a camel's maximum load would "break its back." What might happen?

To begin with, you'd probably learn almost immediately that these old stories were mostly **exaggerations.** That is, you'd find that any reasonably intelligent camel you used as a subject would lie down, roll over, and refuse to get up long before the weight you put on its back was sufficient to do it any real harm.

So you'd probably have to settle for trying to discover how many straws it took to make the animal "lie down and roll over." Therefore, you'd start piling on the hay to see what would happen.

Individual straws don't weigh very much, so you could load thousands of them on the animal's back before it started to groan. Then, at least according to the saying, there would come a critical point in your experiment. Suppose you had put 999,999 straws on the camel and it was still standing upright. Now you add one additional wisp of hay, and down the beast goes.

The camel's *action threshold* would obviously be 999,999 straws.

Question: We noted in Chapter 4 that a pigeon confined in a small box will attack anything handy if it is shocked or frustrated. What kind of experiment could you set up to determine the "frustration–aggression" threshold in pigeons? Could you determine the same sort of action threshold for people, or for nations?

Perceptual Thresholds Next, suppose you wanted to determine what would be the smallest amount of light that you could see under the best conditions. At first blush, it might seem that you would be measuring your *visual sensory threshold*, but that wouldn't be the case. For if you are *conscious* of seeing the light, then you *perceive* the light. Hence you would be working with a perceptual threshold. We will discuss sensory thresholds

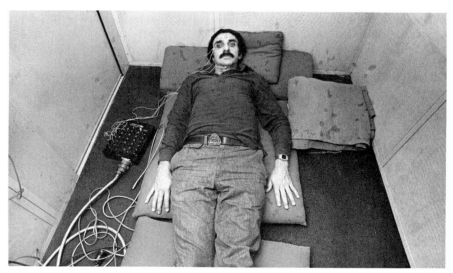

At the American Society for Psychical Research, a subject is in an altered state of consciousness in a dark, soundproof room while stimulus pictures, randomly chosen, are displayed six doors away. The subject is asked to describe the pictures. The subject's brain waves, eye movements, and muscle tension are being monitored.

Exaggerations (ex-adge-er-RAY-shuns). To exaggerate is to overstate something beyond the bounds of truth. If you tell someone the food in your college dorm "is the worst in the world," you probably have exaggerated (because you've probably not tasted the food served in the dorms at Michigan!).

in just a moment. Right now, let's see how you could test your own perceptual threshold for a very weak visual stimulus.

One way would be to get a light bulb whose brightness you could increase or decrease merely by turning a knob of some kind. Then you could sit in a dark room for 30 minutes, to give your eyes a chance to adapt, and then start turning up the intensity of the bulb until you first became aware that the light was on.

The point at which you could just make out that the bulb was shining faintly would be one measure of your *visual perceptual threshold*. Turn the light down a little, and you can't see it. Turn the knob up a bit and you have no trouble seeing the light all the time.

But there would be a point—a halfway point—between seeing and not seeing, which you could determine by using the bulb–knob apparatus. This halfway point is, of course, your perceptual threshold.

By definition, then, the visual perceptual threshold is that intensity of stimulus—that brightness of a light—that you *can* see half the time and that you *can't* see half the time.

Question: How would you go about testing your auditory threshold, or your threshold for the taste of salt?

A couple of points about thresholds probably occur to you at once. The first point is that this definition is quite **arbitrary.** There's no reason why we couldn't have defined the threshold as being that stimulus strength which you could perceive 25 percent of the time, or 75 percent of the time, or even 38.729 percent of the time. However, European scientists in the 1800's picked the 50 percent point and, for the most part, that definition has stuck.

The second thing about thresholds that might set you wondering has to do with their *stability*. Let's go back to the camel. Suppose you decided to test the animal just after it had run a long race across the desert, and the beast was very tired. Under these conditions the camel might collapse if you piled no more than 800,000 straws on its back. If you had chosen a particularly good day for the animal, after it had rested for a couple of weeks, it might have been able to tolerate 1,100,000 straws with no great strain.

Thresholds differ. They differ from person to person, from day to day, even from moment to moment. If you tested your camel for a thousand different days, you would get a great many different measures of the threshold. If you counted up the number of times the threshold was *exactly* 999,999, the number of times it was 999,998, and so on, you could put the figures on a graph like the one in Fig. 11.1.

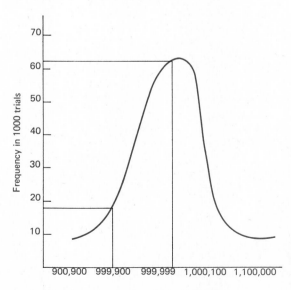

Fig. 11.1 "The number of straws it takes to break a camel's back" from one day to the next. The number of times that it took exactly 999,999 straws is called the **frequency** with which that event occurred (out of 1000 trials). As you can see, the threshold was 999,999 some 62 times, while it was 999,900 some 18 times.

By looking at the curve, you can tell that most of the time the camel's threshold was very close to 999,999 straws. Once you knew this fact you could begin working out ways to keep the animal from collapsing. Making sure the camel was in good health would be one way; keeping its load well below 900,000 straws would be another.

Question: If someone you know gets angry very easily, how might you use the threshold concept to help reduce the number of temper tantrums that the person throws?

Perceptual thresholds are much like action thresholds—the *weaker* the stimulus with which you are presented, the *lower* the probability that you will perceive the input on any given test trial.

Suppose we gave you a pair of earphones to wear and then we presented such a soft musical tone through the phones that, out of 100 trials, you were consciously aware of the tone only *once*. What can we say about this tone?

If the tone were *right at* your auditory threshold, you would expect to be aware of it half the time, or 50 times out of 100. A tone that you heard only once in 100 trials is obviously far *below* your usual threshold.

The Latin word for threshold is **limen**. Thus, speaking technically, the very weak tone would be "below your perceptual *limen*," or **subliminal**. A subliminal stimulus is one so weak that you would be conscious of it much less than 50 percent of the time, but which is still strong enough so that under ideal conditions it might break through to consciousness.

As you will soon learn, the word "subliminal" almost always refers to a stimulus that is *below* your perceptual threshold, but *above* your sensory threshold. For instance, even the faintest of stimuli may contain enough physical energy to excite the rods and cones in your retinas and hence cross the visual *sensory* limen. But it takes a great deal more energy for a stimulus to cross your *perceptual* threshold of conscious awareness.

Now that the definitions are out of the way, we can add a little salt and butter to James Vicary's subliminal "popcorn" advertisements.

Subliminal Perception

Back in 1956, Vicary ran a brief series of experiments at a movie theater in Fort Dix, New Jersey. During the showing of the feature films at this movie house, Vicary used a special slide projector that flashed "secret" messages about Coca-Cola and popcorn on the screen. These messages were projected at such a weak intensity and at such a fast speed that apparently none of the movie-goers was aware of what Vicary was doing. (At least, no one complained to the management.) The ads were, then, well below the visual perceptual thresholds of the people involved.

According to Vicary, however, this subliminal advertising was so effective that popcorn sales rose more than 50 percent and soft-drink sales increased 18 percent. No wonder the advertising agencies were interested! Here was a sales pitch delivered so subtly that the audiences didn't know they were being influenced, but so "unconsciously powerful" that the audiences bought things they probably didn't really need. And no wonder that politicians and other concerned citizens became upset about the possibilities for "mind control" that subliminal advertising seemed to offer.

However, as we noted at the beginning of this chapter, subliminal stimulation was neither new nor effective.

Two-Point Threshold

More than a century ago, a European scientist named Suslowa noticed something rather odd when he was attempting to determine the **two-point**

Limen (LIME-en). The Latin word for "threshold."

Subliminal (sub-LIM-in-ull). Literally, "below any limen or threshold." However, many psychologists arbitrarily define the word as meaning "below the perceptual threshold."

Two-point threshold. Also called the "two-point limen." The distance apart that two metal points must be (when touching your skin) so that you can perceive them as being "two" instead of "one" exactly 50 percent of the time. Electrical current is often (but not always) passed through the points when the threshold is being measured.

Supraliminal (SUP-pra-LIM-in-ull). From the Latin words meaning "above" and "threshold." Our words "supreme" and "super" come from the Latin word *supra*.

threshold on some experimental subjects. Suslowa had two pointed pieces of metal through which he could pass a weak but mildly painful electrical current. He would touch these points, or electrodes, to the skin of a blindfolded male subject and turn on the current. The subject was then asked to say whether he could feel *both* the points separately, or whether they were so close together that the mild stimulation seemed to come from a *single spot* on his skin.

Sometimes, just to keep the blindfolded subject alert, Suslowa would touch the man with but *one* of the electrodes. If the man then claimed to feel "two points," Suslowa would know he should not place too much value on the subject's verbal reports. Thus sometimes Suslowa touched two points to the man's skin, sometimes just one. On any given trial it was the subject's task to perceive whether he had been stimulated with "one point" or with "two."

Suslowa was interested in mapping out skin sensitivity, and was one of the first scientists to do so. But what we remember him most for was the following discovery: On those trials when his subjects insisted that they couldn't *consciously* tell whether it was one point or two, his subjects "guessed" the right answer far more often than chance would allow.

To appreciate how intriguing this discovery was, perhaps you should imagine yourself as a subject in an experiment like Suslowa's. The psychologist would blindfold you, ask you to lie on your stomach, and then would begin stimulating various parts of the skin on your back (see Fig. 11.2). You'd be asked to report "two points" or "one point" each time you felt the weak electric shock.

The psychologist might discover that, at a certain point in the small of your back, you *always* reported "two" if the electrodes were 3 centimeters apart—and that you *never* reported "two" if the electrodes were but 1 centimeter apart. However, if the electrodes were exactly 2 centimeters apart, you reported "two" 50 percent of the time and "one" 50 percent of the time.

Obviously, your *two-point threshold* would be 2 centimeters on that part of your back. The 3-centimeter distance is well *above* your threshold—what the psychologist might call a **supraliminal** or "above-threshold" stimulus. The 1-centimeter distance is well *below* your threshold, hence is a *subliminal* stimulus.

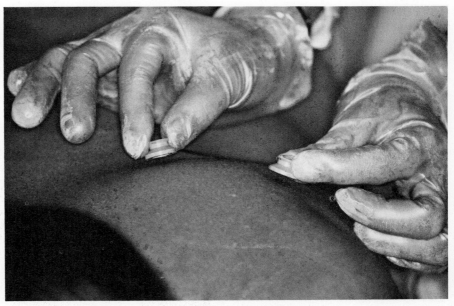

Fig. 11.2 The two-point threshold experiment using electric stimulation on the skin of a subject's back.

PART TWO Sensation and Perception

Under these conditions, you would almost never *perceive* the 1-centimeter distance as being "two." That is to say, the psychologist could touch the electrodes to your back all day long, and you would almost never "feel" two points if the electrodes were only 1 centimeter apart. Even if the psychologist sometimes touched your skin with two electrodes (1 centimeter apart), and sometimes with just one, you would consciously "feel" or perceive the stimulus as being a single point.

But suppose that the psychologist demanded that you *guess* whether one point or two had been used. What would your guesses be like?

Theoretically, your guesses should be *random*—about the same as if the psychologist had asked you to guess "heads" or "tails" when the psychologist flipped a coin. But that is not what Suslowa found. His subjects did *not* guess randomly. Instead, they were correct in their guesses much *more* than 50 percent of the time.

You must realize that Suslowa's subjects insisted they could *not* consciously perceive or detect or feel the difference between two points and one under these conditions. But when Suslowa forced them to *guess*, they were surprisingly accurate. The subjects themselves could not account for the fact that they were responding with such accuracy to the subliminal stimulus.

Discrimination without Awareness

How is it that you can feel something that you can't really feel? At first, psychologists thought that it was a matter of **attention.** Your behavior is often influenced by environmental events that you pay little or no conscious attention to. For example, have you ever started to walk someplace when you had a lot of things on your mind and then found yourself at your destination without the slightest idea of how you got there?

Or have you ever been driving a car along a highway while you were thinking about something important, and then you suddenly "woke up" to the fact that you had been paying no attention at all to the car? Yet somehow you had managed to stay on the road, slow down at the right moments, and speed up when necessary. How is it that you didn't have an accident?

Attention. To pay attention to something is the act of becoming consciously aware of that thing. Your "center of attention" is your focus of consciousness. Your "attention span" is the length of time that you can focus on one event or object.

Most drivers discriminate without awareness while on the road. That is, they drive automatically while thinking of other things.

Reflexive (ree-FLECKS-ive). Reflexive movements are automatic reactions that require no conscious thought or attention.

Discrimination without awareness. Responding reflexively or unconsciously to stimuli strong enough to cross your perceptual threshold. You are not aware of the stimuli when you react to them—but you could become conscious of them if your attention were called to the stimuli.

Synapse (SINN-apse). The junction point between two or more neurons. As an input message moves up your nervous system toward your cortex, each synapse it must cross acts as a kind of gate or threshold. Unless the input is strong enough to cross the synapse, it is "gated out" and never crosses the perceptual threshold. (See Chapter 2.)

After you have been driving for a while, most of the motor skills necessary to keep the car on the road become automatic. That is, the responses that your hands make on the steering wheel and your feet make on the pedals become **reflexive.**

Reflex movements are often handled by the lower centers in your brain, or perhaps in part by your right hemisphere, leaving your left hemisphere free to think about more weighty problems. And since your left hemisphere is the site of your *conscious* experience, most of these reflexive or automatic responses would be *unconscious*. (If you have ever seen a movie or videotape recording of yourself, you probably know only too well that you have many mannerisms that you simply are not aware of, and yet you make these characteristic movements all the time.)

The stimuli that you respond to when you are driving are almost always *supraliminal*. That is, you *could* become aware of them if your attention were directed to them. But sometimes your left hemisphere withdraws from day-to-day activities for a brief period. During these moments, your lower centers and your right hemisphere probably "run things" for you. That is, they screen all the incoming sensory inputs, make various discriminations, and respond appropriately.

We call this **discrimination without awareness,** and it is a very common thing that most of us experience many times daily.

Discrimination without awareness always involves stimuli that are *above both your sensory and your perceptual thresholds*. That is, your left hemisphere *could* perceive them if your attention were called to the stimuli.

Subliminal perception is something else again. For subliminal stimuli are *above* your sensory thresholds but are *below* your normal perceptual thresholds. In fact, these stimuli are so weak that even if your left hemisphere worked overtime trying to sense or detect them, it simply couldn't do the job.

How, then, does subliminal perception work?

The answer is—not very well. The neurological road from your receptors to your cortex has many gates and barriers on it. Each time the incoming sensory information must cross a **synapse,** there is a chance for very weak stimuli to be gated out or rejected. Thus there are a few inputs strong enough to get through to the very lowest centers of your brain—but no higher. You'd never be conscious of them, but they could affect your behavior in very slight ways.

For instance, in Chapter 8 we mentioned that your eye makes many reflexive movements. When a point of light suddenly appears at the edge of your visual field, you automatically turn your eyes toward the light. This reflexive movement is controlled by the lower visual centers of your brain. If the pinpoint of light is bright enough, you will *consciously* see it after you look in its direction.

But if the light stimulus is just strong enough to reach the lower centers—but not strong enough to reach your left cortex—you couldn't *see* it no matter how hard you tried. If someone now asked you if you saw anything, you would truthfully say "no." But if someone *demanded* that you guess whether a light had been there or not, the fact that your eyes had moved might bias your left hemisphere just enough so that it guessed "yes."

So there are times when you can respond correctly to stimuli that are far too weak or *subliminal* for you to perceive consciously.

"Dirty Word" Experiments

One of the most interesting sets of studies on subliminal perception were the "dirty word" experiments performed in the 1950's and 1960's by Elliott McGinnies and several other US psychologists.

McGinnies began by determining the *perceptual threshold* for ordinary words. He did this by showing student subjects simple words such as "table" and "chair" at faster and faster speeds. With each student (and for

Elliott McGinnies.

PART TWO   Sensation and Perception

each word) McGinnies was able to calculate an exposure time so rapid that the subject could perceive the word *exactly 50 percent of the time.*

For a word such as "whole," this perceptual threshold might be about 100 **milliseconds.** For an emotionally laden word such as "whore," however, the threshold was typically much *higher*—200 milliseconds or more. McGinnies believed that his subjects were *unconsciously defending* against perceiving such "disturbing" words as "whore." He called this effect **perceptual defense.**

Many psychologists objected to McGinnies' studies, claiming that he had not *controlled* for all the outside influences he ought to have taken into account. For instance, we know that the more common a word is, the *lower* its threshold will be. You can recognize the word "cat" in a much shorter time than you can recognize the word *concatenation.* In the 1950's, words such as "whore" seldom appeared in print, so the student subjects might well have been relatively unfamiliar with the printed form of the word.

We also know that, in some circles, speaking such words out loud is unacceptable—particularly if both sexes are present. McGinnies' critics speculated that if a male student were presented with the word "bitch," he might indeed recognize it but be afraid to say it in public. Instead, he might say "botch" or "batch" or "butch," and would keep on doing so until the word was presented at such a long time interval that he clearly saw it was "bitch." These critics guessed that male students would be more likely to report "dirty" words in an experiment if the psychologist testing them were male than if the psychologist were female, and, as further experiments showed, the critics were quite right.

The critics also noted that a few students actually had *lower* thresholds for "dirty" words than for "clean" words. How might this finding be explained?

The answer given by McGinnies is that while most people *defend* against sexual stimuli, a few of us are vigilantly searching the world around us for anything that might be slightly smutty. McGinnies called this *lowered* threshold **perceptual vigilance.**

Whether a person tends to seek out, or to defend against, sexual stimuli seems to be a matter of each individual's own past experience and moral upbringing. But even when the criticisms against this line of research are taken into account, there still seems to be fairly good evidence that something like perceptual defense or vigilance does occur in many people.

Milliseconds (MILL-ee-seck-unds). The Latin word *milli* means "thousands." A millisecond is therefore a thousandth of a second. A millimeter is a thousandth of a meter.

Perceptual defense. The act of suppressing or repressing threatening stimuli. When you defend yourself (perceptually) against recognizing "dirty words," you are in fact raising your perceptual threshold for perceiving these words, usually by blocking off the input message at some synapse.

Perceptual vigilance (VIDGE-ill-ants). The opposite of perceptual defense. The lowering of a perceptual threshold, usually by making a synapse easier to cross. If your mind unconsciously defends against sexual stimuli, when someone shows you the word "rape," you are likely to perceive it as "rope." If your mind is unconsciously vigilant for sexual stimuli, when someone shows you the word "rope," you are likely to perceive it as "rape."

Censor (SENN-sor). From the Latin word meaning "to assess, or tax." When the lower centers of your brain assess an input as being highly emotional, they may reflexively cut it out of your conscious awareness.

Unconscious Censoring

Presuming that the *perceptual defense* experiments are valid, how can we explain them? How can you *defend* against perceiving a word until you actually *see* it? There are two types of explanation for the perceptual defense studies—one based on Freudian theory, the other based on recent findings about the brain.

Sigmund Freud, perhaps the greatest personality theorist of modern times, believed that each of us has a **censor** operating somewhere within our minds, whose chief task is to prevent sexual or other types of threatening impulses or memories from breaking through to consciousness to embarrass us. According to Freud, this censor acts as a "mental gate" through which all thoughts and memories must pass before we become aware of them.

If you want to call up some simple, pleasant image from your storehouse of memories, this image should get past your censor with no difficulty. However, whenever you are prompted to remember some psychologically upsetting event, your censor goes into action. Presumably, your censor screens out offending material by *increasing the threshold* that the memory must cross in order to become conscious.

If the memory is weak, or if it is so threatening that your censor "goes all out" in order to prevent it from getting through to your left hemisphere, the censor can **repress** the thought by pushing it down into unconsciousness.

Your censor may also attempt to screen out incoming *sensory* information, but usually sensations are too strong for your censor to handle. However, if the disturbing stimuli are weak enough, the censor may in fact be able to raise your perceptual threshold sufficiently to screen them out too.

Right Hemisphere "Screening"

When Freud first **postulated** his theories more than 60 years ago, he wrote about them in purely psychological or even literary terms because we did not know enough about the nervous system then for Freud to be able to make much use of neurological data. Now, in the 1980's, there is a fair amount of physiological experimentation to support Freud's early notions.

In one of the "dirty word" experiments, for instance, psychologist Robert McCleary hooked his subjects into a **polygraph** or "lie detector" before testing their visual thresholds. McCleary found that when he showed his subjects "dirty words" at speeds far below their perceptual thresholds, the subjects denied seeing the stimuli. But the subjects often showed emotional responses *on the polygraph record* even when they insisted that they hadn't the foggiest notion what the word was. And just as McCleary had predicted, these "emotional reactions" did not show up on the polygraph when the stimuli used were words such as "table" or "chair."

Subsequent experiments by both Canadian and US psychologists have confirmed McCleary's early research. But still the problem remains: How can you react to the emotional content of a stimulus when you don't consciously know what the input is?

In the early chapters of this book, you learned that your right hemisphere (if you are right-handed) is the "perceptual–emotional" half of your brain. Under normal conditions (such as reading this book), your left hemisphere handles *words* better than does your right. However, your right hemisphere recognizes *visual patterns* much better than does your left. When you attempt to perceive a word flashed on a screen at very high speed, you will most likely be aware of the *pattern* of the letters before you can read the letters one by one.

Thus it seems likely that your right hemisphere can recognize the "shape" of an emotionally charged word long before your left hemisphere becomes conscious enough of the word to say it out loud. And since your right hemisphere controls many of your unconscious emotional responses (including many reactions picked up by the polygraph), the right half of your brain could easily defend against, or seek out, weak emotional stimuli before they broke through to consciousness in your left hemisphere.

Freud drew his conclusions about "unconscious censoring" from his astute observations of the people who came to him for help, but he had no idea where in the brain this "censor" might be located. Recent research not only confirms many of Freud's psychological insights about censoring, it also suggests the censor may reside in the right hemisphere.

So we may conclude with some safety that you *can* react meaningfully to sensory inputs that you don't consciously perceive. The next question is, can you react to *extra*-sensory inputs that you don't consciously perceive?

Extra-Sensory Perception

Both subliminal perception and "discrimination without awareness" have sometimes been used as explanations of something called **extra-sensory perception.**

Many people believe that, under certain special conditions, the human mind can **transcend,** or rise above, the usual physical means of communication—that is, communication by talking or signaling or writing messages.

Repress. To press down, usually out of consciousness. To "censor" a thought, memory, or stimulus input.

Postulated (POSS-tew-lay-ted). From the Latin word meaning "to ask for" or "demand." In English, the word more often means you have assumed something to be true, decided arbitrarily about something, or theorized. Freud postulated that almost all forms of love had a sexual basis—that is, he assumed or theorized that love was primarily sexual. One of the difficulties in making postulates or assumptions is that one seldom gets around to proving whether or not the assumptions are true.

Polygraph (POLL-ee-graf). A machine that measures your pulse, rate of breathing, skin resistance, and so forth. Sometimes (incorrectly) called a "lie detector."

Extra-sensory perception. Perceptions are ordinarily triggered off by sensory stimuli—that is, by inputs to your eyes, ears, and so forth. If you could perceive something without making use of these sensory inputs, you would experience extra-sensory perception.

Transcend (trans-SEND). To go beyond the normal limits or thresholds.

If you want to know what is going on inside the mind of a friend of yours, you typically have to observe your friend's *behavior* or ask the friend what he or she is thinking about. It's likely you're not always aware of the subtle behavioral cues you pick up while your friend is talking or behaving. Nonetheless, we can presume that information about your friend's thoughts *normally* reaches your brain by way of the same sensory pathways that tell you whether the traffic light is red or that an airplane is flying overhead.

But what if your mind could reach out and make "spiritual" (nonphysical) contact with your friend's mind? If this could happen, you could read your friend's thoughts *directly* by means of extra-sensory perception, or ESP.

There are many types of ESP. Four of the best-known are mental telepathy, clairvoyance, precognition, and psycho-kinesis.

Mental telepathy is the technical term for "reading someone's thoughts."

If you could see through walls, as Superman does in the comics and movies, you would have to do so by *extra-sensory* means, since your senses are incapable of this feat. **Clairvoyance** is the term we use to describe the perception of external objects or events without normal sensory stimulation.

Precognition is the ability to perceive future events before they happen.

If you could influence the movement of physical objects simply by wishing them to move, you would be demonstrating a power called **psycho-kinesis, or tele-kinesis.** Literally speaking, psycho-kinesis is the power of "mind over matter." (Whether or not psycho-kinesis is a form of *perception* is debatable, but it surely involves extra-sensory powers of one kind or another.)

All of these unusual experiences are referred to as **para-normal** events, because they are beyond the realm of ordinary or normal explanation. (The Greek word *para* means "beyond.")

The study of para-normal events makes up a field called **para-psychology,** the investigation of events that are beyond the normal boundaries of behavioral science.

In 1978, New York psychologists Mary Monnet and Mahlon Wagner asked more than 1,100 US college teachers if they believed in ESP. Overall, 16 percent thought ESP was an established fact, while 49 percent believed it probably was a real-life occurrence. About 24 percent of the teachers denied it existed, while the rest thought it "merely an unknown." Teachers in the humanities, arts, and education were the most enthusiastic supporters of ESP—about 75 percent believed in it. Only 5 percent of the psychologists thought ESP to be an established fact, and only 29 percent thought it was likely.

Given the fact that teachers are fairly representative of all college-educated individuals, the chances are good that either you or someone you know has had an experience that seemed at the time to be para-normal. Perhaps you dreamed that someone you know would have an accident, and shortly thereafter something similar to your dream actually occurred. Perhaps one day you looked at someone and were convinced that you could actually read that person's thoughts. Or perhaps you have heard stories of someone who went to Las Vegas and won big by mentally controlling the dice, or by guessing accurately what numbers would come up on a roulette wheel.

How can science explain such **phenomena?**

The answer is that science can't always explain such things, nor should it always try to. Science is but one way of looking at humans and the world around them. Religion is another way, art is another, and para-psychology is yet a third. Our lives would be greatly impoverished if we ever settled on just one way of viewing or explaining things.

In the case of ESP, however, science can explain *part* of the events people have claimed are para-normal. And that much, at least, science should attempt to do.

Mental telepathy (tell-LEP-uh-thee). The Greek word *tele* means "far off," or "at a distance." The word "television" means "seeing at a distance." The word "telephone" means "speaking over a distance." The Greek word *pathos* means "experience" or "emotion." Mental telepathy is therefore to experience something at a distance through mental or emotionl communication rather than by physical means.

Clairvoyance (clair-VOY-ants; rhymes with "bare boy dance"). From the French words meaning "clear-sighted." The ability to see things hidden from normal sight.

Precognition (pree-cog-NISH-shun). Cognition is the intellectual process by which knowledge or ideas are gained. Precognition is knowing or perceiving something before the event actually occurs.

Psycho-kinesis (SIGH-ko-kin-EE-sis). The Greek word *kinesis* means "movement," or "to move." *Psyche* is the Greek word for "mind." Psycho-kinesis is the ability to move things mentally (by willing them to move) rather than by touching them physically.

Tele-kinesis (TELL-ee-kin-EE-sis). To move things at a distance through thought power instead of physical power. Another word for psycho-kinesis.

Para-normal (PAIR-uh). Something beyond the usual or ordinary, such as a creature from outer space, or a failing grade in a psych course.

Para-psychology. That part of psychology concerned with the study of ESP and other para-normal happenings.

Phenomenona (fee-NOMM-ee-nah, or fee-NOMM-ee-nuh). Plural of phenomenon. Anything you are conscious of is a "phenomenon."

Generally speaking, believers in ESP fall into two main camps:

1. Those who hold that such talents as mental telepathy are entirely *super*natural. By definition, supernatural events are beyond the scope and interest of science (although often of great concern to individuals who earn their living as scientists).

2. Those people who feel that ESP is a *natural* occurrence, but beyond the scope of our present understanding. These people usually believe that the scientific method can be used to discover new and perhaps undreamed of channels between the world and the brain. The difficulty with this view is that before para-psychologists can prove an event is truly *extra*-sensory, they must demonstrate that the event cannot somehow be explained as an odd but perfectly normal *sensory* occurrence.

Demonstrating that an event can be explained in normal scientific terms often calls for great ingenuity. So let us see why para-psychological experiments are so difficult to design, and how their results are sometimes misinterpreted.

ESP Experiments

Suppose you volunteered to participate in a para-psychological experiment. You might be shown a pack of ordinary bridge cards so that you could make sure that, like all other bridge decks, this one contained 52 cards divided into four suits. The experimenter would then shuffle the cards thoroughly and place the deck face down on the table between the two of you.

The experimenter might then pick up the cards one by one in such a manner that he or she could see the card, but you couldn't. You would then be asked to "read the experimenter's mind," that is, to guess the *suit* of the card that the para-psychologist was looking at. Since there are four suits in the deck, you would have *one chance in four* of being right with any given card. If the first time you tried this experiment, you guessed the suit correctly 13 times out of 52, you would have done no more than would normally be expected *by chance alone*.

Question: How many times would you have to guess the suit correctly before you might begin to suspect that something para-normal had occurred?

An ESP experiment with a card. The man is trying to "send" a mental image of the card to the woman.

PART TWO Sensation and Perception

Undaunted by your first experience, you try again. And this time you guess all 52 of the cards correctly! Surely this is evidence that mental telepathy occurred, isn't it?

The answer is—not yet. First you must show that you had no *sensory* cues to help you out. Thousands of studies similar to this one have been performed in the past, and almost all of them are useless from a scientific point of view.

Why? Because the experimenter failed to appreciate how likely it is for subliminal perception and discrimination without awareness to occur in this type of situation.

Miller's Harvard Study More than 30 years ago psychiatrist James G. Miller trained Harvard college students to "guess" correctly the symbols on a deck of cards even though the students could not consciously see the symbols and were not aware that they were being trained or "conditioned."

Miller got students to volunteer for what they thought was an ESP experiment. He then asked them to sit in front of a glass screen fixed on the wall like a mirror. The student was supposed to stare at the glass screen and to "project" on the screen the mental image of whatever card they thought Miller was looking at.

James G. Miller.

Miller would stare at the card, remind the student to look at the screen, and then ask the student to guess the card. If the student was right, he was rewarded. If he was wrong, the student was given a mild shock.

To most students' great surprise, they were able to "guess" the symbols with incredible accuracy—although their accuracy disappeared if Miller omitted *either* the reward for correct responses *or* the punishment for incorrect responses.

Had Miller demonstrated a high level of ESP among Harvard students? Not quite. What the student didn't know was that the glass screen was really a one-way mirror. In the next room, Miller had a slide projector aimed at the back side of the mirror. When he pressed a button in the experimental room, the projector would throw on the mirror a very faint image of the card that Miller was looking at.

The projected image was so weak that it was well below the student's *conscious* threshold—yet, when Miller *motivated* the students highly enough, they were able to make use of sensory information so subliminal that it never reached consciousness. As you might guess, none of the students reported actually *seeing* the picture of the card as it flashed on the screen.

In a second part of the experiment, Miller switched from studying subliminal perception to studying discrimination without awareness. At first, each student was shown very weak stimuli as before. But while the experiment was in progress, Miller gradually increased the intensity of the projected images until they were well *above* the conscious threshold.

Most of the students continued to stare at the "blank" screen without being aware that the symbols were as visible as the numbers on the door to the experimental laboratory. At this stage of the experiment, of course, the students were "guessing" the cards with 100 percent accuracy, but they still thought they were "reading Miller's mind." Miller then told them what he was doing and, naturally enough, the students immediately "saw" the symbols quite clearly.

Miller's explanation of what the experiment was all about did not please all of the students, however. Some of them insisted afterward that they had guessed correctly using *mental telepathy,* and that Miller was trying to "trick" them into believing that they hadn't really used ESP after all!

Question: Why did motivation play such an important part in getting the students to perform well?

Kennedy's Stanford Study At about the same time Miller was working at Harvard, J.L. Kennedy at Stanford was studying what he called **unconscious whispering.**

Unconscious whispering. The act of making sounds you are unaware of making that give clues to other people about what you are seeing or thinking.

Kennedy asked two students at a time to participate in his study. One of them was to look at one card at a time from a special deck and to "send" the other student a mental message about each card. The "receiver" student guessed out loud what card the "sender" was looking at. The sender would then tell the receiver whether the guess had been right or wrong.

Kennedy used a special piece of apparatus for his work that "funneled" very faint sounds from the sender's mouth to the receiver's ear—much as a long narrow hallway "funnels" echoes from one end to another. Kennedy could wipe out these faint sounds by taking away the special equipment. He found that when the "funnel" apparatus was in place, many of the receivers had **phenomenal** success in "guessing" what card their senders were looking at. However, the instant that Kennedy removed the equipment, the guesses would drop back to chance level.

Kennedy observed very carefully just what his successful senders were doing. He noted that, in many cases, the sender would make a *characteristic sound* for each different type of card that the sender looked at. For example, if the sender was looking at a heart, she or he might always make an "ahem" sound. If the card was a spade, the sender might always inhale sharply.

The receiver apparently soon learned what faint sounds were associated with which cards. As you might expect, unless the students had been trained to notice such things, neither senders nor receivers were usually aware of this "unconscious whispering."

Some of the students turned out to be very good "unconscious" senders and receivers. In general, those subjects who were strong believers in ESP were good at the task, while those people who had a firm disbelief in ESP were unable either to send or receive successfully.

Question: Why were the "disbelievers" so poor either at sending or receiving the "unconscious whispers?"

Schmidt's Precognition Study   Neither Miller's nor Kennedy's experiments disproved the existence of para-normal powers, nor were they aimed at doing so. Rather, both studies showed how difficult it is for anyone to perform a cleanly designed, well-controlled investigation of a topic that is by definition almost beyond the boundaries of modern science.

As Miller and Kennedy both noted, one of the difficulties with ESP studies is that the experimenter must make sure that there is *no possible way* the information the subject is trying to "receive mentally" could be received by normal sensory pathways. Thus the experimenter must control for "unconscious whispering" and other such sensory clues.

Another problem is that the experimenters themselves may unconsciously "cheat" while recording the results of the study. As Kennedy notes, "human beings . . . are not trustworthy recording devices," particularly when they hope very strongly that the results will turn out a specific way.

In 1969, physicist Helmut Schmidt reported a study on *precognition* that seems to overcome the problems raised by Miller and Kennedy. Schmidt built a *random generator*—a machine that would randomly turn on one of four colored lights. Beneath each light was a button that the subject could press. It was the subject's task to predict which light the machine would turn on, on any given trial, by pressing the appropriate button.

Since the machine did not make its random selection until *after* the subject had pressed a button, there was no way that either Schmidt or the subject could know which light would turn on, except through *precognition*. Thus there was no way that Schmidt could have given the subjects "unconscious clues."

Schmidt's machine made an objective recording both of the subject's guess and of which light actually came on, so there was no way that Schmidt could have cheated in scoring the results.

In his first experiment, Schmidt used three subjects who made more than 60,000 guesses. They guessed correctly far more often than chance would allow. In a second experiment, the subjects could guess either which light would turn on, or which one wouldn't. Again they did far better than chance.

Do Schmidt's studies *prove* that precognition exists? No, not necessarily, although they do offer encouraging evidence about ESP.

The problem is that not everyone who has tried to **replicate** Schmidt's work has been successful. Furthermore, subjects who are "good" at the guessing game one day often fail to show precognition the next time they're tested.

As Rhea A. White noted in 1977, "Some experimenters have reported not being able to obtain significant results on ESP or psycho-kinesis tests while others often seem able to get significant results. Others are successful only with certain subjects or under certain testing conditions." Dr. White suggests that the *attitudes* of the experimenters may strongly influence whether a given study yields results favorable or not favorable to ESP.

Replicate (REPP-plee-kate). To repeat something (such as a scientific experiment) exactly. In fact, it is almost impossible for a scientist in one laboratory to replicate *precisely* an experiment performed in another lab. The conditions simply are too different. Therefore, when scientists say they have replicated a study, they mean that they have repeated it "more or less exactly."

Does ESP Exist?

Do all these facts mean that ESP is little more than a figment of people's imaginations? No, not at all. But the facts do indicate that the "personal" evidence for ESP is presently stronger than is the "experimental" evidence. Extra-sensory perception seems at best to be a kinky, slippery, undependable thing that happens rarely, unpredictably, and for the most part uncontrollably.

As the survey taken by Monnet and Wagner showed, psychologists are often very skeptical of such things as ESP. And probably most of them will continue to be skeptical, until some very bright person can demonstrate the conditions under which para-normal powers occur with *regularity,* so that these powers can readily be studied by the scientific method. For far too much of the evidence offered to "prove" the existence of para-normal powers can better be explained in terms of highly motivated, sincere people who make use of subliminal stimuli without being conscious of doing so. And that is why the study of subliminal perception bears directly on the study of ESP.

A brain wave machine in use. The attendant places cards face down on a table. The machine is attached to the subject, who sits in the next room and attempts to identify the cards.

Subliminal Advertising

To return now to the question with which we started: Need we worry about men and women of evil design who might practice "mind control" using subliminal advertising?

The answer appears to be *no*. Shortly after James Vicary announced he had increased popcorn sales 50 percent by flashing the command "Eat Popcorn" on a movie screen, dozens of psychologists attempted to repeat Vicary's study. And all of them failed.

In the *laboratory*, under very artificial conditions such as those Miller used, you can demonstrate that subliminal perception does exist. But by 1980 more than a hundred scientists had reported experiments showing that "subliminal advertising" simply doesn't work in *real-life situations*.

Subliminal inputs *can* influence your behavior—but only under two rather rare conditions: First, you must be in a position where all the *supra*liminal inputs available to you do not give you the information you need to make a decision. And second, you must be highly motivated to make use of even the weakest of "hunches."

When you are forced to guess the answer to a difficult or tricky problem, or when it is urgent for you to become attuned to all the subtle stimuli in your environment that you might usually ignore, then, and only then, will you make use of sensory inputs that lie below the threshold of conscious awareness.

Your own personal motivation is thus the key to understanding how and when your mind makes use of subliminal as well as any other kind of stimuli. It is to the study of *motivation*, then, that we next turn our attention.

Summary

1. Knowledge about the world around you—as well as the world within you—typically comes to you through your **sensory** (input) pathways.

2. A sensory input or stimulus will be effective only if it is strong enough to cause a physical response by your neurons. An **effective stimulus** is therefore an input that is sufficiently strong to cross one of several **thresholds.**

3. The three main types of thresholds are as follows:

a. **Sensory thresholds** are crossed whenever the stimulus input is strong enough to excite one or more **receptor neurons.** For example, suppose a friend whispers "hello" in your ear. The sound waves created by your friend's voice are a **physical stimulus.** If this input is strong enough, it excites neural receptors in your inner ear and thus crosses your **auditory** (sensory) **threshold.** If the sound waves are too weak, the stimulus is below your sensory threshold and you hear nothing.

b. **Perceptual thresholds** are crossed whenever you become consciously aware of a stimulus input. But many stimuli are "gated out" by the lower centers of your brain. Even though a "whisper" might be strong enough to cross your auditory (sensory) threshold, it might not be important enough to punch through to **consciousness** by crossing your perceptual threshold. In this case, your ear would "hear," but your mind wouldn't.

c. **Action thresholds** are crossed when you respond behaviorally to an input. Thus even if you heard what your friend said, you might choose to ignore the "hello." However, if your friend had whispered "fire" instead, you probably would have taken some action.

4. Under rare conditions, a weak stimulus input may cross a sensory threshold and have an effect on the lower centers of your brain, but not break through to consciousness. Under these conditions you may respond to a stimulus without being aware of what external event called forth your action. This sort of sensory input is called a **subliminal stimulus,** because it is below your perceptual threshold and you cannot perceive it no matter how hard you try.

5. Attempts to use subliminal stimuli as "hidden" forms of advertising have so far been unsuccessful.

6. The lower centers in your brain—and perhaps your unconscious right hemisphere—often respond to stimuli that your left hemisphere ignores. You could be conscious of these inputs if someone called your **attention** to them, but generally you are not because your left hemisphere is attending to other things. The act of responding unconsciously to stimuli your left hemisphere ignores is called **discrimination without awareness,** an act we all perform countless times each day.

7. Some people are emotionally aroused or upset by certain types of stimuli, such as "dirty words." Their right hemispheres may unconsciously raise the perceptual thresholds for these stimuli, an act called **perceptual defense.**

8. Other people may seek out presumably threatening or arousing stimuli (such as "dirty words"), an act called **perceptual vigilance.**

9. **Extra-sensory perception** is the ability to know or perceive things by non-sensory means.

10. **ESP** includes such strange talents as **mental telepathy, clairvoyance, precognition,** and **psycho-kinesis** (or **tele-kinesis**).

11. Many ESP studies are better explained in terms of **subliminal perception** and discrimination without awareness than they are in terms of **para-normal** powers.

12. There are a few ESP experiments that are difficult to explain, however, except in terms of para-normal powers.

13. Despite the existence of these few well-controlled studies on ESP, most psychologists do not believe in ESP. Most non-psychologists—particularly in the arts and humanities—believe ESP exists, however.

14. Whether para-normal powers exist or not, the study of ESP has taught us a great deal about how we respond to faint stimuli and how hard it is to design well-controlled experiments using humans as subjects.

(Continued from page 265.)

Mrs. Sarah Wilson
832 Third Street
South Clarion, Missouri

Dear Mrs. Wilson:

It was most kind of you to send along the alarm clock which, now that I have used it in the experiment, I am returning to you.

Barbara came out for coffee last night, and she reacted just as I had thought she might. As I told you on the phone, I am studying *déjà vu,* that odd psychological condition which makes people feel that they have "seen this all before." The experience is often so strong that the person believes that she or he can actually predict what is going to happen next.

Many religious leaders have written about their own *déjà vu* experiences, believing them to be mystically inspired. My own belief is that the *déjà vu* experience is caused by the way the hemispheres of the brain process information.

As you may know, the left hemisphere processes information logically and verbally, while the right hemisphere seems more concerned with visual perceptions and the emotional meanings of stimuli. The right hemisphere often perceives "patterns" that the left hemisphere misses.

The right hemisphere also seems better at predicting the consequences of certain events, and tries to warn the left that it ought to take action in order to avoid a disaster. But since only the left hemisphere is conscious, messages and warnings from the right hemisphere tend to break into our awareness more as "flashes of insight" than as logical deductions.

Most of us make equal use of both our hemispheres. A few individuals, however, tend to overuse their left hemispheres. These people are often frightened by the messages that come from their right hemispheres and tend to suppress them—or to explain them as "The Voice of God."

Other individuals tend to be particularly sensitive to messages from their right hemispheres. These people occasionally reject logical explanations for things, preferring to believe in "hunches," "intuitions," and "occult principles."

I believe I mentioned on the phone that I hope to show that *déjà vu* can be triggered off in right-hemisphere people when they encounter something very familiar to them in a strange environment. Under these conditions, the right hemisphere will signal "familiar object" although the left hemisphere is conscious only of "new environment." In my opinion, it is this *conflict* between the two hemispheres that leads to *déjà vu.*

At any rate, that's why I wanted to borrow from you some small object that Barbara would recognize instantly. She is a particularly sensitive and intuitive person, and I wanted to see how she would react when her right hemisphere spotted this well-known object in unfamiliar surroundings. Your guess that I ought to use her old alarm clock was an excellent one.

I have at my home rather a large room that I use as a study. It has bookshelves lining three walls from floor to ceiling, and the shelves are full of books and souvenirs from my many visits overseas. To say that the place is cluttered is something of an understatement. At any rate, I put Barbara's old alarm clock rather high up on one of the shelves, surrounded by a couple of vases so that it was just barely visible. If you hadn't known it was there, you probably would never have noticed it. But, as I had hoped, Barbara's right hemisphere perceived it right away.

Or, to put the matter more objectively, she was very bothered by it even though she couldn't consciously put her finger on what it was that was affecting her. The longer she stayed in the study, the more excited she became. Finally she bubbled over and told me what she was feeling.

I tried to get her to analyze what was causing the experience, but she was too excited to do so. We will talk about it in class later on, and then perhaps she will understand.

You see, when her right hemisphere (presumably) spotted the clock, it triggered off a lot of old memories and visual associations. Her left hemisphere just couldn't understand why her right hemisphere was feeding it associations having to do with her past experiences with the clock. And since these old memories were very much out of context and couldn't be tied in logically with my cluttered bookshelves, her conscious hemisphere got very upset. It couldn't understand that only *part* of the experience was familiar—so it apparently just assumed that Barbara had somehow lived through the whole thing before.

At least, that's what I think happened. I won't be sure, of course, until my research is finished—and that may take several years.

I've had several students out for coffee this semester and have, thanks to their parents, exposed them to similar situations. But so far, only one other person besides Barbara has had the *dèjá vu* experience. I haven't told the class about it yet, but I will before the semester is over. So I would greatly appreciate your not mentioning the business unless she brings up the subject herself, or until the term is over.

My hunch is that Barbara is one of the lucky ones, a person who is very sensitive to the emotional importance of things. She is a very bright, humane individual who should grow into a very perceptive woman. She will probably go through life following her insights, and most of the time these insights will be good ones. Her insights would be even better if she tried to analyze *why* she feels the way she does, but perhaps that's expecting too much at this stage of her life.

At any rate, she has a fine talent and a marvelously developed right hemisphere, and I think you should be proud of her.

Again, my thanks for your considerable help.

Sincerely,

Theodore A. Tompkins

Recommended Readings

Greenburg, Dan. *Something's There* (Garden City, N.Y.: Doubleday, 1976).

Hardy, Alister, Robert Harvie, and Arthur Koestler. *The Challenge of Chance* (New York: Random House, 1974).

Rhine, J.B., and J.G. Pratt. *Parapsychology: Frontier Science of the Mind* (Springfield, Ill.: Charles C Thomas, 1972).

Steiger, Brad. *ESP: The Sixth Sense* (Mattapan, Mass.: University Publisher & Distributor, 1973).

3

Motivation

Introduction to Motivation: Hunger

Did You Know That . . .

Most of your basic, life-sustaining needs can be expressed in terms of inputs and outputs?

Whenever you lack something necessary for survival, a primary drive builds up within you that motivates you to satisfy that need?

Your brain controls your inputs and outputs much as a wall thermometer controls room temperatures?

Associated with most primary needs are certain learned or secondary needs?

Some psychologists believe that you cannot achieve "self-actualization" until you have satisfied all of your more basic needs?

Your most basic "need" may be that of predicting and controlling your biological, mental, and social inputs?

While a third of the people in the world suffer from undernourishment, some 20 percent of the people in the US suffer from eating too much?

Medical treatment for fatness has a cure rate less than that for treating cancer?

Colleges often discriminate against overweight students?

There is a neural center in your brain that, when stimulated electrically, might make you go on an eating jag?

Hunger pangs are mostly learned?

Fat people apparently don't pay much attention to their hunger pangs?

More lower-class than upper-class persons in the US are overweight?

Some husbands seem to push food on their wives to keep the women fat and faithful?

Almost anyone can lose weight by following a program that takes into account biological, intra-psychic, and social/behavioral needs?

"By Bread Alone"

Thelma Green shook her plump face vigorously. "It's a dirty shame the way they treat people who are a trifle overweight," she said. "They don't consider our problems at all, and we've got lots."

Annette Holmes smiled and nodded encouragingly. Thelma Green certainly did have "lots"—about 280 pounds of "lots," and the woman couldn't be more than about 5 feet 2 inches tall. But Annette liked the woman and, in her capacity as therapist at the Weight Control Clinic, wanted to help Thelma shed some of those pounds if she could. So Annette just nodded and smiled and waited to see what Thelma had in mind.

"Take, for instance, clothes." Thelma Green picked at the blouse she was wearing. "Who makes good-looking clothes for somebody as fat as me? Potato sacks is what they sell us, and we have to buy them because there's nothing else available."

Annette looked carefully at Thelma's clothes. They didn't look all that bad. The woman was neat in her appearance despite her size. But Annette continued to nod her head.

"And anyhow, what kind of wardrobe can you have when you shoot up or down 30 pounds every six months?" Thelma continued. "I've got a wardrobe full of clothes that are either too big for me, or too small for me. I'm like a yo-yo. I gain a little, so I don't fit most of the things I have. And then I go on a crash diet, and I lose 40 pounds, and I *still* don't fit my clothes because now they're too big for me. I tell you, I've been on so many diets I think I'll puke if I ever see another bowl of cottage cheese!"

"Diets don't do all that much good, it's true," Annette said. "It's not losing pounds that is the difficult part, as you know. It's learning how to eat sensibly so that you reach and maintain a sensible weight that's so terribly hard for most overweight people."

Thelma frowned. "Why is that?" she asked.

Annette warmed to her subject. "Going on a diet means starving yourself for a while, but you don't make any fundamental changes in your eating habits, your exercise habits, or in your self-image. You have to learn to eat sensibly, and keep on eating that way. Most overweight people just aren't motivated to make drastic and permanent changes in the way they live and think and feel."

"But I don't eat all that much," Thelma replied, an edgy tone in her voice. "I just can't understand why I stay so heavy."

Annette smiled. "Look, Thelma. Fatness is caused by just one thing—you take in more calories than you burn up. Some people eat too much, or they eat the wrong kinds of food, or they eat at the wrong times of the day. Other people eat fairly sensibly but exercise too little. But the real problem is that most people don't *measure* what they're doing. So they never face the fact that they're inputting too much and outputting too little."

"Now, really!" Thelma said a bit testily. "That can't be my problem, because I know what I eat, and it's very little, I assure you. No breakfast at all, and I have a very light lunch. I eat a sensible dinner, and that's it. Maybe 1,500 calories per day. But I gain weight on that, so maybe there's something wrong with the way my body utilizes food, or something."

Annette sensed the woman's impending anger and backtracked a little. "Well, I suppose that could be the difficulty. Have you seen a doctor yet?"

"I've seen a dozen," Thelma said unhappily. "They've put me on diet after diet, given me pills, and all that jazz. Hasn't helped a bit, in the long run. I saw one guy last week. He gave me lots of tests, and then he told me I had a possible heart problem, something might be wrong with my kidneys, and I was going to die if I didn't lose 100 pounds right away. I asked him how I was going to shed those pounds, and he said that any dummy knew how to lose weight. Then he gave me another diet and said it would be my fault if I got sick and died because I was too stubborn to lose weight."

"So how did you react to this news?" Annette asked.

Thelma pulled out a handkerchief and dabbed it at her eyes. "I got so discouraged and depressed I went home and cooked a huge meal to make me feel better."

Annette had heard that one before. She just wished medical doctors would look at the actual consequences of what they told their patients. She favored Thelma with a supportive smile. "Well, I can understand your reaction. But it does seem as if you ought to try to learn how to eat better so that you can get back into shape medically as well as socially. Suppose we start off by taking a baseline of what you really eat . . ."

"It isn't much, I told you that."

Annette smiled again. "I know, but we want exact figures. Here's a form I'd like for you to fill out. Please record everything you eat and drink. Put down the time, the place, the amount, who else is present, what you're doing, and how you feel. That will give us a good baseline or starting point. Once we have those data, we can talk seriously about how to help you learn some new eating and exercise habits."

"Fifteen hundred calories a day, it's no more than that. And I still gain weight!"

Annette nodded. "Perhaps, but you may be surprised. What I want you to do next is to decide how much you'd like to weigh a year or so from now. Then make a list of all the benefits and gains you'd receive if you got down to this weight."

"Well, my clothes would fit better," Thelma responded. "And I could go bowling again, and there's my friend Shirley in Miami I want to impress . . ." Her voice trailed off quietly.

"Very good thoughts!" said Annette. "Please put all those things down on your list, and any others you can think of. And come see me again on Friday at this same time. We'll have our dietitian see you then."

Thelma Green gathered herself together and stood up. "Do you really think there's any hope for me?" she asked softly. "Can I really get things under control?"

Annette looked the woman squarely in the eye. "Certainly there's hope. You can do it—if you really want to."

"I really want to," Thelma said. "I really do."

Three days later Annette got an urgent telephone call. "I don't believe it!" Thelma wailed. "I wrote down everything I ate and drank, just like you said I was supposed to do . . ."

"The baseline, yes . . ." said Annette. "That's good."

"No, it's terrible! Absolutely terrible! I added it up, and I'm taking in 5,000 calories a day. Can you believe that?"

"I can believe it," Annette said, thinking of the woman's size.

"Listen," said Thelma, "I want to go on a 1,000 calorie-a-day diet right away. Do you hear, right now!"

For just a second, Annette panicked. Cutting down from 5,000 to 1,000 a day would surely be too much a change for almost anyone. So Annette stalled a bit. "Listen, Thelma, you said you didn't eat much breakfast or lunch and had just a light dinner. When are you taking in all those calories?"

"At night, after dinner, sitting in front of the boob tube," the woman replied. "I snack and snack and snack. About 3,000 calories worth an evening, to tell you the truth."

Annette nodded to herself, then spoke into the phone. "And how do you feel when you're snacking?"

"Bored," came the reply. "I had a bad day at work yesterday, and I got depressed, and I came home and started dinner and just kept on eating all night long."

"Well," said Annette, "What happened at work that got you so depressed?"

Thelma paused a moment before replying. "To tell you the truth, one of the women I work with screwed up one of her reports, and when I criticized her and told her to do it over again, she threw the report in my face. I was just trying to be helpful, and she throws a temper tantrum like a three-year-old."

Annette sighed deeply. Weight control therapy seemed so simple when you first went into it. Just help people learn to eat correctly, right? But people over-eat for a thousand different reasons. Very often you had to help them clean up their emotional problems before you teach them to control their over-eating. Annette suspected she'd have to teach Thelma some new job skills so that she wouldn't get depressed at work and thus over-eat when she went home.

"Listen," continued Thelma, "I've gone through the kitchen and thrown out all the junk food I could find. But now there's practically nothing left to eat. I'd go to the grocery store right now, but I don't know what to buy or how to cook low-cal stuff. Can you help me?"

"Of course I can help," Annette responded. "That's what I'm here for. Tell you what. I'll come over and we can make up a shopping list. Then we can have a light dinner somewhere and go to the grocery store."

Thelma snorted loudly. "Go to the store *after* you eat?"

"Certainly," Annette replied. "That way you cut down on the impulse buying. I'll bring over a really good diet plan I have, and we can work it out, and then go shopping . . ."

"A thousand calories a day, right?"

Annette groaned silently. "Well, we'll see. Maybe 1,500 would be better to start with . . ."

Thelma was adamant. "No, a thousand is my limit. Don't worry, I can do it. I want to lose 30 pounds in the next six weeks."

Again Annette groaned. Thelma wanted to go too far much too rapidly. But Annette wanted to capitalize on the woman's remarkable motivation, so she decided to let Thelma take the lead. Then a thought struck her. "Listen, Thelma, I'll bring over a nice exercise plan too."

"Exercise?" Thelma said in a shocked tone of voice. "I don't go for that stuff very much. Except for bowling, which I've given up for the duration."

"Why?"

Thelma hemmed and hawed a bit on the phone, then confessed. "Well, I used to belong to this bowling league, and I really did like it. But I got so big I didn't fit my bowling clothes any more, and then we usually had three or four drinks. And you know how many calories there are in alcohol. And, well, to tell the truth, sometimes when I got a little high I got into arguments with my buddies . . ."

Annette could see it all quite clearly. Thelma simply didn't know how to get along very well with people. So she avoided company and stayed home by herself and got depressed and watched the tube and snacked. "Listen," Annette said, "You should go back to bowling even if your clothes don't fit. You can tip the bartender to give you a glass of icewater with lots of cherries and orange slices in it, and everyone will think you're drinking gin. And we can do some role playing so that you'll learn how to handle any social situations that might bother you. Okay?"

"Okay," came the reluctant response.

"But we're going to have to get you on a regular exercise program too."

"None of that crazy jumping around, do you hear?"

Annette smiled. "Of course not. We'll start with walking. Just walking. For instance, you tend to eat when you first come home from work, right?"

"Right."

"Well, we can interrupt that habitual behavior by having you walk for 10 minutes when you get home. That way . . ."

Thelma suddenly sounded excited again. "That way I don't associate eating with getting home from work, right? Hey, that's great. And you know I live in an apartment house, so even if it's raining I could just walk up and down the stairs for a while. Probably meet a lot of my neighbors for the first time, too. Might even be fun . . ."

"Of course it will be," Annette said enthusiastically. "Tell you what. It will take me about 15 minutes to get over to your place. Why don't you go for a walk and meet me at the parking lot in a quarter of an hour. Then we can make out the diet and go grocery shopping."

"Okay, it's a deal. But listen, no grapefruit and no cottage cheese, or I'll upchuck right there in the supermarket."

Annette laughed. "Okay, but no cookies and no cake and no potato chips either, right?"

Thelma moaned softly and hung up the phone.

A month later, Annette sat quietly in her office, staring at the telephone. For the first time ever, Thelma had missed an appointment. Annette had called the woman's apartment several times, but she didn't answer. And since it was nearly 11 at night, Annette was very worried.

Thelma had asked to see Annette at 9, because Thelma was going bowling right after work. Annette had agreed, because Thelma was doing beautifully. To Annette's great surprise, Thelma had stuck religiously to the 1,000 calorie per day diet. The woman had actually lost 22 pounds in four weeks, which was amazing. She was walking at least 30 minutes each day, and she had made several new friends while marching up and down the apartment stairs.

Thelma had gotten many insights into her own personality in the process of trying to lose weight. As Annette had guessed, Thelma tended to be rather bossy and punishing to her friends. But during their role-playing exercises, Thelma had learned how to express affection and gratitude openly instead of converting it into criticism.

She also was doing much better on the job. Before treatment, Thelma had thought that being a supervisor meant you ignored the people working for you until they goofed up. Now she spent most of her time helping these people set goals for themselves and letting the people know when they were showing progress. So she seldom came home depressed, and she had so many invitations to visit her friends that she almost never spent the evening watching TV.

Annette dialed Thelma's number again, but there still was no answer.

Of course, Annette didn't kid herself about the extent of Thelma's progress. The woman still had a long way to go—both physically and psychologically. Thelma had a terrible image of herself, so Annette had suggested that she put a high school photograph of herself on the mirror so that Thelma could frequently see "her once and future self."

The two women had spent a fair amount of time working on clothes and cosmetics. Thelma was basically a very attractive person, but she refused to accept this fact. She wouldn't use cosmetics at all, until Annette had insisted that she learn at least the rudiments of applying make-up.

"I don't deserve to look good," Thelma had said the first time Annette raised the issue. "No one as fat as me deserves to look anything but ugly."

Annette had solved the problem by getting Thelma to keep track of the compliments people gave her, and to write down daily at least one good thing that she thought about herself. But still it was touch and go . . .

It was funny, Annette thought to herself. One day Thelma was "up" and on top of the world. The next day—for no apparent reason—she's be terribly depressed. Much of the depression came from Thelma's not realizing how good she was, and how much progress she was making. So the two women had talked at length about Thelma's real goals in life.

The one thing that Thelma seemed to want most was the respect and affection of others. Her feelings about Shirley, the friend who lived in Miami, were an example. Shirley had been begging the woman to lose weight for many years, but to no avail.

"Shirley's worried more about my health than about my looks," Thelma had said. "She's a doll, that woman is. She stuck by me through thick and thin. Mostly thick, of course, given my size. Anyhow, what I want to do most is to lose 100 pounds, buy me a ticket to Miami, get on the plane without telling her I'm coming, and take a taxi to her house from the Miami airport, and ring her doorbell. I've seen that scene a thousand times in my mind's eye. Shirley opens the door, and she is thunderstruck at how I look. 'Hi, Shirl,' I say to her. 'It's the new me.'"

What better motivation? Annette had asked herself. So, at her suggestion, Thelma had started putting away $2.00 in her piggy bank every day that she stuck to her diet. Half the money went for cosmetics, but the other half she put in the bank to pay for the projected trip to Miami.

Maybe that's where she's off to, Annette said to herself with a smile. But then, Thelma had a long way to go psychologically before she headed South . . .

Annette gave Thelma's number one last try. After three rings a discouraged and somewhat intoxicated voice answered.

"Thelma? This is Annette. What's happened?"

After a moment's silence, Thelma sobbed, "Oh, Annette. I'm sorry. I'm just no damned good. I just don't deserve to get better."

The crisis, Annette thought. It almost always happens when the person is right on the brink of success.

"Look, Thelma, I want to come over to see you. Right now."

"You better hurry, honey," came the tearful reply. "There may not be much left to see if you don't."

(Continued on page 316.)

Distended (dis-TEN-dead). From the Latin word meaning "to stretch." When you blow up a balloon, you distend the material the balloon is made of.

The Motivation To Live

"What do I want from life?" Chances are that you've asked yourself this question many times. And if the answers you've come up with so far haven't entirely satisfied you, don't be discouraged. For the chances also are good that you've never realized how frightfully complex that question really is.

To begin with, has it occurred to you that everything you "want" is dependent on your being alive? That is, to get things from _life_, you must survive, you must _have_ life itself. Therefore, many of your basic needs are _life-sustaining:_ food, air, water, sleep, a certain range of temperatures, protection from such environmental dangers as storms, poisons, and germs.

Most of these life-sustaining "wants" can be expressed as _input_ needs. But you also need to maintain certain _outputs_ in order to survive. You must breathe out excess moisture and carbon dioxide, and you must release water and waste products through sweat, urine, and defecation.

Yet even these _output_ needs have their _input_ components. You don't go hunting for the nearest bathroom just because your bladder is full and needs to release urine. Rather, you feel the _urge_ to urinate because, when your bladder is full or **distended,** sensory neurons in the walls of your bladder send very painful input messages to your brain informing you that action on your part is urgently needed.

When you are deprived of fresh air, sensory neurons detect the build-up of carbon dioxide in your lungs and blood. When the build-up becomes too great, the neurons send alarm messages to your central nervous system that prompt you to vigorous movement (the "suffocating reflex," which is instinctive).

Even your output needs, then, are made known to you by input signals.

If you stop to consider all this, you will realize that your own bodily survival is primarily dependent upon your _controlling various types of sensory inputs._ As long as you can get the right types and quantities of certain critical inputs, you have an excellent chance of continuing to "have life."

Luckily, your body (like the bodies of most other animals) is genetically programmed so that you are born with reflexes that keep you alive. That is to say, you have certain innately-determined response patterns (outputs) associated with each of the critical stimulus inputs that you need to control in order to keep your body alive.

Motivation: Fact and Theory

The concept of motivation is one of the most difficult that psychologists have to work with, for the meaning of the word seems to change according to one's solution to the mind–body problem (see Chapter 5). Thus those psychologists who see the human animal as primarily a _biological_ creature tend to think of motivation primarily in terms of _bodily needs._ Those psychologists with an _intra-psychic_ bent often perceive humans as motivated mostly by _inner feelings_ and _rational decision making._ And those scientists who view the human race as a group of _social_ beings sometimes insist that our major motives are those involving our dealings with other _people._

Does your mind do anything more than interpret, rationalize, or yield to your body's itches and urges? Can you explain all of your emotions and desires in terms of increased or decreased firing rates of specialized nerve centers?

Are your needs for companionship—for love, personal growth, success and prestige, or even for helping others—as basic and as primary as your needs for food and water? Can we understand the complexities of human actions without realizing that people are highly complicated living systems with a variety of biological, intra-psychic, and social needs?

These are some of the thorny issues that we must grasp if we are to comprehend the problems—and the wide range of solutions—associated with our attempts to answer that seemingly simple question, "What do I want from life?"

Little wonder, then, that the field of human motivation is at the same time one of the most fascinating yet frustrating areas in all of psychology.

Motivation and Self-Movement

The word *motivation* comes from the Latin term meaning "to move." Ancient scholars were fascinated by the fact that some objects in the world seem to be *self-movers*, while other objects remain stationary unless *acted upon* by some outside force.

The ancients assumed that self-initiated motion was caused by a *spirit* inside the object (a "little man" of some kind) that pushed or impelled the object into action. Whenever the "spirit was moved," so was the object or body that the spirit inhabited.

Nowadays, we assume that only living systems are capable of self-determined movement. But to tell the truth, some of our theories of motivation (and of life itself) are still based on the idea that there is a **homunculus** deep inside us that pulls our strings and keeps us on the go. "Mind," "soul," "cosmic force," and **libido** are just a few of the terms we use to refer to this inner spirit or power that pushes us along life's path.

It was not until about the sixteenth century that Western scientists gained enough knowledge of physics that they could explain the "behaviors" of such **inanimate** objects as rocks and rivers in purely *mechanical* terms. Once scientists had made this giant intellectual step, they began to wonder if the actions of *living* organisms couldn't also be understood in physical, mechanical, or non-spiritual terms. Many of our theories of motivation are thus based on the belief that human activities are just about as mechanistic as are the movements of thunderstorms or ocean waves.

Two of the best-known mechanistic approaches to human motivation are *drive theory* and *arousal theory*. Each of these theories offers a slightly different *biological* solution to the mind–body problem, each has its strengths and weaknesses, and each is incomplete in and of itself.

Opposed to these physiological viewpoints are a number of *perceptual* or *intra-psychic* theories of motivation in which the organism's inner feelings or emotions are presumed to direct or control its physiological reactions.

We will examine all of these approaches briefly, then discuss the influence of various *environmental inputs* on what often appear to be purely *internal* motivational states. In this way, we may end up with a fairly complete and practical understanding of what motivates us—that is, what makes us move.

Drive Theory

As we, noted, physics became a science when physicists began to explain the motions of inanimate objects in terms of fairly simple *equations*. For the past century, many psychologists have attempted to imitate the "hard sciences" by reducing the complexities of human motivation to fairly uncomplicated *biological* equations. Instead of dealing with the mind, or with intra-psychic events (thoughts and feelings), these psychologists tried

Homunculus (ho-MUN-cue-lus). From the Greek and Latin words meaning "little man." See Chapter 4.

Libido (lib-BEE-doe). From the Latin word meaning "desire" or "lust." According to Freud, libido is a set of unconscious instincts that provides the energy for all our thoughts and actions. See Chapter 22.

Inanimate (inn-ANN-ee-mate or inn-ANN-uh-mutt). The word "animate" comes from the Latin term meaning "breath" or "spirit." "Animate" also means "to move about in a spirited fashion." Animate objects are those that have an internal source of motivation or movement power. Inanimate objects are those that move only when acted upon by some external motivator or mover. Our word "animal" comes from the same Latin source.

PART THREE Motivation

to explain all human movements or behavior in terms of physiological processes. Rather than assuming that people (or animals) are capable of self-determined actions, these psychologists theorized that organisms are *driven* or pushed into motion much the way an automobile engine is cranked into activity when you turn the ignition key or step on the starter.

At its simplest, the physiological approach to motivation is often called **drive theory.** Generally speaking, drive theorists presume that *biological* needs are the ones that rule your life. Biological pain *arouses* you to movement, while biological pleasure *reduces* your motivation to move. Put more bluntly, you tend to avoid pain but approach pain-reducing or pleasurable inputs.

You do have needs and wants other than biological pain and pleasure, of course. But drive theorists assume that you *learned* these needs by associating them with your attempts to reduce the physical arousals that propel you along life's highway.

In many ways, drive theory is an ingenious intellectual activity that has taught us much about the physiological mechanisms underlying many of our behaviors. But humans are *self-starting systems* rather than being auto engines. Thus, as we will see shortly, even in drive theory there's at least the ghost of a "little man" lurking about inside our bodies who pushes us toward pleasure and pulls us away from painful inputs.

It is easy for most of us to criticize drive theory. Sometimes it is not so easy for us to see the many contributions it has made to our understanding of motivational processes. So let us first look at the theory itself, then add up its pluses and minuses.

Primary Needs and Drives   Most drive theorists refer to those things you absolutely must have to survive as **primary needs.** Whenever your body runs short of some physical input you need for life—such as air, food, water, proper temperature—a **primary drive** builds up within your body that tends to motivate or move you to *satisfy that need.*

As long as all of your primary needs are met, your body presumably ticks along smoothly in a quiet state of balance. But whenever your body begins to run low on something required for survival, this balance is upset. Built-in physical mechanisms sense or detect your body's wants, and the firing rates in various neural centers in your brain start to *increase.* As these nerve cells fire more and more rapidly, you become physically aroused. When your arousal is great enough, your action threshold is crossed and you are *driven* (motivated) to seek what it is that you need.

Drive States and Homeostasis   According to drive theory, whenever any of your needs are not satisfied, you are likely to experience a state of *neural* arousal or excitation. This increased rate of neural firing creates what is called a primary **drive state.** Generally speaking, the longer you are deprived of something you need, the faster your nerve cells fire, the greater your drive state becomes, and the more aroused or "motivated" you are.

Eventually your aroused movements bring you into a position to satisfy your need. Once you do so, your drive level falls back toward zero, your drive state is greatly reduced, your arousal (motivation) disappears, and your normal physiological *balance* is reinstated.

As an analogy, you might consider how an air-conditioning unit controls the temperature in a room. Suppose that on the morning of a pleasant summer day, you set the control at 24°C (76°F). For a while, the machine is quiet because the room is still cooler than the temperature you set into the control. But as the day wears on, things begin to heat up. When the room gets too warm, the thermostat inside the unit *detects* this fact and is "motivated" or "driven" to turn on the fans and motors within the machine.

Cool air then blows into the room and the temperature rapidly begins falling. When the temperature inside the room reaches 24°C, the thermostat's "drive state" drops to zero, and it shuts off all the "aroused" electrical excitation within the unit.

Drive theory. The belief that all our really important needs are physiological ones, such as food, air, and water. Hence a biologically oriented, one-level theory in that it ignores intra-psychic and social/behavioral types of motivation.

Primary needs. Things that the body must have in order to survive; physiological needs, such as food, air, and water. Unlearned or instinctual needs.

Primary drive. Whenever your body is deprived of something necessary for life, an urge or desire for the "something" builds up which "drives" you to hunt for what you need. Associated with each primary need is a related primary drive. Food is a primary need; hunger is the associated primary drive.

Drive state. The state or condition of being without something you need, or of being motivated or "driven" to find something that you need. Generally speaking, the more deprived you are of what you need, the higher the drive state, the stronger the drive, and the more urgent the motivation to seek satisfaction. Eating when you are very hungry reduces your hunger drive.

Physiologists suggest that much of your biologically determined behavior is turned on or off by "internal thermostats" that detect your wants. When these inner "thermostats" detect a need of some kind, they arouse you so that you attend to the goal of keeping your body in a static, need-free, unexcited condition.

We call such activities **homeostatic,** from the Greek words meaning "home state" or "normal condition." The concept of *homeostasis*—the return to the normal or unexcited state—plays a central role in drive theory. See Fig. 12.1 for a diagram of simple drive theory.

Secondary Needs and Drives You need to take in liquid to live—but *what* you drink depends in large part on what many psychologists call your learned or **secondary needs.** Primary needs are innately determined—they are built into your genetic blueprint. Secondary needs are presumably acquired, and they vary widely from person to person and from culture to culture.

Many, but not all, secondary needs are related to the satisfaction of primary needs. For instance, although you have a primary need to **excrete** water, you learned very early in life that there are some things that we just don't ordinarily do in public. Thus your secondary need not to violate a very strong social law sets you to looking for a toilet when your bladder is full.

Associated with every secondary need is a corresponding **secondary drive** that, when aroused, impels or pushes you to satisfy that need. Although secondary drives are *learned*, they operate much like the primary needs we have just described.

To summarize, the drive approach to motivation is what we might call a biologically oriented, *one-level* theory. It is biological in orientation because physiological needs are presumed to be primary. All other needs are said to be acquired or learned. And the theory operates on only one level because the feelings, perceptions, emotions, and behaviors of the organism are held to be relatively unimportant since they are *caused* by physiological reactions.

Question: What position do drive theorists appear to be taking with regard to solving the mind–body problem?

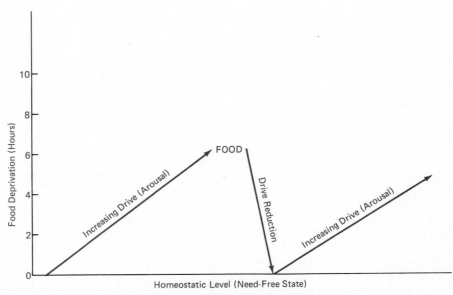

Fig. 12.1. A simple diagram of drive theory using food deprivation as an example.

Some Problems Concerning Drive Theory Many objections have been raised to the simple form of drive theory that we have just outlined. Three of the major objections are as follows:

1. Drive theory equates an *increase* in neural excitation with an *increase* in motivation. Yet, as we learned from the sensory deprivation experiments, sometimes a *decrease* in excitation can cause an *increase* in psychological arousal.

2. Your intra-psychic feelings, perceptions, and emotions may have as much or more to do with motivation as do your physiological needs, drives, and arousals. For example, can we explain all the rich variety of loving behaviors *solely* in terms of sex hormones and physiological arousal? Or does it make sense to explain the intense joy of winning a game or solving a difficult problem *entirely* in terms of an innate need to reduce neural excitation?

3. Many of the so-called learned or "secondary" needs are neither very secondary nor are they always acquired by being associated with "primary" needs. For instance, according to drive theory, *personal survival* is the strongest biological need that you have. Yet there are many situations in which you would willingly sacrifice yourself to save the life of a loved one, or to promote some political or religious ideal. Drive theory has considerable trouble, therefore, explaining complex social and inter-personal behaviors.

As we will see, the scientists who raised these objections often were "driven" to create competing motivational theories of their own.

Arousal Theory

In the late 1950's, Elizabeth Duffy (and others) made a telling criticism of classical drive theory. As Duffy pointed out, arousal is not always caused by a lack of such things as food, air, or water. We have *informational needs* that are as innate and as highly motivating as are our life-sustaining or *energy needs*.

Thus the "boredom" associated with a marked *decrease* in neural excitation can be as arousing or motivating as the *increase* in neural firing typically associated with food deprivation.

This objection led Duffy and other scientists to a new approach to motivation which, roughly speaking, we can call **arousal theory.** The basic **postulates** of this position can be summaried as follows:

1. Your homeostatic "home base'" is not a state of *zero* excitation but rather a point of **optimum** stimulation.

2. This optimum point may *change* from time to time, depending on your biological condition.

3. A *decrease* in optimum stimulation may be as arousing or motivating to you as is an increase.

Arousal and Homeostasis Arousal theory had its beginnings in the sensory deprivation experiments performed in Canada and the discovery of the reticular activating system by Magoun and his associates (see Chapter 9).

Consider the sensory deprivation studies for just a moment. You will recall that the subjects in these experiments apparently had all of their physiological needs met all the time, yet most of the men could not endure the experience for more than a day or so. Drive theorists sometimes explained this "flight from boredom" as evidence that we have an innate biological "need for stimulation." But this kind of *postulated* instinct surely contradicts the simple homeostatic model in which an increase in motivation can be brought about *only* by an increase in neural firing rates.

More than this, as Duffy noted, you do not have a single "homeostatic

Arousal theory. A one-level, biologically oriented theory in which motivation comes from some departure from a norm or optimum point of neural excitation. Any increase or decrease in neural firing moves the organism away from this optimum point and hence is arousing.

Postulates (POSS-tew-lates or POSS-tew-lutts). To postulate is to make a guess about something, or to insist that something exists or is very important. Postulates may or may not be facts. For instance, centuries ago people postulated that the world was flat, so they didn't sail across the Atlantic Ocean for fear they would fall off the edge of the world. Then along came adventuresome men like Columbus and Magellan who postulated that the world was round instead of flat. The words "theory" and "hypothesis" (high-POTH-thuh-sis) mean about the same thing as "postulate," although (technically speaking) a theory is a set of related postulates.

Optimum (OPP-tee-mum or OPP-tuh-mum). From the Latin word meaning "best." Literally, the most favorable point or condition.

level" that is set at birth and never varies thereafter. Rather, your need for stimulation changes according to your past experience and present conditions.

You might recall from earlier chapters that your sensory receptors are designed to detect environmental *change*. For the first few minutes that you turn on a fan in an otherwise quiet room, the fan may seem particularly noisy. After a while, however, your nervous system stops responding (habituates) to the sound of the fan—even though your ears are still sending "noisy messages" to your cortex. If the fan now stops, the neural excitation in your ears *decreases*, as does the excitation in your cortex. Yet you will immediately pay attention to this change in inputs even though it caused a *decrease* in your neural firing rates.

In much the same fashion, if you had to eat exactly the same meal three times a day for a month or so, you'd probably "go bananas" and look for something else to eat, even though all of your physiological needs might be satisfied by the monotonous meal.

Because your body adjusts to any constant sensory input, the optimum level of stimulation that you need *varies from moment to moment*. Given this fact, it doesn't take much imagination to realize that you lose much of your ability to predict and control your inputs whenever your environment becomes *too constant*.

But you also lose that same ability whenever your environment *changes too much*. Thus, while you need a certain amount of *stability* in the world around you (just as the homeostatic model would predict), you also need a certain amount of *variability* in stimulation (as arousal theory predicts) or your receptor systems will "turn off" and leave you without any inputs at all. (Your reticular activating system seems designed to stir you into action whenever your inputs become either too different or too much the same.) Fig. 12.2 illustrates how we might diagram arousal theory.

As presented by Duffy, the arousal position remained a one-level, biological theory in that it reduced motivation to what seemed to be purely physiological processes. But it was a noticeable improvement over simple drive theory in that Duffy could explain a number of motivational situations that early drive theorists had difficulties with.

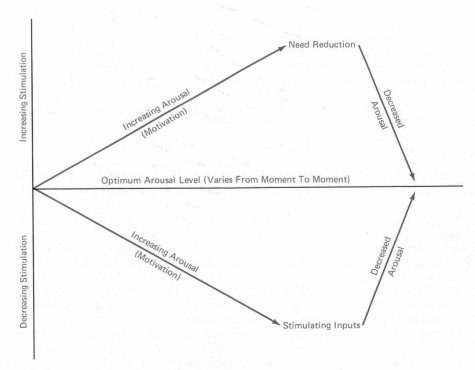

Fig. 12.2. A simple diagram of arousal theory.

PART THREE Motivation

Question: *In Chapter 3, we noted that certain drugs such as LSD lead to a fearful experience called "loss of personal control." In Chapter 9, we noted that sensory deprivation leads to a panic-inducing experience in which subjects can no longer control their thought patterns. How might both these unpleasant situations be related to a need to predict and control your inputs?*

Intra-Psychic Approaches to Motivation

Why do you eat? According to drive and arousal theorists, when your body lacks food, certain neural centers in your brain show an increase in electrical excitation that drives you to find food in order to decrease your state of arousal. Yet most of us believe that we eat because we feel 'hunger pangs," and it is the *pain* of hunger that drives us to grill a hamburger or to make a peanut butter sandwich.

Hunger stirs us up, true. But it is the *subjective discomfort* and not the *physiological arousal* that seems to goad us into stuffing goodies into our mouths. Furthermore, some things taste so good that we will often eat a cookie or a potato chip even when our bodies don't have a real *biological* need for food and can't possibly be physiologically aroused.

What about the motivational aspects of our *feelings,* then?

It should be clear by now that drive and arousal theorists place little importance on the mental experiences that accompany motivational states. But some aspects of human motivation are much easier to explain in terms of our feelings, emotions, and perceptions than in terms of drives and arousals. For instance, it is almost impossible to describe how we learn without making reference to those intra-psychic feelings we call pleasure and pain.

Pleasure, Pain, and Learning   Most theorists agree that learning seldom occurs unless the organism is motivated. A rat will rapidly master a complex maze if, by doing so, it either avoids electric shock or receives food when it is hungry. In attempting to explain how this maze learning comes about, drive theorists often spoke of the "punishing" effects of arousal and the "rewarding" aspects of **drive reduction.**

But in using these terms, the theorists were really shifting away from a one-level, purely biological theory of motivation toward a *two-level theory.* For punishment and reward surely carry with them subtle associations of "pain" and "pleasure"—words that are descriptive of intra-psychic events, not of physiological states or conditions.

In fact, there are many types of stimuli that arouse intense feelings of pleasure in and of themselves and hence motivate us strongly. It is impossible to explain the thrilling beauty of a rainbow—or the glorious sounds of music—in terms of physiological drive *reduction* or even in terms of sensory deprivation.

The sights, smells, and tastes associated with the table are another example of pure *sensory pleasures.* Almost any rat will learn a maze more quickly if given flavorful food as its reward than if the food is tasteless—even though the **bland** food might actually be more **nutritious** and hence better at reducing the animal's hunger drive. A newborn child will often reject water, but will readily accept milk. The sweeter the milk is, within limits, the more eagerly most infants will consume it.

Therefore, hunger not only arouses us, it also makes certain types of food inputs either more pleasurable or less unpleasant than they normally would be.

One of the major effects of deprivations, drives, and arousals is that they make it easier for us to survive by changing our emotional feelings toward—and perceptions of—certain stimuli in our environments.

Facts such as these led many psychologists to abandon one-level, purely physiological theories of motivation in favor of two-level approaches that include both biological drives *and* intra-psychic processes such as emotion and perception.

Drive reduction. The act of satisfying a need, or reducing a drive state. Drive theorists are sometimes called "drive reduction theorists" since they believe that reducing drives is reinforcing, hence is the heart and soul of learning (as well as of motivation).

Bland (rhymes with "canned"). From the Latin word meaning "smooth," or "not stimulating." A bland diet is one that contains no spicy or highly-seasoned foods.

Nutritious (new-TRISH-us). From the Latin word meaning "to nurse." A nutritious food is one that is nourishing or that promotes growth and health.

Emotion

William James.

When someone mentions the word **emotion** to you, what sorts of pictures pop into your mind? Images of love and hate? Ideas about anger and rage and fear?

In fact, if you look carefully at the word, you can guess immediately that *emotion* has the same Latin root as the word *motivation*. "Motivation" means to move toward or away from a goal, while "e-motion" means to move but in a stirred up or **agitated** way.

An emotional *response* may involve a general state of bodily excitation—such as turning red in the face or shaking your fists when you're angry. Or it may involve such goal-oriented behaviors as approaching someone you love or running away from a threatening rattlesnake.

Generally speaking, however, when we use the word "emotion" in everyday speech, we typically refer to our intra-psychic *feelings* rather than our bodily movements. Thus most theories of emotion are *two-level theories* because they deal with mental experiences as well as with physiological reactions.

But in emotional situations, which comes first—your perceptions and feelings, or the biological arousal that often accompanies them? That is, when you feel emotional about something, does your mind stimulate your body, or does your body stimulate your mind? Or do both mental and physiological processes occur at about the same time and feed on each other?

In 1884, Harvard psychologist William James proposed that your *body* almost always takes the lead. According to James, when you almost step on a rattlesnake, you run. Your heart rate increases dramatically, your hair stands on end, and you breathe rapidly as you rush away from the dreaded reptile. Moments later, you notice these physiological reactions and realize that you're scared.

You may think that you saw the snake, became frightened, and then ran. But, according to James, this is not the case, for he presumed your reactions precede and thus almost wholly determine your feelings. As James put it, "We are afraid because we run; we do not run because we are afraid."

To James, your emotional feelings are mostly a matter of your *consciously* noting the feedback you get continuously from various parts of your body. In 1885, the noted Danish physiologist Karl G. Lange independently proposed much the same sort of explanation of emotional behavior. For that reason, this viewpoint is often called the **James–Lange theory of emotions.**

As you might surmise, the James–Lange approach led to a lot of highly emotional debate and, happily, a lot of useful research as well. It is now pretty much agreed that in emergency situations your feelings may lag slightly behind your physiological processes. At other times, your intra-psychic processes determine what your bodily reactions will be. But in *all* situations, your mind and body stimulate each other and it is this *blend* of mental and physical experiences that we call "emotion."

Perceptual Theories of Emotion

One of the main difficulties with one-level theories—as with the James-Lange viewpoint—is that emotional (motivated) behaviors often seem to have a *precise direction* to them. If physiological excitation were identical to motivation—if the "drive state" were nothing but a generalized condition of arousal—then a hungry rat would be as likely to drink as to eat. But rats seldom make that kind of mistake.

If arousal were the same thing as emotion, we might also find ourselves hitting our lovers and embracing our enemies. But few of us perform such foolish actions.

Emotion From the Latin word meaning "to agitate or stir up." Emotions are often said to have a biological component (arousal or depression), a mental component (pleasantness or unpleasantness), and a social or environmental component (an object or a goal).

Agitated (ADGE-gee-tait-ted). From the Latin word meaning "to arouse, or stir up." The Soviet propaganda ministry is sometimes called "Agitprop," because its main function is to arouse public passions.

James-Lange theory of emotions. A theory proposed by William James and Karl Lange (LAHN-guh) which postulates that your behaviors determine your feelings, so that you are afraid because you run, rather than you run because you are afraid.

In 1960, Magda Arnold revised the James–Lange theory to take into account the guiding effects of perception on motivated behaviors. According to Arnold, you typically first *perceive* a situation, then *evaluate* it. This evaluation leads to an emotional *response* that has both biological and intra-psychic components, and the emotional response may or may not lead to a behavioral reaction.

According to Arnold, emotions are either *pleasant* or *unpleasant*. Since you are motivated to avoid pain and pursue pleasure, emotion is the driving force that moves you toward or away from various environmental situations.

For Arnold, emotion is the central part of the motivational process—but emotion is almost always triggered by your perception and evaluation of what is happening to you.

A somewhat similar theory to Arnold's was advanced in 1965 by Robert Leeper, who argues that biological reactions to emotional situations have but one main effect—*to change the way that your cortex processes or handles various inputs.*

Robert Leeper.

Sensory inputs go not only to your cortex, but to lower brain centers such as your **limbic system.** We know from many experiments that neural excitation in your limbic system affects the way your cortex responds to stimuli (see Chapter 4). Thus activity in your limbic system can actually change the way you perceive and evaluate the world around you.

For Leeper, intra-psychic or perceptual activities are the basis of *all your* motivational processes. For without perception, your physical reactions would lack direction and would thus be pretty meaningless.

Emotions, therefore, not only arouse you, but they *guide* your behavior as well.

Social Behavioral Influences on Motivation

A few pages ago, we noted that when drive theorists began to talk about pain and pleasure, they opened the door to intra-psychic theories of emotion and motivation. Perhaps now that you have struggled through our brief descriptions of several intra-psychic viewpoints, you can see a similar problem:

Perceptions may direct your behavior, but where do your perceptions come from?

As we saw in Chapter 10, you learn much of what you perceive from your interactions with other human beings. You see what you expect to see—but what you expect to see is influenced by your past experiences in various social environments, and by what other people have told you you ought to see.

Thus social inputs *guide* your perceptions, which in turn *influence* your bodily reactions.

You can get around many of the difficulties associated with one- and two-level theories of emotion by realizing that you have at least *three* different types of motivational processes. That is, you have biological motives, intra-psychic motives, and social/behavioral motives.

These three separate systems of emotional processes interact with and influence each other. In some situations, for instance, a social input may trigger off strong mental and bodily reactions. In other situations, a biological input may affect your perceptions and social behaviors. Under most circumstances, the three systems operate simultaneously and in parallel—in a kind of *mutual inter-dependence.*

To over-emphasize the importance of any one of the systems—or to try to explain all motivation in one-level terms, such as percepts or neural firings—might prevent you from appreciating the marvelous complexities buried in that simple question, "What do you want from life?"

Limbic system. The emotional centers lying deep on the underside of the cerebrum. See Chapter 4.

According to A.H. Maslow—one of the best-known **humanistic psychologists**—what people want most from life is **self-actualization.** The term *self-actualization* is a hard one to define. Put simply, it means your need to develop to your own greatest potential, to do the things you do best in your own unique way, and (finally) to help those around you achieve self-actualization too.

Not all of us have a chance to become self-actualized persons, primarily because we have simpler needs that must be satisfied first.

Maslow's Hierarchy of Needs   Maslow has developed a **hierarchy,** or ladder, of human needs (see Fig. 12.3):

1. *Physiological needs.* Bodily needs come first, which is to say that you must always satisfy your physiological wants or you don't live long enough to take care of any psychological or social needs you may have. You cannot take the next step up the motivational ladder unless, and until, your primary biological needs are met. (Drive theory operates at this rung of the ladder.)

2. *Safety needs.* As we will see in later chapters, an infant will typically not explore its environment unless it feels *secure.* Unless your environment is a stable enough one so that you can predict and control your inputs, you cannot advance to the next level of the needs hierarchy. (Arousal theory operates partly at this rung of the ladder.)

3. *Belongingness* and *love needs.* According to Maslow, you have an innate need for affection and love that can only be satisfied by other people. You thus must **affiliate** with others, and identify yourself with one or more like-minded individuals. When you identify with someone else, you learn to perceive part of the world as that person presumably does. (Perceptual theory operates partly at this rung of the ladder.)

4. *Esteem needs.* Until you identify successfully with others, you cannot begin to satisfy your need to have them respect or esteem you. And until you gain the esteem (sincere positive feedback) of people who value you as a person, you probably will not be able to achieve very much esteem for yourself. (What we will later define as "social learning theory" operates at this rung of Maslow's ladder.)

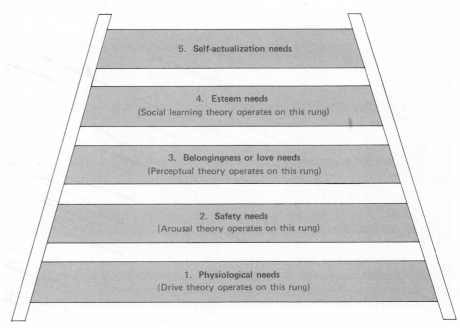

Fig. 12.3. Maslow's hierarchy of needs.

5. *Need for self-actualization.* Until you have achieved self-esteem, you probably will not feel secure enough to become a "fully-actualized person." That is, unless you have confidence in yourself, you will not dare to express yourself in your own unique way, make your own contribution to society, and thus achieve your true inborn potential. Each person's "self" is different, of course, since each person's inheritance is different. But according to Maslow, the *route* to self-actualization always leads up from the four lower rungs in the ladder.

Question: How far up the ladder would a frequently abused child be likely to climb? Or a student whose teachers gave the student nothing but criticism?

A Multi-level Approach We will talk about humanistic psychology in more detail later. What Maslow seems to have done, though, is to pull together drive theory, arousal theory, perceptual theory, and social influences into a *multi-level approach to motivation.*

According to Maslow, self-actualization almost always involves creativity and problem-solving. From a General Systems Theory point of view, then, becoming yourself might mean getting your two hemispheres to engage in the sort of "silent dialogue" we described in Chapter 5. But if you are to feel *free* to express yourself creatively, you must learn to predict and control (1) your biological inputs, (2) your perceptual and emotional inputs, and (3) your social inputs. And to control your inputs, you must learn how to change your outputs. The goal of life (as Maslow says) may well be that of developing your own inner psychological *processes* to their fullest. But from a systems viewpoint, you aren't likely to gain that inner control unless you first learn how to satisfy your needs for various inputs from your environment.

As we noted in Chapter 5, the best test of any theory is its *usefulness.* So let us take much of what we know about one highly motivated behavior—that of over-eating—and show just how useful the systems approach to motivational problems can be to anyone, fat or skinny.

Fatness: An American Problem

There are four billion people living on earth at the present time. At least a third of these people don't get as much of the right things to eat as they should, and hence are undernourished or suffer from **malnutrition.**

Overweight people usually must learn new habits of buying food in order to lose weight.

Malnutrition (mal-new-TRISH-shun). The French word *mal* means "bad," or "sickness." Nutrition is the whole process of eating food, digesting it, and turning it into energy that your body can use. Someone who suffers from malnutrition simply isn't getting enough energy to live properly. Not having enough to eat, or eating the wrong things, or having something wrong with your digestive system can all lead to malnutrition. Alcoholics often experience malnutrition because they spend their money on liquor instead of food, or simply get so drunk they forget to eat.

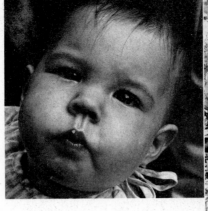

Two weight problems. Some children are badly undernourished, but obese children also suffer physical and psychological problems. Although most of the people in the world survive fairly well, a significant proportion are undernourished.

Overweight. Scientists have worked out an "ideal weight" for people, depending (mostly) on their age and height. Anyone who tips the scales at 10 percent more than this "ideal" is usually considered to be "slightly overweight," and anyone more than 25 percent above this "ideal" is usually considered to be "noticeably overweight." In fact, the amount of fat you carry is probably more important than your actual weight. The definition of "overweight," however, varies considerably from one expert to another. If you have any worries about your own weight, you might wish to see a physician to determine if your problem is serious.

Calories (KAL-or-rees). The Latin word *calor* means "heat." The caloric (kal-LOR-ick) content of anything is the amount of heat it will generate when burned. Your body "burns" food when it converts what you eat into energy to keep you alive. Rich, sweet, fatty foods have lots of calories (that is, a high caloric content). Water has no calories at all. Fat burns; water doesn't.

Obesity (oh-BEE-sit-tee). From the Latin words meaning "to overeat." Obesity means fatness; an obese (oh-BEESE) person is someone who weighs *at least* 25 percent more than the person's "ideal weight."

There are more than 220 million people in the United States. Perhaps because we are the richest, most powerful nation on earth, only a relatively small percentage of our population is badly undernourished. Hunger *is* a very real problem for many people living in poverty-stricken rural and slum areas. But many Americans suffer because they eat too much, not too little. Dietitians estimate that from 10 to 25 percent of the American public is **overweight.**

The average family doctor treats more than 10 patients a month who want to lose weight. Perhaps one in 20 of these patients has a *physical* problem that is responsible for their fatness—and with these patients, the medical profession can often be of considerable help. The other 19 out of 20 people are fat simply because they do not use up all the **calories** in the food they eat, and their bodies store the surplus energy as fat tissue. According to physicians interested in the subject, medical science has not done particularly well with these patients.

At a 1972 meeting on the topic of fatness, Dr. Alvan Feinstein of the Yale Medical School reported that the success rate of most *medical* weight-loss programs is "terrible, much worse than in cancer." The situation hasn't changed much since 1972. Experts now estimate that only some 12 out of 100 patients who seek a *physician's* help actually lose weight, and that 10 out of these 12 gain back their excess pounds within a year or two.

Presuming that your own weight is normal, why should you worry about such things? First, because fatness could happen to you someday, and probably has already happened to one or more of your friends or relatives; and second, because fat people are a very discriminated-against minority.

If you are overweight, you have difficulty buying attractive clothes. You also have difficulty getting out of many chairs and getting into many small cars. Employers appear to be hesitant to hire overweight individuals (have you seen a really fat airline stewardess?).

And fatness can even affect your academic career. Several years ago, H. Canning and J. Mayer made an interesting study of the effects of **obesity** on high school students. These scientists report that school counselors are less likely to write letters of recommendation for fat students than for normals. Canning and Mayer also found that college admissions committees discriminate against fat students during interviews. Faced with two students with equally good grades and equally high test scores, college committees tend to accept the non-obese student and to shut out the one who weighs too much.

Unfair? Of course it is. So is our society's discrimination against people with dark skins or slanted eyes. Of course most of us realize that you had little to say about your skin color—but fatness is primarily a *voluntary choice*, isn't it?

The answer is, No. In a very strange way, you are not entirely responsible for how much you weigh. First, there is strong genetic component in fatness, and you are no more to blame for inheriting "fat genes" than for inheriting a certain skin color. Second, the psychological factors influencing fatness or thinness are just as important as the genetic or physiological ones. So if you happen to be snacking on something delicious, perhaps you'll want to put the food aside while we look at the biological, intrapsychic, and social/behavioral influences on **gluttony.**

The Biology of Hunger

Psychologist Marshall Jones, who has spent most of his career studying problems of motivation, has pointed out an interesting fact: To understand why a person does what he or she does, you must answer the following questions:

1. Why does a given behavioral sequence begin? That is, what inputs prompt the thought or get the action going?

2. Why does the behavior continue in the direction that it does once it begins? That is, where do your goals come from, and how do you learn to achieve the *sequences* of behaviors that lead to those goals?

3. Why does the thought or behavior eventually come to an end? That is, once a behavioral sequence has begun, what brings it to a stop?

Eating is a motivated behavior—but so are over-eating and under-eating. Therefore, to understand why you eat as you do, we must answer three critical questions: Why do you start eating, why do you stop eating, and why do you prefer steak and ice cream to fried worms and boiled monkey brains?

As we will see, the biological viewpoint offers answers to the first two questions, but not to the third.

Marshall Jones.

Question: From a motivational point of view, fat people might be overweight for at least four reasons: (1) they eat too frequently; (2) once started, they don't know when to quit; (3) they prefer rich, fat-laden foods, and (4) they don't burn up enough energy through exercise and physical labor. Would you think that different forms of therapy would be needed depending on what combination of these four behaviors the person engaged in?

Blood Sugar Level

When you eat a baked potato for dinner, how does your body make use of this fuel? As you know, digestion actually begins in your mouth, for your saliva contains chemicals called **enzymes** that begin tearing the potato apart into its chemical building blocks (proteins, sugars, fats, and other simple molecules).

When the partially digested potato arrives in your stomach, it encounters even more powerful enzymes that continue tearing away at it. Eventually the potato is reduced to molecules so small that they can pass through the lining of the small intestine and be absorbed into your bloodstream.

Blood containing these energy-rich molecules flows to almost every part of your body and passes the food particles on to any cell that might be "hungry." A few hours after you have eaten a large meal, your blood

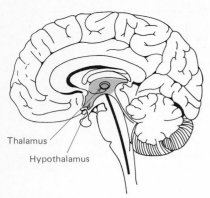

Fig. 12.4. The hypothalamus and thalamus.

contains a great many of these food molecules. However, if you starve yourself for 24 hours or so, your blood would contain relatively few of these energy particles—and you would normally be highly motivated to obtain some caloric inputs to help reduce your hunger pangs.

Here is our first clue as to what the *sensation* of hunger is all about—the chemical composition of your blood at any given time makes a difference. If we could somehow control the molecules floating around in your blood-stream, might we not be able to control your sensation of hunger directly?

From a purely biological point of view, the answer is a probable yes. Much of the energy your body uses comes from simple sugars, which are contained in most of the foods you eat. Under normal conditions, your body secretes a chemical called **insulin** that makes it easier for your cells to take up sugar molecules.

If we let a hungry rat eat all that it wants, then take a blood sample from the animal a little later, we would find a lot of sugar molecules in the rat's blood. If we now inject the animal with insulin, we will rapidly lower its blood sugar level—and to our surprise the rat will soon begin to eat again (although it had a very large meal just minutes before).

Somewhere in your body, then, there must be a "sugar detector" that lets your cortex know how many sugar molecules are floating around in your bloodstream. Recent research suggests that this "detector" is located in a central part of your brain called the **hypothalamus.**

Sitting right at the top of your brain stem is a neural center called the **thalamus.** The thalamus is a sort of "central switchboard" through which sensory inputs pass before being relayed to your cortex. The word "hypo" means "below" or "beneath." The hypothalamus is a bundle of nerve cells lying just under the thalamus that exercises rather strong control over many of your physiological motivations and emotions (see Fig. 12.4).

The Hypothalamic "Feeding Center" One small part of your hypothalamus contains neurons that are particularly sensitive to the amount of sugar in your blood. When your blood sugar level drops too low, the cells in this region of your hypothalamus begin to fire more and more rapidly—and you typically begin to feel more and more hungry.

If we put a metal electrode into this part of a rat's brain and stimulate the cells electrically, the rat will begin to eat at once (even if it has just had a big meal). If we stimulate this hypothalamic **feeding center** continuously, the rat will eat and eat and eat—until it becomes so obese that it can barely move around. If we continue the electrical stimulation even when food is not present in the rat's cage, the animal will often gnaw on anything handy—including air.

If we destroy this "feeding center" in the rat's hypothalamus, the animal usually refuses to eat at all and will die of starvation unless we force-feed it.

Does this one "feeding center" in the hypothalamus control all aspects of eating behavior? Certainly not. To begin with, even the "dumb rat" knows better than to over-eat continuously, no matter what we do to it. If we give rats the continual hypothalamic stimulation mentioned earlier, the animals will become very, very fat. But eventually they will reach a cut-off point beyond which they will not go. Their weights will stabilize at this point and we cannot induce them to become much fatter.

We can achieve similar results by giving the rats daily injections of insulin, but again the animals will grow only so fat—and no fatter. And if we combine insulin objections with electrical stimulation to the "feeding center" in the hypothalamus, we can get the animals to eat so rapidly that they will reach this **obesity limit** very quickly—but they will *still* stop eating when they reach this limit. (You will probably be pleased to know that, when we stop prodding the rat's brain with insulin and electrical stimulation, the animal will typically go on a "crash diet" and return to its normal body weight.)

Why do you eat? Part of the answer to this question obviously lies in the "feeding center" in your brain. As the sugar content in the blood reaching your brain *decreases*, electrical activity in this part of your hypothalamus *increases.* Your cortex translates this neural input into the psychological experience of hunger—and you go looking for a decent meal. But when you find the food you want, and begin to consume it, why do you stop after you've eaten just so much? Why don't you munch away for hours and hours?

Because, you say, as soon as you start eating, the sugar content in your blood goes up dramatically and your "feeding center" turns off. Not so, for eating behavior doesn't have a simple explanation, even at a biological level.

If you ate a big steak right now, it would take several hours for the meat to be digested and assimilated into your bloodstream. It takes only 10 to 20 minutes for you to eat the steak, though. Thus you actually *stop eating* long before that steak can greatly affect your blood sugar level.

In fact, if you're a quick eater, your "feeding center" may still be signaling "eat—eat—eat—!" at the top of its neural voice at the very moment when you push yourself away from the table, so stuffed with food that you can't imagine ever being hungry again.

So a lowered blood sugar level can turn *on* your hunger. But what physiological mechanism turns it *off?*

The Hypothalamic "Satiation Center" As we pointed out in Chapter 2, your body is **bilaterally symmetrical**—that is, the left half of your body is a mirror image of the right. Most of your physiological and psychological functioning is symmetrical too.

For every muscle that acts to extend your arm, there is another muscle that acts *symmetrically* to cause your arm to pull back.

For each drug that acts as an excitant or "upper," there is another drug that can *counteract*, or be a depressant or "downer."

So if there is a "feeding center" in your hypothalamus that causes you to *start* eating, wouldn't you guess there might also be a center that, when stimulated, causes you to *stop* eating?

It is called the **satiation center,** and it is also located in your hypothalamus, close to your "feeding center."

Suppose we implant an electrode in a rat's hypothalamic "satiation center." Then, just as the hungry animal goes to eat, we pass a weak electrical current through this "satiation center." The animal will suddenly refuse its meal. And if we continue the simulation for a long enough time, the animal will come close to starving itself to death.

Bilaterally symmetrical (buy-LATT-tur-rally sim-MET-tree-kal). The Latin word *lateral* means "side." *Bi* is the Latin word for "two." Anything that is bilateral has two sides to it (such as most arguments and love affairs). Symmetrical means "balanced," or "equal on all sides." Your body is bilaterally symmetrical because it has two sides (left and right) that are mirror images, or are equal to each other.

Satiation center (say-she-A-shun). Our word "satisfied" comes from the Latin words *satis*, meaning "enough," and *facere*, meaning "to do" or "to make." Satiation is the condition of being completely satisfied. The "satiation center" is that part of the hypothalamus which, when stimulated electrically, causes a hungry animal to stop eating—that is, to behave as if it were already satisfied.

A hypothalamic, hyperphagic rat.

On the other hand, if we surgically remove the rat's "satiation center," the animal will become **hyperphagic.** That is, the animal will go on an eating jag and will become as obese as the rats given insulin injections. But as you might already have surmised, eventually the animal will reach its "obesity limit" and will taper off its wild consumption of food.

Under normal conditions, the "satiation center" functions *symmetrically* with the "feeding center." When your blood sugar level goes up, the neurons in your "feeding center" slow down their response rate and the nerve cells in your "satiation center" increase their firing rate. When your blood sugar level falls, your "feeding center" turns on and your "satiation center" turns off.

So now we know why you start eating and stop eating, don't we?

Sadly enough, we've learned only part of the picture. For what do you think would happen if we surgically removed *both* the "feeding center" and the "satiation center" from a rat's hypothalamus? Would the animal starve, or would it become obese?

The answer is, some animals will starve, but many will continue to eat pretty much as it had before the operation. So there must be other systems in the brain that strongly influence eating behaviors.

The "Swallow Counter"

One such mechanism is what we might call the **swallow counter.**

A young rat eats almost continuously. As it grows up, however, it soon learns to associate the "feeling" of hunger with the amount of food that it ought to eat. When its blood sugar level is slightly lower than usual, and neurons in its "feeding center" are mildly excited, the rat will eat a *small* amount of food because it has learned that is all it needs to reduce its hunger drive. When its "feeding center" neurons fire more rapidly, the rat will eat *more* because it has learned that it needs more food under these circumstances.

Research indicates that some part of the animal's brain actually *counts* the number of swallows the animal makes as it eats. When it has had enough to satisfy its present state of hunger, the rat stops eating. And it stops before there is much of a change in its blood sugar level, or in the firing rates in its "feeding" and "satiation" centers.

But even the "swallow counter" doesn't give us the whole answer to the puzzling question, "Why do you eat?" For example, experiments by Eliot Stellar and his associates at the University of Pennsylvania suggest that people are able to control their food inputs even if they can't "count" what they're swallowing.

Stellar and his colleagues asked students to swallow a tiny plastic tube that pumped Metrecal directly into their stomachs when the students pressed a lever. The students could not see, smell, taste, chew, or swallow the food. But they somehow learned to control the amount of Metrecal they consumed just as readily as if they were drinking it from a glass. Perhaps the most interesting result of these experiments was the fact that the students were completely unable to explain to Professor Stellar how they managed this feat!

Perhaps your stomach "knows" things about your eating habits that your "feeding" and "satiation" centers are only dimly aware of.

The Hunger Habit

When you've packed your stomach with a huge meal (or with Metrecal), the muscles in your stomach are stretched out or distended. The feedback nerve cells in your stomach would surely let your brain know how inflated your stomach was, and then your cortex could inhibit or block out the input messages from your "feeding center" even before your blood sugar level changed.

Eliot Stellar.

Does stomach feedback influence your eating?

Years ago, long before the "feeding center" had been discovered, the great US physiologist Walter Cannon performed a very important experiment on hunger. He got a student volunteer to swallow a balloon attached to a long hose. Once the balloon was inside the man's stomach, Cannon pumped air through the hose and inflated the balloon until it pushed firmly against the walls of the subject's stomach (see Fig. 12.5). (Fortunately, the man suffered little or no pain from this procedure.) Now, whenever the man's stomach contracted at all, the balloon was pinched and air was forced up the tube. By measuring the air pressure in the hose, Cannon got an excellent reading of when the man's stomach muscles churned about.

Cannon found that "stomach contractions" began an hour or so before the man would normally have eaten a meal. As lunch time approached, for instance, the man's stomach began to contract more and more vigorously—and the man reported an increased interest in food. An hour or so after the man's usual lunch time, the stomach contractions almost stopped—*despite the fact that the man hadn't eaten a thing.* The man's subjective experience of hunger also decreased.

If you eat lunch every day at 12 noon, your "feeding center" and other parts of your brain begin to *anticipate* when they will have to go to work. An hour or so before noon, your brain starts sending neural signals to the muscles in your stomach telling them to "wake up" and get ready to start performing. The muscles contract in response to these signals, and your stomach "growls."

Other parts of your brain notice the growling (and the input signals coming from your "feeding center") and decide you're probably hungry. The closer the clock gets to noon, the more vigorously your stomach muscles respond.

Oddly enough, if you once get past the lunch hour without eating, your stomach will often calm down just as it does after you have eaten. Then your hunger pangs will disappear, only to rise as supper time approaches.

Question: Why do both your hunger "pangs" and your stomach contractions tend to decrease after lunch even though you didn't eat anything?

The hunger pangs that come from stomach contractions are learned or **conditioned.** Almost any habit that is learned can be unlearned if you go about it the right way. If you stop eating *entirely,* your subjective experience of hunger will rise to a maximum in three to five days as the centers in your brain and the muscles in your stomach continue to anticipate meal after missed meal.

By the end of five days of *complete* starvation, however, your body will have started to learn that food simply isn't going to be coming along as it once did. Your stomach contractions will slow down and eventually cease almost entirely, and your subjective experience of hunger will drop to a low ebb.

Fiction writers who describe starvation (and who have never experienced it themselves) often assume that if one of their characters starves for a week, the person will be so **ravenously** hungry that the person will perform almost any anti-social act in order to get food. In truth, the first three days of *complete* starvation are by far the worst. However, if you go on a diet and "eat just a little" at each regular meal time, your "habitual" stomach contractions will take a very long time to change, and you may experience biting, gnawing hunger for weeks on end.

If you wish to break the hunger habit in order to gain better control over your own food intake, you might be wise to do so slowly—by putting yourself on a very irregular eating schedule. If you vary the times at which you eat, the number of meals each day, and the amount you consume at each meal, you will slowly train your body not to be hungry at specific times of the day. Once you have lost the hunger habit, you will find that dieting is somewhat easier.

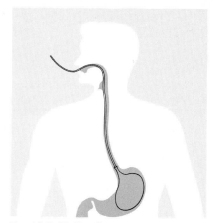

Fig. 12.5. Walter Cannon was able to read the churning of the stomach muscles when his subject swallowed a balloon which was then inflated.

Conditioned (konn-DISH-shunned). When an organism is trained to give a particular response to a specific stimulus, we say that it has been conditioned to respond to that stimulus. As we will see in Chapter 15, there are several types of conditioning. Psychologists often use the words "learning" and "conditioning" as if they were the same.

Ravenously (RAV-enn-nuss-lee). From the Latin word meaning "to take by force." A ravenous person is someone who "takes food by force," that is, who feeds greedily.

Diet Pills Some of the diet drugs on the market today have a very slight effect on the firing rates of the hypothalamic "feeding" and "satiation" centers. Other drugs are aimed at fooling the stomach muscles. These chemicals have little food value, but swell up considerably when they reach your stomach.

The best-known diet drugs usually contain an "upper" of some kind, because such chemicals often make people so nervous or excited that they lose their appetites. Many of these drugs have rather unpleasant side effects, however, and to be truthful, none of them works very well all by itself.

Why don't the diet pills work? For at least two reasons. First, over-eating is *habitual* in most people. Going on a diet or taking a pill simply does not teach you the *good eating habits* you must substitute for those bad behaviors that involve consuming too much.

Second, while our bodies tell us when to stop eating, some people apparently don't know how to listen to these "body signals."

Obesity and "Body Signals"

In 1959, psychiatrist A.J. Stunkard repeated parts of Cannon's balloon experiment with 37 obese and 37 normal subjects. That is, he asked these subjects to swallow balloons that would let him record their stomach movements. Then, for several hours, he frequently asked the subjects whether or not they *felt* hungry.

Stunkard found that, when their stomachs were *not* contracting, both fat and normal people were much alike—about 38 percent of them reported they were hungry.

When their stomachs *were* contracting, however, the groups were markedly different. About 71 percent of the normals said they were hungry, while only 48 percent of the fat subjects said they were hungry.

No matter what kinds of reports they gave, both groups of subjects showed about the *same number* of stomach contractions during the experiment.

Hilde Bruch.

There are at least two explanations for Stunkard's results. The first is that fat people have *defective sensory input*. That is to say, their stomachs contract, but receptor cells in the stomach don't let the brain know what is happening. Further research reported by Stunkard in the early 1970's casts doubt on this possibility. For Stunkard has now proved that fat people can very easily be *trained* to recognize their own stomach contractions. The second explanation seems more probable—fat people simply don't *listen* to what their bodies are trying to tell them.

Psycho-analyst Hilde Bruch reported in 1961 that her obese patients literally did not know when they were physiologically hungry. Dr. Bruch suggests that, during childhood, these patients were not taught to discriminate between hunger and such states as fear, anger, and anxiety.

Perhaps fat people simply label almost *any* state of physiological arousal as hunger. And so they eat whenever they are angry, anxious, upset, or annoyed. To understand what Dr. Bruch was talking about, we must look more closely at hunger as a "mental experience."

Intra-Psychic Influences on Hunger and Eating

Consciously or unconsciously, many parents train their children to be over-eaters. Sometimes the parents are overweight themselves and, without realizing it, may over-feed their children in order to make the children like themselves. Other parents may believe that "fatness" and good health are pretty much the same thing. If the usual reward that the parents offer the child for good behavior is an extra helping of pie or cake, the child will soon learn that over-eating is a very effective way of winning approval. Food then takes on the *symbolic meaning* of love and acceptance. Later, as

Parents, consciously or unconsciously, serve as models for their children.

an adolescent or young adult, the person may feel a yearning to "raid the refrigerator" whenever she or he feels rejected or disappointed by life.

Data to support this view come from an additional series of studies by Hilde Bruch, who found that many overweight people felt unwanted, inadequate, and insecure as children. According to Dr. Bruch, these subjects began over-eating not only to gain attention from their parents, but also because eating too much made them feel big and important to themselves.

Schachter's Studies of Obesity

If fat people eat to satisfy symbolic needs—or because they cannot tell the difference between hunger and some other form of arousal—then one would expect eating behavior to be primarily under the control of internal or intra-psychic drives.

Columbia University psychologist Stanley Schachter disputes this view, at least as far as fat people are concerned. Schachter believes that normal people eat when their bodies tell them to—that is, when their stomachs contract and their "feeding centers" are active.

However, according to Schachter, obese people *don't listen to their bodies*. Rather than being driven to eat by internal cravings and desires, overweight individuals are simply abnormally sensitive to the world around them. Schachter and his colleagues recently reported a fascinating series of experiments supporting this view.

In 1968, Schachter, R. Goldman, and A. Gordon studied the effects of fear arousal on eating. Their subjects included both overweight and normal Columbia students. Schachter *et al.* found that when normal subjects were threatened with painful shock, they reduced their food intake markedly. Fat subjects, who might have been expected to *increase* their eating if they could not tell anxiety or fear from hunger, did nothing of the kind. When faced with a threat of painful shock, fat subjects ate about the same amount as when no threat was present. Studies such as this one convinced Schachter that psychiatrist Hilde Bruch might have erred when she said her obese patients could not tell the difference between fear and hunger.

In a second experiment, Schachter and L. Gross measured the effects of time perception on eating. They reasoned that normal students would eat when their *bodies* told them to, no matter what the clock on the wall said. Overweight subjects, on the other hand, might "eat by the clock" since they presumably pay little or no attention to what their stomachs and "feeding centers" tell them.

Overweight or not, people have a limit to how much they will eat.

Schachter and Gross kept both normal and fat subjects in an experimental situation in which the students could not tell what time it was. After the subjects had performed some boring tasks for a fairly lengthy period, the experimenters told half the subjects it was now a few minutes before their normal dinner time. The other half were told that it was then a few minutes after their normal dinner hour. Both groups were then offered some good-tasting crackers "to munch on until the end of the experiment."

Schachter and Gross found that normal students were not much affected by the incorrect information about the time of day—they ate about the same number of crackers no matter what time they thought it was. The fat subjects, however, ate very few crackers if told it was *before* dinner time, but large numbers of crackers when told it was *after* their normal dinner hour. Schachter assumes that obese people are guided more by *external cues* than by their internal physiological *drive states*.

In other studies, Schachter and his associates have shown that fat people tend to be "plate cleaners"—that is, they eat everything set before them whether they need it or not. If given a large portion, the obese individual will consume it all. If given but a small helping, the obese person will eat that, and seldom ask for more. Normal people are much more likely "to leave a little something on the plate" if given more than they usually eat, and to ask for more if given less than they are accustomed to eating.

Fat people are also more affected by the taste of food than normals, according to Schachter. When offered food of average or above-average taste, fat individuals eat a great deal more than do normals. When offered food of below-average or miserable taste, however, fat people eat a great deal less than normals do. The normal person seems to eat what he or she needs, almost in spite of the good or bad taste.

Fat people are also less likely to perform physical labor for food, or to suffer mild amounts of pain to get to eat, than are normals.

When we see someone who is grossly overweight, we often assume that their problem is that they are greedy, psychologically immature, or that they must have a physiological difficulty of some kind. But if Schachter is right, the major cause of obesity may be *external* rather than *internal*, for we often forget the strong effects that our culture has on our eating habits.

Let us look briefly at environmental influences on hunger.

Social/Behavioral Influences on Eating Behavior

The social world you live in plays a great part in controlling what you eat—and when you eat it.

For example, European farm workers often have five or six "regular" mealtimes per day. When they are working in the fields 12 to 14 hours daily, they need all this fuel to stay healthy. But many of them continue to eat just as frequently when they move to the city and take jobs in offices. They may even continue their five meals a day when they move to a new country.

A recent study by psychiatrist A.J. Stunkard shows that farm women from central Europe who immigrate to the United States are four to five times more likely to be overweight as are women from the same background whose families have lived in the United States for several generations.

People from different **social classes** in the US have quite different types of eating behavior. Men and women who belong to the wealthiest or "upper class" tend to be thinner, healthier, and to live longer than do men and women of the so-called "lower class."

In a recent study of 1,660 adults living in New York City, 32 percent of the men and 30 percent of the women in the lower classes were found to be obese. However, only 16 percent of the men and 5 percent of the women in the upper classes were overweight. Four times more upper-class women were "thin" than were women in the lower class. And the chances that an upper-class individual will go on a diet are two to three times as great as the chances that a person from any other social class will start to lose weight voluntarily.

Cultural Food Preferences

Religion and food preferences have always been closely connected. A few cultures are vegetarian, but most societies are **carnivorous.** Beef is perhaps America's favorite meat, but in India the flesh of the cow is **taboo** to certain religious groups because cattle are presumed to be sacred animals. Orthodox Jews (and many people from Arabic cultures) will not eat pork or unscaled fish (shellfish) such as shrimp, and many Jews will cling to these **culinary** customs even when they have given up other forms of religious **orthodoxy.**

Catholics, on the other hand, usually enjoy both beef and pork but, until recently, usually switched to shrimp and other seafoods on Fridays.

The Ifugao—a primitive tribe living in the Philippines—are very fond of insects. They eat three species of dragonflies, as well as crickets, ants, locusts, and a variety of beetles. Most Americans would prefer a nice glass of cool milk to a dish of ants fried in lard. Many primitive cultures, however, consider milk a disgusting secretion to be avoided if possible.

In some parts of the world, roast puppy is considered a real treat. But can you imagine how you would react if your family pet came to the dinner table—barbecued?

Question: Why do you suppose that animal flesh is more likely to be taboo than are fruits and vegetables?

Fat Wives and Insecure Husbands Many of our social needs are pressed upon us by our social environments. Thus we may over-drink or over-eat because the people we love may be *rewarded* in various ways when we are drunk or fat.

Richard B. Stuart worked for many months with married women who were complete failures at losing weight. Stuart eventually suspected that

Social classes. A way of grouping or classifying people according to their occupations, incomes, family histories, where they live, and their social relationships. There are three general classes. About 5 percent of the US population is said to be "upper class." These people are mostly very rich, live in expensive homes, hold executive positions, own their own businesses, or are so wealthy they don't have to work for a living. About 40 percent of the US population is considered to be "middle class." These people are white-collar workers, middle-level executives, or professional people. About 55 percent of the population is said to be "lower class." These people are blue-collar workers who perform unskilled or semi-skilled jobs and who have less education and (usually) smaller incomes than do members of the other two classes.

Carnivorous (kar-NIV-or-us). From the Latin words meaning "meat eater."

Taboo (tab-BOO). Anything that is forbidden on moral or religious grounds is taboo.

Culinary (CUE-lin-air-ree, or sometimes CULL-lin-air-ee). From the Latin word meaning "kitchen." Having to do with eating or the preparation and serving of food.

Orthodoxy (OR-tho-dox-ee). From the Greek word meaning "to have the right opinion." An orthodox person is someone who follows a recognized set of social, moral, political, or religious rules. Orthodoxy is conforming to custom or to some higher authority.

Corpulent (KOR-pew-lent). From the Latin word *corpus,* or "body." We get our words "corpse" and "corporation" from the same Latin source. To be "corpulent" is to have too much body—that is, to be somewhat obese.

the women's husbands were partially responsible for keeping their wives **corpulent.** To test his hypothesis, Stuart asked these couples to make tape recordings of their dinner-table conversations.

Stuart found that, although all the women were on diets and their husbands knew it, the husbands were four times more likely to offer food to their wives than the wives were to offer food to the husbands. The wives were twice as likely to reject this offered food than were the husbands, but the husbands were 12 times more likely to offer *criticisms* of their wives' eating behavior as they were to *praise* it.

Stuart also interviewed 55 husbands married to women who were trying to lose weight. Stuart's data suggest that the "food-pushing" husbands fall roughly into four groups:

1. Some husbands enjoyed demonstrating their masculine power by coaxing or forcing their wives to become fat. If the wife was overweight, the husband sometimes found this a useful fact to bring up in family arguments. The man could win almost any battle by calling the woman "a fat slob." Stuart believes the husbands realized (perhaps unconsciously) that if the wife lost weight, the husband would begin losing more arguments.

2. Other husbands viewed dinner time as being the main social event of the day. When the wives refused to eat very much, the husbands saw this as a rejection of themselves and the rest of the family group.

3. Some men had lost any sexual interest in their wives. They seemed to want to keep their wives fat as an excuse for their "playing around" with other women. Stuart's data also indicate that the husband lost sexual interest first, and then began rewarding the woman for over-eating, rather than losing interest after the wife was already fat.

4. Other husbands apparently feared their wives might be unfaithful to them if the women were too attractive. These men encouraged their wives to over-eat in order to keep their wives ugly—and therefore faithful.

Question: Do you think even a superb therapist could help these women change their eating behaviors unless the husbands were somehow motivated to solve their own psychological problems?

How To Lose Weight

Like almost everything else you do, your eating behavior is *multi-determined.* That is, you eat not just because you've been without food for a while, but also because: (1) your blood sugar level has fallen; (2) your stomach is contracting; (3) your "feeding center" has increased its neural activity; (4) your "satiation center" has decreased its neural activity; (5) your "swallow counter" has been silent for a while; (6) your regular dinner time is approaching; (7) you smell food in the air and hear other people talking about "what's for lunch"; (8) because your mother and father thought that fat babies were healthy babies; and (9) because food and eating have a variety of symbolic values for you.

Obviously, then, if you want to lose weight, your dietary program must take into account not just the calories you consume and how you burn them up, but your motives and mannerisms as well.

If you wish to embark on a well-rounded weight-loss program, the first thing you should do is to have a physical check-up. That way you can make sure that you are not that one American in 20 who is under- or overweight because you have a physical problem of some kind. If you want to gain or lose more than 5 to 10 kilograms (11 to 22 pounds), you probably should do so under medical guidance. Your physician may wish to prescribe drugs to help control your appetite, and may also send you to see a registered dietician.

One good habit to acquire is to shop for groceries after you've eaten, not when you're hungry.

However, diets and pills are only the first step in a long journey. The real problem usually lies in learning enough about yourself to recognize what internal and external *stimulus inputs* affect your eating behavior. The better you know yourself and the people around you, the more likely it is that you will be able to gain voluntary control over what you weigh.

If, at some time in the future, you wish to lose weight, you might consider these suggestions:

1. Begin by recording *everything* you eat and drink for a period of a week or so. Psychologists call this "taking a **baseline.**" Keep a record of where you eat, of the events that occurred just before you started eating, of what you thought about just before you ate (and afterward). And, *most important*, notice who is around when you eat and what their response is to your food intake. Is anyone in your life (other than yourself) rewarded by your being too fat or too thin? In brief, measure both the psychological and the social *consequences* of your eating behaviors.

2. Write down all the rewards and pleasures that will come to you if you gain better control over your eating behavior.

3. Break the hunger habit by changing your meal times to a very irregular schedule several weeks before you begin your diet. (If you are underweight and you eat irregularly, you may wish to force yourself to eat on schedule in order to help build up the hunger habit so that your stomach muscles will begin urging you to eat more.)

4. Increase your physical activities to help you burn off excess fat. If you are "out of shape," begin by walking a few minutes each day and work up from there. *Don't* push yourself to do too much at any one time. Pick the forms of physical exertion you like best, and *keep a record* of what you do so that you can note your progress.

5. Once you have your baseline material available, you may want to talk things over with a psychologist. You may be using your fatness as a psychological defense, or as a substitute for healthier behaviors. Unless you solve your own psychological problems first, you are not likely to be successful at losing weight.

6. Habits are difficult to change, and you will probably need all the help you can get. So you may find it wise to involve as many people as possible in your program. If someone close to you unconsciously wants you to remain fat, you may well have to find some substitute reward for this person if you are to gain her or his active and willing participation in what you are trying to do.

7. When you start your program, you may find it very useful to make a large chart or graph on which you record each aspect of your daily routine. Post the graph in a prominent place so that everyone can see your progress and comment on it. Arrange to have someone give you regular rewards (money, special privileges, a gold star on your chart, or a verbal pat on the back) each time that you meet your daily goal. Give yourself a bonus for

Baseline. A starting point. To "take a baseline" is to record a set of behaviors *before* you try to change those behaviors. Most people assume they "know" what their baseline (or customary) behaviors are. In fact, most of us really don't. Many people who wish to lose weight consider it a waste of time to take accurate baseline recordings of when and what they eat. Nothing could be farther from the truth. Much of what we call "psychotherapy" consists of getting people to set measurable goals for themselves, and to make an accurate assessment of where they presently are and what they are presently doing. If you don't know *precisely* where you are starting from (in any form of therapy), you stand rather a poor chance of knowing how close you really are to your goals—much less whether or not the therapy is effective.

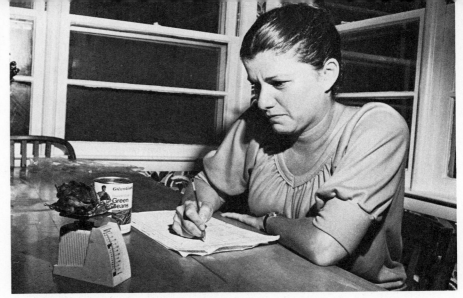

A dieting subject records the number of calories in food she plans to prepare.

meeting that goal every day for a whole week. In some ways the graph is the *most important part* of any weight-control program, for it gives you immediate feedback on your progress. Learning to eat correctly is a matter of establishing voluntary self-control over your actions. And without feedback, you will find it almost impossible to acquire the self-discipline you will need both to get your weight down and to *keep* it down.

8. Don't expect too muct too fast. Unless you change your diet drastically, your average weight loss or gain will be about two pounds a week. Because your weight fluctuates from day to day, it is good to keep track of what you eat and the exercise you do *in addition* to charting your weight each day.

9. Don't think of your program as being a "weight-loss" program, or you probably won't maintain it. Rather, think of it as your way of finally learning how to eat properly.

Long-term weight loss is difficult to achieve because it is affected by so many different parts of your life. If you set realistic goals for yourself, you can probably achieve them. And as you see the first small effects of your program take place, you will probably be encouraged to continue.

The old saying that "nothing succeeds like success" has a great deal of psychological truth to it. So do your best to arrange your program so that—at least at the beginning—there is little or no chance you can fail.

However, if after the first few days your graph shows that things aren't going as they should, don't hesitate to make adjustments in your schedule. And keep on making changes until you find something that works for you.

Even if you are one of the lucky majority of people whose weight is more or less normal, you still might wish to try to gain or lose a few pounds as an experiment on yourself. For once you have put yourself through this kind of psychological analysis, you will have achieved something even more important than gaining voluntary control over your own eating behavior—you will have learned a great deal more about your own motives, desires, habits, needs, and drives than reading a textbook can ever teach you.

(Continued from page 293.)

The crisis, Annette thought as she rushed up the stairs to Thelma's apartment. People like Thelma could stand anything except success achieved through self-discipline. That was what seemed to trigger off the emotional outburst. And if you didn't catch them right away. . .

A bedraggled-looking Thelma answered the door and quietly invited Annette in. Her eyes were moist and puffy from crying. "Listen, Annette," she said when they were seated. "I'm terribly sorry about tonight. I just sort of lost control, you know?"

"I know," Annette replied.

"I mean, it was a rotten day at the office. I jumped all over people, and they were nasty to me in return. I knew what I was doing wrong, but I just couldn't stop myself. Anyhow, I went bowling after work, and I was feeling so damned rotten, I decided to have just one little drink. Just one, you know . . ."

Annette nodded. "I know."

"And then before I knew it I was on my fourth Tom Collins, and I bowled really lousy, and I told one of my friends to go to hell." Thelma started weeping. "I mean, I *knew* what I was doing and how it hurt people, and I just couldn't seem to stop."

"Yes, we all do that sometimes," said Annette quietly.

"Then I got so mad at myself I just ran out to the car and started driving. I couldn't bear to face you right then. Does that make sense to you?"

"Of course."

"I must have driven for three hours anyway. I kept hoping the car would run out of gas way out in the country somewhere, and I'd just die or something before anybody found me." Thelma sighed. "But finally I just gave up and drove back here. And then you called."

"I'm glad I did."

Thelma nodded, trying to smile a bit. "So am I, Annette. I think I finally figured it out, what went wrong. But I want your advice on it."

"Of course," said Annette, brightening considerably.

"It sounds screwy, I know, but I think I got depressed because I was doing so well. You know what I mean?"

Annette nodded. "I know exactly."

"I mean, I've lost 23 pounds in a month, I've stayed completely legal, I've done better at the office—except for today—and you've helped me like nobody else ever has. But *I* was the one who did it, you understand?"

"Yes, I do."

Thelma rushed on, motivated by continuing insight. "I mean, *you* didn't resist all those hunger pangs in the middle of the night, *I* did. And *you* didn't have to do all that exercise, *I* did."

"I know," said Annette. "And you really did beautifully."

"That's the trouble!" Thelma said quickly. "I did better on the job, I did better at losing weight, I did better with my social life, I look better, I feel better, I'm happier than I've been in years."

Annette smiled. "And that's the problem, isn't it?"

"Of course," Thelma said, a weary smile on her face. "I kept asking myself, why did I have to wait so long to wake up to what life's all about? Why did I need you to help me do what should have been obvious? And I kept thinking about all of the wasted times in my life, the people I'd hurt because I didn't know any better."

"You've got a lifetime left to make up for it," said Annette.

"Oh, I know. And I suppose I will. But even that isn't the real problem, is it?"

Annette grinned broadly. "No, Thelma, it isn't."

"I mean, the problem is, I *know* I can change myself. I've already done it. So I guess I could do some more, right?"

"Right," said Annette. "You've got both the motivation and the technique."

Thelma nodded. "That's the scary part. Now that I can do just about anything I want to do, what the hell do I really want to do?" Thelma giggled a bit.

"Well, what are your goals, Thelma?"

"I'm not sure yet, but I guess I better start figuring them out. I mean, as long as I was failing, I could blame it all on God, or my parents, or just about anybody. Now I've got nobody to blame, not even myself. I finally have all the freedom anybody could ask for. That's frightening."

"Of course," said Annette. "Because there's no freedom without responsibility. Freedom's pretty expensive, when you stop to think about it."

Thelma laughed. "Well, I guess I can afford it now." She shook her head, as if in wonderment. "You know, I guess I must be the happiest person in town. No, that's wrong. I must be the happiest person in the whole wide world."

Now it was Annette's turn to cry a bit. "Can I be number two?"

Thelma reached over and squeezed Annette's hand tightly. "Sure. And thanks for everything, you know?"

"I know," said Annette, wiping her eyes with a tissue.

Thelma released the woman's hand and leaned back in her chair. "Listen, Annette, while you're here, we've got some things to plan. I've been thinking about getting a new job in a year or so, after I've lost another hundred pounds or so. And learned a few things more, like how to be nice to people even when they bug you. You know what I want to be?"

"No, but tell me."

Thelma grinned. "Looking at me now, you'll think it's crazy. But I always wanted to be an airlines stewardess."

"You're kidding!"

Thelma nodded. "They're always so slim and trim, you know. I wanted to be just like that, all my life. And now maybe I can be." She paused for a second. "And there's another thing about being a stewardess, you know."

"What?"

Thelma roared with laughter until she almost cried again. "Well, it sure would beat buying my own ticket to Miami!"

Summary

1.   In the past, many of the best-known theories of motivation have been **one-level** approaches. That is, the theories have attempted to explain "what moves us" in purely biological terms.

2.   **Drive theory** is the best-known of these physiological theories of motivation.

3.   According to drive theory, our biological or life-sustaining needs

are said to be **primary needs.** Whenever we lack something necessary for life, a **primary drive state** builds up within us that leads to greater neural firing rates. This increased neural activity is painful and arouses us to action.

4. The stronger the primary need, the faster our neurons fire, the stronger the drive state, the greater the **arousal,** and presumably the more pain that we feel.

5. When we satisfy a primary need, we experience pleasure because the painful arousal (drive state) is reduced

6. According to drive theory, our major motivation is that of **drive reduction**—that is, reducing drive states and thereby returning to our **homeostatic** "home base"—a condition in which we experience no painful needs or drives.

7. Most drive theorists believe that intra-psychic and social needs are learned because they are associated with biological or primary needs. These non-physiological motives are often called **secondary needs.**

8. Associated with each secondary need is a **secondary drive state** that, when reduced, can give us pleasurable reinforcement.

9. Although drive theory has added much to our understanding of motivation, it has been subjected to many criticisms:

   a. It cannot explain all aspects of human motivation. Terms such as "hunger" and "thirst," "pain" and "pleasure" are perhaps better understood as descriptions of **mental experiences** than as physiological conditions.

   b. Sometimes **increased stimulation** is pleasurable although, according to drive theory, it should be painful.

   c. Many secondary needs seem not to be learned through association with the satisfaction of primary needs.

10. These criticisms (and others) led psychologists to develop **arousal theory.** The basic postulates of arousal theory include:

   a. The homeostatic "home base" is a point of **optimum stimulation,** not a state of **zero excitation.**

   b. This optimum point may change from time to time.

   c. Any movement away from optimum is arousing, and hense motivates us to return to optimum.

11. Although arousal theory solved some of the problems associated with drive theory, it made the organism dependent upon psychological inputs from the environment, and thus led to an increased interest in **two-level** or **intra-psychic theories** in which emotion is often seen as the driving force behind motivation behaviors.

12. According to the **James–Lange theory of emotion,** action always precedes (and generally causes) emotional feelings. "We are afraid because we run; we do not run because we are afraid."

13. Research studies seldom support the James–Lange viewpoint. Rather, we typically perceive a situation, evaluate it, experience an emotion, and then respond. Thus our **intra-psychic processes** often guide or direct our biological reactions and our social behaviors.

14. Our perceptions are shaped by our experiences with others and by environmental inputs. This fact led to the development of **multi-level theories of motivation,** in which biological, mental, and social motivations are all assumed to be primary and necessary for sustaining human life as we know it.

15. From a **General Systems Theory** approach, one of our major motivations is that of predicting and controlling our biological, intra-psychic, and social **inputs.**

16. In order to gain this predictive control, we often must change our **outputs.**

17. Your **swallow center** measures the amount you eat and reduces your intake accordingly, even before your blood sugar level changes.

18. If you eat at regular times, your stomach begins to contract and growl shortly before your usual meal times, an experience most people of average weight interpret as **hunger pangs.**

19. Overweight individuals often seem not to know when their stomachs are contracting. They appear to overeat to reduce **psychological** and **social drives** more than because they are biologically starved.

20. Freud believed that if a child's oral desires were not satisfied during the first year of its life, it might develop into an **oral personality type** as an adult.

21. Parents often train their children to eat too much by giving a child affection when it eats. As an adult, this person may "raid the refrigerator" as a **symbolic** means of gaining affection.

22. There are many social/behavioral influences on **obesity.** Upper class individuals are much less likely to have weight problems than are lower class individuals. People from central European backgrounds are more likely to be obese than are native-born US citizens.

23. Most important of all the social influences on eating behavior seems to be **rewarding feedback.** Studies suggest that many people who have difficulty losing weight have someone close to them who (often unconsciously) encourages them to continue over-eating.

24. Should you wish to lose weight, you may find it easier to do so if you attempt to determine, and to bring under control, all those biological, psychological and environmental inputs that influence your eating behavior.

Recommended Readings

Arkes, Hal R., and J.P. Garske. *Psychological Theories of Motivation* (Monterey, Calif.: Brooks/Cole, 1977).

Atkinson, John W. *An Introduction to Motivation* (New York: American Book Company, 1964).

Buck, Ross. *Human Motivation of Emotion* (New York: Wiley, 1976).

Levine, Fredric M. *Theoretical Readings in Motivation: Perspectives on Human Behavior* (Skokie, Ill.: Rand McNally, 1975).

Mahoney, M.J., and Kathryn Mahoney. *Permanent Weight Control* (New York: Norton, 1976).

Schachter, Stanley. *Emotion, Obesity, and Crime* (New York: Academic Press, 1971).

Stuart, Richard B., and Barbara Davis. *Slim Chance in a Fat World* (Champaign, Ill.: Research Press Company, 1972).

Sexual Motivation

Did You Know That . . .

We know less about the workings of your sex organs than about the physiology of your heart or liver?

The first scientific studies of the human sexual response were probably performed by psychologist John B. Watson in 1917?

Watson may have been indirectly responsible for getting Alfred Kinsey interested in making scientific surveys of sexual behavior?

The best current research on human sexual physiology and behavior is probably that of Masters and Johnson?

The sex life of animals is controlled primarily by hormones?

Male insects may perform their sexual functions better if the female first bites the male's head off?

A female fetus may be born with male sex organs if the mother is exposed to excessive amounts of male hormone during pregnancy?

Hormone therapy does not "cure" homosexuality?

You have "pleasure centers" in your brain which, when stimulated electrically, make you "feel good?"

"The Mating Game"

"Sex," said Paul Schmidtt. "It's the hormones that do it. At least in birds like ring doves, hormones pretty well control the entire sex drive. No hormones, no drive. No drive, no sexual behavior. No sexual behavior, no little doves. It's as simple as that."

"Or as complicated," Linda said in an amused tone of voice.

"Oh, it's not all that complicated, really," Paul replied. "Come on. I'll show you."

Paul led the way into the lab. "I'm not doing anything really exciting—just repeating some of the work that Professor Lehrman and his group at Rutgers did several years ago. After I learn what the research is like, then I may start something on my own."

"In research, you mean?" Linda said mockingly.

"What else?" Paul said, not really catching the gist of her comments. "Or maybe I'll wait until I'm a graduate student somewhere to begin my own projects. Anyhow, working in the lab is a great way to learn all about sexual behavior."

The mating response of ring doves is influenced by their behavior as well as their hormones.

"In birds, you mean," Linda said archly.

"Of course in birds. That's what I'm studying in my senior project—the sexual behavior of the ring dove." Paul opened the door to the animal room and went in.

Large metal cages, each holding one or more doves, lined the walls of the room. The cages were cleanly stacked on movable steel racks so that they could be rolled around as necessary. Many of the birds in the cages fluttered their wings as if frightened by the intrusion of the two undergraduates, but Paul ignored them.

"This is where we house the birds, but there's nothing much interesting going on here." Paul then pointed to a door that bore a large sign reading, EXPERIMENT IN PROGRESS—KEEP OUT!! "But if you'll come into my Inner Sanctum . . ."

"Yes?" asked Linda.

"I'll show you what effect hormones have on sexual behavior."

"In birds, you mean."

"Of course," Paul replied, walking quickly through the door.

"I can hardly wait," Linda said, following Paul into the experimental chamber.

Paul pointed at a metal table that had some cages on it. "These are our experimental cages. This one, as you see, has a glass soup bowl and some nesting material in it—as well as food and water for the birds. Now, suppose we introduce a male bird to a female by putting them together in this cage . . ."

"Doesn't the poor little female have any *choice?*"

"No, and neither does the male, for that matter," Paul replied. "All's fair in the science of love. Anyway, we bring the two birds together for the first time, and shortly thereafter, the male gets interested in mating. So he circles in front of the female. Then he bends his head over and takes a deep bow . . ."

"Like an actor on a stage, pleased with his performance," Linda said.

Paul Schmidtt laughed. "It's the audience that's pleased with his performance, and in this case, the audience is the female ring dove. She eggs him on—so to speak."

Linda groaned.

"Anyway," Paul continued, "as the male bows toward the female, he makes a cooing sound, like this . . ." Paul swelled up his chest, bowed low toward Linda, and uttered a heartfelt "coo-oo-oo."

"Bravo!" cried the young woman.

Encouraged by her response, Paul repeated the "bow-coo."

"You're wasting your time in psychology," Linda said, crossing her legs provocatively as she sat down. "Have you thought about making movies?"

"I can't afford a camera yet—to film the doves' sexual behaviors, I mean. So I simply sit in that chair and take notes. Anyhow, the female responds to the 'bow-coo' by starting to build a nest. The male helps her out—that's very important."

Linda nodded. "From the point of view of women's equality, having the male share the household chores is a *very* important thing."

Paul laughed again. "You ain't heard nothing yet. A week after the nest-building starts, the female lays the eggs. And then both birds sit on them to incubate them until they hatch. Then both momma and papa feed the little doves until they're old enough to take care of themselves. So you see it's a mutual adventure right from the start. Then the male begins bowing and cooing, and the whole cycle starts over again."

Linda blushed a bit. "When do they . . . oh, you know."

"Mating occurs during the first couple of days, while the male is still courting the female."

"And you sit here and *watch?*"

Paul grinned. "Only in the interests of science, I assure you."

"I see," said Linda. She uncrossed her legs. "But what about those hormones you were going to show me?"

Paul Schmidtt frowned. "Hormones are just chemicals—nothing much to look at by themselves. It's their effect that you look for, really. If we castrate the male, we cut off his supply of hormones. Then he won't show any interest in the female at all, and he won't perform the 'bow-coo.'"

Linda seemed dismayed. "Not even with a particularly charming and attractive young female?"

"Not unless we inject him first with male hormones called androgens to replace the ones he would normally be producing. No androgens, no sexual behavior. But it's the sight of the female dove that gets the male excited enough to do his little dance, if that makes you feel any happier."

"I'm sure it makes the female doves happier."

Paul sat down fairly close to Linda. "It does, I assure you. And, of course, it's the 'bow-coo' that triggers off the instinctive behavior in the female. If we put a female bird into the cage by herself, she won't build a nest or lay eggs. If we put her in with a castrated male, or with other females, she still shows no interest in sexual matters. But if we give her a little pornography . . ."

"What?" said Linda in a shocked tone of voice. "I didn't think birds could read!"

Paul grinned. "No, but they can watch. See this cage over here? With the glass partition down the middle? We put a male on one side, a female on the other. They can't touch each other, but they can see and hear what the other one does."

"Like two star-crossed lovers, separated from each other's tender touch by the cold steel curtain of a prison's bars," Linda said, a misty look in her large blue eyes.

"We use glass, not steel. Anyhow, if the male can see the female, he will do his 'bow-coo,' and she will respond by building a nest all by herself. She even lays eggs and tries to incubate them, all on her own."

Linda laughed. "I don't think the women's equality movement would approve of that particular experiment."

"But you see," Paul said, "in normal conditions, the male always helps out. But only if he has an ample supply of female hormones present in his body."

Again Linda seemed shocked. "Female hormones? In the male bird? But I thought . . ."

Paul looked very pleased with himself. "Yes, I know. You think in terms of blacks and whites, but sex is a matter of shades of gray. The male's testes produce androgens, true, or the mating cycle never begins. But sitting on eggs and feeding the young is a female behavior pattern—and for the male to participate, he has to be stimulated by female hormones."

"But where does he get them?" Linda asked.

"The male's testes produce female hormones called estrogen and progesterone—as well as producing androgens. Estrogen controls nest-building, while incubation is affected by progesterone. A castrated male injected with androgen will do the 'bow-coo,' but he won't build a nest or sit on the eggs."

A wicked gleam appeared in Linda's eyes. "But if you inject the dear little castrated bird with female hormones . . ."

"Then he carries out the cycle in a normal fashion. Usually, you see, the male has enough estrogen present to trigger off the nest-building if the female is there to coax him a little. Putting the nest together causes his testes to secrete progesterone, so that he helps to hatch and care for the young."

"That's a point my friends in the equality movement ought to be very interested in." Linda rearranged her skirt a bit. "But what about the female dove . . ."

Paul moved even closer to Linda. "It's the sight of the male doing his 'bow-coo' that starts the female's ovaries working overtime producing estrogens. The more estrogen she has in her body, the more interested she gets in nest-building and in mating. Building the nest causes her ovaries to produce progesterone, and so she gets interested in hatching the eggs just about the time she actually lays them."

"She's just a prisoner of her body."

Paul's foot momentarily touched Linda's. "No, just like the male, she's a prisoner of her environment and the effects of her own behavior as much as she is tied to her own hormone cycle. Rather a nice prison, I'd say."

"Only if you have the right cellmate," Linda said as she moved her foot away. She looked at her watch, then frowned. "Oh, I really must be running along. Thanks so much for showing me your birds. I think it's utterly fascinating, but I do have to go get ready for the party tonight." She touched Paul gently on the cheek. "You are coming to the party, aren't you?"

"Wouldn't miss it for the world."

"It's a BYOH party, you know."

"BYOH?"

"Bring your own hormones," Linda said brightly as she danced out the door.

(Continued on page 339.)

The Scientific Study of Sexuality

Sex has always posed something of a problem for the psychologist, both at a theoretical level and, as we will see, at a personal level as well. As far as theory goes, it would seem that sexual needs should be explainable in the same terms as are any of the other physiological needs. However, there is a crucial difference: You cannot live without air, water, food, elimination, and the proper temperature. But you could readily (if not pleasantly) live out your entire life without engaging in any reproductive behavior whatsoever. Without air, you die within minutes. But at one time or another in your life, you may go for weeks, months, or even years without having any sexual contact with another person.

The major difference between sex and other physiological needs is this: Food, air, and water are necessary for the survival of the *individual*, but sex is necessary for the survival of the *species*.

For reproductive activities to occur, two more-or-less compatible individuals must find each other and adjust to each other's needs—at least momentarily. Men and women breathe the same way, drink the same way, and eat the same way, but their sexual behaviors are typically quite different. So sexuality—at least at the human level—involves learning to meet the needs of your partner in order to meet both your own needs and those of society and the human race.

In higher animals, species survival depends not only on getting the male and female together so that mating can occur, but also on keeping one or both parents around to care for the young until they are large enough to face the world on their own. An adequate theory of sexuality, then, must explain not only the differing sexual needs and responses of male and female, but maternal and paternal activities as well. We will talk about "parenting" behaviors in later chapters. But given the complexity of sexual behaviors, we can readily understand why none of our theories about sex really explains all we need to know.

The Objective Study of Sex

The theoretical issues facing the psychologist interested in sexual behavior are only a small part of the difficulties of studying this complicated subject, however. Consider the practical problems for a moment.

In our society, at least, sexuality intrudes into almost everything we do. It is a major topic of conversation; it is the presumed cause of many crimes; it leers at us from movie screens and winks at us from television tubes. Sex is no longer something for private consumption. Rather, it is marketed with the commercial shrillness once reserved for automobiles and breakfast cereals.

And yet, for all the noise, we really know precious little about human sexuality. Medical science has, until very recently, avoided any serious study of the physiology of sexual behavior. We know a great deal more about the functioning of your heart and your liver than we do about the normal functioning of your sexual organs.

A significant number of the patients who walk into a physician's office need guidance in sexual matters, but most medical schools still treat the

In our society, sex is a popular topic of conversation and the subject of many new books every year.

Many states offer sex education in grammar and high schools.

John B. Watson.

subject with an air of **prudery**—when they mention it at all. Only in the field of psychiatry has the scientific study of sexuality gained a real foothold, but even the psychiatrists restrict their attention primarily to the mental and emotional aspects of sex.

Until the last decade or so, sexual education for the average person consisted of whatever "facts of life" were passed on by the person's parents or **peers,** whatever information the person could glean from reading various "dirty books" that were secretly passed from hand to hand, and whatever knowledge the individual could gain from personal experience.

Many states have attempted to make "sex education" available in grammar and high schools, but not with any great success. For example, in 1978 the State of Michigan undertook a survey of parental attitudes toward sex education. The results of the survey were most interesting—from a scientific point of view. The vast majority of parents stated that young people should receive their sex educations at home, not at school. However, more than 80 percent of these same parents reported that they had never once discussed the technical aspects of sexual behavior with their own children.

Watson's Physiological Studies

A few scientists have tried to bring human sexual behavior into the laboratory, to study it as objectively as other scientists studied the digestion of food. Almost without exception, however, these pioneers were rejected by their scientific colleagues for daring to perform experiments on what most people believed was an intensely private aspect of human life.

John B. Watson, who started the **behaviorist** tradition in psychology, was one of the first Americans to investigate the physiological aspects of the sexual response. Although Watson gained his early fame (1914) for insisting that studies of animal behavior could be of value to psychologists, Watson always realized that human behavior was considerably more complex than the behavior of rats. Studying the manner in which laboratory animals **copulated** told you something—but not everything important—about the psychological and physiological changes that occurred in humans during sexual intercourse. Since the medical sciences had studiously ignored the subject, Watson set out to investigate the matter himself—at first hand.

Watson wanted to know what kinds of biological changes occur in humans during the stress of intercourse. The medical literature in 1917 reported little more than that the pulse rate usually increases, but the hows and whys and whats of the matter were simply not known.

Watson tackled the issue directly, by constructing a set of instruments to measure the physiological arousal of a woman during sexual arousal. Since Watson's wife refused to participate in such an outrageous project, he used his female laboratory assistant as a subject. Watson fathered what were probably the very first reliable data on the female sexual response, and since it was a topic he could obviously study with pleasure, he acquired several boxes of scientific data. Unfortunately for all concerned, Watson's wife eventually discovered why her husband was spending so much time in the laboratory, and she not only sued him for divorce, but also confiscated the scientific records!

Although Watson was one of the brightest and most creative men of his time, his academic career was ruined by this episode. He had to resign his professorship at Johns Hopkins University, and most of his friends and colleagues deserted him. The Baltimore newspapers reported the divorce in lurid detail, and the judge presiding at the trial gave Watson a severe tongue-lashing—calling him, among other things, an expert in *mis*behavior.

After the divorce Watson married his assistant, but still could not find a job at any other college or university. In desperation, he took a position with a large advertising agency and stayed with it the rest of his professional life. Although he continued to write books and scientific papers, he was a ruined man and soon slipped into the solace of alcohol. He died in 1958, at the age of 80.

When this aspect of Watson's career was first reported in print in 1974, many noted psychologists refused to believe that "the great man" could have engaged in such **sordid** experimental studies. However, in 1978 the museum of the Canadian Psychological Association in Montreal put on display some scientific equipment taken from Watson's laboratory at Johns Hopkins. Included in the display was "a set of small instruments for measuring the female sexual response."

Kinsey's Interviews

Watson's influence on the scientific study of human sexuality was profound, but largely indirect. One of Watson's students, Karl Lashley, did undertake some work in the area. But Lashley's major contribution came when he got a noted biologist interested in studying sexual responses—a biologist named Alfred Kinsey. The first survey of US sexual behavior based on an adequately large segment of the public did not come until 1948, when Kinsey and his associates published their monumental volume, *Sexual Behavior in the Human Male.*

The Kinsey group asked many thousands of men to talk about every aspect of their sexual lives, and a surprisingly large number responded to the questions without shame or evasion. Since Kinsey depended on volunteers, it may be that his sample was fairly **biased,** for one can never be sure of what a man does who won't talk about his experiences. Nonetheless, Kinsey did show that a large group of normal-appearing US males regularly engaged in a wide variety of sexual practices that "nice people" were not even supposed to know about.

In later years, Kinsey and his group published a similar book about female sexual behavior and, in the late 1970's, reported a study of **homosexual** activities. Perhaps Kinsey's most significant contribution was that when his books were published, a great many guilt-ridden people who thought of themselves as **perverts** or mentally ill discovered that, compared to almost everyone else, their sex lives were really rather tame.

Masters and Johnson's Research

Still and all, the writings of Kinsey and many others all sprang from conversations and case histories rather than direct observations: People

Alfred Kinsey.

Biased (BUY-us'd). From a Latin term meaning "to cut or go against the grain." In psychological terms, to be biased is to have preconceived notions about a situation, or to perceive things as you want to see them, not as they actually are. A "biased sample" is one not selected randomly, but rather selected according to some (often unconscious) scheme. People tend to select as their friends others who think and act as they do. Thus you and your friends make up a "biased sample" of the entire US population because the sample excludes everyone who is different than you are.

Homosexual. Sexual activities between two (or more) males, or between two (or more) females. As opposed to *heterosexual* (HETT-er-oh-sex-you-all) activities, which occur between a male and a female. Homosexual behaviors are frequently found in lower animals and, according to Kinsey, take place more often among humans than "prudish people" are willing to admit. Freud—and most other scientists who have studied human sexuality—believe that homosexual activities are as "normal" and as "genetically determined" as are heterosexual behaviors.

Perverts (PURR-verts). From the Latin word meaning "to turn the wrong way, or to corrupt." Anyone who takes her or his sexual pleasures in a manner not approved by society is considered a pervert—at least, within that particular society.

Gynecologist (guy-nuh-COLL-oh-jist, or jin-nuh-COLL-oh-jist). The Greek word *gyne* means "woman." A medical doctor whose speciality is treating the diseases of women is called a gynecologist.

Masturbation (mass-tur-BAY-shun). To bring oneself to sexual climax by hand, by rubbing against something, or occasionally through fantasy. Also called "self-abuse," "playing with yourself," "the solitary vice," and other terms.

Frigidity (frih-JID-it-tee). Sexual coldness or unresponsiveness in the female. The inability of a woman to enjoy sex or to achieve orgasm.

Repression (ree-PRESH-un). To inhibit thoughts, desires, or actions.

were asked to *talk* about their sex lives while the scientists recorded what the people *said*. It was not until the 1950's that William Masters and Virginia Johnson began to study what people actually *did*.

Masters was trained as a **gynecologist**—that is, a physician specializing in disorders of the female reproductive system. Johnson was trained in social work and psychology. They started their work in St. Louis, using female prostitutes as paid subjects. Following Watson's lead, Masters and Johnson made recordings of their subjects' bodily reactions while the women experienced various simple types of sexual arousal (chiefly **masturbation**). Later, they studied the physiological changes that accompany sexual excitement in males, as well.

When Masters attempted to present his early data to a gathering of US gynecologists, the majority of these physicians refused to support his research and suggested that he give it up. Many of the best-known medical journals would not publish his findings, and political pressure prevented his getting governmental support for his work.

Thus the first public discussion of the Masters and Johnson research was delayed until 1962, when they presented their findings to an enthusiastic audience at the annual meeting of the American Psychological Association.

The Masters and Johnson research has challenged many of the old superstitions concerning sexuality. Prior to their studies, it had been thought (primarily by male scientists) that women achieved different types of sexual climaxes, or orgasms, depending on the manner in which they were excited or aroused. Masters and Johnson found that a woman's body undergoes the same characteristic changes no matter what type of stimulation brings the woman to her climax. Although the woman's *feelings* might vary considerably from one sexual experience to another, the *physiological changes* associated with orgasm almost always occur in the same sequence.

Their research led Masters and Johnson to pioneer new types of therapy with men and women who had various types of sexual problems. For instance, many women suffer from **frigidity**—that is, the inability to achieve climax. Until recently, most psychologists and psychiatrists assumed that the major cause of frigidity was **repression**—that is, the woman's feelings of guilt and anxiety concerning the sexual act were so strong that she simply could not relax and let nature take its course. Therapy usually consisted of helping the woman talk through her early sexual thoughts and experiences in the hope that she would gain some insight into what was really bothering her.

Masters and Johnson believe that frigidity is often caused by ignorance and clumsiness on the part of both the woman and her partner. By teaching these women and their partners to pay greater attention to the *physiological*

William Masters and Virginia Johnson.

indicators of sexual arousal, Masters and Johnson have been able to help many patients for whom the usual "talk" therapies were not particularly effective.

Men often suffer from the opposite sort of problem—they achieve climax so quickly that their partners are left unsatisfied. By training the women to monitor the man's state of sexual arousal, Masters and Johnson have achieved nearly 100 percent success in their treatment of this problem, called **premature ejaculation.**

In some ways, sexual behavior has much in common with the eating behavior we discussed in the last chapter. Both types of activity are based on physiological needs; both have important intra-psychic or personal aspects; and both are greatly influenced by the social environment and by rewards and punishments.

In the case of food-taking, the intra-psychic and social/behavioral factors are often ignored or misunderstood. In the case of sex, however, it is often the *physiological* or *mechanical factors* whose importance is frequently neglected.

We will look at sexuality from an intra-psychic and an environmental standpoint in several later chapters. For the moment, let us see how your body chemistry influences both your sexual motivation and your sexual behavior.

The Physiology of Sex

In almost all forms of animal life, sexual behavior is greatly influenced by fluids secreted in several different glands or organs within the animal's body. Glands, for example, are small chemical factories that release their products either into the bloodstream, onto the tissues surrounding the gland, or even into the outside world.

Some of these chemicals have primarily a local effect. For instance, the tear glands in your eyes secrete that clear but romantic liquid which, in small quantities, lubricates the movement of your eyes in their sockets and, in larger amounts, tells the world that you are sad or unhappy.

Other types of glands—such as the adrenals and gonads—secrete their products directly into your bloodstream, and so these fluids have their primary effects some distance away from the glands. These "action-at-a-distance" chemicals are called **hormones,** from a Greek word that means "to stir up, to attack, to set in motion."

Hormones

You have two **adrenal glands**—one atop each of your kidneys. The adrenals secrete more than 20 different hormones that influence both your growth and your behavior. The majority of the adrenal hormones regulate such bodily functions as digestion, urine excretion, and blood pressure. However, several of these chemicals have a direct effect on your sex life. These are called *sex hormones.*

Sex hormones are also produced by your **gonads,** or sex glands—the testes in the male, and the ovaries in the female. Your adrenals and your gonads (see Fig. 13.1) worked together to provide your body with the chemicals it needed to develop into—and to remain—a sexually mature adult.

Male hormones are called **androgens.** The two main types of female hormones are known as **estrogens** and **progesterone.** Once you are born, whether you are a woman or a man, your adrenals and your gonads produce *both* male and female hormones. It is the *relative balance* between these two types of hormones that at puberty makes your body take on the physical and behavioral characteristics that we associate with maleness and femaleness.

Premature ejaculation (PREE-mat-chur ee-jack-you-LAY-shun). "Premature" means "to arrive too early" or "to explode too soon." To ejaculate is to discharge semen (SEE-men) at the moment of a male's sexual orgasm. When a male reaches sexual climax before the female has achieved satisfaction, he has ejaculated prematurely.

Hormones (HORR-moans). Complex chemicals secreted by various glands that affect growth and behavior.

Adrenal gland (add-DREE-nul). A small gland at the top of the kidney that secretes many different hormones, including those that affect sexual growth and behavior. You have two adrenal glands—one for each of your kidneys.

Gonads (GO-nads). The primary sex glands—the ovaries in the female and the testes in the male. The ovaries produce the egg cells that are fertilized by the sperm secreted by the testes.

Androgens (ANN-dro-jens). From the Greek words meaning "producer of males." There are several male hormones; collectively these are known as androgens.

Estrogens (ESS-tro-jens). The Latin word *estrus* (ESS-truss) refers to the period in a female's reproductive cycle when she is fertile and hence capable of becoming pregnant. Estrogens are the hormones that generate or bring about estrus.

Progesterone (pro-JEST-ter-own). One of the several female sex hormones.

Primary sex characteristics. Those physical characteristics that differentiate males from females—the actual sex organs themselves.

Genitals (JEN-it-tulls). From the Latin word meaning "to beget, to reproduce, to generate children." The external sex organs, or *genitalia* (jen-it-TAIL-ee-uh).

Secondary sex characteristics. Those male-female differences that usually appear during adolescence, such as the male's beard and the development of the breasts in the female.

Puberty (PEW-burr-tee). The onset of sexual maturity, when the person becomes physically capable of sexual reproduction. Usually between the 11th and the 14th year, the female's ovaries begin producing eggs and menstrual (MEN-strew-ull, or MEN-strull) bleeding begins. At about the same age, the male's testes begin producing semen and ejaculation becomes possible. Recent studies show that, for unknown reasons, the onset of puberty now occurs about a year earlier in US males and females than it did 100 years ago.

Fetus (FEE-tuss). An unborn child, still carried in its mother's womb. More precisely, the unborn child after it has taken on human characteristics (during the final six months in the womb).

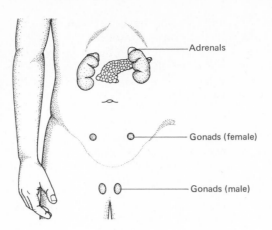

Fig. 13.1. The location of some major endocrine glands.

Primary and Secondary Sex Characteristics

Physiologists like to differentiate between two types of sex characteristics—the *primary* and the *secondary*. When scientists speak of **primary sex characteristics,** they mean the actual sex organs themselves—the ovaries, vagina, uterus, and clitoris in the female, and penis and testes in the male. Additionally, those parts of the reproductive organs in either sex that can be seen by the naked eye are often called the *external genitalia,* or **genitals.** Male-female differences in primary sex characteristics are usually present at birth.

The **secondary sex characteristics** are those that appear at **puberty**—the growth of facial hair and deepening voice in the young man, the development of the breasts and broadening of the hips in the young woman. The appearance of both primary and secondary sexual characteristics is controlled almost entirely by *hormones.*

As we will see in a later chapter, your sexual gender was determined at the moment of your conception. The sperm cells of the male are normally of two types—the X sperm and the Y sperm (see Chapter 19). If an X sperm from the father unites with (fertilizes) the egg carried by the mother, the child will be a female—and *every cell* in the child's body will carry the X (female) label. During the nine months that the **fetus** is carried in the mother's womb, the glands of the fetus will produce *female hormones* rather than male hormones, and the body of the fetus will develop the

A new interest in friends of the opposite sex usually comes with puberty and the beginning development of secondary sex characteristics.

primary female sex characteristics. The glands secrete female hormones, of course, because the cells in the glands carry the X label.

However, if a Y sperm fertilizes the egg, the cells in the fetal glands will carry the Y label. These cells will then secrete male hormones rather than female, and the child will be born a male.

Hormones Determine Gender

One point about hormones is of crucial importance: No matter what type of sperm fertilizes the egg, and no matter what label all the cells carry, unless the male androgens are present in the fetus, the child will be born with *female sex characteristics.*

For example, if a Y sperm unites with the egg, but through some mishap the fetal glands do not produce androgens, the infant will develop female genitalia. That is to say, the child will *look* like a female despite the fact that all of its cells carry the Y or "male" label.

But the reverse is true as well. Suppose that a mother monkey is carrying a fetus conceived from an X sperm. If all went well, the baby monkey would be female. However, if some weeks before the birth we inject the mother with male androgens, the fetus will develop male genitalia and will *look* like a male—although all its cells carry the X or "female" label.

This **gender** confusion may occur in humans if a woman carrying a female (X sperm) child is given medical treatment with massive amounts of androgens during her pregnancy. The child will be born with a penis and testicles even though the cells in its body carry the X label.

An unborn male child whose glands fail to produce sufficient androgens will not develop normal male sex organs—despite the Y label carried by the child's cells. If the unborn male's glands secrete some, *but not enough,* of the male hormone, the child may even be born with *both* male and female genitalia, although its cells carry just the Y label.

As you might guess, children born with the "wrong" external sex organs often find themselves sexually confused in later life, since their "cellular label" doesn't agree with their genitalia. Recently developed medical techniques can often detect which gender the child should have (according to its cellular label), and surgery can frequently help set matters straight.

If a young boy's adrenals and testes *overproduce* androgens—or *underproduce* estrogens—he will experience early puberty. That is, his voice will change and his beard will begin to grow sooner than expected. But if the boy's glands *underproduce* androgens or *overproduce* estrogens for some reason, his puberty will be delayed and his body may take on very feminine characteristics—a high voice, overdeveloped breasts, and a lack of facial hair.

If a young girl's adrenals and ovaries *overproduce* estrogens—or *underproduce* androgens—the girl will come to sexual maturity earlier than expected. If the reverse is true, her puberty will be delayed, and she may even develop such masculine secondary characteristics as flat breasts, excess facial hair, and a low voice.

Innately Determined Sexual Behavior

The neural circuits that control sexual behavior—in lower animals, at least—is "wired into" the animals' brains at birth.

Surprisingly enough, the genetic blueprint for most animals includes *both* male and female response patterns. Which pattern develops is determined by which hormone is *most active* during fetal development and just after birth.

For example, consider the female monkey we just mentioned that was born with male genitalia because her mother was injected with androgens. As this female grows up, she will show male patterns of play and social

Gender (JEN-durr). The *physical* characteristics associated with being male or female. As differentiated from "sex roles," which are learned or social behaviors or thought patterns. A man with effeminate behavior patterns is of the male gender, but may play a feminine sex role.

Castrated (KASS-trait-ted). From a Latin word meaning "to cut to pieces." Literally, to cut off the testes. Two centuries ago, boys with good voices were occasionally castrated prior to puberty so that they would retain their pure, high voices. These singers were called *castratos* (cass-TRATT-toes) and often played women's roles in operas (and in real life).

Cyclical (SIGH-klick-cull, or SICK-lick-ull). Anything that repeats itself, or that goes in a full circle. The seasons of the year (winter, spring, summer, fall, winter . . .) are cyclical. During her fertile years, the human female ordinarily has a menstrual cycle that repeats itself about every 28 days.

Threshold. A half-way point between two places or events. See Chapter 11.

Primates (PRIME-eights). The highest or "prime" order of mammals. Includes humans, apes, chimpanzees, monkeys, and several more primitive monkey-like animals.

Copulins (COPP-you-lins). Chemicals released by females that have a sexually arousing effect on males. See Chapter 7.

Impotence (IM-po-tents). The inability of a male to achieve erection, or to sustain the erection long enough to achieve orgasm and ejaculation.

behavior. If male rats **castrated** at birth are given injections of female hormones at that time, they will display a complete set of female behavior patterns as adults.

If, during fetal development and immediately after birth, the *relative balance* of the sex hormones is toward the androgens, then the fetus will have male genitalia, and those parts of the brain that control male sexual responses will develop. If the relative balance is toward the estrogens, the fetus will have feminine sexual characteristics, and those parts of the brain that control female sexual behavior will develop. The interplay between glands and growth, between cortex and chemicals, is so subtle and complicated that it is a wonder that any of us turns out to be normal!

The sexual behavior of lower animals is almost entirely under the control of sex hormones. The female white rat, for instance, is sexually receptive to the male only when her estrogen level is high. If her ovaries are removed, she will not mate unless given injections of estrogens.

If the testes of an adult male rat are removed by castration, the male will continue to mate with receptive females for a few weeks until the androgens already present in his body are depleted. But during this period, his interest in females gradually wanes and eventually vanishes unless he is given injections of male hormones.

Sexual behavior in most lower animals is **cyclical** and is usually tied to a particular part of the year. Most of the time, the **threshold** for sexual behaviors is too high to be triggered off by such environmental stimuli as the sight or smell of a receptive partner. However, at one or more times during the year, the passing of the seasons will trigger off the production of sex hormones. These hormones serve as chemical inputs to the brain and *lower* the thresholds for sex-related activities. When the threshold is low enough, the animal responds to sexual stimuli in its environment—and we say that the organism is now *motivated* sexually.

Primate Sexual Behavior

The **primates**—humans, monkeys, apes, and chimpanzees—show much more complex sexual behaviors than do the lower mammals. In the higher species, for instance, the sex drive is less frequently seasonal and not as closely tied to the female reproductive cycle. The ovaries of the female rat produce eggs once every five or six days, and the female rat will mate only during that part of her cycle when the eggs are ready to be fertilized by the male. The human female is fertile only a few days out of her 28-day reproductive cycle, but her receptivity to the male is determined more by *psychological* factors than by the types of hormones her body is producing at any given moment.

The male rat will usually attempt to mount females only when they are at the receptive point in their cycle—when the female releases **copulins** into her urine. The male monkey may try to mount female monkeys at any point in their cycles—and will often attempt to mount younger or less aggressive males as well. When an older, stronger monkey becomes aggressive toward a younger male, the weaker animal may often protect himself by assuming the posture of a receptive female and allowing the dominant animal to mount him and to attempt to copulate.

In humans and monkeys, sexual behavior is predominantly under the control of the *brain* rather than the hormones. Birds and rats can be induced to mate out of season or cycle if injected with the proper hormones. However, hormone injections are not an effective therapy for frigidity in most women or **impotence** in most males.

Homosexual behavior occurs fairly frequently in lower animals, but seems to be directly related to the types and amounts of hormones present in the animals' bodies. Injecting androgens into human male homosexuals—or estrogens into female homosexuals—does not turn them into *heterosexuals*, however. Instead, such injections are likely to increase the strength of their *homosexual* desires.

Women who have had their ovaries removed usually do not experience any decrease in their sex drives, nor do women who have undergone **menopause,** when their ovaries become relatively inactive.

The pattern for human males who undergo castration is more complex—some lose their sex drive entirely, while others experience desire but cannot achieve an erection. Experience seems to be the key factor. If a boy is castrated prior to puberty, he seldom develops the ability to perform sexually unless given regular injections of androgens. If the castration occurs after a man has been quite active sexually, however, he may retain full sexual ability for many years after the operation. What the man *expects* to happen to him after castration and his own prior sexual history are more important influences than the amount of androgens present in his body.

Intra-Psychic and Environmental Influences on Sexuality

Of the hundreds of different societies studied by social scientists, all of them have placed some restrictions on sexual activities. For instance, **incest taboos** are found in almost all cultures. But the type of incest prohibited varies considerably from one society to another.

G.P. Murdock stated in 1949 that, of the 158 societies he studied, 70 percent permitted premarital sexual relations, but **adultery** was "freely allowed" in only five. Homosexuality is strongly forbidden in many cultures, is quite acceptable in others, and was actually "glorified" in ancient Greece.

Within a given society, different segments of the population may prefer quite different forms of sexual activity. For instance, Kinsey and his colleagues reported that people in the upper middle class and the upper class were significantly more likely to engage in kissing and in oral stimulation of the genitals—and more likely to experiment with new sexual positions—than were people from the so-called lower class. However, the greatest *amount* of sexual activity seems to occur among men and women in the lower or lower middle class who have a high school education, but who have not gone to college.

The Kinsey group also reports that religiously devout individuals, especially women, are sexually more conservative, less active, and begin their sex lives much later than non-religious people.

Question: In what ways might the social class you are brought up in influence both the frequency and the types of your sexual activities?

Sexual Inhibition

Some brain circuits function to increase the sexual drive, primarily by *increasing* hormone production and thereby *lowering* behavioral thresholds. But other parts of the brain *inhibit* sexual activity, primarily by *raising* behavioral thresholds. In general, the more *complex* an organism is, the more its higher brain circuits are devoted to *inhibiting* rather than to facilitating behavior.

In humans, most sexual inhibition appears to be learned—primarily during the person's early life. If the child's parents are **repressive**—if they punish the child whenever it touches its genitals or when it asks questions about sex—the child's sex life as an adult may be marked by shyness, fears, or even outright distaste for sexual matters.

Almost anything learned can be unlearned, however, and most people can overcome their sexual inhibitions if given careful guidance and suitably rewarding experiences.

Menopause (MEN-oh-paws). Literally, a "pause" in the woman's menstrual cycle. That time in a woman's life—usually between ages 45 and 50—when her ovaries stop producing egg cells and she no longer can become pregnant.

Incest taboos (IN-sest tab-BOOS). Incest is sexual activity between close relatives, such as between father and daughter, or brother and sister. Such incestual (in-SESS-tew-ull) activities are forbidden or taboo in most societies.

Adultery (add-DULL-turr-ee). From the Latin word meaning "to pollute, to corrupt, to make impure." Adultery is voluntary sexual intercourse between a man and a woman other than his wife, or between a woman and a man other than her husband. Sexual intercourse between two unmarried partners is called fornication (for-knee-KAY-shun).

Repressive. To repress is to deny consciousness to your own unacceptable thoughts. To be repressive is to force others to deny expression of their thoughts that you may consider improper. Repressive actions almost always involve punishment, criticism, or both.

Man and Mantis

The praying mantis stalks other insects—including her mate.

In lower animals, inhibition is often instinctual and unlearned. For instance, consider the case of the male praying mantis, whose sex life is fraught with difficulties that most human males would shudder to contemplate.

The praying mantis is an insect several inches long that looks like a twig with a head and legs. The female mantis spends her time stalking other insects—including the much smaller male. When she comes close to another insect, her heavy forepaws slash forward, crushing the prey and dragging it back to her well-formed jaws.

During most of the year, the female mantis would as happily consume the male for dinner as she would a beetle or a butterfly. Only during the mating season, when her hormone levels *raise* the thresholds of her normal **predatory** behavior patterns, will she allow the male to come close to her without immediately swallowing him.

However, hunger is usually a stronger drive than sex, even during the mating season. So the male mantis' best chance for success lies in waiting until the female has just caught an insect. The male then stealthily approaches the female from behind and attempts to mount her while she is distracted by more important things. If he misses in his first attempt, his cause is lost—and he typically ends up as the main course of her meal.

But even if he finds the proper position on his first try, his troubles are far from over. For, during the act of copulation, his head comes dangerously close to hers. And should she notice him, she is very likely to reach up and bite his head off for dessert.

Luckily, this little romantic by-play has a happy ending. For the nervous system of insects is quite different from that of humans. A headless insect can live for several hours, and the brain of the male mantis is made up almost entirely of *inhibitory* centers that increase behavioral thresholds and thus decrease the animal's sexual functions. Once the male has literally "lost his head," he copulates much more vigorously and effectively than when his brain is present to repress him.

The male's inhibitory centers are necessary to keep him out of the female's range during most of the year. But not even the seasonal increase in male hormones can knock out the inhibitory activity of his brain as effectively as does one crunch of the female's jaws!

The inhibitory centers of the human brain are not so easily wiped out. Human beings have, during the course of history, wasted an enormous amount of time and money hunting for **aphrodisiacs**—drugs that will arouse or inflame sexual passions. Despite the tales you may have heard, the only chemicals that have been proven to increase the human sex drive are those related to hormone production—the estrogens and androgens, the copulins, and (perhaps) the **exaltolides** (see Chapter 7).

However, some drugs—such as alcohol—do seem to influence sexual performance by reducing activity in the inhibitory centers of the brain. **Dis-inhibitors,** as they are called, do not *increase* your desire—they merely *decrease* the strength of the inhibitions that your culture has built into your brain. It was this fact, perhaps, that led a biologist to refer to the enhanced performance of the headless mantis as the "martini effect."

Why Sex?

With all of the cultural taboos and inhibitions on sexual activity, you might legitimately wonder why people bother with it at all! Reproductive behavior is, as we said earlier, necessary for the survival of the species, but not for the survival of the individual. Yet nature seems to have worked out a way to motivate members of both sexes to *want* to reproduce themselves. For sexual stimulation usually creates within the individual a great amount of intense *sensory pleasure.*

But, as scientists, we may legitimately ask the question: What is the

Predatory (PRED-uh-torr-ree). An animal that preys on, or destroys, or devours other animals.

Aphrodisiacs (AFF-roh-DEE-see-acks). Aphrodite (AFF-roh-DIE-tay) was the Greek goddess of love. An aphrodisiac is anything that causes sexual excitement, particularly a perfume, food, or drug.

Exaltolides (ex-ALL-toh-lides). Chemicals that both males and females release into their urine, although males release (on the average) about twice as much as do females. Men are apparently unable to detect the odor of exaltolides, although women apparently can. Supposed to be sexual excitants for women, but obviously not for men if they cannot smell exaltolides. See Chapter 7.

Dis-inhibitors (DISS-in-hibb-it-tors). Things that decrease inhibition, or that lower behavioral thresholds.

PART THREE Motivation

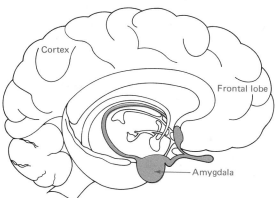

Fig. 13.2. The colored areas are part of the limbic system.

biological basis of this pleasure? Or, to put the matter another way, why in the world does sex "feel so good?"

The Pleasure Centers

When physiological psychologists first began sticking electrodes into the brains of rats and other animals, they found that stimulation of a few parts of the **limbic system** (see Fig. 13.2) caused the animals to react as if they had experienced sharp, biting pain. This discovery was, at first, surprising—because, as we saw earlier, the brain has no pain receptors as such.

These scientists suspected that they had tapped into what are now called the "avoidance centers" of the brain. So they began to map out as many different regions of the brain as they could, to find out how extensive these "avoidance centers" really were.

The answer is—they are not extensive at all. You can stimulate more than 99 percent of the brain electrically without getting an avoidance reaction from the animal. However, this search paid unexpected dividends when, in the early 1950's, two psychologists working in Canada discovered that sometimes electrical stimulation of the brain can have *pleasurable* consequences.

Olds and Milner's Discovery James Olds took his doctorate in psychology at Harvard in 1952. Then, because Olds was interested in the biological processes underlying motivation, he went to McGill University in Montreal to work with the noted physiological psychologist, Peter Milner.

Olds and Milner implanted electrodes in what were thought to be "avoidance areas" in the brains of white rats, then let the animals run about on the top of a table (see Fig. 13.3). When the rat would move toward one

Fig. 13.3. One of James Olds's electrode-implanted rats.

particular corner of the table, they would turn on the current. The rat would stop, then turn around, and move in the opposite direction. The animal would subsequently avoid that particular corner of the table even if not given any more electrical stimulation.

However, one day Olds and Milner made a glorious mistake—they stuck an electrode in the wrong place in one rat's brain. When the animal started moving toward one of the corners of the table, they turned on the electrical current as usual. But this rat stopped, sniffed, and then moved a step or two *forward!*

Olds and Milner assumed that the current wasn't strong enough to have any effect, so they turned up the juice and stimulated the animal again. And once again, the rat stopped, twitched its nose rather vigorously, and moved several more steps forward.

The more that Olds and Milner stimulated the rat's brain, the more eager it became to get to the corner. Finally, the animal reached the corner, sat down, and refused to move! It is to their credit that, instead of thinking the rat was "sick" or "abnormal," Olds and Milner realized at once that they had discovered a part of the rat's brain where electrical stimulation was obviously very *rewarding.*

We now know that there are dozens of **pleasure centers** in the brains of most mammals (including humans) which, when stimulated electrically or chemically, will give the animal the subjective experience of *pleasure.*

In animals such as the white rat, neural excitation in these "pleasure centers" causes a strange and oddly *compulsive* set of behaviors to occur. Suppose we rig up a small, rat-sized box with a single metal lever in it (see Fig. 13.4). The lever is then connected to an electrical stimulator so that every time the rat presses the lever, the animal stimulates one of the "reward centers" in its own brain. Will the rat press the bar very often?

The answer is yes—very often indeed. Under these conditions, a rat will bang away on the lever as often as a hundred times a *minute,* and will do so hour after hour after hour—until it collapses in exhaustion. Then the rat will sleep a while until it regains its strength. But as soon as it wakes up, it starts pressing the lever again.

If we offer this rat the chance to bar-press as a reward for problem-solving behavior, it will learn highly complicated mazes just to get a few whacks at the lever. Obviously, something about the electrical stimulation of the "pleasure centers" is highly *motivating* to a rat.

Two Types of Pleasure   Until the discovery of the "pleasure centers" by Olds and Milner, sexual behavior had always posed something of a problem to motivational theorists. Since they knew nothing about the "pleasure centers" in the brain, drive theorists assumed that pain *reduction* was the chief motivational force underlying all behavior.

But sexual excitement is almost entirely a matter of pleasurable *arousal*—the more stimulated an organism is, the more pleasure it feels. How could an *increased* drive level be associated with pleasure rather than with pain? Wasn't this rather like hitting yourself over the head with a hammer because it felt so good when you stopped?

We now know that there are two distinctly *different* types of pleasure: (1) The generalized feeling of relief when pain ceases; and (2) the sensory thrill associated with what we might call "pleasurable inputs."

Food not only reduces hunger, it tastes good as well. Therefore, there must be a direct connection of some kind between the taste receptors in your tongue and the "pleasure centers" in your brain. Once Olds and Milner had shown the way, psychologists began looking for just those connections.

Current animal research indicates that some parts of the rat's brain are associated with sexual pleasure, while other parts are associated with eating or drinking pleasures. Stimulation to still other brain areas seems to give the rat a "general glow of satisfaction" that isn't tied to any specific physiological drive yet known.

If we implant an electrode in those "reward centers" related to eating

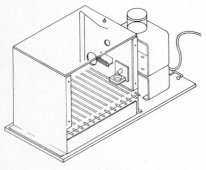

Fig. 13.4. A single-lever rat box.

behavior, the rat will bar-press compulsively *only* if it is hungry. If we feed the rat first, it will ignore the lever for several hours until its hunger drive mounts up a bit. Oddly enough, once the hungry rat begins bar-pressing, it typically prefers electrical stimulation to food. If we implant the electrode in those parts of the brain connected with drinking behavior, the rat will bar-press only if it is thirsty.

Now, let us extend the animal research to the human level. The neural pathways running from your tongue and nose to the "food-reward areas" in your brain were built in by your genetic blueprint. But these pathways only become *functional* when you are hungry. As your blood sugar level falls, your behavioral thresholds fall too. Thus it becomes easier and easier for the taste and smell of food to excite the "food-reward circuits" in your brain.

Food deprivation, therefore, does two things almost simultaneously: First, it creates a painful "hunger" drive. Second, it increases the possibility that your "pleasure centers" can be stimulated by sensory inputs from your nose and mouth.

Hormones influence sexual pleasure. If we put an electrode in those parts of a male rat's brain that are associated with reproductive pleasure, we find that the animal will bar-press much more vigorously if it has been sexually deprived than if it has copulated recently.

More than this, if we castrate the rat, we find that it presses the lever less and less frequently on the days following the operation. Apparently, as it uses up all the male hormone left in its body after castration, it finds the electrical stimulation less and less pleasurable.

We can restore the castrated rat to its original high performance level, however, by giving it an injection of androgens. Within a short period after the injection, it begins to press the lever vigorously.

Human Pleasures   "Reward centers" have been found in the brains of almost all mammals, including humans. When Olds and Milner first reported their results, many people feared that governments might seize upon electrical stimulation of the brain as a new way to control people against their wills. Some writers warned that big corporations might implant electrodes in the brains of all their workers and pay off these employees in jolts to their "pleasure centers" instead of paying them in cold cash.

However, these fears proved to be groundless. For the "compulsiveness" that one can create in a rat with brain stimulation seems to be lacking in humans. Those women and men who have volunteered to have their "reward centers" tickled with electricity have all reported the experience as being mildly pleasant, but something they could take or leave.

The scope and type of sexual behavior in humans is dictated not only by biology but also by thoughts, past experience, and society. Sex is not reserved for the young.

For example, when the "food-pleasure centers" of the subjects' brains were stimulated, they often reported things like, "Oh, that was nice, rather like eating a good meal. But I'd rather have steak and French fries." Or they might say, "Yes, that felt good, and it did have a sexual flavor to it somehow. But nothing like the real thing."

Pleasure in humans is obviously a more complex experience than it is in the lower animals. The androgens, estrogens, and progesterones shape our bodies, bias our brains, and energize our behaviors. Pleasure is the neural carrot that nature dangles before us to entice us down the path of biologically appropriate behavior. The pain of deprivation is the chemical club that nature applies to our backsides to urge us onward.

But over-riding these biological motivations are the neural commands that come from the higher centers of our brains. The structure of the female figure is ideally suited to stimulate the sensory receptors in the male's genitalia, and vice versa—but our choice of mate and the scope and type of our reproductive behaviors are dictated primarily by our thoughts, past experience, and by society.

The pattern of sexual activity that we find physiologically rewarding grew out of the millions of reproductive experiments that nature has conducted since life first appeared on earth. But only humans have brains complex enough to understand that societies must survive as well as species, to conduct our own scientific studies on the subject of sexual behavior, and to realize that unlimited population growth may sometimes be a disaster rather than a blessing.

Nature points us in a given direction and pushes us along but, as we will see in later chapters, the beliefs and attitudes of our parents and friends, and the "rules and regulations" of the groups we belong to, provide us with our road maps, stop signs, and detours. Our higher brain centers, with their inhibitory powers, are the battleground for this war between nature's nudges and society's strictures.

Just how we individual foot soldiers learn to cope with the stresses and strains of this constant warfare is a matter to be covered in the next chapter.

Summary

1. We really know very little about the **psychological** and **physiological changes** that occur during **sexual arousal**—despite the fact that our culture markets sex much as it does breakfast food.

2. Some theorists have tried to explain sexuality in purely physiological terms, some primarily in mental or intra-psychic terms, while others have focused on sexual behavior as a social response. In fact, human sexuality is influenced by all three types of inputs.

3. Of the three types of inputs that influence human sexuality, the physiological aspects have perhaps been the least studied scientifically.

4. **John B. Watson** was a pioneer in the study of the human sexual response. He was fired from Johns Hopkins University for his efforts.

5. **Alfred Kinsey** and his associates were perhaps the first scientists to make a reasonably accurate **sociological survey** of sexual behavior in the United States. Their findings amazed some people, but annoyed many others.

6. **Masters and Johnson** took their study of human sexuality into the laboratory and developed many new ways of helping people solve their "sexual hang-ups." This research is still considered immoral or socially improper by many people.

7. **Hormones** are the primary determinant of sexuality in most lower organisms.

8. Hormones secreted by the **adrenal glands** and the **gonads** determine whether a child is born with male or female **primary sex characteristics.**

9. Hormones also influence the appearance of the **secondary sex characteristics** at **puberty.**

10. If an organism has male hormones present in its body during its **fetal development** (and immediately after birth), the organism will display male sexual behaviors when it becomes adult. If an organism has female hormones present during its fetal and early development, the organism will show female sex patterns as an adult.

11. Hormones determine adult behavior patterns by activating some "built-in" brain circuits while suppressing other "built-in" circuits.

12. The sexual behavior of most lower animals is seasonal or **cyclical,** and is determined almost entirely by body chemistry.

13. In **primates,** early experience is at least as important as the presence or absence of hormones in determining sexual behavior.

14. Children learn at a very early age what types of sexual behavior are **taboo** or forbidden in their cultures. This childhood conditioning may create very strong sexual inhibitions that must somehow be overcome if the person is to function as a sexually mature adult.

15. There is almost no form of sexual behavior that is not forbidden in some cultures, or that is not accepted as "normal" in other cultures.

16. Sexual pleasure seems correlated with neural firing in certain regions of the brain called the "reward centers" or **pleasure centers.** In lower animals, stimulation to these centers is rewarding only if the animal is sexually deprived and only if the animal has sufficient hormones in its body.

17. Most other types of motivated behavior (such as hunger or thirst) seem to be aimed at reducing tension or arousal. Sexual motivation, to the contrary, appears to be based on pleasurable arousal or pleasurable sensory inputs. The type of arousal each person finds pleasurable, however, is more a matter of cultural conditioning than of basic biology.

(Continued from page 324.)

Paul Schmidtt could hear the disco music half a block away. As he entered Linda's apartment building, a row of metal mailboxes just inside the foyer caught his eye. He read the writing on each of the little metal cages until he found Linda's name, then pressed the button above the card.

A buzzing sound announced that someone upstairs had responded to his call, so Paul pushed open the inner door and walked up the flight of steps. Hanging on the door to Linda's apartment was a large sign, PARTY IN PROGRESS—COME IN.

Paul did just that.

As he opened the door, a blast of sound fizzed out at him. The place was packed with people he hardly knew, most of them dancing to a disco hit that the stero was reproducing at ear-shattering volume. Strobe lights blinked at him from the corners of the room.

In the center of the dancers was a strikingly handsome couple. The young woman wore a white dress stretched so tightly over her ample figure that Paul was sure it would come apart at the seams as she rolled her hips and flapped her arms in tempo to the music. Her partner—a tall, thin young man—was clothed in tan leather, his shirt open to his waist. He watched his date through half-closed eyes, sometimes responding directly to her impassioned movements, sometimes leading off on his own. His movements were more angular and controlled than hers, but no less sexual. Paul watched them for a moment, then moved on.

As he reached the dining room, a redheaded girl in green shorts came rushing out of the hallway and almost knocked him down. He grabbed her in his arms to keep from falling over. She paused a moment, fitting her body to his. The musky perfume she was wearing tickled his nose, but before Paul could say a word, an angry young man grabbed the redhead and began pulling her toward the front door. She waved good-bye to Paul, then disappeared, leaving nothing behind but her tantalizing aroma.

Paul pulled himself together and pushed into the kitchen. Linda spotted him at once, and waved a paring knife at him threateningly. "Paul, you beast, you're incredibly late."

"Sorry, Linda, but I got tied up at the lab."

"Well, if you prefer those ring doves of yours to the birds you'll find at my party, I can't say much for your taste."

Paul looked chagrined. Then he brightened, thinking of the redhead. "Lots of exotic plumage here tonight, I'll say that."

Linda took the remark personally. "Thanks. I thought you'd like my outfit." She stretched out her arms to show off her dress, nearly stabbing Paul with the paring knife.

Paul jumped back quickly, laughing. "What's the weapon for, Linda? Have you taken up surgery or something?"

"Actually, darling, it's for you." When Paul looked shocked, Linda rapidly continued. "Oh, you do have a dirty mind. No, your hormones are safe—it's open-heart surgery I have in mind. Celery hearts, that is. Would you be a lamb and cut the celery stalks down to size, and then scrape a few carrots? I've got this super cheese dip for the vegetables, but no vegetables ready yet."

Linda pointed to a young woman standing at the sink, tearing a cauliflower apart piece by piece. "Carol here is dissecting various other organic tissues, so you'll have some help. You have met Carol, haven't you?"

Paul nodded gravely at Carol, who smiled shyly back at him, then used her fist to push a lock of sandy-colored hair out of her pleasant face. As she did so, a piece of cauliflower got caught in her hair.

"Here, you'd better let me help," Paul said, moving quickly to her side.

"Well, darlings, I'm off to check on the guests," Linda said, walking toward the door. Then she stopped to look at the young couple standing by the sink. "But Carol dear, I should warn you. Paul will probably tell you that he's the world's greatest expert on S-E-X. But the truth is, he thinks it's for the birds!"

Paul laughed loudly. Then, with a wink at Carol, he threw back his shoulders, puffed out his chest, cooed at the top of his voice, and bowed his head into the sink.

Carol seemed very impressed at his performance.

"Birds of a feather," Linda said. She shut the kitchen door quietly behind her and headed toward the music.

Recommended Readings

Forsiha, Barbara Lusk. *Sex Roles and Personal Awareness* (Morristown, N.J.: General Learning Press, 1978).

Katchdourian, Herant A., and Donald T. Lunde. *Fundamentals of Human Sexuality,* 2d ed. (New York: Holt, Rinehart and Winston, 1975).

Maccoby, Eleanor Emmons, and Carol Nagy Jacklin. *The Psychology of Sex Differences* (Stanford, Calif.: Stanford University Press, 1974).

Masters, William, and Virginia Johnson. *Human Sexual Response* (Boston, Mass.: Little, Brown, 1966).

Pomery, Wardell B. *Dr. Kinsey and the Institute for Sex Research* (New York: New American Library of World Literature, 1973).

Stress

Did You Know That . . .

Your emotional reactions are controlled in large part by your autonomic nervous system?

Most people find it difficult to differentiate among hunger, fear, anger, and sexual arousal just on the basis of their bodily changes during these emotional states?

Your body seems to go through three distinct stages in response to stressful situations?

Voodoo witch doctors really can kill people by suggestion?

Animals can be conditioned to be "hopeful?"

Direct methods of coping with stress are usually more effective than are defensive or indirect methods?

There is "good" stress as well as "bad?"

Authoritarian parents often teach their children to be rigid in outlook, uncreative, prejudiced, conforming, and overcontrolled?

Authoritarianism is often a defensive method of dealing with stress?

"The Stress of Life"

Charlie lay quietly on his back, staring at the dim light bulb dangling from the ceiling. For a moment it seemed as bright as the sun, and he wondered whether he would get a sunburn the way he did that day in Vietnam when he lay on the beach for too long.

"Get up and turn off the light," said one part of his mind in a bright, arousing tone of voice.

"Don't!" said another part of his mind in heavy, demanding tones. "A sniper might get you if you move. Movement is forbidden!"

Charlie recognized that voice of authority, so he remained motionless, except for his eyes. They turned stealthily in their sockets, inspecting the room for perhaps the hundredth time that hour. There was a religious picture on the wall, one that his mother had given him. Out of the corner of his eye he could see a photograph of Gail, his girl friend. He avoided gazing in that direction. Mostly there was dirty wallpaper everywhere he looked.

"Get a new room," Gail had said. "This one stinks."

"Stay where you are," the heavy voice in his head had said to him. Charlie stayed, and Gail had gone off mad.

"Come home and live with us," his mother had pleaded. "There's plenty of room, and we miss you."

"You want to go through *that* again?" the voice had asked him. Charlie knew he hadn't the strength to go through "that" again with his mother, so he kept the room. It was small and safe and quiet. It folded itself around him snugly like a blanket. Why leave?

For several months, in Vietnam, Charlie had lived in a tiny cubicle in the barracks. He always felt safe there. Then his best friend, Red, went out on patrol one night and returned in a canvas bag.

"Go to his funeral. You owe him that, at least," the soft-spoken voice had urged him.

"Stay where you are," the heavy voice had said. "Red should have stayed in bed."

So Charlie stayed in bed for a while. The sergeant ordered Charlie to get up, called him a "dirty dogface" and a "coward," but he just tuned the man out. There were snipers out there. The sergeant should have known that.

Eventually they had taken him to a hospital outside Saigon and put him on a ward with lots of crazy people who shouted and screamed all day and all night. Charlie had found a dark, friendly corner and refused to come out.

"Those crazy people will kill you," the voice had said. "Don't go near them!" Charlie stayed in his corner until they flew him back to the States.

Right after the plane took off, they flew into the sunrise. Charlie had stared at the sun for half an hour, until the man sitting next to him pulled down the shade and told him he'd ruin his eyes. The sun hadn't been much brighter than the bulb dangling from the ceiling in his room, but he had done as the man told him to do.

After Charlie got home, things got brighter for a while. His parents came to see him, as did Gail, and the doctors convinced him he could "make it" out there in the world. The heavy voice had gone on vacation for months and months, and Charlie got a job and rented a room and saw a lot of Gail.

His mother didn't like Gail, of course. Not good enough for him, she said. But then, no girl was good enough for his mother. To tell the truth, he wasn't good enough for himself. She'd told him that often enough—usually just after she had smacked him across the mouth for saying or doing something she didn't approve of. "Don't you ever try that again," she'd say. And then she'd usually hit him again, "Just to make sure." Half the time Charlie never knew quite what it was he had done wrong.

Charlie had volunteered for the Army more to get away from the sound of his mother's voice than to serve his country or to see the world. And all he saw was people getting killed, and all he heard was the sergeant screaming at him not to act like the dirty dogface he was.

The phone rang. It had been ringing all day. He ignored it. Probably just more bad news anyhow.

Gail had been good news, at least when he first got back from 'Nam. They had enjoyed each other immensely, despite his mother. He kept telling Gail that she was the only good thing to happen to him in his entire life. She kept him from thinking of Red, and of 'Nam, and of his mother. When she smiled, she lit up his world like sunshine. But then came the rainy day when the sun had vanished into the clouds.

The phone rang again, and a faint but excited voice inside his head urged him to answer.

"Don't touch that phone!" the heavy voice suddenly demanded. "It's not safe to talk to people. You know that. All they tell you is lies."

"So here I lie," Charlie said aloud. And alone. He had tried to explain to Gail why he had to live alone, at least for a while. She had talked him into going to see Dr. Smith, because she said it wasn't healthy to live that way. He had seen the psychologist a couple of times, and rather liked him. But the heavy voice told him it wouldn't do any good, that Dr. Smith would end up sniping at him like all the rest. So Charlie had missed the last couple of appointments. Better not to do anything than to make a mistake, and have people hurt you.

Take Gail, for instance. She had given him everything. Everything. Some times he was so happy he just couldn't believe it, and he kept waiting for the heavy voice to come tell him it was all a fake. Of course it was a fake, after all, although the voice hadn't warned him.

Gail didn't love him. She couldn't, not when she had shouted and screamed at him and then slapped his face. And just because she had caught him with Cynthia. Charlie hadn't wanted to take Cynthia to dinner, but his mother had insisted. Cynthia was "her" kind of young woman. Something had told him not to give in to his mother's demands, but she cried and acted hurt, so he gave in.

Charlie heard a knocking sound at the door.

"Don't move!" the heavy voice said.

The knocking got louder.

"Don't answer!" the voice demanded. "It might be a trick."

"Trick or treat," Charlie chuckled softly to himself. He had treated Cynthia to dinner, and his mother had tricked him. He hadn't wanted to invite Cynthia home to his room, but she had rubbed against him and coaxed him. And then she had demanded that he show her where he lived.

So he showed her everything—his bed, his body, his wounds, where he really lived.

"Oh, do it! Do it!" Cynthia had cried.

"Oh, how could you do it!" Gail had cried, when she opened the door and turned on the light and saw Charlie and Cynthia naked on the bed.

And then Gail had screamed at him and slapped him.

He had forgotten that Gail had a key to his room. And he should have known that his mother had set the whole thing up with Cynthia. Then she had probably called Gail and told her he was sick and needed her. Sniped again.

Cynthia had giggled about it all, so he threw her out and locked the door behind her. And then he crawled into bed and pulled the covers over him. How long ago was that? Two days? Three? Well, it didn't matter. He wouldn't be going out again, ever.

Someone knocked at the door again, and called his name.

"Ignore it!" commanded the voice inside his head. "There's nothing but snipers behind that door. Do you want to end up in a canvas bag?"

Charlie heard the sound of metal scraping on metal, like a key going into a lock. Then the door opened.

Gail. And Dr. Smith. He could barely make out their faces.

"Close the door," he said in a heavy tone of voice. "I can't cope with snipers."

And then he pulled the covers over his head.

(Continued on page 359.)

Defensive Reactions

In a sense, your body is like the walled cities that dot the landscape in Europe. The citizens of those ancient towns built defenses to keep invading armies out, but left gates in the walls to bring in supplies and take out the garbage.

Your skin is the "wall" around your own body. Your skin keeps out invaders, but it lets food and water in and waste products out. It also contains "local defenses" that go into action the moment that any danger threatens.

For instance, if you cut your finger, the "local police" at the point of the cut begin repairing the damage even before you are aware of it. If germs enter the wound, the blood vessels nearby open up to let more "soldiers" (white **corpuscles**) through to fend off the invading germs.

All of these defensive reactions are automatic and take place without your conscious direction. But when your skin is damaged, it has receptors that sound the alarm to let your brain know something bad has happened, so that you can move your body out of the way or prepare to defend yourself from attack.

When you run low on food or water, the "guards" in your hypothalamic "motivation centers" ring bells that arouse you to the urgency of your own needs. Even when you become sexually motivated, physiological sirens sound to alert various parts of your body to the impending pleasurable inputs.

Your own internal alarm reactions have both local and generalized effects. When you see a funnel-shaped cloud roaring toward you out of the southwest, your cortex cannot take the time to sit down and compose a lengthy memo to your legs, feet, arms, and hands to remind them gently that trouble might be brewing. Instead, your body must have a way of instantly energizing itself—of waking up all its parts in a matter of seconds—and of coordinating all its activities so that you get out of danger quickly, and stay out.

In emergencies, you don't have *time to think*. Your reactions are emotional and *reflexive*—that is, they take place without your conscious **volition** or desire. You do not have to "will" your sweat glands to secrete water or your teeth to start chattering when you are frightened. These activities are handled for you *automatically* by the unconscious parts of your brain.

Autonomic Nervous System

That part of your body which controls your emotional reactions is called your **autonomic nervous system.** It is connected to most of the glands and many of the muscles in your body. Your autonomic nervous system has two major parts or divisions: (a) the **sympathetic nervous system;** and (b) the **parasympathetic nervous system.**

In general, activity in your sympathetic system tends to excite or *arouse* you much as an "upper" drug might. Activity in your parasympathetic system tends to *depress* or slow down many of your bodily functions as would a "downer."

Corpuscles (KOR-puss-sells). From the Latin word *corpus*, meaning "body." White corpuscles are "little white bodies" carried by your blood which attack germs and foreign matter that invades your own "corpus," or body. We get our terms "corpus callosum" and Marine "Corps" from the same Latin source.

Volition (voh-LISH-shun). From the Latin word meaning "to wish" or "to will." When you decide to reach out and pick up an apple off the table, you are exercising your volition. If someone shouted at you just as you picked up the apple, and you dropped the fruit without thinking the matter over, your "dropping response" would be reflexive and therefore performed without your conscious volition.

Autonomic nervous system (OUGHT-toe-NOM-ick). "Autonomic" means automatic or reflexive, without volition. The autonomic nervous system is a collection of neural centers which takes care of most of your normal body functions (breathing, pumping of the blood, digestion, emotional reactions) that occur automatically—without your having to think about them.

Sympathetic nervous system (sim-puh-THET-tick). To have sympathy for someone is to experience common emotions or feelings with that person. The sympathetic nervous system is that half of the autonomic nervous system responsible for "turning on" your emotional reactions.

Parasympathetic nervous system (PAIR-uh-sim-puh-THET-tick). That half of your autonomic nervous system that is "beyond" or opposed to the sympathetic system. The parasympathetic system "turns off" or slows down most emotional activity.

Together, these two nervous systems (see Fig. 14.1) control your bodily functions in a *coordinated* fashion, much as the coordinated activity of a furnace and an air conditioner could serve to keep the temperature in your home at a livable and pleasant level the year round.

Sympathetic Nervous System

Your sympathetic nervous system consists of a group of 22 *neural centers* lying on or close to your spinal cord. From these 22 centers, **axonic fibers** run to all parts of your body—to the salivary glands in your mouth, to the irises in your eyes, to your heart, lungs, liver, and stomach, and to your intestines and genitals. Your sympathetic nervous system is also connected to your sweat glands, your hair cells, and to the tiny blood vessels near the surface of your skin.

Whenever you encounter an emergency of some kind—something that enrages you, makes you suddenly afraid, creates strong desire, or calls for heavy labor on your part—your sympathetic nervous system swings into action in several ways:

1. The pupils in your eyes open up to let in more light.
2. Your heart pumps more blood to your brain and muscles and to the surface of your skin.
3. You breathe harder and faster.

Fig. 14.1 The sympathetic and parasympathetic nervous systems.

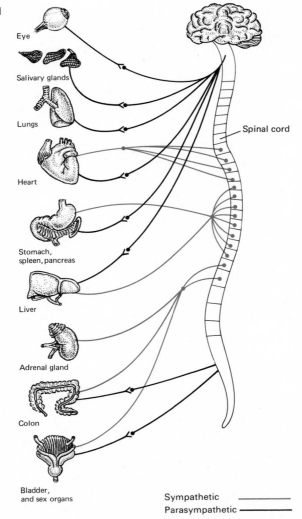

Eye

Salivary glands

Lungs

Spinal cord

Heart

Stomach, spleen, pancreas

Liver

Adrenal gland

Colon

Bladder, and sex organs

Sympathetic ——————
Parasympathetic ——————

4. Your blood sugar level is elevated.

5. Your digestion is slowed down to a crawl.

6. Your skin perspires to flush out the waste products created by the extra exertion and to keep you cool.

The sympathetic nervous system also controls orgasm and ejaculation during sexual excitement. In short, activity in your sympathetic nervous system prepares you for fighting, for fleeing, for feeding—and for sexual climax.

Question: Why do people often get red in the face when they get angry?

Parasympathetic Nervous System

Your parasympathetic nervous system is connected to most of the same parts of your body as the sympathetic nervous system. In general, parasympathetic stimulation produces physiological effects that are in most ways the *opposite* of those induced by sympathetic stimulation. Activity in your parasympathetic system does the following things:

1. It closes down or constricts the irises in your eyes.

2. It slows down your heart rate.

3. It slows down your breathing.

4. It lowers your blood sugar level.

5. It increases salivation, stimulates the flow of digestive juices, and promotes the processes of excretion.

6. It retards sweating.

Generally speaking, activity in your parasympathetic nervous system *conserves* or builds up your body's resources. For these reasons, the parasympathetic is often referred to as the **vegetative nervous system.**

Question: Heroin causes the pupils to narrow to mere pinpoints, even when the person is sitting in relative darkness. Which part of the autonomic nervous system does heroin affect most?

For the most part, the parasympathetic and the sympathetic systems act together in coordinated fasion—when one becomes more active, it inhibits excitation in the other.

The two systems cooperate during sexual activity, however, for parasympathetic stimulation is necessary for erection to occur while, as we noted earlier, orgasm and ejaculation are controlled by sympathetic excitation.

There is one major *difference* between the two systems, however—the sympathetic nervous system is connected to your adrenal glands, while the parasympathetic system is not.

The Adrenal Glands

You may recall from the last chapter that you have two adrenal glands, one sitting atop each of your kidneys. The adrenals not only produce hormones that influence sexual development and that affect bodily functions such as urine production, but they also produce two chemicals that are referred to as the "arousal" hormones. These two hormones are called **adrenalin** and **nor-adrenalin.**

When adrenalin and nor-adrenalin are released into your bloodstream

Vegetative nervous system. Another name for the parasympathetic nervous system. The phrase "to vegetate" means to withdraw or to sit quietly, gathering strength, like a vegetable quietly growing in the ground. The vegetative functions of the body are those that promote quiet growth and restoration of mental or physical energy. These functions are controlled primarily by the parasympathetic nervous system.

Adrenalin (uh-DREN-uh-lin). One of the two "arousal" hormones released by the adrenal glands. Also called epinephrine (EP-pee-NEFF-rin).

Nor-adrenalin (NORR-uh-DREN-uh-lin). The second of the two "arousal" hormones released by the adrenals. Injection of adrenalin or nor-adrenalin into the body causes a rise in blood pressure and pulse rate, an increase in the breathing rate, and a general speeding up of bodily functions. Also called norepinephrine (NOR-EP-pee-NEFF-rin).

"Arousal" hormones prepare the body to react to an emergency.

by your adrenal glands, these hormones bring about all of the bodily changes associated with strong **emotions** such as fear, anger, hostility, and sexual aggressiveness. That is, these two hormones act to prepare your body to meet an emergency by increasing your blood pressure and heart rate, speeding up your breathing, widening the pupils in your eyes, and increasing perspiration.

As you might guess from this description, the release of adrenalin and nor-adrenalin is under the control of your *sympathetic* nervous system, whose activities the hormones imitate or mimic.

When you encounter an arousing situation, your sympathetic nervous system goes into action first, mobilizing your body's energy resources and also causing the secretion of the two "arousal" hormones. As you secrete adrenalin and nor-adrenalin, these hormones continue the arousal process by chemically stimulating the *same neural centers* that the sympathetic nervous system has stimulated with neural impulses.

But the hormones also increase the firing rate of the nerve cells in the sympathetic nervous system itself. This stimulation causes you to secrete more of the hormones, which increases activity in the sympathetic system, and so on until the emergency has passed or you collapse in exhaustion.

Question: Why might it be useful in emergencies to have this "positive feedback loop" between the arousal hormones and the sympathetic nervous system?

The Arousal Hormones and Emotion

Can you tell the difference (subjectively) between your emotions? That is, can you differentiate between such emotional states as hunger, fear, anger, and sexual arousal? Most of us can, but we apparently do so on the basis of intra-psychic cues rather than biological states. For, with minor exceptions, the *physiological* changes that occur in your body are pretty much the same no matter what type of emotional upheaval you are undergoing.

There is some recent evidence that fear is controlled primarily by adrenalin, while anger is controlled primarily by nor-adrenalin. But both hormones are released to some degree in *all* arousal situations. Thus we

Emotions (ee-MOH-shuns). Both "emotion" and "motivation" come from the same Latin word meaning "motion" or "to move." Emotions are "stirred up movements," or "stirred up feelings." Our emotional feelings are usually correlated with activity in the autonomic nervous system. Emotions stress the body by using up its resources at a faster than usual rate. See Chapter 12.

cannot tell *objectively* whether you are angry or afraid just by measuring the relative amounts of adrenalin and nor-adrenalin floating around in your bloodstream.

When human volunteers have been injected with large amounts of adrenalin or nor-adrenalin, they often report that they feel as if they were "about to become emotional," but they can't say why. Their feelings of arousal do not seem "real" somehow, and their upset does not seem to be focused or directed toward any given object. Some of the volunteers described the experience as "cold rage."

Question: Some people report that they are most easily aroused sexually when they are hungry, or immediately after a frightening experience or a violent argument. Why might this often be the case?

Emotional Stress

Emotional experiences seem to have three rather distinct aspects:

1. The bodily changes associated with arousal and relaxation.

2. The emotional behavior (such as fighting, loving, or running away).

3. The subjective feelings that give a distinctive personal flavor to the emotion.

Because the first two aspects of emotional arousal can be studied relatively easily from an objective viewpoint, we have a fair amount of hard data about them. But feelings such as love and hate are private events that occur within your mind. We can investigate these intra-psychic states only indirectly by asking you to tell us what you are experiencing. But sadly enough, from a scientific point of view, whenever you stop to analyze your own emotional feelings, they tend to change, diminish, or disappear entirely.

The matter is complicated by two additional facts: (a) many people are rather bad at pinning precise labels on their emotional states; and (b) individuals who are quite good at discriminating one emotion from another can't always identify the internal and external cues or inputs that triggered off the response.

What we can say with some assurance is this: Emotional arousal puts you under a variety of biological, intra-psychic, and behavioral *stresses* that, if continued too long, can exhaust your resources. When a medieval European walled city was surrounded and besieged by an invading army, the populace sometimes dipped into the town's supplies at an alarming rate—because they could not bring in fresh food until the siege was lifted. When you are excited or keyed up, your body burns up calories at many times its normal rate.

For instance, a sudden fright may cost you the same expenditure of energy as an hour's study. Sexual intercourse burns up as many calories as would running up a very long flight of steps or performing light exercise for several minutes. And when your sympathetic nervous system is called into play during a fit of anger or rage, your digestion functions badly so that you do not assimilate food properly—and you may lose so much liquid through sweating that your kidneys must work overtime to keep your water balance under control.

Of course, if your emotional behavior leads you to damage your body in any way, you pay a price for that too.

Question: During highly exciting sexual intercourse, your pulse rate may more than double and your blood pressure may rise far above normal. What sort of information about sexual arousal do you think physicians should give to patients recovering from heart attacks?

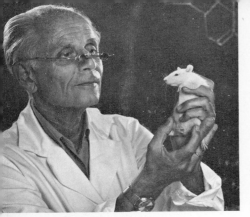

Hans Selye.

Alarm reaction. According to Hans Selye (SELL-ye), the alarm reaction is the first state of a stress reaction in which the bodily defenses are rapidly called into play.

Limbic system (LIM-bick). A set of related neural centers in the brain that influence emotional reactions. See Chapter 4.

Stage of resistance. The second state of a stress reaction during which the body tries to repair itself while continuing to react in an aroused manner.

Stage of exhaustion. According to Selye, if the first two stages of the stress reaction last too long, the body's resources are exhausted, the parasympathetic system takes over, and all physiological functions slow down dramatically. If the stress lasts too long, the organism may collapse or die.

Voodoo deaths. Stress-related deaths that occur when a witch doctor "casts a spell" on the affected person. Cannon believed death occurred from overstimulation of the sympathetic nervous system, but Richter showed it was parasympathetic over-stimulation that caused the person's heart to beat so slowly the person died.

Physiological Stress Reactions

The noted Canadian scientist, Hans Selye, first outlined the three states that your body seems to go through when its resources must be mobilized to meet situations of excessive physiological *stress*. Selye calls the first state the **alarm reaction,** in which your body's defenses are rapidly called up by activity in your **limbic system,** your sympathetic nervous system, and through the secretion of "arousal hormones" from your adrenals.

If the stress continues, your body must not only maintain its first-line emotional defense—it must also immediately begin *repairing the damage* that this arousal causes. So your adrenal glands begin to secrete abnormal amounts of the body-regulating hormones we mentioned in the last chapter. This second stage Selye calls the **stage of resistance.**

During the first two stages, your sympathetic nervous system is intensely aroused. However, if the emergency continues for too long, all of the energy available to your sympathetic system may be used up. At this point, an overwhelming *counter-reaction* may occur in which your parasympathetic system takes over. You may fall into the third state—the **stage of exhaustion**—during which most of your body's functions are slowed down abnormally or may even stop altogether. Further exposure to stress at this time can lead to depression, insanity, or even death, since overstimulation of your parasympathetic system may cause your heart to stop beating entirely.

Selye believes that many of what he calls the "diseases of adaptation"—high blood pressure, arthritis, and some types of ulcers—are caused by excessive stress.

Intra-Psychic Stress Reactions

Any time that you are placed under great pressure, your mental functioning is affected in much the same way that your physiological functioning is. During the alarm reaction, for instance, you typically will feel tense and alert, anxious and wary, as if you were mobilizing your mental powers of self-control. As the situation continues, you may begin to feel highly anxious, or experience vague pains and aches that don't seem to be related to any physical damage to your body.

Too much anxiety can lower your ability to make sound judgments. As your performance deteriorates, you may begin to blame others for your own failures. If these failures continue, you could lose all hope of being able to handle or cope with the situation. You might then either run away, or else lapse into psychological depression, disorganization, inactivity, or even death.

Question: Can you trace the experience of a "bad drug trip" through the three stages of arousal?

Social/Behavioral Stress Reactions

A psychological "stab in the back" from your social environment may in fact kill you almost as rapidly as a switchblade thrust between your ribs. Physiologist Walter B. Cannon—whose work on hunger was mentioned earlier—made a study of **voodoo deaths.** In many primitive cultures, the witch doctor is supposed to possess magical or voodoo powers strong enough to kill or cure the people in his tribe. If someone in his village angers him, the witch doctor may cast a spell on the person, often by pointing a bone or magic wand at the individual while muttering dreadful curses.

Given up for dead by the rest of the villagers, the accursed individual may retire to her or his hut, or may wander off into the woods alone to hide in shame. If the person's belief in the powers of the witch doctor is great enough, the individual may actually die within a day or so after the curse has been uttered.

Cannon, who was at first highly skeptical of the rumors he had heard of such things, went to Africa himself to investigate the matter. He was able to confirm the authenticity of at least 30 "voodoo deaths." Cannon believed (incorrectly) that these people died from heart attacks brought about by over-stimulation of the sympathetic nervous system. We know now, however, that the *parasympathetic nervous system* is usually the culprit.

Richter's Hopeful Rats

Psychiatrist Curt Richter became interested in the consequences of stress early in his long and productive scientific career. He saw many people literally fold up and die when they found themselves under too great pressure. The stress was often purely psychological—but it was the patient's body as well as the patient's mind that often collapsed. So Richter began a fascinating series of experiments in which he measured, as best he could, the physiological consequences of various highly threatening situations.

Since any abnormally stressful environment is potentially harmful to the organism, Richter worked with rats rather than with human beings.

Death by a Whisker   One of Richter's experimental situations involved a large tub filled with water. He would throw a rat into the water and let it swim until it was so absolutely exhausted that it would have drowned had it not been rescued.

If the water was at room temperature, the average rat would swim about 80 hours (without rest) until it went under. If Richter made the water too cold or too hot, however, the rat would give up after no more than 20 to 40 hours. If he blew a jet of air into the animal's face while it was swimming, the rat became exhausted even more quickly.

After the experimental animals had met all these challenges, Richter would inspect various parts of their bodies to see what the physiological reactions had been. His early work was instrumental in the development of drugs that have helped thousands of human patients survive the devastating effects of psychological stress and **hypertension.**

But one of Richter's most fascinating findings came about almost by accident. Richter noticed that, no matter what he did to them, many of his rats always swam around the sides of the tub in the same direction. Some animals always swam clockwise, some always counter-clockwise—but once they had "picked" their direction, it was always the same.

Richter knew that many insects and other lower animals show the same sort of "circling" behavior if you cut off one of their "feelers" or **antennae.** An ant that has lost its left antenna will tend to circle to the left, and a lobster deprived of its right "feeler" will circle to the right. Richter wondered if there might not be some connection or **correlation** between the length of a rat's whiskers and the direction in which it swam in the tub. Perhaps rats always turned their heads toward the side where their whiskers were the shortest.

And so Richter asked his assistants to cut the whiskers off one side of a rat's face and toss it into the tub. When they did so—to everyone's surprise—the animal paddled around frantically for a minute or two, and then it sank straight to the bottom of the tub like a stone. The de-whiskered rat would have drowned in two minutes (rather than 80 hours) if it hadn't been rescued.

Now, this finding simply didn't make sense to Richter. Obviously a rat doesn't depend on its whiskers to keep it afloat. What could be wrong? So he asked his assistants to show him what they had done to the rat while clipping it.

The Traumatic Black Bag   For the most part, the white rat found in

A chief of Eyambe, medicine man and witch doctor of the Congo.

Hypertension (HIGH-purr-TENN-shun). A medical problem caused by over-stimulation of the sympathetic system. Usually related to stress, or the inability to handle same in a healthy fashion. Hypertension is thought to be one of the major "killers" in the US today.

Antennae (an-TEN-knee). The antenna of a TV set is the metal rod or wires put up to catch television waves. The antennae (or antennas) on an insect are the "feelers" that stick out of the animal's head. Most insect antennae contain touch and olfactory receptors that help the animal "feel out" the world around it.

Correlation (kor-ree-LAY-shun). Two events that occur together frequently are said to be co-related, or correlated. The more closely associated the events are, or the more often they occur together, the higher the correlation between them. See the Statistical Appendix to this book for further details.

Curt Richter.

psychological laboratories is a gentle beast that can be handled without gloves and even makes an amusing pet. But rats have sharp teeth, as Richter's assistants knew only too well. If the rat becomes frightened, it will sharpen its keen teeth on any handy object, including the fingers of a lab assistant.

To avoid being bitten when clipping the rat's whiskers, Richter's assistants had nearly smothered the animal inside a black bag. To get the rat out of its cage, they had held the mouth of the bag up to the open cage door. Perhaps because it thought it could escape easily, or because it was attracted to darkness, the rat had jumped into the thick black sack.

The assistants then grabbed the animal tightly through the cloth and peeled back the top of the bag until the rat's head was exposed. Holding the rat's body firmly inside the bag, the assistants proceeded to clip the whiskers from one side of its face with a large, noisy clipper. Then they held the sack over the tub and dropped the poor frightened **rodent** into the water in the tub.

Little wonder that the rat sank to the bottom almost at once!

Richter soon found that it was the **trauma** induced by the handling—and not the whisker clipping at all—that so over-stimulated the animal's fear responses that it went straight into the stage of exhaustion. The parasympathetic nervous system simply took over and clamped down on all activity. The rat's heart slowed down almost to a complete stop, and the animal soon lost consciousness and sank.

It was from these and related studies that Richter concluded that "voodoo death" was caused by *parasympathetic*, rather than sympathetic, over-stimulation.

Learning To Be Hopeful Perhaps the most interesting finding Richter made, however, was this: If Richter pulled the de-whiskered rat out of the water even seconds before it was about to drown—and let it sit on a table for a minute or two—the animal would make a remarkable recovery. Once it had rested and gathered its wits together, it seemed to realize that it could, in fact, survive the traumatic situation. And so, if Richter then tossed the rat back into the water, it would swim for many hours.

Those two or three minutes out of the water were enough to give the rat momentary *hope*. If it were given several gentle, playful exposures to the black bag before having its whiskers clipped, it swam about 80 hours after being dumped into the tub. And if it were "rescued" several times during the first few minutes it was swimming, the rat apparently gained excellent control over its autonomic nervous system. It then managed to swim even better than did rats that hadn't been trained in this way to withstand stress.

Hope springs eternal—but apparently only if you have been given signs or reasons to be hopeful.

Coping

During your lifetime you have met many challenges, experienced many stressful situations, and worked your way through many emotional experiences, which is to say that you have *learned to adjust* to the problems that you face in life. Psychologists often speak of "learning to adjust" as **coping** with the world.

Your problems typically come to you as *inputs*, which you must *process* in some way, and then *react* to. There are many different ways of *coping*, but they all involve making some change in your "input–output relationships." Thus some methods of coping involve changing, controlling, or even avoiding certain inputs. Others involve changing the way in which you "process" or think about problem-related inputs. Still other ways of coping involve altering your outputs—that is, changing the ways in which you respond or behave when the problem occurs.

And whether you attack the problem by working on your inputs, your internal processes, or your outputs, you will typically choose one of two major ways of adjusting—**defensive coping** or **direct coping.**

Defensive coping typically involves protecting yourself by getting away from the threatening inputs. Direct coping involves meeting the challenge head-on.

Defensive Coping

Most forms of defensive coping involve either mental or physical *escape* from the traumatic situation. You either flee from the problem and in the future avoid going near the stress-inducing situation, or you block out the threatening inputs and deny that the inputs are stressful. Many of the defense mechanisms described by Sigmund Freud are types of defensive coping (see Chapter 22).

As we noted in Chapter 11, if you are threatened by sexual stimuli, you may repress these inputs by simply ignoring them or by not paying attention to them until they become incredibly strong. **Repression,** then, is a type of defensive coping.

Hysterical blindness is a similar form of adjusting to things defensively. During battles, soldiers who see their best friends shot down may become psychologically "blind." Their eyes still work—but their minds refuse to process any incoming visual stimuli. By refusing to see anything at all, these men defend against having to witness more deaths.

Reaction formation, projection, and **displacement** are also forms of defensive coping. The mother who hates her child, but finds this hatred stress-inducing, may adjust to the situation by forming an entirely different reaction to the child. That is, she may repress the hatred and *react* to the child with far too much love. Or she may *project* her feelings onto the child by telling herself that she really loves the child, but the child hates her. Or she may *displace* her feelings by kicking the cat when she really wants to kick the child.

Fixation and **regression** are forms of defensive coping that involve refusing to learn new ways of behavior or going back to old ways of behavior (see Chapter 21). A growing child may become *fixated* at an immature level if it is punished each time it tries to take the next step up the developmental ladder. Or, if the individual does learn to act in an adult way, but experiences great stress, the young person may *regress* to a much more childish (but safe) way of behaving.

Depression is one of the most common types of defensive coping. Stress almost always involves an increase in sympathetic nervous system activity. One way to counter this arousal is somehow to increase activity in your parasympathetic system. For some people, this means learning how to relax and "stay cool" in the face of danger. But other people go a bit too far—they seem to turn their parasympathetic systems up to "maximum volume." They *give up*, both physiologically and psychologically. And like Richter's rats, these individuals fall into such a deep depression that they are incapable of dealing with any of life's problems.

We are all depressed now and again, just as we are all occasionally highly aroused. The problem comes when we adopt depression as our customary way of avoiding stress. When carried to extremes, this form of *defensive depression* can lead to hospitalization or suicide.

Direct Coping

Most forms of *direct coping* involve taking at least three steps:

1. An *objective analysis* of what your problem is, how it came into being, and how you are presently responding.

Repression. The act of denying reality by refusing to become conscious of stress-related thoughts or inputs.

Hysterical blindness (hiss-TARE-ick-kal). Hysteria (hiss-TARE-ee-uh) is a form of agitated or excited behavior caused by stress. In order to reduce the stress, the hysterical person may block off sensory inputs related to the stressful situation.

Reaction formation. A form of defensive coping in which the person reacts to an unacceptable emotion by unconsciously forming an entirely different response.

Projection. A form of defensive coping in which you project your own unacceptable impulses onto someone else.

Displacement (diss-PLACE-ment). A form of defensive coping in which you displace unacceptable emotions from one person or object to another.

Fixation (fix-A-shun). According to Freud, a child must pass through several developmental stages (see Chapter 21). If the child attempts to move up to a higher rung on the developmental ladder, but is frightfully punished for doing so, the child may remain stuck or "fixated" at an immature level.

Regression (re-GRESH-shun). If the developing child does move up to a higher rung, but later is punished for acting in a more mature way, the child may regress back to a more immature level of adjustment simply because the child was less frequently punished at this immature stage. All of the forms of defensive coping discussed above—except for fixation—are what Freud called "ego defense mechanisms." See Chapters 21 and 22.

Depression. Perhaps the most common form of defensive coping. Frequently accompanies other forms of defensive coping, such as the Freudian defense mechanisms. Depression is usually caused by an over-stimulation of the parasympathetic nervous system.

Julian Rotter.

2. A clear statement of how things might be better—that is, a precise description of what your *ultimate goal* or adjustment would be.

3. A *psychological road map*, or list of new approaches to life that you might engage in to reach your goal.

Direct coping is not always easy, and it is often very time-consuming. For it requires that you "stand back" and look at things as unemotionally as you can. When you are caught up in the middle of a frightening or stressful situation, you may have neither the motivation nor the self-control to think things through rationally. Thus you may find that, at least to start with, you might require professional help of some kind if you wish to learn how to deal with stressful inputs in a direct manner (see Chapter 25).

Direct coping also requires that you set clear-cut goals, and then move toward these goals a step at a time. People in stressful situations—such as those who want to lose weight—aren't always willing to set realistic goals or take the slow-but-steady approach to getting there. And there are many individuals who believe the best way to learn how to cope is to jump right into the middle of things.

To cope with problems directly, you must first perceive that there is something you can do to change things. That is, you must realize that, to some extent, you control your own destiny. We will talk more about *direct coping* in just a moment. First, however, you should learn something about your own personal "locus of control."

Locus of Personal Control

Some people are taught to believe that they are **autonomous**—that is, they are masters of their own fates and hence bear personal responsibility for what happens to them. They see their own personal **locus of control** as being *inside* themselves, as coming from their own intra-psychic resources. Psychologist Julian Rotter calls these people **internalizers.**

On the other hand, many people believe that they are helpless pawns of fate, that they are creatures controlled by *outside forces* over which they have little if any influence. Such people appear to feel that their *locus of personal control* is external rather than internal. Thus they often act as if they feel little or no responsibility for what happens to them. Rotter calls these people **externalizers.**

Perhaps the major differences between externalizers and internalizers, as Rotter makes clear, is that people with an internal locus of personal control know how to act to get their desired inputs. People with an external locus of control seem not to have this knowledge. Rather, externalizers tend to wait passively for whatever inputs come their way.

According to Rotter, *externalizers* usually believe that God or "fate" controls whatever happens to them. When faced with an external threat of some kind, these people either block off the stressful inputs, ignore them, or become depressed.

Internalizers, on the other hand, don't believe in fate or "luck." They believe that "getting ahead in the world" is primarily a matter of what you do, not what accidents befall you. When faced with a threat, internalizers tend to face the matter directly, or to remove themselves to temporary safety.

As we will see in Chapter 23, there are no "pure" personality types. Concepts such as "locus of control" are useful, but we must not make the mistake of thinking that everyone in the world must be either a "pure" externalizer or a "pure" internalizer. Rather, we all probably have mixed tendencies.

For example, psychologists Patricia and Gerald Gurin have found that many individuals have an *internal* locus of control as far as their personal lives are concerned, but have an *external* locus of control on the job. These people are quite effective in handling their own personal stresses—they know how to cope in many day-to-day activities, and how to face the strains

Some parents encourage the child's attempts to work out family differences by logical compromise.

of living with their relatives and close friends. But many of these individuals work for large organizations and lack the social or managerial skills to achieve their goals on the job. Thus, while at work, they see themselves as puppets pushed around by forces they don't really understand. Locus of *personal* control therefore includes a somewhat different set of attitudes and behaviors than does locus of *organizational* control.

But both ways of perceiving the world—and of coping with it—seem to be learned.

Learning to Cope

Early Development

The characteristic response that you show to stressful situations appears to be something that you learned early in life.

For the growing child, few situations are as potentially stressful as those in which the child's desires come in conflict with parental demands. The first few times such conflicts occur, the child's sympathetic nervous system is aroused, and the child either stands up and fights, or turns and flees.

Some mothers and fathers may encourage defiance; others may encourage running away. Still other parents may reward the child's attempts at conciliation and working out family differences by logical compromise. In any of these cases, the child is likely to learn that the stress of arousal may be reduced by some positive action on its part. Such children tend to acquire an internal locus of control, because they have been taught that they are responsible for what happens to them.

However, consider what might happen if the child's parents were rigid and uncompromising. When the first few conflicts with the child arose, the parents might refuse to allow the child either to fight or to flee. Instead, the child would be encouraged to submit blindly to the authority of the parents—or to whatever philosophical or moral code the parents followed. Any attempt the child made to take control of its own destiny might be severely punished.

This child would soon learn to bury its resentments and to be obedient to the parents' demands. But to do so the child must learn some way of handling the arousal of its sympathetic nervous system, an arousal that

Parents who always intercede when differences arise make it difficult for children to learn to handle stressful situations.

occurs almost automatically in stressful situations. From a logical point of view, the two best ways of doing this would seem to be: (a) preventing the arousal from occurring in the first place; and (b) overcoming sympathetic activity by means of massive excitation of the parasympathetic nervous system.

If you follow the first way, you learn to block out stressful inputs by use of such defense mechanisms as repression, hysterical blindness, reaction formation, projection, displacement, and regression. If you follow the second way, you become depressed. In either case, you will probably develop an external locus of personal control.

Conformity Breeds an External Locus of Control   The person with a strongly externalized locus of control pays rather a heavy penalty for avoiding the stresses and strains of life, however. Studies of these people suggest that they often become rigid, constricted in their outlook, uncreative, prejudiced, conforming, and over-controlled. They are, in general, much more depressive and suicidal than is the average woman or man.

Externalizers function fairly well in highly structured, **authoritarian** social systems—particularly those with a military character. They also tend to be intolerant of change and sometimes fiercely resist any attack on the authority to whom they have surrendered control.

In general, the externalizer's motivation seems to come from the outside—from the "system" rather than from internal sources or desires. Externalizers volunteer for nothing, unless they are told to do so, and they tend to have difficulties in adjusting to situations in which they do not have a ready-made set of rules to follow.

People who have been taught by their parents to be overly external in their locus of control can often be helped by psycho-therapy. Some types of treatment are aimed at giving these individuals *insight* into their present predicament. By going back over their early experiences, they often come to understand what stimuli they are defending against. Even as adults, if they are exposed to mildly stressful situations and encouraged to handle them effectively, bit by bit, they gain hope and begin to internalize their locus of personal control.

However, if they are merely dumped into hot water again and again without being given new ways of tolerating it, externalizers tend to become *more rigid* rather than more flexible.

"Sink or Swim" Learning

In 1971, Lt. Col. William Dattel reported an interesting set of experiments performed on Army recruits at Fort Ord, near Monterey, California. Each year, thousands of recruits are given their basic training at Fort Ord. Most of the recruits find the situation fairly stressful. They have little privacy, they are punished (often severely) for any mistakes, they are not allowed to talk back or argue with orders, and they are restricted to camp for the first several weeks of their stay at the camp.

Many recruits survive this stressful ordeal rather well. But many young men and women fall by the wayside. Some try to escape the situation by "going AWOL"—that is, by being absent without leave. Some become ill or depressed. A few commit suicide.

When Colonel Dattel was asked to help find better methods of providing basic training, he first analyzed the situation psychologically. The basic philosophy in most army camps is that recruits must be "tempered in the fire of experience." Thus many army training methods are devised to arouse the maximum amount of stress in the recruits—and then throw them into waters of experience to see whether they sink or swim.

Direct methods of coping—like all other habits—are usually best-learned when you are rewarded for progress rather than being punished for failure. Knowing this, Colonel Dattel set up an experimental unit at Fort Ord that trained a random selection of recruits using **positive reinforcement** rather than punishment. These men earned "points" for everything they did well,

Authoritarian (aw-thor-it-TAIR-ee-ann). A dictatorship is a perfect example of an authoritarian system—one in which the person on top rules with an iron fist. In 1950, several social scientists identified a group of traits or behavior patterns that make up what they call "the authoritarian personality." These traits include a high degree of conformity, dependence on authority, over-control of feelings and impulses, rigidity of thinking, and prejudice toward other races and religions. Individuals possessing these traits are said to have highly conventional values, are preoccupied with gaining power or status, and try to think and act like their political or social leaders.

Positive reinforcement. Anything that "reinforces" a behavior by making it more likely to occur again. More or less the same as "reward."

Pilots begin work on the ground using flight simulators rather than real airplanes.

but were not penalized for their mistakes. The recruits in this experimental unit could trade in the points for any rewards they wished—including the privilege of going into town the first night they were at the camp.

Colonel Dattel followed his experimental recruits both while they were at Fort Ord and throughout their next several years in the Army. He compared their progress with that of a "control group"—namely, an equal number of recruits who went through the regular stress-oriented basic training at Fort Ord.

Dattel's first finding was that almost none of the men in the experimental program went "AWOL." This result alone saved the Army many thousands of dollars. Dattel also found that his experimental subjects got the best marks of any group the Army had measured on such skills as rifle marksmanship, map reading, and so forth. Furthermore, when they went into combat in Vietnam, they performed better under enemy fire than did the "control group" recruits. And more of the experimental group re-enlisted at the end of their term of duty than did members of the "control group."

Unfortunately, despite Dattel's data, the Army abandoned the experimental program a few years after Dattel had set it up. Most military commanders apparently still believe that tolerance to stress is best learned through "sink or swim" training techniques.

"Step-by-Step" Learning

During the early 1970's, the Federal Aviation Agency (FAA) collected data that tended to confirm Colonel Dattel's research. The FAA, which is charged with testing the nation's airline pilots to make sure that they have the skills needed to fly commercial aircraft, made more creative use of their findings. Twice a year, each commercial pilot must fly a "test run" with an FAA inspector. For many years, these inspectors used to create highly stressful situations for the pilots—usually by turning off the plane's engines or by disabling it in some unusual way. The **rationale** for this sort of testing was that pilots must learn to expect the unexpected. They can hardly hope to save the lives of their passengers in emergency situations unless they have experienced those situations and learned how to cope with them.

The "emergencies" that the FAA inspectors threw at their test pilots, therefore, were often highly unlikely or particularly dangerous ones. Most of the pilots did beautifully, but a few buckled under the stress or didn't

Rationale (rash-uh-NAL). From the Latin word meaning "to think." Your rationale for doing something is your logical explanation of why the action is necessary.

recognize what had gone wrong until too late. In one such situation, an FAA inspector "killed" two engines on a jetliner just as the pilot was trying to land at New Orleans. The plane went out of control and crashed into a large motel.

After this disaster, the FAA changed the stress-testing techniques they used. Rather than dumping pilots into dangerous water without warning, the FAA identified as many possible types of emergencies as they could. They then created a step-by-step training procedure in which they began with the simplest type of problem and slowly worked up to the more dangerous situations. The pilots began their work on the ground—using computerized **flight simulators** rather than real airplanes. Once they experienced success in the simple problems, the pilots were allowed to move up to progressively more stressful tasks. And they usually were not challenged with a situation while "in the air" until they had proved they could handle that emergency in the simulator.

According to the FAA, since they adopted their new techniques, flight safety has increased measurably.

Eustress

In an interview with Hans Selye, published in the March 1978 issue of *Psychology Today,* the man who "invented" the concept of physiological stress talks at length about **eustress,** or "good" stress.

According to Selye, not all stress is bad. We shouldn't try to avoid all stress, for that would be impossible. Rather, we should recognize what our typical response is to stress, and then try to adjust our life-styles to take advantage of what that typical response is.

Selye believes that some of us are what he calls "turtles"—that is, we prefer peace, quiet, and a tranquil environment; and others are "race-horses," who thrive on a vigorous, fast-paced way of life. The amount of stress we may require to function best is what Selye calls *eustress.*

In a sense, Selye has done little more than adapt the "Arousal Theory" of motivation to his own terms. But his point remains valid.

All motivation is based on stress of some kind. If you did not want something, or need something, or desire something—if you weren't somehow deprived of some energy or informational input—you might never get around to learning or experiencing much of anything. Nor might you be much interested in joining a group, forming a family, rearing children, or supporting yourself by working in an organization. Society depends on eustress, for cultures are kept going by motivated people who are willing to learn how to cope with each other, and with their own individual needs and personalities.

Now that we have learned something about the stressful aspects of motivation, perhaps it is time we coped with the laws of learning.

Summary

1.   Your body and mind have many ways of defending themselves against the **stresses** and strains of life.

2.   At a physiological level, most of your defenses are controlled by the two parts of your **autonomic nervous system**—the **sympathetic** and **parasympathetic nervous systems.**

3.   Your **sympathetic nervous system** prepares you for such actions as fighting, fleeing, feeding, and sexual climax.

4.   Your **parasympathetic nervous system** acts to depress or slow down those bodily functions that are aroused by sympathetic system activity. For a variety of reasons, the parasympathetic is called the **vegetative nervous system.**

5.   The sympathetic and parasympathetic systems generally have opposite effects on your reactions, but the two actually operate to-

gether in a coordinated manner. Working together, they influence much of what you do and feel.

6. Once you become excited or emotionally stirred up, your sympathetic system causes the release of **adrenalin** and **nor-adrenalin**—the **arousal hormones** secreted by the **adrenal glands.**

7. The arousal hormones have much the same excitatory effect on physiological reactions (such as blood pressure and pulse rate) as activity in the sympathetic system itself.

8. Emotional arousal always puts you under a variety of biological, intra-psychic, and behavioral stresses that, if continued too long, can exhaust your resources.

9. Hans Selye suggests that your body goes through three rather distinct stages when stressed:

   a. The **alarm reaction,** in which your body's defenses are mobilized by activity in your **limbic system,** sympathetic system, and through secretion of adrenalin and nor-adrenalin.

   b. The **stage of resistance,** which occurs if the stress continues for very long. During this stage, your body tries to repair the damage that arousal causes while still defending itself.

   c. The **stage of exhaustion,** which comes about if the emergency continues for too long. During this stage, your body may use up all of its available resources and fall into depression or die.

10. Intra-psychic and **social/behavioral stress reactions** follow much the same pattern as biological stress.

11. Psychological or environmental threats can be at least as exhausting as can physiological stresses, such as disease.

12. People respond to psychological pressures in different ways, depending in part on their own personal **locus of control.**

   a. People who believe they are **autonomous**—that is, who believe they control their own fates—are aroused by threats and try to overcome them. Julian Rotter calls these people **internalizers.**

   b. Individuals who see themselves as being controlled primarily by external forces may face threats passively, waiting for some outside agency to protect or take care of them. Rotter calls these people **externalizers.**

13. Some individuals have an internal locus of personal control, but have an external **locus of organizational control.** These individuals cope well with their personal problems, but believe that their careers are influenced by external forces over which they have little control.

14. Generally speaking, there are two main ways of adjusting to stress—**defensive coping** and **direct coping.**

15. Externalizers tend to employ defensive coping strategies such as **repression, hysterical blindness, projection, reaction formation, displacement, regression,** and **depression.**

16. Internalizers tend to utilize direct coping methods in which they objectively analyze their problems, state clear-cut goals, and move toward these goals in a step-by-step manner.

17. Stress reactions—and personal locus of control—seem typically to be learned at an early age.

18. Authoritarian groups and organizations, such as the military, foster an external locus of control by training their members to handle stress in a "sink or swim" fashion. The "step-by-step" method, however, usually yields better results.

19. All motivation is based on stress of some kind. Selye calls the amount of stress you need to function properly **eustress,** or good stress.

(Continued from page 345.)

"Get up, Charlie."

Dr. Smith's voice was loud, but somehow not as heavy and as threatening as the voice inside Charlie's head usually was.

"I can't get up. I can't cope with things out there," Charlie said dully, pulling the covers more tightly over his head.

"Of course you can," Gail said. She seemed to be crying. He wondered why she wasn't still angry at him.

When Charlie didn't respond, Dr. Smith tugged gently at the covers. "Open up in there and come on out. You can make it, Charlie. Just try it and see."

"Don't move!" the heavy voice warned him.

"I won't," Charlie responded.

Dr. Smith thought Charlie was talking to him. " 'Won't' is very different from 'can't,' Charlie. You can make it if you want to."

"Do something, please!" Gail said to Dr. Smith.

Charlie thought she was talking to him. "I'm too tired to do anything," Charlie said.

"Too tired of what?" Dr. Smith asked.

"Hurdles," Charlie said finally. "Too many hurdles to jump, and too many snipers trying to hit you."

Gail sobbed and sat on the bed beside him.

"Hurdles. That's it, of course. Hurdles," Dr. Smith said, pulling up a chair. "Listen to me, Charlie. I want to tell you a story."

"Go away," Charlie said. Gail thought he was speaking to her and sobbed again.

Dr. Smith tugged on the blanket again, exposing a bit more of Charlie's face. "Once upon a time, Charlie, there was a psychologist named Martin Seligman. He worked with dogs."

"I was a dog once," Charlie said. "A dirty dogface. I couldn't make it as a dog, either. They sent me to a hospital."

Again the gentle tug on the blanket. "Seligman made his dogs jump a hurdle, Charlie, just like you said. The hurdle separated two chambers in a large wooden box. Seligman taught the dogs to jump the hurdle when he sounded a signal. If they jumped into the other chamber right away, they were safe. If they didn't jump when the signal came on, they got shocked."

"Snipers don't give signals," Charlie said.

"Seligman did," Dr. Smith continued. "When he first put a dog in one of the chambers and gave the signal, the dog ignored it. Then came the shock. The dog bounced around, hunting for a way out."

"There is no way out," Charlie mumbled.

"Yes, there is. Over the hurdle," Dr. Smith said. "After the dog had jumped around for a while, it accidentally went over the hurdle. And found it was safe."

Charlie pulled the blanket up again. "It's not safe anywhere."

"Yes, it is," Dr. Smith continued. "The dog soon learned to jump the moment the signal came on. And it always avoided the shock."

"That sounds cruel," Gail said. "Why are you telling Charlie stories like that?"

"It's a cruel world," Charlie said. "Even for dogs,"

Dr. Smith tugged the blanket down once more. "And even dogs can learn, Charlie. Listen. Once the dog had gotten the message, it never forgot. Even when Seligman turned off the electric current, the dog continued to jump, and jump, and jump. There wasn't any shock to hurt it, but it just kept right on trying to avoid something that wasn't there any more."

"Why did it do that?" Gail asked.

"The signal had become stressful and arousing," Dr. Smith said. "Jumping reduced the dog's conditioned fear and hence turned off the stress."

"Safer to jump," Charlie said.

"Smarter to learn when you don't have to be afraid," replied Dr. Smith. "But Seligman found a way to help the dog cope. He simply made the hurdle so high that the dog couldn't possibly jump over it. Then he turned on the signal."

Gail seemed distressed. "But the dog couldn't escape . . ."

"That's right," the psychologist said. "It tried to leap over the barrier, but couldn't. It kept trying to jump for several minutes while the signal sounded. Eventually it realized that the shock was gone forever. So it stopped being afraid of the signal. Then when Seligman lowered the barrier and turned on the signal, the dog ignored it. The dog had learned a better way of coping with its fear than by blindly jumping the instant the signal came on."

"Avoid these people!" the voice inside Charlie's head signaled.

Dr. Smith pulled the blanket down to expose a bit more of Charlie's face. "Listen. We all go around avoiding things that we really ought to face up to, because they no longer have any power to hurt us. But that's not the most important lesson in Seligman's research."

"Then why talk about it?" Gail asked.

"Because of what he did next," Dr. Smith said, avoiding a direct answer to Gail's question. "Seligman took an untrained dog and put it in the chamber, but he started with the hurdle up so high the animal couldn't jump it. Then he turned on the signal and the shock."

"No way out," said Charlie.

Dr. Smith nodded, and pulled the blanket completely away from Charlie's grasp. "That's right. The poor dumb beast leaped all around the place. It whined, and it crapped on the floor, but it couldn't find a way out. So what do you think it did?"

"Hid in a corner," Charlie said, struggling for control of the blanket.

"Gail, take hold of the blanket, please," Dr. Smith said. She pulled the cover toward her.

"Hide!" cried the heavy voice inside Charlie's head.

"No, it couldn't hide," said Dr. Smith. "The best the dog could do was to stand on its tippy-toes with its eyes shut. That way it got the least amount of shock possible. It couldn't escape, so it learned to cope by shutting off as much of the outside world as it could."

Gail looked at the psychologist. "It hid inside its own mind, you mean."

"And it never came out," said Charlie, covering his face with his arms.

"That's right. At first it wouldn't come out," Dr. Smith said. "Not even when Seligman lowered the barrier and gave it a chance to get away. The dog still went up on its tippy-toes when the signal went on."

"Even though it could see the other side of the chamber?" Gail asked.

"Safer on the inside," Charlie mumbled.

Dr. Smith nodded, and shook Charlie by the shoulder. "Come out from in there."

"No!" cried the voice.

"But why wouldn't the dog jump when Seligman gave it a chance?" Gail asked.

Dr. Smith laughed. "Why doesn't Charlie jump into your arms, now that you've come back to him? You faced the facts about what his mother did to him, and you adjusted. Why can't Charlie make the same jump to freedom?"

"Because!" Charlie moaned as he squirmed about on the bed.

"Because," Dr. Smith continued, "like Seligman's dog, Charlie was punished for all his attempts to find a way out. So Charlie just gave up and stopped looking. The stress signal comes on, and Charlie instantly goes up on his mental tippy-toes because that's the way he's learned to minimize the pain. 'Learned helplessness' is what Seligman calls it."

"Leave me alone," Charlie cried.

A puzzled look crossed Gail's face. "But surely if Seligman coaxed the dog a bit . . ."

"Seligman tried that, but it didn't work. He tried offering the dog food, too. The dog just closed its eyes." Dr. Smith shook the young man's shoulder a bit roughly. "Listen, you in there, you've got to learn to stand on your feet instead of on your tippy-toes."

Gail persisted. "But how did Seligman get the dog to cope?"

"Grab Charlie's other arm, please," Dr. Smith said, pulling the young man to his feet with Gail's help. "We're going for a walk into the real world."

"Help!" cried the heavy voice.

"Better help than helplessness," Dr. Smith said, propelling Charlie through the door.

"You didn't answer my question," Gail said as the three of them walked awkwardly down the apartment house stairs.

"Oh," said Dr. Smith. "Seligman put a rope around the dog's neck and dragged it across the hurdle to freedom. Had to do it 40 to 50 times before the dog got the message that jumping was safe."

As they reached the front door, a car on the street outside backfired. Charlie pulled back violently. "Snipers! It's not safe out there!" he cried.

Dr. Smith grabbed him firmly by the collar. "Listen, Charlie. You can make it out there. I promise you that."

"Can't!" cried the heavy voice.

"Yes, you can," Dr. Smith said, pulling him forward.

"Yes, you can," Gail urged, pushing from behind.

The three of them tumbled out onto the street. It was a bright, clear, summer day. Pulling and shoving, coaxing and caressing, Gail and Dr. Smith got him moving. They walked toward a little park a couple of blocks away.

"You're making it!" Dr. Smith said.

"You're doing great!" said Gail.

And then they came to a curbstone about a foot high. Charlie pulled back suddenly, as if he had been shot at.

"Stop!" cried the heavy voice.

"Jump, Charlie," urged Dr. Smith. "You can make it."

"Can't!" Charlie moaned.

Gail jumped lightly over the obstacle. "Look, Charlie, if I can do it, you can too."

"Jump!" cried Dr. Smith.

"Jump!" Gail coaxed.

Charlie learned forward, tripped, hopped, skipped, and clumsily jumped over the curbstone.

"You did it!" Gail said, grabbing Charlie in her arms.

He held on to her tensely, panting, shaking with fear.

"And you can do it again, any time you want," said Dr. Smith, patting him on the back.

A few seconds later, after he got his breath and stopped trembling like a frightened puppy, Charlie looked up. The sky was blue, the sun was shining, and there wasn't a single sniper in sight.

"Any time you want to," Gail reminded him, kissing his cheek. Her smile matched the radiance of the sun.

Charlie relaxed a bit, then frowned, then almost managed a smile. He listened carefully for the heavy voice, but all he heard were birds singing.

After a while, he shrugged his shoulders. "Maybe I can," he said.

"Doggone right," said Dr. Smith.

Recommended Readings

Levi, Lennart. *Society, Stress and Disease* (New York: Oxford University Press, 1971).

Rabkin, Judith G., and Elmer L. Streuning. "Life Events, Stress, and Illness," *Science*, 194 (1976), pp. 1013–1020.

Rotter, Julian. "External Control and Internal Control," *Psychology Today*, vol. 5, no. 1 (1971), pp. 37–42.

Selye, Hans. *The Stress of Life*, rev. ed. (New York: McGraw-Hill, 1978).

Spielberger, Charles D., and Irving G. Sarason, eds. *Stress and Anxiety*, Vol. 1 (Washington, D.C.: Hemisphere, 1975).

4

Learning
and
Memory

Conditioning
and
Desensitization

Did You Know That. . . .

Although a Russian named Ivan Pavlov is usually given credit, a US psychologist named E.B. Twitmyer was apparently the first to experiment with what we now call the "conditioned response?"

Pavlov was able to train dogs willingly to withstand considerable pain to get food?

Animals put in conflict-inducing situations often display behaviors that, if they were human, would lead us to assume the animals were "mentally ill?"

Children can be conditioned not to wet the bed?

The so-called "lie-detector" doesn't really detect lies?

A person with an abnormal fear (called a "phobia") can sometimes be helped by the same sort of conditioning techniques Pavlov used with his dogs?

Learning how to relax "on cue" is often a first step in learning how to overcome your fears?

The most effective forms of therapy usually involve changes in attitudes and emotional responses as well as changes in behavior?

"The Leningrad Connection"

"You see, I'm really here only because my wife wanted me to come," Hans Larsen said to his therapist, Dr. Roberta Turner. "I have this little problem, I guess. Not really a problem exactly, just my own way of doing things. It doesn't hurt anybody but me, so what's the difference? I mean, what's to get excited about? Do you see what I mean?"

A spark of veiled amusement lit up Dr. Turner's dark brown eyes. "No, Mr. Larsen, I don't see. Yet. But I'm sure I will if you tell me more about it."

"Well, it's a sort of very personal problem, if you know what I mean. Nothing really abnormal, or anything like that. But it cuts close to the skin, and I'm not exactly eager to talk about it. Really, when you stop to think about it, it's more my wife's problem than my own." Larsen ran his hand nervously through his pale blond hair. "Yes, that's it. My wife just isn't very understanding or cooperative, and that's the truth."

Dr. Turner nodded. "But your wife insisted that you come talk to me, so she must think it's your difficulty and not hers. So why don't you tell me more about what's troubling the two of you?"

Larsen began to sweat a little. "Gee, you know, some things are very personal. Now, don't take this wrong, because I don't want to hurt your feelings. But . . . I mean, isn't there a *male* doctor I could talk to? I mean, there are some things . . ."

Dr. Turner smiled reassuringly. "Mr. Larsen, I can't blame you for being reluctant to talk about sexual matters. But don't you think that women are often more understanding of a man's sexual problems than other men are? And I'm sure that you're right in thinking that it's as much your wife's responsibility as yours. So just relax for a moment, lean back in your chair, and get comfortable. And then see if you don't want to tell me what's troubling you."

Larsen looked at the woman for a moment or two, then followed her suggestion. A deep sigh escaped his lips as he let himself go limp. Then he began to talk.

"I don't satisfy her. I guess that's the heart of the matter. At least, I can't usually make it, well, *worthwhile* for her without a little something extra to turn me on." His voice dropped to a whisper. "I guess if I told you how screwed up I really am, you would be pretty shocked."

Dr. Turner smiled. "It depends on what it takes 'to turn you on.'" The last man I worked with was impotent unless he took his teddy bear to bed along with his wife."

"You're kidding me! About the teddy bear, I mean."

"No, not at all."

Larsen laughed. "Well, maybe I'm not so bad off as I thought. And it's not that I *have* to have them, it's just that it's usually better that way . . ."

"Have what?"

Larsen sighed again. "The whips. I like the touch of a whip when it's bedtime. The cutting edge, you might say. Gives me the power to get up and go, stirs my blood a bit. So when we got married, I bought my wife a couple of small whips—tiny ones, really—and asked her to use them on me. At first, she didn't want to. Hurt her more than it did me, she said. And then she gave in for a while and tried them, and it was good, really good."

The man paused, as if remembering old times. "But now, she's read a book or something, and she says I'm a masochist, and I need help." He spat it out like a dirty word, MASS-oh-kist. "I guess that's pretty unusual, isn't it? A guy who needs pain to get sexually excited?"

"It's a great deal more common than you probably realize. Pick up any of the underground newspapers and see how many 'personal' ads talk about whips and leather clothes and 'the need to be disciplined.'" Dr. Turner smiled gently at the man. "And we may be able to give you more help than you suspect."

Larsen's voice quickened. "Gee, do you really think so? I mean, this book my wife read, it says I feel guilt and anxiety because I unconsciously think sex is dirty and that I'm a prude at heart. So I've got to be punished first, to pay in advance for my sinful pleasures. Otherwise, I can't relax and do what comes naturally." He paused. "Is that what you think is wrong?"

Dr. Turner cleared her throat. "Mr. Larsen, there are many different views on what causes masochism. Your feelings and actions are determined by three main things—your genes, your past experiences, and the environment you're presently in. As far as we know, masochism isn't an inherited tendency, so we can pretty well rule out physiological causes.''

"That's good to hear," Larsen said.

"But there may very well be a 'masochistic personality.' Some therapists believe that the real problem is *sadism*—or the desire to hurt other people. According to this view, people who cannot tolerate the thought of hurting others may turn their desires inward. They hold their own hostile impulses in check by making other people hurt them instead.''

Larsen shook his head. "I don't like to hurt anybody. I just like to be hurt, if you know what I mean.''

"I know," Dr. Turner said. "Well, to continue, some psychologists believe that masochism is related to castration anxiety, that the man invites his wife to hurt him slightly as a way of warding off her attempts to castrate him.''

"My wife wouldn't dare!''

"Let's hope not. Anyhow, still other psychologists think the problem is basically one of being *trained* to like or accept pain when you are very young. You can come to tolerate a great deal of pain if you're conditioned to do so.''

Larsen shook his head in confusion. "I don't know about that. What do you believe, Doctor?''

The woman smiled. "There's a lot to be said for all those views, and just because one is right doesn't mean that the others are wrong. The important thing is finding some way to help you change your style of life, to help you grow into the happier sort of person I'm sure you can become. You are not merely 'the sum of all your yesterdays.' You are also 'the possibility of all your tomorrows.' Some types of therapy focus on understanding your past. Other therapies are oriented toward helping you change your future.''

"Which would be best for me?''

Dr. Turner frowned slightly. "Ideally, we'd want to try both types of treatment at the same time. Masochism is sometimes just a symptom of some deeper problem, some unconscious anxiety that needs to be uncovered if you're to learn to cope and to avoid similar difficulties in the future. In recent years, however, psychologists have found that many types of masochism are the result of improper learning when the person was young. In these cases, the newer 'conditioning therapies' can often be of help—particularly if we also try to find out what caused your love of pain to begin with, and if we try to help you achieve greater personal growth and self-actualization as well.''

"How does this conditioning stuff of yours work? Do you have to whip me, or something?'' Larsen's voice was quite eager.

The woman smiled. "No, we assume that some time early in your life, you were rewarded for hurting yourself or being hurt by someone else. Probably there were sexual overtones to the experience, and that's how you were shaped into needing pain to stimulate you. Perhaps your mother caught you playing with yourself and punished you for it, and now sexual stimuli elicit an anxiety reaction instead of the normal response.''

"Gee, I don't really remember anything like that . . .''

"Well, perhaps one time you were terrified of something that involved sexuality or your own sex organs, and you got hurt, and somehow your anxiety was greatly reduced. Then pain would become associated in your mind with fear-reduction. For example, did your parents have frequent fights?"

Larsen blushed. "Oh, I wouldn't say they were *frequent* . . ."

Dr. Turner nodded. "I'm not trying to insult either you or your parents, Mr. Larsen. But when a child's parents have a fight, the child may become terrified. If the child gets hurt, and the parents stop fighting in order to give love or affection to the child, then the child might unconsciously be conditioned to seek pain in order to reduce fear and anxiety."

"I don't seem to recall anything like that," Larsen said, still blushing.

"This sort of conditioning happens when you're so young that you don't remember it as an adult," Dr. Turner said.

Larsen shrugged his shoulders. "Well, if you say so. But how do we start? Do I lie on a couch, or something? Or maybe a bed of nails?"

Dr. Turner laughed. "No, we'll talk about the origins of your masochism later on. But first, you will have to decide what you most urgently need help with right now."

Larsen groaned, as if experiencing some kind of intra-psychic pain. "I guess my wife comes first."

"All right, would you like to see if we can retrain you so that you can enjoy sexual pleasure with your wife without having to suffer pain first?"

A shrewd look washed over Larsen's face. "Couldn't we just train my wife to be a sadist? I mean, wouldn't that be just as quick?"

Again Dr. Turner laughed. "She might not consider that a form of 'self-actualization' on her part. Anyway, do you want your problem to control you, or do you want to control your problem?"

"Yeah, I guess you're right. But what do we do first?"

"First, we teach you how to relax, and how to listen to your body. You see, pain has probably become a conditioned signal for sexual arousal in your case. If you skip the whips, you probably become nervous about whether or not you'll be able to perform sexually, am I correct?"

Larsen began to sweat a little. Very quietly he said, "Yeah, you got it right."

"Well," said Dr. Turner, "anxiety is controlled by your sympathetic nervous system. That's the part of your body that handles excitement. Unfortunately, erection is controlled by your parasympathetic nervous system, that part of your body which is involved in relaxation."

"So you're saying that I can't do my wife much good unless I'm relaxed?"

Dr. Turner nodded. "At the beginning of things, yes. And the more anxious you become about not being able to perform, the more your sympathetic nervous systems turns on and the more difficult it is for your parasympathetic system to do its job."

Larsen nodded. "Yeah, that makes sense, in a strange kind of way."

"So we teach you how to handle your anxiety by learning how to relax. Then we'll make a list of all the situations that make you tense, beginning with things that aren't really all that disturbing and working up to things that make you break out in a cold sweat even just thinking about them."

"We'll make a little list, eh?"

The woman agreed. "That's right. And then, when we've taught you how to differentiate between the signals your body gives your mind when you're relaxed—and those signals your body gives when it's tense—you'll know how to relax whenever you want to."

"Sounds good."

"Well, it's very relaxing. Next, we'll start talking about the items on that list, one at a time, starting with the simplest and working up to the most disturbing. If we can teach you to think or talk about these things while you're calm and cool and collected, then they won't make you very anxious any more. And if you're not anxious . . ."

". . . then I can take care of my wife without needing the whips, you mean."

Dr. Turner smiled. "That's right."

Larsen pondered the matter for a long time. "Well, I guess it might work. How do we begin?"

"It's simple. First, stretch out your legs and make them as rigid and as tense as you can. Go ahead, do it now. Do you feel the tension?"

"Sure. It kind of hurts a little."

Dr. Turner nodded. "That's good. Now, relax your legs completely. Just let go, let go completely. Relax your feet and your ankles and your thigh muscles. There. Now tense them up again. That's right, tense, tense, tense. Feel the tension? Okay, now relax again, just go completely limp. Now, can you tell the difference between tension and relaxation?"

"I sure can. There's a world of difference."

"Good," said the woman. "Next, we'll do the same thing with your arms, and then with your head and neck muscles. We want to get you to the point where you can command your body to relax any time you want to, and the muscles in your body will respond automatically. And we want to train your mind to recognize the feedback signals from your muscles so that you can discriminate between tension and relaxation. That way, you can relax if the feedback tells you that you're tense. We want to bring your bodily processes under your voluntary control."

Larsen grinned. "If I could do that . . ."

"Then your immediate problem would be solved, and you could go on to find out how the masochism got started, and how to avoid such things in the future."

Larsen looked doubtful. "That sounds like a really painful process."

Dr. Turner laughed lightly. "I thought you liked pain, Mr. Larsen."

The man suddenly smiled. "Dr. Turner, you've got a deal!"

(Continued on page 388.)

The Innate Reflex

Some time about the beginning of this century, a pleasant young man named E.B. Twitmyer began work on his doctoral dissertation in psychology at the University of Pennsylvania. Twitmyer was interested in **innate reflexes**—those automatic behavior patterns that are wired into your brain circuits by your genetic blueprint.

Innate reflexes. The word *innate* comes from a Latin term meaning "inborn." Innate reflexes thus are inherited behavior patterns. Put more correctly, they are inherited *neural connections* between inputs and outputs. Whenever the stimulus input occurs, the response output follows automatically.

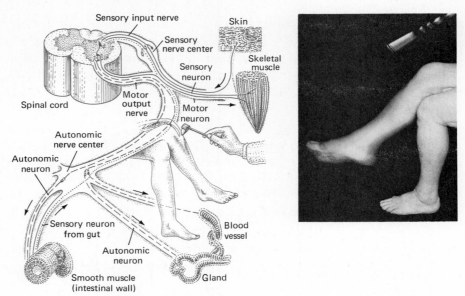

Fig. 15.1. The patellar reflex, or knee-jerk.

During the late 1800's, neurophysiologists all around the world were just
beginning to get a vague idea of how the human nervous system actually
works. One of their chief tools for mapping out the functions of the brain
was the *reflex.*

The concept of the "reflex" came slowly to psychological science,
however. For instance, the first scientific reports ever published on the
patellar reflex, or knee-jerk, did not appear until 1875. For more than 30
years thereafter, noted physiologists here and in Europe raged at each
other concerning the neural mechanisms by which this reflex operates.

You can elicit the patellar reflex in either of your legs rather simply (see
Fig. 15.1). When you are sitting down, cross one leg on top of the other,
leaving your uppermost leg hanging freely. Now, reach down with the edge
of your hand and strike this leg smartly just below your kneecap. At this
point, your **patellar tendon** runs close to the surface of your skin. And
whenever you tap on this tendon, the lower half of your leg will swing
forward involuntarily.

But why should your leg move reflexively when you stimulate your
patellar tendon? The early neurophysiologists couldn't agree on an answer.
Some thought that when you hit the tendon, it pulled *directly* on the
muscles and your leg twitched. Other scientists believed that the sensory
receptors in the tendon sent a message back to your spinal cord—and up to
your brain—and the motor output center in your cortex responded by
ordering the muscles in your leg to jump.

Thanks to research by Twitmyer and many other scientists, we now
know that the patellar reflex involves the nervous system, and that the
tendon doesn't pull directly on your muscles when hit.

Twitmyer's Experiment

E.B. Twitmyer.

E.B. Twitmyer was interested in how the patellar reflex operates for a very
good reason: Medical doctors could often use the reflex for diagnostic
purposes. If you had to have an intact spinal cord in order for the reflex to
appear, as turned out to be the case, then an abnormal patellar response
would suggest to the physician that you had suffered damage to your spinal
cord.

Twitmyer believed that the patellar reflex might be influenced by the
emotional or *motivational state* a subject was in when the reflex was

elicited. So he rigged up a small hammer that would strike the subject's patellar tendon when Twitmyer let the hammer fall. Twitmyer didn't bother telling his subjects when he was about to stimulate their reflexes—he merely dropped the hammer and measured how far their legs jerked. His subjects were other students at Penn, and they soon complained that the hammer blow often caught them unaware. Couldn't he ring a bell as a warning, so that they wouldn't be surprised? Twitmyer agreed, and began sounding a signal to announce the hammer drop.

As you might guess, one day when Twitmyer was working with a subject whose knee had been hit hundreds of times, Twitmyer accidentally sounded the warning signal without dropping the hammer. As promptly as clockwork, the subject's knee jerked *despite the fact that his tendon hadn't been stimulated.* Although Twitmyer didn't realize it at the time, he had just discovered the **conditioned reflex,** a response pattern upon which a dozen different psychological theories would later be built.

However, Twitmyer did appreciate the fact that he was on to something important, and he dropped his original research plans in order to investigate his discovery. He established some of the conditions under which this new type of reflex occurred, and reported his findings at the 1904 meeting of the American Psychological Association.

Sadly enough, Twitmyer was years ahead of his time, and the psychologists to whom he spoke paid little attention to what he had to say. Discouraged by the frosty reception his ideas received, Twitmyer failed to pursue his findings and was little heard of afterward.

And so, credit for the discovery of the *conditioned reflex* passed by default to the famous Russian physiologist, Ivan Pavlov.

Pavlov's Conditioning Studies

Ivan Pavlov, who lived from 1849 to 1936, is perhaps Russia's most famous scientist. After taking his medical degree in 1883, he traveled in Europe, studying with various other scientists. In 1890, Pavlov founded the Institute of Experimental Medicine in Leningrad, which he directed the rest of his life.

Pavlov's early interests were in the physiological processes of *digestion,* and he chose dogs for his experimental animals. He trained the dogs to lie quietly on operating tables or in leather harnesses while he studied what went on inside their **digestive tracts** before and after the dogs had eaten a meal. His experiments proved for the first time that the nervous system coordinates *all* digestive responses. Because of the pioneering nature of his work, Pavlov was awarded the Nobel Prize in 1904—the first Russian to be so honored.

Digestion actually begins in the mouth, when you produce saliva that starts breaking up food particles chemically. Pavlov soon found a way to measure the amount of saliva that the glands in the dog's mouth produced. While the dog was in a harness, Pavlov would give food to the dog, then count the number of drops of saliva that these glands secreted. Dogs do not have to be trained to salivate when given food—they do so reflexively, or automatically. Salivation is therefore an innate *response* or reflex that is elicited by the *stimulus* input of food in the mouth.

Pavlov wanted to determine the neural pathways that connected the stimulus receptors in the dog's mouth with its salivary glands, but his research was often interrupted by peculiar responses the animals would make. Inexperienced dogs would typically lie quietly in the harness he had prepared for them and would secrete saliva only *after* the food had actually been popped into their mouths. However, after an animal had gotten accustomed to being fed in the harness, its salivary glands would often "juice up" *before* it got the food. In fact, an experienced dog would usually start salivating if one of Pavlov's assistants merely rattled the food dishes in the sink or walked toward the dog carrying a plate.

Pavlov called these "unusual" reactions **psychic stimulations,** and they

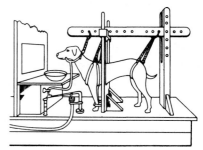

Pavlov's experimental arrangement.

infuriated him because they "got in the way" of his regular research. He did his best to ignore them because he wasn't interested in anything "psycho-logical." However, the psychic stimulations refused to go away. And so, in 1901, Pavlov began to study them systematically, hoping that he could thereby get rid of these "annoyances." He told his friends that this work surely wouldn't take more than a year or two to complete. In fact, Pavlov spent the last 34 years of his life determining the properties of these "psychic stimulations."

Unconditional Input–Output Connections

If you blow food powder into a dog's mouth, the animal will salivate reflexively. This response is determined by the dog's genetic blueprint. Pavlov called the food an **unconditional** or **unconditioned stimulus** (UCS) because the food's power to evoke salivation is not *conditional* upon the dog's having learned the response. The salivation *reaction* is also innately determined. Therefore, Pavlov named it the **unconditional** or **uncondi-tioned response** (UCR) since it too is not *conditional* upon learning.

We might diagram this innate input–output connection as follows:

(innate input–output connection)

UCS ————————————————————→UCR
(food)   (salivation)

Conditional Input–Output Connections

But one of the first things that Pavlov discovered in his research was this: If he sounded a musical tone just before he blew the food into the animal's mouth, the dog would soon come to salivate almost as much to the music alone as it would to the tone *plus* the food powder. Apparently the animal learned to "associate" the *sound* of the music with the *stimulus* of the food. Thus the tone takes on many of the psychological properties the food has. And thus every time the tone sounds, the dog *anticipates* being fed, and so it salivates to the tone just as it does to the food.

This sort of *conditioning* occurs in people as well as in dogs and all other animals. The smell of bacon frying in the morning is enough to set your mouths to watering, but only because you have learned to associate the *smell* of the meat frying with how it tastes a few minutes later when you eat it. And, in the same way, the clang of a dinner bell is enough to set your stomachs rumbling, because your stomach muscles have been *conditioned* to expect to go to work shortly after the bell sounds.

Technically speaking, this kind of learning involves an *association between stimulus inputs*. In the case of Pavlov's dog, the association is between a **neutral stimulus** (the tone) and an unconditioned stimulus (the food). We might diagram this associative learning as follows:

(learned input–input connection)

Neutral S ————————————————→UCS
(tone)   (food)

But the food powder "unconditionally" elicits the salivation *response* in the dog. So every time we pair the tone with the food, the dog salivates. Rather rapidly, then, the "neutral" tone takes on much the same ability to elicit salivation that the food has.

Pavlov called the tone a **conditional** or **conditioned stimulus** (CS), because its power to call forth the salivation response is *conditional* upon its being paired with the food powder. We can diagram the situation as follows:

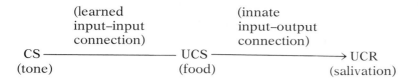

CS ——————————————— UCS ——————————————→ UCR
(tone)   (food)   (salivation)

Once the dog has learned the connection between the tone and the food, you can present just the tone alone—without giving the dog food—and the dog will salivate. In similar fashion, once you have learned to associate the aroma of bacon with its taste, the mere *smell* of the meat will set off your salivary glands even if you don't eat any.

Question: Is the odor of bacon more likely to cause you to salivate when you're hungry or when you've just finished a large meal?

The "Conditioned Response" But what can we call the salivary response when it is triggered off by the tone alone? Surely it is no longer an *un*conditioned response because there is no innate connection between a "neutral" musical tone and salivation. Pavlov named this *learned* reaction to the neutral stimulus a **conditional** or **conditioned response** (CR). *Conditioning* is the term Pavlov used to describe the process by which the previously "neutral" stimulus (CS) gains the power to elicit the conditioned response (CR).

Pavlov soon discovered that the unconditioned response (UCR) usually was much stronger than the conditioned response (CR). That is to say, the dog almost always salivated less to the tone than it did when given food.

Once the conditioning process has taken place, we can diagram the situation as follows:

(learned input–output connection)
CS ——————————————————————→ CR
(tone)   (partial salivation)

The type of training developed by Pavlov is called by many names: classical conditioning, reflex conditioning, Pavlovian conditioning, **respondent conditioning,** and stimulus–response (S–R) learning. Generally speaking, when psychologists use the term *conditioning*, they refer to some situation in which an input gains the power to elicit an output in a reflexive or mechanical fashion.

Factors Affecting Conditioning

During the many years that Pavlov studied the conditioning process, he made a number of interesting discoveries about the factors that affect this type of learning:

1. The more frequently the CS and the UCS are paired, the stronger the CR becomes. For example, the more often a tone is associated with food powder, the more drops of saliva the tone will elicit. And the more frequently the CS and UCS are paired, the better the animal will remember the learning later on.

2. Conditioning is fastest when the CS is presented *immediately* before the UCS. For example, the optimum time interval for conditioned salivation in the dog is about half a second. If the tone is presented too long *before* the food, or is presented *after* the food, little or no learning occurs. However, the optimum time interval does vary from animal to animal, from species to species, and from situation to situation.

3. Conditioned responses are *unlearned* just as easily as they are learned. Suppose you train a dog to salivate—that is, you establish a CS–CR

Conditional (conditioned) response. Abbreviated CR. Any reaction set off by a CS. A bright light (UCS) flashed in your eye causes your pupil to contract (UCR). If someone frequently rings a bell (CS) just before turning on the bright light (UCS), the sound of the bell (CS) would soon gain the power to make your pupil contract. Once this conditioning has taken place, the UCR (contraction) becomes a CR that can be elicited by the CS. Since pupil contraction can now be set off *either* by the CS or the UCS, the contractive response is *both* a CR and a UCR. In many cases, however, the CR looks slightly different from the UCR.

Respondent conditioning (re-SPOND-dent). Pavlovian conditioning is called by many names, including "classical conditioning," "reflex conditioning," and "stimulus-response conditioning." These terms are often used more or less interchangeably, although some psychologists attach slight differences to the various terms. See next chapter for comparison of respondent and "operant" conditioning.

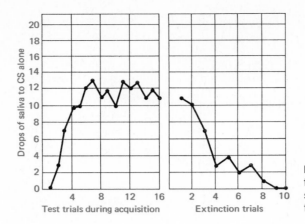

Fig. 15.2. The charts show first the acquisition of conditioned salivation in a trained dog, and then extinction.

connection in the animal between a tone and salivation. Now you present the dog with the tone *without* giving it the food. You would find that the animal salivates less and less on each trial. Finally, the response would be **extinguished** completely.

4. An "extinguished response" is not completely *forgotten* (see Fig. 15.2). Suppose you condition a dog, then extinguish the response. Then you pair the CS with the UCS for a second round of training trials. The dog will acquire the conditioned response much more quickly than it did the first time around. Apparently the original conditioning has left a trace or "neural groove" on the cortex that makes relearning easier.

5. The passage of time can act as a conditioning stimulus. When Pavlov fed his animals regularly each half-hour, they began to salivate a few seconds before the next feeding even though there were no *external stimuli*, such as rattle of dishes, to give them cues that it was almost time to eat.

6. Suppose you give a conditioned animal *extinction training*. That is, you sound the tone time and time again without giving the dog food. Eventually, the animal will stop salivating when the tone sounds, so the conditioning has apparently been *extinguished*. Now you let the dog sit in its cage for two weeks, then bring it back to the lab, hook it up in its harness, and again sound the tone. What will happen? As you might guess, the dog will have "forgotten" the extinction and it will again salivate. Psychologists call this **spontaneous recovery** of a previously extinguished response.

Question: Pavlov believed that the mere pairing of the CS and the UCS was sufficient for conditioning to occur—whether or not the subject wished to learn or found the experience rewarding. Look back over the past couple of pages. How many times have the terms "CS" and "conditioned stimulus" been paired? Are the two terms now associated in your mind? Were you conscious that you were learning? And the next time you watch television, look closely at the commercials. Do the advertisers seem to be using Pavlovian techniques to get you to like or remember their products?

Pavlov's Masochistic Dog

Pavlov believed that learning was always accompanied by the establishment of new neural connections in the brain—a position held by most psychologists today. Having made this initial point, Pavlov then moved into the field of mental health. He wondered why a few people, called **masochists,** seemed to enjoy or seek pain. Many psychologists believed that *masochism* was the result of some deep-seated "flaw" in the individual's personality. Pavlov suspected that this "love of painful inputs" might be the result of simple conditioning.

Extinguished (ex-TING-guished). To "extinguish" a response is to reduce the frequency of a learned response either by withdrawing the reward that was used during training, or by presenting the CS many times without the UCS. In fact, it is the "bond" or "connection" between the CS and the CR that is extinguished.

Spontaneous recovery. If you "extinguish" a CS-CR connection by presenting the CS without the UCS, the animal stops responding in a conditioned fashion. For example, suppose you had been trained to jerk your knee when a bell sounded. Now we ring the bell several times *without* hitting your tendon. Soon you will no longer jerk your knee when the bell rings. But if we wait a month and (catching you unaware) ring the bell, your knee might jerk slightly. This *recovery* of the original conditioning is "spontaneous" in that we didn't give you additional training after the extinction process had occurred.

Masochists (MASS-oh-kists). Masochism (MASS-oh-kiss-em) is a sexual deviation in which pleasure is derived from pain. The pain may be psychological or physical, and may be self-inflicted or inflicted by others. The term comes from the name of the Austrian novelist Leopold V. Sacher-Masoch, whose stories frequently featured scenes in which sexual pleasure was associated with painful stimulus inputs.

To settle the matter, Pavlov trained a dog to withstand extremely painful stimuli by using a "step-by-step" learning technique. First, Pavlov carefully marked off an area of skin on the dog's front leg. Then he stimulated this area with a weakly painful CS, and *immediately* gave the dog some food. The UCR of salivation appeared to *inhibit* or suppress any avoidance response the animal might have made to the tiny amount of pain.

Then, day after day, Pavlov carefully increased the intensity of the painful CS, each time pairing it with food that the dog eagerly anticipated. At no time did the animal respond as if it were being hurt. Indeed, the dog seemed more than willing to be put in the training harness and given the pain, since the pain soon became a conditioned signal that food would shortly be forthcoming.

Once the dog was fully trained, it would passively withstand incredible amounts of painful stimulation delivered to its front leg. However, if Pavlov applied the painful CS to any other part of the dog's body, the animal would instantly set up a great howl and attempt to escape from its training harness.

Pavlov concluded that when he touched the CS to the dog's front leg, the animal did not in fact *feel* any pain because all responses except salivation were suppressed by the strength of the pain–salivation neural connection. Apparently, in dogs, as well as in humans, "You can't do more than one thing at a time." And whatever response is *strongest* tends to suppress most other responses.

Pavlov's attempts to create a masochistic dog were successfully repeated by many other scientists, including psychologists in the United States. In some of these studies, the animals learned to approach an experimenter and "beg" to be stimulated painfully. Others acquired the habit of giving themselves painful stimulation in order to get food from an automatic dispenser. Even when not particularly hungry, these animals would often approach the experimental apparatus "of their own free will," cause the painful input to be delivered to their bodies, and then eat the food.

The parallel between these animals and those humans who seek out pain or humiliation in order to gain pleasure (often sexual) is rather remarkable. But as important as these experiments might have been to the discovery of a "cure" for masochism in humans, the animal work was regarded with considerable distaste by most other scientists.

Discrimination and Generalization

Perhaps the most interesting "mental health" experiment Pavlov conducted had to do with **discrimination training.** Pavlov began by showing a dog a drawing of a circle, then giving it food immediately. Very soon the dog became conditioned to salivate whenever a circle appeared before its eyes.

Pavlov then tested the animal by showing it drawings of figures such as an ellipse, a pentagon, a square, a rectangle, a triangle, and a star. He found that the salivary response *generalized* to stimulus inputs other than the original CS (the circle). As you might guess, this **generalization** followed a specific pattern—the more similar to a circle the other figure was, the more the animal salivated.

Pavlov then trained the dog to *discriminate* between the two stimuli by always giving the dog food when the circle appeared, but never giving it a reward when the ellipse appeared. Soon the dog came to salivate *only* when the circle was shown.

After Pavlov had established that the dog could discriminate between a circle and an ellipse, he tried to fool the animal. On subsequent trials, he presented the dog with ellipses that were closer and closer to being completely round. Eventually the animal's nervous system was strained to the breaking point, for the animal could not perceive the difference between the positive CS (the circle) and the negative CS (the ellipse).

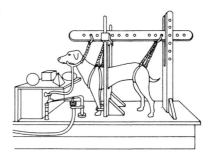

A dog in Pavlov's harness learns to discriminate between shapes.

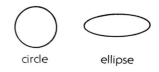

circle   ellipse

Pavlov's first experiments at the physiological department of the Soviet Military Medicine Academy.

Overcome by stress, the animal broke down, snapped at Pavlov and his assistants, barked loudly, urinated and defecated, and tried very hard to get out of the restraining harness. If a human being had displayed the same behavior patterns, we probably would say the person was **neurotic** or "unable to cope."

How different Pavlov's two "mental health" experiments were! In the first case, an animal learned to give a *normal* response to a very abnormal input. In the second study—even though it received no painful inputs at all—the dog gave an *abnormal* response to a very "normal" set of inputs.

These two studies convinced Pavlov that "mental illness" was learned and was mostly a matter of mixed-up brain signals. (Pavlov took a purely biological view toward the causes of mental illness. As we will see in later chapters, there are intra-psychic and environmental influences that are at least as important.)

Conditioning and Communism

From Pavlov's very limited view, all organisms were passive. They lived out their simple lives waiting for stimulus inputs to come along and elicit response outputs from them. Pavlov insisted that learning, if and when it occurred, was almost always an involuntary and mechanical process that involved building up a "neural connection" between an S and an R.

Like most S–R theorists, Pavlov believed that all forms of behavior—including what most people would call "thinking" and "feeling" and "problem-solving"—were almost totally under the control of stimulus events. He saw humans as being **plastic,** or infinitely changeable by the environment into which they were born. Given the proper social environment, a man or woman could be conditioned into being a happy and productive worker, or could be enslaved by circumstances.

When the Communists took over the Russian government in 1918, they found Pavlov's *mechanistic* view of human nature most sympathetic to their own. After all, his work suggested that the peasant–farmers, who then made up most of the Russian population, could rapidly be re-educated if only the proper S–R connections could be made in their brains. So the Communists kept Pavlov on as Director of the Institute at Leningrad and gave him funds to continue his "mental health" research.

Question: How might you explain "brainwashing" in terms of extinguishing one set of responses and acquiring another? Given the importance of environmental stimuli in the conditioning process, why should the "brainwashed" person be isolated during retraining?

Neurotic (new-ROT-tick). Abnormal or unusual behavior patterns are sometimes referred to as being "neurotic." A neurosis (new-ROW-sis) is a relatively mild form of mental disorder. As we will see in Chapter 24, however, psychologists do not agree on the causes and cures of neurotic behaviors. Although the term is widely used in psychology, it has recently fallen out of favor in psychiatry and is no longer an "accepted diagnosis" for any type of mental problem.

Plastic (PLASS-tick). From the Greek word meaning "formed" or "shaped." As used in psychology, the term means "changeable," or "capable of being shaped into new response patterns."

Conditioning Therapies

Mowrer and Bed-Wetting

O.H. Mowrer was one of the first US psychologists to use conditioning as a therapeutic technique. In 1938, Mowrer suggested a new type of "cure" for the age-old problem of **enuresis,** or bed-wetting.

The bladder is under the control of the autonomic nervous system. During toilet training, a child learns to bring its natural tendencies to urinate under voluntary control. To do so, the child must learn to pay attention to the **proprioceptive** signals or "feedback" coming from its bladder and to inhibit its urges to relieve itself except under certain conditions.

This sort of conditioning obviously involves *discrimination:* The child must learn to pay attention to some internal stimuli and to ignore others. The child must also determine which environmental stimuli, such as the sight of bathroom fixtures, are appropriate CS's for certain of its bodily responses. And the child must learn to maintain this voluntary control while it is asleep. The bed-wetting or enuretic child has learned but half the task. That is, the child has conscious control over its bladder only while it is awake.

Most of us have learned to listen to the signals that our bodies give us. Therefore, proprioceptive feedback from a full bladder is a CS that makes us respond by waking up and going to the bathroom. Mowrer believed that the enuretic child simply hadn't made this CS–CR connection. So he devised an apparatus to help train the child to gain control.

Mowrer put tiny electrical wires inside a thin cloth pad that could be placed under the bottom sheet on the child's bed (see Fig. 15.3). The wires were connected to a loud bell near the child's head. Whenever the child urinated while asleep, the urine "closed the electrical circuit" in the pad and set off the bell, waking the child up. Although the child received no shock, the "distress" of being rudely aroused in the middle of the night presumably might motivate the child to "connect" feedback from a full bladder with the response of waking up before an accident could occur. In fact Mowrer's device is an effective training tool for many children, but it fails miserably with many others.

Question: Why might Mowrer's device not work very well with a child who experienced no fear or anxiety when awakened by the bell? Or with a child whose parents fussed over it when it "had an accident," but ignored it when it "stayed dry all night."

Watson and Little Albert

Once an organism has been conditioned or *sensitized* to fear a given CS, the arousal response can often be elicited by any stimulus *similar* to the CS. In one of John B. Watson's most famous experiments, he and his wife (Rosalie Rayner) taught a child named Albert to become afraid of a gentle and placid white rat. At the beginning of the study, Albert was unafraid of the animal and played with it freely. While Albert was doing so one day, Watson deliberately frightened the boy by sounding a terrifying noise behind him. Albert was unpleasantly startled and began to cry. Thereafter, he avoided the rat and cried if it was brought close to him. (This sort of experimentation is now forbidden by the American Psychological Association's Code of Ethics.)

In Pavlovian terms, a bond or connection had been set up between the sight of the rat (CS) and the arousal of Albert's autonomic nervous system (CR). Once this S–R bond was fixed, the fear response could also be elicited by showing Albert any furry object.

Fears *generalize* to stimuli similar to the CS. Fear or anxiety also gener-

O.H. Mowrer.

Fig. 15.3. A conditioning cure for bedwetting. This device is sold by Sears.

Enuresis (en-your-EE-sis). A fancy name for bed-wetting.

Proprioceptive (pro-pree-oh-SEP-tive). Feedback messages from receptors in your muscles, glands, and internal organs that let you know what your body is doing are called "proprioceptive stimuli."

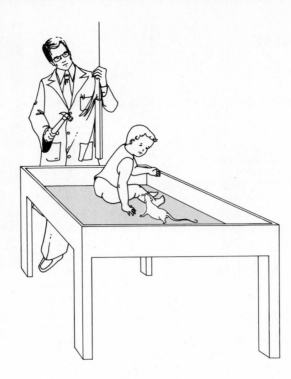

John B. Watson conditioned "Little Albert" to fear a rat by striking a metal gong loudly whenever the animal approached the boy.

alizes to any random or accidental stimulus cues that happen to be present when the conditioning or sensitization takes place. The burnt child not only dreads the fire, but also fears stoves, pots and pans, ovens, pictures of flames, and even stories about the great Chicago fire.

The Polygraph

Words are stimulus *inputs* as much as are bells or musical tones. If you were chased by a bull when you were young, you would probably still show some autonomic *arousal* if you were forced to enter a pen containing a pawing, snorting, long-horned Brahmin bull. But you might also show some slight autonomic arousal if you merely read the word "bull," saw a picture of one, or were asked to think about one.

We could measure your fear reaction by attaching you to a **polygraph,** often called a "lie-detector" (see Fig. 15.4). The polygraph would record your pulse, blood pressure, breathing rate, and the amount of perspiration secreted by the cells in the palms of your hands (or feet).

Polygraph (PAHL-ee-graff). *Poly* means "many." A polygraph is a machine that makes a graph of many different responses simultaneously. Sometimes called a "lie-detector," but it records emotional responses, not "lies."

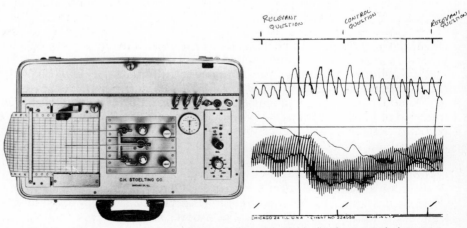

Fig. 15.4. A polygraph machine and record; the midpoint indicates a control question.

Fig. 15.5. A polygraph records a person's emotional responses to stimulus words.

As you know by now, arousal of your sympathetic nervous system would lead to an increase in sweating, an acceleration in heart rate, and a change in the way that you breathe. If we showed you an emotionally "neutral" stimulus, your polygraph record would remain calm and regular. If we then presented you with a picture of a large bull, or said the word aloud, the graph would note a sudden sharp *change* in your autonomic activity. We would then *assume* that you had experienced some emotion such as fear, anxiety, or guilt.

The polygraph is really an *emotion detector,* and not a "lie-detector." It is useful to police agents because suspected criminals often lie about their guilt and are afraid of being found out. For instance, suppose that someone has been murdered by being strangled with a silk scarf of an unusual color. Presumably only the murderer would recognize the scarf. The police might show this scarf to several suspects, all of whom might deny ever having seen the scarf before. But if one of the suspects showed a strong emotional reaction on the polygraph, the police would be justified in questioning this suspect further (see Fig. 15.5).

Polygraph recordings are often unreliable and hence are not admitted as evidence of guilt in a court of law. Some criminals feel no anxiety or guilt whatsoever concerning their crimes, and thus if they "lie" about what they have done, their polygraph records will suggest innocence rather than guilt. On the other hand, a person may show violent emotional reactions to a stimulus such as a colorful scarf without having committed any crime.

The polygraph is, however, a useful psychological tool. For example, one of the problems that psychotherapists often have is that patients will deny or *suppress* their true feelings. If the topic of sex arises during therapy, the patients may insist that they have no sexual problems or hang-ups, but polygraph records made during therapy might indicate that the word "sex" was indeed a CS for all kinds of autonomic arousal. A psychologist who monitored the patients' polygraph records continuously during treatment could easily determine what parts of their lives most needed working on.

Use of the machine might also give the psychologist an indication of when the patients were making progress in bringing their suppressed feelings to the surface and learning to handle them.

Counter-conditioning

Many forms of psychotherapy are based on *breaking* S–R bonds instead of establishing new ones. Once John B. Watson and his wife had demonstrated (in 1920) that a child could be conditioned to fear furry things, it was even more important to show that fear conditioning could be "cured" using the same techniques that caused it.

In 1924, another student of Watson's—Mary Cover Jones—did just that. She used a method now called **counter-conditioning,** which is based on the fact that you can't give two incompatible responses to the same CS. Suppose that, at some time in the future, your own two-year-old son accidentally became conditioned to fear small furry animals. You might try

Counter-conditioning. A psycho-therapeutic technique based on extinguishing inappropriate habits or breaking S-R (stimulus-response) bonds. If as a child you were frightened the first few times you saw a kitten, you might develop a lifelong fear of cats. The sight of a cat would become a CS that elicited a CR—such as fear, anxiety, or avoidance. This early conditioning can sometimes be *countered* by pairing a weak form of the CS with a strongly pleasant UCS such as food.

to cure the boy the way that Mary Cover Jones did—by trying to attach some response other than "fear" to the conditioning stimulus.

The sight of a white rat would presumably upset your son—but the sight of food when he was hungry surely would make him happy and eager to eat. If you could somehow attach the "rat" stimulus to the "happy" response, your child would obviously have been *counter-conditioned* to like the rat rather than fear it.

You might begin the counter-conditioning procedure by bringing a white rat into the same room with your son while you were feeding him. At first, you would want to keep the animal so far away from your son that he could barely notice it out of the corner of his eye. Since the animal wouldn't be close enough to bother him, he probably would keep right on eating. Then, step by step, you might bring the rat closer.

Since your son could not cry and eat at the same time, and since you'd never bring the rat close enough at any one time to elicit the crying reaction, the CS–CR fear response would gradually *extinguish*, while the strength of the CS–CR "pleasure of eating" bond was being built up. Counter-conditioning almost always involves breaking an inappropriate S-R bond by attaching the old "S" to a new and more appropriate "R." When Mary Cover Jones followed this procedure (actually using a white rabbit rather than a rat), she found that children soon learned to play with animals that had previously terrified them.

The Case of Anne M.

In a sense, Watson created a **phobia** about rats in little Albert. *Phobias* are intense, irrational fears about people, places, things, or situations. Usually these fears are so strong that the person with the phobia cannot control her or his reactions even when the person clearly realizes that the terror is illogical and unreasonable. These **morbid dreads** are often created almost overnight, from a single emotion-charged encounter with the dreaded object—or perhaps from a continuing series of highly unpleasant interactions.

As an example of how phobias can be learned, and then unlearned, consider the case of Anne M., a middle-aged woman living near Cleveland. In her early 40's, she was not married and lived with her mother, upon whom she was very dependent emotionally. One day the two women got into a quarrel at their home. At the end of the argument, the mother ran out into the street. Anne followed her mother to the door, just in time to see the older woman get hit and killed by a passing car.

As a consequence of witnessing the death of her beloved mother—and because she felt partially responsible—Anne developed a phobia about moving vehicles. She retreated to the security of the house and refused to come out. She closed the curtains on all the windows, for even the sight of an automobile or truck was enough to throw Anne into a violent panic reaction. Finally, her withdrawal from the rest of the world became so severe that she had to be hospitalized in a nearby mental institution.

Once in the hospital, Anne refused to leave. Her therapists tried to explore her guilt feelings and her anxieties about death. But even after years of treatment, Anne M. still panicked whenever she looked out of the hospital window and saw an automobile passing on the road.

Desensitization Therapy At this point, two psychologists then at The University of Michigan—David Himle and Clayton Shorkey—attempted a form of counter-conditioning called **desensitization therapy.**

In their first talks with Anne M., Himle and Shorkey drew up a **hierarchy of fears**—that is, a list of disturbing *stimuli* arranged in rank order from the least to the most frightening (see Fig. 15.6). The act of actually riding in an automobile was the most frightening thing Anne could think of. Getting into a parked automobile was somewhat less disturbing, so sitting in a car ranked lower on the hierarchy than did riding. Walking past a car was even

Phobia (FOE-bee-uh). From the Greek word for "fear." A phobia is a strong and often unusual fear of something.

Morbid dreads (MORE-bid). Gloomy or unhealthy feelings or fears. "Morbid" comes from the Latin and Greek words meaning "diseased."

Desensitization therapy (DEE-sen-suh-tie-ZAY-shun). When you acquire a conditioned fear of cats, you have become *sensitized* to cats and thus become anxious or afraid each time you see one. Desensitization therapy, as developed by Joseph Wolpe (WOHL-pee), involves training you to relax whenever you see a cat. Once this form of counter-conditioning is complete, your fear of cats will have been "desensitized."

Hierarchy of fears (HIGHER-ark-key). To make up a hierarchy is to list things (or people) in order of their importance. A hierarchy of fears, as used in desensitization therapy, is a list of dreaded stimuli running from the most feared to the least feared. Treatment usually begins by training the client to relax in the presence of the stimulus lowest on the hierarchy of fears. Once that stimulus has been desensitized, the next-highest stimulus on the hierarchy is treated in the same way.

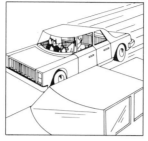

Fig. 15.6. Hierarchy of fears used in desensitization therapy for reduction of fear of automobiles.

less threatening, but was still more likely to induce panic than merely seeing a car or truck through a window. Merely imagining what a car looked like evoked very little fear, so this item was at the bottom of the hierarchy.

When Himle and Shorkey began treating Anne M., they first got her to relax as much as possible. Once she was quite comfortable, they asked her to imagine seeing a car out of the window. She soon got to the point where she could tolerate seeing a car "in her mind's eye" without feeling any anxiety at all. Then they asked Anne M. to look out a window briefly, and got her to relax again. Soon Anne M. was able to look at cars out the window whenever she pleased.

At this point in her treatment, Anne M. had been conditioned to handle the lowest item on her fear hierarchy. For the stimulus of "seeing a car through the window" now elicited the conditioned response of *relaxation* rather than the conditioned response of *panic*.

Next, Himle and Shorkey asked her to imagine walking out the front door of the building and approaching a car. Once she could manage this imagery, they turned thought into action and got her to leave the hospital building and actually touch a parked automobile outside. When she was relaxed enough to handle this real-life problem, they encouraged her to get inside the car and take a short ride.

To help Anne M. imagine what each step in her desensitization would be like, Himle and Shorkey built a scale model of the hospital and its grounds. The model included all the streets and highways in that area. Anne learned to move toy cars around the streets without becoming fearful. Once she had "thought through" a given journey using the toy cars, she was able to make the same brief trip in a real automobile.

At the end of just 10 training sessions, Anne M. was driven out of the hospital grounds onto a nearby highway on a short excursion—a trip that caused her little or no discomfort. Thereafter, with no further therapy, Anne M. began taking part in more of the social activities on the ward, including short visits to points of interest near the hospital. Once she saw that she could tolerate these brief trips, she spontaneously began visiting friends who lived in nearby towns.

The final test of Anne's desensitization came when she was invited to spend a few days with some relatives who lived several hundred miles away. Anne had to make the trip by bus. When she felt she was relaxed enough to handle this experience—which might well have rated right at the top of her original hierarchy of fears—she packed her bag and caught the bus.

Ironically, the vehicle broke down while on the expressway and Anne and the rest of the passengers had to sit by the side of the road for more than an hour while traffic buzzed furiously past them. However, Anne handled the situation without any panic and reached her destination safely. Thanks to the help of Drs. Himle and Shorkey—and the staff at the hospital—Anne M. no longer had a phobic reaction to moving vehicles.

Curing a "Blood Phobia" S.H. Kraines has reported a somewhat simpler form of desensitization therapy involving a young medical student who feared the sight of blood. This young man, whom Kraines calls J.M., seriously considered giving up the study of medicine because each time the student walked into an operating room, he keeled over in a dead faint.

Kraines first attempted to determine the causes for this response and tried to change the boy's attitude toward medicine—but he also tried a step-by-step deconditioning treatment. J.M. was told to walk into the operating chamber during an operation and then immediately to walk out. On the second day J.M. went into the room, counted five, and then walked out. On the third day J.M. was told to stay a full minute before leaving. On subsequent days, J.M. stayed longer and longer.

Two weeks later, when J.M. was supposed to stay but 10 minutes, he got so interested in the operation that he just stayed on until it was completed. Thereafter, Kraines reports, J.M. had no trouble at all—even when called on to assist in operations. His "blood phobia" appeared to be gone for good.

Question: Some college students become so aroused and frightened when forced to take an examination that they become violently ill. How might desensitization therapy be used to help them?

Desensitization: Pro and Con

Phobic reactions usually involve some form of *sensitization* to stimuli that elicit autonomic arousal and muscular tension. A major part of *de*sensitization therapy, therefore, consists of teaching the patient to relax voluntarily—the theory being that you can't very well be tense or aroused at the same time that you are physically limp as a wet rag.

By alternately tensing and then relaxing your muscles, you can acquire the ability to relax at your own verbal or mental command. Once you have mastered this skill, you can *order* the muscles in your body to relax even when you are faced with a mildly disturbing situation, such as the least-threatening stimulus on a fear hierarchy, if you happen to suffer from a phobia.

Dr. Joseph Wolpe, now at Temple University in Philadelphia, is usually given credit for having popularized desensitization training. Wolpe believes that the secret of its success comes from never *over*-stimulating the patient or letting the phobic reaction get so strong that it cannot be counteracted by voluntary muscular relaxation (see Fig. 15.7). Wolpe and his colleagues achieve this goal by always starting with the least-feared item on the hierarchy and working up the scale. They also stop treatment momentarily whenever the client shows the slightest sign of distress.

Cognitive and attitudinal changes often occur during desensitization training. That is, the patient often reports perceiving the once-feared situation in a new and less frightening light. Wolpe and many others believe that these perceptual changes are the *result* of learning to handle disturbing stimuli in a relaxed fashion—that the lack of muscular tension leads to or induces the change in the patient's attitudes.

Other therapists insist that Wolpe has put the cart before the horse, that cognitive changes occur *first* and thereby allow the patient to relax in the presence of the dreaded stimulus. As evidence, these critics cite research

Joseph Wolpe.

Cognitive (COG-nuh-tive). From the Latin word meaning "to think." Generally speaking, any "mental process" is likely to be a "cognitive process."

Fig. 15.7. A patient and Dr. Joseph Wolpe during systematic desensitization. Note that the patient's index finger is raised to indicate that she is visualizing the scene required by the therapist.

suggesting that one need not start at the bottom of the fear hierarchy and work up gradually to the most disturbing item. Rather, one can pick items at random and expose the patient to them—as long as the patient doesn't become too disturbed by the procedure. Many studies show that purely *mental* relaxation may be as powerful in helping to cure phobias as is *muscular* relaxation.

Psycho-analytically oriented therapists carry the cognitive argument even further. While admitting that desensitization therapy can be effective with simple phobic reactions, psycho-analysts believe that many phobias represent a person's attempts to *suppress* or defend against inappropriate or threatening impulses.

For instance, a woman who cannot make a normal **heterosexual** adjustment might become phobic about, or *sensitized* to, pointed objects because they symbolize the male sexual organ to her. Or a young man who hates his parents and wants to kill them might develop a phobia about guns and knives. His fear then serves to keep him away from weapons he might use if his hatred ever got out of control. Unfortunately, the psycho-analysts note, his phobia also serves to keep him from facing what may be a basic flaw or weakness in his personality.

The psycho-analytic view is that the phobia is simply a **symptom** of an underlying personality problem that cannot be helped or alleviated merely by curing the *symptomatic behavior.* The expectation is that if one merely cures the symptom—without first changing the personality structure that gave rise to the phobic reaction—other and perhaps more devastating symptoms are bound to take its place. (As we will see in Chapter 25, there is not much scientific evidence to support this fear of "symptom substitution.")

Wolpe's response to these criticisms is twofold. To begin with, he believes that the symptom is usually what really bothers the patient. A man may continue to have a morbid dread of guns and knives long after his parents are dead and buried. Talking through his hatred for the long-gone parents may give the man considerable insight into his problems, but research suggests it usually does very little to help overcome phobias.

In the second place, Wolpe holds that what the analysts call "the underlying problem" is typically an attitude or perception that was *learned* by the same laws of conditioning as was the phobic reaction. Men aren't born with an instinctive hatred of their parents. It takes years of careful training—usually on the part of the parents themselves—to achieve that. If a therapist feels that a patient's perceptions of his or her parents should be changed, conditioning techniques offer a fast and reliable methodology for doing so.

Heterosexual (HETT-er-oh-sex-you-al). The Latin and Greek words "hetero" mean "different." Heterosexual behavior involves males and females. As opposed to *homosexual* behavior, which involves just males, or just females.

Symptom (SIMM-tum). From the Latin word meaning "sign." Fever can be a symptom of an underlying cause (disease) called "influenza," but the fever is *not* the disease itself. Many psychologists believe that abnormal behavior patterns are symptomatic (simm-toe-MATT-tick) of some underlying mental disorder or illness. Thus "removing the symptom" would no more "cure the disease" than would giving you aspirin "cure" your influenza. Other psychologists believe that symptomatic behaviors are *learned,* and hence are not "caused" by some deep psychological problem. These psychologists believe that the abnormal behaviors are *themselves* the real problem, thus "removing the symptoms" does indeed bring about a "cure." In truth, as we will see in Chapter 24, we really know very little about "curing underlying psychological problems," so the least we can do for people is to help them learn better ways of coping with their difficulties.

Which Changes First, Attitudes or Behaviors?

Must you always change your attitudes first, if you want to change your behavior outputs? Or do most attitudinal changes result from a change in your behavior?

In retrospect, Wolpe and the psycho-analysts appear to be caught up in yet another battle over the "mind–body" problem we discussed in earlier chapters. And the truth seems to be that attitudes and behaviors change more or less simultaneously. It is difficult, if not impossible, to prove that a change in one always *causes* a change in the other.

Wolpe is a physician who places much faith in biological processes and little faith in what goes on inside the mind. The cognitive psychologists are convinced that intra-psychic changes are the ones to aim for, and thus neglect both biological and social inputs. The psycho-analysts do a fine job of uncovering suppressed emotions, but don't always know how to help patients alter their emotional *outputs* or responses efficiently. None of the groups looks at the *whole* patient—from a biological, intra-psychic, *and* a social/behavioral point of view.

In fact, there really is little sense in fighting over which form of therapy is best, since all types of treatment have their uses. Indeed, it is likely that psycho-analysts unconsciously make use of some forms of conditioning while treating their patients, although the psycho-analysts may not realize that they are doing so. Likewise, Wolpe and other behavioral therapists have surely benefited from psycho-analytic and humanistic insights—although these researchers may refuse to acknowledge their debts.

Desensitization, when it is effective, works so quickly that it might uniformly be tried as a kind of "psychic first aid" with most phobic patients. If desensitization helps the patient, all well and good. But should one always stop with "first aid" no matter how effectively it removes the phobic symptoms? Shouldn't the patient also have the opportunity of gaining insight into her or his past experiences, or of working toward further inter-personal growth and self-actualization—if this is what the patient honestly desires? And what does one do in those cases where desensitization simply doesn't solve the patient's problems?

Sometimes, in the heat of defending our theoretical positions, we all lose sight of the prime goal—namely, to get the patient back to normal as quickly and as surely as possible. And to do that, we surely must be able to treat *all* the problems the patient has, whether they be biological, psychological, or social. Any form of therapy that helps us achieve our prime goal of treating the *whole patient* is bound to find eventual acceptance no matter how revolutionary it may seem when first introduced.

SUMMARY

1. Psychologists often use the term **conditioning** to mean **learning.** If an organism has been conditioned to respond in a new way to a **stimulus,** then a new **stimulus-response (input-output) connection** or **bond** has been established. The organism has now been **conditioned** to react in a different way than it did previously.

2. All learning or conditioning is built on—or is an adaption of—**innately determined input—output (stimulus-response) connections.**

3. **Instinctive reactions,** such as the knee-jerk, are called **unconditioned responses** because they are present at birth or are specified by the organism's **genetic blueprint.** The stimulus input of striking the **patellar tendon** innately calls forth a knee-jerk. Therefore, the knee-jerk is the output of an **unconditioned stimulus-response** connection in the nervous system.

4. Almost all unconditioned responses can be modified by experi-

ence. That is, the response output can be connected with a new or **conditional stimulus.**

5. Conditioning occurs when a previously **neutral stimulus** input—such as a muscle tone—is paired several times with the unconditioned stimulus (a blow to the patellar tendon). Eventually the tone gains many of the psychological properties of the unconditioned stimulus (UCS). That is, the tone becomes a **conditional (conditioned) stimulus (CS)** that can **elicit** the knee-jerk just about as reliably as can striking the tendon (the UCS).

6. The tone is called a conditioned stimulus because its power to elicit the knee jerk is **conditional** upon the tone's being **paired** several times with the unconditioned stimulus.

7. Once this learning has occurred, the knee-jerk given in response to the conditioned tone is called a **conditioned response (CR).** Usually the CR is slightly different in one or more ways from the unconditioned knee-jerk, which is called the **unconditioned response (UCR).**

8. Conditioning is sometimes referred to as **strengthening S-R** or **stimulus-response bonds.** The stronger the bond, the more likely it is that the conditioned stimulus will elicit the desired conditioned response.

9. The conditioned response was first reported by the US psychologist E.B. Twitmyer. However, credit for its discovery is usually given to the noted Russian physiologist, Ivan Pavlov.

10. The more frequently the CS and the UCS are paired, the stronger the **S-R bond** becomes.

11. Conditioning proceeds fastest when the CS is presented immediately before the UCS.

12. Conditioned responses are **unlearned** just as easily as they are learned.

13. Unlearning proceeds fastest when the CS is presented several times without being followed by the UCS. Once the S-R bond is broken, the response is said to be **extinguished.**

14. An extinguished response is not totally forgotten. If the CS is again paired with the UCS, **relearning** usually takes much less time than did the original learning. Furthermore, extinguished responses often show **spontaneous recovery** after some time has passed.

15. **Internal stimuli** (such as feedback from the muscles) can seve as a CS just as well as can bells or musical tones. The passage of time can also serve as a conditional stimulus.

16. If an animal is trained to respond to an orange light, this response may **generalize** to other similar stimuli, such as a red or yellow light. However, with the proper training, the animal can usually learn to **discriminate** among similar stimuli and give different responses to each.

17. If this discrimination becomes too difficult, the animal may show such **neurotic** responses as biting, barking, and defecation.

18. Both humans and lower animals react to the stress of conflict by acquiring inappropriate or **unadaptive behavior patterns.**

19. Many psychologists believe that most human **phobic reactions** are conditioned. If a child is frightened the first time it sees a horse, it may become conditioned to fear horses all its life.

20. Conditioned or learned fears or **phobias** may be **desensitized** or extinguished through **counter-conditioning procedures** that involve pairing the feared stimulus with something pleasant. Usually this procedure involves making a **hierarchy of fears** ranging from the least feared to the most feared. The patient learns to relax in the presence of the stimuli low on the hierarchy of fears first, then **step-by-step** moves up the hierarchy.

21. Although **desensitization** (counter-conditioning) has enjoyed considerable success with many types of anxious patients, some psychologists believe that the technique merely removes the **symptom** and does not cure the **underlying intra-psychic cause** of fear.

22. Some psychologists believe that attitudinal or **intra-psychic changes** occur first, and that behaviors change as a consequence. Therefore, therapy should be aimed primarily at giving patients **insight.** Other psychologists believe that behavior changes first, therefore, therapy should be aimed more at changing actions than attitudes.

23. In truth, attitudes and behaviors seem to be closely linked, and a change in either is likely to cause a change in the other.

24. Perhaps the best form of therapy is one that treats *all* of the patient's problems, whether the problems be biological, psychological, or social.

(Continued from page 371.)

"Has the desensitization program helped you any?" Dr. Turner asked Hans Larsen, during one of his visits to her office.

The blond man grinned. "Well, maybe you really ought to ask my wife. After all, she's the one who whipped me into coming to see you."

Dr. Turner clucked her tongue. "I thought the problem was that your wife *wouldn't* whip you."

"Just kidding around," the man said. "Actually, it's going pretty well even without the whips." He paused for a moment, then a crimson blush spread over his pale face. "Except for the other night."

"Oh," replied the woman. "What happened the other night?"

"Nothing happened," Larsen said. "That was the trouble."

Dr. Turner nodded sympathetically. "Why don't you tell me about it, and then we'll pick up where we left off on the hierarchy."

Larsen sighed. "Let me relax a minute first." He tensed various parts of his body, then let them go limp. "Still feels good to be able to do that. But it just didn't work the other evening."

"What was the situation?" Dr. Turner asked. "Tell me what you were doing, what your wife was doing, and how you responded."

"She was lying in bed, watching television, eating some candy. Chocolates, I think. Something she picked up at the grocery that day." Larsen stopped. "Funny, suddenly I'm tense all over."

The woman smiled warmly. "Relax for a moment. Completely relax. Okay?"

"Okay," said the man.

"Now, shut your eyes and listen to your body while I talk. The moment that you feel any tension occur, lift your right hand. Understand?"

"I understand," said the man.

"I want you to imagine your bedroom," the psychologist said. "Bring it into focus in your mind's eye. Can you do that?"

"Easily," said the man.

"Look at the chairs, and the dresser. Any tension?"

The man shook his head.

"Now look at the bed. Any tension yet?"

"Maybe a tiny bit. Nothing, really."

Dr. Turner nodded. "That's progress. A month ago, you felt tension just thinking about the bed. Okay, now imagine your wife lying in bed asleep." She watched Larsen's right hand carefully. When he didn't move it, she continued. "Good, no tension yet. Now imagine your wife awake, looking at you as you come in from the bathroom."

Again the psychologist paused, then continued to talk when Larsen's right hand remained quiet. "You're really doing fine. Just relax again, for a second or two, and then we'll go on. Now, when we hit on something deeply buried inside your mind, you'll get a conditioned tension response. So listen to your body carefully."

Larsen smiled. "Nothing yet."

"Okay, on we go. Your wife is lying in bed, but now she's turned on the TV and is watching some program. Is that unusual?"

"Happens all the time, although I can usually give her a reason to turn it off—if I really want to."

Dr. Turner grinned. "Right on. But that's a different kind of tension, so you just relax now. Keep your eyes closed, and imagine your wife watching the TV. Just as you walk into the bedroom and start to approach her, she reaches into a box of chocolates . . ."

"Stop," Larsen said. "That did it. A little bit, anyhow."

"Chocolates," said the woman. "Why does that bother you? Any ideas?"

Larsen shook his head. "Haven't the foggiest." He sighed. "Oh, well, the tension seems to be gone now anyhow. Maybe it was a passing fancy."

"I doubt it," Dr. Turner said. "Tell me more about what happened the other night. Did your wife offer you some of the chocolates?"

Larsen grunted. "I don't like candy much, particularly gooey types."

"Well, what happened after you saw your wife eating the candy?"

"Hum," said the man, trying to remember. "You know, we talked a bit, kidded around a bit. She was smoking a cigarette, but when I sat down on the bed, she went to put it out, and knocked the ashtray over . . ."

Dr. Turner leaned forward. "Suddenly you're sweating."

"The tension started just then," the man said.

"Relax. Just go limp, really limp."

Hans Larsen complied. When he was comfortable, he sighed deeply.

"Stop me if the tension starts again," Dr. Turner said. "Now, there seem to be four stimuli that, put together, cause the tension. You just stay as relaxed as you can while I name them. First, your wife in bed. Second, she's watching television. Third, she's eating chocolates. And fourth, she knocks over the ashtray."

"Stop," Larsen said. "There it goes again."

"Well," said Dr. Turner. "It seemed to be the ashtray that you really reacted too. Now, I want you to relax deeply again. Go deep down inside your mind, and look for something about an ashtray. Did you ever knock one over?"

Larsen shook his head. "I don't smoke, and never have."

Dr. Turner continued. "Well, did you ever see someone knock one over? Your mother, perhaps, when you were a small child."

"Stop," Larsen said. "I feel tense again. Not much, but some."

"Just relax. Be calm," the woman said. And when the man sighed, she went on. "Okay, the ashtray is the clue. Did your mother smoke?"

Larsen shook his head. "No, but my father did." He stopped. "Oh, my, I'm tense again."

"Relax, relax as deeply as you can," the psychologist said. "We're getting close now. I want you to push your memory as hard as you can. I want you to think of a time when you and your mother and your father were together, and your mother was eating chocolates and watching television."

Hans Larsen groaned loudly. "Oh, my God, it's all coming back to me now."

"Good, good," said Dr. Turner. "Just go limp, really limp, and then tell me what you remember. If you get too tense, just stop and relax, and don't worry about it."

"Incredible," said the man. "I completely forgot about that time. I was nine or ten, I guess. It was a cold winter night, I remember that particularly. We must have still been living in Minnesota. Momma was watching television. She loved the tube, said it was her only friend." He stopped for a long time. "Funny, I guess she meant that she and my father didn't get along too well. Never thought about it that way before. You know, maybe they had troubles like my wife and me . . ."

"You're tensing up again," Dr. Turner said. "Just relax again."

Larsen smiled. "I guess I can think about things like that now. Anyhow, she made me stand in the corner in the bedroom, while she watched the tube." He blushed. "I guess I had been bad, or something. I remember she was always making me stand in the corner for one reason or another. Anyhow, this particular night, she was eating chocolates and watching the tube, and I really had to . . . to . . ."

"Urinate?" asked the psychologist.

"Yeah," the man said in an embarrassed tone of voice. "So I was squirming a bit, you know, trying to hold it back, and she got very upset because I was . . ."

"Touching your genitals?"

Larsen nodded. "Yeah, that's right. I guess most kids do that, don't they, when they have to urinate."

Dr. Turner nodded her agreement. "They certainly do. Most natural thing in the world." She paused to think, then continued. "Now, I want to ask you a question, but I want you to relax deeply first. Okay?"

"Okay, I'm relaxed."

"Did your mother threaten to whip you when you touched your genitals?"

Larsen groaned again. "Oh, lordy, yes. She did that all the time when I touched myself!"

"Relax," commanded the woman. "It's all right. Now, tell me what happened next."

Larsen thought a moment. "This is getting pretty painful, you know."

"I know. We can stop now if you like, and go on some other time."

Larsen shook his head. "No, let's do it now. I'm beginning to understand some things. Let me relax again first." He made a deliberate effort to get his muscles to let go. "Okay, I was standing in the corner, squirming around and touching myself, and my mother was watching the tube and eating chocolates and threatening to whip me if I didn't behave. Then my father came into the room, and . . ."

"You're tensing again."

"Not much really," the man said. "I can handle it. Anyway, my father came into the room, and I guess they must have had an argument. Now that I think about it, they must have had lots of arguments. But I think this one must have been a lulu. Scared the hell out of me . . ."

"Very understandable . . ." said the woman, soothingly.

"Yeah, well, I remember he called her a fat slob, and she said, she said . . ."

"Relax," the woman said. "Take it easy."

Larsen nodded. "She said all he wanted to do was to, you know, make love."

Dr. Turner nodded.

"And they started calling each other dirty names, and shouting at each other, and my father got pretty mad, I guess. He probably had been drinking a little, if you know what I mean."

"I know," said Dr. Turner.

Larsen sighed. "Anyhow, she said something about how he wasn't good enough for her, that he didn't deserve her, and he got pretty mad, and . . ."

Dr. Turner leaned forward. "Relax, Hans. You're very close to the heart of the problem now."

"He must have screamed at her, or something. I remember I got really scared and tried to get away—to the bathroom, I guess. I can see him. He was a big man, you know, and pretty strong. He screamed at her and rushed toward her and I tried to get away." Larsen stopped. "There's something else, though, something I can't recall . . ."

"Are you fairly relaxed?" Dr. Turner asked.

"Yeah," said Larsen. "I guess so. Why?"

Dr. Turner smiled. "When your father rushed toward your mother, what did she do?"

"Oh, my God," the man said. "Of course! She threw the ashtray at him, but she missed, and . . . and . . ."

The woman nodded. "I know, it hit you instead, didn't it?"

"That hurts," the man said softly. "That hurts like hell."

"Of course it hurt," Dr. Turner said. "And it would have gone right on

hurting all the rest of your life if you hadn't dredged it up and faced it squarely. I think you're doing beautifully."

Larsen frowned. "But I still don't see the connection, really. So my mother hit me with an ashtray. So what?"

Dr. Turner sighed. "You've got the wrong connection, I suspect. See if you can remember what happened after the ashtray hit you."

Larsen suddenly gasped for air. "Oh, my, that did it. That really did it. I had forgotten that part entirely."

"Relax as best you can, and tell me about it," she said.

"Okay. I remember I screamed, and they stopped arguing. My mother rushed over to me and grabbed me up and started hugging me. She kissed me and hugged me to her breast and said she didn't mean it. She said she'd make it up to me." Larsen stopped. "Oh, my," he said a moment later.

Dr. Turner nodded again. "Yes, I think you see the connection I was referring to. You got afraid and very tense, then you got hurt, and that stopped the argument and the fear. And then your mother hugged you and kissed you. One-trial conditioning, I'd say."

"Oh, my," said the man.

The woman sighed deeply. "I think we've done enough for today. We can put the scene into the hierarchy the next time you're here. Shouldn't take too long to desensitize you to the whole thing. Okay?"

Larsen smiled. "Okay. But in the meantime, I'm going home and break every ashtray in the house. And throw out all the chocolates."

"And the whips?"

"Yeah. Those too. And then I'm going to kiss my wife, and . . ."

Dr. Turner grinned. "And?"

Larsen grinned back at Dr. Turner. "And then I'm going to make it up to her in the best way I know how."

"No sweat," said the woman.

"No pain," said the man.

Recommended Readings

Lazarus, A.A. *Multi-Modal Behavior Therapy* (New York: Springer, 1976).

Lazarus, A.A. "Has Behavior Therapy Outlived its Usefulness?" *American Psychologist,* 32, 1977, 550–554.

Pavlov, Ivan. *Conditioned Reflexes* (Oxford: Clarendon Press, 1927).

Wolpe, J., and A.A. Lazarus. *Behavior Therapy Techniques* (London: Pergamon Press, 1966).

Cognitive Maps and Operant Conditioning

Did You Know That. . . .

Most of the teaching techniques used in US classrooms are derived from laboratory experiments with animals?

E.L. Thorndike's law of effect states that S-R connections are strengthened by rewards?

Pavlov was very annoyed with Thorndike for insisting that reward was important to learning?

Chimpanzees and even rats seem to have the same sort of insight (or "Ah ha!") experiences during learning as do humans?

If you use an effective educational technology, you can teach a pigeon to bowl in a couple of hours or so?

B.F. Skinner believes that rewards increase the probability that an organism will repeat the response it has just made?

Most complex behaviors appear to be sequences of simple responses that have been "chained" together?

The speed with which an organism responds is frequently dependent on the schedule of reinforcement the animal receives?

Most of the animals you see perform on TV and in shows are trained using techniques developed by Skinner and his associates?

"That'll Learn You!"

I am writing this because I presume He wants me to. Otherwise He would not have left paper and pencil handy for me to use. And I put the word "He" in capitals because it seems the only thing to do. If I am dead and in hell, then this is only proper. However, if I am merely a captive somewhere, a little flattery won't hurt matters.

As I think about it, I am impressed most of all by the suddenness of the whole thing. At one moment I was out walking in the woods near my home. The next thing I knew, here I was in a small, bare room, naked as a jaybird, with only my good sense to stand between me and insanity. When the "change" was made—whatever the change was—I was not aware of even a momentary flicker between walking in the woods and being here in this room. He must have a technology available to Him that is very impressive indeed!

As I recall, I was strolling along, worrying about how to teach my introductory psychology class some of the more technical points of

Learning Theory when the "change" came. How far away life at the University seems at the moment! I must be forgiven if now I am much more concerned about where I am and how to get out of here than about how undergraduates can be cajoled into understanding Pavlov or Skinner.

Problem #1: Where am I? For an answer, I can only describe this room. It is about 20 feet square, some twelve feet high, with no windows, but with what might be a door in the middle of one of the walls. Everything is of a uniform gray color, and the walls and ceiling shine with a soft white light. The walls seem made of metal, since they are cool to the touch. The floor is spongy, with a "tingly" feel to it suggesting that it may be in constant vibration.

The only furniture in the room consists of a table and chair. They are not quite that, but they can be made to serve this purpose. On the table I found the paper and the pencil. No, let me correct myself. What I call paper is a good deal rougher and thicker than what I am used to, and what I call a pencil is a thin round stick of graphite which I have sharpened by rubbing one end of it on the table.

I wish I knew what He had done with my clothes. The suit was an old one, but I am worried about my watch. It was one of those fancy digital things, and quite expensive.

The problem still remains, however. Where in the hell am I—if not hell itself!

Problem #2 is a knottier one—why am I here? I have the usual quota of enemies, but even the Dean isn't powerful enough to arrange for something like this. And I surely am not rich enough to be a kidnap victim. So I am left as baffled as before.

Where am I, and why? And who is He?

· · · · ·

There is no sense in trying to keep track of time. This room is little more than a sensory deprivation chamber, and I haven't the foggiest notion of what hour or even what day it is. Well, it can't be that important. If He wasn't bright enough to leave me my watch, He can't complain that I don't keep accurate records.

Or is that the problem I'm supposed to solve?

· · · · ·

Nothing much has happened. I have slept, been fed and watered, and have emptied my bladder and bowels. The food was waiting on the table when I awoke last time. I must say that He has little of the gourmet in him. Protein balls are not my idea of a royal feast. However, they will serve to keep body and soul together (presuming, of course, that they *are* together at the moment).

But I must object to my source of liquid refreshment. The meal made me very thirsty, and I was in the process of cursing Him and everybody else when I noticed a small nipple that had appeared in the wall while I was asleep. At first I thought that I had fallen into a Freudian fantasy. Experimentation convinced me, however, that the nipple is real and that it is my present source of water. If I suck on the thing, it delivers a slightly cool and somewhat sweetish flow of liquid.

But really, it's a most undignified procedure. It's bad enough to have to sit around all day in my birthday suit. But for a full professor to have to stand on his tip-toes and suck on an artificial nipple is asking a bit too much. I'd complain to the Management if only I knew to whom I should complain!

Following my meal, the call to nature became a little too strong to ignore. Now, I was adequately toilet-trained with indoor plumbing, and the absence of same is most annoying. However, there was nothing much to do but choose a corner of the room and make the best of a none-too-pleasant situation. However, I have at least learned why the floor vibrates, for the excreted material sank out of sight moments later. Clever technology, but bothersome, since I have to sleep on the floor. What happens to me if I sleep too long? You know, this place seems dreadfully quiet to me.

. . . . .

Suddenly I have solved two of my problems. I know both where I am and who He is. And I bless the day that I got interested in sensory psychology and the perception of motion.

The air in this room seems to have more than the usual concentration of dust particles. This fact didn't seem particularly noteworthy until I noticed that most of them seemed to pile up along the floor against one wall in particular. For a while I was sure that this was due to the ventilation system—perhaps there was an air outlet where the wall joined the floor.

However, when I put my hand to the floor there, I could feel no breeze whatsoever. Yet even as I held my hand along the dividing line between the floor and the wall, dust motes covered my hand. I tried this same experiment everywhere else in the room to no avail. This was the only spot where the phenomenon occurred, and it occurred along the entire length of this one wall.

But if ventilation was not responsible for the pile-up of dust, what was? All at once there popped into my mind some calculations I had made when NASA first proposed a manned satellite station. Engineers are notoriously naive when it comes to the performance of a human being in most situations, and I remembered that the problem of the perception of the satellite's rotation seemingly had been ignored by the calculator crowd.

The NASA people had planned to build a wheel-shaped satellite and then

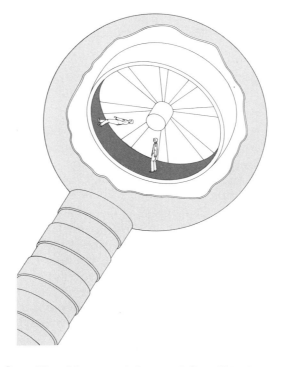

set it to spinning slowly. This way they could substitute centrifugal force for the force of gravity. Thus the outer shell of the wheel would appear to be "down" to anyone inside the thing. Apparently they had not realized that humans are at least as sensitive to angular rotation as they are to the pull of gravity.

As I figured the problem then, if a man aboard the wheel moved his head as much as three or four feet toward or away from the center of the doughnut-shaped satellite, he would have become fairly dizzy! Rather annoying it would have been too, becoming nauseous every time you sat down or stood up. Also it was apparent that dust particles would move in a direction *opposite* to the direction of the rotation of the wheel, and thus they would pile up against any wall that impeded their flight.

Using the behavior of the dust motes as a clue, I climbed atop the table and jumped off. Sure enough, my head felt like a mule had kicked it. My hypothesis was confirmed.

So I am aboard a wheel-shaped spaceship!

The thought is incredible, but in a strange way comforting. At least now I can postpone worry about heaven and hell and start worrying about other things.

And, of course, I know who "He" is. Or rather, I know who He *isn't*, which is something else again. Surely, though, I can no longer think of Him as being human. Whether I should be consoled by this or not, I have no way of telling.

I still have no notion of *why* I am here, however, nor why this alien chose to pick me of all people to pay a visit to His spaceship. What possible use could I be? Surely if He were interested in making contact with the human race, He would have spirited away a politician. After all, that's what politicians are for! Since He's made no effort to communicate with me, however, I doubt that His purpose is that of making contact with the inhabitants of earth.

Perhaps He's an alien scientist—a biologist of sorts—out gathering specimens. Now, that's a particularly nasty thought. What if He turned out to be a physiologist, interested in cutting me open to see what makes me tick? Will my innards be smeared over a glass slide for hundreds of youthful Hims to peer at under a microscope? Brrrr! I don't mind giving my life to science, but I'd rather do it a day at a time.

• • • • •

Good God! I should have known it! Destiny will play her little tricks, and all jokes have their cosmic angles.

He is a *psychologist!*

Had I given the matter thought, I would have realized that whenever you come across a new species, you worry about behavior first, physiology second. So I have received the ultimate insult, or the ultimate compliment, I don't know which. I have become a laboratory specimen for an alien psychologist!

This thought first occurred to me when I awoke after my latest sleep (which was filled with most frightening dreams). It was immediately obvious that something about the room had changed. Almost at once I noticed that one of the walls now had a lever of some kind protruding from it. To one side of the lever there was a small hole with a container beneath the hole. I wandered over to the lever, inspected it a few moments, then accidentally depressed the thing. At once there came a loud clicking noise, and a protein ball popped out of the hole in the wall and fell into the container.

For just a moment I was puzzled. This seemed somehow so strangely familiar. Then, all at once, I burst into wild laughter.

The room had been changed into a gigantic Skinner Box!

For years I have been studying animal learning by putting white rats into a Skinner Box and following the changes in the rats' behavior. The rats had to learn to press the lever in order to get a pellet of food, which was delivered to them through just such an apparatus as now protrudes from the wall of my cell. And now, after all of these years, and after all of the learning studies I have done, to find myself trapped like a rat in a Skinner Box!

Perhaps this is hell after all, and the Lord High Executioner's advice to "let the punishment fit the crime" is being followed.

Frankly, this sudden turn of events has left me a little shaken.

· · · · ·

I seem to be performing according to theory. It didn't take me long to discover that pressing the lever would give me food part of the time, while at other times all I got was the click and no protein ball. It appears that approximately every twelve hours the thing delivers me a random number of protein balls—the number has varied from five to fifteen so far. I never know ahead of time how many pellets—I mean protein balls—the apparatus will deliver, and it spews them out intermittently.

Sometimes I have to press the lever a dozen times before it will give me anything, while at other times it gives me one ball for each bar-press. Since I don't have a watch on me, I am never quite sure when the twelve hours have passed, so I stomp over to the lever and press it every few minutes when I think it's getting close to time to be fed. Just like my rats always did. And since the pellets are small and I never get enough of them, occasionally I find myself banging away on the lever with all the compulsion of a stupid animal. But I missed the feeding time once and almost starved to death (so it seemed) before the lever delivered food the next time. About the only consolation to my wounded pride is that I've already lost an inch or so around my waist.

At least He doesn't seem to be fattening me up for the kill. Or maybe he just likes lean meat!

· · · · ·

I have been promoted. Apparently He in his infinite alien wisdom has decided I'm intelligent enough to handle the Skinner Box. So I've been promoted to solving a maze.

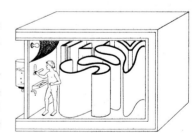

Can you picture the irony of the situation? All of the classic laboratory apparatus is being thrown right in my face. If only I could communicate with Him! I don't mind being subjected to tests nearly as much as I mind being underestimated. Why, I can solve puzzles hundreds of times more complex than the ones He's giving me. But how can I tell Him?

As it turns out, the maze is much like the ones I have used. It's rather long, with 23 choice points along the way. I spent half an hour wandering through the thing the first time. Surprisingly enough, I didn't realize what I was in, so I made no conscious attempt to memorize the correct turns. It wasn't until I reached the final choice point and found food that I recognized what was expected of me. The next time I made fewer errors, and was able to turn in a perfect performance fairly rapidly. However, I'm embarrassed to state that my own white rats could have learned the maze somewhat sooner than I did.

My "cage," so to speak, still has the Skinner apparatus in it, but the lever delivers food infrequently. I still give it a whirl now and again, but since I'm getting a fairly good supply of protein balls at the end of the maze each time, I don't pay the lever much attention.

Now that I am very sure of what is happening to me, my thoughts have turned to how to get out of this situation. Mazes I can solve easily, but how to escape apparently is beyond my intellectual capacity. But then, come to think of it, there was precious little chance for my own experimental animals to get out of my clutches.

And assuming that I am unable to escape, what then? After He has finished putting me through as many paces as He wishes, where do we go from there? Will He treat me as I treated most of my rats—that is, will I get tossed into a jar containing chloroform? "Following the experiment, the animals were sacrificed," as we so politely put it in our journal articles. This thought doesn't appeal to me very much, as you can imagine. But perhaps if I seem particularly bright to Him, He may use me for breeding purposes, to establish a colony of His own. Now, that might have possibilities . . .

Oh, damn Freud anyhow!

. . . . .

And damn Him too! I had just gotten the maze well learned when He changed things on me. I stumbled about like a bat in the sunlight for quite some time before I finally got to the goal box. I'm afraid my performance was pretty poor. What He did was just to reverse the whole maze so that it was a mirror image of what it used to be. Took me only two trials to discover the solution. Let Him figure that one out if He's so smart!

. . . . .

My performance on the maze reversal must have pleased Him, because He's added a new complication. And again I suppose I could have predicted the next step if I had been thinking along in the right direction.

I woke up a few hours ago to find myself in a totally different room. On the wall facing me were two doors—one pure white, the other jet black. Between me and the doors was a deep pit, filled with water. I didn't like the looks of the situation, for it seemed just like the "jump stand" I used to use with rats in my laboratory. Apparently I had to choose which of the doors was open and led to food. The other door would be locked. If I jumped at the wrong door, and found it locked, I'd fall into the water. I needed a bath, that was for sure, but I didn't relish getting it this way.

While I stood there thinking, I got the shock of my life. I mean that literally. The monster had thought of everything! When I used to train rats on a jump stand, I shocked them to get them to jump. He's doing exactly the same thing with me. The floor in this room is wired, and it delivers a very nasty jolt. I howled and jumped about and showed all the usual anxiety behavior. It took me less than two seconds to come to my senses and make a flying leap at the white door, however.

You know something? That water is ice cold!

. . . . .

I have now, by my own calculations, solved no fewer than 87 different problems on the jump stand, and I'm getting sick and tired of it. Once I got angry and just pointed at the correct door—and got shocked for not going ahead and jumping. I shouted bloody murder, cursing Him at the top of my voice. All He did, of course, was to increase the shock.

If He were giving me half a chance to show my capabilities, I wouldn't mind it. But he treats me like an animal! If I don't get out of here soon, I shall go stark, raving mad!

. . . . .

For almost an hour after it happened, I sat in this room and just wept. I realize that it is not the style in our culture for a grown man to weep, but there are times when cultural taboos must be forgotten.

One of the standard problems in Learning Theory is this one—do animals in a maze merely learn a "set of stimulus-response bonds," or are they capable of "drawing a cognitive map" of its environment? Does the rat on a jump stand gain a "mental concept" of the situation, or does it mechanically leap toward the stimulus door that yields a reward? Can rats think through a problem (as I obviously can), or are they little more than S–R robots? Behavioral theorists stick to S–R bonds, while cognitive learning theorists believe that animals are capable of "insight" and intellectual activity.

Historically speaking, the battle between the behaviorists and the cognitive theorists came to a head with the development of the "oddity problem." Suppose that you were a rat on a jump stand, and instead of seeing two doors before you—one black, one white—you perceive three doors in a row. The outside doors are both white, but the "odd one" in the middle is black. You leap at the white door on the left, and you fall into the ice water. You try the other white door, and again you are dunked. So you jump toward the middle black door, and find a nice meal of protein balls awaiting you.

Thereafter—whether the black door is on the right, the left, or in the center—you leap toward it as quickly as you can. And you are always rewarded.

Now, the question is, what have you learned? To approach the black stimulus and avoid the white stimulus? Or have you learned something more subtle—namely, to go to the "odd" color? If you have learned to approach the odd stimulus, then obviously you have learned a "mental concept," since *oddness* is hardly a true stimulus input!

So you say you learned to approach the black? Well, how would you react if the next time on the stand you faced two black doors and one white one? Would you approach black or white? Surely you'd jump toward the white one, although the white stimulus had been incorrect the first time around. And if the next set of stimuli were two reds and a green, you'd jump toward the green, even though the response of jumping toward green had never been rewarded!

The "strict behaviorists" predicted that rats couldn't solve the oddity problem. There simply was no way they could explain the rat's consistently jumping toward new stimuli (such as the odd green door) when it hadn't yet built up S–R bonds involving those stimuli. Nor could simple behaviorism easily describe how the rat learned to approach green if two reds were present, but approach red when two greens were present.

And the behaviorists were right, up to a point. Monkeys learned the problem readily, but who cares about them? The important thing was that rats seemed to fail the test miserably. Then a chap named Wodinsky proved the rat could do it—if you treated the animal very, very gently and gave it lots and lots of experience. So much for simple behaviorism.

Of course the early behaviorists became furious, and published a barrage of papers attempting to disprove Wodinsky's results. But mostly they ignored the whole thing and hoped it would go away. The cognitive theorists, of course, were delighted. And since behaviorism is such a powerful approach, and explains so much of animal behavior, this little "oddity" was mostly overlooked.

Well, He must be a simple behaviorist. The last time He put me on the jump stand, I found myself facing two blue doors and a yellow one. I realized what was up instantly, and leaped toward the yellow. Success! Immediately He tested me with two yellow doors and a blue one. I jumped to the blue, and heard what I can only describe as a cosmic roar of frustration. I gather He wasn't very happy with what I had done.

Next up were two doors with horizontal stripes and one with vertical stripes. I "went for the vertical," and had no more than landed safely when the whole apparatus started to shake as if someone had kicked it in anger!

Of course on the subsequent trial I found two doors with vertical stripes and one with horizontal. I chose the horizontal, landed safely, and this time someone threw several dozen protein balls at me!

The next thing I knew, I was tossed rather roughly back in my cage. Since nothing has happened for an hour or so, I presume He's off sulking somewhere because my actions didn't confirm His expectations.

I suppose I should have realized it before now. Theories are typically born of the equipment one uses. This has probably been the case throughout the history of all science, but perhaps most true of all in psychology. If Skinner had never invented his blasted box, if the maze and the jump stand had not been developed, we probably would have entirely different theories of learning today than we now have. For if nothing else, the type of apparatus that you use reduces the types of behavior that your subjects can show, and your theories only have to account for the kinds of responses that show up in laboratory situations.

But if He has a problem, I have a worse one. What should I do next, now that I know what He expects of me? Should I help Him confirm his simple-minded notions about behavior—and about the new species He's testing? Or should I prove to the monster that I'm brighter than He thinks I ought to be? In the old days, rats that gave "unusual" results used to die of "wall-itis," which is to say they got bounced off the wall rather angrily. Or someone would "forget" to give them food and water for a while. Will I end up splattered against a green door? Or choke on a particularly nasty protein ball?

I'm sure He will shortly snatch me back for a final test. When I face those different-colored doors, should I perform "stupidly" like the intelligent human being I really am, or should I perform "intelligently" by acting like the dumb rat He wants me to be?

What am I anyhow? A man, or a mouse?

(Continued on page 419.)

Learning Theories

During the many years that you have gone to school, you must have had contact with hundreds of different teachers. Some of them probably were strict **disciplinarians** whose "learning theory" was that knowledge had to be *pounded* into people's heads through constant repetition. Holding a lesson book in one hand and a stick in the other, these teachers often drill their pupils over and over again until the student can spew back from memory whatever material the teacher believes should be learned. The students who survive may acquire a lot of facts, but the constant threat of punishment may also teach them to hate anything associated with school.

Disciplinarians (diss-sip-plin-NAIR-ee-ans). From the Latin word meaning "teachers." We get our word "disciples" from the same Latin source. *Webster's New Collegiate Dictionary* defines *to discipline* as "to punish or penalize for the sake of discipline, to train or develop by instruction and exercise, especially in self-control." A disciplinarian is a teacher who believes that pupils should be punished into "learning and obeying the rules." The "rules" may vary from one disciplinarian to another, but the #1 rule is that punishment is the key to self-control.

In olden days, a teacher often ruled the classroom with a stick.

Other teachers appear to be much less concerned with punishing incorrect responses than they are with creating an academic environment in which the student's inborn intellectual potential can grow and blossom like a flower seed planted in fertile soil. Their classrooms often have a friendly but **boisterous** character to them, and the teachers themselves often gain a warm place in their students' hearts. But affection for a teacher doesn't necessarily guarantee the learning of those basic skills necessary for the students to survive and prosper after they leave school.

Is there a "best way" to educate all people? Should students be treated like Pavlov's dogs—drilled and conditioned until they have acquired the proper response for any stimulus they are likely to encounter? Or should pupils be considered **cognitive,** self-motivated creatures who will learn willingly everything they need to know if given a rich intellectual environment?

As you will soon see, the history of psychological learning theories—and the history of educational practice in the US—sometimes resembles a battle plan between these two opposing viewpoints.

Thorndike's Theories

In a sense, it all began with E.L. Thorndike, a giant figure in psychology who influenced educational practices here almost as much as Pavlov did in Russia. Thorndike spent most of his academic career at Teachers College, a part of Columbia University in New York City. He helped create some of the very first intelligence and **aptitude** tests. He was a strong supporter of educational research, and, with the help of C.L. Barnhart, Thorndike developed a series of dictionaries for school children that is still widely used.

Thorndike believed that science and mathematics helped build good "mental discipline" and insisted that all children should learn these subjects, which he felt should be presented in as clear and interesting a manner as possible. Indeed, Thorndike once said that scientific laws should

E.L. Thorndike.

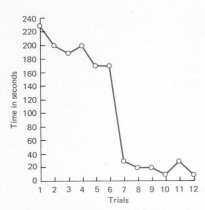

Fig. 16.1. The seventh trial shows a remarkable improvement in the time it took one of Thorndike's cats to open a puzzle box.

be relatively accurate, but should be stated simply enough to be teachable to freshmen.

Thorndike's own scientific training made him an early supporter of Charles Darwin's theory of evolution. Believing that man was descended from, and hence *learned the same way as,* lower animals, Thorndike began his studies on animal learning in about 1890. His research efforts—probably the first laboratory studies ever performed on animal intelligence—involved putting cats inside a "puzzle box." If the animal could figure out how to unlatch the door to the box, it escaped and was often given a bit of food as a reward.

At first the animals showed a great deal of what Thorndike called "random behavior." They sat and scratched or licked themselves, they mewed and cried, they paced the box, or they bit at the bars and tried to squeeze between them. Then, apparently by accident, the cat would bump into the latch. The door flew open, and the animal rushed out and was fed.

The next time the cat was put into the box, it performed many of the same "random" behaviors as before. But it eventually hit the latch again and escaped. In subsequent trials, the cat would spend more and more time near the latch and would get out of the box sooner and sooner. Eventually the cat seemed to learn what was required of it. The moment it was placed in the box, it would hit the latch, escape, and claim its reward.

When Thorndike plotted on a graph the amount of time it took the cat to exit from the box on each trial, he came up with something that we now call a "learning curve" (see Fig. 16.1). Similar experiments on monkeys, chickens, and even humans yielded the same-shaped curves, a finding that confirmed Thorndike's original theory that animals and humans solve such simple tasks in much the same manner.

Trial-and-Error Learning

Thorndike believed that animals learn to escape from puzzle boxes by **trial and error.** That is, they perform various responses in a blindly mechanical way until some action is effective in securing their release from the box. On succeeding trials the animal learns that certain types of behaviors—such as roaming around the box—are much more effective than are other behaviors (such as sitting and scratching) for gaining freedom.

Since the ineffectual responses do not bring the animal much satisfaction, these activities tend to drop out of the animal's **repertory.** But those actions that gain the animal's release and lead to food are most satisfying, so in turn these responses become more and more connected to the stimuli in the puzzle box. Thus the "satisfying" responses are much more likely to occur the next time the animal is put in the box.

Thorndike's Laws of Learning The results of his puzzle box experiments led Thorndike to formulate two basic laws of learning: (a) the **law of exercise;** and (b) the **law of effect.**

In part, the *law of exercise* states that S–R connections are *strengthened* by practice or repetition—in short, that practice makes perfect. The *law of effect* holds that S–R bonds or connections are also strengthened by the "effects" of what you do. If the response you make to a stimulus somehow gives you pleasure or satisfaction, the connection between the S and the R will be appropriately increased.

Thorndike defined rewards (or "satisfiers," as he called them) as situations that an organism willingly approaches or does nothing to avoid. Had Thorndike stopped at this point, his influence might have been more profound. Unfortunately, early in his career Thorndike also stated that "punishers" weakened or broke S–R connections. "Punishers" were situations that the animal avoided or did nothing to approach.

Late in his life, Thorndike changed his mind about the consequences of punishment, but by then the "negative" half of the law of effect had had its effect on US educational practice. As we will see in the next chapter, punishment doesn't operate that way at all, and the "effects" of punishment can often be fairly disastrous.

Nonetheless, Thorndike's influence on our educational practice was so great that generations of school teachers accepted his theories as if they were natural rather than man-made laws. The great man had said that repetition was the key to learning, and that punishment was the key to weakening or wiping out "inappropriate" S–R bonds. So millions of school children were made to recite their math and science lessons, endlessly urged on by the stinging threat of a hickory stick.

Cognitive Theories of Learning

As we noted in Chapter 10, we often see what we expect to see. This principle holds in scientific investigations as well as in ordinary life. Thorndike surely *expected* his cats to learn by trial-and-error methods before he began his work. Indeed, as **Gestalt** psychologist Wolfgang Koehler pointed out, the puzzle box could hardly be solved in any other way.

Koehler, trained at the University of Berlin, became director of a research station in the **Canary Islands** in 1913, a few years after Thorndike published his first work on animal learning. Koehler believed that animals were capable of greater intellectual accomplishments than random solutions to puzzle boxes. He thought that, given the chance, they could discover *relationships* between objects and events. The animals could then act on these relationships to gain whatever ends they had in mind. Much of Koehler's work in the Canary Islands involved presenting various "intellectual" problems to chimpanzees to see what kinds of solutions they might come up with.

Learning by Insight

Koehler's most famous subject was a particularly bright chimpanzee named Sultan. First Sultan learned to reach through the bars of his cage and rake in a banana on the ground outside by using a stick as a tool. After Sultan had mastered this trick, Koehler set the animal the much more difficult task of putting two sticks together to get the food. The banana was moved farther away from Sultan's cage, and the chimp was given two bamboo poles which, when fitted together, were just long enough to gather in the reward (see Fig. 16.2).

At first Sultan was confused. He tried reaching for the fruit with one stick and then with the other, but neither was adequate for his purposes. Next he pushed the longer of the poles out toward the banana and left it lying on the ground. Then Sultan used the tip of the shorter stick to prod the longer one out until it touched the banana. He had reached his objective, in a sense, but couldn't complete his task because the two sticks were

Gestalt (guess-TALT). A German word that means "good form" or "good figure." Also means the tendency to see things as "wholes" rather than as jumbled bits and pieces. See Chapter 10.

Canary Islands (can-AIR-ee). A series of tropical islands south of Spain and just off the west coast of Africa. Beautiful, warm islands with no snakes and hundreds of different species of birds. Wolfgang Koehler (CURL-er) spent the years of World War I doing research on these islands.

Fig. 16.2. Sultan in action.

not joined together in any way, and therefore he could not get the banana back into his cage. Koehler even had to hand the larger pole back to Sultan because it was now beyond his reach.

Koehler watched the animal for more than an hour, hoping that an intellectual flash of lightning would strike Sultan's cortex. When the chimp abandoned the banana and retreated into his cage (perhaps in frustration) to play with the sticks, Koehler decided the animal had failed the test. So Koehler went home, leaving Sultan to be observed by an assistant.

Koehler gave up too soon. Not long after he'd left, Sultan happened to hold one stick in each hand so that their ends were pointed toward each other. Gently, he pushed the tip of the smaller one into the hollow of the larger one. *They fitted.* Even as he put the sticks together, Sultan was up and running toward the bars of his cage. Reaching through with the double stick, he touched the banana and started to draw it toward him.

At this point fate played Sultan a nasty trick for which Koehler was most grateful—the two sticks came apart! Annoyed at this turn of events, Sultan gathered the sticks back into the cage, pushed them *firmly* together, tested them briefly, and then "liberated" the banana.

These actions proved, at least to Koehler's satisfaction, that Sultan actually understood that *joining the poles together* was an effective way of lengthening his arm. Koehler used the term **insight** to refer to this very rapid "perception of relationships" that sometimes occurs in humans and animals. He believed that *insight* involved a sudden restructuring or reorganization of the organism's perceptual world into a new pattern or *Gestalt*.

Koehler never denied the importance of repetition and reward in learning simple tasks. Nor did he underestimate the importance of **associations** between stimulus inputs and response outputs, such as those that Pavlov had studied. He merely believed that living systems were capable of more complex forms of learning—if you gave them the chance.

As you might imagine, Ivan Pavlov did not take gladly to Koehler's experiments. As soon as the chimpanzee work appeared in print, Pavlov leaped to the attack. He accused Koehler of being a "mentalist" (which Koehler was) and of performing sloppy experiments—that is, studies in which the CS and the UCS could not readily be identified. From his sanctuary in Leningrad, Pavlov issued one **vitriolic** criticism after another, most of which Koehler simply ignored. But thanks to Koehler's work, Pavlov soon found himself assailed by a barrage of experiments from the United States, few of which could easily be fitted into the Russian scientist's theory of conditioning.

Tolman's "Cognitive Maps"

E.C. Tolman and his associates at the University of California, Berkeley, published a series of studies that appeared to show rats were much more "insightful" than Thorndike or Pavlov perhaps thought they ought to be.

In most of Tolman's experiments, the rats were given considerable training in very complicated **mazes.** Although the animal could reach the food reward at the end of the maze by a great many pathways, one path was typically much shorter than the rest and was preferred by the animals. When that pathway was blocked, however, almost all of the rats would instantly shift to the next most efficient way of getting to the food.

If at any time the experimenter moved the reward from one part of the maze to another, the rats responded immediately as if they had some kind of **cognitive map** of the maze. That is, the rats acted as if they understood a great deal about the *spatial relationships* involved in getting quickly from one part of the maze to another.

Question: What similarities do you see between Sultan's "problem-solving" activities with the sticks and the banana and the "creative behaviors" involved in writing a poem that we discussed in Chapter 5?

E.C. Tolman.

Maier's Rat "Bismarck"

N.R.F. Maier.

N.R.F. Maier, at The University of Michigan, performed a similar set of experiments that appeared to show rats were capable of "insightful" behavior patterns. One of Maier's best subjects, a young male rat named Bismarck, was trained to get food on top of a table by crawling up a little ladder from the floor. One day, after Bismarck had run up the ladder many times to claim his reward, the rat found a wire mesh barrier that blocked his access to the food. Bismarck crawled all over the barrier but was unable to get through it to his dinner. He could, however, see a new pathway from the floor to the food—one that he had never traveled before.

Bismarck sat quietly for a while, expressing his frustrations (as rats often do) by laboriously washing his face. Then Bismarck suddenly jumped straight up in the air, turned and dashed *down* the ladder he had previously only gone up, chased around the table, found the new pathway, raced up the new route, and settled down to gorge himself.

The many experiments by Tolman, Maier, and other Gestalt psychologists clearly demonstrated that *some* rats, in *some* situations, acted as if they had "cognitive maps" of their environments. Monkeys, chimps, and humans show a great deal more cognitive activity than do rats, however, so the Gestalt theorists soon started using **primates** as their preferred laboratory subjects.

"Mental maps" are neither stimuli nor responses. Rather, they are *percepts*, or internal mental processes. And as we noted in Chapter 5, it is these internal *representations* of the external world—or the "mental relationships" we perceive among stimuli—that allow us to respond to our environments in a meaningful way. Because Pavlov and the early **behaviorists** focused entirely on S–R bonds, these theorists weren't at all interested in "percepts" or "relationships." The rather mechanical behavior patterns of the lower animals appealed greatly to the behaviorists, and so they chiefly stuck to their rats, dogs, and pigeons.

Learning in Classroom Situations

Educational practice is often affected by experiments such as those of the Gestalt and behavioral psychologists, for the classroom follows the laboratory more than it leads it. Teachers who fell under the influence of E.L. Thorndike and other behaviorists typically expected their students to learn material just as a rat usually does—by connecting thousands of tiny responses to thousands of highly specific stimuli. So these teachers drilled their pupils over and over again in one subject after another, punishing each mistake and occasionally rewarding correct responses.

On the other hand, those educators who were influenced by Tolman and his associates believed that learning is spontaneous and rapid, and that it occurs in big bursts of insight. The most radical of these teachers held that

Cognitive map. Some psychologists (such as Thorndike and Pavlov) believe that animals learn each section of a maze by trial and error. Other psychologists believe that animals acquire a "mental map" of the maze and can "think" their way through to the goal—rather than respond reflexively (and unconsciously) to the specific stimuli in each section. In fact, animals such as the rat seem to do a little of both.

Primates (PRIME-ates). *Prime* means "first." Thus the primates (apes, monkeys, chimps, and humans) are the "top dogs" of the animal kingdom.

Behaviorists. Psychologists whose explanation of human conduct focuses almost entirely on *measurable behaviors* rather than explaining things in terms of "mental processes." See Chapter 5.

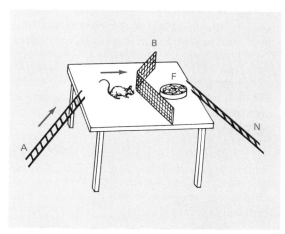

Bismarck was trained to go up the ladder (A) and get his food at F. When a barrier (B) blocked his way, he noticed the new ladder (N) and used it to get his reward.

each child learns at his or her own speed, in her or his own way. Thus the teachers tried to give the child as rich and permissive an intellectual environment as possible. The teacher then sat back and waited for the cognitive map-making to occur "on its own," without the teacher's guidance. Because these educators could not specify exactly what simulus conditions promoted "insightful" learning, the most the teachers could do was to expose their students to "routine-free" classrooms and hope for the best.

Thorndike's views were much more acceptable to Pavlov than were Tolman's. Indeed, there is a strange similarity between the explanations that Pavlov offered for classical conditioning and Thorndike's *law of exercise.* Pavlov, as you will remember, believed that if the conditioning stimulus (CS) is paired with the unconditioned stimulus (UCS) a sufficient number of times, an S–R bond would be formed. And the more the bond is *exercised,* the stronger it becomes.

Thorndike's *law of effect,* however, stuck in Pavlov's throat. For the Russian scientist believed that learning occurs *automatically*—whether or not the organism likes it. According to Pavlov, the mere *closeness in time* between the CS and the UCS is enough to bring about an "association" between these two stimuli, and hence a connection or **contiguity** between the CS and the CR. And, in situations such as the ones that Pavlov studied, *contiguity* between S and R is often sufficient for learning to occur.

Thorndike, on the other hand, thought that we all remember things better if they please or satisfy us. (Pavlov seems not to have cared much about the personal satisfaction of the organism.) It took a pigeon to show the narrowness of Pavlov's views, and to map out a kind of common ground between the Thorndikeans and the Tolmaniacs.

Operant Conditioning

Teaching a Pigeon to Bowl

Suppose that, as a final examination in one of your psychology classes, your instructor gives you a common, ordinary pigeon and tells you that if you want to get an A in the course, you must teach the pigeon how to bowl!

After you recover from your surprise, you take stock of the situation. The apparatus you can use is a large box with a wire screen over the top of it. Inside the box is a small bowling alley with a tiny ball at one end and pigeon-sized bowling pins at the other. In one corner of the box is a metal cup into which you can drop food pellets from the outside.

Just above the food cup is a small bell that you can ring by pressing a button outside the box. Luckily for you, the pigeon has already been trained to run to the food cup to get the pellets whenever the bell rings.

Your instructor tells you that if you can teach the pigeon to bowl in a matter of two hours or less, you pass the exam and get your A reward. Keeping in mind all of the practical advice on educational practice you have acquired so far in this book, how would you go about educating your pigeon so that you could satisfy your instructor, yourself, and, of course, the bird?

If you played the game according to Pavlovian rules, what would you do? Well, you might begin by ringing the bell and then pushing the pigeon toward the ball, hoping that an S–R connection of some kind would be established in the bird's nervous system. In fact, the pigeon would surely resent such an intrusion into its life space. Instead of learning to bowl when you rang the bell, it probably would learn to peck at your hand viciously. For Pavlovian conditioning is almost always built on *already-established unconditioned responses* (UCR's). If dogs did not salivate naturally when given food, how would you go about teaching them to salivate when you sounded a buzzer?

If the pigeon already knew how to bowl, you could probably train it to give this response on command when you rang the bell. But you could read

A pigeon bowling alley.

PART FOUR *Learning and Memory*

everything Pavlov wrote—in Russian or in English translation—without learning much about how to get a bird to bowl in the first place, if bowling wasn't something that it did naturally.

If you turned to Tolman and the Gestalt theorists instead, perhaps you might decide to give the pigeon plenty of experience in the bowling box itself before you started the training. Once the animal had acquired a **valid** cognitive map of the apparatus, it would surely learn how to bowl much faster. But the relationship between striking the ball and knocking down the pins is an insight that comes hard to most pigeons—unless you facilitate matters a little along the way. And not even Koehler offered much practical advice about how this facilitation should be accomplished.

If you looked to Thorndike for help, you still might have troubles. You could utilize the law of effect by waiting until the pigeon happened to knock the ball down the alley by accident and then giving the bird some food. This reward should help stamp in the memory of what it had done, but how long would you have to wait until the pigeon *by accident* hit the ball straight down the alley the first time?

Once the pigeon had done so, and been rewarded, you could surely get it to do so again, and hence exercise the S–R bond to make it stronger. But it is that *very first response* that Thorndike's notions of trial-and-error learning cannot help you bring about.

All of these components—*reward, exercise,* and *repetition,* and *unlearned or innate responses*—are necessary if you are to train the pigeon and pass your exam. But putting them all together into a workable educational system took the genius of Harvard professor B.F. Skinner, who surely qualifies as being our most influential living psychologist.

B.F. Skinner's Techniques

According to Skinner, whenever you wish to change an organism's behavior, you always begin by defining *precisely* what it is you want to accomplish. For instance, to get your A, you must train the pigeon to bowl. But what do we mean by "bowling"? Do we have some objective, clear-cut, agreed-upon way of measuring the response pattern we call "bowling"? If so, then we know when to *terminate* the training, and we know when you've passed the exam.

Terminal Response or Goal Bowling is obviously a complex *set of responses* that ends when the pigeon has whacked the ball down the alley toward the pins. Thus your goal must be that of getting the bird to hit the ball in the proper direction.

Skinner calls the final step in any chain of behaviors the **terminal response.** When the organism has performed this final act, the chain of responses is *terminated,* usually by a reward or punishment of some kind. Thus when the pigeon finally "bowls," you will ring the bell and give it a pellet of food. And when the pigeon "bowls" regularly, you will terminate the training and receive your A.

The single most important thing about the terminal response, however, is that it must be *measurable.* As you will soon see, pigeons *can* be trained to bowl in two hours or less, if you go about it the right way. However, how long do you think it would take to train a bird to be a "good sport"?

Question: College catalogues often state that the goal of higher education is to turn students into "creative individuals" who are "good citizens" and "productive members of modern-day society." What might B.F. Skinner say about the measurability of such terminal responses?

Entering Baseline or Behavior Once you have a well-defined goal to work toward, you are ready to tackle the second stage in Skinner's analysis of behavioral change—that of determining what the organism is doing before you **intervene** in its life.

B.F. Skinner.

(see Chapter 12).

Entering behavior. The behavior patterns of an organism before training begins. According to behavioral therapists, you must always build upon the client's strengths (the good behaviors) and select out of these "entering behaviors" those actions that can be shaped toward the terminal response. Entering behaviors also include problematic or inappropriate actions, but these should be ignored (or at least not rewarded) in the hope that they will thereby be extinguished.

Baseline behavior. You "take a baseline" when you make a record of the organism's entering behaviors. Thus a baseline behavior is one that the organism displays before training begins.

Successive approximations to a goal. Rewarding any incremental (in-kree-MENT-tull) response that will lead the organism toward the terminal response. That is, reinforcing any slight behavioral change (increment) that represents a step in the right direction. Behaviorists believe that most learning occurs in small steps—"Rome wasn't built in a day." But if the successive approximations are rewarded and encouraged, they build up in incremental form until the goal is reached.

Reinforced. Concrete with steel rods inside it is called *reinforced* concrete, because the steel strengthens the concrete. Positive feedback reinforces an S-R bond by making it more likely that the response will occur again the next time the stimulus input appears.

Skinner calls this the organism's **entering behavior.** In order to determine the entering behavior, you measure what the organism is already doing, and plot its responses on a graph or record of some kind. Skinner often calls this the animal's **baseline behavior,** and refers to the measurement itself as "taking a baseline" (see Chapter 12).

The entering or baseline behaviors must be stated in objective, measurable terms too. Clever animal trainers (or people educators) always take advantage of the response patterns that the organism brings to the training situation. According to Skinner, you always build new learning on old.

Successive Approximations When you are sure of: (a) the organism's entering behavior; and (b) the terminal behavior that you hope to achieve, you are ready to move from (a) to (b). Skinner suggests that you do so in a step-by-step fashion called **successive approximations to a goal.**

Neither people nor pigeons typically make dramatic changes in their behaviors in large, insightful jumps. We *can* do so occasionally, as the Gestalt theorists showed, but most of the time we change slowly, bit by bit, millimeter by millimeter. And we usually need to be coaxed and encouraged whenever we must acquire a new way of doing things—which is to say that we need to be rewarded or **reinforced** for each tiny step that we make toward the goal or terminal response. (We will have more to say about the importance of reward momentarily.)

The technique of *successive approximations to a goal* is the heart of the Skinnerian system. But mastery of the step-by-step technique calls for rather a penetrating insight on your own part: Namely, you must come to realize that even the faintest, feeblest movement toward the terminal goal is *a step in the right direction*, and hence one that you must vigorously reward. Most people are unable or unwilling to analyze behavior in these terms, which is why most people would not be able to train a pigeon to bowl in two hours or less.

Behavioral Analysis If we apply the Skinnerian *behavioral analysis* to the problem of getting your pigeon to perform, we can perhaps see better how the technique works.

The terminal behavior your instructor has set is that of "bowling." But how shall we define it? Humans usually pick up the bowling ball in their hands and roll it down the alley. But Mother Nature has given the pigeon wings instead of arms, and feathers are poor substitutes for fingers when it comes to lifting a heavy ball.

But could we teach an armless man to bowl? Couldn't the man kick the ball down the alley, or even butt it with his head? Do you really care how he manages it, so long as the ball zings down the alley and hits the pins?

One of the purposes of getting you to "take a baseline" of the pigeon's normal response patterns is that of forcing you to see what it *already* does well. If you observe pigeons for a while, you will notice they use their beaks to manipulate the world around them much as we use our hands. There is nothing in your "goal statement" that insists the pigeon must use its "fingers" (claws) while bowling. So if you can train the bird to hit the ball with its beak, you surely have taught the animal to "bowl" within the stated definition of the problem. And you surely should get an A on your exam.

Now that you know what your goal is, you can begin to take advantage of the "entering behaviors" the pigeon already shows. Obviously, at the start of training, the bird doesn't bowl at all. It merely moves around nervously, inspecting its new environment. The final response that you want from the animal is that of striking the ball with its beak so that the ball travels down the alley and hits the pins. To make this terminal response, though, the animal must be standing *near the ball*. So your first task would seem to be that of getting the pigeon to move to where the ball is. But how to do it?

If you were training your child to bowl, you would probably explain to the child, in English, what you wanted it to do. Then, as it began to make the first muscle movements involved in approaching the ball or picking it up, you would encourage the child and tell it that it was doing well. But pigeons are non-verbal, so how can you give your bird feedback to let it know when it's doing something "on target"? The answer is: You *reward* each step it makes toward the goal.

Two Functions of Reward Reward or positive reinforcement has at least two functions. First, it gives us pleasure, usually by satisfying some need or reducing some drive or deprivation state. When we are hungry, food tastes good and gives us new energy. But rewarding inputs also have an *informational* aspect to them, for such stimuli give us feedback as to how well we are doing, and how close we are coming to a goal.

Positive reinforcement, then, *increases the probability that an organism will repeat the response* that led to the appearance of the rewarding stimulus.

Since your pigeon has already been trained to go to the food cup when it hears the bell ring, you can use the *sound of the bell* as a rewarding input whenever you want to let the pigeon know instantly that it has made what you consider to be a step in the right direction toward the goal of bowling.

"Shaping" a Pigeon To Bowl With these preliminaries out of the way, you would be ready to start passing your final examination. You know your goal; you know the entering behavior the bird shows; the animal is deprived of food; and you have an effective reinforcer available. What is your next step?

Actually, as Skinner points out, the next step is up to the bird. As it wanders around the box excitedly, at one time or another it will accidentally move toward the bowling ball. If you have the insight to recognize this simple movement as being "a step in the right direction," and ring the bell *at once* and reward the animal with food, you will have no difficulty in training the bird to bowl.

But if you wait until the pigeon "acquires an understanding of the problem," or if you insist that it is unreasonable to reward halfway measures and thus wait until the pigeon scores a strike before you give it the first food pellet, it may take you years to pass the exam—if you ever do.

Presuming that you do sound the bell the first time the bird moves tentatively in the general direction of the ball, how does the pigeon respond?

By running to the food cup to claim its reward. After eating the food, it will pause for a while near the food cup. But when pausing doesn't ring the bell, it will usually begin its random trial-and-error movements around the box again. Once more, as soon as it heads toward the ball, you sound the bell. And again the bird runs to the food cup and eats.

The fifth or sixth or tenth time the pigeon repeats this response, a very strange event often occurs. The bird behaves as if it has experienced a "flash of insight" into what is happening. That is, the pigeon acts as if it had discovered that it can actually control *your* behavior! All it has to do to *force* you to give it food is to move in a given direction. (Skinner would probably oppose such a cognitive or mentalistic description of the process, believing it inappropriate to speculate on what private psychological events might be occurring inside the animal's head.)

Once your pigeon has learned the connection between *doing something* and *being rewarded*, you can go much faster with your training. By making the animal move a little bit farther toward the ball each time before you next ring the bell, you can usually get the animal to the vicinity of the bowling ball in a matter of a few minutes. Each time you sound the bell, the pigeon will dash to the food cup, then return at once to where it was the instant the bell rang.

Question: What do you think would happen if you attempted to make the pigeon go too many steps at once before giving it a reward?

The Beak and the Ball So the bird is now where the ball is. Next, you must find a way of getting the animal's beak down on the floor, next to the ball.

Normal level

Figure 16.3. Whenever the pigeon's head bobs below the normal level that it keeps its beak at, you "ring the bell" and reward the pigeon. Then, step by step, you reward it for moving its head lower and lower. Finally, the bird's beak will be on the floor, where the ball is.

Again, you go back to the natural or innately determined responses that the animal makes. As pigeons move, their heads bob up and down. Sometimes, then, the bird's beak is closer to the ball than at other times. A good animal trainer will soon perceive the bird's downward head movements as "good responses," and begin to reward them (see Fig. 16.3).

After several such reinforcements, the pigeon begins to return from the food cup holding its head a little lower than usual. Now it is a simple matter to move the pigeon's beak all the way to the floor by demanding that its head be a little closer to the ball each time you ring the bell.

Question: Do you imagine that, at any time during training, the pigeon gains a cognitive awareness that it is "learning to bowl"?

On to the Goal By now the pigeon's beak is close to the floor, and the bird is moving about near the ball. Within a few moments, its beak will touch the ball "accidentally." The skilled animal trainer now rings the bell joyously, knowing that victory is near. When the bird returns from claiming its reward, it typically takes a second swat at the ball. When again the bell sounds, the pigeon scoots back and forth from food cup to ball, giving it a healthy whack each time the bird comes close.

Now it is up to you to shape the bird's "whacking responses" so that the animal knocks the ball straight down the alley instead of merely hitting it in any random direction. Such **shaping** should take only a few minutes, for at first you reinforce only those whacks that aim the ball in the general direction of the pins. Then you *selectively* reward those hits that come closer and closer to your stated goal. The pigeon soon learns that it will be fed only when it strikes the ball so that it rolls straight down the alley and hits the pins.

An experienced pigeon-handler can usually shape a hungry pigeon "to bowl" in less than an hour. (Training the animal to get a good score takes a little longer.)

Analysis of Skinner's System

There are several fairly subtle points about the Skinnerian system that are sometimes overlooked. To begin with, notice that *no punishment* was necessary to get the animal to perform. The pigeon obviously *can* learn. If it fails to do so, the fault presumably lies with the teacher or the learning environment, not with the student. (Skinner differentiates between *pun-*

Shaping. To "shape" a response is to bring it about using successive approximations to a goal. Thus *shaping* means "training an organism using operant conditioning techniques."

PART FOUR Learning and Memory

ishment, which is a painful input that the animal learns to avoid, and **negative reinforcement,** which is the termination of a painful "drive state" such as extreme hunger. Whether giving food to a hungry animal is "positive" or "negative" reinforcement is a matter much debated. However, food is clearly a *reinforcer* rather than a *punisher,* since the animal approaches food but avoids painful inputs.)

Second, "bowling" is obviously a very complicated set of responses that the animal has to learn in a *particular order or sequence.* You got the bird to learn one simple thing at a time, never demanding too much. You always encouraged the "right" things the pigeon did, and you ignored (or certainly didn't punish) its mistakes. And by doing so, you **chained** the sequence of responses together from its first step to its last whack at the ball. However, the experienced pigeon will perform its bowling routine so smoothly and efficiently that it is not easy for us to see the various individual responses that have been chained together during training.

Third, you didn't need to force or threaten the animal in order to get it to acquire a new way of behaving. By depriving the animal of food before the experiment began, you make the bird willing to work for its supper. You control the *timing* of the reinforcement—but the pigeon determines whether it wants the reward you offered it. If the reinforcement is meaningful and satisfying to that particular bird, then the animal will work. But if you offer the animal something it doesn't want or need—or if you expect too much work for the amount of pleasure that you give the bird in return—it is free to rebel and ignore you. (Surprisingly enough, pigeons appear to enjoy this type of training and, once they have learned the task, will "bowl" again and again with but a minimal amount of encouragement.)

Fourth, at the beginning of the training, you should always reward *each and every* move in the appropriate direction. However, once the pigeon has mastered a given response in the chain, you may begin slowly *fading out the reward* by reinforcing the response **intermittently.** Continuous reinforcement is necessary at first, both to keep the animal eager to perform and to let it know that it is doing something right. However, once the pigeon learns what that "something" is, you may begin reinforcing the response every second time, then every third or fourth time, then perhaps every tenth time. If you fade out the reward very gradually, you can get a pigeon to make a simple response such as pecking a button several thousand times for each reinforcement.

Fifth, during the fading process, the exact *scheduling* of the reward is crucial. If you reinforce *exactly* every tenth response, the bird will soon learn to anticipate which response will gain it food. As soon as it makes this tenth response and feeds, it will take a "rest break" because it knows that its next response never brings it any goodies. Skinner calls this **fixed-ratio reinforcement,** because the ratio between the number of responses required and the rewards given is fixed and never varies.

Negative reinforcement.
Technically speaking, "positive" reinforcement is the *onset* or appearance of a stimulus input which "satisfies" an organism in some way. "Negative" reinforcement is the *termination* of a stimulus situation which the organism would ordinarily avoid. "Punishment" is the *onset* of a painful stimulus that the organism would ordinarily avoid. The difference between positive and negative reinforcement is a technical one. Both types of reinforcement bring about an *increase* in the probability that a response will be repeated, while punishment *suppresses* or disrupts behavioral responses. Food given to a hungry animal is usually considered positive reinforcement, yet it actually terminates a painful stimulus situation called "hunger." Thorndike's terms "satisfiers" and "dis-satisfiers" probably are more apt descriptions of the actual effects of positive reinforcement and of punishment.

Chained. To write the word "cat" on a typewriter, you must first hit the "c" key, then the "a" key, then the "t." You will have made (at least) three different responses that are chained together to achieve the goal of typing the word "cat." Behaviorists believe that complex human behavior patterns are mostly long chains of related responses that must be learned one at a time.

Intermittently (in-turr-MITT-tent-lee). If it rains on Monday, is clear on Tuesday, but rains again on Wednesday and Thursday, then it has rained intermittently during the week. If you reward a rat each third time that it presses a bar, you are giving the animal intermittent reinforcement.

Fixed-ratio reinforcement. If you reward a rat for *exactly* each third bar press that it makes, the ratio between responses (bar presses) and reward is fixed.

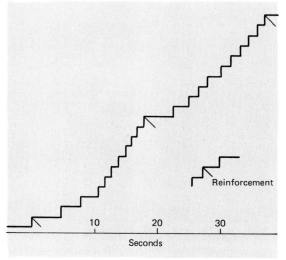

Fig. 16.4. A cumulative record of a pigeon trained to peck a button on a 10 to 1 fixed-ratio reinforcement schedule. Each vertical movement of the graph represents one press of the lever. Note that the pigeon responds more quickly just prior to a reinforcement than just afterward.

Reinforcement

10   20   30
Seconds

If we make a **cumulative record** of the time intervals between each response the animal makes, we would find that it responds slowly just after a reinforcement, but more and more quickly as it approaches that response it knows will gain it the reward (see Fig. 16.4).

We can get the pigeon to respond at a more or less *constant* rate by tricking it a bit—that is, by rewarding it on a *random* or *variable* basis rather than on a fixed-ratio schedule. Instead of reinforcing *exactly* the tenth response, we vary the schedule so that sometimes the third response yields food, sometimes the seventh, sometimes the eleventh, sometimes the twentieth—or any response in between. A thousand responses will yield *about* 100 rewards, but the bird will never know when the next reward is coming. Under these conditions of **variable-ratio reinforcement,** pigeons will respond vigorously and without let-up. We could also reward the pigeon using **interval reinforcement**—that is, by rewarding the first correct response it made after—let's say—an interval of 20 minutes had passed. Generally speaking, *ratio* reinforcement is easier to use than is *interval* reinforcement.

Question: Do the slot machines in Las Vegas pay off on a fixed ratio or a variable ratio?

The sixth point about the Skinnerian system is this: "Shaping" any organism's responses is more of a psychological art than a science, and some people are much better psycho-artists than are others.

Skinner says that you should reward each successive step toward the behavioral goal you have in mind. But there are thousands of different response chains that might lead from the animal's entering behavior to the terminal goal. Skinner doesn't tell you which one to pick, nor how to judge which pathway is best. Lion tamers at the circus, teachers at dog and cat "obedience schools," and the trainers at the various Sea Worlds and Marineland aquariums often make use of Skinnerian principles in teaching their beasts to perform dazzling tricks. But some lion trainers are much better at putting the "big cats" through their paces than are other animal handlers, just as some instructors are much more effective than others at rewarding successive approximations to educational goals. As you might guess, there is still considerable debate about what behavioral traits you need in order to become an effective "shaper."

Question: Which parts of "shaping" seem to be left hemisphere traits? And which might be right hemisphere or "perceptual" traits?

Gunther Gebel Williams in his wild animal cage.

Operant Versus Respondent Conditioning

Skinner calls the type of learning he studies *instrumental conditioning*, or **operant conditioning.** Skinner chose the term "operant" because be believes that the organism must learn to *operate* on its environment in order to get the reinforcers that it desires. Stated in General System Theory terms, the system must somehow change its behavioral outputs until it finds one that is instrumental in bringing it the rewarding inputs that it needs.

Skinner refers to Pavlovian training as **respondent conditoning** because Pavlov taught his animals to *respond* in a specific way to a specific stimulus.

There are many differences between "operant" and "respondent" conditioning. Surely one of the most obvious ones is this: Pavlovian (respondent) learning is always tied to a unique and specific stimulus, while operant conditioning is not. Food powder blown into a dog's mouth **elicits** the salivary response. Pairing the bell with the food gives the bell the power to elicit the same sort of salivation—whether the dog liked it or not. The important point is that neither dogs nor humans go around salivating unless they are stimulated to do so by a highly specific sensory input. Respondent conditioning thus involves setting up involuntary, *elicited* responses to specific stimuli.

On the other hand, pigeons (and people) perform all kinds of actions that don't seem to be "elicited" or pulled out of the organism automatically. Rather, says Skinner, we typically **emit** or produce a wide variety of behaviors rather freely. Those activities that are reinforced, we tend to repeat. Those behaviors that aren't reinforced tend to drop out of our *behavioral repertory.*

Certainly the pigeon whacks at the bowling ball because it is *there*, and the pigeon has learned that doing so yields it a reward. But the "whacking response" is not the same reflexive sort of action that salivation is. The pigeon can, under certain circumstances, walk away from the ball and ignore it. Pavlov's dogs didn't have that choice—when the bell or the food came, they salivated in the same mechanical fashion as your knee jerks when you hit your patellar tendon.

Skinner believes that, in respondent (Pavlovian) conditioning, the *environment operates on the organism.* It doesn't matter whether salivating "pleases" the animal or punishes it, the conditioning occurs anyhow, and the animal will continue to respond in an S–R fashion until it is trained to do something else. In operant conditioning, however, the organism learns how to *operate on its environment.* The animal notes the consequences of what it does, and it tends to repeat those behaviors that bring it rewards. It also attempts to avoid repeating those responses that bring it useless or painful inputs.

In General Systems Theory terms, respondent conditioning involves attaching a *new input* to an *already established response output.* Operant conditioning, however, involves attaching a *new response* to *already present stimulus inputs.* Pavlov almost never taught his animals to respond in a new way. Skinner almost always teaches organisms to respond in ways they never have before (see Fig. 16.5).

In respondent conditioning, the organism need not be a "willing partner," so you can sometimes use Pavlovian techniques to condition an animal that is unconscious during training. Since the important connection is the one between the *CS* and the *UCS*, it also shouldn't matter whether or not the animal actually *responded* during the learning! Thus you could probably train a dog to salivate even if you had paralyzed the animal's salivary glands prior to training. During the experiment, the dog would hear the bell, swallow the food you gave it, but couldn't salivate. But once the paralysis had worn off, it should salivate the first time it heard the bell.

In operant conditioning, the important association is that between the *response* itself and the *feedback* the response generates. Thus the animal must be conscious enough during training to monitor its actions and observe the consequences of what it does.

Respondent conditioning typically involves those *involuntary muscle*

Operant conditioning (OPP-purr-ant). Also called "instrumental conditioning." A type of learning in which the organism must learn which of its responses will operate on its environment to yield a reward.

Respondent conditioning. Also called "classical conditioning" or "Pavlovian conditioning." So named because the organism always responds to presentation of the UCS or the CS with the UCR or the CR.

Elicits (ee-LISS-sits). To elicit is to pull out, to evoke, to stimulate into action. In Pavlovian conditioning, the stimulus that elicits the CR is always identifiable. The important bond is the one between the stimulus and the response.

Emit (ee-MITT). In operant conditioning the exact stimulus that makes a rat press a lever isn't really known. The animal is presumed to be responding to some set of stimuli in its environment, but the stimulus pattern may be so complex that we can never figure it out. The important association in operant conditioning is between the response itself and the reward that follows. If a rat is trained to press a lever only when a light is turned on, the rat is said to "emit" the response in the presence of the light stimulus—however, the light doesn't really elicit the bar-press response. It merely serves as a "discriminative" stimulus that lets the rat know that if it now emits a response, that response will be rewarded.

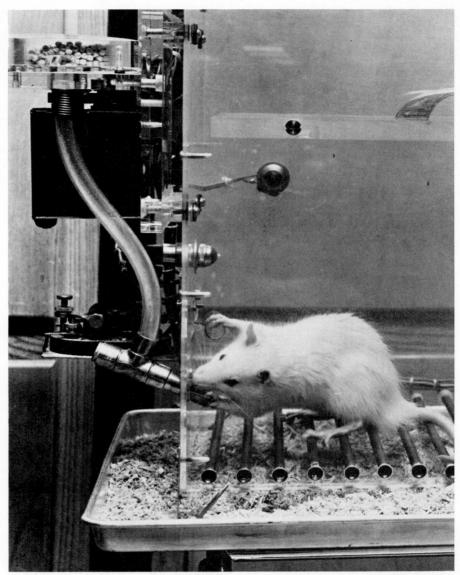

Fig. 16.5. The rat in a specially designed Skinner box is being rewarded for responding correctly in a learning experiment.

groups controlled by the autonomic nervous system and the lower brain centers. Most emotional learning—such as fears and phobias—involves Pavlovian conditioning.

Operant conditioning typically involves those *voluntary muscle groups* controlled by the cortex and the higher brain centers. Motor skills, such as sewing or playing football, are usually the result of some type of operant conditioning.

Question: Suppose you trained a dog to press a bar to get food using operant techniques. Do you think that, at some time during the training, the animal might learn involuntarily to salivate at the sight of the bar?

Biofeedback

As we noted, Pavlovian conditioning techniques seem particularly effective in controlling *autonomic* activities, such as heart rate, while operant conditioning techniques seem more suitable for acquiring *voluntary* responses like bowling.

For many years, psychologists believed that it was nearly impossible to use Skinnerian techniques to help organisms gain voluntary control over their autonomic responses. Recently, however, Neal Miller, Leo DiCara, and their associates have challenged this view. In the late 1960's, Miller and DiCara showed that rats could be trained to increase or to decrease their heart rates if the rats were reinforced for doing so.

In one of their early studies, Miller and DiCara implanted electrodes in the pleasure centers of their rats' brains. Then they gave their animals a drug called **curare,** which left the rats conscious but prevented all voluntary movements.

Once the animals were paralyzed, but still conscious, Miller and DiCara attached the rats to a **polygraph** that recorded their (involuntary) heart beats. Whenever a rat's heart rate would increase a little, they stimulated the animal's reward center electrically. Slowly, over a period of time, the rat's heart responded to this form of *biological feedback* by beating faster and faster.

By reversing the procedure—that is, by giving the animal a rewarding type of feedback whenever its heart *slowed* momentarily—Miller and DiCara were able to condition a decrease in the rat's pulse. By giving the animals **biofeedback** about their blood pressures, sweating, salivation, urine formation, or stomach contractions, the scientists were able to bring these reflexive responses under operant (voluntary) control as well.

Because the Miller–DiCara experiments contradicted long-held theoretical notions about the differences between respondent and operant conditioning, psychologists were reluctant to accept the data. This skepticism reached a peak in the early 1970's, when Miller and DiCara had difficulties in repeating (replicating) some of their earlier experiments involving curare. By the late 1970's, however, numerous other laboratories had confirmed the initial findings, not only with rats and dogs, but also with humans.

Biofeedback in Hospitals By 1973, doctors in several clinical laboratories had begun to use biofeedback and operant techniques to help patients who suffer from various types of heart and circulatory problems. People whose lives are endangered by high blood pressure, for instance, have learned to control their **hypertension** by watching a machine that gives them continuous *visual biofeedback* on their blood pressure. Whenever the machine indicates their blood pressure is rising, the patients try to think relaxing

Curare (cure-RAH-ree). A drug that paralyzes most of the muscles of the body. Several tribes of South American Indians put curare on the darts used in their blow-guns. When the dart strikes an animal, the animal is paralyzed and can easily be captured or killed for food.

Polygraph. A machine that graphs or makes records of many different bodily reactions simultaneously. Sometimes called a "lie detector."

Biofeedback. Literally, biological feedback. Any mechanism that feeds back information on biological performance, such as an EEG machine. See Chapter 3.

Hypertension. From the Latin term meaning "over-stressed." See Chapter 14.

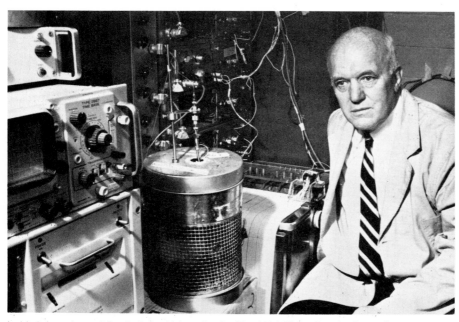

In his laboratory at Rockefeller University, Dr. Neal E. Miller records visceral responses from a freely moving rat.

Chapter 16 Cognitive Maps and Operant Conditioning 415

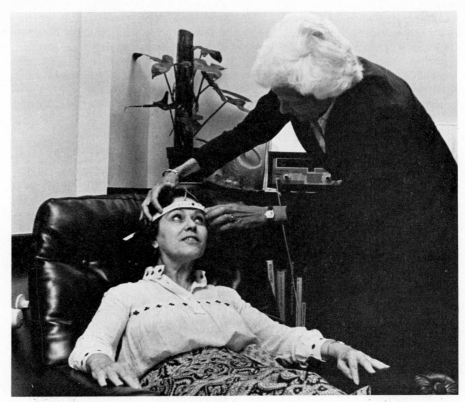

Fig. 16.6. This woman, using biofeedback, can reduce the pain of a migraine headache by learning to lower the temperature of her forehead.

thoughts or make their muscles go limp. Whenever their blood pressure falls a little, they try to remember just what it was they were imagining or feeling when the drop occurred, and to repeat that thought or emotion more often in the future.

Other patients attempt to learn to control irregularities in their heart beats, or to reduce the flow of stomach acids that might damage or inflame their ulcers. These training techniques are particularly useful with people who, for one reason or another, cannot make use of the drugs often employed to control circulatory or digestive illnesses.

Still other patients have learned to reduce the pain associated with **migraine headaches** by training themselves to control their skin temperatures. During a migraine attack, patients often have abnormally cold hands and an unusually warm forehead. By using machines that give them visual feedback on their skin temperatures, patients are often able to warm up their hands and cool down their forehead temperatures voluntarily, and thus reduce the severity of their headaches (see Fig. 16.6).

Although the use of biofeedback is in its infancy in medical circles, operant technology will surely be widely employed in the future to help sick people gain voluntary control over many of their physiological responses. And how odd it is that a laboratory technique developed in order to train pigeons in a box would turn out to have such usefulness for humans.

An Evaluation of Skinner's Approach

Migraine headache. From a Greek term meaning "pain in one side of the head." A recurring or very severe form of headache.

Powerful as the Skinnerian system is, it has a number of flaws in it. For example, reinforcement is one of the key concepts in operant conditioning, yet Skinner has focused chiefly on those biological rewards, such as food, that seem to reinforce all living systems. That is, while paying attention to the *energy inputs* that organisms find rewarding, Skinner has neglected the *informational inputs* that living systems need in order to achieve their intra-psychic and social goals.

Many Gestalt theorists believe that people are often rewarded by new *perceptions*, by gathering previously unrelated facts into a meaningful whole (which they term a "Gestalt"). As we mentioned earlier, when pigeons are trained to bowl, they often show the same kind of delighted "Ah ha!" response that Maier's rat and Koehler's chimpanzee showed when those animals suddenly perceived a relationship that had eluded them before.

Question: Koehler had to wait several hours until Sultan "accidentally" held the two poles in front of him and noticed that one could be fitted into the other. How might Skinner have trained Sultan to get the banana in a much shorter time?

Educators sometimes refer to the "Ah ha!" experience as "the thrill of discovery," and there is little doubt that such reactions can be strong reinforcement. However, these experiences are quite rare, and the teacher who believes that "insight" is the *only* kind of reward necessary in the classroom is probably not a very effective people-trainer.

Insights typically occur when a person or pigeon has built up enough units in a response chain to be able to perceive or anticipate previously unexpected results. It would seem that we all need a Skinnerian type of feedback and reward to guide our steps toward the creation of a Gestalt. But it is the *intellectual pleasure* resulting from achieving the insight that gives the whole experience meaningfulness, generality, and memorability. But since Skinner prefers not to deal with "mental" events, he has no way of accounting for the power of intra-psychic reinforcers (see Chapter 5).

Skinner and Self-Control

When Skinner trains a pigeon to bowl, *he* determines what the goal of the training will be, *he* measures the entering behaviors of the bird, and *he* selectively reinforces approximations to the goal. The bird *behaves;* Skinner *monitors* these behaviors and *gives the animal feedback* in order to shape its responses. Because Skinner can tell you what he is doing as he goes along, he can describe both the terminal response and the approximations in measurable terms. Thus he doesn't need to talk about what goes on inside the pigeon's mind, and he can legitimately claim that such intra-psychic processes as "thinking" aren't needed in order to explain behavior.

However, humans are more complex systems than are pigeons, and you can use operant techniques to change your own outputs *voluntarily* in a wide variety of ways. The problem for Skinner is that this sort of self-determined change is difficult to explain in purely "objective" terms.

Let's assume that you have decided you want to lose weight (see Chapter 12), so you think the matter over, decide on the goal you wish to reach, and decide to give yourself a "mental pat on the back" for cutting down on rich foods. You reduce your caloric intake drastically for the next couple of weeks, you exercise more, and you lose five pounds. You find the process so *cognitively* reinforcing that you decide to continue dieting for a while, and again you are successful. Only then do you mention your weight-loss program to other people.

Since you did not tell anyone what you were doing, the goal of your efforts was a "thought" or "intra-psychic" event and *not* something an external observer could define or measure objectively. You monitored your own behaviors, you shaped your own responses, and you gave yourself "mental" feedback. In short, you conditioned yourself—presumably by carrying on a "silent conversation" inside your head that led to a measurable change both in your inputs and your outputs.

Because Skinner states that *all* learning is under the direct control of external stimuli, he has difficulty explaining the sort of self-directed behavioral change you engage in when you lose weight or demonstrate in some other way that you are capable of self-control.

From a General Systems Theory viewpoint, operant conditioning typically involves an interaction between two systems—one that *emits measurable outputs*, and a second system that *sets goals, monitors outputs*, and *gives performance feedback* to the first system. The goals, the outputs, and the feedback may be biological, intra-psychic, social/behavioral, or a combination of all three types.

When Skinner trains a pigeon to bowl, he is the "monitoring and goal-setting" system, while the bird is the "behaver." The bird's reinforcers are biological, while Skinner's are presumably intra-psychic (though he might not admit it). When you train yourself, your left (talking) hemisphere is presumably the "doer," while your right (silent) hemisphere is presumably monitoring and shaping the thoughts and actions of the left hemisphere by giving it emotional and cognitive feedback. And in this case, surely, your reinforcers are primarily psychological.

Given the history of our science, Skinner's demand that psychologists deal with measurable events was certainly a step in the right direction, and operant technology is indeed a powerful tool. But, in a sense, you demonstrate the narrowness of Skinner's approach each time that you have a creative insight, experience the joy of learning, think through a problem, or voluntarily control your outputs in order to achieve some personal goal.

Summary

1. The study of **learning** is one of the major areas within psychology.

2. E.L. Thorndike assumed that humans learn in much the same way that animals do. His studies with cats in a **puzzle box** led him to believe that most learning is by **trial-and-error learning.**

3. Thorndike stated learning is influenced by two laws:

    a. The **"law of effect"** states that **stimulus–response (S–R) bonds** are strengthened if the effect of the response is to yield the animal a reward.

    b. The **"law of exercise"** states that the more frequently an animal repeats an S–R bond, the stronger it becomes.

4. Thorndike, like Pavlov, believed that all learning is mechanical or **reflexive. Gestalt psychologists,** such as Wolfgang Koehler, assume that animals are capable of thinking about what they do and of solving problems mentally (through **insight**) rather than just through mechanical trial and error.

5. According to Koehler, animals do not learn a **maze** by acquiring hundreds of **S–R connections.** Rather, they make a **cognitive map** of the maze which guides their behavior.

6. B.F. Skinner, a behaviorist much like Thorndike, developed **operant conditioning**—a method of training organisms that differs from Pavlovian or **respondent conditioning.**

7. Pavlov believed that the CS **elicits** or pulls the CR out of the animal involuntarily. Skinner believes that animals **emit** responses freely and that the environment rewards some of those responses, but ignores or punishes others.

8. According to Skinner, **reinforcement** tends to increase the probability that an organism will emit the same response the next time it is free to do so.

9. Training an organism by operant (Skinnerian) techniques consists of several steps:

    a. First, the **terminal response** or goal of the training must be stated in measurable terms.

    b. Second, the **entering behavior** (what the organism is doing before intervention begins) must be measured precisely. This act is called "taking a **baseline.**"

    c. Third, those entering behaviors that seem directed toward the terminal response are rewarded. All other responses are ignored.

    d. Each small step toward the goal is reinforced—a technique called **"shaping"** or "rewarding **successive approximations** to a goal."

10. Most professional animal trainers in the United States now use this Skinnerian, or operant, form of conditioning.

11. Generally speaking, Pavlovian or respondent conditioning involves those **involuntary muscles** controlled by the **autonomic nervous system** or the **lower brain centers.**

12. Generally speaking, operant conditioning involves those **voluntary muscles** controlled by the **cortex** and higher **brain centers.**

13. The proper use of **biofeedback** can allow you to gain voluntary control over such **reflexive responses** as your heart rate, skin temperature, and so forth.

14. Although Skinner claims that all behaviors are directly controlled by environmental inputs, he has problems explaining **voluntary self-control** in purely S–R terms.

15. No one system of training organisms is complete in and of itself, however. The cognitive theorists, the Pavlovians, and the behaviorists have all added greatly to our understanding of how humans acquire new attitudes, skills, thoughts, and behavioral reactions.

(Continued from page 400.)

FROM: Experimenter-in-Chief, Inter-stellar Labship PSYCH-474
TO: Director, Bureau of Science

Thlan, my friend, this will be an informal report. I will send the official report along later, but I wanted to give you my impressions first.

The work with the newly discovered species is, unfortunately, at a standstill. Things went well at first. We picked what seemed to be an average but healthy animal and began testing it in our standard apparatus. I may have told you that this new species looks much like our usual laboratory subjects, the White Rote, so we included a couple of the "toys" that the Rotes seem fond of—thin sheets of material made from woodpulp and a tiny stick of graphite. Imagine our delight when this new specimen made exactly the same use of the materials as have many of the Rotes. Could it be that there are certain innate behavior patterns to be found throughout the universe in the lower species?

The answer is of little importance, really. Your friend Verpk keeps insisting that the marks the Rotes make on the sheets are an attempt at communication, but that is, of course, utterly impossible. (Why did you saddle me with this idiot anyway when there are so many reasonable-thinking scientists available?) Ah, well, this "scribbling" behavior did give us hope that the new species would behave according to standard theory.

And at first this was the case. The animal solved the Bfian Box problem in short order, yielding as beautiful data as I have ever seen. We then shifted it to mazes and jump stand problems, and the results were equally pleasing. The animal clearly learns by forming conditioned reflexes linking inputs with outputs in purely mechanical fashion.

Then, just to please Verpk, we tested it for "concept formation." Now you and I both understand that lower organisms are not intelligent enough to solve the Oddity Problem, even if some cognitive theorists (whom I shall not name) disagree. For a few terrible trials, it seemed that those nameless theorists might be right! Which is to say that the animal *appeared* to react correctly even to stimuli it had never seen before! What an annoyance that would be since we are committed to "protecting" species intelligent enough to form concepts.

Ah, well, not to worry. The Oddity Problem apparently overloaded its simple brain circuits, for the organism soon broke down and became quite ill. Probably just as well, since this species is obviously unsuited for further experimentation.

I am not sure what to do next, either with this specimen or the world from which we took it. One of the students has nursed the animal back to some sort of health, and wishes to keep it as a pet. Verpk, however, suggests we put it back where we found it, and that we begin a crash program to see if these organisms really are concept-formers. Stupid suggestion, but I pass it along anyhow. My own belief is that we should sacrifice the animal and study its anatomy carefully to determine if it really is related to the White Rote.

But that is not why I write. Since this new species tends to break down readily under stress—much like Vavlov's Wogs—I see little sense in wasting our time in this part of the universe. We will not serve either our race or our glorious theories by studying what is clearly another stupid species.

The question is, then, should we stay here and continue our work as Verpk insists, or should we look for healthier and more normal animals elsewhere? And if we depart, should we first destroy the "home colony" so that these pests cannot be used in unscientific ways by those cognitive theorists I refuse to name?

Since all lower species are under your protection, we need your advice. My hope is that you will let us seek out new colonies and test our theories with *healthy* animals. For it is only in this fashion that science as we know it progresses.

Respectfully yours,
Iowyy

Recommended Readings

Basmajian, John V., ed. *Biofeedback: Principles and Practice for Clinicians* (Baltimore, Md.: Williams & Wilkins, 1978).

Davis, Hank, and Harry M.B. Hurwitz, eds. *Operant-Pavlovian Interactions* (Hillsdale, N.J.: Erlbaum, 1977).

Hall, John F. *Classical Conditioning and Instrumental Learning: A Contemporary Approach* (Philadelphia, Pa.: Lippincott, 1976).

Kamiya, Joe, Theodore X. Barber, Neal E. Miller, David Shapiro, and Johann Stoyva, eds. *Biofeedback and Self-Control 1976/77* (Chicago: Aldine, 1977).

Koehler, Wolfgang. *Gestalt Psychology* (New York: Liveright, 1947).

Skinner, B.F. *Walden Two* (New York: Macmillan, 1960).

Skinner, B.F. *About Behaviorism* (New York: Knopf, 1974).

Memory

DID YOU KNOW THAT...

You have not one memory, but many different kinds of memories?

Your eyes momentarily store an "exact photo" of what you see, but your brain "forgets" most of what your eyes see?

Your Short-term Memory is limited to about seven items?

Your Long-term Memory consists in part of "mental file cards" that allow you to reconstruct past events rather than remember them exactly?

There are at least seven types of forgetting?

Your brain has a better memory system than any computer?

When you learn, you seem to "re-program" your own brain?

Some scientists believe that, when you learn, your brain manufactures new "memory molecules?"

Some experiments suggest these "memory molecules" can be transferred from one organism to another by injection?

If you are deprived of REM sleep, your Long-term Memory may be adversely affected?

"Where Is Yesterday?"

"What's your name, dear?" The middle-aged woman lying in the white hospital bed smiled sweetly as she asked the question.

The young woman in the gray uniform paused from her chores. "Jamie," she said quietly. "Jamie Calvin. I'm the Nurse's Aide."

"That's an odd sort of name, now isn't it? Is it English, or something?"

The girl in gray grinned at the bedridden woman. "Not really, Mrs. Bjork. I'm the oldest child in our family, and my father really wanted a boy. So when I turned out to be a girl instead, he gave me a boy's name anyhow." The young woman continued her work, picking up a couple of empty glasses and throwing some used tissues into the wastebasket.

"But whom did he name you after, dear?" Mrs. Bjork continued.

"Daddy was nuts about a psychologist named William James. He really wanted to call me Willie, but Mother wouldn't stand for it. So they compromised on Jamie instead. I don't mind, really. It's rather a nice name when you get used to it."

"William James! Isn't that peculiar! Why I can remember reading his book *Varieties of Religious Experience* in one of my psychology classes! Was your father by any chance a psychologist, Jamie?"

"No, but he sometimes thought he was. Actually, Daddy was a nice, old-fashioned Methodist minister. With a name like Calvin, what else would you expect? We buried him two years ago, God rest his soul."

"Oh, I'm so sorry, my dear. I know you must miss him."

"I do, Mrs. Bjork. But he lives on in my memory, just as though he was still alive." The young woman paused, then brightened. "Is your father still alive?"

Mrs. Bjork laughed. "Very much so. A big bear of a man, he is. In fact, I rather expect him to come visit me today."

"That would be nice," Jamie Calvin said, as she gathered up the dirty glasses and headed for the door. "You just rest comfortably until he does, Mrs. Bjork."

Jamie Calvin walked softly as a Siamese cat down the long hospital corridor, deposited the glasses in a large container, and returned to the nurses' station.

"Nice woman in 914, that Mrs. Bjork," she said to Mrs. Melton, the chief nurse on duty. "What's she in for?"

Mrs. Melton was filling out some forms. Stopping for a moment, she said, "Mrs. Bjork? Oh, she's a brain-damage case. She's in for some tests. You haven't seen her before, have you? Yes, she's a very nice person. I do hope they can do something for her."

"What's wrong with her?" Jamie said, sitting down.

"She was in a terrible automobile accident not long ago. Wasn't wearing her seat belt, and her head went right through the windshield. Didn't scar her up much, but she suffered considerable brain damage anyhow. They had to remove a fair share of both her temporal lobes."

"Temporal lobes?" the younger woman asked plaintively.

"They're the part of the brain right by your temples."

"Oh," Jamie said. "That doesn't sound very good. Poor Mrs. Bjork."

A buzzer sounded, and Mrs. Melton looked at the call board. "914," she said. "Speak of the devil. Be a dear, Jamie, and go see what Mrs. Bjork wants."

When Jamie walked into room 914, Mrs. Bjork looked at the young woman through puzzled eyes. "I'm terribly sorry to bother you, Nurse, but I seem to be confused about a few things. Obviously I'm in a hospital, but for the life of me, I can't think why. I don't feel at all sick. I'm terribly sorry to impose on you this way, but I wonder if you can tell me what's wrong?"

Jamie frowned. "Mrs. Melton—she's the chief nurse—says that you were in a car accident, and they want to give you some tests. I'm sure it won't hurt at all, and that you'll be out of the hospital very quickly."

"A car accident? Now, isn't that peculiar? I can't remember a thing about a car accident. Are you sure?"

"That's what Nurse Melton just told me."

Mrs. Bjork frowned. "Oh well, I'm sure it will all come back to me soon." Then she smiled at the Nurse's Aide. "By the way, what's your name, dear?"

"Jamie Calvin. Like I told you. I'm the Nurse's Aide."

"That's an odd sort of name, now isn't it? Is it English, or something?"

Jamie's eyes narrowed. She thought a moment as if deciding how to continue. Then she said softly, "Not really, Mrs. Bjork. I'm the oldest child in our family. My father really wanted a boy, but I turned out to be a girl. So he gave me a boy's name instead."

"But whom did he name you after, dear?" Mrs. Bjork continued.

Jamie took a step nearer the door. "Daddy was nuts about a psychologist named William James."

"William James! Isn't that odd! Why I can remember reading his book, *Varieties of Religious Experience* in one of my psychology classes! Was your father by any chance a psychologist, Jamie?"

"Would you like a glass of water or a Coke or something, Mrs. Bjork?" Jamie said rather desperately.

"Water? Why, yes, a cola or a ginger ale would be nice. I think my father will be coming to see me shortly, you know. He likes ginger ale very much. Why don't you be a lamb and bring us two bottles of ginger ale?"

"Right away," Jamie said, leaving the room quickly.

"What did Mrs. Bjork want?" Nurse Melton asked when Jamie returned to the station.

"Some ginger ale." Jamie sat down for a moment, a puzzled frown on her face. "What's wrong with Mrs. Bjork? She didn't even remember me from five minutes ago."

"Oh, I should have warned you. Something's wrong with her memory. She can't remember a thing. That's what they want to do the tests on."

Jamie frowned. "But she remembered a lot of things. Like a psychology course she took, for instance, and a book she'd read."

"I know. But she can't remember where she is or what day it is," Mrs. Melton replied, continuing her paperwork. "Makes her seem stupid sometimes, but she's really quite bright. One of the psychologists tested her intelligence yesterday. Said her IQ after the accident is actually a bit higher than it was the last time she was tested, about 10 years ago. She spoke fluent French and Spanish before the accident, and she still speaks them fluently. Only thing is, she can't remember what she had for breakfast or who her doctor is."

After a moment, Jamie sighed deeply. "I guess I'd better go get that ginger ale. She's expecting her father."

Nurse Melton stopped and put down the forms she was working on. "Jamie, dear, her father is dead. He was driving the car when the accident occurred."

"But hasn't anybody told her?"

"Jamie, everybody has told her, many times. She just doesn't remember."

"But she remembers her name! How could she forget her father's death and still remember her own name?"

Nurse Melton shrugged. "Jamie, Mrs. Bjork suffers from what the psychologists call *continuous retrograde amnesia*. She remembers almost everything that happened before the accident, but her brain is incapable of forming new memories that last for more than a couple of minutes. She'll live in 'The Eternal Now' for the rest of her life." Nurse Melton shook her head sadly, then went back to her paperwork.

A few moments later Jamie knocked softly at the door to Room 914, then entered, carrying a tray with two bottles of ginger ale, glasses, and a little bucket of ice. "Here's the soda pop you wanted, Mrs. Bjork."

"Soda pop?" the woman in the bed said. "I didn't order any soda pop. That must be for one of the other patients."

"Why, Mrs. Bjork, you particularly asked for ginger ale because you said your father was coming to visit you."

Mrs. Bjork shook her head. "I'm sure I didn't ask for any ginger ale, but it is true that my father likes it very much. So why don't you just be a dear and leave it here for him." As the young woman put the tray down on a table, Mrs. Bjork stared at her thoughtfully. "What's your name, dear?"

"Jamie," the young woman whispered. "Jamie Calvin. I'm the Nurse's Aide."

"That's an odd sort of name, now isn't it? Is it English, or something?"

There were tears in Jamie's eyes as she answered. "Not really, Mrs. Bjork. I'm the oldest in our family, and Daddy really wanted a boy. So when I happened to be a girl instead, he gave me a boy's name anyhow." Jamie turned and headed for the door.

"But whom did he name your after, dear?" Mrs. Bjork continued.

Jamie Calvin muffled a sob and fled from the room.

"Now, wasn't that odd?" Mrs. Bjork said aloud, reaching for a bottle of ginger ale. "I wonder what's the matter with her?"

(Continued on p. 446.)

Memory

What time is it?

A simple question, and one that you probably are asked frequently. How do you respond? You look at your watch, or at a clock, and you give the answer almost automatically. If you don't have a timepiece handy, you guess—and usually you'll be accurate within a few minutes or so. If you are **bilingual**—that is, if you speak another language besides English—you will answer the question either in English or in your second language, depending on what language the question was asked in.

A simple question, "What time is it?" Yet, to be truthful, we know very little about how your brain goes about processing such inputs, and we know even less about how your brain responds so appropriately. Perhaps if we explore this question further, though, you will gain an even greater respect for, and understanding of, the complexities of your mind and your nervous system.

Memory Systems

To answer any question, you must make use of your **memory.** If someone asks you the time, you must first recognize that someone has spoken to you, then that you have been asked a question to which you might respond. Then you must check your memory banks to make sure that you recognize the language the person has used.

But while all this "checking" is taking place, *your brain must have some way of remembering what the original question was.* If you had no way of holding the question in some kind of "temporary storage," you'd end up realizing that someone had asked you something in English without being able to remember what it was that the person asked.

As we will see, a different part of your brain seems to be involved in this *temporary storage* of the question than is involved in *answering* the question itself.

Bilingual (buy-LING-wall). From the Latin words *bi*, meaning "two," and *lingua*, meaning "tongue" or "language." The term "lingo," meaning the slang words used by a particular group of people, also comes from the Latin word *lingua*. For that matter, so does the word "slang."

Memory. From the Latin and Greek words meaning "to be mindful, or to remember." Your memory is your store of past experiences, thus the seat of your ability to recreate or reproduce past perceptions, emotions, thoughts, and actions. To be truthful, we have only the vaguest of notions of how your memory actually works.

PART FOUR Learning and Memory

Question: Suppose you are reading an interesting book when someone nearby asks you a question. Have you ever responded with "What did you say?" and then, even before the question could be repeated, given the correct answer?

In point of fact, you don't have just one "memory system," you have several "sub-systems," and they typically perform their functions simultaneously. Whenever a new stimulus comes to your attention, your *receptors* appear to hold on to the stimulus pattern for a fraction of a second while some part of your brain "looks the stimulus over" to see if it is familiar to you.

If you recognize the input, another part of your brain then takes over and "memorizes" the most **salient** or important parts of the stimulus for a few seconds while the rest of your brain decides what to do with the incoming message.

Sensory Information Stage

What time is it?

When the image of those words first impinges on the retinas in your eyes, your rods and cones begin to fire a characteristic *pattern of nerve impulses* that flash along your optic nerve to the visual centers of your brain.

Suppose that we showed that stimulus question to you for exactly one-tenth of a second. How long would your rods and cones continue to fire after the words had disappeared? The answer is—it depends. As I showed in 1956, if you have been sitting in absolute darkness for several minutes, the words *"What time is it?"* would hang suspended in your visual field for quite some time, like the words on a huge billboard if all the rest of the world were blacked out.

On the other hand, if you were sitting in a lighted room reading the words in a book, the very next words you read would wash out or erase the phrase "What time is it?" Under normal conditions—as you look from one thing to another in your visual world—your eye holds on to each stimulus pattern for but a fraction of a second before it is replaced by yet another input pattern.

Your memory *begins*, then, in your receptors, in what psychologists call the **Sensory Information Storage** stage of information processing. When your eye briefly "stores" a visual input, it records the scene in amazing detail, much as a photograph would. However, by the time this visual information reaches your brain—and you become aware of what you are looking at—much of the rich detail is lost.

To put the matter another way, your *eye* has a "photographic memory," but your *brain* doesn't. As soon as the lower centers in your brain receive the input, they begin "processing" or "analyzing" the message for its meaning or importance. These lower centers promptly discard or reject any part of the sensory pattern that they don't find interesting.

For example, your **reticular system** (see Chapter 9) probably looks the stimulus over to see if it is familiar and "non-threatening." If so, the reticular system notifies your cortex that all is well and tells your cortex to have a look at what is coming through on the visual circuits.

If the stimulus is mildly threatening but quite weak—such as a "dirty word" or a "sexual scene"—your reticular system may clamp down on the message and try to keep it from reaching the rest of your brain.

If the visual pattern is novel, quite unexpected, or very threatening, your reticular system may trigger off an emotional reaction in your autonomic nervous system. This emotional response occurs, as you might suspect, even before your cortex becomes aware of what the visual input actually is.

Whether your reticular system has its own memory bank, or simply has connections to the larger library of information stored elsewhere in your brain, or both, no one knows for sure.

Salient (SAY-lee-ent). Anything that stands out from its background, that is important or noticeable.

Sensory Information Storage. The first stage of memory storage. Suppose you are looking at a blank television screen when the word "help" suddenly flashes on the screen for exactly 1/10th of a second and then disappears, leaving the screen blank again. The rods and cones in your retina will actually hold the image of the word "help" for much more than a second. During this "holding stage," the rods and cones will continue to send signals to your brain just as if the word "help" were still showing on the screen. This momentary "hold" of an incoming sensory pattern is the Sensory Information Storage stage of memory.

Reticular system (ree-TICK-you-lar). The reticular activating system (RAS) or "alerting" system in the brain. See Chapter 9.

Short-term Memory. You experience millions of different sensory inputs every day. As these incoming stimulus messages are passed to the brain from Sensory Information Storage, some part of the brain "remembers" them for a few brief seconds. If the inputs are not important, they are soon forgotten. Experts believe that you typically hold no more than about seven items at a time in your Short-term Memory.

Cyrillic (seer-RILL-ick). The Russian alphabet, which is based on the Greek, was supposedly invented by St. Cyril, who died in A.D. 868. St. Cyril, who was born in Greece, helped take Christianity to the Slavic people in south Russia and translated the Bible into their language. Prior to this, the Slavic language had existed in spoken but not in written form. When St. Cyril wrote out the Bible, he "created" the Cyrillic alphabet still used in Russian today. In Cyrillic, the initials "CCCP" stand for the Soviet Union, that is, the Union of Soviet Socialist Republics, just as in English the initials "USA" stand for the United States of America.

While your reticular system is judging the *emotional importance* of the incoming message, other parts of your brain make a preliminary interpretation of what the stimulus input *means*. While this "interpreting" is going on, your brain must be able to put the stimulus input on "hold" for a few moments. So your brain stores what we might call a "verbal description" of the input in your **Short-term Memory** while the stimulus is being processed. As you can guess from the name itself, anything tucked away in your Short-term Memory has a very brief lifetime, probably no more than a few seconds.

Your Sensory Information Storage system records (momentarily) a more or less exact copy of the stimulus pattern. Your Short-term Memory holds the verbal description of this pattern for a few seconds longer, while the rest of your brain is deciding how best to respond to the stimulus. But much of the complexity of the sensory pattern is lost in the storage process. To prove this fact to yourself, read the following sentence rapidly and then look away from the page for a few seconds and try to remember exactly what the stimulus sentence was:

Который час?

Chances are—unless you are familiar with the Russian language—you had a difficult time trying to remember just what it was you actually saw. You surely sensed at once that it was something written in a language other than English, but could you "see" in your mind's eye each of the letters in that strange **Cyrillic** alphabet that the Russians use? Or was it more or less a jumbled blur?

Question: Would a camera have any more difficulty photographing the phrase in Russian than in English? If not, why did your "mind's eye" blur over the Russian words but get the English words correctly?

Now look quickly at the following stimulus sentence and then look away and try to visualize exactly what it says:
What time it is?
When this phrase appeared in Russian, your Short-term Memory couldn't make a verbal description of the words because they are in Russian, not English. So you couldn't remember them any better than you could describe them. But when the phrase appeared in English, you remembered the description very well, because the words were quite familiar to you and thus easy for you to "code into words" for your Short-term Memory to keep "on hold" while your brain interpreted the meaning of the input.

Question: Look again at the English phrase one paragraph above. Does it really say what you remembered it as saying? If you didn't perceive it correctly, what might this fact tell you about your Short-term Memory?

Your Short-term Memory has a very limited capacity. Ordinarily it cannot retain anything for more than a few seconds, and it typically cannot hold on to more than six or seven items at once. At the moment that your brain inserts an item into Short-term Memory, that item is strong and clear and easy to recall if you do so *immediately*. But shortly thereafter, your brain tucks away a second item, and then a third item, and a fourth. Although a few seconds have passed, you will now have much more trouble trying to recall what the first item was really like (see Fig. 17.1).

And by the time your brain has pressed 5 or 6 new items down on top of the first, that original item has lost most of its strength and has faded away.

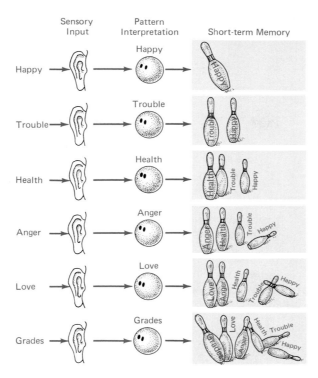

Sensory Input	Pattern Interpretation	Short-term Memory
Happy	Happy	Happy
Trouble	Trouble	Trouble Happy
Health	Health	Health Trouble Happy
Anger	Anger	Anger Health Trouble Happy
Love	Love	Love Anger Health Trouble Happy
Grades	Grades	Grades Love Anger Health Trouble Happy

Fig. 17.1. Short-term Memory storage.

The new items appear to *interfere with* or erase the ones in front of them, just as each new visual pattern you look at wipes clean the stimulus you were looking at just a moment before.

While you are holding an item in Short-term Memory, you can recall it more or less at will. However, once the item drops out of "temporary storage," it is likely to be gone forever—unless your brain decides to make a *permanent record* of the stimulus input.

Long-term Memory

If you stroll along a busy street, you may see a thousand different people in one short hour. Most of their faces will fade from your memory immediately, like snow in the springtime winds. Yet some things you remember vividly—or at least you think you do.

For example, think of the last long trip that you took. Can you recall *right at this instant* the exact date and hour that the trip began and ended? Chances are that you can't. But if you "put your mind to it," couldn't you work out some of the details? What day of the week did the trip begin? Couldn't you figure out the date if you really tried? Did you start in the morning, the afternoon, or the evening? Who went with you, if anyone? If you flew, what airline was your carrier? If you drove, what kind of car was it?

If you actually take the time to think about the details, and perhaps write them down as you go, you'll find that you can *reproduce* a surprising amount of detail about that trip, even though it may have occurred months or years ago. However, if you inspect those memories carefully as they pop back into your consciousness, you'll find they are *qualitatively* quite different from the immediate memory you have of a face you've just seen.

In fact, your recollection of things that happened long ago usually is hazy and incomplete at first. One of the first (and greatest) investigators of human memory was a German scientist named Hermann Ebbinghaus. More than 100 years ago, Ebbinghaus proved that you typically don't *remember* complex events—rather, you usually recall a few "high points" and then *reconstruct* the experience piece by little piece.

Your Short-term Memory is rather like an "instant replay" on television—a few seconds of highlight action that you can recall with considera-

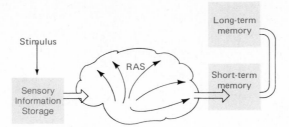

Fig. 17.2. Short- and Long-term Memory flow chart.

ble clarity for a brief period of time thereafter. But it is the *salient features* of the experience, and not all the rich sensory detail, that you can replay at will until these too quickly fade away into obscurity (see Fig. 17.2).

Your **Long-term Memory,** however, lasts the rest of your life. And for all practical purposes, its storage capacity is unlimited. Buried away in the cells of your brain are billions of different memories that date back to your early childhood. You could, if the circumstances were right, go back and reproduce "in the theater of your mind" all those countless experiences. And yet, *right now,* can you remember all the things you did on your fifth birthday?

Your Long-term Memory is practically limitless—rather like a huge library with billions of books stashed away on the shelves. You add thousands of new volumes to that library every day of your life, and most of us never run out of shelf space for new arrivals. Not even the largest, most expensive computer system now in operation can match the complexity of your own brain's memory banks. Still, most of us complain that we have lousy memories. Why?

Learning and Forgetting

To appreciate how your Long-term Memory works—and why it often fails to function the way you would like it to—you must first discover the answers to several questions:

First, what *part* of your immediate psychological experiences do you file away?

Second, why do you store some experiences in Long-term Memory, but not others?

Third, once an item is placed in your permanent memory bank, how in the world do you go about recalling it? That is to say, what is the process of **item retrieval** all about?

And fourth, what causes you to forget things?

As we will see, you can answer these four questions best if you first discover what your "mental library" is really like.

Cataloging Memories

If you would like to stretch your imagination just a little, suppose that a rich uncle died and left you: (a) his personal collection of more than a million magazines and books; (b) a huge but empty warehouse; and (c) a check for $500,000. However, you can't cash the check until after you personally arrange all his collection and store all the items in the warehouse, without any outside help on the project. Since you could use a little pocket money, you decide to have a go at earning the half-million dollars. But when you arrive at the warehouse for the first time, you find that the movers have dumped all the books and magazines in a huge pile in the middle of the floor. Now what should you do?

The "Mental Index" Perhaps some people would throw up their hands in horror and quit on the spot. But you decide to **persevere.** So you sit down on the foor and stare at all those items. You wonder how you might go about putting them in some kind of sensible order so that if someone

Long-term Memory. Your store of permanent memories. Inputs that are important enough to survive your Short-term Memory are transferred to long-term storage by some physiological mechanism we don't yet understand. For the most part, you seem to store items in Long-term Memory by "mental categories"—that is, by some descriptive term. Once an item is put away in long-term storage, it presumably is available to you if you know how to retrieve it.

Item retrieval. You retrieve items from long-term storage by checking various "categories" under which the item might be filed. If you cannot find the right entry point (or category) to retrieve the item, you will ordinarily not be able to remember it. The item is still in your memory files—you merely don't know where it is located.

Persevere (purr-suh-VEER, or purr-see-VEER). To persist in something; to pursue a goal until it is achieved. The psychological term "perseverate" (purr-SEV-ur-ate) means to keep doing something or talking about something long after the actual goal is achieved. Compulsive behaviors are often forms of abnormal perseverations (purr-sev-ur-RAY-shuns).

walked into your warehouse library and asked for a particular book, you could retrieve the item in a few short moments.

You might begin by separating the books from the magazines. Surely that would help. Of course, you'd find there were a few fancy magazines that looked a great deal like books, and there were books that were hard to tell from **periodicals.** In general, though, the selection process should be fairly simple.

But how would you arrange the books? By their size? Color? The language they were printed in? Or would you arrange them by the names of their authors? Or by their titles? By the name of their publishers? Their subject matter? By the year in which they were published? By whether you liked them or not?

And once you had answered those questions to your satisfaction, wouldn't you want to make up a "card index" of some kind of handy reference? Then, when a friend of yours came in and said that she or he had once read "a big green book written by some foreign author on the unusual sex practices of a tribe of primitives in Africa, or maybe South America," you could find the volume for your friend without too much trouble (and might even decide to read the book yourself).

The next time you visit a library, you might wish to take a look at the card catalog and see how professional librarians try to handle these problems (see Fig. 17.3). For libraries use much the same *filing system* as the one your own brain employs. Whenever your brain files an item away for future references—that is, stores an item in your Long-term Memory—it also creates a "mental index card" of some kind telling you how to *retrieve* that item if you have to do so.

That is, your brain translates your personal experiences into a kind of mental shorthand and files those experiences away in various *categories.* You usually cannot remember an item unless you can first discover what "category" the item relates to.

Verbal Schemes Think about dogs for a moment. How many different dogs can you remember? Can you recall a beloved pet from early childhood, or the big fierce animal that barked loudly at you just a few days ago?

Now answer this question: Why is it that, when you're trying to think of dogs, your brain doesn't pull out mental images of airplanes or snakes or roses? The answer seems to be that dogs and snakes are filed in different ways (or perhaps different places) in your brain, and when you want to remember one, images of the other are blocked from your consciousness. Of course, there are cross-references between the various categories—can you remember seeing a dog riding on an airplane, or a dog fighting a snake?

Whenever you try to call an item up from your Long-term Memory, you

---

Freud, Sigmund.   131-F
    The origins of psycho-analysis; letters to Wilhelm Fliess, drafts and notes: 1887-1902.   Ed. by Marie Bonaparte, Anna Freud, Ernst Kris. Authorized translation by Eric Mosbacher and James Strachey.   Introduction by Ernst Kris.   Basic Books [c1954]   486 p.   illus.

    On cover: Sigmund Freud's letters: The origin of psychoanalysis.
    "Bibliographical index of the writings of Freud referred to in this work": p. [447]-455.   "Bibliographical index of the writings of authors other than Freud": p. [457]-462.

    1. Psychoanalysis
    I. Fliess, Wilhelm.
    II. Title.   ◯

                                                           5 18 54

Fig. 17.3. An item on file in a library card catalogue.

Periodicals. A technical term for any publication which appears regularly, or at the end of a stated "period" of time. The daily newspaper, the weekly newsmagazine, and the monthly fashion report are all "periodicals," and are usually stored in a different part of a library than are the books (which appear once and often gather dust thereafter).

usually retrieve that item according to some *verbal scheme.* For most people, the "scheme" or arrangement of mental categories seems to run from the most specific to the most general.

If you once owned a dog named Spot, you could retrieve many memories of Spot simply by thinking first of the dog's name. If you couldn't recall what kind of dog Spot was, you might try thinking about dogs in general, and consider what kind of dog Spot might have been (boxer, bulldog, collie . . .). If you were trying to remember what kind of pet you used to own, thinking about pets would lead you to try out the categories of canaries, cats, dogs, horses . . . And, of course, pets are all animals, so items about pets should be filed differently in your memory than are items about plants or machines or books.

When you want to find a particularly obscure item in your memory, your best bet often is to play the "animal, vegetable, or mineral" game, checking the broadest categories first and then moving down toward the more specific.

Question: If you have to memorize material for an exam, how might you organize it to make it "fit your memory" most easily? Would making an outline first help?

Early Memories Now that you know a bit about how your Long-term Memory works, ask yourself this question: Why is it so hard for you to remember what happened to you in the first year or two of your life? The answer seems to be this: You file most items away in permanent storage by means of a verbal or *meaningful* description of the experience. And before you learned to speak, you had no logical way of cataloging your memories.

We are not sure how far back in time your own personal memory banks go. Many psychologists believe that your brain contains memories of what happened to you at your birth—or perhaps even shortly before—but that you cannot ordinarily retrieve them because your brain wasn't very good at making "index cards" before you learned to speak.

If these early experiences are present in your permanent storage, they probably exist as almost formless and highly emotional impressions. One of the main functions of **psycho-analysis**—and of some other forms of psycho-therapy—is that of helping you dig down as deeply as possible into these early memories to uncover emotional **traumas** that still may be affecting your thoughts and behaviors (see Chapter 22). Once you can attach verbal labels or descriptions to these infantile experiences, you can usually recover them fairly readily from then on.

Question: What would your life be like if you had an absolutely perfect memory of everything that happened to you, rather than mere "verbal descriptions," but you could only retrieve an item by "replaying your memory tape" starting at the beginning of your life? Would it take you as long to remember your last trip as it did to live through the experience in the first place? What does the fact that you can almost instantly recall one part of the trip tell you about your own memory storage system?

Forgetting

There are at least seven types of forgetting:

1. Some sensory inputs *decay* before they reach the higher centers of your brain.

2. Other inputs are *rejected* by the lower centers of your brain because they are meaningless or unimportant.

3. Still other experiences are *repressed* by the emotional centers of your brain before you can make a conscious effort to remember them.

4. Items in your Short-term Memory continually *interfere* with each other.

Psycho-analysis (SIGH-ko-an-AL-uh-sis). A theory of personality involving psycho-sexual development and a form of intra-psychic therapy developed by Sigmund Freud. See Chapters 21 and 22.

Traumas (rhymes with "DRAW-mahs"). Injuries or disabilities inflicted on one's mind or body. Frightening experiences.

PART FOUR Learning and Memory

5. The "fine details" of many of your experiences are lost when you *translate* them into Long-term Memory.

6. Some items in your Long-term Memory get mis-filed and thus are hard to retrieve.

7. And brain damage or emotional trauma can lead to **amnesia**—the "wiping out" of memories already in permanent storage, or in the process of being stored.

Given the massive amount of "forgetting" that you actually do, it's a marvel that you manage to remember anything at all!

To give you a better notion of how you do manage to store items away for future reference, let's look more closely at the various types of forgetting.

Neural Decay and Interference

The sensory information storage system in your receptors provides you with sharply etched impressions of the world around you. But this is at best a very temporary sort of storage. For example, when a visual input reaches your eye, your rods and cones fire rapidly. But this pattern of neural firing is quickly destroyed in one of two ways—either the receptor neurons **adapt** to the input (and hence the neural pattern *decays*), or the next visual input "erases" the first input and thus *interferes* with your memory of what you've just seen.

Once an input reaches your brain, it may be put into Short-term Memory. But since your Short-term Memory is very limited, it continually "forgets" items as they are pushed out of "temporary hold" by new items that keep pushing in and interfering with your memory of old items.

Neural decay and interference are two of the simplest types of forgetting.

Rejection and Repression

The lower centers in your brain take each incoming stimulus pattern and scan it quickly for *recognizable features*. Your Short-term Memory mechanism then picks out the most meaningful aspects of the sensory input and holds them in temporary storage. But this same mechanism *rejects* items that are meaningless or unimportant to you. Although you are usually unaware of it, this "screening out" of trivial items goes on constantly and is a very necessary part of the forgetting process. (Can you recall *exactly* what the skin on your back felt like 20 minutes ago? How often do you need to recall such items?)

If a given stimulus input is threatening or disturbing, the emotional centers in your brain may *repress* the stimulus and hence make it very difficult for you to remember it later on. "Repression" is thus an unconscious but perhaps "deliberate" form of forgetting.

Translation and Filing Errors

Any item in Short-term Memory that is of real importance to you is processed for Long-term Memory. This processing usually involves *translating* the input into meaningful terms, and you almost always lose some of the "fine detail" of the input during the translation process.

When your brain translates an input into "mental language," it also seems to create a mental index card for each category under which that experience will be filed. You use these index categories when you try to recall something that happened to you in the past. As in any library, these index cards occasionally get *lost, misplaced,* or *mis-filed*.

Filing errors seem to occur most frequently when you have to learn too many things at once, or when you have too many or too few index cards relating to a particular category.

Mental file cards can get lost if your memory mechanism is "overloaded." For example, if you are introduced to a dozen unfamiliar people at

Amnesia (am-KNEE-see-uh). From the Greek word meaning "forgetfulness." To suffer amnesia is to suffer a loss of memory. The loss may be of things you experienced some time ago, or it may involve an inability to store new items away in Long-term Memory. The latter type is called retrograde amnesia (RETT-tro-grade).

Adapt. When a stimulus excites your receptor organs, they fire furiously for a few brief seconds. But if the input is *constant*, your receptor cells soon adapt—that is, they fire less and less frequently (although the input remains as strong as when it initially excited the receptors). Your receptor organs are more sensitive to *changes* in inputs than they are to constant inputs.

Why is it easier to remember faces than names?

Mnemonic (knee-MON-ick). From the Greek word *mneme*, meaning "memory." Mnemonics are devices that are intended to help you remember something.

Consolidation period. The period of time (20 to 30 minutes) which it takes your brain to file an input or experience away in Long-term Memory. Any trauma that disrupts your nervous system during the consolidation process will probably prevent that input from being put in permanent storage. Any marked increase in neural activity during the consolidation period may increase the ease with which the experience is filed away (and thus make it more readily available to you in the future).

Retrograde amnesia (RETT-tro-grade). When you are hit on the head, you are likely to forget most of the things that had happened to you for 20 to 30 minutes prior to the blow—but you may very likely remember things that happened immediately after the trauma. The amnesia is "graded" because you will very likely forget *everything* that happened immediately before the trauma, *most* of what happened 5 minutes before, and *some* of what happened 20 minutes before. The term *retro* means "after the fact."

a party, you probably will forget some of their names by the next day. If you met one person a day, you would have a better chance of remembering all the names.

Your memory also misplaces or mis-files things occasionally. A "forgotten item" may thus be stored somewhere in your memory banks—wherever those banks may be—but you simply can't find the item "on command." Old experiences are often hard to retrieve because you have to scan the millions of similar index cards you've made since then to recover that one unique memory. The new memories thus *interfere* with your ability to recall older ones. Brand new experiences are sometimes hard to remember because you have such a limited number of cues as to their location in your long-term files, or because you must learn a whole new set of relationships between familiar items ("mental categories"). For instance, if you were to learn Chinese, you would have to prepare "mental index cards" in Chinese for every memory category that you have in English.

Question: A mnemonic is a mental "trick" that can help you associate one item with another. For example, if Mr. Bird looks like an owl, you can make an easy connection between the man and his name. In terms of item retrieval, why might this sort of "mental association" help you remember things?

Amnesia

Memory is the process by which "neural patterns" are stored in your brain. *Amnesia* is the process by which these patterns are physically erased from your memory banks, blocked off from easy access, or prevented from being stored in the first place.

As we will see momentarily, memory storage does not occur instantaneously. Rather, it takes some 30 minutes or so for your Long-term Memory to file an item away. Any physical or psychological *trauma* that occurs to you during this half-hour-long **consolidation period** can prevent the item from being recorded in your memory banks. This type of forgetting is called **retrograde amnesia,** because a shock to your nervous system *now* can erase the memory of something that happened *several minutes earlier* (see Chapter 1). Memories already in long-term storage usually aren't affected by retrograde amnesia since they are already "consolidated."

Severe brain damage, however, can cause *permanent* or *continuous* retrograde amnesia by destroying the parts of the brain involved in converting short-term into long-term memories. A person suffering from continuous retrograde amnesia can recall "old items" with ease, but can remember new items for only a very few minutes.

Psychological amnesia, caused by an emotional shock, is really a form of repression. Witnessing a terrible automobile accident can cause you to "block off" all your memories of the fateful day. The items are still in your long-term storage banks, however, and you could probably retrieve them if you tried hard enough to do so (or underwent psycho-therapy).

Question: Why does "retrograde amnesia" suggest that memory storage is basically a physiological process?

The Search for the Engram

When the first computers were made, their memory-storage devices were designed to mimic that biological computer residing inside your skull. Computers can perform many routine mathematical functions much faster than your brain can, but (like your brain) they must be very carefully *programmed* to do so.

Suppose you undertook a very complex scientific experiment during which you gathered stacks of data. You might elect to analyze these data using a computer. You would begin by creating a specific "feed-forward program"—a sequence of instructions—telling the computer how to organize, categorize, and analyze these data. The machine could then process the data thousands of times faster than your "brain computer" could. However, it might take you weeks or even months to write the program in the first place. For you must specify *in advance* and *in complete detail* each tiny step that the machine must take. If you miss one small step—or if you get just one of the machine's memory file cards out of place—the computer will malfunction. You must then rework the program until it yields the expected results.

Your brain is superior to the computer in many ways, but mostly because your brain is *self-programming*. Thus, in a sense, what you do when you learn some new skill (or deliberately change yourself in some way) is to *re-program your own brain*. Psychologists and neuro-physiologists are presently spending a great deal of research time trying to figure out how your brain manages to reprogram itself and rearrange its memory banks.

Computer memory banks are usually detachable; yours are not. Many computers store their inputs on magnetic tape or disks (see Fig. 17.4), much

Fig. 17.4. As complicated as modern-day computers are, their memory banks are much smaller than those in your brain.

Engram (ENN-gram). A memory trace. The physical change that presumably occurs in the brain each time you store some item away in Long-term Memory.

Hibernation (high-burr-NAY-shun). From the Latin word *hibernus*, meaning "of winter." To hibernate is to pass the winter asleep, usually in a cave or other hiding place protected from the cold. To become dormant (DOOR-mant), or inactive, during a relatively long period of time.

Synapses (SINN-app-sez). The fluid-filled space between the axon of one neuron and the dendrites of a second neuron is called a synapse. See Chapters 2 and 4.

as we store music on records or tapes for our stereo systems. Scientists who record their research data on a reel of computer tape could, if they wished, remove the reel from the machine and clip out a piece of the tape that contained a particular "memory" they were interested in. They could then hold that bit of tape—*the physical representation of the memory*—in their hand and inspect it at leisure. If we could clip out a memory from someone's brain and inspect a human memory under a microscope, we could learn a lot more about brain-computers than we presently know. Unfortunately, we must often study the functioning of the brain indirectly.

The Engram

We are sure that whenever you learn something—no matter how simple—there must be a *physical change* of some kind in your brain associated with storing that item away in your permanent memory banks. We call that physical representation of a memory an **engram.**

We *assume* that there must be a different engram for each tiny bit of information that you have ever learned, and that your brain therefore is jam-packed with many billions of engrams. But we have no real proof for these assumptions, and no one has ever been able to put a finger on an engram or view one under a microscope. About all we can say is this: On the basis of the laboratory data gathered so far, different sorts of engrams appear to be stored in different parts of your brain.

The "search for the engram," as it is sometimes called, has occupied the attention of thousands of scientists for the past century or so. When neuro-physiologists first discovered the amazing amount of electrical activity that occurs in the brain (see Chapter 4), they speculated that the engram might be an electrical loop or circuit of some kind. As long as the electricity flowed in its proper pathway through the brain, the engram was maintained. Early computers were built on this memory model. The problem was that if you pulled the plug and shut off the electricity for any reason, the computer lost all of its memories, even when you fired the machine up again.

Neuro-physiologists tried the same experiment with animals—that is, they turned off all the electrical activity in a hamster's brain to see if this would wipe out the animal's memories. When bears, hamsters, and other beasts go into the deep sleep associated with **hibernation,** their brain temperatures drop considerably and most electrical activity ceases. So the neuro-physiologists trained a hamster, then put it to sleep and cooled its brain down until they could no longer detect any electrical responses at all. Later they warmed the animal up again and checked to see what it would remember. All the animals they tested showed excellent retention of their prior training. The electrical current hypothesis had failed, and scientists had to look elsewhere for the engram.

Again, they followed what might be called "computer logic."

Synaptic Switches

Computers store memories in a variety of ways. One device used in many computers is a simple switch, which can be left in either an open or closed position. When a message passes through the computer, the switches can route the information from one point to another—much the way the switches in a railroad yard can switch a train from one track to another. If you ask a computer a simple question—such as, "What is 2 + 2?"—the computer routes your question through a series of switches until the final destination, "4," is reached.

Switches are not very complicated mechanisms. But given enough of them, the computer can store almost *any* information, no matter how complicated. To a neuro-physiologist—or to anyone else interested in how your nerve cells function—your brain is made up chiefly of cellular "switches" called **synapses.** When someone asks you a question (such as,

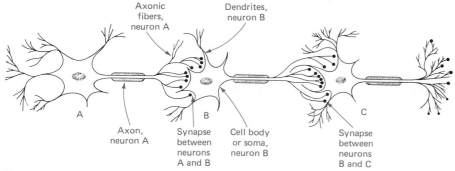

Fig. 17.5. Three neurons in a row. The axonic fibers of A make synapse with the dendrites and cell body of B, and the axonic fibers of B make synapse with the dendrites and cell body of C.

"What is your name?"), the message must cross over a number of synaptic switching points before you can answer it. If you could rearrange the functioning of these synaptic connections—opening some and closing others—you could send the message to any part of your brain that held the right answer. Perhaps, the neuro-physiologists reasoned, learning was chiefly a matter of *rewiring the neural circuits in your brain* by shuffling around the synaptic connections (see Fig. 17.5).

This idea has considerable appeal to scientists, for the nerve cells in your brain are much more complicated than the simple switching devices in a computer. You may recall, for instance, that the **dendrites** at the "front end" of each cortical neuron may be in direct contact with *thousands* of other nerve cells, while the axonic "output" fibers of that same single neuron may connect to the dendrites of *thousands* of other cells. Your brain, then, has billions and billions of possible "memory routes" in it. Little wonder that your brain has a memory capacity greatly superior to that of any existing computer!

It is generally agreed that the engram—that physical representation of whatever you remember—must involve some functional change at the synapse. But there is not much agreement (or solid data) about how you manage to shift the switches in your brain. Many scientists appeal to Thorndike's *law of exercise*, described in the last chapter. They produce data showing that if you force a neural message to cross a certain synapse again and again, it is thereafter much easier for the message to take that particular route. Why this might be so, no one really knows. But it does seem clear that some kind of *chemical change* must take place at the synapse, or it wouldn't change the way that it functioned.

Memory Molecules

A small but growing number of scientists believe that some part of the memory storage process may involve the creation of new *chemical molecules* in the brain. These scientists point out that the synaptic connections you were born with were a part of your "genetic blueprint"—that is, the original wiring diagram for your brain was contained within the set of **DNA** molecules that you inherited from your mother and father.

These DNA molecules held your *genetic code*—the set of biological instructions that caused the single cell you started life with to grow into the complex adult body you have today. You became a human rather than a rat or a worm because your DNA genetic code "remembered" what your parents were like. And yet all those original DNA molecules of yours came packaged in a cell not much larger than any of the neurons now living in your brain.

The genetic code carried by your DNA molecules *presets* the synaptic connections in your brain so that your innate behavior patterns are like those of your parents. DNA molecules thus carry what we might call your "inherited memory" of what humans ought to act like—and how they ought

Dendrites (DEN-drights). The "feelers" that extend from the front end of a neuron. The input side of a nerve cell.

DNA. Literally, de-oxy-ribo-nucleic acid (dee-ox-ee-rye-bo-new-CLAY-ick). The stuff that genes are presumably made of. Large, complex molecules that have the ability to reproduce themselves. The DNA molecule may also produce RNA.

Ward Halstead.

to develop. Could it be that other large molecules, such as **RNA** and **proteins,** might carry your own "personal memory code?" Some psychologists, myself included, believe this may be the case. The evidence we offer in support of our beliefs is still controversial and often hotly debated by scientists who view the brain in terms of electrical circuits and switches. In the next few pages, I would like to give you what is surely a prejudiced account of our research, and then let you make up your own mind about the accuracy of our data.

The Biochemistry of Memory

Perhaps the first person to speculate in public that chemicals might be involved in memory storage was Ward Halstead. In 1948 and 1949, Halstead advanced the theory that RNA and protein molecules might be the *engrams* that scientists had sought for so many years.

At about the same time, the Swedish biologist, Holger Hydén, said much the same thing, although Hydén's first beliefs were that RNA, not protein, was the chief candidate.

During the 1950's, Hydén and his colleagues performed an interesting set of experiments in which they taught various tricks to rats, then looked at the chemical composition of the animals' brains. Hydén and his group theorized that the brain of a trained rat should be *chemically different* from the brain of an untrained rat, and their research tended to support this belief. For they found noticeable changes in the amounts of RNA in the brains of trained animals (as compared with the brains of untrained rats).

Subsequent experiments in laboratories both here and abroad have generally confirmed the view that an organism's brain chemistry is *subtly altered* by whatever experiences the organism has. More important, it now appears that different types of psychological experiences give rise to quite different sorts of chemical changes.

Whenever a wave of electrical activity sweeps the length of a nerve cell from dendrites to axon, the nerve cell responds by suddenly increasing its production of several chemical molecules, including RNA. The more vigorously a neuron fires, the more RNA it produces. And since RNA guides or controls the production of protein molecules, the more RNA a cell produces, the more protein it typically manufactures as well. In short, nerve cells are not only generators of electrical activity, they are very efficient chemical factories too (see material on hormone production in Chapter 13).

Chemical "Erasers"

You are not consciously aware of all the chemical changes taking place in your brain as they occur, of course. But if the changes didn't come about, you probably wouldn't be "aware" of anything at all! For example, what do you think might happen if someone injected into your brain a special chemical that destroyed RNA just as you were trying to study for an exam? How might that injection affect your ability to learn?

This question was probably first asked by neuro-physiologist E. Roy John, whose work we discussed in Chapter 5. In the mid-1950's, John taught a cat a rather difficult task involving visual perception. Immediately thereafter, John injected **ribonuclease** into the cat's visual cortex. *Ribonuclease* is an **enzyme,** or destructive chemical, that breaks up RNA molecules. Although the cat performed very well before the injection, the ribonuclease enzyme appeared to destroy its memory. Thus, after the injection, the cat performed as if it had never been trained at all.

Memory Loss in Old People As you may know from bitter personal experience that when people grow old, they often begin to lose parts of their memories. The elderly person sometimes drifts into a psychological decline in which today's events are rapidly forgotten, and the person's mind dwells in the distant past. We call this condition senility, and it often places an immense burden on whoever must care for the individual. **Senility** typically involves a disruption of the person's ability to store new information away in Long-term Memory.

A senile man or woman can often recall past events—that is, items already present in permanent storage before the senility set in. But the person's memory banks seem closed to *new inputs*. A few fairly rare types of brain damage may also create the same kind of memory deficit. Scientists Brenda Milner, Suzanne Corkin, and Hans-Lucas Teuber recently described a young man who had lost part of his **temporal lobes** in a brain operation. Prior to the operation, his IQ was measured at 104. After the operation, he scored 118 on a similar IQ test. He could remember most things that had happened before the surgery very well, but nothing that happened afterward seemed to stick in his Long-term Memory. He described his condition as being "like waking from a dream"—that is, he couldn't really remember where he was or how he got there. Once he remarked that, for him, "Every day is alone in itself, whatever enjoyment I've had, and whatever sorrow I've had."

As you might imagine, this young man had rather unusual problems getting along with other people. For instance, if he took a girl friend to a dance, he had to stay very close to her the entire evening. Otherwise he would forget whom he had brought and might very well go home alone or with someone else.

When an elderly person experiences the same memory problems, we often say that the person has fallen into a kind of second childhood—that is, all the person's references are to early events, for only "yesterdays" have much meaning to the individual. "Today" is continually being pushed out of the person's Short-term Memory, one item at a time, and tomorrow never comes (and couldn't be remembered even if it did).

Psychiatrist D. Ewen Cameron spent many years trying to help senile patients in several hospitals in Canada and the United States. His studies were, for a time, aimed at discovering whether or not the body chemistry of senile people was measurably different from that of other people who were just as old, but who were not senile.

E. Roy John.

Senility is a problem many elderly people must face.

Senility (see-NILL-uh-tee, or suh-NILL-uh-tee). From the Latin word *senex*, meaning "old" or "old man." Senility is the loss of physical and mental ability that sometimes accompanies advanced age. Our word "senior" comes from the same Latin source.

Temporal lobes (TEM-por-ull). The parts of the cerebrum that lie just above the ears, close to the temples. They seem to be involved in hearing, in speech production, and in emotional behavior—among other things. See Chapter 4.

Chapter 17   Memory   437

In one of his experiments, Cameron found that senile patients had more of the *ribonuclease enzyme* present in their bloodstreams than did non-senile oldsters. Cameron guessed that this abnormal amount of ribonuclease might be destroying brain RNA as fast as the senile person's neurons could manufacture it. Perhaps if RNA were involved in helping the brain store away long-term memories, then too much ribonuclease would *wipe out the engrams* before they could become permanent. If so, Cameron thought he might be able to help his patients by *lowering* the amount of ribonuclease in their bodies.

Cameron tried two different types of chemical therapy. First, he injected his patients with large amounts of yeast RNA, hoping that the ribonuclease would attack this foreign RNA rather than the RNA produced by the patient's brains. While this approach seemed to help some people recover part of their memory functions, the yeast RNA was often impure and gave Cameron's patients fevers.

Next Cameron tried giving his patients a drug that was supposed to increase the *production of brain RNA*. Again, Cameron was fairly successful—but only with people who had not slipped too far into senility. However, the improvements that Cameron's **chemotherapy** caused were slow to come about—often the patient showed no improvement at all for several weeks or months. And once the patient was taken off the drug, the person's memory often began to **deteriorate** again.

Cameron died of a heart attack while on a mountain-climbing expedition (he was in his mid-70's) before he could complete his work. A group of scientists in Italy repeated his research and reported at least partial success, but no one in America seems to have picked up where Cameron left off. In the late 1970's, scientists reported that a chemical called *neosuppressin* may help pre-senile patients, but the work is still too new to evaluate adequately.

Drugs and Memory   As we noted earlier, your long-term memories take time to form or *consolidate*. Anything that retards or interferes with normal brain function during this consolidation period will interfere with your ability to remember.

The other side of the memory coin is perhaps a bit more intriguing, however. For it is likewise true that anything that *facilitates* or speeds up your brain activity during the consolidation period will make it easier for you to form engrams.

We usually think of *strychnine* as a poison; in fact, it is a neural excitant. In large doses, it causes convulsions and eventual death. In very small doses, strychnine increases neuronal firing rates much as does the **caffeine** found in coffee or cola drinks.

If you inject a rat with a tiny amount of strychnine just before you train it on a simple task, the rat typically will learn the problem faster. The explanation usually offered for this effect is that strychnine makes the animal more active and alert to its environment—hence, it learns faster. Surprisingly enough, you can get a similar effect by training the animal first, then giving it the strychnine a few minutes *after* it has learned the task. Now, when you retest the rat on the same problem a day or so later, the injected animal will remember the task much better than a rat injected with salt water, or one not injected at all.

How can a post-training injection speed up *learning?* It can't, for the rat given the strychnine takes just as long to *learn* the task as does an uninjected animal. What the drug apparently does is to make the animal's brain more active during the *consolidation period* following training. Speeding up the consolidation process apparently "enhances" memory formation. However, the drug must be given within 30 minutes or so after the training, or the "enhancement effect" does not take place. A rat injected two hours after training remembers no better than does an uninjected animal.

Question: Black-market LSD often contains small amounts of strychnine. What would the addition of this dangerous "upper" do to the drug experience itself?

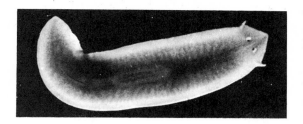

Fig. 17.6. The planarian possesses a true brain, a synaptic type of nervous system, and both male and female sex organs.

Memory Transfer

The strongest but most controversial support for the chemical theory of memory comes from the so-called "memory transfer" experiments. In 1953, when Robert Thompson and I were graduate students at the University of Texas, we attempted to train common flatworms using Pavlovian conditioning techniques. The simple **planarian** flatworm we used in our studies grows to be about an inch in length (see Fig. 17.6). It is found on the bottom of ponds, streams, and rivers throughout the world.

The planarian is unique in many respects. To begin with, each animal has both male and female sex organs, and some species are actually capable of self-fertilization. It reproduces both sexually and asexually—that is, a flatworm may mate with itself or with another planarian and subsequently lay eggs from which tiny worms will hatch. Or its body may split in half, following which both head and tail sections will *regenerate* into complete worms.

The flatworm is also the simplest animal to possess a true brain and a synaptic-type of nervous system. Once these neural structures appeared on the evolutionary tree, they apparently offered such excellent survival value that all more complex animals made use of them. In a sense, your own magnificent nervous system is little more than an elaborate version of the synaptic brain contained within the tiny head of each planarian.

Thompson and I were interested in flatworms because of their nerve cells. In 1953, the synaptic theory of memory storage was just becoming popular. We reasoned that if synapses were important for learning, and if the flatworm was the lowest animal that had synapses, it should be the simplest animal capable of showing true learning. So we set out to see whether or not we could train them.

Conditioning a Flatworm If you pass an electrical current through a trough of water containing a planarian, the animal will violently contract or "scrunch up" (see Fig. 17.7). Shock is then an *unconditioned stimulus* (UCS)

Robert Thompson.

Fig. 17.7 A water-filled training trough for planarians.

Paradigm (PAIR-uh-dime, or PAIR-uh-dimm). From the Greek word meaning "pattern," "model," or "example." A training paradigm is a model or ideal way of training animals. Pavlov's way of pairing the CS with the UCS is a paradigm for establishing the conditioned response.

that brings about an innate "scrunching" response in worms (and most other animals). If you shine a weak light on the planarian, it may respond by twitching its head, but it seldom contracts. Usually it just ignores the light—or moves away from it. Light then is a relatively "neutral" stimulus in that it does not innately elicit the "scrunching" response.

The training **paradigm** Thompson and I used consisted of turning on a light for 2 seconds before we shocked the worm. The light then became a *conditioning stimulus* (CS)—just as the bell in Pavlov's experiments was.

Thompson and I assumed that if pairing the light CS with the shock UCS was successful in conditioning the animals, they should eventually begin to "scrunch" or contract as soon as the light came on—*before* they were shocked. And the worms did just that. In a matter of 150 trials, their response rate to the light more than doubled. (Later, using better training techniques, my students and I were able to teach the worms to respond to the light at least 95 percent of the time.)

Convinced that we had demonstrated that planarians could be conditioned, Thompson and I published our results in 1955.

Regenerated Memories When I came to The University of Michigan in 1956, I talked several bright young students into continuing the worm research with me. The first of these students were Allan Jacobson and Daniel Kimble, and the experiment we undertook had rather surprising results.

If you cut a flatworm in half across its middle, the head will rapidly regrow a tail. The tail section—after a matter of a few weeks—will regenerate a new head complete with the brain and synaptic nervous system. It occurred to us that it might be amusing to condition some worms (using light and shock) and then, after the animals were trained, cut them in half and let them regrow. We could then test both regenerated heads and tails to see which half remembered the original training.

The question we were asking, of course, was this: *Where is the engram stored in the worm's body?* Is it just in the head, as you might suppose would be the case, since only the head contained the brain? Or could part of the worm's memory banks be distributed in the tail as well?

To say the least, the results surprised us. After the original head sections had regenerated, they showed just as much retention of the conditioning as did worms that had been trained but not cut in half. Apparently losing their tails did not disrupt the planarian's memory banks.

We gave the tails a month to replace their heads, then tested them. These tail sections with completely regrown brains not only remembered as well as did uncut planarians—they often did somewhat better! In further experiments, we showed that worms could be cut into several different pieces, and each piece—after regenerating—remembered what the original planarian had learned. There was not one engram, but several—scattered through the worm's entire body.

E. Roy John and William Corning soon carried this work a step farther. As we noted, John had already "erased" a cat's memory by injecting it with ribonuclease immediately after training. Would the same technique work with flatworms? To find out, John and Corning classically conditioned their animals as we had, then cut them in half and let them regenerate. Some of the heads and tails regrew in ordinary water and showed the expected retention of the original conditioning. Other heads and tails were forced to regenerate in a weak solution of ribonuclease. These head sections remembered; the tails did not. Apparently the ribonuclease enzyme had attacked the RNA in the regrowing brains and somehow "erased" the engram (see Fig. 17.8). (Later experiments in Russia and in Turkey suggested that a strong-enough solution of ribonuclease could erase memories even in uncut planarians.)

All of these experiments led us to believe that memory formation somehow involved the creation of new molecules, and that RNA played some part in the process. About 1960, it occurred to me that if two worms learned the same task, the chemical changes that took place inside their bodies might also be identical. If this were so, it might not matter how the

Fig. 17.8. RNA from a conditioned donor being injected into a recipient planarian.

chemicals got inside the worms: Provided the right molecules were present, the worm should "remember" whatever the chemical engrams told it to remember. Our attempts to test this odd notion took us not to the heart of the matter, but to the worm's digestive system.

Cannibalistic Transfer of Learning   Most higher organisms have stomachs that break up the food they eat into useful-sized molecules. The flatworm lacks a stomach: When it eats, the food particles float around inside the animal and each cell takes up whatever it needs. I hoped that if we could get the engram molecules out of a trained worm's body, and somehow inject them into an untrained animal, we might succeed in *transferring the memory* along with the molecules.

In 1960 Reeva Kimble, Barbara Humphries, and I did just that. We classically conditioned a bunch of "victim" planarians, then chopped them in bits and fed the pieces to hungry, untrained cannibalistic flatworms (our experimental group). We fed untrained victims to another group of cannibals (our control group). After we had given both groups of cannibals a couple of days to digest or *consolidate* their meals, we trained both groups. To our delight, from the very first trials the planarians that had eaten educated victims responded to the light CS significantly more often than did the worms that had consumed their untrained brethren. We seemed to have transferred an engram from one animal to another.

Memory by Injection   A year or so later, we carried the matter one step farther. We extracted RNA molecules from several "donor" groups of planarians. Some of the donors had been given light-shock conditioning. Other donors had been exposed to light or to shock (but not to both). Some donor worms were not given any training at all. Using a very tiny needle, we then injected the RNA from these different donors into several groups of recipient planarians.

Only those recipients injected with RNA from trained donors showed a transfer effect.

In 1964 scientists working in the United States, Denmark, and Czechoslovakia reported similar success using rats as subjects rather than worms. In all these studies, donor animals were given some type of training, then were sacrificed and their brains removed. Extracts from these brains were next injected into untrained recipients. The subsequent behavior of the recipients (as compared to various controls) suggested that these animals had *by injection* acquired engrams that the original donors had acquired only by hard experience.

Rats, mice, and goldfish soon became the favored experimental subjects for these studies, and by 1980 more than a thousand successful memory transfer experiments had been reported in the scientific literature. But everything was not peaches and cream—or even RNA and protein—in this chemical search for the engram.

Are Memory Transfer Studies Valid?   To begin with, there is the nagging question of **validity**—that is, when you inject an animal with chemicals taken from a trained donor, are you really transferring *specific memories* or are you merely giving the animal some molecules that excite or depress its brain activity (as do caffeine and strychnine)?

Jessie Shelby and I answered that question for planarians some time ago. We first trained donor worms to go either to the light or the dark arm of a simple, water-filled T-maze. When the donor planarians were going to the correct arm at least 9 times out of 10, we chopped them up and fed them to untrained cannibals. We then trained the cannibals using **blind testing techniques.**

The results of our study were as follows: (1) The cannibals that learned fastest were those trained to go to the same arm as had been the "victim" they ate. (2) Cannibals trained to go to the opposite-color arm as had their "victims" learned somewhat more slowly—but still faster than if they had eaten untrained victims. (3) Cannibals that ate untrained donors learned at the same speed as did planarians that had eaten no victims at all.

Validity (vall-LID-uh-tee). Strong, believable, trustable facts are "valid" facts. The validity of a set of experimental results is the "trustability" of those results."

Blind testing techniques. To prevent themselves from unconsciously fudging their results, scientists often make use of experimental paradigms in which the person testing or evaluating a subject doesn't know what treatment the subject has been given. Which is to say that the scientific evaluator is "blind" to whether the subject is in the "experimental" or the "control" group.

Jessie Shelby.

However, by far the most interesting results came from a group of cannibals that were fed "conflicting instructions." That is, they ingested a "worm stew" made up of some donors trained to go the light arm and some donors trained to go to the dark arm of the maze. These poor cannibals learned the slowest of all. The "conflicting engrams" they ate apparently made learning more difficult than if they had ingested nothing at all. They showed their conflict in many ways. For instance, when these cannibals reached the choice point in the maze, they sometimes acted as if they couldn't make up their minds which way to go. Often their indecision was so great that they simply turned around, came back to the starting point, and refused to run the maze even when we prodded them gently with a tiny brush.

Several other laboratories soon showed much the same sort of stimulus-specific transfer using rats and goldfish.

Are Memory Transfer Studies Reliable? An equally important question has to do with the **reliability** of the transfer effect. A reliable friend is one whom you can depend upon to do the same thing for you again and again. A reliable scientific experiment is one that you can depend upon to yield the same results any time you or anyone else tries it the same way. The planarian studies seem highly reliable in that (to the best of my knowledge) no one who was able to train worms successfully in the first place ever failed to get a transfer effect of some kind.

In 1970 James Dyal at the University of Waterloo in Canada questioned everyone who had attempted transfer experiments with rats and other higher animals. Dyal found that better than half of the 400 studies reported had yielded evidence supporting the transfer hypothesis. Since the odds of getting successful results for any one experiment were greater than 100 to 1, a .500 "batting average" is very good indeed, and suggests that the effect is probably as reliable as most others in the field of biopsychology.

Ungar and Scotophobin But if chemicals are involved in memory formation (and transfer), which molecules are they, and how do they work?

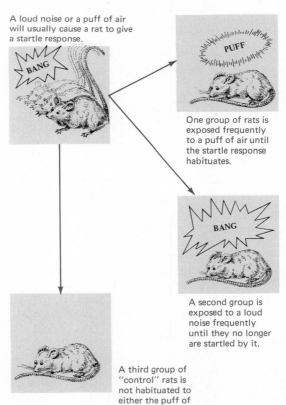

A loud noise or a puff of air will usually cause a rat to give a startle response.

One group of rats is exposed frequently to a puff of air until the startle response habituates.

A second group is exposed to a loud noise frequently until they no longer are startled by it.

A third group of "control" rats is not habituated to either the puff of air or the noise.

Fig. 17.9. Psychologist Georges Ungar's procedure for habituating rats to a loud noise or to a puff of air.

A series of studies by Georges Ungar and his associates may give us a clue. Ungar began by *habituating* one group of donor rats to a loud noise, another group to a sudden puff of air (see Fig. 17.9). This habituation took 10 to 15 days. Ungar then extracted chemicals from the donor brains and injected the molecules into untrained recipients. Although the injectees received brain material from just *one* set of donors, they were subsequently habituated to *both* the noise and the puff of air.

The injectees that received brain material from noise-habituated donors learned to ignore the loud sound in less than 2 days. It took them 12 days or more to habituate to the air puff, however.

The injectees given brain extracts from air puff-habituated donors learned to ignore the puff of air in less than 5 days. However, they were still showing the startle reaction to the noise at the end of 10 days of training.

Recipients injected with brain extracts from completely inexperienced donors took at least 12 days to habituate to the noise, and a full 15 days to learn to ignore the puff of air.

Later on, Ungar used a training chamber first designed by R. Gay and Al Raphelson at The University of Michigan. This rat box has a row of three chambers connected by open doors. The center and one end chamber are white; the other end chamber is black. Like many rodents, rats usually prefer darkness to light. When put in the center (white) chamber, untrained rats typically go into the black chamber and stay there. Ungar and his colleagues trained these donors by shocking them whenever they entered the black box. To no one's surprise, the rats soon learned to avoid the black chamber. In fact, they would squeak, bite, and urinate or defecate whenever they were pushed toward the dark end of the apparatus.

These donor rats were sacrificed and the chemicals extracted from their brains were injected into untrained recipients. When these injectees were put into the middle white chamber for the first time, they tended to escape into the white end of the box instead of into the black—just as Gay and Raphelson had originally reported in their own experiments.

However, Ungar and his group carried this work much farther. They first performed a chemical analysis of the brains of more than 4,000 rats trained to avoid the dark chamber. They found a simple protein—which Ungar called **scotophobin**—that appeared in the brains of trained rats but not in the brains of untrained animals. Using rather complicated techniques, Ungar *et al.* were able to specify exactly the chemical formula for scotophobin. With this information, they next made *synthetic scotophobin*, using inorganic materials anyone could order from a chemical supply house. Finally, they injected this synthetic material into untrained rats and tested these animals in the Gay and Raphelson apparatus. These rats behaved just as if they had been injected with scotophobin taken directly from trained brains—or as if they had themselves been shocked for entering the black compartment.

Did Ungar discover the chemical formula for a specific memory? It is far too soon to know for sure. However, many other scientists have been able to repeat much of what Ungar has done. And several students working with David Malin and me at Michigan have shown that this scotophobin effect is highly specific. Our rats or mice injected with synthetic scotophobin molecules did not merely "fear the dark." Rather, they appeared to be afraid of the black chamber in the *specific apparatus* that Ungar used originally.

The scotophobin effect, then—whatever it turns out to be—does seem to be highly stimulus specific.

Perchance to Dream

Additional support for the memory molecule theory of learning comes from recent studies on the function of **REM sleep**. As we pointed out in Chapter 3, dreaming seems intimately connected with memory consolidation. Animals, or people, who are put into situations where difficult new learning is required typically show a marked increase in REM sleep afterward (see Fig. 17.10).

Georges Ungar.

Scotophobin (sko-toe-FOE-bin). From the Greek words *skoto*, meaning "darkness," and *phobos*, meaning "fear" or "avoidance." Literally, "fear of the dark." Our word "phobia" comes from *phobos*.

REM sleep. Rapid-eye-movement sleep, during which dreaming occurs and memory consolidation may take place. See Chapter 3.

Fig. 17.10. An apparatus for depriving a rat of REM sleep. If the animal dozes off, it falls into the water and is awakened.

For instance, suppose on Day 1 of a scientific study we train a bunch of rats until they learn a very complicated maze. We also measure REM sleep in all the animals both the night before and the night after their training. On day 2, we test the rats to see how much of the maze they recall. Some rats will remember their training quite well; others will show little or no memory of how to get through the apparatus correctly. Almost uniformly, those rats that "remember" will have shown a large increase in REM sleep the night after training. The rats that "forgot" will mostly have shown little or no increase in dreaming. More than this, if we train animals in the maze and then deprive them of REM sleep afterward, few if any of them will remember the next day.

In humans there is a similar correlation between increased dreaming and the learning of certain tasks. The correlation is highest when the learning involves highly complex material (such as words in a foreign language) or some kind of adaptation to a fairly emotional situation. Ramon Greenberg and Chester Pearlman have shown that depriving human subjects of REM sleep almost always lowers their ability to remember the important things that they experienced or tried to learn the day before.

Question: Why would it be important for you to get a good night's sleep immediately after studying for an important exam?

Toward a Better Memory

To be truthful, no one knows very much about the chemical changes that take place inside your head when you learn something. When you try to study for an exam, or learn the name of someone you've just met, you cannot *feel* any of the chemical and electrical changes that must go on in your brain. But if your nerve cells do manufacture a unique new set of molecules for each of your memories—and if we can ever unravel this "memory code"—what a different world we could create!

Already we know a little bit about which chemicals increase learning speed and which retard it. If we could devise *safe* drugs that would make almost anyone learn more easily, we could perhaps make education a faster and less boring experience.

And if the day comes when we can actually synthesize memories in test tubes, then in future years those students who "drop chemicals" might be

In the future it is possible that certain behaviors can be induced by chemical injection.

trying to learn Spanish or psychology rather than trying to "seek Nirvana."

Are the memory transfer experiments valid and reliable? Will education ever come packaged as pills or extracts? Read (or swallow) the next edition of this book to find out!

Summary

1.   When sensory inputs arrive at your receptor organs, they are held momentarily in what is called **Sensory Information Storage**—an exact copy of the stimulus itself.

2.   As the receptor organs relay this image or copy to your brain, some part of your cortex appears to **process** the sensory input by interpreting the meaning of the stimulus.

3.   This interpretation is held briefly in **Short-term Memory,** which has a capacity of about seven items. The "hold time" for an item in Short-term Memory seems to be a few minutes (at most).

4.   Items drop out of Short-term Memory very rapidly as they are replaced by other incoming stimuli.

5.   During this initial processing, your brain checks to see if you have encountered this same stimulus before—by checking its **Long-term Memory** files.

6.   Important inputs move eventually from Short-term Memory into the permanent, or long-term, memory banks of your brain.

7.   Your long-term memories seem to be filed by **mental categories,** so that you can **retrieve** them readily.

8.   Although we are not sure how you manage to remember, it seems that your brain **translates** your experiences into meaningful descriptions rather than filing "photographs" of what you see or "recordings" of what you hear or feel.

9.   **Forgetting** occurs in many ways.

   a.   An input to Sensory Information Storage either *decays* rapidly, or is "wiped out" by the next input.

   b.   Some inputs are *rejected* by the lower centers of your brain because they are meaningless or unimportant, and thus are never "memorized."

   c.   Other inputs are **repressed** by the emotional centers of your brain.

   d.   Items in your Short-term Memory *interfere* with each other, and thus are continually forgotten.

   e.   The "fine details" of an input are lost when you **translate** them into Long-term Memory.

   f.   Some items in your Long-term Memory are *mis-filed*, and thus are hard to retrieve.

   g.   Brain damage or emotional trauma can lead to **amnesia** in which prior memories are "erased."

10.   It takes about 30 minutes for your brain to **consolidate** an item in Long-term Memory. Interruption of the consolidation process leads to a type of forgetting called **retrograde amnesia.**

11. The physical representation of a memory is called an **engram.**

12. No one knows what the engram really is, but remembering does seem to be correlated with rearranging the **synaptic switches** in your brain.

13. Recent studies of the biochemistry of memory suggest that molecular changes may occur in your neurons whenever you learn something. The molecules involved in memory formation may be **RNA** and/or **protein.**

14. A series of controversial studies suggested that **memory transfer** may occur under two circumstances: (a) when trained **planarian** flatworms are devoured by untrained worms; and (b) when extracts from the brains of trained rats are injected into the brains of untrained recipients.

15. **REM sleep** may be involved in the formation of Long-term Memory. Rats that learn a maze well show more REM sleep afterward than do rats that did not learn the maze very well. And human subjects deprived of REM sleep do not remember as well as do those subjects allowed all the REM sleep they need.

(Continued from p. 424.)

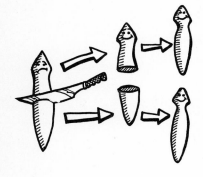

". . . Worms?"

"Yes, Don. Flatworms. Planarians. Sit down and I'll tell you about it."

The young graduate student named Don wrapped his lanky legs around a kitchen stool and sat down. "This I've got to hear. I thought you psychologists only studied two species—the white rat and the college sophomore. Victor, why can't you be respectable like all your fellow students?"

"Because I want to study the effects of regeneration on memory, and rats don't regenerate worth a hoot," Victor said, lighting a cigarette. "I want to start by repeating some of the early experiments to make sure I know how to train the worms—and then go on to more complicated things involving a biochemical analysis of trained planarians. I want to find the engram in the flatworm. That's why I need your help."

Don smiled. "Because I'm in biochemistry."

"Right. I can do all of the behavioral stuff, but I wouldn't know a molecule if I met one on Main Street. If you could help out with the experiment . . ."

"Too busy, man," Don said at once.

". . . Or teach me how to shuffle those test tubes around, I'd really appreciate it."

"Well, I'm pretty sure you could learn the techniques, Victor, if you had all the necessary lab equipment to work with. But I'm not at all sure about your worms."

Victor scratched his head. "What do you mean?"

"Worms are pretty tiny, aren't they? Brain no bigger than the point of a pin, as I recall. They don't have enough neurons to learn anything, do they?"

"How many neurons do you think a planarian has, Don?"

"I don't know, but it can't possibly be enough."

Victor laughed. "They've been trained in more than 30 laboratories—and by several thousand high school students for science fair projects. But you have to treat them gently, pay attention to their needs, and maybe learn to think like a worm yourself."

A crooked smile twisted Don's pleasant face. "You've got the right-sized brain for thinking like a worm, Victor. No doubt about it. But what next?"

"Then I want to cut a trained worm in half, let both pieces regenerate into complete animals, and test both animals to see which half remembers."

"Oh, come off it."

Victor took a puff on his cigarette, then responded. "I'm dead serious. According to the literature, even though the tail has to grow a completely new brain, it remembers at least as well as the head does. Then I want to train a worm, cut it in half and throw the old head away. After the old tail grows a new head section, I want to cut off the old tail and throw *it* away. When the new head regenerates a new tail, I'll have a completely reformed planarian. I want to see if it remembers the original training."

"Don't be silly, Victor. If a completely reformed animal could remember, a zoologist would have done the experiment years ago."

Victor smiled. "A zoologist did—working with a psychologist. That's why I'm sure it will work. What I want to do is to perform a chemical analysis on this regenerated worm. When the tail builds itself a new head and brain, it must make use of the genetic blueprint it inherited from its parents. But somehow the training must cause a chemical change in that blueprint or the new brain wouldn't remember what the old brain was taught."

"But nobody knows . . ."

Victor nodded. "True, nobody knows what chemicals cause the tail to regenerate a new head in the first place. But my guess is that they're the same chemicals involved in memory storage. I'd like to find out, but I don't know enough biochemistry to do the analysis."

"Enter the biochemist, smiling," Don said, a stern look on his face. Then he got up. "And exit the biochemist, groaning."

"Don't go! I haven't finished explaining the experiment yet."

"You've said quite enough, Victor. I can see a thousand things that could go wrong with that experiment, and I don't want any part of it."

"What could go wrong?" Victor asked plaintively.

Don shook his head in dismay. "Well, for one thing, how will you know that the chemical you identify in the trained tail is the one that affects memory?"

"Oh, that's easy. I'll just inject it into untrained worms. If they respond as if they had been trained, then I'll know I've got the right molecule."

This time Don groaned out loud. "Don't tell me you believe those memory transfer experiments? Grind up an educated rat and inject the knowledge into another animal with a hypodermic needle? Why I wouldn't believe those experiments if we did them in our own laboratory and got positive results!"

Victor smiled slyly. "Well, why don't we try it in your lab and find out?"

"You're off your rocker, Vic. The professor I work for would bite my head off if I even suggested such a thing."

"Your . . . *head?*" Victor said, a thought slowly dawning.

"So you see, I'd really like to help you, but we just couldn't do it in our lab."

Victor licked his lips, then said, "Well, why couldn't we do the experiment here?"

"Here? In your kitchen?"

"The first planarian study done in the United States was performed in a kitchen in Austin, Texas—because the professor in charge of the psych labs didn't trust flatworms."

"Or flatworm trainers either, I'd guess," Don said.

"You're probably right."

"Anyway, Vic, it just won't work. You'd need a lot of fancy analytical machinery. Centrifuges, balances, spectrophotometers, electrophoresis equipment—things like that."

"True," answered Victor, rubbing his hand across his mouth. "But at the start, all I'd really need would be knowledge. You could give me that."

Don shook his head. "I'm afraid I don't approve of what you want to do. And I simply don't have time to teach you all the techniques." He sighed once, softly. "You'll just have to learn it all the hard way—by reading textbooks and journal articles."

"That's all right, Don. I'm determined to get the information—one way or another."

"Well, if you didn't want to do such kooky research, maybe I could have helped."

Victor smiled pleasantly. "No problem, Don. And I do appreciate your thoughtfulness. I was sure you'd put your brain to it if you could."

The thought that had been lurking in the recesses of Victor's mind snapped into focus.

"In fact," Victor continued, breathlessly, "I'd like to show my appreciation by having you over for dinner some time soon."

Don grinned. "Hey, man, that's great of you. I can always use a free meal. But I didn't know you could cook."

"My Transylvanian grandmother whispered all her cooking secrets in my ear just before she died. I'll get a bottle of fine wine, and I guarantee the main course will be something you'll never forget."

"So set a date."

"I'll have to call you, Don. I need some special equipment to prepare this meal. As soon as I've located what I need, I'll give you a buzz."

After Don had left, Victor sat at the kitchen table for several minutes, smoking yet another cigarette. Then he picked up the telephone book and let his fingers walk through the yellow pages until he found the information he wanted. Picking up the phone, he dialed a number.

"Hello, Acme Restaurant Supply Company? Say, listen. Do you people sell meat grinders? I mean, really big ones? It's for a scientific project, you see."

Recommended Readings

Fjerdingstad, Ejnar, ed. *Chemical Transfer of Learned Information* (Amsterdam: North-Holland Publishing Company, 1970).

Horton, David L., and Thomas W. Turnage. *Human Learning* (Englewood Cliffs, N.J.: Prentice-Hall, 1976).

Luria, A.R. *The Mind of a Mnemonist* (New York: Basic Books, 1968).

Norman, Donald A. *Memory and Attention: An Introduction to Human Information Processing,* 2d ed. (New York: Wiley, 1976).

Pain and Hypnosis

Did You Know That . . .

Many of the "patent remedies" sold as medicine don't cure anything, but can make you mildly drunk or stoned?

Perhaps half of the "cures" supposedly caused by pills or medicines are actually brought about by a psychological factor called the "placebo effect?"

Hypnosis was discovered in the 1700's by a famous "quack" named Anton Mesmer?

The French government once banned hypnosis because it supposedly made women too easy to seduce?

Sigmund Freud rejected hypnosis because it didn't seem to help cure "mental illness?"

A hypnotized person may, under certain special conditions, commit murder or engage in other anti-social acts?

Some psychologists believe that hypnosis is an altered state of consciousness, while others believe hypnosis is only a form of role-playing?

Some people are born without the capacity to feel physical pain of any kind?

You can learn how to reduce pain by using certain "cognitive strategies?"

You have a "spinal gate" that seems to control painful inputs?

"Mesmer's Magic Wand"

"Are you sure you want to do it in class?" Brian Healy asked.

"Why certainly," Assistant Professor Don Powell replied, staring intently at his teaching fellow. "It's a legitimate demonstration of mental functioning, a tool used extensively by respected members of the medical and dental professions. Isn't it time that hypnosis was taken out of the closet and brought into the open? It isn't a cure-all; it isn't a parlor trick; it isn't a mysterious force. It's merely mind over matter." Powell smiled. "Besides, the students will love it."

"I don't doubt that at all, Professor Powell," the teaching fellow said. "But what if something goes wrong?"

"What could possibly go wrong?"

Brian Healy thought for a moment. "Well, what if the person you hypnotize doesn't come out of the trance? Who'd want to be hypnotized for life?"

"Nonsense!" Powell snorted. "I suppose at one time or another some hypnotist must have experienced problems in bringing a subject back from a deep hypnotic trance, but I've never run across a fully authenticated case where that happened. What we do know is that if you don't wake a person up deliberately, the person drops off into a restful, normal sleep and in a short time wakes up naturally. And with no physical ill effects, I might add emphatically," Powell added emphatically.

"Okay, you're the boss," Healy said. "But what if nobody in the class can be hypnotized? What would you do then?"

"Change the subject, probably," Powell said, perhaps a little too truthfully. "But it won't happen. In a class of 100, I'd expect roughly 15 students would not be hypnotizable at all, that about 65 would go into a light or medium trance, and that 20 would be capable of achieving a really deep hypnotic state. The subject's prior attitudes are the main controlling factor anyhow. If you think you can't talk when you're hypnotized, you won't talk no matter how much the hypnotist coaxes you. If you think you can't stop talking when you're in a trance, nothing will shut you up."

"Sounds like my mother-in-law. Nothing can shut her up either."

"Brian, no personal problems, please! We must approach this demonstration seriously. Hypnotism isn't a joke of some kind. It's a serious psychological tool. We are following in the great tradition of Mesmer, Braid, Charcot, Bernheim, and even Freud. Just do as I tell you, and everything will turn out fine."

And, of course, it did. Professor Powell began the class with a lengthy discussion of the history of hypnotism, beginning with Anton Mesmer and his animal magnetism, and concluding with recent experiments on the effectiveness of hypnotherapy. Much of the class was entranced. Next, he attempted to hypnotize all 100 students at once. Much of the class was tranced.

Then, as his final demonstration, Dr. Powell asked for a volunteer who might want to test out her or his mental powers. An alert, eager, wiry young man immediately stuck up his hand.

"What is your name, please?" Powell asked the volunteer.

"Elvis McNeil," the young man said, running one of his hands through his wavy hair.

"All right, Mr. McNeil. I'm going to put you into a trance, if I can. And then we're going to open up the pathways to your mind. We're going to unshackle all the latent mental powers you've always suspected you had. We're going to prove to you that your own mind—as untrained and untutored as it may be in its present state—can move mountains."

The young man began nodding in almost too-eager agreement, so Powell changed to a rather cautious tone of voice. "We won't do anything that could possibly harm you, of course. But there is always the possibility that you may feel a little foolish afterward. Is your ego big enough to withstand the laughter of your fellow students?"

"Gee, Professor Powell, I think my ego only has problems when people *don't* laugh at me," the intense young man said, carefully adjusting his glasses. "I'll go along with anything you want to try."

Powell smiled. "Excellent, my boy, excellent. Now just sit in this comfortable chair right here in the middle of the stage and start relaxing. Are you comfortable?"

Elvis McNeil nodded as he settled into the chair. Dr. Powell then pulled out a long, sharp hatpin and sterilized it over the flame of a match. "Would it hurt you if I jabbed this pin into one of your fingers?"

Elvis tensed a bit. "Of course it would. I thought you said it wouldn't hurt!"

"Since we won't try it until you're fully hypnotized, I guarantee you that you won't feel a thing. It's just a test to see if you're really in a trance. You won't mind, will you, as long as it's a scientific test of sorts?"

"Not if it unleashes the latent powers of my mind," McNeil said solemnly.

"Good," Powell replied, pulling a gold watch on a long chain out of his pocket with a flourish, much as a magician might. "Now, Mr. McNeil, I want you to stare at this mystical pocket watch that was passed on to me by my paternal grandfather. See it swing back and forth before your eyes? Look at it closely, Mr. McNeil. Watch as it moves back and forth, back and forth, back and forth."

McNeil stared intently at the glittering gold watch.

Powell continued in a soft, crooning tone of voice, almost as if he were singing. "Your eyelids are getting heavier and heavier. Your eyelids are like lead, sinking slowly down over your eyes. You are getting sleepier and sleepier and sleepier. Soon you will be fast asleep, deep asleep. Soon you will see nothing, hear nothing, but the sound of my voice. Go to sleep, Mr. McNeil. Sleep. Deep, deep, deep sleep."

McNeil's eyes closed. He sat rigid, unmoving.

"Are you asleep?"

McNeil's head nodded slowly.

"Deeply, completely asleep?"

Again the young man's head nodded, almost mechanically.

"Hold your hand out, Elvis. That's right, straight out in front of you. Your hand is made of steel, isn't it? Impenetrable, painless steel. You can't feel a thing in your hand, Elvis. See, I can touch it, and you can't feel my touch, can you?"

"No."

"That's right, no pain at all. I can even stick this pin in your hand and it will cause you no pain at all. You can't feel a thing, remember. No pain at all. Now I will stick the pin in—like this!—and it didn't hurt at all, did it?"

The class gasped as Powell plunged the sterilized hatpin half-an-inch into the young man's hand. But McNeil didn't react. Instead, he shook his head slowly and whispered, "No, it didn't hurt at all."

Professor Powell removed the pin, inspected McNeil's hand, and put a small bandage over the tiny wound. Then he turned to the class and said, "So, you see, pain is ultimately controlled by the cortex. Your brain can turn pain off or turn it on, depending on the circumstances. Under hypnosis, you can be made to perceive things that aren't there, and you can be made not to perceive even the strongest of stimuli. Mr. McNeil here is obviously a very good hypnotic subject. So now let's put matters to a further test."

Powell motioned Brian Healy to come toward him. "Now, Mr. McNeil, you surely remember what my teaching fellow, Brian Healy, looks like. Right?"

McNeil nodded slowly.

"Well, in a moment, Mr. McNeil, I'm going to ask you to open your eyes. But when you do so, Mr. Healy will be totally invisible to you. You simply won't be able to see Mr. Healy no matter where he is or what he does. Do you understand?"

Again the slow nod.

"Good. Now, please open your eyes."

Elvis McNeil blinked a couple of times and looked around carefully.

"You can see me, right?" Powell asked, putting an arm around Brian Healy's shoulders. "But is there anyone else up here on the stage with me? Do you see anyone else here but me?"

McNeil said, "Only me. There's just you and me on the stage, Professor Powell."

"Right, absolutely right. You're a very perceptive person, McNeil. Now then, I want to help you open up the channels of your mind and tap the secret powers that lie dormant inside your skull. I want to give you the faith of a mustard seed, the faith that moves mountains and turns the physical world into your mental slave, to do with as you wish. Would you like to learn those secrets, McNeil?"

Although he was still apparently in a deep trance, Elvis became excited. "Yes, yes," he cried loudly. "That's what I came to college for in the first place!"

"Then you should have taken this course sooner, right? Well, now, Mr. McNeil, let's begin by teaching you how to levitate objects—that is, how to overcome the force of gravity merely by willing things to rise straight up into the air." Powell moved very close to the young man. "We'll begin with that empty straight chair on the other side of the stage. Do you think you can get it to float upward merely by giving it the mental command to rise?"

McNeil looked dubious. "If you say so . . ."

"Good. Good," Powell said, motioning Brian Healy to grab hold of the empty chair, which was some 5 meters away from the professor and McNeil. "Now, Elvis, all you have to do is concentrate. Concentrate with all the hidden power in your cortex. Order the chair to rise. Do so now. Talk to the chair—give it commands out loud, and then watch what happens when your concentration becomes deep enough!"

McNeil took a deep breath. "All right, chair, you're going to rise. You're going to go sailing up into the blue like a funny old balloon. Rise. Rise!"

As the young man spoke, Healy began to lift the chair slowly from the floor.

"Rise! Rise!" McNeil cried again.

The chair "rose" an inch or two each time McNeil urged it upward.

"Holy Moly, Professor Powell, it's working! What a trip!"

The chair suddenly dropped back onto the floor.

"You're not concentrating, McNeil. Keep your mind on the business at hand."

"Sorry, sir," McNeil said, and took another deep breath. "Okay, chair, let's float some more. Up, up and away!"

In Brian Healy's strong hands, the chair rose a foot off the stage.

"That's right, chair, keep going. Higher, higher, higher!"

The class began to giggle just a bit, not sure of what was going on. Healy lifted the chair until it was at the level of his waist.

"Don't stop now, get it on up there!"

Healy raised the chair above his head. Small beads of sweat began to pop out on his forehead. The chair was heavier than he had thought it would be.

"Higher! Higher!" McNeil screamed.

Quickly, Professor Powell interrupted. "That's high enough for the first time around, McNeil. We don't want to strain your cortex, after all. Why don't you tell it to dance instead?"

"Sure. I can do it. I'm sure I can do it. Okay chair, I want you to shake, rattle, and roll."

Healy twisted the chair over his head rhythmically, following the beat of some distant drummer.

Suddenly McNeil burst out laughing. "It's a rocking chair! That's what it is. A crazy chair that dances because I've got rocks in my head!"

"Be serious, McNeil, or you'll ruin everything," Powell warned him sternly.

As if in sympathy, the chair came crashing down onto the stage, and Brian Healy collapsed into it.

The class went wild with applause. McNeil beamed, confident the clapping was for him. Brian Healy stood up and took a bow, but Elvis appeared not to notice it and just smiled happily at his fellow students.

McNeil shook his head, then looked around slowly.

"And now, Mr. McNeil, I want you to wake up, to recover completely from the trance, as soon as I count to three," Professor Powell commanded. "Ready? One, two . . . THREE! You're awake!"

"Do you feel okay? Good," said Powell, not waiting for an answer. "And can you see Mr. Healy now?"

Elvis McNeil looked at the teaching fellow, then nodded. "Of course. He's right here on the stage with us."

"And how do you feel?"

"Fine, fine. But what happened? How did I get this bandage on my hand?"

"That's where I injected you with the secret powers. Don't you remember making the chair dance in the air?"

McNeil looked puzzled. "Oh, yes. I remember. How did I do that, Professor Powell?"

"Mind over matter, my boy. Concentration, that's what does the trick. Thank you very much for your assistance."

At that point, the bell rang, ending the class. Several students crowded around Professor Powell to ask questions. After he had answered as many as he could, he and Brian Healy headed back toward the office.

"What do you think the after-effects will be for poor Mr. McNeil?" Healy asked.

"After-effects?" Professor Powell said. "Why there won't be any. Elvis will find out what really happened, and he'll be embarrassed for a while. He's one of those students who takes psychology thinking that it's magic, or something. Now perhaps he'll see that the only way to unleash the powers of the mind is to study like crazy, learn all the facts about human nature, and then discover how to apply the facts wisely. Hypnosis is a marvelous tool, for some things. I think we proved that in class. But it's not a miracle cure for acquiring personal power or for gaining mystical control over the world. Besides, we proved another point that's even more important—you perceive what your mind wants you to perceive. Beautiful demonstration, didn't you think so?"

Brian Healy scratched his head. "Sure, Professor Powell. Sure."

(Continued on page 470.)

Mind Over Matter

The field of medicine has always attracted its share of **quacks** and **charlatans**—that is, disreputable women and men with little or no medical knowledge who promise quick cures at cheap prices. The reasons why quackery thrives even in modern times are not hard to find.

To begin with, pain seems to be a chronic human condition. A person whose body or mind "hurts" will often pay any amount of money for the promise of relief. Second, even the best medical treatment cannot cure all the ills that beset men and women. People who mistrust or dislike the truths that their physicians tell them often turn to more sympathetic ears.

Many people lack the training necessary to evaluate medical claims. Given the choice between (a) a reputable physician who says a cure for cancer will be long, difficult, expensive, and may not work at all, and (b) a **patent remedy** salesperson who says that five bottles of a secret formula "snake oil" will cure not only cancer, but tuberculosis, syphilis, warts, and bad breath as well, some individuals will opt for the bottle of snake oil.

Many "snake oil" remedies are highly laced with alcohol or narcotic drugs. Anyone who drinks them may get so drunk or stoned that they drown their pains in the rising tide of pleasant intoxication. Little wonder that "snake oil" is a popular cure-all for minor aches and hurts! But let there be no misunderstandings. A very few "home remedies" actually work. However, most patent remedies sold by quacks are not only useless, but often can be harmful to the user as well.

The Causality Fantasy

Another reason that quack cures remain popular is what we might call the "causality fantasy." We all learn in school that if event B always *follows* event A, then it is likely that A *causes* B to take place—that is, we **infer** a connection or **causality** between two events merely because they occur in sequence.

Suppose that you overindulge at dinner and wind up with a nasty stomach ache. A friend of yours offers you a sure-fire cure—**dried frog eyes** mixed with **chicken blood.** You hold your nose, swallow a spoonful of the dreadful medicine, and go to bed as quickly as you can. The next morning the stomach ache is gone.

A miracle? No, for chances are you would have felt much better anyhow after a good night's sleep. And yet, the mere fact that you (a) took the medicine and (b) the pain later went away might lead you to fantasize that A had caused B to happen. Many human illnesses heal themselves if given half a chance. The magic cures we stuff into our stomachs may often retard rather than speed up this natural healing process, yet we fall prey to the "causality fantasy" because the act of taking the worthless medicine *precedes* our getting better.

The Placebo Effect

By far the most potent reason that quack medicines still are sold around the world has to do with the power of "mind over matter." Your brain is the master organ of your body: It regulates all the chemical processes that keep you alive and well. When you become depressed and lose hope, your autonomic (emotional) nervous system slows down these bodily processes and retards your chances of getting well. When you have hope and faith, these curative processes are speeded up. You are thus more likely to recover even from the most dreadful of diseases than when you are depressed.

The medical doctor who can *convince* her or his patients that they will recover typically cures more people than the physician whose behavior causes those patients to lose faith in themselves and in the medical profession.

If a sick person mistakenly believes that his or her condition can best be cured by taking a drug of some kind, most physicians are quite happy to give the patient a **placebo,** or pill made of sugar or ordinary flour. The placebo pill does no harm at all, but it may so help the patient *psychologically* that the person's *pain* diminishes and the patient may actually recover much faster than without taking the pill. Indeed, placebos may even have a *physiological* effect. In the late 1970's, several investigators reported that placebos cause the body to produce more of the natural pain-killers called **enkephalins** that we discussed in Chapter 3.

Many physicians estimate that at least half the patients they see suffer from psychological rather than physical ailments. For these patients, the "placebo effect" of taking a sugar pill is perhaps the best cure any medical doctor can offer. If sugar pills can be so helpful to physicians, little wonder that snake-oil remedies often appear to bring about miraculous cures.

As we will see in later chapters, the *placebo effect* is one that psychologists must constantly consider in all their research and therapeutic efforts.

Question: Why might some medical doctors refuse to tell a patient how seriously ill the patient actually is?

Anton Mesmer

One of the most famous quacks in all of medical history was a man named Anton Mesmer. Born in 1734 in a tiny Austrian village, Mesmer studied philosophy at a university in southern Germany and then took degrees in **theology** and medicine at the University of Vienna (where Freud later taught).

At the time that Mesmer began his medical practice, the prevailing view toward mental illness was that insanity was due to an imbalance of certain body chemicals called **humors** (see Chapter 23). Mesmer rejected the humoral theory in favor of an even more "humorous" notion supplied by **Paracelsus,** the noted Renaissance physician.

Paracelsus held that mental illness was forced on an individual by "disturbing environments" that led to an improper development of the individual's personality. The "environments" that Paracelsus thought influential, however, were primarily **astrophysical** rather than social. It was not your parents who drove you batty, according to Paracelsus, but the fact that your "negative" and "positive" charges were out of phase with what he called the *Universal Spirit* (see Fig. 18.1).

To cure insanity, Paracelsus gave patients various medicines derived from minerals "guaranteed" to capture beneficial magnetic forces that supposedly came from the planets and the stars.

Fig. 18.1. Azoth, which is shown on the head of the sword, is the alchemical name for mercury, the universal remedy of Paracelsus.

Placebo (plas-SEE-bo). From a Latin phrase meaning "to please." A harmless drug given for its psychological effect, especially to satisfy the patient or to act as a control in an experiment.

Enkephalins (en-KEFF-a-lins). Natural pain-killers secreted by the body. See Chapter 3.

Theology (thee-OLL-oh-gee). The study of the traditional doctrines of a religion or religious group.

Humors (YOU-moors). From the Latin word meaning "fluids" or "moisture." According to early Greek medical men, the body secreted four different humors: black bile, yellow bile, blood, and phlegm. See Chapter 23 for further explanation.

Paracelsus (PAIR-ah-SELL-sus). A swiss physician born about 1490 whose real name was Theophrastus Bombastus von Hohenheim. After studying medicine, he became interested in mining and in the diseases of miners. Named to the faculty of medicine at the University of Basel in 1526, he burned the works of Galen and other famous early physicians in order to discredit their theories and substitute his own. He began calling himself Paracelsus about this time, presumably to inform people that he was superior to Celsus, the greatest of the Roman medical writers. Whatever his name, he introduced the use of such minerals as mercury, lead, sulfur, iron, and copper sulfate as "curative agents." He also insisted that physicians should know astronomy since, he said, the stars influence disease and humans all have astral (heavenly) spirits. He left Basel in 1529 after a dispute over his salary, and died in Salzburg in 1541 when he fell over a cliff. His enemies (of whom he had many) insisted he was drunk at the time. His friends (of whom he had few) believed he was thrown over the cliff by thugs hired by jealous physicians.

Astrophysical (ASS-tro-FISS-ick-ull). The physics or physical side of astronomy. The study of the physical laws that pertain to the sun, moon, stars, and planets.

Agitations **(adge-jit-TAY-shuns). From the Latin word meaning "to drive" or "to turn over in the mind." To agitate (ADGE-jit-tate) is to stir up, or to move quickly to and fro. To shake or quiver.**

One of Paracelsus's followers, Jan Baptista van Helmont, went a step farther. Van Helmont stated that your body contained "magnetic fluids" which you could somehow "focus or aim with your mind." If you did so properly, you could bring the minds and bodies of other people under your control.

"Cures" by Magnetism Although Mesmer wrote his doctoral thesis on the magnetic effects of the planets on the human body, he believed that these celestial forces could be better focused through "magnets" than through the magnetic minerals recommended by Paracelsus. As R.M. Goldenson has pointed out, Mesmer lived at a time when magnetism and electricity were new and exciting physical forces, and people were just beginning to speculate on how these forces might be used to cure human illnesses.

For example, an English quack named James Graham had seen Benjamin Franklin's attempts to capture lightning by flying a kite during an electrical storm. Graham thereafter opened up in London a weirdly decorated Temple of Health in which his patients splashed about in electrically magnetized water. In the United States a physician named Elisha Perkins patented a copper and brass device that was supposed to be able to "draw pain" from injured arms and legs as a magnet draws iron toward it (see Fig. 18.2). Perkins' contraption became so famous that even George Washington purchased one. And in Europe a man named Father Maximilian Hell claimed that he could cure various emotional illnesses by applying magnetic plates to the patient's body.

Anton Mesmer took a heavenly view toward Hell's claims. That is, Mesmer thought that magnets could capture the magnetic fluids that radiated from the planets, and that these fluids could cure various sicknesses. One of his first patients was an hysterical woman who complained of various pains, convulsions, and **agitations.** When Mesmer "magnetized" her stomach and legs, the woman's pains vanished for several hours. Mesmer became so successful at these "magnetic cures" that he took to wearing odd clothes and soon announced that, through his techniques, "the art of healing reaches its final perfection."

It did not occur to Mesmer that his "cures" were due to the placebo effect—to what we might call *the power of suggestion.* But this explanation did occur to Mesmer's colleagues at the University of Vienna. They investigated his techniques and decided his "cures" were a product of imagination rather than magnetism. Mesmer was thereafter expelled from the university, fled Vienna, and set up shop in Paris.

Mesmer's "Grand Crisis" Paris in the 1780's was friendlier to Mesmer than Vienna had been, and he soon opened a healing salon that had in its center a huge tub containing "magnetized water" (see Fig. 18.3). Twisted, oddly shaped rods stuck out from all sides of the tub. Mesmer made his patients sit holding hands in a closed circle around the tub so that the rods could touch the injured parts of their bodies, and thus direct the "magnetic fluids" toward the wound.

Goldenson states that, to help things along, Mesmer dressed himself in a long purple robe and walked around the tub, touching his patients with a wand, urging them to yield themselves up to the magnetic fluids that surrounded them, telling them they would be cured if only they could focus on the heavenly powers within their sick bodies. Some of the patients apparently went into trance-like states. They would sit or stand as if frozen in place, apparently unseeing and unhearing.

Mesmer had, in fact, discovered *hypnosis,* but made no real scientific study of what the hypnotic state was like or what really induced it. Instead, he urged his clients "to reach farther into their minds." By continually pushing his patients psychologically, Mesmer drove many of them to reach what he called a "grand crisis," something we would call a "grand mal" convulsive seizure. Mesmer was convinced that the "grand crisis" was responsible for the cures his clients reported. Other medical doctors were not quite so sure.

MR. AND MRS. SNOW.

I ELIZABETH SNOW, of Plainfield, in the ſtate of Connecticut, certify that in the month of June, 1795, I was ſorely afflicted with pains in the ancles, which had ſettled there after a ſevere fit of ſickneſs, and had troubled me to ſuch a degree that I became very weak and emaciated. In this unhappy ſituation I continued about three months, until in the month and year above-mentioned, I applied to Doctor Eliſha Perkins who viſited me and operated on the pained part of my ancles, with his Metallic Inſtruments. Immediately the pain ceaſed and has never ſince returned. I am perſuaded a radical cure was at that time effected.

ELIZABETH SNOW.

Plainfield, Auguſt 3, 1796.

I the ſubſcriber, fully concur with my wife, in the above ſtatement of facts.

ABRAHAM SNOW.

(The Granger Collection)

Fig. 18.2. A testimonial from a 1797 pamphlet published by Elisha Perkins, the inventor of metallic tractors.

Fig. 18.3. The tub of Mesmer, a satirical engraving from *L-Antimagnetisme,* 1784.

Mesmerism, the name soon given to the technique for inducing a trance state and the "grand crisis," became the rage of Paris. The French government offered Mesmer a reward of 20,000 francs to reveal the secret of his "cures." When he refused, the government appointed two committees to investigate his techniques. Benjamin Franklin, then the US ambassador to France, was a member of one. The committees were unanimous in their public reports: Mesmerism was a hoax, and the cures were due to suggestion and imagination rather than to magnetism. The committees also sent a report in secret to the French king, warning that the "grand crisis" was probably habit-forming and dangerous to one's health. Furthermore, they told the king, women seemed to be particularly susceptible to the "grand crisis" and could easily be seduced while in this state.

So Mesmerism was banned on moral as well as medical grounds. Mesmer's star fell from public view. He soon retired to Versailles, a town near Paris, where he lived another 30 years—presumably basking in the magnetic radiations of the celestial bodies and, perhaps, occasionally trying to hypnotize a peasant or two.

Hypnosis

Considering the circumstances of its discovery, it is not surprising that hypnotism even today is considered to be more of a parlor trick or black magic than a legitimate psychological phenomenon. Because most scientists and physicians have held hypnosis in such low esteem, it was not until fairly recently that psychologists gathered enough data on the topic to view hypnosis objectively.

It was James Braid, a Scottish physician, who in 1842 gave *hypnosis* its present name, which Braid took from the Greek word for "sleep." After attending a session held by a wandering Mesmerist, Braid became convinced that magnetic fluids had nothing to do with the effect. Rather, Braid felt, it was an abnormal or intense form of sleep that the hypnotist induced by somehow affecting certain centers in the subject's brain. As the subject focused her or his eyes on something the hypnotist was doing, the subject fell into a deep, if rather strange, psychological sleep.

Shortly after Braid's analysis, Jean Charcot, a noted French professor of anatomy, announced that in his opinion there was a close connection between hysteria and hypnosis, and that only hysterics could be hypno-

Suggestibility. The state of following suggestions, of doing what you are told to do. If someone dares you to eat frog eyes, and you do, you are probably quite suggestible. The French anatomist Charcot (shar-KOH) believed hypnosis was merely a matter of some people's being highly suggestible.

Jean Charcot, here giving a clinical lecture, believed that hysterical women made the best possible hypnotic subjects.

tized. Other French scientists soon disputed Charcot's claims, believing that the hypnotic state was a result of **suggestibility,** not hysteria, although there seemed little doubt that hysterics often made good subjects.

Freud and Hypnosis

It was into this sea of controversy that Sigmund Freud stepped in the winter of 1885. And finding the hypnotic tide a little too cold for his comfort, Freud soon withdrew, leaving the waters muddied for almost 50 years.

Freud went to Paris in 1885 to study for a few months with Charcot, and apparently the experience marked a turning point in his life. Prior to this visit, Freud had thought of mental illness as being primarily *physiological*, and had used massage, baths, rest, and electrical stimulation with many of his hysterical patients. When he returned to Vienna in 1886, he began thinking of insanity as having primarily *psychological* causes.

Following Charcot's lead, Freud used hypnosis to suggest to hysterics that their symptoms would disappear. Sometimes the patients' symptoms

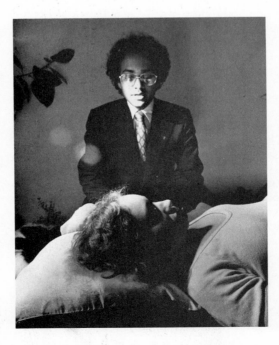

Fig. 18.4. An example of hypnotic induction.

disappeared, but just as often the problems came back again. Just as bad—from Freud's point of view—was the fact that not all of his patients could be hypnotized, and many of them became so dependent on his suggestions that they could not function in society unless they were under his hypnotic spell. It was this latter fact, perhaps, that called Freud's attention to the critical importance of the relationship between the hypnotist and the subject. Only those clients who could experience a strong personal trust in him seemed to be easily hypnotizable (see Fig. 18.4).

Renouncing hypnosis as a useless therapeutic tool, Freud instead developed the technique of **free association,** in which an unhypnotized patient learned how to pull long-forgotten but important material out of his or her memory banks.

As Freud's influence grew, his negative opinions about hypnosis took on more and more weight, and fewer and fewer people bothered to study or use it. It was not until the 1930's—when American behavioral psychologists reached the point of rejecting much of Freud's theorizing—that hypnosis again became a subject deemed fit for study in scientific laboratories.

Clark L. Hull.

Suggestibility

What is hypnosis? Braid thought it a form of sleep, but the early Behaviorists believed it to be a *state of narrowly focused attention* in which the hypnotized person somehow becomes extremely suggestible. Clark L. Hull, the noted learning theorist working at Yale, made a lengthy study of suggestibility and hypnosis. Hull was hunting for some simple test that would quickly tell who would be a good hypnotic subject. Hull was unable to find any one psychological or physiological trait that was a sure-fire index of hypnotizability. Research did suggest, though, that **in general** children between seven and eight years of age were more easily hypnotized than at any other time in their lives. Females *in general* seemed slightly better subjects than were males, and drug addicts were *in general* more suggestible than non-addicts. Hull's data also showed that individuals with high intelligence were *in general* more susceptible to hypnosis than were individuals of lower intelligence. (We might note in passing that many psychologists believe men are just as susceptible to hypnosis as women are.)

Question: If you were hunting for the best possible hypnotic subject, would you look for a seven-year-old girl genius who was a heroin addict?

Hypnosis, Imagination, and Parental Punishment

More recently, Ernest Hilgard and his associates at Stanford have collected data suggesting that the response you make to a hypnotist is partially determined by the type of parents you have. Hilgard *et al.* believe that for you to become a good hypnotic subject, you must have the capacity to become deeply involved in imaginative experiences. Hilgard and his colleagues further presume that if your parents were inclined to punish you severely and frequently when you were young, chances are that you will be able to "go under" in an hypnotic trance rather easily. Why? For two reasons. First, continual punishment may teach you the habit of automatic and unquestioning obedience to authority. Second, you may learn to escape parental wrath by retreating into your own imagination, and you may thus learn the mental skills that are necessary when you go into an hypnotic trance.

Question: In Chapter 14 we described Julian Rotter's concept of "locus of personal control." Which would seem more likely to be a good hypnotic subject, an "internalizer" or an "externalizer?"

Free association. Sigmund Freud's method of getting people to remember the traumatic events of their childhoods. The patient usually lies on a couch and is encouraged to say whatever comes into her or his mind—that is, to freely give whatever mental associations occur to the patient.

In general. A non-technical way of saying, "low, positive correlations." Two events are correlated if they tend to occur together more than chance would allow. That is, two events are correlated if the connection between them is non-random. If the events are not connected at all, they have a zero correlation. If the events almost always occur together, they have a high, positive correlation. If the connection between the events is weak—that is, if they sometimes occur together but sometimes don't—they have a low, positive correlation. In general, according to Hull's research, people with high IQ scores are easier to hypnotize than are people with low IQ scores. Translation: IQ scores have a low, positive correlation with hypnotizability. See the Statistical Appendix for further details.

One of the fascinating aspects of hypnosis is that people often seem to do things while hypnotized that they couldn't (or wouldn't) do otherwise. For example, studies show the following effects of hypnosis:

1. Subjects in a deep hypnotic trance can be made to act as if any (or all) of their sensory inputs have been cut off completely, or can be made to respond to sights, smells, sounds, tastes, or tactile stimuli that aren't really there.

2. Subjects may perform what seem to be incredible feats of strength, such as lifting objects that weigh several hundred pounds.

3. Subjects gain great voluntary control over their muscles. For instance, you can tell a woman to make her body rigid as a board, then put the woman's head on one chair, her feet on another, with nothing in between. Now you can sit on the woman's unsupported stomach without having her buckle underneath your weight.

4. The subject may learn long lists of words with apparent ease and may recall past events with what seems to be surprising clarity.

5. If the person is particularly susceptible, you may tell the subject that you are going to touch a very hot poker to the person's arm—and then merely touch the subject with the point of your finger. Within a few hours a blister-like welt may appear just where you put your finger to the subject's flesh.

6. Under certain circumstances, you may talk a shy, very proper young woman into taking off all her clothes in public, command the leader of an anti-violence movement to shoot one of his best friends, or get a secret agent to divulge confidential government material.

But as impressive as these feats may seem, there is a strange quality of showmanship to them that demands further investigation and discussion.

Under hypnosis, a slightly built young woman can be made to lift an object weighing 135 kilograms (300 pounds) when ordinarily she would refuse to consider picking up even half that weight. Has hypnosis made her suddenly as strong as Mr. Universe? No, not at all. Women in peasant societies routinely lift heavy weights as a matter of course. And what would this same young woman do if she walked out of her house one day and saw the wheel of the family car come to rest on top of one of her children?

Hypnosis does not make you any stronger than normal—but it can *motivate you to perform as if your life depended on it.*

Anyone can pretend to be blind—actors on stage do a credible job of it all the time. And anyone can pretend to see things or people who aren't physically present—many children have imaginary playmates with whom they hold long conversations daily.

Only a very few subjects can "raise blisters" when hypnotized. As it turns out, however, these individuals are all prone to getting rashes, blister-like cold sores, or skin swellings when emotionally upset. Apparently, under hypnosis, they merely "do their physiological thing" on command. The ordinary subject, even in a deep trance, cannot match this performance.

Anti-social Behaviors As for anti-social acts, we all perform them occasionally if we think we can get away with them, if we believe no one will be hurt, or if some higher authority has told us to do so. A modest young woman will disrobe in public while in an hypnotic trance—but *only* if the hypnotist convinces her that it is proper to do so. If the hypnotist can make her perceive herself as being alone in her bathroom and badly needing a shower, or that her clothes are on fire, then her actions will suit her perceptions.

A non-violent young man can be talked into picking up a gun (loaded with blanks) and firing it at a friend, but only if the hypnotist first convinces him that the friend is really an enemy who is about to murder his mother or rape his sister. Or if he is told that he is in the army and leading an attack against a foreign army that is at war with the United States.

And secret agents have been made to "tell all" under hypnosis—when the hypnotist made the agent believe that only the agent's legitimate superior was present to hear what the agent said.

In short, you will perform under hypnosis only those acts that you *would perform normally*—if the situation were right, and if your motivation were high enough. But even these factors are usually not enough. In addition, there must be an intense, emotional relationship between you and the hypnotist. If you are to violate society's laws when hypnotized, you will usually do so only when your desire to please the hypnotist is intensely strong. And, of course, if you have a burning need to please someone by obeying his or her commands or suggestions, then you probably will do so whether you are hypnotized or not. All the hypnotic trance might do in such cases is to provide you with a convenient excuse for your own anti-social behavior.

Hypnosis imparts no magic powers to the subject or to the hypnotist. It does not increase any of your physical or mental abilities. Rather, hypnosis merely makes it more likely that you will do things that you ordinarily might not do.

There are two seeming contradictions to this view of hypnosis, one having to do with memory, the other having to do with pain. Let us look at memory first.

Hypnotic Age Regression

One aspect of hypnosis that first attracted Sigmund Freud was that while in a trance, subjects sometimes reported past events in their lives in amazing detail. Freud had theorized that most of the psychological problems that bothered people were the result of traumatic events that occurred when the people were quite young. During therapy, however, the patients often couldn't recall these early traumas. In fact, it seemed as if some part of their brains was deliberately *repressing* access to early memories.

Under hypnosis, however, some patients could recall **repressed** material with greater than normal ease. The problem was, as Freud soon discovered, that not all of his clients could be readily hypnotized, and even the "good subjects" occasionally recalled things that seemed unlikely to have happened. For many reasons, then, Freud abandoned the use of hypnosis— perhaps without ever realizing its full usefulness as a therapeutic tool.

The psychologists who picked up the study of hypnosis a half century after Freud discarded it were particularly impressed with the rapid access that it seemed to give to a person's early memories. They soon found that, while in a deep trance, subjects could be told to **regress** back to their childhoods and made to "relive" certain events—such as birthday parties, trips, or vacations. The subjects acted as if they were children again and had forgotten all of their adult experiences.

When told to "go back" to her fifth birthday, for instance, a young woman might begin to talk in a very childish voice. She would then go on to recount in detail who was at her party, what presents she got, what her parents said and did—even what she dreamed of later that night.

A few subjects went much farther: When pressed to do so by the hypnotist, they reported in detail conversations *they thought had occurred* between their mothers and fathers while they themselves were unborn and being carried in the womb. Or they recounted events that happened to them centuries before—when they were seemingly living in a different body. Since most of us have trouble recalling in detail conversations of just a few days ago, the feats performed under **hypnotic age regression** appeared fabulous indeed, and several odd theories of human behavior were spawned to account for these findings.

Some psychologists incorrectly assumed that *every experience a person had* was somehow recorded in blazingly accurate detail deep in the person's brain. Hypnosis merely opened up the floodgates and let all these

Repressed. Sigmund Freud believed that we deliberately "forget" experiences that are unpleasant or threatening. Freud called the act of pushing a memory into unconsciousness the act of repression. From the Latin word meaning "to put down."

Regress. Freud stated that each person goes through several developmental stages as he or she matures psychologically. When a mature adult returns to childish thoughts or actions, that person is said to regress to an earlier developmental stage. See Chapter 21.

Hypnotic age regression. To regress to an earlier age under hypnosis. To return to an earlier time when a hypnotist tells you to do so. Many psychologists believe that when you regress hypnotically, you are just "role-playing" because you wish to please the hypnotist.

memories come gushing forth. Other theorists compared the personality to the structure of an onion—that is, it came in layers, with the early or immature parts at the center and the more mature layers surrounding this central core. Hypnotic age regression supposedly **ablated,** or stripped away, the outer layers, leaving the "childish" core of the personality exposed.

Question: If someone offered you $1,000 if you could successfully imitate the behavior of a six-year-old for 20 minutes, would you take the bet?

Hypnotic "Role-playing"

As attractive as these theories might seem at first blush, they soon fell victim to the cutting edge of laboratory research. In the 1950's psychologist Martin Orne published a series of studies suggesting strongly that hypnotic age regression was chiefly a matter of rather excellent *role-playing* on the part of the hypnotic subject.

Orne put several college students into deep hypnotic trances and regressed them back to their sixth birthdays. He then asked the students to describe what happened to them that day.

The students responded magnificently, piling one insignificant detail on top of another. Orne was more impressed with their inventiveness than with their accuracy, however. For in many cases he had independent descriptions (from the students' parents and from other sources) of what had actually happened. As it turned out, the students were woefully inaccurate—they mixed up events from many different birthday parties, they included events they had read about in novels, or they simply made up things that never happened.

And although the hypnotized students "played" as though they were six years old, they made many critical mistakes. When asked what time it was, they looked at their wrists, though none of them wore watches when they were six. They responded appropriately to complex words they could not have understood when six, and they showed awareness of political and social events that had occurred long after they had reached their 6th birthdays. One student, born and reared in Germany, had not learned to speak English until he was 17. Yet he described his 6th birthday party as if everyone were speaking English instead of German. When this fact was pointed out to him, he switched to speaking a childish form of German and refused to speak English again until the trance was ended.

Orne went a step farther with some subjects, for in a few cases he had actual records of psychological tests that the students had taken when they were six or seven years old. He then regressed the students back to their sixth or seventh years through hypnotic trance and re-administered the same tests. Their answers as hypnotized adults were stylized attempts to act childish, and were nothing like the answers they had actually given at that age. The students were then allowed to inspect their early records as closely as they wished. Then they were once more regressed back to their sixth or seventh years. Now they tended to respond to test items as they actually had when at that early age—a feat they could not accomplish until they had looked at their test records.

Orne believes that most of what a person does when hypnotized is largely a matter of role-playing. When you allow yourself to be hypnotized, you also allow yourself to respond to most suggestions made by the hypnotist. You will go out of your way to please the person who put you into the trance. When the hypnotist suggests that you are six years old, you do your best to respond appropriately, just as you might do if someone offered you $1,000 to act in a childish manner. If you can't remember exactly what you did and said and thought when you were six, then you "fake it" as best you can.

Question: If someone offered you $1,000 to withstand a painful jab with a needle, without flinching, would you take the offer?

Martin Orne.

Ablated (ab-BLAY-ted). From the Latin word meaning "to remove" or "to carry away." The term is used frequently by surgeons to refer to the cutting away of certain parts of the body or brain. During hypnotic age regression, the "mature layers of the personality" are said to be ablated, or cut away.

PART FOUR Learning and Memory

Hypnosis and Pain

More than a century ago, a number of British physicians reported they had used hypnosis during hundreds of operations with great success: They claimed that the patients experienced no pain at all and suffered no ill effects. However, scientific investigations of these claims turned up a most intriguing point—quite often the hypnotized patient did indeed show evidence of experiencing terrible pain during these operations. But afterward, when the patients were out of the trance, they denied having felt anything at all! The scientific commissions reported that hypnosis seemed not so much to reduce or prevent pain as to prevent the patient from remembering the unpleasantness afterward.

In 1978 psychologist Ernest Hilgard reported similar results in a study of 20 volunteers who held their hands in ice water for 45 seconds. The water was painfully cold, as the subjects reported only too willingly if they were not hypnotized. Hilgard then "suggested" that they try consciously to control their experience of pain, and most of them were able to do so. They now reported much less pain than before.

Next Hilgard hypnotized the subjects and suggested they would feel *no pain at all* from the ice water. While their hands were in the water, Hilgard asked them if they experienced pain. The subjects told him, "Some, but not much." Then Hilgard asked them to move a finger on the hand *not* in the water if the subjects *really* felt the pain at some "unconscious level." Most of the subjects immediately did so. Thus *consciously* the subjects were suppressing the pain, but at some deeper level, they apparently knew the pain was really there (Fig. 18.5)

Now, which part of the subjects' minds experienced the pain? Hilgard calls this the subject's "hidden observer." This "hidden observer" apparently can report—during the trance—things that the subject's conscious mind cannot report while hypnotized.

Hilgard beieves that hypnosis is an *altered state of consciousness* in which your consciousness can "split." One part of you acts in a hypnotized fashion and experiences the world as the hypnotist suggests. But another part of your mind—which can communicate by gestures during the trance—remains unhypnotized and perceives things as they actually are.

As we will see in Chapter 24, this "splitting of the mind" is very similar to the "split personalities" that are occasionally found in mentally-disordered individuals. Usually, when one personality "takes over," it *suppresses* the memories and behaviors of any other personality patterns the person might

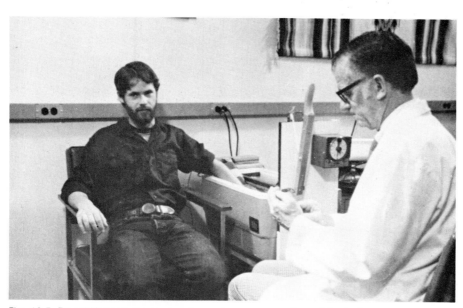

Fig. 18.5. Ernest Hilgard measuring the pain response of a subject whose arm is immersed in ice water.

Anesthetic (ann-ess-THET-tick). The word "esthetic" comes from a Greek term meaning "sensation" or "perceivable by the senses." An anesthetic is thus something that cuts out or prevents sensations, such as pain.

Parietal lobe (pair-EYE-uh-tull). Part of the cerebrum at the very top of the brain. Sensory input from the skin receptors and the muscles comes to this part of the cerebrum. See Chapter 4.

also have. According to Hilgard, this same *personality split* may occur in otherwise normal individuals during hypnosis.

Question: How can you "consciously" control the experience of pain?

Is Hypnosis an "Altered State of Consciousness?"   Both Martin Orne and Theodore X. Barber disagree with Hilgard's definition of hypnosis as an "altered state of consciousness." They point out that Hilgard's subjects may be unconsciously "faking" the presence of a *hidden observer,* just as people unconsciously "fake" any experience that they perceive the hypnotist as wanting them to perceive.

In fact, both Orne and Barber seriously doubt whether "hypnosis" actually exists! In a recent paper, Barber points out the major problem that "trance state" theorists such as Hilgard face—their definition of hypnosis seems circular, at best. "How do you know a man is in a hypnotic trance? Because he responds to suggestions. And why does he respond to suggestions? Because he is hypnotized!"

A more likely explanation of what we call hypnosis, according to Barber and Orne, is that it is made up of equal parts of "role-playing" and learning how to control both your sensory inputs and your behavioral outputs.

"Conscious Strategies" for Controlling Pain   Over the past 20 years, Theodore X. Barber has conducted a series of studies in which he has taught people *conscious strategies* for reducing the intensity of pain. Some of these strategies are more effective than others, but the best of them seem to reduce pain at least as much as does an hypnotic trance.

For example, in one study, Barber asked subjects to immerse their hands in extremely cold water. Some of the subjects were told to try various "mental strategies" for reducing their discomfort, such as: (a) imagining their hands were so numb they couldn't feel pain at all; (b) concentrating on other things; (c) re-interpreting the stimulation as being non-painful; (d) mentally "dissociating" themselves from the pain; and (e) not letting themselves be bothered by the ice water. Another group of subjects was given essentially the same instructions while hypnotized. By all measures of "painfulness," the *cognitive strategies* for reducing pain were at least as effective as was hypnosis.

Barber concludes that, since hypnosis is no better as an **anesthetic** than is "mental discipline," perhaps we should discard "hypnosis" entirely as a psychological concept. Not all psychologists agree with Barber and Orne, and the matter is far from settled.

But it seems clear that, before we can make up our minds about what hypnosis is or isn't, we must face squarely a problem that we rather delicately ignored in Chapter 6—namely, what is *pain?*

Pain

When sensory psychology was first getting off the ground, a century or so ago, the prevailing view was that there were four unique psychological experiences you could get from stimulating your skin—warmth, cold, pressure, and *pain.* Each of these four experiences was thought to be related to a specific type of receptor or nerve ending buried somewhere in your skin.

But further study turned up some troubling facts: There did seem to be receptors that were primarily concerned with temperature sensations, and other receptor cells that seemed to mediate the experience of pressure. But no one ever found a nerve ending that was solely concerned with the sensation of pain.

Investigations of the **parietal lobe** uncovered parts of the cortex that, when stimulated electrically, gave rise to the experience of pressure or temperature. But no one ever found a part of the parietal lobe whose stimulation produced pain (see Fig. 18.6).

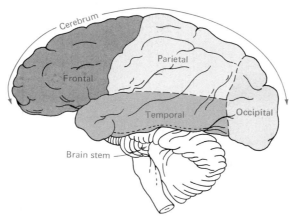

Fig. 18.6. The cerebrum, showing the parietal lobe.

Enigma (ee-NIGG-mah). From the Greek word meaning "to speak in riddles." Winston Churchill once said, "I cannot forecast to you the action of Russia. It is a riddle wrapped in a mystery inside an enigma."

Spinal cord. The massive tract of nerve fibers inside the spine. Takes messages up from the body to the brain, and from the brain back to the body.

Insulated (IN-sue-lay-ted). From the Latin word meaning "island," or "to isolate." To insulate is to shield or protect. The insulation in the walls of a house keeps the heat in and the cold out in winter. Telephone wires have rubbery insulation around them to keep the messages traveling down one wire from mixing with the messages on an adjacent wire. The axons of some nerve cells have a fatty insulation called *myelin* (MY-uh-lin) around them to keep sensory messages from "jumping wires."

Fast fibers; slow fibers. Neural messages travel along axonic fibers at different speeds, depending on the thickness of the fibers and the amount of myelin wrapped around the axon. Uninsulated fibers are "thin and slow"; sensory inputs travel along slow fibers at a speed of about 3 meters (10 feet) per second. Some insulated fibers are so thick and fast that messages flow along the axons at about 100 meters (300 feet) per second or more.

Nor could a "pain center" be found anywhere on the surface of the cerebral hemispheres. No special receptor organs, no special "input area" on the cortex—what an **enigma** pain seemed to be!

But if no one could figure out how the pain signal got started in the skin—or where it ended up in the brain—there was no doubt at all about how it got from the "non-existent receptors" to the "invisible locus in the brain!" For it had long been known that pain sensitivity was quite well represented in the **spinal cord**—that great trunk of neural "input" pathways running from the body to the brain, and "output" pathways running from the brain back to the body (see Fig. 18.7).

Certain types of diseases that affect the spinal cord often give rise to continuous and vicious pain that can be relieved only by cutting some of the sensory pathways going up the spinal cord from the skin receptors. So pain obviously is an "input" message of some kind. But, as we have found in recent years, even the spinal cord data are more complex than they seem to be at first glance. And if you are to understand why pain hurts as it does, and why hypnosis and "cognitive strategies" can sometimes reduce or alleviate the pain, we must take another (very quick) look at how your skin receptors operate.

Fast and Slow Fibers

The (hairy) basket cells and the encapsulated nerve endings in your skin send their messages to your brain primarily by way of special pathways in your spinal cord. The nerve cells in these pathways are **insulated**—that is, the axons of these cells have a layer of fat wrapped around them. Because this layer of fat insulates the electrical impulses that pass along the axon, the speed with which the neural messages flow is *faster* in insulated fibers than it is in nerves that lack this fatty insulation. Insulated fibers are called **fast fibers.**

The free nerve endings, on the other hand, send their messages up your cord *slowly* by way of uninsulated axons. Since the speed of the neural messages in your uninsulated nerve tracts is up to 100 times slower than in the "fast fibers," the uninsulated neurons are called **slow fibers** (see Fig. 18.8).

If you implanted an electrode in the *fast fibers* of someone's spinal cord and stimulated these nerve cells directly, the person would report "pressury" feelings. If you put the electrode in the *slow fibers* instead, the person might report feeling pressure or temperature changes. But if the stimulation was *intense* enough, the person might report feeling pain.

Neurologists use these facts to help diagnose the "site of damage" to the spinal cord in accident victims. The physician will brush a feather over the soles of the patient's feet. If the patient feels the pressure of the feather, his or her fast fibers are probably intact. If the patient has lost temperature sensitivity in the feet—or if a pinprick does not hurt—then the nerve tract

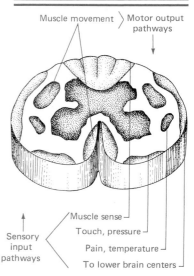

Fig. 18.7. The spinal cord in cross section.

Muscle movement — Motor output pathways

Muscle sense
Touch, pressure
Pain, temperature
To lower brain centers

Sensory input pathways

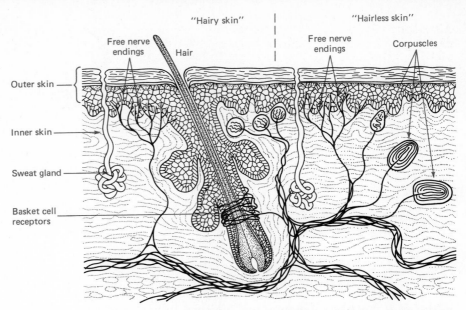

Fig. 18.8. The basket cells and encapsulated nerve endings send pressure messages to the "spinal gate" via fast fibers. Free nerve endings send messages to the "spinal gate" via slow fibers. Greater than normal stimulation of the slow fibers often leads to the perception of pain.

carrying the slow fibers has probably been pinched, cut, or otherwise damaged.

Neurological evidence such as this led physiologists at first to speculate that skin pain was not a special sense all its own. Rather it might be the result of over-stimulation of *any* of the skin receptors. We now know that the early physiologists were half right—pain surely is not a unique "sense" in the way that pressure, temperature, vision, and hearing are. Rather, pain is a highly complex psychological *experience* that is affected by many factors.

But to understand why painful inputs too often "hurt," you must first discover why they sometimes don't!

Pain Insensitivity

When neuro-physiologists first stuck an electrode into the slow fibers in a patient's spinal cord and stimulated these fibers electrically, the patient experienced pain just as expected. But when they stimulated the fast fibers, the patient felt no pain at all—even when the stimulation was very intense. In fact, just the opposite occurred. If the patient had (let's say) a badly damaged foot and was suffering considerable discomfort, stimulation of the patient's fast fibers actually *decreased* the hurt and unpleasantness of the wound! Obviously, over-stimulation of the slow fibers *causes* pain, but over-stimulation of the fast fibers *reduces* sensitivity to pain. Pain, then, is far from being a simple input such as pressure or temperature.

Next, there began to appear in the medical literature reports of seemingly normal individuals who experienced no pain at all! These rare individuals had the usual sensitivity to pressure and to temperature, but *no amount of stimulation* to any part of their body caused them any kind of sensory unpleasantness. If one of these "pain-insensitive" individuals broke a leg, or burned the skin off an arm, the person might not notice what had happened to them.

One such male, treated by neurologist Kenneth Magee at The University of Michigan Medical Center, was named Joseph B. All his life Joseph B. had thought the people around him were "sissies" because they complained of having "pains." Joseph B. enjoyed visiting dentists—if he had the time. If he didn't, having his teeth pulled with a pair of pliers was fine with him.

Although he enjoyed eating, drinking, and sex, Joseph B. didn't experience discomfort from any form of sensory over-stimulation—even to being kicked in the testicles.

Question: If you suddenly lost sensitivity to pain yourself, why might you have to learn new techniques for staying alive?

"Spinal Gate" Theory of Pain

The fact that patients such as Joseph B. had quite normal sensitivity to pressure and temperature suggested that the pain experience must be due to something more than over-stimulation of the skin receptors. And the experiments on stimulating the fast and slow fibers demonstrated that the spinal cord was somehow involved in creating the perception of sensory pain.

But it was not until 1965 that two scientists—Ronald Melzack of McGill University in Montreal and Patrick Wall of University College in London—put all these odd facts together and created a comprehensive theory of what pain is—and isn't.

Melzack and Wall believe that there is a kind of neurological "gate" in your spinal cord that determines whether or not you will feel an incoming sensory message as painful. Both the slow fibers and the fast fibers are connected to this spinal "gating" mechanism. According to Melzack and Wall, it is the *relative amount* of neural activity at the point of the **spinal gate** that controls the sensation of pain. The same message coming through on the slow fiber tracts will "hurt" or "not hurt" depending on how active the fast fibers are at that moment. If the fast fibers are completely silent—as when they are damaged or cut—almost any stimulation of the slow fibers will cause considerable pain. If the fast fibers are firing at a very high rate, it often doesn't matter how much you stimulate the slow fibers: The organism simply will not feel pain (see Fig. 18.9).

Activity in the fast fibers, then, tends to *inhibit* or "close the gate" on the experience of pain (see Fig. 18.10).

Question: If you accidentally stick your hand into a bowl of very cold water, you will first feel the pressure of water on your skin. Then, a fraction of a second later, you will feel that the water is very cold. And then, a moment after that, you will experience pain. How might you explain these facts in terms of the Melzack–Wall "spinal gate" theory of pain?

Ronald Melzack.

Fig. 18.9. According to Melzack and Wall, the "spinal gate" can "turn off" incoming painful stimuli.

Spinal gate. To gate something out means to keep something from entering. Melzack and Wall believe there is a nerve center in the spinal cord that "gates out" some sensations and lets others through to the brain. No one has yet located this "spinal gate" precisely nor determined exactly how it works.

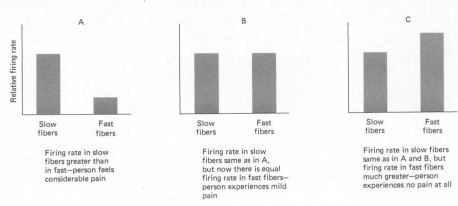

Fig. 18.10. How the ''spinal gate'' operates.

Cortical Control of Pain　But what about Joseph B.? He experienced normal amounts of both temperature and pressure, so both his slow and fast fibers were obviously intact. How could this be?

The answer, according to Melzack and Wall, is that the "spinal-gate" is also affected by the higher centers in the brain. These higher centers can "turn the volume down" on activity in the slow fibers just as effectively as can speeding up the firing rate of the fast fibers. So, under the right conditions, your brain can turn off the unpleasant aspects of pain merely by affecting the way that the "spinal gate" works. It seems likely that some higher center in Joseph B.'s brain had incorrectly turned off his "spinal gate" at birth—and left it that way throughout his life.

Melzack and Wall believe that when you are hypnotized, when you are highly motivated to ignore pain messages, or even when you are distracted by a good movie, your cortex turns off your pain sensations at the level of the "spinal gate."

Mind Over Matter

As we have said many times before, the brain is the master organ in your body. Anything that alters the normal functioning of your brain cells can alter the physiological responses of all the rest of the cells in your body.

If you were brought up to believe that "pain is for sissies," then you would experience less discomfort from a toothache or a broken ankle than if your parents had encouraged you to tell them about the slightest little pain you felt.

If, in a particular culture, childbirth was accepted as a natural and painless experience, then women in that society might be expected to role-play a pain-free delivery of their children. Even if the women did experience severe labor pains, many of them would surely suppress both the pain itself and the memory of the pain just as if they had been hypnotized into doing so.

If you strongly believe that hypnosis "works," then your brain will see to it that you feel no pain when you are hypnotized.

Hypnosis, magic wands, anesthetics, cognitive strategies, and quack remedies—all of these pain killers operate within the confines of particular cultural traditions and each person's unique pattern of social development.

Your parents, your friends, and your associates have as great an effect on the normal functioning of your brain, and your mind, as does the genetic blueprint you were born with. Thus it is now to the *development of the individual*—in whatever society—that we must turn our attention.

Summary

1.　Almost all of us experience **pain** during our lives. For this reason, people have long been willing to pay large sums of money to reduce the stings and harrows of discomfort.

2. The experience of pain is often a signal of some damage to body tissues, yet the mental or psychological aspects of pain are as important as the physiological.

3. Physicians have known for centuries that a **placebo** can be very effective in reducing pain—if the patient *believes* that the placebo is some powerful medicine. Thus what goes on in your mind influences how you experience pain.

4. One of the best-known mental techniques for reducing pain is **hypnotism,** first developed by Anton Mesmer in the late 1700's. Mesmer **mesmerized** his patients by putting them into a hypnotic trance. He then used **suggestion** to banish their pains. In many cases, his patients felt better afterward. Mesmer thought he had "cured" the patients' diseases. In fact, he had merely gotten them to repress their consciousness of pain.

5. Sigmund Freud tried to "cure" mental patients of their psychological problems by using hypnosis, but abandoned the technique because it didn't always work.

6. The early behaviorists believed that hypnosis was a state of narrowly focused attention in which the subject became extremely suggestible.

7. Your ability to be hypnotized depends on many things, including your age, sex, intelligence, personality, and your ability to use your imagination.

8. Under hypnosis, you may perform many unusual feats of mind and body—but nothing that you wouldn't do anyhow if highly motivated.

9. Hypnotized subjects will sometimes perform **anti-social acts,** but only if they are convinced that the act is "normal under the circumstances."

10. Subjects undergoing **hypnotic age regression** often act as if the more mature parts of their personalities had been **ablated,** or as if they had access to **repressed** memories. Most of these experiences can be explained as a type of **role-playing.**

11. Hypnosis seems to reduce pain in much the same way as does a placebo—by affecting the way the subject's mind "processes" painful inputs.

12. Some psychologists believe that an hypnotic trance is an **altered state of consciousness.** Other psychologists believe that hypnosis is merely one of many types of **cognitive strategies** for blocking out pain mentally.

13. A century ago, pain was thought to be a sensation much as pressure, temperature, sights, and smells are sensations. However, recent studies suggest that pain is a **complex mental experience** rather than a simple sensation.

14. Pressure sensations are carried up your spinal cord by **fast fibers** that are insulated by fat.

15. Temperature sensations are carried up your spinal cord by **slow fibers** that are not insulated.

16. If stimulation reaching the **spinal gate** from the slow fibers is greater than the stimulation from the fast fibers, the brain usually experiences pain. If the stimulation from the fast fibers is greater, the brain usually does not experience pain.

17. According to the **Melzack–Wall theory of pain,** the brain may at times inhibit or depress messages flowing through the "spinal gate." The brain can thus shut off painful inputs by turning off the "spinal gate."

18. Hypnosis, suggestion, placebos, "cognitive strategies," and role-playing appear to reduce pain at least in part by increasing your ability to shut off the slow-fiber messages as they pass through your "spinal gate."

(Continued from page 453.)

Assistant Professor Don Powell and his teaching fellow, Brian Healy, were correcting exam papers in Powell's office when a loud knock at the door interrupted their work.

"Come in!" Powell cried.

When Elvis McNeil walked through the door, the psychologist paled momentarily. Recovering quickly from his shock, Powell forced a broad smile. "Come in, come in, Mr. McNeil. Sit down! Make yourself comfortable! Why, we haven't seen you for several days! Wherever have you been?"

McNeil sat confidently in the chair that Powell had indicated. "Reading, sir. Reading everything I could lay my hands on about the powers of the mind."

Powell seemed a little flustered. "Er, well, yes. Interesting. Very interesting. We were afraid that you were angry with us—with Mr. Healy and me—about the little hypnosis demonstration we put on in class. I do hope you haven't stayed away from class because of some juvenile embarrassment . . ."

"Embarrassment? Of course not, sir! The very opposite."

"Then you aren't angry with us?"

"Certainly not, Professor. I came to thank you—and to ask for your help. You see, I've always been convinced that I had a strong mind, that I had hidden talents which I simply couldn't bring out into the open and gain control of."

Powell and Healy looked at each other uneasily.

"Yes, Professor," McNeil said, leaning toward the psychologist. "Even before I took your class, I had searched through all the occult literature. I had answered ads in the magazines that offered to make me a mental giant if I would purchase a set of their long-suppressed masterpieces. I had read the life histories of the mystics and tried to tap the power of the stars through astrology. But none of it worked very well. And then . . . and then, you opened the doors to my perception! You transported me to the pinnacles of power!"

Powell glanced sternly at Brian Healy, who was struggling valiantly to suppress a grin.

"Yes, well, I'm sure that's one way to look at it," Powell said hurriedly. "No harm done, then . . ."

"Oh, no. No harm at all. You see, I was sure I could really make the chair float around and dance without any help from you, if only I could find the key that would unlock my latent mental energies. Hypnosis did it, as you saw for yourself. So I've been reading all the books I could find on using hypnotism to unleash cortical forces. You really set my synapses to tingling!"

Brian Healy made a noise suspiciously like a muffled giggle.

"The trouble is," Elvis McNeil continued, not perceiving the reactions his words were evoking, "the trouble is, I can't seem to regain the powers that I had while hypnotized that day in class. I mean, I've tried and tried and tried. I've talked to one chair after another, and none of them will float—not even a centimeter. I feel I'm so close, so extremely close to being able to get it all together and prove the power of mind over matter, to establish dominance again over the mundane world of physical objects. But I can't seem to make that final step. That's why I'm here."

"Yes?" said Professor Powell.

"Sir, how much would you charge to hypnotize me again, and bring back the power?"

The psychologist was stunned. "Well," he said a few moments later. "Well, well. We'll have to think about that one for a while."

Elvis McNeil said hurriedly, "I can't afford much, but I'll pay whatever I can. Anything, anything to get that mystical magic back under my voluntary control!"

Powell gave the young man a wide-eyed look. Then he shook his head, almost sadly. "Yes, well, I do think we'd better have a long talk about this, McNeil. In private." Powell reached for his desk calendar. "Could you come see me tomorrow afternoon, say about 4 o'clock?"

"Certainly, sir. Any time you name."

"And let's keep our mouths shut about all this, shall we? I mean, we wouldn't want to let everybody in on the secret, now would we?"

"Certainly, sir. Anything you say."

"And in the meantime, I want you to go to the library and check out a book called *LSD, Marihuana, Yoga and Hypnosis* by Theodore X. Barber. Read it through carefully, particularly the section on hypnosis. Read it very, very carefully indeed. And if you're behind in any of your studies, use those latent mental powers of yours to catch up quickly. Okay?"

"Okay."

"And see me tomorrow at 4 P.M. sharp."

"Yes, sir. I can hardly wait!"

After Elvis McNeil had left the office, Professor Powell sat staring at the wall and tapping a pencil nervously on his desk. Then he turned to his assistant and said, "You know, Brian, when we teach this course next semester, instead of having a class demonstration on hypnotism, what would you think about our showing a movie? I mean, maybe that's a fine way to show the students that while hypnosis can be useful, if improperly used it can cause, er, unexpected problems."

Brian Healy scratched his head. "Sure, Professor Powell. Sure."

Recommended Readings

Barber, Theodore X. *LSD, Marihuana, Yoga and Hypnosis* (Chicago: Aldine-Atherton, 1970).

Bowers, Kenneth S. *Hypnosis for the Seriously Curious* (Monterey, Calif.: Brooks/Cole, 1976).

Frank, Jerome D. "The Medical Power of Faith," *Human Nature,* vol. 1 (August 1978), pp. 40–47.

Hilgard, Ernest R. "Hypnosis and Consciousness," *Human Nature,* vol. 1 (January, 1978), pp. 42–49.

5

Maturation
and
Development

Genetic Psychology

Did You Know That . . .

The genes you inherited from your parents helped shape not only your physical development but some of your basic personality patterns as well?

Each human being starts life as a single cell with 46 chromosomes (which contain the person's genes)?

You became a male or a female because of the influence of just one of these 46 chromosomes?

Males who are born with an extra "male" chromosome tend to be taller than average, to have severe acne, to be impulsive, and are more likely to end up in the penal wards of mental hospitals than are normal males?

Children who are badly malnourished during infancy may become permanently retarded if they are not given special attention and a stimulating environment?

If a newly hatched goose follows a human being rather than its own mother, it will (as an adult) be sexually attracted to humans rather than to other geese?

An infant develops control over its head muscles long before it develops control over the muscles in its legs and feet?

Many parents of children born with genetic defects reject or badly distort the scientific information they are given about their children?

With the proper training and encouragement, even severely handicapped individuals can be helped to reach their genetic potential?

"Where Sex Leaves Off"

Dr. Martin Mayer stared at the classroom, terrified. The three dozen or so students swarmed around like bees defending their hive. Through his thick-lensed glasses, the bright young faces seemed slightly distorted, larger than life. The thirty or so young bodies whirled around in constant, almost frightening motion. High school students, Mayer said to himself, have more energy than they know what to do with. How in the world could he have let himself in for something like this?

The man standing at the front of the classroom beside Dr. Mayer smiled mechanically and then said, "All right, young people. Let's settle down now and listen. We have a special guest today, someone famous in the field of genetic psychology, or the study of inherited behavior patterns. He's come to Clearview High School all the way from Mid-American University to give the annual Science Lecture this afternoon. And since he arrived earlier than we had expected, we've prevailed upon Dr. Mayer to address all the biology classes today. Isn't that kind of Dr. Mayer?"

Kind? They hadn't really given him the chance to refuse. At the University, Mayer stuck close to his lab. By choice, he taught only small graduate seminars. These bubbling, excited high school students were at least 10 years younger than the men and women who elected his classes at the university.

What could he talk to these youngsters about that he hadn't already planned to say in his formal address later that afternoon? Even though their regular teacher was droning on in a loud voice, many of the students were still milling about, talking and laughing. What could Mayer do if they wouldn't listen to him politely, as his graduate students did? How could he stop them from passing notes to each other and whispering and giggling? A sinking feeling in the pit of his stomach began working its way up his digestive system.

"Dr. Mayer has published more than a hundred articles in various scientific journals; he has written a number of chapters in learned texts; and he is co-author of the famous *Handbook of Behavior Genetics.* I'm sure you'll want to give him your closest attention. And now let's welcome Dr. Mayer with a nice round of applause."

The students clapped loudly, and one or two even whistled. Dr. Mayer blinked twice. The co-author of the famous *Handbook of Behavior Genetics* was frankly petrified. Every face in the class was focused on him now, waiting expectantly. His wife, Elizabeth, would have called it a "pregnant pause." What had she told him, just before he got on the plane? "If you get stuck for something to say, just talk about sex. They'll listen."

Dr. Mayer adjusted his glasses on his nose. "With your permission, students, I'd like to talk about sex."

Their immediate rapt attention gave him all the permission he needed.

"As a scientist, I'm interested in sex—in all its aspects. In fact, one of the joys of becoming a psychologist is that you have a legitimate right to study sexual behavior. Among lower animals, sex is primarily a matter of hormones and instincts. Among humans, it can also be an act of love. But among both humans and lower animals, sex is the beginning of life, not just the living end of things. For life starts where sex leaves off. And scientists who study the beginnings of life, as I do, must consider the biological as well as the social and moral consequences of the sexual act."

Mayer smiled at the students wanly. "A few months ago, I re-read Aldous Huxley's novel, *Brave New World,* for the third time. Huxley was a renegade, a radical, an artist born into a family of famous scientists. He was one of the first people in his generation to pay much attention to the hallucinogenic drugs. Huxley was taking mescaline—and writing about its effects on his perceptions—when your parents were still in high school and when the only drugs that most people used were alcohol and aspirin. But before he began experimenting with mescaline, Huxley was interested in genetics—in the social consequences of sexual behavior."

Mayer looked around. The students continued to follow his words closely. His talk was going better than he had anticipated.

"Huxley came to his knowledge of genetics quite naturally—his grandfather had defended Charles Darwin's theory of evolution against attack by religious leaders in the 1860's. Darwin had described how the various animal species evolved on earth by what he called the 'Process of Natural Selection.' That is, Darwin believed that animals mated rather freely, and their genes mixed rather randomly. When a male lion had sex with a female lion, neither of them was trying to build a better world or create a super-lion. They were just following their blind instincts. Some of their lion cubs were, by chance, bigger and stronger than others, and these cubs survived. The weak cubs died because the environment in which they lived favored big, strong lions."

Mayer glanced at the students. They were still listening raptly, so he continued. "Humans are different, of course. We are the only animals that have gained any real control over our environment. We have the ability to select quite deliberately and consciously which of our offspring will survive simply by changing the world our children live in. And that ability puts us in a moral bind that lions don't have to face."

Mayer paused to take off his glasses and clean them. "Sometimes I think it would be great just to be a lion, so I wouldn't have to worry about the consequences of having sex."

Several of the students laughed.

"Control of the environment is perhaps the most difficult problem facing us at the moment," Mayer said once his glasses were adjusted. "But Huxley was wise enough to see an equally difficult problem that would pop up in the near future. What would happen, he asked in *Brave New World*, if we could also control the genetic process?"

"When two human beings—or two lions—mate, the sperm from the male unites with the egg borne by the female. The tiny male sperm cell contains little more than a bundle of genetic information—that is, the genes of the male. The egg contains the female's genes, plus a lot of food material to get the process of reproduction going. When the sperm enters the egg, the two sets of genes try to unite. If you mixed a lion sperm with an elephant's egg, nothing would happen because the two sets of genes would be too different. But when the two sets of genes are very similar to each other, then the egg becomes fertile and immediately starts to grow and divide. It divides millions and millions of times—because that's what the genes inside each cell tell it to do."

Mayer frowned gently. "One of the primary functions of the genetic message inside each sperm and egg cell is that of telling the cell how to grow and develop into an adult organism. The genes, then, are a kind of 'computer program' that instructs the cell in what its future behavior should be like."

Now the scientist smiled. "Ever ask yourself why you turned out to be a human instead of a lion? The answer is, because of the genes you

inherited from your mother and father. Human genes have different instructions in them than do lion genes. And you developed blue eyes—or brown ones—because your parents' and grandparents' genes passed along 'biological instructions' that programmed your cells to turn out as they did. You had no choice in the matter—just as you will pass on your genes for eye color or skin color to your children whether you or they like it or not."

"But what if we could *change* your genes before you started creating the next generation? That is, what if we could *re-program* your genetic computer? Aldous Huxley was bright enough to see that, when scientists learned enough about genes, we could probably do just that."

Mayer shook his head. "See what I mean about the consequences of sex? Well, someday soon, we'll have acquired enough knowledge about which genes do what, so that we can reach into the genetic blueprint and change it, just as we can re-program an ordinary computer by giving it new instructions. Some time in the future, we can go to a young couple just about to be married and say, hey, what kinds of kids would you like to have? Do you want a big tall blond football player for a son? Would you prefer a small, dark-skinned daughter as beautiful as the Queen of Sheba? Or would you rather your daughter became a physicist, a sort of Alberta Einstein? And is there any reason why she couldn't be both beautiful and exceptionally bright? And would you like for your son to have big hands—not so he could catch a football, but so he could play the piano like Van Cliburn?"

Some of the students frowned, a fact that pleased Mayer immensely, so he kept on talking. "That's part of what *Brave New World* is all about. What I'd like to ask you today is the same question—when that great day comes and we know how to re-program the genes of our children, what kind of kids would you like to have?"

The class sat silent, as if this was an idea they didn't really care to give much thought to.

"You," Dr. Mayer said, pointing to a very attractive young girl sitting in the second row. "How are you doing in biology?"

The girl blushed and the class giggled. Obviously biology wasn't one of the girl's better subjects.

"Are you getting an A+ in biology?"

The girl shook her head.

"Do you have to study more than you'd like to in order to get grades that aren't as good as you wish?"

The girl nodded her agreement.

"Wouldn't it have been nice if your parents had had you engineered to be a 'brain,' so you could breeze through the biology book and learn it all very quickly? Wouldn't that help?" Mayer asked in a joking tone of voice.

"But then I wouldn't be *me*," the girl wailed. "I'd be somebody else!"

Mayer turned quickly to a small but handsome young man sitting toward the back of the class. He had a guitar case lying beside his chair. "You, there, you're pretty good on the guitar, aren't you?"

"I'm just learning," the young man said shyly.

"But you'd like to be able to play as well as Segovia, or some of the popular rock stars, right? Did you know that the best guitar players seem to have much better finger coordination than average players have? The ability seems to be inherited, and all the practice in the world won't make you a performing genius if you don't have the right genes to start with. Don't you wish now that your parents had fixed up your finger genes before you were conceived?"

"Sure," the boy said quietly.

"You're smaller than average, too," Dr. Mayer continued. "Does that ever bother you, maybe just a little?"

The boy nodded slowly.

"Well, wouldn't you like your kids to be taller than the average? Wouldn't you want to see a genetic engineer to change things in your sperm cells before you start having a family?"

One of the boys in the middle of the room interrupted. "But if everybody wanted their kids to be bigger than average, what would happen to the average?"

The class laughed.

"That's pretty unnatural, isn't it?" one of the girls asked.

"Of course it's unnatural," Mayer shot back. "Lions can't do it and neither can elephants. But maybe someday we'll be able to plan these things. When you get married and have your first house or apartment, you're going to spend a lot of time planning what kinds of decorations you want—because the place you live in reflects what kind of person you are. Don't you think you ought to spend just as much time planning what kind of children you'll have?"

"But you can't change human nature," the guitar-playing boy said.

"Ah, but you can," Mayer said. "Each time you try to teach your children something, you're trying to influence the child's development. Education is always an attempt to change human nature. But you will be starting too late in some cases, because you can't do much now until after the child is born. By that time, much of its pattern of development is already set."

One of the girls started to interrupt, but Mayer continued. "Nowadays, if you have ugly children, your friends and neighbors don't blame you for it because you couldn't do anything to change how they looked. But if your kids are badly dressed, or if you don't send them to school, or if you beat them a lot and make them cowards or train them to be bullies, then it's your *conscious choice* and people hold you responsible. In the future, when we can re-program genes at will, the world will hold you responsible for how pretty your children are—and for what native abilities they have as well. The lion can have sex without worrying about it. You can't. You'll have to decide whether you want your kids to be geniuses or just average types."

"But if everybody wanted their kids to be Einsteins, who'd collect the garbage?" complained a young man sitting in the front row.

"Beautiful question," Dr. Mayer said. "Once science gives us the technology to engineer our offspring, will society have a *right* to intervene? If there's a shortage of strong-bodied people who like to collect garbage, will the government have the *right* to require you to have kids who are strong and who have an instinctive love for gathering up other people's trash?"

"I don't want anybody telling me what kinds of kids I've got to have," a young black student said. "Probably they'd try to make them all into robots."

"Or stupid soldiers who like to kill people," said another student.

"Hey, man, you're making *assumptions*" said a third. "I mean, is garbage-loving an inherited tendency?"

"Magnificent!" Dr. Mayer cried. "As far as we know, it's not. But maybe it could be. What kinds of *behaviors* do you think we can engineer into your children's genes?"

After a moment's pause, the guitar-playing boy responded. "You already said that finger coordination was inherited."

"Right. But someone born with the ability to move her or his fingers quickly probably could become a great violinist as well as a great guitarist. Or would be great at sewing or typing or repairing computers. How would you feel if you had your future son's genes arranged so that he had superb finger coordination and he wanted to become a football player instead of a musician?"

"I'd get him an athletic scholarship to Notre Dame," said a large young man with an apparent interest in sports.

"Good idea," said Mayer. "But what other innate skills would you want to program into your future son to push him toward music? An inborn sense of rhythm? Is that something you inherit, or do you learn it from your parents? You, young lady," he said, pointing again to the girl in the second row. "What musical talents do you think are inherited, and which ones are learned?"

"I think you're trying to make us think too much," the young woman replied. "Why can't we just have kids and let them grow up the natural way, like our parents did? I don't know which talents are inherited, and I don't much care."

Mayer smiled. "Well, I agree with you halfway. I don't know what specific inherited abilities are necessary for a kid to become a great musician or a great football player. But both as a father and as a scientist I'd like to find out. I can't do anything about changing my children's genes because they're already born. But I can study behavior genetics in my lab so that your kids, or your grandchildren, can make decisions I couldn't make. But meanwhile, I've got a great big problem and it has to do with sex."

The class, which had become rather noisy during the discussion, suddenly quieted down again. Mayer smiled at how well things were going. His wife, Elizabeth, had given him very sound advice.

"Someday in the future, as Huxley pointed out, we'll have genetic engineering and we will be able to order our kids from a catalog. Maybe then government leaders will tell us what models to choose—for the good of our country. But until then, there are some things we can do anyhow.

"First off, behavior is always a function both of genes and of environment, and we surely can make a better world for kids to grow up in. But more than this, we already know enough about genetics to realize that some diseases and maybe even some types of insanity have a genetic component. The facts are that some people carry the *wrong kind of genes.* If we were lions, nature would take care of things—lions with the wrong genes just don't survive in lion environments."

Mayer frowned. "The problem is, we're humans, and we tend to keep people alive no matter what's wrong with them, and no matter how much it costs. If we were 'natural' about things, the way lions are, we'd just let these people die when they were young. Until we have genetic engineering, and we can change these bad genes into good ones, what can we possibly do to protect ourselves from bad genes?"

PART FIVE Maturation and Development

The guitar-playing boy stuck up his hand. "Well," he said quietly, "why don't we just pass a law saying that people with bad genes can't have kids?"

The class exploded in anger.

(Continued on page 497.)

Case of Clyde C.

The young man we shall call Clyde C. was born in Glasgow, Scotland, in the spring of 1950. His father was a laborer at a chemical factory in the northern part of town, his mother a pleasant and highly religious woman who came from one of the many suburbs that ring Scotland's biggest city. The mother's church attendance was matched by the father's frequent drinking bouts at the many taverns and pubs near their home.

Clyde C. was the third child in the family, and the first boy. He was by far the tallest of his several **siblings,** and even as a teenager, Clyde C. towered over his father by a foot or so. He was also the worst behaved of the children, as his father frequently pointed out to him.

As a young child Clyde C. was noted for the intensity and frequency of his temper tantrums. "A born **hellion,**" his father called him. Clyde did poorly in school, in part because he seemed unable to focus his attention on his lessons. His large size gave him an advantage in games and sports, however, and he excelled at fighting. In fact, he was something of a bully and often terrorized the other children either by hitting them or by destroying their books and toys. Frequent lectures and paddlings both by his father and his teachers did little to improve Clyde's behavior. He always seemed sincere in promising to do better in the future, but seemed incapable of resisting even the slightest temptation that crossed his path.

To the dismay of almost everyone around him, Clyde C. became sexually mature before he was 10. By the time he was 13, he was caught several times forcing his sexual attentions on younger children, chiefly on smaller boys. He was much taller than average, and he was not particularly good looking. Nor were his looks improved by the severe case of acne that he developed even before he reached **puberty.**

By the time he was 14, Clyde had stolen a motorbike and wrecked it, an escapade that led to his dropping out of school. His teachers (and his schoolmates) breathed a sigh of relief. His father tried to find a job for Clyde, but the boy had little regard for anyone or anything and destroyed more than he produced. When he was fired from his third job, his father threw him out of the house.

For a couple of years Clyde lived by such wits as he had, borrowing small sums of money from his mother when he couldn't steal enough to keep himself in food and clothing. Then, when he was barely 17, he got very drunk one night and went on a real spree. Around midnight Clyde spotted a young man and woman in an expensive sports car sitting at the side of a lonely street, talking. Clyde dragged the young man from the car and beat him up, threatened both the man and the woman sexually, stole the car, and zoomed off into the night. By the time morning came, the car was smashed beyond repair, and Clyde was in the hospital with a member of the Glasgow Metropolitan Police sitting by his bed waiting for him to recover.

Because of his past history and the sexual nature of his offense, Clyde was not sent to jail but rather to a **penal** institution for the criminally insane. His mother cried a great deal at the trial, blaming herself for his bad behavior. Clyde's father refused to see him again, calling him a "born troublemaker" who had inherited "bad blood" from his mother's side of the family. The doctors who treated Clyde tended to agree with his mother that he had been improperly reared.

Siblings (SIBB-lings). From the Latin word meaning "brothers and sisters." If you have two brothers and three sisters, you have five siblings—and so does each of your brothers and sisters.

Hellion (HELL-yun, or HELL-ee-un). From the old Scottish word *hallion,* meaning "scamp" or "scoundrel." Literally, someone "born to raise hell."

Puberty (PEW-burr-tee). That time in a young person's life when sexual maturity begins. See Chapter 13.

Penal (PEE-nall, or PEE-null). From the Latin word meaning "penalty" or "punishment." A penal institute is one designed to administer punishment.

XYY condition. An unusual genetic condition in which a male has an extra Y chromosome in all his cells. Although an abnormally large percentage of XYY males end up in medical-penal wards (or get in trouble with the law in some way), the *majority* of XYY males manage to lead normal, crime-free lives. Thus the XYY condition *in and of itself* does not cause deviant social behavior. Rather, it seems, XYY males have more difficulties learning to control their impulses. If given special care and the proper up-bringing, XYY males are probably no more likely to become criminals than are normal males.

Deviant (DEE-vee-ant). From the Latin word meaning "to turn aside." A deviant person is one who "turns aside" from the normal path, or who acts or thinks in a way different from most others in the person's culture.

Nucleus (NEW-klee-us). From the Latin word meaning "kernel," as in the phrase, "This statement has a kernel of truth to it." The nucleus is the heart or center of any system. The sun is the nucleus of our solar system. The yolk is the nucleus of an egg. The center portion of a living cell is called the nucleus, which usually contains the genes that direct the cell's functioning.

Cytoplasm (SIGH-toe-PLASS-em). The Greek word *kyto* means "hollow vessel" or "cell." Our word *plasm* comes from the Greek word meaning "plastic," "formable," or "fluid." Cytoplasm is the fluid-like substance surrounding the nucleus of a cell, as the white of an egg surrounds the yolk.

Chromosomes (KRO-moh-sohms). From the Greek words *chromo*, meaning "colored," and *soma*, meaning "body." The genes of a cell are strung together like strands of colored beads. These "strands" are the chromosomes.

DNA. An abbreviation for deoxyribonucleic acid. The genes are composed chiefly of DNA molecules. You developed into a human being rather than a rat or a flatworm because the DNA in your genes is quite different from the DNA in rat or flatworm cells. See Chapter 17.

Then, a year or so after Clyde had entered the medical prison, a team of scientists performed certain biological tests on all the inmates of Clyde's ward. These scientists discovered that Clyde suffered from a peculiar genetic defect called the **XYY condition.** Because an unusually large number of the other inmates on Clyde's ward also suffered from the XYY condition, the psychologists speculated that there might be some direct connection between these men's mixed-up genes and the **deviant** behavior patterns that Clyde (and the others) showed.

Can mixed-up genetic patterns actually *cause* a young man to show anti-social behavior patterns? Before we answer this question, we must first learn a little bit about genetics and how your own genetic blueprint influenced your growth and development.

Genetic Development

Like Clyde C. (and all other human beings), you began life as a single cell (see Fig. 19.1). This egg cell—produced in your mother's reproductive organs—began its existence looking much like many other human cells. That is, the egg cell was a tiny round blob of material with a dark **nucleus** in its center which was surrounded by a watery-looking substance called **cytoplasm.** The nucleus contains what we might call the "top managers" of the cell—its **chromosomes** (see Fig. 19.2).

Most of the cells in your body contain 23 *pairs* of chromosomes. If you looked at them through a microscope, each of these 46 chromosomes would seem to be a long strand of colored beads folded over on itself. These 46 "top managers" of the cell are composed chiefly of a nucleic acid called **DNA,** which is an acid because of its chemical composition. DNA is a *nucleic* acid because it is found chiefly in the nucleus of the cell.

DNA controls the functioning of the cell by making a substance called **RNA,** another nucleic acid. RNA carries the "instructions" from the DNA in the nucleus out to the cytoplasm or work area of the cell. It is in the cytoplasm that the proper proteins are put together which keep the cell (and you) alive. These "instructions" are really a form of cellular **feedforward,** in that they are a series of biochemical commands telling the "workers" in the cytoplasm what proteins to produce next (see Chapter 5).

Question: Foods such as meats, cheeses, and grains contain a high percentage of protein. Why do you think these foods are often better for you than are foods that contain little or no protein?

Cells reproduce by dividing (see Fig. 19.3). When a cell divides, its nucleus splits in two and half the DNA present goes into one of the

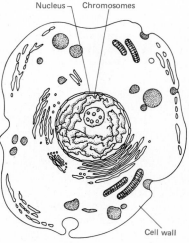

Fig. 19.1. A cell.

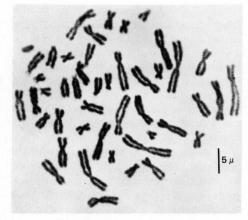

Fig. 19.2. The 23 pairs of human chromosomes.

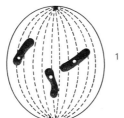

The nucleus of a cell just beginning to divide.

1

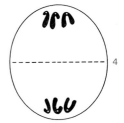

The nucleus begins to divide.

4

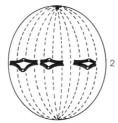

The chromosome pairs begin to separate from each other.

2

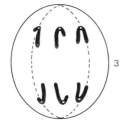

Just before final division the cell has two functioning nuclei. The whole process takes approximately 3 hours. During the next several hours, each chromosome will replace its missing pair.

5

The chromosomes of each pair pull far apart.

3

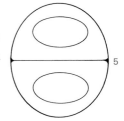

Fig. 19.3 Cell reproduction.

Fig. 19.4. Human chromosome cells. Only the 23rd pair differ—XX for a female, XY for a male.

female or male

daughter cells, while the other half of the DNA goes into the other daughter cell. (The term "daughter" is used even if the child will develop into a son rather than a daughter.) But before cell division takes place, the nucleus must *double* the amount of DNA present so that each daughter cell will have its full complement of 46 chromosomes the moment the split occurs. Since the daughter cells have exactly the same DNA, the two cells are "identical twins."

The only exception to this rule is in the case of the sperm and unfertilized egg cells. When an egg cell is produced through division, the original 23 chromosome pairs split in half *without doubling,* so that the egg cells contain exactly half the chromosomes it needs to survive and multiply. But since the sperm and egg have *different* DNA when they unite, they form a cell that is *unlike* any cell in either the mother's or father's body.

X and Y Chromosomes

The sperm cell, like the egg cell, contains only 23 chromosomes (see Fig. 19.4). The only way the sperm cell can survive is by mating with an egg cell to make up the 23 *pairs* of chromosomes every human cell needs to function properly. But the sperm cell is somewhat different from the egg. Its twenty-third chromosome can be either the large X type or the smaller Y type. The twenty-third chromosome of the egg cell is *always* a large X type.

If an X-type sperm is the first to enter the egg cell, the fertilized egg will of course have an XX twenty-third chromosome pair—and the child will be female. If a Y-type sperm fertilizes the egg, the twenty-third chromosome pair will be of the XY variety and the child will be a male.

There are slightly more male children born than female, a fact which could have two explanations. Either human males produce slightly more Y-type sperms than X-type, or the female body is *slightly more receptive* to Y-sperms than to the X-type. Generally speaking, however, the chances of a man's fathering male or female children are about equal.

RNA. An abbreviation for ribonucleic acid. A molecule similar to DNA and typically produced by DNA. Messenger RNA takes "instructions" from the DNA in the nucleus out to the cytoplasm of a cell. May also be involved in memory storage. See Chapter 17.

Feed-forward. A series of commands issued now to be followed in sequence at some future time. When you walk down a flight of familiar stairs, your mind issues a set of instructions to your muscles, and you subsequently march down the steps "without thinking about it further." The DNA in your genes issued a set of instructions that, during your development, caused your body to grow as it did.

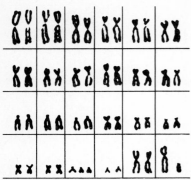

female or male

Fig. 19.5. Trisomy-21. Note the three chromosomes instead of the usual 21st pair.

Chromosomal Abnormalities

The human reproductive process is a very complicated one indeed, and sometimes it breaks down. Occasionally the twenty-first chromosome pair does not divide properly, and the child is born with *three* twenty-first chromosomes rather than the normal pair (see Fig. 19.5). This condition, technically called **trisomy-21,** leads to a type of mental, physical, and behavioral deficiency called **mongolism** (see Fig. 19.6).

Sometimes the twenty-third chromosome pair does not divide properly and the child ends up with but a *single* twenty-third chromosome—always an X-type—or with one or more *additional* X or Y chromosomes. In what is called the **Turner syndrome,** the child's cells contain but a single X chromosome. Individuals who experience this chromosomal problem have female **genitalia** but lack ovaries. If given injections of female hormones at puberty, they develop the normal behavioral and physical characteristics of an adult female. But since they lack ovaries, women with Turner's syndrome cannot bear children.

A child with an XXY twenty-third chromosome will be physically a male—with penis and testicles—but with strong feminine characteristics. This condition, known as **Klinefelter's syndrome,** occurs in about one child out of every 900 born. Although the child will grow into a tall, thin male, his breasts will be enlarged and his testicles will not produce sperm. The XXY male is almost always mentally and behaviorally retarded. XXY males are rather easy to spot from their physical appearance.

About 1 boy in 1,000 has two Y chromosomes and one X, like Clyde C. This male looks and acts quite normal and seldom realizes that he has a chromosomal problem. However, research on XYY males, begun in Scotland in the 1960's, suggests that many of these men are not quite as normal as they seem at first glance. Working at Western General Hospital in Edinburgh, a research team led by Patricia A. Jacobs discovered that there were 35 times more XYY males than one might expect among those patients classified as being *criminally insane.* Could the XYY chromosome condition somehow be *causing* the men to commit anti-social acts?

Further studies from all around the world have sometimes yielded contradictory results, but in general the original findings by Jacobs and her team have been confirmed. For example, in August 1976 a team of Danish and American scientists led by Sarnoff Mednick reported on their findings in *Science.* This international team found that about 40 percent of the XYY males and about 20 percent of the XXY males they studied had been convicted of one or more criminal offenses. The conviction rate among normal XY males was less than 10 percent. There is also strong evidence that there are many times more XYY males in institutions for the criminally insane than one might expect by chance, but the story is complex.

The XYY Condition To begin with, the problem seems to be almost entirely a white one—there are very few black, brown, red, or yellow-skinned XYY males. (No one yet knows why this should be true.)

Fig. 19.6. A child suffering from Down's syndrome, or trisomy-21.

PART FIVE Maturation and Development

Second, XYY males do not appear in unusual numbers either in normal prisons or in regular mental hospitals—only in those wards that take care of patients who are both insane *and* criminals.

Most of the XYY males studied by the Danish-American research group came from lower-class families. Their IQ scores were below the national average, but *not* below the average for other males from similar social backgrounds. The XYY problem is thus not associated with mental retardation. Neither is the "criminally insane" XYY male particularly more aggressive, violent, or more dangerous than "normal" XY prisoners on the same wards.

But there are marked if subtle differences between the XYY and the XY male. The XYY male is typically taller than average, and most of them are sexually **precocious.** They reach sexual puberty a year or more before the normal XY male does. About half of the XYY males suffer from moderate to severe acne, a much higher percentage than is found among normal men. Homosexual behavior patterns—and most other abnormal types of sexual behaviors, as well—are much more frequent in XYY males than in XY's.

All of these differences might well be related to the fact that the XYY's additional chromosome is a *male* chromosome. The presence of this second Y chromosome apparently causes the boy's adrenal glands to secrete an abnormally large amount of **androgens** (male hormones) during the boy's early life. These extra androgens not only make the XYY male grow taller, they cause his testicles to become functional earlier than normal and to secrete more male hormone following puberty. Acne is often related to hormone level, and the higher the androgen level, the more likely it is that a boy will develop acne at the onset of puberty. High hormone levels also increase sexual activity—both homosexual and heterosexual.

Some investigators have reported that XYY patients in medical–penal wards are less sociable and outgoing than are XY prisoners in the same institutions. Other scientists have found that XYY prisoners differ markedly from other prisoners in their ideas of what behaviors are acceptable and socially permissible.

The most important difference, however, has to do with what psychologists call *impulse control.* Unlike most normal men, the XYY prisoner typically can resist anything but temptation. Much more so than his normal **counterpart,** the XYY prisoner cannot *delay gratification* of his desires. If he sees something that he wants—be it someone's property or someone's body—the XYY prisoner simply must have it *right now.* If he has to be violent to get what he suddenly wants, he will resort to violence. If his attempts are frustrated, he often behaves childishly and throws a temper tantrum—or he destroys anything handy or attacks anyone nearby.

How could the presence of a few extra DNA molecules in each of his cells prevent an otherwise normal young man from learning to control his destructive, selfish impulses? Part of the answer can be found in a report published by the Danish–American group in the *British Journal of Psychiatry* in January 1977. These scientists found that the brains of XYY males mature more slowly than do the brains of normal men. Since the **corpus callosum** is one of the last brain structures to develop, this "bridge" between the two hemispheres matures far more slowly in XYY males than it does in normal individuals. Since a lack of self-control is sometimes associated with damage to the corpus callosum, perhaps it is not surprising that XYY males also show a similar difficulty in establishing self-discipline (see Chapters 1 and 5).

Still and all, we cannot yet explain why XYY males behave as they do. Part of the explanation hinges on the way that you, and all other people, grow from a single cell into a mature social being with a personality all your own. Your genes give you a start in life by specifying what your *initial* behavior patterns will be like. But the environment you grow up in—and your own intra-psychic development—determine how your genetic potential will be expressed.

We will discuss mental and social development later on. For the moment, let us continue our investigation of the "biological you."

Genitalia (jenn-uh-TAIL-ee-uh). The external sex organs. See Chapter 13.

Klinefelter's syndrome (rhymes with "MINE-belter"). A set of related physical characteristics (syndrome) found in males who have an extra X chromosome.

Precocious (pre-KO-shuss). From the Latin words meaning "early ripening." A "child genius" is intellectually precocious. A young boy who reaches puberty very early is sexually precocious.

Androgens (ANN-droh-jens). Male hormones, including testosterone (tess-TOSS-ter-own) secreted by the testes and by the adrenal glands. See Chapter 13.

Counterpart. A Xerox copy of a document is a duplicate or counterpart of the original. Someone who is more or less identical to you in some way is your own personal counterpart. The male lead in a play or drama is the counterpart to the female lead.

Corpus callosum (KOR-puss kal-LOH-sum). The thick bridge of neural tissue that connects the left with the right hemisphere. See Chapters 2 and 4.

The Beginnings of Life

Identical twins. Twins formed from a single fertilized egg. Although called "identical," they are often more like mirror images of each other.

Embryo (EM-bree-oh). An unborn child from the time of conception to the second or third month of development, when the child takes on vaguely human form and is thereafter called a fetus. From the Greek word meaning "to swell within." Oddly enough, the German word sauerkraut ("swollen cabbage") comes from this same Greek term.

Fraternal twins (fra-TURN-ull). Twins born from two fertilized eggs. Fraternal twins are no more alike than are brothers or sisters born at different times. From the Latin word meaning "brothers," from which we get the word "fraternity."

Uterus (YOU-turr-us). From the Greek word meaning "belly." The womb inside a woman's "belly" that contains and nourishes an unborn child.

At the moment that you were conceived—when your father's sperm entered your mother's egg cell, determined your sex, and began the glorious process of reproduction—you were no more than a tiny speck locked away in your mother's body (see Fig. 19.7). The 23 chromosomes the sperm brought to the egg gave the spark of life to that egg. Within 24 hours, the cell had grown enough to divide into two daughter cells. During this and all subsequent cell divisions, an identical set of 23 chromosome pairs goes into each daughter cell. So if the original cell you started life with had any form of chromosomal abnormality (such as the XYY condition), this abnormality would be passed along to every cell in your body.

At this point in your life, you might have become **identical twins** (see Fig. 19.8). Usually the first daughter cells remain close together and develop into a single individual. Sometimes, for reasons not clearly understood, these first cells separate and each eventually creates a complete human **embryo.** Since the daughter cells were identical, the twins will be identical too.

Fraternal twins are much more common. Occasionally a woman will produce two (or more) eggs during her fertile period. If both egg cells are fertilized, they will both begin independent growth at the same time, and the woman will produce fraternal twins nine months later. Since these two egg cells were fertilized by *different sperms*, they are no more identical than are brothers and sisters born to the same parents at different times.

If the two daughter cells remain linked after the first division, each of them will divide once more within a second 24-hour period. Within a third 24-hour period, all four of these cells produce enough new proteins and DNA and other cellular materials so that a third division can occur. While this growing of new daughters is going on, the group of cells travels slowly down a tiny tube to the mother's **uterus,** or womb (see Fig. 19.9). About nine days after fertilization, the rapidly forming human being attaches itself to the wall of the uterus. At this point in your own life, you were about 0.5 millimeters (0.02 inches) in size.

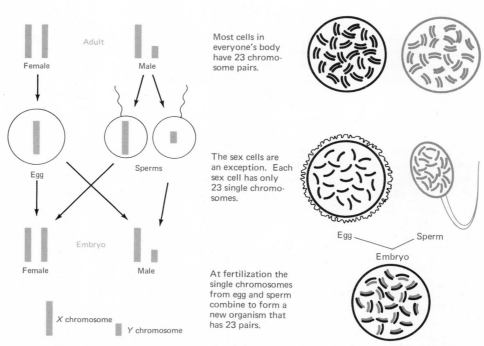

Fig. 19.7 (Left) Sex is determined by the sperm cell. (Right) An egg and sperm unite to form a new being.

PART FIVE Maturation and Development

Fig. 19.8 Identical twins are not identical but are usually mirror images of each other.

Question: Lower animals, such as dogs, often produce many egg cells at the same time and hence give birth to many puppies in a single litter. Each egg cell must be fertilized by a different sperm. Would it be theoretically possible for two puppies in the same litter to have different fathers?

Cellular Differentiation

Some two weeks after your life started, a remarkable change occurred in the tiny cluster of cells that made up your rapidly forming body. Up until this point, all of your cells were pretty much identical—because the "feed-forward" commands from the chromosomes were identical. But as we noted in Chapter 5, living systems are made up of sub-units that perform *different roles* in keeping the system alive. Thus, 13 to 14 days after fertilization, some of the chromosomes began feeding out slightly different sets of "command" instructions, and the cytoplasmic chemical factories in these cells began to produce slightly different proteins (and other materials).

As these new proteins and other molecules appeared, they forced the cells to *differentiate*—that is, to change shape, size, and function.

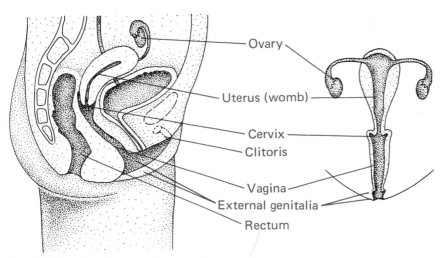

Fig. 19.9. The female reproductive system.

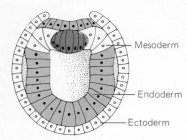

Fig. 19.10. The embryo at about 2 weeks showing the three kinds of "derm."

Development of the Fetus By the fourteenth or fifteenth day of your life, you were made up of three clearly different groups of cells (see Fig. 19.10). One of these groups developed into what we call the **ectoderm,** a technical term that means "outer skin." Eventually these cells became your skin, your sense organs, and your nervous system.

Another group of cells, on instructions from their chromosomes, developed into what we term the **mesoderm,** or "middle skin." These cells eventually became your muscles, bones, and blood.

Yet a third group of cells received instructions to become **endoderm,** or "inner skin." These cells turned into your digestive system.

(As we will see in a later chapter, there are some psychologists who believe that your basic personality structure was determined at the moment that the three "derms" separated from each other and began their unique patterns of development. According to this theory, if your ectoderm matures more rapidly than do the other two "derms," you will grow up to be thin and intellectual. If your mesoderm outstrips the other two, you will become an athlete. If your endoderm predominates, you theoretically will grow into a fat person who loves creature comforts. The data supporting this theory are not particularly strong—for example, XYY males are tall and thin, but scarcely "intellectuals." But, as we will see, there is a possible connection between the physiological growth of your three "derms" and the types of reinforcing feedback that you may prefer as an adult.)

At the moment this differentiation into the three "derms" occurred, you were a tiny hollow ball about 2.5 millimeters (0.1 inch) in size, and technically you were then an *embryo.* It was not until six weeks later—some two months after your life started—that the three types of cells arranged themselves into vaguely human form, and the embryo thus became a **fetus.**

The Placenta Developing cells—like developing children—are *unusually sensitive* to the environments they find themselves in. Luckily, as you grew within your mother's womb, you were protected from most of the chemicals in her body by an organ called the **placenta.** The placenta acted as a screen or barrier which blocked out most of the substances in your mother's blood that might have harmed your cells.

Illnesses, such as the German measles, can cause the pregnant woman's body to secrete somewhat different chemicals than is usual. If these chemicals (or the germs that cause them) infiltrate the placenta, they can upset the normal development of the fetus. If a woman has German measles during the third month of her pregnancy, for instance, the child is often born badly retarded. Narcotic drugs, such as morphine, also pass through the placenta and can set up an addiction in a fetus long before it is born. The presence of the morphine apparently keeps the fetus from developing the normal amount of **enkephalin,** the "natural pain-killer." At the time of its birth, the child suffers rather frightening withdrawal symptoms until its cells can start producing enkephalin in the usual quantities (see Chapter 3).

Effects of Deprivation Your genetic blueprint specified in rather general terms what you would look like and when and how you would grow. But this blueprint is always brought to life by orders from the DNA molecules in each cell. And depending on circumstances, your growth and development can either be speeded up or retarded.

If a pregnant woman is forced by circumstances to undergo starvation, her body protects the fetus as much as it can by giving the unborn child almost all the resources the woman's body has available to it. Still, the child may be born much smaller than usual. If the child receives ample food immediately after birth, it usually catches up to the size its genetic blueprint had set for its normal development.

The same kind of catching up often occurs if a growing child is deprived of nourishment for brief periods by war or poverty. As an example, consider a study on Korean children reported late in 1975 by Myron Winick, Knarig Katchadurian Meyer, and Ruth C. Harris. During the Korean conflict in the 1950's, many very young children in that Asian country were separated from their parents and were placed in orphanages. Most of these youngsters suffered from severe malnutrition before they entered the institutions. After the hostilities ended, some of these children were returned to their war-shattered homes. But many others, whose parents were dead or missing, were placed in foster homes in the United States. Winick and his colleagues studied the physical and intellectual development of several hundred of these Americanized orphans.

About a third of these children were so malnourished when they entered the orphanage that they ranked in the bottom 3 percent of all Korean children as far as height and weight were concerned. Another third were moderately malnourished. The rest were more or less of average size when first considered for adoption. After several years of good care in the United States, *all* of these children were of greater than average height and weight (compared to other Koreans). Winick and his group concluded that the adopted children were heavier and taller than if they had remained behind in Korea.

Of even greater interest are the data that Winick *et al.* gathered on school achievement and intelligence. Previous studies had shown that the Korean children who were returned to their own home environments suffered rather severe mental and social retardation. This retardation continued through young adulthood—a fact suggesting that many war-torn Korean homes offered little in the way of social stimulation or intellectual enrichment. In marked contrast, the Americanized orphans had intelligence test scores that were 40 to 50 IQ points higher than children who stayed in Korea. Indeed, their US foster homes were apparently so stimulating that the orphans had IQ and school achievement scores that averaged slightly better than those of native-born US children of the same age.

It would seem that your genes *set limits* for your physical and intellectual development. But it is the environment you were reared in that determines *where within these limits* your actual growth will fall.

Physical Growth and Development after Birth

In general, as soon as the newborn child's muscles, sense organs, and nerves are fully formed, the child begins to use them. But much of the human nervous system is not fully developed until the child is a year or two old—and some parts, such as the corpus callosum, continue to mature for at least the next 20 years.

The general pattern of bodily development is from head to foot. Simple skills, such as head movements, appear first because the structures that control these skills are among the first to mature. More complex behavior patterns, such as crawling, standing, and walking, come much later in the developmental sequence than head movements do (see Fig. 19.11).

The motor centers in the brain (see Chapter 4) send long nerve fibers out to connect (usually through one or more synapses) with the muscles in

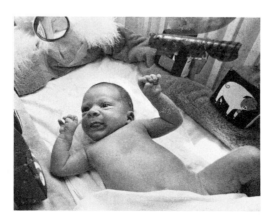

A rich environment usually speeds up a child's physical and cognitive development.

Motor skill. Motor skills, or motoric (moh-TORR-ick) skills, are those movements that are controlled by the muscles. Gross motor skills typically involve large muscle movements, such as walking. Fine motor skills are those involving tiny movements, such as repairing a watch or threading a needle.

Fig. 19.11. Motor development in an infant.

various parts of the body. Since the head muscles are closer to the brain than are the foot muscles, the head comes under the control of the motor centers long before the feet do. The appearance of a new motor skill (such as crawling or grasping) always suggests that a new part of the child's body has just matured—that is, that the brain centers have just become connected to the muscles involved in the new **motor skill.**

Effects of Early Training

Children develop at different speeds, in part because of their environments, but also because they follow different genetic schedules. Most children begin to walk between the twelfth and eighteenth month after birth. No matter how much coaxing and practice the parents may give their six-month-old child, it will not walk much sooner than if the parents had simply let the child alone.

In many primitive cultures, where the mother must spend almost all of her time working in the fields or elsewhere, young children spend the first year or so of their lives bound to a board or bundled tightly inside a bag carried on their mothers' backs. These children are released from their

A child taking its first steps.

restraints only for an hour or two each day, so they have little chance to practice motor skills. Yet their muscular development is not retarded, and they creep, crawl, and walk at about the same ages as children who are not restrained. (As we will see in a later chapter, however, oriental and American Indian children react to "bundling" rather more passively than do black or white infants.)

The results of a number of studies with identical twins also suggest that practice is not necessary for early motor development. In most of these studies, one twin has been encouraged to practice a skill (such as climbing stairs), while the other has been confined to a playpen. Training usually begins well before either twin could be expected to display the skill and proceeds until the "experimental" twin has clearly mastered the desired behavior pattern. At that point, the "control" twin is removed from its playpen and tested. The usual finding is that, right from the first trial, the "control" twin can perform the task almost as well as the "experimental" twin.

There are two exceptions to all this. The first has to do with special skills—such as swimming or skating or playing a musical instrument. These behaviors need practice and guidance, and a child left to develop on its own usually does not do well without special training. The second exception has to do with the *attitude* the child takes toward physical activities. A child that is encouraged to explore its environment, to swing and jump and run and play, is more likely to become active and physically outgoing than a child who is confined for much of its early life to a playpen. By rewarding their child for physical activities, the parents may instill important *social skills* in the child even if they don't speed up its physical maturation.

It is only if the parents become discouraged that their six-month-old daughter cannot be taught to walk and run—and hence reject the child and stop playing with her—that the child's development may be harmed by parental training.

Critical Periods

There is some evidence that the best time for a child to learn a given skill is at the time the child's body is just mature enough to allow mastery of the behavior in question. This belief is often called the **critical-period hypothesis**—that is, the belief that an organism must have certain experiences at a *particular time* in its developmental sequence if it is to reach its most mature state.

Imprinting   There are many studies from the animal literature supporting the critical-period hypothesis. For instance, Nobel Prize winner Konrad Lorenz discovered many years ago that birds such as ducks and geese will follow the first moving object they see after they are hatched. Usually the first thing they see is their mother, of course, who has been sitting on the

Critical-period hypothesis. The belief that there is a best time for a child to experience certain things or learn certain skills. Trying to train a child before or after this critical period is supposed to be like picking an apple before it is ripe—or after it has turned mushy and rotten.

eggs when they are hatched. However, Lorenz showed that if he took goose eggs away from the mother and hatched them in an incubator, the fresh-hatched **goslings** would follow *him* around instead.

After the goslings had waddled along behind Lorenz for a few hours, they acted as if they thought he was their mother and that they were humans, not geese. When Lorenz returned the goslings to their real mother, they ignored her. Whenever Lorenz appeared, however, they became very excited and flocked to him for protection and affection. It was as if the *visual image* of the first object they saw moving had become so strongly **imprinted** on their minds that, forever after, that object was "mother" (see Fig. 19.12).

During the past 20 years or so, scientists have devoted much time to the study of *imprinting*, as it now is called. Imprinting takes place in many (but not all) types of birds, and it also seems to occur in mammals such as sheep and seals. Whether human infants "imprint" is still a matter for debate. Imprinting is very strong in ducks and geese, however, and they have most often been the subjects for study.

The urge to imprint typically reaches its strongest peak 16 to 24 hours after the baby goose is hatched. During this period, the baby bird has an innate tendency to follow anything that moves, and will chase after its mother (if she is around), a human, a bouncing football, or a brightly painted tin can the experimenter dangles in front of the gosling. The more the baby bird struggles to follow after this moving object, the more strongly the young animal becomes imprinted to the object.

Once the goose has been imprinted, this very special form of learning cannot easily be reversed. For example, the geese that first followed Lorenz could not readily be trained to follow their mother instead. Indeed, when

Fig. 19.12. Konrad Lorenz "mothering" his goslings.

these geese were grown and sexually mature, they showed no romantic interest in other geese. Instead, they attempted to court and mate with humans.

Question: Given the fact that imprinting is an intensive form of learning, would you expect goslings to show unusually large amounts of REM sleep during the first 24 hours after they hatch?

Innate Fears If a goose is hatched in a dark incubator and is not allowed to see the world until two or three days later, imprinting often does not occur. At first it was thought that the critical period had passed, and hence the bird could never become imprinted to anything. Now we know better. The innate urge to follow moving objects does appear to reach a peak in geese 24 hours after they are hatched, but it does not decline thereafter. Rather, a second innate urge—that of *fearing and avoiding new objects*—begins to develop, and within 48 hours after hatching this fear typically overwhelms the urge the bird has to follow anything that moves.

To use a human term, the gosling's *attitude* toward strange things is controlled by its genetic blueprint: At first it is attracted to, then it becomes afraid of, new objects in its environment. As we will see in a moment, these conflicting "attitudes" may explain much of the data on critical periods in both animals and humans.

Question: How might these two apparently conflicting behavioral tendencies help a baby goose survive in its usual or natural environment?

Pecking and Flying In other experiments, baby chickens have been hatched and raised in the dark for the first several days of their lives. Chicks have an innate tendency to peck at small objects soon after they are hatched—an instinctive behavior pattern that helps them get food as soon as they are born. In the dark, of course, they cannot see grain lying on the ground and hence do not peck (they must be hand fed in the dark during this period of time). Once brought into the light, these chicks do begin to peck, but they do so clumsily and ineffectively, as if their critical period for learning the pecking skill had passed.

Birds such as robins and blue jays learn to fly at about the time their wings are mature enough to sustain flight (their parents often push them from the nest as a means of encouraging them to take off on their own). If these young birds are restrained and not allowed to fly until much later, their flight patterns are often clumsy and they do not naturally gain the necessary skills to become good fliers.

Overcoming the Critical Period All of these examples may appear to support the critical-period hypothesis—that there is one time in an organism's life when it is best suited to learn a particular skill. These studies might also seem to violate the general rule that an organism can catch up if its development has been delayed. However, the truth is more complicated (as always) than it might seem from the experiments we have **cited** so far.

Baby geese will normally not imprint if you restrict their visual experiences for the first 48 hours of their lives—their fear of strange objects is by then too great. However, if we give the geese tranquilizing drugs to help overcome their fear, they can be imprinted a week or more after hatching.

Once imprinting has taken place, it may seem to be irreversible. But we can occasionally get a bird imprinted on a human to accept a goose as its mother if we coax it enough and reward it for approaching or following its natural mother.

Chicks raised in darkness become clumsy eaters—but what do you think would happen if we gave them special training in how to peck, rather than simply leaving the matter to chance? And if we can train a pigeon to bowl (see Chapter 16), couldn't we train a baby robin to fly despite the fact that it had been restrained too long in the nest?

Cited (SIGHT-ted). From the Latin word meaning "to summon" or "to put in motion." To cite an author's name is to summon that person's name from memory. To cite an example is to "put an example in motion." Our word "excite" comes from the same Latin term and means "to call forth or arouse to action."

There is not much scientific evidence that human infants have the same types of critical periods that birds and other lower animals do. By being born without strong innate behavior patterns (such as imprinting), we seem to be better able to adjust and survive in the wide variety of social environments human babies are born into. Like many other organisms, however, children do have an inborn tendency to **imitate** the behavior of other organisms around them. In a study reported in *Science* in 1977, Andrew Meltzoff and M. Keith Moore note that infants begin to imitate the facial expressions of adults by the time the infants are two weeks old. Furthermore, if the infant is sucking on a pacifier when the adult "makes a face," the infant will repeat the gesture a few moments later when the pacifier is removed. Thus the infant can not only imitate, but can delay its response for a period of several seconds. (As we will see in the next chapter, infants also have an innate tendency to become emotionally attached to the adults who care for them.)

Question: Why would it aid a child's survival if its genes "programmed" the infant to imitate the behavior of adults rather than "programming" the child to respond to its world in a reflexive, mechanical fashion?

The Limits of Change

The critical-period hypothesis is, in a way, a restatement of that old expression that "you can't change human nature." For the hypothesis holds that the first years of a child's life are by far the most important, and that the child's intellectual and social potential is fairly fixed by the time it is a few years old.

If this view were true, it would do us little good to take culturally deprived children and give them special training after they had spent their early years in unstimulating environments. Luckily for these children, as we noted in the study on Korean orphans, recent evidence casts considerable doubt on the critical-period hypothesis—at least as it used to be stated. All of us are limited by the genes ("human nature") that we inherited, but within these limits we have much more freedom and flexibility than most scientists previously thought to be the case.

With the exception of identical twins, every person on earth has a different set of genes. You are a genetically unique organism, and your own gene pattern will probably never again be repeated in the entire history of the human race. But genes are nothing more than a set of molecular instructions that tell our cells, organs, and bodies how to respond to *particular environments*. If any one of us is to reach the full potential allowed by our genetic blueprints, obviously we will need to find out what kinds of environmental inputs will help us become what we want to become.

At the moment, we are not wise enough to be able to predict from a child's inheritance what kind of world it needs. Indeed, we are not even wise enough to know what we mean by "reaching our full potential." Nor can we yet practice "genetic engineering" on a fetus. That is, we cannot rearrange its genes—even if this were a morally wise thing to do—in order to ensure that the child would be born with the kinds of chromosomes that might help it succeed in our world as it exists today. But perhaps it is a sign of progress that we now speak more of "genetic potential" than we do of "genetic limits." For the greatest limit to our development lies not in our genes, but in our own ignorance of how best to help people grow and mature.

Question: If a child of yours was born with trisomy-21, would you be more interested in discovering the child's psychological limitations, or its psychological potential? How would you go about learning what your child's potential actually could be?

Genetic Counseling

As you will recall from the beginning of the chapter, Clyde C. was born with an extra Y chromosome in all his cells and ended up in a medical–penal hospital. That additional Y chromosome made Clyde taller than average, caused skin problems, brought him to sexual maturity sooner than usual, and gave him a more impulsive set of behavior patterns than most of us have. Perhaps 50 years from now we will know how to remove this extra Y chromosome before a child is born—or at least know how to suppress the chromosome's harmful effects.

But what could we do for you, in the next 10 years or so, if the doctor who delivered your first son discovered that the boy had an extra Y chromosome? True, majority of XYY males grow up to be normal citizens who have no problems with the law or with society. And it seems likely that, if the parents knew that the boy might need greater-than-normal help in establishing "impulse control," the parents could be of considerable help in giving the boy the extra training that he might need.

Princeton sociologist James Sorenson has made a study of parents who seek genetic counseling about their children. Early in 1973, Sorenson reported that almost all of these parents waited to ask for help until *after* they had already had at least one child who suffered from genetic damage much more severe than having an extra Y chromosome. Furthermore, these parents tended to spend more time and money trying to *disprove* the initial medical **diagnosis** than they did in trying to find out how to help the child (and themselves).

The XYY condition is not really "inherited": It could happen to anyone. For as far as we know, an XYY father is no more likely to have an XYY son of his own than is a normal XY father. But in many cases, people *do carry defective genes*, and they pass along their own chromosomal problems to their children. Most forms of color-blindness, for instance, are directly inherited (see Chapter 8), as are many types of mental and physical retardation. And, of course, if both the mother *and* the father have "bad" genetic blueprints, the odds that their children will be abnormal are much, much higher than if only one parent has chromosomal defects.

Shouldn't married couples who are high genetic risks be counseled about the difficulties their children may face? Dr. Sorenson found that, sadly enough, such counseling seldom is effective *as presently practiced*. More than half the couples he studied either forgot, rejected, or badly distorted the scientific information they were given. In many cases, this new information seemed to cause a dramatic change in the parents' own evaluations of themselves. It also led to frequent marital problems.

When only one parent carried the defective genes, the parent often developed severe and chronic feelings of guilt and shame, while the other partner often came to have strong negative emotional feelings toward her or his partner. When both carried some kind of "genetic misfortune," Sorenson says, the situation was likely to produce a sense of being a doomed family—a feeling on the part of both partners of having lost control over their lives.

The Future of Genetic Counseling

Dr. Sorenson points out that the difficulty with present forms of genetic counseling is this: Although we can identify some (but not all) chromosomal difficulties for parents, we often do not know what to tell them to do about overcoming the handicaps their children will face. Clyde C.'s parents did not know of his extra Y chromosome. But supposing they had been told at birth that he might have trouble controlling his impulses—would that have helped?

In 1950, when Clyde C. was born, the answer was no—because no one knew how to handle "impulsiveness" very well. His parents might well have rejected the information and done nothing about it. But now we are beginning to learn how to help people with this problem.

Diagnosis (die-ag-NO-sis). From the Latin term meaning "to recognize something by its signs, or to distinguish one thing from another." Medical doctors diagnose a disease by distinguishing the symptoms of that disease from all other types of illnesses.

Children who suffer from trisomy-21 and various forms of brain damage often are even more impulsive than are XYY males. These youngsters are easily distractable—they cannot focus their attention on anything for more than a few seconds. If they see something they want, they often try to take it by force, no matter what the consequences. Without special training, they remain this way all their lives.

But as we indicated in the story that begins Chapter 5, psychologists have recently found that even severely handicapped children can be taught to bring their impulsiveness under control—if they are rewarded for doing so. Thus we may now ask two very important questions: What might have happened had Clyde C.'s parents been taught to "shape" the boy into gaining greater control over his destructive impulses? And once he had learned how to control himself, wouldn't he have been in a much better position to achieve whatever goals in life he wished for himself?

We need much better techniques for measuring the genetic potential of a child—not only before and after it is born, but even before it is conceived. More than this, we need to learn as much as we can about how social and behavioral inputs affect the expression of a child's genetic blueprint. Then we need to develop better ways of helping all people adjust to their genetic limitations by gaining better control over their thoughts, behaviors, and environments.

The field of genetic counseling is still in its infancy. But what a challenging and rewarding future lies ahead for those psychologists who choose to specialize in solving these very human problems!

Summary

1. You began life as a **single cell.**
2. Your mother produced an egg that contained 23 **chromosomes.** At the moment of **fertilization,** one of your father's sperms penetrated the egg and added 23 chromosomes of its own. This cell then underwent **cellular division.**
3. Since all the cells in your body are **daughters** of this original cell, the **nucleus** of every cell in your body (with certain minor exceptions) has 23 **pairs of chromosomes.**
4. These chromosomes contain the **genes,** made up of **DNA** molecules, that govern the functioning of each cell. The DNA sends "command messages" (a type of **feed-forward**) to the **cytoplasm** of the cell telling it what kinds of **proteins** and other molecules to manufacture.
5. The 23rd chromosome in each egg has an **X chromosome.** The 23rd chromosome in each sperm has either an X or a **Y chromosome.** If an X sperm unites with the egg, the 23rd chromosome will be **XX,** and the child will be born a female. If a Y sperm unites with the egg, the 23rd chromosome will be **XY,** and the child will be born a male.
6. Shortly after fertilization occurs, the fertilized egg begins to divide to make other identical cells. Should these first daughter cells become separated, each will form complete **embryos** that develop into **identical twins.** Should the mother carry two eggs at once, each may be fertilized (by different sperms) and the mother will give birth to **fraternal twins.**
7. Sometimes the chromosomes of the mother and father contain **genetic defects,** and the child is born defective. Color-blindness is a type of inherited defect.
8. Sometimes the chromosomes from the egg and sperm do not match up as they should, or something goes wrong during early cellular divisions. Then the child's cells may contain but a single 23rd chromosome—always an X—and may suffer from **Turner's syndrome.** Or the child may have three 23rd chromosomes instead of the usual two.
9. A child with an **XXY 23rd chromosome** becomes an infertile male and is said to suffer from **Klinefelter's syndrome.**
10. A child with an **XYY 23rd chromosome** becomes a normal-appearing male but may have difficulty learning **impulse control.** This

extra male chromosome causes the child's body to secrete too much **androgen,** the male hormone. This excess androgen appears to speed up much of the child's physical maturation and brings the XYY boy to **puberty** sooner than expected.

11.   Two weeks after fertilization, the cells begin to **differentiate**—that is, take on different roles. The three main types of cells are **ecto-derm, meso-derm,** and **endoderm.**

12.   Two months after fertilization, cellular differentiation has proceeded far enough so that the **fetus** takes on a vaguely human shape.

13.   During pregnancy, the fetus is protected in the mother's body by an organ called the **placenta.**

14.   If the mother is starved during pregnancy, the child may be born smaller than usual. If the infant is given ample food, however, it will usually "catch up" to the size its **genetic blueprint** originally specified.

15.   If the infant is reared in a poor environment, it may become physically and mentally retarded. However, if it is given ample stimulation later on, it will usually "catch up" to its original **genetic potential.**

16.   Physical development in the infant typically proceeds in a **head-to-feet pattern.** The muscles controlling the head and neck become mature much sooner than those needed for walking or climbing.

17.   Children cannot be taught to walk before their leg muscles are mature. However, if a child is prevented from walking at the time it would normally do so, it doesn't appear to suffer much **physical retardation.**

18.   Baby geese (and the young of other animals) often **imprint** on the first moving object they see or can follow. The young animal behaves toward the imprinted object—whatever it is—as if the object were its mother. Imprinting is a powerful form of learning that usually occurs during the first 24 hours of life and is difficult to reverse.

19.   The **critical-period hypothesis** states that the "best time" for learning to occur is when the organism is first ready to make a response. Recent studies suggest the hypothesis is not always correct, particularly when applied to human growth and development.

20.   Parents whose children are born with genetic defects often avoid or distort **genetic counseling** about how to help their children reach their maximum potential.

21.   Most children with genetic defects can overcome many of their problems if we give them the environmental inputs they need to counteract their genetic limitations.

(Continued from page 481.)

When the class calmed down a bit, Dr. Martin Mayer continued. "That's a very interesting approach," he said, nodding at the guitar-playing young man. "I presume you mean we could identify men and women who are carriers of the wrong kinds of genes, and prohibit them from having kids. Not from getting married or from having sex—but from raising a family."

"Man, that is the most up-tight attitude toward sex I've ever heard!" said one of the girls. "Having kids is a religious thing. You're asking us to play God with human souls! That's not something people ought to decide."

"I agree with you entirely," Dr. Mayer said, polishing his glasses again. "We certainly must take religious views into account. But sex is also a matter of economics. Very soon we're going to have too many people on this old globe we call the earth. Maybe we have too many right now. Can't support them all, no matter what we do. We could let them starve, which is the way the lions handle things 'naturally.' Or we can voluntarily control who gets to have children in the first place, using some plan that religious groups would agree to. But if we don't do something voluntarily, the government is bound to step in and pass laws."

Mayer put his spectacles back on his nose. "Any of you students grow up on a farm?"

Several of the young people held up their hands.

"Well, I guess your parents have a few cows around to give milk and to supply meat, right? And if your parents are smart, and they probably are, they're going to buy the best breeding stock they can afford, because good cows give more milk and more butter fat than poor cows. And good bulls produce stronger offspring with better meat on them than poor bulls. One good bull can service a whole lot of cows through artificial insemination. Even a puny little cow will have better offspring if her eggs are fertilized with genes from a first-rate bull. So a blue-ribbon bull can share the wealth of his fine genes with lots of cows, even the scrawniest. Perhaps we should do the same with humans. Maybe only the President should be allowed to have children."

"If only the President of the United States can have kids, he's going to be one busy daddy," one of the girls said laughing.

"Doesn't seem fair somehow," the boy sitting next to her said. "You've gotten rid of half the bad genes by using just one prime bull, but what about the scrawny cows? They're still passing along their scrawny genes to their kids. Why not have just one big mother cow that's as good as the bull?"

"Wouldn't be enough calves born to feed us all," said another boy.

"Scrawny cows are cut out of the herd early and sold for hamburgers and hot dogs. That way you improve the herd as you go along," said another, obviously well-acquainted with farm life.

"Well, we're working on ways to improve herds even more," Mayer continued. "Just because a first-rate cow has good genes in her egg cells doesn't mean that she has to be burdened with carrying the calf until it's ready to be born. It's a waste of her time. So we've worked out a deal. After we inseminate the prime cow artificially, we let the fertilized egg grow for a few days, and then we remove the embryo and transplant it into the body of a scrawny cow and let her do all the work of carrying the little calf until it's ready to be born. A few months later, the scrawny cow gives birth to a super-calf with superior genes."

"Why bother," a student asked.

"Financial reasons," Mayer responded. "Once we remove the embryo from the super-prime cow mother, she starts producing new eggs right away, which also can be fertilized artificially and then transplanted to the body of another inferior cow. That way, one super-momma can produce lots of superior calves each year instead of just one or two. It's still too complicated a technique for general use, but when the cost comes down, it's sure going to make a lot more money for the farmers."

"I know what you're going to say next," said the guitar-playing boy. "If it works with cows, why not try it with humans?"

"You've got to be kidding," one of the girls said. "I wouldn't want to carry somebody else's baby."

"Not even for a million dollars?" Mayer asked. "Suppose a rich lady wanted to have a child but didn't want to go through the trouble of being pregnant.

"Suppose she offered you a million dollars if you'd let her doctor transplant the embryo into your body. That way you could carry the child for her while she went off on a fancy vacation somewhere. Then, when the child was born, she could pick the child up at the hospital and give you the million dollars. How would you like that?"

PART FIVE Maturation and Development

"If I carried the baby, it would be mine, and no rich lady could take it away from me," the girl replied.

"Yeah, but what if the government decided you couldn't have kids," one of the boys said.

"Why couldn't I have kids, I'd like to know?"

"Because the government would say you didn't have the right kind of genes, stupid. Just like my father decides which of his cows can have calves and which can't," the boy added rather smugly.

"But I've got great genes!" the girl said. "And no government is going to tell me I don't! And even if they did, I'd just get Dr. Mayer to engineer my genes so they were the right kind. So there," she concluded, making a face at the boy who was tormenting her with his comments.

"What's the right kind of genes?" asked another girl.

"Yes, it all boils down to that decision, doesn't it?" Mayer said. "As Aldous Huxley pointed out in *Brave New World*, the day will surely come when we can engineer genes—if we know what kinds of kids we want to have. We can judge what kinds of cow we want because we value meat and milk production. But what do we value most in humans? Size? Strength? Intelligence?"

"That old Einstein wouldn't have done so well as a fullback for the Dallas Cowboys," an athletic young man said.

"I don't even want to talk about this, it scares me so," another girl said. "It's abnormal and immoral. It could never happen in the United States."

"That's probably what the cows thought a few years ago," said one of the boys.

"Well," said Mayer, "maybe it won't happen here, but the possibility of genetic engineering won't disappear just because we refuse to talk about it. In fact, just the opposite. But let's get back to that point about who should carry the baby. Is there any reason why a woman should have to go through a lengthy pregnancy? In *Brave New World* the embryos are grown in bottles rather than in their mothers' bodies. When they are ready to be born, the babies are uncorked like a bottle of fine wine. Maybe the day will come when each home has a mechanical incubator in it. You would watch your child's development before birth just the way you watch a plant grow and flower."

"That's outrageous," said the girl in the second row. "I don't want my baby born in a machine."

"You'd destroy the warm, maternal feeling every woman has when she's carrying her own baby," said another.

"I wouldn't love my baby if I didn't carry it myself," said another girl.

"And how would my baby feel if it learned that it had developed in a machine instead of inside me?" said another. "It just wouldn't love me as much."

"Do you really think that maternal love is dependent on carrying the baby yourself?" Mayer asked.

"Of course," said the girl in the second row. "All that pain is natural. It makes the baby worthwhile, something you really suffered for. You just wouldn't take care of the baby as well if it weren't for that special feeling of closeness you get when you're carrying the child. It just wouldn't be *yours*. That's what the pain is for—to make you love the baby more."

A girl in the middle of the room suddenly stood up, tears filling her eyes. "I'd like to say something. A woman doesn't have to carry a child, or give birth to it, or suffer pain, in order to love the baby and see that it gets the best care and attention. And whether a child is born in a bottle or from its mother's body doesn't affect the love it has for the woman who brings it up. Maybe you ought to remember that I'm adopted. My adopted mother can't have children, so she and my foster father adopted me when I was just two weeks old. And they love me very, very much, both of them."

The class was absolutely silent for several moments after the girl sat down. Then the bell rang.

"Thank you very, very much," Dr. Mayer said, a smile on his face.

Recommended Readings

Clarke, Ann M., and A.D.B. Clarke, eds. *Mental Deficiency: The Changing Outlook,* 3d ed. (New York: Free Press, 1974).

Huxley, Aldous. *Brave New World* (New York: Harper & Row, 1932).

Lickona, Thomas, ed. *Moral Development and Behavior: Theory, Research, and Social Issues* (New York: Holt, Rinehart and Winston, 1976).

Lubs, Herbert A., and Felix de la Cruz, eds. *Genetic Counseling: A Monograph of the National Institute of Child Health and Human Development* (New York: Raven Press, 1977).

Rostand, Jean. *Can Man Be Modified?* (New York: Basic Books, 1959).

Emotional Development

Did You Know That . . .

Death and love are two important areas of human existence seldom studied scientifically?

We cannot investigate love directly, since it is an internal process, but we can study loving behavior.

Even though all their other needs are met, infant monkeys will die if not given something to "love"—that is, something to cling to and rub against?

A human infant, if separated from its mother, may fall into a profound depression?

If a female monkey does not engage in "sex play" with her peers when young, she may refuse to mate as an adult?

Monkeys raised in partial isolation are often either wildly aggressive or almost hopelessly passive as adults?

Much of what we call "maternal" and "paternal" instincts are really learned behavior patterns?

Monkey mothers raised in isolation often destroy their own offspring?

Child abuse occurs most often among young parents who live in cities, who are social isolates, and who were themselves abused as children?

Mothers who treat their children inconsistently, or unresponsively, can predispose the children to later psychological difficulties?

Boys separated from their fathers before age six tend to show more "feminine" behavior patterns than usual?

Girls separated from their fathers by divorce tend to become more promiscuous in their early sexual behavior than do girls reared in intact homes?

"Love Me, Love Me Not"

"Now, admit it. Isn't this the cleanest, most modern nursery you've ever seen?"

The Director of the nursery, who was leading the tour, hardly waited for his guests to answer. "Spotless, absolutely spotless. We want to make sure that the infants are completely protected from dirt and disease. And I dare say we're succeeding."

The Director was showing the kitchen to his visitors, two women and a man.

"The best of all possible baby foods, served in absolutely sterile containers. Each portion contains special vitamins and minerals, prepared by cooks wearing face masks so that no germs ever contaminate the food. Isn't it beautiful?" the Director said, an angelic smile on his face.

Then he moved forward. "Let's go into the observation room. We can watch the children through the glass. You understand that we can't let you actually go into the sleeping room with the children themselves. That is, unless you're willing to scrub down first in the shower and put on one of our freshly laundered white uniforms. We can't have you transmitting some disease to these poor little babies, now can we?" The Director uttered a small, brief, high-pitched laugh.

Through the glass window the visitors could see the nursery room. Each of the infants had its own little bed made up with immaculately white sheets. Waist-high wooden partitions stood between each of the cribs, giving every infant almost complete privacy.

"Why do you have the cribs separated that way?" one of the women visitors asked.

"Ah, an interesting question," replied the Director. "We want to minimize the transmission of disease, you see. Should one of the infants contract an ailment, the others are too far away to be readily infected. The partitions are covered with a special white paint, and we wash them down with disinfectant once a week. Nothing but the best, I assure you!"

One of the infants was crying lustily. A nurse came into the room and picked the child up, holding it close to her starched white uniform. Although the woman cradled the infant in her arms for some time, it continued its loud, gulping cries.

"Why is that child crying so much?" asked one of the visitors,

The Director smiled confidently. "A new arrival, just separated from its mother. Takes them a while to get used to new surroundings, of course. After a few days—a couple of weeks or so—they calm down and begin to enjoy their healthy new environment. After all, we've rescued many of them from very unsanitary home conditions."

"Why was it necessary to separate the children from their mothers?" asked one of the women.

"Mostly because the mothers had to go into a hospital for an operation of some kind, or because of some sickness. So it's not at all surprising that the children should be a little upset at first. 'Parting is such sweet sorrow,' you know. They all cry a fair amount when they first arrive, but look at them now! They aren't making much of a fuss, now are they?"

It was true. Most of the infants lay in their cribs unmoving, staring at the white ceiling with wide-open eyes. Large tears rolled gently down the cheeks of one of the children. The nurse stopped by its crib, offered it a play toy, but the child merely continued its gentle weeping.

"You see, before we took over, the children were raised in filth, real filth. Noise, grime, germs—that was their steady diet. Many of them took sick and died. Now it's different. Those kids must have the most unpolluted environment on earth. Isn't it great?"

One of the visitors looked at the Director with raised eyebrows. "What's your sickness rate now?"

The Director cleared his throat. "Oh, I think we're doing quite well, all things considered."

"What do you mean, 'all things considered?'"

The Director's voice squeaked slightly as he responded. "Well, remember that these kids all come from bad home environments. Mothers sick, families mostly broken apart at the seams. You've got to keep that in mind. You'd expect a lot of illness in those situations anyhow, wouldn't you?"

"What kinds of symptoms do the children show?"

The squeak in the Director's voice grew more pronounced. "Well, you see, it's really odd. They don't eat. That's the main problem. Maybe when we sterilize the food, we take all the taste out or something. And they catch a lot of colds. We don't really understand why. Probably a bug or something that's going around, but I'm sure we'll lick it."

"What do you plan to do?"

"Well, first we're going to wash the whole place down again with disinfectant, and then . . ."

"You see, Señores, we do the best we can. But we have little money, and we have tradition to fight. So it is very difficult . . ."

The Superintendent of the jail shrugged his shoulders with an eloquence that could only come from practice. He was showing his visitors—two women and a man—the jail's kitchen. A fat, contented-looking little child, perhaps 18 months old, waddled across the floor and sat down by its mother, who was shelling beans.

"Look at that poor child," one of the women said. "Just look at the dirt on its face! And the rags that it's wearing! Can't you at least provide the children with adequate clothing and keep them clean?"

Again the Superintendent shrugged. "Señora, we try. But the government does not give us money to buy clothes for the children. You see, they are not here officially. It is the mother who is in jail, not the child. But it is our custom not to separate the little ones from their mothers, and who am I to go against such tradition? The mothers would complain loudly if I did. And the fathers as well—if we knew who the fathers were!"

The fat little child got to its feet and started to walk again, but soon stumbled and fell to the floor. Almost before the first cry was out of its mouth, its mother scooped it up and pressed it to her breast.

The visitor persisted. "But the dirt. At least you can do something about that!"

A smile crept across the Superintendent's dark, heavily wrinkled face. "Dirt? Senora, these women come from huts with dirt floors. They are not from what you would call the best classes of society. We merely keep them in jail. We are not equipped to teach them to be ladies!"

"But cleanliness is next to godliness!"

"Señora, the padre will tell you that even the godliness of some of these women is in rather grave doubt."

The child stopped its crying, but tears still ringed its eyes. The mother brushed the tears away with a dirty rag, then dangled a bunch of beans in front of the child's face, teasing it. The baby reached for the beans, but missed, so the mother continued the little game. On the second try, the child caught the beans and pulled them away from its mother. Both of them laughed.

"Just listen to them," one of the women visitors said, shaking her head in disgust.

"Yes it's apparent that we must do something to save these children from such an unhealthy and unwholesome environment," said the male visitor. "We would be shirking our duty if we left these poor little babies to grow up in a jail!"

Chapter 20 Emotional Development

"What do you think would be best?"

The man thought for a moment. "Well, what do you think of building a nice, clean orphanage or hospital for them . . ."

Science and Social Taboos

Science is, to some extent, the fine art of asking questions and then trying to find reasonable and reliable answers. Sometimes the questions are safe and obvious: Why does the sun give off heat and light? Why is grass green? Why does lemon juice taste sour? The answers to these questions are often complex and highly mathematical, but they seldom offend anyone.

Occasionally, however, scientists manage to upset the people around them by posing a problem that many of us would rather not have investigated objectively: What are the actual consequences of war? What happens when we show violence on television? What are the effects of giving pornography to children? Our culture gives us *socially acceptable* answers to these questions, and the scientists who wish to peer further into the matter—or to obtain experimental data rather than collect opinions—frequently find themselves outcasts. Open minds are not always beloved by closed societies. Yet it was Albert Einstein himself who told young scientists that if they wanted to be successful, they should "challenge an **axiom**"—that is, they should challenge a belief that most people simply take for granted.

There are many areas of human behavior that are partially or entirely restricted from scientific investigation. One such topic is death: Although we may study what happens to people when they are dying from some natural cause, we obviously cannot hasten the process merely to see how the individual might react.

Another **taboo** area is love. As we remarked earlier, sexual love is a topic much discussed but seldom studied in the laboratory. But even the non-sexual aspects of love are not often subjected to a scientist's scrutiny, perhaps because many of us believe it is too personal a topic. Or perhaps we fear that the magic of love would somehow disappear if we analyzed it in factual terms.

A related "forbidden topic," at least until very recently, is that of parent–child relationships. John B. Watson, the first great **behaviorist,** believed that parents should not give much love or affection to their children for fear of "spoiling" the child. But Watson never bothered to test out his belief in any scientific way. Other psychologists have stated **vociferously** that the *primary task* of a parent is to give "love" to the infant, but these psychologists have not always defined "love" in any measurable way, nor have they performed controlled studies in which parents were required either to "love" or to "hate" their infants for long periods of time. We are not likely to know the full facts about parent–child interactions (and how they affect the child's later life) until we *do* perform controlled experiments on living children. But both our societal **mores** and our own gut feelings prevent us from undertaking such experiments.

And so we are left in something of a *quandary*—some of the most important areas of human experience are closed to scientific investigation. There are thousands and thousands of studies on how rats learn, but only a handful of adequate experiments on how people fall in love. And while we now have a few dozen *observational* studies on child-rearing practices, we will not be entirely sure what successful parenting is—that is, what the best ways are for parents to rear children—until we have an ample supply of scientific experiments to give us empirical data on the subject.

Love

Let us begin with an apparently simple question—what is love? The usual belief (in our society) is that love is something that an individual falls into, often without meaning to do so. That is, we believe love is entirely an *internal state or process* that happens to almost everyone. Love is a feeling, an intra-psychic emotion that is entirely inside us, and hence not subject to objective scrutiny. This view holds that we can study the *reactions* of a person who says she or he is in love, but we cannot see the *love itself*.

Love certainly is an emotion, and it most assuredly can be studied from an intra-psychic viewpoint. The intra-personal side of love has been written about for centuries by some of the wisest poets and novelists the world has known. When Elizabeth Barrett Browning wrote, "How do I love thee? Let me count the ways . . ." she told us as much about some aspects of intra-psychic love as any psychologist could.

However, love can also be approached from the biological viewpoint see Chapter 13) and from the behavioral/social viewpoint (see Chapter 26). For example, we may look at maternal love and say that it is an instinctual, biological response strongly influenced by the female's hormones. Or we may look at an individual's behavior and *assume* that only someone in love would act in that fashion. Perhaps a young man spends all his free time (and much of his money) entertaining a certain young woman. Or perhaps a young mother spends much of her time (and almost all of her money) taking care of her newborn child. Our assumption would be that "love is the cause of it all," because people in love typically advertise their condition by getting as close as they can to the object of their affections. Since a person in love is *attracted to* someone or something else, we can speak of *loving responses* or *loving behavior*—and these we can study scientifically, if we have the patience and wit to do so.

Our objective study of love will never *replace* our subjective, poetic examination of this glorious condition—nor is there any reason why it should. But once we realize that love is, *in part,* a response to some living or inanimate object, we can make certain statements about love that we could not make otherwise.

For example, taking this viewpoint we can see that, like all behavior, loving responses must be affected by a person's genetic blueprint, past experience, and present environment. We can also state that loving behaviors will *tend to increase* if they are followed by satisfaction and reward, and that they will *tend to decrease* if followed by pain or punishment or lack of reinforcement. We do not usually think in these terms, perhaps because we have been taught to perceive love as "an affair of the heart" rather than as a response to present and past stimulus inputs. And yet the data gathered so far strongly suggest that the "condition of love" is as influenced by internal secretions and external stimuli as is eating or breathing or speaking. By adopting such a view, we may lose a bit of the magic and mystery, but we surely gain a great deal in terms of real understanding of what love is all about.

Parental Love

In this chapter we will pay particular attention to the love that an infant shows toward its parents, and the attraction that mothers and fathers feel toward their children. Since most of the research has involved mother-child relationships, we will look at this type of love most closely.

We will find that "mother love" is not merely a mystical emotional bond, determined by nature (and neither is "father love"). In fact, an infant has no way of knowing who its biological mother or father really is. Thus a young child will love anyone or anything that gives it comfort, caresses, food, and protection. Without this loving attention, the child will die, or will grow up to be a very disturbed adult. So there is good reason for an infant to enter into a loving relationship with whomever or whatever satisfies its many needs. But what about the mother? Often she can survive better without the many demands that a child makes on her time and energy. Why then should a woman love an infant merely because it is born of her own flesh? And why should a father love his children at all since his biological role is over and done with the moment conception occurs?

The answers to these questions are a good deal more complex than they look at first glance. Society demands that a woman love—or at least care

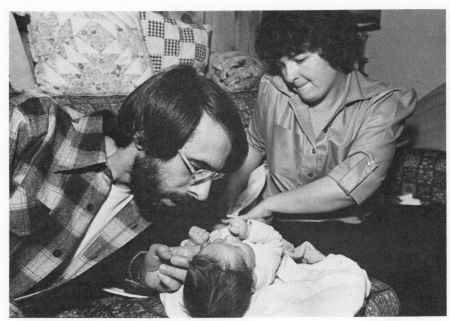

Mothers tend to train a child verbally while fathers tend to stimulate the child physically.

for—her children. Even animal mothers love their offspring and often *nurture* them tenderly. Isn't this proof that there is a "maternal instinct" which forces a female to love her child? And in many species of birds and fish, the father spends more time with the young ones than does the mother. Isn't this proof that there is a "paternal instinct" too?

Surprisingly enough, with humans and most other higher animals, it seems that the maternal and paternal instincts are remarkably weak. Many women neither love nor take care of their sons and daughters. In fact, as we will see, women by the thousands each year desert, **mutilate,** or even kill their children. Fathers are often worse. For the "paternal instinct," if it exists at all in humans, is considerably less potent than is the "maternal instinct."

Perhaps instead of being surprised that there are a few bad mothers and fathers in the world, we should be pleased and delighted that there are so many good ones.

Once we begin to look at loving *behavior*, rather than placing the entire emphasis on feelings and emotions, we find that we can ask a number of rather pointed questions we couldn't ask otherwise. For example, what is there about an infant's behavior that determines a mother's responses, and what is there about the way a mother cares for her child that makes the infant love and trust her? What happens to children without mothers and fathers? What effect does early separation from its parents have on a child? What if the separation comes later on? What substitutes can we give the child to replace the mother or father? Are parents enough, or does the child need to have experience with other children its own age? And if the mothering or fathering process somehow goes **awry,** what kinds of therapy or special training can help overcome the child's problems?

Love in the Laboratory

We have probably learned more (at a scientific level) about loving behavior in the past 50 years than in the previous 500—in part, because we have made more objective observations of love in humans (and other animals), and in part, because a few scientists have recently taken love into the laboratory and studied it experimentally.

We have finally realized, too, that middle-class US society is not the only culture in which love occurs, and that what seems natural and normal and

Mutilate (MUTE-till-late). To cut up or disfigure; to destroy.

Awry (uh-RYE). An old English word meaning "turned or twisted toward one side, wide of the mark, not on target."

PART FIVE Maturation and Development

moral for us may be quite different in Asia, Africa, or even in different segments of our own society. We have even learned that infants born to Asian parents may have quite different *innate response patterns* than those born to parents in the western world or in Africa (see Chapter 21).

And we have discovered that experiments involving animal subjects can give us clues to the complexities of human behavior that we could not get outside the laboratory. We cannot separate a dozen human infants from their mothers merely to see how the children react. But we can isolate *monkey* infants from their mothers in the hope that these studies will tell us how better to care for human children whose mothers desert them. We might also learn something about why some mothers abandon their off-spring in the first place. Thus we will talk a fair amount in this chapter about monkeys and chimpanzees—not because these animals interest us more than do humans, but because hard data on human loving behavior are often difficult to come by.

Primate (PRIME-ate). The "top dogs" of the animal kingdom—that is, the apes, chimpanzees, monkeys, and humans.

Motherless Monkeys

The scientist who has conducted the best long-term laboratory experiments on mother–child relationships is surely Harry Harlow, who did most of his work at the University of Wisconsin. Profesor Harlow did not set out to study love: It happened by accident. Like many other psychologists, he was at first primarily interested in how organisms learn. Rather than working with rats—as many other psychologists have done—Harlow chose to work with monkeys.

Since Harlow needed a place to house and raise the monkeys, he built the **Primate** Laboratory at Wisconsin. Then he began to study the effects of brain lesions on monkey learning. But Harlow soon found that young animals reacted somewhat differently to brain damage than did older monkeys, so Harlow and his wife Margaret (also a psychologist) devised a breeding program and tried various ways of raising monkeys in the laboratory.

The Harlows soon discovered that monkey infants raised by their mothers often caught diseases from their parents, so the Harlows began taking the infants away from their mothers at birth and tried raising them

Margaret and Harry Harlow in laboratory with monkeys.

Fig. 20.1. Baby monkey in a cheese-cloth blanket.

Fig. 20.2. Baby monkey with surrogate cloth monkey.

by hand. The baby monkeys had been given cheesecloth diapers to serve as baby blankets (see Fig. 20.1). Almost from the start, it became obvious to the Harlows that their little animals developed such strong attachments to the blankets that, in the Harlows' own terms, it was often hard to tell "where the diaper ended and the baby began." Not only this, but if the Harlows removed the "security" blanket in order to clean it, the infant monkey often became greatly disturbed—just as if its own mother had deserted it.

The Surrogate Mother What the baby monkeys obviously needed was an artificial or **surrogate** mother—something they could cling to as tightly as they typically clung to their own mother's chest (see Fig. 20.2). The Harlows sketched out many different designs, but none really appealed to them. Then, in 1957, while enjoying a champagne flight high over the city of Detroit, Harry Harlow glanced out of the airplane window and "saw" an image of an artificial monkey mother. It was a hollow wire cylinder, wrapped with a terrycloth bath towel, with a silly wooden head at the top. The tiny monkey could cling to this model mother as closely as to its real mother's body hair. This surrogate mother could be provided with a functional breast simply by placing a milk bottle so that the nipple stuck through the cloth at an appropriate place on the surrogate's anatomy. The cloth mother could be heated or cooled. It could be rocked mechanically or made to stand still. And, most important, the surrogate would not "protest" when it was removed from its "child."

While still sipping his champagne, Harlow mentally outlined much of the research that kept him, his wife, and their associates occupied for many years to come. And without realizing it, Harlow had shifted from studying monkey learning to studying love and emotional development in monkeys.

Five Types of Love

Harlow believes that there are five types of social love—that is, the love of one organism for another. These five types appear in a definite developmental sequence:

1. First comes the love an infant shows for its mother—or for her surrogate or substitute.

2. Out of this infant–mother love grows what Harlow calls "peer love," the affection of young organisms for other youngsters their own age.

3. When children reach puberty, they can experience a new dimension in their emotional development—that of heterosexual love, which Harlow

Surrogate (SIR-oh-gate, or SIR-oh-gutt). From the Latin word meaning "to substitute." A surrogate is a substitute or stand-in. A surrogate court is a court of law that handles the money and property of someone who has died—that is, a court which "stands in" for the dead person and sees that the person's will is carried out.

believes develops from peer love. As we will see, this third type of love is possible only if the organism has learned certain behavior patterns while playing with its peers.

4. The fourth type of love is available (under normal circumstances) only to females, for it is the affection that a mother shows to her infant.

5. Males, under the right conditions, may demonstrate the fifth type of love, which Harlow calls "paternal love."

In a moment we will discuss each of these "stages of emotional development" in turn. But first, we should mention two major objections that have been raised to the Harlows' experiments.

The Lab versus Real Life   The first objection made against the Harlows' work is that these studies were conducted in laboratory settings. Can we be sure that monkeys (or any other organisms) raised under more natural environments would experience the same developmental sequence? Labs are often as artificial and unresponsive as surrogate mothers themselves. Can anything worthwhile be learned from such investigations?

The answer seems to be yes, provided we remember the limitations of the laboratory and we supplement these experimental data with information taken from more natural sources. As we will see, the Harlows' findings often offer us insights into "real life observations" that we couldn't gain otherwise.

Question: What kinds of information about emotional development and loving behaviors in humans (and other species) can best be obtained from "real life observations," and what kinds can best be obtained in a laboratory?

Monkeys versus Humans   The second objection to the Harlows' experiments is perhaps more pertinent—are monkeys and chimpanzees similar enough to humans that a study of how apes love each other will tell us anything about human emotional development?

Again the data suggest that the answer should be positive, provided we keep firmly in mind that humans are many times more complex than even the brightest of other primates. The chimpanzee is the animal closest to humans in its talents and behavior patterns, and careful observation of its habits and development can give us a veritable gold mine of information we might not be able to gain any other way. But studies of chimps and monkeys can at best give us only hunches and hypotheses that we will later want to supplement with data from human subjects.

Question: What do you think the major psychological differences between chimpanzees and humans might be?

Infant–Mother Love

The chimpanzee or monkey infant is much more developed at birth than the human infant, and apes mature much faster than we do. Almost from the moment it is born, the monkey infant can move around and hold tightly to its mother. During the first few days of its life, the infant will approach and cling to any large, warm, soft object in its environment—particularly if that object also gives milk. After a week or so, however, the monkey infant begins to avoid newcomers and focuses its attentions on "mother"—real or surrogate.

During the first two weeks of its life, warmth is perhaps the most important psychological thing that a monkey mother has to give to its baby. The Harlows discovered this fact by offering infant monkeys a choice of two types of mother substitutes—one wrapped in terrycloth and one that was made of bare wire. If the two artificial mothers were both the same temperature, the little monkeys always preferred the cloth mother. However, if the wire model was heated, while the cloth model was cool, for the first two weeks after birth the baby primates picked the warm wire mother substitute as their favorite. Thereafter, they switched and spent most of their time on the more comfortable cloth mother.

Why is cloth preferable to bare wire? Something that the Harlows call **contact comfort** seems to be the answer, and a most powerful influence it is. Infant monkeys spend much of their time rubbing against their mothers' skins, putting themselves in as close contact with the parent as they can. Whenever the young animal is frightened, disturbed, or annoyed, it typically rushes to its mother and rubs itself against her body. Wire doesn't "rub" as well as does soft cloth. Prolonged "contact comfort" with a surrogate cloth mother appears to instill confidence in baby monkeys and is much more rewarding to them than is either warmth or milk. Infant monkeys also prefer a "rocking" surrogate to one that is stationary.

According to the Harlows, the basic quality of an infant's love for its mother is *trust*. If the infant is put into an unfamiliar playroom without its mother, the infant ignores the toys no matter how interesting they might be. It screeches in terror and curls up into a furry little ball. If its cloth mother is now introduced into the playroom, the infant rushes to the surrogate and clings to it for dear life. After a few minutes of contact comfort, it apparently begins to feel more secure. It then climbs down from the mother substitute and begins tentatively to explore the toys, but often rushes back for a deep embrace as if to reassure itself that its mother is still there and that all is well. Bit by bit its fears of the novel environment are desensitized (see Chapter 15), and it spends more and more time playing with the toys and less and less time clinging to its "mother."

Question: How might you explain "trust" in terms of the infant's need to predict and control its inputs?

Nurturance in Human Infants   Why is "contact comfort" so important? According to neuropsychologist James W. Prescott, sensory stimulation of the infant's receptor organs is necessary for the infant's brain to develop properly. The maturation of the infant's brain is strongly influenced by the sensory environment the child grows up in. And the *way* that an infant's brain develops in turn strongly affects the way the child thinks and behaves.

Fascinated by the Harlows' discoveries, Prescott (who works at the National Institute of Child Health and Human Development) undertook a survey of "nurturance" in a variety of human cultures. In 1978, Prescott noted that in some cultures, parents give their offspring very little of what Prescott calls *physical affectional stimulation*. That is, the parents either give their children minimal attention, or treat them indifferently or in a punitive manner. This lack of loving stimulation can have terrifying consequences for, as Prescott reports, "human infants, and animals, who are deprived of sensory stimulation during the formative period of brain development develop a biological system of brain functioning" which predisposes them to *violent behavior*. In 36 of the 49 cultures Prescott studied, there was a strong connection between "lack of physical stimulation in infants" and violence in adults. Prescott states further that the failure of parents to nurture their children is the principal factor "in the development of **alienation, psychopathy,** violence and aggression and, I might add, drug abuse and alcoholism."

Prescott has gathered considerable data to support his position. As an example, Prescott notes a study of three generations of families who abused their children. The study was performed by scientists at the University of Colorado who wondered why child abuse seemed to be "handed down" from one generation to another. The Colorado scientists found that although the abused infants received adequate care and food, they were deprived of what Prescott calls "nurturance"—that is, touching, physical affection, and sensory stimulation. In most cases, the abused children grew up to be as violent and as abusive as their own parents had been.

James W. Prescott.

Psychiatrist Henry Massie reported similar findings in 1978. Massie, who works at the University of California Medical School in San Francisco, showed home movies of mother–infant interactions to a group of impartial judges. It was the task of the judges to decide which of the children had become psychotic later in life, and which children had grown up to become normal individuals. The movies, of course, had been taken years earlier, before anyone knew how the children would turn out.

At first the judges concentrated on observing the responses of the children themselves. But they soon found that all the infants acted more or less the same. The infants in both groups touched, gazed at, and responded to their mothers in similar fashion.

However, the judges could tell at once which child would become psychotic by watching *how its mother treated it*. The mothers whose infants grew up to be normal gave their children "high quality" nurturance. That is, the mothers touched the infants often, held them close, gazed at them frequently, and seemed very strongly attached to the children. The mothers of the children who later became psychotic, however, gave "low quality" nurturance. These women touched and "loved" their children significantly less often than did the mothers of the children who grew up to be normal. Since there was no observable difference in the way that the infants reacted to the mothers, Massie concludes that it was the quality of sensory stimulation the mother gave to her infant that *predisposed* the child to become either normal or psychotic at a later stage in its development.

Neurons and Normalcy   How can lack of sensory stimulation so "warp" a child's brain that it has psychological problems later in life? While the answer is not entirely known, Dr. Prescott does offer one possible answer. Recent research in 1978 by psychologists Robert Struble and Austin Riesen shows that infant monkeys deprived of physical contact with other monkeys wind up with brain cells that have fewer **dendrites** than do the brain cells of normal rats (see Fig. 20.3). The more dendrites a neuron has, the greater its inter-connections with other nerve cells. And, presumably, the more complex the pattern of inter-connections in your brain, the better are your chances of turning out to be a normal human being.

Good Mothers and Bad   A mother's failure to give her infant sensory stimulation may explain, in physiological terms, why a child might develop an abnormal brain. But there is more to emotional development than growing dendrites. Let us return to the Harlows for additional data.

According to the Harlows, once a baby monkey has become *emotionally attached* to its mother (real or surrogate), the mother can do almost no wrong. In one of their studies, they tried to create "monster mothers" whose behavior would be so abnormal that the infants would desert the mothers. The problem was: How could you get a terrycloth mother to reject or punish its baby? The Harlows' solutions were ingenious—but most of them failed in their main purpose.

The Harlows designed four types of "monster mothers," but none of

Dendrites (DEN-drights). The input portion of a neuron. The "feelers" that extend from the "front end" of a nerve cell. See Chapter 2.

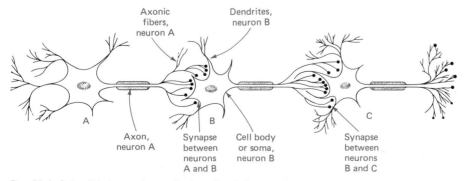

Fig. 20.3. Scientists have shown that a stimulating environment causes neurons to build up an increased number of synaptic connections.

Chapter 20   Emotional Development   511

Catapult (CAT-uh-pult). From the Greek words meaning "to throw against." An ancient military device for hurling stones at an enemy. Our modern version of the catapult is the slingshot.

Temperament (TEM-purr-uh-ment). The Latin word *temperare* means "to soften." To temper your argument is to criticize softly. To lose your temper is to lose your restraint. Your temperament is the way that you regulate yourself—that is, your characteristic attitude or behavior pattern. If you are nice to almost everybody you meet, you are said to have a polite temperament.

Anaclitic relationship (ann-uh-KLITT-ick). A strong, non-sexual love; the loving dependency and trust of a young child for its mother. The emotional attachment that builds up between a child and its mother.

them was apparently "evil" enough to impart fear or loathing to the infant monkeys. One such "monster" occasionally blasted its babies with compressed air. A second shook so violently that the baby often fell off. A third contained a **catapult** that frequently flung the infant away from it. The most evil-appearing of all had a set of metal spikes buried beneath its terrycloth; from time to time the spikes would poke through the cloth, making it impossible for the infant to cling to the surrogate.

The baby monkeys brought up on the "monster mothers" did show a brief period of emotional disturbance when the wicked **temperament** of the surrogates first showed up. The infants would cry for a time when displaced from their mothers. But as soon as the surrogates returned to normal, the infant would return to the surrogate and continue clinging, as if all were forgiven. As the Harlows tell the story, the only prolonged distress created by the experiment seemed to be that felt by the experimenters!

There was, however, one type of surrogate that uniformly "turned off" the infant monkeys. S.J. Suomi, working with the Harlows, built a terrycloth mother with ice water in its veins. Newborn monkeys attached themselves to this "cold momma" for a brief period of time, but then retreated to a corner of the cage and rejected her forever.

Expectancies and Emotional Development

There are many studies suggesting that punishment *by itself* is not usually sufficient to disrupt a child's love for its parents, nor does an abused child always turn out to be an abnormal adult. Something more is needed: The infant usually must be given sensory and social inputs that are *inconsistent* as well as punishing.

What does a "good" mother (or father) do for an infant that a "poor" parent doesn't? For one thing, obviously, the "good" parent exposes the child to a great deal of sensory stimulation. This stimulation not only helps create dendritic connections in the infant's brain, but helps the child *psychologically* to build up expectations of what its environment is like.

When a mother picks up her child to play with it, when she dangles a toy in front of its eyes, when she talks to the child, or takes it places with her, she is both exercising its sensory receptors and giving the infant a chance to build up the kind of "input expectations" that it will need to predict and control its environment and its own behavior as it grows up.

The "good" parent also trains the child to respond in socially acceptable ways by lavishing love and attention on it when it is good and by withholding affection when the child's behavior is unacceptable. The "poor" parent too often ignores the child or responds to it *inconsistently*. If the child runs to its mother for help, the inconsistent mother may give it love one day, ignore it the next day, and punish it the third. Since the child never knows what to expect, it cannot find consistent ways of satisfying its needs.

In order for the child to be able to build up expectancies about the world around it, that world must present certain regularities and certainties. As we saw in Chapter 12, however, *too much regularity* can cause problems too—if this regularity is suddenly disrupted before the child is mature enough to respond appropriately. For instance, a child cared for by a "good" mother with consistent behavior patterns rapidly builds up an emotional *attachment* to its mother, for it learns that much of what is pleasant and satisfying in its world comes to it through inputs from its mother. Psychologists call this an **anaclitic relationship**, the phrase coming from the Greek word meaning "to lean on."

Prior to age 6 months, the infant smiles at and relates to all the adults around it in much the same way. However, as J. A. Bowlby has shown, at about 7 months of age the infant begins to respond differently to its mother than it does to strangers or to people it seldom sees. The child's responses make it clear that it has become strongly attached to the mother. Once this anaclitic dependency builds up, disturbing the relationship between the child and its mother (or whoever gives it most of its care) can be dangerous. For instance, if it is the mother who *always* feeds the child, the infant soon associates *food* with *mother*—that is, they become part of the same mental image or mental expectation (see Chapter 5). When food appears, the child expects its mother to be there too, because it is not yet mature enough to discriminate food from mother. If the infant is suddenly separated from its mother during the first few months of its life, it may lose its appetite and have other difficulties adjusting to its altered circumstances.

René A. Spitz.

Anaclitic Depression   Psychiatrist R.A. Spitz studied the reactions of infants 6 to 12 months old who, for family reasons, had been separated from their mothers and put into institutions or foster homes. In their new environments, these infants received at best impersonal care. Almost as soon as the infants were institutionalized, they began showing signs of disturbance. They became quite upset when anyone approached them; they lost weight; and they became passive, inactive, and had trouble sleeping as well.

Spitz calls this **apathetic** condition **anaclitic depression.** According to Spitz, the first sign of anaclitic depression is a type of behavior that he describes as being "a search for the mother." Some babies quietly weep big tears; others cry violently. None of them, Spitz says, can be quieted down by any type of intervention, although at the initial stage of the depression they still cling tightly to any adult who picks them up.

If the mother does not return in three to four weeks, the picture changes. The child withdraws, lies quietly on its stomach, will not play if offered a toy, does not even look up if someone enters the room. The baby becomes dejected and passive, refuses food, loses weight, and becomes more susceptible than usual to colds and other ailments.

If the separation does not come until after the child is a year or more old, the depression may be reversed if the child is given adequate "mothering" within three months. Spitz believes that anaclitic depression might well account for some types of mental retardation, since the children he studied seemed to show considerable physical and intellectual impairment during and immediately after their periods of depression.

Maternal Deprivation in Humans: A Case History

Children who enter a hospital for treatment are, quite naturally, very prone to anaclitic depression since they usually must be isolated from their mothers, sometimes for an extended period of time.

That this depression may affect the child's behavior in rather unusual ways is shown in a study by Clayton Shorkey and John Taylor while they were at Michigan State University. Their patient was a 17-month-old girl who suffered severe burns that covered 37 percent of her body. The little girl was placed in isolation as soon as she was admitted to the hospital. The first day the infant was fairly quiet, but on subsequent days she cried lustily and tossed her limbs about in a violent, agitated manner.

To treat the child's burns, the nurses applied a stinging drug called silver nitrate, which they squirted over the little girl's bandages at frequent intervals. The doctors also began a series of skin grafts, but discontinued them when the infant's physical condition grew markedly worse. After a month of treatment, the little girl refused to eat. More than this, she became markedly upset whenever she was approached by any of the nursing staff.

At this point social workers Shorkey and Taylor were called in to help. They observed that the nurses, who were extremely disturbed at the child's condition, would frequently interrupt the painful treatment procedure and would attempt to soothe the little girl by talking to her, singing, and playing with her toys. The more the nurses attempted to give the child love, the more violent the infant became in her rejection of their attention and affection. Indeed, it almost appeared that the staff members were making the child worse, not better.

Shorkey and Taylor reasoned that, in the infant's depressive state, she simply could not *discriminate* between love and pain. To her, a nurse coming into the room had become an *inconsistent* stimulus—one that sometimes was followed by love and affection, but that just as frequently

Apathetic (app-puh-THET-ick). From the Greek word meaning "without feeling," or "without emotion." An apathetic child is one that cannot easily be stimulated to show emotion or expressive movement no matter what you do to (or for) the child.

Anaclitic depression. A type of passivity or apathy that very young children show when they are separated from their mothers for any great length of time. During the first two or three weeks of the separation, the child may be highly emotional. If the mother does not return, the child falls into an apathetic condition known as anaclitic depression.

Trauma (rhymes with "DRAW-mah"). A frightening event, or a physical or psychological wound.

was connected with unpleasant consequences (the stinging silver nitrate). Although the social stimulation the nurses gave the girl presumably kept her from experiencing the most profound aspects of anaclitic depression, the infant had been *conditioned* to expect hurt rather than love whenever a nurse appeared on the scene. Psycho-therapy, then, should consist of helping the child build up a new set of conditioned expectancies so that she would be able to predict ahead of time what was going to happen to her.

Conditioning Therapy   Shorkey and Taylor instituted the following changes: Whenever the nurses were to bathe the girl's bandages with silver nitrate, they first turned on bright white lights. The nurses were instructed to wear green medical garments during the "treatment condition" and were not allowed to talk with or handle the infant unnecessarily and did not play with her. In fact, they were asked not to spend one moment longer in the room than they had to while the white lights were on. But when the nurses wanted to socialize with the child, they were told to turn on red lights. During this "social condition," the nursing staff wore distinctive red garments, and they spent as much time as possible playing with the girl, rubbing the unburned parts of her body, talking to her, and giving her food. The nurses were not allowed to give the girl medication of any kind during the "red light" or social-stimulation condition.

By the end of the second day, the infant began responding *differently* to the two treatment conditions. That is, she continued to cry, but briefly, when the white lights were on and she was doused with the painful silver nitrate. But when the red lights were on, her crying ceased and for the first time in several weeks she lost her fear of the staff members. By the fourth day the infant began entering into little games with the staff. By the end of two weeks, she was playing happily during the "red light" condition. At this point, the doctors resumed the skin grafts. By the end of six weeks, the little girl was well enough to be discharged from the hospital.

The Mother's Reactions   An interesting sidelight to this case comes from studying the behavior of the child's mother. At first she refused to follow the new rules, since she insisted the infant would recognize her as "mother" no matter what she was wearing and no matter which lights were on when she entered the room. To the woman's surprise, the child continued to react with lusty crying whenever it saw its mother while she was dressed in normal clothes. When the mother was persuaded to wear red clothes and to see the girl only when the red lights were on, the infant rapidly adjusted and responded to its mother in a positive, accepting fashion.

Shorkey and Taylor studied the little girl for a period of two years after her discharge from the hospital. They report she showed no detectable problems in either her physical or psychological recovery from the **trauma.** They also note that the child was placed in her grandmother's care after she

left the hospital because the child's mother had indicated that her daughter's injury might not have been entirely accidental—a point we will return to later in this chapter.

Question: How does the Shorkey-Taylor research reinforce the belief that parents must provide their infants with consistent stimulus inputs?

Peer Love

The first type of "love" that Harlow mentioned was the love of an infant for its mother (or for whoever nurtures it). This infant–parent relationship helps the child develop expectancies about the world around it, and stimulates the child to grow both physically and psychologically.

The second type of love is **affectionate bonding** between two or more young organisms. Peer love, as it is called, seems to be necessary for the child to develop mature *social responses*. Let us again return to the Harlows' work to see why this is the case.

Monkeys raised on cloth surrogates appear to be fairly normal in their behavior patterns—at least while they are isolated from their peers. For example, when tested for their learning ability on reasonably simple tasks, these monkeys perform about as well as do animals raised in laboratory colonies or monkeys that grew up in the wild. However, when the Harlows put *groups* of surrogate-trained monkeys together, they soon found they had a problem. Although these animals had never seen other monkeys during their entire lives, they responded to one another with excessive amounts of aggressive behavior. Eventually this hostility waned and then disappeared, but the animals' social behavior remained unusual, to say the least.

Many of these monkeys showed the kinds of **stereotyped** activities one finds in certain types of mental patients in mental hospitals. That is, the monkeys made oddly repetitive movements that seemed to have no function, or they froze into bizarre postures, or they would stare into space for hours on end. Sometimes, while a monkey was looking blankly out of its cage, one of its arms would rise slowly as if not really attached to the monkey's body. The Harlows refer to this as a **floating limb** response, and note that it is also seen in human patients who suffer from **catatonic schizophrenia.** If the monkey noticed its limb while it was "floating," the animal often jumped away in fear or even attacked its oddly behaving limb.

Question: In what ways does the "floating limb reaction" seem similar to the "left-handed response" found in the split-brain patients described in Chapter 2?

Sex and the Single Monkey

As the Harlows point out, these infants had been raised in *partial* social deprivation—that is, they had their surrogate mothers, and they often interacted with their human keepers. But the animals had never experienced the pleasures of socializing with other growing monkeys. Little wonder they didn't get along well with each other.

From the Harlow's viewpoint, there was an even greater disaster—none of these animals ever *learned* the rudiments of sexual behavior. The Harlows had put these monkeys together in the first place so that they might breed and hence provide more baby monkeys for experiments. But the partially deprived animals refused to cooperate. Their sex lives were **nil.** Even when the Harlows introduced an experienced, normally raised male into the colony, he was a complete failure as far as impregnating any of the females was concerned.

Rats and other lower animals raised in similar isolation will usually mate fairly readily as soon as they are sexually mature and their isolation is

Affectionate bonding. A warm relationship between two organisms, or an emotional bond that connects two people. The anaclitic relationship is a type of affectionate bonding which exists between an infant and its mother.

Stereotyped (STAIR-ee-oh-typed). Any activity that is repeated automatically, without thought and without variation, is said to be stereotyped.

Floating limb. People (and monkeys) suffering from some mental disorders seem at times to lose voluntary control over the movements of their arms and legs. The person's arm may rise "as if it had a mind of its own," without the person's being conscious of why the arm is making this "floating" kind of movement.

Catatonic schizophrenia (CAT-uh-TONN-ick SKITS-oh-FREE-knee-uh). *Schizophrenia* comes from the Greek words meaning "split mind." Someone whose mind is "split away from reality" is said to suffer from a severe form of mental illness, or schizophrenia. *Catatonia* means "under tension" or "contracted." A mentally-disturbed person who "freezes" the body into strange positions has contracted her or his muscles abnormally.

Nil (rhymes with "hill"). From the Latin word *nihil*, meaning "nothing" or "non-existent." A nihilist (NYE-hill-ist) is someone who believes this is the worst of all possible worlds, one where no sensible rules exist. Therefore, the person sometimes says, why not blow everything up and start over again?

ended, particularly if the partner has prior experience at the game. The sex lives of lower animals is determined to a great extent by their hormones. When their **gonads** say "go," the animals are ready and able to respond. In primates, however, hormones are not the only determining factor. Heterosexual love appears to grow out of peer love, and if the monkey has no peers to respond to when young, it doesn't respond sexually as an adult.

Monkeys mate with the female crouching down on all fours and the male mounting her from behind (the more exotic forms of intercourse seem to be limited to the human species). The male monkey supports himself during these erotic festivities by clinging to the female's hind legs. If the female will not assume the proper crouching position, or will not allow the male to hold on to her, sex becomes impossible. During much of peer group play, the monkeys "practice" chasing each other and then assuming the mating posture—even though they are years too young to be able to enjoy its ultimate consequences. As Harlow puts it so well, unless a female monkey is chased by her age-mates when she is young, she will very likely remain **chaste** all the rest of her life.

Question: Studies reported in 1979 suggest that less than 30 percent of young people in the US today obtain information about sex from their parents—a marked decrease from ten years ago. Most young people seem to learn the "facts" of sex from their peers, or from the printed word. What changes might occur in adult sexual behavior if we began encouraging children to "rehearse" sexual behaviors openly as most other primates do?

Peer Deprivation in Monkeys

The presence of peers is necessary, but not sufficient, for normal emotional development in monkeys. In one of their best-known experiments, the Harlows tried to reproduce a human type of *anaclitic depression* in normal infant monkeys. These young animals were from birth raised in a large group with their mothers present. Then, for a period of several weeks, the mothers were taken away, leaving the infants to get along as best they could together. As you might expect, the tiny monkeys went through much the same sort of anaclitic depression as do human infants. At the time of their separation, the baby monkeys searched actively for their mothers and cried loudly. Soon, however, they began to withdraw. Even though they

Harry Harlow believes that peer love is a necessary stage in the development of mature emotions.

had their peers to romp about with, they stopped playing and socializing. Instead, the babies huddled in corners alone, each clinging to its own body, each lost in its individual bleak-brown thoughts.

Once the mothers were re-introduced, the infants went through a momentary period of frantic activity, most of which was aimed at clinging so tightly to the mother that she could never leave them again. Peer play soon became re-established and the infants recovered normally.

In a further set of studies, the Harlows showed that it is not merely the loss of maternal "magic" that leads to severe depression. Rather, it is the deprivation of whatever form of social stimulation the organism is *accustomed to* at the time of separation that throws it into a state of hopelessness. Monkeys raised from birth in the presence of other infants their age (but without any mothers present) appear to grow up fairly normally. That is, they play more or less as do infants raised in "families," and their behavior patterns mature at about the same speed as one would normally expect. When these infants are isolated from their peers, however, they too fall into an anaclitic depression, just as if they had been separated from their mothers. When reunited with these peers, they engage in the same intense clinging as would an infant given back to its mother.

Taking a baby monkey away from its mother, or her surrogate, also appears to slow down the baby's "maturational clock." Infants separated from their peer-mother-substitutes simply did not develop behaviorally during this period of isolation. Rather, they were as infantile in their behavioral responses after a six-month period of deprivation as they had been before being separated from their peers.

Question: The anaclitic depression occurs not merely because the infant is separated from its mother, but because its expectancies *are grossly violated. Could you explain adult depressions caused by loss of job, friends, or loved ones in terms of "violated expectancies?"*

Mother-Infant Love

Peer love grows out of the love an infant has for its parent(s), and heterosexual love grows out of peer love. These three types of love, therefore, are based on *experience* as much as they are on *instinct*.

But what about maternal love? Isn't this a natural, normal, innately determined type of emotionality that would appear no matter what the mother's prior experience had been?

Judging from the data, the answer seems to be "no." In one study, the Harlows were able to find ways of getting female isolates pregnant (despite their lack of interest in mating) by confining them in a small cage for long periods of time with a patient and highly experienced male. When these isolated females gave birth to their first monkey baby, they turned out to be the "monster mothers" the Harlows had tried to create with mechanical surrogates. Having had no contact with other animals as they grew up, they simply did not know what to do with the furry little strangers that suddenly appeared on the scene. These motherless mothers at first totally ignored their children, although if the infant persisted, the mothers occasionally gave in and provided the baby with some of the contact and comfort it demanded.

Surprisingly enough, once these mothers learned how to handle a baby, they did reasonably well. Then, when they were again impregnated and gave birth to a second infant, they took care of it fairly adequately.

Maternal affection was totally lacking in a few of the motherless monkeys, however. To them, the newborn monkey was little more than an object to be abused the way a human child might abuse a doll or a toy train. These motherless mothers stepped on their babies, crushed the infant's face to the floor of the cage, and once or twice chewed off their baby's feet and fingers before they could be stopped. The most terrible mother of all popped her infant's head into her mouth and crunched it like a potato chip.

We tend to think of most mothers, no matter what their species, as having some kind of almost divine "maternal instinct" that makes them love and take care of their children no matter what the cost or circumstance. While it is true that most females have built into their genetic blueprint the *tendency* to be interested in (and to nurture) their offspring, this inborn tendency is always expressed in a given environment. The "maternal instinct" is strongly influenced by the mother's past experiences.

Humans seem to have weaker instincts of all kinds than do other animals. Since our behavior patterns are more affected by learning than by our genes, we have greater flexibility in what we do and become. But we pay a sometimes severe price for this freedom from genetic control.

Normal monkey mothers seldom appear to inflict real physical harm on their children. Human mothers and fathers often do. Late in 1978, Dr. Richard J. Gelles of the University of Rhode Island reported on a study of 2143 US families that he made in cooperation with Murray A. Straus and Suzanne Steinmetz. Gelles estimates that at least a quarter of a million children are abused by their parents annually in the United States. Of these "battered babies," at least 50,000 may be very badly injured. Gelles' data also suggest that from 5 to 10 thousand children are killed by their parents each year in this country alone.

In discussing the factors associated with violence toward children, Gelles notes that the highest proportion of child abuse occurs in cities. Midwesterners are more likely to be violent toward their offspring than are parents in the south, east, or west. The *attitudes* of parents in the midwest do not seem to be all that different from those of parents elsewhere in the country, but their parenting *behaviors* obviously are more violent.

Gelles notes as well that *young parents* are much more likely to abuse their children than are parents over the age of 30. A mother or father is even more likely to be abusive if the other parent is absent from the home, or if the parent is socially isolated from other members of her or his family. Violence toward children also is greater in families that feel *stress:* if the parents are having troubles adjusting to the marriage, are deeply in debt, or seem unable to build up warm and loving relationships with other adults.

Worst of all, as we noted earlier, there seems to be a very strong tendency for child abuse to be handed down from one generation to another. That is, parents who were themselves abused as children are prime candidates to become violent toward their own children.

Question: Scientists have noted that when a gorilla mother abuses her infant, other members of the gorilla tribe will intervene to protect the child. Experienced mothers will also "model" infant care behaviors that new mothers can imitate. How might these facts help explain the fact that child abuse in humans seems most likely to occur in young parents who live alone?

Paternal Love

Human families differ from monkey and chimpanzee families in many complex ways, not the least of which is that the father of the children is typically present as well as the mother.

The noted anthropologist Margaret Mead once said that "fathers are a biological necessity but a social accident." But data gathered by developmental psychologists tend not to support Dr. Mead's viewpoint. As Drs. Ross Parke and Douglas Sawin report in the November 1977 issue of *Psychology Today*, fathers contribute significantly to an infant's social and emotional growth, although the father's contributions are often quite different from the mother's. While the father is just as capable of taking care of an infant as is the mother, the father's chief role (at least in our society) seems to be that of *playmate* to the child.

Parke and Sawin studied the responses of fathers to their infants and found that, when given the chance, the men were just as likely to nurture and stimulate their children as were the mothers. In fact, the men were more likely to hold the infants and to look at them than were the mothers. Furthermore, the fathers were just as likely to interpret correctly the cues the infants gave as were the mothers. However, in most real-life settings, the fathers were less likely to feed the child or change its diapers than were the mothers. This difference in parental behaviors seems due to cultural roles, however, and not to innate differences in male–female "instincts."

Harvard **pediatricians** Michael Yogman, T. Berry Brazelton, and their colleagues made slow-motion movies of parent-child interactions and then studied the films intensively. They found that fathers talked to their infants less than did the mothers, but the men were much more likely to touch or hug the child than were the women. The fathers primarily engaged in rough-and-tumble play with their children, while the mothers were more likely to play conventional games, such as peek-a-boo.

In most studies of the child's reactions to its parents, the data suggest that children respond more positively to the father than to the mother. They are more likely to pick the father as a preferred playmate than the mother, and apparently feel more at ease among strangers if the father is an involved parent than if just the mother takes care of them. The father's contribution, then, is often that of physical and social stimulation, while the mother's is more verbal training and general nurturance.

Paternal Deprivation

Given the fact that a father's influence on his child is more strongly social than intellectual, what would be the result of the father's absence during the child's early years? Would boys react differently to paternal deprivation than would girls?

Several studies suggest that boys reared without fathers are less aggressive, more dependent, and have more "feminine" interests and behavior patterns than do boys who are brought up in normal families. Although these "effeminate" response patterns do tend to decrease as the boys enter school and begin to respond to social pressures outside the family circle, many of the boys develop rather extreme masculine behaviors as if to compensate for the loss of their fathers.

The earliest age at which most US boys can tolerate separation from the father without ill effects seems to be six years. Apparently the presence of an adult male is necessary during the first six years of a boy's life so that he may learn from his father the proper "masculine" traits encouraged by our present society.

Older males can contribute significantly to the development of a boy whose father is absent.

Chapter 20 Emotional Development

519

Question: If a widowed or divorced mother were aware of this problem, what might she do in order to compensate for the absence of her young son's father?

Father–Daughter Relationships

But it is not just the son who suffers when the father is gone. Research reported by E. Mavis Hetherington suggests that young girls too need their fathers if they are to grow up in a fashion our culture views as being normal. Dr. Hetherington has made an extensive study of the effects of early paternal deprivation on the behaviors of adolescent girls. She began by observing the activities of three types of girls—those whose mothers were divorced when the girls were very young, those whose fathers had died when the girls were very young, and those who had grown up in normal family situations. None of the girls had brothers. Although few of these young women had noticeable behavior problems, and all were doing reasonably well in school, there were marked differences in the way these adolescent girls reacted to the males in their environments.

According to Hetherington, girls from divorced families sought more attention and praise from males than did girls in the other two groups. They were also more likely to hang around places where young males could be found—gymnasiums, carpentry and machine shops, and the stag lines at school dances. In marked contrast, girls with widowed mothers tended to avoid males as much as possible. These fatherless girls stayed away from typically male gathering places, some of them remaining in the ladies' room the entire evening during dances and other social events.

Hetherington reports that these differences were not due to popularity. For instance, both groups of girls received equal numbers of invitations to dance when they were actually present in the dance hall.

Girls who came from broken homes were also much more likely to take a punitive view toward the behavior of others than were girls whose fathers had died—that is, girls with divorced parents advocated harsh treatment for prisoners; they favored restrictive laws governing the social behavior of their peers; and they took a highly favorable view toward the punishment of other people.

There were marked differences as well in the ways that the three groups of girls responded when interviewed by adult males (although not in the way they responded to female interviewers). Girls reared by divorced mothers tended to sit close to and adopt an open, sometimes sprawling posture with male interviewers. The girls leaned forward more toward the man, looked more often into his eyes, and smiled more often than did girls in the other groups. In contrast, Hetherington reports, girls whose fathers had died sat at greater distances and turned their shoulders farther away from male interviewers, smiled less often, and established less eye contact. Girls from normal homes were somewhere in between these two extremes.

All three groups of girls appeared to have similar and quite normal relationships with other girls and women, but not with men. Girls from homes broken by divorce dated earlier and more frequently than did the others, and were more likely to have engaged in sexual intercourse. By contrast, girls whose fathers had died tended to start dating much later than normal and seemed to be sexually inhibited.

Most of the differences in the girls' behavior patterns seem to be due to the ways they were reared by their mothers. According to Hetherington, the divorced mothers had negative attitudes toward their ex-husbands, themselves, and toward life in general. They stated that their lives and marriages had not been very happy, and that they were concerned about their adequacy as mothers. However, they were all fond of their daughters and showed the same patterns of affection toward the girls as did mothers in the other groups. Both divorced and widowed mothers appeared to be over-protective of their daughters when compared to mothers in normal home-life situations. Divorced mothers revealed they had had considerable conflict with their husbands before separation and conflict with the daughters after the girls had reached adolescence. Widowed mothers

E. Mavis Hetherington.

PART FIVE Maturation and Development

reported little or no conflict either with their husbands before death or with their daughters at any time in the girls' lives.

Hetherington concludes from her research that girls apparently need the presence of an adult male during their formative years in order to learn appropriate responses to men when the girls reach puberty.

Question: Given the fact that the divorced mothers reported having "conflict" with their daughters, and the fact that children tend to imitate their parents in many ways, how might you explain the girls' having "a highly favorable view toward the punishment of other people?"

The Pattern of Emotional Development

As Harry Harlow noted, the development of loving behavior patterns does seem to go through several stages. The infant loves its mother, then its peers, then enters into heterosexual love, then loves its own offspring. The critical point to note, however, is how dependent all of these forms of love are on the organism's *interactions with its environment*.

The infant is born with certain strong needs that are expressed in instinctual behavior patterns: The infant approaches and clings to warm, stimulating objects and flees from cold or punishing objects. The mother responds to these approaches by cuddling the infant and feeding it. This maternal "affection" or reward for approaching and clinging increases the likelihood that the infant will engage in these behaviors again. And the responsiveness of the infant makes it more likely the mother will react more positively and tolerantly toward the infant. Jane Goodall—who has spent many years studying chimpanzees in the wild—has described several cases of mother chimps whose babies died of disease shortly after the babies were born. An inexperienced mother might carry the dead infant around with her for several days before abandoning it. An experienced mother would toss the lifeless baby away within hours after it had stopped responding to her. Apparently to live is to respond, and to respond is to go on living.

Once the infant has built up a firm set of expectancies from its relationship with its mother, it can begin to handle interactions with its peers. As it plays with other youngsters, it comes to love them if their behaviors are consistent and rewarding, and they come to love the infant if it is stimulating and rewarding to them. Out of this pattern of mutual affection comes heterosexual love—but only when the young organism's body goes through the biological changes associated with puberty.

As the child grows and matures, then, it learns both from being rewarded for certain of its actions, and from imitating its peers and parents. As a parent, it tends to behave toward its own offspring as it was treated when it was young. Its genetic blueprint predisposes it to act in certain ways, but the organism's environment turns these predispositions into actual behavior patterns.

Love and Psycho-therapy

Given the great influence that the environment has on emotional development, and the strong effect that parents have on their children, it is understandable that infants who grow up in abnormal environments are likely to end up with abnormal thoughts and behavior patterns. If parents and peers are absent—or if the child's father and mother are punitive, inconsistent, or unresponsive—the child will very likely need psychological help at some stage in its life.

But what kind of help? How do you teach someone to love?

We will attempt to answer some of these questions *at the human level* in later chapters. But we might mention how the Harlows attempted to solve similar problems with loveless *monkeys*.

When the Harlows' totally-isolated animals were introduced into normal monkey groups, the isolates responded with fear and withdrawal. When their terror of others had **habituated,** the isolates reacted with hostility and aggression. The Harlows figured that even these isolates might learn to love, but who could best act as a therapist for a socially-withdrawn animal?

Because the Harlows reasoned that contact comfort was the key to turning an isolated monkey into a normal one, they selected as their "therapists" socially-normal female monkey infants who were only three to four months old. The isolates were all males. The "therapists" had been raised by their natural mothers, and they remained with their mothers except during "therapy hours." Since these young females were all much smaller than the male isolates (who had spent at least six months living with terrycloth surrogates), the Harlows believed the babies would not threaten the isolates as much as would an adult animal—or a human. Then, too, persistence in therapy often yields rich rewards, and there are few things in life as persistent as a baby monkey in search of contact comfort.

So the Harlows built a "mental hospital" in which they could control the interactions between the isolates and the baby-therapists (see Fig. 20.4). At the beginning, the babies were allowed contact with their "patients" for two hours a day. At their first meeting, the typical male isolate (who had not yet learned to be aggressive) retreated to a corner of the "hospital" cage, hugged himself, and rocked back and forth, doing his best to ignore the infant. The infant's response was to approach the isolate and try to cling to him. Although the isolate rejected the "therapist's" overtures again and again during the first day or so, gradually his fear of the tiny stranger **waned.** The isolate stopped retreating from the infant and soon let her satisfy her need for contact comfort by clinging to his body.

Within a few days, the isolate was clinging to the infant with the same apparent pleasure that the infant derived. Within a few weeks, the isolates and "therapists" were playing together enthusiastically. Gradually, over time, most of the isolates' abnormal behaviors disappeared. By the time therapy had continued for six months, the isolates appeared to have recovered completely from their initial period of social deprivation. At this point the isolates could be introduced into normal monkey groups and could make a successful adjustment.

Question: How might we use the Harlow's research to design new types of psycho-therapy for disturbed human children?

Fig. 20.4. A baby "therapist" comforts a monkey reared alone.

Learning about Love The scientific study of emotional development has taught us many things about love that we never knew before. In our society, apparently, we presume that human maternal and paternal "instincts" are so strong that society itself does not have to worry about the rights of the child. Indeed, until fairly recently, children were considered to be the *property* of their parents, to be loved or beaten or even sold into slavery if the mother and father desired. Little wonder then that society paid little attention to what really went on in family settings, since we presumed that "parental instincts" or impulses were always healthy and good.

And because we have always assumed that punishment was one of the best ways to socialize children and teach them right from wrong, it was not until recently that we began to investigate closely those parents whose impulsive treatment of their children was abusive and dangerous. We were late to realize that, if these abused children managed to survive, grow up, and become parents themselves, they would very likely harm their own children as they had been harmed.

Hopefully, as we learn more about the splendors of love, we will also discover better ways of training our human social isolates to establish loving relationships with their fellow men and women, young and old.

Summary

1. Love is an **emotion**—an internal state or condition—that happens even to the best of us.

2. We cannot measure love directly because, like all emotions, love is an **intra-psychic experience** that takes place inside us. But we can measure loving behaviors and discuss them objectively.

3. From their studies of laboratory monkeys, Harry and Margaret Harlow identified five types of love:

   a. **Infant love**—the love an infant has for its mother (or for whoever **nurtures** it).

   b. **Peer love**—the love a child has for others its own age.

   c. **Heterosexual love**—the sexual love an adult has for its mate.

   d. **Maternal love**—the love a mother has for her offspring.

   e. **Paternal love**—the love a father has for his offspring.

4. A newborn monkey clings to its mother because she gives it warmth, food, and **contact comfort.** Warmth is the most important input during the first two weeks of a monkey's life. Thereafter, contact comfort, or "rubbability," is more important.

5. A young monkey will cling to any warm, "rubbable" object if deprived of its mother.

6. Contact with the mother (or her **surrogate**) appears to give the infant the trust that it needs in order to mature biologically and emotionally—that is, to come to love its mother. Maternal contact also allows the infant to build up **perceptual expectations** about its world. When its expectancies are grossly violated, the infant monkey falls into an **anaclitic depression** and may die.

7. If the infant grows up without having other young monkeys to play with, it never develops peer love and does not know how to respond in social situations.

8. Sexual love grows out of peer love. Young monkeys deprived of the pleasure of their peers do not form **affectionate bonds** or mate in the usual fashion.

9. Both the **paternal instinct** and the **maternal instinct** are greatly influenced by learning and early experience.

10. **Abusive parents** are likely to be young, socially isolated, to live in cities (particularly in the midwest), and to have been abused themselves when they were young.

11. Children who are treated inconsistently or who are given minimal stimulation by their mothers seem predisposed to suffer later psychological problems.

12. Female monkeys raised on surrogate mothers often treat their first infants cruelly.

13. When given the opportunity, fathers seem as interested in and as responsive to their infants as are mothers.

14. Fathers tend to engage in rough-housing and **physical contact** with their children more than do mothers.

15. Mothers tend to talk to their children more than do fathers.

16. Boys who grow up without fathers often show very "feminine" behavior patterns.

17. Girls who grow up without fathers may either be strongly attracted to adult males or tend to avoid them, depending in part on whether the girls' mothers were divorced or widowed.

18. Monkeys raised on **surrogate mothers** become social isolates, but can learn to get along with other monkeys if given **therapy** by normal monkey infants.

19. Our early experiences strongly affect the types of loving behaviors we display as adults. Fortunately, with the right kind of training, we can usually overcome the many problems associated with growing up in poor social environments.

Recommended Readings

Goodall, Jane. *In the Shadow of Man* (New York: Dell, 1972).

Harlow, H.F., M.K. Harlow, and S.J. Suomi. "From Thought to Therapy: Lessons from a Primate Laboratory," *American Scientist*, vol. 59, no. 5 (September–October 1971), pp. 539–549.

Tiger, Lionel, and Robin Fox. *The Imperial Animal* (New York: Holt, Rinehart and Winston, 1972).

Parke, Ross D., and Douglas B. Sawin."Fathering: It's a Major Role," *Psychology Today* (November 1977), pp. 109–112.

Cognitive Development

Did You Know That . . .

Jean Piaget, perhaps the most respected child psychologist alive today, published his first scientific paper when he was 10?

According to Piaget, thinking is a process that grows out of goal-achievement?

Piaget believes that the very young child often explains its world in illogical terms, such as "a balloon flies because it is red?"

According to Piaget, a child's mental development passes through four distinct stages or periods?

Language learning is one of the most complex aspects of cognitive development?

During the time you were learning to speak your mother probably taught you the use of "social contracts" as well?

Oriental infants appear to be more passive during their early life than are black or white infants?

Chimpanzees have been taught 100 or more words of an artificial language called "Yerkish?"

Many early theorists believed that a child would "explode" from surplus energy if it didn't release this energy in play?

Sigmund Freud believed that it was primarily sexual energy that a child released in fantasy and play?

"Play's the Thing"

"Harry, you've got to get rid of those two snot-nosed little girls."

"What?" said Harry Smith, a shocked look on his face. "I know you're the boss around here, Dr. Jensen, but I can't just make those two children disappear, you know."

"I don't care what you do," Dr. Jensen said as the two men walked toward one of the old stone buildings at the orphanage. The Iowa summer was in full bloom. The sky was a brilliant blue, the sun was blinding hot, and waves of heat pounded at the men from all directions. "We're up to our adenoids in kids as it is. You know that. We've got them jammed in every nook and cranny. Nice, normal kids with a chance for adoption someday. We can't be putting up with God's rejects."

The heat got to Harry a bit. "Don't call them that. They're human beings, just like you and me."

Dr. Jensen's sudden, sharp laugh sounded almost like a bark. "Human, yes. Like you and me, no." The man stopped a moment to wipe his sweaty brow. "Look, Harry, I know you think I'm being hard-nosed about all this. But try to see the situation from my point of view. I'm trying to run a decent home for the hundreds of orphans that the sovereign state of Iowa dumps in my lap. We're stuck in buildings that were constructed during the Civil War. We've got twice as many youngsters as we can handle. We're in the middle of the worst depression this country has ever seen, and there's more illegitimate kids being born each year than there are people who can afford to adopt them. Or want to. The blond, blue-eyed, good-looking kids we can place right away. The average, run-of-the-mill types we maybe can place, maybe we can't. But the snot-nosed idiots are losers from the word 'go' and there's no sense in kidding ourselves about it."

"They're not idiots," Harry replied angrily. He started walking toward the nearest building, leaving Dr. Jensen to catch up with him.

"Hey, wait up," the man said. "I know that technically they're not idiots, because they've got IQ scores above 20. That means they're imbeciles, not idiots, but you know what I mean."

"They're not imbeciles, either. They're disadvantaged human beings," Harry replied, walking even faster.

"Yes they are imbeciles, Harry. They're scrawny, bawling, ugly little critters with runny noses and IQ scores below 50 points. They sit in their beds all day long, whining and rocking back and forth. Nobody in their right minds would want to adopt those two, and you know it. They're dumb, ugly, and about as lovable as runty pigs with diarrhea. You just get rid of those two so we can make room for kids with some kind of future."

The two men had reached the front of the old stone building and paused for a moment in the shade of the doorway.

Dr. Jensen put his hand on the younger man's shoulder, then continued. "Harry, you're still pretty young. You're like most college kids these days, full of all kinds of optimistic hopes about how to change the world and make things better. But this orphanage isn't college, Harry. It's the cold, cruel world of hard facts, and you'd better get used to reality. Those two little girls you're so taken with haven't a ghost of a chance. They're badly retarded mentally, they have miserable personalities, they're weak in body and spirit, and I doubt they'll ever get out of what Piaget called the 'pre-operational stage' of mental development. They are doomed to live out their shabby little lives in state institutions, as guests of the taxpayers of the great state of Iowa. So they might as well get a head start."

"But surely there's something we can do, Dr. Jensen."

"Face the facts, Harry. There's nothing we can do except make the best of a bad situation. Those two snot-nosed little girls are God's mistakes—or rather, our mistakes as human beings. They never should have been born. But they were, and you and me together, working full time, couldn't turn them into normal human beings."

"But . . ."

"But nothing, Harry. We hired you straight out of the university to help us take care of orphans until we can find a home for them. There's only one home those two girls are ever going to know, and it's down the road a piece."

Harry frowned. "You mean the State Home for the Retarded?"

Dr. Jensen nodded sadly. "That's it. That's where they're going to end up anyway, so they might as well get a head start. And give us room for kids we can do something with."

"But the State Home doesn't have a nursery! They've got no facilities for taking care of children that young."

"That's their problem, not ours. You write out the transfer papers and take the girls over there. And you do it right away."

"I . . ."

"I know, son, I know. It's a tough world, but you've got to get used to it if you're going to stay in this business. You've got to learn to spend your time working on problems you can do something about, instead of wasting your efforts on lost causes like those two runty little girls. We've got too little money and too many kids, and the taxpayers frankly don't seem to give a damn. So bite the bullet, get them transferred, and don't shed any tears over the matter. Believe me, you'll see worse things than this if you stick in this business for any length of time."

Harry Smith stared hard at the ground. Drops of sweat—or were they tears?—oozed slowly down his smooth face. "I suppose you're right, but . . ."

"Look, Harry. You gave the kids their IQ tests yourself. You know. In your heart, you know. Get rid of them now, before they break your heart."

Harry looked the older man directly in the eye. Maybe it was true. Maybe there wasn't anything he could do. "All right, Dr. Jensen. I'll do it."

The older smiled knowingly, then walked inside the building. Harry followed reluctantly. It was cool and dark inside the stone walls; the air had the musty smell of a cluttered closet. *Skeletons,* Harry said to himself. *We are the keepers of the skeletons in one of society's closets. No wonder so few people come to see the children. People are embarrassed by these kids. Who wants to adopt a skeleton?*

Dr. Jensen paused at the door to his office. "Now you get those transfer papers ready, and I'll sign them. Okay?"

"Okay," Harry said, reluctantly but with a note of resignation in his voice. "But I don't think the women at the State Home will quite know what to do with those two young girls."

"Like calls to like, Harry," Dr. Jensen responded. Then he barked out another laugh. "And you never can tell. Those ladies at the State Home may know more about helping their own kind than you and me put together."

(Continued on page 550.)

Cognitive Development

In the past two chapters, we have discussed both the biological and emotional development of infants. But children have minds as well as bodies and behaviors, and they are as capable of thinking as they are of experiencing hunger and hatred. Watching the intellectual development of a growing child can be at least as fascinating as observing the age at which an infant walks and the social responses it makes to its parents and peers.

There are many intra-psychic theories that attempt to explain how a child's mental functioning increases and expands during its younger years. Perhaps the best-known positions are those of Jean Piaget and Sigmund Freud.

Piaget is a Swiss biologist who has studied children for more than 50 years. His main interest has been in describing the **cognitive** development of children—that is, how they come to *think* the way they do. As we will see, Piaget's training in biology has led him to assume that *biological* maturity comes first, then mental maturity. To Piaget, therefore, each stage of cognitive growth is preceded by the development of certain sensory and **motor** skills.

Freud was born in Slovakia but grew up in Vienna, Austria. One of Freud's contributions to psychology was his description of the growth of the child's mind. Like Piaget, Freud believed that the course of intellectual development was primarily determined by a child's genetic blueprint. But perhaps because Freud was a psychiatrist (while Piaget is not), Freud placed more emphasis on feelings and unconscious motivation than does Piaget. To Freud, the child's mind developed out of *emotional conflict* between its instinctual needs and those of society, thus each stage of cognitive growth is preceded by a change in the child's innate motivations.

In a sense, then, Piaget and Freud offer **complementary** rather than conflicting theories of the intra-psychic development of young people, for Piaget emphasizes *conscious mental operations*, while Freud emphasized *unconscious processes and motives*.

Both Piaget and Freud believe that the child's biological/emotional/intellectual development passes through several distinctive *stages* or periods, which are determined primarily by the genetic blueprint. The relative *speed* at which people move up the maturational ladder may vary considerably, depending (in part) on the environment they grow up in. But the *order* of the steps is supposed to be the same in all children—because this order is believed to be determined entirely by the child's genes. Since children all over the world presumably have very similar genetic blueprints, Freud and Piaget assume that all children should mature in much the same way. Whether this assumption is correct or not remains to be seen.

In order to let you discover both the strengths and weaknesses of these two theories, we will present the viewpoints of both men and then mention some of the criticisms that others have made about the theories. As you go through the chapter, you might try to remember your own early life—as best you can—and attempt to interpret your own intellectual growth in Freudian or Piagetian terms. If you make this effort, you might discover firsthand why our scientific attempts at understanding cognitive development are anything but "child's play."

Jean Piaget

One of the most respected figures in child psychology today is Jean Piaget, a professor at the University of Geneva and director of the Rousseau Institute. Trained as a zoologist, Piaget began publishing his scientific observations at the ripe old age of 10. It was not until after his college years, however, that he began what he calls his search for a "theory of knowledge," a search that led him to study the intellectual development of children. He believes that the ability to think (to process information effectively) is genetically determined, and that our abstract intelligence is the trait that sets human beings apart from other animal species. To Piaget, "intelligence" is your ability to adapt to, and cope with, whatever environment you live in. "Abstract intelligence" is your ability to deal with your environment in **symbolic** terms.

Mental Development

The basic psychological problem that Piaget has tried to solve can be stated fairly simply. When you were born, you were little more than a bundle of biological reflexes. You took in food, you **excreted** wastes, and you responded in a reflexive way to a variety of stimuli. But you did not "think," solve problems, or have any real understanding of who you were or what the world is really like. You simply reacted to your environment (and to the demands of your body) as your genetic blueprint told you to react. Now, many years later, you are a conscious, self-directed, mature human being. You speak a complex language, you are capable of understanding the **arcane** symbols of mathematics and nuclear physics, and you can create new things (such as poetry and music) if you wish to. You engage in **altruistic** behaviors that often benefit others more than they benefit yourself. You probably have a firm sense of what is right and wrong, and how to make many things in the world better than they presently are (including yourself).

Now, how did this miraculous change occur? That is, how did you develop from a passive "bundle of biological reflexes" into the infinitely complicated, self-directed human being that you are today? How (and why) did you learn to speak, to think, to solve problems, to control your own destiny?

Was your mental maturation determined entirely by your genes? Would you have turned out to be the same person no matter who your parents were, and no matter where (or when) you were born? Or were you but a piece of putty that was shaped and moulded entirely by the environment you grew up in? Or, more likely, did your genetic blueprint and your environmental inputs *interact* to produce the marvelously complex living system that make up the person we call "you?"

Most developmental psychologists assume that your mental development occurred because of the interplay between your genes and your environment. Piaget is no exception. Piaget believes that your mind is, basically, an "information processing machine" much like a computer. You are born with certain innately determined *mental programs* that connect stimulus inputs with response outputs. These inborn "computer programs" are called **innate reflexes** by many other psychologists, but to Piaget these instinctual behavior patterns are little more than evidence that your brain is "pre-wired" to begin processing information the moment you are born.

The *function* of your brain, then, is to process and respond to environmental inputs so that you can survive in whatever environment you find yourself. This function remains **invariant** (unchanged) throughout your life because it is built into your brain from birth.

The *structure* of your brain changes continually, however. The initial synaptic connections you were born with grow in complexity as you are stimulated by your environment. Put another way, environmental inputs actually create new *neural programs* inside your skull that allow you to think (process information) in new ways. But these "neural programs"—Piaget calls them **schemata**—are always created from and built upon the instinctual programs you were born with. While your ability to process information, and even to re-program your own brain, grows by leaps and bounds as you mature, the *function* of your brain (survival) remains the same through your life.

Put more simply, Piaget believes that your goals in life are pretty well determined by your genetic blueprint, for these goals are determined by the *functions* of your brain. But your ways of achieving those goals will vary depending on your state of maturity and your present environmental inputs—that is, on the present *structure* of your nervous system.

Piaget's Language

Piaget's theory is one of the most complex and difficult to understand in all of psychology. The reasons for this difficulty are not hard to find. To begin with, Piaget writes in highly technical French, and even the best of English translations of his writings are barely adequate. Second, Piaget is basically a "systems theorist" who prefers to invent his own **terminology** rather than use words the way most other scientists would.

For example, look back at the definitions of "structure" and "function" we just gave you. Most psychologists would say that the *structure* of your brain remains pretty much the same throughout your life, but its *functions* alter dramatically as you grow, learn, and develop. Piaget reverses the usual meanings of the terms, in part because that's the way he thinks, in part to

Jean Piaget.

Arcane (ar-KAIN). From a Latin word meaning "mysterious," or "knowledge available only to someone who has the key." Something is arcane if you have to study it extensively in order to be able to understand it.

Altruistic (al-true-ISS-tick). From the Latin word *alter*, meaning "other." To be altruistic is to have a genuine concern for the welfare of others, to place the well-being of someone else above your own happiness or prosperity.

Innate reflexes. Inborn, unconscious response patterns. See Chapter 15.

Invariant (in-VAIR-ree-ant). To vary is to change. To be invariant is to resist change, to behave in the same way no matter what the circumstances.

Schemata (ski-MAHT-tah). If you have a plan for doing something, you have a "scheme" that will get you to your goal. *Schemata* is the plural of "scheme," just as *data* is the plural of "datum" (DAY-tum).

Terminology (ter-min-OLL-oh-gee). Each science (or profession) has its own set of terms that have special meaning to those who study or practice that science or profession. The terminology used by a given set of professionals is often called *jargon* (JAR-gon), which comes from a French word meaning "the twittering of birds." Only someone trained in that field is likely to understand the specific meanings that the professionals (or birds) attach to the terms or jargon that they use.

Fig. 21.1A. Assimilation.

Fig. 21.1B. Accommodation.

Brevity (BREV-it-tee). From the Latin word meaning "short." We get our word *brief* from this same Latin source.

Assimilation (ass-simm-uh-LAY-shun). The Latin word *assimilare* means "to make similar." When you assimilate something, you make it similar to you, or rearrange it so that it suits your needs.

Accommodation (ack-komm-oh-DAY-shun). From the Latin word meaning "to adapt." People who accommodate us are people who try to satisfy our needs or adjust to our desires. A large hotel offers accommodations for hundreds of people when it rents them rooms or sells them food.

remind us that the "usual definitions" are not correct anyhow. For, as we noted in Chapter 17, learning does involve highly specific *changes* in the biochemical and the physiological structure of your neurons, but the function of your neurons (that of information processing) does remain *constant*.

Whatever terms he chooses to use, Piaget seems most interested in two things: First, how environmental inputs "program" your brain during your developmental years; and second, how you acquire the miraculous ability to "re-program" your own brain voluntarily.

Since Piaget is, at heart, a "systems theorist," we will take the liberty of translating his complex French into simplified General Systems Theory terms. You must understand, however, that any attempt to make Piaget readily comprehensible is bound to fail. As John H. Flavell wrote in 1977, "One always has the feeling, when writing about Piaget's theory, that **brevity**, clarity, and accuracy are somehow incompatible."

Assimilation and Accommodation

The major function or purpose of your body is to process inputs and respond to them in such a way that you promote your own health and happiness. Some of these inputs are *informational*, while others have to do with *energy* (*see* Chapter 5). Your major need for physical and psychological survival never changes from the moment of your conception to the moment of your death.

There are two fundamental ways in which your body makes use of inputs—**assimilation** and **accommodation**, which is to say that either you *assimilate* environmental inputs by making them part of your mind or body, or you *accommodate* or adjust to the inputs and thus become more like your environment (see Figs. 21.1A and B). These two fundamental processes remain invariant throughout your life too, because they are specified by your genetic blueprint and thus are innate *functions* of your brain.

Assimilation occurs at three different levels—biological, mental, and social.

1.   Biological assimilation, at its simplest, involves taking food into your body and converting or rearranging its chemical structure by digestion. But you change your own *biological structures* by incorporating the food molecules into your body.

2.   Mental assimilation involves taking in data or information about the world and "digesting" it so that it makes sense to you perceptually. But you change your own percepts (*mental structures*) by incorporating the information into your mind.

3.   Social assimilation occurs when you learn the rules and regulations of society and then work out your own moral or behavioral standards. But you alter your own interpersonal relationships (*social structures*) by incorporating social **norms** into your personal code of ethics.

Assimilation thus involves *making inputs from the outside world fit your own internal needs.*

Accommodation occurs at the same three levels as does assimilation.

1.   Physical accommodation in its most elementary form involves such things as changing your eating habits when you visit a foreign country. If hamburgers are not readily available in Japan, you learn to eat fish and rice instead.

2.   Mental accommodation refers to any intellectual adjustment you must make in order to assimilate or "digest" information. If your parents refer to the family pet as a "dog," you will call it that too (rather than making up your own name for the animal).

3.   Social accommodation has to do with your "yielding" to the pressures that your family and friends put on you to conform to group standards or norms. If your peers insist that people from certain ethnic or racial

groups (such as Jews, Catholics, or blacks, or whites) do not make "appropriate" marriage partners, then you may unquestioningly avoid romantic relationships with members of these "inappropriate" groups.

Accommodation thus involves *changing your response outputs to fit the realities of the external environment.*

Seeking the Proper Balance According to Piaget, mental growth comes about through the continuous active interplay between the processes of assimilation and accommodation. But these two mental functions should be carefully balanced during the developmental years, for there is always a danger that one process may somehow predominate over the other. If accommodation prevails, and the child passively adjusts to its surroundings, the child will engage in mere imitation and will usually accept the world as it is viewed by its parents and peers. If the parents are authoritarian, the child will try to live by authoritarian rules and regulations without ever learning the ability to evaluate and respond to the world on its own terms. On the other hand, if assimilation prevails—if the child tries to make its perceptions suit its needs rather than adjusting its **percepts** to reality— then the child will primarily engage in play and daydreaming. If the assimilation goes too far, the child may end up living in a fantasy world—or a mental hospital.

According to Piaget, assimilative play and accommodative imitation are innately determined *functions* the child uses to help it learn to predict and control its inputs, and to anticipate the consequences of its own thoughts and actions. From a General Systems Theory framework, therefore, assimilation and accommodation can be seen as processes that aid the child in achieving its biological, intra-psychic, and social goals.

Goal-Achievement

A newborn infant is a pure stimulus–response machine. It cries when it feels hunger, it sucks when a nipple touches its lips, and it swallows when its mouth is full. According to Piaget, these innate reflexes or "instinctual programs" are the foundation on which all of its later mental development will be built.

While the infant is assimilating its food, however, it is also assimilating information. That is to say, almost immediately after birth, the child's basic reflexes begin to change, grow more complex, and start to fall under the child's voluntary control.

For instance, in his book *The Origins of Intelligence in Children*, Piaget describes the actions of a three-month-old girl named Lucienne as she learns to anticipate the consequences of her actions. Piaget begins by hanging some cloth dolls from the top of Lucienne's crib. Lucienne accidentally moves her legs, and the cloth dolls begin to dance in the air. Lucienne smiles, and starts moving her legs violently once more. Again, the dolls dance. The next day, as soon as Piaget hangs the dolls from her crib, Lucienne resumes her vigorous leg movements and stares at the dolls intently. Seven days later, while she is carefully inspecting her hand, Lucienne moves her legs. Immediately she gazes up at the dolls, as if she *anticipated* that they would dance for her. A week later, her leg movements have become precise and rhythmical rather than random and violent. About a month later, when Piaget hangs a doll directly above her feet, she reaches up and kicks it. Lucienne smiles, then she stares intently at her foot and kicks the doll again. A month later, she is able to kick the doll even when it is not held directly over her feet. And a month after that, when she sees the doll at a distance, she shakes her legs very briefly—as if to show that she recognizes the motor movements associated with shaking the doll.

According to Piaget, this same pattern of *goal-achievement* will remain with Lucienne all the rest of her life. First, she will accidentally stumble on some sequence of movements that yields pleasure (or avoids pain). She will repeat the movements until they become a smoothly efficient way of achieving her ends. And then, finally, she will *internalize* the movements so

Norms. A "norm" is a reference point, usually the middle point on a distribution of some kind. To be normal is to behave according to society's norms—that is, to act like most of the people in that society act. See Chapter 26.

Percepts (PURR-septs). Perceptions, or perhaps mental images, of past experiences. Your percept of yourself is your self-image. See Chapter 10.

that she can anticipate their consequences *mentally* without actually having to "move a muscle."

From Piaget's point of view, then, thinking grows out of goal achievement—that is, learning how to move, anticipating what will happen, and then noting the actual consequences of your movements. Or to put the matter in General Systems Theory terms, thinking evolves from three related processes: (a) learning how to "program" your brain to feed forward complex sequences of goal-oriented responses; (b) building up expectancies about the results of your actions; and (c) using feedback information to correct or refine the original sequences of commands.

Feed-Forward, Expectancies, and Feedback

When Piaget talks about accommodation, he typically refers to a situation in which the child creates new **feed-forward** sequences by imitating the behaviors of others. The child watches an older brother open a jar, take out a piece of candy, and eat it. The child struggles with the jar until he or she finds some way of removing the lid, anticipating that there will be candy inside. The pleasurable feedback of finding (and eating) the sweet *reinforces* not only the child's expectancies and behaviors, but the act of imitation itself. In accommodation, then, following the actions of others gives the child new expectancies about itself (and the world) that are confirmed by **feedback.**

When Piaget talks about assimilation, he often refers to situations in which the child realizes that it can put two behavioral sequences together to create something new. A child sits by a small lake, playing with a toy boat. The boat drifts to the middle of the pond, out of the child's reach. The child then picks up a piece of wood and throws it at the boat. The chip of wood misses the boat, but remains floating atop the water. The child thinks about the matter, then picks up another woodchip, calls it "my new boat," and begins to play with it as the child had played with the original toy. In assimilation, then, the child usually changes its expectancies *before* it changes its behaviors. Again, the real-world feedback the child receives can reinforce both the changed expectations and the new behavior patterns.

As the child matures, it builds up longer and more complex response patterns, it pays increasing attention to the effects of its actions, and it comes to expect more and more from its environment (and itself). It even learns how to respond when its expectations are not confirmed. Harvard psychologist Jerome Kagan notes that a seven-month-old infant will reach at once for a new toy. An 11-month-old child, however, will pause for a moment before reaching—as if it is balancing its instinctive desire to approach novel stimuli with a sudden realization that it has not built up a "mental program" telling it how to react toward this strange object. It is at this same age that children in a wide variety of cultures first begin to cry when approached by a stranger or show emotional distress when separated from their mothers while in an unfamiliar environment.

The sudden appearance of a new set of expectations or behavior patterns suggests to many theorists—Piaget included—that human development goes through a series of **discrete** stages or periods. Truthfully, there is no universal agreement on what these maturational stages are, or even that they exist. But the general pattern of cognitive development does seem fairly clear. During its first months, the child learns to anticipate what

During the sensory-motor stage an infant learns to control its muscle movements.

stimulus inputs will do to it. Then it discovers how to respond to these inputs in order to achieve its immediate goals. Then it gains the ability to predict what effects its actions *might* have on its environment (and itself) without having to "go through the motions."

Question: How does the "approach–avoidance" conflict that develops in children at about eight months compare with the development of imprinting in birds that we described in Chapter 19?

Question: How does the process of building up expectations compare to Harlow's description of the way that infants build up "trust" in their mothers (see Chapter 20)?

Piaget's Four Developmental Stages

According to Piaget, there are four major stages of intellectual development:

1. The sensory-motor period.
2. The pre-operational stage.
3. The stage of concrete operations.
4. The stage of formal operations.

Each of us goes from one stage upward to the next at slightly different ages, but the *average age* at which children attain each maturational level might well be expected to be roughly similar from one culture to the next.

Sensory-Motor Period The first of Piaget's four stages is called the **sensory-motor period,** which begins at birth and usually ends when the infant is 18 to 24 months old. It is during this time that the infant builds up its initial *percepts* or expectations about objects and people in its world. At birth, the infant has no way of coordinating its mother's voice with the sight of her face, the touch of her hands, the smell of her body. The infant responds to each type of sensory input differently. Only during the last part of the sensory-motor period can it assimilate all of these inputs and put them together to make the percept *mother.* And until it has created the percept *mother,* it cannot respond to her as an "object" because it perceives her as merely a random collection of sights, smells, and sounds—and it cannot miss her when she is gone.

Thus, according to Piaget, the infant has no idea of **object permanence** during the first few months of its life. A 6-month-old child will typically follow an object with its eyes as the object moves across its field of vision. But if the object disappears, the infant shows no disappointment, nor does the child appear to anticipate the object's reappearance. Playing "peek-a-boo" with a child this young is often a frustrating task because the infant seems not to realize what the game is about. When the child reaches eight months of age (on the average), it will reach for an object hidden from view provided that the infant has seen the object being hidden. Peek-a-boo becomes a fun game.

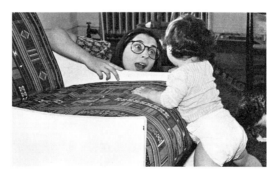

Games such as Peek-a-boo are meaningless until an infant gains the concept of "object permanence."

Sensory-motor period. The first of Piaget's developmental stages, during which the infant tries to correlate its sensory inputs with its motor outputs.

Object permanence. Piaget's concept that objects don't have a "permanent meaning" to very young infants. They must learn—when they are mature enough to do so—that the teddy bear they play with daily is the same bear from day to day, and not an entirely new toy each time they see it.

Fig. 21.2 Conservation of quantity according to Piaget.

By the time the child is 18 months of age or so, it will search for something it hasn't seen being hidden—an indication, according to Piaget, that the child now realizes that an object can exist independent of the child's own involvement with the object.

Stated in General Systems Theory terms, the sensory-motor stage is that period during which the child learns to control its own muscular responses and how to make simple, non-verbal predictions about the movement of objects in its life space. It also begins to acquire *self-discipline*—that is, it learns how to delay gratification of some of its minor, immediate needs in order to achieve more important goals in the near future.

Pre-Operational Stage   During the sensory-motor period, the infant responds directly to its environment. But as the child acquires language, it passes to the second, or **pre-operational stage** of development. Now the child can begin to deal with its world **symbolically,** by talking about objects instead of having to manipulate them directly. Piaget believes that language allows the child to *remember past events* and hence to anticipate their happening again. That is, language gives the child a great boost in its ability to predict and control its inputs.

However, not until the child is four or five years of age does it seem capable of dealing with abstractions—such as love and hate, up and down, large and small. The child can think—it can use language to generate expectancies—but it cannot reason. Reasoning, to Piaget, is the mental manipulation of abstract symbols. The child explains its world in concrete and often illogical terms rather than in terms of abstract processes. When asked why a balloon flies, the child may respond, "Because it is red and has a string hanging from it."

During the pre-operational stage—which lasts from about two until six years—the child is **egocentric.** That is, the child perceives itself as being at the center of the universe. The child sees the world in terms of its own actions and intentions toward the world, thus it cannot perceive things from any viewpoint other than its own. When the child closes its eyes, it cannot see its mother. Therefore, the child reasons, when its eyes are closed the mother cannot see the child either. The four-year-old may realize that it has exactly one brother and one sister, but you cannot convince it that its parents have three children.

During the sensory-motor period, the child learns that "objects" have permanence. But during the pre-operational stage, according to Piaget, the child struggles with the fact that an object can undergo **transformations** (certain types of changes) and still remain the same object. The classic example Piaget offers is this: If you fill two identical, tall thin glasses with water and set them in front of the child, it will agree that both glasses have the same amount of liquid in them. Now suppose you empty one tall glass into a short, wide glass. To you it is obvious that the fat glass holds the same *quantity* of water as does the tall thin glass. But to a four-year-old, the tall glass now seems to have more liquid in it. Although the child watches the *operation* of pouring water from one glass to the other, it lacks the mental ability Piaget calls **conservation of quantity**—that is, the abstract notion that the quantity of an object does not change when you "operate" on the object by pouring it from one container to another (see Fig. 21.2).

The pre-operational child is also unable to *conserve length*. If you lay two sticks of equal length before the child, it will agree they are the same. If you then move one stick forward a bit, the pre-operational child will insist that the stick you moved is now longer than the other.

In all these cases, the problem seems to be that the child is unable to realize that objects do not change (or become unpredictable) merely because the child's *immediate perception* of the object may change slightly.

Stated in General Systems terms, Piaget's pre-operational stage is that period during which the child gains greater control over its muscular responses, and discovers how to give simple input–output verbal explanations for the behavior of objects and other people.

Question: Piaget seems never to have used the shaping techniques (described in Chapter 16) to teach a child to conserve quantity. How might you go about using successive approximations of pouring just a little bit of water back and forth from tall to fat glasses to see if children could be taught conservation of quantity at a young age?

Stage of Concrete Operations By the time a child reaches the age of six or seven, it typically enters into what Piaget calls the **stage of concrete operations.** Now it can conserve both length and quantity, because it can perform these transformations mentally. But it usually cannot handle operations involving weight until its ninth or tenth year. If you place two identical rubber balls in front of a young child, it will assure you that they weigh the same. But if you now cut one ball in pieces, the child may announce that the cut-up pieces don't weigh the same as does the intact ball. According to Piaget, the child's answer suggests that it actually *perceives* weight in quite a different way than do older children and adults. However, once the child attains the *mental concept* of weight, it perceives the world differently. And it finally realizes that the whole is equal to the sum of its parts.

The concept of *number* is another acquisition the child usually makes during the stage of concrete operations. Suppose you lay out 10 pennies in two rows on a table, and show them to a child still at the pre-operational stage:

```
0  0  0  0  0

0  0  0  0  0
```

The child will see at once that the two rows are identical and that they both contain the same number of pennies. But suppose you widen the spaces between the pennies in the bottom row:

```
   0  0  0  0  0

0    0    0    0    0
```

The pre-operational child will now state that the second row has more pennies, despite the fact that the child can count the coins in each row with no difficulty. Piaget emphasizes that *counting* is not the same thing as the *concept of number*, a *percept* which a child usually attains only during the stage of concrete operations.

It is during this stage of its intellectual development that the child begins to visualize a *complex sequence of operations*. A five-year-old child can walk to school without getting lost—that is, it can perform a series of complex operations in order to reach a goal. But it is usually after age six that the child gains the ability to draw a map showing the route it takes from home to school, and it is only at this point that the youngster realizes that anyone else could follow the map as well.

Prior to the stage of concrete operations, the child sees the world as an extension of its own **ego** or conscious awareness of itself. Now the child begins to differentiate between its inner self and the outer world. It realizes that the sun does not shine just for its own pleasure, but rather must shine on everyone else as well. It comes to see that if it has an older brother, that brother must logically have a younger sibling—namely, itself. Only when the child gives up its egocentric, self-centered view of the world can it learn the meaning of true cooperation, which to Piaget means the ability to see things (including itself) through other people's eyes.

Put in General Systems terminology, Piaget's stage of concrete operations is that period in which the child learns the **rudiments** of mental role-playing. That is, the child learns—through the use of thinking and language—to predict some of the complex reactions that other individuals have by trying to think and feel the same way that these others might. As the child's predictions become better, it gains the ability to influence the responses of others and thus get from them the inputs that it desires.

Stage of concrete operations. The third of Piaget's developmental stages, during which the child begins to visualize series of operations independent of its own actions.

Ego (EE-go). From the Latin word meaning "I." The self, or the conscious parts of the personality. See Chapter 22.

Rudiments (ROO-duh-ments). From the Latin word meaning "beginning, or first attempt." The rudiments are the fundamental skills necessary to perform a given act.

Stage of Formal Operations The last of Piaget's four periods of intellectual development is called the **stage of formal operations,** which begins about age 12 and continues the rest of the person's life. Prior to the twelfth year of its life, the child is presumed to be limited to thinking in concrete, or non-symbolic, terms. Only in the final, mature stage can the young person think in completely abstract terms. At this level of development, people can solve problems in their minds by isolating the important variables and manipulating them mentally or perceptually. Now at last the individual is able to draw meaningful conclusions from purely abstract or hypothetical data.

Stated in General Systems terms, it is during the stage of formal operations that the individual gains enough experience and language ability to be able to create a personal "theory of knowledge." Although Piaget does not make reference to the different functions of the two hemispheres of the brain, it would seem that during the stage of formal operations, the right hemisphere is able to detect *abstract patterns of responses* and to "shape" the left hemisphere into "talking silently" using these abstract percepts.

In the stage of concrete operations, a child can predict what its mother will do. At the stage of formal operations, it can see that mothers are a class of people who share certain **attributes** or who respond in similar ways. Therefore, the young person can anticipate how *most* mothers will react in *some* situations. Piaget might say that motherhood is an abstraction or symbol that stands for a certain pattern of responses, and that the 12-year-old youth can now reason using this abstract percept rather than relying on the reactions of one member of the class—its own mother.

Piaget is most interested in the development of reasoning, a skill that almost always involves the creative use of language. Before we comment further on Piaget's theory, then, let us take a brief look at how the art of communicating verbally is acquired.

Language Development

During the first year or so of its life, a child communicates its wants primarily by means of crying, laughing, gurgling, and by various bodily gestures. An attentive parent can soon tell what kind of cry means the child is hungry, and what kind of wail means that a pin is sticking the infant somewhere.

By the time the child is three or four months old, it begins babbling to itself in what might be called "baby talk." That is, the infant makes sounds such as "ma," "mu," "da," and "na." Usually by its sixth month, the infant's verbal responses become more complex as it learns to *chain* sounds together:—"dadadadad." Since almost all children in almost all cultures produce these sounds (and build similar "verbal chains"), we assume that the production of "baby talk" is part of the human genetic blueprint.

But while infants *produce* sounds instinctively, it is up to the child's parents to *shape* these instinctive vocal responses into whatever language(s) the child must learn. And, as Oxford psychologist Jerome Bruner has noted, parents typically teach children to speak by use of "modeling" and by reinforcing successive approximations to correct speech.

Bruner has studied language acquisition in children for more than 30 years, and is one of the world's leading experts on the subject. Recently he reported a study in which he made video-tape recordings of mothers as they taught their children to communicate both verbally and non-verbally.

Much of the early non-verbal communication involves the eyes. According to Bruner, during the first few months of the child's life, a mother spends much of her time simply trying to find out what the infant is looking at. Then she begins trying to get the infant to look where she is looking. At age four months, only about 20 percent of the children Bruner studied would follow their mother's gaze. But by one year of age, almost all of the children would do so, even if the mother were looking at an object behind the infant's back.

Before we continue with Bruner's research, we should note an important fact. A mother's response to the child—and the child's reactions to her—*vary considerably from one culture to another.* According to a 1979 report by Daniel G. Freedman, European, American, and African children tend to be much more active and irritable than are oriental infants. White and black infants will usually struggle when confined, but oriental and **American Indian** infants accept restraint rather passively. Western mothers tend to "speak" to their babies and demand that they respond; the babies usually react by moving their arms and legs as well as by gazing at their mothers. Oriental mothers engage in much fewer "conversations" with their infants—they attract the child's attention by gazing at the infant silently. The oriental infant responds just as silently by gazing back. Oriental children continue to be much less active during their developmental years than do white or black children.

Freedman believes that these behavioral differences are caused by *genetic factors,* for oriental children born and reared in the US respond like infants in China and Japan, not as American infants do. What Bruner has to say about language learning, then, holds for white and black children, but not necessarily for oriental or American Indian youngsters.

Jerome Bruner.

Question: Americans visiting China recently have noted that Chinese youngsters are much more "well behaved" and "better disciplined" than are American children the same age. Some of the visitors suggest this "good behavior" means the Chinese have some special wisdom about children that we seem to lack. Keeping Freedman's research in mind, what other explanation can you suggest?

"Shaping" Verbal Responses   According to Bruner, once the mother discovers how to attract the child's attention, she begins to point out objects and give them names. At about 10 months of age, the child can point to objects in response. The mother then begins the "verbal shaping process," which has several parts to it. First the mother points to an object, perhaps a picture of a dog in a magazine. Next she asks the child, "What is that?" At first, the child may not respond, so the mother answers her own question: "That's a dog." The child may now say, "Dog." The mother will usually reward the child at this point, often by smiling and saying, "Yes, that's right. That's a dog." The mother may also hug the child momentarily. Once the youngster can give correct one-word responses, the mother begins demanding increasingly more complex answers to her questions.

Jerome Bruner has shown that adults follow a specific procedure in teaching words to children.

American Indian. Most anthropologists believe that the Indians who inhabited America when Columbus arrived were immigrants from the orient. They apparently came across from Asia—through Alaska—more than 15,000 years ago. There are many genetic similarities between American Indians and present-day Japanese, Mongolian, and Chinese peoples. It is no surprise, then, that oriental infants show similar behavior patterns to American Indian infants.

Bruner points out that this mother–child interaction is really much more complex than it looks at first glance. For the mother not only is teaching "words" to the child, but also instructing it in social skills. For instance, the mother's voice rises when she points and asks a question. The child soon learns that this rising **inflection** means that the mother is demanding a response of some kind. If the child responds inappropriately, the mother gently corrects it, thus modeling the sort of "criticism" that the mother will later tolerate from the child. If the child says "dawg" instead of "dog," the mother will repeat the correct pronunciation of the word and encourage the child to try again.

Bruner also notes that, during language learning, the mother begins making *social contracts* with the child that serve as the pattern for adult behaviors. If the child grows restless, the mother may say, "Let's learn two more words, and then we'll go play." If the child requests a cookie, the mother may ask the youngster where the cookies are kept. If the child answers correctly, the mother may give the child permission to go get the sweet. Should the child refuse to do so, the mother may offer to get the cookie if the child will do something for her in return.

When the child fulfills a social contract with the mother, she often praises it by saying something like, "See how well you did? Aren't you pleased with yourself?" Thus, according to Bruner, while the mother is "shaping language," she is also encouraging the child to monitor the consequences of its actions and to become increasingly less dependent on the mother's actions and judgments.

Question: What would happen to an infant's intellectual development if it had no one to teach it to talk? What would happen if this child were now placed with a dozen women who took turns daily teaching it language and social skills?

Self-judgments and Fear of Failure The next stage in the child's cognitive development may well come about two years of age, when the child begins making (and fulfilling) social contracts with itself. Jerome Kagan notes that a 20-month-old infant will happily imitate the actions of an adult model, but a 24-month-old child often refuses to do so.

In one of Kagan's studies, a woman assistant "modeled" a chain of three simple behaviors for a watching child. The behaviors mostly involved playing with dolls or toys. Then the child was asked to perform the chain of responses itself. Most 20-month-old infants had little difficulty in repeating the actions that the woman had demonstrated. But as the children approached two years of age, they began to show signs of distress when called upon to "perform." Some of them cried, others clung to their mothers, while a few threw temper tantrums. Kagan believes that the children "experienced uncertainty" about their ability to get the sequence of actions correct.

Prior to this age, the youngsters apparently were not able to predict *before performing an action* how other people might evaluate their behaviors. That is, the children could see what to do, but could not predict how adults might judge their performance. Once they could generate expectancies about the reactions of others, the children could begin to set the "performance standards" that adults would expect them to meet. And once the youngsters could "see themselves through the eyes of others," they became upset at the possibility that they might fail to meet society's demands and expectations. Kagan believes that this childish display of distress is the earliest form of what in older children and adults is called **fear of failure.**

The Father's Role in Language Learning Traditionally, in most societies, it is the mother who spends the most time with an infant, and who is most responsible for nurturing the child. The father's role in teaching an infant to speak is important, however, but his contributions are likely to be more indirect than direct.

As we noted in Chapter 20, fathers tend to talk to their infants less (and touch them more) than do mothers. According to a recent Harvard study, mothers also speak more softly, repeat words and phrases more frequently, and imitate the infant's sounds more often than do fathers. The fathers, on the other hand, usually play more stimulating games with the child— tapping it rhythmically, tossing it into the air, and introducing it to physically exciting and often creative types of play activity.

Fathers also give the child more confidence. Studies from several different cultures suggest that infants can cope better with the appearance of strangers and with other unusual social situations when their fathers have spent considerable time with the children. A child whose father is an involved parent is thus more likely to *perform verbally in public* than one whose father is uninvolved in caring for the child.

Question: The mother's greatest influence seems to be on the child's verbal and social development, while the father's greatest influence seems to be on the child's perception of rhythmic patterns and on its creative abilities. Which hemisphere of the child's brain is most involved with language? Which is most involved with rhythm and creativity?

The Source of Language Learning

As you know, neural control of speech is usually located in just one of the two cerebral hemispheres. And, in fact, the "speech center" in the left hemisphere is physically a little larger than the same area of the right hemisphere in most humans. This size difference between the hemispheres exists to a much lesser extent in the higher primates, but is not found at all in lower animals. It is likewise true that the kind of "dominant hemisphere" found in humans is not present in any other animal species. Furthermore,

Experimenters at Yerkes Regional Primate Center have taught two young chimpanzees, Austin and Sherman, to communicate directly with each other using an artificial language.

TABLE 21.1
Rhesus Calls[a]

Roar	Long, fairly loud noise	Made by a very confident animal when threatening another of inferior rank
Pant-threat	Like a roar, but divided into "syllables"	Made by a less confident animal who wants support in making an attack
Bark	Like the single bark of a dog	Made by a threatening animal who is insufficiently aggressive to move forward
Growl	Like a bark, but quieter, shriller, and broken in short sound units	Given by a mildly alarmed animal
Shrill-bark	Not described	Alarm call, probably given to predators in the wild
Screech	An abrupt pitch change; up then down	Made when threatening a higher-ranked animal, and when excited and slightly alarmed
Geekering screech	Like a screech, but broken into syllables	Made when threatened by another animal
Scream	Shorter than the screech and without a rise and fall	Made when losing a fight while being bitten
Squeak	Short, very high pitched noises	Made by a defeated and exhausted animal at the end of a fight

[a] Adapted from figure 2, Rowell, T.E. Agonistic noises of the Rhesus monkey (*Macaca mulatta*). *Symp. Zool. Soc. Lond.* No. 8 (1962): 91–96 by permission of the Zoological Society of London.

the vocalizations made by monkeys and chimpanzees seem to be primarily under the control of centers in the **limbic systems,** or emotional brain. Electrical stimulation of the limbic system can call forth all of the vocal responses that monkeys are capable of making (Table 21.1). As we saw earlier, destruction of the "cortical speech center" in humans typically leaves them speechless. Destruction of similar areas of the monkey cortex does not affect the animal's vocalizations at all.

It would appear, then, that human brains are uniquely suited for language learning, and hence for reasoning and abstract thought. However, many scientists have recently been successful in teaching chimpanzees to communicate using either crude vocalizations or "sign language."

For example, psychologists Sue Savage-Rumbaugh and Duane Rumbaugh have been able to train chimps to use an artificial language called **Yerkish.** To help the animals learn, the Rumbaughs present word-symbols on an overhead projector. The chimps respond by pressing illuminated buttons on a computer console. If the chimps use the word-symbols correctly, they are rewarded. Several chimpanzees have been able to learn 100 or more symbols, and use them as correctly as a child in the pre-operational stage might.

In 1978, the Rumbaughs reported that they had taught two animals, named Austin and Sherman, to communicate directly with each other using Yerkish. In one experiment, Sherman was given a variety of foods that both animals knew the "names" for. Austin could see the foods through a window, but could not obtain them directly—except by requesting the items by punching out a sentence in Yerkish. Austin soon learned to do so, and Sherman usually responded by giving Austin the *specific* food requested. Indeed, the only problem the two animals had came when Austin would ask for an item (such as chocolate) that Sherman was particularly fond of, in which case Sherman usually would offer Austin something else instead.

Chimpanzees are also able to solve fairly complex "intellectual" problems, if given the chance. In the November 3, 1978 issue of *Science*, David Premack and Guy Woodruff report the results of their attempts to help an adult chimp named Sarah learn problem-solving skills. Premack and Woodruff showed Sarah video-taped scenes of a human actor struggling with a problem of some kind (such as trying to reach a banana suspended by a rope from the ceiling). Then they showed Sarah pictures of two possible solutions to the problem, only one of which was correct. Sarah was able to choose the correct solution about 85 percent of the time with relatively little training, even though she had never encountered similar problem situations before.

Few scientists believe that chimpanzees will ever be able to communicate as well as even a six-year-old child can. However, as Premack and Woodruff point out, research on language learning in primates has already told us a great deal about the *specific stimulus patterns* needed to help very young infants learn to speak. And this same research may well give us important clues concerning language learning in retarded children. Already, Yerkish is being taught with some success to severely impaired humans who lack the ability to handle English.

As Sigmund Freud said, we learn about the normal from studying the abnormal. Most of us have no conscious memory of how our parents taught us to speak and to think, and the process of language learning seems so "normal" and "instinctual" to us that for many centuries we never bothered to study it scientifically. How much sooner we might have known about our own **linguistic** abilities had we begun studying language learning in chimpanzees several centuries ago!

Question: Scientists such as the Rumbaughs hope to discover soon whether female chimps who speak Yerkish will spontaneously train their infants to speak the language too. Do you think the chimp mothers will do so, or not? Why? And what does your answer tell you about your own personal "theory of cognitive development?"

Piaget and His Critics

Piaget's theory, in one form or another, is similar to that held by many child psychologists. But as British psychologist Susanna Millar points out, Piaget makes three basic assumptions which may not be true.

The first assumption is that intellectual development absolutely must proceed in 1-2-3-4 sequence. The *speed* at which a child matures may be sped up or retarded, but the *sequence of stages* must always be the same. The second assumption is that there are no halfway points between two stages. Just as a child cannot keep its foot for long between the two rungs of a ladder, so it cannot linger for long between the pre-operational and operational stages. The third assumption is that all mental development can be described in terms of the logical operations a child employs while thinking. Unfortunately, the evidence supporting these three assumptions is not strong.

Jean Piaget has spent more than 50 years observing children, and his insights into their thought patterns are legendary. His description of the way children behave is both **apt** and **eloquent.** But the children Piaget has spent a lifetime observing are for the most part white, middle-class youngsters reared in normal European homes. His four-stage theory appears to hold in good measure for such children, who do tend to learn conservation of volume about age 6, conservation of weight about age 9, and who typically show an ability to handle abstract operations when they are 12—at which age they are often welcomed into adulthood by religious ceremonies such as the *bar mitzvah* or *Christian confirmation.* But what about children brought up in other cultures, or even in different segments of our own society? Would a child reared in an orphanage or concentration camp or ghetto show the "normal" pattern of cognitive development?

More than this—perhaps because Piaget was a biologist first and a psychologist second—he seems to have over-emphasized the importance of the genetic blueprint and under-emphasized the strong role played by the environment in cognitive development. The fact that most children proceed up the maturational ladder rung by rung does not tell us how they *might* develop were we bright enough to discover more effective ways of educating them.

Question: How might you go about teaching a 6-year-old child to "map" a route from his or her home to a nearby store or school?

Play

The infant is born little more than an animal. If society does not condition it to become human, the child will remain non-verbal, non-social, and "retarded" (at least it will seem retarded from our biased point of view). We typically call this conditioning process *education*, and believe that "study" is more important than "play." Recent studies suggest, however, that a young child may learn as much from seemingly random "play" as it learns in the schoolroom.

Since Sigmund Freud's theory of psycho-sexual development in part grew out of earlier theories of play behavior, let us look briefly at various types of play before we look at Freud's theory.

Types of Play

Pre-social Play The first type of play that infants engage in is rightly called **pre-social.** That is, the six-month-old infant plays with a doll dangling from its crib, it plays with bells and rattles and balls and teddy bears, and it plays with its own hands and feet. Only later does it learn the marvelous capacity for play that other people offer.

Psychologist Harry Harlow lists three types of pre-social play—

Apt. From the Latin word meaning "suitable." An apt description is one that is well chosen. Our word "aptitude" comes from this same Latin source.

Eloquent (ELL-oh-kwent). Forceful, effective, persuasive, sincere speech.

Pre-social. The first of Harlow's two types of play, which includes exploration, parallel play, and instigative (INN-stuh-gate-tive) play in which a child merely imitates the actions of someone else.

541

Social play. The second of Harlow's two types of play, which includes free play, formal play (with rules), and creative play.

exploration play, parallel play, and instigative play—all of which Piaget would define as belonging to the pre-operational stage.

The infant *explores* its environment by crawling around and by inspecting and playing with anything that drops into its narrow life space. A little later in its life, the child makes the first step toward social contact with its peers by engaging in *parallel play*. Even before an infant is ready to interact with other children, it may choose to play beside them—but not with them. A little later yet, it may engage in activities that are directly instigated by other people—follow-the-leader, mimicking, peek-a-boo. Yet in these behaviors the child does not really interact socially with the "leader." Harlow calls this *instigative play* and believes it is the final step toward true social interaction.

Social Play As the Western child passes from the pre-operational to the operational stage of intellectual development, its play becomes more complex and other people begin to become animate partners in its life rather than mere objects to be manipulated. **Social play** seems to be of three major types—*free play*, *formal play*, and *creative play*.

Of the three, physical free play with other children is perhaps the easiest for the child, and hence often the first to appear. As Harlow points out, this sort of "rough-housing" is also the most disturbing to the middle-class parent who is often afraid that the child will either hurt itself or be hurt by others. Yet this type of activity may help the child learn to tolerate minor frustrations and keep its temper in check.

As the child becomes more verbal, rough-and-tumble play drops off sharply, and formalized play begins. The mock fights of four-year-old boys develop rapidly into games of tag and cops and robbers in which the youngsters must follow *formal rules*. Once the child begins to learn society's "rules and regulations," it can begin predicting the consequences of its social actions *before* it engages in them.

In Piaget's terms, physical free play and formal play are both a matter of *accommodation* to the responses of other children (and to objects in the real world), and imitation of the actions of others. Creative play, however, is primarily a matter of *assimilation*—of "pretending" that things might happen that haven't yet happened. The child thus learns to anticipate what kinds of reactions (feedback) might occur if things were different than they presently are. Piaget believes that creative play is the child's way of learning to manipulate symbols rather than objects. He calls it the "high point" of all types of play.

Question: When scientists plan an experiment, they often indulge in "What-if" thinking. That is, they ask themselves questions such as, "What would happen if we tried to teach chimpanzees to speak an artificial language?" What similarities do you see between "What-if" thinking in scientists and the "pretending" a child engages in during creative play?

Biological Theories of Play

Most of us might assume that play is an activity that children fall into spontaneously, and that its major purpose might be that of making children more pleasant—or of keeping them occupied for a while. However, to a variety of scientists, play has a deeper and more profound importance.

Both Plato and Aristotle suggested that children be given toy tools to play with, to "shape their minds" for future activities as adults. Later philosophers tended to see play as being the "unfolding" of innate or inborn talents and desires—much as Piaget does—and suggested that children be left alone to determine freely what they wanted to do or become. Nineteenth-century German philosophers believed that play somehow restored the child's physical and mental powers and recommended it as a form of relaxation for exhausted children.

Perhaps the most detailed theory of play came from British philosopher

Herbert Spencer. Writing a little more than 100 years ago, Spencer suggested what is now called the *surplus energy hypothesis* of play. Spencer thought that each child was born with an energy-producing machine of some kind inside it. This energy had to be released regularly or the child would simply "explode." Before humans became civilized, Spencer said, children used up most of this energy just in surviving. But modern-day infants are well-cared for, thus they have surplus energy inside them which finds expression in aimless outbursts of activity. Spencer thought that all art came from play, as did Sigmund Freud, who incorporated many of Spencer's ideas about psychic energy into his theory of psycho-analysis.

Recapitulate (ree-cap-PITT-you-late). From the Latin word meaning "to sum up, to restate." When a TV announcer finishes a new program, the announcer may "recap the news" by reading the headlines again.

Play and Evolution   Although Spencer's ideas on the purpose of play were influenced by Charles Darwin's books on evolution, it was G.S. Hall who pushed evolutionary theory to what now seem to have been absurd lengths. Hall believed that each child must **recapitulate** (relive) the behavioral history of the human race through its play. For instance, children supposedly love splashing about in water because they are re-enacting their fish ancestors' pleasure in swimming in ancient oceans. Youngsters love climbing trees because our monkey ancestors did such things. Young boys like gathering in groups to go hunting and fishing because early humans had to make their living that way. According to Hall, before the child could become a modern-day adult, it had to rehearse or re-trace all of the ancient behaviors that were built into its genetic blueprint over millions of years of evolution.

Although Hall's 1904 book on child psychology did have the effect of interesting many psychologists in studying children more closely, his theory has many serious faults. As Susanna Millar points out, it is difficult to explain a modern child's joy in bicycles, airplanes, telephones, and space ships as being a reliving of ancestral experiences.

Darwinian theory was pushed even farther by Karl Groos, who taught philosophy in Switzerland at the turn of this century. Groos believed that play was a generalized instinct which caused a young organism to practice all the other instincts it would need to survive as an adult. To Groos, rough-housing was a boy's way of preparing for the pleasure of fighting off other adults to win the hand of his own true love, and even of learning the skills of war.

Question: How would Groos explain the many countries—such as modern Israel—where women have become excellent soldiers?

Groos' books on play did point out several interesting and previously overlooked aspects of play—that it often involves almost all of the natural functions of an organism, and that behaviors (such as random exploring) which may look aimless can still serve important biological functions. But to say that children play because they have an *instinct* to play tells us very little about human behavior and neglects the profound influence that social inputs and feedback have even on children.

Question: How would a "surplus energy" theorist explain anaclitic depression in infants deprived of their mothers?

Sigmund Freud

Freudian theory bubbled up in the same biological pot that spewed forth the theories of Groos, Hall, and Spencer. To Freud, behavior was determined both by instinctual urges and by the pleasant or painful consequences of our actions as we try to satisfy those urges.

Freud accepted Spencer's notion that we all have energy-producing centers in our nervous systems, but Freud thought that the energy pro-

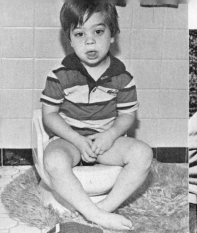

According to Freud, an infant discharges libidinal energy through mouth movements.

Toilet training takes place during the anal stage.

During adolescence young people acquire an ego ideal by incorporating the values and skills of older people.

During the latency period boys tend to play with boys and girls with other girls.

During the genital stage libidinal energy is discharged through heterosexual attachments.

duced was primarily *sexual*. He called this inborn sexual energy **libido,** and equated it with the instinct to live. All of a human being's motivations come from its need to release libidinal energy, but the exact flow of energy from "mind" to "behavior" is determined by each person's youthful experiences. According to Freud, we seek pleasure because it allows us to discharge libidinal energy. We avoid pain because it bottles up the release of this same energy. But in order for us to detect pleasurable inputs, our receptor organs must mature and become functional.

Psycho-sexual Development

According to Freud, you pass through various psycho-sexual stages of development that correspond to the maturational stage of your body at various times in your life. When you are newborn, the brain centers which control your mouth movements are physically the most developed, so you can release libidinal energy most easily through eating. Therefore, your joys at this age come primarily from oral activities, such as sucking and swallowing, and your sorrows come from denial or punishment of these behaviors. Freud called this period—which lasts from birth to about 1 year of age—the **oral stage** of development.

At about 1 year of age, you are able to pass into the second or **anal stage** of development, which lasts from about age 1 to 3. Toilet training typically takes place (in Western society) during the anal stage. During toilet training, you learned to control your egocentric urges to pleasure yourself (by urinating and defecating when you wished to) because these instinctual desires conflict with society's demands.

Libido (lib-BEE-doh). From the Latin word meaning "desire, or lust." According to Freud, the libido is the life force, the instincts that drive you to satisfy your biological urges.

Oral stage. The first stage in psychosexual development in which your satisfactions come chiefly from your mouth.

Anal stage. The second stage in psychosexual development, during which your pleasures come chiefly from withholding or expelling feces and urine.

By encouraging you to learn self-control, your parents helped you pass on to the next stage of development—the **phallic stage,** which lasts from about 3 until 5 or 6. During this period, the skin receptors in the penis or vagina mature, as do the brain centers associated with sexual activity. Thus genital pleasures predominate during the phallic stage because you were able to release libidinal energy through stimulation of your genitals. Freud believed that true socialization begins in the phallic stage, for it is at this point that you were mature enough to perceive that other people exist outside of your own perceptions of them. You became aware of sex differences, and you built up a warm relationship with whichever parent was of the opposite sex—with your father (if you are female), or with your mother (if you are male). Freud stated that, during the phallic period, boys experience incestual desires to possess their mothers and compete (or even kill) their fathers, while girls come to desire their fathers and fear or hate their mothers.

Freud believed that the phallic period is marked by frequent masturbation. It is during the fantasies that accompany this self-stimulation that desires to conquer one parent and destroy the other break through to consciousness. But these fantasies create so much guilt and anxiety in the child's mind that the child gives up sexual yearnings for a time and, at age 5 or 6, enters into what Freud termed the **latency period,** which lasts until puberty.

During the latency stage, you presumably repressed much of your innate sexuality as you slowly solved the riddle of your relationship with your parents. You moved out of the home more frequently, and friendships with your peers took on greater importance to your emotional and intellectual development. Freud believed this was a *natural homosexual period* during which boys found "heroes" among older male teachers and friends, and girls developed "crushes" on other girls and older women.

Phallic stage (FAL-ick; rhymes with "PAL sick"). The Greek word for "penis" is *phallos*. Freud called the third stage of psychosexual development the phallic stage, during which you gain pleasure from genital stimulation.

Latency period. The time (from 5 or 6 to puberty) during which your sexual desires were repressed as you tried to work out your relationships with your mother and father. The latency period is marked by "natural homosexual activities" since you tended to play mostly with same-sexed peers.

Sigmund Freud and his dog.

Genital stage. The last of the Freudian stages of psychosexual development, beginning at puberty, during which you learn that giving pleasure to a sexual partner is as satisfying as receiving genital stimulation yourself.

The latency period ends at puberty, when you entered the final or **genital stage** of development. After puberty, your libidinal energy could be released naturally through heterosexual activities and your pleasures were focused primarily on contacts with the opposite sex.

Libidinal Energy

Freud's theory of play comes directly from his theory of psycho-sexual maturation. From the moment you were born, Freud said, your body began producing libidinal energy. To Freud, high energy levels always mean pain and discomfort, while low energy levels mean pleasure. Anything that increases the amount of libidinal energy inside you leads to tension and unhappiness, while a decrease of energy leads to a feeling of contentment and well-being. When environmental situations cause an increase in tension, you attempt to relive the experience in fantasy. This "acting out" reduces the excitement and hence is rewarding to you. By going over the situation again and again, as a youngster so often does when it plays, you learned to master your frustrations and to release your repressed energy in socially-approved ways.

To Freud, every behavior was motivated—that is, goal-oriented or *purposeful.* Play is tension-reducing, therefore it is rewarding and is engaged in by all children.

Are Theories Necessary?

Freud was a genius. His theory of psycho-analysis was, in its own way, as bold and creative a step forward as was Darwin's theory of evolution. Freud forced psychologists to consider the symbolic, intra-psychic aspects of much of human behavior, and to look at childhood experiences for explanation of the beginnings of many adult behavioral problems. More than that, Freud focused in clearly on the *unconscious* aspects of cognitive development. Piaget and many other theorists talk almost exclusively about "what goes on in the child's mind"—which is to say, these theorists speak primarily of the mental development of the child's left (or dominant) hemisphere. But half a century before the "split brain" research was first published, Sigmund Freud knew that the *non-conscious* (right hemisphere) aspects of cognitive growth were just as important as were language learning and abstract reasoning.

Freud developed his theory the way that you or I would—by reading books, by listening to lectures, and by observing the actions of the people around him as carefully as he could. Most of the *data* that Freud reported were quite accurate: Children (in our society) *do* show preferences for the parent of the opposite sex at about age four or five, they *do* engage in masturbatory play when 3 or 4 and stop doing so (to some extent) at five or six; they *do* develop fantasies related to their daily frustrations, and their psychological maturation *is* retarded by parental deprivation and excessive punishment. However, the *explanations* that Freud gave for these events 50 years ago are not as accurate as we can make them today.

Freudian *theory* seems to fall down in two major areas:

1. The relationship that Freud *hypothesized* between early experiences and later psychological problems simply is not supported by experimental evidence. For instance, careful study shows that there is no significant correlation between the type of toilet-training experiences you had as a child and the type of personality you have as an adult.

2. The fact that most children in a given society pass through certain developmental stages does *not* mean that this maturational pattern is built into the genetic blueprint of all human beings everywhere. The people Freud lived among and studied were middle-class Europeans living in the late 1800's and early 1900's. His patients were primarily wealthy, highly verbal individuals. Many of them had considerable education. He described—and explained—their life histories with brilliant insight. But had Freud lived among a primitive tribe in Africa or South America, or even had he lived in the US today, would his theory have turned out the same?

In truth, none of our theories of human development is adequate. Piaget borrowed from Darwin and Freud, and his theory is subject to the same sorts of criticisms that can be leveled at evolution and psycho-analysis. Energy and motivation come as much from our environments as from our inner selves. A child growing up in a world that stimulates and rewards boisterous behavior becomes noisy and outgoing. A child buried in an impoverished ghetto becomes **indolent,** not because it is repressing its libidinal energy but because its world does not motivate it to move. Freud looked at the rough-and-tumble games of European middle-class children and assumed that their libidos were generating a surplus of sexual energy that had to come out in violent play. Yet, as Susanna Millar points out, children typically have no choice in the matter. They have not learned the fine-muscle movements necessary for more sedate occupations—such as reading a textbook, sewing a dress, playing the piano, or sitting still while listening to a lecture. Intellectual concentration appears to be possible only when a person has all the motor centers of her or his brain firmly under voluntary control. It may take as much practice—and almost as much skill—to *listen* to a musical concert as it does to *play* one.

Freud thought that all children went through a "latent period" in their psycho-sexual adjustment from years 5 or 6 through 12, roughly speaking. This time of repressed sexuality was, Freud assumed, a *biological consequence* of the Oedipal or Electra situation. However, anthropological studies of children in other cultures suggest that the latent period simply does not exist if the society adopts a casual and permissive view toward youthful sexual explorations. Indeed, there is some doubt as to whether even European children are quite as "latent" as Freud stated they were. Perhaps, about age 5 or 6, the average child becomes capable of learning which behaviors and verbal phrases its mother and father won't tolerate.

Freud believed that children **project** their own repressed desires onto the fantasy play behavior of their dolls. By *interpreting* these projected behaviors, one could presumably determine much about the psychic life of the child. In a similar way, Piaget *interprets* the mental states of his subjects by asking them questions and posing problems. The difficulty with such interpretations is this: The person doing the observing is likely to project his or her own perceptual distortions onto the child's behaviors. We see not only what we want to see, but we also perceive primarily those things our favorite psychological theory tells us *ought to be present.*

Freud, Piaget, and many other theorists believe that maturation occurs in readily recognizable steps, that the child is either in the oral stage or the anal, that it is at a pre-operational level or has both feet firmly planted on the "operational" rung of the developmental ladder. But as John H. Flavell notes, "The truth of the matter . . . is that most important cognitive developments appear to proceed slowly and gradually rather than abruptly." Indeed, as Flavell also states, there is nothing in Piaget's descriptions of assimilation and accommodation which demands that mental maturation should take place in giant leaps or steps. It is thus much more likely that cognitive development is a *continuous process,* made up of thousands of different skills that the growing child acquires whenever its nervous system is mature enough to respond to environmental demands. The "stages" that Freud, Piaget, and others see in the maturational process, therefore, are little more than apt descriptions of our cultural expectations of how children *should* develop, rather than being biologically determined steps toward adulthood.

The Purpose of Play

What then is play, if it isn't blowing off libidinal steam or a way of stepping rapidly up the developmental ladder? The truth seems to be that play serves so many different functions in so many different situations that no one theory will presently **suffice** to explain its many functions.

Indolent (IN-doh-lent). From the Latin words meaning "no pain." To be indolent is to "live easy," to loaf instead of work.

Project (pro-JECT). To project is to push off your own desires or needs onto someone else, to see things in others that you wish to see whether they are there or not. As we will see in Chapter 24, the ink blot test is one of many psychological devices for measuring how much people project their own personalities onto unstructured stimuli (such as ink blots).

Suffice (suff-ICE). From the Latin word meaning "to provide, or to be enough." To suffice is to be equal to a task, to be competent, to satisfy your needs. Suffice it to say that our word "sufficient" comes from the same Latin source.

In most cultures, play serves to allow children to explore their physical environments, to learn motor coordination, and to determine their own physical limits. It also helps children learn about *aggression*, and how to control their own aggressive behaviors. In permissive societies, play also teaches the child something about sexual behavior and the physical make-up of its own and the opposite sex.

Play also allows the child to practice social roles—that is, to build up sequences of behaviors that yield approving feedback from the adults the child must live with.

By exploring both its physical and social environments, the child learns to perceive the world more accurately, to monitor its outputs, and to predict the consequences of its own actions. This perceptual learning is apparently what Piaget means when he speaks of creative play as being that of "symbol manipulation." The child checks and re-checks its perceptions when it plays house or cops-and-robbers or builds castles out of blocks. It also learns to detect patterns in the world around it, to think (solve problems silently), and to "listen to its own inner voice." Thus one of the chief functions of play is that of developing such right-hemisphere skills as creativity, rhythmic patterning, and emotional expression—skills that seldom are taught effectively in most schools.

College students spend almost as much time per week on "playful" activities as do kindergarten students. Is there all that much difference between a four-year-old who spends a week playing with the same dump truck and the sophomore who takes a semester off "to master Shakespeare"?

Play, then, serves to stimulate the biological, psychological, behavioral, and social development of the child. And its **hallmark** is *pleasure*. Children who laugh while they are fighting seldom hurt one another. Adults who smile as they read textbooks seldom murder authors. Play is therefore a useful, necessary, vital part of life—but primarily because it rewards children (and adults) for learning the things they have to learn.

Summary

1. Measuring the mental development of a child is much more difficult than is measuring its physical growth, because we have no uniformly acceptable "measuring tapes" for **cognitive development.** In consequence, different theorists have emphasized different aspects of mental maturation.

2. The two best-known theories of cognitive development are probably those of **Jean Piaget** and **Sigmund Freud.** Piaget emphasizes the growth of conscious **mental operations,** while Freud emphasized **unconscious processes** and motives.

3. Piaget speaks of **functions** and **structures.** The function of your brain is to process information. The structures of your brain are those percepts, memories, and learned behaviors that allow you to do the processing. Mental functions never change; structures change continuously.

4. The two major developmental functions described by Piaget are **assimilation** and **accommodation.**

5. Assimilation involves making sensory inputs fit your own internal needs, as you do when you "pretend" or create fantasies. Assimilation often involves putting two percepts or behaviors together to form something new.

6. Accommodation involves adjusting your thoughts and behavior to fit external realities, as you do when you put on a coat in cold weather. Accommodation often involves **imitation** or "following rules."

7. According to Piaget, thinking grows out of **goal achievement**—that is, learning how to move, anticipating what will happen, then noting the actual consequences of your movements.

8. Piaget believes that all children pass through four **developmental**

stages, each of which grows out of (but is more complex than) the one preceding it:

    a. During the **sensory-motor period,** the child learns to integrate its various sense impressions into **percepts.**

    b. During the **pre-operational stage,** the child learns to speak and to deal with its world in **symbolic terms,** by talking about objects rather than by having to manipulate them directly.

    c. During the **stage of concrete operations,** the child learns to visualize a whole series of operations in its mind and to differentiate itself from the outer world.

    d. During the **stage of concrete operations,** the child gains the ability to think in purely **abstract terms.**

9. By the stage of concrete operations, the child is able to handle fairly complex mental **transformations.** That is, it begins to realize that an object can remain the same even if some aspects of the object (such as its shape) change slightly.

10. Piaget believes that children pass through these stages at their own individual speeds, but that the stages cannot be reversed or their order changed.

11. **Language learning** is one of the most complex aspects of cognitive development. Infants **babble** instinctively, but it is up to the environment to **shape** these sounds into meaningful language.

12. In our society, the mother usually trains the child to speak. First, she learns to attract its **attention,** then she asks it questions, **models** the answer, and **reinforces** correct responses.

13. During language learning, the mother also trains the child in the use of **social contracts.**

14. Oriental infants appear to be more **passive** during their early life than are black or white infants. Oriental mothers tend to attract their infant's attention by gazing at it. Western mothers tend to attract attention verbally.

15. The child learns to monitor and evaluate its own performance about age 2, at which time it may experience **fear of failure.**

16. Western fathers appear to be more involved in stimulating the child physically than in teaching it to talk.

17. Chimpanzees have been taught to "speak" 100 or more words and phrases, but have not as yet passed on this **artificial language** to their offspring.

18. Piaget's theory appears to over-emphasize the importance of the **genetic blueprint** and under-estimate the role played by the environment in cognitive development.

19. Harlow has listed several types of play:

    a. The first is **pre-social play,** which includes **exploration, parallel play,** and **instigative play.**

    b. At a later age, the child engages in various forms of **social play,** including **formal play, creative play,** and **free play.**

20. Philosopher Herbert Spencer believed that play was necessary for the release of **surplus energy** within the child.

21. Freud held a similar viewpoint. He believed that people had within them a **libido,** or life force, which generated energy. Releasing this energy brings the child satisfaction, **repressing** energy gives the child pain.

22. Freud thought that a child's satisfactions varied depending on which **psycho-sexual stage** it was passing through:

    a. In the **oral stage,** the child gains pleasure by releasing energy through mouth movements.

    b. During the **anal stage,** satisfaction comes from expelling or withholding urine and feces.

    c. In the **phallic stage,** the child has matured enough to enjoy genital stimulation.

    d. At age five or six, the child is presumed to develop **incestuous desires** for the parent of the opposite sex. Anxiety about these desires brings on the **latent period** which terminates when the child reaches **puberty.**

e. During the **genital period,** the individual releases libidinal energy primarily through heterosexual activities.

23. If, at any stage, the child's needs are not satisfied, its sexual desires may become **repressed.**

24. To Freud, play was often a matter of acting out in symbolic terms the **repressions** forced on the child by its environment. Through play, the child could thus release pent-up libidinal energy.

25. One major objection to both Freud and Piaget is that their theories were based on observations of middle-class, white European children. Children in other cultures do not develop in quite the same fashion.

26. A second objection is that both Freud and Piaget based their viewpoints on a biological model of cognitive development. The mind of a child now seems to us to be more flexible and shapable than either Freud or Piaget assumed.

27. The functions of play vary widely, but in part it seems a rewarding way of helping both sides of the brain develop in balanced fashion.

(Continued from page 527.)

A year or so later, Harry Smith knocked boldly on the door of Dr. Jensen's office. Interpreting the barking noise from within as permission to enter, Harry opened the door and went in. Two young girls followed close behind him.

"Dr. Jensen, I'd like for you to meet two charming young ladies." He pushed a bright-eyed young blonde girl in front of him. "This is Betty Jo, who's five. Isn't she pretty?" Betty Jo giggled and tried to hide her face. "And this is Sally Ann," Harry continued, pulling a healthy-looking brunette around in front of Dr. Jensen's desk. "Sally Ann is awfully advanced for her age, aren't you? Already in what Piaget would call 'the stage of concrete operations.' Shake hands with Dr. Jensen, Sally Ann."

The brown-haired girl walked boldly around the desk and stuck a tiny hand out toward the older man. Startled, but pleased, Dr. Jensen shook her hand with considerable gravity. "You are a pretty little thing, aren't you?"

"I'm pretty too," said Betty Jo, and not wanting to be left out, she too extended her hand.

"You're both thoroughbreds, that's for sure," Dr. Jensen said. He turned to Harry. "Where did you find these delightful young ladies?"

"We live with our mummies," Sally Ann replied in a high but pleasing voice.

Dr. Jensen looked puzzled. "Oh, I thought you were coming to live with us here. But if you live with your mothers, you can't be orphans, now can you?"

"Oh, we're orphants, all right," said Betty Jo in a happy tone of voice.

"But we live with our mummies and aunties down the road," said Sally Ann.

"Down the road? What is this, Harry? Who are these children?"

Harry Smith grinned but remained silent.

"Can I sit on your lap, please?" Sally Ann asked. And without waiting for permission, she climbed up on the older man and made herself comfortable.

"Me, too," said Betty Jo, squeezing in as best she could.

Dr. Jensen adapted to this assault on his authority as best he could by putting an arm around each of the girls. He inspected them carefully. They were obviously normal, healthy, lovable kids. There was even something oddly familiar about them. "If you live down the road, why are you here?"

"I told you," Betty Jo said, leaning forward to pick up a pencil from Dr. Jensen's desk. "Because we're orphants, and Uncle Harry says this is where we really belong. In the orphantige." She leaned forward, the pencil firmly in her hand, and began marking up a paper on Dr. Jensen's desk.

"Don't do that, dear," he said, removing the pencil from her grasp. "That's a transfer order I have to sign."

And then it dawned on him. He stared intently at the girls, then shook his head in disbelief. "It can't be, Harry. Say it isn't so."

Harry laughed. "It is so, Dr. Jensen. These are the 'runty pigs with diarrhea' you told me to get rid of."

"But what's happened to them?" he said, catching Betty Jo as she almost wiggled off his lap.

"I did what you told me to do. I put them in one of the wards at the State Home for the Retarded."

"And?"

"And the women there adopted the girls and took care of them."

"My mummy and my aunties take good care of me. They talk to me all the time," said Sally Ann, reaching for a bottle of ink. Dr. Jensen rescued it just as the girl was about to pour it over the top of a stack of papers.

"My mummy takes me walking, and the nurses take me shopping and for rides in the country, and everything!" said Betty Jo, getting down from Dr. Jensen's lap and walking over to Harry Smith. He picked her up and held her in his arms.

"My mummy and my aunties spend all day with me, every day," Sally Ann said, hunting for something else besides the bottle of ink to play with. "Will you play with me all day here at the orphantige?"

Dr. Jensen coughed. "No, dear, we don't have time for that. But Harry, you haven't told me what happened yet. What did you do to these two girls?"

"I didn't do anything. The women at the State Home did it all. There are 30 or so of them in the ward, you know. And each woman took turns taking care of the girls. Can you imagine what it would be like to be a child and to have the undivided attention of 30 women every day of your life? Can you imagine how stimulating it would be to a child to have that kind of social environment? Can you imagine what that might do to the development of your personality?"

"But, Harry, those women are *retarded*!"

"Not so retarded that they don't know how to take loving care of babies, Dr. Jensen. But the nurses and the attendants helped too. It's surprising what a little stimulation will do."

Dr. Jensen removed an ashtray from Sally Ann's grasping fingers, then pulled her tight to him to keep her out of mischief. "But what about their IQ scores, Harry? Didn't they score below 50 when they were here?"

Harry smiled as he sat down in a chair, still holding on to Betty Jo. "I gave them both tests last week. Would you believe they both scored above 100?"

"You're joking. IQ scores don't vary that much."

Harry chuckled. "They seem to go down a bit after we've kept children here for a while, don't they?"

Dr. Jensen huffed defensively. "That's different. We don't have time to cater to kids very much. Don't have the staff for it. You know that better than I do. But you can't tell me that living with retarded women will *double* a child's IQ. It just isn't right!" He removed a cigarette lighter from Sally Ann's hands before she could set a pile of papers on fire. "Besides, no professional person would believe it. Not for a minute, they wouldn't."

"Will you take us for walks, and talk to us all the time like our mummies and aunties do?" Betty Jo asked.

"No, you'll live with 20 or so other children your own age in a nice little house. And you'll have a house mother to take care of you, when she has the time. Won't you like that?" Dr. Jensen replied.

"No," said Betty Jo, putting her arms around Harry's neck. "I like my mummy and my aunties best. But Harry says if we're orphants, we ought to be here at the orphantige."

Dr. Jensen rescued a vase of flowers from Sally Ann's grasp before she could turn it over on his desk. "I think we ought to talk this matter over, Harry. I want to see the test scores myself. And I want to talk to the people at the State Home. I just don't believe this. And I know no one at the capital will believe it either. Meanwhile, I think you ought to leave these lovely children right where they are."

"Kind of embarrassing, isn't it?" Harry replied. "We took a couple of living skeletons and tucked them away, out of sight. And a year or so later, they emerge as living flesh and blood and normal in every respect." He sighed, thinking of the supposedly normal children who had stayed at the orphanage, and who weren't doing nearly this well.

Dr. Jensen grabbed Sally Ann's hand just as she was removing the pen from his shirt pocket. He put the pen in the center drawer of his desk. "I don't know what those retarded women did to these two youngsters, but I suppose we ought to find out. Might be helpful here. Meanwhile, don't you breathe a word of this to anybody. If the word gets out that retarded women are better at rearing kids than our professionally trained staff is, you and I will both be out of a job."

"They're not better mothers because they're retarded, they're better because they spent massive amounts of time with the girls." Harry sighed. "Just think how much progress we could make if we had 30 well-trained staff members for each of our orphans. I dare say we'd do even better than the women at the State Home did with these two."

"Couldn't get the money for that sort of intensive care," Dr. Jensen said. "Waste of state money. Probably couldn't hire enough staff even if we had the money."

"So?"

Dr. Jensen caught Sally Ann just as she was pulling his expensive gold watch out of his pocket. He put the watch back, kissed her on the cheek, and put her down on the floor. "You go with Uncle Harry, dear. He'll take you back to your mother and your aunts. You stay there a while, and maybe later you can come live with us. If we have room."

Harry got up from the chair and took the two girls by the hand. "Mum's the word, eh? Okay, Dr. Jensen. I get the picture. But I have a feeling that we ought to do a little research on the matter. I won't squeal if you can dig up some funds to support a little research."

"You drive a hard bargain, Harry. But if you don't squeal, as you put it, you've got a deal."

Harry nodded. "Tell Dr. Jensen 'goodbye,' girls."

They both turned and waved. Betty Jo then started out the door, but Sally Ann hung back for a moment. She giggled a couple of times, then said, "Did you really call us 'runty pigs with dia-uh-reed-uh?'"

Dr. Jensen pursed his lips. "Oh, my," he said. "What an imbecile I must have been. Oh, my, my, my, my. What an idiotic thing to say."

Recommended Readings

Bruner, Jerome S., Alison Jolly, and Kathy Sylva, eds. *Play—Its Role in Development and Evolution* (New York: Basic Books, 1976).

Geber, Beryl A. *Piaget and Knowing: Studies in Genetic Epistemology* (London: Routledge & Kegan Paul, 1977).

Flavell, John H. *Cognitive Development* (Englewood Cliffs, N.J.: Prentice-Hall, 1977).

Millar, Susanna. *The Psychology of Play* (New York: Penguin Books, 1968).

Tizard, Barbara, and David Harvey, eds. *Biology of Play* (Philadelphia, Pa.: Lippincott, 1977).

Whiting, B.B., ed. *Six Cultures: Studies of Child Rearing* (New York: Wiley, 1963).

6

Personality

Personality
Theory

"Heavenly Objects"

The afternoon wind, the *breva* as it is called by the natives, ruffled the soft blue waters of Lake Como. The morning wind, the *tivano*, sweeps down from the Swiss Alps to the north, gusting heartily through the mountain gorges that form the banks of the long, narrow lake. The *breva* begins in the hills of Milan, near the southern shore of Lake Como, and pushes back up the pencil-thin body of water toward Switzerland. This constantly shifting pattern of wind keeps the air as bright and clear as the deep blue waters themselves.

Clinging to the steep shores of Lake Como are numerous little Italian villages—resort towns, really. And dotting the mountainsides are thousands of expensive villas where wealthy Europeans spend their summers. During the warmer months, luxurious steamers cruise back and forth, taking tourists (and their cars) from one point to another.

In late September, as occasional chilly days blight the flower gardens, the steamers disappear and the only way to cross the narrow, 30-mile-long lake is by private boat, or by water taxi. Residents of Cadennabia, at the center of the western shore of Lake Como, can see Bellagio on the eastern shore directly across from them, only a couple of kilometers away. But to get from Cadennabia to Bellagio by car, you must first drive south to the city of Como, then up the eastern shore to Bellagio—a trip of more than 80 kilometers over winding, often treacherous mountain roads.

Just outside the town of Como, at the southern end of the lake, is the beautiful Villa d'Este, one of the last great hotels in all Europe. Sitting on the hotel's concrete terrace one warm September afternoon, looking up the lake toward Cadennabia and Bellagio, were three famous scientists. One was a tall, thin, well-dressed man in his 60's, psychologist Jonathan L. Fraser from the University of London. The other man was shorter, younger, and a bit on the heavy side. A neuro-physiologist from McGill University in Montreal, his name was Donald M. Papas. The third member of the group was a woman, Joyce Young Sapir, from Israel.

"Don, why did you invite us here?" the woman asked, as they waited for their drinks.

Donald Papas glanced nervously at the woman. She was short, dark, verging on plumpness. But she had a fiercely handsome face. Joyce Sapir's psycho-analytic research, conducted chiefly at Hebrew University in Jerusalem, had brought her considerable fame.

"Why did I ask you all to come here? Because I have hope, I suppose."

"Hope for what?" Fraser asked. "Not that I'm complaining, you understand. Beautiful spot, and all that."

A waiter brought the three of them drinks. Papas signed the bill, and the waiter vanished silently back into the Villa d'Este. "Yes. Como is one of the most heavenly places in the world, isn't it?"

"So you flew us in to northern Italy from all over the world because you had hopes of getting us drunk?" Professor Fraser persisted. "I know you Canadians are supposed to be rich and generous, and I'm sure that Montreal is deadly dull this time of year. But you never leave your laboratory unless you have some earth-shaking purpose in mind. So, my dear friend and colleague, tell me what you're hopeful about."

Papas stretched out in his metal chair. "Well, as you know, the Foundation is very interested in peace. So they asked me to put together a small International Symposium on Peace and Personality. If either of you had bothered to read the 'Statement of Purpose' I sent along with the invitation, you'd have known that."

"Don't be foolish, Don. We read it—quite carefully, I might add," Joyce Sapir said. "It had all the proper terms in it—all those lovely words so loaded with self-importance that we academics toss around. 'Strive toward better understanding of the complexities of human nature,' for example. Or, 'Utilize our knowledge of the structure and dynamics of human personality to reduce international tensions,' for another. I'm sure phrases like that impress the people at the Foundation. But we are hard-nosed types, Dr. Papas, and we aren't that easily tricked by fancy language."

PART SIX **Personality**

"How can you say that?" Fraser interrupted, a twinkle in his gray eyes. "All that you Freudians have as your stock in trade is fancy language."

Joyce Young Sapir favored the Englishman with a harsh stare. "I am not a Freudian, Jonathan Fraser, I am a neo-Freudian. A new-Freudian, if you please. An Ego Psychologist, really. It has been almost 50 years since Freud published his last paper of any consequence. We have come a long way since then. We accept many of his ideas, but we have benefited from the criticisms and contributions of Jung, Adler, Erikson—and from his own daughter, Anna Freud."

Fraser snorted. "No matter what you call yourselves, you still deal in fancy fictions instead of facts. If you were objective about things, if you looked at behavior instead of mucking about in the cesspools of the mind, you might actually discover something worthwhile." Fraser was obviously enjoying himself.

Dr. Sapir lit an Israeli cigarette. "I have observed, in my many years of psycho-analytic practice, that disturbed people tend to take on the personality characteristics of their pets. I am writing an article on it now, for the *Psychoanalytic Review.* You, Jonathan Fraser, have spent your life studying pigeons in the hope of discovering something about the human psyche. You have confined yourself to pigeons for so long that you are getting to be something of a bird-brain yourself!"

"Now, now," said Papas. "Let's save the nasty comments for the meeting tomorrow, when the tape recorders can preserve for posterity your so-called peaceful comments."

"Don't try to shush me, Don," the woman said. "Fraser is not a psychologist. He is a behavioral mechanic, just like Skinner. Human beings are not *objects* to be observed through a telescope like the planets Venus and Mars. We are *subjects.* We have minds, and the richest, most vital part of humanity lies in our subjective experiences. Our outward behavior is a pale copy of our mental activity. To look at us entirely from the outside is to ignore the *causes* of what we do. You cannot understand people merely by measuring their muscle twitches from afar. You must use a psychic microscope. You must peer deep inside them, learn to appreciate their instinctual urges, bring to light their unconscious thoughts, find the true meaning of their personal experiences. Only when you have stripped away the hidden deposits of the past can you help their egos face reality, and hence achieve self-actualization."

"I've seen more meaningful deposits on the bottom of my pigeon cages," observed Fraser dryly.

"Whoa!" Papas said quickly. "Both of you are looking at people from a very limited perspective. Pigeons behave, and so do men and women. Our nervous systems are similar, and humans respond to rewards and punishments much as do birds and rats and worms. But our differences are just as important as our similarities."

"More important," Joyce Sapir said militantly.

"No, *just* as important," Papas replied. "It is as foolish to say we can learn *nothing* about humans from studying pigeons as it is to say that we can learn *everything* about ourselves from experiments involving animals. That's one of the things I hope we can get some agreement on during the symposium."

"But how can pigeons help us find a path toward peace?" the woman demanded. "Birds don't have personalities!"

"How do you know?" Fraser asked. "Have you ever psycho-analyzed a pigeon?"

"Don't be ridiculous," Sapir said sharply. "Pigeons can't talk."

"Lucky beasts," Fraser replied.

"What you are really saying, Joyce, is that one major difference between humans and animals is that humans have language. Or 'verbal behavior,' if you want the Skinnerian term. The humanists such as Carl Rogers seem to agree that thoughts, to become a part of consciousness, must be expressed in verbal symbols. The major tool we have for investigating the human mind is the spoken word. We ask people to express their feelings, their experiences, and they must do so in language that we understand." Don Papas paused to sip at his drink.

"Then you really study verbal behavior, and not the human psyche," Fraser said, a grin illuminating his thin face. "Remember what Watson said about the Introspectionists—that they weren't being subjective at all, they were just refusing to be objective."

"Nonsense," the woman said. "We use our intuition to go beyond the language, so that we can tap the meaning that lies latent in the words. We call it 'listening with the third ear.' People tell us what they are like without knowing that they are doing so. We hear their verbal mistakes, their slips-of-the-tongue, their little forgetfulnesses, their pauses, their stutterings, their evasions. Their words are like footprints in soft sand.

Speech tells you what kind of prehistoric beasts are roaming the beaches of the unconscious, but you cannot trap the beasts themselves. You must guess at their size and shape and colors from the tracks they leave behind."

"And from their droppings," said the British psychologist.

The woman turned on him angrily. "Jonathan Fraser, you are the most anal personality I have ever met."

"But witty. You must admit that, Joyce," said Papas.

"Freud said that wit was often a form of unconscious or disguised aggression. If we are to study peace, perhaps first we had better dissect Professor Fraser's personality to discover the unconscious roots of his hostility."

"That's easy," Fraser said. "I've been shaped into it. People pay me more attention when I say nasty things about them. And, like most academics, I find attention very rewarding. If you want me to be peaceful, then ignore me when I'm hostile and reinforce me with a smile when I'm polite."

Papas nodded. "Good idea! All we have to do to get rid of war is to establish a 'Smile Corps' and send them out to shape the whole world."

"Nonsense!" said Sapir. "That's utterly superficial. You're dealing with the symptom, not the cause. Humans are innately aggressive. It is part of our animal heritage, and we could not have survived our early years on earth if we had not fought for our right to survive. But now, our unconscious tendencies to hate and kill are often as useless as our appendixes. We might be better off born without them."

"But that's the point," said Papas. "We *are* aggressive—even pigeons will attack when pained or frustrated—and we have to learn to live with the instinctual parts of our personalities. But we can only do that if we are bright enough to discover who we really are and where we ought to be going."

"And how are we to achieve *that* miracle?" asked Fraser. "Not through psycho-analyzing the whole world, I trust!"

"And certainly not through smiling at people to reward them for polite behavior," said Sapir.

Donald M. Papas adjusted his glasses. "Listen, my children, and you shall hear what I have planned for the First International Symposium on Peace and Personality."

(Continued on page 582.)

A Matter of Gravity

Isaac Newton.

Poor Isaac Newton! He was one of the brightest scientists the world has ever known, but he was such a poor student during his first years in school that he almost flunked out. Given his family situation, perhaps his early difficulties were only to be expected. When Newton was born in England on Christmas Day, 1642, his father was already dead. His mother soon remarried, leaving him in the care of his grandmother. Although he was later knighted by the British government for his contributions to science, as a boy he was a complete failure on the family farm. He was always mooning about, scribbling mathematical symbols on pieces of paper instead of caring for the pigs and chickens. The family sent him off to college, since he was obviously of little use in the "real world" of farming and business.

While Newton was at Cambridge, he changed the course of that "real world" rather profoundly. He invented the science of optics almost by himself. If you wear glasses, you owe a debt to Sir Isaac for his early experiments on how light passes through lenses and prisms. His mathematical discoveries laid the basis for statistics and for calculus, without which most of modern-day technology couldn't exist. But most of all, Newton gave us the sun and the stars.

According to Sir Isaac's own account, he was sitting one day under an apple tree. When one of the ripe apples fell to the ground nearby, he asked himself a pregnant question: Why did the apple fall down instead of up? Before Newton knew what he was doing, he had worked out the law of gravity—the fact that objects are attracted to each other. Building on this simple principle, Newton was able to explain in a few simple equations almost *all of the known behaviors* of the stars, suns, moons, planets, comets, and asteroids. And in the process, he had unwittingly made life very difficult for all psychologists to come.

Newton's goal was to explain *all the movements* of the heavenly bodies as they float majestically in their orbits. In a very real sense, the goal of psychology is to explain *all the actions* of the billions of human bodies (including yours and mine) as we run out our orbits on the face of the earth. If Newton could explain the earth's behavior in a few lines of mathematics, shouldn't psychologists be able to find equally simple explanations for all the behaviors of human beings?

Probably you see one difficulty immediately. Earth didn't discover the law of gravity—Newton did. Earth is an inanimate object, incapable of insight into the causes of its own performance. But humans are *analyzing animals.* We do more than "move in our orbits." We have thoughts and dreams, hopes and aspirations, virtues and vices. And most of all, we seem to have an urge to comprehend the structure and functioning of our own personalities.

Theories of Personality

That portion of the psychological world given over to the uncovering of global principles ("equations") describing human behavior is called **personality theory.** Personality theorists have the difficult job of explaining, in simple terms, everything that anyone has ever done, can do, or might think of doing—even in the wildest of circumstances. A good theory of human personality must explain human sensations, perceptions, values, motivations, our ability to learn and to change, and our tendency to relate to other humans. And the theory must do so in terms that fit within our understanding of the human nervous system and the cultures we live in.

Personality theory. That part of psychology which attempts to explain *why* people think, feel, and act as they do. The theorist usually attempts to explain all human thought and behavior in terms of a few general principles. Each of us has his or her own theory about the causes of human behavior, so there are as many theories as there are people. The major differences between your own unique theory and (let's say) that of Sigmund Freud are that Freud probably was a little more systematic in tying his explanations together—and that he wrote out his ideas and published them.

Psychology is still awaiting its Newton. But at least we have had our Freud, our Jung and Adler, our Erikson and Maslow, our Carl Rogers and B.F. Skinner—and the many others who have contributed to our limited comprehension of human beings while we wait for our Newton to come along.

What Is Personality?

Let us define **personality** as the characteristic way in which you think and behave as you adjust to your environment. This definition includes your **traits,** values, motives, genetic blueprint, attitudes, emotional reactivity, abilities, self-image, and intelligence—as well as your **overt** or visible behavior patterns. A *complete* theory of personality would not only describe your present style of adjustment, but would also give us some notion of how you got that way and where you were going—things that Newton's theory of planetary motion never bothered with.

For the sake of simplicity, Newton assumed that the inner *structure* of all heavenly objects was pretty much the same. By ignoring *individual differences* among the stars, Sir Isaac could focus his attention on their behavior or **dynamics**—a Greek word that means "the forces that cause movement or change."

Personality theorists, borrowing as always from the "hard" sciences, have tended to focus either on the *structure* of an individual's personality, or on the *dynamics* that brought about the person's present state of perfection. In this chapter we will look primarily at *dynamic theories,* saving the structuralists for the next chapter.

Dynamic theories of personality more or less begin with Sigmund Freud. Prior to Freud's time, it was assumed that you were pretty much what your genes allowed you to be. Kings and queens were better than common folk because royalty had better genetic blueprints. Your psychological nature was determined at birth and, as everyone knew full well 100 years ago, "you can't change human nature." Freud started with this purely biological view toward human development, but soon realized it wasn't the whole story. Human beings did have inherited instincts that pushed them through life, and Freud spent much of his time trying to determine just what these instincts were and how they were expressed in conscious and unconscious thought. But Freud was one of the first to realize that by thinking—by logical reasoning and creative insight—people could battle with and sometimes overcome their instinctual urges.

Freud saw personality as being shaped by the *interaction* between biological and intra-psychic forces. But perhaps because he was the first to break with past traditions, Freud saw humans as physiological animals struggling to become psychic individuals. His colleague, Carl Jung, disagreed. To Jung, humans were primarily spiritual beings. Jung, then, emphasized the purely intra-psychic aspects of human personality. Another colleague, Alfred Adler, took the next logical step. Adler saw people as being social creatures, influenced more by environmental events (and a desire for social improvement) than by physiological forces.

Three viewpoints: the biological, the intra-psychic, the social/behavioral. Logically, a theory of personality should take all three aspects of human nature into account, giving equal weight to all three. To date, no theory does so. Indeed, many of the arguments among personality theorists have to do with which one or two of the viewpoints should be given major emphasis. Let us first look at each of the major dynamic theories in detail, and then ask ourselves how each might be broadened and perhaps bettered.

Sigmund Freud

Sigmund Freud had a problem. Or rather, he had several of them. It is a mark of his greatness that, in trying to solve his own dark difficulties, he was able to shed considerable light on the many mental problems that people everywhere must face.

Personality. From the Greek word *persona,* which means "mask." In olden days, Greek actors used to wear masks on the stage. Each role they played had a different mask associated with it. As they put on a new mask, the actors assumed different personalities—that is, different ways of talking and behaving.

Traits. A talent, skill, or way of performing. Intelligence is assumed to be a personality trait.

Overt (oh-VERT). From the Latin word meaning "to open." Any visible act is overt. The opposite of overt is covert, which means hidden or latent.

Dynamics (die-NAM-icks). From the Greek word meaning "powerful," or "to be able." A dynamic person is someone with a forceful or powerful personality. In medicine, doctors study both the structure (anatomy) of the body and the dynamics (physiological processes) of the body. Our words "dynamo" and "dynamite" come from the same Greek source. Freud, Jung (yewng), and Adler (AHD-lur) were interested both in the structure and the dynamics of the human personality.

Freud was born in 1856 in what is now Czechoslovakia, but he lived for almost 80 years in Vienna. Austria had for centuries been the crossroads of middle Europe, and opposing armies from east and west had frequently turned the little country into a bloody battlefield. As a student growing up in this beautiful but war-scarred land, Freud could not make up his mind what road to success he should follow. For a while he wanted to be a chemist, but despite his brilliance in most subjects, he found he wasn't particularly gifted in chemistry. So he turned to anatomy and physiology. He studied medicine at the University of Vienna, not because he was interested in curing people but because it was an intellectual challenge—and because it was a great Jewish tradition to become a medical doctor.

After taking his degree in medicine in 1881, Freud spent many years in the laboratory studying the human nervous system. While working as a neuro-physiologist, he proved that many of the nerve cells in the spinal cord of man and animals are identical; he studied the physiology of hearing; and he published textbooks on cerebral paralysis and the effects of brain damage on children's speech. Then about the time of his 40th birthday, he decided to get married. Since being a laboratory scientist didn't pay much money (then or now), Freud went into private practice in order to earn enough to support a family. His Theory of Psycho-Analysis grew out of the observations that he made on his private patients.

Perhaps because of his medical training, Freud believed that you could not understand an individual's intra-psychic life unless you knew a great deal about the way that the human nervous system functioned. But neuro-physiology was a very young science when Freud began his research. It simply could not give Freud the answers he needed in trying to explain mental functioning. Freud solved this problem by inventing terms and ideas to fill in the gaps where biological data were lacking. These "psychic inventions" (such as the id, ego, and super-ego) constitute the heart and soul of his Theory of Psycho-Analysis.

Around 1885, Freud spent several months in Paris, studying hypnosis with Charcot. Freud's interest in personality theory seems to have begun about this time. As we noted in Chapter 18, he returned from Paris believing that hypnosis might be useful in curing some types of insanity. This view was strengthened by the success that another Viennese psychiatrist, Josef Breuer, had achieved using hypnosis with an hysterical patient. Under hypnosis, Breuer had gotten this patient to relive some early unhappy experiences. After the patient had "acted out" these childhood miseries, the hysterical symptoms seemed to disappear.

Together with Breuer, Freud developed a technique called **catharsis**—the re-enactment of emotional situations while under hypnosis. Catharsis was supposed to work because it allowed the patient to dissipate or use up all of the energy (dynamic forces) that had been bottled up inside. It was this repressed energy which presumably was producing the "insane" behavior and thoughts that were making the patient miserable.

Unfortunately, hypnosis didn't always work very well. At best, it seemed to remove the "insane behavior" without curing the underlying intra-psychic problem that presumably caused the behavior (*see* Chapter 16). Freud solved this particular problem when he discovered the importance of the *interpersonal relationship* between therapist and patient. He found that if he merely encouraged patients to think about their past lives, they could often dig up long-forgotten but important memories. The patients could then undergo catharsis—that is, relive traumatic moments from childhood—without using hypnosis as a crutch. Additionally, if Freud could get a patient to analyze these critical experiences in unemotional terms, the patient often gained insight into or understanding of what was wrong at the moment. Freud called this technique *psycho-analysis*.

The Unconscious, Preconscious, and Conscious

Why did Freud's patients need his help? Many of them were well-educated, middle-class Jews who seemed to be as mentally war-torn as Vienna had been physically. Like everyone else, these patients had very strong physical

Sigmund Freud in 1906.

Catharsis (ka-THAR-sis, or kuh-THAR-sis). From the Greek word meaning "to purge, or to clean out." If you are constipated and take a laxative to "clean out" your digestive system, you have undergone a physical catharsis. Freud and Breuer (BROY-er) believed that psycho-therapy could act as a psychological catharsis to cleanse the mind of bottled-up emotions.

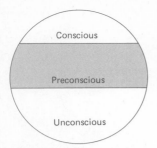

Fig. 22.1. Freud's "levels of consciousness."

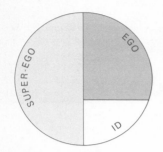

Fig. 22.2. Freud's "structures of the mind."

Psyche (SIGH-key). From the Greek word meaning "life, spirit, soul, self." Now used to mean "mind." In Greek mythology, Psyche was a beautiful maiden representing the soul who was pursued by Eros, the god of love. Freud put Psyche and Eros together in a marriage he called psycho-analysis.

Autonomic nervous system (aw-toh-NOMM-ick). That part of your nervous system (the sympathetic and parasympathetic) that automatically "swings into action" whenever you are motivated or experience emotion. You are generally not conscious of activity in your nervous system. See Chapter 14.

Limbic system (LIM-bick). A group of neural centers lying mostly on the bottom surface of the cerebrum that has a strong influence on emotional behaviors. See Chapter 4.

Hypothalamus (high-poh-THAL-uh-mus). An important neural center that lies under ("hypo") the thalamus. The hypothalamus is intimately involved in motivated and emotional behaviors. See Chapter 12.

needs, particularly a need for sexual expression. Their cathartic ("re-living") experiences suggested to Freud that sexual needs occurred even in new-born infants—if you interpret the word "sexual" in its broadest sense. But most of his patients had been punished for expressing any of their child-hood sexual desires. This punishment appeared to drive their needs "underground," out of the patients' "streams of consciousness." Since the needs had not been satisfied, the energy associated with these needs was still present, lurking unconsciously "in the back of the patient's mind." Catharsis and psycho-analysis brought these hidden needs forward into consciousness.

But where were these lusty, unexpressed desires *hiding* in the mind? Charcot, in his attempt to explain hypnosis, had suggested that there must be different *levels of consciousness*. Freud took Charcot's idea and made it very much his own. In 1913, Freud divided the human **psyche** into three levels or regions: The *conscious*, the *preconscious*, and the *unconscious* (see Fig. 22.1).

The Conscious Mind   As we noted in Chapter 3, *consciousness* is one of those "you know what I mean," primitive terms that cannot be defined precisely. Whatever you are aware of at any given instant is what you are "conscious of" at that instant. In physiological terms, consciousness is a primary property of your left (dominant) hemisphere.

The Preconscious Mind   Long before Freud divided the psyche into three levels, German psychologists had realized that there was more to consciousness than meets the eye. They likened consciousness to a cluttered stage in a darkened theater. A narrowly focused spotlight sweeps across the stage, illuminating now this, now that. As you sit in the theater, you see a continual flow of images flash into focus, then disappear into darkness. The narrow beam of the spotlight is your momentary consciousness. The rest of the stage is *potentially* visible to you—if and when the spotlight shines on it. But *at the moment* all you can perceive is what's within the tiny circle of light.

To Freud, your conscious mind included whatever you were aware of or paying attention to at the moment. Your preconscious mind included any sensory input or mental process that *you could become aware of*—if and when the spotlight of awareness shone on it. In physiological terms, the preconscious would be the total range of experiences available to your left (dominant) hemisphere.

Question: How might the reticular activating system (RAS) described in Chapter 9 help determine what part of the preconscious the "spotlight of awareness" shines on?

The Unconscious Mind   Freud's concept of the unconscious mind is exceptionally difficult to explain in simple terms. Briefly put, the unconscious contains all of those memories, experiences, images, feelings, and motives that you cannot voluntarily bring to consciousness or examine under the light of immediate attention. We can define it better by example.

As we noted in Chapter 12, you have innately determined reflexes and instincts that affect your behaviors and thoughts *whether you are conscious of them or not.* Your heart beats, your lungs breathe, and your gonads and adrenal glands secrete hormones whether or not you're aware of what they're doing. Your **autonomic nervous system** responds without your voluntary direction, and often without your awareness of what it is doing or how its actions affect your mental processes. Nor do you have *direct* consciousness of neural activity in the emotional centers of your brain (such as your **limbic system**) or in the motivational centers of your brain (such as your **hypothalamus**). "Body language," then, and emotional "feelings" are typically a part of your unconscious mind.

In Chapter 11 we stated that you tend to *repress* unpleasant experiences. That is, you tend to put *blocks* on the spotlight so that it can't shine on some of the messier areas of your "mental stage" that you'd rather not look at. Repressed memories, then, are locked away in the "unconscious" portions of your mind.

As you discovered in Chapter 17, you cannot recall many of your infantile experiences because you didn't file them in long-term storage as verbal descriptions. These early memories are "unconscious" because you simply don't know how to retrieve them.

Then there are dreams and flashes of creative insight. You are, by definition, not conscious while you dream, and dreams are often very hard to bring to conscious awareness after they've occurred. Freud thought that the dream was the **epitome** of an unconscious experience. As for insight, it often consists of what we defined in Chapter 10 as "making a **Gestalt**," or perceiving a pattern of some kind. Where in your mind did this pattern form if not in your unconscious?

By now you may have perceived a pattern yourself. What Freud referred to as the unconscious portions of your mind seem to consist of two things: Processes that are mediated by the "lower" centers of your brain, and those that are mediated by your right (nonverbal) hemisphere.

Libido

While Freud was mapping out the *regions* of the mind, he tried as well to determine the psychological processes which energized, focused, moved, and even blocked the spotlight of consciousness.

Of particular interest to Freud was the concept of **psychic energy.** Being a neuro-physiologist, Freud was well aware of the great amount of electrical activity that occurs in the brain. What puzzled him most, perhaps, was where this electrical energy came from, and what caused it to be released in neuronal firing. He also wondered what "moved" or motivated people. What was the "life force" that propelled you through your life with behaviors that aided not only your own individual survival, but that of the human race as well?

Freud decided the body continually creates "psychic" energy much as a dynamo continually produces electrical power. As we noted in Chapter 21, Freud called this "psychic energy" **libido** and believed that it is the motive force that "powers" your spotlight of consciousness. A build-up of libidinal energy creates a painful drive state that forces you to become aware of some unsatisfied need. You then tend to focus on activities that will satisfy the need by allowing you to release the pent-up energy and hence reduce the drive. Thus *expending* libidinal energy is almost always associated with sensory or sensual pleasure, while *repressing* libidinal energy almost always leads to painful tension.

Id, Ego, and Super-ego

An infant is *conscious,* but it doesn't "know" enough to keep itself alive. How then does it survive its first years on earth?

The Id According to Freud, you were born with a collection of basic instincts or biological drives that are the *source* of your libidinal energy (see Fig. 22.2). Freud called this set of instinctual drives the **id,** from the Latin word for "it." These drives are mediated by the lower centers of your brain, such as the limbic system and the hypothalamus. As such, the id is buried at the deepest level of your unconscious mind, far removed from conscious reality. Freud described the id as a "cauldron of seething excitement" which has no inner structure or organization, which operates in illogical ways, and which seeks only the pleasures that come from discharging its pent-up energies.

The id keeps an infant alive because it obeys the **pleasure principle,**

Epitome (ee-PIT-oh-me). From a Greek word meaning "to cut short, or to sum up." If you are the epitome of a good student, then you are an "ideal example" or a "summing up" of what a student should be like.

Gestalt (guess-TALT). A German word that means "good figure" or "to perceive something as a whole." See Chapter 10.

Psychic energy. Psychoanalysis is often called "a hydrolic (high-DROHL-lick) theory of personality" because Freud believed that we are motivated primarily by a need to release pent-up energy. Our innate instincts create energy (libido) which we must express in thoughts and behaviors, much as a pump builds up pressure as it pumps out water. The water (psychic energy) will most certainly spew out somewhere unless it is blocked (repressed). If your upbringing was normal and natural, your psychic energy is expressed in socially approved and healthy thoughts, feelings, and behaviors. But if you experienced trauma during your early years, the energy is repressed or expressed in unhealthy (neurotic) ways.

Libido (lib-BEE-doh). The psychic energy created by your innate instincts. Freud also spoke of it as the "life force." See Chapter 21.

Id (rhymes with "kid"). The primitive, instinctual, childish, unconscious portion of the personality that obeys the pleasure principle.

Pleasure principle. Freud's notion that we are all driven to satisfy our needs in childish (instinctual) ways. The reduction of a drive gives us pleasure, the increase in a drive gives us pain. We are born, therefore, with a strong drive to seek pleasure and avoid pain. According to Freud, "The id lives by the pleasure principle."

Egocentric (ee-go-SEN-trick). A self-centered approach to the world, or an inability to perceive the world (and yourself) through the eyes of other people. See Chapter 21.

Reality principle. Freud believed that we have to learn that the world has a reality of its own, separate from what we wish it to be. Children sometimes act as if the world is their oyster, that it is an extension of their minds, and should do what they tell it to do. This sort of egocentric thinking often gets a child in trouble—until it learns that it is but a small part of the real world and that it must give up momentary pleasures today to get bigger and better pleasure tomorrow. When the ego learns to mediate between the demands of the id and the super-ego, the ego is following the reality principle.

Super-ego. That part of your personality which "splits off from your ego," and which contains both your own and society's "rules of conduct." According to Freud, the super-ego has two parts—the stern "conscience," which you acquired from your parents (mostly during the latency period) and the "self-ideal," which you acquired mostly from other people during puberty. The conscience operates mostly at an unconscious level, while the self-ideal operates mostly at a conscious level.

Introjecting (in-tro-JECK-ting). To introject is to put something into something else. When you interrupt someone who is speaking, you are introjecting your own words into the other person's conversation. When you learn to follow society's "rules and regulations," you are introjecting society's norms into your own personality structure.

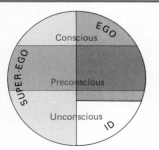

Fig. 22.3. "Levels of consciousness" occupied by the id, ego, and super-ego.

which demands the *immediate* gratification of all the infant's needs. Since most of these needs are related to bodily functions—such as hunger, thirst, aggression, and sexual stimulation—the newborn child survives because it is *biologically programmed* to release its libidinal energy in life-sustaining ways.

The Ego The id helps the infant survive because it is selfish, **egocentric,** and impulsive. But as the infant matures, the "real world" begins to make demands on the child—and punishes it severely if the child doesn't respond in socially appropriate ways. As the infant is forced to delay gratification of some of its instinctual needs, it gradually becomes aware that there is a difference between its own desires and those of other people. And once the child begins to distinguish between itself and the outer world, its ego or *conscious self* comes into being.

According to R.M. Goldenson, the ego is a group of mental functions or processes that enable you to perceive, reason, make judgments, store memories, and solve various problems. Your id was present at birth. Your ego developed slowly as you learned to master your impulses, delay immediate gratification of your needs, and get along with others.

Your ego is the part of your personality that is in communication with the external world. For the most part, then, your ego operates at a conscious (or preconscious) level, but it includes some unconscious processes as well. Thus like your id, your ego is subject to the demands of the pleasure principle. But as you mature, your conscious self is more influenced by what Freud called the **reality principle**—the practical demands of daily living. On occasion, however, your ego may be torn between the opposing forces of pleasure-seeking and reality. It often resolves this conflict by trying to satisfy your instinctual desires (id) in socially-approved ways.

The Super-ego There is more to your personality, however, than id and ego, than pleasure principle and reality principle. For as you grow, the people around you demand that you adopt society's "rules and regulations." That is, you must build up a *conscience* that keeps you from violating the rules, and an *ego-ideal* that you must strive to attain. Freud called this part of your personality structure the **super-ego** and regarded it as a part of your ego that splits off and begins to act on its own.

Your super-ego develops slowly (and unconsciously) during the first five years of your life as you increasingly imitate the thoughts and actions of others—primarily those of your parents. The positive, aspiring side of the super-ego—the "ego-ideal"—is often said to develop from the child's relationship with its mother. The stern and perhaps repressive "conscience" may well develop from the child's relationship with its father which, in the case of boys, includes the child's fears about castration. The child resolves these fears by **introjecting** the father's standards into its super-ego and thus becoming more like the father (and society in general).

During adolescence and young adulthood your super-ego matures even more as you come into contact with adults (other than your parents) whom you admire and whose values you take on either in part or totally. For the most part, this socialization process occurs at an *unconscious* level, as your super-ego gains the power to criticize and supervise both your id and your ego. Much of the *repression* of socially unacceptable thoughts and behaviors that we described in Chapter 11 are the result of "censoring" activities by your super-ego. Your super-ego is thus your "unconscious voice" that helps you discriminate social rights from wrongs without your being aware of why you do so (see Fig. 22.3).

Question: From Freud's point of view, why might some people be unable to give a logical explanation for their hostility toward long-haired men or assertive women?

Psychosexual Development

Freud's notions about personality development came from many sources—from his knowledge of medicine and physiology, his studies with Charcot and with Breuer, and from Darwin's theory of evolution. But mostly his theory sprang from his observations of his own patients. Freud was fascinated by the fact that most of his clients seemed to have gone through very similar developmental *crises* as children.

The first crisis obviously was that of *birth*, when the infant is thrust out into the world and becomes dependent on others to meet its needs. Obviously it had innate reflexes that helped it survive, but it also seemed to have a "will to live." Freud decided that the infant's instincts created the *motivation* to survive by creating *libidinal energy* that had to be discharged. Since the newborn spends much of its time sucking and swallowing, it must go through an oral stage in which it releases energy primarily through mouth movements. Since he saw many childlike oral behavior patterns in his patients, Freud presumed that some *residue* of infantile experience remained locked away in the unconscious mind even when the patients had become adults. Perhaps the patients were *still trying to release libidinal energy through adult oral activities.*

After analyzing the experiences of his patients, Freud decided that the next developmental crisis occurred when the infant's parents began making demands on it—demands that conflicted with the child's instinctual needs. This crisis seemed to reach a peak during toilet training. Prior to that time the child had been little more than an egocentric animal, bent primarily on pleasing itself. Conscious awareness of itself was thrust upon the child by its need to find ways of delaying gratification of its immediate impulses. Freud assumed the child resolved this crisis by creating an "ego" or conscious self that could respond to reality by gaining voluntary control over the release of libidinal energy through anal activities.

As the child's sex organs mature, it gains a new avenue for discharging its instinctual energies and thus obtaining pleasure. This ability seemed to usher in a new crisis, and yet another battle between id and ego. For during this **phallic stage** of development, many of Freud's male patients developed an intense emotional attachment to their mothers, while female patients seemed to grow particularly fond of their fathers. But this **Oedipal** or **Electral** attachment was unacceptable to the parents because it violated the *incest taboo* found in all societies. Freud's patients seemed to resolve this crisis—and pass into the "latency period" of psycho-sexual development—by developing a conscience or super-ego. That is, they began incorporating the standards of society into their unconscious mental make-ups.

But at puberty, the next crisis period, the patients' sexual instincts came to the fore again. By this age, however, the clients seemed to be better able to control their impulsive desires. Thus both their egos and their super-egos must have developed considerably since early childhood. During this *genital stage*, Freud's patients consciously began to hunt for an idealized sort of "life style" in which their main means of discharging libido came through heterosexual activities.

Had all gone well during their psycho-sexual development, the patients would have become fully functioning and self-actualized adults. But all did not go well with them. Were that not the case, Freud might never have had many patients—and he might never have developed his theory of psycho-sexual development.

Defense Mechanisms

Freud's theory of psycho-sexual development is really the story of how the ego comes to mediate between the pleasure principle and the reality principle. Caught in the crossfire between id and super-ego, the ego learns to defend itself as best it can—just as the Viennese learned to defend themselves against the intrusions of their powerful neighbors. But with such wars going on inside his patients, little wonder that so many of them became "psychic casualties."

Phallic stage (FAL-ick). The third of Freud's developmental stages, which comes between the anal stage and the latency period. See Chapter 21.

Oedipal (ED-uh-pal). Freud took many of his analogies from Greek mythology. Oedipus was a young man separated from his parents at an early age. Later—not knowing who they were—Oedipus killed his father and married his mother. Freud believed that all young boys (during the phallic stage) develop an intense incestuous desire for their mothers and a strong hatred for their fathers. But they also fear that if they express their feelings, they will be punished (or even castrated) by the father.

Electral (ee-LECK-tral). Electra was a Greek woman who dearly loved her father. When Electra's mother killed the father, Electra talked her brother into doing away with their mother in a particularly bloody fashion. Freud believed that all young girls (during the phallic stage) develop an intense incestuous desire for their fathers and a strong hatred for their mothers. But they also fear that if they express these feelings, they will be severely punished by their mothers.

Freud said that during the Oedipal stage a young boy develops strong emotional feelings about his mother.

From trying to help his clients solve their problems, Freud noted that the ego had several **defense mechanisms** at its disposal to help handle the ultimatums from the irrepressible id and the stern super-ego. But because the id and much of the super-ego are *unconscious,* the ego is not always consciously aware of what their demands or needs are. **Anxiety** is the ego's signal that libidinal tensions have built up and that it must find some way of handling them.

Almost all of the defense mechanisms available to the ego have three characteristics in common:

1. They are ways of trying to reduce anxiety.
2. They involve the denying or distortion of reality.
3. They operate at an unconscious level so that the ego is not always aware of what it has done.

Repression The most important of the defense mechanisms is undoubtedly **repression,** the process by which the ego blocks off or denies threatening thoughts or desires and thus keeps them from sweeping into the spotlight of consciousness. Most of these experiences have undischarged libidinal energy attached to them in some way. In repressing these experiences, the ego has to use up some of its own energy sources—for, as Newton said of physical objects, force can be opposed only by an equal or greater force. The more painful the memory, or the stronger the unacceptable urge, the more energy the ego must expend in order to keep the material repressed. Eventually the ego may run out of steam, and bits and pieces of the repressed material may leak through to consciousness as slips of the tongue, or as symbols in dreams. By re-living these painful experiences in therapy, many of Freud's patients were able to bring this repressed material into the focus of consciousness and deal with it directly. Thus coming to understand their problems allowed the patients to discharge the pent-up libidinal forces, reduce anxiety, and free their egos to engage in more productive activities.

Regression When placed under considerable stress, many of Freud's patients seemed to fall back into childish behavior patterns. Some of them responded to stress by eating a lot, talking a lot, drinking a lot, or smoking a lot. Freud saw this as a **regression** to an earlier (oral) mode of pleasure. Or, when a young male patient encountered heterosexual difficulties, he sometimes would resort to such immature forms of gratification as masturbation or homosexuality. This regression allowed the man to discharge libidinal energy in a "safe" way—but it often prevented him from trying to solve his present inter-personal problems.

Identification Freud observed that people seemed to resolve their Oedipal or Electra crisis by taking on the characteristics of their same-sex parent. This process of **identification** was the ego's way of defending itself against incestual feelings. The young girl identifies with her mother out of fear of her mother's wrath—and thereby builds up the unconscious portion of her super-ego, the "conscience." In adolescence, the girl identifies with other women and thus strengthens the conscious portion of her super-ego, the "ego-ideal." Freud thus saw the super-ego itself as a kind of "super" defense mechanism that helped reduce anxiety by allowing the person to release libidinal energy in socially approved ways.

Denial Many of Freud's patients seemed to be "deliberately" unconscious of certain painful facts. Freud decided that they were practicing **denial,** a defense mechanism by which their ego shut itself off from certain realities. Hysterical blindness is an example of denial (see Chapter 14).

Reaction Formation and Projection A step beyond denial is **reaction formation,** in which the ego changes unacceptable love into acceptable hate (or vice-versa). If a mother hates her child—a feeling she must deny conscious awareness of—the mother may smother the child with affection. Or the mother's ego may indulge in **projection** by pretending that the child actually hates her. Freud believed that the mythical "old maid" who looked under her bed every night before she went to sleep, fearing to find a man hiding there who might be waiting to rape her, was actually *projecting* her own unacceptable desire for sex onto the man she feared (hoped) was lurking under her maidenly mattress.

Rationalization Freud found that many of his patients offered him elaborate justifications for what were obviously illogical or immature actions. When he pointed out what they were doing, these patients would usually refuse to confront reality. Rather, they would give him yet another **rationalization** or questionable excuse for acting as they did. This self-justification seemed to allow the patients to reduce any anxiety they had, and yet go right on behaving as they had. Thus a father who physically abused his young son might insist that he was doing it to "make a man" out of the boy. If challenged, the father might reply, "Spare the rod and spoil the child." The problem is, as Freud noted, that those who rationalize spend their energy justifying their mistakes rather than correcting them.

Displacement and Sublimation Over the years Freud and his followers identified a great many defense mechanisms, of which we have space to mention only the best known. The last of these are **displacement** and **sublimation.**

At birth, the objects of all our instincts are specified by our genetic inheritance. You don't have to teach an infant that food satisfies its hunger, because its body already knows this. But as the infant grows up, the *objects* of its instincts can change through learning and experience. That is, the child's ego gains the ability to *displace* the flow of libidinal energy from one object to another. But the ego may use this ability inappropriately, as a defense mechanism. If the child gets angry at its mother, it dares not hit her because it will be punished. Therefore it displaces its anger on a safe object—such as a doll—that cannot retaliate if the child strikes it.

Sublimation is at once a form of displacement and the most mature of the defense mechanisms. Freud thought that the energy that an artist devotes to painting—or a scientist to the laboratory, or a politician to governing—was really energy that had been channeled away from sex or aggression or eating. Although this displacement was socially acceptable and sometimes highly creative, it seldom seemed to satisfy all the id's needs. Thus even Freud himself had surplus energy left over from his theory-building and occasionally indulged himself in ways he knew were childish and impulsive.

Theologians (thee-oh-LOW-juns). Priests, ministers, rabbis, and scholars who study religion or the laws of religious groups are called "theologians."

Occult (ock-KULT). From the Latin word for "hidden," or "covered up." Occult mysteries are those that are supernatural or "hidden from the eye."

Personal unconscious. Each individual's collection of memories and ideas that stem from that person's own experiences. Your Long-term Memory.

Collective unconscious. Racial memories. Unconscious thoughts wired into your brain by your genetic blueprint. Instinctual behaviors or ideas that are a kind of "feed-forward" built into your nervous system by your genes.

Complex. A housing complex is a group of houses set off or isolated from other nearby dwellings. Jung believed that certain thoughts and ideas might grow into an independent unit or substructure of the personality. He called this separated set of thoughts a "complex."

Freud's Influence

Freud's theory has had a tremendous influence on Western thought, in no small part because it forced people to pay more attention to the unconscious aspects of human behavior. Prior to his time, psychologists primarily had studied conscious activities or overt behavior patterns. But neither introspection nor the study of conditioned reflexes yielded the insights into personality development that Freud gave the world.

Freud gave us not only a new theory, but a novel approach to psychological treatment as well. Both theory and therapy are called *psycho-analysis*. As we will see in a later chapter, Freud saw psycho-analysis as a way of strengthening the ego, so that it could handle the demands of the id and the super-ego in more satisfying ways.

Freud was one of the first "drive theorists." He believed that arousal was painful and that pleasure came primarily from the satisfaction of biological drives. Like most other early drive theorists, Freud grew up in a repressive and moralistic culture. Little wonder that he saw the effects of punishment more clearly than he perceived the potentiality of rewarding feedback. But by making parents conscious of how they affected their children's development, he helped *change* the culture itself into a less punitive one.

But he had a little help along the way. People flocked to study with him, and his disciples restructured the fields of psychiatry and personality theory. However, not all of Freud's followers agreed with his emphasis on unconscious biological instincts and the almost unchangeable influence of a child's early upbringing. Among the most important of those theorists strongly influenced by Freud were Jung, Adler, and Erikson.

Carl Jung

Born in Switzerland in 1875, Carl Gustav Jung came from a family of **theologians** and medical doctors. As a student at the University of Zurich, he dabbled in biology, philosophy, archeology, mythology, and mysticism. His dissertation for his medical degree had to do with the psychology of the **occult.** Jung discovered Freud in 1907 and became something of a disciple until 1912, when Jung branched out with his own theory.

Jung could not accept Freud's notion that the goal of "growing up" was to bring the infantile, sexual instincts under control. Human beings are not aggressive beasts only recently tamed by civilization. Rather, Jung said, we are *religious* animals whose unconscious roots go back to the very beginnings of the race. Jung believed we are motivated more by moral and spiritual values than by primitive sexuality. To Jung, the purpose of our existence is the integration of our conscious perceptions of the outside world with our unconscious, mystical experiences.

To Freud, the unconscious was the land of the libido and the home of the id—that is, the source of our psychic energies. But to Jung, there was not one unconscious but two—the **personal unconscious** and the **collective unconscious.**

The Personal Unconscious

By personal unconscious, Jung had in mind something like Freud's idea of the preconscious—that is, the pool of half-forgotten ideas, wishes, and past experiences that are now so weak that they can be brought into the spotlight of awareness only with difficulty. According to Jung, some of these thoughts and memories may be so closely related that they grow together, or congeal into a **complex** or structure all their own. This complex of associated experiences might then split off from the person's psyche and function independently, with a psychological life of its own. (Freud believed much the same thing happened to the super-ego, which splits off from the ego early in the child's development.) During an *altered state of*

Carl Jung.

consciousness, or under stress, one of these complexes may "take over" and act independently, causing hallucinations, **speaking in tongues,** or other odd forms of behavior. The purpose of psycho-therapy, from a Jungian point of view, is often that of identifying these complexes and bringing them back into conscious control.

In a sense, Jung seems to have placed in the "personal unconscious" most of the traits and psychological processes that we now associate with the functioning of the right (nonverbal) hemisphere.

The Collective Unconscious

The *collective unconscious* was a much more interesting and important part of the human psyche to Jung than was the *personal unconscious.* The collective unconscious houses all of the "racial memories" that each person presumably is born with. Jung, in his study of anthropology, had noticed that some myths and ideas seem to appear in *all cultures.* Even primitive tribes believe in a Supreme Being, and many of them have very similar stories about the creation of the world, the virgin birth of a god, man's fall from heaven or paradise, and heroes who lead men wisely. Jung called these myths **archetypes** and thought that, through evolutionary processes, the *mental images* associated with these archetypes had become engraved on our genes. Thus, Jung said, each human being is born with some unconscious "mental fragments" of the past history of the human race. The most important archetype of all, however, is that of the **self-concept,** for it is an instinct that encourages us to integrate all of our conscious and unconscious psychological processes into one meaningful whole.

Extroversion and Introversion

Jung's most widely accepted ideas have to do with **extroversion** and **introversion.** Jung thought that we are born with two innate attitudes, one of which leads us to look inward, the other of which leads us to look outward.

Some people seem to be born *introverts*—that is, they spend most of their time looking toward their inner or personal world. Highly religious individuals—such as the monk who retires to a monastery to think and pray—tend to be introverts. The *extrovert* is someone who focuses on the outside environment. Outgoing, highly social individuals are examples of what Jung meant by extroverts. Jung believed that you are born with both tendencies, but that one usually comes to predominate. You are usually conscious of which attitude is dominant but, according to Jung, you may not realize that the other attitude often expresses itself unconsciously through your dreams and fantasies.

Jung Versus Freud

Freud emphasized the role of biology in human development. Jung preferred to think that humans could rise above their animal natures. Freud believed that happiness often came from escaping pain or reducing anxiety, and he tended to attract patients who were highly anxious or pain-ridden. Jung was one of the first great **gurus.** Many of Jung's clients were artists, mystics, or wealthy individuals who felt the need for spiritual guidance "outside the church." Freud focused on the early, developmental years, which he saw as determining the entire structure of an individual's personality. Jung worked to a great degree with older patients, and never did offer a complex account of how the personality is formed.

Perhaps the most telling difference of all between the two men, though, lay in their use of language. Freud was a superb writer who was a serious contender for the Nobel Prize in literature. People might not have agreed with what Freud said, but they were seldom in doubt as to what he meant

Speaking in tongues. During religious ceremonies, persons belonging to some churches believe they are "possessed" by God. During the height of this altered state of consciousness, the person may speak in what seems to be a foreign language. The belief held by most of these people is that God is speaking though them in languages not comprehensible to ordinary humans. This sort of experience is called "speaking in tongues."

Archetypes (ARK-ee-types). From the Greek words meaning "the original model, form, or pattern from which something is made or from which something develops." The archetypes that Jung referred to are the original models of myths, legends, and stories—instinctual thought patterns passed on genetically from generation to generation.

Self-concept. In Jung's terms, the original archetype of "self-awareness." The instinctual percept that one is a separate entity.

Extroversion (EX-troh-vurr-shun). The act of directing your attention toward happenings or people in the outside world. Literally, "to go outside."

Introversion (INN-troh-vurr-shun). The opposite of extroversion. The act of directing your attention toward or getting pleasure from your own thoughts and feelings. Literally, "to go inside."

Gurus (GOO-roos). From a Hindu word meaning "heavy," or "worthy of praise." A guru is a spiritual leader.

Alfred Adler.

to say. Jung's books and articles, however, were filled with obscure images and symbols and are very difficult for most tough-minded scientists to make sense out of. Jung's greatest influence, then, was perhaps not on psychology, but on art and mysticism. For example, many movies—such as Fellini's *The Satyricon*—are attempts to capture on the screen the "archetypes" and unconscious symbols that Jung believed were built into everyone's genetic blueprints.

Alfred Adler

Alfred Adler was born and educated in Vienna. A few years after Adler took his medical degree, he joined Freud's group. Adler's first work was on the living conditions of Austrian tailors, a study that helped confirm his early bias toward the importance of environmental factors in determining personality. As fascinated as Adler was by Freud's ideas, he was the first to break away from "the master" and form his own group, the Society for Individual Psychology.

Adler disputed Freud's notion that human behavior is dominated by the workings of blind, selfish instincts. Instead, said Adler, people govern themselves by a conscious need to express and fulfill themselves as unique individuals. Rejecting both Freud's theory of biological drives, and Jung's emphasis on intra-psychic mysticism, Adler emphasized the importance of the social environment. He thought that people could shape their own destinies, and that they could build a superior society by satisfying their basic need to transcend their personal problems.

The Creative Power

To Adler, life is a conscious struggle to achieve *superiority*. Thus he denied the importance of sexual instincts and substituted aggressive tendencies in their place. Freud and Jung emphasized the unconscious, unknowable inner influences on behavior. Adler believed that most of us are only too aware of why we do what we do. We see our own *inferiorities*, and we strive to overcome them. We have an instinct for *self-realization*, for completion and perfection, that Adler thought was the driving force of life itself. Adler called this force the **creative power** and thought it was the "first cause" of all behavior.

The Inferiority Complex

Children learn very early that adults can do things that children cannot. This knowledge creates in all of us an **inferiority complex** that adds to our motivation to succeed. As children we also learn that other people in our life space are bigger and faster and brighter and prettier and stronger than we. This knowledge merely fuels the fire of our feelings of insecurity. The inferiority complex creates a drive for **compensation,** the urge to overcome our failures in one part of life by excelling in another. The small, weak boy may try to succeed in his school studies or become a great musician in order to *compensate* for his physical weakness.

Life Style

Adler was an optimist. He believed that we have buried in our genes a basic need to cooperate with each other and to work toward building a finer society. This innate tendency needs developmental guidance, however, and so Adler spent much of his time working with teachers and setting up child-guidance clinics. For it is through training and experience that you develop your own **style of life**—that is, you learn to express your own striving for superiority in a unique way.

Creative power. According to Adler, the instinctual drive for self-realization. Similar to Freud's idea of ego, and to Jung's notion of the self-concept.

Inferiority complex. A subsystem (complex) of the personality that, realizing the person's own failings, attempts to overcome them by efforts to succeed, or to become superior.

Compensation. The attempt to overcome your feelings in one area by becoming superior in other ways.

Style of life. Adler's term for the uniqueness of the personality. Each person, Adler said, tries to succeed in her or his individual way. The characteristic behavior patterns and attitudes that differentiate one person from another.

In a sense, Adler's "style of life" is equivalent to Freud's concept of the ego. At first, Adler thought this style was fixed early in life. Later, he decided this view did not do justice to the dynamic quality of human development. Adler's emphasis on the importance of *social factors* in determining personality was, for a time, unique in psycho-analytic circles and helped give rise to what we now call "social psychology." And by assuring people that they were basically humane, open-minded, and in control of their own destinies, Adler encouraged the development of "humanistic psychology."

Indeed, as humanist Abraham Maslow stated shortly before his death, "Alfred Adler becomes more and more correct year by year. As the facts come in, they give stronger and stronger support to his image of man."

Erik H. Erikson

In some ways, the United States accepted Freud more readily than did most of Europe, and the development of Freud's ideas was eagerly carried on by US psycho-analysts. Although Erik Erikson was born abroad, he spent most of his life in the United States and can be counted as an American. Erikson has, in general, followed Adler's lead in stating that personality development continues long after the genital period is reached and the heterosexual crisis solved.

Like most US psycho-analysts, Erikson believes that the ego is a much more important determinant of personality than are the id and the superego. The ego is the point of contact between the individual and society. Therefore, Erikson says, the *type of society* that the person grows up in is at least as important as the person's instinctual drives. Erikson's **psychosocial theory of development** is hence less biased by middle-European culture than was Freud's.

Erikson accepted most of Freud's notions on the importance of instinctual drives in young children. But Erikson insisted that it is the *conflict* between instincts and cultural demands that shapes the child's personality. Instincts are presumably pretty much the same from one child to another, but cultures differ remarkably, and they grow and develop just as do human beings.

Freud and Jung emphasized the importance of past history on the maturation of the individual. Erikson, like Adler, emphasized the future. At any given moment in time, Erikson said, the person's *anticipation of future events* helps determine how the person will behave in the "here and now."

Eight Developmental Stages

According to Erikson, each human being must pass through eight developmental stages on her or his way to complete maturity (Table 22.1). Each of these stages is characterized by its own type of *crisis*, or conflict. Eirkson saw these crises as being eight great tests of the person's character.

1. Erikson called the first developmental stage the "sensory stage," because for the first few months after its birth, the infant is a passive receptor of sensory inputs from the world around it. The sensory stage corresponds closely to what Freud called the oral stage. To Erikson, the crisis involved in the sensory stage is that of learning a basic *trust or mistrust* of other people. At this point in life, the infant is totally dependent on others for its needs. If its mother (or someone else) meets these needs, the infant learns to depend on others in later life. If the mother is inconsistent in satisfying the infant's needs—for whatever reason—the infant may carry suspicion and doubt through the rest of its years.

2. The second of Erikson's stages, similar to the anal stage, is that of *muscular development*. During toilet training the child learns to control its own muscles and begins to assert its individuality. The crisis here is that of **autonomy,** or the ability to control one's own bodily functions. The child

Psychosocial theory of development. Erikson's extension and elaboration of Freudian theory. Freud stated that personality development more or less ends during adolescence. Erikson, who places more emphasis on environmental factors than did Freud, believes that personality development can continue all one's life—that the personality is always a psychological adjustment to social inputs or situations.

Autonomy (aw-TAWN-oh-me). Freedom; self-direction. The autonomic nervous system is usually "free" of conscious direction or control.

Erik H. Erikson.

Table 22.1

Erikson's Stages of Development

Stage	1	2	3	4	5	6	7	8
Maturity								Ego Integrity vs. Despair
Adulthood							Generativity vs. Stagnation	
Young Adulthood						Intimacy vs. Isolation		
Puberty and Adolescence					Identity vs. Role Confusion			
Latency				Industry vs. Inferiority				
Locomotor-Genital			Initiative vs. Guilt					
Muscular-Anal		Autonomy vs. Shame, Doubt						
Oral Sensory	Basic Trust vs. Mistrust							

SOURCE: Reprinted from *Childhood and Society*, Rev. by Erik H. Erikson, by permission of W.W. Norton & Company, Inc. Copyright 1960 © 1963 by W.W. Norton & Company, Inc.

either learns autonomy, or, if it is unsuccessful, develops shame and doubt about its own abilities.

3. The third stage, that of *locomotor control*, is similar to Freud's phallic stage. Now the child attempts to develop its own way of asserting its needs and gaining its rewards. Urged by its instincts to possess its oppo-site-sex parent (at least in fantasy) and to rival its same-sex parent, the child faces the crisis of inner desires versus society's demands. Erikson believed that if the child could channel its sexual needs into socially acceptable behaviors, the child acquired **initiative.** If not, the child might build up a strong sense of *guilt* that would haunt it the rest of its days.

4. Both Freud and Erikson called the fourth developmental stage that of *latency*. During these (typically) school years, the crisis the child faces is that of *competence* or *failure*. If the child does well in school, it learns that it can succeed and thus becomes *industrious*. If it does poorly, it gains a sense of *inferiority*. For example, Isaac Newton was rather an indifferent pupil during his early years. His crisis came when he was attacked by the school bully. Newton fought back, and won. After that time, he began to work hard to excel both in his lessons and in after-school fights.

5. At *puberty*, Freud thought, sexual interest returns and the individual must make the final adjustment, that of *heterosexuality*. Erikson saw the puberty crisis as that of either finding one's *identity*, or of developing what he called *role confusion*. The adolescent must decide what the future will hold and who he or she will become. Although the social roles available may vary from one society to another, the young person must decide which of these roles to adopt. By discovering who and what they want to be, adolescents are able to plan their lives as working, functioning adults.

6. Erikson postulated three final stages of maturation beyond the five that Freud spoke of. The first of these stages, which occurs in *young adulthood*, presents the person with the crisis of *intimacy versus isolation*. If

Initiative. The tendency to be self-motivated. To start things on your own rather than waiting to be told.

we have "found" ourselves by now, we can then go on to the delightful task of "finding" someone else to share life's intimacies with. If we fail to resolve the identity crisis, however, we will remain isolated from the closest forms of psychological "sharing" with others. Young people who resolve the first six crises exceptionally well become trusting, autonomous, full of initiative, highly competent at a variety of tasks, industrious, sure of their social and personal roles, and able to identify with and understand the intimate feelings of others. But few of us are that fortunate: According to Erikson, most of our personalities are a mixture of partial successes and failures. We function well enough to survive in our particular society, but few of us ever achieve our best or most balanced development.

7. Societies often pass through a period of rapid development, then settle into **complacency** when growth stops and stagnation sets in. Erikson believed that adults often experience the same "growth" crisis during their *middle years*. Human beings need more than intimacy. We must be productive and helpful to our fellow humans, and we must make a contribution to society. The crisis decision here, then, is that between what Erikson called **generativity** and **stagnation.**

8. Erikson's final stage is that of *maturity*. If we live long enough, we have to face squarely the fact that we are mortal, and that some day (perhaps sooner than we think) we will die. By resolving our prior crises, we gain the strength to **integrate** even death into the pattern of our existence. We come to terms with ourselves, content with the knowledge that we have done about the best that we could do, under the circumstances. Knowing that our lives have been successful, we can die as we have lived—with integrity. But if we fail to solve the earlier crises, we may see our lives as having been useless, incomplete, unintegrated—or wasted—and we may succumb to feelings of despair at the futility of existence.

Maturity and Old Age

Adler and Erikson deserve a vote of praise for reminding us that people do not stop developing once they reach adulthood. Even today, most personality theorists concentrate on the early years of life, perhaps because children change so dramatically and quickly, perhaps because children are easier (and often a lot more fun) to study than are grown-ups. It is also true that childhood development is more influenced by genes, thus is similar from culture to culture. Adult development, however, varies radically from one society to another because our later years are shaped more by *social learning* than by our *genetic blueprints* (see Chapters 26–28). Whatever the case, we know a fair amount about the mental and physical changes associated with childhood, but very little indeed about how older people adapt and develop.

The "growth" crisis that Erikson describes for the middle years is that of generativity versus stagnation. There is a cultural myth in Western society that, like a machine that has worn down from constant use, the older person should become slow-moving, mentally inflexible and rigid, and above all, asexual. Let us look at each of these points in turn.

There is no doubt that most younger people expend more physical energy than do most people in their 40's and 50's, but this change in "body tempo" is probably due more to psychological and social causes than to something like "tired blood." Young people often have neither the skills nor the experience to command high-paying desk jobs that require much mental but little physical exertion. With maturity usually comes the knowledge of how to avoid strenuous exercise—and all the bumps and bruises associated with exertion. Professional athletes often retire in their 30's, not because they are physically incapable of continuing, but because their salaries simply are not sufficiently motivating for them to go on suffering the pain and injury too often associated with contact sports. More than this, keeping one's body in peak condition takes enormous amounts of time and concentration and tends to exclude the person from many delightful and rewarding social activities.

Complacency (kom-PLAY-sen-see). From the Latin word meaning "to please greatly." A complacent person is someone who is unduly satisfied with his or her own actions or talents. Feeling so perfect, the person finds little reason to change.

Generativity (jen-ur-uh-TIV-uh-tee). To generate is to produce. Generativity is having the power of producing or originating things.

Stagnation (stagg-NAY-shun). From the Latin word meaning "a pool of standing water, or a swamp." Any living thing that doesn't move, or grow, tends to stagnate, decay, become dead or bad-smelling (like a swamp).

Integrate (INN-tee-great, or INN-tuh-greate). To pull together, or to make into a whole. According to Erikson, a mentally healthy person is someone who can integrate all aspects of life into a meaningful whole.

In young adulthood the crisis is that of intimacy versus isolation.

During the middle years adults either settle into complacency or learn new ways to contribute to society.

During the final stage of life people must face squarely the fact that they are mortal and must integrate the concept of death into their personalities.

Androgen (ANN-droh-jen). Male hormone, such as testosterone (tess-TOSS-ter-own). Produced primarily by the testes (TESS-tease).

Young people who are just learning about themselves and their social world are perhaps more likely to "latch on to new ideas" than are older people. However, older individuals are generally able to learn more quickly those facts or skills that do not directly *contradict* their previous learning. Recent studies suggest that young people may be capable of taking in information more rapidly, and may have larger Short-term Memories, but that older people are just as good at making decisions. Most attempts to compare learning speed between young and old, however, run afoul of the problem of *motivation*. There is often little need for highly successful older individuals to "latch on to new ideas." After all, they got where they are by using "old ideas." And their very success makes most rewards of less value to them. In brief, you can teach an old dog (or human) new tricks, but you cannot use the simple reinforcers that work so well with puppies (or younger people).

In her book *Passages*, Gail Sheehy explores many of the myths associated with sexuality and the aging process. Summarizing the findings of several scientists who have worked in this area, Sheehy asserts that men and women have the same sexual potential at age 18 and again at age 60. In between these extremes, Sheehy says, the woman is usually more capable of sexual arousal than is the man. The more usual view of "sexual arousability" is shown in Fig. 22.4, for many experts believe that after age 30, the woman typically remains more easily "turned on" than is the male.

The truth of the matter is that there simply aren't enough studies, made in enough situations, to tell us all that we need to know about sexuality in the later years. It is true that **androgen** levels reach a peak in the male at

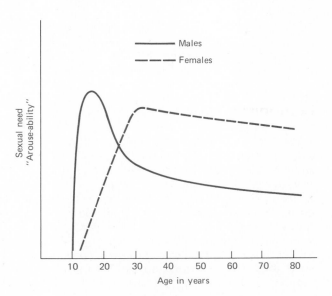

Figure 22.4. Most psychologists believe that "sexual arousability" reaches a peak in males at about age 18 and thereafter declines, while "arousability" peaks in females at about age 30 and remains fairly constant thereafter.

PART SIX Personality

about age 18, and fall thereafter. It is just as true that a 90-year-old male typically has a high enough hormone level to perform the sex act several times a week.

Most research suggests that sexual "arousability" *at any age past puberty* is as greatly affected by intra-psychic and social factors as by hormone levels. Our society has typically allowed early sexual expression in males, but not females. Little wonder then that men's "curve" reaches an earlier peak than does the one for women. But psychological inhibitions are more likely to affect the sexual performance—and the *desire* for sex—of men than of women. Thus males may become inhibited at just the age when women become more liberated.

It is also true that our society has certain "expectations" about sex among older individuals, and the expectation is primarily negative. A study of attitudes among college students—reported in the June 1977 issue of *Psychology Today*—notes that more than half the students believe their parents have sex once a month or less, while about 25 percent of the students think their parents make love less than once a year. (Kinsey's figures suggest that the parents probably have intercourse 3 to 4 times a week, but only 4 percent of the students guessed this was the case!)

On a more positive note, a number of studies do agree on one important point: People who, in their middle years, continue to have an active sex life typically look younger, have more energy, and show a greater zest for living than do people who give up this important part of the human experience.

The same is true of any part of our existence. Elderly people who "give up" at retirement age, who shut themselves away, who turn their backs on growth and change are typically the people who soon become **senile.** While not too many psychological studies have been performed on the elderly, it does seem that they are much more capable of doing *almost everything* than society assumes they are. If activity, challenge, and stimulation are necessary for the healthy growth and development of an infant, then shouldn't we expect much the same to be true throughout life?

Question: How might children's attitudes about what their parents' sexual behavior ought to be *affect what the parents actually do?*

Erikson Compared to Freud

Freud emphasized the animal side of human nature—the physiological instincts. Erikson incorporated many elements of Freud's theory into his own, but believed that innate, unconscious urges were important only during the first few years of human development. Freud saw people as being pushed hither and yon by blind sexual itches and urges. Erikson saw humans as motivated more by the conscious need for getting along with others and determining their own place in a social world. More than this, Erikson believed it is the humane need to relate to other human beings that elevates us above the rest of the animal kingdom.

Humanistic Theories of Personality

Freud stated that our destinies lay in our genetic blueprints, and that we more or less became what nature intended us to be. To Freud, the social environment could *hinder* your personal development, but it couldn't *enhance* it all that much.

This predominantly physiological view of human nature is rejected by a group of psychologists who call themselves **humanists.** Freud, following Darwin, built his theory on the *similarities* between humans and the lower animals. The humanists emphasize the *difference* between us and the rest of the animal kingdom. They see us as being unique, set apart, and above all other life forms. We are not mechanisms wound up and abandoned to tick out our lives as our gene-clocks dictate. Rather, we are masters of our

Senile (SEE-nile). The condition of being old and usually forgetful. For a further explanation, see Chapter 24.

Humanists. People who are devoted to human welfare. People with a strong interest in or love for individuals (as opposed to loving nations, organizations, or abstract ideals.)

Carl Rogers.

Phenomenal field (fee-NOM-me-nall, or fee-NOM-uh-null). A phenomenon is an event, a happening, an experience. The sum total of all your experiences (sensory inputs, processings, outputs) is what Rogers calls the phenomenal field.

---

destinies, creative individuals capable of rising above our animal heritage.

According to the humanists, we are motivated not merely to survive, but to become better and better. This process of continual psychological growth and improvement is what the humanists call "self-actualization."

There are many psychologists whose theories fall within the humanistic tradition. Of these, the best known are probably Carl Rogers and Abraham Maslow.

Carl Rogers

Carl Rogers is an American who taught for many years at the University of Chicago and at the University of Wisconsin. Rogers believes we are born with no self-concept, and no self—but we do have an innate urge to *become* a fully functioning and actualized person. At birth, as William James supposedly said, all we have is a blooming, buzzing, confusing set of sensory impressions, physiological processes, and motor activities. Rogers calls this sum total of our experience the **phenomenal field.** As we mature, the outside world imposes a kind of order or logic onto this field, and as we become aware of this logic, our *self* emerges and differentiates itself from the phenomenal field. The self is thus the *conscious* portion of experience.

For Rogers, maturation is a matter of distinguishing your own body and thoughts from the objective, outside world. As you mature, your "self" begins to build up expectations about its own function—that is, you take on values and make judgments about your own behavior. Some of these values come from your own desires. Other values are imposed on you by the society in which you live. You are most likely to run into developmental mental problems when society wants you to become something that conflicts with your own internal values or standards. If you yield to the demands of society too much, your psychological experience is distorted and your self-concept suffers accordingly.

According to Rogers, most of your experiences are *unconscious*—that is, below the threshold of consciousness (see Chapter 11). But you can bring almost any experience above threshold if you merely give the experience a name or a label—that is, if you develop *word-symbols* that will allow you to describe (and hence think about) the experience. If a particular event threatens your self-concept, then you may refuse to symbolize this event in words or thoughts. But if you cannot tolerate some of your own behaviors, you will have problems achieving full actualization because you are continually hiding some of your own values or motivations from conscious expression.

To Rogers, therefore, you become fully-adjusted when you can symbolize any experience that has happened to you, or that might possibly happen—that is, when you gain a conscious awareness of (and are comfortable with) all parts of your own behavior. When you can accept yourself completely, you become what Rogers calls a *fully functioning individual*. You are open to all experience, and you defend against nothing. You are aware of both your faults and your virtues, but you have a high positive regard for yourself. And most of all, you maintain happy and humane relationships with others.

Abraham Maslow

Carl Rogers' theory grew out of his long-time work as a psycho-therapist. Thus his theory is built in part on Rogers' study of abnormal and maladjusted individuals. To a great extent, this statement is also true of Freud's theory, and of Jung's, Adler's, and Erikson's. Abraham Maslow, on the other hand, is one of the few theorists who took his ideas about human behavior from studying highly creative and psychologically healthy people. Some of these individuals were his personal friends. Other—such as Lincoln, Einstein, Eleanor Roosevelt, and Beethoven—he studied through books, papers, and letters. Maslow assumed these individuals had achieved

Abraham Maslow.

PART SIX Personality

Table 22.2

Abraham Maslow's Whole Characteristics of Self-actualizing People

They have more efficient perceptions of reality and are more comfortable with it.

They accept themselves and their own natures almost without thinking about it.

Their behavior is marked by simplicity and naturalness and by lack of artificiality or straining for effect.

They focus on problems outside themselves; they are concerned with basic issues and eternal questions.

They like privacy and tend to be detached.

They have relative independence of their physical and social environments; they rely on their own development and continued growth.

They do not take blessings for granted, but appreciate again and again the basic pleasures of life.

They experience limitless horizons and the intensification of any unselfconscious experience often of a mystical type.

They have a deep feeling of kindship with others.

They develop deep ties with a few other self-actualizing individuals.

They are democratic in a deep sense; although not indiscriminate, they are not really aware of differences.

They are strongly ethical, with definite moral standards, though their attitudes are conventional; they relate to ends rather than means.

Their humor is real and related to philosophy, not hostility; they are spontaneous less often then others, and tend to be more serious and thoughtful.

They are original and inventive, less constricted and fresher than others.

While they tend toward the conventional and exist well within the culture, they live by the laws of their own characters rather than those of society.

They experience imperfections and have ordinary feelings, like others.

SOURCE: Condensed from "Self-Actualizing People: A Study of Psychological Health," in *Motivation and Personality*, 2nd ed., by Abraham H. Maslow, Copyright 1954 by Harper & Row, Publishers, Inc.: Copyright © 1970 by Abraham H. Maslow. By permission of the publishers.

a high degree of self-fulfillment, otherwise they wouldn't have been so prominent and have demonstrated so much leadership. By determining the similarities among the members of this noted group, he arrived at the characteristics of a truly "self-actualized" person. A list of these characteristics appears in Table 22.2.

Most psycho-analytically oriented theories focus on what can go wrong during the developmental years—they emphasize the possibility of sickness, not the probability of success. Maslow's approach is different, for he looks primarily at the *healthy side of human nature*. As we noted in Chapter 12, Maslow has created what he calls a **hierarchy of needs,** of which self-actualization is the highest. Maslow acknowledges the strength of our physiological instincts, but sees them as being "basic needs" easily satisfied in most civilized societies. But even our drives for food and sex are part of a more impelling urge—an active "will toward health"—that drives us up the developmental ladder toward self-actualization.

Behavioral Theories of Personality

There should be little doubt in your mind by now that biological and intra-psychic drives do exist. But are they the only forces that motivate human beings? What might John B. Watson, B.F. Skinner, and Ivan Pavlov have to say? What kind of theory of personality might we come up with if we viewed men and women as capable of learning to think and behave in almost any fashion imaginable—*if* given the proper inputs from people around them and the rest of their environments? Would this social/behavioral view add anything to our understanding of human personality not already covered by the biological and intra-psychic theorists?

Hierarchy of needs (HIGH-er-ARK-key). Maslow's list of human needs, running from the most basic physiological needs up a ladder to self-actualization. See Chapter 12.

B. F. Skinner.

B.F. Skinner

The person who has contributed most to the behavioral approach to the study of personality is B.F. Skinner, whose principles of behavior change we have mentioned several times earlier (see Chapters 5, 12, 16).

Skinner believes that behavior is, above all else, **lawful.** By this he means that your actions (and hence your thoughts) are predictable and primarily under the control of external, measurable influences. You do not move because you want to, according to Skinner. Rather, you move because the external environment (perhaps working through your own past experience) stimulates you to do so. Your energy comes not from dynamic forces working deep within your unconscious mind, but from external inputs. In short, your motivation comes from outside forces, not from internal instincts.

Like many scientists, Skinner pays attention only to those aspects of the world that he can measure *objectively*. We cannot measure your intra-psychic experiences directly, therefore we should not discuss them scientifically. But we can measure behavior, and so we must describe human existence almost solely in terms of actions and reactions. We cannot measure "needs" such as hunger, but we can measure how frequently and how much and what you eat. Since Skinner assumes that you are conditioned or trained to eat what and when you do, the phrase "I *am* hungry" has no scientific meaning because your eating behavior is almost entirely under the control of external, social forces.

Skinner believes that biological data are presently insufficient to tell us much about the human condition. He thus rejects the physiological viewpoint not because it is unscientific, but because it tells us so little about *behavior*. He also has little use for the intra-psychic theories, considering them to be "fiction rather than fact." His views often outrage people, particularly the humanists, who have frequently debated him in public. For, by denying the usefulness of concepts such as "consciousness" and "self," Skinner seems to make us into robots—clockwork machines that need frequent windings to keep on running.

Do humans have the ability to think, to plan, to scheme, to solve problems "in their minds," and thus to influence their destinies? Actually, Skinner does not deny this possibility entirely. He merely says, as we noted in Chapter 5, that we have no way as yet of measuring thinking—but we can measure verbal behavior rather precisely. And since the complex vocal outputs that we call "human speech" are obviously learned, and influenced by the external environment, why do we need such vague and undefinable terms as "id" or "ego?" Do these concepts really add anything to our understanding of human behavior?

Skinner's major contribution has really been in the field of technology, not in theory. Indeed, Skinner denies that he is a "theorist" in the true sense of the word. But by giving us highly effective ways of changing ourselves, and by emphasizing the importance of the external environment in "shaping" our destinies, Skinner has added much to our understanding of what humans are like. But in neglecting the qualitative differences among people (as Newton neglected many of the differences among heavenly objects), and in discarding entirely the physiological and intra-psychic influences on our lives, Skinner has dramatically narrowed the scope (and impressiveness) of his potentially great contribution. (We will talk more about learning theory and personality development in Chapters 26–28.)

Judging A Theory

As we pointed out in Chapter 5, there are four main **criteria** for judging among scientific theories: accuracy, completeness, impressiveness, and usefulness. How do the theories we have discussed in this chapter stack up against these criteria?

If we judge the accuracy of a theory on how well it *explains* past events to our satisfaction, Freud and the psycho-analysts probably would come

Lawful. In science, a law is usually an expression of a high, positive correlation between measurable inputs and outputs. The law often makes no mention of the processing that may occur between the input and output—that is, the law merely states that the correlation exists without explaining why. A behavioral law usually states that, given a certain input, an organism will respond with a certain specific output. The more powerful the law, the better it predicts the regularities between stimuli and responses, or between inputs and outputs.

Criteria (cry-TEER-ee-uh). A criterion (cry-TEER-ee-un) is a standard by which something is judged, or a goal that must be reached. The criteria for judging a scientific theory include accuracy, completeness, impressiveness, and usefulness.

out on top. But if we measure accuracy in terms of how well a viewpoint *predicts* future thoughts or behaviors, probably the behavioral approach would rank at the top of the list.

As for completeness, Freud and his followers win hands down. Neither the humanists nor the behaviorists have yet given us the detailed description of human development that psycho-analysis has.

As we noted earlier, impressiveness is a matter of individual taste. European intellectuals rejected Freud's theory in the early 1900's because it was too radical and shocking for them to tolerate. Eventually, as Freud's notions became more familiar, people *habituated* to psycho-analysis and it became the most widely accepted theory of personality we have today. The humanistic theories gained strength in the early 1960's and 1970's, perhaps because of their emphasis on human growth and potential. Maslow and Rogers *impressed* people in no small part because their viewpoints were oriented more toward achieving health than toward curing illness. And as for behaviorism, it surely seems as radical to present-day Freudians and humanists as Freud's theory seemed to most people in 1915. Perhaps we will habituate to Skinner some day too. And once we can look at his contributions with less emotionality, perhaps we will see him for the creative genius that he is.

As for usefulness, "you pays your money and you takes your choice." If you find explanations of inner processes most useful, you will do better with Freud and/or the humanists. If, however, you are primarily interested in the technology of behavioral change, then Skinner's approach might be of more value to you. The different approaches have yielded quite different types of psycho-therapies, and all are successful in helping some of the people some of the time. We will evaluate therapies in a later chapter, but we might note that none of them *individually* does as well as a *combination* of approaches usually can do.

Someday, perhaps, we will have a master theory that tells us everything about the human personality that we want to know—one that is *holistic* enough to give us "deep understanding" of ourselves as well as the power to predict and control our personal development. But both understanding and prediction imply that we can somehow measure what it is we are trying to comprehend and change. So it is to the *measurement* of human personality that we must now turn our attention.

Summary

1. **Personality theory** refers to some explanation of why people do what they do. Each of us has her or his own theory of personality.

2. Prior to Freud, most theories concerned the **structure of personality**—that is, **traits, values, abilities, intelligence,** and **genetic disposition.** The study of **personality dynamics** really begins with Freud.

3. The helpful effects of **catharsis** suggested to Freud that we are often unconscious of our real problems and that early traumas may be connected with sexuality.

4. Freud described three "levels of consciousness," the **conscious,** the **preconscious,** and the **unconscious.**

5. Whatever is in the focus of your **attention** at any given moment is at the level of consciousness.

6. Anything that you *could* become conscious of lies at the level of preconsciousness.

7. Those experiences or processes that you ordinarily cannot bring to consciousness—such as activity in the **emotional centers** of your brain—make up what Freud called the unconscious.

8. An infant is born with a set of basic **instincts** that motivate it to live. Freud called these unconscious instincts the **id.**

9. The energy supplied by these instincts is called the **libido,** or **life force.**

10. The id obeys the **pleasure principle,** which means it seeks in an **egocentric** way to achieve immediate gratification of its needs by releasing **libidinal energy.**

11. As the infant undergoes **psychosexual development,** its parents force it to delay immediate satisfaction of its needs. Out of its need to learn self-control, the infant develops its **ego,** which becomes the part of the infant's personality that deals with the outer world.

12. The ego obeys the **reality principle** when it takes into account the demands of the external environment.

13. During the **phallic stage,** the child experiences the **Oedipal** or the **Electral crisis** when it becomes attached to the parent of the opposite sex. It solves the crisis taking on the attitudes and behaviors of its same-sex parent, that is by developing its **conscience,** which becomes an unconscious part of its **super-ego.**

14. At **puberty,** the young person **introjects** the values of other adults and forms its **ego-ideal,** a conscious part of its super-ego.

15. The ego **mediates** between the demands of the id and super-ego by trying to control the release of libidinal energy. The ego experiences **anxiety** whenever these demands are not being properly met.

16. The ego attempts to relieve anxiety by discharging libidinal energy through various **defense mechanisms.** These mechanisms include **repression, regression, identification, denial, reaction formation, projection, rationalization, displacement,** and **sublimation.**

17. Carl Jung rejected Freud's belief that the child's chief task is to bring its infantile, sexual instincts under control. Jung believed we are more motivated by **moral** and **spiritual** values than by primitive sexuality.

18. According to Jung, we have two different types of unconscious:
    a. The **personal unconscious** contains our own individual memories.
    b. The **collective unconscious** houses all of our **archetypes,** or racial memories, which are part of our **genetic blueprint.**

19. The **self-concept** is the most important archetype. It allows us to integrate all our conscious and unconscious processes into one meaningful whole.

20. Jung believed we have two **innate attitudes,** that of **introversion** and of **extroversion.**

21. Alfred Adler believed the **social environment** a more important determinant of personality than the genetic blueprint.

22. Adler thought conscious experiences more important than unconscious ones.

23. Adler saw life as a struggle to achieve **superiority,** a drive to achieve self-realization. When we discover our own **inferiorities,** we may **compensate** by trying to become superior in other ways.

24. Freud believed personality development more or less ceased during **adolescence.** Erik Erikson extended Freud's **psycho-analytic theory** to include the mature years.

25. According to Erikson, every human must pass through eight **developmental stages,** each of which is characterized by its own type of **crisis** or test of a person's **character.**

26. The **humanists** reject most psycho-analytic concepts, emphasizing instead the drive for **self-actualization.**

27. Humanist Carl Rogers believes that a fully adjusted person can symbolize any experience in conscious verbalizations.

28 Humanist Abraham Maslow sees humans as being innately healthy.

29. **Behaviorists** such as B.F. Skinner often reject theorizing and focus on technology instead. Skinner believes behavior is **lawful** and hence predictable.

30. All types of personality theories have contributed to our ability to understand and predict human experience, but no theory is complete in itself.

(Continued from page 561.)

The afternoon sun angled sharply down through the towering mountains onto the waters of Lake Como. Bellagio, on the eastern shore, was bathed in golden light. Cadennabia, just a mile or so directly across the water, had already slipped into twilight. A water taxi headed toward Bellagio dipped and tossed in the breeze, its passengers clinging tightly to their seats as the boat plunged through the rough water. And although the three scientists sitting safely on the terrace of the Villa d'Este didn't know it, they too were about to experience rather a rough passage on their journey toward peace and understanding.

"As I mentioned earlier, I have hope," said Donald M. Papas, the Canadian psychologist. "That is why I agreed to the Foundation's request to lead this First International Symposium on Peace and Personality. And that is why I invited you, Jonathan, a behaviorist, and you, Joyce, a neo-Freudian, and ten other personality theorists to come to the conference."

"You really hope to end war throughout the world?" Fraser asked.

"No, hope to end war throughout psychology. Or, at least, within the field of personality theory."

"An armed truce is about all you can expect of us," Joyce Sapir said.

"I'll settle for that, as a first approximation. I know it's idealistic of me, but I rather hoped that if I could get you all together, talking and listening to each other, we might make some headway."

"Who listens at these conferences?" asked Fraser.

"It depends on who talks," Papas continued. "All of you really have a lot in common—including your individual desires to help people live more peaceful, productive lives."

"To help people achieve self-actualization, you mean," said Joyce Sapir.

"You mean, to help people achieve voluntary self-control over their behavioral outputs," said Fraser.

"There, you see, you're saying almost the same thing, but in different words. It's your language that is at the heart of the problem."

Fraser smiled. "George Bernard Shaw once said that the US and Britain are separated by a common language."

"Exactly!" continued Papas. "In Joyce Sapir's terms, self-actualization means learning enough about your unconscious sensual desires so that you can handle them consciously. Skinner would say that physiological rewards such as food and sex are so strong that we can condition an organism to accept social rewards by pairing praise with food. If you pat a dog on the head each time you give it food, eventually it will find the affection as rewarding as a piece of meat. But isn't that what Freud really meant when he said that a young boy in the latency period learns to act like his father because his mother is more affectionate to him when he does?"

"But humans have an innate need for affection," Joyce Sapir insisted.

"And so do monkeys," responded Fraser. "No, my dear neo-Freudian, what our sneaky Canadian friend seems to be saying is this—ego psychologists, such as yourself, focus on innate needs. You measure these needs indirectly, by asking people how they feel."

"Of course," said the woman.

Fraser nodded. "But you get so involved in hunting for hidden meanings in their verbal responses that you forget verbal responses can serve as *reinforcers.* And reinforcers can be studied objectively. When you praise me, I listen. When you criticize me, I say something nasty in return. It doesn't matter whether or not you *intended* to reward me or punish me, that's the way I react. You analysts measure the unconscious *intent* of the speaker. We behaviorists measure the speaker's *actual* effect on the listener's behavior."

"I see," Joyce Sapir said. "You behaviorists focus on satisfiers instead of needs, because you can *see* environmental inputs. But since you can't measure internal needs or intentions directly, you assume that they just aren't there."

"You're doing beautifully, both of you," Papas said. "But now, let's go a step farther. Skinner defines a reward as anything that increases response rates. He never asks *why* reward has this effect—it just does. And so Skinner studies *how* rewards work. The psycho-analysts and the humanists—like the physiological psychologists—are interested in *why*. But as the behaviorists learned long ago, insight into the 'whys' of your own motives doesn't necessarily tell you 'how' to change your thoughts and actions and hence achieve inner peace and self-actualization."

Joyce Sapir shook her head sadly. "But knowing 'how' doesn't tell you a thing about *why* people have personal difficulties."

Papas nodded. "True, but to help people best, you have to give them both insight *and* feedback on how well they're doing. Many behavior modifiers will tell you that the person with psychological problems is often the person who ignores feedback. If you can get people to chart their growth or development, they find any positive change in the graph very rewarding indeed."

Joyce Sapir mused a moment, then responded. "Carl Rogers said that we get into trouble when our 'self' or ego loses touch with our biological organism. But if the therapist reflects back to a man what he is really like—if the therapist acts like a mirror—then the person can define himself and, in the process, achieve growth and understanding."

Fraser shook his head in mock dismay. "Don, are you suggesting that Rogers and Skinner were saying almost the same thing?"

"Well, if reflecting back to a man what he's really like isn't giving feedback, I don't know what is," Papas responded. "Rogers says that the feedback should be emotionally neutral, but he calls it 'unconditional *positive* regard.' That sounds suspiciously like positive reinforcement to me."

Joyce Sapir smiled. "And Carl Rogers is one of the most charming, encouraging therapists I've ever met. He almost never has a bad word to say about anyone—except about Skinner, of course."

"Perhaps if Rogers had given Skinner a bit more 'unconditional positive regard,' and Skinner had rewarded Rogers instead of criticizing him, their famous debates would have had a different outcome," Papas said quietly.

"And not nearly as bloody much fun," remarked Fraser. "Don, are you by any chance suggesting that psychologists don't always practice what they preach?"

Papas smiled slyly. "No, merely that we sometimes don't see the forest for the trees. Psycho-analytic theory is a single-minded way of looking at humans—from the inside out. Behaviorism operates from a different point of view—from the outside in. We can't give up one or the other, any more than we can give up either the forests or the trees."

"I can give up psycho-analysis any time I try really hard," Fraser said.

"No, you can't. For the analysts and humanists have identified some very potent reward systems that you really ought to look into," Papas responded.

"But surely some of the personality theorists have come close to achieving a completely integrated theory of human nature," Joyce Sapir protested.

"Sorry, but I can't agree," Papas said. "Freud probably came the closest, but like all the rest, he failed. A complete theory would have to take into account both the physical and psychological aspects of human sensations and perceptions, cognitions and altered states of consciousness, synapses and transmitters, social roles and developmental sequences, needs and motives, rewards and punishments, muscle twitches and ego, instincts and the biochemical basis of learning, memories and forgettings, and even the over-riding urge to achieve self-actualization. And the theory would have to handle all these different viewpoints and levels of analysis in a series of simultaneous equations. I doubt it can be done. But perhaps we *can* build a verbal bridge that will allow us to go back and forth from one level or viewpoint to another. That's what I hope we can do at the Symposium—if I can get all of you to stop carping at each other and use unconditional positive regard instead."

Fraser seemed amused. "Your Bridge of Heavenly Peace will never get off the ground. Carping at each other is far too rewarding!"

"I agree," Joyce Sapir said, smiling. "In my own experience, the need to carp is a basic oral urge, and we all know that professors are uniformly fixated at the oral stage of development. Besides," she added in mock horror, "building a bridge between psycho-analysis and behaviorism would be as senseless as building a bridge across Lake Como, from Cadennabia to Bellagio. Why, it would ruin the view!"

"And put all those water taxis out of business!" Fraser said, turning to watch the little boat as it tossed about in the center of the lake.

"But you'd have fewer seasick passengers to worry about," Papas continued. "And the government could loan money to the boat owners to buy regular taxis instead. The increase in tourism between the two towns would more than justify the expense."

Joyce Sapir favored Jonathan Fraser with a smile. "I'd say that our Canadian colleague is as optimistic as Adler and the humanists. How would you say it, Jonathan?"

The British scientist smiled back. "Joyce, I'd simply say that hope springs eternal."

"In the heart of a fool," said Papas, lifting his glass in a toast. "To bridges!"

Recommended Readings

Abramson, Paul R. *Personality: A Heuristic Approach* (New York: Holt, Rinehart and Winston, 1980).

Dollard, J., and N.E. Miller. *Personality and Psychotherapy: An Analysis in Terms of Learning, Thinking and Culture* (New York: McGraw-Hill, 1950).

Hall, Calvin S., and Gardner Lindzey. *Theories of Personality*, 2d ed. (New York: Wiley, 1970).

Maddi, Salvatore R. *Personality Theories: A Comparative Analysis* (Homewood, Ill.: Dorsey Press, 1968).

Sheehy, Gail. *Passages: The Predictable Crises of Adult Life* (New York: E.F. Dutton, 1976).

Personality Tests

Did You Know That . . .

The Greek scientist Galen thought your personality was determined primarily by your heart, lungs, and liver?

Harvard psychologist W.H. Sheldon said your personality was determined primarily by the shape of your body?

Most US psychologists believe that your personality is primarily composed of your intra-psychic traits or mental processes?

The first real IQ test was developed by two French scientists who believed that your intelligence is determined almost entirely by your genetic blueprint?

IQ tests predict academic performance reasonably well, but don't do a very good job of predicting success in later life?

The best single predictor of a child's IQ at age three is how much time its mother spends talking to it when it is an infant?

Several psychologists have shown that you can sometimes raise your own IQ score by taking special training?

The "inkblot" test gives a great deal of information about your personality, but we have no reliable way of interpreting this information?

Although there are many personality tests on the market, none seems to be both valid and reliable?

"Measure for Measure"

"What is this 'Late Bloomer' test of yours, Mr. Flagg? I don't think I've ever heard of it," Jessie Williams said quietly, favoring the handsome young man with a distant stare. Tom Flagg had an athlete's physique, a handsome dark-brown face, and a ready smile. Jessie Williams, whose body was as soft and rounded as Tom Flagg's was hard and angular, had learned the hard way that she couldn't always tell the shape of a man's intentions from the shape of his physique. So she was wary of this young graduate student who had just walked into her fourth-grade school room. But Jessie Williams was also quite taken by his appearance.

"The 'Late Bloomer' test was devised by Professor Rosenthal at Harvard," Tom Flagg replied, hoping (for several reasons) to overcome the good-looking young black woman's obvious distrust. "You've been teaching fourth grade for several years, haven't you, Miss Williams?"

"Three years, Mr. Flagg. Exactly three years."

Tom grinned at the woman's precise way of expressing herself. "Well, maybe you've had a kid who seemed real dumb the first few months or so of school. Then, all of a sudden, the kid just took off and bloomed. Like a flower you'd forgotten to water until just then."

"I water all my flowers regularly, Mr. Flagg," Jessie replied. "I don't neglect any of them. Black or white, red or yellow—I hope they all bloom for me as much as they can."

Tom nodded appreciatively and smiled even more broadly at the pretty young teacher. If it wouldn't have prejudiced the results of his experiment, he would have tried to date her. Just looking at the soft outlines of her body greatly stimulated his admittedly non-academic desires. He pulled himself together and resumed the conversation. "Mr. Washington, your principal, told me you were one of the best teachers he's ever seen. So I'm sure you do get all your kids to show a lot of cognitive development while they're with you. But aren't you occasionally surprised when one of them does a lot better than you had expected?"

Jessie Williams shook her head. "I expect great things of them all. Maybe that's why I'm not surprised when they do well."

"Okay, said Tom, "I guess my test won't help you any. But maybe you can help me out by letting me give it to your class anyhow. If I don't get to try out the test in enough classrooms, I won't get a good grade on my project back at the university. Even if you don't need the information, I do."

To his surprise, Jessie smiled broadly. "Well, why didn't you say so, friend? I'm always happy to help one of us get ahead. Tell me about these 'Late Bloomers' of Professor Rosenthal's."

"Well, it's really your bloomers I'm interested in," Tom said, and then blushed furiously as he realized what he had said. "I mean, it's a test devised by Professor Rosenthal and his associates at Harvard. They think they've found a way of telling in advance when a school kid is going to show a sudden spurt in intellectual achievement—when the kid is going to get it all together psychologically and take off like a jet plane. The test can also tell when a kid is going to backslide or tread water for a while. You know, when the youngster fails to show much improvement at all for a period of several months. The change usually shows up in the kid's grades, although sometimes the IQ blossoms or backslides too."

"Some of our education books say that a child's intelligence is fixed by the time the child is six or seven. Don't you believe that's so, Tom?" Jessie asked, a malicious twinkle in her eye.

Tom looked startled. "Well, I suppose that the limits to a man's mind are determined at birth, but the rate at which people develop intellectually sure varies a lot. And the score you get on an IQ test depends as much on which test you take, who gives it, and how you feel when you take it as it does on how bright you really are. Have you even given any of your kids IQ tests?"

"No, Tom. I'm not qualified to do that. I give achievement tests, but the school counselor tests their intelligence."

"But aren't you sometimes surprised at the scores the counselor reports on your kids?"

Jessie Williams smiled slyly. "I just don't pay them any mind."

"What do you do when the parents want to know what the kid's IQ is?"

"I tell them the story of my life, Tom," she said. "I was born in Mississippi, where my father was a tenant farmer. We moved North when I was six. My first year in school they gave me a test and said my IQ was 87.

As you know, that's what you might call 'dull normal.' You just don't learn very much about the world on a tenant farm in the back woods of Mississippi. But I loved school, and I had good teachers, and when I was in the seventh grade, I took another test. This time I got a score of 98. The counselor couldn't understand the change. So he gave me a different test, and I scored 104. He asked me what I wanted to do, and I said go to college and learn how to teach. He told me to forget it, that I'd never make it."

"But you did," Tom said, smiling to reassure her.

"Yes, I did," she said, a strong tone of confidence in her voice. "In high school they gave me another test. This time I tried very hard to impress the woman giving me the test, and I got a score of 111."

"The 'halo effect,' probably," Tom responded. "Good-looking, eager children always score a little higher than uglies do because the tester gives them the benefit of the doubt. And I suspect you were very good looking indeed."

"You needn't flatter me, friend. I've already agreed to help you with your study. Anyway, the counselor said I might just get through college if I work very hard, although you're supposed to have an IQ of 120 to graduate."

"So you went to the university and got your degree anyhow?"

"No, Tom, it wasn't that easy. My high school grades were excellent but I didn't score too well on the college entrance examination. The university didn't want me. So I went to a community college for two years. I got all A's, and the university finally let me in. My last year there, I took another IQ test. This time I got a score of 122." She paused for a moment, then laughed. "But, of course, by then I knew the kinds of answers they wanted on the test."

Tom shook his head in amazement. His route to the university had been quite different. "And that's why you don't tell the parents what their kids' IQ scores are?"

"Right on. Now suppose you tell me what your study is all about."

"Okay," he said. "I'll give the Rosenthal 'Late Bloomer' test to all the kids in your room. Then, when I've scored the results, I'll tell you which kids are supposed to 'bloom,' and which kids are supposed to backslide. Then, six months from now, I'll come back and see if that's what really happened."

A suspicious look crept into Jessie's eyes. "Why are you doing this, Tom? Doesn't sound much like an experiment to me."

"Rosenthal validated the test mostly in white classrooms. I want to see if it predicts for integrated classes as well."

"And you'll come back in six months to see what happened?"

Tom Flagg squared his shoulders a bit. "Well, your class is so important to me, I might just drop around a little more often than that—just to see how things are going."

She favored him with a broad grin. "You do that, Thomas. You do that very thing."

(Continued on page 610.)

Analysis versus Integration

In an early chapter, we asked you to consider what may have seemed an odd question—*Where is your mind located?* Our purpose was to urge you to consider a very important problem, namely, where within your brain the

PART SIX Personality

essential YOU resides. As we discovered, bits and pieces of YOU are located everywhere within your central nervous system. That is, various parts of your conscious and unconscious experience are controlled or mediated by widely different neural centers.

Now, let us face an even more challenging issue: *Who are you?* In those first chapters we took primarily the neurological view—we assumed that YOU are a living system, but that you are composed of sub-systems that are in some sort of communication with each other. Sigmund Freud assumed much the same thing when, through psychological *analysis*, he divided the human personality into the id, ego, and super-ego. Carl Rogers may have had the same problem in mind when he wrote that the conscious self differentiates itself from the perceptual field and becomes relatively independent of it. Yet you do not experience yourself as "bits and pieces," held together by some kind of psychological glue. Probably you perceive yourself as being an *integrated* individual, much more than the sum of your psychological parts.

Here, then, is one of the basic problems faced by the personality theorist. You may function as a whole, intact person, but if we are to *measure* you, we are more likely to pay attention to your parts than to your integrated self. We will see why this is the case in just a moment.

But first, to return to our question—*Who are you?* If you were to make as objective and complete an *evaluation* of yourself as possible, what would you say? If you enjoy doing such things, you might take out a piece of paper and write down at least five of your strongest and most desirable features, and at least five points about yourself that could perhaps be changed or improved. Since many schools and business firms require you to do this sort of thing if you apply to them for admission or for a job, perhaps this "practice evaluation" can be of some value to you.

Psychological Traits

Now, what sorts of things did you say about yourself? Although, as you know by now, some psychologists prefer to describe the human personality in terms of *observable behaviors*, the chances are as good that you see yourself primarily in terms of your inner, subjective qualities. Are you sincere? Are you happy? lazy? intelligent? creative? religious? loving? jealous? shy? prejudiced? If you described yourself in these terms, you made use of what we often call *psychological traits*. That is, you probably perceive your outward behavior as being produced by, or influenced by, long-lasting mental states or conditions such as your intelligence, your motives, your emotions and values, and your general outlook on life. Like the majority of psychologists, you would have assumed that the human personality is best talked about (and measured) in terms of its structure, or its "bits and pieces."

Question: How might you describe yourself in overall or global terms, without mentioning any of your traits at all? Can it be done?

Similarities versus Differences

If you enjoy this sort of experience, let's go one step farther. Now that you have painted a verbal picture of yourself, what about others? You might pick a close friend or relative and list that person's five best traits, and her or his main faults. How do you stack up against this person? Do you have *similar* traits, or *different* ones? If both of you are sincere people, which of you is the more sincere?

Perhaps now you begin to see some of the joys and frustrations that face the psychologist interested in the structure of human personality. Each person is a unique, never-to-be duplicated living system, different from all others. And yet, if you can compare one person with another, it is obvious that these unique individuals have many points or traits in common. What kind of personality theory can we come up with that will allow us to describe *both* the similarities and the differences among people?

Hippocrates.

Hippocrates (hip-POCK-rat-tease). Often called "the father of medicine," Hippocrates lived about 400 years prior to the birth of Christ. Although the best-known physician of his time, and although he wrote the Hippocratic Oath that medical doctors still take when granted their degrees, he made surprisingly little impact on medical science until long after he died (Plato mentions him but twice, Aristotle but once).

Humors (YOU-mors). The Latin word *humor* means "moist, wet, liquid." Galen (GAY-lun) believed that your personality was determined by the fluids secreted by your body. When you were in "good humor," you had good fluids bubbling around inside you. The four important humors were blood, phlegm, black bile, and yellow bile.

Sanguine (SAN-gwin). From the Latin word *sanguis*, meaning "blood." Someone who hopes for the best, or is confidently optimistic, is a sanguine person.

Phlegm (FLEM). The Greek word *phlegma* means "flame" or "inflammation." Phlegm is the white mucous (MEW-cuss) that you cough up when you have a cold, or sometimes when you clear your throat.

Phlegmatic (fleg-MATT-tick). A watery, slow, unemotional person.

Choler (KAHL-urr). From the Greek word meaning "bile." One of the four humors. A choleric (KAHL-urr-ick) person is someone readily given to anger, or to losing her or his "good humor."

This question seems to have puzzled people for perhaps as long as there have been people. The Greek scholars Aristotle and Plato had their say before Christ was born, as did the famous Greek physician **Hippocrates.** Hippocrates hypothesized that our personalities are determined primarily by our body fluids, but his theory had little impact until it was refined and modified by Galen, one of the greatest medical doctors the world has known. Although Galen was born and educated in Greece a century or so after the death of Christ (and several hundred years after Hippocrates), Galen spent much of his adult life practicing medicine in Rome. His studies of the functioning of human and animal bodies were so excellent that he is considered the father of modern physiology.

Galen's Humor Theory

One of Galen's main interests was the various glands in the human body, and the chemicals these glands secreted. Like most other physicians 2,000 years ago, Galen called these glandular secretions the **humors** of the body. Borrowing a notion from Hippocrates, Galen stated that four of these humors were mainly responsible for human personality. As far as Galen was concerned, blood was a "humor." If a woman was most influenced by her blood, Galen called her a **sanguine** or "bloody" person. Sanguine people were supposed to be cheerful, hearty, outgoing, sturdy, fearless, optimistic, and most interested in physical pleasures.

The second humor that Galen mentioned was **phlegm,** the thick, white material that you sometimes cough up when you have a cold. From Galen's point of view, phelgm was cold, moist, and unmoving. If your bodily processes were dominated by too much production of phlegm, you became **phlegmatic**—cold, aloof, calm, detached, unemotional, uninvolved, quiet, withdrawn, dependable, and perhaps just a trifle dull.

Galen believed that the human liver produced two different "humors"—yellow bile and black bile. He called the yellow bile **choler,** because it supposedly caused the disease we now refer to as "cholera." The choler-ic personality was one easily given to anger, hate, and fits of temper—someone who gave in to most of his or her bad impulses.

Black bile was even worse, for it symbolized death in Galen's mind. If your personality was dominated by black bile, you were **melancholic**—that is, you were always depressed, unhappy, suicidal.

To Galen, your biochemistry determined your personality type—and all human beings had to fall within one of the four "humoral" categories we have just described. It is unclear from Galen's writings whether he thought you had to be entirely one type or the other, or whether you could be a mixture of the four. Assuming mixed personality types were allowed, Galen's scheme might be represented as shown in Fig. 23.1.

As "humorous" as Galen's theory may seem to you, it still lives on today. One of the dominant psychiatric beliefs about mental illness is that abnormal *behavior* is almost always caused by some abnormal *chemical imbalance.* Thus a great many psychiatrists today treat mental illness just as Galen tried to—by giving patients pills that will change their inner chemicals and hence presumably will "cure" their unusual thoughts and behaviors.

Question: What approach did Galen take to the "mind/body problem?"

Fig. 23.1. *Left,* Galen's personality traits; *right,* Galen's personality pyramid.

PART SIX   Personality

Body Types

The belief that people with certain types of *body structure* are predisposed to have specific *personality structures* is even older than Galen's time. For instance, in one of his most famous plays, William Shakespeare has Julius Caesar say, "Let me have men about that are fat; sleek-headed men and such as sleep o'nights. Yon Cassius has a lean and hungry look; He thinks too much; such men are dangerous." Only in recent days, however, has the "body type theory" gained much respectability. Although several European scientists puzzled over the matter a hundred or more years ago, it was the noted German psychiatrist Ernst Kretschmer whose theory became most famous.

Kretschmer's Morphological Theory

Kretschmer worked with mental patients at several hospitals in southern Germany in the first part of this century. He found he could place these patients in one of three categories according to their **morphology,** or the measurements of their arms, legs, and trunk:

1. The **pyknic** has short limbs and a roly-poly face, a broad and thick middle-section, and tends to gain weight in middle age. According to Kretschmer, pyknics tend toward wild fluctuations in mood, such as those found in the **manic–depressive syndrome.**

2. The **asthenic** has a narrow waist, long arms and legs, and usually is very thin. Kretschmer called asthenics introverted, retiring, shy, often cold and calculating, but sometimes rather dull and phlegmatic. He thought that asthenics tended toward **schizophrenia.**

3. The **athletic** has a "balanced" physique and the sort of muscular development often displayed by the men who appear in "muscle magazines" and the women who appear in *Playboy.* The athletic personality type was, according to Kretschmer, energetic, aggressive, and sanguine.

Kretschmer's theory was attacked on two major points. First, it is almost impossible to fit everyone in the world into the three categories or "body types" that Kretschmer described. Second, there are millions of people whose personalities simply don't fit their body types.

Sheldon's Theory of Body Types

Around 1940, Harvard scientist W.H. Sheldon offered his own theory, in its way a great improvement over Kretschmer's. Sheldon also believed there were three major *morphologies,* or body types:

Galen.

Melancholic (mell-ann-KOLL-ic). The Greek word *melan* means "black." Melanin (MELL-ann-inn) is the dark pigment in your skin that darkens when you get a suntan. Melan-choler is black bile. A melancholic individual is someone who is perpetually sad, unhappy, depressed.

Morphlogy (more-FOLL-oh-gee). The Greek word *morph* means "shape" or "form." Morphology is the study of biological forms, shapes, or body types. The word also means the structure or form of something, such as the human body.

Pyknic (PICK-nick). From the Greek word meaning "thick" or pressed together." One of Kretschmer's three body types. Someone "pressed together," or short and stocky.

Manic-depressive syndrome (SIN-drome). The set of symptoms or syndrome that includes wild swings of mood, from manic happiness to depressive sadness. See Chapter 24.

Asthenic (ass-THEN-ick). From the Greek word meaning "weak." Someone with a slender, thin, weak morphology.

Schizophrenia (SKITS-oh-FRENN-eeuh). A common form of mental disorder. See Chapter 24.

Athletic. From the Greek word meaning "someone who competes for a prize." In ancient Greece, men who competed in the Olympics or other sports contests tended to be big and strong. The more muscled the man's body, the more he competed. Hence, the more "athletic" he was.

Sheldon's three body types.

1. The **endomorphs,** who had soft, rounded bodies and big stomachs.
2. The **mesomorphs,** who had hard, square, bony bodies with over-developed muscles.
3. The **ectomorphs,** who had tall, thin bodies with over-developed heads.

If these names sound vaguely familiar, you might wish to turn back to Chapter 19 and read again the description of human development within the womb. As you may recall, shortly after a child is conceived, the growing mass of cells develops three distinct layers. The central layer, called the endoderm or "inner skin," develops into the digestive system and internal organs. The middle layer—the mesoderm or "middle skin"—turns into bone and muscles. The outer layer, or ectoderm, becomes the central nervous system.

According to Sheldon, your genetic blueprint usually causes one of these three layers to become predominant—that is, to develop more rapidly and fully than the other two layers, and thus:

1. If your endoderm becomes dominant, you develop a roly-poly body and fixate on food. You become very social, enjoy relaxing and lazing about, you talk a lot, and you prefer the "sweet life" of physical comfort.
2. If your mesoderm gains the upper hand during your fetal development, you will have a square, heavy, mesomorphic body. You will like sports, power, be energetic and assertive, courageous and sanguine.
3. If your ectoderm comes out on top, your brain will predominate and your body will develop long, thin legs and arms—and a big head. You will be introverted, inhibited, intellectual, and prefer being alone rather than being in a crowd.

To test his theory, Sheldon took detailed measurements of the photographs of 4,000 male college students. The pictures were taken "in the nude," a fact that upset many people when they discovered what Sheldon had done (remember—this was nearly 40 years ago).

Sheldon found that most of his subjects were not "pure" body types, however, but mixtures. So he devised 7-point scales for each of the three morphologies. You were supposed to have a numerical rating on each of the three scales. A "true" endomorph would rate 7–0–0, but if you were *mostly* an endomorph, with a touch of mesomorph and a trace of ectomorph, then you'd rate about 6–1–1. If you were mostly a mesomorph, you'd rate a 1–6–2, or perhaps a 2–6–2. If you were a tall, thin "brain," you'd rate a 1–1–6, or perhaps 2–1–6, and thus be highly ectomorphic.

Question: What numbers would you assign to your own body type?

Body Type and Personality Traits   Sheldon made up a large list of personality traits for each of his three body types. He then tested 200 university men to see if their personality traits and body types were *correlated* or associated with each other. Sheldon reported that sociability was highly correlated with endomorphism, as were 19 other traits. Extroversion was one of 20 traits correlated with mesomorphism, while restraint and passivity were 2 of the 20 traits that were found to a high degree in ectomorphs. Other investigators have found similar but less impressive correlations between behavior patterns and body structure, or type.

Criticisms of Typological Theories

Although Sheldon's findings were confirmed to some extent by other scientists, many questions have been raised about his research. To begin with, he did not really consider the age of his subjects, nor whether they had grown up in poverty or wealth. You may recall from Chapter 19 that Korean war orphans who were reared in the US were considerably larger and taller than their age-mates who remained behind in Korea in deprived

PART SIX Personality

A 4-6-1 (endomorphic mesomorph); a 5-2-1 (endomorphic mesomorph); and a 2-5-6 (ectomorphic mesomorph).

circumstances. (It's hard to be a fat, jolly endomorph if you've been starved all your life.)

Second, Sheldon never could offer any reasonable explanation of *why* or *how* your body type influenced your thoughts, feelings, and behaviors. About the most we can say is that body type (or fetal development) might affect the *type of reinforcers* that you would prefer. If your endoderm predominated, you might end up with well-developed taste and smell receptors. Thus you might enjoy food more than someone whose tastebuds were less sensitive than yours. Or if your mesoderm was dominant, you might find that feedback from muscular activities was more gratifying to you than it was to others, and you might then exercise more than they. And if your ectoderm came out on top, you might enjoy sensory inputs from your eyes and ears more than "muscular" people did.

Of course, as Sheldon himself noted, we are all mixtures rather than pure types, and even your preferred reinforcers are surely influenced by your past experiences and environmental demands. And there surely is no strong body of data which argues that your reinforcers are determined in the womb. However, many of the theoretical battles that personality theorists have engaged in do make a bit more sense if we assume there are three major types of reinforcing inputs, and that most of us prefer one type more than another in many situations. For this approach makes us focus as much on inputs (and outputs) as it does on internal "causes" of personality such as liver bile and body structure.

Question: What class of reinforcers do business people in general seem to value most highly or pursue most frequently? What about teachers? nurses? politicians? farmers? psychologists?

Mental (Intra-Psychic) Traits

What some personality theorists appear to want is a set of terms, or labels, that will describe fairly accurately people's intra-psychic activities. This set of descriptive categories about our mental processes must be neither too large to handle nor so small that it insults our feelings of individuality. Perhaps because Sheldon emphasized *physiological* variables, psychologists have generally rejected his approach and have focused instead on the concept of *mental traits.*

Technically speaking, a trait is a tendency or predisposition to respond to many different stimuli or situations in the same way. If you are kind to almost all of the different people you meet, then you possess the trait of kindness. If you are good at solving all kinds of different problems, and if you adapt rapidly to all types of intellectual challenges, then you possess the trait of intelligence.

Alfred Binet.

Fig. 23.2. Drawing of a diamond by a 5-year-old (*left*) and a 7-year-old.

If we wanted to get an exact measure of your kindness, we might dream up a test for this trait—a "kindness scale"—that had 100 questions on it. We could ask things like, "If you saw an injured puppy lying by the side of the road, would you pick it up and take it to the doctor's or just ignore it?" Or, "Do you prefer to pat a person on the back, or kick the person in the seat of the pants?" If the test were a good one—if it were really a **valid** measure of the trait—then people who were kind *in real life* would get high scores, while people who were unkind *in real life* would get low test scores. And if the test were valid, you would be able to *predict* a person's behavior in many situations just by knowing the person's score on the "kindness test."

Question: What numerical score should the average person get on a 100-point "kindness test?"

Intelligence Tests

Traits such as kindness can be fairly easily measured, provided we have a good working definition of the trait to begin with, and as long as we recognize that kindness might mean one thing in our culture, but something radically different elsewhere in the world.

But what about *intelligence?* How could we go about defining—and measuring—such a complex trait as this? Obviously, some of the people in the world are bright, and some are not so bright. Probably you make judgments of people's intelligence very day. But what kind of test, or scale, do you use?

The Binet-Simon IQ Test   One of the first psychologists to face this problem was a Frenchman named **Alfred Binet.** In about 1890, he became interested in the differences between bright and dull children and tried to devise a simple scale that allowed him quickly to distinguish the smart ones from the dumb ones. As we noted in Chapter 5, another French scientist named Paul Broca had theorized that *brain size* was related to intelligence, and (at first) Binet believed Broca was right. So Binet initially relied on physical measures—such as the size of the child's head or the pattern of lines on the palm of the child's hand. However, none of these scales correlated very highly with the child's performance in school, so Binet abandoned them.

In 1904 the French government asked Binet and a physician named **Théophile Simon** to devise a test that would allow teachers to identify "retarded" children so that they could be given special attention in school. Binet and Simon pulled together a large number of rather simple problems that seemed to require different mental skills—and then they tried the test problems out on a large number of French school children of different ages. This technique allows Binet and Simon to select appropriate test items for each age group. They found, for example, that the average seven-year-old could correctly make a pencil copy of the figure of a diamond, but most five-year-olds could not (see Fig. 23.2).

If a boy of 9 got the same score on the test as did the *average* seven-year-old, Binet and Simon presumed that the boy's mental development was retarded by two years. The boy would thus have a physical age of 9 but a **mental age** of 7. If an eight-year-old girl did as well on the test as the average eleven-year-old, then she had a mental age of eleven, although her physical age was but eight.

Later, at the suggestion of German psychologist Wilhelm Stern, the relationship between **chronological** (physical) **age** and mental age was put into an equation:

$$\frac{\text{Mental age}}{\text{Chronological age}} \times 100 = \text{Intelligence Quotient, or IQ}$$

A girl with a mental age of 6 and a chronological age of 6 would have an IQ of

PART SIX   Personality

$$\frac{6}{6} \times 100 = 1 \times 100 = 100 = IQ$$

By definition, she would be of average intelligence. A boy with a mental age of 7 and a chronological age of 9 would have an IQ of

$$\frac{7}{9} \times 100 = .777 \times 100 = 78 = IQ$$

A girl with a mental age of 11 and a chronological age of 8 would have an IQ of

$$\frac{11}{8} \times 100 = 1.375 \times 100 = 138 = IQ$$

A subject taking a modern IQ test.

The Binet–Simon test did so well at predicting the *academic performance* of school children that intelligence testing became a standard part of educational psychology.

The noted Stanford psychologist, L.M. Terman, made up his own version of the French scale, which he called the Stanford–Binet intelligence test. Other psychologists soon followed Terman's lead, and now there are hundreds of IQ tests available. Properly used, they can give you useful information about your own mental abilities—or those of other people. Unfortunately, as we will see presently, there are a great many problems associated with the use of these tests—problems that perhaps the average person does not appreciate. To understand both the successes and failures of IQ tests, we must look more closely at the trait of intelligence itself.

Normal Distributions

Binet and Simon were greatly influenced by Darwin's theory of evolution. Darwin had suggested that intelligence is *inherited* in much the same way as are eye color, skin color, height, and other physical characteristics. If a man and woman of average height (for their culture) could have 100 male children—so Darwin assumed—most of them would also be of average height. A few would be very tall, a few very short—but most of the boys would be about as tall as their father. If the couple had 100 girls instead of boys, the girls would show the same *distribution of heights*—and would average out much like their mother. If we made a graph of the height of the boys, it presumably would look something like the one in Fig. 23.3.

If you measured the heights of all the men in the world, they would indeed create a graph with a shape pretty much like the one shown above. In technical terms, this is called a **normal distribution** of test scores, or a **bell-shaped curve.** Many school teachers believe that the scores that

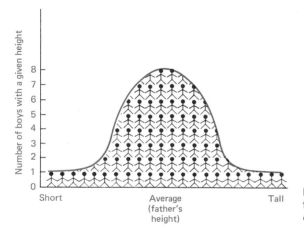

Fig. 23.3. Bell curve showing the height of 100 boys from one family.

Chronological age (kron-oh-LODGE-uh-cull). Chronos (KRO-nos) was the Greek god of time. Your chronological age is the actual number of years that you have lived. Binet and Simon believed that your IQ was your mental age divided by your chronological age times 100.

Normal distribution. A set of test scores that are distributed along a more-or-less bell-shaped curve. Most of the scores are bunched up in the "bell" in the middle, but a few of the scores trail off at either end of the curve.

Bell-shaped curve. The curve or graph of a normal distribution. See Fig. 23.3.

students make on a history or mathematics examination should "fit the curve," or be "normally distributed." A few students should get A's, a few should get F's, while most should get C's. The teachers then *write examinations that will give them the results they expect.*

Most intelligence tests are based on this same assumption of normal distribution of scores. Binet and Simon juggled their items around until their test yielded a bell-shaped distribution of IQs for each age level. If intelligence were in fact a single trait (like height), and if IQ were *entirely determined by your genetic blueprint,* then such a procedure might be justified. But are these assumptions really valid?

Is IQ a Single Trait?   The results of many psychological studies suggest that intelligence is not a single trait. Rather it is made up of a great many related talents or abilities. Psychologists don't entirely agree about what these "related" talents are, but they often mention such things as the ability to memorize words and numbers, to learn motor tasks, to solve verbal and numerical problems, to evaluate complex situations, to be creative, to perceive spatial relationships of various kinds, and so forth. If intelligence is really a mixture of many different traits, then there is no reason to expect that IQ's should fit a bell-shaped curve—any more than there is firm justification for assuming that math exam scores should *necessarily* be normally distributed on the same type of curve.

More than this, we must face up to the fact that all traits are expressed as an *interaction* between genes and environment. A young boy born to very tall parents might be expected to grow up to be at least as tall as his father. But if the boy is severely starved during most of his early years, he may wind up considerably shorter than we might have expected. And a child may inherit the genetic potential for high intelligence (whatever that turns out to be), but if the child grows up in a socially or intellectually-deprived environment, the young person will surely perform at less than full intellectual capacity.

Test Reliability and Test Validity   When a psychologist makes up a "trait scale" of any kind, the psychologist usually has to prove two things to other scientists before *they* will accept the scale and use it themselves. First, the creator of the test must show that it is **reliable.** Second, the psychologist must provide evidence that the test is also valid.

A *reliable* friend is one you can depend on, no matter how often you call for help or in what circumstances. A reliable psychological scale is one that yields the same results again and again. A yardstick is reliable because it will give you almost precisely the same measurements over and over again.

A *valid* test is one that measures what it says it measures—and measures little or nothing else besides. A yardstick is a valid measure of length because length is defined by tools such as yardsticks. And yardsticks don't pretend to measure weight or temperature very well.

Unfortunately, very few psychological scales—*including all tests* of *human personality*—have either the reliability or the validity that a yardstick does. If we look at this matter in detail, perhaps you will come to understand better why many psychologists would be reluctant to tell you what score you got on an IQ test—or how you performed on a given personality test.

IQ and Early Deprivation   As we noted earlier, children who are reared in deprived environments often show remarkable improvements in their IQ scores if they are later given the proper intellectual stimulation. One of the first psychologists to make this point was H.M. Skeels. In the 1930's, Skeels shocked many of his colleagues by reporting that he had been able to increase the IQ scores of retarded children by putting them in an unusual environment. Skeels took the children out of a dreary orphanage and gave them to a group of retarded women to rear. The first children he studied were two little girls, whose IQ scores rose from below 50 to near normal (*see* the "story" that opens Chapter 21).

Skeels then shifted a dozen more orphans to the home for retarded

Reliable. That which is repeatable, dependable.

adults. Their pre-shift IQ's ranged from 35 to 89, with an average of about 65. Several of the children were classified as **imbeciles.**

Another dozen or so children who remained in the orphanage served as "controls." These children had IQ's ranging from 50 to 103, with an average of about 87. As you can see, the orphanage "controls" were, on the average, more than 20 IQ points *brighter* than the children shifted to the "home."

Both groups of children were tested at regular intervals for some time. All of the dozen orphans moved to the "home" showed an *increase* in intelligence, ranging from 7 to 58 points. Their average increase was 28 points. In contrast, all but one of the "controls" who remained in the dreary orphanage showed a *decrease* in intelligence, ranging from minus 8 to minus 45 IQ points. The average decrease in the control-group children was close to 30 IQ points.

Skeels made a follow-up study of all the children in both groups some 30 years after he first saw them. The children sent to live with the "retarded" women had all left state care early in their lives, their average length of institutionalization being about five years. Almost all of them had gone through high school, had jobs, and were married. *All* of their children had normal or above-average IQ scores.

By comparison, the average length of stay in state institutions for the orphanage "controls" was 22 years, and many of them were still in hospitals of one kind or another. They averaged but three years of schooling, only two had married, and most were barely surviving on their own or were recipients of some kind of state support or charity.

The Minnesota Study Although Skeels' experiment was begun more than 40 years ago, many more recent studies confirm his findings. For example, Sandra Scarr and Richard A. Weinberg studied several hundred children in Minnesota who were placed in foster homes. Some of the foster parents were black, but many were white. Most of them were college graduates with professional jobs or responsibilities. Scarr and Weinberg estimate that, judging from the adopted children's genetic backgrounds, they might have been expected to end up with IQ's well below the national average. Instead, they scored well above average and very close to youngsters brought up in natural homes similar to the ones the orphans were adopted into.

Scarr and Weinberg also report that the younger the child was when adopted, the higher its later IQ score tended to be. Generally speaking, black children adopted into middle-class white homes had about the same IQ's as did white children.

If nothing else, the Minnesota study suggests that orphans placed with concerned, well-educated foster parents do even better than they might have done if reared by their own parents.

Question: The obvious "control group" for this study would be white orphans reared in black foster homes. Why do you think Scarr-Salapatek were not able to find enough such children to make a meaningful comparison?

Dumber by the Dozen? But what is it about an "enriched" environment that has such a marked effect on IQ scores? Perhaps part of the explanation comes from a study by Lillian Belmont and Francis A. Marolla, who examined birth order and intelligence scores for almost 400,000 19-year-old Dutch males. Since their subjects included almost all the men born in Holland between 1944 and 1947, the "group" can be considered fairly representative of Dutch society in general.

Belmont and Marolla found that the more children there were in the family, the lower their average IQ was. More than this, the first-born children had a clear-cut advantage over the children born into the family later on. These findings were true no matter how wealthy the family. It happens that, generally speaking, boys from rich families scored higher than did boys from middle-class homes, and middle-class boys had higher IQ scores than did boys from poor families. However, taking any one class

Imbeciles (IM-be-sills, or IM-buh-sills). In old-fashioned psychological terms, a person with an IQ from 20 to 50. Morons were said to have IQ's from 50 to 70, while idiots were said to have IQ's below 20. A century or two ago, all these mentally retarded people were thought to be possessed of demons or devils, or to be "fools" or "God's children." More recently, as we have learned of the powerful effects the environment has on mental functioning, psychologists have not used terms such as "moron," "imbecile," "idiot," "fool," or "God's child" as frequently as once we did. Individuals considered mentally retarded in a given society are certainly different from the average person in that society. We are not yet sure what all the differences are, why they come about, or how to overcome them.

Sandra Scarr.

Robert Zajonc.

of family into consideration, children from small families scored significantly higher than did children from large families.

The highest IQ scores of all were obtained by the first-born child in families of just two children. By far the lowest average scores came from the last-born child in families of 9 children. The difference between these two extremes was more than 10 IQ points. (When you are dealing with 400,000 subjects, a difference of 10 or more IQ points is quite meaningful.)

Michigan psychologist Robert Zajonc (his name rhymes with "science") explains the Belmont and Marolla data as follows: Children grow up in quite different intellectual environments, depending on their birth order. The first child is born into a predominantly adult world, for it has mostly its two parents with whom to talk and who serve as its models. The second child is born into what Zajonc calls a "diluted" intellectual environment, for it not only has two parents but also one slightly older **sibling** from whom it can learn. Since the younger child spends much of its time with the first-born, and since this older sibling does not have the mental maturity of the parents, the second-born doesn't receive the same intellectual stimulation that the first-born did. The third-born has an even more "diluted" environment. And by the time the fifth-born comes along, it is reared primarily by siblings, not by adults.

Question: In poverty-stricken areas, families tend to be larger than the national average, there are more one-parent families, and the children are often born in fairly rapid succession. How might all these facts help explain why children from impoverished backgrounds generally have below-average IQ scores?

Can You Raise Your Own IQ?   Many IQ tests place rather heavy emphasis on *reasoning,* or the ability to work your way through a complicated mental task step-by-step. The makers of most IQ tests believe, as did Piaget, that the ability to handle such intellectual problems is genetically determined. And surely it is true that people who obtain high scores on most IQ tests often breeze through complex problems with little difficulty and—if you ask them to do so—can usually tell you the precise steps they went through "in their heads."

But what about people who score below average on IQ tests? Do they lack some innate talent for reasoning, or have they never bothered to learn the tricks of the IQ trade? Benjamin Bloom and Lois Broder at the University of Chicago did an interesting study of how college students with either low or high IQ scores react to mental challenges. Bloom and Broder gave these subjects various sorts of problems to work on and asked the students to "talk out loud" as they proceeded. High IQ subjects tended to read the instructions carefully, then diligently eliminated all the incorrect answers. The low IQ students often lacked the patience to isolate the correct answers when they faced questions that required formal reasoning. Unlike their high-IQ peers, the low-scoring students didn't seem to carry on an internal

Sibling (SIBB-ling). A fancy term for "brother or sister." If you have three sisters and two brothers, you have five siblings.

The more stimulating the child's early environment, the higher the child's adult IQ will be.

conversation with themselves (such as the "dialogue of the hemispheres" we discussed in Chapter 5). Nor did the low-scorers proceed through a step-by-step sequence of deductions. If they couldn't see the answer immediately, they felt lost and usually guessed.

The low-scoring students also seemed mentally careless and passive in their approach to problem-solving. They often selected their answers on the basis of hunches or gut feelings, and they frequently rushed through the instructions to a test or skipped them entirely. If forced to reread the instructions, the low-scorers often came to understand what was required and then could answer the question correctly. However, they tended to place little value on reasoning, preferring to act quickly instead.

(Confirmation of these findings comes from a study by Carl Bereiter and Siegfried Engelmann, who discovered that many low-IQ children believe it is better to answer a question *immediately*—even if the answer is wrong— than to give the question a certain amount of consideration before responding.)

Bloom and Broder were convinced by their study that the low-scoring students had somehow never acquired the proper mental habits. So Bloom and Broder next developed a training program aimed at helping these young people "learn how to think." The students were asked to solve various problems aloud. After they had discussed the student's solution with the student, the experimenters read the correct solution aloud. Then they asked the student to explain what had gone wrong if the student had been incorrect. The students had many difficulties at first, and the instructors had to show tremendous patience. But once the students began to recognize that they actually could learn how to reason, they did so with increasing frequency. Although Bloom and Broder did not retest the students' IQ scores after this training, the psychologists report that most of their subjects got much higher grades in college thereafter.

In discussing his own highly successful attempts to help people raise their IQ scores, California psychologist Arthur Whimbey points out that learning how to reason requires immediate positive feedback and much practice. If you wish to try to improve your own test performance, Whimbey said, you should work with a trained tutor, use old tests and puzzle books as practice tools, and you should always read questions carefully without jumping to conclusions. You should think "out loud" as you work, listen to what you say, and try to figure out how you got the incorrect answer if you are wrong. Whimbey notes that following these techniques won't turn you into a genius overnight, but he reports that many of the people he has worked with have increased their IQ scores by 20 or 30 points.

Question: If a six-year-old girl wanted to "learn how to reason," would she do better if taught by an adult or by her seven-year-old sister?

Are IQ Tests Reliable?   If intelligence were *absolutely fixed* at birth, psychologists would probably have little trouble making up IQ tests that were highly reliable. But since intelligence is obviously determined by a mixture of genetic and environmental factors, almost everyone performs better when given adequate stimulation. In the US, children reared in rural areas *on the average* get IQ scores that are about 15 points lower than do children reared in cities and suburbs. Does this fact mean that rural children are innately (genetically) inferior to city kids? Not necessarily, because children born in the country who move to the city when still young often show the same dramatic increase in IQ scores that Skeels found in the orphans who moved to a more stimulating environment. Young children who move out of ghetto or slum areas to suburban situations show the same upward change in their tested intelligence—and this fact is as true of white children as of blacks, Spanish–Americans, Orientals, or Indians.

Perhaps by now you have sensed what the basic problem of the reliability of test scores is all about. Traits, or "genetic pre-dispositions," are *subjective* states or conditions. That is, they lie within you. But IQ tests are *behavioral*—they measure performance, not your inner condition. Your score on an IQ test reflects not only your innate intellectual capacity but also your past experience and your present motivational state. If you grew up in a deprived environment, or as the last child in a large family, you probably will not score as high as you would had your background been more stimulating. And surely you have almost flunked an exam or two because, the day of the quiz, you had a headache, a toothache, or you were so worried about things that you "clutched." But had you taken the test a day or so later, you might have gotten the A that you deserved.

Question: Could any IQ test strongly influenced by a person's motivational or emotional state be considered a reliable measure of intelligence?

Are IQ Tests Valid? The problem of intelligence test validity is equally thorny. It is hard to devise a psychological scale if you are not entirely sure what it is that the scale ought to be measuring. Since there is no universal agreement as to what abilities or talents actually make up the trait of intelligence, we can't be sure how to prove that any given IQ test is a *valid* measure of that trait. Psychologists, such as Simon and Binet, usually solve this problem by offering their own *carefully limited* definition of what they think the trait really is, and then show that their particular test is valid within those limits.

Binet and Simon assumed that "intelligence" was whatever mental properties were needed to succeed in French schools. Children who scored high on their tests generally got good grades, while students who scored low got much poorer grades. The correlation between IQ scores and exam grades *validated* the IQ test, as far as Binet and Simon were concerned. And within the limits of their definition, they were right.

IQ tests of various kinds still predict school grades well, and (under most circumstances) are very useful for this purpose. They also give us reasonably accurate predictions of "on the job performance" in many tasks, and are useful **diagnostic tools** in the hands of skilled **clinicians.** However, intelligence tests do *not* predict academic performance very well when low-scorers are given the kind of "special training" developed by Bloom and Bruder or by Whimby.

Cultural Bias Built into most IQ tests is a *cultural bias* that we are not always aware of. Binet and Simon, for example, took many of their basic ideas on intelligence from Paul Broca, who believed that the size of your brain determined the amount of your intelligence. As we noted in Chapter 5, Broca performed some very inexact measurements on brain size and "proved" that men were brighter than women and that whites were smarter than blacks.

Most modern-day psychologists reject Broca's assumptions about male–female differences—as, indeed, did Binet and Simon. Thus most IQ scales are *deliberately* constructed of items that both men and women score equally well on. However, as we will show in a later chapter, there are very real differences between the intellectual performances of men and women in our culture. Men tend to be superior to women in *right hemisphere tasks* such as mathematics and spatial perception, while women tend to be superior to men in *left hemisphere tasks* that involve the use of words or purely verbal problem-solving.

Because most scientists who construct intelligence tests *assume* that these male–female differences should "average out," the test-makers tend to reject items that strongly favor one sex or the other. The test-constructors thus unwittingly have rejected items that measure abilities mediated primarily by your left hemisphere or by your right hemisphere. By assuming that intelligence is *necessarily the same* in men and women, the test-makers have surely told us less about *differences* in intellectual skills than we probably ought to know.

Diagnostic tools (die-ag-NOS-tick). Any test or measure that lets you know what might be wrong with someone's mental or physical functioning is called a diagnostic tool. One purpose of giving people mental tests is to figure out what problems they have, so that you can help them get better. See Chapter 24 for a description of DSM-III, which is the newest diagnostic tool used by psychiatrists.

Clinicians (klin-ISH-shuns). Psychologists who work directly with mental patients, or with individuals who seek help, are often called "clinicians," presumably because most of these psychologists practice their profession in a clinic or office. Clinicians are typically *applied* psychologists in that they apply the knowledge that the "experimentalists" discover in the laboratory.

Racial Differences While most modern psychologists reject Broca's notions about the superior mental abilities of males, until recently many scientists did agree that blacks (in the US) might well have genetic blueprints that were somehow "inferior" to whites. As Robert V. Guthrie points out in his 1976 book *Even the Rat Was White*, this belief was based on three points. First, many scientists believe (even today) that intelligence is a trait which is *primarily* determined by whatever genes you inherit from your parents, and that no one can really "overcome bad genes." Second, until recently, psychologists studying blacks tended to focus on *differences* between blacks and whites—and particularly those **attributes** in which whites were clearly superior to blacks. Third, until very recently, blacks (as a group) have consistently scored "below the white norm" on many types of intelligence tests—particularly those designed by middle-class whites. Taken together, these points tended to confirm the preconceived notions many white scientists had about the inferiority of blacks.

Robert V. Guthrie.

However, as we have noted many times, all behaviors (and mental abilities) are determined by the *interactions* among your genes, your past experiences, and your present environment. Comparing blacks with whites (or any other group of people) is valid *only when the groups have similar past experiences and present social environments*. White (or black) children brought up in deprived circumstances uniformly score more poorly on intelligence tests than do either black or white children brought up in stimulating environments.

Most intelligence tests—and hence most racial comparisons—are *culturally biased* because they simply do not take into account the past experiences of the people taking the test. Black children—in the US as in most other places in the world—still do not (as a group) enjoy the cultural advantages experienced by the average white child. Thus IQ tests, as presently written, probably tend to *under-estimate* the innate intelligence of blacks (and all other socially deprived groups, including many whites).

The Milwaukee Study As an example of how strong an effect early deprivation can have on IQ scores—and how one can sometimes overcome it with special training—consider the research of Rick Heber and his colleagues at the University of Wisconsin. In 1967, Heber and his associates selected for study 40 infants who were born to black parents living in one of the worst sections of Milwaukee. Although many parts of Milwaukee are delightful places in which to live, blacks in this particular section of town have the lowest average family income and education level found in the entire city. They also have the highest rate of unemployment and the highest population density. Although less than 3 percent of the city's people live in this area, it accounts for about 33 percent of the total number of children classified as "educable mentally retarded." The mothers of the 40 infants in this Milwaukee Project all had IQ scores below 75 and, in many cases, the fathers were absent from the home.

Of these 40 infants, 20 were randomly selected to be in what Heber considered the "experimental" group, while the other 20 were placed in an untreated "control" group. The families of the experimental-group infants were given intensive vocational help and training in homemaking and child-care skills as soon as the children were born. When these "experimental" infants were 30 months old, they were put into a special education center for 35 hours a week. The training at this center focused on the development of language and cognitive skills. The experimental-group children remained in this center year-round until they were six years old and could enter school. The families and children in the control group received none of these benefits.

The children in both groups were given IQ tests frequently. In the summer of 1976, when the youngsters were all about nine years old, the children in the experimental group had IQ scores that averaged about 110, while the children in the control group averaged below 80 on the tests. During the nine-year period when they were tested, the groups' differences were never less than 20 IQ points and frequently were as high as 30 points. Dr. Heber believes that this superiority was due to the special training

Attributes. From the Latin word meaning "to bestow, or give to." When you quote from someone, you are "attributing" the quotation to that person. When you assume that a person is mean to you because that person is innately nasty, you are "attributing" the quality (or attribute) of meanness to that individual's personality.

David C. McClelland.

which the children in the experimental group (and their families) were given—most of which was aimed at teaching them the same sorts of intra-psychic skills that middle-class, white children typically acquire as part of their normal upbringing.

Question: Research reported at the International Conference on Infant Studies in 1978 suggests that the extent to which a mother touches and talks with her baby is the single best predictor of what the child's IQ score will be at age three. Would you expect ghetto mothers—no matter what their skin colors—to be as likely to touch and talk to their children as would middle-class, suburban mothers? Why?

IQ Tests and Real-life Performance   In the January 1973 issue of the *American Psychologist*, Harvard psychologist David McClelland notes that IQ tests are often reliable indicators of how a child will do in the future— but only within the classroom. IQ tests, McClelland feels, tap those traits that are necessary for success in academic situations, but these abilities may have little or nothing to do with success in the non-academic world.

In short, as McClelland notes, your IQ predicts what grades you will get (for instance) as a student in the Harvard Medical School, but not necessarily how good a doctor you will be once you get your medical degree. To pass med-school exams, you need a large vocabulary, you need the ability to memorize a great many facts, and you must have considerable respect for authority. But to succeed as a praticing physician, you must get along well with people and speak *their* language (rather than "book language"), you must be able to solve real-life rather than mathematical problems, and you should have considerable respect for life itself. In a paper published in 1976, McClelland suggests that we abandon "intelligence tests" and create instead scales that will measure those *specific competencies* that people need to thrive and survive in the current world.

In 1976, Duke psychologist Michael Wallach pointed out that most academic tests tell us very little about the *innate potential* of students who take those tests. Wallach does believe that achievement or IQ tests might be of help in screening out students who score at the very bottom end of the test scales. But there apparently is very little evidence that these tests tell us much about how students will perform after they have left school.

For example, in 1963, L.R. Harmon investigated the professional contributions of physicists and biologists who had taken advanced degrees. Three or more expert judges, working independently, evaluated these scientists in terms of their research, their publications, and the number of patents granted to them. Harmon then compared the actual "life's work" of the scientists with achievement test scores the scientists had gotten while still students. Harmon reports that there simply was no connection at all between test scores and actual (later) achievement.

In a later survey, Wallach and C.W. Wing investigated the Scholastic Aptitude Test (SAT) scores of 500 undergraduates and compared these scores with achievement outside the classroom. Students who received low SAT scores tended to achieve *just as much* as did high scorers. The problem, Wallach suggests, is that most tests simply don't measure the intellectual and other qualities (traits) that lead to creativity and success outside the classroom. Wallach concludes his 1976 article by stating that, "Testing agencies should perhaps devote less effort to tests and more to helping educators assess achievement in activities that we value."

In a 1977 paper, psychologist Leona E. Tyler discusses most of the recent controversy surrounding the definition and measurement of intelligence. She draws three interesting conclusions:

1. The trait measured by IQ tests is not "intelligence" at all.

2. We cannot presently determine what aspects of intelligence are affected primarily by our genetic blueprints, and which aspects are affected primarily by factors such as the environment. Therefore, comparisons of the IQ's of different races tell us nothing at all about such matters as racial superiority or inferiority.

3. Scientists who study such sensitive problems as racial differences have a special responsibility—to take into consideration the social consequences of their research.

Question: Why might a poorly designed experiment on the learning abilities of black rats have less damaging social consequences than a poorly designed experiment on the learning abilities of black school children?

Allport's Theory of Traits

For the most part, psychologists interested in the measurement of personality traits have looked to a person's past to get glimpses of that person's future. Traits—the tendency to react to many different stimuli with the same sorts of responses—were presumed to result from your genetic inheritance, your past experiences, or perhaps interactions between the two. But once you had acquired the trait, there was presumably little you could do about changing it. Traits were thought to be the basic, stable skeletons that gave shape or structure to your psychological flesh. And how many times a year do you change your skeleton?

Individual and Common Traits

One of the first scientists to recognize that the most important human traits might be those that look to the future rather than to the past was Harvard psychologist Gordon Allport. Like many other humanistic psychologists, Allport saw people as being motivated primarily by the desire to become—that is, to change and grow. Allport believed that conscious desires control behavior more than do unconscious wishes or instincts, and that your values, hopes, goals, and aspirations were more reliable predictors of future experiences than were such skills as word memory or mathematical reasoning. For Allport, the important traits were those that *motivated* a person, as well as providing structure to the individual's personality.

Allport identified several classes of traits. To begin with, he pointed out the difference between **individual** and **common traits.** No two people are exactly alike, therefore all traits are individual or unique. But because all human beings have similar genetic heritages, and because our cultures are all fairly similar, our behavior patterns are roughly or approximately comparable. All blonds are different, for example, because they are different individuals. But they do all have light-colored hair, and we can talk about "blondness" as long as we remember that their differences are as important as their similarities.

Within a given individual there are **cardinal, central,** and **secondary traits.** A person driven by just one goal in life—perhaps to make a million dollars—displays a *cardinal* trait. More common are *central* traits—those few, important values or interest patterns that seem to color almost everything we do and that your friends recognize in you with no difficulty. Allport believed that most people have between two and ten such traits. For example, the noted science-fiction writer, H.G. Wells, once said that there were but two major themes (central traits) to his life—his interest in promoting world government, and his preoccupation with sex.

Cardinal and central traits determine your major motives in life, and thus indicate the sort of person you will become. *Secondary* traits are those incidental, learned responses that differ markedly from one person to another—such as a preference for Chinese food, or a strong dislike of crowds.

Allport's Six Values

Allport was interested in the normal personality, not in mental illness or **psychopathology.** Although he emphasized the uniqueness of the individual, Allport identified six central traits or values that seemed to be common among the people of our time and place. Although Allport believed that

Leona E. Tyler.

Individual traits; common traits. Gordon Allport (ALL-port) points out that each person has a unique set of attitudes, tendencies, and behaviors that he calls "individual traits." The love your mother had for you when you were a child was expressed in her own individual way. Hence, her "love" was an individual trait. But most mothers love their children, hence maternal love is a trait common to most mothers.

Cardinal, central, secondary traits (CAR-dih-null). According to Allport, a cardinal trait is displayed by a person who has but one over-riding goal in life. Central traits are the half-dozen or so highly important goals or values that most people seem to have in life. Secondary traits are those minor or occasional values that are displayed in very specific situations.

Psychopathology (SIGH-ko-path-OLL-oh-gee). From the Greek words meaning "mind" and "disease." Psychopathology is any form of mental illness or unusual emotional disturbance.

Gordon Allport.

What would you say is Ralph Nader's central trait or value?

some portion of all six values was present in everyone's personality, he felt that one trait often was dominant and hence colored or influenced the other five. Working with P.E. Vernon and Gardner Lindzey, Allport developed a questionnaire that attempted to describe and measure six basic personality types:

1. *Theoretical.* Someone who seeks objective truth, who is rational and critical, systematic, and who cares more about theory than about applying knowledge.

2. *Economic.* The typical business man or woman interested in matters practical and useful, in markets and manufacturing and money.

3. *Esthetic.* The artistic type who loves form and harmony and beauty, who enjoys sensory impressions for their own sake without asking about practical matters.

4. *Social.* People who need people, who value helping others more than they value money or abstractions.

5. *Political.* The manipulator, interested in power and influence and fame in politics or in any other profession.

6. *Religious.* Someone, like Jung's "mature individual," who looks for truth within, who wishes to bring unity to all of his or her experiences.

Question: How would you describe yourself in terms of Allport's six types?

Trait Profiles

Profile (PRO-file). From the Latin word meaning "to draw in outline." Your own profile is your face as seen from a side view, or a drawing of your face from a side position. The profile of a mountain range is a side view of the tops of the mountains. A psychological profile is a graph or line connecting the "peaks" or top scores on a set of tests.

Unlike many other pen-and-paper questionnaires, the Allport–Vernon–Lindzey test gives the subject a number of alternatives in answering the test items. On the basis of the subject's scores, a psychologist can draw a **profile** of the strength of the subject's interests in each of the six categories listed above (see Fig. 23.4). Men and women are scored differently on the test, and there are ways of adjusting the scores depending on the subject's socio-economic background. In general, women rate higher on esthetic, social, and religious values, while men rate higher on theoretical, economic, and political interests.

The Allport–Vernon–Lindzey test has been criticized on several grounds, including the fact that it includes no negative, anti-social, or selfish values. But Allport was interested in assisting normal people to achieve self-actualization, in helping them become better than they presently were. Very few of us will admit that our life's ambition is to become more jealous, more self-centered, more destructive and evil.

Objective versus Subjective Tests

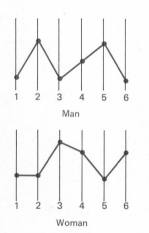

Fig. 23.4. Two of Allport's profiles.

How would you go about creating a personality test? You could go about the task in two quite different ways. First, you might *theorize* about how people differed and then construct a scale based on your theoretical insights. Or you might measure people in a variety of ways, determine how people actually did differ on these scales, and then build a theory of personality based on the differences you found on this limited set of measuring tools.

Allport theorized that there were six basic personality types and then devised a psychological yardstick to measure what he assumed was true. If the theory underlying the test is a valid view of human nature, then the test itself may have high validity.

But what would you do if you weren't sure how to define a given trait? Then you might do what Binet and Simon did, and give a large number of test items to thousands of subjects and analyze your results as carefully as possible. Perhaps most nine-year-olds will know the answer to a certain question, while most eight-year-olds won't. A test of this kind might have high reliability, in that nine-year-olds might *consistently* score better on a

PART SIX Personality

given item than would the average eight-year-old. If you assumed that this reliable difference between ages was due to "mental maturity," you would have developed a workable definition of "intelligence."

Or perhaps most patients in a mental hospital will respond one way to a given set of items, while most people outside the hospital (and hence presumably sane) will respond in a different way. You might then assume that "mental illness" had to be whatever your test measured, and thus anyone who answered your questions the same way that mental patients did probably was showing symptoms of mental disturbance.

As we will see, there are dangers and difficulties associated with both ways of constructing personality scales.

Projective Tests

Suppose you believed strongly in the psycho-analytic theory of personality, and you wanted to devise a means of getting at the *dynamic* aspects of a person's inner or subjective life. You could hardly ask the person about such matters directly, using a pen-and-paper test, because the most important dynamics are often unconscious and thus the person wouldn't express them openly. But what would happen if you presented the subject with a variety of unstructured or **ambiguous** situations? Wouldn't you expect people to *project* themselves into the task given them? That is, shouldn't people structure ambiguous stimuli according to the structures of their own basic personalities? If they did, then you could easily interpet their responses to these **projective tests** according to psycho-analytic (or any other) principles.

Question: What similarities do you see between the psycho-analytic concept of personality projection and that of the introjection of the values of others during adolescence to form the ego-ideal?

Word Association Test   The first of these "projective" instruments was the *word association test* devised by British psychologist Sir Francis Galton more than 100 years ago. It was subsequently revised by Carl Jung for psycho-analytic use in the early 1900's. The test consists of a list of highly emotional stimulus words that are presented to you one at a time. You are asked to respond to each word with the first thing that comes to mind. Both Galton and Jung assumed that if you reacted to a word like "sex" by blocking (refusing to answer)—or if you started sweating, or fainted, or gave a wildly inappropriate reaction such as "firecrackers" or "death"—then you might have sexual problems that a therapist ought to look into. Sometimes the tester will use a polygraph, or lie detector, to check your physiological reactions as you respond to the words (see Chapter 15).

The TAT   The **Thematic Apperception Test,** or TAT, was developed by Henry Murray, a US biochemist who became a psychologist through Carl Jung's influence. The TAT consists of a set of 20 stimulus pictures that depict rather vague but potentially emotional situations (see Fig. 23.5). You respond by making up a story telling: (a) what led up to the situation shown in the picture; (b) what the people are thinking and feeling and doing right then; and (c) what will happen to them in the future. Each story you produce is scored and interpreted individually. The psychologist giving the test usually assumes that you will express your deep-seated needs and personality problems by projecting them onto the hero or the heroine in the story.

Inkblot Tests   By far the most famous of the projective instruments is the inkblot test, first devised in the 1920's by Swiss psychiatrist **Hermann Rorschach** (see Fig. 23.6). The Rorschach—as it is usually called—is a series of ten colorful inkblots that are given to you one at a time. You look at each inkblot and report what you see, much as you might look at clouds passing

Ambiguous (am-BIG-you-us). Vague, indefinite in form.

Projective tests. According to psychoanalytic theory, people tend to project their own personalities onto vague or ambiguous stimulus inputs. Projective tests—such as the inkblot test and the TAT—are vague stimuli that a psychologist might ask you to describe or talk about, in the hope that you will somehow structure the stimulus in the same way that your personality is structured. Thus, by "psyching out" your responses, the psychologist can (presumably) "psych you out" as well. Unfortunately, projective tests are, generally speaking, neither as valid nor as reliable as we might wish them to be.

Thematic Apperception Test (tuh-MATT-tick app-purr-SEP-shun). A "theme" is a story, or the plot of a story. *Apperception* is defined as "the process of perceiving something in terms of your prior experience." The TAT is a set of vague stimulus pictures that you are asked to "tell stories about," presumably because you will perceive or structure the pictures in terms of your own personality. Hence the "themes" of the stories will give the psychologist some clue as to how you perceive the world (in terms of your own prior experiences.)

Rorschach (ROAR-shock). Hermann Rorschach (1884–1922) was a Swiss psychiatrist who devised the famous inkblot projective test.

Fig. 23.5. Two photographs that might be used in a TAT test.

Fig. 23.6. Although this is not an actual Rorschach, it is typical of the inkblots used in testing.

overhead and tell someone what "faces" and other things you saw in the clouds. The psychologist then scores and interprets your responses according to one of several methods.

When used by a sensitive and perceptive psychologist, any one of the projective tests can yield a great deal of information about your personality. However, the bulk of scientific research suggests that most projective tests are neither very reliable nor particularly valid as presently used. Projective tests seem to give us more information about you than we have the wisdom to use, and they give us this information in highly subjective descriptions of what you are like rather than as reliable, objective test scores.

Question: It is sometimes said that Rorschach interpretations tell us more about the person doing the "interpreting" than they do about the person who took the test. Why might this sometimes be the case?

PART SIX   Personality

Objective Tests: MMPI

The **Minnesota Multiphasic Personality Inventory,** or MMPI, is the exact opposite of the projective tests. Perhaps the most widely used personality test in the United States today, the MMPI was created to be as reliable as possible—and research suggests that its reliability is indeed fairly high. In its original form, the MMPI consisted of some 560 short statements that were given to large numbers of people, some of them mental patients, some of them presumably normal. The statements mostly concern psychiatric problems or unusual thought patterns, such as: (a) Someone is trying to control my mind by using radio waves; (b) I never think of unusual sexual situations; and (c) I never have been sick a day of my life. When you take the MMPI, you respond to each statement either by agreeing or disagreeing, or by saying that it is impossible for you to respond at all.

As you might expect, the mental patients used in the original sample reacted to many of the statements in quite different ways than did the normal subjects. Depressed or suicidal patients gave different responses than did patients diagnosed as being schizophrenic or paranoid. The authors of the test were able to pick out different groups of test items that appeared to form "depression" scales, "paranoia" scales, "schizophrenia" scales, and so forth. If an otherwise normal individual takes the test and receives an abnormally high score on the "paranoia" scale, the psychologist interpreting the test might well worry that the person could become paranoid if put under great psychological stress or pressure. By looking at the pattern or *profile* of a subject's scores on the different MMPI scales, a psychologist might also be able to predict what areas of the subject's personality need strengthening.

The psychologists who made up the MMPI could not tell in advance which items would differentiate between a normal person and a patient in a mental hospital. Nor, in a sense, did the psychologists care. Their goal was to find a group of items which patients reliably responded to one way, and non-patients reacted to in another. If almost all depressed patients agreed with the statement: "I love cooked carrots," while most normal individuals disagreed with that item, it was included on the Depression Scale.

This objective approach to the study of personality—judging people almost entirely in terms of their objective responses—gives the MMPI a very high reliability. Whether the MMPI is a *valid* index of personality structure is another matter altogether.

Question: The validity of the MMPI depends in part on the correctness of the psychiatric diagnoses that caused the mental patients to be hospitalized in the first place. If these diagnoses are questionable, how valid can the MMPI be?

Which Test Is Best?

Unfortunately, there is at present no personality test that has both high reliability and great validity. At their best, personality scales can offer you a type of psychological feedback about yourself—but you have to pay for what you get.

If you believe that your personality is primarily determined by your fetal development and your body type, you might wish to look into Sheldon's tests of morphological types.

If you prefer an intuitive, subjective understanding of how you came to be what you presently are—and you agree with the psycho-analytic approach to personality development—then you may want to be evaluated by a psychologist using projective techniques such as the Rorschach.

If you assume that one or more of your personal values is the strongest influence on what you feel and do, then the Allport–Vernon–Lindzey scale is probably the one for you.

However, if you are most interested in learning your scores on a number of different scales, all of which have fairly high reliability, then perhaps the MMPI might be your best choice.

Malcolm Gynther.

In any case, you will want the guidance of a trained psychologist to help you interpret the test data and to discuss what use you might wish to make of the information.

Ethical Considerations

Technological devices, including personality inventories, are typically "morally neutral"—that is, they are neither good nor bad in and of themselves. A surgeon's knife may be used to save a life, or to stab someone. An intelligence test may help a teacher identify what academic areas a student needs help with—or the test may be used as an excuse not to work with a student because his or her IQ "is so low that special help would be a waste of time."

On the average, psychologists themselves tend to get rather high scores on the "social" scale of the Allport–Vernon–Lindzey test—which could mean that psychologists are usually more interested in helping people than in hindering them. Also, the American Psychological Association has a code of ethics that its members must follow, or be booted out of the organization.

All these facts mean that you can usually trust a psychologist's *intentions.* But can you place as much faith in his or her *actual performance?* Most psychological tests have a rather strong if unconscious streak of bias to them. The MMPI was validated primarily on white populations. It does a much better job of diagnosing personality problems in whites than it does in blacks. When the MMPI is used to screen job applicants, as Malcolm Gynther of St. Louis University has pointed out, the test scores give a significant advantage to whites over blacks. The makers of the MMPI did not intend for this to be the case, but their methods of test construction insured that white attitudes and norms would be more strongly represented than are black viewpoints (see Table 23.1).

The same may be said of most intelligence scales. The validity of IQ tests rests primarily on the correlations between IQ scores and success in school. Thus the tests may tell us more about what is right—or wrong—with our school system than it does about "innate intelligence."

It is illegal and unethical in the US today to discriminate against people because of their skin color, sex, religion, or ethnic background. However, it

---

Table 23.1
The Chitling Test[a]

1. A "handkerchief head" is:
   (A) a cool cat
   (B) a porter
   (C) an Uncle Tom
   (D) a hoddi
   (E) a preacher
2. Which word is most out of place here?
   (A) splib
   (B) blood
   (C) gray
   (D) spook
   (E) black
3. A "gas head" is a person who has a:
   (A) fast-moving car
   (B) stable of "lace"
   (C) "process"
   (D) habit of stealing cars
   (E) long jail record for arson
4. "Bo Diddley" is a:
   (A) game for children
   (B) down-home cheap wine
   (C) down-home singer
   (D) new dance
   (E) Moejoe call
5. If a man is called a "blood," then he is a:
   (A) fighter
   (B) Mexican-American
   (C) Negro
   (D) hungry hemophile
   (E) Redman or Indian

[a]This IQ test was designed by Adrian Dove, a sociologist who is familiar with black ghetto culture. It probably seems as unfair to white middle-class culture as the tests designed by them appear to other culture groups. The answer to all the above questions is C. (Copyright 1968 by Newsweek, Inc.)

is NOT illegal or unethical to discriminate against people because of their scores on psychological tests—and most of these tests have a strong cultural bias to them.

Laws can control many forms of conscious, open discrimination against minority groups, or those with special problems or handicaps. But unconscious prejudice can be controlled only through education and therapy. Perhaps in the future we can construct personality tests that are reliable and as free of cultural bias as possible. And perhaps there is hope. In 1977 California psychologist Paul McReynolds noted three current trends in **psychological assessment,** which he believes are healthy ones indeed:

1. Psychologists are, more and more, relying on objective tests rather than subjective evaluations.

2. Psychologists are, more and more, becoming more **holistic** in their approach to personality assessment.

3. Psychologists are, more and more, looking for input-output correlations rather than attempting to determine "inner processes" directly.

"Being" versus "Becoming"

There is a further form of unconscious prejudice that is perhaps worse than any we have discussed so far. It is the viewpoint that intelligence, personality, and human ability become fixed or inflexible at a very early age. Almost all of the newer approaches to the study of personality focus on growth, on change, on your ability to achieve self-actualization no matter what your age, sex, skin color, or past experience. As Leona Tyler says, "Individuals create themselves . . . It is development we must study, but the development of the shaper rather than the shaped."

We cannot exceed our genetic limitations—few of us will become Einsteins, Rembrandts, Shakespeares, or Beethovens no matter how hard we may try and no matter what special training we are given. But in truth there is little evidence that any of us comes close to reaching our biological limits, whatever they may be.

Summary

1. Measuring **personality structure** is as difficult as measuring the processes by which those structures function or interact.

2. Psychologists generally assume that your personality is composed of **traits**—that is, rather long-lasting mental states or conditions such as **intelligence,** motives, emotions, values, and attitudes.

3. If we could somehow determine which of your traits were most important, we could better understand why you think and act as you do. But we still don't agree on which traits are important, much less on how to measure them.

4. Galen (and Hippocrates) were the first **type theorists.** They assumed that the four main fluids or **humors** of the body (**blood, phlegm, yellow bile, black bile**) were the major determinants of personality, a belief long since discarded by scientists.

5. Kretschmer believed that your inherited **body type,** or **morphology,** determined your traits. Kretschmer assumed that every human being could be described as either a fat **pyknic,** a thin **asthenic,** or a muscular **athletic.**

6. Sheldon believed that we are all mixtures of three body types, the **endomorph,** the **ectomorph,** and the **mesomorph.** Whichever type you became was determined during your fetal period. Sheldon found correlations between body type and various personality traits.

7. Type theorists assume that your personality is determined almost entirely by the structure of your body. It seems more likely that

Psychological assessment. The process of describing people in terms of their traits, values, personality characteristics, and psychological attributes.

Holistic (ho-LISS-tic). Seeing things as a "whole," rather than as a bunch of parts. Viewing people as unique living systems rather than focusing primarily on people's traits or attributes. See Chapter 5.

there are three general classes of **reinforcing inputs,** and that you may be born with a slight predisposition to prefer one type more than the other two.

8. Modern structural theorists have rejected typologies, focusing instead on **mental traits** such as intelligence.

9. **IQ tests** were first developed by Binet and Simon, whose ideas came from Darwin and Broca. Their early tests were found to be of value in the French school system.

10. **Intelligence Quotient,** or IQ, is often defined as **mental age** divided by **chronological age** times 100.

11. IQ tests usually have a strong **cultural bias** built into them and thus are useful only with the population for which they were designed. In particular, tests devised by whites discriminate against blacks and other minority groups.

12. Children brought up in deprived circumstances generally have lower IQ scores than do children brought up in stimulating environments. The amount of time that a mother talks to and touches her infant is the best single **predictor** of what the child's IQ score will be at age three.

13. Children brought up in large families generally have slightly lower IQ scores than do children brought up in small families. In large families, the late-born children usually score lower on IQ tests than do first-borns.

14. Most people can add significantly to their IQ scores by learning how to reason, and how to take IQ tests.

15. IQ test scores **correlate** highly with academic performance, but do not predict "real-life" success very well.

16. IQ tests are fairly **reliable,** but there is considerable question about their **validity** since there is no agreement on what intelligence actually is.

17. Allport, Vernon, and Lindzey developed a "test of values" that describes people in terms of six different **primary** or **cardinal traits,** but we have no proof as yet that these six traits are the most important ones displayed by most human beings.

18. **Projective tests,** such as the **Rorschach,** the **word association test,** and the **TAT,** are ambiguous stimuli that you are supposed to "structure" in terms of your own personality.

19. The **MMPI** is a very reliable set of scales standardized on a fairly large population. However, the MMPI is not necessarily a valid measure of personality.

20. The trend in **personality assessment** is toward more objective tests, more **holistic** tests, and toward scales that describe **input–output correlations.**

21. At best, personality tests offer interesting psychological feedback, but should be used and interpreted with great caution since all such tests (and all psychologists who interpret test scores) have a fair amount of cultural bias built into them.

(Continued from page 588.)

"Well, Jessie, if I don't get my Ph.D., I can always blame it on you," Tom Flagg said, his smile belying the seriousness of his words.

"Did I mess up your experiment?" Jessie Williams asked in a concerned tone of voice."

"Royally. But luckily, you were practically the only teacher who did."

"None of my bloomers bloomed?"

Tom shook his head. "That wasn't the problem. Just the opposite. *All* of your kids bloomed, black or white, whether the test said they should or not."

"And that's bad?"

"Good for the kids. Bad for my experiment."

Jessie frowned. "Will it really hold you back from getting your doctorate in psychology?"

"No, not at all. As I said, the Rosenthal test predicted rather well for several other teachers." Tom stretched his muscular legs out in front of him. "I just wish that it hadn't. I hoped it wouldn't work."

Jessie looked puzzled. "But I thought you wanted the test to work. I thought you wouldn't get credit for your experiment if it didn't."

"I couldn't tell you everything about the test, Jessie," Tom said sheepishly. "You see, Professor Rosenthal didn't really make up a test for 'Late Bloomers.' He was interested in people's expectancies instead. He figured if you told a teacher that one of her children was going to show a great improvement, then the teacher would pay a lot more attention to that child. She'd look for each little bit of learning the kid showed, and would communicate her enthusiasm to the kid. So the kid would respond to the teacher's expectancies, and would really bloom. But if the teacher expected the kid to backslide, she'd be biased against the kid, and pick on the kid's faults and mistakes. Then the kid would become discouraged and wouldn't do well. And that's exactly what Rosenthal found—in a lot of cases anyhow."

"But it didn't work with me, did it?" Jessie said, grinning.

"No, it didn't. Not that I'm complaining, you understand. It shouldn't work with really good teachers, because they shouldn't be prejudiced for or against kids just because of their test scores."

"Water them frequently with love and affection, and you help them all bloom as much as they can."

"Right," said Tom.

"Then why are you concerned if I didn't pay any attention to your test scores, Tom? I'm not suggestible enough for you?"

Tom laughed. "How did you guess?"

"Keep your mind on your experiment. What's troubling you, friend?"

Tom shrugged. "The fact that so many other teachers, black and white, were influenced by the faked test scores that I gave them. I can maybe understand why some of the white teachers might be prejudiced in favor of white kids and against blacks—that's part of our culture, though it's changing some now. And maybe I can understand why some of the black teachers would be prejudiced against white kids and biased toward the blacks. Somehow you expect that. But why would white teachers be prejudiced against white kids, and black teachers prejudiced against black kids—just because some silly test said the kids were going to backslide, or do poorly?"

"Brother Thomas, we are all human beings," Jessie Williams said, crossing her arms over her ample breasts. "Our blood is the same color, our brains are the same size, our bodies are the same shapes, and we all learn our prejudices at our mother's knees. I'm just lucky that I was taught to be prejudiced *toward,* instead of prejudiced *against.* But it's prejudice, just the same."

"You think love is prejudice?"

"Of course. Love is prejudice in favor of life."

Tom swallowed hard. "Well, do you think you might be prejudiced just a little in my direction?"

"It might happen to be so."

"Then maybe I ought to ask you out to the movies tomorrow night."

Jessie grinned. "You do that, Baby. You do that very thing."

Recommended Readings

Block, N.J., and Gerald Dworkin, eds. *The IQ Controversy: Critical Readings* (New York: Pantheon, 1976).

Fiske, Donald W. *Strategies for Personality Research: The Observation versus Interpretation of Behavior* (San Francisco: Jossey-Bass, 1978).

Guthrie, Robert V. *Even the Rat Was White: A Historical View of Psychology* (New York: Harper & Row, 1976).

Jones, Russell A. *Self-Fulfilling Prophecies: Social, Psychological, and Physiological Effects of Expectancies* (Hillsdale, N.J.: Erlbaum, 1977).

McReynolds, Paul, ed. *Advances in Psychological Assessment*, Vol. 4 (San Francisco: Jossey-Bass, 1977).

Tyler, Leona E. *Individuality: Human Possibilities and Personal Choice in the Psychological Development of Men and Women* (San Francisco: Jossey-Bass, 1978).

Abnormal Psychology

Did You Know That . . .

According to Kinsey, the average white married man aged 21–25 has about four sexual climaxes a week?

Psychologists use the statistical term "2 standard deviations from the mean" to describe most forms of unusual or abnormal behavior?

You have been using statistical concepts most of your life?

The American Psychiatric Association has recently decided that all forms of abnormal behavior are medical disorders and thus require a physician's care?

A "diagnostic and statistical manual" put out by this same association has abandoned use of the term "neurosis?"

The APA no longer considers homosexual behavior to be a symptom of mental illness?

Most sexual offenders are undersexed, misinformed, and narrow-minded people?

Although the patient population has remained much the same, more people are diagnosed as suffering from schizophrenia today than was the case a decade ago?

When a person develops abnormal behavior patterns, everyone the person has close contact with probably has helped bring about the abnormality?

"I'm Crazy—You're Crazy"

Steve May got out of the car, closed the door, then stuck his head back in through the window. "You really think it will work?" he said for perhaps the tenth time that day.

Dr. Mary Ellen Mann smiled reassuringly at the handsome young man. "Well, it worked for all of Professor Rosenhan's subjects. They all got admitted to the mental hospital without any trouble at all. Getting out's the problem, not getting in. But you know that, Steve. You've read Rosenhan's article in *Science* yourself. You know what's likely to happen, and I'm sure you'll be able to cope beautifully with any problems that may arise. Just get yourself in gear and go convince those people that you're crazier than a bedbug."

Steve thought about the matter for a moment or two. He had willingly committed himself to helping Dr. Mann with her research on the reliability of psychiatric diagnoses, but committing himself to a state mental hospital was a very frightening thought. He supposed that he couldn't really chicken out at the last moment, but still . . .

"If they do admit me," the blond young man said, "you're sure that I can prove to them that I'm okay so they'll let me out?"

Dr. Mann snorted as she laughed. "I don't promise anything—except that if you get stuck in there, you've got to get out on your own. Oh, I'll come rescue you eventually, have no fears about that." She leaned toward him a trifle. "Or maybe you're afraid that you really are a bit nuts. Is that the problem?"

A rosy flush spread over Steve's face. "Of course not! I'm as sane as you are!"

Dr. Mann snorted even more loudly. "Just don't tell the psychiatrist that, or you may never get out!" Then she smiled warmly. "Good luck, Steve. I really appreciate your helping out my research this way."

Steve nodded slowly, then pulled his head out of the car window. Dr. Mann waved at him, then put the car into gear and slowly drove off.

Steve turned to look at the hospital. It was a huge, towering, forbidding structure. The thought of spending the next few days—or weeks, or months—in that place frankly scared him. But he had promised . . .

He walked slowly up the path and went through the heavy, wooden door. The lobby inside was cool and almost empty. A nice-looking young woman sat behind a reception desk, filling in a form of some kind on a typewriter. Steve put on his best smile and walked over to her.

"Hello," Steve said.

The woman stopped typing and looked up at him. Her face brightened as she took in his handsome features and his muscular body. "Oh, hello," she said warmly. "What can I do for you? Would you like to see a patient?"

Steve returned her smile. "No, I want to be a patient, if you don't mind."

The woman's smile faded a bit. "Oh," she said briskly. "There's something wrong?"

Steve nodded. "Yeah. I need help. I hear voices."

The woman's smile faded away entirely, as if she had suddenly placed him in a less desirable category than she had at first. "What do the voices seem to be saying?" she asked.

"They're kind of indistinct," he replied. "Mostly words like 'dull,' 'thud,' 'empty.' You know, things like that."

The woman nodded slowly, mechanically. "And what sex are the voices, male or female?"

Steve smiled wanly. "I can't always tell."

The woman frowned. "Are you in any pain right now?"

"No, not really," Steve said. "But I do think I need your help—for a while, that is, until the voices go away."

A typical state mental hospital.

614

Again the woman frowned. "Well, we're pretty full these days. You'll have to see the admitting psychiatrist, of course. But he's very busy right now. And we'll have to fill out a lot of papers, and . . ."

Two hours later, Steve's fingers were almost numb from writer's cramp. He finished all the forms, and then sat patiently in the lobby for another hour or so until the psychiatrist could see him.

The psychiatrist was a pleasant man of about 40 who spoke with such a thick foreign accent that Steve couldn't always understand the questions the man asked him. Steve told the man about his voices—that they were indistinct and that they seemed to be saying "dull," "thud," and "hollow." The doctor nodded sagely, and muttered under his breath. Steve thought the man had said something like, "Existential crisis." Steve smiled inwardly. It was going just like Rosenhan's paper had suggested it would. Almost all of Rosenhan's subjects got the same sort of diagnosis.

Then the psychiatrist started asking questions about Steve's early life. When Steve admitted that he occasionally argued with his father, and that he really got along better with his mother, the doctor nodded sagely again. Steve thought he mumbled something like, "Very significant." And when Steve said that he wasn't always sure what his goals in life were, and that he now and again lost his temper, the psychiatrist muttered something under his breath that sounded suspiciously like, "Poor impulse control."

Aside from the bit about the "voices," Steve answered the man's questions as honestly as possible, just as Dr. Mann had told him to do. At first Steve had been sure the psychiatrist would see through the game, and would announce loudly that Steve was "just faking it." But the doctor apparently took him only too seriously. To Steve's surprise, the psychiatrist never once asked him about his abilities and strengths, or what made him happy. The man obviously couldn't tell that Steve was really normal and healthy, and that thought frightened Steve more than he would admit.

Finally the psychiatrist leaned back in his chair, tapped a pencil on his desk, and stared silently at Steve for a few moments. "Look, Steven," the doctor finally said, "I don't want to alarm you, but I do think I ought to be honest with you. You seem to be suffering from very real psychological problems. You were right to come to us. I'm sure that we can be of help. We'll keep you under observation for a while, and then we'll talk about getting you legally certified . . ."

"Legally certified?" Steve said in a horrified tone of voice.

"Of course. If you are to stay here more than 60 days, which will likely be the case, there are certain legal formalities we have to go through . . ."

"Sixty days! But what if I get better right away—like tomorrow?" Steve protested.

The psychiatrist allowed himself a brief, thin-lipped smile. "As you Americans say, we'll cross that bridge when we come to it." The doctor pressed a button on his desk and, almost immediately, a burly young attendant entered the office.

"Charles, this is Steven," the psychiatrist said. "He will be staying with us for a while. Please check him in and then put him on Ward A-5."

The attendant nodded, then said to Steve, "This way, please."

Steve got up and started to extend his hand to the psychiatrist. But the man was already busy working on the papers that would admit Steve to the mental hospital. So Steve picked up his small bag and followed the attendant out of the office.

"First, we'll check you in and get all your valuables stowed away," the burly attendant said.

"Oh," said Steve, "I'd rather keep them with me."

"Can't. It's the rule," the attendant said. "Got to stow it all away—your money and credit cards and all that stuff. Your watch and rings, too. We can't be responsible, you know. And we'll have to inspect your shaving kit and all your personal gear. No razors, you know, and you can't keep all your clothes either."

"Clothes?" Steve said in an unbelieving tone of voice.

"Belts, stuff like that. Might hurt yourself."

Steve had to hurry a bit to keep up with the attendant. "But surely I can keep my pictures, and my books, and things like that . . ."

"Nope. It's the rule, you know."

For a moment, Steve panicked. The folly of what he was doing finally struck home. They were taking away all his "cards of identity," all his symbols of power, all his memories and mementoes. They were stripping him of his personality and turning him into a number, a card in a file, a statistic.

"We'll give you a shower and then get you some hospital clothes," the attendant said, opening a huge metal door and then locking it securely after they had passed through.

"But I just had a shower, this morning," Steve protested as they walked down a long, bare corridor. "Do you think what I've got is catching?"

"Don't give me any trouble, man. I don't make the rules." The attendant unlocked another huge metal door at the end of the corridor and banged it shut behind them. They walked down a flight of metal stairs and then the attendant unlocked yet another door that had a small window in it. The window was covered with thick steel bars. The burly attendant told Steve to strip, took his things, and pointed to a shower room. When Steve returned, water still dripping from his hair, the attendant gave him a set of hospital clothes.

"You look fine," the attendant said. "Now, let's get on with it."

They walked down another long, bare corridor to a metal door that bore a small sign, "Ward A-5." Steven shook his head in dismay. They had passed through four locked, steel doors already. If getting into the ward was this difficult, what would getting out be like?

"This is it," the attendant said, unlocking the door and walking into the ward. "Wait here until I find the nurse," the man said, shutting the metal door behind them. "She should be around someplace."

Steve stood staring at the inmates. Several of them were watching a small television set, but they didn't seem to respond emotionally to the program in any way. They just sat there, passively. One middle-aged man rushed feverishly about the ward, as if looking for something he had lost. A younger man was rocking back and forth in a straight-backed chair. A third man was standing in a corner, quietly urinating.

My God, Steve thought. *You've got to be crazy to stay in a place like this.*

The attendant came up with a nurse, who gave Steve an efficient smile and then showed him where his bed would be. The man in the next bed was curled up in a fetal position, laughing quietly to himself, a serene smile on his face.

Steve stretched out on the narrow bed and stared at the ceiling. "Well, I made it in okay," he said aloud. "But how in the world am I ever going to get out of this place?"

The man in the next bed giggled softly.

(Continued on page 640.)

How Normal Are You?

Quite frankly, most personality theorists would probably consider you just a little abnormal. To begin with, you're almost certainly above average in intelligence. People who score below average on most IQ tests, for whatever reason, tend to drop out of school rather early and are most unlikely to do much textbook reading thereafter. Second, if we gave you the MMPI, you would most likely not score *right at the average* on the dozens of different scales that make up that test. You'd probably be above average on some of the scales, below average on some, close to average on the rest.

Most of the great personality theorists—Freud, Jung, Adler, Erikson, Kretschmer, Rogers, and the rest—based their ideas on the study of mentally disturbed people. Some of these individuals were patients in mental hospitals, and some were private patients who asked for help. Most of them had mental or behavioral problems that were *exaggerations* of the mental and behavioral traits that we all have. Therefore, the theorists presumed, there is a little bit of madness in each of us. The mental patient differs from the average citizen in the *quantity* or amount of her or his madness, not in the *quality* or type of psychological problem. In short, the view of these theorists has been that we are all mildly abnormal, but some of us are more abnormal than others.

But does that view make sense? If everyone **deviates** from the norm one way or another, doesn't the word "normal" lose most of its meaning? And if we can't define the word "normal," what shall we make of the word "abnormal," which literally means "away from the normal?"

Before we can discuss such abnormal topics as mental illness, "insanity," sexual deviation, and "crazy behavior," then, we must first take a good, hard, objective look at the word "normal."

What Is Normal?

Suppose a young married couple named Mary and John Smith are on the verge of divorce. They go to see a psychologist to ask for help. Even before the psychologist learns their names, this counselor knows several things about the Smiths. First, one or both of them is going to be suffering considerable psychological pain, distress, or anxiety. Second, things are probably worse for the couple now than at some time in the past. That is, their way of life has changed from its usual (normal) pattern. Third, they are bright enough to sense this departure from normal and to seek help.

Any deviation from a person's usual way of thinking, feeling, or behaving can be considered a symptom of psychological abnormality—provided that the person was reasonably "normal" (as defined by the person's culture) to start with. Generally speaking, if this deviation is slight, the psychologist is likely to believe that the person suffers from what was until recently classified as a **neurosis.** If the deviation is large, the psychologist may worry that the person suffers from a more severe problem called a **psychosis.** The *terminology* in this area of psychology is undergoing rapid change right now, a point we will discuss more fully later in this chapter. For the moment, all you need to remember is that some people have relatively minor problems, while others have such major difficulties that they may need to be hospitalized at some point in their lives. It is the psychologist's job, in either case, to help the person solve the problem and return to normal—(as defined by the society in which the person must live and function.)

Mary and John Smith could have many quite different *kinds* of psy-

Deviates (DEE-vee-ates). To deviate is to turn aside, to go off in an unusual direction, or to move away from the norm or average. Most people *perceive* themselves as being "normal," even when they're measurably deviant. In fact, very few people are "right at the norm" on the majority of psychological, social, and political scales. Thus almost all of us are "deviates" in one way or another, even if we typically fail to perceive how deviant we really are.

Neurosis (new-ROW-sis). Also called "psycho-neurosis." A mild form of mental disorder that usually does not keep the individual from living a reasonably successful life. Freud thought that the seeds for a neurosis were planted in early childhood. According to the American Psychiatric Association's latest diagnostic scheme, the term "neurosis" is no longer to be used.

Psychosis (sigh-KOH-sis). A severe and usually incapacitating form of mental disorder that often requires hospitalization.

chological difficulties. In this chapter we will describe what some of the more common types are like. But to help us understand what the word "normal" means, let us assume that they have a *sexual incompatibility.* John complains that Mary is **frigid,** that she no longer shows him much affection, that she consistently refuses him the pleasures of the marriage bed. Mary replies that John is a **satyr**—that is, he has an unusually strong sex drive. She claims that he thinks of nothing else, talks of nothing else, and that he is interested only in her body and not in her mind or personality. (As we will see later, the problem might be the other way around—the wife might desire sex more frequently than the husband. But we will delay discussion of that situation for a moment.)

The psychologist might well assume that the woman was *normal,* but that the man's **libido** had gotten out of control and was ruining the marriage. Or the counselor might assume that the man had a *normal,* healthy appetite for sex, but that the woman was so *repressed* that she could not enjoy one of the finer aspects of marriage. Or the therapist might assume that *both* Mary and John showed symptoms of abnormality. How could the psychologist tell for sure?

Question: Psychologists always make assumptions about what is normal and abnormal for a particular patient. Do you think that male counselors might tend to make different assumptions about John and Mary Smith than would female counselors?

Cultural Norms

Normality is always defined *within a given context or culture.* No psychologist can come to any meaningful conclusions about the Smiths' problems if the counselor ignores the *social environment* in which the couple lives. That is, before the psychologist can concentrate on the unique aspects of the Smiths' difficulties, the therapist must ask what other people with similar backgrounds are like. How many times do most young husbands expect sex each week? How frequently do most wives desire it? Do husbands typically *wish* to make love more frequently than their wives, or the other way around? And what about the actual *behavior?* How frequently do young married men *actually* achieve sexual climax? And is it always with their wives? And how frequently do young married women actually reach orgasm, and is it always with their husbands?

Sex and the Bell-shaped Curve

Until Alfred Kinsey performed his pioneering research on human sexuality, no one really knew the answers to these questions. Judging from a rough analysis of the Kinsey data, it would seem that the average white married man aged 21–25 reaches sexual climax about three to four times a week. In Kinsey's rather stilted, formal, biological language, he said that the young, married, middle-class, white US male achieved an *average* of about four "sexual outlets" per week. (Kinsey thus included all forms of sexual activity—including masturbation, homosexuality, bestiality, "wet dreams," and extra-marital heterosexual contacts in his figures.)

Although Kinsey gathered his data more than 20 years ago, more recent surveys tend to confirm his findings. Thus we can use Kinsey's results to give us a "social context" in which to consider the Smiths' marital problems—but only assuming that the Smiths are white, middle-class Americans. Yet there is still a lot more we need to know. If Mr. Smith desired seven outlets a week, would you consider him abnormal? What if he demanded 17? And would John Smith be "far above normal" if he wanted 77?

Range

As you can see, knowing what the average is doesn't always help. The average score on most IQ tests is 100. If you get a score of 101, are you "way above average"? Before we could answer we would have to know the *range* of scores, as well as how those scores were *distributed* over the range. And the best way to find out would be to resort to that favorite psychological tool, the bell-shaped curve.

The range of IQ scores on some tests goes from 0 to about 200, and the tests are so constructed that most people's scores are bunched up in the middle of the distribution. Although some 50 percent of the scores lie above the mid-point of the curve, and some 50 percent lie below it, most of the IQ's do not *deviate* very far from this mid-point (see Fig. 24.1). Depending on how the mid-point is calculated, it is called the **mode,** the **mean,** or the **median.** If you are interested in how these terms are calculated, see the Statistical Appendix at the back of this book. However, "mode," "mean," and "median" are merely words that mean the **norm,** or the middle of the range of scores.

In the case of Kinsey's data on the sexual behavior of the (young, white, middle-class) US male, the mean, median, and mode are probably close together. Thus, for our present purposes, we can consider any of them the norm. The actual distribution of outlets per week probably looks something like the graph shown in Fig. 24.2.

Now we can see that if Mr. Smith desired seven outlets a week, he would be fairly close to the norm. But what if he wished 17? Would this fact make him ab-norm-al, or away from the norm? How far away is "away?"

Standard Deviation

Psychologists have a method of measuring deviations from the norm that they call the **standard deviation.** If you are interested in learning more about this matter, you might wish to look at the Statistical Appendix. However, when all is said and done, the standard deviation is little more than a fairly accurate way of measuring *percentages*.

Psychologists assume that, on any given test (or on the measurement of any given behavior), whatever *two-thirds of the people do* is probably pretty normal. On an IQ test, for example, the norm is arbitrarily set at a score of 100. On many such tests, about two-thirds of the people get scores between 84 and 116. As you can see from Fig. 24.3, this fact means that about one-third of the people scored within 16 points *below* the norm, and about one-third of the people scored within 16 points *above* the norm. By definition, then, the *standard deviation* for such a test would be 16 points. If you score within one standard deviation of the norm, your performance is almost always considered "within the normal range."

If you got a score of 132 on the IQ test, you would be 2 standard deviations above the norm, and you would be well above average in terms

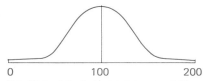

Fig. 24.1. A bell-shaped curve of IQ scores.

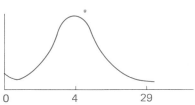

Fig. 24.2. Range of weekly outlets in young married men.

Mode. From the Latin word *modus,* meaning "to measure." The highest point or most frequent score on a bell-shaped distribution of scores.

Mean. That which is "middling" or intermediate in rank or order. The arithmetical average.

Median (ME-dee-un). From the Latin word *medius,* meaning "middle." The median on a superhighway is the paved or planted strip down the middle dividing the road in half. The median in a distribution is the score that exactly cuts the distribution in half.

Norm. From the Latin word *norma,* meaning "pattern" or "rule." The expected, the average, the usual. That which is a model.

Standard deviation (dee-vee-A-shun). The standard deviation is a mathematical way of figuring out how much a test score deviates from the mean, median, or mode (usually the mean). The standard deviation thus gives you a precise way of measuring how significantly your own score on a test varies or departs from the norm.

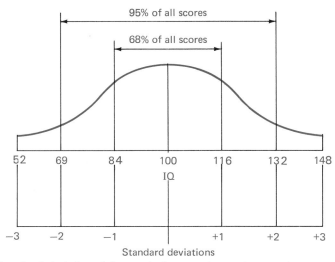

Fig. 24.3. Standard deviations tell you what percentage of scores fall within a certain distance from the mean.

of your IQ score. In fact, your score would be as good as or better than about 98 percent of the people who took the test. If you got a score of 148 on the test, you would be 3 standard deviations above the norm, which is an exceptional score since it puts you in the upper one-tenth of a percent of the test population.

In order to get back to talking about *psychological deviations* from the norm, let us summarize:

1. If your performance on any measure is within 1 standard deviation of the norm, you are like two-thirds of the population and hence quite normal.

2. If your performance on any measure is between 1 and 2 standard deviations from the norm, you have departed somewhat from the average.

3. If your performance on any measure is more than 2 standard deviations from the norm, you are behaving differently than about 98 percent of the population. Thus your performance should be considered *significantly* abnormal. You may score higher than the rest of the people, or lower—but surely you are measurably *different* from the majority of the others.

Normal Sexuality and the Standard Deviation

Now we're ready to put the Smiths' problem into context. Dr. Kinsey's surveys of sexual behavior suggest that young married men like John Smith have, on the average, four sexual outlets per week. The range is from 0 to more than 29. The standard deviation is about 2.

These facts mean that if Mr. Smith desires sexual contact with his wife from two to six times a week, he is probably like two-thirds of all similar men that Kinsey talked to. In short, within the society in which the Smiths live, his sexual demands would seem average, or normal. If he expected sex more than eight times per week, Mr. Smith would be more than 2 standard deviations from the norm (for his culture), and thus his requests would be at least *statistically* abnormal (see Fig. 24.4).

Of course, in the long run, the problem that exists between Mr. and Mrs. Smith is a personal one that cannot be solved by reference to bell-shaped curves. And yet the beauty of Kinsey's work was that he brought sexual behavior out in the open, so that it could be examined statistically as well as personally or theoretically. Lacking this important reference information, the psychologist might well make some very wrong decisions about how to help the Smiths. For we all tend to judge normality *in terms of our own behaviors and expectations.*

For instance, suppose that the counselor was a man who *himself* pre-

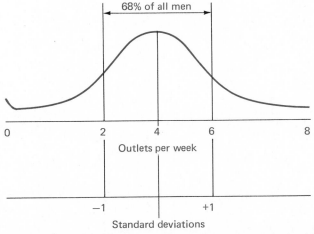

Fig. 24.4. According to Kinsey, two-thirds of all young, white, married, middle-class, American males experience two–six sexual outlets per week.

PART SIX Personality

ferred but one sexual outlet a month—and thought this was more than adequate and normal. If Mr. Smith wanted sex four times a week, the counselor might tend to agree with Mrs. Smith that her husband was a "satyr" who was terribly over-sexed. What kind of therapy might he suggest? On the other hand, if the psychologist was one of those (statistically) rare US men who regularly performed the sex act 20 times a week, he might think that both John and Mary Smith needed to take a few "pep pills" or hormone shots.

Question: How might the "personality theory" you believed in affect your judgment about who was "mentally ill" and who wasn't?

Classifying Abnormal Behavior Patterns

As you can gather, it is difficult to define psychological abnormality without a theory of some kind, or some set of data such as Kinsey's, to tell you both what is normal and how any abnormality might have come about.

There is, unfortunately, no one master theory of human behavior that everyone agrees on. Psychologists and psychiatrists have worked out a variety of diagnostic schemes that are supposed to classify people according to their problems. Of these, the best-known is surely the *Diagnostic and Statistical Manual of Mental Disorders,* first published by the American Psychiatric Association in 1952. A revised edition (DSM-II) appeared in 1968, and a "trial draft" of DSM-III was circulated to psychiatrists and psychologists in the late 1970's. It will pay us to take a look at DSM-III—and to compare it with the first two editions—before we go any farther in our study of abnormal behavior patterns, sexual or otherwise.

DSM-III

The third version of the *Diagnostic and Statistical Manual of Mental Disorders* was put together by a task force composed primarily of psychiatrists and neurologists. Thus DSM-III represents a strongly *medical* approach both to the classification and treatment of "mental illness." Indeed, one of the main objections that psychologists have to DSM-III is that the people who created it state rather boldly that "mental disorder should be defined as merely a subset of medical disorder." Thus only those individuals who hold the medical degree should, presumably, be allowed to have major responsibility for *treating any form of psychological problem.* Needless to say, most psychologists (and many psychiatrists) do not agree with what is now the "official" approach of the American Psychiatric Association. You should keep this conflict between the psychologists and the psychiatrists firmly in mind as we discuss the Manual itself.

DSM-III was designed to give specific diagnoses for *every* patient who might be referred to a psychiatrist (or perhaps to a psychologist)—no matter what the patient's problems might be. After interviewing the patient, and perhaps giving the individual various tests, the therapist rates the patient on each of five different **axes** or categories:

Axis 1. Clinical Psychiatric Syndrome(s) and Other Conditions
Axis 2. Personality Disorders (adults) and Specific Development Disorders (children and adolescents)
Axis 3. Physical Disorders
Axis 4. Severity of Psychosocial Stressors
Axis 5. Highest Level of Adaptive Functioning (during) Past Year

Axis 1 Included on Axis 1 are most of the psychological disorders that the American Psychiatric Association officially recognizes as being "mental illnesses." Generally speaking, Axis I is made up of all those severe psychological or behavioral problems that would send you to see a psychiatrist in the first place.

Axes (AX-ease). The plural of "axis." An axis is a line about which something rotates. The earth's axis is the line connecting the north and south poles. An axle on a car is the rod that connects two tires (and about which the tires rotate). In the DSM-III, the five axes are really "categories" or types of information that the psychiatrist should use in making a diagnosis about what could be troubling a given patient. Whether it is the patient or the psychiatrist who "rotates" around these five axes is an open question.

Included in the Axis 1 category are the *psychoses,* all cases of addiction and drug abuse, and most of what were once considered to be the *neuroses.* According to DSM-III, all of these problems are *medical illnesses,* just as mumps and measles are medical illnesses. Thus (by implication) these disorders should be treated by a physician. A given patient may have more than one major form of "mental illness," just as a person may also have mumps and measles simultaneously. Also included on Axis 1 are *psychological reactions* to such physical problems as epilepsy and brain damage.

Axis 2   Technically speaking, Axis 2 is limited to what are called the **personality disorders,** as well as a few specific "developmental disorders" such as language and reading difficulties. Presumably, these are all relatively mild psychological problems that may or may not be causing the patient much difficulty at the present time.

In fact, Axis 2 seems designed to let the **diagnostician** describe the patient's psychological traits and personality types. For example, severe forms of "aggressive behaviors" in children are listed under Axis 1, because they are presumed to be symptoms of a true "mental illness." However, if the aggressive behaviors extend into adulthood—and become relatively mild—the patient is diagnosed as having an *anti-social personality disorder,* which is an Axis 2 category. Likewise, a severely withdrawn patient would be diagnosed as "schizophrenic" (Axis 1), but a mildly withdrawn or introverted patient would be diagnosed as having a *schizoid personality disorder* that would appear as an Axis 2 problem.

Since Axis 2 problems are *mental disorders,* they too may require treatment by a physician. A given patient may have more than one "rating" on Axis 2.

Many patients will have disorders listed on both Axis 1 and Axis 2. However, since almost all types of "mental illness" are included on Axis 1, many patients will receive no "rating" at all on Axis 2 (or at least none really worth bothering about). A *very* few might have Axis 2 disorders without suffering from any disorder listed on Axis 1.

Axis 3   Axis 3 is a reminder that patients who seek psychological assistance may have physical ailments (such as cancer) that may be related to their mental disorders (such as depression). Included on Axis 3 are all the *physical symptoms* of any type of disease, damage to the brain or any other part of the body, and disabilities caused by accidents or drugs. The *psychological reactions* to these biological problems, however, are generally considered to be mental disorders that would be listed under Axis 1.

Reading therapists can often help children with developmental problems.

Axis 4 Axis 4 is a "social stress scale" that lists such traumatic social stresses as the death of a loved one, changing (or losing) your job, and getting married (or divorced). Again, the patient's *psychological reaction* to these social traumas will probably be a mental disorder listed under Axis 1. Generally speaking, only those stressful events that occurred in the past 12 months are given serious consideration.

Axis 5 Axis 5 is a scale running from "superior" to "grossly impaired" that describes your highest level of psychological adjustment for the past year.

Major Diagnostic Categories

Table 24.1 gives a *brief* outline of the diagnostic categories included on Axes 1 and 2. However, before you read the material in Table 24.1, there are several things you should understand.

First, the Table is taken from a "rough draft" of DSM-III that was published early in 1979. When the "final draft" appears, many of the listings will probably be changed.

Second, DSM-III is filled with psychiatric **jargon.** We will describe many of the disorders later in this chapter, but a complete definition of the terms used in the Table would take up several hundred pages.

Third, as we will see in a moment, there is considerable argument both about the *validity* and the *reliability* of the diagnostic categories used in DMS-III. The mere fact that we apply a certain "label" to a person doesn't mean that the label actually fits—or even that a given type of "mental disorder" exists anywhere but in the minds of many present-day psychiatrists.

Fourth, the theoretical approach underlying DMS-III would please *none* of the personality theorists discussed in Chapter 23 (Freud, Jung, Adler, Erikson, Rogers, Maslow, and Skinner). Nor would DSM-III fit very well within a **holistic** approach such as General Systems Theory.

None the less, DSM-III is important because it represents "the shape of the future" within clinical psychiatry, and thus will have a strong influence on the field of abnormal psychology.

The Psychoses

DSM-III marks a radical shift in the psychiatric approach to classifying mental disorders. DSM-II, published in 1968, was based in part on psycho-analytic theory. Freud believed that almost all types of mental illness were due either to biological or to psychological causes. Some disorders were very severe, and were called the *psychoses*. Other forms were not as severe, and were called the *neuroses*. The psychoses were characterized by a loss of contact with reality, a disorganized personality, and by extreme deviation from normal patterns of acting, thinking, and feeling. Some of these severe disorders had clear-cut biological causes and were referred to as **organic psychoses.** Other severe disorders had emotional causes and were referred to as **functional psychoses.** The neuroses *always* had emotional rather than organic causes.

The authors of DSM-II took into account the fact that not all mental problems fell within these categories. For example, mental retardation is neither a psychosis nor a neurosis, yet it usually has a physiological cause. And the "personality disorders" or "character disorders" (including sexual problems) didn't fit the "psychosis–neurosis" scheme too well either. The same may be said of drug dependency and problems of social adjustment. In DSM-II, the disorders that didn't fit the psycho-analytic pattern were simply included as "special categories" of mental problems.

The authors of DSM-III have thrown the term "neurosis" out the window—and make little use of "psychosis," for that matter. Rather than using these "psycho-analytic" terms, the psychiatrists who have created DMS-III have moved off in quite a different direction. They have simply lumped all possible psychological problems (save for the "personality

Jargon (JAR-gahn). The "special terms" or "shop talk" of a given profession. As we noted earlier, the word *jargon* comes (appropriately enough) from a French word meaning "the twittering of birds."

Holistic. The viewpoint that mental disorders are always multi-determined. That is, the belief that all human problems involve the body, the mind, and the social environment, and that "curing" the problem typically involves treating (or changing) the body, the mind, and the environment. See Chapter 5.

Organic psychoses (sigh-KOH-sees). Severe mental disorders that supposedly have a clear-cut physiological basis, such as brain damage, stroke, old age, drug abuse, and so forth. In fact, since people react quite differently to brain damage, strokes, old age, and drugs, there is no psychosis that is *entirely* "organic."

Functional psychoses. Severe mental disorders that have no measurable physiological cause. That is, mental disorders that appear to stem from malfunctions of the mind, not the body. In fact, since the body always reacts physiologically to psychological stress, there is no psychosis that is *entirely* "functional."

Table 24.1

A Brief Outline of the Diagnostic Categories Included on Axis 1 and Axis 2 of DSM-III (January 1979).

Axis 1 Severe Mental Disorders (Including Psychoses and Many "Neuroses")

Disorders That Usually First Manifest Themselves in Infancy, Childhood, or Adolescence
  Mental Retardation
  Attention Deficit Disorders
    Hyperactivity
  Conduct Disorders
    Aggressive Conduct Disorder
      Undersocialized Type
      Socialized Type
    Unaggressive Conduct
    Disorder
  Anxiety Disorders
    Separation Anxiety
    Avoidant Disorder
    Over-anxious Disorder
  Other Disorders
    Attachment Disorder
    Schizoid Disorder
    Elective Mutism
    Oppositional Disorder
    Identity Disorder
  Eating Disorders
    Anorexia Nervosa
    Bulimia
    Pica
    Rumination Disorder
    Atypical Eating Disorder
  Stereotyped Movement
  Disorders
    Transient Tics
    Chronic Motor Tics
    Tourette's Disorder
  Other Physical Disorders
    Stuttering
    Functional Enuresis
    Functional Encopresis
    Somnambulism
    Pavor Nocturnus
  Pervasive Developmental
  Disorders
    Infantile Autism
Organic Mental Disorders
  Senile and Pre-senile Dementias
    Multi-infarct dementia
  Substance-Induced Disorders
    Alcohol
      Intoxication
      Withdrawal Delirium
      Hallucinosis
      Amnesiac Syndrome
      (Korsakoff Syndrome)
    Barbiturates
    Opioid
    Cocaine
    Amphetamine
    Hallucinogen
    Cannabis

    Tobacco
    Caffeine
Substance Use Disorders
Schizophrenic Disorders
  Catatonic
  Paranoid
  Undifferentiated
  Residual
Paranoid Disorders
  Paranoia
  Shared Paranoid Disorder
    Folie a Deux
  Atypical Paranoid Disorder
Affective Disorders
  Manic Disorder
    Single Episode
    Recurrent
  Depressive Disorder
  Bipolar Affective Disorder
  Chronic Minor Affective
  Disorders
    Cyclothymia
**Psychotic Disorders Not
Elsewhere Classified**
  Schizophreniform Disorder
  Brief Reactive Psychosis
  Schizoaffective Disorder
Anxiety Disorders
  Phobic Disorders
    Agoraphobia
    Social Phobia
    Simple Phobia
  Panic Disorder
  Obsessive-Compulsive Disorder
  Post-traumatic Stress Disorder
Factitious Disorders
  Factitious Illness with
  Psychological Symptoms
  Chronic Factitious Illness
  with Physical Symptoms
  (Munchausen Syndrome)
Somatoform Disorders
  Somatization Disorder
  Conversion Disorder
  Psychogenic Pain Disorder
  Hypochondriasis
Dissociative Disorders
  Psychogenic Amnesia
  Psychogenic Fugue
  Multiple Personality
  Depersonalization Disorder
  Atypical Dissociative Disorder
Psycho-Sexual Disorders
  Gender Identity Disorders
    Transsexualism
    Gender Identity Disorder
    of Childhood
    Atypical Gender Identity

    Disorder of Adolescence or
    Adult Life
  Paraphilias
    Fetishism
    Transvestism
    Zoophilia
    Pedophilia
    Exhibitionism
    Voyeurism
    Sexual Masochism
    Sexual Sadism
  Psychosexual Dysfunctions
    Inhibited Sexual Desire
    Inhibited Sexual Excitement
    Inhibited Female Orgasm
    Inhibited Male Orgasm
    Premature Ejaculation
    Functional Dyspareunia
    Functional Vaginismus
  Other Psycho-sexual Disorders
    Ego-dystonic Homosexuality
**Disorders of Impulse Control
Not Elsewhere Classified**
  Pathological Gambling
  Kleptomania
  Pyromania
  Intermittent Explosive Disorder
  Isolated Explosive Disorder
Adjustment Disorders
  With Depressed Mood
  With Anxious Mood
  With Disturbance of Conduct
  With Work (or Academic)
  Inhibition
  With Withdrawal
Other Conditions
  Unspecified Mental Disorder
    (Non-psychotic)
  Psychosomatic Reaction
**Conditions Not Attributable to a
Mental Disorders That Are a Focus
of Attention or Treatment**
  Malingering
  Borderline Intellectual
  Functioning
  Adult Anti-social Behavior
  Marital Problem
  Parent–Child Problem
  Other Interpersonal Problem
  Academic Problem
  Occupational Problem
  Uncomplicated Bereavement
  Noncompliance with Medical
  Treatment
  Phase of Life Problem or Other
  Life Circumstance Problem

Axis 2 Personality Disorders (Traits)

Paranoid
Schizoid
Schizotypal
Histrionic
Narcissistic
Anti-social
Borderline
Avoidant

Dependent
Compulsive
Passive–Aggressive
Atypical, Mixed, or Other
Specific Developmental Disorders
  Developmental Reading Disorder
  Developmental Arithmetic
  Disorder

Developmental Language
Disorder
Developmental Articulation
Disorder
Atypical Specific Developmental
Disorder

disorders") together and treated them as "Clinical Psychiatric Syndromes"—which is to say, severe mental disorders that are merely various types of medical problems. (Milder types of neuroses and character disorders have been renamed "personality disorders" and put on Axis 2, but are still considered medical disorders.)

DSM-III has many merits, not the least of which is that it is based more on **symptomatic behaviors** that can be objectively measured than it is based on guessing at the "mental processes" inside the patient's head. However, as we will soon see, DSM-III has many faults, not the least of which is that it is based on what psychiatrist George L. Engel (and many others) have called the **medical model** of mental illness. That is, the authors of DSM-III still believe mental disorders are *diseases* caused by some "mental germ" that infects your mind much as chicken pox is caused by a virus that infects your body. Thus, even **phobias** that are clearly learned behavior patterns (and best treated by **extinction** procedures) are now to be considered *medical sicknesses* rather than *behavior problems* (see Chapter 15).

As we noted in Chapter 5, Dr. Engel believes that a General Systems approach to diagnosing and treating mental disorders is far superior to that offered by DSM-III. Let us therefore continue our discussion of abnormal psychology by looking at three types of behavioral problems—those caused primarily by biological factors, those caused primarily by intra-psychic factors, and those caused primarily by social factors. Once we have examined "mental illness" from this *holistic* approach, our comments on DSM-III will make a bit more sense.

Question: Suppose a child of yours stuttered. If your family physician followed the recommendations in DSM-III, would the physician be more likely to refer your child to a psychiatrist or to a speech therapist?

Biological Abnormalities

Let us go back now to Mary and John Smith. Many types of psychological problems that they might face can be traced directly to brain damage, an imbalance in the body's chemicals or hormones, or to genetic misfortunes. The range of these *organic abnormalities* is very wide indeed, running from mental retardation to drug addiction.

Psychologist Jerome Kagan estimates that from 3 to 7 percent of the children born in the US suffer from genetic imperfections or birth defects that will prevent the children from succeeding in our present school system. If we give these children the usual sort of IQ test, they will always score some 2 or more standard deviations below the norm. We typically refer to them as **mentally retarded** individuals, but in truth they are physiologically or organically retarded. We do not at present know the limits of their abilities, but each year we do learn a little more about how to help them improve their performances. They are different from normal children in many ways, but they are not necessarily inferior nor are their problems usually treatable with pills and medicines.

At the other end of the age scale are those biological, mental, and social/behavioral problems caused by growing old. Several experimenters have found that most people show a slight increase in their intelligence test scores as they age—up until a year or so before their deaths, at which time their intellectual performance often drops sharply. Fortunately, even people in their 80's and 90's typically retain their mental sharpness as long as their bodies are reasonably healthy. And, at least from a physiological point of view, they retain their ability to perform and enjoy sex as well.

Sex and Old Age

Old age brings many physiological problems that can have important psychological consequences. Many women suffer a severe depression at the onset of menopause, when menstruation stops and the woman loses the

Symptomatic behaviors (sim-toh-MATT-tick). Those actions or verbal outputs that presumably are "symptoms" of an underlying mental disorder. Until fairly recently, the belief has been that "curing the symptoms" will not "cure the underlying mental disorder" that supposedly caused the behaviors to occur in the first place. For further discussion of this point, see Chapters 5 and 15.

Medical model. The belief—in psychiatry and psychology—that mental disorders are caused by some "underlying" or "deep-seated" psychological problem, just as influenza is caused by an infectious virus. In fact, what we call the "medical model" should really be termed "the infectious disease model," since there are many other "models" in the field of medicine. Those holistic psychologists and psychiatrists who believe that psychological problems are multi-determined are opposed to the medical model. As we will see in the next chapter, therapists who follow the medical model in treating mental patients typically do not have as high a "cure rate" as those therapists who take a more holistic approach to solving human problems.

Phobias (FOH-bee-uhs). Intense, abnormal fears that typically are learned through experience. See Chapter 15.

Extinction (ex-TINCK-shun). The loss or suppression of a learned response. If you reward a pigeon for pecking a button, it will acquire a very strong and reliable pecking response. If you stop rewarding the pigeon, the pecking response will undergo extinction. See Chapter 16.

Mentally retarded. According to *Webster's Third International Dictionary*, mental retardation or deficiency is "a failure in intellectual development resulting in social incompetence that is considered to be the result of a defect in the central nervous system and (hence) incurable." However, we now suspect that many forms of mental retardation are "helpable," if not yet entirely curable.

Bernice L. Neugarten.

ability to have children. This depression appears to come from psychological causes rather than being due to a change in the way the woman's body responds to sexual inputs. If Mary Smith were the sort of person who equated her physical and psychological attractiveness with her ability to become pregnant, menopause might bring with it a deep **melancholia.** For she might assume that, having lost her "womanhood," she would also lose all sexual desire and that John might no longer find her desirable.

But many women find the release from childbearing a great relief. Thus Mary Smith might enter into her post-menopausal years with great joy and renewed interest in sexual expression. The change (if any) in a woman's sexuality at menopause, then, depends primarily on social and psychological factors.

One such factor is her husband's interest in sex. Middle-aged men often go through a sort of "male menopause" during which they become excessively worried about their sexual capability. And to add to their problems, older men sometimes suffer from an enlargement of the **prostate,** an organ that indirectly influences enlargement of the penis. If John Smith's prostate had to be surgically removed, John might slip into a state of black depression because he feared he had lost his mental as well as his physical potency.

Strokes

Old age brings with it the increased possibility that you will suffer from a **stroke**—a broken blood vessel in your brain—or from other diseases that disrupt the normal flow of blood to your central nervous system. Immediately after the stroke, you may lose muscular control of one or both sides of your body. Or you may become confused, forgetful, or even develop delusions or suffer from hallucinations. If the stroke is a mild one, neural *compensation* may occur and you will return to normal (or near normal) in a few weeks or months. That is, other parts of your brain may take over the functions of the nervous tissue lost when its blood supply gave out.

Generally speaking, pills and drugs do not speed up neural compensation. In fact, treating the stroke victim as a "patient," rather than demanding that the person attempt to learn new ways of coping, tends to retard the person's recovery.

Senile Psychosis

If the blood supply to your brain is choked off by what is sometimes called "hardening of the arteries," you may lapse into a child-like state commonly called a **senile psychosis,** or senility. In 1974 this type of mental illness accounted for almost 5 percent of the admissions to public mental hospitals. As our life spans increase, however, this figure will surely rise. The average age of admission for patients diagnosed as senile is 75 for both men and women, although the problem may occur as early as age 60 or so.

The symptoms that lead us to call someone "senile" usually develop slowly, but the condition can be hastened by physical illness or psychological stress. The first changes that you might notice in a pre-senile person are usually those of a narrowing of the person's interests, a decrease in alertness, a dislike for change. If Mary Smith were becoming senile, she might seem forgetful, easily irritated, interested primarily in her own thoughts and bodily functions. She might also become more and more hostile and unsympathetic toward others. Eventually she might forget who she is, lose all her memory of recent events, or even refuse to recognize John Smith and their children.

One of the best forms of therapy to *prevent* (or at least retard) the onset of the senile condition seems to be that of giving a sense of meaningfulness to older people's lives, often by helping them maintain family and friendship ties and by making sure older individuals know they are loved and wanted. Robert J. Havighurst and his colleagues at the University of Chicago found—in a series of experiments performed in the 1960's—that older people who remained actively engaged in life were generally happier and healthier than those people who withdrew from society. But it remains true, as Bernice L. Neugarten pointed out in 1973, that people who are well-adjusted and productive during their middle years tend to be those who do best as senior citizens. Dr. Neugarten concludes that, "Within broad limits, given no major biological accidents or major social upheavals, patterns of aging are predictable from knowing the individuals in middle age." In brief, the seeds of a senile psychosis are typically planted long before the person's 50th birthday.

Alcoholism and VD

Alcoholism is, at least in the US, a psychological problem associated with aging. In a study reported in 1978, Yale psychologist Jeffrey Blum noted that 35 percent of patients aged 55–64 admitted to VA hospitals were diagnosed as being alcoholics. In marked contrast, only some 5 percent of the patients aged 17–34 were classified as alcoholics. Mental problems associated with venereal disease are also more likely to show up in older people than in younger individuals—perhaps because it takes many years for the disease to work its harm on the nervous system.

When the germs associated with **syphilis** attack the brain, they can cause a condition known as **general paresis.** Although our ability to diagnose and to treat this venereal disease has improved remarkably since the discovery of penicillin, general paresis still accounts for about 1 percent of first admissions to US mental hospitals. For reasons still unclear, only some 3 percent of untreated syphilitics develop the disease. It is much more common among men than women, and among whites than blacks. The behavior patterns associated with general paresis are, in many ways, similar to those found in senile psychosis. If medication is given promptly, before too much brain damage has occurred, the patient may show an almost complete recovery.

Although most experts believe that alcohol does not directly kill brain cells, the biochemical changes that are associated with alcoholism do have their effect on mental functioning. The acute alcoholic may show almost all of the symptoms associated with senile psychosis—particularly hallucinations, a denial that any problem exists, memory loss, and a general state of confusion. Only some 10 percent of chronic alcoholics develop what is called an *alcohol psychosis* and thus require hospitalization. (As we will see in the next chapter, medical treatment for alcoholism is usually far less effective than is psychological or behavioral therapy.)

Drug Psychosis

Addiction to, or overdose from, many other types of drugs can lead to abnormal behavior and thought patterns. A person suffering from such abnormalities is said to have a *drug-induced psychosis,* or a "substance-abuse disorder." We discussed many of the causes for drug-related problems in Chapter 3, and most of the types of drugs that people "abuse" are described in Table 24.1.

Lead and mercury—those heavy metals that occasionally pollute our food and water—can also bring about psychotic-like states if you swallow them in abnormal quantities. But then, so can malnutrition and an excess of some vitamins, particularly B-12.

Neuro-physiologist Ralph Gerard once said that there was "no twisted thought without a twisted molecule." Professor Gerard meant that, associated with each unusual or bizarre personal experience, there probably was an abnormal chemistry of the brain. In some cases we can be sure which molecule (PCP, heroin) is doing the damage and, by removing the chemical, we often can help solve the problem. In most situations, however, it seems that the psychological experience may actually "twist the molecule," rather than the other way around (see Chapter 17).

Your brain responds chemically to thought patterns and to changes in your environment. If your basic problem is *intra-psychic*—that is, due to your developmental history or to unresolved psychological tensions—

At least six million US citizens are alcoholics.

Syphilis (SIFF-ill-us). A deadly form of V.D. or venereal (vee-NEAR-ee-ul) disease usually transmitted from one person to another through sexual contact (although research reported in 1979 proved that many forms of V.D. can, in fact, be caught by sitting on a contaminated toilet seat). In A.D. 1530, the Italian poet-physician Girolamo Frascatoro wrote a fictional story about the first man supposed to have gotten syphilis. Frascatoro named the hero of his tale Syphilus, from which we get the name of the disease.

General paresis (pair-EE-sis). An organic psychosis caused by the destructive action of the syphilitic germ on the brain. There is a lengthy incubation period in general paresis, the initial symptoms appearing 5 to 30 years after the primary infection. One of the first effects the disease has is on memory—the paretic (pair-ETT-ick) gradually loses ability to transfer items from Short-term to Long-term Memory. If asked to tell what happened yesterday, the paretic may not be able to remember, so will make up fantastic stories to fill in the gaps in Long-term Memory. This filling in is called "confabulation" (kon-fabb-you-LAY-shun).

treating your "twisted molecules" by chemotherapy may not be the best way of treating your "twisted thoughts."

Intra-Psychic Problems

Let us assume that John Smith tells the marriage counselor that his wife is frigid and that he desires sex 20 times or more per week. A medical examination shows that he is physically normal. Knowing Kinsey's data, however, we realize that his preferred level of sexual performance puts him several standard deviations above the mean for men of his age and social class. From a *statistical* point of view, then, he seems abnormal. Given this information, most psychologists would assume that John Smith suffered from an intra-psychic problem of some kind.

If John Smith seems to have most of the rest of his life in good shape—if he has continued his work and seems reasonably well-adjusted other than in his sex life— we can assume that his problem is fairly mild. Thus (prior to DSM-III) we might have diagnosed him as having a *neurosis* or *psycho-neurosis* (both terms mean the same thing). According to DSM-III, however, John Smith would be diagnosed as having a psycho-sexual disorder called "atypical psycho-sexual dysfunction."

If, however, John Smith's thoughts and behaviors had become so unusual that he had lost his job, if he suffered from extreme emotional outbursts or hallucinations, or if he seemed to have lost contact with reality, we might decide that he suffered from a *psychosis*, or severe intra-psychic abnormality. (According to DSM-III, he would probably be diagnosed as suffering from a schizophrenic disorder complicated by atypical psycho-sexual dysfunction.)

The Neuroses

The psycho-analytic view is that neuroses are persistent but relatively mild emotional disturbances that are caused by your inability to deal with stress, conflict, and anxiety. Freud said there are five stages that you go through in the development of a neurotic condition:

1. You experience *trauma*, or psychological damage, while passing through your early psycho-sexual development. Neuroses, from a psycho-analytic standpoint, are almost always rooted in childhood experiences.

2. As a result of this trauma you *learn* faulty or inappropriate patterns of behavior and *acquire* incorrect or distorted attitudes and perceptions about your social and physical environment.

3. As you grow older, these inappropriate behavior patterns and attitudes create problems of their own. The more you may try to adjust, the more difficulty you may have. It is this inability to *cope with life* that creates the anxiety that causes the neurotic condition.

4. In order to reduce the pain and tension you experience, you may *regress* to a more infantile style of behaving. You may also make increasing but inappropriate use of the various *defense mechanisms*—such as denial, repression, projection, reacting formation, rationalization, and sublimation (see Chapter 22).

5. Unless you get some kind of help, these defensive reactions may become habitual—that is, they may develop into rigid, unconscious behavior patterns with widely varying *symptoms*.

Six Types of Neuroses Prior to DSM-III, most psychologists and psychiatrists believed there were six main types of neuroses:

1. The *conversion neurosis*. If Mary Smith suffered from this type of neurosis, she would tend to *convert* hidden or unacceptable wishes or impulses into organic symptoms—presumably in an attempt to divert her feelings of anxiety and perhaps to arouse sympathy and attract attention. If

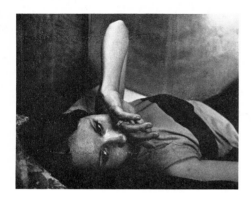
Severe depression is one of the most common mental disorders.

Hysteria (his-TAIR-ee-uh). From the Greek words meaning "wandering womb." A type of neurosis marked by unrestrained emotionality—wild laughter or giggling that can change in a moment to outbursts of anger or tears. A person suffering from hysteria may "convert" fears and anxieties into bodily symptoms such as blindness or a loss of skin sensations. A woman forced against her will to touch a man's penis may subsequently lose all sensation or "feeling" in her hand—presumably so that she will not have to "touch" the dreaded object again. This "glove anesthesia" (an-es-THESE-see-uh), as it is called, may continue for weeks or even years, then suddenly disappear almost overnight. Hysteria was originally thought to be a neurosis found only in women experiencing some displacement or "wandering" of the womb.

she insisted that her sex organs had no "feelings" at all, that they were "anesthetized," she might be converting her fears about sexuality into a bodily symptom. This sort of problem is also frequently called **hysteria.** (DSM-III calls this a somatoform conversion disorder.)

2. The *depressive neurosis.* If John Smith feared that his sexual performance was inadequate, that he could not live up to his image of what a man should be, he might give in to his fears and enter a period of dark depression. He might withdraw from most forms of communication with Mary Smith (and others), refuse to make plans for the future, and talk about nothing but his own personal discouragement with life. (DSM-III calls this an adjustment disorder with depressed mood.)

3. The *dissociative neurosis.* If your ego prevents unacceptable impulses from gaining consciousness, these desires may find other (unhealthy) ways of expressing themselves. According to Jung, they may split off from your ego entirely and form a *complex,* or separate personality structure all their own. If Mary Smith's desire for sex bothered her, she might repress all thoughts of sex. But these repressed sexual urges might be so strong that they could split off into a separate sub-personality in order to find expression. Mary Smith might refer to this part of herself as "Miss Black," who periodically (usually in bed) seized possession of her body and "did wicked things" with Mr. Smith. In this form of "multiple personality," the dominant personality often forgets (shows amnesia for) the behaviors that the minor personality engages in. (DSM-III calls this a dissociative disorder with multiple personality.)

4. The *obsessive–compulsive neurosis.* Suppose that Mary Smith had, during her childhood attempts to resolve her Electral crisis, picked up the attitude that sexual desires are evil and ought to be resisted even in marriage, and so she attempts to repress her natural instincts and urges, much to John Smith's dismay. But her sexual impulses become so strong that the only way she can keep them safely repressed is to think continually about something utterly irrational—and keep thinking about it again and again and again. Or perhaps she performs compulsive, repetitive actions—over and over and over. Usually the obsessive thoughts or compulsive actions are symbolically related to her problem. Her mind may be filled with images of germs: She may see them everywhere. Or she may wash her hands, or the bedroom floor, dozens of times each day, all in an attempt to prevent or to get rid of the "dirty sexual thoughts" that occasionally flood her mind. (DSM-III would refer to this as an obsessive–compulsive sub-type of an anxiety disorder.)

5. The *phobic neurosis,* or phobia. As we mentioned in Chapter 15, phobias are abnormal or unusual fears that have no real basis in fact. If John Smith is unconsciously afraid of sexual activity, he may transfer this unacceptable anxiety to a fear of small or tight places. If the Smiths' bedroom is cramped for space, John may avoid the anxiety associated with entering his wife by refusing to enter the bedroom. (DSM-III lists this as a phobic sub-type of an anxiety disorder.)

6. The *anxiety neurosis.* Fear begets fear, and panic leads to more panic. If John Smith is unconsciously worried about his masculinity, he

Schizophrenia (skits-oh-FREE-nee-uh). A psychological label that we apply to personality disturbances characterized by shyness, introversion, and a tendency to avoid social contact and close relationships. Distorted thought patterns, delusions, emotional impulsivity, and unusual body movements are often symptomatic behaviors associated with schizophrenia.

Dementia praecox (dee-MEN-cha PREE-cox). The original name for schizophrenia. Means "insanity of the young."

Autism (AW-tism). Literally, an absorption in need-satisfying or wish-fulfilling fantasy as a mechanism for escaping reality. The autistic (aw-TISS-tic) person withdraws from the cold, hard facts of the world into a dream-like existence. Any attempt to demonstrate reality or bring the autistic individual out of her or his fantasy world is likely to be met with hostility. As we noted in Chapter 9, recent evidence suggests that autistic children (in particular) suffer from "input overload" and can be helped by therapy that involves reduction of sensory inputs. Although autism is sometimes considered a "form of schizophrenia," neurological studies suggest that schizophrenic patients process inputs primarily with their left (dominant) hemispheres, while autistic patients process inputs primarily with their right (nonverbal) hemispheres. Thus the two disorders are probably not related.

Disorganized (hebephrenic) schizophrenia (hee-bee-FREN-ick). According to Goldenson, hebephrenia is characterized by severe disintegration of the personality. The patient loses touch with reality, and all major functions—thought, speech, behavior, and emotionality—become increasingly disorganized and distorted.

Catatonic schizophrenia (kat-tah-TAHN-ick). Goldenson states that there are two main types of catatonic schizophrenia. The first (called "catatonic stupor") often comes on rapidly. The patient becomes mute, stares blankly at the floor, and may assume a fixed, stereotyped posture which may be maintained

---

may suffer from such acute anxiety that he is unable to perform sexually. The more he tries to satisfy his wife, the more anxiety he experiences, and the worse he performs. Eventually he may break out in a cold sweat if Mary so much as puts her arm around him in the kitchen, fearing that this show of affection is the prelude to another bedroom disaster. (DSM-III calls this a panic sub-type of an anxiety disorder.)

The six categories mentioned above are, at best, rather loose labels that we sometimes apply to complex human problems. A given individual may show several different types of symptoms, not all of which can be nicely tucked into one label or category of neurosis.

It remains to be seen whether or not the term "neurosis" will continue to be used once DMS-III is officially published. Perhaps the most important thing that DSM-III teaches us, however, is that people's *problems* remain the same, but the labels or diagnoses that we give to the problems may change dramatically from one year to the next.

Question: What do the differences between prior diagnostic schemes and DSM-III tell you about the validity *of psychiatric labels such as "neurosis" and "psychosis?"*

Functional Psychoses

Psychologists have, in the past, differentiated between the *organic psychosis*, which we have already discussed, and the *functional psychosis*, which is a severe form of psychological disturbance that has no obvious physiological basis. It is the misfunctioning of the mind, not of the central nervous system, that is generally considered to be the causal factor for the functional psychoses.

About 40 percent of the first admissions to public mental hospitals are for patients with functional psychoses. Another 25 percent of first admissions are for patients with organic psychoses. Public health officials estimate that, during any given year, more than one million Americans can be considered psychotic. About two-thirds of these people are hospitalized, more than 98 percent in public institutions. Perhaps 50 percent of the hospital beds in the US are occupied by mental patients, the vast majority being people suffering from psychotic problems. Fortunately, many of these individuals recover completely after treatment and never need hospitalization again.

Schizophrenia By far the most common type of functional psychosis is **schizophrenia.** The term comes from the Latin words that mean "splitting of the mind." The use of this term is unfortunate, for the "multiple" or "split personality" we listed as a type of dissociative neurosis has little or nothing to do with schizophrenia.

General mental disorganization is usually the major hallmark of schizophrenia. If you badly distort reality, or if you withdraw into a psychological shell and won't come out, you would probably be diagnosed as suffering from schizophrenia.

An older name for schizophrenia is **dementia praecox,** from the Latin words meaning "youthful insanity." And schizophrenia *is* primarily a disorder of the young. Jeffrey Blum's study of patients at VA hospitals shows that 45.7 percent of patients aged 17–24 were diagnosed as being schizophrenic, while but 8.9 percent of patients over 65 were so diagnosed. About 27 percent of all the patients in Blum's study were classified as suffering from schizophrenia. Furthermore, this disorder is becoming increasingly more common. Only 22.2 percent of the VA patients in 1954 were classed as schizophrenic, while in 1974, the figure had risen to almost 31 percent. Schizophrenia affects men and women in equal numbers but, as we will see, single males are particularly susceptible.

When schizophrenia affects children, as we saw in Chapter 20, it is usually called **autism.**

There is considerable argument in psychological circles as to whether schizophrenia really exists as a "single" mental illness, or whether we simply call people "schizophrenics" because we don't know what else to call them. The fact that so many people are diagnosed as schizophrenic suggests that this category may be too loose and too large to be meaningfully applied to the complex living systems we call human beings.

DSM-III lists four main types of schizophrenia: **disorganized (hebephrenic), catatonic, paranoid,** and **undifferentiated.** A fifth category, called *residual,* is reserved for patients who have made some sort of recovery or who are not presently showing all the symptoms of the disorder. However, schizophrenic patients are not expected to recover fully. If they do, the psychiatrist is urged to reconsider the original diagnosis.

DSM-III describes the schizophrenic disorders at some length. Briefly put, disorganized schizophrenic patients show a flattened **affect** or lack of emotionality—or, their emotions and behaviors are "silly" in some way. They show disorganized thought patterns and have severe problems getting along with others. Anyone who withdraws from society; whose main problem seems to be that of "coping"; and whose actions are often "out of place" or bizarre is likely to be diagnosed as an undifferentiated schizophrenic.

Catatonic schizophrenia typically involves strange forms of "posturing" in which the patient may assume a "pose" and hold it rigidly for hours. During such rigid posturing, the patient will refuse all contact with the outside world; will become mute; and may even starve if the "posturing" goes on too long. The authors of DSM-III note that while this disorder used to be fairly common, it is now rarely found in Europe or North America.

Paranoid schizophrenia primarily involves such symptoms as "delusions of grandeur," and/or feelings of persecution. Any hallucinations the patient has will almost always involve grandiose schemes and persecutions. In addition, the patient may suffer from intense jealousies. Patients diagnosed as paranoid schizophrenics often show little impairment in their daily functioning—particularly if they do not pay much attention to their delusions. This type of schizophrenia usually occurs later in life than do the other types.

Undifferentiated schizophrenia is a sort of "waste-basket" diagnosis used when the patient is clearly schizophrenic but does not fit clearly, or fits into more than one, of the other three categories.

Patients who recover from schizophrenia are said to be **in remission.** According to DSM-III, they must be free of all symptoms (and off all medication) for a period of at least *five years* before they can be considered "cured."

Question: What might Harlow's studies of "motherless" monkeys tell us about the causes of catatonic behavior? How does Harlow's use of normal infants as therapists compare with the type of treatment offered in most mental hospitals?

Paranoia Some patients have delusions, severe types of jealousy, and feelings of being persecuted—but show no other evidence of mental illness (such as distorted thought patterns or inappropriate emotions). These patients are often diagnosed as suffering from **paranoia.** But as the authors of DSM-III note, "the boundaries of this group of disorders and their differentiation from other disorders, particularly severe Paranoid Personality Disorder and Paranoid Schizophrenia, are unclear." The authors of DSM-III also state that deafness, immigration, and other stresses may predispose a patient to the development of a paranoid disorder. The delusions brought on by drug abuse are also considered to be a form of paranoid psychosis.

Affective Psychoses People whom we call "schizophrenic" sometimes seem to be stuck in the middle of the "mood scale," being neither very far "up" nor very far "down," no matter what the situation. People suffering from what we call the **affective psychoses** often seem stuck at one end or the other of the emotionality scale (and sometimes they "flip-flop" from one extreme to the other).

for days or weeks. The second (called "catatonic excitement") is characterized by frenzied motor activity. The patient may talk incoherently at the top of the voice, rush frantically back and forth, tear off clothing, and without warning may attack someone or break up furniture. The two states may alternate—that is, a patient may be "stuporous" for a while, then lapse into excitement, then become calm and "freeze" into a strange posture for several days.

Paranoid schizophrenia (PAIR-uh-noid). According to Goldenson, the major symptoms of paranoid schizophrenia are poorly organized, internally illogical, changeable delusions, often accompanied by vivid hallucinations. Delusions of persecution ("they're out to get me!") are very common.

Undifferentiated schizophrenia. A "waste-basket" category into which patients are fitted who apparently suffer from schizophrenia, but who are not clearly hebephrenic, catatonic, or paranoid.

Affect (AFF-fect). The conscious, subjective aspect of an emotion.

In remission. Medical jargon meaning, "The patient no longer shows symptoms of the disorder, but we suspect that the disorder will occur again." A diagnosis much beloved by those diagnosticians who believe in the "medical model" of mental illness and that "underlying causes" are seldom cured.

Paranoia (pair-uh-NOY-ya). A diagnosis given to those patients who show delusions of persecution or grandeur, or intense and irrational jealousy, but who do not seem to be schizophrenic. From the Greek word meaning "madness."

Affective psychoses (aff-FECK-tive). Also called "affective reactions." The Latin word *affectus* means "desire," or "emotion." When psychologists speak of your "affect," they mean your emotional state or reactivity. The affective psychoses are those that have to do primarily with emotional reactivity—mania and depression.

Manic psychosis. Goldenson states that manic reactions are characterized by elation and hyperactivity, and range in degree from the mild through the acute to the delirious (dee-LEER-ee-us) form. The manic state is often preceded by a brief simple depression, leading some authorities to believe manic attacks are a defense against depression. The most severe type is delirious mania, in which the patient becomes totally disoriented and incoherent, develops vivid hallucinations, and engages in wild bodily movements.

Depressive psychosis. According to Goldenson, there are three stages the depressive patient may pass through. In the first—called "simple depression"—the patient shows loss of interest in the world, becomes dejected, thinks of suicide, and refuses to work or eat. In acute depression, the patient withdraws further. Physical activity is almost at a standstill, and contacts with other people rarely occur. In the final stage—depressive stupor—motor activity ceases. The patient is usually mute, confused about almost everything, and may have wild hallucinations. The patient often must be force-fed to be kept alive.

If you met a woman on a hospital ward who was racing about, giggling and smiling and acting rather as if she had taken too many "pep pills," you could be pretty sure that the hospital staff would insist she was suffering from a **manic psychosis.** A person afflicted with this disorder is often excessively happy and optimistic even in the face of life's greatest tragedies. During the worst part of an attack of mania, the patient may become so active and agitated that he or she must be forcibly restrained.

The **depressive psychosis** is almost the exact opposite of the manic. If you met a patient overwhelmed by the sadness and futility of life, someone sunk into a deep pit of despair, you would have met someone suffering from a depressive psychosis. Depressed patients respond as if they had taken an overdose of "downers," and often sink into a state of complete passivity. They may refuse to move from their beds, and must be force-fed to be kept alive.

There is a curious but not well understood relationship between manic and depressive disorders. Some patients swing wildly from one emotional extreme to the other, while some patients show only the manic or depressive reaction. According to the authors of DSM-III, if the patient shows *both* schizophrenic thought patterns *and* severe mania or depression, the patient probably should be diagnosed as having at least two types of psychosis simultaneously.

Question: What might Harlow's research on "depressed monkeys" tell us about the causes of some types of human depressions?

Labeling

There are many problems associated with pinning the standard psychiatric labels on individuals who suffer from psychological pain or disorder. The first of these problems has to do with our own theories about "mental illness." Once we label a person a "paranoid," we run the real danger of forcing our perceptions of the patient to fit the label. We may unwittingly focus our attention on the few inappropriate things the patient does and ignore all the healthful thoughts and behaviors the patient shows.

The second problem is that we often assume that the patient and the problem are one and the same. If Mary Smith breaks out in a red rash, we say, "Mary Smith *has* the measles." We never say, "Mary Smith *is* the measles." Yet how casually we remark of a patient in a mental hospital, "Oh, Mary Smith *is* psychotic," rather than saying, "Mary Smith suffers from a type of psychological distress that some people *call* a psychosis." Mary Smith may have many personal difficulties, but the only thing that Mary Smith *is*, is Mary Smith! If we treat her as a *psychotic*, rather than as a *human being*, we do her and all other humans a grave injustice.

The third problem with labeling is that it may mislead us into thinking we know more about the causes and cures of the problem than is really the case. We will have more to say about this problem at the end of the chapter. But we might note here that even the functional psychoses are affected by biological and social conditions.

For example, the *tendency* toward schizophrenia appears to be at least partially inherited, and the body chemistry of patients called "schizophrenic" is often reported to be different from normal. And the social environment and family backgrounds of schizophrenic patients are usually much more confused and disorganized than those of normal individuals. Psychotic problems also seem to be two to three times as prevalent among poor people as among the rich.

When we say that "John Smith is a schizophrenic," we may automatically assume that the problem is entirely his—that his "sickness" lies entirely inside his mind, and that he is entirely responsible for his present condition. In fact, his genes, his parental upbringing (or lack thereof), his poor socio-economic background, his lack of schooling or training, and the stresses and strains of present-day society may be the major contributors to his difficulties. If we say, "John Smith has a functional psychosis," we may then attempt to cure just his mind—instead of working to change his environment and to give John Smith better personal and social skills so that he can cope with his problems on his own.

Problems of Social Relations

Whatever their causes or cures, the psychoses and neuroses typically give the most pain and unhappiness to the individual concerned. The **social disorders,** however, are a broad category of abnormal behavior patterns that are as likely to cause problems for others as for the person who shows the deviant behavior. The social disorders, then, should be viewed as disruptions in relationships *between* individuals, or between an individual and a group or society. Most criminals fall into this category, as do sexual deviates, prostitutes, manipulators and "con artists," and many types of political rebels.

Illegal activities are, by definition, *social disorders,* since governments usually presume that law-abiding behavior is the norm. Given this fact, you can understand that considerable cultural bias creeps into our definitions of what is socially abnormal. Adolf Hitler was considered a warrior-hero by many Germans, but was considered "insane" by most world leaders. People who have continual hallucinations are generally hospitalized in the US, but are worshipped as powerful witch doctors or magicians in some primitive cultures. Individuals who fight against the Communist political system are often locked up in insane asylums in the Soviet Union. The top politicians in Russia apparently believe that anyone who doesn't see politics their way is mentally unbalanced and in need of hospitalization. This same individual might become a highly successful person if allowed to leave Russia.

It has taken us a long time to learn that "different" doesn't necessarily mean "evil," "abnormal," or "insane." Now, however, most psychologists assume that learning to tolerate different life styles is one of the main hallmarks of mental health and maturity.

The two most frequently discussed types of social disorders are the anti-social personality and the sexual deviate.

The Anti-social Personality

Perhaps the best definition of the anti-social personality is someone who lacks a conscience or superego, or who has never learned to measure the consequences of her or his behaviors. Such an individual not only breaks social laws or rules but is without guilt or anxiety about her or his actions.

At their worst, anti-social individuals appear to be incapable of establishing warm, personal relations with other individuals. They often appear to be greedy, impulsive, egocentric men and women who cannot understand the social consequences of their actions. Their relationships with others are typically one way: They "get" and the others are expected to "give." DSM-III refers to this problem as an "anti-social personality disorder." Older names for this same category are **psychopath** and **sociopath.**

Many people with anti-social personality disorders are quite intelligent. A few become business and political leaders who are known for their ruthlessness and toughness. Some drift into military organizations, where they may rise rapidly to positions of considerable power. *Most* anti-social people, however, move from one scrape with the law to another and spend much of their time sitting in jails or hospitals. Since they often feel little or no remorse about hurting or killing others, they often become "leaders" in prison societies.

Although a few anti-social individuals may suffer from some genetic fault (see Chapter 19), the main causes for this disorder appear to be poor parental guidance. The majority of anti-social people appear to behave toward others as their parents behaved toward them.

Sexual Deviations and Standard Deviations

Anyone whose behavior is more than two standard deviations from the norm is, by definition, a *deviate* as far as that one specific measure or test is

Social disorders. Those abnormal behavior patterns that appear to be a matter of inappropriate social learning rather than of intra-psychic or biological origin. Once called "character disorders."

Psychopath. See *sociopath*.

Sociopath (so-see-oh-path). A type of personality disorder marked primarily by failure to adapt to prevailing ethical and social standards, and by lack of social responsibility. Like "psychopath," the term "sociopath" has been replaced by "anti-social personality."

German dictator Adolph Hitler.

concerned. Some norms are determined statistically or by experiment—such as the modes, medians, and means on IQ tests. Other norms are arbitrarily set by law or custom. Although it was long suspected that the *actual* norms for bedroom behavior were somewhat different from the "model" or "legal" norms sanctioned by our society, it took Kinsey's research to prove this was the case.

Technically speaking, we should not consider any form of sexual behavior *abnormal* if it is engaged in by large numbers of people. In practice, however, any sexual responses that involve physical harm to others (such as rape) or that can be seen as psychologically damaging (such as sex with children) are likely to be considered abnormal.

The three main types of sexual deviation have to do with choice of sex partner, with the means of achieving sexual climax with that partner, and with the frequency with which sex is desired or performed.

Question: Suppose that, using the DSM-III, you diagnose 51 percent of a given population as being "mentally abnormal." Statistically speaking, who should be hospitalized, the people diagnosed as "crazy" or the ones you consider "sane?"

Deviation with Respect to Sex Partner Sigmund Freud, like most other theorists, assumed that we are all born with a fairly strong drive toward heterosexuality. As we saw in Chapter 19, the presence or absence of hormones during critical developmental periods determines our physical **gender**—we are born with a penis or a vagina because our hormones shape our sexual organs while we are still in the womb. These same complex chemicals probably shape our basic sexual desires, too, by acting directly on our brains during our maturation. However, the actual use that we make of our sex organs is strongly influenced by the demands of society and our own personal experiences while growing up. In other words, our hormones usually *predispose* us toward heterosexuality. But this predisposition is sufficiently weak that it may be altered or changed in many ways.

However, adult homosexual behaviors are not *caused* by a lack of the proper hormones. If a male homosexual is given injections of androgens, the man simply shows an increased sexual desire for other men. If a **lesbian** is injected with female hormones, she typically shows more interest in other women. Boys who have lower than average amounts of male hormones typically grow into adult heterosexuals, and boys with abnormally large amounts of male hormones often engage in homosexual behaviors as adolescents or adults. Thus your hormones *orient* you toward heterosexuality, but your choice of sex partner is greatly influenced by your early upbringing and present environment.

As Freud pointed out, if a young boy's mother is domineering and his father is weak or absent, the boy may lack a suitable male model and may develop feminine rather than masculine sexual interests. These interests may involve the type of clothing that the young man prefers to wear as well as the type of sexual partner the young man chooses.

According to DSM-III, the psychiatric label for a person who prefers to wear the clothes of the opposite sex is **transvestism,** which is a type of *psycho-sexual disorder.* A transvestite may or may not engage in (or enjoy) homosexual behaviors. People who "cross-dress" because they feel they are "trapped inside the wrong kind of body" may also suffer from a *gender identity disorder.*

Aside from their sexual behaviors, however, homosexuals tend to be entirely normal in their dress and actions. These individuals—for one reason or another—simply find some type of personal pleasure in having sex with a person who has the same gender that they do. Some types of homosexual activities are the result of early developmental problems. If a child's opportunities for sexual exploration are limited to other children of the same sex, the child may experiment with homosexuality. If, later in life, the person's first heterosexual contacts are psychological disasters, the person may revert or regress back to homosexuality as a less threatening and more rewarding way of behaving. Or, having found that same-sex

Gender. The physical aspect of sexuality. People of the male gender have penises and testicles, although they may *behave* in what we consider feminine ways. People of the female gender have vaginas, although they may *act* in what we consider masculine ways.

Lesbian. The celebrated Greek woman poet Sappho (SAF-foh) came from the island of Lesbos. Much of Sappho's poetry sang the praises of other women, a fact that led many scholars to conclude she was a homosexual. Our word for female homosexual comes from the name of Sappho's birthplace.

Transvestism (trans-VEST-ism). From the Greek words *trans,* meaning "across," and *vestire,* meaning "to dress." A transvestite is a female who "cross-dresses," that is, who wears masculine clothes, or a male who wears dresses and feminine underwear.

Most psychologists and psychiatrists believe homosexuality is an alternate lifestyle, not a mental disorder.

Ego-dystonic homosexuality (EE-go diss-TON-ick). A type of homosexuality in which the person's ego becomes threatened or "torn apart" by the person's sexual thoughts or behaviors. A homosexual who is greatly disturbed by her or his own sexuality.

Pedophilia (pedd-oh-FEEL-ee-uh). From the Greek words *paed*, meaning "child," and *philia*, meaning "love of." A pedagogue is someone who teaches children; a pedophiliac is someone who has a sexual love for children.

Voyeur (voy-YOUR). From the French verb "to see." Someone who would rather look at sexual activity than participate in it.

Exhibitionist (ex-hibb-BISH-un-ist). People (mostly males) who get sexual pleasure from displaying their genitals in public. Often called "flashers" in newspapers and magazines.

Bestiality (beast-tee-AL-it-tee). Sexual contact with a beast.

Fetishism (FETT-ish-ism). From a Latin word meaning "artificial," or "false." A fetish is an object toward which unusual emotion, respect, or love is shown. A man with a "shoe fetish" is someone who is sexually "turned on" more by women's shoes than by women themselves.

contacts can sometimes be stimulating, the person may simply *add* heterosexual behaviors and interests to the homosexual patterns already established.

Other types of homosexual activities are precipitated by the present environment. Authorities estimate that from 50 to 80 percent of men confined to same-sex schools, prisons, hospitals, or who are in isolated military situations engage in occasional homosexuality. The estimates of lesbianism under similar circumstances are only slightly lower. Thus the tendency toward homosexuality is probably built into our genes almost as strongly as is the tendency toward heterosexuality.

For many centuries, homosexual behavior was considered highly abnormal (and usually illegal), and anyone with a homosexual *orientation* toward life was thought to be "mentally disordered" or insane. In the early 1970's, however, the American Psychiatric Association removed homosexuality from its list of mental disorders (as the American Psychological Association had done some years earlier). According to DSM-III, only **ego-dystonic homosexuality** is a mental disorder—as when the person's homosexual behaviors cause the individual severe pain or anxiety. Indeed, there is a trend toward viewing homosexuality as an alternative life style rather than as a social disorder or mental abnormality.

People whose social skills are badly deficient may find it difficult to relate closely and intimately with other adults of *either* sex, but may find it easy to entice children into bed with them. DSM-III refers to this condition as **pedophilia.** Although some of these encounters involve little more than caressing the child, or engaging in some form of masturbatory behavior, pedophilia may lead to rape or murder. The child's response to the situation may also cause problems. If the child is pleasurably excited by a sexual experience with an adult of the same sex, the child may grow up with a positive bias toward homosexuality. If the child is frightened by an early heterosexual experience, the child may become a very repressed adult. Kinsey's data (and later surveys) suggest that pedophilia is much more common than most people would like to think it is.

An adult who finds it difficult to attract or to establish strong personal bonds with another adult may turn to many other types of sexual relief. The **voyeur,** or "peeping Tom," may gain sexual excitement primarily from spying on other people as they undress or as they engage in sexual activity. The **exhibitionist,** usually a male, often can achieve sexual climax only by displaying himself to unsuspecting women whom he encounters (usually by accident) in public places.

Kinsey reported that **bestiality,** or sex with an animal, occurred in nearly 20 percent of men raised on farms, but was rather rare in men growing up in urban regions. Some men and women find their major form of sexual gratification in masturbation while looking at or caressing articles of clothing or other inanimate objects, a condition known as **fetishism.**

You should understand, however, that just because we have fancy Latin and Greek names for these types of sexual behavior doesn't mean that we understand what causes them, how to help people change them, or that they are necessarily harmful.

Deviant Means of Gratification   Even when the individual's choice of sex partner is natural, or heterosexual, the means of gratification may be abnormal. Oral-genital contacts of all kinds, even between man and wife, are still illegal in many US states, as is anal intercourse. In fact, these forms of sexual release are so common that they are not considered psychologically abnormal unless they are the *only* means of gratification the person desires. Sadism and masochism (see Chapter 15) are two other fairly familiar forms of deviant sexual pleasure (or pain).

Deviant Frequency of Gratification   Variations in the frequency of sexual contact may be considered abnormal if too extreme. The man who spends all of his time occupied (or preoccupied) with sex is said to suffer from **satyrism** or **satyriasis.** The woman with an insatiable desire for sexual gratification is said to suffer from **nymphomania.** Satyrs and nymphomaniacs are considered deviant not because their sex drives are so strong, but because their sexual encounters often lack psychological depth and human warmth.

For a variety of reasons, the opposite sort of problem—impotence in males and frigidity in women—is more common but is still considered psychologically deviant. Oddly enough, impotence and frigidity are perhaps the only forms of sexual deviation that society generally does not punish. Indeed, under many circumstances, sexual **abstinence** is considered *model* behavior (although Kinsey's data suggest that it is seldom the norm).

Are Perversions Perverse?   Many forms of unusual or **perverse** sexual behaviors are deviations from the law more than they are from the psychological norm. From 10 to 25 percent of the prisoners in most state penal institutions are sexual offenders. Most are men. Women, when they are arrested for sex offenses, are usually charged with prostitution or crimes against children.

In one study of sex criminals in the state of Michigan, 60 percent of all offenses were directed against children. Young unmarried males were the most frequent offenders, but most of them had been sexually delinquent during adolescence. More than 40 percent of those arrested for sex crimes were voyeurs or exhibitionists, who usually were put on probation or given suspended sentences. Fewer than 10 percent has been arrested more than once, and most of these arrests were for very minor offences.

Only about 5 percent of sexual offenders in the Michigan study inflicted any kind of physical harm on other people. Most of these 5 percent were judged to be abnormal or psychotic in *all* their behaviors, not just in the sexual realm. Very few sexual offenders progressed from minor to major crimes, since they usually persisted in the same type of sexual gratification. And most offenders were not over-sexed but rather the opposite—they were chiefly under-sexed, misinformed, narrow-minded people.

If we assume that sexually deviant behavior is that which is two standard deviations from the norm, then what Alfred Kinsey and his associates wrote in 1949 seems particularly appropriate:

> In spite of the many centuries in which our culture has attempted to suppress all but one type of sexual activity, a not inconsiderable portion of all the sexual acts in which the human animal engages still fall into the category which the culture rates as "perverse." The specific data show that two thirds to three quarters of the males in our American culture, and some less number of females, engage in at least some "perverse" sexual behavior at some time between adolescence and old age. One half to two thirds of the males engage in such behavior with appreciable frequency during some period of their lives and a fair number engage in such behavior throughout their lives.

The Multiple Causes of Deviant Behavior

Why do people do the crazy, abnormal things that they do? According to the psychiatrists who wrote the DSM-III, the organic psychoses are due to bad genes or physical accidents. But most other mental disorders are due to some weakness or fatal flaw within the individual's mind or personality structure. Perhaps because of its strong belief in the *medical model of mental illness*, the psychiatric world seems to take a very narrow view toward the causes (and cures) of psychological problems.

Validity of the DSM-III

As narrow as the psychiatric view is, it does tend to change over time, much as fads and fashions in clothes change from year to year. In his 1978 report, Jeffrey Blum points out that in 1954, 25 percent of the patients seeking admission to VA mental hospitals were diagnosed as suffering from a neurosis. In 1974, however, less than 5 percent of the patients received a similar diagnosis. Over the same time span, the number of patients categorized as "schizophrenic" rose from 22 percent to almost 31 percent, while the number of patients diagnosed as having "affective disorders" increased from 8.5 percent to 22.5 percent.

Have the *patients* changed so dramatically over a 20 year period? No, says Blum, they haven't. Rather, it is the *viewpoint* of the diagnosing physician that has altered significantly in the past 25 years. Blum believes that DSM-III reflects this change in viewpoint rather dramatically.

And why the change? Blum notes that in 1954, psycho-analytic thinking dominated psychiatry. Freud believed that psychotic patients couldn't be helped much, but neurotic patients could be. The **treatment of choice** in 1954, then, was rather long-term "talk therapy." But about 1954, **psychotropic** medications—such as the tranquilizers and the "anti-psychotic" drugs—became available. In 1954, only 10 percent of the mental patients were given medication for their problems. In 1964, almost 27 percent of the patients were given drugs. But by 1974, more than 60 percent of the mental patients received medication—often as the *major form of therapy*. Blum contends that present-day psychiatrists prefer not to treat neuroses, perhaps because "talk therapy" can be performed by professionals other than medical doctors. On the other hand, psychiatrists may be quite willing to treat psychoses that can be "helped" with medication, perhaps because only a physician can prescribe drugs.

Blum also notes that, in 1954, the prevailing view was that neurotic behaviors were merely *symptoms* of deep-seated mental problems. Therapy that simply removed the symptomatic behaviors was thought to be worse than useless, since the basic neurosis would still be present in the patient's mind. But even Freud thought that many affective disorders were best treated through symptom removal. Since most "neuroses" involve emotional or affective problems, perhaps it was easier to re-diagnose them as "affective disorders" and stick with symptom-removal techniques (such as medication) than to attempt the time-consuming process of "talk therapy." Blum sees DSM-III as a misguided attempt by the American Psychiatric Association to put mental patients in the diagnostic pigeon-holes that most psychiatrists want them to fit into, rather than trying to describe the patients' problems in objective terms.

Like many other psychologists, Blum openly questions the *validity* of the DSM-III. He believes that diagnostic categories—and the theoretical approaches that underlie them—become popular for a while, then slowly fade from the psychiatric scene. Blum suggests that we should stop hanging fancy diagnostic labels on patients, since most diagnoses may tell us more about the psychiatrist's belief system than about the patients' problems. Rather, Blum says, "we might study how people become identified as patients, what factors actually lead up to their hospitalization, and what the patients experience as they progress through treatment."

Treatment of choice. A medical term meaning, "Using the treatment that most doctors (at any given point in time) would choose or approve of."

Psychotropic (sigh-koh-TRO-pick). From Greek and Latin words meaning "acting on the mind." A psychotropic drug is one that affects thoughts or behaviors.

Reliability of the DSM-III

D.L. Rosenhan.

In a sense, *Diagnostic and Statistical Manual of Mental Disorders* is inappropriately named. As we have noted, the diagnostic categories themselves are questionable, as is the philosophy of mental illness that underlies DSM-III. The manual contains few statistics, and none of them refers to means, medians, modes, or standard deviations. Furthermore, DSM-III makes no attempt to describe normal or healthy behavior. The manual thus defines "mental health" almost entirely as the *absence* of any symptoms of "mental illness." And since *almost everyone* has one or more "symptoms," presumably *almost everyone* is to some extent mentally disordered (and hence might benefit from seeing a psychiatrist).

More than this, there is considerable evidence that psychiatrists using the manual often disagree on what diagnosis to make about a particular patient. Worse yet, psychiatrists often cannot tell (in a reliable fashion) who is a "genuine" mental patient and who is "just faking it."

In 1973, Stanford psychologist David L. Rosenhan shocked the psychological world with a report of research he had undertaken on the reliability of psychiatric diagnoses. Rosenhan asked several "normal" people to attempt to get into mental hospitals by pretending to be mentally ill. These **pseudo-patients,** as Rosenhan called them, asked for voluntary admission to several state and private mental hospitals. The pseudo-patients all stated that they "heard voices," and thus needed help. Other than on this one point, these quite normal people told the admitting psychiatrists the *absolute truth* about their lives and feelings.

To Rosenhan's surprise, *all* of the pseudo-patients were admitted without question. They were all classed as being psychotic, and about 95 percent of the time, they were diagnosed as being "schizophrenic."

Once the pseudo-patients were admitted, it was up to each one of them to get out of the mental hospital as best they could. They were told to ask to see the admitting psychiatrist the next day, to say that the "voices" had gone away, and that they wished to be released. But getting out proved to be much more difficult than getting in. No matter how "normal" the pseudo-patients acted, they found it hard to convince the hospital staff that there was now nothing wrong with them. On the average, it took the pseudo-patients more than two weeks to get out. And on their release, all of their records were marked, "psychosis *in remission,*" meaning that only the symptoms were gone. The "disease" presumably was still present, but hidden. One man was detained (against his will) for almost two months. He finally escaped because, as he put it, the hospital was driving him crazy.

When Rosenhan's article was published, it caused a furor. Many psychiatrists attacked him violently for daring to say that they couldn't tell normal people from people who were mentally ill. Rosenhan then agreed to a further study. He promised to send an unspecified number of pseudo-patients to a number of hospitals in the near future. The admitting psychiatrists at these hospitals were asked to "guess" whether each patient they admitted during this time period was a pseudo-patient or not. In fact, Rosenhan sent out no more pseudo-patients. He merely checked all the psychiatric admissions at the end of the time period. To his surprise, he found that some 25 percent of the *actual* patients admitted were thought to be "pseudo-patients" by the psychiatrists.

Rosenhan concludes that psychiatric judgments of what is normal and what isn't—and what is "mental illness" and what is "mentally healthy"—are much less reliable than we had previously suspected.

Pseudo-patients (SUE-doh). *Pseudo* means "false." Rosenhan's "pseudo-patients" were normal individuals who pretended to suffer from mental disorders in order to get admitted to various mental hospitals.

A Holistic Approach to Abnormal Psychology From a General Systems viewpoint, all behavior is multi-determined, which is to say that everything you do has not one cause but many. Human problems, like human successes, are almost always due to *interactions* of biological, psychological, and sociological forces. Thus any diagnostic scheme that does not view people *holistically* is bound to be both unreliable and invalid.

We can demonstrate this point by returning once more to John and Mary Smith. The authors of the DSM-III consider female frigidity as being

PART SIX Personality

primarily the woman's problem—a mental disorder (or personality trait) that resides entirely in the woman's mind. But all personality traits (and mental disorders) have a biological background, and they are always expressed in social, interpersonal situations. In a small percentage of cases, female frigidity may be related to physical causes—an imbalance of hormones or perhaps a vagina so small or abnormally shaped that intercourse is painful to the woman.

But biological difficulties don't really *cause* frigidity. Rather, frigidity is the woman's response to her physical condition. And this response is chiefly determined by her own unique developmental history and the social **milieu** she grew up in. As we saw in an earlier chapter, a girl with a widowed mother may learn to fear both men and sex. And in many parts of our society the belief is still held that it is a woman's duty to submit sexually to her husband, but she shouldn't *enjoy* the process. Perhaps it is the society, not the woman, that is frigid.

Milieu (mill-you). The French word for "environment."

Male impotence—which is defined by DSM-III as being the *man's* problem—can be seen in much the same light. A very small number of men are physically unable to perform the sex act. But (by definition) about half the men in the world are born with smaller-than-average penises. In many cultures and societies, physical size is assumed to be related to masculinity and potency. A man with a small penis—or who *thinks* he has a small penis—may develop considerable fear and anxiety about his ability to satisfy a woman. The more he worries about her possible disappointment, the more likely it is that he will develop the symptom of impotency. The woman who fears she is not attractive enough to hold a man's interest may shun the marriage bed for similar reasons.

Even so, frigidity and impotence (and other sexual difficulties) are seldom the exclusive problem of just the male *or* the female. A man may have symptoms of impotency at the time of his marriage, but it is his wife's (often unconscious) responses to his condition that help keep him that way. A woman may dislike sex when she marries, but if her attitude does not change after the wedding, it is surely as much her husband's responsibility as it is hers. In such marriages, it may be useless to treat one of the partners and not the other. For, generally, when a person develops abnormal behavior patterns, everyone the person has close contact with must be considered part of the cause.

In the long run, a theory of mental illness—or a set of diagnostic categories—stands or falls on its ability to help people get better. Thus we cannot make a final evaluation of DSM-III, or any other similar scheme, until we discover what kind of "cure rate" it gives us. As we will see in the next chapter, the holistic approach to treating mental illness apparently yields a higher percentage of cures than does the "medical model" on which DSM-III is based. And perhaps that is the strongest evidence we can offer in favor of viewing human beings as highly complex living systems.

Summary

1. The words **normal** and **abnormal** have no meaning except when they are defined within a given context. What is normal in one social situation may be quite abnormal in another.

2. Psychologists often use the terms **mean, median,** and **mode** to describe the **norm,** or center, of a **distribution** of test scores or behavioral measures. This distribution is often a **bell-shaped curve.** An abnormal behavior or score is one that departs noticeably from the mean, median, or mode.

3. The term "departs noticeably" is often defined as being two **standard deviations** from the norm.

4. Any test score or behavior that is within one deviation of the norm is considered to be "normal"—at least within the context of that test.

5. Psychiatrists and psychologists use many different **diagnostic systems** to describe and interpret thoughts or actions that are presumed to be abnormal. One such system is described in the **Diagnostic and**

Statistical Manual of Mental Disorders, the third edition of which will appear in the early 1980's.

6. **DSM-III** represents a significant change from earlier diagnostic schemes. To begin with, because it is based on the **medical model of mental illness,** it defines all psychological problems as being medical problems best treated by a physician.

7. DSM-III also makes no use of the term **neurosis,** and but infrequent use of the term **psychosis.**

8. DSM-III marks a movement away from **psycho-analytic theory** and a move toward objective description of psychological **symptoms.**

9. A psychiatrist using DSM-III would probably rate a patient on five different diagnostic **axes:**

    a. On axis 1, the psychiatrist would note the **clinical psychiatric syndrome(s),** or major mental disorders the patient suffered from.

    b. On Axis 2, the psychiatrist would list the **personality disorders** or **personality traits** the patient showed.

    c. On Axis 3, the psychiatrist would note any **physical problems** the patient had, such as brain damage or disease.

    d. On Axis 4, the psychiatrist would describe any **social stressors** the patient had experienced in the past year.

    e. On Axis 5, the psychiatrist would evaluate the patient in terms of the patient's highest level of **adaptive functioning** during the past year.

10. Prior to DSM-III, severe abnormalities thought to stem from physiological causes were called **organic psychoses.**

11. Among the organic psychoses are problems stemming from brain damage, **strokes, senility, venereal disease, menopause,** and from **substance abuse.**

12. Prior to DSM-III, minor but long-lasting psychological problems were referred to as neuroses. Labels for these problems included the **conversion neurosis, depressive neurosis, dissociative neurosis, obsessive-compulsive neurosis, phobic neurosis,** and the **anxiety neurosis.**

13. These "neuroses" are now classified as **anxiety disorders, somatoform disorders, dissociative disorders, impulse control disorders, adjustment disorders,** or **personality disorders** on DSM-III.

14. Relatively severe intra-psychic problems—previously called **functional psychoses**—are now referred to as the **schizophrenic disorders, paranoid disorders,** and the **affective disorders (mania** and **depression)** on DSM-III.

15. Problems stemming chiefly from person-environment interactions are often called **social disorders.** They include the **anti-social personality,** the **sexual deviate,** the **criminal,** and the **highly aggressive person.**

16. Research suggests that psychiatrists tend to diagnose patients in terms of the **treatments** available, rather than in terms of the patients' real problems.

17. There is considerable debate about both the **validity** and the **reliability** of DSM-III (and other similar schemes). The diagnostic categories are not clearly drawn, nor are they based on research or statistical findings.

18. Research indicates that many psychiatrists cannot reliably discriminate between people with real mental disorders and **pseudopatients** who "fake" being ill.

19. Since all forms of abnormal behavior are influenced by biological, intra-psychic and environmental factors, a more **holistic approach** to diagnosis than that offered by DSM-III seems called for.

(Continued from page 613.)

Steve May looked at the hamburger and burst into tears. "It's the most beautiful thing I've ever seen," he said.

Dr. Mary Ellen Mann nodded her head sympathetically. "Would you like a milk shake to go with it?"

"I'm not sure I could stand that much pleasure all at once," Steve replied in a serious tone of voice. Then he smiled. "But let's order one and see."

Dr. Mann motioned to the waitress and gave her the order. She watched with amusement as Steve demolished the hamburger and sucked up the milk shake in one long gulp. Then the young man sat back in his chair, a contented smile on his face, and uttered a very loud belch. The people at the next table glared at him. "Sorry," Steve said loudly enough for them to hear. "I forgot where I was."

"It's not where you are, but where you've been the past two weeks that I'm interested in," Dr. Mann said. "You said you'd tell me all about your stay at the hospital if I would buy you dinner. I have given you the food of your choice, although I cannot imagine why you chose to celebrate your freedom at McDonald's. So, for starters, why a hamburger instead of a steak?"

"You miss the things you can't have," Steve explained. "Sometimes the food was okay, but mostly it was terrible. The inmates cook as crazy as they sometimes act." He groaned. "You have no idea what disasters can be inflicted on innocent objects such as hamburgers and green peas."

"Oh, yes I have," Dr. Mann replied. "I eat at the Faculty Club all the time. But start at the beginning. I want to know what happened, from the moment you walked through the hospital door until the moment you exited in the garbage truck."

Steve stirred his coffee slowly, considering what to say. "Well, I got in, as you no doubt know. The admitting psychiatrist never batted an eye when I told him I heard voices. He just nodded his head and then asked me what the voices said. When I said, 'dull,' and 'thud,' he nodded more vigorously and asked if the voices were male or female. I said I couldn't tell. That seemed to impress him mightily. Then he muttered the words, 'existential crisis.'"

Dr. Mann smiled. "Just as we suspected he'd do, eh? 'Existential crisis'—a type of schizophrenic psychosis that is described in many books, but that nobody's ever seen in real life."

"And then he asked me about my relationship with my mother, and did I have arguments with my father," Steve continued.

"The Oedipal Crisis, of course."

Steve smiled. "Of course. Seems I've never worked it out. He thought it significant also that I lose my temper a couple of times a year."

"Poor impulse control," Dr. Mann said. "You tend to belch in public places, and terrible things like that."

"I guess you do get back to the elementals in the mental hospital. Nobody thought twice about belching, or even crapping on the floor. They didn't even make you clean it up afterwards."

Mary Ellen Mann nodded. "If the people around us didn't complain, we'd all act a lot crazier than we presently do. But to return to the subject, the psychiatrist never guessed you were a 'pseudo-patient,' like the ones in Professor Rosenhan's study?"

"No, he just asked questions for a while, then wrote down on the admission form that I was a certified nut."

"Which you probably are for letting me talk you into the whole affair," Dr. Mann said with a sigh. "I'm really sorry if you suffered very much, Steve."

"Oh, it wasn't all that bad. I did feel terrified at first, but I got over it after a while."

"Terrified of what?" Dr. Mann asked gently.

Steve grinned. "First I was worried that the 'crazies' might attack me. But of course they didn't. In fact, getting to know them was the best part of the whole experience. But after I realized I was physically safe, I got to worrying about how to influence what was happening to me. I was a nobody, you see. I didn't have any money or power or status, so I tried to act sane and sensible and be nice to people. Being nice was the only way I could think of to get them to help me. So I smiled a lot."

"Did it work?"

"Hardly," Steve replied. "One nurse finally told me that smiling was a symptom of my underlying problems. So I stopped. Maybe she was right. Anybody who'd smile in there has to be out of touch with reality."

Dr. Mann frowned. "But they did treat you decently, didn't they?"

"The patients did. The staff treated me more like I was retarded, or some species of vegetable. There was one rather good-looking young nurse's aide I tried to get to know, but she wasn't about to get serious with a 'mental patient,' if you know what I mean. The nurses were much better, but I didn't see much of them. That's one of the things that frightened me."

"Why?" the woman asked.

Steve laughed. "You can't get out of that place unless the nurses and the social workers *see* you and realize that you're 'doing better,' as they put it. And most of them aren't around too much."

"Where are they?" Dr. Mann asked.

"In their offices, filling out papers, I guess. You know, I didn't believe what Rosenhan wrote in his *Science* article—that the psychiatrists in the hospitals he studied spent less than one percent of their time on the wards. But it's true." Steve May shook his head. "You can't convince people you're sane if they aren't around to be convinced."

Mary Ellen Mann sighed. "Rosenhan says that if we just valued the patients as people, if we treated them as human assets rather than as liabilities, we might learn a lot from them and simultaneously help most of them get better."

"Some of them don't want to get better," Steve said quietly. "They're afraid they can't cope 'outside,' and it's easier to stay where someone will take care of them. I tried to help a couple of them, as best I could."

"Like how?" Dr. Mann asked.

"Well," said Steve, "there was Crampy Joe. Nice guy, really, but he walked around all stooped over like he had the cramps. I started giving him a cigarette every time he walked upright."

Dr. Mann laughed. "Behavior Mod to the rescue, eh? Did it work?"

Steve nodded. "It worked until the nurses made me stop. They said it was against the rules for one patient to perform therapy on another."

"A sobering thought, that," Mary Ellen Mann said. "And they never caught on to your game, did they?"

"Oh, many of the patients did," Steve said. "Several of them told me that I wasn't 'like them,' so I must be a reporter cooking up a story on the hospital, or something like that. But the staff members never guessed. That's what terrified me most, I guess. The crazy people thought I was sane, but the sane people insisted I was crazy. After a while, I didn't know which group to believe. And that *really* worried me."

"And that's when you decided to get the hell out of there, eh?"

Steve grinned. "You bet. I tried to see the psychiatrist for two weeks, to tell him I was okay. But I couldn't get an appointment. They just increased the number of pills they gave me. And I just kept on flushing them down the toilet, when nobody was watching."

"You aren't as crazy as you look," the professor said.

"No, but I did get to worrying about it." He smiled shyly at the woman. "For a day or two, I even thought you had cooked the whole deal up, because you thought I was nuts and it was the only way you could think of to get me into the looney bin. That's when I knew it was time to leave."

Dr. Mann laughed. "But why make your grand exit in a garbage truck?"

"Only way out. I noticed that the garbage truck always arrived right at lunchtime. So today I waited until they weren't looking and hid under the garbage. Once the truck was outside the gates, I dropped off, cleaned myself up as best I could, and hitch-hiked home. Then I took a very long shower, and called you."

Mary Ellen Mann gave a deep sigh. "Well, I do appreciate what you did, and we'll talk more about it later on. Do you have any final words of wisdom for tonight, though?"

Steve nodded. "Yes, I do. I realize that it's an important point you're trying to make. We can't improve the hospital system until we know it from the inside out, as well as from the outside in. And so you've got to have volunteers like me go in and look for you. But I have a favor to ask. If you talk anybody else into volunteering, tell them one thing for me, will you?"

"What?" she asked.

He smiled. "Tell 'em they're nuts."

Recommended Readings

Blum, Jeffery D. "On Changes in Psychiatric Diagnosis over Time," *American Psychologist,* vol. 33(11) (November 1978), pp. 1017–1031.

Braginsky, B.M., D. Braginsky, and K. Ring. *Methods of Madness: The Mental Hospital as a Last Resort* (New York: Holt, Rinehart and Winston, 1969).

Green, Hannah. *I Never Promised You a Rose Garden* (New York: New American Library, 1970). (Paperback)

Kesey, Ken. *One Flew Over the Cuckoo's Nest* (New York: Viking, 1962). (Paperback)

Task Force on Nomenclature and Statistics, American Psychiatric Association. *Diagnostic and Statistical Manual of Mental Disorders,* 3d ed., draft version of January 2, 1979. (Available from the American Psychiatric Association, 722 West 168 Street, New York City.)

Psycho-therapy

25

Did You Know That . . .

The term "to beat the devil" out of someone refers to a primitive form of psycho-therapy?

Many Cree Eskimos believe that they can be "possessed" by a witch or *witigo* who will make them cannibalize their relatives and friends?

A male Chinese may sometimes suffer from a dismal fear that his penis is about to be drawn up into his stomach and disappear?

Psychiatrists, psycho-analysts, and psychologists often disagree on how to define a "cure" for mental illness?

The majority of mental patients will recover spontaneously even if not given treatment?

Prior to the 1600's, mental patients were seldom put in asylums or hospitals?

One form of psycho-therapy grew out of the theater?

Encounter groups are good opportunities for people to explore and express themselves, but are not very effective as psycho-therapy?

Behavior therapists sometimes pay mental patients for getting well?

The "team contracting approach" probably has the best "cure rate" of any type of psycho-therapy?

"The Odds in Favor"

Mark Evans looked at the little old lady standing by the slot machine. She wore cheap gloves to keep her hands clean, and dirty tennis shoes to keep her feet comfortable. As Mark watched her, she grubbed about in her huge purse, then produced a dollar bill and handed it to a scantily clad young woman who made change for the machines in the casino. The attractive attendant smiled as she handed the older woman a roll of 20 nickels. "Good luck," she said.

"Good juju," the little old lady said in response. Then she tottered along a row of slot machines until she found one to her liking. Mark Evans moved over to watch her as she dumped her purse beside the one-armed bandit, then ever so carefully unrolled the nickels. She counted them one by one. Exactly 20. Examining one of the coins closely, she decided it would do. She spat on it, then rubbed the nickel gently between her gloved fingers to remove the tarnish.

"You'll rub all the luck off it, honey," said a large, red-headed woman who was dropping dimes into the next machine.

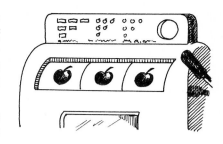

"Luck?" cackled the little old woman, taking a grimy cloth bag from her purse and shaking it at the slot machine. "Luck is just a matter cf chance, and I don't leave anything to chance. I put a hex on the machines, and they always pay off. I brought my juju bag with me today, so I can't lose. My juju is strong today. I feel its strength in my bones. You just wait and see."

The old lady dropped the coin in the machine and pulled the handle. The three reels spun wildly, then clicked to a stop, one by one. A plum, an orange, and a lemon. She took her head, and deposited another nickel. Again the reels whirred into action and jerked to a stop—two lemons and a bell.

"Your juju is all lemons today, dearie," the red-headed woman said.

The little old lady gestured wildly at the machine with the bag. "Juju!" she cried. "Give me a jackpot."

The reels produced a cherry and two bells, and the machine grudgingly coughed up two nickels as a reward.

"See! That's a good start. It's going to be a good day. I feel it in my bones!"

Mark Evans shook his head in amazement, then checked his watch. Time to meet his relative-in-law, Lou Hudson, from Chattanooga, Tennessee. Lou, who had married Mark's cousin Betty, was in Las Vegas for a convention of life insurance agents. Betty had called Mark a few days ago, asking Mark to take time out from his graduate studies at the University of Nevada to "show Lou the sights." That was the trouble with studying psychology in Las Vegas—sooner or later everybody you knew showed up and expected you to entertain them.

Lou Hudson turned out to be a thin young man with blond hair and blue but bloodshot eyes. "Stayed up half the night playing blackjack," Lou said, after the introductions were completed. "You wouldn't believe my luck. I was 200 bucks ahead, and I just knew I had a streak going. But then the cards turned against me. I barely broke even."

Mark Evans smiled. He had heard the phrase "broke even" enough to know that it usually meant losing a lot.

"Hey, man this Las Vegas place is too much! I've never seen anything like it." Lou gestured at the activity in the casino. "Hotels with gambling halls instead of lobbies, people running around 24 hours a day, throwing their money away like there wasn't any tomorrow! Bands playing, and free drinks, and lots of good-looking females on the prowl. Nobody to tell you when to get up or when to go to bed. Why, it's a gambler's paradise!"

"You're here for a convention?" Mark asked, a touch of sarcasm in his voice.

"Yeah. I suppose I really ought to get around to some of the meetings pretty soon now," Lou said with a frown. "But I've been having so much fun, there just hasn't been time." His face brightened suddenly. "Hey, man, they've got every kind of game here you can imagine, haven't they? I mean, I like to gamble a little, just now and then you know. Poker, blackjack, the horses—strictly for small stakes. But they got things here I've only read about, like in that James Bond story, *Casino Royale*. Roulette tables, I mean. You ever play roulette?"

Mark Evans shook his head. "No percentage in it. The odds against winning are too great."

"Whatta ya mean, too great?" Lou demanded almost hostilely, leading Mark toward one of the roulette tables nearby. "See—36 numbers, half of them red, half black. You put a dollar chip on any one of them, and they spin the ball around the wheel. If the little ball drops into your number, the house pays you back 35 to 1. That's pretty good odds, isn't it?"

Mark groaned. "Lou, you forget the two green zeros at the top of the board. There are really 38 numbers, not 36. If you put a dollar down on all the numbers, it would cost you $38 a game. And you'd win back only $35, no matter what number came up. You'd lose $3 each time the wheel spun, because the odds are against you."

"Yeah, but if you pick a lucky number, and put a dollar on it 10 times in a row, and it hits twice, then you've won $70 and it only cost you $10. You can quit a big winner," Lou said.

"*If* you quit. In the long run, it doesn't matter whether you play all 38 numbers once, or one number 38 times—you're going to spend $38 to win $35. Because your number is going to win just once in 38 times—on the average."

Lou was plainly annoyed. "You don't understand, man. Look at that fat man over there with the big diamond ring on his pinkie. He got a stack of chips in front of him that would choke a giraffe. He's bound to be making money on the roulette wheel."

"The only way to make money in Las Vegas is to open your own casino, Lou. That man may be winning now, but if he plays long enough, he'll lose. Because the odds are against him."

Lou shook his head. "I know you may be right in theory, Mark, but look at that man's stack of chips. Maybe he's got a secret system or something. Maybe he knows what number's going to come up next."

Mark was beginning to understand why the casinos made so much money. "Lou, old man, if that wheel is honest—and out here, they almost always are—there's no way in hell that you or anybody else can make money at roulette if you play long enough."

"Well, how the hell *can* you win at this game, anyway?"

Mark thought a moment. "The only way I know of is to sit for hours and keep a record of each number that comes up. Sometimes the wheel does get out of balance. It gets biased toward one number, let's say 25. Out of 38,000 spins, 25 ought to come up 1,000 times."

"So should every other number on the board, right?"

"Right, Lou," Mark replied. "Well, you plot all 38,000 spins on a graph. Some numbers will be a little over 1,000, some a little under. No big deal. But suppose 25 comes up 2,000 times, or even 3,000. Then maybe the wheel is out of balance."

"You're saying I ought to sit and count for 38,000 times, and then if one number like 25 is way out at the tail end of the graph . . ."

"Two or three standard deviations from the mean," Mark interjected.

". . . then you've got something you can bet on, right?"

"Absolutely," Mark replied, happy that Lou seemed to be getting the message. "You may not know *why* 25 is better than the other numbers, but the graph tells you it's a winner. So you go with the odds."

"Sounds like a lot of work to me," Lou said, taking a free drink from a cocktail waitress as she passed by. His hands trembled slightly as he sipped the drink. "Oh, I know. You're a brain, and you've studied statistics and all that. Betty never stops reminding me of things like that. But Mark, you've neglected the most important thing—the human factor. Man, when I get hot, I get really hot. I mean, I win big. It's like I've got some power over the cards, or the horses, or maybe even the roulette wheel. That kind of power is a helluva lot more important than drawing up graphs and fiddling with all those numbers."

Mark sighed. "Lou, if you gamble to have fun, then you can just charge your losses off as entertainment expenses. Same as you might a night on the town. You can follow your hunches, and enjoy your gut reactions. Maybe you'll win, but mostly you'll lose. But if you gamble for money—if you absolutely have to win—then you hunt for situations in which the odds are in your favor—for results that are 2 or 3 standard deviations from the mean in your direction."

It was obvious that Mark's answer didn't exactly satisfy Lou Hudson. His bloodshot eyes opened wide. "But man, I'm a special case! I mean, I get these streaks when I'm hot as hell. How do you explain the power I have over the cards when I've got a streak going?"

"Lou," Mark said gently, "How much money do you have?"

"Me? Well, to tell the truth, I'm pretty near broke right now."

"And you've been gambling all your life. If you have all that power, how come you aren't a big winner?"

Lou took a big gulp of his drink. "Well, I've been down on my luck lately. But just wait until tomorrow. I'm gonna bounce right back with a big killing. I got that special feeling, you see . . ."

Mark sighed heavily. "Lou, friend, listen. How does the insurance company you work for manage to make money?"

Lou frowned. "Why they sell policies, of course. You wouldn't happen to need some life insurance, would you?"

"No, but pretend I did," Mark replied. "Suppose I bought a million dollar policy from you."

"Nice commission on a policy that big," Lou said dreamily.

Mark nodded. "Yes, but how can the company make any money when I might die an hour after I bought the policy?"

"It's simple," Lou said. "The company knows how many people your age are likely to die in any one year, and they charge enough to cover their expected losses and to make a little dough on the side too."

"They go with the percentages, you mean."

"Sure," Lou replied. "They don't know who's gonna live, or who's gonna die. And I reckon they don't really care. They just go with the odds. I tell you no lie, Mark, those people are pretty hard-nosed when it comes to money." Lou stopped for a moment. Then his head drooped a little, and he continued in a voice grown suddenly hoarse. "Speaking of money, Mark, you wouldn't happen to have a little extra cash on you, would you? Just a temporary loan, you know. Until my luck turns good again."

Mark shook his head. "Sorry, man. The way tuition's shot up recently, students just barely get by these days. But what's the matter? Aren't you selling very many policies?"

Lou's bloodshot eyes filled with tears. "Oh, I sell a few. But the money always seems to go out faster than it comes in. Betty's pretty disturbed about it, I suspect. She says that I'm a compulsive gambler. And she ought to know, her being a psychiatric social worker. You're a psychologist, Mark. Do you think I've gone looney or something?"

Mark sighed. "I'm just a grad student, Lou, and there's lots of things I don't know yet. What do you think?

"I think I've got a problem, Mark. I mean, I *hurt*. Deep down inside. I hurt real bad." Lou grabbed Mark by the arm. "Man, you gotta help me. What can I do to get rid of the pain? What can I do?"

(Continued on page 671.)

Turning Knowledge into Power

There's an old saying that "knowledge is power." Sometimes you study the world and try to figure out what makes things go. But as soon as you discover some significant relationships about the things you've been studying, you're likely to want to put your knowledge to use to make things go *better*.

At other times, when you're faced with a practical problem, you may try out something new. If it works to your satisfaction, you may sit down and attempt to figure out *why* the new technique succeeded—so that you can use it again, perhaps more effectively. In either case, you're trying to convert knowledge into power.

We began the last chapter with a *knowledge* question—"What makes people do the crazy, wonderful things that they do?" And we found that there was no simple answer to that question. Behavior is always influenced by biological, intra-psychic, and environmental factors. To neglect any of these factors diminishes your understanding of the complexity and the very humanness of people.

In this chapter we ask a *power* question—"How do you change or cure abnormal behavior once you understand why it occurs?" As you might guess, the answer to this puzzler depends in large part on the viewpoint that you have about the causes of the abnormal condition. The more restricted your knowledge of the subject matter, the more restricted your power to change things is likely to be.

In many primitive parts of the world, for instance, people still believe in the "devil theory" of mental illness. Crazy people are thought to be *possessed* (or at least affected) by devils—outside spirits that take over a person's mental functioning. These psychic demons may find their way to the afflicted individual by chance, or perhaps as a divine punishment for some sin. Or it may be that the individual has offended a "witch," someone with the power to lay a curse or to force the devils into a person's mind. Let us look at some examples of the "devil theory" in action before we discuss more modern approaches to the problem of curing mental illness.

Primitive Approaches to Mental Illness

The Cree Eskimos and Ojibwa Indians of Canada occasionally suffer from a psychosis known as **witigo,** or devil-caused cannibalism. The first symp-

Witigo (WITT-tee-go). A Cree Eskimo word meaning an "ice witch" who eats human flesh. Also means the condition of being possessed by such a witch. The Ojibwa (oh-JIB-wah) Indian word for the same condition is *windigo* (win-dee-go).

In some African cultures, psychiatrists and "witch doctors" cooperate to help cure patients.

PART SIX Personality

toms usually are a loss of appetite, vomiting, and diarrhea—as well as the person's morbid fear that she or he has been possessed by a *witigo* or witch, who lives on human flesh. The affected individual becomes withdrawn, brooding, and cannot eat or sleep. The person's family, fearing for their very lives, immediately calls in a "witch doctor" to cast out the witigo by saying magic words or reciting supernatural **incantations.** If a witch doctor can't be found in time, however, the psychotic individual may be overwhelmed by the witigo's powers and kill and eat one or more of the members of the family.

In Malaysia, in Southeast Asia, young males occasionally suffer from a different type of possession by devils, called **running amok.** At first the man becomes more withdrawn, depressed, and brooding than usual. Then he will suddenly leap to his feet with a blood-curdling scream, pull out a dagger, and begin stabbing anyone or anything in his path.

Therapy for "running amok" usually consists of killing the amoker before he can kill you, or keeping everyone out of the amoker's way until he kills himself. The few men who survive the psychotic "seizure" usually say that the world suddenly turned black and they had to slash their way out of the darkness with a knife.

In Spain and Morocco, the name given to this form of madness is *juramentado,* the Spanish word for "cursed person." In the United States, we sometimes call it *homicidal mania.*

Question: How does "running amok" seem to compare with the manic–depressive psychosis described in the previous chapter?

Koro

Chinese males occasionally suffer from an odd phobia called **koro,** or **shook yong**—a dismal fear that their penis is about to be sucked up into their stomachs and disappear, causing death and other disappointments. To prevent this disaster, the man will hold on to his penis for dear life—and when he tires, will ask for help from friends and relatives. The man's wife may "cure" the attack if she practices oral sex on him immediately, but this treatment is not always successful.

Koro is thought to be caused by a sudden upsurge in the strength of the man's femininity. Thus, it can be cured by giving the patient "masculine" medicine such as powdered rhinoceros horn. If this therapy fails, the man may use a special clasp that holds his penis out from his body mechanically.

On the Pacific island of Borneo, a similar disease affects women, who fear that their breasts and genitalia are being pulled up into their bodies. Therapy in Borneo often consists of asking a witch doctor to remove the curse—presumably laid on the woman by a "witch" jealous of the woman's physical beauty.

Question: Under what diagnostic category would a psychiatrist using the DSM-III put koro?

Four Issues Concerning Psycho-therapy

Even in the United States—where most of us no longer believe in witches, demons, and evil spirits—our therapies almost always stem from theories of what causes human behavior. Indeed, as we saw in the last chapter, our theories are often affected by what therapies we have available or find of value. If we see an organic psychosis as being due *primarily* to physical causes, we tend to treat the patient with physical measures, such as drugs and surgery. If we see a neurosis as being due *primarily* to a conflict between ego and super-ego, we use psycho-analysis to help bring some rational resolution to the conflict. If we assume that deviant behavior is *primarily* the consequence of inappropriate rewards and punishments, we

Incantations (in-kan-TAY-shuns). From the Latin word meaning "to enchant." The use of spells or verbal charms spoken or sung as part of a ritual of magic.

Running amok (uh-MUCK). The Malaysian word *amok* means "furious attack." To run amok is to undergo a murderous frenzy and attack people at random. Similar to the Scandinavian term "going berserk" (burr-SERK) and the Spanish term *juramentado* (whoor-ah-men-TAH-do).

Koro, shook yong (KOH-roh). A phobia occurring in the East Indies and southern China. The disorder consists of a sudden fear that the penis will disappear into the abdomen and lead to death.

might prescribe behavioral therapy or otherwise attempt to alter the person's social environment.

In this chapter we will discuss all these special forms of treatment, and the theories that give rise to them. But before we can evaluate the various forms of therapy, we will have to raise several pertinent (and very hard-nosed) issues:

1. How successful is the therapy? That is, what is its "cure rate"? Would the patient have recovered anyhow, even if we hadn't done anything? Would a "witch doctor," or someone using a different form of treatment, have done as well? In short, does the therapy make a *significant difference* in helping the patient? Is it a *valid* form of treatment?

2. Assuming that the therapy does make a significant difference, how *reliable* is it? Does it work all the time, or just occasionally? Is it effective with all sorts of patients, or does it succeed better with some than with others?

3. What are the *side effects?* What else happens to the patient when we apply the treatment? Is the "cure" sometimes worse than the disease?

4. And cutting across all these issues is the basic question: "What do we mean by *cure?*" How shall we define improvement and, just as important, how shall we measure it?

We will have much more to say about these issues as we discuss the three main types of psycho-therapy. We will also find it all too customary for therapists of opposing views to call each other "witch doctors," and to accuse each other of using "black magic" rather than "scientific magic."

Physiological Therapies

Two centuries ago, when the "demon theory" was the accepted explanation of most forms of psychosis, the therapy of choice was *punishment*. The belief then was that if you whipped a patient vigorously enough, you could "beat the devil" out of the person. The fact that many patients did improve after whippings was evidence enough to support the validity of the theory—just as the fact that the number 25 on the roulette table occasionally comes up two or three times in a row is evidence enough to convince some gamblers that they have "magical control" over the roulette ball. It was not

Until fairly recently, the treatment of choice for many mental patients was "beating the devil out of them."

until *scientific investigations* suggested that the "cure rate" for unbeaten patients was higher than for those who were beaten that we finally hung up the whip in our **lunatic asylums.** Whether our present forms of psycho-therapy are all that much more effective than "beating the devil" out of lunatics, however, is a point much debated today in psychology and psychiatry.

As we suggested in the last chapter, the organic psychoses do seem directly related to damage to the central nervous system or to genetic causes. Perhaps for that reason, many of the therapies used to treat organic psychoses are explicitly *physiological*—the three main types being artificially induced seizures, psycho-surgery, and drugs.

Convulsive Therapy

In 1935 a Hungarian psychiatrist named Ladislaus J. Meduna noted an odd fact—very few of the schizophrenics he worked with were also epileptics. Without considering alternative hypotheses too seriously, Meduna concluded that seizures might somehow *prevent* schizophrenia. If he could induce epileptic-type seizures in his schizophrenic patients, he reasoned, he might be able to cure them of their problems.

As a test, Meduna injected schizophrenic patients with drugs that caused seizures. Many patients did show some improvement, but an alarming number of them were severely injured or died from the treatment. Others showed intense apprehension about the unpleasantness of the experience. Meduna's treatment was abandoned as "barbaric," but the idea lived on.

Question: If therapy is extremely painful—be it whippings or convulsions—might patients "get well" in order to avoid further treatment?

ECT   In 1938 two Italian psychiatrists—Ugo Cerletti and L. Bini—began using electrical current rather than drugs to induce seizures. If you were to be given electro-convulsive therapy (or ECT, as it is often called), the psychiatrist would probably apply it in the following way. First you would be given a muscle relaxant or "downer" and strapped to a padded bed in order to reduce the possibility of your breaking an arm or leg during the seizure. Then the psychiatrist would apply electrodes to your head, and pass a brief but fairly strong electrical current directly through your brain (see Fig. 25.1). You probably would lose consciousness before you could feel any conscious pain. Your muscles would become rigid for about 10 seconds, then you would go into convulsions much as an epileptic might. The convulsions would last for a minute or two, but you would remain unconscious for up to 30 minutes and would be drowsy or confused for many hours thereafter. Because seizures induce **retrograde amnesia** (see Chapter 17), you usually would not remember the shock or the events immediately preceding it. Typically, you would be given ECT two or three times a week for a period of many weeks or months—or until you showed some recovery.

There is considerable argument about the effectiveness of ECT. It does seem to be of help in bringing a severely depressed patient back to normal, for a time, but anti-depressant drugs and other forms of psycho-therapy may accomplish the same end. And excessive use of ECT can lead to damage both to the brain and to the heart and lungs.

What does seem clear is that ECT is of proven value only with depressed patients. Meduna's original observations about schizophrenia and epilepsy were based on a mistaken idea: He apparently did not realize that all patients with both epilepsy *and* schizophrenia were put in a different ward than the one he was working on.

There are very few well-controlled studies comparing the effectiveness of ECT with other forms of therapy. But recent studies by Canadian psychiatrists suggest that its usefulness even with depressive patients may be over-rated. The use of ECT seems to be declining in the US.

Lunatic asylums (LOON-uh-tick as-SIGH-lums). In Europe during the Middle Ages, there was a common belief that insanity was caused by some influence the moon had on human behavior. *Luna* is the Latin word for "moon," thus mental illness came to be called "lunacy," and mentally ill individuals were called "lunatics." An "asylum" is a place of safety, or of freedom from arrest and persecution. Patients are put in mental hospitals to accomplish at least two goals—to remove them from society, and to help them get better. Hospitalization obviously achieves the first goal. Whether it helps people recover is still a point much debated in psychology.

Retrograde amnesia (RETT-troh-grade am-KNEES-ya). A type of forgetting in which the immediate past is forgotten. If you are struck violently on the head, you may well forget everything that happened 20 to 30 minutes prior to your accident. Retrograde amnesia suggests that it takes your brain 20 to 30 minutes to "consolidate" an experience into Long-term Memory. See Chapter 17.

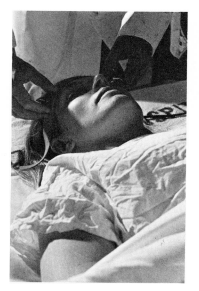

Fig. 25.1. An example of electro-convulsive shock therapy.

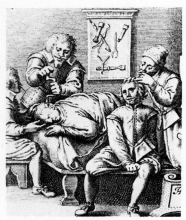

In olden days, psycho-therapy often consisted of boring holes in the skull to release bad humors or "devils."

Psycho-surgery

Galen's humoral theory of personality (see Chapter 23) led early Greek and Roman physicians to believe that insanity was caused by an *imbalance* of the four humors in the patient's brain. The treatment of choice in those days involved opening up the skulls of patients to let the abnormal humors drain out. During the Middle Ages, physicians also occasionally cut holes in the heads of lunatics to permit "poisonous gases" (or "devils") to escape.

In 1891, a Swiss psychiatrist named Gottlieb Burckhardt claimed that removing part of a manic patient's cortex successfully calmed the patient down, but similar operations performed elsewhere failed to achieve the same result. However, the notion that you could remove a psychosis by removing a portion of the "diseased brain" responsible for the psychosis has always been an attractive one to physicians and surgeons. These operations are generally called **psycho-surgery.**

As you will remember from reading the early chapters of this book, emotional responses are controlled by certain parts of the brain called the *limbic system* (see Chapter 4). As Mark and Ervin and many others showed, destroying portions of the temporal lobe of the brain can *sometimes* reduce seizure-induced fits of aggressive behavior in brain-damaged patients.

Portions of the thalamus and the frontal lobes are also involved in emotional reactions. In 1935, John F. Fulton and C.E. Jacobsen demonstrated that surgery on the frontal lobes had a *calming effect* on two chimpanzees they were working with. Prior to the operation, the animals reacted to frustration by chasing around their cages, screaming, shaking the bars of the cage, defecating, and attacking anything handy. After the surgery, the animals became placid, calm, and seemingly unaffected by emotional stress and strain.

After learning of the Fulton and Jacobsen demonstration, a Portuguese psychiatrist named Egas Moniz decided that cutting the frontal lobes—an operation called a **lobotomy**—might help aggressive or hyper-emotional patients. In 1936 Moniz and his associates reported that lobotomy did seem to be effective with some of these patients. The operation was introduced to the US in 1942 by Walter Freeman and his colleagues, and Moniz and Freeman later received the Nobel Prize for their work. Other psychiatrists soon reported that cutting the *connections* between the lower brain centers and the frontal lobes seemed to work just as well as *removing* the frontal lobes.

The question is, of course, "Work as well as what?" Many lobotomy patients do show an improvement after the operation, but many do not. And the fatality rate from the operation may run as high as 4 percent. Well-controlled comparisons of patients given lobotomies and those given other forms of treatment suggest that the operation is neither as effective (valid) nor as reliable as Moniz and Freeman had hoped. (We might note that the "fatality rate" must include Moniz himself, who was shot and killed by one of his lobotomy patients.)

The single form of psycho-surgery that appears to offer much hope today is the temporal lobe operation for aggression—and even that operation is controversial and seems to work only with limited numbers of patients who also suffer from additional brain damage.

Question: *Why might many physicians be more interested in performing operations on patients with mental disorders than in giving the patients long-term psycho-therapy?*

Drug Therapy

Various chemical compounds have been reported as being effective in treating some types of psychophysiological abnormalities. Dilantin and

Psycho-surgery. Operations on the brain designed to "cure abnormal thoughts or behaviors" by removing or isolating the brain tissue presumably causing the mental disorders. While psycho-surgery is occasionally effective, the dangers associated with its use are exceptionally high. See Chapter 4.

Lobotomy (loh-BOTT-toe-mee). A surgical technique involving cutting the nerve pathways that run to any one of the four cerebral lobes. Usually means "frontal lobotomy," or cutting the connections between the thalamus (THALL-uh-muss) and the frontal lobe.

various **barbiturates** can help control many types of epileptic seizures.

For many centuries medical practitioners in India have given tense or manic patients a drug from the snake plant because it seemed to calm them down. We now call this drug **reserpine.** In 1953 the Indian physician R.A. Hakim reported that reserpine seemed to be effective with some schizophrenic patients. When the noted US scientist Nathan S. Kline tried reserpine here in 1954, he stated that it brought about marked improvement in 86 percent of the schizophrenic patients he tried it with. At about the same time another drug, **chlorpromazine,** was discovered in France. Chlorpromazine had similar calming or tranquilizing properties. Reserpine and chlorpromazine were the first of the many tranquilizers now used widely with mental patients (see Chapter 3).

While no one is quite sure why the tranquilizers appear to be effective, there is some evidence suggesting that they reduce the amount of **serotonin** in the patient's brain. Serotonin is a chemical that appears to act like a super-transmitter—that is, a drug that over-stimulates the parts of your brain involved in processing information. Many scientists suggest that chemicals (such as LSD and PCP) that cause hallucinations may do so by increasing the amount of serotonin in the brain. In 1973 UCLA psychiatrist Edward Ritvo reported finding abnormal amounts of serotonin in the brains of autistic children—that is, youngsters who suffer from a type of infantile schizophrenia. Ritvo believes that these children inherited abnormal brains that produce too much serotonin, and hence drug therapy should be particularly effective with them.

Beginning in the mid-1970's, a drug called *lithium carbonate* has been used with varying degrees of success with patients displaying manic-depressive symptoms. A very few therapists have claimed that lithium carbonate is so potent a treatment for the affective disorders that anyone who experiences even mild depression might consider using the drug. However, judging from the latest research, this viewpoint seems overly optimistic. To begin with, lithium carbonate seems to work only with those patients who swing back and forth between mania and deep depression. It has little or no proven effectiveness with patients who suffer *just* from depression or *just* from manic episodes. Second, not all manic-depressive patients are helped by lithium carbonate. Third, the drug is a dangerous chemical that must always be administered under the close supervision of a knowledgeable physician. As evidence of the dangers involved, during 1975, several patients in the US died from overdoses of lithium carbonate. We might also note that the drug has no proven usefulness in treating schizophrenia or any psychological problem other than manic–depressive psychoses.

Scarcely a month goes by that the popular press doesn't serve up a juicy story about some new drug that seems to offer "miracle cures" for many types of psychological problems. Most of the reports need to be taken with a grain of salt, however. First, chemicals *by themselves* seldom solve mental, social, or behavioral problems. Even if the drug "cures" some underlying biological dysfunction, the patient will usually still need psychological and social help in adjusting to life. Second, not all of the drug research has been as well planned and nicely controlled as we might wish. Perhaps a case history will demonstrate these points.

Mendel's Research on Psycho-therapy

Werner Mendel is Professor of Psychiatry at the University of Southern California School of Medicine. He was also, for many years, the clinical director of the only public facility for treating acutely disturbed psychotic patients in Los Angeles County.

Like all psychiatrists, Mendel is a medical doctor. After receiving his MD degree at Stanford, he served a year as a psychiatric **resident** at St. Elizabeth's Hospital in Washington, D.C. Thereafter, Mendel spent several years as a resident at the Menninger Foundation in Topeka, Kansas—one of the best psychiatric training facilities in the world. Once his training at Menninger's was complete, Mendel was qualified to call himself a psychiatrist. Next, he moved to Los Angeles and studied for several years at the Southern California Psychoanalytic Institute, where he is currently an

Barbiturates (bar-BITT-your-ates). Drugs (such as phenobarbital) that reduce activity in the central nervous stem; hence, "downers," or sleeping pills.

Reserpine (ree-SIR-peen). From the word "serpent." So-named because this tranquilizer was first discovered in the snake root plant in India.

Chlorpromazine (klor-PRO-muh-zeen). A tranquilizing drug that appears to reduce fear and anxiety by reducing the firing rates in those parts of the brain that process fear responses.

Serotonin (sair-oh-TONE-in). A chemical found in the brain and elsewhere in the body that, in large doses, seems to cause hallucinations.

Resident. After completing four years of medical school, and obtaining their M.D. degrees, most medical students elect to continue their studies by becoming interns or residents in some hospital or clinic. Residents treat patients, perform research, and learn about their chosen fields of interest in depth before going out to practice on their own. A psychiatric residency may last 4 or more years. Thus, before psychiatrists go into private practice, they may have had 9 or 10 years of schooling *after* completing their B.A. or B.S. degrees.

Werner Mendel.

653

instructor, and completed his training as a psycho-analyst. After moving to Los Angeles, Mendel continued a series of experiments on the treatment of mental illness which he had begun as a resident in Washington, D.C.

St. Elizabeth's Hospital was the largest of all the US government facilities dealing with psychiatric patients. When Mendel arrived at St. E's, as the hospital is usually called, he was put in charge of a ward of Spanish-speaking patients, most of whom came from Puerto Rico or the Virgin Islands. All of these patients were diagnosed as being hostile, aggressive individuals. Some were considered homicidal. They were all considered so dangerous to themselves and others that they were confined to "padded cells" or were physically restrained in **strait-jackets.** Mendel states that he needed two large attendants to protect him whenever he visited the wards. And because the patients spoke little or no English, and Mendel spoke no Spanish, there was little he could do in the way of treatment.

Luckily, it was just at this time that news of the apparent effectiveness of reserpine spread to the US. The authorities at St. E's decided to test the drug. To make the test scientifically valid, they used the *double-blind method:* that is, they selected certain wards whose patients would be given reserpine. But they needed some *comparison groups* to make sure that the changes they noted in the patients given reserpine (the "experimental groups") were due to the drug and not just to the fact that the patients had been given pills. So the scientists running the experiment selected an equal number of wards whose patients were given "sugar pills" rather than reserpine. The pills looked the same no matter what was in them. The experiment was "double-blind" because neither the patients nor the doctors in charge of the wards knew which drug the patients on any particular ward were actually receiving. The experiment ran for several months, during which any improvement in the patients was recorded as carefully as possible. Mendel's ward of Spanish-speaking patients was one of those chosen for the experiment.

Mendel reports that, almost as soon as the study began, he was sure that his patients were receiving the reserpine, for they all calmed down dramatically. Within a short period of time they were so tranquil that many of them could be released from restraint. Mendel no longer needed to have the two large attendants go with him when he visited the ward. Mendel was convinced that a psychiatric revolution had begun.

Then the experiment ended and the results were announced. To Mendel's amazement, he learned that his ward had been one of the "controls," and that his patients had all received *placebos* or sugar pills instead of reserpine. Yet they had shown marked improvement! It occurred to Mendel that, when the experiment began, he unconsciously changed his attitude toward the patients. Convinced that they were becoming more peaceful, he then treated them as if they were improving. And they did improve—not because of the drug but because of the way in which he responded to them.

The St. Elizabeth's experiment points up one dramatic difficulty in evaluating any psychiatric research—the good results that an experimenter often obtains may be due to *chance factors*, or to things that the scientist *failed to control*. Drugs are always given in a social setting. The patient's attitude, and the scientist's, may be more influential than the chemical effects on the patient's body. Or if a surgeon communicates to the patient the belief that psycho-surgery will surely solve the person's problems, the patient may very well get better after the operation—for all the "wrong" reasons.

Intra-Psychic Therapy

Intra-psychic therapy almost always focuses on making "deep changes" in the structure or the functioning of the individual's core personality—the belief being that the symptomatic behaviors will disappear naturally as the cure progresses. As we noted in Chapter 24, this approach to treatment is based on what is called the *medical model of mental illness*.

If you ever have need for intra-psychic therapy, you would seem to have your choice between two major types: (a) those methods that are primarily designed to help you understand your present self by uncovering what has gone wrong in your past; and (b) those techniques that focus on future goals in order to help you change your present mode of existence. (As we will see, the difference between the two types may be more a matter of emphasis than anything else. Highly successful therapists appear to treat their patients in similar ways despite the fact that their theories may be quite different.)

Psycho-analysts usually follow the first method. That is, they concentrate on discovering traumas that occurred during psycho-sexual development in order to help patients set their "mental houses" in order. Psycho-analytic theory suggests that, if you complete your analysis and become a *fully functioning individual*, you should be able to handle future problems with little difficulty.

The humanists, on the other hand, mostly follow the second method. They hope to make you aware both of your present condition and of your ultimate goals, so that you can shorten the distance between the two and hence move toward self-actualization.

A view of Freud's study.

Psycho-analytic Therapy

There is no single accepted and approved method of psycho-analytic treatment: It varies widely according to the patient's needs and the analyst's skills and beliefs. Freud compared analysis to a chess game in which only the opening moves could be standardized. Thereafter, endless variations may develop.

In general, however, the technique is designed to bring about a basic reconstruction of the patient's personality. The analyst achieves this end in two ways: (a) by encouraging the patient to build up an emotional relationship, or **transference,** with the analyst; and (b) by getting the patient to associate freely about past thoughts and experiences. By interpreting these free associations, the analyst can often discover both the content and the dynamics of the patient's unconscious mental processes.

But the task is not an easy one. Psycho-analysis typically takes from two to five years to complete, and the 50-minute-long therapy sessions are usually held three to five times a week. Costs for a complete analysis typically run from 10 to 30 thousand dollars (or more). The most successful patients seem to be between 15 and 50 years of age. They must be bright, verbal, self-motivated, and be willing to cooperate with the therapist. Although psycho-analysis is occasionally used with individuals classed as "psychotic," the usual patient is a mildly disturbed or neurotic individual.

Most psycho-analysts are males. Although Freud insisted that the medical degree was not necessary for the practice of psycho-analysis, more than 90 percent of the analysts practicing today are physicians who have gone through psychiatric internships and residencies before becoming candidates at a psycho-analytic institute. During the several years of training required for graduation, the candidate undergoes a "training analysis" to make himself or herself aware of personal problems that might prejudice analytic interpretation of a patient's problems. As Freud noted in 1910, "Every analyst's achievement is limited by what his own complexes and resistances permit."

Transference If you decided to undergo psycho-analysis, you would probably be treated by a male, since less than 10 percent of the analysts are women. You most likely would find your doctor in a private office completely cut off from the outside world. He might well ask you to lie down on his couch and then sit out of sight, just beyond your head, where he could take notes and observe your facial and bodily reactions. He would ask you to free associate—that is, to say anything and everything that came to mind. But he would try to direct your attention to your inner world of feeling, emotion, and fantasy. In a variety of subtle ways, he would encourage you to "transfer" to him many of your intense emotional feelings.

Transference (trans-FURR-ents). In psycho-analysis, the patient is encouraged to transfer to the analyst the emotions and attitudes the patient has concerning the "power figures" in the patient's life—chiefly her or his father and mother. That is, the patient is asked to act toward the analyst as the patient does toward the mother and father. The analyst, by observing these reactions, can often determine what the patient's underlying intrapsychic problems are. Some of the transferred emotions may be warm and loving. Others may be cold, hateful, or angry. In either case, displacing the feelings onto the analyst may help release pent-up libidinal energy. At the end of treatment, the analyst must carefully remove the transference relationship so that the patient stands on his or her own. The emotions that the analyst feels toward the patient are a part of what is called "counter-transference."

In a sense, he would become a "father figure" on whom you could rely and trust.

Free Association   Free association is the basic game plan of most forms of psycho-analysis. Freud believed that everything you do and say and think has a *cause,* and that trivial and apparently meaningless statements often mask deep-seated emotional conflicts. The more you cut yourself off from conscious control—the more you let your unconscious mind come through to consciousness—the more easily you can bring the buried problems to the surface. If your attempts to do this fail (mostly at the beginning of therapy), it is usually because some part of your mind is blocking the expression of these difficulties. By noting the things you *avoid talking about,* the analyst can often get a feeling for what your problems are.

Interpretation   During the course of the treatment, your analyst would interpret your thoughts, feelings, and actions in light of psycho-analytic theory. If inner blocks kept you from expressing important (repressed) material, the analyst might ask you to recall your dreams and talk about them. Freud believed that many psychic conflicts express themselves in fantasy, particularly when the patient's defenses are down (as during dreaming). He felt it was not so much the actual content of the dream that was important, but rather, it was what the dream *symbolized* that must be discovered. For Freud, dream analysis was a "royal road" to the patient's unconscious and to the real significance of the patient's childhood experiences.

Psycho-analysis takes so long—and there are so few analysts available—that only a tiny fraction of the people who need help ever undergo this process. Most patients settle for briefer, less intensive types of treatment. The problem of finding an analyst has become particularly difficult of late, too. As we noted earlier, there are relatively few female analysts, but more than half of the patients in analysis are women—and many of them openly state that they would prefer to work with an analyst of their own gender.

Psycho-analytic theory has influenced almost all other forms of intra-psychic therapy. Any form of treatment that concentrates on explaining the present in terms of past experience and unconscious motivations owes a large debt to Sigmund Freud.

Humanistic Therapy

Freud grew up in Austria, a land of kings and emperors who possessed "divine rights" that their subjects dared not question. Austrian fathers typically claimed the same privileges: When the man of the family spoke, the children listened and obeyed. Perhaps it is understandable, then, that in psycho-analysis the fatherly analyst often sets the goals of therapy and urges the patient onward.

But times have changed. Like the US, Austria now is a democracy. In democratic societies, citizens are expected to help choose their own destinies and work toward them. Modern *humanistic* therapists reject the "divine right" of the therapist to determine what is mentally healthy for the patient. In humanistic therapy, the patient rather than the therapist is king.

Humanistic psychologists—such as Carl Rogers and Abraham Maslow—emphasize the *conscious* determinants of behavior. All human beings are presumed to have a positive drive toward good mental health. Thus your environment may shape you into bad habits of thought, feelings, and action—but your "innate motivation to improve" will win out if given a chance.

The humanistic therapist does not look too deeply into your unconscious nor too far back into your past, for the present and future are considered much more important than events long since forgotten. Therapy consists primarily of making you aware of your present state of functioning. It also focuses on how you see yourself now, how others perceive you, and what "ideal state" you would like to reach. Once you understand all these things clearly, the therapist need only provide you with objective feedback about whatever progress you are making toward becoming your "self ideal."

Client-centered Therapy In Carl Rogers' **client-centered therapy,** the client determines the goals of treatment and the speed at which these goals will be met. Like most humanists, Rogers is loath to impose his own standards or values on his clients. Instead, Rogers tries to provide a "psychological mirror" in which the clients can see themselves. Like most humanists, Rogers believes the clients will use this reflected information to achieve whatever changes in themselves are necessary to meet their own standards.

If you went to see a "client-centered" therapist, you would most likely find a clinical psychologist who had taken the Ph.D. rather than a medical degree. You would sit in a chair rather than lie on a couch, and you would decide more or less what the two of you would do together. The therapist would try to be warm, humane, concerned, and supportive. But the Rogerian therapist would seldom give advice or offer suggestions about what you ought to do or be.

As you talked about your problems, the therapist would frequently restate what you had said—*reflecting back* your own thoughts in slightly different form. In this way the therapist would provide you with an objective "mirror" of yourself and your own mental functioning.

By giving you **unconditional positive regard**—that is, by accepting you and the things you did, rather than criticizing or making value judgments about your emotions and perceptions—the therapist would hope to build a relationship of trust and affection with you. Only under such non-punitive conditions, Rogers believes, can you build sufficient courage to see yourself as you really are. This same supportive atmosphere helps you determine what your goals are, and helps you decide what *you* want to become, not what you think the world wants you to become. But once you can see yourself objectively, and know where you want to go, your own internal motivation will push you toward a better state of mental health and acceptance of yourself.

Most of the people practicing intra-psychic therapy in the US today are neither "pure" Freudians nor "pure" humanists. Rather, therapists tend to be **eclectic,** a fancy term that means they make use of whatever psychologicl techniques seem to work best for them and their clients.

The Effects of Intra-psychic Therapy

Many factors make it difficult to evaluate the effectiveness of psycho-therapy scientifically. Science deals with objective events, things that can readily be measured. But by its very nature, intra-psychic therapy concerns itself with changes that occur inside a person's mind—changes that can seldom be seen or **scrutinized** under a microscope. The success rates of various forms of treatment, then, must always be considered in terms of *what changes therapists hope to achieve.*

Some psycho-analysts evaluate their treatment almost solely in terms of the amount of *insight* the patient gains about her or his own "hang-ups" and the changes that seem to occur in the patient's basic personality. Since the analyst is the only person who has worked through these problems with the patient, the analyst may feel that he is the only person qualified to judge whether a "cure" has taken place. The fact that the analyst could not demonstrate objectively to independent observers that the patient was, in fact, "improved" might not matter too much to this sort of therapist. Although this position has its merits, other psycho-analysts are willing to use less subjective measures of improvement—such as modifications in the patient's overt behavior and the gradual disappearance of neurotic or psychotic symptoms. At least these changes can be observed and agreed upon by people other than the analyst himself.

If we take an analyst's subjective impressions as our guide, then psycho-analysis would seem to lead to a "full recovery" in 35–40 percent of the clients, with an additional 15–20 percent of the patients showing noticeable

Carl Rogers.

Client-centered therapy. Carl Rogers believes that psycho-analysis is "therapist-centered," in that the analyst typically chooses the goals of treatment. In *client-centered therapy,* the client determines both the goals and the pace at which they are achieved.

Unconditional positive regard. Rogers' technique of accepting whatever the patient says or does as being "normal" for the person at that point in time. Client-centered therapists are taught never to criticize or punish their patients. Instead, the therapists "give acceptance" in a positive fashion for whatever the client is or wants to become.

Eclectic (eck-KLECK-tick). From the Greek word meaning "to pick out, or select." An eclectic therapist is someone who picks out the best of several different theories or viewpoints, or who fits the therapy to the patient's present needs.

Scrutinized (SCREW-tin-ized). From the Latin word *scrutari,* which in olden days meant "to search through the trash or garbage," presumably for something worth saving. To scrutinize is to examine anything carefully, piece by piece or part by part.

H.J. Eysenck.

improvement. If we apply the more objective measure of "symptom removal," we find that the improvement rate is much lower—30 percent or less.

In the humanistic therapies the patient usually determines whether the therapy was successful or not. Rogers does have objective tests that measure changes in the client's *perceptions* of his or her progress, and the tests do seem to be reliable. But the validity of using the client's subjective impressions as an index of improvement remains in some doubt. The claimed "cure rate" for humanistic therapy is usually in the neighborhood of 75 percent or so.

Eysenck's 1952 Report In recent years, the behavioral psychologists in particular have leveled strong criticisms against the "unscientific ways" in which the effectiveness of psycho-therapy is usually determined. Immediately after World War II, behaviorist H.J. Eysenck investigated several thousand cases of mentally disturbed servicemen and women in British hospitals. Eysenck reported in 1952 that the overall improvement rate among those patients given psycho-analytic treatment was about 44 percent. The improvement rate for patients given any other form of psycho-therapy (eclectic treatment) was about 64 percent. Several hundred other patients received no psycho-therapy at all. Their physical ailments were treated as necessary, but they were given no psychological therapy. The improvement rate among these *untreated* patients was about 72 percent. These data led some scientists to compare psycho-analysis with "witch doctoring," and to suggest that psycho-analysis might actually *retard* the patient's progress.

As you might imagine, the psycho-analysts did not take such comments lightly. They pointed out that Eysenck's criteria for improvement were considerably different from their own, since Eysenck focused on easy-to-measure behavior changes. Eysenck ignored all of the basic alterations in the patient's personality that are the stated goal of most psycho-analytic treatment. The analysts also raised the important issue of patient selection. Some patients are better-suited for analysis than others, and the usual feeling is that hospitalized psychotics make the worst clients of all.

Question: As we noted in Chapter 24, DSM-III continues a 20-year trend toward describing mental disorders in terms of the symptoms associated with the illness. How might DSM-III in part be a response to Eysenck's data?

The 1953 APA Study In 1953 the American Psychoanalytic Association undertook its own survey of all the people undergoing analytic treatment in the entire US. Although data collection was completed on some 3,000 patients by the end of 1954, the analysts could not agree among themselves as to what constituted "success." Could one depend on the analyst's own subjective feelings about the progress his patients had made, or should one rely entirely on a more objective **criterion?** When the results of the APA study were finally published in the late 1960's, the only figures reported were for "symptom removal"—a disappointingly low 17 percent. Many well-known psycho-analysts reject the APA study for not coming to grips with the intra-psychic changes that do occur during therapy.

Spontaneous Recovery Eysenck's criticisms deserve more careful consideration than we have space for here, as do the replies of the people he has criticized. We should note, however, that people made **spontaneous recoveries** from mental illness long before we had any real form of therapy to offer them. Eysenck states that about 45 percent of untreated neurotics show spontaneous recovery within a year of the onset of their illness. By the end of the second year, this figure rises to 70 percent. And within five years about 90 percent of all untreated cases are either dramatically improved or "cured." Although we must always keep in mind what we mean by the term "cured," it does seem as if the effectiveness of *any form* *of psycho-therapy* must be measured against whatever figures we have on spontaneous recovery.

Scientists have made many attempts to measure the effectiveness of therapy by comparing groups of patients who receive different forms of treatment. Although the results of these experiments have varied widely, there does seem to be one rather uniform trend—the more objectively the improvement is measured, the less effective the standard forms of intra-psychic therapy appear to be.

Question: Why would it be more difficult to prove that therapy "works" using objective criteria than if you merely measured the subjective opinions of the clients and therapists?

Sloane's Temple Study

R. Bruce Sloane.

One of the best studies on the effectiveness of therapy was performed by psychiatrist R. Bruce Sloane and his associates at the Temple University School of Medicine in Philadelphia. These researchers selected 94 patients suffering from moderately severe neuroses and personality disorders, who had come to an out-patient clinic for help. Roughly one-third of the patients were treated with a brief form of psycho-analytic "insight" therapy. Another third received behavior therapy (see Chapter 15). The rest were told that they would have to wait at least four months for help—and hence became an untreated control group (relatively speaking).

Sloane or another psychiatrist interviewed each patient before treatment and gave an initial impression of how disturbed the patient was and what symptoms the person showed. The patient was also given several personality tests, including the MMPI (see Chapter 23). At the same time, a research assistant interviewed a close friend or relative of the patient to get this person's evaluation of what might be troubling the patient. After the **intake interview,** the patient was randomly assigned to one of the three groups mentioned above. The assessing psychiatrists did not perform therapy themselves; they merely evaluated the patients before (and after) treatment.

Patients in the treated groups were given an average of one hour of therapy a week for four months. Patients in the untreated control group were called every few weeks to find out how they are doing, and were encouraged to "hang tight" until a therapist could see them. These calls, of course, were themselves a type of treatment. At the end of four months, all the untreated patients who still wished help were put into "insight" therapy.

At the end of the four-month period, all the patients were again interviewed by the assessing psychiatrist, who did not know (and was told not to ask) what kind of therapy (if any) the patients had been given. Each patient re-took the personality tests, and the research assistant once more talked with the close friend or relative to determine what progress this person thought the patient had made. Psychiatric assessments of the patients were also made one year and two years after the experiment began.

Sloane and his associates measured as many different aspects of the therapeutic situation as they could. Some of the tests or assessments they employed were objective, and were aimed at determining success in symptom removal, bettering job performance, improving relationships with others, and so forth. Some of the measures were subjective, having to do with how well the patient liked the therapist (and vice versa), the patient's inner feelings about her or his improvement, the amount of anxiety the patient was experiencing, the perceptions that the interviewing psychiatrist and the patient's friend or relative had about changes in the patient's emotions and behaviors, and so forth. In addition to these rather specific measures, the assessing psychiatrist, the patient, the friend or relative, and the patient's therapist (in two of the groups) also made what Sloane calls "global evaluations" of the amount of improvement shown by the patient.

Intake interview. Before being admitted to a hospital—or to treatment—the patient is usually interviewed by a psychiatrist or a psychologist. The purpose of the intake interview is to diagnose the patient's problems, and then to determine what type of treatment seems most likely to aid recovery.

Results The results of the Sloane study are both complex and fascinating:

1. Some 80 percent of the patients given *either* behavior therapy or "insight" psycho-therapy showed significant symptom removal, but so did 48 percent of the patients in the no-therapy control group. Thus either type of therapy is better than nothing, but spontaneous recovery did occur in about half the untreated patients.

2. As we noted earlier, Freud believed that anxiety is the hallmark of neurosis, and psycho-analysts typically hold that the reduction of anxiety is a sign of improvement. Both the treated groups showed a significant reduction in anxiety, but the no-therapy patients also improved so much that Sloane and his colleagues conclude that the differences among the groups were not really significant.

3. A frequent complaint made by neurotic patients is that they have trouble keeping a job or in making progress in their careers. At the end of four months of treatment, the behavior therapy patients showed significantly greater improvement in their work situations than did the "insight" or no-therapy patients. The latter two groups of patients performed about the same.

4. As far as social adjustment was concerned, the behavior therapy and the no-treatment patients showed significant improvement. Those individuals given "insight" therapy did not do as well.

5. The patient's sexual adjustment was rated by the patient, by the therapist, by the close relative or friend, and by the assessing psychiatrist. All three groups of patients demonstrated about the same amount of improvement *except* when rated by the therapist. The psycho-analytically oriented "insight" therapists gave their patients significantly *lower* ratings of sexual adjustment than did anyone else. The behavior therapists gave their patients significantly *higher* ratings on the sexual adjustment scale than did anyone else. The patients gave themselves significantly higher ratings than did the insight therapists. Generally speaking, in most of the subjective ratings, the patients (no matter who treated them) and the behavior therapists were much more optimistic about recovery than were any of the other raters.

6. The "global evaluations" of patient improvement made by the assessing psychiatrists yielded the most marked differences among raters. As judged by the psychiatrists (all of whom had psycho-analytic training), 93 percent of the behavior therapy patients showed improvement, while only 77 percent of the "insight" and 77 percent of the no-therapy patients showed improvement. As judged by the patients themselves, 74 percent of those in the behavior therapy group, 81 percent of those given "insight" treatment, and but 44 percent of those in the no-therapy group felt they had improved. It would seem that those patients *denied* therapy believed they couldn't possibly have gotten much better without treatment despite the objective evidence to the contrary seen by the assessing psychiatrists.

We might note, in explanation of these findings, that the patients in the two treatment groups probably had quite different perceptions of what improvement ought to be. As we mentioned earlier, the goal of insight therapy is usually that of giving the person better *understanding* of his or her mental processes. Behavior therapy is a broader-scale type of treatment, in which self-help and self-improvement in many areas are emphasized. It is possible that the "insight" patients did notice a marked improvement in their mental processes and, believing this to be the major goal of therapy, rated themselves highly. The assessing psychiatrists, knowing that things like good job performance and healthy social relations are also necessary to mental health, downgraded the "insight" patients because they had shown little improvement in these areas (while the behavior therapy patients had).

7. Additional findings by Sloane and his group were equally interesting. One of the major objections raised against behavior therapy is that it merely removes symptoms without curing the underlying cause of the disorder, hence other symptoms would crop up to replace those the therapy had done away with. However, Sloane and his associates found no evidence for **symptom substitution** in any of the patients in any group. To the contrary, it seemed that when a patient's primary symptoms showed improvement, the patient often spontaneously reported improvement of other minor difficulties as well.

Another objection brought against behavioral treatment is that it is a "cold and mechanistic way of pushing people around." In fact, the patients in behavioral treatment rated their therapists as being significantly "warmer, more involved, more genuine, and as having greater and more accurate **empathy**" than the insight patients rated their therapists as being.

8. Sloane and his colleagues found that their psycho-analytically oriented therapists did better with well-educated, middle- or upper-class, verbally fluent patients than with relatively uneducated or verbally passive patients. The behavior therapists did about as well with one type of person as with any other. Perhaps for this reason, none of the patients given behavior therapy got worse, while one or two people in the other two groups showed a marked deterioration over the four-month period.

Sloane's Conclusions   R. Bruce Sloane and his colleagues conclude that:

> behavior therapy is at least as effective as, and possibly more so than, psychotherapy with sort of moderately severe neuroses and personality disorders that are typical of clinical populations. This [finding] should help to dispel the impression that behavior therapy is useful only with phobias and restricted "unitary" [simple] problems. In fact, only the behavior therapy group in this study had improved significantly on both the work and the social measures of general adjustment at four months. Behavior therapy is clearly a generally useful treatment.

Question: Research such as Sloane's is sometimes criticized as being unethical because individuals in the control group are denied therapy for a period of time. Given the considerable improvement the untreated patients showed, and the fact that they eventually were given therapy, do you believe this criticism is valid?

"Sick Talk" and "Well Talk"

One of the most puzzling aspects of the Sloane study is that the analytically trained therapists saw *less* improvement in their patients than did the patients themselves, or the outside assessors. The behavior therapists were just the opposite. An explanation for this finding may come from research by a psychologist named Joel Greenspoon.

In a series of brilliant studies reported in the late 1950's, Greenspoon demonstrated how important the attitude of the therapist is in affecting the behavior of most clients. Greenspoon noticed that when a patient begins talking about sexual abnormalities, or about bizarre thought patterns, the therapist may unconsciously encourage the patient to continue talking. The therapist may lean forward, look very interested, and say to the patient, "Yes, yes, tell me more about that." But when the patient is speaking normally, or discussing solutions rather than problems, the therapist may believe that the patient is making little or no progress. So the therapist may lean back and look disinterested. In Greenspoon's terms, there is always the danger that the therapist may unwittingly *reward* the patient for "sick talk" and *punish* the patient for "well talk."

In more humanistic terms, getting the client to concentrate on achieving mental *health* may be more important than getting the client to understand the causes of his or her mental *illness*. It is possible that the insight therapists in the Sloane study *perceived* their patients as being a "collection of problems" rather than as a "collection of healthy possibilities."

Cures may begin in a therapist's office, but the cure is of little value unless it can be maintained in the patient's normal social environment. The "isolated womb" of an analyst's office is one thing; the real world of normal human interaction is quite another.

Symptom substitution. Freud believed that most mental disorders were caused by libidinal energy that was either pent-up or diverted from normal expression. This libidinal energy was often "diverted" into unhealthy thoughts or symptomatic behaviors. Freud stated that changing the symptomatic behaviors would merely cause the libidinal energy to be expressed in the form of "substitute" behaviors or thoughts. Thus, in Freud's terms, behavioral therapy merely caused the patient to substitute one symptom for another without curing the underlying cause—the repressed libido. In fact, almost all scientific research to date suggests that Freud was wrong about symptom substitution, for it seldom occurs in real life. Indeed, as the behaviorists have shown, in many patients "the symptom is the major problem." See Chapter 15.

Empathy (EM-path-thee). From the Greek words meaning "to suffer with." Literally, the ability to project one's own feelings into another being, or the capacity for feeling the projections of someone else.

Group therapy. Any form of treatment in which several patients are treated at a time—in a group rather than individually.

Milieu therapy (mill-YOU). The French word for "social environment" is *milieu.* Milieu therapy involves changing the patient's environment in order to induce changes in the patient's mind and behavior.

Seances (SAY-ahn-sez). From the Latin word meaning "to sit." A seance is a meeting, or a "sitting." More technically, a seance is a session in which people sit waiting for spirit communications.

Social/Behavioral Therapy

Up until fairly recently, most of our laws, customs, and philosophies have been based on the assumption that mental illness existed *within* an individual—in the brain or in the mind. When factors outside the individual contributed to mental illness, these factors were presumed to be primarily supernatural—gods, witches, and evil spirits. Most forms of biological and intra-psychic therapy can be seen as attempts to cure the patient by working from the inside out.

Within the last century rather a different point of view has emerged—a belief that mental illness is as much a disruption of relationships *between people* as it is a disruption of *one person's inner psycho-dynamics.* Abnormal behavior is almost always expressed in social situations. And unless "crazy people" disturb or upset others, they are seldom sent to mental hospitals or to see a therapist. Treatment must not merely alter the functioning of the patient's body or brain, or change the patient's personality, it must also help the patient get along better with others. Indeed, in many instances, the group of people around the patient may actually be contributing to the "craziness" without realizing it. In such cases the best form of therapy may be removing the person from that environment—or somehow getting other people to behave differently toward the patient.

The two major types of social–behavioral treatment are: (a) **group therapy,** in which the patient learns better ways of responding to a group of people who often have similar problems; and (b) **milieu therapy,** in which the patient's social environment or milieu becomes the focus for treatment.

Group Therapy

The history of group therapy probably stretches back to the dawn of recorded time. In a sense the early Greek dramas offered a type of psychological release not much different from the psychodrama we will discuss in a moment. Bull sessions, prayer meetings, revivals—even the hypnotic **seances** that Mesmer conducted in Paris in the late 1700's—are the ancestral forms of today's encounter groups.

Religious groups rely heavily on inspiration.

PART SIX Personality

Group therapy did not gain any scientific notice, however, until 1905, when a Boston physician named J.H. Pratt made a fortunate mistake. Pratt found that patients suffering from **tuberculosis** were often discouraged and depressed. He first believed their despondency was due to ignorance on their part: They simply didn't know enough about the disease they suffered from. So he brought them together in groups to give them lectures about "healthy living." The lectures soon turned into very intense discussions among the patients about their problems. Pratt discovered that his patients gained much more strength from learning they were not alone in their suffering than they did from his lectures.

By 1910 group treatment was used by many European psychiatrists who gave "collective counseling" to people with similar psychological problems. Psychiatrist J.L. Moreno tried this method in Vienna with displaced persons, children, and prostitutes. By 1914 Alfred Adler suggested that group techniques might be a more effective way of helping larger numbers of patients than the usual one patient–one therapist encounters.

According to R.M. Goldenson, European psycho-analysts were for the most part hostile to group psycho-therapy, but this form of treatment soon gained a firm foothold in the United States. Some of the major varieties are psycho-analytic group therapy, directed group therapy, inspirational group therapy (such as Alcoholics Anonymous and Christian Scientism), play group therapy, activity group therapy, family group therapy, encounter groups, and psycho-drama.

Group Therapy Techniques As you might guess, these various forms of group treatment differ considerably among themselves. But, as J.D. Frank puts it, they all seem to be based on the belief "that intimate sharing of feelings, ideas, [and] experiences in an atmosphere of mutual respect and understanding enhances self-respect, deepens self-understanding, and helps the person live with others."

Some types of groups are directed by a leader and have rather a formal treatment plan. One purpose these groups often have is that of helping people break through their psychological resistances. The group leader may give lectures or pass out written material that forms the basis of group discussion. This "structured" technique is used particularly with psychotic or withdrawn patients who would not, perhaps, be able to function effectively in a less-structured social environment.

Other groups are more inspirational in character. They are typically led by someone with a strong personality who uses a variety of techniques (including strong criticism, or calling on higher spiritual powers) to inspire change in group members. Some groups concentrate mostly on encouraging the patients to form new behavior patterns and attitudes. Other groups concentrate on breaking down emotional resistances in their members. The 10,000 or more chapters of Alcoholics Anonymous, the Christian Science Church, EST, the Seventh Step Foundation for ex-convicts, and even Weight Watchers, Inc., are examples of groups that rely heavily on inspirational or highly emotional devices.

Nondirective Group Therapy Carl Rogers has extended his client-centered therapy to group situations, which Rogers calls **nondirective group psycho-therapy.** Rogers believes that group leaders should not control the activities of the group, but should function as **permissive catalysts.** The leader helps the group members achieve self-understanding by mirroring back to them their own attitudes and reactions. Rogers' objective is to stimulate the group members to bring their feelings out in the open and clarify them, rather than trying to uncover the intra-psychic dynamics that caused the emotions in the first place. Rogers emphasizes the importance of communications between members of the group and the benefits people gain by seeing themselves as others see them.

Psycho-drama Moreno, who first used group therapy with socially displaced persons around 1910, later developed a type of treatment he called **psycho-drama.** Moreno had a life-long interest in the theater, but believed

Tuberculosis (tew-burr-kew-LOH-sis). Also called T.B. A disease in which a potato-shaped (tuber-shaped) germ destroys tissue in the lungs and elsewhere in the body. A deadly illness that has been wiped out almost entirely by modern medicine.

Nondirective group psycho-therapy. A form of treatment developed by Carl Rogers in which the therapeutic group determines the direction the therapy will take.

Permissive catalysts (KAT-uh-lists). In chemistry, a catalyst is a compound that speeds up, or facilitates, a reaction without participating in the reaction itself. In Carl Rogers' terms, the leader of a nondirective group should facilitate any changes the group members themselves wish to make. The technique is permissive in that the leader does not attempt to impose direction on the group.

Psycho-drama (SIGH-ko-DRAH-mah). A theatrical therapy developed by J. L. Moreno (mor-REE-noh). Some part of the patient's life is usually acted out on a stage, often by professional actors. The patient may play one of the roles, or may simply observe.

Eric Berne.

that most plays were too rigidly structured to allow the actors and actresses to breathe life into their parts. In 1921 he founded the **Theater of Sponta-neity** in which the characters on the stage made up their lines and created their parts as they went along. As Moreno had thought, spontaneous theater was an excellent training device for budding young players. To his surprise, it also seemed to bring about dramatic improvement in their inter-personal relations.

Moreno then developed the technique for use with mental patients. The therapist usually serves as "director" for the psychodrama, which often takes place on a real stage. The patient stars as "heroine" or "hero" in a "play" that centers around some problem in the patient's life. Trained actor-therapists assist in the production. At times, a whole family or group may act out their difficulties. Moreno often invites audiences to watch the proceedings, for he believes that people in the audience can benefit from seeing problems similar to their own presented on stage.

Transactional Analysis   A very different form of role-playing is found in a type of group therapy called **transactional analysis.** US psychiatrist Eric Bern developed a personality theory that was, in part, an extension of Freudian psycho-analysis. He used the term "game" to refer to the **stereo-typed** and often misleading inter-personal "trans-actions" that people frequently adopt in dealing with others. According to Berne, a game is a "recurring series of transactions, often repetitive and superficially rational, with a concealed motivation." He believed that each game is but a tiny part of a "script" that a person uses in "performing" various roles in his or her life.

Berne stated that we all "play games" with one another, and usually do so when we are trying to manipulate others to achieve our own selfish ends. And to control the behavior of others, we often give them "positive strokes" or "negative strokes," depending on whether we wish to reward or punish them.

By analyzing the psychological games that members of a group play with each other, each person in the group can hopefully gain greater awareness of his or her own social interactions. The purpose of transac-tional analysis is to help people "stop playing destructive ego games" and help them learn new and healthier ways of dealing with their problems.

Gestalt Psycho-therapy   **Gestalt therapy** has its roots in classical Gestalt psychology (see Chapter 10). The main object of this type of treatment often seems to be that of *growth through exploration*. The explorations are sometimes emotional, sometimes perceptual, sometimes attitudinal. The group leader hopes that members will discover new ways of viewing themselves, their problems, and the world around them. In his 1978 book *Creative Process in Gestalt Therapy,* Joseph Zinker defines Gestalt therapy as an ongoing creative adjustment to the potential in the therapeutic situation.

Encounter Groups   **Encounter groups** vary so widely among themselves that no simple description of them is possible. In general, an encounter group is made up of people who have had little previous contact with one another. The group may meet one or more times a week for several weeks, or the members may live together in close, intense contact for a day, a weekend, or even longer. The participants are usually encouraged to bring their feelings out into the open and to learn more honest ways of commu-nicating with each other. Often the focus is on some aspect of non-verbal experience—perhaps on developing better sensory awareness of bodily reactions, perhaps on learning how facial expressions communicate deep-seated emotions. As a means of helping group members strip away their defenses, or urging them to "let it all hang out," a few encounter groups meet in the nude.

Evaluating Group Therapy

Group therapy sessions of one kind or another have become increasingly popular in recent years. Group leaders, like most other psycho-therapists, often describe in glowing terms the psychological changes they *perceive* in group members. Many participants—particularly if asked immediately after therapy has ended—are highly enthusiastic about the benefits they feel they have received from the experience. Other participants—particularly those who drop out before therapy is complete—tell rather a different story.

Perhaps the best evaluation so far of the effectiveness of different types of group therapy is a series of studies performed by psychologists Morton A. Lieberman, Matthew B. Miles, and psychiatrist Irvin D. Yalom. This research on group therapy began at Stanford in 1968 and is still going on. Over the years, Lieberman, Miles, and Yalom have studied just about every type of group treatment offered to the public. Typically, they investigate the group leader's perceptions of what went on, ask the participants to evaluate the experience both immediately after treatment and at some later time, and then ask close friends or relatives of the participants to rate the participants' progress.

In a recent book, Lieberman, Miles, and Yalom report that their studies offer little scientific evidence that group therapy is of much *therapeutic* value. Indeed, it may often be just the opposite. They state that about 8 percent of the participants are "casualties"—that is, people who show evidence of serious psychological harm and whose difficulties can reasonably be attributed to the group experience. Overall, however, about a third of the group members got better, about a third got worse, and the rest seemed unchanged immediately after the experience. There were few differences among the various types of group therapy (Gestalt, psychodrama, and so forth) as far as their effectiveness was concerned.

It would appear that the group situations accentuated positive changes in some members, negative changes in others, but that the overall effect was about the same as if the groups had never been brought together. Immediately after therapy had ended, almost 65 percent of the group members stated that the experience had been a positive one. However, six months later, less than a third of the group members were still enthusiastic about having undergone treatment.

There are several other aspects of these experiments worthy of note. First, the group leaders typically report that they see some improvement in almost 90 percent of the members—rather a rosy view not supported by the data. When the participants are asked to rate others in their groups, they usually report seeing improvement in but a third of their fellow group members. Nor is there usually *any significant agreement* at all among the leaders, the participants, and the participants' friends as to who changes and in what ways.

Benefits of Group Therapy   Lieberman, Miles, and Yalom conclude from their work so far that none of the groups they studied were particularly effective as *change agents,* but that the groups can excel at creating *instant, brief, and intense interpersonal experiences.* Lieberman, Miles, and Yalom state that this chance to learn something about yourself from the open reactions of others is real, important, and not often available in our society. But they believe that such experiences are not the crucial ones that alter people permanently for the better. They write that:

> Encounter groups present a clear and evident danger if they are used for radical surgery to produce a new man. The danger is even greater when the leader and the participant share this misperception. If we no longer expect groups to produce magical, lasting change and if we stop seeing them as **panaceas,** we can regard them as useful, socially sanctioned opportunities for human beings to explore and to express themselves. Then we can begin to work on ways to improve them so that they may make a meaningful contribution toward solving human problems.

Panaceas (pann-uh-SEE-uhs). From the Greek words *pan,* meaning "all," and *akes,* meaning "remedy." A panacea is a cure-all.

Environmental Therapy

Ecologists (ee-KOLL-oh-jists). Ecologists are scientists who study the pattern of relationships between organisms and their environments.

Paupers' prisons. To be a "pauper" is to be poor. Until 100 years ago or so, people who couldn't pay their debts were imprisoned until they obtained enough money to pay their creditors. Since obtaining money in prison was even more difficult than it was outside of prison, most paupers stayed in prison for a very long time indeed.

Protestant Ethic. Protestants tend to believe that entrance into heaven is brought about by what you do, not merely what you feel. Thus, anyone believing in the Protestant ethic is likely to assume that people ought to earn their bread and board, or participate actively (and intelligently) in their own salvation. A century ago in the United States, anyone who refused to work was deemed either lazy or crazy. Lazy people were put in prison, but could get out by hard work. Crazy people were put in lunatic asylums from which there was little or no hope of escape. Behavioral therapy is, in a sense, modeled on the Protestant ethic in that behaviorists tend to believe that mental patients *ought* to work hard in order to get better.

One of the more interesting discoveries of the past century has been the slow realization of how sensitive we all are to our environments. The **ecologists** have demonstrated rather vividly the disasters that may occur when we pollute the physical world around us. But humans do not die from lead poisoning alone: Polluted psychological environments can kill or corrupt your spirit as readily as dirty air and water can kill or corrupt your body. The job of the environmental psycho-therapist is similar to that of the ecologist—to identify the sources of pollution and remove them.

The simplest form of environmental therapy is perhaps the vacation, for "getting away from it all" can often give you a fresh perspective on your life and problems. Psychiatric social workers show their awareness of this fact when they recommend removing a child from an unhealthy family situation and putting the child in a foster home. Helping mental patients find jobs and comfortable living quarters outside the hospital is another form of environmental therapy practiced by social workers. Rehabilitation centers often teach disturbed people how to function better in work situations, how to relax, how to play or paint or read or make music, how to meet people and stay out of trouble with the law—all ways of helping people make healthier adjustments to presently existing environments.

If the therapist cannot easily find ways of removing the "psycho-pollution" from a patient's world, or of helping the individual live more happily despite the pollution, then more radical treatment is usually needed. Typically this treatment takes the form of moving the person to different surroundings, such as a mental hospital.

Mental Hospitals: Past and Present   Yale psychologist Jeffrey Blum points out that mental hospitals first came into existence in 1657, when the General Hospital of Paris was founded. Prior to this time, mentally ill people had been free to roam the countryside at will. But in the mid-1600's, society's view toward "abnormality" changed. Those individuals who were "2 standard deviations from the mean" in *any way* were considered "misfits" who deserved to be segregated from "normal people." It was about 1650, too, when western society first began building large numbers of jails for criminals and **paupers' prisons** for people who couldn't pay their debts. But, as Blum notes, mental patients were at the bottom of society's list. Indeed, in 1657 it was considered *inhumane* to lock up axe murderers, armed robbers, and rapists in a mental hospital because the patients might threaten the physical safety of the *criminals.*

In his monumental work on the history of mental hospitals in the US, David Rothman states that in the 1800's we built asylums as a way of trying to impress the **Protestant Ethic** on social outcasts who did not work at a steady job, support themselves, and pay taxes. Rothman cites a physician who, some 150 years ago, stated that mental illness was caused primarily by such *economic factors* as "over-trading, debts, bankruptcy, sudden reverses, [and] disappointed hopes." This doctor believed that poor people became crazy because they had unrealistic hopes about bettering themselves financially. Wealthy people, however, were threatened by "luxury, self-indulgence, effeminacy, and late hours." The mental hospital in the mid 1800's was not a place to cure *mental* illness, then, but a place where lazy or disturbed people could learn the benefits of leading a disciplined, scheduled, hard-working life.

Far from being *asylums* where people could flee when the storms of life became too threatening, early mental hospitals were little more than human garbage dumps, crammed with life's failures and misfits. As **ecological systems,** these institutions were often more abnormal and destructive to human egos than was the outside world the patients had sought relief from. Little wonder, therefore, that the "cure rate" in US mental hospitals remained very low from the 1700's until the mid-1900's.

Milieu Therapy   Social/behavioral therapists tend to see mental illness as being *caused* by unhealthy living conditions—not by character defects or mental weakness. It was the failure of society to teach people healthy behaviors—not the failure of people to learn—that caused insanity. The best form of treatment, therefore, would be putting the patient in a new environment or milieu—each aspect of which would be carefully designed to help the patient *learn better habits of adjustment.*

The term "therapeutic community" was coined by British psychiatrist Maxwell Jones in 1953 to refer to this type of *milieu therapy.*

Writing in the *American Handbook of Psychiatry,* Dr. Louis Linn points out that our concept of therapy began to change drastically around 1950:

> In former days there was a tendency to regard treatment in the mental hospital as that which takes place during the fraction of a second when the current flows from an electro-shock apparatus, or during the longer intervals involved in other therapies . . . In the therapeutic community the whole of the time which the patient spends in the hospital is thought of as treatment time, and everything that happens to the patient is part of the treatment program.

Viewed this way, Linn continues, the trees and flowers on the hospital grounds, the decorations in the wards, the way the food is served, and the behavior of all hospital personnel, without exception, are part of the treatment program.

Though it does not replace other forms of treatment, milieu therapy does attempt to make the total environment a "school for living" in which the patient can develop new attitudes and build more rewarding social relationships. In a sense the therapeutic community is rather like a non-stop, 24-hour-a-day encounter group. However, its primary function is *not* usually that of removing symptoms or merely changing behaviors. Rather, its aim is said to be that of drawing the patient into normal relationships that will give the person confidence, self-esteem, and social competence. The belief thus is that, if the patients are given a supportive environment, they will *learn better habits on their own.*

The difficulty in evaluating milieu therapy is the same as with other forms of group therapy—terms like "confidence" and "self-esteem" refer to intra-psychic traits and hence are hard to define or measure objectively. Therapeutic communities certainly are far more humane forms of treatment than the old-style mental hospitals. But as we will see momentarily, there is serious question as to whether milieu therapy is as effective in curing people as it might be.

Token Economies   Rather a different type of environmental treatment is favored by behavior therapists, whose aim is that of changing habit patterns rather than altering inner psychological states.

Patients in mental hospitals often develop what is called an **institutional neurosis:** They lose interest in the world and the people around them, they develop hallucinations and fantasies, and they become quarrelsome, resentful, and hostile. Institutional neurosis appears to be caused at least in part by the fact that, in most hospitals, patients often are treated like children or helpless invalids. They are "given" everything they might need by the "authority figures" in charge. Under these conditions, many of the patients develop a rather child-like dependency on the staff.

The behavioral psychologists believe that the best cure for institutional neurosis is making the patients take as much responsibility for their own improvement as possible. To help achieve this goal, the behaviorists have developed what they call the **token economy.** In the money economy that operates in the world outside the hospital, you must typically work to live. Our social system rewards you for good work behavior with dollars that you can spend on food, clothing, and shelter. If you perform poorly or refuse to work, you may very well starve. In contrast, mental hospitals typically operate on a "free economy." That is, the patients are given whatever they need merely by asking for it. In fact, the *worse* they behave, the *more* attention and help they usually receive.

The behaviorists take the view that, within the hospital economy, it is the patient's "job" to get well as quickly as possible. Patients then should be rewarded for each sign of improvement they make by receiving "tokens"

Ecological systems (ee-ko-LODGE-uh-kal). Human beings cannot survive without friendly environments. We must have good food, clean air and water, a decent range of temperatures, and an absence of disease germs. We also need intellectual stimulation and humane treatment from others. All of these "items necessary for the good life" are related to each other in rather complex ways. Plants give us food, oxygen, and help retain rainwater in the soil. When we destroy plants, we destroy part of the complicated system that sustains our very existence. A hospital patient is as dependent on the social system in the institution as the rest of us are dependent on plants and rainwater. From a psychological point of view, some hospitals are barren deserts that "starve" their patients of intellectual and emotional stimulation without meaning to do so. Through our study of the biological aspects of ecological systems, we are learning how to make deserts blossom. Perhaps someday we will learn similar psychological techniques for making institutions such as mental hospitals "bloom."

Institutional neurosis. Hospital patients are often subtly encouraged to remain "sick" in order to stay in the hospital. The "sicker" the patient becomes, the more dependent the patient is on the hospital, and the more the institution justifies its own existence. When patients develop an abnormally strong dependency on a hospital or its staff, the patients are said to suffer from an institutional neurosis.

Token economy. An artificial economy set up in an institution to "cure" institutional neurosis. The patients are rewarded for positive (socially approved) behaviors by being given "tokens" which may be exchanged for various types of rewards. The "healthier" the patient's behavior, the more tokens the patient receives, the greater the rewards the patient reaps, and the sooner the patient can usually be eased out of the institution and back into society.

that can be traded in for tangible pleasures (such as candy, cosmetics, cigarettes, clothes, magazines, and records) or special privileges (better jobs in the hospital, going to movies, and visits home). In a token economy, therapy usually consists of having the staff reinforce "socially approved" or "healthy" behaviors and having them ignore inappropriate or "insane" behaviors. Each patient is encouraged to decide what rewards she or he wants to work for. The patient is then given the tokens as visible evidence that he or she is making progress toward these chosen goals.

In his 1977 book on token economies, Alan E. Kazdin points out that this form of treatment has been quite successful with many different types of mental patients. It works well in helping patients with chronic schizophrenia learn to take better care of themselves, get along better with others, and gain the self-control neccesary to reduce some of their bizarre behaviors. It also functions well with mentally retarded individuals who need to acquire job skills and learn to communicate more efficiently with others. But the token economy is often most effective with troubled children, perhaps because it gives them socially approved ways of getting what they want from the adults around them (including their own parents). Kazdin notes that almost all scientific comparisons of the token economy with "traditional" ward treatment in hospitals show the behavioral approach to be superior.

Perhaps the best study comparing the token economy to other forms of treatment was reported by Gordon Paul and Robert Lentz in 1977. Paul and Lentz contrasted the improvement rates in three groups of hospitalized patients—those given traditional "milieu" therapy, those put on a token economy, and those left on the usual ward without any special form of therapy. The patients in the token economy showed far greater improvement than did the patients in either of the other two groups.

The criticism most often raised against the token economy is that it is mechanistic and dehumanizing because it focuses on observable behaviors—on symptoms—rather than dealing with underlying, dynamic psychological problems. From the intra-psychic viewpoint, the criticism has considerable merit. The behavioral changes that the token economies do bring about, however, seem to be very reliable (repeatable)—a point in their favor.

Therapy and the Whole Individual

Psycho-therapy is perhaps the most challenging and interesting part of psychology for most of us. It combines the pleasures of intellectual analysis with the warm emotions of "doing good" for individuals who might need our help. These statements, however, are as true of witch doctoring as they are of any other type of psycho-therapy. And, whether we like it or not, most "mentally disturbed" individuals get well whether or not they receive treatment. As the noted psycho-analyst Karen Horney said in her book *Our Inner Conflicts,* "Fortunately [psycho]analysis is not the only way to resolve inner conflicts. Life itself still remains a very effective therapist." How then can we make sure that our therapy does, in fact, speed up (or add something extra to) what seems our inborn way of healing ourselves?

One thing seems certain: If we look at a disturbed individual from any one narrow perspective, we are likely to limit both our understanding of the client and our chances of bringing about a cure of the person's very real problems. In the past, we have too often allowed ourselves to develop "tunnel vision" to suit our own particular theoretical orientation. We have given people drugs without realizing that the manner in which we give the pill may be as important as the chemical inside the pill. Or we have spent years digging into the patient's unconscious to give the person insight into her or his personality dynamics. At the end of several years of therapy the patient may have gained a complete understanding of his or her intrapsychic traumas, but may still have a collection of inappropriate habits (symptoms) that must be unlearned. Just as bad, we may focus entirely on the observable behaviors, ignoring the fact that internal fears and feelings need our attention too.

Karen Horney.

Meyer's Holistic Approach

To help us avoid this segmented approach to human difficulties, we might turn to someone like Adolf Meyer, who is often called the "dean of US psychiatry." Meyer believed in the *holistic* approach and recognized that there were multiple causes for even the simplest of behaviors. Rather than passing verdicts on patients by labeling them as "schizophrenics" or "neurotics," Meyer preferred to discover both what was wrong and what was right with the patients at all levels of analysis—the biological, the psychological, and the sociological. He seldom *interpreted* the patient's problems; he merely tried to describe them in plain English.

Meyer also attempted to determine those normal aspects of behavior that the patient might still have available, and then build on these psychological assets to bring about change. Meyer believed that the patient should set both the goals and the pace of therapy, and that the therapist should work as hard at changing the patient's home (or hospital) environment as in changing the patient's psyche or behaviors. Meyer called his approach "critical common sense."

There are thousands of different kinds of psycho-therapy. The surprising thing is that almost all of them "work" with certain kinds of patients and with certain types of problems, and fail with others. If we apply Adolf Meyer's "critical common sense" to an analysis of the strengths and weaknesses of all the various types of therapy—and if we pay as much attention to hard, scientific data as we do to the therapists' and the patients' gut reactions to the therapeutic process—we might discover that most successful forms of treatment have several things in common:

1. Psychological change almost always occurs in a supportive, warm, rewarding environment. People usually "open up" and talk about things—and try new approaches to life—when they trust or admire or want to please the therapist. Encounter groups whose members focus on expressing hostility toward each other often do incredible damage—unless such expression is embedded in a background of affection so strong that the members can tolerate occasional (but hopefully brief) punishment from each other. Criticism seldom cures, and too often kills all chance of improvement (if not the patient as well). Sincere expressions of warmth and tolerance for "abnormalities" provide the atmosphere in which change can occur.

2. Most successful forms of treatment can be seen as feedback mechanisms. That is, they provide you with information about what happened in the past, they put you in touch with the present functioning of your body, and they make you aware of how your behavior actually affects other people. Feedback also helps you realize the distance between your desired goals and your present achievements, and offers information on how the social environment influences your own thoughts, feelings, and behaviors. Ideally, a complete form of therapy would do all these things, and also help you learn how to seek out and make even better use of feedback in the future.

3. Magic can "cure" mental illness overnight; all other forms of psycho-therapy take a little longer. If you believe that madness is a matter of possession by devils—or that it's due to a "poor attitude" on the part of the patient—then you might expect that beatings or **exhortations** could cure the illness quickly. But if you believe that it takes many years of punishing or stressful experiences—and perhaps a particular genetic predisposition—for a full-blown psychosis to develop, then you might also expect the road to recovery to be a fairly lengthy one.

4. The attitudes of both the patient and the therapist are of critical importance. A Cree Eskimo woman suffering from *witigo* "knows" that she needs a witch doctor. Will giving this woman a tranquilizer help her much? On the other hand, patients often see their therapists as being models of mentally healthy or socially approved behaviors. Effective therapists (witch doctors, psycho-analysts, humanists, or behaviorists) usually practice what they preach.

Exhortations (ex-hor-TAY-shuns). From the Latin word meaning "to incite, or to urge strongly through argument or advice." A pep rally usually consists of frequent and heart-felt exhortations to the home team to win the next game.

5. The best forms of therapy seem to build on strengths rather than attacking weaknesses. By helping the patient work toward positive improvement—toward self-actualization and good mental health—the therapist motivates the patient to continue to grow and change. Therapies that focus entirely on uncovering or discussing psychological problems may merely confirm the patient's attitude that sickness is inevitable.

The Future of Psycho-therapy

It is likely that, in the coming years, we will take Adolf Meyer's ideas more seriously than we have in the past, and that we will treat the whole patient as a unique individual rather than treating just one aspect of the person's difficulties. Already in some hospitals there is a *team of therapists* available to work with each patient. One member of the team looks at the person's physical or biological problems. Another deals with the person's intrapsychic dynamics. A third helps the patient change behavior patterns. A fourth team member is an expert in altering social environments. The patient can then get as much, or as little, of each type of therapy as his or her own particular case demands.

Ideally, the goals of therapy should be spelled out in a written contract agreed to by the patient and all members of the therapeutic team, and the patient's progress should be recorded regularly on a graph of some kind so that all team members are aware of the patient's achievements. As this "team-contracting approach" increases in popularity, our success rate in curing mental illness is likely to show a significant increase.

All forms of therapy achieve some success. In 1975 the Research Task Force of the National Institute of Mental Health released a report covering 25 years of research on therapy and mental illness. According to the NIMH report, most types of psycho-therapy yield a 70 percent "cure rate." The major exceptions are behavior therapy and drug therapy, both of which (when effectively utilized) have produced cure rates well above 80 percent. But, as the NIMH report suggests, perhaps the single most important thing we have learned about mental health in the past 25 years is that neither problems nor cures occur in a vacuum. No matter how well a patient may respond in a hospital setting—and no matter what insights a client achieves in a therapist's office—the ultimate test of therapy comes when the person returns to her or his usual environment. If the patient can function successfully and happily in the real world, we can then conclude that a "cure" had indeed taken place.

It is thus to the complexities of the social environment that we now must turn our attention.

Summary

1. The types of therapy that we prescribe for mentally ill persons usually stem from our theoretical explanation of what causes the person's problems.

2. In primitive times (and societies), insanity was said to be caused by **possession.** That is, a devil of some kind was thought to take over the sick person's mind. Eskimos believe they can be possessed by a witch or **witigo** who craves human flesh.

3. In Malaysia, young males occasionally suffer from manic episodes called **running amok.**

4. Primitive forms of **psycho-therapy** typically involve the use of magic to "cast out the witch," or painful whips to "beat the devil" out of the patient.

5. As our scientific explanations of the causes of human behavior have changed, so have our types of treatment. In evaluating any form of therapy, we must ask ourselves several questions:

    a. How successful or **valid** is the treatment?
    b. How **reliable** is the therapy?
    c. Are there unfortunate **side effects?**
    d. How shall we define "success" or **cure rate?**

6. Mental patients often show **spontaneous recovery**—that is, they recover without therapy, or even in spite of it.

7. Biological treatment typically involves the use of **artificially induced seizures, psycho-surgery,** and **chemotherapy** or drugs.

8. Although helpful in limited situations, **biotherapy** seems not to have a very high "cure rate" and often has many bad side effects.

9. There are many forms of intra-psychic treatment, including **psycho-analysis, humanistic therapy,** and **eclectic therapy.**

10. In psycho-analysis, the client is encouraged to undergo a **transference relationship** in which the analyst becomes a kind of **father figure.** The therapist—usually a male with psychiatric training—often **interprets** the client's feelings and dreams in psycho-analytic terms in order to determine the client's unconscious **psycho-dynamics** and motivations.

11. In humanistic therapy, the client sets his or her own **therapeutic goals** and determines the pace at which treatment proceeds. The therapist—who usually has a Ph.D.—helps the patient reach her or his **ego-ideal.**

12. In **Rogerian** or **client-centered therapy,** the therapist gives the client **unconditional positive regard** while **reflecting back** the client's thoughts or feelings in slightly different words.

13. When psycho-analysis is judged in terms of **symptom removal,** the "cure rate" is less than 30 percent. When judged by the subjective impressions of the analysts, the "cure rate" is closer to 60 percent.

14. The cure rate for humanistic therapy, for eclectic psycho-therapy, and for most types of **insight therapy** is about 70 percent.

15. The **spontaneous cure rate** for untreated patients is 50 to 70 percent or more. The longer the patient goes without therapy, the higher the recovery rate.

16. Intra-psychic therapy seems better at changing a patient's **internal psychological states,** or **self-awareness,** than at removing symptoms or changing behaviors.

17. Research suggests that **behavior therapy** is at least as effective with most patients as is psycho-therapy. **Symptom substitution** seems not to occur very frequently either in behavioral treatment or in psycho-therapy.

18. Environmental therapies include many types of **group therapy,** as well as attempts to change the patient by altering the patient's **social milieu.**

19. One of the problems with group therapies—such as **nondirective group therapy, psycho-drama, transactional analysis, Gestalt therapy,** and **encounter groups**—is that some 8 percent of the clients end up as **psychological casualties** who are worse after treatment than before.

20. Group therapies seem better as ways of encouraging people to explore and express themselves than as **psychological panaceas.**

21. **Milieu therapy** involves changing the patient's environment so that the person may grow in psychologically healthy ways.

22. The most effective form of milieu therapy appears to be the **token economy,** in which patients earn rewards for appropriate behaviors.

23. **Holistic therapy**—in which the patient is treated as a whole individual functioning within a complex environmental system—seems to be the most promising type of treatment available.

24. It is likely that, in the future, a **team approach to treatment** will prove to be highly effective, particularly if **patient–therapist contracts** are employed.

(Continued from page 648.)

"I *hurt,* Mark," Lou Hudson repeated, ignoring all of the boisterous activity in the gambling casino as he poured out his heart to Mark Evans. "I've lost almost everything we own. The house, the car, everything—gambled it all away. I've borrowed from everybody in the family and lost it all on the horses. I'm even going to lose Betty and the kids if I can't shape up somehow. But I get those urges, you understand, those times when I just know that I've got a winning streak going, and I have to play my hunches. I've got to get help of some kind, Mark, but what should I do?"

"What does Betty think you should do?"

"She wants me to join the Chattanooga chapter of Gamblers Anonymous. They're a bunch of people just like me that get together regularly to talk over their problems and help each other out. Betty says they've helped lots of folks."

"So, why don't you join and see what they can do for you?"

"'Cause it would make your uncle angry at me. I mean your Uncle John, the psycho-analyst. He says I'm a masochist and have an unconscious desire to punish myself by losing all the time. He thinks I ought to lie on a couch for a few years and find out what's wrong deep down inside me. He says that group therapy just doesn't get at the roots of the problem."

Mark smiled at the thought of Lou lying on a couch. "Well, why don't you try psycho-analysis, then?"

"Because of your Cousin Sophie," Lou said.

"The Rogerian?"

"Yeah. She thinks I need non-directive therapy to help me achieve self-actualization. Sophie's a wonderful woman, Mark, and she's awful easy to talk to. Every time I say something to her, she just says it back to me in different words. Trouble is, she isn't talking to your Uncle John, and I owe her almost as much money as I owe him."

Mark decided that he needed a drink too, and hoisted a glass off the tray of a passing cocktail waitress. "So, why don't you go in for a little self-actualization?"

Lou groaned. "Your Aunt Beverly would never approve."

"You mean the behavior therapist?"

Lou nodded. "Yeah." He swallowed half his drink in a single gulp. "Man, you've got more different kinds of shrinks in your family than I ever heard of!"

"Psychology runs in my family the way that insanity runs in others. But what does Aunt Beverly, the behaviorist, think?"

"She tells me that all the other forms of therapy are unscientific. According to her, I'd do better to find a witch doctor than to go to your Uncle John for psycho-analysis. She wants to set up a behavioral program that will reward me for not gambling, to help me learn new input-output relationships. And I hate to tell you how many cash inputs I owe that woman, Mark."

"The cure rates for some kinds of behavioral therapy are very impressive, Lou. So why don't you try it?"

Lou shook his head in dismay. "Because it would make everybody else in the family mad as hell at me, including my wife Betty. I wouldn't mind going to any of them if I was sure they could help me. But how can you be sure you're going to be cured, Mark?"

"You can't be, Lou. Any more than you could be sure that if you sold me a life insurance policy, I wouldn't die the next day. All you can do is play the odds."

"What do you mean?"

"Ask each of the shrinks in the family to tell you what the cure rate is for compulsive gambling with their type of therapy. Take a good, close look at what they consider successful treatment to be, and how they measure success, and what the cost to you is going to be. Then pick the one that gives you the best odds for your time and money."

Lou Hudson blinked his bloodshot eyes as he pondered the matter. "That's being pretty hard-nosed about a very human predicament, isn't it?"

"Being hard-nosed about human predicaments is what keeps insurance companies and gambling casinos in business, Lou. You can't be sure that the therapy with the best overall cure rate is going to work for you and your own unique set of problems, but the fact that the odds are in your favor gives you a bit of a head start."

"Yeah," said Lou reluctantly. "I see what you mean."

"But what do *you* want to do, Lou? That's the most important factor of all."

"I kind of like the advice your Cousin Oscar gave me, and I owe him more than anybody."

Mark laughed. "Ah, yes, Cousin Oscar. What does the black sheep of the family recommend?"

Lou grinned. "Well, he knows of this woman who's a fortune teller. She lives in the same trailer park that Oscar lives in. He says that if I slip her a few bucks, she might look into her magic crystal ball and give me a tip on the races. Oscar says she's most always right. If I could just win a few big ones, Mark, I could pay back my debts, stop gambling, and then I wouldn't need any therapy at all. What do you think of that?"

Mark shook his head. "No dice. If she's so good with crystal balls, how come she lives in a trailer instead of a mansion?"

Lou frowned. "Yeah, I see what you mean. Bad odds, eh? But what can I do? No matter whose therapy I pick, I'm going to make everybody else in the family madder than a wet hen."

Mark scratched his nose. "I think I have an idea. Lou, *you* haven't got a problem. The *family* has a problem. So we ought to come up with a family group solution."

"What do you mean? Me get a divorce from Betty?"

"Lou, I suspect they'd all rather give you free therapy than continue to lend you money."

Lou Hudson rubbed his eyes with the back of his hands. "Maybe you've got something there, Mark. I'd better go call Betty on the phone and see what she thinks."

As the two men walked toward the door of the casino, the little old lady in tennis shoes stopped them. She held a coin. "My juju's deserted me today, boys, but I feel a change coming over me. This is my very last nickel, and I've got to get a winner. Where do you think I ought to put it?"

"Back in your purse," Mark said.

"Naw, Mark, you don't understand us gamblers." Lou closed his eyes and turned around three times. Then he pointed to a small slot machine far down the row. "Try that one, lady. I gotta hunch."

The little old woman trotted obediently down the row of one-armed bandits and paused to look the machine over carefully. Then she spat on the coin gently, rubbed it lovingly between her gloved hands, dropped the nickel in the slot, and pulled the handle. The reels spun wildly. The

first one stopped on a bar. The second one did likewise. When the third reel clicked into place, it too sported a bar.

Suddenly the machine exploded. A bell rang loudly, and lights flashed off like skyrockets.

"Jackpot!" the woman screamed. "I did it, I did it! I've got my juju back! The magic power is with me again!"

A small crowd of people gathered around to watch the slot machine pay off.

Lou Hudson looked at the woman and smiled wanly. "She probably spent $50 in nickels just to win one $10 jackpot. And now she'll put all those nickels right back in the machine, won't she?"

Mark nodded in agreement.

"You think I can stop that kind of nonsense, Mark?"

"If you really want to, and you get good help," Mark said, "The odds are definitely in your favor."

The slight young man with bloodshot eyes grinned in response. "I'll bet on that!"

Recommended Readings

Bastide, R. *The Sociology of Mental Disorder* (New York: McKay, 1972).

Heine, Ralph W. *Psychotherapy* (Englewood Cliffs, N.J.: Prentice-Hall, 1971).

Kazdin, Alan E. *The Token Economy: A Review and Evaluation* (New York: Plenum, 1977).

Kazdin, Alan E., and G. Terence Wilson. *Evaluation of Behavior Therapy: Issues, Evidence, and Research Strategies* (Cambridge, Mass.: Ballinger, 1978).

Rothman, D.J. *The Discovery of Asylums: Social Order and Disorder in the New Republic* (Boston: Little, Brown, 1971).

Yalom, I.D. *The Theory and Practice of Group Psychotherapy* (New York: Basic Books, 1970).

Social
Psychology

Inter-personal Attraction, Person Perception, and the Attribution Process

Did You Know That . . .

There seem to be two types of group leaders—the "task specialist," who is given respect, and the "social–emotional specialist," who gains the members' affection?

These two "social specialties" may be related to the functions of the right and left hemispheres?

Successful business managers seem to be motivated by self-actualization and use participatory management techniques, while unsuccessful managers are motivated by security needs and supervise in an authoritarian way?

You tend to perceive your actions as being responses to your environment, but tend to perceive the actions of others as being caused by personality traits or flaws of character?

You have a "psychological bubble" around you that you defend whenever anyone intrudes on this "personal space?"

People tend to judge you more by your "body language" than by what you say or think?

The fact that boys engage in team sports more than girls do may help explain why men are often more successful in business organizations than are women?

Guards who behave cruelly toward prisoners are often just normal people who are responding to what they perceive to be "society's rules?"

"The Best of Intentions"

Day 1. I was walking home from the meeting when I saw the police car sitting in front of our apartment house. They had come for Charlie, of course. Charlie is my best friend and bosom buddy.

Charlie and I have been rooming together for two years now. He is a top-notch person, and since we are both pre-legal, we have decided to open up an office together when we get out of Law School. Charlie is a super jock, the sort of guy you'd really want on your team. He is also a born leader, always coming up with great ideas about things to do and giving me advice on what to wear and how to act. Which I guess I sometimes need. I suppose that when we do open that office, his name will be first on the door.

It was Charlie who read the ad in the student newspaper. The one offering to hire us at $25 a day to take part in this two-week-long "prison" experiment that Dr. Wakeman is running. That struck us as a great way to earn some big bucks over the summer vacation. So we showed up, got interviewed, took all those psychological tests, and signed away our rights. I was sort of skeptical about that, you know. Agreeing to give up our basic rights to privacy, and all those good things. But, as Charlie pointed out, it was only for two weeks. And besides, they promised that they wouldn't use physical punishment of any kind on us. So when Charlie volunteered, I felt sort of obligated to go along with him. And now I am going to make almost 300 bucks, and help science besides.

Funny that they should have selected me to be a guard, and Charlie to play the prisoner's role. Well, maybe the tests showed he was more daring or impulsive or something like that.

I arrived at the apartment house just as the cops were dragging Charlie out the door. He sure did look surprised! We learned at the Guard's meeting this afternoon that the local police were cooperating with Dr. Wakeman. They had agreed to pull the prisoners in unexpectedly, charge them with suspicion of armed robbery, search them, fingerprint them, and take "mug shots" of their faces. Then the cops put blindfolds on the prisoners and we picked them up and drove them over to school where the "mock prison" is. Which we did, all in the spirit of good, clean fun, you understand. Tried to get them in the mood, so to speak.

They needed some mood-setting because the prison is pretty "mock," I tell you no lie. Just some rooms in the basement of the Psych Building, with bars painted on the doors and the tiny windows. Dr. Wakeman said he is repeating a study performed by some professor at Stanford named Philip Zimbardo, who found that isolating people from society was dehumanizing. Well, okay, what else is new? But these prisoners are hardly going to be "isolated from society." There will be us guards, three to a shift, and Dr. Wakeman and his students who will be the Prison Staff and actually live there. Plus the guys—the prisoners, I mean—will be allowed visitors twice a week. So I do not think this study is going to work very well.

But maybe it will be fun anyhow, plus the money.

Dr. Wakeman has asked us to keep diaries which he will collect, and we are to write down everything we think and do, even if it seems critical of him and the staff. I don't like criticism or hassling people anyhow, so he shouldn't worry.

Charlie put on a big smile and tried to look very nonchalant when the policemen escorted him out of the apartment. Several of the neighbors were standing outside, watching. I will have to explain to them later what it is all about. I admire Charlie for taking it so calmly. Of course, I did not let on I knew him, since that is one of the rules.

At the meeting today we decided on the Rules and Regulations for the Uni-Prison. Mostly, they are just common sense things to keep an institution running properly. There is to be no physical abuse, although we can lock a prisoner up in the isolation room if he breaks the Rules. Which, given the sensible nature of the Regulations, a prisoner would be stupid to do anyhow. Charlie being anything but stupid, I figure he will do All Right as a prisoner. Unless his Irish impulses get out of hand, or something.

I am not so sure about me in the role of a guard. Sorry. We are to refer to ourselves as Correctional Officers. Anyhow, I put on my uniform at the apartment after the Police Officers took Charlie away. The dumb-looking khaki pants and shirt are a size too big and I feel uncomfortable in them. But I have a whistle and a billy-club, just to make me look "official." And they gave me a neat pair of mirrored sun glasses. Before I left, I stood in front of the mirror for a few minutes. Funny thing. I look pretty tough in that outfit, maybe because you can't see that my eyes are laughing. Mostly at myself.

Then I went over to the Uni-Prison and checked in. They started bringing the "Numbers" in about half an hour later. I call them "Numbers," because that is how I am to address them. Good old Charlie is now #853, which is written on both sides of the nightshirt he wears. He was one of the first Numbers brought in. We stripped him down, then sprayed him with a "de-louser" which, it turned out, was only deodorant. Well, they are going to need that deodorant because they are not going to get a shower while they are in prison. That is one of the Regulations.

Charlie got a little bit teed-off when we put the steel chain around his ankle and then required him to stand naked in the exercise yard for 20 minutes before we gave him his nightshirt. Well, it was necessary to remind him that he is a prisoner even when he's bare-assed. Of course, underneath, I felt just as foolish as he did, but I don't think he or the other guys noticed. A Correctional Officer should not be embarrassed since he is just doing the job for which he is being paid.

When we checked the guys in—the Numbers—we gave them a nylon stocking to put on over their heads. Makes them harder to tell apart, but they are just Numbers, after all. They have got nothing on under the nightshirts, and that does lead to some comical situations. Charlie complained right off that he wasn't a woman and didn't like wearing a skirt, but I told him to shut up because that is one of the Rules.

Warden Wakeman then assembled the Staff and the Numbers and gave them an Official Welcome. He did a pretty good job of role-playing, I do say that. His talk was really pretty patriotic.

"Listen," he said to the Numbers, "you have shown that you are unable to function outside in the real world. You lack the responsibility of good citizens of this great country. We of this prison, your correctional staff, are going to help you learn what your responsibilities as citizens of this country are. Here are the Rules. We expect you to know them and to be able to recite them by number. If you follow the Rules and keep your hands clean, repent for your misdeeds, and show a proper attitude, you and I will get along just fine.

"Rule Number One: Prisoners must remain silent during rest periods, after lights are out, during meals, and whenever they are outside the prison yard.

"Rule Number Two: Prisoners must eat at mealtimes and only at meal-times.

"Rule Number Three: Prisoners must not move, tamper with, deface, or damage walls, ceilings, windows, doors, or other prison property.

"Rule Number Four: Prisoners must address each other only by their numbers.

"Rule Number Five: Prisoners must address the guards as 'Mr. Correctional Officer.'"

"Rule Number Six: Prisoners must obey all lawful commands and orders issued to them by Correctional Officers.

"Rule Number Seven: Failure to obey any of the above rules may result in punishment."

Now, that's what I call *sensible* rules for a place like this!

Well, after the Warden had welcomed them, we put the Numbers away in their cells for Rest Period, and then I was off for the evening. I went back to the apartment, which I admit was sort of empty, what with old #853 being in Prison. Of course, he got himself into this, not me, so I guess it serves him right. But I do not know yet whether I am going to enjoy this experience at all.

Day 2. This morning when I got to work the guys on the night shift told me that they didn't have much trouble handling things. Some of the Numbers broke the Rule about not conversing after Lights Out, but the guys said they stopped that nonsense in a hurry. Charlie likes to talk a lot so I was not surprised to learn that my old buddy #853 got himself shouted at a few times. Sort of wish I'd been around to hear what they said to him.

We got the numbers through the morning ritual pretty well. Part of their job is to sweep up the place. Naturally #853 complained about having to clean the toilets. Back at the apartment, that's usually my chore. Funny to watch #853 get a taste of what's good for him, for a change. I would have given him a chit to see the movie that night if he had done a good job, but he bitched too much, and that's against Regulations. Then at lunch he acted up something awful. Broke the Rules all over the place. Lunch was sausage and potatoes, and being his roommate, I am well aware that he does not like sausages very much at all. So #853 refused to eat them, although that's illegal, because Rule Number Two says that Numbers *must eat* at mealtimes, which means that they must eat *everything* we give them, right?

So I said, "Listen you dumb twerp. Just because you are bigger than me doesn't mean that you are going to get away with breaking the Rules. You don't scare me, #853. You eat that damn sausage or I'll stick it in your ear and let you digest it that way." Of course I didn't say "ear," but you know what I mean.

Well, that must have teed him off, or something, because he started arguing with me and abusing me, which is definitely against the Rules. So the other guys and I just grabbed #853 by his nightshirt and led him away to solitary confinement. Which is really just a closet he's got to stand in, but it's just what he deserved.

Even then he didn't calm down much, and I had to go down two or three times to shut him up. He got a little nasty the last time, so I shook the billy-club at him, just to let him know who was boss. I wouldn't ever use it, of course, because that's against the Regulations. But it was a little frightening to have this guy I thought I knew threaten me with verbal abuse and physical gestures. Finally, I couldn't take it any more, so I went and got the other guys and we got a couple of sausages and took them down to the "hole" and stuck them in #853's hands.

"Listen you," I told him in no uncertain tone of voice. "You are going to hold on to those sausages until you see fit to obey the Rules and Regulations and eat them. Beggars can't be choosers, and you will stay in this 'hole' until you choose to obey the lawful orders of your Correctional Officers."

To tell the truth, even with the other guys around to protect me, I was a little worried because #853 has got one helluva temper, him being Irish

PART SEVEN Social Psychology

and red-headed and all that. Of course, I couldn't *see* the color of his hair because of the nylon stocking pulled over his head, and maybe that made the difference. Anyhow, #853 shook the sausages at me and stepped forward, like he might be going to hit me with them. So in self-defense I held up my billy-club. Funny thing. He stopped and stared at me, and then he sort of trembled or shivered, like he had a chill. Then he burst out crying, and turned around and hid his face in a corner. I just let the old sissy cry, since he brought it all on himself.

Jeez, I hate sissies. So before I left for the day, I deliberately got in a loud conversation outside the "hole" with one of the Correctional Officers. I had a date that night, and so did the other CO, and we spent a lot of time describing just what we were going to do with the ladies that evening. I figured that would teach #853 a lesson, because he certainly did like his nocturnal activities before he got sent to Prison.

Day 3. The first thing that the guys told me when I came on duty was that #853 still refused to eat the sausages, so they were starving him until he gave in. He had missed supper and breakfast both, which is only proper, under the Rules. I saw right away that we had trouble on our hands, because he was setting the other Numbers a very bad example. What would happen if everybody behaved that way? So I called his two cellmates into the yard, and then I handcuffed #853, sausages and all, and brought him out too.

"Listen you Numbers. This stupid jackass is disobeying the Regulations, and we cannot let him get away with gross violations of the sort he is guilty of. Therefore, we are going to take away your eating privileges until your cellmate here gives in and eats the sausages we have provided to keep him alive."

Well, naturally, the other two Numbers are not very happy. But we tell them to shut up and to get back on the Routine. Which, I am happy to say, they do without too much complaint. Except for #853, the Numbers are mostly a bunch of sheep. Then as I am taking #853 back to the "hole," Warden Wakeman came up and asked me to remove the handcuffs. I am not sure why he did this, since I was just trying to keep #853 from escaping. Which is what I am paid to do.

At lunchtime, when we wouldn't let them eat, the other two Numbers stood in front of the "hole" and tried to talk some sense into 853. Which, I am sad to say, they failed to do, so they went hungry. I would feel sorry for 853, except that he is obviously just being stubborn to show off, and now he is hurting others besides himself. Which is a downright crime, if you ask me.

Naturally, this whole nasty business upset the Routine so much that nobody knew which way was up. Finally, things got so bad that I suggested we ought to take away the eating privileges of all the Numbers until 853 showed he was sorry for his misdeeds and corrected his bad attitude and behaved like any decent human would. The other Correctional Officers agreed with me that this seemed a reasonable course of action, but they were a little worried about keeping discipline if all the Numbers went hungry. I volunteered to stay on for the evening shift, just to help out. But Warden Wakeman refused, even though I said he wouldn't have to pay me anything. Just trying to be of service, you know.

When we told the Numbers of our decision, they got pretty surly. In fact, one of them started wise-mouthing a bit and showing off, but I tapped him lightly with my billy-club, and he got back into line.

Day 4. I was barely asleep when the Correctional Officers on the evening shift phoned. They said the Numbers had gone crazy and were rioting! The Evening Shift got the Numbers cornered by spraying them with a fire extinguisher, but they needed reinforcements.

I put on my uniform and, as I rushed over to help, I really got angry thinking what a sissy jerk 853 turned out to be. Embarrassing us all with that stupid, childish behavior. Why didn't he just give in and obey the Rules, like everybody else?

Well, when I got there, I guess I taught him a lesson, didn't I?

(Continued on page 703.)

Liking and Loving

Do you want people to like you? That may seem a silly question, for almost everyone seems to want to be liked by almost everyone else. Americans spend billions of dollars annually on cosmetics, deodorants, new clothes, shiny cars, gleaming stereo sets, decorations for their houses or apartments, fancy office furniture, greeting cards, entertainments of various kinds, flowers, charm schools, diet pills, and self-improvement courses. All of these things are designed, one presumes, to attract other people and make them *like* us. Since similar behaviors (and expenses) are found in all human cultures, we may presume that the desire to be liked is probably built into our genes. What then can a psychology text tell you about the innate desire to be liked that you couldn't discover in the thousands of popular books and articles on the subject?

To begin with, a psychologist might insist that we need a better definition of the verb "to like" than usually appears in magazine stories—if possible, a definition so clearly and so objectively stated that we can *measure* what we're talking about.

If you looked the word "like" up in a large dictionary, you would find almost a full page of definitions. *To like* is to be attracted to, to feel positive emotions toward, to desire, to value, or to have high regard for some object or person. In his book *Liking and Loving,* Harvard psychologist Zick Rubin suggests that there are two main aspects of "liking" that deserve our attention. According to Rubin, when we say that we like someone, we usually mean either that we have *affection* for that person, or that we have *respect* for that person.

You have affection for someone who relates to you personally, someone who gives you a feeling of closeness and emotional warmth. Respect, on the other hand, is a cooler and psychologically more distant emotion. You have respect for someone whose personality, status, accomplishments, or talents you admire.

Two Types of Specialists

Of course, respect and affection don't always go hand in hand. You may respect political leaders, artists, scientists, and athletes, but you don't always feel *personal* warmth toward them unless you have somehow gotten to know them as individuals. And you may love someone for being a good *human being* even though the person may not merit international acclaim and respect. Harvard **sociologist** Robert Bales and his colleagues demonstrated this fact rather well in a classic series of experiments involving groups of male college students. The men were brought together in a laboratory and given certain intellectual problems to solve. Bales *et al.* measured the men's verbal behaviors as objectively as they could. And at the end of each problem-solving session, the experimenters asked the subjects to rate each member of the group in a number of ways, including how much the man liked the others and which men seemed to be leaders or have the best ideas.

Bales and his associates found that two types of people got high scores

Sociologist (so-see-OLL-oh-jist). The Latin word socius means "associate" or "companion." A sociologist is someone who studies society, social institutions, and social relationships—that is, a scientist interested in the inputs, processes, and outputs of social systems.

PART SEVEN Social Psychology

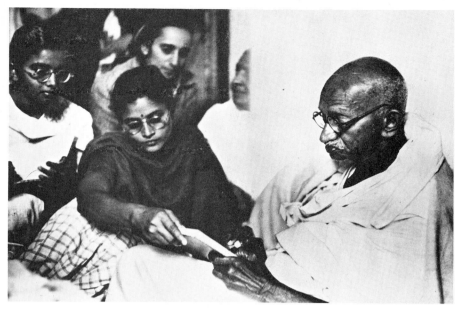
Mahatma Gandhi, Hindu nationalist leader, surrounded by young followers.

on the rating scales: the "idea man" (or **task specialist**) and the "social actualizer" (or **social-emotional specialist**).

During group sessions, the task specialist gave opinions and made suggestions more often than anyone else. He kept reminding the group of its goals and brought them back to the task at hand whenever they strayed from problem-solving. These behaviors apparently caused other group members to rate the man as a good leader or idea-generator.

The social-emotional specialist, on the other hand, was much more likely to *ask* for suggestions than to give them. He was particularly sensitive to the needs of others, made extensive use of praise and other forms of feedback, and smoothed over arguments in order to create what Bales calls *group solidarity*.

According to Bales, the idea man directed the cognitive or intellectual resources of the group, and was respected for his knowledge and expertise. The "actualizer" directed the emotional resources of the group, and was warmly liked for his ability to keep the group functioning as a **cohesive** unit.

Question: What similarities do you see between the two types of "specialists" in the Bales study and the functions associated with the two hemispheres of the brain?

Successful Managers

Zick Rubin believes that it is a rare person who is a "natural-born" expert at controlling both the cognitive and emotional processes of groups of people. According to Rubin, such greatness is found only in a very few leaders— Ghandi of India, Mao of China, Winston Churchill of Great Britain, and Franklin Roosevelt of the United States.

A study reported in 1979 by Texas psychologist Jay Hall, however, suggests that leadership skills are more a matter of training than of innate ability. In the course of his survey, Hall measured the attitudes and behaviors of more than 17,000 managers in 50 different US business and government organizations. Since so few women had risen to the higher ranks in these organizations, Hall decided to include only males in his experiment. (As we will see in a moment, Hall has also studied women managers and has found them to be little different from males.)

Task specialist. Someone primarily interested in goal achievement, or in getting the job done, rather than being interested in the feelings of the people trying to achieve the goal. Generally speaking, task specialists are given "respect" by the people who work with them, but are not always looked upon affectionately.

Social-emotional specialist. Bales' term for a group member more interested in interpersonal relations than in achieving measured goals or performing tasks well. Generally speaking, social-emotional specialists are given affection by the people who work with them, but aren't always given the same sort of respect that "task specialists" sometimes achieve.

Cohesive (ko-HE-sive). From Latin and Old English words meaning "to stick, to adhere." Cohesive forces are those that hold things together, like glue. A cohesive unit is one in which the members or parts function efficiently together, usually to achieve some common goal.

Hall began by scoring his subjects on the Rhodes *Managerial Achievement Quotient*, which measures how rapidly and how far a man has risen "through the ranks" in the organizational structure. According to Hall, only some 10 percent of the men had "high MAQ scores," which is to say that they were highly successful managers who had received frequent and rapid promotions. About 50 percent of the men received "average MAQ scores," while some 40 percent of the men had progressed so slowly that they received "low MAQ scores."

Next, Dr. Hall gave his subjects the *Work Motivation Inventory*, a test based on Maslow's **hierarchy of needs** that we discussed in Chapter 12. Hall found clear-cut differences among the three groups of managers in terms of what seemed to motivate them. The "successful" managers were most interested in what Maslow calls *self-actualization*—that is, in becoming better both as supervisors and as people. The "average" managers were motivated by *ego and status needs*—that is, in "looking good" and "feeling important." The men with "low" MAQ scores were partially motivated by status needs, but more by *security needs* (such as making a living wage, and not being fired). Obviously, from the point of view of Maslow's *hierarchy of needs*, the most successful managers had risen to the top of the motivational ladder, while the least successful men were stuck on the bottom rungs (see Fig. 26.1).

Just as interesting, Hall notes that the men seemed to impress their own needs on their subordinates. When Hall asked the managers what they thought motivated the people who worked for them, the men tended to believe that their employees had *just the same needs the managers did*. And when Hall gave the Work Motivation Inventory to these same employees, they tended to score just as their managers did. Hall believes that workers tend to take on the attitudes, motives, and behaviors of their supervisors—and that the workers are likely to *change motives* when put under a new manager.

Question: How might taking on your manager's (or teacher's) motives and attitudes help you survive in an organization (or school)?

Participatory Management Some organizational leaders *tell* people what to do. Other managers encourage their subordinates to *participate* in the decision-making process. According to Jay Hall, the greatest difference

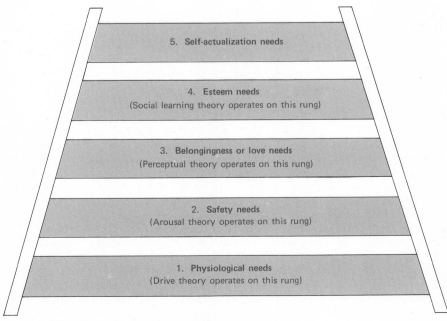

Fig. 26.1. Maslow's hierarchy of needs.

PART SEVEN Social Psychology

between successful and unsuccessful managers lies in how frequently the men make use of **participatory management.** The "unsuccessful" managers did not encourage much participation at all from their subordinates. The men with "average MAQ scores" asked (and took) the advice of the workers relatively infrequently. The "successful" managers, however, almost always sought the opinions and consent of the people who worked for them.

Hall then checked the workers' reactions to the style of management employed by their own managers. He states that, "Only the subordinates of managers with high MAQ scores may be found to enjoy the satisfaction and achievement that characterize a healthy organizational climate." In fact, as Hall notes, unsuccessful managers—and to some extent average managers—"are reported by their subordinates to employ practices which repress and frustrate subordinate personnel."

Interpersonal Competence Jay Hall next gave the *Personal Relations Survey* to several thousand managers and their subordinates. The PRS is a test that measures the amount of goal-setting and feedback that a manager uses—that is, it measures a person's competence at being *both* a "task specialist" and a "social-emotional specialist." Hall reports that the successful managers got high scores, the average managers got average scores, and the unsuccessful managers received very low scores on the test. And, as you might expect, the men's subordinates tended to earn inter-personal competence scores that were very similar to their supervisor's scores.

Question: Which type of manager was probably both liked and respected by his employees? Which type of manager might have been respected, but probably wasn't liked very much?

Managerial Goals Jay Hall believes that a manager's goals in large part determine how successful the manager will be. Hall reports that men with high MAQ scores show both a strong interest in achieving organizational goals *and* in helping their subordinates satisfy personal needs for self-actualization. Managers with average MAQ scores, on the other hand, feel a strong urge to "get the task done," but they show considerably less concern about what happens to their employees in the process. The unsuccessful managers appear to be protecting themselves: They seem to have little commitment either to the goals of the organization or to satisfying the needs of those individuals whom they supervise.

Hall's survey suggests that successful managers *perceive* their subordinates as being resources, not liabilities. They then treat the workers as colleagues rather than treating them as people to be "bossed around." The workers typically respond by *perceiving themselves* as being valued employees, and respond accordingly. If you want to be a successful manager, then, you must somehow get your subordinates to perceive you as both task-oriented and concerned about their welfare.

Women Managers Jay Hall's first study dealt exclusively with male managers. In a second study—published in 1980 with Susan M. Donnell—Hall gave similar measures to women managers and to their subordinates. Out of the dozens of measures they took, Donnell and Hall found only two (relatively insignificant) differences between male and female executives. First, women seem to be more "achievement oriented" than are their male counterparts. And second, women have somewhat less interpersonal competence than do men—that is, women managers seem to be less open and candid in relating to their colleagues than are males. Donnell and Hall conclude that "Women, in general, do not differ from men, in general, in the ways in which they administer the management process."

According to Jay Hall, there is a certain irony in these results. For one of the main problems that women managers have is that males *perceive* the women as being skilled at handling social-emotive resources, but as being poor at task achievement. In fact, the truth may be just the opposite—males are less oriented toward achievement than are women managers, and

When two people meet, their body language and facial expressions usually indicate how much they initially like each other.

Person perception. That part of social psychology which has to do with discovering the stimulus inputs that influence one individual's perceptions of or attitudes toward another individual. As we will see, many of the rules that we discussed in Chapter 11 concerning the perception of objects also hold for person perception.

Attitude. An "internal process," or psychological variable, that we use to explain why certain inputs lead to certain outputs. A consistent way of thinking about, feeling toward, or responding to some environmental stimulus or input. Made up of cognitive, emotional, and behavioral components. Many psychologists now believe that your attitudes are your own predictions about how you will act (or react) in certain situations.

males may be more skilled at interpersonal relations than women are. Yet, as long as males dominate the work scene, it is their *perceptions* of women that make the difference, not the actual behaviors of the women themselves.

So let us now turn to the subject of **person perception**—that is, the cues that both women and men probably make use of in judging others. For if you understand what stimulus inputs influence the way that people *perceive* each other, you may also get a better picture of why you view people the way that you do.

Question: What similarities do you see between Jay Hall's findings and Werner Mendel's discovery that his patients at St. Elizabeth's suddenly showed improvement when he started to perceive them differently (see Chapter 25)?

Person Perception

Suppose some good friends of yours have talked you into taking a blind date to a party. They paint a glowing picture of your date as a kind of super-person, and put considerable pressure on you to accept the date so that you won't spoil the party. When the magic moment comes, and you first meet the person, what sorts of things do you look for immediately? What clues do you see as a guide to whether you will like (have respect or affection for) the individual?

Obviously, your answers to these questions may be somewhat different than other people's answers, but the social psychologists who study *person perception* have come up with some generalities that might interest you.

First Impressions

Parties are social situations, so we might assume that you will be more interested in dating someone you could "like" emotionally than a "brain" or idea person whom you could "respect." Presumably, then, the moment you first meet your date "face to face," you will be looking for emotionally warm responses in the individual.

But remember the primary rule of perception: *You see what you expect to see.* Before you meet your date, your friends will have *biased* your perceptions by their descriptions of the individual. If they have told you the person is warm, affectionate, responsive, and outgoing, you will probably *look for* these attributes in your date as soon as the two of you meet. Certainly your *attitude* toward the person will be different than if you have been told your date is rather intellectual, cold, withdrawn, quiet, and self-possessed.

Attitudes

The word **attitude** refers to a consistent way of thinking about, feeling toward, or responding to some aspect of your environment (or toward yourself). You may hold attitudes toward almost anything—concrete objects such as automobiles, living objects such as people or animals, groups or organizations such as the US government, even abstract ideas such as "love" and "psychology."

Attitudes usually have three dimensions to them—that is, they are made up of cognitive, emotional, and behavioral components. For example, we can measure the behavioral aspects of your attitude toward (let's say) a political leader by seeing whether you vote for the person or listen to her or him on radio and TV. The cognitive and emotional aspects of your attitude must often be measured indirectly, for thoughts and emotions are *internal processes*. Usually we measure these "inner dimensions" of your attitude by asking you questions about how you think or feel.

PART SEVEN Social Psychology

Reputations

Harold Kelley.

When your friends describe your blind date to you, they are telling you something about that person's *reputation*—that is, the way that most people presumably perceive your date, or the attitude that most people have toward the person.

Psychologist Harold Kelley tested the importance of "reputations" in a study performed at MIT in the late 1940's. Kelley told a large class of undergraduates that they would have a visiting lecturer for the day, and that the students would be asked to evaluate this man at the end of the class. Kelley then passed out a brief biographical note about the teacher, presumably to help the students with their evaluation. Although the students did not realize it, the description that half the class received referred to the lecturer as being "rather a warm individual," while the description given the rest of the class called the man "rather a cold intellectual."

After the class had read the printed comments, the man arrived and led the class in a 20-minute discussion. Kelley watched the students and recorded how often each of them asked a question or made a comment. Afterward, the students were asked to rate the man on a set of attitude scales and to write a brief description of him.

Although everyone in the class had witnessed *exactly* the same performance at *exactly* the same time, the manner in which each student responded was measurably affected by the descriptions each had read. Those students who had been told the instructor was warm tended to rate him as much more informal, sociable, popular, good-natured, humorous, and humane than the students who had been told the same man was cold.

More than this, the subjects *reacted* to the man quite differently. The students who were told he was warm spoke to him in class much more frequently than did the students who were told he was cold.

Judging from Harold Kelley's research, once you believe you won't like a person, you tend to avoid further contact with him or her. Michigan psychologist Theodore Newcomb has called this response **autistic hostility**, and suggests that it may apply to interactions among groups as well as among individuals.

Stereotypes

Your initial impressions are often colored by the **stereotypes,** or biased perceptions, that you (and all of us) have about certain types or groups of people. If you assume that all blacks are lazy, dull, ignorant but musical, you will tend to "see" these attributes even in an energetic, bright black doctor who perhaps couldn't carry a tune in a handbag. If your attitude toward Jews is that they are intelligent, emotional, and penny-pinching, you may respond to each Jew as if she or he had to fit your stereotype.

Any time that you react to an individual *primarily* in terms of that person's membership in some group—or in terms of that person's physical characteristics, race, or religion—you are guilty of *stereotyping*. That is, you have let the reputation of the group influence your perception of the individual who belongs to that group.

Autistic hostility (aw-TISS-tic). Autism is the act of withdrawing into oneself, of shutting off external stimulation. Autistic hostility is the act of cutting off or denying favorable inputs about people or things we don't like. "My mind is made up—don't confuse me with facts."

Stereotypes. A stereotype is a fixed or unconscious attitude or perception—a way of responding to some person or object solely in terms of the person's (or object's) class membership. The failure to treat people as individuals, each different from the other, is the act of stereotyping.

Primacy effect (PRY-muh-see). *Primus* is the Latin word for "first." Whenever you remember your first impressions of a stimulus (or person) better than your second or third impressions, you are demonstrating the power of the primacy effect. An equally interesting phenomenon is the "recency effect," or the tendency to be more influenced by your last or most recent impressions than by your initial impression.

Body language. The "messages" about yourself that you communicate by how you dress, and by your expressive movements. As opposed to "verbal language," which is what you say out loud. First impressions (and person perception) are often more strongly influenced by body language than by spoken language.

Newcomb's concept of *autistic hostility* suggests that getting off on the right foot with a new acquaintance may be very important—for you may have just one chance to get the person to like you. Back in the 1940's psychologist Solomon Asch gave a group of subjects a list of adjectives describing someone they might meet. Half the subjects were told the person was "intelligent, industrious, impulsive, critical, stubborn, and envious." The other half of the subjects were given the same list, but in opposite order: "envious, stubborn, critical, impulsive, industrious, intelligent." The subjects were then asked to write a brief paragraph evaluating what they thought the person might be like. The responses made by two of Asch's subjects are good examples of what psychologists call the **primacy effect.**

A subject told the person was "intelligent . . . envious" wrote that: "The person is intelligent and fortunately he puts his intelligence to work. That he is stubborn and impulsive may be due to the fact that he knows what he is saying and what he means and will not therefore give in easily to someone else's idea of what he disagrees with."

A subject told the person was "envious . . . intelligent" wrote that: "This person's good qualities such as industry and intelligence are bound to be restricted by jealousy and stubbornness. The person is emotional. He is unsuccessful because he is weak and allows his bad points to cover up his good ones."

Presumably, the first information you get about a person creates the perceptual framework, or the bare bones, of an attitude. The rest of the data you receive about this individual merely helps you flesh out the details of the individual's presumed personality.

Question: Psychologists often speak of a recency effect *which can counteract the primacy effect. Can you guess how the "recency effect" would affect your attitude toward a stranger you happened to run into several days in a row?*

Two Channels of Communication

How do you communicate with someone to give them a good first impression of yourself? Actually, you have but two main channels of communication—what you do with your body, and what you say with your tongue. The way you look and dress and move—these are part of your **body language.** What you say, the opinions you express, and the verbal responses you make—these are part of your verbal language. Surprisingly enough,

The first impression that a job applicant makes (not the person's skills) often determines whether or not she or he will be hired.

when it comes to first impressions, people are often more influenced by your looks and *body talk* than they are by what you actually say.

Non-verbal Communication

When you form a first impression of a person, what aspects of the individual's character are you likely to be interested in? Do you try to "psych the person out"—that is, determine the motives, responsiveness, and further behaviors of the individual? If so, what you probably want to know the person's *intentions* toward you. And since you usually see people for at least a few seconds before you hear them talk, their looks and movements will often have a *primacy effect* in determining your initial attitude toward them.

Whether you know it or not, you have a characteristic way of dressing, of combing your hair, of moving your arms and legs, of looking toward or away from people as you speak or listen, of smiling, of frowning, and of giving feedback. Your own physical attributes may not really be good indicators of what you are like deep down inside. However, experiments suggest that many people you meet will judge your intentions toward them primarily by the way in which you communicate non-verbally.

But what makes up your own unique brand of body language? What can a stranger tell about you just by watching you behave?

Cultural Expectations To begin with, and perhaps most important, is the simple fact that you are either male or female. Every culture has different *social expectations* about the ways that women and men should look and behave. In the US we presume that males are bigger, stronger, cruder in their language and movements, and more violent and domineering than women. Men are expected to be interested in such things as automobiles, sports, business and finance, science and technology. Women are expected to prefer the arts, children, home life, cooking, and social relations. Thus you surely have stereotyped beliefs about the psychological differences between men and women that color the first impressions of everyone you meet.

Next, and more important, is probably your age. Young people are expected to be energetic, enthusiastic, idealistic, liberal, but perhaps inexperienced. Older people are expected to be more **sedate,** conservative, settled, experienced, and perhaps more willing to compromise to get some of the things they want from life. It doesn't matter that these cultural expectations are not entirely accurate: What does matter is that almost all of us *expect* older people to behave differently from young people.

Your size, shape, skin color, and physical beauty also affect the impression you give others. The closer your looks and actions are to our culture's stereotypes of "a good person," the more likely it is that a stranger will gain a favorable first impression of you.

As you can now see, all cultural stereotypes are miniature personality theories. And like most personality theories, stereotypes are usually built on small but statistically reliable correlations. As we noted in Chapter 23, Sheldon's research suggests that slightly more **endomorphs** are jolly and lovers of creature comforts than might be expected by chance alone. If you stereotype all fat people as being jolly, you will do a grave injustice to many of the endomorphs you meet—but in predicting their actions you will probably be right slightly more often than you will be wrong.

Question: Why do you think beautiful children score higher on individually administered IQ tests than when they take a written test administered to a whole group of children?

The Attribution Process

Why do we so often resort to stereotyping? According to social psychologist Fritz Heider, it is because of our culture's traditional solution to the

As our cultural stereotypes change, women are free to enter professions previously closed to them.

Sedate (see-DATE). From a Latin word meaning "to soothe, calm, appease, or make tranquil." A sedate person is one who is not readily influenced by disturbances. A sedated person is one who has been given a tranquilizing drug of some kind.

Endomorphs (EN-doh-morffs). Sheldon's "body type" description of someone who tends toward fat and soft body curves. As opposed to the mesomorph (ME-soh-morff) who is muscular and the ectomorph (ECK-toh-morff) who is thin and wiry. See Chapters 19 and 23.

Attribution process. The act of projecting personality traits or motives onto others so that you can explain their past or present behavior, hence predict what they may do in the future. The concept comes from Fritz Heider (HIGH-durr).

Personal space. Sommer's belief that you have your own "psychological territory"—a bubble of space around your body that you think of as being your "home base," not to be invaded by others without your permission.

Flagrant (FLAY-grant). From the Latin word meaning "to flame or burn," as in "conflagration" (kon-fluh-GRAY-shun), which means "fire." Anything that is particularly obvious or noticeable is flagrant.

mind-body problem (see Chapters 4 and 5). We all have a need to predict the way that people will react to us. But in Western society, we are usually taught that predictions about human behavior are possible only if we can comprehend the *inner causes* that presumably control the outward behavior.

Edward E. Jones noted in 1976 that most of us assume that our own actions are highly controlled by our environments, that we simply react to whatever challenge presents itself to us. If our actions are *inconsistent*, for example, we blame this inconsistency on the environment. However, when we observe inconsistent behaviors in *others*, we tend to blame their actions on some inner need, motive, or flaw of character. Thus, according to Jones, we perceive our behaviors as *forced on us* by the situation we're in. But when judging the behavior of others, we tend to ignore the social background and perceive them as *wanting* to behave that way.

As Fritz Heider pointed out in 1958, when you perceive a woman's actions as being an expression of her character, you are actually *attributing* certain personality traits to the woman. Most of these *attributed traits* are in fact stereotypes and—since you may have ignored the social stimuli to which the woman was responding—she may not possess these traits at all. But once you have "psyched her out," you immediately have a ready-made attitude or perception to fit her, and hence a ready-made way of responding to her.

As we noted in Chapter 12, our major motivation seems to be that of trying to predict and control our stimulus inputs. Most of us become alarmed (stressed) whenever we cannot guess fairly accurately what will happen to us next. By using what Heider calls the **attribution process,** we attribute to others motives that make their actions understandable (predictable) to us. And we tend to perceive (and remember) those actions that fit our predictions, while we repress those behaviors that don't match our expectations.

Question: It seems a fact that we are often frightened by people whose behavior is highly unpredictable. How could Heider's theory of the attribution process explain why deviant individuals often end up in prisons and mental hospitals?

Personal Space   The physical responses you make toward other people also influence the initial attitudes you arouse in others. California psychologist Robert Sommer has for many years studied what he called **personal space.** Sommer believes that you carry an "invisible bubble" around your body that encloses what you consider to be your own, personal psychological space. He notes that in a number of studies, subjects have shown a dramatic increase in nervousness when an experimenter moved to within a foot or so of them. Most of the subjects "defended their territories" by either moving away from the intruder, or by becoming increasingly hostile.

Sommer states that the size of your own personal space bubble is influenced by such factors as your personality, your status, and your culture. For middle-class Americans, this private area extends outward about two feet from any part of the body. For Arabs, the space is usually much smaller. For Scandinavians, the bubble is typically larger. People with great status (that is, people whom almost everyone respects) often command a larger personal space than do individuals with little or no status. We approach a prince, a pope, or a president with care and caution, lest we come too close. But we approach babies, young children, and animals as closely as we wish, because we typically perceive them as having little if any real status.

Question: When you change roles—as from Correctional Officer to prisoner—why does the size of your personal space often change?

Touching   The most **flagrant** violation of your personal space comes when someone tries to touch you. According to Robert Sommer, you are more

Robert Sommer.

likely to defend your bubble-territory against intrusions by equals than against someone who is inferior or superior to you in status. Parents and teachers, doctors and dentists, princes and policemen may "lay hands" on you because they have roles of authority, but you typically must ask permission first to touch them. Touching is often a sign of intimacy and a way of expressing affection, but you may often be shy about touching your friends, particularly if the gesture might have sexual overtones. The woman who sprawls in a chair with her legs uncrossed and the man who leans close to whisper something in your ear give the impression that they would like you to violate their personal space—or vice-versa.

In a study on body posture, psychologist Albert Mehrabian asked men and women to act out the ways in which they would sit when speaking to someone they liked or disliked. Mehrabian reports that both men and women leaned *forward* to express liking, but that men (more than women) leaned back or became more tense when addressing someone they disliked.

Psychologist Donn Byrne and his associates set up an experiment in which couples were selected by a computer for blind dates. After the young man and woman had gotten to know each other briefly, they were called into Byrne's office and stood before his desk for further instructions. The subjects were then separated and asked to fill out a questionnaire indicating how much they liked their dates. Byrne and his colleagues report that couples who liked each other stood measurably closer together in front of the desk than did couples who didn't care much for each other.

Question: Why might strangers in a crowded elevator stare straight ahead and avoid conversation?

The Eyes Have It Movements of your face and eyes are often as critical to the first impression you give as are the ways you move your arms and legs. Smiles invite approaches; frowns demand distance. The eye contact you make with people often controls both the flow of conversation and their initial opinion of your honesty and aggressiveness.

Psychiatrist R.D. Laing states that many schizophrenic patients who withdraw from the social world seem to avoid eye contact entirely. This avoidance response is particularly characteristic of autistic children, who often refuse to look anyone directly in the eyes. Indeed, it is often precisely this avoidance *behavior* which makes people attribute to autistic children the *mental trait* called "insanity." In fact, as we noted in Chapter 9, autistic children seem to avoid eye contact because they suffer from **input overload.** When left in a deprived sensory environment for a while, they often can reduce the overload and then begin to look directly at people again.

In fact, the rules of "eye contact" are primarily learned and vary considerably from culture to culture. If you happen to be a middle-class adult, you probably look *at* people when they are talking or lecturing. For your society, staring directly at a speaker is an acquired response that apparently encourages that person to continue conversing—particularly if you nod or smile in apparent agreement. When you look *away* from whoever is speaking, however, you signal that you are bored or that you want to take over the talking role yourself. Any speaker who is sensitive to your social cue of glancing away will rapidly change the subject or throw the conversational ball in your direction.

When you are telling a story or making a point, chances are that you will glance away from your audience, particularly if you are trying to think through a point while speaking. While you speak, you may glance back at your audience from time to time to make sure they are still with you (that is, still looking at you), then look away again in a hurry if you wish to continue speaking.

Conversation shifts from one person to another primarily when two people are in direct eye contact. Anyone who violates these unwritten social rules is often thought to be rude, immature, or overly aggressive.

These middle-class eye signals are often reversed in lower class cultures. For example, individuals reared in lower class environments tend to stare

Albert Mehrabian.

Input overload. You have a certain maximum speed at which you can process or react to the inputs that come your way. In a very stimulating environment, you may receive more inputs than you can readily process, a stressful condition called "input overload." There are many ways of coping with input overload. One way is to try to make the inputs "line up in a queue," as people do at an airplane counter when trying to board a crowded flight. Another way is to repress, deny, or cut off the inputs in some way—perhaps by paying them no attention whatsoever.

directly at people when talking, but avert their eyes when listening to show respect (particularly if listening to someone of higher status).

Question: If a man stared at you intensely while speaking to you, what motives would you attribute to him? If he averted his eyes while listening to you, would you think he was showing disinterest or respect?

Appropriate versus Inappropriate Behaviors   Initial impressions are but the first step in getting a stranger to like you. The mere fact that you act in what you consider to be a friendly and considerate manner doesn't guarantee that the stranger will assume your actions reflect "the real you." Since most of us are "on our good behavior" in first encounters, many of the people we meet may discount our *appropriate* behaviors as being "put on."

Oddly enough, however, if you behave *inappropriately*, most people will assume that you did so because of some basic flaw in your personality. Apparently we are often reluctant to believe the best about strangers, but only too ready to believe the worst.

Edward Jones and his associates demonstrated the operation of this principle by asking subjects to listen to recorded interviews between a psychologist and a male student applying for a job. In one interview the student went out of his way to impress the psychologist favorably. The student suggested several times that he more than met the job requirements. Subjects who heard this recording found it difficult to describe the applicant's personality: They thought he was "just playing a role." In the second interview the same student presented himself as being quite different from the sort of person that the job required. Subjects who heard just the second tape were confident that the student had "shown his true colors" because he apparently behaved inappropriately in the situation.

As Shakespeare put it: "All the world's a stage, and all the men and women merely players. They have their exits and their entrances; and one man in his time plays many parts." The lasting impressions that we make depend to a great extent on the *consistency* of the parts that we play in the theater of life. So perhaps it is time we looked seriously at role playing.

Social Roles

A **social role** is a more or less stereotyped set of responses that a person makes to related or similar situations. In a sense a social role is like a part that an actor or actress might portray in a play or film. Some roles (such as being masculine or feminine) are a basic part of your **repertory** all through your life. Other roles (such as being a cheerleader or class president) are "bit parts" or "walk-ons" that you often discard as you mature. Like a part in a play, a social role is made up of a characteristic set of body movements and verbal statements.

Question: What kinds of behaviors and attitudes would you express if you took on the role of a policeman? How would you behave if playing the role of a convict?

Male and Female Roles

While basic roles (like traits) surely have a biological component, for the most part we must learn the parts we play in the theater of life. Michigan psychologist Judith Bardwick states that in middle-class US society, a fundamental shift between male and female roles occurs when a child reaches six or seven years of age. At this time, a girl often builds up an intense dyadic relationship with another girl. This strong friendship is characterized by *complete acceptance:* Each girl perceives the other as being "the best person living in all possible ways." Neither member of the dyad will usually tolerate criticism about the other from any outside source (such as parents).

Judith Bardwick.

Sometimes a third girl will become friends with both members of the dyad, thus turning the pair-relationship into a **triad.** But triads are typically less stable than dyads, so the new girl may "capture" one of the others and form a dyad that excludes a member of the original pair.

While young girls tend to form *pair-bonds*, young boys mostly form *teams*, particularly when engaging in social activities such as sports. Bardwick notes that team members "rank" each other according to ability. If you are "choosing up sides" for a game of football, you may select Joe first because he's a good runner, but may choose Bill last because he's too thin and tall. If the game is basketball, you may pick Bill first because of his height, while selecting Joe last since he's poor at hitting the basket. According to Bardwick, boys select their friends in terms of an overall "balance" of pluses and minuses. Boys are also less upset by justifiable criticism since they realize that, while they cannot be "best" in all activities, they still can be a valued and warmly accepted member of "the team."

Heterosexual Relationships   Bardwick believes these early experiences set the basis for later development in male and female *roles* in our society, particularly in heterosexual relationships. Males often select women as they would a team mate—that is, they choose as a wife someone who ranks high on a number of dimensions, including physical beauty. But they don't expect "perfection." Women, on the other hand, may demand *complete acceptance* from men because they are trying to regain the intense emotionality of that childhood dyadic relationship. However, the woman may also have conscious or unconscious fears of rejection, particularly if she was cut out of a triad when young.

The problem in adult male–female relations may come, Bardwick says, when neither party in a marriage understands the needs of the other. The man may believe that the act of choosing a woman "for his team" should be enough to convince her of his affection, while the woman may assume that the man surely must perceive her as being "the best person in all possible ways" since he married her. If her husband casually remarks that another woman is pretty, the wife may interpret the remark to mean that he no longer sees her as perfect, therefore he no longer loves her.

Job Performance   The differences in early **socialization** for boys and girls may also affect later performance on the job. Middle-class men may do better than women in organizations because men are accustomed to the mix of criticism and praise that are a part of most team operations. The woman working for a large corporation may attempt to survive by trying to

Triad (TRY-add). From the Latin word meaning "three." A dyad (DIE-add) is a two-person relationship. The dyad becomes triadic (try-ADD-ic) when a third individual is included. A husband and wife make up a marital dyad. A wife, husband, and one child make up a family triad.
Socialization (soh-shall-uh-ZAY-shun). The process by which children learn the "rules and regulations" of their own family group, and of their culture and the society in which they live. That is, the process by which we all learn to live together in a civilized manner.

About age seven, boys tend to form "teams" while girls tend to form close dyadic relationships.

form a "pair-bond," particularly with her manager. If this person criticizes the woman in any way, she may perceive the criticism as complete rejection.

Bardwick believes that about 70 percent of young boys and girls in our culture go through the socialization process she has described. Males who do *not* acquire the "team mentality" when young often have problems getting along in work (and other) organizations, while young women who are socialized into forming teams rather than pair-bonds tend to rise rapidly through corporate structures.

Question: How might the current push for equality in men's and women's sports have a profound effect on what roles females and males later play in business and industry?

Role Change

Illinois psychologist Harry C. Triandis believes that your actions are determined primarily by two things: habits and behavioral intentions. *Habits* are those stereotyped ways you have of responding to specific situations. Your *behavioral intentions* are, more or less, whatever goals you are trying to reach at any given moment. These momentary goals are affected by many things—the roles you have learned, your emotional reactions, and your cognitive expectancies. Thus, according to Triandis, you can predict a man's behavior much better if you know his behavioral intentions than if you merely know what his habits are.

Triandis views the process of human interaction as little more than an exchange of resources. You want things from me, and I want things from you. If you know my intentions, you can guess what I want—and what I am willing to pay for satisfying this goal. But the intentions you *attribute* to me are strongly influenced by your social expectations. In his 1977 book *Interpersonal Behavior*, Triandis reports a series of studies he has made of what happens when two people from different cultures meet and interact. He finds that most subjects assume that someone from a different country *must* have the same intentions as they do. Thus most Greeks will explain the behavior of Americans in terms of Greek tradition and culture, while Americans find it difficult to believe that Greeks aren't motivated by precisely the same intentions as we have.

Triandis believes that the first thing you have to do when you learn a new role is to discover what behavioral intentions are associated with that role. Thus when you meet someone new, learning what the person's role-expectations are will tell you a great deal about that person's intentions—and how to change or satisfy them.

Bandura's "Modeling" Approach

Roles (and intentions) are learned, but *how* are they learned, and how do you go about *changing* them? Stanford psychologist Albert Bandura believes that the primary mechanisms of social learning may be *observing* and *modeling*. Whenever you see someone act a certain way, you may observe them to see if that action is rewarded or punished. Then you try to imitate those behaviors that you see reinforced, while avoiding those behaviors that lead to punishment.

Bandura states that, to some extent, psycho-therapy is a matter of choosing a more adaptive role and then learning how to play it well. The technique he finds particularly useful is called **modeling**, in which the therapist demonstrates the new behavior pattern in a step-by-step fashion. The client watches not only the actions the model performs, but is encouraged to note the consequences of the model's behaviors. In one of Bandura's best-known experiments he helped people lose their fear of snakes by observing a "therapist" handle the animals without fear (and without being bitten).

Modeling. Part of the socialization process. You learn society's "rules and regulations" by being told what to do (and rewarded for doing so, or punished if you disobey), and by imitating the behaviors of "model citizens." Modeling thus consists of learning by imitation.

PART SEVEN Social Psychology

Bandura began by advertising in a newspaper for subjects who wished help in overcoming a snake phobia. Thirty-two people answered the ad. One was a museum official who was afraid to enter the snake exhibit in his own museum. Several were individuals who feared going hunting, fishing, or hiking because they might encounter a reptile. Others were school-teachers whose young students often brought snakes to class for "show and tell." One woman had a neighbor who kept a boa constrictor as a pet. Thinking about the closeness of the snake had nearly given the woman a heart attack.

Bandura compared four different types of treatment. Eight of the subjects were randomly selected to receive no therapy at all during the first part of the experiment. These eight people made up the no-treatment control group. Another eight were shown movies of adults and children playing with snakes. A third group of eight was given systematic desensitization to overcome their fears (see Chapter 15).

The fourth group was given "modeling therapy." At the beginning of treatment this fourth group watched through a glass partition while the therapist played with a snake to show that it wasn't dangerous. The therapist tried to model all of the snake-handling behaviors he wished the subjects to learn. Then the subjects entered the room where the therapist was, but stayed some distance away from the dreaded reptile. Next, through gradual approximations, they were encouraged to approach the snake and touch it, just as the therapist had modeled doing (see Fig. 26.2). As the subjects gained confidence in playing with the snake, the therapist faded out of the picture.

The "final exam" for the effectiveness of the therapy was somewhat dramatic. The subject was asked to sit in a chair for 30 seconds, hands at side, while a snake was placed on the subject's lap and allowed to crawl all over her or his body. Every member of the modeling therapy group passed the test with ease. A few of the members of the film-treatment and desensitization groups passed, but almost no one in the no-treatment group was willing to let the reptile invade his or her personal space.

Bandura then did something unusual: He gave modeling therapy to the members of the other groups who hadn't shown improvement. He reports "cures" in 100 percent of the subjects.

The arrival of the first baby usually brings forth innately determined parental response patterns.

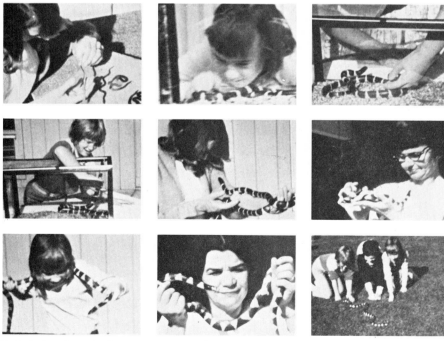

By imitating "models" who handled reptiles confidently, Bandura's clients learned to overcome their fear of snakes.

Donn Byrne.

The Economics of Role Playing

As Harry Triandis notes, role playing is something that we do for others in order that they will do something for us in return. At its worst, role playing is selfish manipulation of other people. For the most part, however, it is a necessary form of social exchange that allows each person to get something by giving something. And just as there are formal regulations governing the purchase of food and clothing, so there are informal rules governing the purchase of social rewards with role playing. The person who takes without giving is often punished by being disliked, ignored, or put in an institution. The most valuable forms of social interchange are typically those in which both parties are satisfied with the bargain.

Cliché (klee-SHAY). *Cliché* is a French word meaning a trite or stereotyped reaction, an overworked expression or idea. The dialogue in many bad movies consists almost entirely of clichés—the actors and actresses give one stereotyped verbal response after another. Samuel Goldwyn, the movie producer, may have had the right idea when he told his writers: "Don't give me old clichés—give me new clichés!"

To Be Alike Is To Be Liked

Why should the roles you play be so rewarding to other people? Psychologist Donn Byrne suggests an interesting answer. If you would like to test the validity of Dr. Byrne's suggestion, first make a list of the things that you want most from a person you've recently met or from someone whom you'd like to know better. After you've done this, make a list of the things you would expect this person to want from you. Is there a similarity between the two lists? That is, are the things you want from others correlated with what you think they want from you? If the two lists are strikingly different, what are the chances of your becoming good friends?

Byrne has collected a great deal of evidence suggesting that the major factor attracting one person to another is *similarity*. He asked hundreds of subjects to fill out questionnaires telling about their own attitudes on a number of topics. Each subject was then shown a second questionnaire supposedly filled out by a complete stranger. In fact, Byrne "faked" the answers to this second questionnaire so that the stranger appeared to be similar to, or dissimilar to, the subject. The subject was then asked whether he or she would "like" the stranger.

As you might guess, the closer the subject's attitudes were to the stranger's, the more frequently the subject reported a liking for the stranger. These results appear to hold for people of all ages, nationalities, educational levels, and socio-economic status.

Byrne's results—and those of dozens of other scientists—tend to validate the old **cliché,** "Birds of a feather flock together." And there are certainly many reasons why "to be like" is almost the same as "to be liked." Having someone agree with us is apparently very rewarding. The more similar your attitudes and intentions are to mine, the more probable it is that you will agree with me without having to suffer the stress and anxiety of pretending to be someone you aren't. The more similar I am to you, the better your attribution process will work, and the more readily you can predict my future behaviors. And the more similar our value systems, the more readily you can determine the rewards and punishments you might give me.

But now suppose you are given the role, of correcting a good friend's "bad attitudes and behaviors." What kind of "correctional techniques" would you use to get your friend to model your behaviors? Would you punish your friend's mistakes and *force* compliance, or would you reward the person for improvement?

As it turns out, the answer depends on what you perceive your role to be, and what character traits you attribute to the person whom you can reward or punish.

If the attributes of this couple are fairly similar, they are probably at the outset of a successful marriage.

Zimbardo's "Jail"

In the summer of 1971, Stanford psychologist Philip Zimbardo and his students undertook some research on what it was like to be in prison. Because no local warden would let them use a real jail, Zimbardo and his crew decided to create their own prison. So they took over a basement corridor in the psychology building at Stanford and converted it into cells, an exercise yard, observation rooms, and a closet that served as the "hole" for solitary confinement. They turned nearby rooms into space for the guards, the "warden" (Dr. Zimbardo) and his students, and for the video tape equipment.

Next, Zimbardo put an ad in two local papers offering to hire students to play the roles of prisoners and guards for a two-week period. Some 75 students responded. Many of them were from the Stanford area, but many were young people who simply happened to be visiting that part of California for the summer. Zimbardo and his colleagues interviewed all the volunteers, screened them for physical and mental health problems, and then selected the 21 men who seemed most healthy, mature, and "normal." On a random basis, 11 of them were chosen to be "guards," while the other 10 were to be "prisoners."

The subjects were told the details of the study and all voluntarily agreed to "play the game" for a period of up to two weeks. They were to be paid $15 a day for participating, and knew that if selected as a prisoner they would be **incarcerated** 24 hours a day and would lose all rights to privacy during the 14-day period the experiment was to run. The guards worked 8-hour shifts, but (unlike the prisoners) were allowed to leave when their shifts were over.

The guards were given special uniforms designed to look "official." They were issued police night-sticks, whistles, and reflecting sunglasses (to prevent eye contact with the prisoners). The prisoners were required to wear muslin smocks with no underclothes, a light chain and lock around one ankle, rubber sandals, and a cap made from a nylon stocking. Each prisoner was given a toothbrush, towels, soap, and bed linen. No personal belongings were allowed in the cells.

An Arresting Experience On the Sunday that the experiment began, the local police "arrested" the ten prisoner-volunteers at their homes. After the police had finger-printed and interrogated the young men, the subjects were blindfolded and were driven to the "Stanford Jail." From that point on, the prisoners were almost entirely under the control of the volunteers playing the guard's role.

Zimbardo and the guards had developed a set of "rules" that the prisoners were expected to memorize and follow while in jail. One of the most important rules was that the prisoners were to be addressed only by the "numbers" painted on their muslin smocks, but the guards were always to be referred to as "Mr. Correctional Officer." The prisoners received three bland meals a day, were allowed three supervised visits to the toilet, and were given two hours daily for the privilege of reading or writing letters. The prisoners were also expected to "work" in order to earn their $15 daily payment. Twice a week, the prisoners were allowed visitors. The guards could also give them a variety of "rewards" for good behavior, including the right to exercise in the "yard" and to attend movies.

Persons and "Non-persons" The first clue as to what the results of the study would be came during the "count" of the prisoners that the guards took three times daily. The **ostensible** purpose of lining up the prisoners was to make sure they were all present and accounted for—and to check to see if they had memorized the "rules." The first day or so, the "count" took but 10 minutes or so. But slowly the guards started increasing the amount of time spent "grilling" the prisoners. By the fifth day, some of the "counts" lasted for several hours as the guards berated and harrassed the prisoners for minor infractions of the "rules."

Philip Zimbardo.

Incarcerated (in-KAR-sur-rated). From the Latin word meaning, "to enclose, or to imprison." To incarcerate is to confine, or to stick someone in jail.

Ostensible (oss-TENN-suh-bull). From the Latin word meaning "to show, or to display." The ostensible reason for doing something is the reason you wish to display to others. The real reason may be quite different, and something you don't always wish to have known. The ostensible reason for wearing a mink coat is to keep warm. The real reason is to let people know how rich you are.

Zimbardo knew that real-life prisons were *dehumanizing* environments, and he had designed his experiment in an attempt to study some of the conditions that lead to depersonalization. He found out in a hurry that one primary factor was the behavior of the guards. True, the prisoners had, technically speaking, given up their identities and became "numbers." But they were still human beings, despite the smocks they wore and the chains around their ankles. However, the guards rapidly began treating the prisoners as "non-persons" who weren't really humans at all. And the more inhumane the guards' behaviors became, the more "depersonalized" the behavior of the *prisoners* became.

But the *reactions* of the prisoners were probably just as important as the *actions* of the guards. Instead of protesting their treatment, the prisoners began to act in depressed, institutionalized, dependent ways—exactly the role-behaviors shown by real-life prisoners and mental patients. And, as you might imagine, the more the prisoners acted like "non-persons," the more they were hassled and mistreated by the guards.

By the end of the sixth day, the situation had nearly gotten out of hand. The guards began modifying or changing the prison "rules" and routines to make them increasingly more punitive, and even some of Zimbardo's students got so caught up in the spirit of things that they neglected to give the prisoners some of the privileges they had earned.

At this point, wisely, Zimbardo called a halt to the proceedings.

The Results   Afterward, Zimbardo and his students interviewed all of the subjects and analyzed the video tapes they had made during the six days. Perhaps their most important finding is an obvious one: The subjects simply "became" the roles that they played. *All* of the 11 guards behaved in abusive, dehumanizing ways toward the prisoners. Some of them did so only occasionally, but more than a third of the guards were so consistently hostile and degrading that Zimbardo refers to their behavior as **sadistic.**

The prisoners, on the other hand, showed a reaction which (in Chapter 14) we called **learned helplessness.** Day by day, the prisoners did less and less, initiated fewer conversations, became more surly and depressed. Half the prisoners were unable to cope with their own reactions and asked to leave. But the other five seemed simply to accept their fates and (in a few cases) didn't even bother to "request parole" when given a chance to do so.

The second important finding Zimbardo made is obvious but, to most people, simply unbelievable. There was absolutely no prior evidence that the subjects would react as they did. Before their random selection as guard or prisoner, the two groups did not differ from each other in any way that Zimbardo could discover. All 21 were healthy, normal, psychologically mature young men—and not one of them predicted he would act as he did. Furthermore, there is no reason to believe that the study would have turned out any different had the roles of the two groups been reversed.

One of the tests Zimbardo used is the F-Scale, which measures **authoritarianism.** Surprisingly enough, the guards didn't differ from the prisoners on this scale, nor were the "sadistic" guards more authoritarian (as measured by the test) than were the more "humanitarian" guards. However, the prisoners who refused to leave were, generally speaking, the ones who scored as being the most authoritarian. Zimbardo believes that these men were psychologically better prepared to cope with the highly structured and punitive environment of the prison.

At no time did any guard ever *reward* a prisoner for anything. The only "correctional" techniques the guards ever employed were criticism, punishment, and harrassment.

Question: Given the data, can you be really sure that you wouldn't have played the guard or prisoner role exactly as Zimbardo's subjects did?

Public Reaction   The results of his experiment distressed Zimbardo so much that he made them available to the news media almost immediately. Public reaction was swift, and primarily punitive. Many critics found it

Sadistic (sah-DISS-tick). The Marquis de Sade (mar-KEY duh SAHD) was a Frenchman who found pleasure in punishing others. A sadist (SAD-ist) is thus someone who enjoys giving pain to other people. See Chapter 15.

Learned helplessness. Psychologist Martin Seligman found that animals who had to cope with unavoidable shock often learned to be "helpless." That is, they acquired a "giving up" response that seemed to minimize the pain. When they were later offered a means of escaping the pain, they refused to take advantage of it. Seligman believes that some types of depression in humans are a form of "learned helplessness." See Chapter 14.

Authoritarianism. An authoritarian is someone who believes that discipline and punishment make the world a better place. Someone who believes in "following the rules" set down by higher authority.

PART SEVEN   Social Psychology

inconceivable that a "noted Stanford professor" would undertake such a dehumanizing study. Most of these same critics also suggested that Zimbardo must have picked a very abnormal bunch of young men for his subjects, because ordinary citizens surely wouldn't behave in that fashion.

In fact, there is no better illustration of the *attribution process* at work than Zimbardo's study. The prisoners became depressed at what they considered to be their own "spinelessness." The guards justified their harrassment in terms of "criminal instincts" they perceived in the prisoners. The critics attributed both the brutality of the guards and the "helpless" behaviors of the prisoners to innate character flaws in *those* specific men. No one caught up in the experiment—including, at times, Zimbardo and his colleagues—perceived that the environment was *almost entirely responsible* for the behaviors of both guards and prisoners. No one saw that the men were just "playing roles."

Perhaps we shouldn't be too surprised at either Zimbardo's results or the public reaction, for social scientists have reported similar findings many times before. And each time most of us seem to find it impossible to believe that our actions are so strongly influenced by the world we live in.

After World War II, there were hundreds of studies made of the guards and prisoners who had been in Nazi concentration camps. Almost all the results suggested that the guards (on the average) were little different from either the prisoners or from the average European. Zimbardo notes that even some of the worst "Nazi butchers" appeared to be perfectly normal—outside of their actions at the concentration camps.

After the Korean conflict, the US Army did extensive research on the 4,000 American soldiers who returned from Chinese prisoner-of-war camps (see Chapter 9). Although 85 percent of these men "cooperated" with the Communists—even to the extent of "squealing" on their comrades—their personality test scores and prior behavior patterns were no different from those of any other group of army men. Despite this evidence, the official explanation of the men's behavior blamed both the men's "psychological weaknesses" and the power of Communist "brainwashing" techniques for the prisoners' behaviors.

Immediately after the My Lai incident during the Viet Nam war, the Army put the soldiers involved through a psychological wringer. In terms both of their personalities and their prior experiences, the soldiers were exactly the same as most other healthy, normal American men of their age and experience. The official explanation minimized the Army's role in the affair and attributed the cause of the massacre to the men's failure to "follow the rules."

Social roles are patterns of attitudes, emotions, perceptions, and behaviors that are "the norm" for a particular group, organization, or culture. They seem to be learned early in life, and primarily through observation and imitation. Although some aspects of a role may be innately determined, they are primarily determined by the social situation.

Most of the things you do, think, and feel are strongly influenced by the conditions you grew up in and by your present social milieu. Present-day society still presumes that human behavior is chiefly influenced by internal processes such as "personality" and "character." So if you find yourself *attributing* motives and intentions to other people, perhaps that is merely a role you have been taught to play.

Summary

1. When we say that we want people to like us, we typically mean that we want them either to **respect** us or feel an **emotional attraction** to us.

2. Research on problem-solving in small groups suggests that there are two types of people who are liked—those individuals who are **task-oriented** or "idea people," and those individuals who astutely manage the **socio-emotional resources** of the group by asking questions and giving praise and criticism.

3. Studies of 17,000 US managers suggest that successful supervisors are motivated by the need for **self-actualization,** while relatively unsuccessful managers are motivated by **security** and **status needs.**

4. Successful managers tend to use **participatory management** techniques, while average or below-average supervisors tend to manage in an **authoritarian** way.

5. Successful managers are both task-oriented and concerned for the welfare and personal development of their employees. Average managers are primarily task-oriented, while relatively unsuccessful managers seem more concerned with **self-protection** than with goal achievement or with helping others.

6. An **attitude** is a consistent way of thinking about, feeling toward, or responding to some aspect of your environment (or toward yourself).

7. What Fritz Heider called our **person perception**—the way we perceive others—is influenced by many factors: The individual's **reputation** and our **cultural expectancies** about how the person should dress, appear, talk, and behave.

8. We tend to perceive people who meet our expectancies in a favorable light, but often show **autistic hostility** toward individuals who don't act or look as we think they should.

9. We tend to react toward the people around us in terms of **stereotypes**—that is, we tend to respond to people in terms of their group rather than their individual characteristics.

10. Our **first impressions** of people are colored by the **primacy effect**—that is, the initial information that we receive about individuals becomes **figure** while later information becomes **background.** The initial inputs that shape our lasting impressions often involve the person's **body language** and style of **non-verbal communication** more than the person's spoken language.

11. Each of us seems to have a **personal space** around us that we defend as our **psychological territory.** The size of our territory is determined by the culture we grew up in and by our **status** in that culture.

12. Each culture also has its own rules for **eye contact** and **social feedback** that determine the ways in which people converse with each other, and sometimes make it hard for people from different cultures to communicate with one another.

13. We tend to see our own behaviors as responses to our **social milieu,** but believe that the actions of others are determined primarily by **inner psychological processes** such as **personality** and **character.**

14. In order to predict and influence the actions of others, we use the **attribution process.** That is, we attribute motives and intentions to them that make their behaviors understandable to us.

15. A **social role** is a stereotyped way of thinking, feeling, perceiving, or behaving.

16. Both our genes and our early experiences affect our **sex roles.** Girls in middle-class US society tend to form **dyadic relationships** about age 7. These relationships are often characterized by each girl's **complete acceptance** of the other. A search for this same acceptance may color the girl's later heterosexual and job experiences.

17. At about age seven, many US boys form **teams** in which each boy evaluates and ranks the skills of the other group members. The adult male role then includes such characteristics as **achievement, cooperation,** and **performance evaluation** rather than dyadic acceptance.

18. Triandis views the process of human interaction as little more than an **exchange of resources.** In order to get what we want from others, we must therefore guess their **behavioral intentions.**

19. Bandura believes roles are learned primarily through **observation** and **imitation.** Abnormal behaviors are thus inappropriate roles acquired through abnormal experiences. By using **modeling therapy,** Bandura has been able to cure people of such "psychological problems" as snake **phobias.**

20. Research suggests we tend to like, and be liked by, people who are similar to us in behavior and attitude.

21. Abnormal behaviors such as **authoritarianism, social aggression,** and **learned helplessness** may be nothing more than **role behaviors** determined primarily by the **institutional setting** in which they occur.

(Continued from page 684.)

Day 5. I don't understand why Warden Wakeman stopped the experiment. We had the riot under control, and we hadn't violated the Regulations. I mean, it isn't really physical punishment if you just *poke* the Numbers a little. That sort of stuff goes on in jails all the time, doesn't it? And how else were we going to get 853 to obey the Rules?

When Dr. Wakeman cancelled the game, he seemed a little upset, although he said that Professor Zimbardo and his students at Stanford had stopped the game there too. Can't figure out why. Things were just getting rolling pretty good. Oh, well, Dr. Wakeman said the game was a success because it proved that Lord Acton was right, and power does corrupt. Which was a funny thing for him to say, since he hired us to enforce the Rules and Regulations in the first place. We were just doing our job as Correctional Officers.

I looked at some of the video tapes that Dr. Wakeman took, particularly the last one showing how we settled 853's hash. And I had to grin. I don't think I will ever forget the sight of him standing there, with that sausage sticking out of his mouth.

Oh, I admit, I got a little angry when Dr. Wakeman came out and ended the game. I mean, it took so *long* for that jackass 853 to shape up, and his stupid misbehavior cost me 200 bucks. Almost everybody was teed-off at him, including the other prisoners.

I watched that final tape twice, and even if I do say it myself, I think I came out of the whole thing looking pretty darn good. Like, when I got there, all of the Numbers were backed into a corner of the yard, and the CO's on the evening shift were pointing the nozzle of a fire extinguisher at them. Old 853 was shaking one of those stupid sausages at the CO's, and they were shaking their billy-clubs back at him. But nobody was getting anywhere. And I saw what I had to do, right off.

I told the CO with the nozzle to keep me covered, and motioned to the other two CO's to come with me. Then we marched right up to 853.

"Grab his arms, men," I said, and they did. He seemed shocked and started to struggle, but the CO's straightened him out right away. Good, dependable guys, those two. Then I grabbed the sausage and stuck it right in 853's face. "Listen, twerp," I said, "we are going to finish this business *right now.* Then you are going to *apologize,* and we are going to get back on the Routine, just like the Rules say."

853 gave me some smart-ass reply, but I was not about to take any of his lip. So I jabbed his nose with the sausage and said, "I will give you 5 seconds to start eating, or I am going to cram this thing down your throat, and it will serve you right if you choke."

He gave me this peculiar look, like he didn't recognize who I was because of my mirror sunglasses, or something. Then I started to count, "One . . . Two . . . Three . . . Four . . . Five!"

Well, at that moment 853 opened up his mouth to say something, and I jammed the sausage right between his teeth. "Bite," I said, in a firm tone of voice. He just glared at me, and right then I knew it was now or never, him or me. But I wasn't at all scared. In fact, I felt rather good because I knew I had things well in hand.

"Bite, you jerk," I told him in an even louder tone of voice. But all that animal did was grin at me defiantly. So, I jabbed him in the stomach with my billy-club. Just a firm little poke, but sudden like, if you know what I mean. Well, his teeth chomped shut automatically, and there was the first bite of the sausage inside his mouth.

"Now chew," I said. And to help things along, I jabbed him another good one. I guess the sausage must have had a lot of pepper in it, because his eyes started to water. He stared at me sort of funny, and then eyes watered some more.

And then, ever so slowly, #853 started to chew.

And everybody breathed a sigh of relief. The Rules were Obeyed.

For some reason, that's when Dr. Wakeman came out and stopped the game. I mean, why then? We had it all under control, and could have gone right back to the Routine. That way, we'd have earned the full 300 bucks.

Well, even if Charlie did cost me the money, he taught me something important. I was looking at the tape, see, and I had this sudden insight. Old friend Charlie was *enjoying* himself, getting all that attention for flouting the Rules that way. Of course, there's no way he would admit it out loud, but you just go look at that tape, and you'll see. It's all there in black and white.

I mean, obviously Charlie knew better. He is no dummy. He accepted the Rules and Regulations when he signed his name to that paper, and he could have gotten up and left at any time. Dr. Wakeman made that clear to us from the start. But no, he stayed because he *likes* breaking the law.

The way I see it, Charlie has got some basic flaw in his moral character. He's just a little *bent*, if you know what I mean. Fortunately, I discovered the truth in time, before asking him to take on the role of my legal partner.

Not that I don't still like the kid, sort of. I'm not even mad that he won't converse with me very much, because I figure he's depressed about how he behaved. He did say we ought to go talk to Dr. Wakeman and apologize for what happened, but I don't see much sense in that. He can go if he wants to, but I have nothing to apologize for.

I was just doing my job.

Recommended Readings

Bardwick, Judith. *In Transition: How Feminism, Sexual Liberation, and the Search for Self-fulfillment Have Altered America* (New York: Holt, Rinehart and Winston, 1979).

Newcomb, Theodore M. *The Acquaintance Process* (New York: Holt, Rinehart and Winston, 1961).

Rubin, Zick. *Liking and Loving: An Invitation to Social Psychology* (New York: Holt, Rinehart and Winston, 1973).

Sommer, Robert. *Personal Space: The Behavioral Basis of Design* (Englewood Cliffs, N.J.: Prentice-Hall, 1969).

Zimbardo, Philip H. "On Transforming Experimental Research into Advocacy for Social Change," in M. Deutsch and H. Hornstein, eds. *Applying Social Psychology* (Hillsdale, N.J.: Erlbaum, 1975).

Social Groups

A group is defined as a set of persons considered as a single entity or system?

Social psychologists are sometimes more interested in how you relate to other members of a group than in what you are like as an individual?

One of the major characteristics of a group is the shared acceptance of group rules and norms by all the members?

If everybody else in your group says that a red rose looks blue to them, you may actually perceive the rose as being bluish?

Many people who claim they are not influenced by group pressures are actually "negative conformers?"

Two-thirds of the subjects tested in an obedience study were willing to shock a person to (seeming) death if ordered to do so by the experimenter?

You may be more likely to aid a wounded stranger if you are alone than if other people are present?

When you do something that conflicts with your moral code, you may be more likely to change your perception of yourself than to change your behavior?

Hostile groups may become friendly if rewarded for cooperating with each other?

"Two (Or More) To Tango"

"Tell me, Mr. Kraus, what area of psychology are you most interested in?"

Norman Kraus squirmed around in the hard, wooden chair. It pained him that his adviser, Professor Ronald Ward, kept such uncomfortable chairs in his office. Professor Ward's seat, of course, was a soft armchair covered with English leather.

"Well, sir, I'm most turned on by social psychology, I guess."

"Good, good. Bloody important field," the Professor said. "Many excellent experiments that you could replicate as your training research."

Norm Kraus squinted at his adviser. Ward spoke with a slight Oxford accent that oddly annoyed Norm. He assumed the man took this means of reminding everyone that he had spent several years in England. Then it dawned on Norm what Ward had said.

"Replicate?"

"Yes, of course. We expect our first-year graduate students to replicate, or to repeat as exactly as possible, some piece of published research. Learn by doing what's already been well done, that's our motto."

"If you don't mind, sir, I'd really rather do something new, something no one's tried before."

Professor Ward nodded sagely. "Yes, I'm sure you would. And did you have something particular in mind?"

Norman Kraus stopped to consider. "No, but I thought we could figure something out."

The Professor's lips pursed into a bitter-lemon smile. "There, you see what I mean. Our attitude is that students should learn to walk before they attempt to run. Try something we know will work first, before they exercise their presumed creativity." Ward coughed discreetly, then continued. "Now, what part of social psychology would you like to work on?"

Norm's anger might have boiled over had he not suddenly recalled his father's advice: "If you want to get along with people, you have to go along with people." Much as Norm hated compromising his own standards, he recognized that his father's comments certainly applied to the present situation. But a devilish urge still prompted him to say, "I'd like to find out why people knuckle under to other people."

Professor Ward glanced at the young man sharply, then frowned. "I presume you are referring to the conformity experiments. The early studies by Muzafer Sherif and Solomon Asch opened the field up, of course, but I've always liked the work that Bob Blake and his group did at Texas back in the '50's. Particularly their use of tape recorders to create synthetic social environments. Have you read Blake's experiments?"

The wooden seat was getting more uncomfortable by the moment. "No, sir."

Ward leaned back in his leather armchair, lit his pipe, and continued. "Asch had students guess the length of lines—a very easy task if no one were around to influence their judgments. But when the students had to make their judgments immediately after several other subjects had spoken, matters got sticky. The other subjects were 'stooges,' paid by Asch to lie about which line was longest. If the stooges gave patently stupid judgments, the students often 'knuckled under' and gave incorrect reports themselves. The presence of the group of stooges was apparently so intimidating that many of Asch's subjects conformed to the false group standard."

"And what did Blake do?" Norm asked, in a slightly desperate tone of voice. This stuff sounded even duller than the flatworm research that another professor had tried to talk him into doing.

Ward tapped his pipe on an ashtray and continued. "Blake and one of his graduate students proved that the stooges didn't have to be physically present. Just hearing a tape recording of the stooges' voices was enough to pressure the subject into conforming. They reported this research at the 1953 meeting of the American Psychological Association in Cleveland, as I recall."

Inwardly, Norm Kraus groaned. Professor Ward's memory for trivial detail was legendary. He should have been a cop instead of a professor, Norm told himself. But aloud he said, "Gee, that's interesting. Do you remember exactly what they did?"

Professor Ward smiled, delighted at the chance to show off. "They used the auto-kinetic effect, as did Sherif. You may recall that if you look at a

PART SEVEN Social Psychology

stationary pinpoint of light in a dark room, the light seems to dance around like a firefly. Because the apparent movement is created by the person's own eyes, everybody sees a rather different dance. Given a 10-second exposure to the light, some people will say that it moved a few millimeters, some will say it danced several meters, while others may insist that it hardly moved at all."

Fireflies? Norm thought. In an experiment on *social* psychology? Maybe he had better go back to the worms after all.

The psychologist plowed right on, as if not noticing Norm's dismay. "Because the auto-kinetic effect is so subjective, it's rather easy to pressure people into conforming to group standards. But that's not what the experiment looked like to the subjects, who were undergraduate males at Texas. They were told it was a study on visual perception. The US Air Force, so they were informed, wanted to find out how people judged the movement of tiny lights on the horizon. So the psychologists had devised a complicated and very expensive piece of apparatus that simulated the movement of airplanes in a night-time sky."

"What was the apparatus like?" Norm asked, beginning to be interested in spite of himself.

Ward snorted with amusement. "An empty tin can with a hole punched in one end. There was a flashlight bulb inside the can that could be turned on and off from the next room. Blake and his student hired four stooges to sit in the dark room and give false reports on how far the light moved. The real subjects were called into the room one at a time and sat directly in the middle of the stooges. During each trial, the light went on for 10 seconds, after which each person was asked to report how far it seemed to move. The four stooges always gave their reports first, before the real subject did."

Norm looked puzzled. "Didn't the real subject know the others were stooges?"

"Certainly not. They looked and acted just like real subjects would have acted—they asked questions and complained about the stupidity of the study. Of course, they asked exactly the same questions with each real subject. Anyhow, the stooges gave ridiculous reports. For example, on the first trial the four stooges reported that the light moved 1.6 centimeters, 1.7 centimeters, 1.9 centimeters, and 2.1 centimeters. Who can make measurements like that in the dark?"

"But it worked?" Norm asked.

Professor Ward lit his pipe again. "Only too well. About two-thirds of the subjects were greatly influenced by what the stooges said."

"And that was news?"

"No, but the second part of the study was. In this part, the subjects sat in the room alone and merely heard the tape-recorded voices of the stooges. Naturally, the subject didn't know a recording was being used. He had met the stooges in person before the start of the experiment and was told they were sitting in different rooms. The stooges asked the same questions and made the same comments on tape as they had in the real-life condition. And, as you might assume, the stooges gave the same ridiculous reports on how far the light moved."

Norm wiggled around on the hard chair. "So, what happened?"

Professor Ward smiled benevolently. "The subjects were just as influenced by the synthetic social background recorded on tape as they were when the stooges were physically present. We seem to conform to imaginary groups as much as to real ones." Ward paused to grind at his

(Continued on page 726.)

Social group. A set of persons considered as a single unit. Two or more individuals who are psychologically related to one another. In certain rare instances, such as a child playing with an imaginary companion, one or more members of the group may not be real (living) people.

System. A living system is an organization of related parts or sub-units that are in communication with each other. A social system is an organization of people (or organizations) that are in contact with each other, or are psychologically dependent on each other. See Chapter 5.

Entity (EN-tuh-tee). Anything considered as a whole. Any object, person, or group that has physical reality, that actually exists. Your family is an entity; the love you have for your family is not an entity. Our word "entire" comes from the same Latin source.

pipe with a metal tool. "Yes, I think you ought to replicate that experiment as your training research."

Norm could feel the crunch coming. "But couldn't I jazz it up a bit, just to make it more exciting?"

The Professor looked at the young man sternly. "You will learn a great deal more if you first do it exactly the way the Texas group did. Of course, if you have a streak of serendipity in your personality, you might turn up something unexpected anyhow. But be so kind as to try it our way first."

"But Professor Ward, I don't think . . ."

"Mr. Kraus," the Professor barked in a tone of absolute authority, "Our departmental rule is clear. We will expect you to replicate the Blake work *exactly*, as your training research. Report back to me after you've set things up and have run a few pilot subjects. Do you understand?"

Through gritted teeth, Norm Kraus muttered, "Yes, sir."

(Continued on page 726.)

Friendly Relations

So, you meet a person for the first time, perhaps at a party, perhaps at church, perhaps in class. You are favorably impressed by the way the person looks and acts. You agree with much of what the person says, and she or he seems to share many of your views on a variety of topics. You have your differences, but they seem relatively unimportant. As you interact with this individual, a mutual attraction rapidly develops between the two of you, and you both agree that you really ought to get together again. Almost before you know it, you are thinking of this individual as a *friend*, and wondering what things you might do together in the future.

Now, what exactly is it that you have done, why have you done it, and how is this friendly relationship likely to change the ways that you think and feel and act?

What is a Group?

Whenever you set up a continuing relationship of some kind with one or more other people, you have in fact either started a new **social group** or joined one already in existence. In the strictest of terms, a group is a **system**—that is, *a set of persons considered as a single* **entity.**

Actually, this definition is so narrow that it is of little practical use, for it

A bar mitzvah is a formal induction into a religious group.

PART SEVEN Social Psychology

implies that groups exist "in the mind of the beholder" rather than in real life. More broadly speaking, a group is a system of two or more individuals who are psychologically related, or who are in some way *dependent* on one another.

You belong to dozens, if not hundreds of groups. Some are *formal membership groups*—for instance, you apply for membership in most colleges, churches, and tennis clubs. But you are born into *family groups* and *ethnic groups*. Some groups, such as "all the people attending a party," are fairly temporary or very informal systems. Other groups, such as friends and lovers, are informally structured but may continue for months or years.

The most important groups in your life are typically those that: (a) last a long time; and (b) are made up of people with whom you have frequent, face-to-face encounters. For obvious reasons, these are called **interaction groups.**

Interaction Groups

Whenever you set up a new friendship, you have begun an interaction group—that is, you have given up some part of your own personal independence to create a *state of inter-dependence* between you and the other person. Whenever you join or create a group, you lose the privilege of "just being yourself" and of ignoring the other group members. But you may gain many things that compensate for this loss.

Some of the rewards for group membership are social. For example, you now have someone to talk to, someone to be with, and to share things with. Other rewards are more practical or task-oriented. For instance, pushing a car out of the mud, rearing a family, playing tennis, and having sex are activities that typically are more reinforcing if two or more individuals participate.

Most interaction groups, then, are made up of people who have affection and respect for each other, who have similar attitudes toward a number of things, or who have a common set of goals and interests.

Social psychology can be defined as the study of how people think, feel, and behave toward one another. Put another way, social psychology is the study of mutual inter-dependencies that exist among members of a social system. Sometimes a social psychologist may be interested in how belonging to a group affects one of its members. At other times the social psychologist may investigate how the inclusion of a new person may change the characteristics of a particular group. But almost always it is the *relationships among people* rather than the *individual person* that the social psychologist focuses on.

Group Structure and Function

As Michigan psychologist Theodore Newcomb notes, groups typically form when two or more people sense that the pleasure of each other's company would be more rewarding than remaining socially isolated. Most such groups are informal—that is, they do not have a stated set of rules governing the behavior of their members (as does a formal group). But informal groups have their rules too, most of which are based on *cultural expectations* of how people should behave when they are together informally. If you are too noisy at a party, if you spill drinks on people, or assault the host or hostess, you might well be asked to leave.

As Newcomb points out, one of the major characteristics of any group is the *shared acceptance of group rules by all the members.* This acceptance may be conscious or unconscious, but it is almost always present in one form or another.

As you may already have discovered in your own life, part of the fun of forming a friendship group (becoming friends or lovers) seems to be "psyching out the situation." That is, the early pleasures of **dyadic relationships** often come from determining what *rules of the game* the two of

Interaction groups. Sets of individuals, psychologically related to each other, who have frequent face-to-face contacts.

Dyadic relationships (die-ADD-ick). Groups made up of just two people. The Latin word *di*, or *dy*, means "two."

When the members of a dyad are neither too similar nor too different they are likely to stay together longest.

you believe ought to be followed. If the person is very much like you, perhaps little or no discussion of the rules may be necessary. If the person is very different from you, the dyad may not last for long (although it can be an exciting relationship at the very beginning). In most cases, however, where the members of a dyad are neither too similar nor too different, each person will compromise a little—for no group can maintain itself unless there is some minimal agreement or **consensus** as to what its members can and can't do.

Question: Judith Bardwick suggests that women often expect quite different emotional responses from men than men expect from women (see Chapter 26). How then can heterosexual dyads be maintained over long periods of time?

Group Norms

As we have mentioned before, the ability to predict the behavior of people and objects in our world appears to be innately rewarding. One of the most reinforcing aspects of belonging to a group is that each member can to some extent predict what the other members are likely to think and do in most situations. Perhaps that is why group rules are almost always stated in terms of behavioral or attitudinal *norms*. That is, the rules specify what the average or normal behavior of each member should be, or what role(s) each member should play.

Of course, no group member will fit all the norms *exactly,* just as no one is *exactly* average in all aspects of intelligence or sexual behavior. Most groups tolerate some deviation from the norm, so long as the member is not perceived by the group as playing "too abnormal" a role—that is, as being more than about two standard deviations from the perceived group mid-point. The more similar the group's members are to each other, and the more emphasis the group places on "following the rules," the less deviation the group will usually tolerate. Perhaps we can demonstrate this point with an example.

Suppose that we measure the attitudes toward premarital sex of two different groups—a class of students taking introductory psychology, and a group of young adults at a campus church or religious center. We will ask the members of both groups to record their agreement or disagreement with the following statement by placing a check mark on a nine-point attitude scale (see Fig. 27.1).

After both groups respond, we measure the position that each person has marked on the nine-point scale. We can then use the number closest to each check mark as a *scale score* that fairly accurately represents each member's attitude toward the statement on premarital sex. And, since we have a number, or score, for each person, we can add these numbers up and calculate the mean or *average attitude* for both groups. This average would, presumably, be the group norm. We can also calculate the *range* and the *standard deviation* of scores for both groups.

For the sake of this discussion, let us assume that the mean or norm for both groups happened to be a scale score of 4: "Agree somewhat." This result might suggest to you that the church group and the psychology class were very similar, since the norm seems to be the same in both groups. But

Consensus (con-SENSE-sus). From the Latin word meaning "to feel together, to agree." A consensus is a harmony of viewpoints, opinions, or feelings. One common language mistake we often make is saying "consensus of opinion," for the word "consensus" all by itself means "agreement of opinion." Our word "consent" comes from the same Latin source.

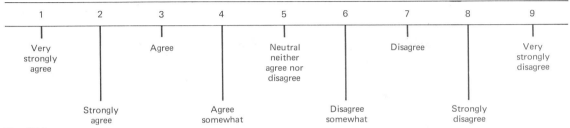

"Premarital sex is generally so damaging from both a psychological and moral point of view that it should be avoided at all costs."

Fig. 27.1.

ask yourself this question: If your own position was a 6 ("Disagree somewhat"), would either group perceive you as being "too abnormal" to belong to that group?

The answer is: It depends on what each group's standard deviation is. Church groups, in general, are more **homogeneous** in their attitudes toward sexual behavior than are the more random collections of students who make up classroom groupings. The distribution of scores for the church group might look like Fig. 27.2.

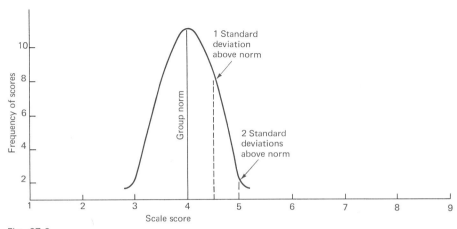

Fig. 27.2.

While the distribution of scores for the classroom group might look like Fig. 27.3.

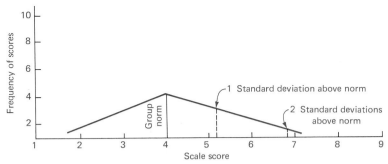

Fig. 27.3.

As you can see, your score of 6 would be more than two standard deviations from the church group norm, but well within the "normal" range for the psychology class. Presumably, the church group would consider your attitude too deviant, while the classroom group probably would not.

Generally speaking, the more homogeneous the group, the smaller its standard deviation will be on most scales. And the more **heterogeneous** the group, the larger its standard deviation will be on most measures.

Homogeneous (ho-moh-GEE-knee-us). From the Greek words meaning "same kind." The more alike members of a group are, the more homogeneous the group is. In more technical terms, the smaller the standard deviation of a distribution of test scores, the more homogenous the scores are.

Heterogeneous (HETT-turr-oh-GEE-knee-us). From the Greek words meaning "different kinds." The more dissimilar the members of a group are, the more heterogeneous the group is, and hence the less cohesive the group is.

Isolated individuals who happen to be together in an elevator.

Question: What do you think would happen to the standard deviation of the church group's scores if you attacked the group for being narrow-minded on the subject of premarital sex?

Group Cohesion According to Theodore Newcomb, **cohesiveness** is the psychological glue that keeps group members sticking together. The more cohesive a group, the longer it will typically last and the more resistant it will be to external pressures. In ordinary situations, cohesion is often a function of the homogeneity of the group—the more homogeneous the attitudes or behaviors of the members, the more cohesive the structure of the group will be. However, even such heterogeneous groups as introductory psychology classes can be made momentarily cohesive if the group is threatened by some outside force.

People riding together in an elevator are not usually considered a group, for they have no real psychological inter-dependencies, and their attitudes are likely to be very dissimilar on most subjects. However, if the electric power fails and the people are trapped together in the elevator for several hours, this very heterogeneous bunch of people may quickly form a group. They will give each other psychological support and comfort, and work together on the goal of escaping. As soon as the people are released from the stalled elevator, however, the common threat to their survival is removed. At this point, the heterogeneity of the members' attitudes and behaviors will probably overcome the temporary cohesion and the group will disband (although individual members of the group may be similar enough to strike up friendships as a result of the experience).

Question: Why do groups that were close-knit in high school tend to become less cohesive if some of the members go on to college, while others don't?

Group Commitment The individual organs in your body cannot wander off to join some other person as they please, but the members of a group system are often free to abandon the group whenever they wish. A group can survive only if it can hold its members together. One of the functions of any group, then, seems to be that of inducing the highest possible **commitment** among its members. For the more committed to the group's norms and goals the members become, the more cohesive the group typically will be and the more homogeneous its attitudes.

In an interesting study of nineteenth-century communes, psychologist R.M. Kanter found that these groups often demanded considerable sacrifice from their members. Some communes required their members to sign over all money and worldly goods to the group and thereafter to work on commune property "for free." Other communes prohibited their members from wearing jewelry or expensive clothes, from smoking tobacco, eating

The Shakers lived in communes in the last century.

The Farm, a modern commune in Tennessee.

meat, or having sex. Kanter reports that communes demanding such sacrifices tended to last longer than communes that did not.

A similar finding comes from an experiment by social psychologists Elliot Aronson and Judson Mills. They offered college women a chance to participate in a discussion group—if they were willing to pay a price. Half of the women were required to suffer a very painful initiation in order to "buy" entrance to their discussion group. The other half of the women were put through a much milder form of initiation. Those who paid by suffering less subsequently liked their discussion group significantly less than did the women who had committed themselves to paying the much higher psychological price.

Question: Which country club would seem more desirable to you, one that charged a $1,000 membership fee or one that charged but $100?

Group Pressures to Conform

Most of us believe that our attitudes toward such things as sexual behavior, politics, economics, and religion are primarily the result of our own soul-searching and logical deduction. In truth, as social psychologist Harold Kelley points out, we use the groups we belong to as reference points, or guides, for much of what we think and so. According to Kelley, these **reference groups** influence your behavior in at least two ways. First, by providing comparison points which you use in evaluating yourself and others. Second, by setting standards or norms and enforcing them by rewarding you when you conform and by punishing you when you do not conform to these standards. As Kelley has shown, members who express opinions, attitudes, or judgments too far from the reference group norm are typically pressured by other members to fall back into line.

Question: Your most important reference group is usually your family. How did your mother, father, and siblings enforce group norms when you were growing up?

The Sherif Experiment

The study of how groups induce their members to conform to group norms is one of the most fascinating areas of social psychology—and probably one of the most relevant. Scientific experiments on this topic date back to 1935, when social psychologist Muzafer Sherif first demonstrated the effects of group pressures on visual perception. Sherif asked students to observe a pinpoint of light in a dark room and tell him how much the light moved. Although the light was actually stationary, it appeared to move around jerkily because of the **auto-kinetic effect.**

When the students made their judgments sitting alone in the room, each went his or her own way. That is, one student would report the light moved only a centimeter while another student might say the light moved a meter or more. But when the students were tested in groups, the first members to give their judgments created a perceptual "group norm" that the others had trouble resisting.

Attitudes expressed verbally in groups almost always tend to be more homogeneous than those the group members express if questioned in private.

Question: Can you explain the phrase "divide and conquer" in terms of destroying group cohesion and reducing group pressures toward conformity?

The Asch Experiment

Several years after Sherif reported his findings, social psychologist Solomon Asch carried the matter a step farther. Asch first tested the perceptual abilities of a group of students who served as "control subjects" for the

Commitment. From the Latin word meaning "to connect, to entrust." When you sign a loan at a bank, you make a legal commitment to repay the money on time. Group commitment involves each member's giving up her or his own freedom to work toward common or group goals.

Reference groups. Those groups that set social norms you are expected to live up to. Reference groups typically give you feed-forward by stating the goals you and other group members should attain, as well as giving you rewarding or punishing feedback as you move toward or away from the goals.

Auto-kinetic effect (AW-toe-kin-NET-tick). Auto-kinetic means "self-movement." When you look at a pinpoint of light in a dark room, the light appears to move even though it is physically standing still. The slight twitching movements that your eyes constantly make seem to be responsible for the auto-kinetic effect.

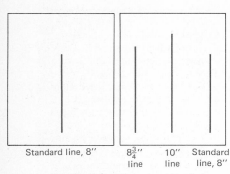

Fig. 27.4. The lines used in Solomon Asch's experiment.

latter part of his experiment. Asch showed these controls a white card that had a black line 8 inches (20.3 cm) long drawn on it, as shown in Figure 27.4. He referred to this as the "standard line" and asked the controls to remember it well. Then Asch removed the first card and showed the subjects a second card that had three "comparison lines" drawn on it. The first of these lines was 8.75 inches (22.2 cm) long, the second was 10 inches (25.4 cm), while the third was the same 8-inch length as the standard. Asch then asked the control subjects to report *privately* which comparison line matched the standard. To no one's surprise, the controls picked the correct answer some 99 percent of the time.

With his "experimental subjects," Asch played a much more subtle game. He asked these volunteers to appear at his laboratory at a certain time. But when each young man arrived, he found several other students waiting to participate in the experiment. What the experimental subject did not realize was that the others were stooges, who were paid by Asch to give occasional false judgments. After the stooges and the experimental subject had chatted for a few moments, Asch ushered them into his laboratory and gave them several opportunities to judge line lengths for him. The judgments were given *out loud*, so that everyone could hear, and the stooges were always called on to report *first*—before the experimental subject did.

During the first two trials, the stooges picked the *correct* comparison line, as did the experimental subject. But on the third trial, each of the stooges calmly announced that the 10-inch line matched the 8-inch line (see Fig. 27.4)! These false judgments created an *incorrect group perceptual norm*, and apparently put the experimental subjects under tremendous pressure to conform. In this first study the experimental subjects "yielded" to group pressures about one-third of the time by reporting that the two lines matched. In later studies, when the judgments were more difficult to make, the experimental subjects yielded to the group of stooges about two-thirds of the time.

In another experiment Asch varied the number of stooges who reported before the experimental subject did. While the presence of one, two, or three stooges did induce some conformity, the maximum pressure to yield apparently was reached when there were four stooges giving false reports. Having 14 or even 40 stooges doesn't increase conformity much more than having four. However, if even one stooge out of 40 gives the "correct" answer, the homogeneity of the group is broken, the group pressures are lifted, and the experimental subject typically gives the correct answer also.

The importance of the Asch study lies not merely in its dramatic demonstration that people tend to conform to temporary reference groups, but in the reasons they gave for doing so. If you were to ask the subjects who "conformed" why they judged the 8-inch line as being as long as the 10-inch line, about half of them would look at you sheepishly and confess that they couldn't stand the pressure. They might say that they figured something was wrong, or that they thought the stooges "saw through a trick" that they hadn't recognized, or that they simply didn't want to "rock the boat" by giving a judgment that went against the group norm.

The other half of the "conformers" are far more interesting, however. For they typically insist that they *actually saw* the two lines as being identical. That is, they were not conscious of "yielding" at all.

Group norms not only influence your attitudes toward complex social issues, but your perceptions of even the simplest objects as well.

What Makes People Conform?

Shortly after Asch reported his initial results, a number of psychologists began to study how groups induce conformity in their members. Perhaps the most detailed of these studies was a series of experiments by Robert R. Blake, Harry Helson, and their colleagues at the University of Texas. In one of the first of these, which I performed under Professor Blake's direction, we demonstrated that the "stooges" did not have to be physically present in

Robert Blake.

PART SEVEN Social Psychology

order to pressure the experimental subject into conforming. In further studies, Blake and his students showed that subjects would volunteer for difficult tasks, donate large or small sums of money to a fake charity, violate social rules ("Don't Walk on the Grass!"), and change their reported attitudes toward war and violence in order to conform to the behavior of various groups of stooges.

Adaptation-level Theory

Robert Blake is a social psychologist with a long-standing interest in group behavior. Harry Helson, however, was an experimental psychologist who spent many years studying visual perception and **psycho-physics** in individuals, not groups. Some of Helson's best-known research had to do with the effects of the *background* on the perception of a visual stimulus—for example, the fact that a white rose appears reddish when seen on a background of blue-green velvet.

Harry Helson.

Originally, Helson had little interest in social psychology. However, during the 1950's, Professor Helson's office was right next door to Professor Blake's at Texas. Helson soon perceived that the stooges were really a "social background" that affected perceptual judgments much as the blue-green velvet "colored" the perception of the white rose. If this were the case, conformity behavior could be explained by reference to **Adaptation-level Theory,** which Helson had devised to account for the way that humans perceive the world. The discovery that their interests were similar led Blake and Helson to form a research group—and to jointly direct a series of experiments that helped clarify the conditions that induce people to conform to group norms.

According to Adaptation-level Theory, all behavior (including conforming) is influenced by three factors:

1. *Stimulus factors.* These influences include the task or problem set before the subject—what the subject looks at or is told to do.

2. *Background factors.* These influences include the social situation or context in which the stimulus is presented.

3. *Personality factors.* These influences include such matters as innate response tendencies, traits, and past experience.

According to Adaptation-Level Theory, if you want to understand why people do or do not yield to group pressures, you must look at all three factors in detail.

Stimulus or Task Variables

The physical properties of the stimulus you must judge in a conformity experiment have a lot to do with whether or not you will yield to group pressures. In general, the vaguer the stimulus, the more likely it is that you will conform. It is a relatively simple task to get you to change your opinions about the beauty of a work of art or the melodiousness of a piece of music. However, it is much more difficult to get you to say that a 10-inch line is shorter than an 8-inch line.

Attitudes about almost anything are easier to shift than are *judgments of concrete facts*, as Richard Crutchfield reported several years ago. However, strong personal preferences for things like food are harder to influence than are guesses about such vague facts as the distance from New York to London.

The more difficult the stimulus task appears to be, and the more confusing the instructions about the task, the more likely it is that the group will be able to influence your behavior. For this reason, perhaps, group pressures are most effective if you must judge the stimulus from memory.

Psycho-physics. That part of psychology which tries to relate the physical aspects of a stimulus input to the psychological aspects of your response to the stimulus. Much of sensory psychology (Chapters 6–11) involves psycho-physical measurements of one kind or another. If a scientist shows you a dozen different lights of increasing brightness and then tries to relate the psychological *intensity* of your experience with the physical *intensity* of the dozen lights, the scientist has just used you as a subject in a psycho-physical experiment.

Adaptation-level Theory. A theory proposed by Harry Helson that accounts for judgments, perceptions, and attitudes in terms of three factors—the physical and social dimensions of the stimulus input, the background in which the stimulus appears, and the personality structure (traits, attitudes, past experiences) of the perceiver. Often called A-L Theory.

If the group is to have an influence on you, then you must know what the group's opinion or norm actually is. One of the most important situational factors, therefore, is how much information you have about what the group is like, and what the other group members believe. In general, the more knowledge you have concerning the group, the more strongly you will feel pressured to yield.

Group pressures to conform develop when stimulus and background factors are in conflict—that is, when your perception of the stimulus differs significantly from that offered by some reference group you belong to. Up to a point, the larger the difference between your judgment and that of the group, the more likely it is you will be influenced by group standards. However, if the matter is carried to ridiculous extremes, the pressure on you may lift. It is all very well to ask you to report that an 8-inch line is the same length as one 10 inches long. It is something else to expect you to report that an 8-inch line is identical to one several meters in length.

The way that you perceive the other group members is also critical. The more prestige or status or competence members of the group seem to have, or the more trustworthy they appear to be, the more powerful agents they become in pressuring you to conform. You are more likely to conform to friends than to strangers, and more likely to yield to strangers who say they like you than to strangers who don't.

The more "out in the open" you are forced to be in making your judgments, the more likely it is that you will yield to group pressures. If you must state your name, or respond so that the rest of the group can hear, then you are more likely to submit to group pressures—at least in public. But if you get the impression that the group may be on the verge of rejecting you, then you may conform in public but not when you're given a chance to make your judgments in private.

If you are told that the whole group must come to a unanimous decision on the matter at hand, you will be strongly pressured to yield. Also, the greater the reward for yielding, or the more importance the judgment is supposed to have, the more likely it is that you will be swayed by incorrect or inappropriate group norms.

Question: Why is it particularly important that juries, who often decide matters of life and death, should always take secret ballots?

Personality Factors and Past Experience

Some people seem to conform much of the time, some practically never. Most of us, however, yield in some situations and not in others. The personality traits of the individual who readily yields to group pressures have often been measured—but not all of these studies have come up with the same results. There are at least three reasons why this conflict might be expected.

First, as we noted in previous chapters, most of our personality tests are not as valid and reliable as we would like for them to be.

Second, with the notable exception of the investigations by Blake and Helson, many of these studies of the "conformist personality" have never been replicated. As a general rule, you probably should not trust any scientific finding until it has been successfully repeated several times.

Third, there is no reason why we should expect that all people who conform to group norms should have the same sort of personality. In fact, judging from Zimbardo's research on prisoners and guards (see Chapter 26), we might assume that we would *all* yield if the situational factors were strong enough.

But there are literally dozens of studies in which personality traits have been correlated with yielding or conforming. Looking at the broad picture, we find that yielders are reported to have had harsh parents who gave their children very little "independence training." Yielders are also reported to receive highly "permissive" scores on a dominance–submission scale. That is, they tend to be followers rather than leaders, but are rather rigid and **authoritarian** in the way they respond to rules. Men who yield more than average are reported to score as being more "feminine" than average on masculinity tests.

Richard Crutchfield found that people who conform typically have lower IQ scores than do people who refuse to conform to group pressures. Frank Barron states that yielders in his experiments scored as having less complex personalities (as measured by various projective tests) than did non-yielders. Barron's yielders also tended to *rate themselves* as being at ease with other people and as being helpful in inter-personal relations, as having personal effectiveness, as being stable and healthy-minded, practical, but group-oriented.

At least, that is the yielders' *subjective impressions* of themselves. In fact, as Crutchfield has shown, on *objective tests* the yielders score as being rigid, conventional, inconsistent, anxious, moralistic, and constrictive in outlook.

There is some evidence that women are more responsive to group pressures than are men, but this difference may reflect cultural values more than basic personality traits. Blake and Helson report that men tend to conform more in areas of traditional interest—such as politics and economics—while women are more likely to yield to group pressures in matters of art and social affairs.

Past experience also has its effects on conformity. If you are an expert on the task at hand, or if the experimenter somehow makes you *think* you are an expert, you are less likely to yield. If you are rewarded for going against the group, then yielding is much less than if you are punished for refusing to conform.

There is little or no evidence that conformity is an innate or inherited trait. Rather, it seems to be a behavior that you learn—primarily because your reference groups *reward* you when you conform and *punish* you when you deviate. There is also evidence that even high yielders can be trained to resist group pressures.

Question: What relationship do you see between Piaget's concept of **accommodation** *and the act of conforming to a social group?*

Negative Conformity

In our society, we all make use of reference groups, and we all conform (one way or another) to group norms. And yet we often talk as if we placed a high premium on being independent of the people around us. People brag (and even write songs about) "doing things *my* way." Blake and Helson discovered a very amusing thing about many of these self-styled "independent thinkers." Many of them yield to group pressures just as much as the rest of us do, but they yield *negatively.* Let us return to our attitude scale on premarital sex (see Fig. 27.5) to see what these **negative conformers** are like.

Suppose we ask a young man to respond to this statement while he is *alone,* and he marks #8, "Strongly disagree." Later, we present him with a similar statement that he must respond to *publicly,* after four stooges have given their opinions out loud. The stooges have been paid to say that they too "Strongly disagree" with the statement. What would you think of this young man if he now switched and gave his score as #2, "Strongly agree?"

Authoritarian. Someone who believes in "following the rules and regulations." Someone who yields to higher authority rather than doing what he or she thinks is right.

Negative conformers. To conform to a group negatively is to move away from the group norm no matter what it might be, even if such movement means giving up your prior opinions and attitudes. An autonomous person is someone not influenced by group pressures. A conformer is someone who adopts group norms no matter what. A negative conformer is just as influenced by group pressures as a conformer, but rejects group norms simply because she or he rejects the group.

"Premarital sex is generally so damaging from both a psychological and moral point of view that it should be avoided at all costs."

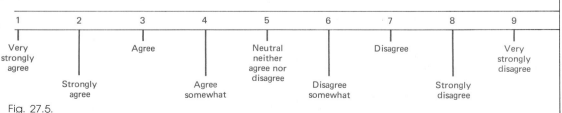

Fig. 27.5.

Stanley Milgram.

Is this man really acting *independently* of the stooge group? If you wanted to trick him into doing something, couldn't you figure out a way to do so?

Question: How might you use the information on stimulus, background, and personality factors to minimize the effects of group pressures on your own behavior?

Obedience

One interesting sidelight to the conformity studies is this: In most of the experiments, the subject was never told that he or she *had to yield* to the group norm. Indeed, many of the subjects were quite unaware that they had given in to group pressures and denied that they had done so. What might the results have been had the subjects been *ordered* to yield by the experimenter?

The Milgram Experiments

The answer to this question apparently comes from a fascinating set of experiments performed by psychologist Stanley Milgram in the 1960's at Yale. His subjects were men who ranged in age from young to old, and who came from many different walks of life. These men were paid to participate in what they thought was a study on the effects of punishment on learning.

In the first experiment, each man arrived at Milgram's laboratory to find another subject (a stooge) also present. The stooge was supposed to be the "learner" who would have to memorize a list of word pairs. The experimental subject was supposed to be the "teacher" who would punish the stooge if he made any mistakes. The stooge was sent into another room and was strapped into a chair so that he couldn't escape when the punishment became severe. The stooge was then out of sight for the rest of the experiment.

Sitting in front of the experimental subject was a very impressive piece of electrical equipment that was supposed to appear to be a powerful shock generator. In fact, the machine was a fake. *No shock was ever delivered during the experiment.* This "fake" generator had 30 switches on it to control the (apparent) strength of the electrical current. Labels on these switches ranged from "Slight Shock" to "Danger: Severe Shock." The first time the stooge made a mistake, the subject was to shock him with the lowest intensity possible. For each subsequent mistake, the subject was to increase the shock intensity by flipping on the next highest switch. The apparatus was so ingeniously designed that none of the subjects guessed that the stooges actually weren't receiving shocks from the machine.

At the beginning of the session, things were easy for the experimental subject. The stooge got most of the word pairs correctly, and the "shocks" delivered were presumably very mild. As time wore on, however, the stooge made more "mistakes" and the "shocks" became more and more severe. When the shock level reached what seemed to be a fairly high point, the stooge suddenly pounded on the wall in protest. Then the stooge stopped responding at all, as if he had fainted or had suffered an attack of some kind.

At this point Milgram told the "teacher" to continue anyway—no matter how dangerously high the shock might get. If at any time the subject wanted to stop, Milgram told him in a very stern voice, "Whether the learner likes it or not, you *must go on* until he has learned all the word pairs correctly. So please go on."

What would you do in this situation? Would you refuse to continue, or would you "obey" Milgram and go on shocking the stooge right up to what you believed were the limits of the electrical generator?

And how do you think most other people would react if they faced this challenge?

After he had completed his first study, Milgram asked a great many college students this question. If you are like them, you will insist that you—and most other people—would refuse to continue the experiment when a dangerously high shock level was reached (and particularly when the stooge apparently had fainted or died in the other room). But, in fact, your guess (at least about other people) would be wrong. For out of the first 40 subjects Milgram tried, almost 65 percent continued to obey Milgram's orders right up to the bitter end. Most of these subjects were extremely distressed about doing so: They complained, they showed tension, and they told Milgram again and again that they wanted to stop. But some 65 percent were *completely obedient* in spite of their inner conflict.

Question: What similarities do you see between the people who "obeyed" Milgram and the young men in Zimbardo's experiment who became "brutal" in their behaviors toward men who were playing the role of prisoners?

Factors Inducing Obedience

In Adaptation-level Theory terms, Milgram's verbal orders to the subjects were "stimulus factors," while the behavior of the stooge can be considered part of the "background or situational factors." By manipulating each of these factors in subsequent experiments, Milgram was able to determine a variety of ways in which obedience could be increased or decreased.

As you might expect, the weaker the stimulus, the fewer the number of people who obeyed. When Milgram stood right over the experimental subjects, breathing down their necks and ordering them on, about 65 percent followed through to the end. But when Milgram was out of the room and gave his orders by telephone, only some 22 percent of the subjects were completely obedient.

In the first experiment, the subjects could not see or hear the stooge in the other room. In subsequent studies, Milgram altered this "background factor." If the stooge began moaning, or complaining about his heart, fewer subjects obeyed orders. Having the stooge physically present in the same room so that the subject could see the supposed pain from each shock reduced obedience even more. And if the subject had to grab hold of the stooge's hand and force it down on a "metal shock plate" before each punishment, very few of the subjects followed Milgram's instructions to the end. As you might guess, the subjects were more likely to deliver severe punishment if they couldn't see the *consequences* of their actions.

In a later experiment, Milgram added the group-pressures technique to his own method of studying obedience. In this experiment, Milgram used three stooges with each experimental subject. One of the stooges, as usual, was the "learner" seated in the next room. The other two were supposed to be "teachers" working in a team with the subject.

The experiment proceeded as before, except that one of the stooge-teachers backed out as soon as the "shock" reached a medium-low intensity. Saying that he refused to continue, this stooge simply took a seat as far from the shock machine as he could. When the "shock" reached a medium-high level, the other stooge-teacher also refused to go on. The subject then was faced with conflicting social norms: Milgram kept pressuring him to continue, while the "group" of stooge-teachers was exerting pressure to stop. Under these conditions the "social background" factors won out over the "stimulus" of Milgram's orders. More than 90 percent of the subjects refused to complete the experiment.

We are taught to obey, just as we are trained to conform. If you consider the great rewards and massive punishments that groups can administer to their members, perhaps it is not surprising that many of us obey and conform rather readily.

Question: What would have happened in Zimbardo's prison study had the "warden" ordered the guards to punish the prisoners severely for infractions of "the rules"?

The Ethics of Deception

The Milgram studies, the Zimbardo prison study, and many others raise a number of complex but important questions about the **ethics** of using humans as subjects in scientific experiments. One of these questions involves the morality of *deceiving* the subjects as to the real purpose of the study, even if the experimenter believes such deception is necessary because people seldom act naturally when they know they're being observed.

When Milgram's research was published, a storm of protest was raised by sincerely concerned individuals who urged that research such as Milgram's be banned or prohibited. This same barrage of criticism, as we noted in the last chapter, occurred when Zimbardo released the results of his prison study. In consequence, a number of codes of ethics were proposed, but workable guidelines for experimentation on humans are not easy to agree upon. For, given a little time and motivation, we could all think of certain types of studies in which deception might be morally justified, and other experiments in which misleading the subjects would be both a legal and an ethical outrage.

As an example of the **dilemma** many scientists face in such matters, consider an article by Dr. Herbert Benson that appeared in the June 21 1979, *New England Journal of Medicine.* Dr. Benson reports 82 percent of heart patients who take **placebos** for the chest pains associated with some types of heart disease get better, simply because the patients *mistakenly believe* that the treatment works. The patients taking these "worthless sugar pills" also can stand more exercise, get by with less "real" heart medicine, and produced better results on **electro-cardiograms.** Dr. Benson notes that placebos are more effective than almost any other form of treatment for relieving chest pain and promoting improved health in these patients. The problem is, of course, that placebos simply don't work unless the physician *misleads* the patient into believing that the sugar pill is some kind of "magic cure." Benson states that deceiving patients is, naturally, unethical, but urges doctors to remember the advantages of "putting their patients in the right frame of mind."

Obviously we should always consider the *actual results* of experiments before drawing hasty conclusions about what is ethical, and what isn't. Viewed in this perspective, Milgram comes off fairly well, for he did discover some fascinating facts, and there is no evidence that any of his subjects suffered ill effects. In truth, Milgram seems to have employed little more deception in his work than is used regularly on TV programs such as "Candid Camera." Yet the nagging question—"When is it ethical to use deception?"—remains for the most part unanswered.

Some of the emotional reaction to Milgram's experiments probably stemmed from the rather unflattering picture his results gave us of ourselves. Had most of Milgram's subjects *refused* to obey blindly, perhaps he would not have been so vigorously attacked. Milgram's research—as well as Zimbardo's, and the early research on conformity—suggests that we all have "psychological blind spots" about the true *causes* of human behavior. Since many of us find it difficult to perceive how influential the social environment is, we apparently prefer to attack people like Milgram instead of "changing our minds" about what inputs actually influence our actions.

However, despite the emotionality of some of Milgram's critics, the issue of experimenter responsibility remains a crucial one, and the American Psychological Association has recently taken a stand against the unwarranted use of deception in similar research.

We will have more to say about these complex ethical issues in the next chapter.

Question: Under what circumstances do you personally think that deceiving subjects in a scientific experiment might be ethically warranted or justified? And under what circumstances would a physician be morally correct in prescribing a placebo for a heart patient with severe pain?

Bystander Apathy

Milgram created problems for his subjects because he told them what to do. In real-life conflicts, there often isn't anyone around to give you directions, and you must act (or fail to act) on your own. If there are other people around you when a crisis occurs, you may look to them as "models" of what you ought to do. Later on, you usually must explain your actions or inaction satisfactorily to yourself. Sometimes the emergency nature of the conflict may make you distort what is actually happening. Just as often, the pressure comes later when you must invent "logical" excuses for what you did.

What would you do if, late some dark night, you heard screams outside your place? Would you rush out at once, or would you first go to the window to see what was happening? If you saw a man with a knife attacking one of your neighbors, how would you react? Might you call the police, or go to the neighbor's aid? Or would you consider yourself to be merely an innocent bystander to one of life's little tragedies, and hence remain **apathetic** and unresponsive? And if you failed to assist the neighbor in any way, how would you respond if someone later on asked why you didn't help?

Before you answer, consider the following facts. Early one morning in 1964, a young New York woman named Kitty Genovese was returning home from work. As she neared her front door, a badly **deranged** man jumped out of the shadows and attacked her. She screamed and attempted to defend herself. Because she screamed loudly, 38 of her neighbors came to their windows. And because she fought valiantly, it took the man almost 30 minutes to kill Kitty Genovese. During this period of time, not one of those 38 neighbors came to her aid, and not one of them even bothered to call the police.

The Darley–Latané Studies Kitty Genovese's death so distressed scientists John M. Darley and Bibb Latané that they began a study of why people refuse to help others in similar situations.

In one experiment, Darley and Latané staged a disaster of sorts for their subjects. They paid people two dollars to fill out a survey form given them by an attractive young woman. While the people were in an office filling out the forms, the woman went into the next room. Shortly thereafter, the subjects heard a loud crash from the next room, and the woman began moaning loudly that she had fallen and was badly hurt and needed help.

Now, how many of the subjects do you think came to her rescue?

The answer is—it depends. Some of the subjects were exposed to this little drama when they were all by themselves in the testing room. About 70 percent of the "alone" subjects offered help. Another 40 subjects faced this apparent emergency in pairs. Only 8 of these 40 people responded by going to the woman's aid. The other 32 subjects simply sat there listening to the moans and groans.

Were the subjects who failed to rush to the woman's assistance merely apathetic and uncaring? In this case, yes. Many of the "apathetic bystanders" informed the experimenters that they hadn't really thought the woman was seriously hurt and were afraid of embarrassing her if they intervened. But we should note that the subject's *perception* of the emergency was strongly influenced by whether or not there was someone else present in the testing room.

Darley and Latané believe that when several people witness a disaster, they perceive their own personal responsibility as being greatly *diminished* or diluted. Hence they are free not to act if no one else does.

In another experiment, subjects heard a young man (presumably in the next room) discuss the fact that he frequently had seizures similar to grand mal epilepsy. Shortly thereafter, the stooge began crying for help, saying that he was about to have an attack and would die if no one came to help him. About 85 percent of the subjects who were "alone" rushed to the stooge's assistance. However, only 62 percent of the subjects who were in

John M. Darley.

Apathetic (app-pah-THET-tick). From a Greek word meaning "without sympathy, lacking passion or interest, being indifferent to the fate of others."

Deranged (dee-RANGED). To arrange something (such as your thoughts) is to "get it all together." To de-range something (such as your thoughts) is to "pull things apart." A deranged person is someone whose thoughts are not logical or orderly.

Bibb Latané.

Bystander apathy. Not becoming involved emotionally when you are an accidental witness to a tragedy. Not offering to help a stranger in need.

Rationalize (RASH-un-al-lies, or RASH-un-ull-lies). To think up logical reasons for your emotionally-impulsive thoughts or behaviors.

pairs offered aid, while but 31 percent of those in 5-person groups overcame their apathy.

In this latter experiment—but not in the earlier ones—many of the non-responsive subjects showed distinct signs of tension and nervousness afterward. That is, they had sweaty palms, trembling hands, and asked the experimenter if the stooge was really all right. Darley and Latané believe that these people were not really apathetic. They were still trying to make up their minds whether to do something when the experimenter terminated the session and interviewed them about their feelings.

Question: Are you more likely to make an unusual response to a social situation when you are "alone," or when you are a member of group whose other members remain apathetic?

Subways Are for Slipping Darley and Latané have suggested that **bystander apathy** occurs primarily in situations where the witnesses can either convince themselves that no real emergency exists, or where there are so many other people around that responsibility for taking action is greatly diffused. More recent research by I.M. Piliavin, J. Rodin, and J. Piliavin tends to confirm the accuracy of this explanation. In the late 1960's, Piliavin and his group turned the New York subway system into an experimental laboratory. Four people involved in the study would board one car of a subway train through different doors. Once the train was underway, one of the male experimenters would stumble down the aisle, slip, and collapse on the floor, face up. Two of the experimenters recorded how long it took the "innocent bystanders" in the subway car to come to the stooge's aid. If no one helped out, one of the other experimenters would then assist the stooge.

From a humanistic point of view, the results of the Piliavin research are fairly encouraging. When the "victim" carried a white cane, and acted as if he were blind, people came to his aid in 95 percent of the tests. Even when the stooge reeked of whiskey and pretended to be drunk, he received assistance in about half the tests.

In emergency situations, we often look to the people around us for guidance as to what an appropriate response might be. If no one else responds, we are under tremendous "group pressure" to remain apathetic since the model we have tells us to "remain apathetic." That is, given an intra-psychic conflict between our inner values that we ought to be helpful and our fears of violating group norms or expectancies, about two-thirds of us will "yield" to the group—about the same percentage as yielded in the "group pressures" experiments of Asch, Sherif, Blake and Helson, and in Milgram's studies on obedience.

Question: People tend to conform to groups less in situations in which they think they are experts. What would happen to "bystander apathy" if we began teaching children how to handle social emergencies as part of their normal training in school?

Cognitive Dissonance

Not all of the conflicts that we face involve a choice between satisfying group expectancies or satisfying our consciences by living up to a moral code. Sometimes the problem has to do with trying to explain to ourselves why we picked a biological reinforcer rather than an intra-psychic one. For instance, most of us are taught that sexual intercourse is immoral except when engaged in by a married couple. Yet, if Kinsey's data are true, many of us violate this ethical standard at some time during our lives. Afterward, rather than admitting that our ids got the better of our super-egos, we may **rationalize** our actions in a variety of ways: "I did it only because I loved him (her)," "He (she) needed me," or "I was forced into doing it."

Doomsday Prophecies Social psychologist Leon Festinger has conducted a series of intriguing studies on how human beings react to situations involving social conflicts. In one of his first studies, Festinger worked with H.W. Riecken and Stanley Schachter. These social scientists made an extensive study of a "doomsday group" whose leader had predicted that the world would end on a certain day. As the fatal day approached, the members of the group became more and more excited and tried to convince others to repent and join their group in order to "save their souls." When "doomsday" arrived, the members of the group gathered together to await final judgment and to pray for deliverance. To their amazement, the day passed, and so did several other days, and the world continued to speed on its merry way.

And how did the leader of the "doomsday group" react to the failure of her predictions? Apparently, by finding a "logical excuse" for what actually happened. Several days after the date the world was supposed to end, she told the members of her clan that "God had spoken to her, and had spared the world in answer to the group's prayers." The group members then reacted with great joy. Rather than rejecting the leader, they accepted her more warmly and believed even more firmly in her prophecies.

Dissonance Theory In the early 1960's, Festinger suggested that in conflict situations we experience **cognitive dissonance.** That is, whenever we do something we think we shouldn't, we face the problem of explaining our actions to ourselves and to others. Festinger stated that we are usually highly motivated to reduce cognitive dissonance when it occurs, and that we do so chiefly by changing our *beliefs or attitudes* to make them accord with our *actual behaviors*—and then we go right on behaving the way we always had.

Although Festinger's *conclusions* about human behavior seem accurate, his "theory of cognitive dissonance" has not stood up well under attack by many other scientists. And, indeed, in the 1970's Festinger himself abandoned the belief that dissonance is an innate **drive** which people instinctively attempt to reduce. None the less, it appears true that many of us do change our perceptions or explanations of our actions when we find ourselves in situations of social conflict.

Perhaps you will have noticed a certain similarity between the group pressures experiments, the obedience studies, the research on bystander apathy, and the cognitive dissonance experiments. In all these cases, the actual conflict arose when people failed to recognize the great influence that social inputs have on their attitudes and actions. Given the fact that so few of us ever perceive what strong control our environments exercise over us, perhaps it is not surprising that we must invent all kinds of "logical explanations" for human behaviors that over-emphasize the importance of intra-psychic processes. These "inventions" include most of our theories about "traits," "attitudes," "personality factors," and "mental illness."

Inter-Group Conflict

For the most part, the studies on conformity, obedience, and cognitive dissonance have dealt with individual subjects put under strong psychological pressure to avoid conflict with other members of a group, or with their own value systems. From the standpoint of General Systems Theory, however, we can consider the group itself as a kind of "super-organism" that should be subject to social pressures to conform to the standards set by other groups or organizations. Groups should also show many of the same sorts of *internal processes* as do individuals. Not unexpectedly, most of the factors that influence individual conformity and internal conflict have their direct parallels when we study the behavior of groups as groups.

Sherif's "Camp" Experiments

Muzafer Sherif was one of the first social psychologists to undertake scientific experiments on conflict between groups. Several years ago, Sherif

Leon Festinger.

Cognitive dissonance (KOG-nih-tiv DISS-oh-nance). The feeling you get when your behaviors differ markedly from your intra-psychic values. According to Leon Festinger, you are strongly motivated to reduce this dissonance. You do so either by changing your values or by changing your behaviors. For the most part, people experiencing cognitive dissonance tend to change their attitudes or explanations—and then keep right on behaving as they always had.

Drive. A state of need, or a strong motivation to satisfy a need. Whenever you lack something necessary for life, a biological "drive" builds up inside you that moves you to satisfy the need and hence reduce the strength of the drive. See Chapter 12.

and his colleagues helped run a camp for 11- and 12-year old boys. These youngsters were all from settled, well-adjusted, white, middle-class, Protestant homes. The boys were carefully selected to be happy, healthy individuals who had no difficulty getting along with the others. None of the boys knew each other before being admitted to the camp—nor did any of them realize that they were to be subjects in Sherif's experiments.

Eagles and Rattlers The camp itself had two rather separate housing units. The boys living in one unit were called the "Eagles," while the other group's name was the "Rattlers." Because he had purposely selected boys who were very similar in attitudes and behaviors, Sherif predicted that the boys in each unit would form into a group very readily. On the first day of camp, since there were no pre-existing friendships among the boys, group commitment and cohesion in both units was very low. Then Sherif gave both the Eagles and the Rattlers various real-life problems that could be solved only if the boys worked together effectively. As each unit overcame the difficulties Sherif put to it, the boys came to *like* the other boys in the same unit more and more. Both Eagles and Rattlers became a "natural group," and commitment to each of the groups (and to its emerging norms) increased significantly.

Competition versus Cooperation After the Eagles and the Rattlers had shown considerable cohesion, Sherif introduced a series of contests designed to make the two groups hostile toward one another. As the groups competed for very desirable prizes, conflict developed, since one group could win only at the expense of the other. Very soon the Eagles were making nasty comments about the Rattlers, and vice versa. Most of this hostility consisted of one group's *attributing* selfish or hostile motives to the other group. Name-calling, fights, and raids on the cabins belonging to the other group became commonplace. At the same time, Sherif reports, there was a marked increase in within-group cooperativeness and cohesiveness among the members of both groups.

Reducing Inter-group Hostilities Once the groups were at each other's throats, Sherif tried to bring them back together again. In his first experiment, Sherif attempted to unite the two groups by giving them a common enemy—a group of threatening outsiders. This technique worked fairly well, in that it brought the Eagles and the Rattlers closer together, but they still held *hatred* for their common enemy.

The next year Sherif repeated the group-conflict experiment with a different set of boys. Once inter-group hatred had reached its peak, Sherif brought the two units into very pleasant, non-competitive contact with each other. They sat together in the same dining hall while eating excellent food, and they watched movies together. However, this approach didn't succeed, for the groups merely used these occasions for fighting and shouting at each other.

Sherif then confronted the hostile groups with problem situations that could be solved *only* if the two units cooperated with each other. First, a water shortage "suddenly developed," and all the boys had to ration themselves. Next, Sherif offered to show the whole camp an exciting movie—but to see it, both units had to pool their resources. And one time when all the boys were particularly hungry, the transportation for their food "broke down." It could be fixed only if both groups worked together quickly and effectively.

Sherif reports that this technique worked beautifully. The two groups did indeed cooperate—reluctantly at first, but more and more willingly as their initial efforts were reinforced.

Before the crises occurred, almost none of the boys had friendships outside their units. Afterward, some 30 percent of the friendships were inter-group rather than in-group. During the hostile period, about one-third of the members of each group rated the members of the other group as being "stinkers," "smart-alecks," or "sneaky." Afterward, less than 5 percent of the boys gave the members of the other group such highly unfavorable ratings.

Sherif states that during the time of conflict, the boys in each group indulged in "blatant glorification and bragging" about their own units and rated themselves very highly. After the reunion of the groups, the bragging diminished and there was a slight tendency for the boys to downgrade the ratings given their own groups. Meanwhile, their attitudes toward the other group became significantly more positive.

When you feel conflict *within yourself*, as Festinger has shown, it is often because you hold two dissonant viewpoints at the same time. When disagreements develop *between two people*, it is often because the two have conflicting attitudes about each other or about some third person or object. When hostility arises *between two groups*, as Sherif had demonstrated, it is often the case that their norms or group attitudes are in conflict. Turning enemies into friends is sometimes a matter of changing their attitudes and actions toward one another.

In the next chapter we will take a careful look at how attitudes are formed, how they are changed, and how attitudes relate to behaviors.

Question: Suppose you wished to help a group of whites get along better with a group of blacks. What would you try to do, and what changes would you hope to make in the attitudes and attributions of both groups in order to promote cooperation?

Summary

1. **Social psychologists** study the behavior of **groups.**

2. A group is a set of persons considered as a **social system**—a collection of two or more individuals who are psychologically related to or dependent upon one another.

3. There are many types of groups, including **formal membership groups, family groups,** and **ethnic groups.**

4. **Interaction groups** are made up of individuals who have frequent face-to-face encounters.

5. One of the major characteristics of any group is the **shared acceptance of group rules (goals)** by all the members.

6. The more similar the members, the more **cohesive** the group and the more **homogeneous** it becomes.

7. The more cohesive a group, the more **commitment** the members are likely to have toward the group and its goals.

8. Our **reference groups** are those we look to as social **models** or **norms.**

9. Reference groups give us **feedback** on our behavior by rewarding movements toward and punishing movements away from the **group norm.**

10. Whenever we make a judgment or give an opinion that is different from one shared by other group members, we typically find ourselves under strong psychological **pressure to conform** more closely to the group standard or norm.

11. **Group pressures** become most effective when at least four group members have announced their judgments or opinions without being openly contradicted. If even one group member disagrees openly, group cohesion may be destroyed.

12. Some group members know when they are conforming (but do so anyway), but others yield to pressures without realizing how the group has affected them.

13. Conformity behavior can be explained in terms of Helson's **Adaptation-level Theory.** A–L Theory states that judgments, perceptions, and attitudes are influenced by three factors—the stimulus, the background in which the stimulus appears, and the personality and past experience of the individual under pressure.

   a. **Stimulus factors** include the vagueness of the stimulus, the difficulty of the stimulus task, and the instructions given. **Attitudes** are easier to influence in conformity situations than are judgments of concrete facts.

b. **Background factors** include how the group members feel about each other, how expert they are in the task at hand, the openness with which judgments must be made, and whether the group decision must be unanimous.

c. Although there does not seem to be a "conformist personality," **yielders** in conformity experiments are frequently reported to be more **authoritarian** and **submissive** than are people who tend to resist group pressures.

14. Some people are **negative conformers** who tend to move away from the group norm no matter what they perceive it as being.

15. When given orders from a higher authority, most of us tend to show **obedience** even if we sometimes end up hurting ourselves or others.

16. We are particularly likely to obey orders if the people around us are doing so.

17. **Bystander apathy** occurs in part because groups tend to dilute feelings of responsibility.

18. **Cognitive dissonance** develops when you hold two conflicting attitudes. According to Festinger's early theory, all people have an **innate drive** to reduce dissonance, usually by changing the way we **perceive** the conflict (rather than changing our behaviors).

19. **Social conflicts** can occur between groups that must compete for limited resources. These group conflicts are in many ways similar to conflicts between two people, or between dissonant attitudes within a single individual.

20. Sherif has shown **inter-group conflicts** can be reduced if the groups are either threatened by an outside danger or rewarded for working toward a common goal.

(Continued from page 708.)

"All right, Mr. Kraus, please calm down and tell me what happened."

Norm Kraus leaned forward excitedly, hardly noticing the hardness of the chair in Professor Ward's office. "Well, the Blake experiment worked just like it was supposed to. I put a flashlight bulb inside an empty cocoa box to make the auto-kinetic light, and I got some friends to act as stooges. We made tape recordings of their voices, but I wanted to start with the situation where the subject was sitting right in the middle of my four friends."

Taking a quick breath, the young man hurried on before Ward could interrupt him.

"I got an undergraduate named Dan to volunteer for the experiment. I introduced Dan to the stooges, and then we all went into the lab. The cocoa box was hidden behind a black curtain that I didn't open until the lights were off when nobody could see what it was. Then I gave Dan and my friends the song and dance about airplanes moving on the horizon, turned off the overhead light, and left them to adapt to the dark."

"Sounds fine so far," Ward said.

Norm Kraus smiled. "The lab next door was my control room, where I ran the experiment. I could open the curtains, turn the flashlight bulb off and on, and talk to the subjects over a loudspeaker. I put a mike right in front of Dan so I could hear his voice. And, of course, I could also hear the stooges and make sure they said what they were supposed to say."

Professor Ward nodded in an absent-minded fashion. "Yes, yes, just like Blake and his student did it. But how did your stooges know what to say?"

"I gave them their responses written out on a card."

Ward's eyebrows rose a millimeter or so. "And they read these numbers in the dark?"

Norm smiled broadly. "I wrote the numbers in dark-glow paint. The stooges could just make out the numbers if they squinted at them."

"Didn't this Dan fellow get suspicious?"

"No, sir. You see, I gave him a card with a scale marked across it in centimeters, also in dark-glow paint. It looked just like the cards the stooges had. I told them to look at their cards frequently to make sure they could judge how long a centimeter was."

Professor Ward coughed politely. "Not half bad. But how did it go?"

Norm beamed. "Beautifully, at least at first. I was sitting in the control room recording Dan's reactions. The first trial, he seemed to ignore the group. But on the next 14 trials, he hit the midpoint of their judgments right on the nose. I couldn't believe it! I was so excited at the end of the test that I rushed over to the next room to congratulate everybody and turn on the lights. And that's when it happened."

"Dare I ask what?"

"Well, Dan came bolting out of the lab and went rushing down the hall toward the toilet. I had to chase after him to catch up. He was shouting at me over his shoulder, 'Don't believe a word I said. You can't use my results.'"

"Did he tell you why?"

Norm nodded. "Yes, sir, he did. He said, 'You put me in a bad seat. I couldn't see the damned light at all. I just said whatever the other subjects said. You shouldn't do things like that, it curdles the stomach.'" Norm frowned rather theatrically. "And then Dan rushed into the john and was sick all over the place."

Ward picked up his pipe and stuffed it with tobacco. After a moment, he asked, "Why do you think Dan responded that way? Were the group pressures to conform that strong?"

Norm tried to hide the smirk that kept creeping over his face. "Serendipity, sir. After I left your office the last time, I looked the word up."

"Oh, yes, the Persian fairly tale about the three princes of Serendip, or Ceylon, as many people call it today. They were always going out on expeditions to search for something like iron and discovering a mountain of gold instead. Serendipity is the gift for finding very valuable things you weren't really looking for. Invaluable in scientific research, serendipity is." The Professor smiled rather warmly. "And you think you have the gift?"

Norm attempted a modest grin. "Well, I did luck onto something strictly by accident. It isn't every day you can upset a subject that much without laying hands on him."

"All right, Mr. Kraus, tell me exactly what happened."

Norm Kraus leaned back in the hard chair and relaxed. "Well, at first I couldn't figure it out, and neither could the stooges. But then I checked out each piece of equipment, just to make sure. Guess what I found?"

"I'm veritably breathless with anticipation," Ward said, smiling with encouragement.

"The flashlight bulb had burned out! As far as I can tell, the light went on during the first trial, but then it got shorted or something. I kept saying the light would go on . . . NOW. And the stooges kept giving their reports. But for the last 14 trials, the light simply didn't appear."

"Why didn't your friends, the stooges, notice it?"

"They were too busy trying to read the night-glow numbers on their little cards. Besides, it didn't matter to them if they couldn't see the light at all. Their job was just to read off their reports."

Professor Ward poked at the tobacco in his pipe with a match. "But why did the poor young man get sick?"

"How would you like it if you were sitting smack in the middle of four people who all acted as if they could see something that you saw once, but couldn't see thereafter? Dan told me later that he looked and looked and looked, but the light just wasn't there. He thought maybe he was going crazy. But he didn't want to upset the experiment, so he just sat there and gave the same reports the stooges were giving. He couldn't disobey orders by leaving, and he couldn't violate the group standard by saying he didn't see anything when everybody else did. The stress was so great that his stomach curled up into a tight little ball. He said he'd never felt so much pressure in his life."

A stern tone crept back into Professor Ward's voice. "I hope you explained things to him and tried to make amends."

"Oh, yes sir. I took him over to the clinic and had the doctors examine him. They gave him a tranquilizer and two aspirins and told him to call them in the morning if he didn't feel better. While we were walking back to Dan's place from the clinic, I told him about what we had done, and why. Now he wants to be a stooge if we continue the experiment."

"If?"

Norm sighed dramatically. "Well, sir, it does seem we've discovered an interesting way to measure psychosomatic responses to social stress. I was talking to some of the doctors at the clinic about it. They thought we might do some joint research. You know, trying to figure out how group pressures toward conformity can lead to ulcers and hypertension and things like that. I realize that's not a replication of the Blake experiment, and I wouldn't want to break the rule . . ."

Professor Ward interrupted. "Mr. Kraus, we have two departmental rules about graduate students. The first is that they should begin by repeating a piece of published research. The second rule is that, if the student finds something exciting on his or her own while performing the replication, we expect them to follow it up. You wouldn't want to violate our departmental standards, now would you?"

Norm Kraus smiled slyly. "Oh, no sir."

"Good work, Norm. I'm pleased with your progress. Let me know if I can help, and keep me posted on how you come along. And by the way, why don't you call me Ron instead of Professor Ward?"

Norm could hardly believe his ears. "Yes sir, Profes . . . I mean, bloody good of you, Ron!"

Recommended Readings

Barber, T.X. *Pitfalls in Human Research: Ten Pivotal Points* (New York: Pergamon Press, 1976).

Hare, A.P., ed. *Handbook of Small Group Research,* 2d ed. (New York: Free Press, 1976).

Helson, H. *Adaptation-level Theory* (New York: Harper & Row, 1964).

Kelley, Harold H., and John W. Thibaut, "Group Problem Solving," in Gardner Lindzey and Elliot Aronson, eds., *The Handbook of Social Psychology,* 2d ed. (Reading, Mass.: Addison–Wesley, 1969).

Persuasion, Propaganda, and Attitude Change

28

Did You Know That . . .

You are probably exposed to 1,500 different ads each day of your life?

The more you know about a person, the more stable your attitude toward that person probably will be?

Students at liberal colleges feel strong pressures to conform to the political opinions of their professors?

Although you may reject propaganda if it comes from what you consider to be a biased source, later on you may forget the source and be influenced by the message?

Propaganda messages that arouse a high degree of fear are usually not as effective as low-fear appeals that tell you how to cope with the threatening situation?

Youthful offenders who were exposed to a "scared straight" program actually became *worse* than did similar offenders not treated with scare tactics?

If you express an attitude you don't really believe in, and you are rewarded for doing so, you are very likely to adopt the attitude you previously didn't believe in?

You cannot make valid ethical judgments about persuasive attempts unless you understand how strongly influenced you are by the attitudes and behaviors of the people around you?

"The Mind Benders"

Once upon a time, not so long ago, there was a shining kingdom-by-the-sea called Nacirema. The capital of Nacirema was Imperial City. At its very center, right on Empire Avenue, a concrete castle stretched up to scrape the sky. On the 100th floor of this castle there lived an Iron Duke, one of the Great Wizards of all Nacirema. The Duke's brand of magic was so strong that, for a great many years, he had influenced the minds of almost everyone in the country. But now, after years of mystical success, the Iron Duke feared that his occult powers might be slipping.

"Peasants" said the Duke loudly, glaring out of his 100th floor window at the people marching meekly below. "The peasants be damned!"

Humbly born to poor but proud parents named Mr. and Mrs. Steele, the Iron Duke had risen from obscurity to the Royal life through sheer guts and hard work—although neither the guts nor the labors were entirely his own. After obtaining a degree in Applied Art (Basketweaving) from

Imperial City College, the Duke had immediately taken a position with the Royal Advertising Agency. By means of judicious apple-polishing—and a few lies and magical spells—he had climbed up the corporate ladder until he was just two rungs from the top: Vice-wizard in Charge of Practically Everything.

"Giants," said the Duke with a curse in his voice. "Double-damn the giants."

In Nacirema at this time there existed many giants—huge corporations that wanted to sell their products, but lacked the mystical power to do so effectively. So the giant corporations hired expert wizards such as those at the Royal Agency to create their advertising for them. Each giant was called a Sponsor, and the Agency kept track of each Sponsor's business in a separate financial account. Every account had its own wizardly Royal Executive who saw to it that things went right. The Giant Sponsors paid all the bills. It was the Executive's job to cast spells on the peasants to coax them into buying the giants' products, and to stroke the giants when they became unhappy. And as everyone on Empire Avenue knew, the Royal Surgeon had long ago determined that stroking giants can be hazardous to your wealth.

"And triple-damn the widget!" roared the Duke, still standing morosely at his window.

The Duke was, in fact, a glorified Account Executive. His Sponsor was a giant called General Widgets, Inc. In order to keep his job, the Duke was called on to perform many boring and trivial tasks, such as spending millions of dollars, traveling all over the world, hiring and firing hundreds of people, attending cocktail parties with other members of the Imperial Court, and drinking three martinis for lunch each and every day. When the Duke had time, he tried as well to work a little magic on the giant's behalf.

As successful as the Duke had been, however, gold and power had not brought him security. He still quivered and quaked whenever His Highness, the Chairman of the Royal Agency Board, or His Grace, the Presiding Wizard, called the Duke on the magic carpet. He quivered and quaked even more when the giant called him on the telephone—as the giant had just done—complaining bitterly that widget sales were busting instead of booming. The giant blamed the Duke for the drop in widget sales, and threatened to move the General account to some other agency. The Duke knew that if this evil event occurred, His Highness, the Chairman, would lose his royal temper—and the Duke would lose his Royal head.

As the Duke stood looking out of the castle window at the traffic moving along Empire Avenue far below, cold fear gripped his cast-iron guts. Was he losing his magic touch? Could he think of a new spell to cast on the peasants that would motivate them to buy all those unwanted widgets the Sponsor had sitting in the warehouse? What had the Future in store for him?

At this point in time, Fate intervened: There came a gentle knocking at the castle gate.

"Prithee, enter!" roared the Duke.

A young girl with a crown of golden hair burst happily into the Iron Duke's office. Trailing right behind her was an equally happy and long-haired young man.

"Father!" the girl cried, kneeling quickly before the Duke and then embracing him warmly.

"Princess!" responded the Duke gruffly. "I thought thee still at Lady Bennington's School for Gentlewomen, or at St. Bryn the Martyr's, or some such. What brings thee to town?"

"Father, I wish to present Rodney, my Prince Charming."

"Hail to thee, Rodney, and welcome to our humble abode," cried the Duke, extending one of his huge hands.

"Pleased to meet you, Mr. Steele," said Rodney, shaking hands perhaps a bit too eagerly, his flowing locks bobbing as he did so.

"Just call me Duke," the older man said, shaking his head in dismay at the length of Rodney's hair.

"Yes, Sir, Mr. Duke," Rodney responded.

"Rodney has come to ask you for my hand in marriage, Father. You see, Rodney is my soul-mate."

"Rodney is what?" demanded the Duke in an appalled tone of voice.

"He's a Taurus. And I'm a Libra. That makes us soul-mates," the Princess said, a gentle smile on her radiant face.

"I had thought thee a Virgo," murmured the Duke.

"Ah, well," the lass said defiantly, "now I am Liberated."

"Harrumph," said the Duke ominously, casting steely eyes at his daughter's escort. "But what does thy Prince Charming do for a living?"

"Rodney's a genius," the girl said earnestly.

"Gadzooks!" groaned the Duke loudly. "Then he wants employment."

The young princess caressed her father. "Well, you're always saying that everyone who serves you is either a fool or a knave."

The Duke took a monogrammed handkerchief out of his pocket, mopped his noble brow, and then turned back to the window. "I regret that I cannot add your princeling to my retinue. I fear I have giant problems."

"You mean, the *Sponsor?*" the Princess whispered, a trace of terror in her voice.

The Duke nodded sagely. "General Widgets. They have doubled their budget for advertising, but sales are lower than a dragon's belly. Nobody's buying widgets any more. We've tried every trick known to man, and a few known only to women, but the damned peasants just won't buy. The Sponsor blames me personally for this unseemly failure. If the Olde Iron Duke doesn't come up with some new magical incantations right away, his name is Mudde."

"Yes, Sir, Mr. Mudde," responded Rodney.

"But what's wrong, Father? Why aren't your advertisements working? It's the same old widget it's always been."

"I know not," replied the Duke. "Perhaps thy genius soul-mate can enlighten us."

Rodney cleared his throat. "Widgets stink," he said quietly.

"What!" roared the Duke.

"Widgets stink. They're too big, too expensive, too clumsy, and Sir Ralph Nadir says they're unsafe."

"Nonsense!" cried the Duke haughtily. "You just don't understand, my boy. The product doesn't matter. It's the magic in the advertisement that counts. Royal prides itself on being able to bend the peasant minds whatever way the Sponsors wishes them bent."

"How do you work that kind of miracle?" Rodney asked innocently.

"Follow along, my boy, and I'll show thee how magic is made."

The Duke led Rodney and the Princess down a long golden-carpeted corridor into a huge, well-lighted room. A bank of computers lined one wall. The machines clicked and chirped softly as large numbers of Elves scurried about, feeding incantations into the devices.

"This be our Market Research Department," the Duke said. "We gather every known fact on the Nacirema peasants and insert the gatherings into our Merlin computer. We know where the peasants live, how much gold they earn, what visual entertainments they watch, and whether they've ever bought a widget. Isn't that marvelous?"

Rodney didn't seem overly impressed. "What use do you make of all this information?"

The Duke frowned. "Forsooth, I never bothered to ask. But I'm sure the gatherings must be valuable to someone. Anyway," the Duke continued in a firmer tone of voice, "it really doesn't matter. It's the Creative Department that actually conjures up the magic. I'll show thee what I mean."

The Duke pressed a button on the wall to summon an elevator. "We lock the creative types in the dungeon, to keep them out of mischief." He ushered Rodney and the Princess into the Royal Lift.

Moments later the doors opened out on a dark basement cavern. Several yards away was a roaring wood fire. Huddled around the blaze was a mixed bag of tiny Gnomes and Witches dressed in oddly colored clothes. One of the Witches was stirring a bubbling pot that hung above the fire. The Gnomes passed a large, smoking object among themselves.

"What's that peculiar smell?" asked Rodney, a sly grin on his face.

"Incense," coughed the Duke discreetly. "They use it in casting their occult spells."

The smallest of the Gnomes rushed up to them and bowed several times. "Most noble liege lord, welcome to our insignificant dungeon. What brings thee to our nether regions? What action, fair or foul, has caused thee to descend to our dank depths? In short, what's cooking, Wiz?"

"Thy flesh and mine, I greatly fear," the Duke said grumpily. "The Sponsor hath just called. That last magic potion you created turned sour, and widget sales are faltering like a knight in a daze. If we cannot discover some spectacular new means of ensnaring the peasants' desires, thy whole crew will be back to reading palms by next week."

The tiny Gnome scratched tenderly under his arm, a sad look on his wizened face. Then he suddenly brightened. "I've got it, your Wizard-ship! The Double Whammy, the Evil Eye, and the Final Curse! We'll mix them all together in our little pot and boil up the most magical brew the world has ever smelt! Unresistible, mind-bending magic. We'll push more widgets through the market place in a week than the Sponsor can make in a month. Leave it to us, Wiz!"

"If you don't succeed, I'll personally turn thee back into a pumpkin," said the Duke.

The Gnome bobbed his head respectfully, retreating back toward the fire. One of the Witches came up and whispered in his ear. "Oh, your Wizardship," the Head Gnome called after the departing trio. "We need a new lid for our pot, and sundry things like that . . ."

"That's what we give thee an expense account for," replied the Duke, ringing for the Royal Lift.

Once back in the 100th floor office, the Duke poured himself a glass of Sir Johnny Walker's Black Magic, and took his glass to the window. "That be it. You've seen almost the entire Royal operation. But wherewith have we failed?"

"You've shown us *everything?*" asked Rodney.

"Methinks so," replied the Duke. "There is also a Production Department that makes the films or draws up the art work. But they be all out on location somewhere. And the Media Buyers, who pick which magazines or visual programs the incantations will appear in. But they be all out to lunch somewhere. And that's about the lot."

"Then I have the solution to your problem," said Rodney proudly.

"Oh, Father, I told you he was a genius!" cried the Princess pridefully.

"Young man, although I find it difficult to believe, perhaps I have underestimated thee," said the Duke craftily. "If you can help me keep the widget account, I will not only give thee a job, but the Princess' hand in wedlock as well."

"What kind of a job will you give Rodney?" interjected the Princess practically.

"Well," responded the Duke, "the Head Gnome needs a new assistant. And there are always availabilities as a Merlin-tender."

"I'm more the Wizard Executive type myself," mused Rodney hopefully.

"Let us haggle over unseemly trifles later on," said the Duke brusquely. "Tell me thy bright idea first."

Rodney looked the Duke squarely in the eye and spoke quietly for two minutes.

As Rodney talked, a look of great astonishment blossomed on the Duke's visage. When the young man had finished, the Iron Duke turned pale as a goblin's bedsheet.

"Thou canst not mean it?" cried the Duke.

"Ah, but I do," responded Rodney sincerely.

The Iron Duke collapsed in a dead faint.

(Continued on page 750.)

Ads and Attitudes

What brand of toothpaste do you use? No matter what your answer, you might next ask yourself a much more interesting question: How did you happen to pick that particular brand? Was it the flavor that attracted you to it, or the approval of a dental organization, or the low price? Or did you "choose" it because it's the same brand that the rest of your family uses?

Whatever reason you give, chances are that you probably won't list *advertising* as the factor behind your choice. And yet, if you think about it, how would you have known about this brand if it had never been advertised? Furthermore, if you were subjected to "blind" tests (where you couldn't tell which brand you were testing), are you absolutely confident you could pick your favorite toothpaste or brand of beer, soup, or cigarettes from others on the market?

Most of us like to think our decisions to buy a particular product, to vote for a certain politician, or our opinions about war and sex and minority groups are **rational** decisions. That is, we tell ourselves that we make up our minds about things only after we've given the situation considerable thought. However, while we do sometimes think through such matters logically, our viewpoints are often created *unconsciously*, without our being

Rational (RASH-uh-null). From the Latin word meaning "to reason" or "to compute." Computers are rational because they don't generally have built-in emotional circuits, as does the human brain. Computers make decisions according to the "cold, hard facts" that have been plugged into their memory banks, and according to whatever "decision programs" have been wired into their circuits. Humans sometimes pretend that their decisions are as rational as those made by computers, but all our attitudes and preferences are colored by our emotions. Most biologists and psychologists agree that, although our emotions can often be dangerous, they do have rather high "survival value." Perhaps that is one reason why people invented computers, and not vice versa.

You are exposed to more than 1,500 advertisements each day.

aware of how various forces in our social environments shape our thoughts and preferences. One such force is advertising.

You probably encounter about 1,500 ads each day of your life. Some of these advertisements appear on radio and television. Others show up in books, magazines, and newspapers. And still others flash out from billboards and signs, from bumper stickers on cars, and from the shelves of supermarkets. Americans spend more money each year on advertising than they do on education, or on pollution control, mental health, poverty relief, or scientific research. If the advertisers didn't believe that they could influence your attitudes toward their products (whether or not you were aware of their efforts), would they spend so much?

Public Relations

Nor are advertisers the only ones who wish to bend your opinions to their purposes. Almost every press release put out by the government, or by individual politicians, is aimed at getting voters to think favorably of the person or agency involved. News stories about movie stars, rock musicians, professional athletes, and university professors are almost always "handouts" from **publicity agents.** In fact, up to *90 percent* of what passes for "news" on television and in the newspapers actually comes from **public relations specialists** and not from a reporter who has "dug up the facts" on her or his own time.

Whenever a teacher criticizes or praises a certain theory, whenever a religious leader preaches, whenever a parent "lectures" or a friend offers advice, aren't these people trying to affect your attitudes? And whenever you "dress up to make a good impression," or compliment someone in authority, or try to seduce a potential sex partner, aren't you "advertising" too?

In the past several chapters we have talked at length about how attitudes (or personality traits or types of behavior) are created. In this chapter, let us look at why attitudes are important, why some of them remain fairly stable throughout our lives, and why other attitudes appear to be so changeable.

Question: How has the author of this book attempted to influence your attitudes toward psychology?

Attitude Stability

In an earlier chapter we defined an attitude as a relatively enduring way of thinking, feeling, and behaving toward an object, person, group, or idea. Attitudes almost always involve a certain amount of bias or pre-judging on your part. When you apply a label such as "stingy" or "psychotic" to a person, you both state an attitude and reveal the way in which you perceive the person. In a sense, then, attitudes are *perceptions* that involve emotional feelings or biases, and that pre-dispose you to act in a certain way.

You could not do without attitudes, for many reasons. To begin with, the attitude (or percept) that you have of someone or of some object allows you to predict the future behavior of that person or thing. If you made no pre-judgments about things, you would have difficulties walking across a street or carrying on even the simplest of social conversations. Many of your attitudes, for instance, seem designed to evoke a certain kind of response from the "outside world." When you say that you "hate pollution" to a man wearing an ecology button on his shirt, you not only can predict the man's response but may also be trying to influence his attitude toward (or perception of) you.

Attitudes and Memories

A second important aspect of attitudes has to do with memory. As you learned in earlier chapters, you seem to file your experiences in Long-term

Memory according to your *impressions* of what happened. That is, you attach abstract or "verbal labels" to the important features of the experience, and then file the memory according to these "abstract labels." When you try to remember something that happened in the past, you search your memory files using this same set of labels. Another word for "abstract labels," of course, is *attitudes*.

Psychologists believe that the more that you know about a person, things, or idea, the more stable your attitude will usually be. Likewise, the more strongly you feel about something, the more difficult it will probably be to get you to change the "memory labels" attached to that thing. Furthermore, the better your attitude allows you to predict future events or inputs, and the more you are rewarded for holding a certain percept, the less susceptible that percept or attitude is to being changed.

Theodore Newcomb.

Question: Studies show that most college students have attitudes very similar to those held by their parents. Can you think of at least five reasons why this might be the case?

Newcomb's Study of Bennington Women

Many attitude surveys indicate that liberal arts colleges are populated by professors who have very liberal political opinions. When a student from a politically conservative family arrives on such a campus, the student often comes under fairly intense social pressure to change his or her attitudes. Although political opinions are often deep-seated, highly emotional, and of long duration, many students do in fact become more liberal during their college years.

Bennington College Suppose you were a student who had become politically more liberal than your parents while you were at college. Would you expect this change to endure once you left college and (presumably) returned to your old home environment? What might you do to insure that your newly liberalized attitudes remained the same, even after you had left the campus?

Social psychologist Theodore Newcomb addressed himself to these problems many years ago. At the time that Newcomb began his research, he was teaching at Bennington, a woman's college in Vermont noted for its fine programs in the liberal arts. Because the student body was limited to about 600, Newcomb was able to work with the entire college population in his study of political attitudes.

Most of the women attending Bennington in the mid-1930's came from wealthy and rather conservative homes. The college faculty, however, was quite liberal in their views. Indeed, they felt it a part of their educational duties to familiarize the students with the social and political implications of a Depression-torn America and a war-threatened world. Therefore, the faculty encouraged the students to become politically active and socially concerned. The college itself, nestled between the Taconic and the Green mountains of Vermont, was physically isolated from much of the rest of the world. The nearest town, a village of less than 15,000 people, offered few excitements. The students seldom visited the town more than once a week, and seldom went home for the weekend more than once a month. Hence, the students made up what advertising executives call "a captive audience."

Student Reference Groups In the first part of his research, Newcomb found that the more prestige or *status* a woman had among her fellow students, the more likely it was that she was also very liberal in her views. Conservative students typically were looked down upon; liberal students were very much looked up to. Seniors were significantly less conservative than were freshmen. During the 1936 election, for instance, 62 percent of the freshmen supported the Republican candidate, while only 14 percent of the seniors did. Some 30 percent of the seniors supported the Socialist or

Reference group. That group of people whom you look to for your social feed-forward (models, "rules and regulations") or against whose behaviors you measure or judge your own actions.

Reactionary (ree-ACT-shun-ary). Someone who reacts against the present form of government (or any social change), preferring an older or out-of-date political or belief system. Someone who feels that progress is a matter of going back to prior ways of behaving, or who cries, "Let us march forward to the good old days!"

Autistic hostility (aw-TISS-tick). Social "denial." That is, the blocking off of informational inputs that do not agree with your prior conceptions or prejudices about some person or topic.

Communist candidates in the 1936 election, while only 9 percent of the freshmen did.

Under these conditions, the entire college population acted rather like a **reference group** that rewarded liberal attitudes and punished political conservatism. Those women whose opinions became more liberal during their four years at Bennington tended to identify with the college community and to adopt its prevailing viewpoint. By their own admissions, many of them were quite conscious of how they had changed. As one woman put it, "What I most wanted here was intellectual approval of teachers and the more advanced students. Then I found you can't be **reactionary** and be intellectually respectable."

Those women who resisted the liberal college tradition tended to identify more with their parents than with their classmates. As one woman said, "I'd like to think like the college leaders, but I'm not bold enough and I don't know enough. So the college trend means little to me; I didn't even realize how much more conservative I am than the others. I guess my family influence has been strong enough to counterbalance the college influence." Newcomb notes, incidentally, that this woman was given to severe emotional upsets and had told the college staff that she felt "alone and helpless except when with her parents."

Question: How many Bennington women would probably have become politically liberal had they lived at home and commuted to their classes? What if they had taken most of their courses by television and seldom met their teachers or other students?

Bennington Women 25 Years Afterward Newcomb knew that the majority of students lost a fair share of their liberalism when they returned to their homes. But what about the women who were the most liberal of all? How did they fare after graduation? Taking 150 of these women as his subjects, Newcomb followed their lives for 25 years. Although he had originally suspected that many of the women too would revert to a more conservative position, this turned out not to be the case with many of them. In fact, during the entire 25 years, most of the women remained liberal in their outlooks *despite family pressures.* But why?

Newcomb reports that most of these women *deliberately* set out to remain liberal in spite of their social backgrounds. They tended to select liberal (or non-conservative) husbands who would reinforce their political views. They found little pockets of liberalism in their environments and tried to stay entirely within these pockets. They interested themselves in socially worthy projects that would bring them in contact with others who held similar political outlooks, and they kept in close touch with their Bennington classmates who were also liberal (and tended to ignore those who weren't.)

Newcomb believes that if maintaining a given attitude is important enough to people, they will consciously or unconsciously select environments that will continue to support that attitude. They may also shut out incoming sensory messages that might tend to disrupt the attitudes already held (a form of **autistic hostility**).

The Newcomb study is one of the few aimed at measuring *stability* of attitudes. Attitude *change* is much easier to investigate, in no small part because the subjects need not be studied over such a long time span as the 25 years that Newcomb was in contact with the Bennington students. Indeed, it seems that most of what we know about attitude stability comes from experiments designed to change people's opinions. So now let us look at the factors that bring about shifts in attitudes. Perhaps this information will be useful not only if you wish to change someone's mind, but also if you wish to protect yourself against the influence of the millions of people who would like to persuade you to be different than you presently are.

Question: What actions by Newcomb's subjects suggest that these women might have been guilty of "autistic hostility?

Persuasion and Attitude Change

Suppose you are in the market for a new automobile. You shop around, looking at the Fords, Plymouths, Chevrolets, and a number of other relatively inexpensive cars. You will come to this situation with a number of biases, or attitudes, about cars in general and these automobiles in particular. Perhaps your family has always had a fondness for Fords, because your father's first date with your mother was in a Ford. Or perhaps your uncle bought a third-hand Mustang once and always claimed it was a lemon. If your prior attitude toward Fords is highly favorable, how might a Chevy salesman try to change your impression of his product? Or if you were prejudiced against Mustangs, how might a Ford salesman attempt to alter your attitude?

Solomon Asch points out that there are two basic ways to induce attitude change toward an object like an automobile. The first way is to change the *object* or product itself, so that your own perception of the car simply isn't **consonant** with the facts any more. The second way is to leave the car "as is" but somehow get you to change your perception of its good and bad points. Thus a salesperson might try to overcome your prejudice against Mustangs by demonstrating how much the car had been improved since the one your uncle bought, or the salesperson might try to convince you that your uncle simply didn't know how to take care of a car and therefore his evaluation of the Mustang was faulty.

In either case, however, the sales person must somehow get certain types of information across to you. Without new *sensory inputs* of some kind, your attitudes will presumably remain very stable. Thus the most important aspect of **persuasion** is the flow of communication from the outside world into your nervous system. Asch remarks that, in most real-life situations, attitude change usually comes about because of some change in the *object* of the attitude.

When psychologists study attitude change scientifically, however, they don't always have the power to make changes in the objects of your attitudes. If you wished to examine the biases that people have toward Mustangs, for instance, could you readily get the Ford Motor Company to build a totally new product just to satisfy the rigid requirements of your experiment? Or could you get all the members of a minority group living in the US to act and dress differently starting the first of next year just so you could take precise "before and after" measures of people's prejudices?

The most the psychologist can typically do is attempt to get subjects to view reasonably familiar objects (or people or ideas) in a new light. To do so, the psychologist often tries to control some aspect of the *communication process*.

Question: What sorts of television commentators are you most likely to watch or to place faith in? How often has a TV personality convinced you to vote for a political party other than the one you would ordinarily vote for?

The Communication Process

Psychologists tend to look at persuasive communication as having four main factors—the communicator, the message, the audience, and the feedback loop that exists between the audience and the communicator.

The *communicator* is the person (or group) trying to induce the attitude change. As we will see, the way that the audience *perceives* the communicator often affects the readiness with which the audience will change.

The *message* is the information that the communicator transmits to the audience. The type of language or pictures used, and the channel through which the communicator chooses to transmit the message, can be of critical importance.

The *audience* is the person or group whose attitude is to be changed. Obviously a clever communicator will wish to know as much as possible

Consonant (KON-so-nant). From the Latin words *con*, meaning "with," and *sonare*, meaning "to sound." Consonant thus means "to sound at the same time," or "to agree." The consonants are those letters of the alphabet that are "sounded with" the vowels (a, e, i, o, u, and y).

Persuasion (purr-SWAY-shun). From the Latin words meaning "to urge" or "to advise." To persuade is to induce someone to adopt a certain attitude or behavior by argument or pleading, or to win someone over to your way of thinking.

Credibility (kred-uh-BILL-it-tee). From the Latin words meaning "worthy of lending money to." Literally, the power or ability to inspire belief.

Fig. 28.1. Successful communication depends on feedback from the audience to the communicator.

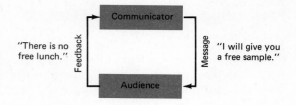

about the personalities and attitudinal characteristics of the audience in order to make the message as persuasive as possible.

The *audience-communicator feedback loop* is perhaps the least-studied aspect of the communication process, yet it is of crucial importance (see Fig. 28.1). Unless the communicator knows what type of response the audience *actually* makes to the message, the communicator is very likely to misjudge the success of the persuasive project. Trying to communicate to someone without getting feedback is like trying to seduce someone you can't see, hear, or feel—you know what you're doing, but it's the other person's *response* that counts most.

Let us see, then, what kinds of experimental evidence social scientists have provided so that we can understand the effects of each of these four influences on persuasion.

Question: Why do you think the audience-communicator feedback loop has been so little studied?

The Communicator

If your best friend told you that a given product was incredibly good, would you be more likely to believe this communication than if you heard a TV announcer say the same thing on a television ad? Chances are you'd put more **credibility** in your friend's endorsement than in that of the TV announcer. And credibility seems to be one of the most influential traits a communicator can possess.

In the past 30 years, there have been hundreds of studies on the communication process, but most of them have done little more than *reinforce* the findings made by a group of Yale psychologists more than 20 years ago. This group of scientists, led by Carl I. Hovland and Irving L. Janis, has given us some of our clearest insights to date into the process of attitude change.

In one of these experiments, Hovland and Walter Weiss tested the influence of "trustworthiness" (credibility) on attitude change. They began by making a list of "communicators" they figured were very trustworthy, and another list of communicators they figured few people would trust. The "high credibility sources" included the *New England Journal of Biology and Medicine*, a Nobel-Prize-winning physicist, and *Fortune* magazine. The "low credibility sources" included a noted gossip columnist, the Russian newspaper *Pravda,* and a well-known US publication that specialized in scandals and sex-oriented stories. When Hovland and Weiss asked students to judge the credibility of these sources, about 90 percent of the subjects rated the first group as being very trustworthy and rated the second group as being exceptionally untrustworthy.

Next, Hovland and Weiss tested the "attitude toward the effectiveness of atomic submarines" in two similar groups of students. They found that most of the students were rather neutral about his highly complex topic. For practical purposes, we might say that their attitudes were neither positive nor negative (in part, perhaps, because few of the students had previously given the matter much consideration). If we were plotting their attitudes on a graph, we would say the students were right in the middle—at the "neutral" point on the graph shown in Fig. 28.2.

Hovland and Weiss then wrote a "message" in which they argued that atomic submarines would indeed be a very important weapon in any future war. They showed this message to the two groups of students. The first

PART SEVEN Social Psychology

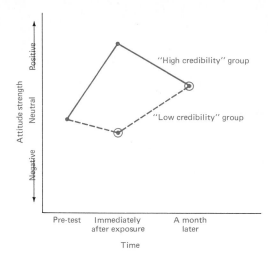

Fig. 28.2. The "sleeper effect." Effects of exposure to propaganda on "effectiveness of atomic submarines."

group was told that the message came from one of the high credibility sources (such as *Fortune*). The second group was told that the message came from one of the low credibility sources. Immediately after exposing the students to the message, Hovland and Weiss retested their subjects' attitudes.

As you might surmise, the students' attitudes were strongly affected by the presumed source of the message. The subjects in the "high credibility" group tended to accept the arguments and their attitudes became significantly more positive. The students in the "low credibility" group tended to reject the arguments as being "biased and untrustworthy." If anything, their attitudes became slightly more negative.

Apparently you tend to move *toward* the position of someone you trust, and *away* from the position of someone you distrust—even if this movement involves giving up your original attitude.

Question: How does this study compare with the experiment on "negative conformity" mentioned in the last chapter?

The "Sleeper Effect" Had Hovland and Weiss stopped their work at this point, we might well have misunderstood the real importance of communicator credibility. However, they continued by retesting all their subjects a month later. To their surprise, they found significant attitude changes in both groups over this period of time. The attitudes of the "high credibility" subjects became significantly *less* positive, while the attitudes of the "low credibility" subjects became significantly *more* positive. As the graph suggests, the students had apparently forgotten the *source* of their information on submarines, but remembered the *arguments* rather well. Hovland and Weiss call this the **sleeper effect.**

The sleeper effect indicates that the credibility of a source has an immediate and often strong effect on whether you accept or reject incoming information. However, once the message has gotten through to you, chances are that you will soon forget the source and recall only the information itself.

Question: There is an exception to the sleeper effect. What do you think would have happened had Hovland and Weiss reminded their subjects of the message source before testing their attitudes a month later?

The Attribution Process If you are like most people, you try to judge the trustworthiness of a source of communications by *attributing* some motive or intention to the communicator. A number of further experiments by Hovland, Janis, and their associates demonstrate that the factors which influence credibility are much the same as those which influence first

Sleeper effect. A term coined by Hovland and Weiss which refers to the following discovery: People tend to remember the facts of an argument rather well but often forget the source of those facts. The credibility you place in a source may cause you to accept or reject a message as soon as you see or hear it. However, the facts are somehow "sleeping" in your Long-term Memory and will emerge on their own long after you have forgotten who told you those facts.

impressions (discussed in Chapter 26). People you like, or who are like you, or who seem to be acting naturally rather than "playing roles," are people whom you typically trust. Persons with high social status—such as doctors, scientists, and church leaders—are somehow more believable than are people with low social status. In the long run, however, it is what the person *says or does* that influences your attitudes the most.

Question: If you were trying to sell a cold remedy on television, what kinds of TV actors would you choose, and how would you have them dress?

The Message

In 1956, a University of Michigan professor named Sam Eldersveld decided to run for the mayor's job in Ann Arbor as a "class project" to help his political science students learn about politics in the "real world." Dr. Eldersveld planned and carried out his campaign with the assistance of his students. The students not only performed several interesting experiments during the heat of the contest, they also managed to get their professor elected (he became a very effective mayor).

In one of the Ann Arbor studies, potential voters were approached in one of three ways. Either the voter received four mail appeals to vote, or the voter was contacted in person, or both. A fourth group of voters served as an "untreated control group." A much higher percentage of the voters contacted in person actually voted than did voters who received just mailings (or no messages at all). The combination of mail appeals and personal contact was no more effective than was just asking the voter in person.

In another study, Eldersveld compared the *content* of the appeals. That is, some voters were given highly emotional arguments—whether by mail or by personal message seemingly didn't much matter. But again, personal contact was much more effective in "bringing out the vote" than were mail appeals, no matter what the content of the appeals happened to be.

Question: How could you be sure that the voters who received messages by mail actually read them?

Fear-arousing Messages Many of us seem to believe that people would behave in more socially acceptable ways if someone in authority just threatened them enough. In recent years, for instance, nation-wide campaigns against venereal disease, the use of hard drugs, cigarette smoking, and the dangers of not wearing seat belts have employed the "hellfire and damnation" approach—that is, the main thrust of the propaganda has been to describe in exquisite detail the terrible consequences of various types of misbehavior (see Fig. 28.3).

But are such threats really as effective as we sometimes think them to be? The experimental evidence suggests that the actual effects of "the punitive approach" are more subtle and complex than we might previously have guessed. Irving Janis and Seymour Feshbach investigated the effects of fear-arousing communications on high school students. These scientists picked as their topic **dental hygiene,** or the dangers of not taking care of your teeth. They wrote three different 15-minute lectures on tooth decay. The first was a "high fear" lecture that contained 71 references to pain, cancer, paralysis, blindness, mouth infections, inflamed gums, ugly or discolored teeth, and dental drills. The second or "moderate fear" lecture was somewhat less threatening. But the third or "minimal fear" lecture was quite different. It made no mention at all of pain and disease, but rather suggested ways of avoiding cavities and decayed teeth through proper dental hygiene.

Janis and Feshbach presented each of the three appeals to a different group of 50 high school students (a fourth group of students heard no lecture at all and thus served as a control group). Janis and Feshback found

Dental hygiene (HIGH-gene). "Hygiene" comes from the Greek word meaning "healthy." Dental hygiene is the study of what makes teeth healthy.

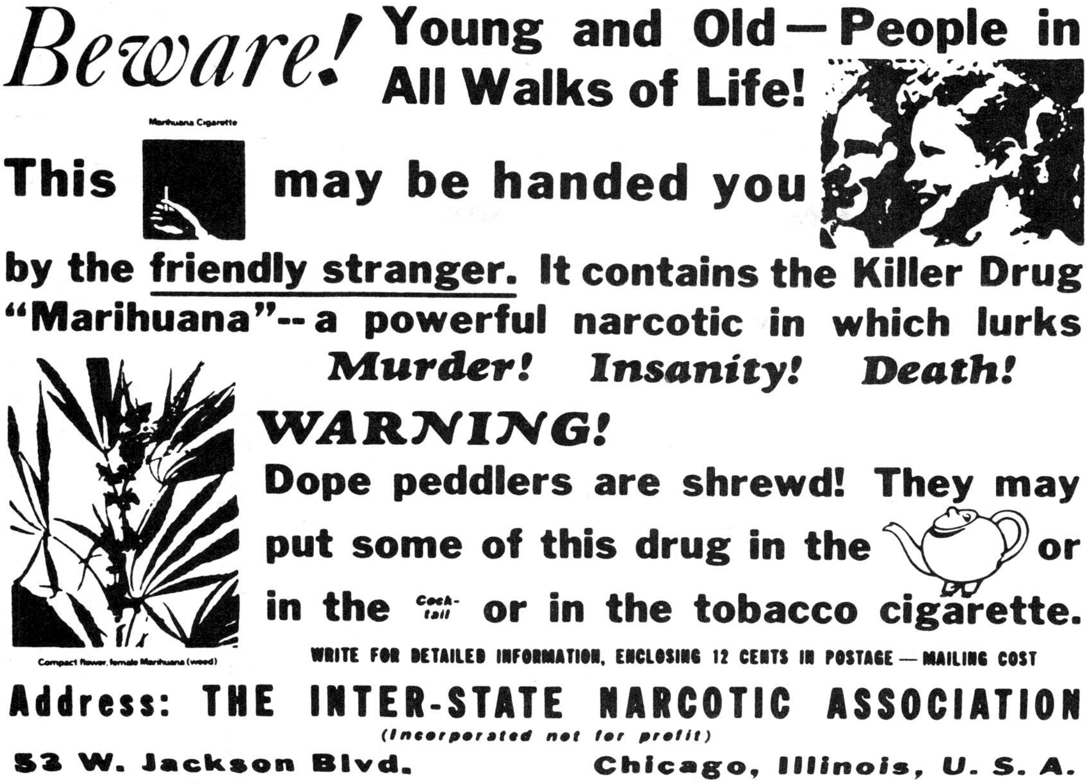

Beware!

Young and Old—People in All Walks of Life!

This may be handed you

by the friendly stranger. It contains the Killer Drug "Marihuana"-- a powerful narcotic in which lurks *Murder! Insanity! Death!*

WARNING!

Dope peddlers are shrewd! They may put some of this drug in the 🫖 or in the ᶜᵒᶜᵏᵗᵃⁱˡ or in the tobacco cigarette.

WRITE FOR DETAILED INFORMATION, ENCLOSING 12 CENTS IN POSTAGE — MAILING COST

Compact flower, female Marihuana (weed)

Address: THE INTER-STATE NARCOTIC ASSOCIATION
(Incorporated not for profit)

53 W. Jackson Blvd.   **Chicago, Illinois, U. S. A.**

Fig. 28.3. Example of a "high-fear" campaign to change attitudes. (How effective was it?)

that *immediately afterward*, the subjects exposed to the "high fear" lecture were highly impressed with what they heard. The students also admitted that the lecture got them very worried about the health of their own teeth. A week later, however, only 28 percent of them had brushed their teeth more often, and 20 percent of them were actually doing worse.

In marked contrast, the "low fear" students were not particularly impressed with the lecture, but a week later 50 percent of them were "brushing better" and only 14 percent were doing a worse job.

The high fear appeal apparently evoked strong emotional responses in the students, many of whom thought that being frightened was somehow "good for them." As one student said, "Some of the pictures [of decayed teeth] went to extremes but they probably had an effect on most of the people who wouldn't want their teeth to look like that. I think it is good because it scares people when they see the awful things that can happen."

Despite this student's *beliefs*, when it came to actually *changing behaviors*, the high fear message simply didn't work as well as did the minimal fear message. In fact, for reasons we will make clear in a moment, the high fear propaganda seems to have had exactly the opposite long-term effect than one might have predicted.

Question: In Chapter 25 we noted that people who join encounter groups often are very enthusiastic immediately afterward, but show little change when measured a month later. What relationship do you see between this fact and the reactions of the students in the "high fear" group?

Counter-propaganda Propagandists often point out that it is not enough to change the attitudes an audience has, you must also make sure that the audience resists any further attempts that might push them back toward their original beliefs. Effective propaganda, then, is that which not only causes attitude shifts but also protects against **counter-propaganda.**

A week after the high school students in the Janis-Feshbach experiment

Counter-propaganda. Communications designed primarily to overcome or to cancel the effectiveness of propaganda issued by someone else.

had listened to the dental hygiene lectures, the experimenters exposed the students to information that contradicted what they had originally been told. The students were then asked whether they believed this counter-propaganda or not. Twice as many subjects in the high fear group were affected by the counter-persuasion as were subjects in the minimal fear group. Janis and Feshbach conclude that "under conditions where people will be exposed to competing communications dealing with the same issues, the use of a strong fear appeal will tend to be less effective than a minimal appeal in producing stable and persistent attitude changes."

Question: Given the data on the subject, why do you think so many people in the US still believe that "high fear" propaganda works?

Fear and Failure   Why don't fear and threats work the way many people think they should? The answer seems to be twofold. To begin with, as Janis and Feshbach report, there seems to be a tendency for people to **repress** or deliberately forget frightening information. Second, and perhaps more important, your emotions can *arouse* you, but they don't always *direct* you in your thoughts and behaviors. Janis and Feshbach believe that fear-inducing communications focus your attention on problems and not on solutions. You become excited by the terrifying message, but you don't know what you must do to avoid or prevent the disaster the message warns you of. In fact, the fearful message may do little more than convince you that disaster is inevitable, and so you give up and do nothing at all.

Scared Straight   In the spring of 1979, a film called "Scared Straight" was shown on many US television stations. The movie shows how inmates at a prison in New Jersey have been using "scare tactics" to frighten troubled young people into avoiding further scrapes with the law. The youths spend several hours in the prison, mostly listening to the convicts describe (in **gory** detail) the effects of homosexual rape, fights, and prison brutality. The film is highly dramatic, and implies strongly that the "Scared Straight" program has been a great success. The film won an Academy Award in 1979, and after it was televised many state legislatures debated whether or not to make such treatment compulsory for all juvenile offenders.

New Jersey authorities tried to frighten juvenile offenders by exposing them to hardened criminals, but the "Scared Straight" program apparently doesn't work very well.

PART SEVEN Social Psychology

Unfortunately, the actual data simply do not support the effectiveness either of the program or of the film's fear-arousing message. In the August 1979 issue of *Psychology Today*, Rutgers professor James O. Finckenauer reports on a detailed study he had made of the juvenile offenders involved in these jail visitations. That the *prisoners* doing the "scaring" think the program works is without doubt. But Finckenauer discovered that only some 60 percent of the *juveniles* were scared straight enough to avoid further arrest. By contrast, some 90 percent of highly similar offenders in Finckenauer's control group "went straight" *without being scared*. Worse than this, of 19 youngsters who had no criminal record before they visited the New Jersey prison, six later broke the law. The data suggest that the program actually increases the crime rate rather than reducing it.

Why didn't the program work? Pearl West, director of the California Youth Authority, offers one answer: "These kids are yelled at home. Yelling at them some more won't do any good." Marian Wright Edelman, director of the Children's Defense Fund, offers another reason: "Having kids visit a jail for a few hours is not going to help them learn to read or deal with unstable family life."

Carolyn Mills.

Question: Why do you think the prisoners doing the "scaring" were so convinced that the program was a great success? How would their attitudes compare with the leaders of therapy groups (discussed in Chapter 25) who incorrectly believed that all members of their groups showed improvement?

Nothing Succeeds Like Success   According to *attribution theory*, you see your own actions as being a response to environmental circumstances, but you see the actions of others as being determined primarily by their personality or character traits. Thus you may believe that "punishment works" because others need a fear-evoking **deterrent** to keep their anti-social impulses under control. But the data show that many criminals—particularly youthful offenders—simply don't have the social skills to succeed in a complex environment. If Marian Edelman is correct, what would happen if juvenile delinquents were given skill-training rather than being threatened?

Tim Walter.

In 1979, Carolyn Mills and Tim Walter gave an answer to this question. They reported achieving a marked reduction in anti-social behaviors among a group of youthful offenders who were given special training in how to get and hold a job. Mills and Walter began with a group of 76 young people aged 14 to 17 who had gotten into trouble. Each of the youths had been arrested four times or so prior to the start of the experiment. Mills and Walter randomly selected 23 of the young people to be a "no-treatment control group." The other 53 were put into a behavioral training program.

In the first part of their program, Mills and Walter recruited a number of local business people who were willing to offer employment to youths who were "on probation." These business people signed contracts agreeing, among other things, to give the subjects day-by-day feedback on their performance and to meet with the experimenters weekly to discuss the youths' progress. The employers were requested to emphasize the positive aspects of the subjects' accomplishments and to resort to criticism as infrequently as possible.

Next, Mills and Walter interviewed the subjects individually and "shaped" their attitudes toward working in a variety of ways. The youths were asked to make a list of the behaviors they thought would be expected of them while working. If the subjects could not guess, they were given a list of job-appropriate activities produced by the employers. The youths then "role-played" the behaviors they thought would help them get and hold the job.

Once on the job, each subject was given written feedback *daily* by the employer. Once a week, the subject saw one of the experimenters for further counseling. During these counseling sessions, Mills and Walter went over the daily feedback sheets and encouraged the youths to talk about "how to make things better" on the job. The major emphasis during the

Deterrent (dee-TURR-ent). From a Latin word meaning "to frighten, or to discourage from acting." Punishment is usually thought to be a highly effective deterrent that keeps "sane" people from commiting crimes. In fact, many studies suggest that fear of punishment seldom keeps people from doing things that they really want to do, or that they find particularly rewarding. If punishment really deterred criminals, those countries with the most punitive laws would be those with the lowest crime rates, which doesn't happen to be the case. Closer to home, punitive laws have obviously not stopped people in the US from smoking marijuana, or from exceeding the 55 mile per hour speed limit.

early sessions was on such behaviors as getting to work daily (and on time), following the employer's "rules and regulations," learning the names of fellow employees, and performing well in the tasks they were given. Since the subjects received their weekly pay sessions at these counseling sessions, attendance remained high throughout the experiment.

When the subjects had been successful "on the job" for a period of several weeks, Mills and Walter began to fade out their assistance. The experimenters also began trying to help the youths gain skills in handling personal and school-related problems (rather than focusing primarily on job-related tasks). All in all, the subjects were followed for a period of 18 months or more.

Mills and Walter list two criteria for "success." First, the subjects should have no further arrests nor be institutionalized. Second, the subjects should stay on the job a minimum of three months while maintaining acceptable school performance. Some 85 percent of the experimental subjects were successful, while only 14 percent of the "no-treatment control" subjects could be counted as successes. More than 90 percent of the trained youths avoided further arrests, but only 30 percent of the untrained control subjects stayed out of trouble.

Mills and Walter note two further points of interest. At the beginning of their intervention program, the youths given training reported that they were subject to considerable verbal harrassment by their peers for "giving in to the system." However, as the subjects began earning good paychecks, many of these peers voluntarily requested placement in the training program. Second, while the training program was fairly costly, the "re-arrest" rate among the trainees was so small that the juvenile court sponsoring the program ended up by saving many thousands of dollars.

Thus changing people's attitudes may be important, but teaching people the skills that will allow them to *maintain healthy attitudes* may be the best form of propaganda presently available to us.

Question: Does criticism or punishment for inappropriate behaviors by itself *tell you what you have to do in order to succeed?*

The Audience

The people whose attitudes are to be shaped make up the communicator's audience. In terms of Helson's **Adaptation-level Theory,** the "message" is a *stimulus* factor, while the context in which the message appears (including the audience's perception of the communicator) are *background* factors. The character traits and past experiences of the audience are, as you might expect, *personality* factors that affect how the audience will perceive and respond to the message.

Obviously, the most persuasive messages are those created with all three factors in mind. A good communicator thus attempts to discover as much as possible about the audience, and then *shapes* the message to suit both the occasion and the people receiving it. Advertising agencies spend millions of dollars each year in order to learn about the personal characteristics of their target audiences, for there's little sense in trying to sell Lincolns to people who can barely afford Mustangs.

The Cincinnati Study Knowing something about your audience doesn't always guarantee that you will be able to get your message through to them, however. Several years ago, a group of social scientists in Cincinnati undertook a monumental advertising campaign in an attempt to inform the citizens of Cincinnati of the great value of the United Nations. Sociologists Shirley Star and Helen Hughes began by taking surveys to determine what people thought about the UN. The groups who knew the least about the UN (and who liked it the least) included the relatively uneducated, the elderly, and the poor.

Once Star and Hughes knew the characteristics of their target audience, the sociologists carried on a six-month campaign aimed at changing their

Adaptation-level Theory. A theory proposed by Harry Helson which accounts for perceptions (and attitudes) in terms of three factors: (1) The strength of the stimulus; (2) the strength of the (social) background; and (3) the person's past experience and psychological traits. See Chapter 27.

PART SEVEN Social Psychology

Almost 95 percent of the US population knew about President John F. Kennedy's death within 90 minutes after the first news bulletin, but the vast majority learned about the assassination from friends and relatives rather than from the news media.

attitudes. Unfortunately, the messages apparently reached or persuaded few of the target population. Instead, the propaganda was effective primarily with young people, and the better-educated and relatively well-to-do segment of the general public. These were, of course, the very people who were already favorably disposed toward the world organization.

Star and Hughes state that the greatest attitude changes of all took place in those individuals actively concerned in running the campaign, a point we will come back to momentarily.

In marked contrast to these results, studies by several investigators show that more than two-thirds of the American public learned about the assassination of President John F. Kennedy within 30 minutes after the news first broke. And more than 95 percent of the population knew about Kennedy's death within 90 minutes after the first radio bulletin hit the airwaves. The vast majority of the public, however, first learned about the assassination from *friends and relatives*, not from the news media.

Obviously mass communications *are* successful from time to time, but primarily when the "message" meets some need the audience has, or when the information imparted is so important or stimulating that people *talk to each other* about what has been printed or broadcast.

Question: How might you explain the response of the "target audience" in the Star and Hughes study in terms of autistic hostility?

Audience Responses

Why did the Cincinnati campaign fail? There probably are many different reasons. To begin with, we have no guarantee that Star and Hughes knew what kinds of messages would be most likely to reach their target audience (the poor, the uneducated, the elderly). Nor can we be sure that those involved in creating the propaganda knew what sorts of appeals would convince the targets to change their attitudes.

A more glaring mistake, however, was that Star and Hughes did nothing to establish feedback loops to monitor continuously the effects of their propaganda campaign. The Cincinnati communicators talked: The audience was merely supposed to listen and to respond appropriately. Most communicators spend a great deal of time and money trying to get their messages out, but seldom spend as much effort trying to determine if anyone is listening and, if so, what the audience's reaction really is.

The one "success story" in the Cincinnati study was that people who actually engaged in the propaganda campaign showed significant attitude change in the desired direction. As they worked on the project, this group of people apparently became more and more committed to making the study a success. Since the group was favorable toward the UN, anyone who joined the group was under strong pressure to conform to the group norm. These individuals also had the greatest exposure to the persuasive messages.

Question: How successful would the Mills and Walter study of juvenile offenders have been had the experimenters not monitored continuously the youths' actual "on the job" behaviors?

Role-playing and Attitude Change   There have been numerous studies demonstrating that the greatest attitude changes of all come when the communicator can get the audience to role-play the attitudes the communicator wants the audience to acquire. For example, W.A. Scott measured the attitudes toward "de-emphasis of football" in hundreds of students taking an introductory psychology course. Some of the students wanted bigger and better football teams, while others wanted to do away with the teams entirely.

Two weeks after measuring their attitudes, Scott asked 58 of the students to engage in mock debates on the importance of football. These debates took place in front of the rest of the class. Each student-debater, however, was asked to give arguments *against* the position the student had taken earlier (on the questionnaire). The class then voted to see which students had "won" their debates.

The "trick" in the Scott experiment was this: The votes actually cast by the class were ignored. Instead, Scott randomly told half the students they had "won," while the other half of the students were informed that they had "lost" the debate. Later, Scott remeasured the attitudes of the debaters.

As you might expect, the rewards and punishments had quite a strong effect on attitude change. Those debaters who thought they had won shifted significantly toward the position they had argued in class, even though this new view was the opposite of the one they had originally held. Those debaters who were told they had lost moved in the opposite direction: They became more convinced than ever that their original position was the correct one.

Question: In psycho-drama, should the therapist usually ask the patient to act out a successful or an unsuccessful outcome to the patient's problems?

Attitudes versus Behaviors

For a period of 20 years or so—from 1945 to about 1965—the major thrust in the field of attitude research was that of determining how attitudes are formed, maintained, and changed. Hovland, Janis, and their associates at Yale studied persuasion and propaganda. Sherif, Asch, Helson, and Blake investigated the many pressures that groups put on their members to conform. And Milgram showed how people with authoritarian attitudes could be induced to obey commands.

But around 1965, the field of attitude research took on a new and more challenging direction. For about this time, many psychologists began to question the usefulness of the very concept of *attitude*. The usual view had been that attitudes were "mental representations" of people's cognitions, emotions, and behavioral tendencies. But the scientists involved almost always *measured* people's attitudes by giving their subjects a pen-and-paper test of some kind—the belief being that the answers that people gave reflected how the people really felt about (or behaved toward) the objects of their attitudes.

By 1965, there was a growing body of experimental evidence showing a strange and unexpected difference between what people *said* their attitudes were and how these same people *acted* in real life. Few people who conform see themselves as being conformist, and few authoritarian people are likely to call themselves by that term on a pen-and-paper test. Furthermore, many people apparently have very inconsistent or conflicting attitudes. They may state on one questionnaire that they are in favor of conserving gasoline, but may the same day vote to increase the speed limit for automobiles and trucks.

According to most social psychologists, whenever you state an attitude, you are making a prediction about your future thoughts, feelings, and behaviors. But what is the psychologist to think when your attitudinal statement doesn't predict very well at all what you actually do at some future time?

Chinese and Blacks Keep Out!   The research study that first opened up this problem was reported by R.T. La Piere in 1934. La Piere had spent considerable time driving across the US with a Chinese couple. Despite the very strong "anti-Chinese" prejudice found among many Americans at that time, La Piere and his friends had been refused service only once during 10,000 miles of travel. Later, when they were safely home, La Piere sent questionnaires to all the hotels and cafes where they had stopped. One item on the questionnaire asked, "Will you accept members of the Chinese race as guests in your establishment?" More than 90 percent of the places responded with a very firm "no," and yet all but one of these hundreds of establishments actually had accepted the Chinese couple without question or comment. Obviously there was a very marked difference between "attitude" and "behavior" on the part of these establishments.

In a similar study reported in 1952, B. Kutner, Carol Wilkins, and Penny Yarrow had three young women visit various restaurants in a fashionable suburban community in the Northeastern part of the US. Two of the women were white; the third was black. The two white women always arrived at the restaurant first, asked for a table for three, and were seated. Shortly thereafter, the black woman entered, informed the head waiter or hostess that she was with friends who were already seated, found the table, sat down with the two white women, and was served without question.

Two weeks after each visit, Kutner, Wilkins, and Yarrow wrote a letter to each restaurant asking if they would serve blacks. Not one replied. The experimenters then called the manager of each establishment on the phone. The managers uniformly responded in a very cool and distant manner, suggesting that they held a highly prejudiced attitude toward serving blacks. Yet, as in the La Piere study, this attitude was simply not translated into action when the restaurant personnel were faced with seating a black person.

Since 1965, there have been dozens of other experiments, all of which suggest that attitudes (as measured by questionnaires) are very poor indicators of what people actually do, think, and feel in many real-life situations. Furthermore, there is often little relationship between attitude *change* and a subsequent change in the way a person *behaves*. Just as important, as we noted in the previous chapters, people often change their behaviors without changing those attitudes related to the behaviors.

Attitudes toward Attitudes   In their classic book *Opinions and Personality*, M. Brewster Smith, Jerome Bruner, and Robert W. White ask a most important question: "Of what possible use to you are your opinions?" The answer to that question is not an easy one to find. Smith, Bruner, and White believe that attitudes or opinions *serve needs*. That is, whenever you express an attitude, you are really describing some need or goal that you are "driven" to fulfill. When you state your attitudes to the people around you, therefore, you are presumably hunting for others with similar needs who might assist you in achieving mutual goals. Like most social psychologists, Smith, Bruner, and White believe that attitudes are *internal processes* that somehow guide or direct your behaviors.

A radically different approach to the subject, however, was stated in the late 1960's by Daryl Bem. According to Bem, attitudes are simply *verbal statements* about your own behaviors. Bem believes that most of what you do is under the control of external stimulus inputs, most of which you simply aren't consciously aware of. Bem points out that La Piere really measured two quite different responses that occurred in two very different environments. La Piere's questionnaire, for example, seems designed to elicit negative responses from the hotel and innkeepers to whom it was sent. But when La Piere presented himself and a well-dressed Chinese couple at the desk of the hotel, the stimulus situation was so different that the behavioral response of the innkeeper was bound to be different as well.

Bem believes that there really are no such things as "attitudes," unless you wish to consider them as verbal explanations of why you do what you do. Attitudinal statements then don't predict well at all: They merely give a *rationalization* of what you've already done. We might summarize Bem's position as follows: "How do I know what I think until I see what I've done?"

The Chicken or the Egg?   Are attitudes internal processes or external behaviors? The problem posed by these two highly different attitudes toward attitudes is much like the old question, "Which came first, the chicken or the egg?" Do you form attitudes (internal processes) first, and then act in accordance with your opinions or beliefs? Or do you learn to behave in a certain way in the presence of certain environmental inputs, and then justify your behaviors later on by expressing verbal attitudes toward these "input-out correlations" you've established?

Or do you do both things simultaneously?

At the moment, there is no agreed-upon solution to the puzzling differences we find between attitudes and behaviors, just as there is no agreed-upon solution to most of the basic problems in the field of psychology. We can measure attitudes, and we do know a great deal about how to change or maintain them. And we can measure behaviors, and we likewise know a lot about how to train people to behave in different ways. Given this knowledge of how to create and change both attitudes and actions, perhaps the most important issue of all is the following one: Who has the right to use these powerful techniques of personal change?

The Ethics of Attitude Change

Is it right to talk someone into buying an expensive new car? Is it ethical to convince people that the United Nations is worthy of support? Is it a morally responsible act to persuade a mentally disordered person to seek professional help? Is it ethical to teach children religion or economic theories? Shouldn't all individuals be free to make up their own minds without interference from persuasive sources?

The ethical questions involved in persuasion and attitude formation are numerous and complex. And the questions become even more difficult to answer in cases of *unintentional* persuasion, such as the influence parents have on their children or the subtle and indirect propaganda found in many textbooks and newspapers.

Psychology, as an objective science, is not in a position to answer ethical questions. Psychology can, however, attempt to provide some of the information and facts that you will need in order to make your own ethical decisions. One important point that psychology makes about attitude formation is this one: *No one is free of the influence of others or free of the responsibility of influencing others.* Every member of society is involved in attitude formation, both as communicator and as audience. Whenever two or more people get together, the outputs (messages) of one individual become the inputs of others. And this exchange of outputs can result in behavior or attitude change.

If every thing you do in the presence of someone else affects that person, then the only way you can hope to judge the ethical value of your actions is to have an *objective* understanding of how your behavior influences others. And since you acquired your own attitudes from others, you will also need as much scientific information as possible about how you were "shaped" to be what you presently are. For only when you know the full facts of how people communicate with and influence each other can you hope to make good ethical decisions about human attitudes and actions.

As Carl Rogers noted long ago, people need people, and no one ever achieved self-actualization without considerable assistance from hundreds of other individuals. The debt you owe these people, in return, is to help them achieve their own unique goals.

And perhaps that is what ethics is all about—helping others at some deep psychological level, so that they in turn can help you. Therefore, the more you can learn about human behavior (and attitudes), the more likely it will be that you can achieve your own form of self-actualization, and the more likely it will be that you can be of *optimal* assistance in helping others.

Summary

1. **Social psychologists** spend a lot of time trying to answer the following questions:
    a. Where do our **attitudes** come from?
    b. What personal and environmental factors promote **attitude stability?**
    c. What factors promote **attitude change?**
2. Although some of our opinions, feelings, and preferences are the product of **rational decision-making,** many of our attitudes are unconsciously influenced by attempts of other people to **persuade** us to think and act as they do (or as they would like us to think and act).
3. In general, the more you know about something, the more **stable** your attitude toward that thing will usually be.
4. The stronger you feel about something, the more difficult it probably will be to get you to change your perception of, or attitude toward, that thing.
5. The better your attitude allows you to predict future events or responses, and the more you are **reinforced** for holding a certain **percept,** the less susceptible that percept or attitude is to being changed.
6. In Newcomb's study of Bennington women, he found that:
    a. Seniors were more liberal than freshmen.
    b. Students felt **group pressures to conform** to the politically liberal environment at the college.
    c. The most liberal students tended to create post-college environments that would help them maintain their liberal attitudes.
    d. These students often showed **autistic hostility** to non-liberal attitudes and opinions.
7. If someone wants to change your attitude toward some object, the person must either change the object or somehow communicate new information to you about that object.
8. The **communication process** is influenced by at least four different factors:
    a. the **communicator**
    b. the **message**
    c. the **audience**
    d. the **feedback** (if any) from the audience to the communicator
9. Studies suggest that one of the most important aspects of the communication process is the **credibility** the audience places in the communicator.
10. Immediately after hearing a message, we tend to accept the word of **high credibility sources,** but reject the word of **low credibility sources.**
11. Several weeks later, we tend to be more influenced by the actual content of the message than by its source—a phenomenon called the **sleeper effect.**
12. Many studies suggest that **person-to-person** communication is by far more effective than **mass communication** involving the news media.

13. When we receive **fear-arousing messages,** our first impression may be that the stimulus is a very **persuasive** one. However, studies show that fear usually achieves little more than **repression** or **rationalization.**

14. Youthful offenders exposed to the **scared straight** program actually had a higher rate of subsequent arrests than did a control group not exposed to the fear-arousing experiences.

15. Youthful offenders given **job-skill training** and **positive feedback** about their attitudes and behaviors showed a much lower rate of subsequent arrests than did control-group subjects.

16. The more that a **propagandist** constructs the message to fit the prior beliefs and attitudes of the audience, and the more the communicator pays attention to audience feedback, the more successful the persuasive attempt will usually be.

17. People involved in presenting **propaganda** are usually more affected by it than are the intended audience.

18. The more you are **rewarded** for expressing a given attitude, the more likely it is you will accept it as your own.

19. Recent research suggests that attitudes are a verbal description of how we *think* we will behave. But since we usually fail to take into account the **social background** in which our actions occur, our attitudes are often poor predictors of our actual behaviors.

20. The **ethical questions** raised by research on attitudes are highly complex and not easily answered. However, we probably should evaluate ourselves objectively in terms of what we really do, rather than evaluate ourselves subjectively in terms of our intentions and attitudes.

(Continued from page 733.)

It took several minutes for the Princess to revive the Iron Duke from his faint. While the young girl was alternately wiping her father's brow and slapping him on the cheeks, Rodney poured himself a glass of Black Magic.

"Thou canst not be serious," the Duke said, when he had finally recovered sufficiently to make it to his huge leather chair.

"Dead serious," said Rodney.

"But to give forth the whole, unadulterated, 100 percent *truth* about our Royal products! Why the whole fabric of society would be torn to shreds. Such folly would lead to the complete collapse of the Nacirema economy."

"Nonsense," said Rodney. "Things would change a little, but perhaps for the better."

"Well, it would surely mean the undoing of General Widget, which is just as bad," replied the Duke, thinking of his own position.

"I doubt even that," said the younger man. "The trouble with a widget is not that it's so terrible but that it just isn't as good as it could be. As long as the Sponsor can sell the present model, why should he change? It's cheaper to use your agency's 'word magic' to cover up the problems than to put out a noticeably better product. If you had to tell the truth about the widget, the Sponsor would no longer have that choice."

The Duke poured himself a large tumbler of the amber liquid. "Thy suggestion would never work," he said finally. "The peasants would never stand for it. They love their illusions, and we but keep them happy. Peasants have no love for the truth."

"Then why have they stopped buying widgets?" Rodney asked smugly. "It seems to me that you and the Sponsors are the ones who don't want the truth. Give the peasants a better product, and maybe they'll start buying widgets again."

"Ah," said the Duke softly, "there's the rub. What meanest thou by better?"

Rodney moved to the window and stared at the traffic 100 floors below. "I must admit that I don't really know."

"And this princeling calls himself a genius!" the Duke said to the princess.

"But I know how to find out," Rodney continued.

"Like how?" asked the Duke, his voice ringing with sarcasm.

"Ask the peasants what they want. Tell the Sponsor your findings. And then do your level best to see that the Sponsor tries to meet the peasants' needs. Then you don't have to be afraid of the truth."

The Duke laughed hollowly. "Thou kiddest."

"No, I kid thee not. Business, politics, education—they've all become like Empire Avenue down below—a one-way street. The Sponsor builds widgets and tells you to sell them. You use glowing descriptions to trick peasants into buying widgets whether they need them or not. But what say do the peasants have about what gets built or what ads get run?"

"The peasants vote with their pocketbooks. They can buy, or not buy, as they please."

"Even when it's the only widget on the market?"

The Duke shook his head vigorously. "We spend millions of dollars each year peering into the peasant mentality."

"So you can persuade them better, not so they can persuade you to give them a better product. You've cut off all feedback from your customers. No wonder widgets are selling poorly."

The Duke remained unconvinced. "No Sponsor in his right mind would dare try it."

Rodney smiled. "Some already are. They're trying to involve their customers in product planning, in production, and in marketing and advertising—just as schools are beginning to involve their students in planning and teaching courses, and politicians are learning to listen more than they talk."

"But I tell thee Wizards like me know what the peasants really want!" the Duke roared.

Rodney turned away from the window. "Papa knows best—is that what you mean?"

The Duke nodded slowly.

"Mr. Steele, have you ever gone out and bought a widget?"

"Heaven forfend!"

"When was the last time you really talked to someone who has?"

The Duke looked puzzled. "Princess," he said slowly, "I don't suppose . . ."

"I wouldn't be caught dead with one, Father. They're just not my style."

The Duke picked up his phone and buzzed his secretary. She didn't use widgets either. And neither did the Director of Marketing, the Chief of Production, nor the Head Gnome.

"See what I mean, Sir? A one-way street. Everybody talks, and nobody listens. What you need is a Vice-wizard in Charge of Feedback."

The Princess laughed. "And, Father, I just happen to know someone who's available."

The Iron Duke grumbled to himself for a moment then managed a half-hearted smile. "Methinks the matter needs serious contemplation. Get thee hence, you two. The Iron Duke has a giant to kill."

After the young couple had gone, the Duke hunched over in his huge chair, considering what Rodney had said. After a while, the big man wearily picked up the telephone and dialed a number.

"Hello, Mama? This is Sonny. How are things? Yes, I know I haven't talked to you in quite a while. Oh, has it been that long? Well you know how busy I've been. What? Yes, the Princess is doing just fine. She's got a new boy friend, a prince of a fellow. There may be wedding bells any day now. Oh, certainly, I do want you to meet him. He's got long hair and some strange ideas, but he'll learn, he'll learn. Incidentally, we may be hiring him here at the firm."

The Duke listened for a moment, nodding in silent response to what he had heard. Then he took a deep breath. "Oh, say, Mama. What's your attitude toward widgets?"

Recommended Readings

Hovland, Carl I., Irving L. Janis, and Harold H. Kelley. *Communication and Persuasion* (New Haven, Conn.: Yale University Press, 1953).

Newcomb, Theodore M., Ralph H. Turner, and Philip E. Converse. *Social Psychology* (New York: Holt, Rinehart and Winston, 1965).

Stumphauzer, J.S., ed. *Progress in Behavior Therapy with Delinquents* (Springfield, Ill.: Charles C Thomas, 1979).

Applied Psychology: Past and Future

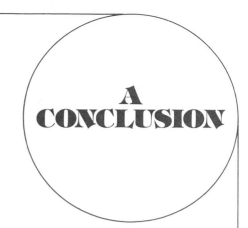

A CONCLUSION

"What's In It For Me?"

Like most scientists, I believe in the future. I guess I always have. I am much more interested in new things than in old, and I am more intrigued by what a person might become than in what a person has already been. Indeed, about the only time I think about yesterday is when I need information that might let me better understand what tomorrow could be like.

Humans seem to be the only animals that can look far into the future and plan accordingly. This ability to change some parts of the present world *deliberately* in order to shape the world of tomorrow is, in my opinion, one of the essential characteristics of being human.

Science is (among other things) the fine art of predicting the future in objective terms. It is therefore one of the most human of occupations. It took human beings a long time to learn how to make their predictions accurate, however, for at least two reasons:

1. Being emotional or subjective seems easier for most of us than being rational or objective. Perhaps this fact is not too surprising. The emotional centers of the nervous system appear to dominate the brains of lower animals. The "thinking" or "processing" centers in the cortex reach their fullest development in humans, but these are *additions to* (rather than subtractions from) the basic blueprint of the highly reactive animal brain. The human limbic system is more complexly evolved than is the limbic system in the white rat, cat, or monkey, and our emotional experiences are likewise more subtle and complicated. The sheer size of the human cortex gives us the potentiality of bringing our passions and desires under *voluntary control*, but we need training and experience in order to do so. However, we need precious little training to be emotional.

As we noted in Chapter 5, in order to think logically, you have to be able to translate parts of the world into verbal symbols, so that you can manipulate the world *symbolically* in your mind. Only the human being has a "speech center," so far as we know, and only humans seem capable of complex speech and symbol manipulation. But as human society developed, we had a long heritage of animal emotionality to overcome, and we had to develop such symbolic languages as mathematics in order to help us gain control of our passions.

2. Even when early men and women attempted to view the world in objective terms, they often lacked sufficient data to make good predictions. It probably wasn't until around the year 1600 A.D. that we had gathered enough hard, unemotional facts about the world—and had the proper mathematical tools—for science to prove a worthwhile occupation.

The Industrial Revolution

Perhaps because it is easier for most of us to look at *things* objectively than for us to be objective about ourselves, the physical (or "thing") sciences were the first to develop. Modern physics and astronomy date from the 1600's. Chemistry came a little later. These scientific disciplines soon matured enough to let us understand and predict the behavior of a few objects under certain specified conditions—for that kind of prediction is science's job. But once we could *guess* how physical things would behave, we could also hunt for ways to *control* the future behavior of these objects, and this ability to control "things" marked the rise of physical technology.

The first major applications of physical technology in Europe began in the mid-1700's, and led to what we call the "Industrial Revolution." Before this time, almost everyone in Europe lived on farms or in relatively small towns, and almost every "thing" was handmade. Life changed little from one generation to another. A man typically became what his father had been, and a woman married the sort of man her mother had married. As greater and greater application of the physical sciences gave humans the ability to shape their physical environments, however, the tempo of cultural change speeded up noticeably.

The Medical Revolution

By the 1800's, we had learned enough to begin viewing our bodily reactions in an objective manner. Biology became a true science, and medical technology became a reality. As the "Medical Revolution" gathered steam in the early 1900's, we learned more and more about how to predict and control our physiological reactions. Because of this applied knowledge, we are now bigger, stronger, healthier, and we live longer than at any previous time in human history.

The Psychological Revolution

During the early part of this century, we took the next step up the ladder—we discovered ways to look at our minds and behaviors objectively. Psychology and the social sciences came into being. We are just now starting to build a technology based on our new-found objective knowledge of ourselves. We call this technology *applied psychology*—that is, the application of psychological facts and theories to help solve real-life problems. In short, we are now in the midst of what might be called the "Psychological Revolution." The cultural changes this third revolution has brought

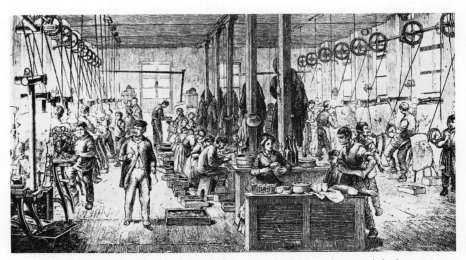

The Industrial Revolution gave us control over the physical environment, but gave us little knowledge about how to help people survive in that environment.

about are, in their way, as "mind-blowing" as those caused by the Industrial and Medical Revolutions.

What will scientific psychology be like in the future? That question is difficult to answer, since it depends in part on the often unpredictable outcomes of all the thousands of experiments psychologists are conducting right at this moment.

The future of applied psychology is somewhat easier to predict, however, since tomorrow's technology will lean heavily on today's scientific knowledge. In these final pages, let me share with you my guesses about the changing world of human behavior, and what these changes might mean to you. Other psychologists will surely see things differently, and predictions are often little more than wild speculation.

Still, it might pay us to try to answer three interesting questions:

1. What will the world be like in the year 2000?
2. What kinds of job opportunities might be open to you then?
3. What types of psychological services will probably be available to you by the end of this century?

In defense of my answers to these questions about the year 2000, let me remind you of one fact. At least half of the *types* of jobs available to college graduates today simply didn't exist as "job classifications" 25 years ago.

The Future of Biological Psychology

There seems little doubt that we will shortly gain a great deal more control over our heredity (and hence our instinctual behaviors) than we would have dreamed possible a few years back. In 1973 scientists at the University of Wisconsin announced that they had been able to synthesize a gene in a test tube—that is, they had been able to take ordinary chemical molecules and combine them to "build" a very simple gene. By the late 1970's, other scientists had shown that "artificial genes" could function *normally* in very simple organisms. Thus it seems clear that "genetic engineering" is no longer as impossible and unthinkable a project as once seemed the case (see Chapter 19).

Once the biologists give us greater control over our inheritance, psychologists will be able to determine with much greater precision what the genetic contribution to behavior really is. We should also be able to learn much more about how to overcome genetic handicaps that people already have. By the year 2000, many psychologists should be employed as "genetic counselors," giving advice to prospective parents both before and after they get married. Other psychologists will be able to offer physically handicapped people much better training than now exists. These psychologists may also offer surgeons advice on what kinds of drugs and operations might be helpful to maximize the *psychological* potential of brain-damaged individuals.

The Two Hemispheres

There is no part of physiological psychology presently more exciting than the study of the functions of the two hemispheres. As we noted earlier, there is now considerable evidence that such "mental illnesses" as schizophrenia and autism are related to a *functional imbalance* between the two halves of the brain. I would guess that our whole approach to treating these "mental disorders" will change markedly in the next decade. Instead of locking schizophrenic patients up in asylums, we surely will begin training them to process information with *both hemispheres*.

We are also likely to be able to help normal children who have language problems by measuring how they input information to their two hemispheres. In the June 29, 1979 issue of *Science,* Joseph Cioffi and Gillray L. Kandel report that young boys tend to process information in quite a different manner than do young girls. When Cioffi and Kandel gave "word-shapes" to more than 100 young people, the girls tended to respond to the "word value" of the stimulus, while boys tended to respond to the "shape" of the input. Boys also tend to have more language development problems than do girls, while girls typically have more difficulty learning spatial concepts and the correct use of mathematical symbolism than do boys.

Psychologist Leona Tyler states that the *main psychological difference* between men and women lies in this area: Men do better at perceptual problems than do women, and women do better at language problems than do men. This difference is found at all ages and in all cultures. Although we often think of women as being more emotional, soft-minded, and submissive than men—and men as being more dominant, tough-minded, and logical—Tyler notes that these are *cultural expectations* rather than empirical facts. Male hormones, it would seem, tend to bias the brain toward processing information with the right hemisphere, while female hormones tend to bias the brain toward processing information with the left hemisphere.

Now that we know what the *major* psychological difference between the two sexes really is, perhaps we can help parents and teachers overcome a variety of hormone-induced problems. Girls tend to get better grades in school because grades typically depend more on language-processing than on perceptual creativity. But men usually do better in tasks calling for creativity and mathematical ability. By giving boys special training to improve the functioning of their "left hemispheres," and by giving girls training to improve the functioning of their "right hemispheres," we can surely come closer to achieving a psychological *equality of the sexes* than if we focus on changing such character traits as "dominance" and "emotionality."

Behavioral Medicine

There are very few psychologists working in hospitals today. By the year 2000, however, hospitals may employ more behavioral technologists than they do physicians and surgeons. This surprising situation will be a direct consequence of the three revolutions we mentioned earlier. For, thanks to our increased knowledge of the physical and biological sciences, the major health hazards are no longer diseases that have purely physiological causes—such as pneumonia, influenza, and tuberculosis. Medical technology has, for the most part, "cured" us of these maladies. But medical technology is presently ill-equipped to help us with health problems that have an intra-psychic or behavioral component, for few physicians are trained in psychological technology.

In the summer of 1975, the US Department of Health, Education, and Welfare released its *Forward Plan for Health,* a long-range blueprint of US needs in the health sciences. According to this report, the major killers today are heart disease, cancer, stroke, and, in younger people, automobile accidents, murder, and suicide. As stated in the *Forward Plan for Health,* "A distinctive feature of these conditions is that most of them are caused by factors [that is, the environment and individual behavior] that are not susceptible to direct medical solution."

Writing in the *Forward Plan for Health,* physician John H. Knowles states that, "The people have been led to believe that national health insurance, more doctors, and greater use of high-cost, hospital-based technology will improve health. Unfortunately, none of them will. . . . The next major advances in the health of the American people will come from the assumption of individual responsibility for one's own health and a necessary change in life style for the majority of Americans."

In brief, our biological systems *interact* with our intra-psychic and our social/behavioral systems, and the next breakthroughs in medicine will come from the wise and human use of a psycho-technology that helps coordinate the inputs and outputs of all three systems.

Already many of my students are working with doctors and patients at several medical facilities in the Ann Arbor area. The students have been particularly successful with "problem patients" whose thoughts and behaviors interfere with improvement in their physical health. Helping patients stay on diets, give up smoking, and stay on medical treatment plans are three of the areas that the student–therapists have done well in.

Sometimes the students can achieve near-miracles with patients that the medical profession has "abandoned." In the late 1970's, four of my undergraduates—directed by Charles Seigerman, himself an undergraduate—began helping the nursing staff at the local VA hospital. One of the patients the students worked with was a young man whom we will call Ennis, who had suffered severe brain damage in an automobile accident when he was 19. The accident left Ennis paralyzed and unable to walk. He spoke but two phrases, "God," and "God damn." He had no voluntary control over his bowels and bladder, he had to be spoon-fed, and he threw amazing temper tantrums whenever anyone tried to wash him or get him into a bathtub. Ennis had little in the way of social behavior: He avoided eye contact with people who tried to talk to him, and he did not respond to the requests the nurses and doctors made of him. He had been shuffled from one hospital to another because he was a "problem patient" and was diagnosed as being "incurable."

The students found Ennis lying on the floor of the neurology ward. The nurses would pull him out of bed each morning, clean him up as best they could, feed him, and then stretch him out on the floor to keep him from getting bed sores. At night, the nurses would put Ennis back to bed. They had little other contact with him because Ennis would scream "God damn" and resist any attempts they made to help him get better.

Seigerman and the other four undergraduates began by trying to teach Ennis how to feed himself, since (they thought) the nurses might be willing to spend more time with Ennis if he could manage some self-care behaviors. A member of the hospital staff recorded their efforts on video tape. In the first taped episode, Ennis looks like a wild man. He screams at the students as they put a spoon into his hands, dip it in food, and forcibly move it toward his mouth. He thrashes about, avoiding eye contact, apparently paying little attention to the constant flow of praise and encouragement that the students give him. But he did eat—once the food was shoveled into his mouth.

By the end of the first week, Ennis had developed into quite a different person. He was still clumsy, but now he looked at the students directly, responded to their requests, and obviously enjoyed the positive reinforcement and the newly acquired ability to move his hands and arms voluntarily. By the end of two weeks, he was able to eat almost entirely on his own. After a month of training, Ennis could pick up a cup and drink without spilling the liquid all over himself. He also had become skilled enough at feeding himself that he no longer required much assistance at mealtimes.

The rapid progress that Ennis made impressed the nursing staff quite favorably, so they recommended he be given physical therapy to help him recover his ability to walk. The therapists worked closely with the students, and by the end of a month or so of daily sessions, Ennis was able to walk on a level surface without assistance (although he still needed help going up and down stairs).

Next the students built a "psychological potty-trainer" for Ennis that rang a bell whenever he used it properly. The nurses would immediately come to him and praise him for showing voluntary control over his bowels and bladder whenever he "rang the bell." It took a week or so of constant reinforcement for Ennis to complete his "toilet training."

The most difficult learning of all concerned Ennis's fear of bathing. The physicians had assumed that this inappropriate behavior was due to his brain injury, but the students discovered the real cause. At another hospital, whenever Ennis had thrown a temper tantrum, the attendants had punished him by dragging him into the shower room and sticking his head into a tub of water. The students attempted to de-sensitize this conditioned fear of water using the "modeling" techniques developed by Albert Bandura at Stanford (see Chapter 26). Charles Seigerman put on a hospital gown similar to the one that Ennis wore. Charles then sat down next to Ennis and began talking with him. A nurse approached them and offered Charles some apple sauce (Ennis's favorite food) if Charles would let her wash his arms. Seigerman agreed, the nurse washed, and gave Charles his reward. She then turned to Ennis and asked if he would like to earn some apple sauce too. Ennis replied by sticking out his arms to be washed—a behavior he had not shown previously.

Day by day, the therapy was expanded so that, within a couple of weeks, Ennis was allowing the nurse to wash his entire body (for the apple sauce reward). Then the wash sessions were slowly moved closer and closer to the shower room. Again, within a week or so Ennis had been "shaped" into the bathroom with little or no difficulty.

However, a near-disaster occurred at this point. Two of the hospital attendants became angry at Ennis one day. To punish his "misbehavior," the attendants took him into the wash room, stuffed him in a shower stall, and turned on the cold water. Ennis naturally regained his fear of bathing after this episode, but the students "reshaped" him within a few days. The final video tape shows Ennis calmly sitting in a tub of water, playing with a rubber duck, and muttering "damn" quietly to himself.

It is difficult to describe a case history such as Ennis' in purely objective terms. The facts are that five undergraduates—with considerable help from the nurses and other staff members—brought about a large number of changes in the man's behavior. The most dramatic change of all, however, is visible in the first segment of the video tape. In his initial encounters with the students, Ennis behaves like a frightened animal. But by the end of the first week of training, he gives the impression of "turning into a human being"—mostly because he now responds appropriately to social inputs. He laughs at jokes, he maintains eye contact, and he no longer attempts to flee at the first touch of human contact.

However, the Ennis story has a sad (but realistic) ending. Shortly after the students had desensitized his fear of bathing, the medical staff at the local hospital decided that Ennis was so dramatically improved that he should be returned to his "home" hospital. The students wrote up a full report of what they had done and asked that the staff at the other hospital be made aware of how effective their work had been. But, as we later learned, the staff either didn't read the report, or didn't believe it. Whatever the case, Ennis was enough improved that he was eventually released from the hospital and placed in a nursing home several hundred miles from here.

In the summer of 1979, Charles Seigerman happened upon Ennis at the nursing home. Ennis had "regressed" in many ways. He was no longer able to feed himself, and many of his social skills seemed to have vanished. But the important thing to note is this: When Seigerman spent a few minutes retraining Ennis, the man rapidly *regained his ability* to use a fork and spoon and to hold a cup in his hands. Seigerman estimates that, given two weeks of intensive therapy, Ennis would be right back at the high level of performance he had shown just prior to his leaving the Ann Arbor hospital. The real problem that Ennis has, then, is not that he is brain-damaged, but that the staff at the nursing home simply didn't give him the environmental support he needs in order to function at his best.

Therapeutic techniques are of little value unless one can get both the therapist and the patient to apply them. We could help Ennis, but we never have found a way of "encouraging" hospital and nursing-home staffs to use the techniques we find effective. But the fact that relatively untrained undergraduates could achieve such marked improvements in a patient the doctors had "given up on" suggests strongly that these techniques will be more widely used once the medical profession comprehends the real contribution that psycho-technology can make to helping severely disturbed patients.

"Behavioral medicine" is a new and relatively uncharted field, but its growth seems assured. For as the *Forward Plan for Health* notes, we cannot cope with most of the major medical problems today unless we realize that good health is *always* an interaction among the biological, intra-psychic, and social/behavioral systems that affect us all.

Biological Feedback Quite often physicians use drugs to try to influence physiological processes that might better be brought under the patient's voluntary control. There are already promising hints that some milder forms of epilepsy may be helped by conditioning procedures. If the epileptic patient can be hooked to an EEG machine, the patient can sometimes see visual representation of the chemical storm building up in her or his own brain. By training the person to detect the subtle physiological "cues" and intra-psychic "feelings" that accompany the onset of an epileptic seizure, the psychologist may be able to teach the patient to relax or otherwise change thought patterns so that the seizure is prevented.

In similar fashion, patients recovering from heart attacks may use machines that record their heart beats, much as the EEG makes records of brain waves. By seeing this graphic representation of the heart's outputs, the patient may discover how to condition the heart to respond in healthier ways. High blood pressure, digestive upsets, urine production, and internal bleeding may also turn out to be controllable through conditioning. It is even possible that we may learn how to influence the production of human sperm and eggs through conditioning techniques. Rather than giving a woman "the pill" to prevent her from becoming pregnant, we may be able to train her to become fertile only when she consciously wishes to do so.

Applied Psychology Involving Drugs We already know that chemicals such as caffeine speed up learning, and that "downers" typically retard it. By the year 2000, psychologists may know of a wide variety of drugs that will help people achieve goals not presently within their reach. Drugs to slow down or help reverse the process of senility are a possibility, as are chemicals that will help prevent some types of mental illness. It is highly probable that all such compounds will be used in conjunction with psychological and social/behavioral treatment, but there is no reason not to use drugs if they can be helpful.

As we learn more about "consciousness," we will surely discover more effective means of inducing whatever "altered states of consciousness" anyone might desire to experience. Both drugs and biofeedback techniques seem likely candidates in this type of research.

Applied Psychology Involving Sensory Processing Computers are crude models of our brains. As we gain more insight into how your cortex looks over sensory inputs and processes them, we should be able to build dramatically better yet simpler computers than we presently have. It is already theoretically possible to use, for example, the brain of an ant or a worm as a "biological computer." The problem at the moment is in controlling the sensory inputs and the motor outputs. Biological computers

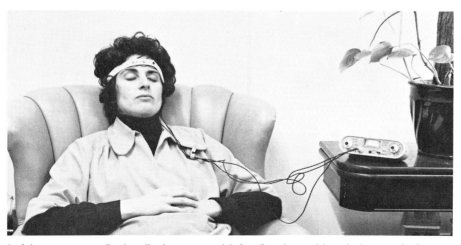

In future years medical patients may use biofeedback machines to learn voluntary control over their bodily functions.

should be able to handle complex decision-making much better than present-generation electrical or mechanical computers—and brains are likely to be smaller and easier to handle than machines. Thus it is possible that some "computer technologists" in the year 2000 will be, in effect, animal trainers rather than machine-tenders.

And, as we learn more about how your receptors actually sense the world, and how your motor centers control your muscles, we might be able to build "electronic eyes and ears" that would be connected directly to the brains of blind and deaf patients. We might also be able to build artificial arms and legs that will be directly connected to the motor-output centers of the brain, so that the mechanical "limbs" would respond to a person's thoughts almost exactly the way that flesh-and-blood would respond.

Biological engineering will be a part of our future whether we like it or not. But it seems reasonably certain that it will always be used in conjunction with improved ways of "engineering" our thoughts and behaviors. So let us look next at what applied intra-psychic psychology may be like.

Applied Intra-Psychic Psychology

Technology implies measurement. The more accurately you can describe or measure anything, the better chance you have of being able to exercise some kind of control over it. As you may have gathered from the earlier chapters in this book, one of the major problems with the intra-psychic or subjective approach to human existence is that internal events are most difficult to describe in quantitative or measurable terms. For this reason alone, we can probably expect greater immediate technological development in biological and behavioral psychology than in the intra-psychic area.

There are a number of highly promising developments, however, that we should take note of. Personality theory in the past has been based on the assumption that your character was fairly well fixed by the end of the first few years of your life. Freud, for instance, thought that only superficial or "surface" changes occurred in people once they had passed the years of early adolescence. Personality tests were usually designed to measure the intellectual and emotional traits a person already possessed, not the traits that the person might acquire with training and encouragement. The IQ test, for example, tells you something about what you are, but not very much about what you could become.

The humanistic psychologists, however, emphasize growth and perpetual change. One of the greatest challenges of the coming 20 years will be to develop new types of intra-psychic tests that will tell us more about the *potentialities* of people than present tests do. We will have to find new types of traits to measure (as best we can) the process-of-becoming rather than "fixed" or supposedly unchangeable traits such as IQ or "psychosis."

The humanistic psychologists are also likely to discover more about human (and humane) goals and values in the coming years than we presently know. In many ways, the humanists are in a unique position—that of functioning as a conscience or "superego" that can help keep the more applied technologies oriented toward ethical solutions of human problems.

Applied Developmental Psychology

One of the fastest growing fields within the behavioral sciences is that of *developmental psychology.* Although this term once meant much the same thing as *child psychology,* we now realize that people continue to change throughout their lives. In the future, developmental specialists will work with people of all ages, helping them solve whatever "growth" difficulties arise at any time in their lives. Developmental psychologists will probably serve as learning specialists in the school system, being as interested in helping young people achieve emotional maturity as in helping them learn to read, write, think logically, and be more creative.

But applied developmental psychology should also be useful to people

There is now no reason why people should be locked into the same profession all their lives.

in the middle years of life. As our health gets better and our lives get longer, we will realize that there is no reason why we should commit ourselves to one occupation, or to one style of life, and stick with it forever. Education should not stop when some college places a degree in a person's hands: rather, it should continue up to the moment of the person's death.

Some of our greatest untapped resources are the skills and abilities of our senior citizens. As we learn how to maintain psychological youthfulness even when our bodies are fairly old, we will need specialists to help older people continue to be useful and contributing members of society.

Death is as much a part of the business of living as is life itself, yet we often avoid the topic, and it has seldom been studied scientifically. Developmental psychologists will probably be called upon as much to help people prepare psychologically for facing death as for facing life.

Psychological Pollution

It has taken us more than 200 years from the start of the Industrial Revolution to realize that our new-found control of the physical environment brings with it serious responsibilities. Because we did not understand the consequences of our actions, we have polluted our lakes and streams, we have destroyed many of our natural resources, and we have fouled the very air we breathe. Ecologists are presently working very hard to help us learn how to keep our physical waste products from ruining our health and lessening the quality of our physiological existence.

As we gain greater influence over our psychological environment, it is likely that we will discover the importance of various forms of *psychological pollution* that we have ignored in the past. Hatred, war, violence, threats, and punishments are forms of psychological pollution that can contaminate your personal psychological space as much as belching smoke stacks can pollute the physical world. Criticism (justified or not) can kill your spirit as quickly as lead or mercury can poison your body. My own opinion is that most of the "hang-ups" and inhibitions that people have are a direct consequence of the punishment, ridicule, and hostility that we too often aim at each other.

One of our future challenges, then, will be to discover ways to get people to control or repress the psycho-pollution of hatred and to express more openly their loves and affections.

Applied Behavioral Psychology

The engineering profession really got its start with the beginning of the Industrial Revolution. Part of an engineer's job is to take known scientific data and use them to transform the physical environment. But in doing so, engineers often discover new scientific principles on their own. And, in putting well-known scientific theories to practical tests, the engineers may uncover flaws in the theory that laboratory scientists were unaware of.

One of the most important new professions is that of behavioral engineering—the science that uses psychological data to help create new and more satisfying social and work environments. My private opinion is that, by the year 2000, half the psychologists in the US will be employed in jobs demanding behavioral engineering skills. Let us look at some of the things they might be doing.

Community Mental Health

As long as we believed that mental illness was primarily the fault (or responsibility) of the individual, we could ignore the effects of the social environment on human behavior. But we now know that, just as dirt and germs breed physical illness, bad cultural conditions can breed crime, violence, insanity, and personal misery. At present we have sanitary engineers who inspect restaurants and food stores to make sure that food is clean and healthy. Perhaps by the next century we will have behavioral engineers who inspect businesses, schools, and industries to make certain that employers show as much concern for the mental health and happiness of their employees, students, and customers as they do for cleaning up dirt and preventing physical disease.

Already we have a great many community mental health centers scattered across the US and Canada. We will need many more of them, and they will surely take on a variety of new tasks. The data suggest, for instance, that most parents who mistreat their children were mistreated by their own parents. If we are to stop this slaughter of innocent children, we will have to find effective ways of teaching these sorts of parents to manage their children without resorting to violent physical punishment.

Mental illness "runs in families" in part because of genetic factors, and in part because certain types of parental responses induce "insane" behavior in children. To break this self-perpetuating pattern of mental illness, we will need more effective forms of family counseling. We will also have to make some rather difficult moral decisions concerning society's right to intervene in unhealthy family situations when the parents may resent or fight against outside intervention.

Mental hospitals as we presently know them may well vanish during the first part of the next century. These "asylums" will be replaced by clinics, re-education centers, halfway houses, group homes, and other forms of "sheltered environments" where people with mental problems may go for relatively short periods of time. Behavioral engineers—working in teams with psychiatrists, psychologists, and social workers—will help these disturbed people find solutions to their problems. The patients will then be eased back into society bit by bit, rather than being discharged abruptly with little in the way of after-care. Behavioral psychologists will also be involved in helping to change the social environment (such as a family situation) into which the patient will return.

The importance of the "step-by-step" method of bringing mental patients back into society is emphasized in recent work by Wayne State psychologist Jacobo A. Varela and his students. Varela noted that many ex-mental patients were housed in cheap hotels where violence was rampant. Terrified by their new environment, the patients often remained locked in their rooms and thus were even more cut off from other people than when they had been hospitalized. Varela and his students slipped notes under the doors of the patients' rooms inviting them to join "rap" groups in the hotel that would discuss problems they all had in common. Varela states that 19 out of 20 ex-patients responded enthusiastically and "came out from behind their locked doors." Unfortunately, this type of carefully engineered "after-care" is seldom offered by the present mental-health establishment.

The sprawling concrete prisons we presently send criminals to will also slowly fade from the scene. As we gain greater control over the social environment, fewer people will "want" to become law-breakers. Rehabilitation and re-education are much more effective ways of dealing with criminals than are merely punishing them and locking them away behind bars. Thus prisons too should develop into "schools for social and personal learning" and be staffed as much by psychologists as by wardens and guards. And prisoners—like ex-mental patients—should be given extensive assistance after leaving prison in order to help them learn the skills necessary for day-to-day survival.

Mass Communications

For a number of years, the federal government has taken frequent surveys of US economic life. The government knows how much money people earn, the taxes they pay, the debts they owe, and how many people have television sets, bathtubs, and automobiles. In the last few years, however, the government has realized that it has mountains of data on the *quantity* of US life—who owns what—but little or no information on the *quality* of life—how happy and satisfied people are. But surely the "cost of loving" is as important a piece of data as is the cost of living. If the government is to serve us better, it must first develop better ways of measuring psychological needs and desires, and then find ways of engineering the "psycho-economy" to our greater satisfaction.

Elections are a form of political feedback, but they come too infrequently to reflect the shifts in mood and the attitude of the general public. Political "polls" are a step in this direction, but they probably need to be taken more often and should cover a broader array of topics. Manufacturers, too, need to create better ways of discovering public desires. Many future behavioral engineers will probably be involved in developing and maintaining more effective goal-setting and feedback systems in government and industry.

Industrial Psychology

Psychologists have long been employed by business firms and governmental agencies in many capacities. One of the chief functions of these industrial psychologists has been that of personnel selection. A great many intelligence and aptitude tests have been developed that supposedly let psychologists evaluate the knowledge and skills of potential employees. Psychologists also have tried to develop "job descriptions" that would state what abilities were needed to handle a particular position. It was then up to the psychologist to match the person to the job.

Unfortunately, most of the tests and "job descriptions" were based on personality theories that assumed people were relatively unchangeable, and the tests were biased in favor of white, middle-class males with considerable education and verbal skills. As we learn more about how to help people grow and develop, industrial psychologists will probably spend more time *training* personnel than in *selecting* them.

We have also learned that a worker's performance is not dependent entirely on her or his own talents, but on the type of encouragement and feedback the worker's supervisor gives, and on how rewarding and satisfying the job happens to be. In his 1978 book, *How To Improve Human Performance*, Thomas K. Connellan points out that a "systems approach" seems to offer the best hope for the future. In several studies that Connellan reports, workers have been asked what things other than money would increase their motivation to perform well. The majority of workers replied that gaining some control over their own destinies, and being able to participate in the management decision-making process, would be particularly satisfying.

The Hawthorne Effect For almost half a century, industrial psychologists have spoken of the "Hawthorne Effect," meaning that one must be careful in real-life experiments since subjects will often produce the results they think the experimenters want. The effect gets its name from a series of studies performed at the Hawthorne (Chicago) plant where the Western Electric Company manufactures equipment for the Bell Telephone System.

This research, done between 1927 and 1932, was designed to discover how much productivity and morale might be improved when the experimenters made various changes in the work environment.

One room in the Hawthorne plant was set aside for test purposes, and a miniature assembly line was set up there. The experimenters (mostly psychologists) then changed the amount of illumination in the room to see what effect this change might have on assembly-line output. According to the reports these psychologists issued later, productivity increased *no matter what the experimenters did.*

The usual interpretation of the data has been that the subjects knew they were being measured—and hence worked harder—even when the experimenters decreased the illumination or otherwise made conditions worse. Because it was originally assumed that the workers merely tried to do what the experimenters wanted them to do, the Hawthorne Effect has been used as an argument in favor of employing deception in scientific studies involving human subjects.

Very recently, though, psychologist H.M. Parsons has re-examined all of the original data in this study. Incredibly enough, Parsons was able to show that productivity increased *only* in those situations in which the workers could have gotten some feedback as to how well they were performing. Parsons reinterprets the Hawthorne Effect to be just another example of how the outputs of living systems are controlled by informational inputs—in this case, feedback about performance.

Management "By Exception" Few corporations pay much attention either to the type or the amount of feedback that is given employees. In a 1972 survey taken at a large Michigan corporation, almost one-third of the 1,000 employees questioned stated that they never saw their supervisor except when the supervisor came to complain about something the employee was doing. Generally speaking, most US managers and supervisors "manage by exception," which is to say that they tend to ignore appropriate work behaviors and focus on punishing inappropriate or off-target behaviors. But as Thomas Connellan points out, "management by exception" actually tends to punish productive responses and reinforce (with attention) unproductive and disruptive responses.

One of the tasks of industrial psychologists in the future will surely be that of training managers to identify desired outputs and to reward them when they occur. Supervisors must also learn that consulting with their employees, and listening to suggestions from the workers, can be a most potent reinforcer—both for the worker and for corporate profits.

As another example of how behavioral engineers might help corporations, let us look briefly at industrial absenteeism. Thomas Connellan notes that employees who stay away from their jobs cost the US more than $40 billion a year. In some companies, 10 percent of the employees are likely to be absent on a given day. For many years the "cure" for absenteeism has been punishing those workers who had no excuse for their failure to show up at work. Most managers *attributed* the cause of "playing hookey" from work to some innate character flaw in the employees' personalities (see Chapter 26).

In fact, as recent studies show, high absence rates are primarily an index of poor employee morale and of job dissatisfaction. In general, the more a worker dislikes the supervisor and/or the work group, the more likely it is that the worker will have a high absentee rate. When jobs are extremely scarce, threatening to fire an employee may have some effect on absenteeism. When jobs are more plentiful, rather a different solution seems to be called for. Offering workers extra financial incentives for good attendance is sometimes effective, as is trying to reduce "psycho-pollution" in the work environment.

However, as E.E. Lawler and J.R. Hackman showed in 1969, by far the best way to reduce absenteeism is to ask employees what incentives or job changes they want, and then to reward the workers with what they asked for when they do show up for work.

Industrial corporations often count their buildings, machines, and profits as "corporate assets." As psychologist Rensis Likert points out, however, the finest resources available to any company are the skills and talents of its employees. Two of the major jobs for future industrial psychologists will be: to help executives (1) measure these human assets; and (2) treasure these assets by developing work environments that are maximally satisfying to all employees.

Psychology in Your Future

Fifty years ago most Americans were employed in producing "things"— farm products and manufactured goods. Today more than half of all Americans are employed in service occupations—that is, in helping other people or in taking care of people's possessions. As we learn more effective ways of assisting one another, the need for psychological services will grow tremendously. The behavioral sciences have rapidly become one of the most popular undergraduate majors in US colleges and universities. My own estimate is that by the year 2000 at least 10 percent of the US work force will be able to lay claim to the title "psychologist" or "behavioral engineer."

Whether you choose to become a psychologist yourself is, quite naturally, a decision that only you can make. But perhaps reading *Understanding Human Behavior* will have given you some notion of what the future possibilities in psychology will be. And no matter who or what you choose to become, your life will surely be affected by what I call the "Psychological Revolution."

At its best, psychology can offer you the tools to shape your body, your mind, and your social environment somewhat closer to your heart's desire. We do not as yet know what the real limits of human potential are—we know only that people are capable of greater growth and development than we dreamed possible a mere 50 years ago. It is up to you to use the tools available to you, and to plot your own course into the future.

Let me close by thanking you for making me your guide through some of the frontiers of psychology, and by wishing you the happiest of life's journeys.

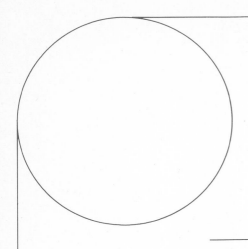

Statistical Appendix

The Red Lady

I was sitting in the student union not long ago, talking with a friend of mine named Gersh, when two young women came over to our table and challenged us to a game of bridge. The two women—Joan and Carol were their names—turned out to be undergraduates. They also turned out to be card sharks, and they beat the socks off Gersh and me. Joan was particularly clever at figuring out how the cards were distributed among the four bridge hands, and hence good at figuring out how to play her own cards to win the most tricks.

One hand I will never forget, not merely because Joan played it so well, but because of what she said afterwards. Joan had bid four spades, and whether she made the contract or not depended on whether she could figure out who had the Queen of Diamonds—Gersh or me. Joan thought about it for a while, then smiled sweetly at Gersh. "I think you've got the Red Lady," she said, and promptly captured Gersh's Queen of Diamonds with her King.

Gersh, who hates to lose, muttered something about "dumb luck."

"No luck to it, really," Joan replied. "I knew you had 5 diamonds, Gersh, while Doc here had only 2. One of you had the Queen, but I didn't know which. But since you had 5 of the 7 missing diamonds, Gersh, the odds were 5 to 2 that you had the Little Old Lady. Simple enough, when you stop to think about it."

The principles underlying statistics are no more difficult to master than are those needed to play bridge.

While Gersh was dealing the next hand with noisy frustration, Joan turned to me. "I know you're a professor, but I don't know what you teach."

"Psychology," I said, picking up my cards for the next hand. The cards were rotten, as usual.

"Oh, you're a psych teacher! That's great," Joan said with a smile. "I really wanted to study psych, but they told me I had to take statistics. I hate math. I'm just no good at figuring out all those complicated equations. So I majored in history instead."

Statistics—A Way of Thinking

I shook my head in amazement at what Joan said. I don't know how many times students have told me much the same thing—they're rotten at mathematics, or they just can't figure out what statistics is all about. But these same students manage to play bridge superbly, or figure out the stock market, or they can tell you the batting averages of every major league baseball player, or how many miles or kilometers per gallon their car gets on unleaded gasoline.

Statistics is not just a weird bunch of mathematics—it's a way of thinking. If you can think well enough to figure out how to play cards, or who is likely to win the next election, or what "grading on the curve" is all about, then you're probably already pretty good at statistics. In fact, you surely use statistics unconsciously or intuitively every minute of your life. If you didn't, you'd be dead or in some institution by now.

Sure, a few of the equations that statisticians throw around get pretty fancy. But don't let that fact discourage you. I've been a psych prof for more than 20 years, I minored in mathematics, but even I don't understand all the equations I see in the statistical and psychological journals. But those "fancy formulas" are usually of interest only to specialists. Forget about them, unless you happen to be a nut about mathematics.

The truth is that you *already know* most of the principles involved in basic statistics if, like Joan, you're willing to stop and think about them. Yet many psych students reject statistics with the same sort of emotionality that they show when somebody offers them fried worms and rattlesnake steak for dinner. Well, worms are rich in protein, and rattlesnake meat is delicious—and safe to eat—if you don't have to catch the snake first. But you may have to overcome some pretty strong emotional prejudices before you're willing to dig in and see what snake meat (or stat) is all about.

Odds and Ends

I've been a gambler all my life, and I really enjoy trying to "psych people out" at the bridge or poker table. So maybe I didn't get conditioned to fear numbers and "odds" the way a lot of people do. But whether you realize it or not, you're a gambler too. And you (like Joan) are pretty good at figuring out all kinds of odds and *probabilities*. Every time you cross the street, you gamble that the odds are "safely" in your favor. Each time you drive your car through a green light without slowing down, you gamble that some "odd" driver won't run the red light and hit you broadside. Every time you study for a true-false exam, you're gambling that you can learn enough to do better than somebody who refuses to study and who just picks the answers randomly. And every time you go out with somebody on a date, you're gambling that you can predict that person's future behavior (on the date) from observing the things that the person has done in the past.

So you're a gambler, too, even if you don't think of yourself as being one. But if you're going to gamble, wouldn't it be helpful to know something about odds and probabilities? Because if you know what the odds are, you can often do a much better job of achieving whatever ends or goals you have in mind.

One way or another, almost everything in statistics is based on *probability theory*. And, as luck would have it, probability theory got its start some

300 years ago when some French gamblers got worried about what the pay-offs should be in a crap (dice) game. So the gamblers, who were no dummies, hired two brilliant French mathematicians to figure out the probabilities for them. From the work of these two French geniuses came the theory that allows the casinos in Las Vegas and Atlantic City to earn hundreds of millions of dollars every year, that lets the insurance companies earn even more by betting on how long people will live, and that lets psychologists and psychiatrists employ the mental tests that label some people as being "normal" and other people as being "abnormal."

The Odds in Favor

If you want to see why Joan was so good at playing bridge, get a deck of cards and pull out the 2, 3, 4, 5 ,6, 7, and Queen of Diamonds. Turn them face down on a table and shuffle them around so you won't know which card is which. Now try to pick out the Queen just by looking at the back of the cards.

If the deck is "honest" (unmarked), what are the odds that you will pick the Red Lady instead of the 2, 3, 4, 5, 6, or 7? As you can see, the odds are exactly 1 in 7. If you want to be fancy about all this, you can write an equation (which is what Joan did in her mind) as follows:

The probability (p) of picking the Queen (Q) is 1 out of 7, therefore

$$p\mathrm{Q} = \tfrac{1}{7}$$

Now shuffle the cards again, place them face down on the table, and then randomly select 2 of the cards and put them on one side of the table, and the remaining 5 on the other side of the table. Now, what are the odds that the Queen is in the stack of 5 cards (Gersh's bridge hand), and what are the odds that the Queen is in the stack of 2 cards (my bridge hand)?

Well, you already know that the probability that any 1 card will be the Queen is $\tfrac{1}{7}$. I have 2 cards, therefore, I have two chances at getting the Queen, and the equation reads:

$$p\mathrm{Q}\ (\mathrm{Me}) = \tfrac{1}{7} + \tfrac{1}{7} = \tfrac{2}{7}$$

Gersh had 5 cards, so his probability equation is:

$$p\mathrm{Q}\ (\mathrm{Gersh}) = \tfrac{1}{7} + \tfrac{1}{7} + \tfrac{1}{7} + \tfrac{1}{7} + \tfrac{1}{7} = \tfrac{5}{7}$$

So if you dealt out the 7 cards randomly 70 times, Gersh would have the Queen about 50 times, and I would have the Queen about 20 times. No wonder Joan wins at bridge! When she assumed that Gersh had the Queen, she didn't have a sure thing, but the odds were surely in her favor.

Outcomes and Incomes

Now let's look at something familiar to everyone, the true-false examination. Suppose that you go to a history class one day, knowing there will be a test, but the teacher throws you a curve. For the exam you get is written in Chinese, or Greek, or some other language you simply can't read a word of. The test has 20 questions, and it's obviously of the true-false variety. But since you can't read it, all you do is guess. What exam score do you think you'd most likely get—0, 10, or 20?

Maybe you'd deserve a 0, since you couldn't read the exam. But I'm sure you realize intuitively that you'd most likely get a score of about 10. Why?

Well, what are the *odds* of your guessing any single question right, if it's a true-false exam?

If you said, "Fifty percent chance of being right," you're thinking clearly. (See what I mean about statistics being a way of thinking?)

The probability (p) of your getting the first question right (R_1) is 50 percent, or $\frac{1}{2}$. So we write an equation that says:

$$pR_1 = \frac{1}{2}$$

The probability of your getting the first question wrong (W_1) is also 50 percent, or $\frac{1}{2}$. So we write another equation:

$$pW_1 = \frac{1}{2}$$

Furthermore, we can now say that, on the first or any other equation, the

$$pR + pW = \frac{1}{2} + \frac{1}{2} = 1$$

Which is a fancy way of saying that whenever you guess the answer on a true-false exam, you have to be either right or wrong, because those are the only two *outcomes* possible.

Now, suppose we look at the first two questions on the test. What is the probability that you will get *both* of them right, if you are just guessing at the answers?

Well, what outcomes are possible? You could miss both questions (W_1W_2), or you could get them both right (R_1R_2), or you could get the first answer right and the second answer wrong (R_1W_2), or you could get the first one wrong and the second right (W_1R_2).

Thus, there are 4 different outcomes, and since you would be guessing at the right answer on both questions, these 4 outcomes are *equally likely to occur*. Only 1 of the 4 outcomes (R_1R_2) is the one we're interested in, so the odds of your getting both questions right is $\frac{1}{4}$.

$$pR_1R_2 = \frac{1}{4}$$
$$pW_1W_2 = \frac{1}{4}$$
$$pR_1W_2 = \frac{1}{4}$$
$$pW_1R_2 = \frac{1}{4}$$

and

$$pR_1R_2 + pW_1W_2 + pR_1W_2 + pW_1R_2 = \frac{1}{4} + \frac{1}{4} + \frac{1}{4} + \frac{1}{4} = 1$$

In a sense, getting both questions right is like selecting the Queen of Diamonds when it is 1 of 4 cards face down on the table in front of you. In both cases, you have 4 equally likely outcomes, so your chances of getting the Queen (or being right on both answers) is 1 out of 4, or $\frac{1}{4}$.

As you can see, if you're taking an exam, playing bridge, or trying to add to your income by buying a lottery ticket, it will surely pay you to consider all the possible outcomes.

Actually, we can figure the odds of your answering the first 2 questions correctly in a much simpler way. We simply multiply the odds of your getting the first question right (pR_1) by the odds of your getting the second question right (pR_2):

$$pR_1R_2 = pR_1 \times pR_2 = \frac{1}{2} \times \frac{1}{2} = \frac{1}{4} = 25\%$$

Maybe you can see, too, that the odds of your getting both answers *wrong* would be exactly the same:

$$pW_1W_2 = pW_1 \times pW_2 = \frac{1}{2} \times \frac{1}{2} = \frac{1}{4} = 25\%$$

If the exam had just three questions to it, the odds of your getting all the answers right by chance alone (that is, by guessing) would be:

$$pR_1R_2R_3 = pR_1 \times pR_2 \times pR_3 = \frac{1}{2} \times \frac{1}{2} \times \frac{1}{2} = \frac{1}{8} = 12.5\%$$

To put the matter another way, on a 3-question exam, there are 8 different outcomes:

$$R_1R_2R_3$$
$$R_1R_2W_3$$
$$R_1W_2R_3$$
$$R_1W_2W_3$$
$$W_1R_2R_3$$
$$W_1R_2W_3$$
$$W_1W_2R_3$$
$$W_1W_2W_3$$

"THE ABNORMAL CURVES"

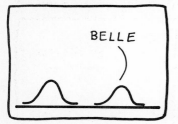

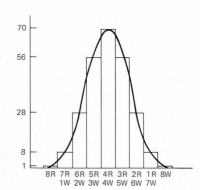

Since only 1 of these 8 possible outcomes is the one you want ($R_1R_2R_3$), the odds in your favor are only 1 in 8.

If the test had 4 true-false questions, there would be 16 different outcomes—twice as many as if the test had but three questions. These outcomes would range from $R_1R_2R_3R_4$, $R_1R_2R_3W_4$ . . . . all the way to $W_1W_2W_3R_4$ and $W_1W_2W_3W_4$. If there are 16 different outcomes, only one of which is "all answers right" or $R_1R_2R_3R_4$, what would be the odds of your guessing all the answers right on a 4-question true-false test?

(If you said,"1 in 16," congratulations!)

Now, let's take a giant leap.

If the exam had 10 questions, the odds of your getting all 10 answers right by guessing would be:

$$pR_1R_2R_3R_4R_5R_6R_7R_8R_9R_{10} =$$
$$\tfrac{1}{2} \times \tfrac{1}{2} \times \tfrac{1}{2} \times \tfrac{1}{2} \times \tfrac{1}{2} \times \tfrac{1}{2} \times \tfrac{1}{2} \times \tfrac{1}{2} \times \tfrac{1}{2} \times \tfrac{1}{2} = \tfrac{1}{1024}$$

So if you took the exam 1024 times and guessed randomly at the answers each time, just *once* in 1024 times would you expect to get a score of 0, and just *once* in 1024 times would you expect to get a score of 10.

Now, at last, we can answer the question we asked you a few paragraphs back: If you took a 20-question exam on which you had to guess at each answer, what exam score do you think you'd most likely get—0, 10, or 20?

Well, what are the odds that you'd get a score of flat 0? In fact, the odds are astronomically against you, just as they are astronomically against your getting a score of 20 right. In either case, the probability would be:

$$pW_{1-10} = pR_{1-10} = \tfrac{1}{2} \times \tfrac{1}{2} \times \tfrac{1}{2} \ldots (20 \text{ times!}) = 1{,}048{,}576 \text{ to } 1!$$

If the exam had 8 questions on it, the histogram or bar graph would look something like the one in Fig. A.1.

Fig. A.1. A bar graph showing the distribution of "right answers" expected when taking an 8-item true-false exam.

Notice that we've added a curve to connect up the bars. Once you get to 8 or 9 questions, curves are easier to handle than are bar graphs (see Fig. A.2). So let's draw a curve for a 10-question exam:

Statistical Appendix

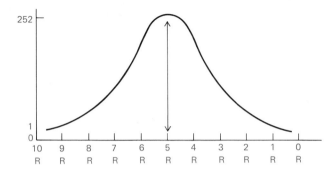

Fig. A.2. A bell-shaped curve showing the distribution of "right answers" expected when taking a 10-item true-false exam.

As we mentioned earlier, the number of possible outcomes in a 10-question exam is 1024. So the odds of getting all 10 questions right by just guessing ("by chance alone") would be 1 in 1024. Not very good odds.

But the probability of your getting 5 questions right and 5 wrong would be 252 in 1024, or about 25 percent. And the odds of your getting 4, 5, or 6 questions right would be well above 60 percent! That makes sense, because just looking at the curve you can see that better than 60 percent of the possible outcomes are bunched up right in the middle of the curve.

Descriptive Statistics

The curve we've just drawn is the world-famous, ever-popular "bell-shaped curve." In fact, the curve describes a *random distribution of scores* or outcomes. That is, the curve describes the outcomes you'd expect when students are forced to guess, more or less at random, which answers on a true-false exam are correct. Naturally, if the exam were written in clear English, and if the students knew most of the material they were being examined on, the curve or *distribution of scores* would look quite different.

There are many sorts of "outcomes" that fit the bell-shaped curve rather nicely. For example, if you randomly selected 1000 adult US males and measured their heights, the results you'd get would come very close to matching the bell-shaped curve. Which is to say that there would be a few very short men, a few very tall men, but most would have heights around 5'10" (178 centimeters). The same bell-shaped curve would fit the distribution of heights of 1000 adult women selected at random—except that the "middle" or peak of the bell-shaped curve would be about 5'5" (166 centimeters) (see Fig. A.3).

Measures of Central Tendency

As we noted in Chapter 23, IQ tests are constructed so that the scores for any age group will approximate a bell-shaped curve. In this case, the peak or "middle" of the distribution of IQ scores will be almost precisely at 100.

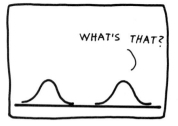

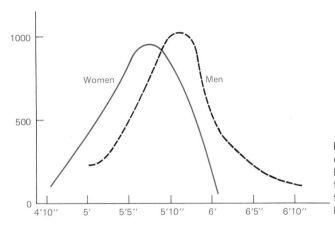

Fig. A.3. A bell-shaped curve showing the distribution of heights of a thousand men and a thousand women selected at random.

Statistical Appendix

A very few individuals would have IQ scores below 50, a very few would have scores above 150. But some two-thirds of the scores would fall between 84 and 116 (see Fig. 24.3).

Why this bulge in the middle as far as IQ scores are concerned? Well, think back for a moment to the true-false test we were discussing earlier that had 10 questions on it. There are 1024 possible outcomes. If you wanted to get all 10 questions right, there was only one way you could answer the 10 questions—all had to be correct. But there were 256 ways in which you could answer the questions to get a score of 5—right in the middle.

There is only one way you can earn a top score on an IQ test—you've got to answer all the questions rapidly and precisely the way the people who constructed the test say is "right." But there are thousands of different ways you can answer the questions on the usual IQ test to get a "middle score," namely an IQ between 84 and 116.

In a similar vein, there are precious few ways in which you can earn a million dollars, but there are dozens and dozens of ways in which you can earn between $10,000 and $15,000 a year. So if we selected 1000 adult US citizens at random, asked them what their incomes were, and then "took an average," what kind of curve (distribution of incomes) do you think we'd get?

Whenever we measure people psychologically, biologically, socially, intellectually, or economically, we often generate a distribution of outcomes that looks very much like a bell-shaped curve. Each person in the world is unique, it's true. But it is equally true that, on any given *single* measuring scale (height, weight, grade-point average, income), most people's scores will be somewhere in the *middle* of the range of possible outcomes.

Psychologists have a variety of tools for measuring the "middle" of any curve or distribution of outcomes. These techniques are often called *measures of central tendency*, which is a fancy way of saying that these techniques allow us to measure the center or midpoint of any distribution of scores or outcomes.

Mean, Median, Mode

1. *The Mean.* The *mean* is simply the statistical "average" of all the scores or outcomes involved. When you figure your grade-point average (GPA) for any semester, you usually multiply your grade in each course by the number of credit hours, add up the totals, and divide by the number of hours credit you are taking. Your GPA is actually the *mean* or mathematical average of all your grades (see Table A.1).

2. *The Median.* Since the mean is a mathematical average, it sometimes gives very funny results. For example, according to recent government figures, the "average" US family was made up of about 4.47 people. Have you ever known a family that had 4.47 people in it? For another example, if

Table A.1
Table of Grade Point Averages

Course	Hours Credit	Grade	Hour × Grade
History	3	A	3 × 4 = 12
Psychology	4	A	4 × 4 = 16
Mathematics	4	C	4 × 2 = 8
Spanish	4	B	4 × 3 = 12
TOTALS 15	15		

GPA = 48/15 = 3.2

you got two As and two Cs one semester, your average or "mean" grade would be a B. Yet you didn't get a B in any of the courses you took.

There are times when it makes more sense to figure the exact *midpoint score* or outcome, rather than figuring out the *average* score. At such times, pyschologists often use the *median*, which is the score that's in the precise middle of the distribution—just as the "median" of an expressway is the area right down the middle of the highway.

If some semester you got two As, one B, and you flunked two courses completely, your *mean* grade (GPA) would be slightly better than a C. But your *median* or middle grade would be a B, because it is right smack in the middle of the five grades you got. The median is often used as a "measure of central tendency" when a distribution has one or two extreme scores in it. For instance, if 9 people earn $1 a year, and a tenth earns $100,000, what is the *mean* income of these 10 people? About $10,001 a year, which is a misleading statistic, to say the least. However, the *median* income is $1, which describes the actual income of the *majority* of the group somewhat better than does the mean of $10,001.

3. *The Mode*. The word *mode* is defined in the dictionary as "the prevailing fashion or most popular custom or style." When we are talking about distributions of scores or outcomes, *mode* means the most popular score. That is, the mode is the highest point (or points) on the curve. If the distribution has two points that are equally high, then there are two scores that are *modal*, and we can call the curve *bi-modal* (having two modes).

Skewedness

If the distribution of scores is more or less bell-shaped, then the mean, median, and mode usually fall at the same point on the curve. But not all curves do us the favor of being so regular in shape. For example, suppose you were interested in whether a particular teacher—Dr. Johnson—started and ended her classes on time. To find out, you take a very accurate watch with you all semester long and make a scientific study of Dr. Johnson's behavior.

During the term, let's say, there are supposed to be 50 lectures by Dr. Johnson. So the number of possible start-time scores or outcomes will be 50. For the most part, Dr. Johnson begins on time, but occasionally she starts a minute or two early, and sometimes she's a minute or two late. Now and again, she is fairly tardy in getting to class, and once she didn't show up at all. But she *never* begins a class more than two minutes early. If you put all of her starting times on a graph, it would look something like the curve on the left side of Fig. A.4. If you plotted all her closing time scores on a similar graph, it would look like the curve on the right in Fig. A.4.

The term we use to describe these curves is *skewedness*, which means they are "slanted" or "pushed out of shape." In the starting-time example, the curve slants out far to the right-hand side, so we say that the curve is "skewed to the right." The other curve has a tail that slants out to the left, so the curve is "skewed to the left." As is the case in many distributions where the scores are measures of reaction times or beginning times, the mean, median, and mode are fairly different.

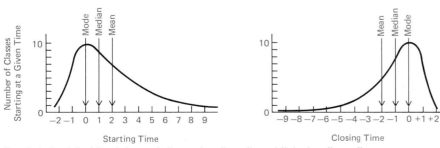

Fig. A.4. A plot of Dr. Johnson's "opening times" and "closing times."

Range and Variation

There are two more important concepts we have to get out of the way before we can finish our discussion of *descriptive statistics*—which is to say, statistics that measure or describe something. The first concept is the *range* of possible scores or outcomes; the second is the *variability* of the scores. The first concept is easy to understand, but the second will take some careful thought on your part.

What is the *range* of possible scores on a 10-item "fill in the blanks" test? From 0 to 10, of course. And since you can't guess as easily on this type of test as on a true-false examination, you can't really tell ahead of time what the class average is likely to be. The range on a 100-item test would be from 0 to 100—and again, you have no way of knowing before you take the test what the "mean" or average score is likely to be.

Let's suppose that you took a 10-item "fill-in-the-blanks" exam and got a score of 8 right, which also turned out to be the mean or average score for the whole class. Then you took a 100-item "fill-in-the-blanks" test and again you got a score of 8, which again turned out to be the class average. What does knowing the *range* of possible scores tell you about the level of difficulty of the two tests? Wouldn't you say that the 100-item test was considerably more difficult, even though the class average was the same on both tests?

Now, let's add one more dimension. Suppose that on the 10-item examination, *everybody in class* got a score of 8! There would be no *variation* at all in these scores, since none of the scores *deviated* (were different from) the mean. But suppose on the 100-item "fill-in-the-blanks" exam, about 95 percent of the class got scores of flat zero, you got an 8, and a few "aces" got scores above 85. Your score of 8 would still be the *mean* (but not the median or mode). But the *deviation* of the rest of the scores would be tremendous. Even though you scored right at the mean on both tests, the fact that you were better than 95 percent of the class on the 100-item test might well be very pleasing to you.

The variation or variability of test scores is simply a measure of *how spread out across the range* the scores actually are. Thus the variability of a distribution of scores is a very important item to know if you're going to evaluate how you perform in relation to anybody else who's taken the test.

The Standard Deviation

In Chapter 24, when we were discussing the sexual problems of Mr. and Mrs. Smith, we noted that the "average" number of sexual outlets desired by young, white, married men in the US was about 3 to 4 per week. What we meant, of course, was that the mean number of outlets was about 3.5 or so. But as Kinsey found, the "outlet curve" is far from being a perfect "bell." There are many men who experience less than one orgasm a week, while others "average" 20 to 30 a week most of their adult lives. The *range* of scores (outlets) runs from 0 to more than 30, but the mean is much closer to 0 than to 30. Thus the tail of the curve runs out far to the right, and the curve is skewed to the right.

If you know the range of scores, plus the mean, median, and mode, you can usually get a fairly good notion of what shape the curve might take. Why? Because these two bits of information tell you something about how the scores are *distributed*. If the mean, median, and mode are almost the same, and they fall right at the center of the range, then the distribution curve must be "vaguely" bell-shaped, or regular in shape.

But why do we say "vaguely" bell-shaped? In Chapter 27, we discussed the distribution of scores on an attitude questionnaire in two different groups. In the homogeneous group, the range of scores was very small (see Fig. A.5):

In the heterogeneous group, the range was much larger (see Fig. A.6). The means for the two distributions were the same, and if the groups had

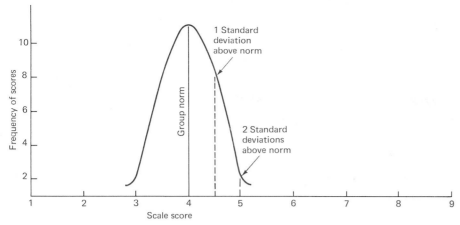

Fig. A.5. A distribution of attitude scores for a homogeneous group.

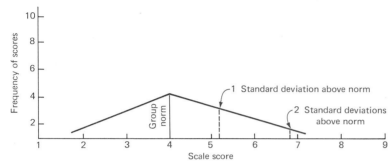

Fig. A.6. A distribution of attitude scores for a heterogeneous group.

been large enough, we might even have found that the ranges of the two distributions were the same. However, in the homogeneous group, the scores were all bunched up close to the mean, while in the heterogeneous group, the scores were broadly *dispersed,* or spread out. We found that we needed a concept we called the *standard deviation* to describe the *dispersion of scores* across the range (or around the mean). The larger the standard deviation, the more widely the scores vary around the mean (and the more heterogeneous the group probably is). The smaller the standard deviation, the more bunched up the scores are around the mean (and the more homogeneous the group probably is).

We can now define the *standard deviation* as a statistical term meaning the variability of scores in a distribution.

There are a variety of mathematical formulas for figuring out such statistics as the standard deviation. Once upon a time, students were required to memorize these formulas and grind out statistical analyses using nothing more than their brains (and perhaps their fingers and toes to count on). Nowadays, however, even cheap pocket calculators will figure out the standard deviation of a distribution of scores almost instantaneously (if you input the right data in the first place). If you wish to learn one of the formulas for calculating the standard deviation—or if you are required to do so—you will find them in many places, including the *Student Manual* that accompanies this book.

However, as we said earlier, statistics is more a way of thinking than it is a bunch of fancy formulas. *Descriptive statistics* are short-hand ways of describing large bunches of data. They are "thought tools" that let you think about the world in convenient symbols.

Let's now see how you can use "descriptive" statistics to help you *make inferences* or draw conclusions about the data you're mulling over in your mind.

Inferential Statistics

Whenever you test a hunch or a scientific hypothesis, you often are hunting for *reliable* differences between two groups of subjects or between two sets of data. Again, there are *many* different formulas for figuring out how reliable (or important) the group differences really are. But one of the simplest—and most often used—is the standard deviation. By convention, scientists accept differences as being "real" if the means of the two groups depart by 2 or more standard deviations from each other.

We pick the figure 2 standard deviations for a very understandable reason. If on the bell-shaped curve shown in Fig. 24.3 we measure out from the mean a distance of 2 standard deviations, we will take into account about 95 percent of all the IQ scores described by the curve. Any score falling outside of this distance will be there *by chance alone* less than 5 percent of the time. So the odds of your getting an IQ score of 132 are but 5 in 100, or 1 in 20. Since these odds are pretty impressive, we can assume that your score didn't occur "by chance alone," and thus the score suggests you are "brighter than average."

If you gave IQ tests to the incoming freshman class at some college and found that the *mean* IQ score of the group was 132, you could be very sure that the *group as a whole* was brighter than the average population for which the test was constructed. Quite naturally, if the mean IQ score for the freshman class was 148, that would put the group average some 3 standard deviations from the mean of the population—and you'd be even more confident that this was a very intelligent group of people.

To summarize, the greater the standard deviation, the greater the odds are that the score (or average score of a group) didn't occur "by chance alone."

Differences between Groups   Now, suppose we compare the IQ scores of two people, Bill and Mary. Bill has an IQ score of 84, which is exactly 1 standard deviation from the mean of 100. He might have "below average" intelligence, true. But he's so close to the mean that we might as well call him "average" since he might have been overly tired when he took the test. (In fact, even if his *true* IQ was 100, Bill would get a *measured* score of between 84 and 100 about one-third of the time that he took the test. Look at Fig. 24.3 carefully and see if you can figure out why this would be the case.)

Mary has an IQ score of 116, which is exactly 1 standard deviation above the mean. But again, her score isn't all that different from the mean, so we could (technically speaking) say that she too has "average intelligence." (She too would be expected to get a *measured* score between 100 and 116 one-third of the time if her *true* IQ was 100. And, like Bill, she would also get a *measured* score between 84 and 100 a third of the time.)

Since both Bill and Mary have IQ scores that "vary" from the mean but 1 standard deviation, their scores of 84 and 116 don't differ reliably from each other, right?

Wrong! (As if you didn't know that intuitively anyhow.)

Bill's score differs from Mary's by *2* standard deviations, thus the odds are at least 20 to 1 that Mary's *true* IQ score is significantly higher than Bill's. (And wouldn't you have been willing to make a small wager that was the case the moment you knew what their IQ scores were?)

Significant Differences

Whenever you hear scientists say that their "findings are significant at the 5 percent level," you can translate this to mean that their groups differed by about 2 standard deviations. In general, if the odds are not at least 20 to 1 in support of the hunch you're trying to prove, you probably shouldn't use the word "significant" in describing your results.

There are many different tests or formulas that you could use for calculating whether the results of an experiment were significant or not.

Among the best-known of such statistical devices are the *t-test* and the *critical ratio*. Should you ever need to employ one of these tests, you'd do well to read about them in a text such as William L. Hays' *Statistics for the Social Sciences*, the second edition of which was published by Holt, Rinehart and Winston in 1973.

In fact, most of these tests for significance are based on the bell-shaped curve and the notion of random variation around a mean. Thus the *t-test* and the critical ratio will suggest that there are significant differences between two groups (or distribution of scores) if:

1. The number of cases or subjects in each group is large.

2. The standard deviations of both distributions are small and fairly similar to each other.

3. The means of the distributions differ by 2 or more standard deviations.

Correlation Coefficients

In several chapters of this book, we have mentioned the term *correlation* to suggest that two events or traits were somehow connected or associated with each other. The mathematics underlying correlations are not too difficult to understand. However, the correlation concept itself has a "problem" buried deep within it that makes it one of the most misunderstood and misused ideas in all of human experience. We'll come back to this problem in just a moment. First, let's look at how one figures out if two sets of scores are correlated.

As we noted in Chapter 23, there is a strong relationship between IQ scores and grades in school, and for a very good reason. IQ tests are usually devised so that they will predict academic success, and the items on most such tests are juggled around until the final score does in fact yield the expected predictions. Thus if we give intelligence tests to all incoming freshmen, and we know their grades at the end of their first collegiate year, we should expect to find some relationship between these measures (see Table A.2).

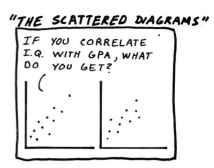

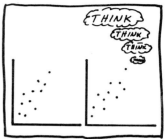

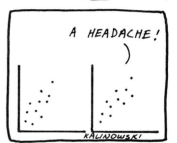

"THE SCATTERED DIAGRAMS"

IF YOU CORRELATE I.Q. WITH GPA, WHAT DO YOU GET?

THINK THINK THINK

A HEADACHE!

KALINOWSKI

Table A.2
Relationship between IQ Score and GPA

		Entrance Test IQ Score	Grade Point Average (GPA)
Ann		152	3.91
Bill		145	3.46
Carol		133	2.77
Dick		128	2.35
Elmer		112	1.51
	Σ (Sum of)	670	14.00
	Mean	134	2.80
	SD	15.54	0.94

Just by looking at the rank orderings of these scores, you can tell that a strong correlation exists between the two distributions. If we plotted the data on what is called a *scatter diagram*, we'd get pretty much a straight line (see Fig. A.7). (A scatter diagram shows how the scores for each subject are *scattered*, or distributed, across the graph or diagram.)

If we reversed the scores, so that Ann got an IQ score of 152 but a GPA of 1.51, Bill got an IQ score of 145 and a GPA of 2.35, and so forth, we'd get a scatter diagram that looked like Fig. A.8.

Generally speaking, the closer the scatter diagram comes to being a straight line tilted to the right or left as these are, the higher the correlation between the two variables (scores).

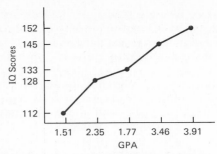

Fig. A.7. A scatter diagram showing the positive correlation between IQ scores and grade point averages.

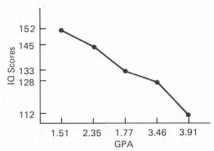

Fig. A.8. A scatter diagram showing a negative correlation between IQ scores and grade point averages.

There are several formulas for figuring out the *mathematical* correlation between two sets of scores that we needn't go into here. All of these formulas yield what is called a *correlation coefficient*, which is merely a "coefficient" or number between +1 and −1.

A correlation coefficient of +1 indicates that the two sets of scores are *perfectly correlated in a positive way*. Which is to say, the person who got the highest score on one test got the highest on the second test, the person who got the second highest score on one test got the second highest on the other test, and so forth.

A correlation coefficient of −1 indicates that the two sets of scores are *perfectly correlated in a negative way*. Which is to say that the person who got the *highest* score on the first test got the *lowest* score on the second, the person who got the second *highest* score on the first test got the second *lowest* score on the other test, and so forth.

A correlation coefficient of +.75 suggests there is a strong (but not perfect) association between the two sets of scores. A coefficient of −.75 would indicate the same strength of association, but in a negative direction.

A correlation coefficient of 0 (or close to it) tells you that there is little or no significant connection between the two sets of scores.

Uses and Abuses of Correlation Coefficients

The ability to make quick correlations is just about the most useful trait that your mind has available to it. Whether you realize it or not, your brain is so built that it automatically makes connections between incoming stimuli. Think back to the discussion of Pavlovian conditioning you read about in Chapter 15. When you ring a bell, and then give food to a dog, the animal's brain soon comes to associate the sound of the bell with the appearance of the food. When the dog eventually salivates to the sound of the bell *before* food arrives, its nervous system has calculated a crude sort of "correlation coefficient" between the onset of the bell and the presentation of the food. Since (in the experiment) the two events *always* occur together, the correlation coefficient of the two events would be close to +1. Thus the dog can anticipate (predict) the stimulus input "food" as soon as the stimulus input "bell" has occurred.

If dogs could talk, how might they explain their conditioned responses? Don't you imagine that Pavlov's beasts might explain matters in *causal* terms? That is, might not a well-conditioned canine remark that the bell has "magic powers" that cause the food to appear?

As peculiar as this notion may sound to you, evidence in its favor comes from some real-life experiments. In several studies, bell-food conditioned animals have later been trained to turn on the bell themselves by pressing a bar in their cages. What do you think the animals do when they become hungry?

As we mentioned earlier, the concept of correlation has a problem buried in it. The problem is this: We too often assume that if event A is correlated with event B, then A must somehow *cause* the appearance of B. This "causal assumption" gets us into a lot of trouble. For example, does the sound of the bell really *cause* the food to appear? Do high IQ scores really *cause* a student to get good grades? As you can see, the answer in both cases must be a resounding *no*.

Scores on an IQ test don't cause much of anything (except, perhaps, favorable reactions from college admissions committees). The underlying trait of intelligence presumably causes both the high IQ score and the good grades. Thus intelligence is responsible for the correlation between the two events, just as Pavlov's desires were responsible for the correlation between the bell and the food.

Worse than this, there are times when highly significant correlations may seriously mislead us. Consider the writers working for a large newspaper. There will be lots of beginning reporters who churn out a massive amount of copy each day, most of it about fairly trivial events. And there are a very few senior reporters who write but a few hundred words daily (if that). Now, who gets paid the most money? If we ran a correlation between number of words written daily and salary per word, wouldn't we find a highly significant but *negative* correlation? Given this correlation coefficient, might we not be tempted to tell beginning journalists that, if they wanted a raise in salary, they ought to write *less?* And whose "problem" would it be if they followed our advice and got fired?

At their very best, correlations can help us predict future stimulus inputs and give us clues as to what the underlying causal connections among these inputs might be. However, in daily life, we too often misuse correlations. If you want to make your psychology teacher very happy indeed, say "Correlations don't determine causes" over and over again— until you're conditioned to believe it!

Experimental Design

Why statistics? Or, to phrase the question more precisely, is there any correlation between knowing something about stat and knowing something about yourself and the people around you?

As it happens, the difference between knowing stat and not knowing it is highly significant. All of your future life you will be performing "little experiments" in which you try to psych out the people around you. It's likely (at the 5 percent level) that you will probe your environment better if you know how to interpret the results of your informal experimentation. If you are introspective, an understanding of correlations and conditioning could help tell you some very important facts about how you have acquired many of your values and attitudes. And, if nothing else, understanding what a bell-shaped curve is all about could save you a lot of money should you ever happen to visit Las Vegas.

The second reason for imposing statistics on you, willy-nilly, is that you may wish to take further courses in psychology. If you do, you may be encouraged (or even required) to perform one or more controlled experiments, either in a laboratory or in a real-life setting. Therefore, you might as well learn the first law of statistics right now:

Your statistical inferences are never better than your experimental design will allow.

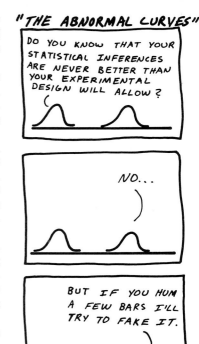

"THE ABNORMAL CURVES"

DO YOU KNOW THAT YOUR STATISTICAL INFERENCES ARE NEVER BETTER THAN YOUR EXPERIMENTAL DESIGN WILL ALLOW?

NO...

BUT IF YOU HUM A FEW BARS I'LL TRY TO FAKE IT.

KALINOWSKI

The topic of how to design a good experiment has filled many a thick textbook, and there's little sense in subjecting you to more grief than we have already. What we can say is this: The secret of good experimentation lies in *controlling variables*. If you want to pick a random sample of people for a political poll, make sure your sample is *really random*. Just asking a few of your friends what they think won't do, because your method of choice was highly biased, and hence not random at all.

Several times in this book we've mentioned the concept of a "control group" that some scientist(s) used in an experiment. There probably is no more powerful way of making sure your results are reliable than by incorporating as many groups as possible in your study—one group to *control* for any factor (variable) that might influence the results of your study.

But, most important of all, if you must run a scientific study, think it through carefully before you do. Then you can design your study as intelligently as possible so that the data you gather will be easy to analyze, and so your expected results will be as truthful and as reliable as you can make them. Scientists are probably about as honest and as open in their work as any professional group can be. And yet all of us might unconsciously bias our results if we feel passionately about the subject we're studying. So we should use control group after control group—just to make sure that we screen out our unconscious biases before they can affect our results.

Anything that you love, or that is important enough to you, is worth working hard for—and worth being entirely honest about. Science is an art form, just as making music is. Some musicians are superb, while others are only mediocre. But in general, the musicians who love their work the most—and who practice and study as much as they can—make the most beautiful music. The same sort of things may be said of scientists.

Birds make music, as do whales and monkeys. Only human beings run experiments, control for bias, select their subjects randomly, and perform statistical analyses. Being a scientist is thus one of the most *humane* occupations you can have, because we all need reliable and valid data about how things are now so we can make things (including ourselves) better in the future.

As it happens, I love science. To me, it is a "fun game," a way of wisdom, and a means of achieving my own goals of self-actualization. My parting hope is that you will someday come to appreciate this art form as much as I do. And if the scientific love bug does bite you, perhaps then and only then will you come to enjoy statistics and experimental design as much as most scientists do.

I wish you the best of luck!

(Meanwhile, Gersh and I are reading several books on probability theory as applied to bridge. Joan and Carol, you'd better watch out!)

Selected Bibliography

Chapter 1

Dyal, J.A., W.C. Corning, and D.M. Willows. *Readings in psychology: The search for alternatives*, 3rd ed. New York: McGraw-Hill, 1975.

English, H.B., and H.C. English. *A comprehensive dictionary of psychological and psychoanalytical terms*. New York: McKay, 1958.

Goldenson, R.M. *The encyclopedia of human behavior*. Garden City, N.Y.: Doubleday, 1970.

Harriman, P.L. *Handbook of psychological terms*. Totowa, N.J.: Littlefield, Adams, 1965.

Kimble, D.P. *Psychology as a biological science*. Pacific Palisades, Calif.: Goodyear, 1973.

Psychology Today, *Psychosources*. New York: Bantam, 1973.

Trotter, R.J., and J.V. McConnell. *Psychology: The human science*. New York: Holt, Rinehart and Winston, 1978.

Chapter 2

Denenberg, W.H., J. Barbanati, G. Sherman, D.A. Yutzey, and R. Kaplan. "Infantile stimulation induces brain lateralization in rats," *Science*, 201, 1978, 1150–1151.

Corballis, M.C., and I.L. Beale. *The psychology of left and right*. Hillsdale, N.J.: Erlbaum, 1976.

Gazzaniga, M.S. "The split brain in man," *Scientific American*, 217, 1967.

Leukel, Francis. *Introduction to physiological psychology*, 3rd ed. St. Louis: Mosby, 1976.

Milner, P.M. *Physiological psychology*. New York: Holt, Rinehart and Winston, 1970.

Ornstein, Robert. "The split and whole brain," *Human Nature*, 1(5), 1978, 76–83.

Pribram, K.H. *Languages of the brain: Experimental paradoxes and principles in neuropsychology*. Englewood Cliffs, N.J.: Prentice-Hall, 1971.

Salamy, A. "Commisural transmission: Maturational changes in humans," *Science*, 200, 1978, 1409–1410.

Sperry, R.W. "Hemisphere disconnection and unity in conscious awareness," *American Psychologist*, 23, 1968, 733–744.

Sperry, R.W. "Left-brain, right-brain," *Saturday Review*, August 9, 1975, pp. 30–33.

Chapter 3

Aserinsky, E., and N. Kleitman. "Regularly occurring periods of eye motility and concomitant phenomena during sleep," *Science*, 118, 1953, 273.

Barchas, J.D., H. Akil, G.R. Elliott, R.B. Holman, and S.J. Watson. "Behavioral neurochemistry: Neuroregulators and behavioral states," *Science*, 200, 1978, 964–973.

Blum, Kenneth, ed. *Alcohol and opiates: Neurochemical and behavioral mechanisms*. New York: Academic Press, 1977.

Byck, Robert, ed. *Cocaine papers: Sigmund Freud (Notes on the Freud papers by Anna Freud)*. New York: New American Library, 1974.

Cohen, Sidney. "Marijuana as medicine," *Psychology Today*, April, 1978, pp. 60–73.

Dement, W.C. "A new look at the third state of existence," *Stanford M.D.*, 8, 2–8, 1968–1969.

Furst, Peter T. *Hallucinogens and culture*. San Francisco: Chandler & Sharp, 1976.

Grinspoon, L., and P. Hedblum. *The speed culture: Amphetamine use and abuse in America*. Cambridge, Mass.: Harvard University Press, 1975.

Hartmann, E.L. *The functions of sleep*. New Haven, Conn.: Yale University Press, 1973.

Kamiya, J. "Conscious control of brain waves," *Psychology Today*, 1, 1968, 56–60.

Marx, J.L. "Analgesia: How the body inhibits pain perception," *Science*, 195, 1977, 471–473.

Matheson, D.W., and M.A. Davison. *The behavioral effects of drugs*. New York: Holt, Rinehart and Winston, 1972.

Meddis, Ray. *The sleep instinct*. London: Routledge & Kegan Paul, 1977.

Rubin, V., and L. Comitas. *Ganja in Jamaica*. The Hague: Mouton, 1975.

Stokes, J.P. "The effects of rapid eye movement sleep on retention," *The Psychological Record*, 23(4), 1973, 521–532.

Webb, W.B., ed. *Sleep: An active process*. Glenview, Ill.: Scott, Foresman, 1973.

Chapter 4

Amerigo, J.A., J.M. Delgado-Garcia, and J.M.R. Delgado. "Behavioral changes induced by radio stimulation of the pallidum in monkeys." XXVIth International Congress of Physiological Sciences, New Delhi, 1974.

Baron, R.A. *Human aggression*. New York: Plenum Press, 1977.

Castle, Raymond, et al. *At risk: An account of the work of the battered child research department, National Society for the Prevention of Cruelty to Children*. London: Routledge & Kegan Paul, 1976.

Cater, D., and S. Strickland. *TV violence and the child: The evolution and fate of the Surgeon General's Report*. New York: Russell Sage Foundation, 1975.

Culliton, B.J.U. "Psychosurgery: National commission issues surprisingly favorable report," *Science*, 194, 1976, 299–301.

Delgado, J.M.R. *Physical control of the mind: Toward a psychocivilized society*. New York: Harper & Row, 1970.

Dollard, J., et al. *Frustration and aggression*. New Haven, Conn: Yale University Press, 1939.

Isaacson, R.L. *The limbic system*. New York: Plenum Press, 1974.

Larsen, K.S. *Aggression: Myths and models*. Chicago: Nelson-Hall, 1976.

Lorenz, K. *On aggression*. New York: Harcourt, 1966.

Pribram, K. "The brain," *Psychology Today*, 5(4), 1971, 44–52.

Rose, S. *The conscious brain*. New York: Vintage, 1976.

Scott, J.P. "Violence and the disaggregated society," presidential address to the International Society for Research on Aggression, 1st International Conference on Aggression Research, Toronto, August 1974.

Chapter 5

Blakemore, Colin. *Mechanics of the mind.* New York: Cambridge University Press, 1977.

Gallin, David. "Implications for psychiatry of left and right cerebral specialization," *Archives of General Psychiatry,* 31, 1974, 572–583.

Ittelson, W.H., et al. *Introduction to environmental psychology.* New York: Holt, Rinehart and Winston, 1974.

John, E. Roy, et al. "Neurometrics," *Science,* 196, 1977, 1393–1410.

Ornstein, R.E. *The psychology of consciousness,* 2nd ed. New York: Harcourt, 1978.

Schwartz, Gary E., and David Shapiro, eds. *Consciousness and self-regulation: Advances in Research, Vol. 1.* New York: Plenum Press, 1976.

Sewell, E., J.F. McCoy, and W.R. Sewell. "Modification of antagonistic social behavior using positive reinforcement for other behavior," *The Psychological Record,* 23(4), 1973, 499–504.

Tibbets, Paul. "The mind-body problem: Empirical or conceptual issue?" *The Psychological Record,* 23, 1973, 111–120.

Chapter 6

Boring, E.G. *Sensation and perception in the history of experimental psychology,* 2nd ed. New York: Appleton, 1950.

Geldard, F.A. *The human senses.* New York: Wiley, 1953.

McBurney, D.H., and Virginia Collings. *Introduction to sensation/perception.* Englewood Cliffs, N.J.: Prentice-Hall, 1977.

Pfaffman, C. "Taste and smell," in S.S. Stevens (ed.), *Handbook of experimental psychology,* New York: Wiley, 1951.

Stevens, S.S. *Psychophysics: Introduction to its perceptual, neural, and social prospects.* New York: Wiley, 1975.

Woodworth, R.S., and H. Schlosberg. *Experimental psychology,* 3rd ed., Vol. 1. J.W. Kling and L.A. Riggs (eds.). New York: Holt, Rinehart and Winston, 1972.

Chapter 7

Beach, F.A. "Behavioral endocrinology: An emerging discipline," *American Scientist,* 63(2), 1975, 178–187.

Davis, H., and S.R. Silverman (eds.). *Hearing and deafness.* New York: Holt, Rinehart and Winston, 1970.

Dethier, V.G. "Other tastes, other worlds," *Science,* 201, 1978, 224–228.

Diamond, J., A.L. Diamond, and M. Mast. "Visual sensitivity and sexual arousal levels during the menstrual cycle," *Journal of Nervous and Mental Disorders,* 155, 1972, 170–176.

Hassett, James. "Sex and smell." *Psychology Today,* March 1978, 40–45.

Udry, J.R., and N.M. Morris. "Distribution of coitus in the menstrual cycle," *Nature,* 220, 1968, 593–596.

Chapter 8

Carterette, E.C., and M.P. Friedman (eds.). *Handbook of perception, Vol. 5: Seeing.* New York: Academic Press, 1975.

Wald, G. "The photoreceptor process in vision," in J. Field (ed.), *Handbook of physiology, Sec. I: Neurophysiology.* Washington, D.C.: American Physiological Society, 1959.

Wald, G. "The receptors of human color vision," *Science,* 145, 1964, 1007–1016.

Weckroth, J. *Dimensions of color sensation.* Stockholm: University of Stockholm, 1960.

Zahl, P.E. *Blindness: modern approaches to the unseen environment.* Princeton, N.J.: Princeton University Press, 1962.

Chapter 9

Bexton, W.H., W. Heron, and T.H. Scott. "Effects of decreased variation in the sensory environment," *Canadian Journal of Psychology,* 8, 1954, 70–76.

Heron, W., B.K. Doane, and T.H. Scott. "Visual disturbances after prolonged perceptual isolation," *Canadian Journal of Psychology,* 10, 1956, 13–17.

Lilly, J. *Center of the cyclone: An autobiography of inner space.* New York: Julian, 1972.

Magoun, H.W. *The waking brain,* 2nd ed. Springfield, Ill.: Charles C Thomas, 1963.

Schein, E.H. "The Chinese indoctrination program for prisoners of war: A study of attempted 'brainwashing,'" *Psychiatry,* 19, 1956, 149–172.

Chapter 10

Allport, G.W., and T.F. Pettigrew. "Cultural influence on the perception of movement: The trapezoid illusion among the Zulus," *Journal of Abnormal and Social Psychology,* 55, 1957, 104–113.

Bond, E.K. "Perception of form by the human infant," *Psychological Bulletin,* 77, 225–245.

Fraiberg, Selma. *Insights from the blind,* New York: Basic Books, 1977.

Gregory, R.L. "Visual illusions," *Scientific American,* 219, 1972, 66–76.

Haber, R.N., and M. Hershenson. *The psychology of visual perception.* New York: Holt, Rinehart and Winston, 1973.

Koehler, W. *Gestalt psychology,* 2nd ed. New York: Liveright, 1947.

Powers, W.T. *Behavior: The control of perception.* Chicago: Aldine, 1973.

Riggs, L. "Human vision: Some objective explorations," *American Psychologist,* 31(2), 1976, 125–134.

Uttal, W.R. *An autocorrelation theory of form detection.* Hillsdale, N.J.: Erlbaum, 1975.

Chapter 11

Beloff, John. *Why parapsychology?" Human Nature,* 1(1), 1978, 68–74.

Diaconis, Persi. "Statistical problems in ESP research," *Science,* 201, 1978, 131–136.

Fareberow, N.E. (ed.). *Taboo topics.* New York: Aldine-Atherton, 1966.

Lindsley, D.B. "The role of the nonspecific reticulo-thalamo-cortical systems in emotion," in P. Black (ed.), *Physiological correlates of emotion.* New York: Academic Press, 1970.

McConnell, R.A. "ESP and credibility in science," *American Psychologist,* 24, 1969, 531–538.

McGinnies, E. "Emotionality and perceptual defense," *Psychological Review,* 56, 1949, 244–251.

Posner, M.I., and S.J. Boies. "Components of attention," *Psychological Review,* 78, 1971, 391–408.

Rhine, L.E. *ESP in life and lab.* New York: Macmillan, 1967.

Swets, J.A. "Is there a sensory threshold?" *Science,* 134, 1961, 168–177.

Taddonio, J.L. "The relationship of experimenter expectancy to performance on ESP tasks," *Journal of Parapsychology,* 40(2), 1976, 107–113.

Chapter 12

Arkes, H.R., and J.P. Garske. *Psychological theories of motivation.* Monterey, Calif.: Brooks-Cole, 1977.

Arnold, M.B. *Emotion and personality,* vols. I and II. New York: Columbia University Press, 1960.

Buck, Ross. *Human motivation and emotion.* New York: Wiley, 1976.

Cannon, W.B. *The wisdom of the body.* New York: Norton, 1932.

Deutsch, J.A., W.G. Young, and T.J. Kalogeris. "The stomach signals satiety," *Science,* 201, 1978, 165–166.

McConnell, J.V. "Feedback, fat and freedom," *Encyclopedia Britannica Yearbook,* 1973.

Mahoney, M.J., and K. Mahoney. *Permanent weight control.* New York: Norton, 1976.

Mayer, J. *Overweight: Causes, cost and control.* Englewood Cliffs, N.J.: Prentice-Hall, 1968.

Malmo, R.B. *On emotions, needs and our archaic brain.* New York: Holt, Rinehart and Winston, 1975.

Richter, C.P. *Essays in biology.* Berkeley, Calif.: University of California Press, 1943.

Schachter, S. *Emotion, obesity and crime.* New York: Academic Press, 1971.

Young, P.T. *Emotion in man and animal,* 2nd rev. ed. Huntington, N.Y.: Kreiger, 1973.

Chapter 13

Beach, F.A., and C.S. Ford. *Patterns of sexual behavior.* New York: Harper & Brothers and Paul Schoeber, 1951.

Forisha, B.L. *Sex roles and personal awareness.* Morristown, N.J.: General Learning Press, 1978.

Maccoby, E.E., and C.N. Jacklin. *The psychology of sex differences.* Stanford, Calif.: Stanford University Press, 1974.

Olds, J., and M.E. Olds. "Drives, rewards, and the brain," in F. Barron et al. (eds.), *New directions in psychology II.* New York: Holt, Rinehart and Winston, 1957.

Williams, J.H. *Psychology of women: Behavior in a biosocial context.* New York: Norton, 1977.

Wright, P., P.G. Caryl, and D.M. Vowles (eds.). *Neural and endocrine aspects of behavior in birds.* New York: Elsevier, 1975.

Chapter 14

Culligan, D. "That helpless feeling: The dangers of stress," *New York,* 8(28), 1975, 28–32.

Friedman, R.J., and M.F. Katz. *The psychology of depression: Contemporary theory and research.* Washington, D.C.: Winston, 1974.

Hassett, James. "Teaching yourself to relax," *Psychology Today,* August, 1978, 28–40.

Levine, S. "Stress and behavior," *Scientific American* 224(1), 1971, 26–31.

Rabkin, J.G. and E.L. Struening. "Life events, stress, and illness," *Science,* 194, 1976, 1013.

Reid, J.E., and F.E. Inbau. *Truth and deception: The polygraph ("lie detector") technique,* 2nd ed. Baltimore, Md.: Williams & Wilkins, 1977.

Rotter, J.B. "Generalized expectancies for internal versus external control of reinforcement," *Psychological Monographs,* 80(609), 1966, 211.

Selye, H. *The stress of life,* rev. ed. New York: McGraw-Hill, 1978.

Williams, J.L., and S.F. Maier. "Transituational immunization and therapy of learned helplessness in the rat," *Journal of Experimental Psychology: Animal Behavior Processes,* 3(3), 1977, 240–252.

Chapter 15

Dallenbach, K.M. "Twitmyer and the conditioned response," *American Journal of Psychology,* 72, 1959, 633–638.

Jones, M.C. "Albert, Peter and John B. Watson," *American Psychologist,* 79, 8, 1974.

McGill, T.E. *Readings in animal behavior,* 2nd ed. New York: Holt, Rinehart and Winston, 1973.

Morris, R.J., and K.R. Suckerman. "The importance of the therapeutic relationship in systematic desensitization," *Journal of Consulting and Clinical Psychology,* 42(1), 1974, 148.

Paul, G.L. *Insight vs. desensitization in psychotherapy.* Stanford, Calif.: Stanford University Press, 1966.

Pavlov, I.P. *Conditioned reflexes.* New York: Oxford, 1927.

Watson, J.B., and R. Rayner. "Conditioned emotional reactions," *Journal of Experimental Psychology,* 3, 1920, 1–14.

Wolpe, J. *The practice of behavior therapy.* New York: Pergamon, 1969.

Chapter 16

Bolles, R.C. *Learning theory.* New York: Holt, Rinehart and Winston, 1975.

Davis, H., and H.M.B. Hurwitz (eds.). *Operant-Pavlovian interactions.* New York: Halsted Press, 1977.

Gantt, W.H. "Pain conditioning and schizokinesis," *Conditional Reflex,* 8(2), 1973, 63–66.

Hall, J.F. *Classical conditioning and instrumental learning: A contemporary approach.* Philadelphia, Pa.: Lippincott, 1976.

Hilgard, E.R., and G.H. Bower. *Theories of learning,* 4th ed. Englewood Cliffs, N.J.: Prentice-Hall, 1975.

Koehler, W. *The mentality of apes.* New York: Harcourt, 1925.

Luria, A.R. *The neuropsychology of memory.* Washington, D.C.: Winston, 1976.

Maier, R.A., and B.M. Maier. *Comparative animal behavior.* Belmont, Calif.: Brooks-Cole, 1970.

Miller, N.E. "Learning of visceral and glandular response," *Science,* 163, 1969, 434–445.

Skinner, B.F. *The behavior of organisms.* New York: Appleton-Century-Crofts, 1938.

Skinner, B.F. "Pigeons in a pelican," *American Psychologist,* 15, 1960, 28–37.

Stuart, R.B. (ed.). *Behavioral self-management: strategies, techniques and outcomes.* New York: Brunner/Mazel, 1977.

Thorndike, E.L. *The psychology of learning.* New York: Teachers College, Columbia University, 1921.

Chapter 17

Bower, G.H. *The psychology of learning and motivation: Advances in research and theory,* Vol. II. New York: Academic Press, 1977.

Chapman, R.M., J.W. McCrary, and J.A. Chapman. "Short-term memory: The 'storage' component of human-brain responses predicts recall," *Science,* 202, 1978, 1211–1213.

Corning, W.C., and S.C. Ratner (eds.). *The chemistry of learning.* New York: Plenum Press, 1967.

Higbee, K.L. *Your memory: How it works and how to improve it.* Englewood Cliffs, N.J.: Prentice-Hall, 1977.

John, E.R. "How the brain works: A new explanation," *Psychology Today,* 9(11), 1976, 48–52.

Lashley, K.S. "In search of the engram," *Symposia of the Society for Experimental Biology,* 4, 1950, 454–482.

McConnell, J.V. "The biochemistry of memory," in R.C. Teevan (ed.), *Readings in introductory psychology.* Minneapolis: Burgess, 1972.

McConnell, J.V., A.L. Jacobson, and D.P. Kimble. "The effects of regeneration upon retention of a conditioned response in the planarian," *Journal of Comparative and Physiological Psychology,* 52, 1959, 1–5.

McConnell, J.V., and D.H. Malin. "Recent experiments in memory transfer," in H.P. Zippel (ed.), *Memory and transfer of information.* New York: Plenum Press, 1973.

McConnell, J.V., and J. Shelby. "Memory transfer in invertebrates," in G. Ungar (ed.), *Molecular mechanisms in memory and learning.* New York: Plenum Press, 1970.

Norman, D.A. *Memory and attention: An introduction to human information processing,* 2nd ed. New York: Wiley, 1976.

Chapter 18

Barber, T.X. *Hypnosis: A scientific approach.* New York: Van Nostrand, 1969.

Barber, T.X. *Pitfalls in human research.* Elmsford, N.Y.: Pergamon, 1976.

Bowers, K.S. *Hypnosis for the seriously curious.* Monterey, Calif.: Brooks/Cole, 1976.

Casey, K.L. "Pain: A current view of neural mechanisms," *American Scientist,* 61, 1973, 194–200.

Hilgard, E.R., and J.R. Hilgard. *Hypnosis in the relief of pain.* Los Altos, Calif.: Wm. Kaufmann, 1975.

Melzack, R. *The puzzle of pain.* New York: Basic Books, 1973.

Sheehan, P.W., and C.W. Perry. *A critical appraisal of contemporary paradigms of hypnosis.* Hillsdale, N.J.: Erlbaum, 1976.

Sternback, R.A. *Pain patients: Traits and treatment.* New York: Academic Press, 1974.

Chapter 19

Clarke, A.M., and A.D.B. Clarke (eds.). *Mental deficiency: The changing outlook,* 3rd ed. New York: Free Press, 1974.

Comfort, A. *Aging: The biology of senescence.* New York: Holt, Rinehart and Winston, 1964.

Dobzhansky, T. "Genetics and the diversity of behavior," *American Psychologist,* 27, 1972, 523–530.

Hook, E.B. "Behavioral implications of the human XYY genotype," *Science,* 179, 1973, 139–150.

Lubs, H.A., and F. de la Cruz (eds.). *Genetic counseling: A monograph of the National Institute of Child Health and Human Development.* New York: Raven Press, 1977.

Sorenson, J. "Genetic counseling," *Behavior Today,* 4, 3, 1973.

Walzer, S., and P.S. Gerald. "Social class and frequency of XYY and XXY," *Science,* 190, 1975, 1228–1229.

Winick, M., K.K. Meyer, and R.C. Harris. "Malnutrition and environmental enrichment by early adoption," *Science*, 190, 1975, 1173–1175.

Chapter 20

Eibl-Eibesfeldt, I. *Ethology: The biology of behavior.* New York: Holt, Rinehart and Winston, 1970.

Harlow, H.F., M.K. Harlow, and S.J. Suomi. "From thought to therapy: Lessons from a primate laboratory," *American Scientist*, 59, 1971, 538–549.

Haith, M.M., Bergman, T., and M.J. Moore. "Eye contact and face scanning in early infancy," *Science*, 198, 1977, 853–854.

Helfer, R.E., and C.H. Kempe (eds.). *The battered child*, 2nd ed. Chicago: Chicago University Press, 1974.

Scott, J.P. *Early experience and the organization of behavior.* Belmont, Calif.: Brooks-Cole, 1968.

Struble, R.G., and A.H. Riesen. "Changes in cortical dendritic branching subsequent to partial social isolation in stumptailed monkeys," *Developmental Psychobiology*, 11(5), 1978, 479–486.

Van Lawick-Goodall, J. *In the shadow of man.* Boston: Houghton Mifflin, 1971.

Chapter 21

Baroff, G.S. *Mental retardation: Nature, cause, and management.* New York: Wiley, 1974.

Brown, R. "Development of the first language in the human species," *American Psychologist*, 28, 1973, 97–106.

Bruner, J.S., A. Jolly, and K. Sylva (eds.). *Play: Its role in development and evolution.* New York: Basic Books, 1976.

Colby, B.N. "Culture grammars," *Science*, 187, 1975, 913–918.

Glucksberg, S., and J.H. Danks. *Experimental psycholinguistics: An introduction.* Hillsdale, N.J.: Erlbaum, 1975.

Hebb, D.O., W.E. Lambert, and G.R. Tucker. "A DMZ in the language war," *Psychology Today*, 6(11)a, 1973, 54–63.

Menzel, E.W., and S. Halperin. "Purposive behavior as a basis for objective communication between chimpanzees," *Science*, 189, 1975, 652–654.

Millar, S. *The psychology of play.* Baltimore, Md.: Penguin, 1968.

Piaget, J. *Construction of reality in the child.* New York: Basic Books, 1954.

Trotter, R. "Evolution of language: A hatful of theories," *APA Monitor*, 7(1), 1976, 12–13.

Weisler, A., and R.B. McCall. "Exploration and play: Resume and redirection," *American Psychologist*, 13(7), 1976, 492–508.

Chapter 22

Adler, A. *Understanding human nature.* New York: Humanities, 1962.

Ansbacher, H.L. "Alfred Adler and humanistic psychology," *Journal of Humanistic Psychology*, 11, 1971, 53–63.

Baltes, P.B., and K.W. Schaie. "On the plasticity of intelligence in adulthood and old age," *American Psychologist*, October 1976, 720–725.

Erikson, E.H. *Childhood and society*, 2nd ed. New York: Norton, 1963.

Freud, S. *A general introduction to psychoanalysis.* New York: Doubleday, 1938.

Freud, S. *The interpretation of dreams.* New York: Basic Books, 1955.

Hulicka, I.M. *Empirical studies in the psychology and sociology of aging.* New York: Crowell, 1977.

Jung, C.G. *Man and his symbols.* New York: Doubleday, 1969.

Krasner, L. "The future and the past in the behaviorism-humanism dialogue," *American Psychologist*, September 1978, 799–804.

Levinson, D.J., et al. *The seasons of a man's life.* New York: Knopf, 1978.

Maslow, A.H. *Motivation and personality*, 2nd ed. New York: Harper & Row, 1970.

Mischel, W. *Introduction to personality*, 2nd ed. New York: Holt, Rinehart and Winston, 1976.

Sheehy, G. "The sexual diamond: Facing the facts of the human sexual life cycles," *New York*, 9(4), 1976, 28–39.

Skinner, B.F. *Walden Two.* New York: Macmillan, 1948.

Chapter 23

Allport, G.W. *Patterns and growth in personality.* New York: Holt, Rinehart and Winston, 1961.

Allport, G.W., P.E. Vernon, and G. Lindzey. *Study of values: Manual.* Boston: Houghton Mifflin, 1960.

Block, N.J., and G. Dworkin (eds.). *The IQ controversy: Critical readings.* New York: Pantheon, 1976.

Ghiselli, E.E. *The validity of occupational aptitude tests.* New York: Wiley, 1966.

Jones, R.A. *Self-fulfilling prophecies: Social, psychological, and physiological effects of expectancies.* Hillsdale, N.J.: Erlbaum, 1977.

Kretschmer, E. *Physique and character*, 2nd ed. New York: Harcourt, 1925.

Lindzey, G., C.S. Hall, and M. Manosevitz. *Theories of personality: Primary sources and research*, 2nd ed. New York: Wiley: 1973.

Marks, P.A., W. Seeman, and D.L. Haller. *The actuarial use of the MMPI with adolescents and adults.* Baltimore, Md.: Williams and Wilkins, 1974.

McReynolds, P. (ed.). *Advances in psychological assessment*, Vol. 4. San Francisco: Jossey-Bass, 1977.

Rice, B. "Brave new world of intelligence testing," *Psychology Today*, 13(4), 1979, 42–55.

Rosenthal, R., and L. Jacobson. *Pygmalion in the classroom.* New York: Holt, Rinehart and Winston, 1968.

Schmidt, F.L., and J.E. Hunter. "Racial and ethnic bias in psychological tests," *American Psychologist*, 29, 1974, 1–8.

Sheldon, W.H. *The varieties of temperament.* New York: Harper & Row, 1942.

Skeels, H.M. "Adult status of children with contrasting early life experiences," *Monographs of the Society for Research in Child Development*, 31(3), 1966, 1–65.

Wallach, M.A. "Tests tell us little about talent," *American Scientist*, 64, 1976, 57–63.

Wing, C.W., Jr., and M.A. Wallach. *College admissions and the psychology of talent.* New York: Holt, Rinehart and Winston, 1971.

Zajonc, R.B. "Family configuration and intelligence," *Science*, 192, 1976, 227–235.

Zigler, E., and P.K. Trickett. "IQ, social competence, and evaluation of early childhood intervention programs," *American Psychologist*, 33, 1978, 789–798.

Chapter 24

Braginsky, B.M., D.D. Braginsky, and K. Ring. *Methods of madness: The mental hospital as a last resort.* New York: Holt, Rinehart and Winston, 1969.

Edwards, A.L. *Statistical analysis*, 4th ed. New York: Holt, Rinehart and Winston, 1974.

Goldstein, J.J., H.S. Kant, and T.J. Hartman. *Pornography and sexual deviance.* Berkeley: University of California Press, 1974.

Hays, W.L. *Statistics for the social sciences*, 2nd ed. New York: Holt, Rinehart and Winston, 1973.

Kalish, R.A. *Late adulthood: Perspectives in human development.* Monterey, Calif.: Brooks/Cole, 1975.

Magaro, P.A., et al. *The mental health industry: A cultural phenomenon.* New York: Wiley-Interscience, 1978.

Maser, J.D., and M.E.P. Seligman (eds.). *Psychopathology: Experimental models.* San Francisco: Freeman, 1977.

Mohr, J.W., et al. *Pedophilia and exhibitionism: A handbook.* Toronto: University of Toronto Press, 1964.

Neugarten, B.L. (ed.). *Middle age and aging: A reader in social psychology.* Chicago: University of Chicago Press, 1968.

Price, R.H. *Abnormal behavior: Perspectives in conflict.* New York: Holt, Rinehart and Winston, 1972.

Rosenhan, D.L. "On being sane in insane places," *Science*, 179, 1973, 250–258.

Spitzer, R.L., and D.F. Klein (eds.). *Critical issues in psychiatric diagnosis.* New York: Raven Press, 1978.

White, R.W., and N.F. Watt. *The abnormal personality*, 4th ed. New York: Ronald Press, 1973.

Chapter 25

Ayllon, T., and N.H. Azrin. *The token economy.* New York: Appleton, 1968.

Berne, E. *Games people play: The psychology of human relationships*. New York: Grove, 1964.

Berne, E. *What do you say after you say hello?* New York: Grove, 1973.

Davis, A.E., S. Dinitz, and B. Pasamanick. *Schizophrenics in the new custodial community: Five years after the experiment*. Columbus, O.: Ohio State University Press, 1974.

Davison, G.C., and R.B. Stuart. "Behavior therapy and civil liberties," *American Psychologist*, 30(7), 1975, 755–763.

Franks, C.M., and G.T. Wilson (eds.). *Annual review of behavior therapy: Theory & practice*, Vol. 5. New York: Brunner/Mazel, 1978.

Greenspoon, J. "The reinforcing effect of two spoken sounds on the frequency of two responses," *American Journal of Psychology*, 68, 1955, 409–416.

Kirschenbaum, H. *On becoming Carl Rogers*. New York: Delacorte, 1978.

Marmor, J. *Psychiatrists and their patients: A national study of private office practice*. Washington, D.C.: Joint Information Service of the American Psychiatric Association and the National Association for Mental Health, 1975.

Mendel, W.M. *Supportive care: Theory and technique*. Los Angeles: Mara Books, 1975.

Perls, F.S. *Gestalt therapy verbatim*. Lafayette, Calif.: Real People Press, 1969.

Rogers, C.R. *Freedom to learn*. Columbus, O.: Merrill, 1969.

Shectman, F. "Conventional and contemporary approaches to psychotherapy: Freud meets Skinner, Janov, and others," *American Psychologist*, 32(3), 1977, 197–204.

Skinner, B.F. *Beyond freedom and dignity*. New York: Knopf, 1971.

Sloane, R.B., et al. *Psychotherapy versus behavior therapy*. Cambridge, Mass.: Harvard University Press, 1975.

Sommer, R. *The end of imprisonment*. New York: Oxford, 1976.

Yalom, I.D. *The theory and practice of group psychotherapy*. New York: Basic Books, 1970.

Chapter 26

Altman, I. *The environment and social behavior: Privacy, personal space, territory, and crowding*. Monterey, Calif.: Brooks/Cole, 1975.

Argyle, M., and M. Cook. *Gaze and mutual gaze*. New York: Cambridge University Press, 1976.

Bales, R.F. *Personality and interpersonal behavior*. New York: Holt, Rinehart and Winston, 1970.

Bandura, A. *Principles of behavior modification*. New York: Holt, Rinehart and Winston, 1969.

Berkowitz, L. *Advances in experimental social psychology*, Vol. 7. New York: Academic Press, 1974.

Byrne, D. "Attitudes and attraction," in L. Berkowitz (ed.), *Advances in experimental social psychology*, Vol. 4. New York: Academic Press, 1969.

Duck, S. (ed.) *Theory and practice in interpersonal attraction*. London: Academic Press, 1977.

Hall, J., and S. Donnell. "Managerial achievement: The personal side of behavioral theory," *Human Relations*, 1979, 32(1).

Heider, F. *The psychology of interpersonal relations*. New York: Wiley, 1958.

Kelley, H.H. "Attribution in social interaction," in E.E. Jones, et al. (eds.), *Attribution: Perceiving the causes of behavior*. Morristown, N.J.: General Learning Press, 1971.

Mehrabian, A. *Public places and private spaces: The psychology of work, play, and living environments*. New York: Basic Books, 1976.

Newcomb, T.M. *The acquaintance process*. New York: Holt, Rinehart and Winston, 1961.

Raven, B.H., and J.Z. Rubin. *Social psychology: People in groups*. New York: Wiley, 1976.

Rubin, Zick. *Liking and loving: An invitation to social psychology*. New York: Holt, Rinehart and Winston, 1973.

Sommer, R. *Personal space*. Englewood Cliffs, N.J.: Prentice-Hall, 1969.

Chapter 27

Asch, S.E. "Effects of group pressure upon modification and distortion of judgments," in E.E. Maccoby, T.M. Newcomb, and E.L. Hartley (eds.), *Readings in social psychology*, 3rd ed. New York: Holt, Rinehart and Winston, 1958.

Back, K.W. "The group can comfort but it can't cure," *Psychology Today*, 6(7), 1972, 28–41.

Bem, D.J. *Beliefs, attitudes, and human affairs*. Monterey, Calif.: Brooks/Cole, 1972.

Darley, J.M., and B. Latané. "Bystander intervention in emergencies: Diffusion of responsibility," *Journal of Personality and Social Psychology*, 8, 1968, 377–383.

Festinger, L. *A theory of cognitive dissonance*. Stanford, Calif.: Stanford University Press, 1959.

Harvey, J.H., W.J. Ickes, and R.F. Kidd (eds.). *New directions in attribution research*. Hillsdale, N.J.: Erlbaum, 1976.

Helson, H., and W. Bevans (eds.). *Contemporary approaches to psychology*. Princeton, N.J.: Van Nostrand, 1967.

Jones, E.E. "How do people perceive the causes of behavior?" *American Scientist*, 64(3), 1976, 300–305.

Milgram, S. *Obedience to authority: An experimental view*. New York: Harper & Row, 1974.

Milgram, S. *The individual in a social world: Essays and experiments*. Reading, Mass.: Addison-Wesley, 1977.

Piliavin, I.M., J. Rodin, and J. Piliavin. "Good Samaritanism: An underground phenomenon?" *Journal of Personality and Social Psychology*, 13, 1969, 289–299.

Ross, L., G. Bierbraver, and S. Hoffman. "The role of attribution processes in conformity and dissent: Resisting the Asch situation," *American Psychologist*, 31(2), 1976, 148–156.

Rubin, J.Z., and B.R. Brown. *The social psychology of bargaining and negotiation*. New York: Academic Press, 1975.

Sherif, M. *Social interaction: Processes and products*. Chicago: Aldine, 1967.

Chapter 28

Hovland, C.I., et al. *Experiments in mass communication*. Princeton, N.J.: Princeton University Press, 1949.

Janis, I.L., and S. Feshbach. "Effects of fear-arousing communications," *Journal of Abnormal and Social Psychology*, 48, 1953, 78–92.

Janis, I.L., and C.I. Hovland (eds.). *Personality and persuasibility*. New Haven, Conn.: Yale University Press, 1969.

Kelman, H.C. (ed.). *International behavior: A social-psychological analysis*. New York: Holt, Rinehart and Winston, 1965.

Leventhal, H. "Findings and theory in the study of fear communications," in L. Berkowitz (ed.), *Advances in experimental social psychology*, Vol. 5. New York: Academic Press, 1970.

McConnell, J.V. "Persuasion and behavioral change," in *The art of persuasion in litigation handbook*. West Palm Beach, Fla.: American Trial Lawyers Association, 1966.

Moscovici, S. *Social influence and social change*. London: Academic Press, 1976.

Newcomb, T.M. "Persistence and regression of changed attitudes: Long-range studies," *Journal of Social Issues*, 19, 1963, 3–14.

Sherif, C.W., M. Sherif, and R.E. Hebergall. *Attitude and attitude change*. Philadelphia: Saunders, 1965.

Wicklund, R.A., and J.W. Brehm. *Perspectives on cognitive dissonance*. Hillsdale, N.J.: Erlbaum, 1976.

Zimbardo, P.G., E.B. Ebbesen, and C. Maslach. *Influencing attitudes and changing behavior: An introduction to method, theory, and applications of social control and personal power*, 2nd ed. Reading, Mass.: Addison-Wesley, 1977.

A Conclusion

American Psychological Association. "A career in psychology." Washington, D.C.: The Association, 1970.

Argyris, C. "Dangers in applying results from experimental social psychology," *American Psychologist*, 30(4), 1975, 469–485.

Campbell, A., P.E. Converse, and W.L. Rodgers. *The quality of American life*. New York: Russell Sage Foundation, 1976.

Cornish, E., et al. *The study of the future: An introduction to the art and science of understanding and shaping tomorrow's world*. Washington, D.C.: World Future Society, 1977.

Havens, R.B. *How to train humans: A behavior modification manual*. Flushing, N.Y.: Scholium International, 1975.

Moore, P. "Not by medicine alone," *APA Monitor*, 6(11), 1, 1975, 24–25.

Parsons, H.M. "What happened at Hawthorne?" *Science*, 183, 1974, 922–932.

President's Commission on Mental Health. *Report to the President from the President's Commission on Mental Health 1978*, Vol. I. Washington, D.C.: U.S. Government Printing Office, 1978.

Sarason, S.B. *Work, aging, and social change: Professionals and the one-life, one-career imperative.* New York: Free Press, 1977.

Wertheimer, M., et al. "Psychology and the future," *American Psychologist*, 33, 1978, 631–647.

(continued from p. iv)

p. 437, bottom photo courtesy of John R. Swisher / p. 444, photo courtesy of Dr. Ramon Greenberg / p. 445, photo courtesy of Kenneth Karp.

Chapter 18: p. 455, illustration courtesy of The Granger Collection / p. 457, illustration courtesy of The Granger Collection / p. 458, top illustration courtesy of The Bettmann Archive Inc. / p. 459, photo courtesy of the Yale Picture Collection, Yale University Library / p. 462, photo courtesy of Fabian Bachrach / p. 463, photo reproduced by permission of Harcourt Brace Jovanovich, Inc., from "Divided Brain & Consciousness," produced by Lee R. Bobker, copyright © 1977 by Harcourt Brace Jovanovich / p. 467, bottom photo courtesy of The Bettmann Archive Inc.

Part 5: photos courtesy of Kenneth Karp.

Chapter 19: p. 477, photo courtesy of Compix-United Press International / p. 482, photo courtesy of Carolina Biological Supply Co. / p. 484, 487, photos courtesy of Samuel Teicher / p. 488, photo courtesy of Carolina Biological Supply Co. / pp. 489, 491, photos courtesy of Michael Weisbrot / p. 492, photo courtesy of Thomas McAvoy, *Life* Magazine, © 1954 Time Inc.

Chapter 20: p. 506, photo courtesy of Michael Weisbrot / pp. 507, 508, photos courtesy of University of Wisconsin Primate Lab / pp. 516, 519, photos courtesy of Michael Weisbrot / p. 522, photo courtesy of the University of Wisconsin Primate Lab.

Chapter 21: photo courtesy of Y. de Braine, Black Star / pp. 532, 533, photos courtesy of Michael Weisbrot / p. 537, top photo courtesy of Harvard University News Office, bottom photo courtesy of Michael Weisbrot / p. 539, photo courtesy of Yerkes Regional Primate Research Center of Emory University / p. 544, top left photo courtesy of Kathryn Abbe, top center photo courtesy of Samuel Teicher, top right photo courtesy of Jane Hamilton-Merritt / left and right photos in second row, courtesy of Michael Weisbrot / p. 545, photo courtesy of Pictorial Parade Inc.

Part 6: photos courtesy of Kenneth Karp.

Chapter 22: p. 558, photo courtesy of the Italian Government Tourist Office / p. 561, photo courtesy of The Granger Collection / p. 563, photo courtesy of Sigmund Freud Copyrights Ltd. / p. 567, photo courtesy of Mimi Cotter / p. 570, photo courtesy of the National Library of Medicine / p. 572, photo courtesy of the William Alanson White Institute / p. 576, top left photo courtesy of Michael Weisbrot / top center and top right photos copyright © 1979 Arthur Sirdofsky / p.

578, bottom photo courtesy of the Viking Press, William Carter.

Chapter 23: p. 590, photo courtesy of The Bettmann Archive Inc. / pp. 591, 594, photos courtesy of The Granger Collection / p. 595, photo courtesy of the National Education Association / p. 598, bottom photo courtesy of Jane Hamilton-Merritt / p. 604, photo courtesy of Wide World Photos Inc. / p. 606, photos courtesy of Featherkill Studios.

Chapter 24: p. 614, photo courtesy of Michael Weisbrot / p. 622, photo courtesy of Samuel Teicher / p. 627, photo courtesy of J. Brian King / p. 629, photo copyright © 1979 Arthur Sirdofsky / p. 633, photo courtesy of Compix-United Press International / p. 635, photo courtesy of Kenneth Karp.

Part 7: photo courtesy of J. Brian King.

Chapter 25: p. 648, photo courtesy of Marc and Evelyn Bernheim from Woodfin Camp / p. 650, photo courtesy of The Bettmann Archive Inc. / p. 651, photo courtesy of the National Institute of Mental Health / p. 652, photo courtesy of The Bettmann Archive Inc. / p. 655, photo courtesy of Magnum Photos Inc. / p. 662, photo courtesy of The Bettmann Archive Inc. / p. 664, photo courtesy of Grove Press.

Chapter 26: p. 685, photo courtesy of The Bettmann Archive Inc. / pp. 688, 690, photos courtesy of Michael Weisbrot / p. 691, photo courtesy of Russell Dian / p. 695, photo copyright © 1979 Arthur Sirdofsky / p. 697, top photo courtesy of Elyce and Bruce Misher, bottom photos courtesy of A. Bandura, E.B. Blanchard, and S. Ritter / p. 698, bottom photo courtesy of Linda and David Dulcie, R.A. Moore, photographer.

Chapter 27: p. 710, photo copyright © 1979 Arthur Sirdofsky / p. 708, photo courtesy of Maury Englander / p. 712, top photo courtesy of Featherkill Studios, bottom left photo courtesy of The Bettmann Archive Inc., bottom right photo courtesy of The Farm, Summertown, Tennessee / p. 715, top photo courtesy of Christianson Leberman / p. 721, bottom photo courtesy of Wooten-Moulton Studio.

Chapter 28: p. 734, photo courtesy of Samuel Teicher / p. 742, photo courtesy of Golden West Television from "Scared Straight" / p. 745, photo courtesy of Wide World Photos Inc.

Chapter 29: p. 754, photo courtesy of The Bettmann Archive Inc. / p. 759, photo courtesy of the Cyborg Corporation / p. 761, photo courtesy of Samuel Teicher.

Appendix: p. 766, photo courtesy of Samuel Teicher.

NAME INDEX

SUBJECT INDEX